The Canadian Law and Practice of International Trade

with Particular Emphasis on Export and Import of Goods and Services

SECOND EDITION

J.-G. Castel, OC, OO, QC, FRSC
General Editor
Distinguished Research Professor
Osgoode Hall Law School
York University, Toronto

William C. Graham, QC, DU
Chairman of the Standing Committee on Foreign Affairs and International Trade, House of Commons, Ottawa

Susan Hainsworth, LLB, MAES
Legal Affairs Officer
Appellate Body Secretariat
World Trade Organization, Geneva

Armand L.C. de Mestral, BCL, LLM
Professor of Law
Faculty of Law
McGill University, Montreal

Mark A.A. Warner, MA, LLB, LLM
Division of Policy Interrelations
Trade Directorate
Organisation for Economic Co-operation and Development, Paris

1997
EMOND MONTGOMERY PUBLICATIONS LIMITED
TORONTO, CANADA

Printed in Canada

Produced by WordsWorth Communications of Toronto, Canada.

Canadian Cataloguing in Publication Data

Main entry under title:

The Canadian law and practice of international trade with particular emphasis on export and import of goods and services

2nd ed.
Includes bibliographical references and index.
ISBN 0-920722-91-1

1. Foreign trade regulation — Canada. 2. Canada — Foreign economic relations. 3. Canada — Commercial treaties. I. Castel, J.-G., 1928-

KE1940.C28 1997 343.71'087 C97-930277-3
KF1609.C28 1997

Preface

The second edition of this book contains a general introduction to the most important public and private law aspects of international trade. It is designed for Canadian readers as it deals specifically with Canadian law and practice with particular emphasis on export and import transactions involving goods and services.

National legislation and international agreements and practices are discussed in detail as they reflect underlying policies. Their study should enable practitioners and students to relate the detailed rules to broader perspectives.

For a country whose political survival and economic well-being depend in great part upon international trade, it is very important to adopt policies and laws that will expand Canada's exports. Yet, few Canadian lawyers have a good understanding of the major problems and issues in world trade and of the legal techniques that have been devised to deal with them. As a result of this lack of expertise, most of the legal aspects of the export and import business have been handled by customs brokers, freight forwarders, insurers, or bankers on behalf of their clients. Only at the litigation stage do lawyers come into the picture. It is the authors' opinion that advising clients with respect to international trade is an area that can be expanded at a time when the legal profession is seeking new challenges.

The role of the practising lawyer in international trade differs greatly from his or her role in domestic trade. It requires a special approach to legal analysis that is based on a broad understanding of political, economic, and business problems. He or she must be thoroughly familiar with the business objectives of his or her clients and the practical alternatives for reaching them abroad. Thus, coordination of business and legal issues is essential. A successful business method in Canada may be impractical in France or Mexico. Since a Canadian lawyer cannot become an expert on foreign laws or keep up with changes in these laws, he or she needs the services of skilled foreign lawyers. This is essential in order to minimize the risks of legal difficulties in the future. For this purpose, he or she must be able to translate, for the foreign lawyer, the range of business issues affecting a Canadian business enterprise that is planning to expand its activities abroad.

In general, a practising lawyer in international trade will spend more time negotiating with foreign business people, lawyers, and government officials than on litigation abroad, which will be handled by his or her foreign confrères.

On the governmental and international levels, conflicts often arise when the economic policies of the various nations of the world interact in relation to trade practices.

Other problems may also result from differences in economic development or from the fact that, on the national level, the government may not agree with private business as to the policies that should be adopted to develop the economy. Finally, while the national policies are subject to the paramount control of a law-making body, this is not the case on the international level. Thus, special techniques must be used to secure agreement and compliance. In this complex world of international trade, it is very important to be well versed in a number of disciplines, such as economics and political science, and areas of the law, such as commercial law and private and public international law, to name but a few.

Every practising lawyer knows that professional success is not determined exclusively by knowledge of the law. It is also the result of human qualities, personality, sensitivity, and a wide range of other knowledge that makes a lawyer aware of the social issues with which he or she comes into contact in his or her daily practice. Indeed, these additional qualities probably determine one's specialty.

This book, to some extent, attempts to recognize the extra-legal factors that are relevant to the practice of international trade law. A lawyer who is familiar with the GATT, the WTO, the North American Free Trade Agreement, or the domestic law relating to extraterritoriality, bills of lading, or letters of credit, etc., is to some extent prepared for the practice of international trade law. But he or she is not as prepared as someone who, in addition to having the purely "legal" knowledge, is familiar with present political, social, and economic structures on a world level within the parameters of which the other rules are evolving. Thus, the Canadian lawyer, both to understand better the present foundations of the legal world order and to advise his or her clients intelligently, must be aware of the many issues that are not part of the normal law school curriculum. In this respect, a sensitivity to the plight of developing countries and their need for transfers of wealth and technology in order to redress the striking imbalance that threatens the very world order on which the law is founded is an essential element to that understanding.

The authors would like to believe that this book will enable law students and practising lawyers to get a better grasp of the evolving process of international trade law.

The second edition of this book covers a number of important new developments affecting the public and private law regulating Canadian international trade in goods and services, such as the North American Free Trade Agreement, the World Trade Organization, and the General Agreement on Trade in Services.

Part I introduces the subject. Part II, which is devoted to the GATT, WTO, and the North American Free Trade Agreement, contains an analysis of the most important international aspects of international trade law. However, some topics that are dealt with in the GATT and GATS and in domestic legislation (for example, intellectual property rights, government procurement, trade in services, dumping, subsidies, etc.) are analyzed in greater detail in other parts of the book. In a book of this scope, some overlap is inevitable due to the nature of the topics. However, much overlap has been kept to a minimum.

Part III deals with international and national legal considerations with respect to export and import transactions. Part IV covers government regulation of export and import transactions. Part V addresses the question of the settlement of international trade disputes.

The authors wish to emphasize that international trade law is a very complex and evolutive subject in need of constant updating, and where international treaties and national laws and regulations are innumerable and extremely complicated. The case law should not be overlooked either. This is why the authors have not dealt with every topic exhaustively. Some sacrifices had to be made. Furthermore, space considerations required that some related topics be omitted entirely—for instance, the importance of taxation in international trade, the regulation of direct foreign investment, foreign or domestic securities transactions, and international monetary matters including the International Monetary Fund, the World Bank, and international banking. These omissions are not too serious, however, as excellent books on such topics are readily available.

Each chapter has a selected bibliography that should be consulted to supplement what is contained therein.

Chapters 1, 2, 3, 4, 13, 14, and 20 were prepared by Professor A. de Mestral, of the Faculty of Law of McGill University, Montreal. Chapters 9 and 18 were prepared by Mr. W.C. Graham, QC, MP, Chair of the Standing Committee on Foreign Affairs and International Trade, House of Commons, Ottawa, with the assistance of Mr. Neil Milton and Ms Leslie Milton. Chapters 5, 7, 8, 10, 11, 15, and 19 were prepared by Ms S. Hainsworth, Legal Affairs Officer, Appellate Body, Secretariat, World Trade Organization, Geneva, Switzerland. Chapters 16 and 17 were prepared by Mr. M. Warner of the OECD Trade Directorate, Paris, France. The introduction and chapters 6, 12, and 21 were prepared by Professor J.-G. Castel, Distinguished Research Professor, Osgoode Hall Law School, York University, Toronto, who acted as general editor.

The authors wish to thank all those who have given their permission to reproduce documents for which they hold the copyright.

The views expressed by Ms Hainsworth and Mr. Warner are their own and not those of the WTO or the OECD.

January 31, 1997
Toronto

Table of Contents

PART IV GOVERNMENT REGULATION OF EXPORT AND IMPORT TRANSACTIONS

PART V THE SETTLEMENT OF TRADE DISPUTES

Detailed Table of Contents

PART V THE SETTLEMENT OF TRADE DISPUTES

List of Selected Abbreviations

AAA	American Arbitration Association
AALCC	Afro-Asian Legal Consultative Committee
ACN	Air Consignment Note
AD/CVD	Antidumping and Countervailing Duties
Adp	Automatic data processing
AID	Agency for International Development (US)
ANCOM	Andean Sub-Group within LAFTA
APEC	Asia Pacific Economic Committee
ASEAN	Association of South-East Asian Nations
Auto Pact	Agreement Concerning Automotive Products between the Government of Canada and the Government of the United States of America 1965
Auto Pact base year	August 1, 1963 to July 31, 1964
Auto Pact	Status attained by automobile manufacturers in Canada by maintaining required production to sales and Canadian value added ratios entitling them to remission of duty
AWB	Air Waybill
BIRPI	United International Bureaux for the Protection of Intellectual Property
BPT	British Preferential Tariff
BTN	Brussels Tariff Nomenclature
CACM	Central American Common Market
C and F	Cost and Freight
CAP	Common Agricultural Policy (EEC)
CARDIS	Cargo Data Interchange System
CARICOM	Caribbean Common Market
CARIFTA	Caribbean Free Trade Association
CCC	Customs Co-operation Council
CCCN	Customs Co-operation Council Nomenclature
CCT	Common Customs Tariff (EC)
CEA	Canadian Export Association
CFR	Cost and Freight
CFS	Container Freight Station
CIDA	Canadian International Development Agency
CIF	Cost, Insurance, and Freight
CIF and C	Cost, Insurance, Freight, and Commission
CIF and C and I	Cost, Insurance, Freight, and Commission and Interest
CIF and E	Cost, Insurance, Freight and Exchange
CIFFA	Canadian International Freight Forwarders Association

CIME	OECD Committee on International Investment and Multinational Enterprises
CIP	Carriage and Insurance Paid to
CISG	UN Convention on Contracts for the International Sale of Goods (1980)
CITT	Canadian International Trade Tribunal
CMEA	Council for Mutual Economic Assistance Council of Europe (also: COMECON)
CMI	Comité Maritime International
CMIT	OECD Committee on Capital Movements and Invisible Transactions
COCOM	Co-ordinating Committee for Multilateral Export Controls
COMECON	(also called CMEA) Council for Mutual Economic Assistance
Commission	Free Trade Commission, established under NAFTA, art. 2001
COMPRO	Common Market Facilitating Procedures Committees (for the other Member States of the EEC)
CPT	carriage paid to
CT	Combined Transport
CTC	Centre for Transnational Corporations
CTO	Combined Transport Operator
CTS	Canada Treaty Series
CV	Countervailing
DAC	Development Assistance Committee of OECD
DAF	Delivered at Frontier
DCP	Freight/Carriage Paid to
DDP	Delivered Duty Paid
DDU	Delivered Duty Unpaid
DEQ	Delivered Ex Quay
DES	Delivered Ex Ship
DRIE	Department of Regional Industrial Expansion (Canada)
DSB	Dispute Settlement Body (WTO)
e. and o.e.	Errors and omissions excepted
EAEC	East African Economic Community
EC	European Community
ECA	(United Nations) Economic Commission for Africa
ECAFE	(United Nations) Economic Commission for Asia and the Far East
ECE	(United Nations) Economic Commission for Europe
ECLA	(United Nations) Economic Commission for Latin America
ECOSOC	Economic and Social Council of the United Nations
ECOWAS	Economic Community of West African States
ECSC	European Coal and Steel Community
ECU	European Currency Unit
EDC	Export Development Corporation (Canada)
EDI	Electronic Data Interchange
EEC	European Economic Community
EFT	Electronic Fund Transfer
EFTA	European Free Trade Association
EMCF	European Monetary Co-operation Fund
EMS	European Monetary System
EPO	European Patent Organization
ESCAP	(United Nations) Economic and Social Commission for Asia and the Pacific
EU	European Union
EUA	European Unit of Account
Euratom	European Atomic Energy Community
Eximbank	Export-Import Bank of the United States

EXQ	Ex Quay
EXSR	Ex Ship
EXW	Ex Works
FAS	Free Alongside Ship
FBL	FIATA—Negotiable Combined Transport Bill of Lading
FCA	Free Carrier
FCL	Full Container Load
FCN	Treaties of Friendship, Commerce and Navigation
FCR	Forwarder's Certificate of Receipt
FIATA	International Federation of Freight Forwarders Association
FIRA	Foreign Investment Review Agency
FOA	Free on Airport
FOB	Free on Board
FOR	Free on Rail
FOSFA	Federation of Oils, Seeds and Fats Association
FOT	Free on Truck
FRC	Free Carrier
FTA	Canada-US Free Trade Agreement
g.a.	General Average
GAFTA	Grain & Free Trade Association
GATT	General Agreement on Tariffs and Trade
GATS	General Agreement on Trade in Services
GPT	General Preferential Tariff
GSP	Generalized System of Preferences
Harmonized System	Harmonized Commodity Description and Coding System
HS	Harmonized Commodity Description and Coding System
IATA	International Air Transport Association
IBA	International Bar Association
IBRD	International Bank for Reconstruction and Development (World Bank)
ICA	Investment Canada Act (Canada)
ICAO	International Civil Aviation Organization
ICC	International Chamber of Commerce
ICS	International Chamber of Shipping
ICSID	International Centre for the Settlement of Investment Disputes Between States and Nationals of Other States
IEP	Agreement on an International Energy Program
IMC	International Maritime Committee
IMCO	Inter-governmental Maritime Consultation Organization
IMDG	International Maritime Dangerous Goods Code
IMF	International Monetary Fund
IMO	Inter-govermental Maritime Organization
INCO Terms	International Chamber of Commerce Trade Terms 1990
ISO	International Organization for Standardization
ITA	International Trade Administration (US Department of Commerce)
ITC	Department of Industry, Trade & Commerce (Canada)
ITC	International Trade Commission (US)
ITO	International Trade Organization
LAFTA	Latin American Free Trade Association
LASH	Lighter Aboard Ship
LCL	Less than Full Container Load
LDC	Less-Developed Country

MFA	Multi-Fibre Arrangement
MFN	Most-Favoured-Nation
MITI	Ministry of International Trade and Industry (Japan)
NAFTA	North American Free Trade Agreement
NEB	National Energy Board (Canada)
NEP	National Energy Policy
NIC	Newly Industrialized Country
NIEO	New International Economic Order
NT	national treatment
NTB	Non-Tariff Barrier
NVD	No Value Declared
OAU	Organization of African Unity
OCL	Ocean Container Lines
OECD	Organisation for Economic Co-operation and Development
OPEC	Organization of Petroleum Exporting Countries
PCT	Patent Co-operation Treaty
SDR	Special Drawing Rights, a unit of value defined in the Articles of Agreement of the International Monetary Fund
SEC	Securities and Exchange Commission (US)
SIMA	Special Import Measures Act (Canada)
TCT	Canadian Trade & Commodity Tax Cases
TMB	Textile Monitoring Board (GATT)
TPRB	Trade Policy Review Body (WTO)
TRIMS	Trade-Related Investment Measures
TRIPS	Trade-Related Aspects of Intellectual Property Rights
TSB	Textile Surveillance Body (GATT)
UCC	Uniform Commercial Code
UCP	Uniform Customs and Practice for Documentary Credits (1983 Revision), ICC
UN	United Nations Organization
UNCITRAL	UN Commission on International Trade Law
UNCTAD	UN Conference on Trade and Development
UNDP	United Nations Industrial Development Organization
UNIDROIT	International Institute for the Unification of Private Law (Rome Institute)
UNITAR	United Nations Institute for Training and Research
USTR	Office of the US Trade Representative
VAT	Value Added Tax
VER	Voluntary Export Restraints (or OMA—Orderly Marketing Agreements)
WIPO	World Intellectual Property Organization
World Bank	International Bank of Reconstruction and Development
WTO	World Trade Organization

Important International Conventions and Other Documents of International Trade Law

1883	International Convention for the Protection of Industrial Property (Paris; revised 1925 at The Hague, 1934 at London, 1958 at Lisbon and 1967 at Stockholm)
1891	Madrid Agreement for International Registration of Trade Marks
1923	Protocol on Arbitration Clauses (Geneva)
1924	Hague Rules relating to Bills of Lading. For amendments, see Brussels Protocols of 1968 and 1979
1927	Convention on the Execution of Foreign Arbitral Awards
1929	Warsaw Convention relating to the Unification of certain Rules relating to International Air Carriage. For amendment, see Hague Protocol of 1955
1930	Geneva Conventions on the Unification of the Law relating to Bills of Exchange
1931	Geneva Conventions on the Unification of the Law relating to Cheques
1941	Revised American Foreign Trade Definitions (US)
1944	Bretton Woods Agreements
1948	General Agreement on Tariffs and Trade
1950	Convention establishing the Customs Co-operation Council (CCC)
	Brussels Nomenclature (full title: Protocol of Amendment of the Convention signed in Brussels on December 15, 1950, for the Classification of Goods in Customs Tariffs)
1951	Uniform Commercial Code (US)
1955	Hague Convention on the Law applicable to International Sales of Goods (amended by the Hague Convention on the Law applicable to Contracts for the International Sale of Goods 1985)
	Hague Protocol amending the Warsaw Convention
1956	Convention dealing with the issue of ECS Carnets (Customs Co-operation Council)
	Convention on the Contract for the International Carriage of Goods by Road

1957 EEC Treaty (Treaty of Rome)

Euratom Treaty

1958 Convention on the Recognition and Enforcement of Foreign Arbitral Awards (United Nations, New York)

1959 Convention of Stockholm creating the European Free Trade Association

1961 European Convention on International Commercial Arbitration (Economic Commission for Europe on the United Nations, Geneva)

Convention dealing with the Issue of ATA Carnets (Customs Co-operation Council)

Convention supplementary to the Warsaw Convention for the unification of certain rules relating to international carriage by air performed by a person other than the contracting carrier (Guadalajara)

International Agreement on Railway Transports

1962 Agreement relating to the Application of the European Convention on International Arbitration (Paris)

1964 Convention relating to a Uniform Law on the International Sale of Goods (The Hague)

Convention relating to a Uniform Law on the Formation of Contracts for the International Sale of Goods (The Hague)

1965 Convention on the Settlement of Investment Disputes between States and Nationals of other States (Washington)

Convention on the Service Abroad of Judicial and Extraterritorial Documents in Civil and Commercial Matters (The Hague)

1966 UN Commission on International Trade Law (UNCITRAL)

Economic Commission for Europe's Arbitration Rules

European Convention providing a Uniform Law on Arbitration (Council of Europe)

1967 Convention establishing a World Intellectual Property Organization (WIPO) (Stockholm)

Revision of the International Convention for the Protection of Industrial Property (Stockholm)

1968 Brussels Protocol amending the Hague Rules relating to Bills of Lading (1924)

Convention on Jurisdiction and the Enforcement of Judgments in Civil and Commercial Matters (Full Faith and Credit Convention) (EEC)

1970 Patent Co-operation Treaty (Washington)

Convention on the Taking of Evidence Abroad in Civil and Commercial Matters (The Hague)

1971 Protocol relating to the Brussels Convention on Jurisdiction and Enforcement of Judgments in Civil and Commercial Matters 1968 (Luxembourg)

1973 Trade Mark Registration Treaty

Society for Worldwide Interbank Financial Telecommunications (incorporated as a co-operative Company under Belgian law, Brussels)

1974	Convention on the Limitation Period in the International Sale of Goods (UNCITRAL)
	Multi-fibre Arrangement
	York-Antwerp Rules on General Average
	The Problem of Clean Bills of Lading (ICC)
	Convention on a Code of Conduct for Liner Conferences (Geneva, UNCTAD)
1975	Court of Arbitration Rules (ICC)
	Rules of Conciliation and Arbitration (ICC)
	Uniform Rules for Arbitration Tribunals (CMEA)
	Uniform Rules for a Combined Transport Document (ICC)
	Montreal Protocols Nos. 3 and 4 (relating to the Warsaw Convention on International Air Carriage, 1929)
1976	Arbitration Rules (UNCITRAL)
	Guidelines for Multinational Enterprises (OECD, Paris)
1977	Conditions of Contract (International) for Works of Civil Engineering Construction (FIDI) (Contract)
	Extortion and Bribery in Business Transactions (ICC)
1978	Convention on the Carriage of Goods by Sea (Hamburg Rules) (UNCITRAL-UNCTAD)
	Uniform Rules for Collection (1978 Revision) (ICC)
	Uniform Rules for Contract Guarantees (ICC)
	Adaptation of Contracts (ICC)
	International Maritime Dangerous Goods Code
1979	GATT Agreements resulting from Tokyo Round
	Brussels Protocol Amending the Hague Rules relating to Bills of Lading 1924 as am. in 1968
	Protocol Amending the International Convention of 1957 relating to the Limitation and Liability of Owners of Sea-going Ships
	General Conditions of Specialization and Co-operation in Production between Organizations of CMEA
	General Conditions of Delivery of Goods 1968-1975 (1979 version, CMEA)
	ICC-CMI Rules of Arbitration (ICC and CMI, Paris)
1980	Incoterms (International Rules for the Interpretation of Trade Terms) (ICC)
	Court of Arbitration Rules Amended (ICC)
	Convention on Contracts for the International Sale of Goods (UNCITRAL, Vienna)
	UNCITRAL Conciliation Rules
	UN Convention on International Multimodal Transport of Goods
	Convention on International Carriage by Rail (COTIF, Berne)
	Convention on the Law Applicable to Contractual Obligations (EEC, Rome)

1982	Combiterms (System for Cost Distribution between the Seller and the Buyer according to Incoterms 1980)
1983	Uniform Customs and Practice for Documentary Credits (ICC)
	Convention on Agency in the International Sale of Goods (UNIDROIT, Geneva)
	Commercial Agency. A Guide for the Drawing up of Contracts between Parties Residing in Different Countries (ICC)
	ECE Guide for Drawing up International Contracts on Consulting Engineering, Including Some Related Aspects of Technical Assistance (UN, New York)
1984	Standard Trading Conditions of the Institute of Freight Forwarders Ltd.
	Regulation on the Creation of a European Economic Interest Grouping (EEIG) (EEC)
1985	Convention on the Law Applicable to Contracts for the International Sale of Goods
	Force Majeure and Hardship (ICC)
	Model Law on International Commercial Arbitration (UNCITRAL)
	Guide to Documentary Credit Operations (ICC)
	Transnational Data Report (TDR, UNCITRAL)
	Simplification of Patent Co-operation Treaty
	Rules of the London Court of International Arbitration
	Commercial Arbitration Rules, supplemented by the Supplementary Procedures for International Commercial Arbitration issued by the American Arbitration Association (AAA)
1986	Standard Forms for issuing Documentary Credits (ICC)
1987	EEC Treaty, Single European Act amending 1957 Treaty of Rome
1988	Rules of Conciliation and Arbitration Amended (ICC)
	UNIDROIT Convention on International Factoring
	UNIDROIT Convention on International Financial Leasing
1989	Canada-US Free Trade Agreement, entry into force (FTA)
	UN Convention on Liability of Operators of Transport Terminals in International Trade
1990	Incoterms Amended (ICC)
1992	Maastricht Treaty creating the European Union
1993	Uniform Customs and Practice for Documentary Credits (Revised)
1994	North American Free Trade Agreement, entry into force
1994	North American Agreement on Environmental Cooperation, Entry into force
1994	North American Agreement on Labour Cooperation, entry into force
1995	GATT 1994 and Agreement establishing the World Trade Organization, entry into force
1995	General Agreement on Trade in Services, entry into force

PART I

Introduction

I. THE CANADIAN CONTEXT

The field of international trade constitutes a relatively new area of specialization for Canadian lawyers. In law schools, the establishment of specialized courses on the topic is an equally recent phenomenon.

Why this should be the case is not easy to determine, since Canada has been a major international trading country for many years and Canada's international trade has been conducted within a framework of international law, domestic regulation, and private ordering by contract. Lawyers can hardly have been absent from this process. However, until recently, lawyers do not appear to have played a central role either in developing trade policies or in ordering Canada's international trade, and, even where strict points of law were involved, there has been some tendency to refer legal questions either to counsel in a foreign head office or to specialized law firms in the United States or the United Kingdom.

Whatever the causes of the limited presence of Canadian lawyers in international trade matters in the past, the situation appears to be changing rapidly. In private practice, corporations, and government departments, there is a growing awareness in Canada of the importance of law in international trade and a consequent demand for legal advice. This book attempts to meet the need for a general commentary on the law applicable in Canada to international trade with particular emphasis on export and import transactions involving goods and services.

A. Basic Outline of the Subject

The law of international trade can usefully be divided into three general areas. First, the general rules of public international law governing the economic relations of states. This law, which is derived both from general principles and treaty law, sets the framework within which states may legislate and under which international trade is conducted. Second, the law of contracts by which persons, companies, and state trading enterprises order their trading relationships. These contracts include sales, agency, licensing, insurance, transportation, banking, and financing. Third, the laws governing the importation and exportation of goods to and from Canada. These laws include legislation on export controls, tariffs, customs, countervailing duties, anti-dumping duties, and the support of exports.

To these basic divisions, the authors feel it important to add two further dimensions. Fourth, the law, both international and domestic, governing the activities of transnational corporations. This law includes domestic statutes such as those dealing with unlawful restraints of trade, as well as the statutes mentioned above, the principles of domestic and international law governing the extra-territorial application of laws, and a growing body of international law, state practice, and codes of conduct directed toward the operations of transnational corporations. Fifth is the area of law dealing with the resolution of disputes. The most signficant body of law here is that governing the private arbitration of international business disputes, although there is a growing body of international law also applicable.

It should be noted that the authors have decided to exclude any treatment of the taxation of international trade, the law governing direct foreign investment, security transactions, international banking, and monetary matters, including the International Monetary Fund (IMF) and the World Bank, due to their specialized character, although the inclusion of these subjects would be fully justified since they affect export and import transactions.

B. Historical Background

The law governing Canadian international business transactions and economic relations is drawn from a rich historical background going back thousands of years. Maritime commerce in the pre-Roman days in the Mediterranean witnessed the beginning of commercial rules governing sales to foreigners and maritime carriage. The *lex mercatoria* of Rome constituted, in a sense, the most universal element of Roman law, being applicable to all traders, Roman and non-Roman alike. In the Middle Ages, the revival of international trade, first in Italy and gradually in Flanders and North Germany, stood in remarkable contrast to the general immobility of society. The law governing merchants, administered by their own city tribunals, dealt with such matters as international banking, sales, and transportation. At no time in history had commercial law stood so much apart from the laws governing the great majority of society. The 16th, 17th, and 18th centuries witnessed the emergence of legal systems more able to cope with commercial matters and hence the assimilation of commercial law into the general law. However, the existence of associations of international traders continued to be a feature of international trade. In the 19th century, despite strong pressures toward the "nationalization" of all legal systems, laws governing maritime carriage of goods, insurance, banking, and even international sales continued to develop along similar lines.

The 20th century has seen the law governing international commercial transactions and economic relations subject to many conflicting "nationalizing" and "internationalizing" pressures. At one level, there has been a series of revolutionary movements that sought to bring about radical economic change within states, thus seeking to restrict any special privileges of foreign traders, to submit them to new rules of law and even, at times, to withdraw from much international commerce. At the same time, this century has seen the emergence of a genuinely international economy where the relative importance of international exchanges in virtually every national economy has grown tremendously. The emergence of new technologies, manufacturing techniques, transportation systems, and global systems of communications has greatly contributed to the increase of international trade. These same factors have contributed to the increased uniformity of legal rules governing international commercial transactions and have forced states to a realization that many decisions about international economic relations can be taken only in common, hence, the development of law making and negotiation in international organizations.

II. OVERVIEW OF THE LAW

A. The Law in Canada

Canadian law governing international trade is the product of the factors outlined above. Canada is a major trading nation; domestically, it is governed by the common law in nine provinces and the civil law in Quebec. Having two official languages, English and French, and a population drawn from across the world, it is almost uniquely open to the rest of the world. However, an examination of Canadian law does not reveal any coherent set of policies, legal principles, or body of statute law designed to gear Canada to international trade. Private law rules are largely inspired by British, American, or French law and the practices and principles followed in those states. At the private law level, there is, as yet, little indigenous thinking or philosophy either in court decisions or writing. In the field of statute law, largely federal, there exists a growing body of law designed to promote and regulate international trade. Unfortunately, this legislation does not reflect coherent and consistent policies.

B. Significance of International Law and International Organizations

It is arguable that the basic rule of international law governing the economic relations of states is that of the complete freedom of each state to act at its sovereign discretion.

However, in practice, interstate economic relations are governed by a complex network of bilateral and multilateral treaties. The rules of public international law speak in many significant respects to the treatment afforded foreign traders and their property by states. At the present time, bilateral treaties are used to deal with matters not covered by existing multilateral agreements, or to deal with relations between states not party to such international agreements. Bilateral agreements have been the source of international law "standards" of treatment of foreign persons and property, such as the most-favoured-nation (MFN) standard or the national treatment (NT) standard, which are now at the heart of many multilateral commitments. Bilateral treaties are also used to establish special arrangements between states such as the Canada-EEC Accord-Cadre.

The General Agreement on Tariffs and Trade (GATT) is the most important multilateral convention governing international trade today. Originally destined to be part of a larger convention governing all aspects of world trade and administered by an international trade organization, the GATT was adopted in 1947 on an interim basis. With the demise of the original plan, the GATT gradually became the structure for international negotiations on tariff reductions. It has also provided a limited code of rules governing international trade practices and has developed as a forum for the resolution of trade disputes and the conduct of international trade negotiations. Many developing states are now willing to apply the MFN and NT standards of the GATT that they had found to be too onerous in the past. The application of these standards, as well as the reciprocity principle enshrined in the GATT, have been considerably attenuated over the last 25 years insofar as developing countries are concerned. Finally, numerous rounds of trade negotiations conducted under the auspices of the GATT have displayed the capacity of the GATT to adapt to new challenges. Thus, the Uruguay Round resulted in the adoption of GATT 1994, which completes GATT 1947. A General Agreement on Trade in Services (GATS) was also adopted in 1994. It is patterned after GATT 1947 and 1994. January 1, 1995 saw the birth of the World Trade Organization (WTO) after 47 years of gestation. The headquarters of this new organization are in Geneva, Switzerland. The GATT-WTO membership now comprises over 135 states with many more requesting accession. The important task facing the WTO is that of making the new multilateral trading system truly global in scope and application. It provides the common institutional framework for the conduct of trade relations among its members and in matters related to agreements and associated legal instruments, such as the GATT 1947 and 1994 and the GATS and a forum for the settlement of international trade disputes.

The states producing raw materials and exporting foodstuffs have long been concerned with the difficulties caused to their balance of payments by the irregular fluctuations in world prices for such commodities. Developing states have complained of the decline in the terms of trade between raw material-producing states and developed states that produce a wide variety of manufactured goods. One of the principal means adopted internationally to protect the earnings of raw material-producing states has been the conclusion of commodity agreements. Many techniques have been employed in different agreements to stabilize commodity prices and to ensure a fair return to producers, while protecting consumers against dramatic price increases. The political and economic pressures under which commodity agreements operate has meant that their effective life has not been long. A recent development has been the negotiation, in 1980, of a UN "common fund" designed to increase the resources available to commodity funds. The most successful commodity agreement in 1981 was clearly the agreement concluded within the Organization of Petroleum Exporting Countries (OPEC), which involved producers only.

Other forms of state international economic regulating arrangements that have a profound impact on the world economy are free trade areas, common markets, or economic unions. A number of examples exist today both in the developed and the developing world. Clearly, the most successful is the European Community (EC) now part of the European Union (EU), which has eliminated tariffs between a number of states; requires free movement of goods, persons, and capital within its territory; maintains a common tariff barrier; and has developed a number of common institutions to implement these and other rules of its constitution, the Treaty of Rome 1957, as amended in 1987 and 1992. Another example is the North American Free Trade Agreement (NAFTA).

The general rules of public international law speak to the problems of the economic relations of states both directly and indirectly: directly in the form of rules governing state responsibility for the treatment of aliens and their property, and indirectly insofar as the rules governing sovereignty grant authority to states to regulate commercial activities and leave states free to determine the basis of their economic relations with other states.

Since the early 1960s, developing states have been urging that the law governing international business transactions and economic relations should be altered to ensure that their interests are fully protected. Much of the debate on this question has been conducted within the United Nations and more particularly within the UN Conference on Trade and Development (UNCTAD). Many of the ideas first launched within UNCTAD, such as the loosening of the reciprocity requirement in trade negotiations and the granting of preferential tariff treatment to certain exports of developing states, were subsequently implemented within the GATT. The culmination of this effort by developing states has been the adoption of the New International Economic Order (NIEO) resolutions by the UN General Assembly in 1974. These resolutions called for a completely new international economic order characterized by rules of international law and international institutions that would promote the welfare of developing countries and ensure equality between rich and poor states. One important feature of the NIEO was the negotiation of codes of conduct governing the activities of transnational corporations and the transfer of technology. The NIEO has clearly had an impact upon state practice and upon the rules of international law. Whether it will come to represent international law in its entirety is very much in doubt.

Finally, the role of international organizations in promoting the development of international law in this area must be noted. Be it the United Nations, a specialized agency such as the World Intellectual Property Organization (WIPO), or a regional organization such as the Organisation for Economic Co-operation and Development (OECD), these organizations play an ever more significant role in developing international trade law.

C. Significance of Private Contracts

Private contracts play a key role in the law of international trade today. The law governing international sales and international banking transactions has been largely untouched by government and, with a few notable exceptions, legislative intervention. The special character of international trade has been reflected by the fact that the law governing private transactions has evolved slowly from private commercial practice to the degree that it has become custom, and has attained judicial and, on occasion, legislative recognition. The classic example of this process is in the area of marine insurance, where the practices of London underwriters, especially the group originating in Lloyds Coffee House in the 17th century, have come to dominate the world marine insurance market. The Lloyds S. & G. (Ship and Goods) Policy is, in all probability, the most widely used standard-form contract in the world. Its only equal may be the international airline ticket used by International Air Transport Association (IATA) carriers. While one contract is very ancient and the other relatively recent, the process of development of the law is the same. In this field of international commerce, a major private commercial association has developed a standard contract that, through wide usage and judicial interpretation and recognition, has come to reflect the state of the law.

The role of private associations in the development of standard-form contracts and, hence, in the fashioning of the law, can hardly be underestimated. Not only in the field of transportation, but equally in the area of foodstuffs and raw material commodity trading, international associations have been responsible for the development of standard-form contracts governing the sale of such commodities. In recent years, a similar process has been at work in such areas as the licensing of technology and the sale of plants or the providing of engineering services. The International Chamber of Commerce (ICC) has been active in promoting the acceptance of standardized terms of sale and insurance and standard conditions of contract in international banking. International organizations, such as the Economic Commission for Europe and more recently the UN Commission on International Trade Law (UNCITRAL), have also played a role in the development of international contracts.

Finally, governments through the conclusion of international conventions providing for the unification of international contract terms, or the establishment of model laws and procedures, have also been active in the promotion of uniform international contracts. The most notable examples of this phenomenon are the "Hague Rules," soon to be superseded by the "Hamburg Rules" of 1978, governing the contractual terms of maritime bills of lading, and the 1980 United Nations Convention on Contracts for the International Sale of Goods.

The essential function of such uniform international contracts is the allocation of risk in the light of the special difficulties of international trade. Such difficulties include distance, culture, language, unfamiliarity with trading partners, transportation, time, delays, currency fluctuations, and the many problems of moving goods through different jurisdictions governed by different legal systems. For this reason, it can be strongly argued that courts and legislators should do their utmost to respect the solutions reached by the international business community, often after long periods of trial and error.

D. Significance of Government Regulation

Governments throughout history have taken an interest in trade across their borders. The purposes and techniques of regulation differ, although virtually all states today possess legislation requiring information concerning international trade in goods and services. Most states also have laws allowing restriction of the flow of trade in and out of their territory. Among the avowed purposes of such laws are the protection of local manufacturers from international competition, the development of new industries, the promotion of secondary manufacturing, the maintenance of an adequate supply of locally produced goods, and the protection of national security. Another range of objectives characteristic of the laws of many states is the protection of a free market in international trade, or at least the elimination of practices of other states that are perceived as discriminatory or unfair.

Customs legislation in virtually all states is designed to oversee the movement of goods in and out of a state and to apply whatever conditions are set for entry or exit. Customs legislation in Canada antedates Confederation, and the Department of National Revenue (Customs and Excise) continues to be a major department of the federal government. The principal means of taxing and controlling the flow of goods into Canada is the customs tariff. Other means such as outright bans, quotas, and surtaxes are available to the federal government, but the indiscriminate and retaliatory use of these means during the 1930s contributed so seriously to the Depression, that Canada, like all other major trading states, limits recourse to these techniques to exceptional situations. Today, the tariff has lost much of its significance, although it continues to be a serious barrier to the importation of certain agricultural and industrial commodities. In recent decades, legislation has been adopted to deal with distortions created in the market by the dumping of foreign goods. Special legislation deals with the problems caused by imports to the troubled sectors of the clothing, textiles, and footwear industry. A number of laws exist in Canada that allow for the restriction of exports. Since 1984, many changes have been made to the Canadian customs tariff and anti-dumping legislation with a view to modernizing the law, and also to bring it into conformity with the latest GATT-WTO agreements.

The effort to make the contents and the administration of domestic legislation relate to international trade has been a major preoccupation of international economic policy since the end of the World War II.

E. Significance of the Transnational Enterprise

Although by no means the sole participants in international trade, transnational enterprises dominate the field. The participation of transnational enterprises in international trade, the special problems that this poses to governments, and the rules of domestic and international law that have been developed to regulate their conduct in international trade, are therefore of particular interest to lawyers concerned with international economic and business law. On the international level, the United Nations has sought to promote the adoption of rules of law or codes of conduct concerning restrictive business practices, trading policies, and investment policies of transnational enterprises. On the domestic level, these enterprises present special problems concerning the extra-territorial application of domestic law designed to regulate their activities.

F. Significance of International Monetary Order

Although it is beyond the scope of this book to deal with the international monetary order, one has to acknowledge that the monetary policies of states have a direct influence on international trade. For instance, a devaluation of the Canadian dollar will raise the price of imported goods and decrease the price of domestic goods that are exported abroad. All monetary restrictions, such as exchange controls, lack of convertibility, etc., also have a direct impact on the import and export of goods and services. Thus, money can be used as an indirect barrier to trade. To encourage the harmonious development of international trade, methods of financing that are adequate and acceptable to all states must be followed. In 1944, the Bretton-Woods Agreements created the IMF and the International Bank for Reconstruction and Development (IBRD) for this purpose. This institutionalized monetary system, as well as cooperation between members of the OECD and the European Monetary System (EMS),[1] play a significant role in international trade since business enterprises must act in conformity with monetary rules applied by the states in which they carry on their activities. The financing of daily international trade transactions has to operate within these international and regional monetary systems.

G. Significance of the Regulation of Foreign Direct Investment

Because this book is devoted to international trade with particular emphasis on export and import transactions, it does not deal with the national and international regulation of foreign direct investment. However, it must be pointed out that such regulation has an impact on market entry. In some instances, it may be more advisable to set up a subsidiary abroad or enter into a joint venture agreement with a foreign party to produce goods abroad than to export them directly from Canada. Various declarations, codes and international agreements dealing with foreign investment, the role of offshore markets, and the protection of foreign investments are relevant to international trade, but not directly at the level of an import or export transaction.

H. Significance of Taxation

The taxation of income earned in Canada by non-residents and income earned abroad by Canadian individuals and business enterprises, affects decisions they make with respect to the way in which and the place where they will carry out business activities. The effects of Canadian tax policy on trade and international flows of capital, and the interaction of the Canadian system with the tax structure of other countries, including the role of treaties for the avoidance of double taxation, cannot be ignored by Canadian and foreign business enterprises. Wealth taxes, capital gains taxes, value-added taxes, excise taxes, etc., are also of concern to the international business community. The various market entry modes, whether by direct export, which involves not only sales but also distribution and agency agreements; contract entry, which involves licensing and contract manufacturing; and direct investment, which includes branches, subsidiaries, and joint ventures, are often determined by tax considerations.

Unfortunately, due to lack of space, it has not been possible to deal with this very specialized aspect of international trade.

---

1 To be replaced in 1999 by a single EC currency, the ECU.

I. Significance of Dispute Settlement Techniques

Given the many legal difficulties in obtaining jurisdiction over foreign enterprises and enforcing judgments against them, private dispute settlement techniques—in particular arbitration—play an important role in international trade. Many national arbitration associations provide effective procedures for solving international commercial disputes. The ICC administers the most extensive system of international commercial arbitration. Recently, the UNCITRAL has adopted a model law on international commercial arbitration, which has been widely adopted in Canada. Arbitration of disputes between governments or between governments and foreign investors, is also very important.

III. SELECTED GENERAL BIBLIOGRAPHY OF BOOKS AND PERIODICALS ON THE LEGAL FRAMEWORK OF WORLD TRADE AND THE EUROPEAN COMMUNITY

A. General

Abbott, *Law and Policy of Regional Integration: The NAFTA and Western Hemisphere Integration in the World Trade Organization* (1995).

Bhagwati, *The New International Economic Order* (1977).

Folsom and Gordon, *International Business Transactions* (1995).

Jackson, *Legal Problems of International Economic Relations* (3rd ed., 1995).

Jackson, *World Trade and the Law of GATT* (1969).

Jackson, *The World Trading System: Law and Policy of International Economic Relations* (1989).

Johnson, *The North American Free Trade Agreement: A Comprehensive Guide* (1995).

Kline, *International Codes and Multinational Business* (1985).

Langen, *Transnational Commercial Law* (1973).

Neale and Stephens, *International Business and National Jurisdiction* (1988).

Paterson, Band, Finlayson, and Thomas, *International Trade and Investment in Canada* (2nd ed., 1994).

Petersmann, *Constitutional Functions and Constitutional Problems of International Law* (1991).

Sarcevic and van Houtte, *Legal Issues in International Trade* (1990).

Schmitthoff, *Schmitthoff's Export Trade: The Law & Practice of International Trade* (9th ed., 1990).

Trebilcock and Howse, *The Regulation of International Trade* (1995).

Wiegley, *Export Trade and Finance* (1996).

B. The European Community

Bulletin of the European Economic Community, monthly.

Breakley and Quigley, *Completing the Internal Market of the European Community: 1992 Handbook* (1989).

Breakley and Quigley, *Completing the Internal Market of the European Community: 1992 Legislation*, vols. 1 to 6 and supplements (1990-91).

CCH, *Common Market Reporter*. Chicago: Commerce Clearing House, 1962-

Hafbauer (ed.), *Europe 1992: An American Perspective* (1990).

Hartley, *The Foundations of European Community Law. An Introduction to the Constitutional and Administrative Law of the European Community* (3rd ed., 1994).

Folsom, *European Union Business Law* (1995).

Kapteyn, *Introduction to the Law of the European Communities after the Coming into Force of the Single European Act* (1989).

Lasok and Bridge, *Law and Institutions of the European Union* (6th ed., 1994).

Mathijsen, *A Guide to European Community Law* (5th ed., 1994).

Wyatt and Dashwood, *European Community Law* (3rd ed., 1993).

C. Major Specialized Periodicals and Reports

Arbitration International

Australian Business Law Review

Banking Law Journal

Canada-United States Law Journal

Canadian Business Law Journal

Canadian Customs and Excise Reports

Canadian International Lawyer

CCH, European Community Cases

Columbia Journal of Transnational Law

Common Market Law Reports

Common Market Law Review

Comparative Law Yearbook of International Business

European Business Law Review

GATT FOCUS, GATT Newsletter

Harvard International Law Journal

ICC International Court of Arbitration Bulletin

International and Comparative Law Quarterly

International Business Law

International Lawyer

Journal of Air Law and Commerce

Journal of Business Law

Journal of International Arbitration

Journal of International Business Law and Practice

Journal of International Law and Economics

Journal of Law, Policy and International Business

Journal of Maritime Law and Commerce

Journal of World Trade

Lloyd's Maritime and Commercial Law Quarterly

Minnesota Journal of Global Trade

PART II

The International Framework

INTRODUCTION

Canada has entered into a number of multilateral and bilateral trade agreements. The most significant ones are the General Agreement on Tariffs and Trade (GATT) dealt with in chapter 1, which applies essentially to trade among states that have a free market economy, and the North American Free Trade Agreement (NAFTA), which is the object of chapter 2 and governs most of Canada's foreign trade. Canada's bilateral trade treaties are examined in chapter 3. Chapter 4 deals with the trade relationship existing between Canada and the European Union (EU) and other regional trading organizations.

CHAPTER ONE

The World Trade Organization and the General Agreement on Tariffs and Trade 1994

I. GENERAL

A. Historical Background of the GATT

The origins of the World Trade Organization (WTO) lie in the establishment of the family of UN institutions created as part of the post-World War II settlement. To complement the Specialized Agencies designed to promote political, social, and transportation policies, a number of economic institutions were also planned. Thus, the International Monetary Fund (IMF) and the World Bank were established to deal with monetary matters. International trade matters were to be the responsibility of the International Trade Organization (ITO). The ITO was founded by the Havana Charter in 1948 but it failed to find adequate support from major trading countries, and when the US Senate failed to ratify the treaty in 1953, all hope of immediate entry into force disappeared.

The GATT emerged originally in 1947, as an interim measure, designed to fill the gap until the Havana Charter could be adopted and to ensure a timely start of the process of post-war reconstruction in Europe. The GATT was drafted largely by taking certain parts of the draft Havana Charter, especially those parts dealing with tariff negotiations and ensuring most-favoured-nation (MFN) and national treatment (NT) of goods traded between GATT contracting parties. Unlike the Havana Charter, the GATT, as originally conceived, was not an international organization but only a meeting of CONTRACTING PARTIES.[1] The original GATT was not meant to have an independent rule making or dispute settlement function because those functions were to have been fulfilled by the ITO. However, when the ITO failed to materialize, state practice and, ultimately, a fundamental revision of the treaty, incorporated these functions into the GATT.[2]

Since 1947, the GATT has undergone slow but remarkable growth and change. With originally 27 contracting parties, composed largely of developed states, there are now more than 120, representing a great variety of stages of development.[3] The original legal text has witnessed tremendous expansion: while the core text of the GATT has been amended only incrementally, GATT law is now composed of a large number of agreements supplementing the original text, now known as the "GATT 1994." The total corpus of GATT law is further supplemented by a large number of understandings, practices, and dispute settlement reports, all the result of the institutional life of the GATT, which itself has developed slowly and incrementally over the years. This institutional dimension of the GATT was finally formalized in 1994 with the establishment of the WTO, membership in which carries the obligation to abide by the GATT 1994. Most important of all, as a result of eight rounds of multilateral trade negotiations, the GATT has come to define the most important trading obligations of its contracting parties concerning trade in goods and increasingly concerning trade in services, investments, and the protection of intellectual property. The GATT 1994 is thus the central legal instrument in the world today defining the international trading system.

B. The Texts

The GATT is a multilateral treaty signed by Canada and 22 other countries in 1947.[4] The GATT entered into force on a provisional basis on January 1, 1948 since it was then expected that the GATT would be shortly superseded by the much more comprehensive constitution of a future International Trade Organization. Such a constitution has never fully emerged, although a fully fledged international organization was finally created on January 1, 1995 in the form of the WTO.

The text of the GATT 1947 remained in force on a provisional basis until 1996 when it was superseded by the GATT 1994. The text of the GATT 1947 is made up of four parts. Part 1 sets out the basic obligations of MFN and NT of goods. Part 2 incorporates a

1 The capitalized version indicates the plenary meeting of the contracting parties to the GATT envisaged in arts. XXII and XXV.

2 See Jackson, *World Trade and the Law of the GATT* (1969), chapter 8, *infra*.

3 Up to 20 more states now apply the GATT in their relations with other states. Among the major states of the world which, for historical reasons, were not contracting parties by 1996, both China and Russia and other members of the former USSR had applied for membership or had been granted observer status in anticipation of a bid for membership.

4 Can. TS 1948, no. 31, also reprinted in BISD, vol. IV (1969).

number of other basic rules governing the treatment of goods. Part 3 covers the duties of transparency, consultation, and joint decision making of the contracting parties. Part 4, added in 1965, covers the treatment of goods from developing countries.

The GATT 1994 includes both the original articles of the GATT 1947, as supplemented by various amendments made to that text over the ensuing years. However, the major part of the GATT 1994 is now composed of four annexes. Annex 1 includes a number of agreements supplementing the basic text. These agreements deal with such matters as trade in agricultural goods and textiles, sanitary and phytosanitary measures, technical barriers to trade, anti-dumping duties, subsidies, customs valuation, preshipment inspection, rules of origin, import licensing, safeguards, and trade-related investment measures. The GATT 1994 also includes a number of understandings that govern the interpretation and application of a number of GATT articles, including those dealing with the settlement of disputes. Annex 2 contains the General Agreement on Trade in Services (the GATS), which for the first time extends the disciplines of the GATT to services. Annex 3 sets out the Agreement on Trade-Related Aspects of Intellectual Property Rights. Annex 4 contains the Plurilateral Trade Agreements on Government Procurement, Civil Aircraft, Dairy Products, and Bovine Meat.

WTO members are required to accept all the obligations of the GATT 1994, except the Plurilateral Trade Agreements of Annex 4, which are only binding on those states that accept them.

The formal text of the GATT 1994 is completed by the schedules of concessions on goods and services deposited by contracting parties with the Director General. These tariff schedules and the schedules on services are part of the GATT and the GATS and, as such, are binding on the contracting parties; they form the basis of the customs tariff and service commitments of each country.

A number of other texts complete the full picture of the GATT-WTO law. Since the early years, it has been the practice of the CONTRACTING PARTIES to adopt "interpretations" of the text of the GATT. These interpretations are authoritative.[5] The GATT, and now the WTO Secretariat maintains numerous official records of the plenary meetings of the CONTRACTING PARTIES, the GATT Council, and other GATT deliberative bodies.[6] The most important decisions, reports, and documents are reprinted in an annual supplement to the *Basic Instruments and Selected Documents.* Among the documents reprinted are the reports of working parties formed to study applications for admission to the GATT and the subsequent protocols of accession of new contracting parties. Of particular significance are the reports of working parties on broad policy questions, and of panels responsible for the hearing and settlement of trade disputes between contracting parties. Decisions of various GATT decision-making bodies and deliberative organs are selectively reproduced in the *GATT Analytical Index.*[7] All these

5 *Ibid.* They are reprinted as Annex I.

6 Unfortunately most of these records have been restricted for considerable periods of time. In 1996, it was decided to make many WTO documents public.

7 The 6th edition was issued in 1995. This volume does not have authoritative status in its own right but it does reproduce decisions deemed to reflect authoritative GATT practice.

practices have been carried forward by the WTO. Finally, the GATT 1994 is completed by a number of ministerial decisions and declarations concluding the Uruguay Round of Multilateral Trade Negotiations, made in the Trade Negotiations Committee at its meetings on December 15, 1993 and on April 14, 1994.[8]

Also relevant to understanding the GATT-WTO law is the domestic legislative and regulatory practice of WTO members. Beyond this, there exists extensive literature on both the broad economic policies followed by the GATT and on the many technical rules of customs administration.

C. The Functions of the GATT

The GATT 1994 is a complex phenomenon. It is above all the most important treaty regulating the conduct of international trade and indeed one of the most significant treaties in the world today. But the GATT is much more than a treaty. The GATT has traditionally been described as having four functions: (1) the negotiation and setting of tariffs; (2) a code of rules governing international trade between contracting parties; (3) a forum for negotiating and resolving international trade disputes; and (4) an international institution that exists to facilitate the discussion and making of the rules governing international trade between the contracting parties. These traditional functions have been both clarified and expanded with the creation of the WTO and the adoption of the GATT 1994.

The first function reflects the traditional task of liberalizing trade in goods, which the original contracting parties sought to perform in 1947 as part of post-war reconstruction. The GATT has performed its mission of tariff reduction with extraordinary success. In eight successive rounds of trade negotiations, the average developed-country tariff on manufactured and semi-manufactured goods has been reduced from over 50 percent to a level close to 4 percent. Large categories of goods now enter the WTO members free of any tariff. For developed market economy countries, the tariff has ceased to be a significant barrier to the entry of such goods. However, even after the Uruguay Round, tariffs continue to be higher in developing and non-market countries. The successful completion of the Uruguay Round and the adoption of the GATS has added the liberalization of trade in services to the functions of the WTO. Barriers to service trade remain much higher than tariff barriers, but an important first step has been taken by the WTO members.

The drafters of the GATT concentrated on tariff questions but also succeeded in taking a minimum of rules dealing with non-tariff barriers from existing drafts of the ITO Constitution. The result is that the GATT has always served as a code of rules for the conduct of international trade, although on a more modest scale than that originally envisaged in 1947. A further limitation on the GATT system was that most of the rules set out in part II of the GATT were only binding on the original signatories subject to legislation in place at the time of signature. This has changed with the adoption of the GATT 1994. GATT rules are binding in their entirety and the many agreements on the

8 See *The Results of the Uruguay Round of Multilateral Trade Negotiations: The Legal Texts* (1994). For a history of the Uruguay Round see Croome, *Reshaping the World Trading System* (Geneva: WTO, 1995); and Preeg, *Traders in a Brave New World* (Chicago: University of Chicago Press, 1996).

elimination or the disciplining of non-tariff barriers contained in the first three annexes to the GATT 1994 are binding on all WTO members, and are subject to a common form of compulsory dispute settlement. Only the plurilateral trade agreements of Annex 4 contain obligations that are limited to the states that assume them. The GATT's function as a code of rules has thus been immensely strengthened by the adoption of the GATT 1994.

The GATT rapidly became a forum for dispute resolution during the early years, as the practice developed of referring a trade dispute between two contracting parties involving the alleged violation of GATT obligations or "nullification or impairment of benefits" accruing under it, to a panel of experts drawn from the GATT diplomatic community. The purpose of the process was to facilitate a settlement of the dispute rather than to adjudicate, and GATT panel proceedings and their conclusions were marked by a high degree of pragmatism and a concern for sound economic policy over the letter of the law. But panel reports came, over the years, to represent something close to a body of authoritative interpretation of the GATT. The adjudicative function is now one of the central aspects of the GATT having been the object of constant concern and comment over the years.[9] The GATT 1994 Understanding on Dispute Settlement, administered by the WTO Dispute Settlement Body, is the culmination of 40 years of incremental development based on this practice. The GATT 1994 also brought about a major change in the nature of the dispute resolution system with the addition of an appellate body charged with delivering decisions in response to appeals on points of law.

D. Parties to the GATT

Until the 1980s, the GATT was viewed as a rich man's club. The major developing countries remained outside and were subject neither to the disciplines nor to the advantages of GATT membership. This changed through the 1980s with the reappraisal of economic policies in those countries, and in 1996 the WTO has more than 120 members, including all the major developing states except those of the Middle East. A number of other states are reported to be following the rules of the GATT without being formally bound. In 1996, some 30 states were seeking WTO membership. China had sought to reassume its GATT membership but as of 1996 only enjoyed observer status. The countries of Central Europe and some Eastern European states have joined or have reconfirmed their membership on the basis of new protocols of adhesion since 1990. As of 1996, the former USSR enjoyed observer status with a view to eventual entry. This dramatic extension of the GATT membership is indicative of the fact that the WTO, and the GATT before it, have become the centre of international trade policy making.

Despite the fact that the GATT 1947 was not based on any institutional structure, over the years a modest institution did in fact emerge on an ad hoc basis complete with a modest budget, deliberative committees, and a Secretariat led by a director general. But it was not until the GATT 1994 laid the foundations of the WTO that a genuine international

---

9 See, for instance, *Understanding Regarding Notification, Consultation, Dispute Settlement and Surveillance*, BISD, 26th Supp. 210 (1978-79) and Mid-Term Review Agreements, 21 April 1989, GATT Doc. MTN.TNC/11 (MIN) analyzed in chapter 15, *infra*.

organization emerged. The WTO still falls short of the model of the ITO, it is simply an institutional structure and does not possess all the attributes of the UN specialized agencies, and the obligations of membership are defined in Annexes 1, 2, and 3 of the GATT 1994. Among the benefits of the new institutional structure are the creation of a wider range of standing deliberative bodies, the better administration of a long-term work program, and the consolidation of a comprehensive dispute settlement system.[10]

E. What Does GATT-WTO Law Cover?

First and foremost the GATT 1994 covers international trade in goods, reportedly worth over $4,800 billion US in 1995. One of the objectives of the Uruguay Round of Multilateral Trade Negotiations was to extend the GATT to cover trade in services. International trade in services was reportedly worth $1,200 billion US in 1995.[11] A further objective of the Uruguay Round was to conclude new agreements under the GATT covering certain aspects of trade-related investment measures and the protection of intellectual property rights.

The core concern of the GATT-WTO continues to be the removal of barriers to the trade in goods, especially the reduction and fixing of tariff barriers. However, since the early 1970s, the GATT contracting parties were preoccupied with non-tariff barriers—tariffs having ceased to be the principal barrier to international trade as a result of the great reductions that have occurred. The principal focus of Annex 1 of the GATT 1994, as already stated, is now upon non-tariff barriers and deals with dumping, subsidies, import licensing, customs procedures, customs valuation, safeguard measures, and other non-tariff barriers in great detail. The Uruguay Round negotiations went beyond tariff and non-tariff barriers and also resulted in extensive new provisions on trade in services and the protection of intellectual property.

Although originally all negotiations were conducted on the basis of economic equality, the GATT has attempted in various ways to adapt itself to the special problems posed by different levels of international economic development. This was evident in part IV of the GATT, adopted in 1965, and the special provisions of the codes of 1979. With the increase in membership of the GATT, economic development came to be one of the central themes of all multilateral trade negotiations, although this no longer necessarily takes the form of broad exemptions of LDC contracting parties from the provisions of the GATT.

II. RELEVANCE OF THE GATT TO CANADIAN LAW

A. How the GATT-WTO Affects the Domestic Legal Order

The GATT-WTO serves both as a source of law and as a restraint on domestic law making, thereby having a profound influence on the law governing Canada's international

10 The Delegation of Canada to the Uruguay Round of Multilateral Trade Negotiations was among those most active in proposing the new institutional structure of the WTO.

11 WTO Press Release, 22 March 1996, no 96-0999.

trade. While Canadian courts and administrative tribunals[12] continue to maintain the very conservative position that treaties do not per se create rights in Canadian law, the GATT-WTO is the true basis for Canada's international trade law.

The GATT is the basis for much of the legislation that presently governs the movement of goods in and out of Canada. Thus, the Customs Tariff established under the Customs Tariff Act is largely the result of negotiations conducted under the aegis of the GATT. The Brussels Customs Nomenclature upon which the current customs classification system is based was adopted by Canada and the United States as a result of pressure exercised by GATT contracting parties. The rules of the Customs Act[13] governing customs valuation were first adopted as a consequence of Canada's ratification of the GATT Valuation Code of 1979 and subsequently amended to conform to the Agreement on Implementation of Article VII of the GATT 1994.[14] Trade retaliation against dumped or subsidized goods is governed by the Special Import Measures Act,[15] which was first adopted subsequent to Canada's ratification of the GATT Anti-Dumping and Subsidies codes of 1979 and subsequently amended to bring it into conformity with the GATT 1994.[16] Other retaliatory measures are taken pursuant to the Customs Act, but the application of these trade remedies is governed by the limits set by the appropriate articles of the GATT 1994. Further, the right of foreign companies to bid for federal contracts in Canada is governed by rules made pursuant to the GATT 1994 Agreement on Government Procurement, to which Canada is a party.[17] Since 1995, both the federal and provincial governments, have undertaken the process of implementing their commitments with respect to trade in services.[18]

In many respects, the impact of the GATT goes beyond the legislative process and has an important effect upon administrative policies. The GATT dispute settlement process can reach out to the domestic Canadian regulatory and administrative process. For example, the policies of the former Foreign Investment Review Agency (FIRA) had to be altered as a result of the GATT panel report in response to a US complaint.[19] Similarly, the decision of the Canadian Import Tribunal against EC ground beef imports,[20] in

---

12 Most recently in *Tomato Paste,* [1993] CITT no. 49 (QL).

13 RSC 1985, c. 1 (2nd Supp.), as am. See chapter 10, *infra.*

14 See an Act to implement the Agreement Establishing the World Trade Organization, SC 1994, c. 47, ss. 70-72.

15 RSC 1985, c. S-15, as am. RSC 1985, c. 23 (1st Supp.), c. 1 (2nd Supp.), c. 47 (4th Supp.), and SC 1988, c. 65. See chapter 11, *infra.*

16 See the Act to implement the Agreement Establishing the World Trade Organization, *supra,* note 14, ss. 144-89.

17 See the amendments to the Canadian International Trade Tribunal Act in ss. 27-47 of the WTO Agreement Implementation Act.

18 See chapter 9 on services.

19 *Canada—Administration of the Foreign Investment Review Act* (FIRA), BISD 30th Supp. 140 (1984); *Canada—Import Restrictions on Ice Cream and Yohgurt,* BISD, 36th Supp. 68 (1989). See s. 46 (Repeal of FIRA) Investment Canada Act, SC 1985, c. 20.

20 *Boneless Manufacturing Beef Originating in or Exported from the EEC* (1986), 12 CER 62.

response to the complaint of western beef producers, gave rise to a GATT panel which held that primary beef producers had no standing to make a dumping complaint against ground beef imports.[21] The successful EC complaint against the markups placed upon European wines sold by provincial liquor boards[22] has had a significant impact upon the pricing policies of these institutions, as has the GATT panel report on Canadian practices governing the sale of beer.[23]

Beyond the formal dispute settlement process, the decisions taken within the many GATT standing committees concerning the resolution of international trading problems or the solutions negotiated within GATT by Canadian representatives, have a profound impact on the development of Canada's domestic policies affecting international trade. Under the WTO, discussions have begun on a wider and more diverse range of issues including the impact of trade on environmental and labour policies, trade in waste products, investment protection policies, and competition policies. In time, it is to be expected that the results of these deliberations will have their impact on governmental policies and legislation.

Since the parties to the GATT 1994 are sovereign states, private individuals and corporations have no standing to participate directly in WTO debates or in WTO dispute settlement proceedings. The primary way for private interests to make their views known in WTO circles is to influence their governments.

B. How Is the GATT Invoked?

The GATT 1994 is an intergovernmental agreement and, as such, it binds only those states that have accepted it. The GATT 1994 is binding on all contracting parties; only the plurilateral trade agreements of Annex 4 are restricted to those states that specifically accept them. This being the case, does the GATT 1994 have any direct applicability to corporations or individuals in Canada? The answer to this question depends very much on the status that is accorded to treaties in Canadian law.

Unlike certain jurisdictions where it is at least theoretically possible for nationals to resort directly to the terms of a treaty,[24] the position in Canadian law is that a treaty

---

21 *Imposition of Countervailing Duties on Imports of Manufacturing Beef from the EEC*, SCM/85, 13 October 1987. Canada resisted formal adoption of this report.

22 *Canada—Import, Distribution and Sale of Alcoholic Drinks by Canadian Provincial Marketing Agencies*, BISD, 35th Supp. 37 (1989) (*EEC v. Canada*).

23 *Canada—Import, Distribution and Sale of Certain Alcoholic Drinks by Provincial Marketing Agencies*, BISD, 39th Supp. 27 (1992) (*US v. Canada*).

24 See Hilf, Jacobs, and Petersman (eds.), *The European Community and GATT* (Boston: Kluwer Law Int'l., 1986) for a discussion of the situation in several European jurisdictions and in the United States. For recent developments as to the status of GATT law before the jurisdictions of the EC (i.e., the Court of Justice and the Court of First Instance), in particular the largely policy-based rulings by the EC jurisdictions that deny GATT law the status of directly applicable and effective provisions and thus deprive individuals of relying on them before the EC courts, see Castilly de la Torre, "The Status of

(The footnote is continued on the next page.)

must be incorporated into domestic law by formal legislative action. The law is to be found in the statute itself rather than the treaty, unless the treaty is reproduced or referred to in the statute.[25] This leaves little room for direct application of the GATT. There has been some attenuation of this rule in that the courts are increasingly willing to look to a treaty for assistance when the text of the statute is ambiguous, and more generally when it is necessary to understand the true nature and purpose of such a statute.[26]

Although the direct application of GATT rules to private persons and corporations in Canada is not the rule, the GATT has an ever-increasing influence on persons and decision making in Canada. Major interest groups, be they customs brokers, lawyers, accountants, farmers, bankers, exporters, manufacturers, or consumers, must take WTO policies into account. Frequently, such groups feel called upon to make representations to the Canadian government as to present or future developments within WTO. During the Uruguay Round of Multilateral Trade Negotiations, certain interest groups joined forces with their US counterparts to lobby foreign delegations to the negotiations. The WTO Secretariat is prepared to meet with private parties from member states in order to be informed of their views but is in no position to respond to their wishes since it plays a strictly neutral role and has no direct regulatory function. The WTO Secretariat will not receive representations from private parties relating to a dispute pending before a panel procedure.

In the normal course of events, private interests in Canada desiring to influence the WTO must deal with the Department of Foreign Affairs and International Trade and, in particular, those officials answering to the Minister of International Trade. If a panel dispute is involved, representations on the appropriate course of action can be made to the Minister of International Trade. Ultimate responsibility for the conduct of the panel rests entirely with the federal government and not with the provincial governments or the private parties whose interests are involved.

C. Constitutional Authority for Implementing GATT Obligations

As a general rule, the central government of a federal state is responsible for the implementation of all the international obligations of the state and it is not allowed to plead constitutional limitations as an excuse or to diminish its obligations. The Government of Canada, having signed the GATT in 1947 and adhered to all subsequent obligations on

---

24 Continued …

GATT in EC Law, Revisited. The Consequences of the Judgment on the Banana Import Regime for the Enforcement of the Uruguay Round Agreement" (1995), 29 *J of World Trade* 53-68 and Kuilwijk, *The European Court of Justice and the GATT Dilemma: Public Interest Versus Individual Rights?* (Beuningen, NL: Nexed ED, 1996) (Crit. Eur. Studies, vol. 1).

25 See, for instance, Special Import Measures Act, *supra*, note 15, s. 2(1) definition of Subsidies and Countervailing Duties Agreement.

26 *R v. Crown Zellerbach*, [1988] 1 SCR 401; *American Farm Bureau Federation et al. v. Canadian Import Tribunal et al.*, [1990] 2 SCR 1324, 74 DLR (4th) 449.

behalf of Canada, and claiming, as it does, sole authority to conduct Canada's international relations, is subject to this rule. In principle, other contracting parties to the GATT look to the federal government to implement Canada's obligations.

More specifically, article XXIV of the GATT contains the following ambiguous rule:

> 12. Each contracting party shall take such necessary measures as may be available to it to ensure observance of the provisions of this Agreement by the regional and local governments and authorities within its territory.

This provision can be read to mean that the federal government is only under an obligation of means, but under no obligation of result, as to provincial respect for the GATT, and this has been the historical position of the Government of Canada. This interpretation is certainly plausible,[27] but it does not preclude the argument that if the provinces fail to respect the GATT, Canada will be internationally responsible for nullification and impairment of other contracting parties' rights.[28] This appears to be the thrust of the GATT panel reports in the 1985 Gold Coins complaint by South Africa against Canada,[29] and the 1988 decision of the panel on *Import, Distribution and Sale of Alcoholic Drinks by Canadian Provincial Marketing Agencies*, on the complaint brought by the EC,[30] as well as the subsequent panel report on the sale and distribution of beer.[31] In these cases, the foreign contracting parties looked to Canada to alter the offending practices. This has happened with the cooperation of the provincial governments, since they generally realize that they have a strong interest in ensuring the compatibility of their policies and legislation with the GATT 1994.

The question remains, however, of the extent of the legislative jurisdiction of Parliament to regulate Canada's international trade. Some authors, particularly in English Canada, continue to argue that Parliament has broad jurisdiction to implement any international treaty.[32] This view flies in the face of the statement of the Privy Council in 1937 that "... there is no such thing as treaty legislation as such ... ."[33] Although the treaty argument is not convincing, there is a very strong argument to be made that Parliament enjoys broad jurisdiction to regulate international trade and general trade and

27 Bernier, "Le GATT et le Commerce d'état dans les pays à économie de marché: Le cas des monopoles provinciaux des alcools au Canada" (1975), 13 *Can. Ybk. Int'l. L* 98.

28 de Mestral, "L'application aux gouvernements et administrations régionaux et locaux de l'Accord général sur les tariffs douaniers et le commerce et des accords et décisions issus des négociations commerciales multilatérales" (1984), 1 *Rev. Q Dr. Int'l.* 105.

29 Canada has refused to accept this report. It therefore remains confidential and unpublished but not unknown.

30 *Supra*, note 22.

31 *Supra*, note 23.

32 For a forceful contemporary restatement of this position see Ziegel, "Treaty-Making and Implementing Powers in Canada: The Continuing Dilemma," in *Contemporary Problems of International Law: Essays in Honour of Georg Schwarzenberger* (1988), at 333. For a remarkable statement of the provincial position see Morin, "La Personnalité Internationale du Québec" (1984), 1 *Rev. Q Dr. Int'l.* 163.

33 *Labour Conventions Reference,* [1937] AC 326, at 351.

commerce, under section 92(2) of the Constitution Act 1867, and that this power embraces much, if not all, that is covered by the GATT with respect to goods and the conditions of their entry and access to Canadian markets.[34] But as the ambit of the GATT 1994 has been expanded to cover services and investments, the question of provincial legislative jurisdiction over the implementation of these GATT rules remains open, and it is perhaps significant that the GATT 1994 implementing legislation did not purport to bind the provincial crowns or give the Governor in Council the power to impose respect for GATT obligations upon reluctant provincial governments.[35] It would seem difficult to assert that Parliament could unilaterally impose obligations upon provincial crowns with respect to their procurement policies and, as the WTO expands its consideration of environmental and labour questions, this uncertainty in respect of the scope of federal jurisdiction can only increase.

Irrespective of the international or constitutional law position, the practice in Canada is now for the federal government to resort to consultation and close cooperation with the provinces on the implementation of Canada's WTO obligations, the conduct of disputes involving provincial law or policies, and on the negotiation of new obligations. Since 1988, industry consultation on international trade policy questions has been instituted through a network of consultative groups representing the different sectors of Canadian international industry and commerce. These consultative arrangements have remained in place after the conclusion of the Uruguay Round.[36]

III. TRADE IN GOODS—HOW THE WTO OPERATES

A. General Principles

The law of the WTO continues to be grounded in the original GATT text that sets out a number of basic principles that continue to be of central importance. These principles

---

34 de Mestral, "L'évolution des rapports entre le droit canadien et le droit international un demi-siècle après l'affaire des conventions internationales du travail" (1987), 25 *Can. Ybk. Int'l L* 301.

35 See ss. 4 and 13 of the WTO Agreement Implementation Act on the one hand and s. 20 of the North American Free Trade Agreement Implementation Act on the other.

36 For a more recent criticism of the Labour Conventions doctrine, see Howse, "NAFTA and the Constitution: Does Labour Conventions Really Matter Any More?" (1994), 5 *Const. Forum* 54-59; Howse, "The Labour Conventions Doctrine in an Era of Global Interdependence: Rethinking the Constitutional Dimensions of Canada's External Economic Relations" (1990), 16 *Can. Bus. LJ* 160 and Strom and Finkle, "Treaty Implementation: The Canadian Game Needs Australian Rules" (1993), 25 *Ottawa L Rev.* 39; for the opposite view, arguing against the adoption of Australian precedents to overturn the ILO case and subsequent cases decided by the Supreme Court of Canada see Struthers, "Treaty Implementation ... Australian Rules": A Rejoinder" (1994), 26 *Ottawa L Rev.* 305. Richards, "The Canadian Constitution and International Economic Relations" in Brown and Smith (eds.), *Canadian Federalism: Meeting Global Economic Challenges?* (Kingston, Ont.: Institute of Intergovernmental Relations, 1991), at 57-67 and Bernier, "L'Impact de l'internationalisation sur le fonctionnement de l'état: le partage constitutionnel des compétences" in *ibid.* (both authors arguing against major revision of division of powers with respect to treaty implementation).

are now extensively fleshed out and in many cases expanded by the Multilateral Agreements on Trade in Goods of Annex 1A of the GATT 1994. They are also affected by the Understanding on Dispute Settlement Procedures of Annex 2, and the Trade Policy Review Mechanism of Annex 3. The first section of this part reviews some of these general principles and the second section is devoted to a review of the operation of the GATT 1994 agreements and understandings.

1. Most-Favoured-Nation Treatment

Non-discriminatory treatment of foreign goods is the fundamental norm of the GATT. In order to ensure respect for the principle of non-discrimination, two basic standards are enshrined in the GATT: the MFN and the NT standard.

The MFN standard of the GATT is set out in article I.1:

> With respect to customs duties and charges of any kind imposed on or in connection with importation or exportation or imposed on the international transfer of payments for imports or exports, and with respect to the method of levying such duties and charges, and with respect to all rules and formalities in connection with importation and exportation, and with respect to all matters referred to in paragraphs 2 and 4 of Article III, any advantage, favour, privilege or immunity granted by any contracting party to any product originating in or destined for any other country shall be accorded immediately and unconditionally to the like product originating in or destined for the territories of all other contracting parties.

No other article of the GATT has such a significant and wide-reaching impact. By virtue of this article, any tariff concession made by one WTO member to another is immediately and unconditionally made available to all other WTO members. A single concession is transformed into 120 concessions without the others having to offer any reciprocal benefit, thus creating potentially new trading opportunities for all of the states. Furthermore, once the concession lowering a tariff barrier is made, all WTO members have an interest in ensuring that it is not subsequently raised. The operation of the MFN standard is thus both simple and extraordinarily effective.

The practical result of article I.1 has been the lowering of the average industrial tariffs of developed countries from over 50 percent in 1947 to close to 3 percent in 1996. Arguably, this is and continues to be the cornerstone of the whole WTO edifice. The scope of the WTO MFN clause is extremely broad, covering not only imports but exports and a host of charges apart from tariffs, including the conditions of sale, taxation of imported goods, and the full range of administrative procedures involving exports.

In principle, the MFN clause prohibits all discriminatory treatment of imported goods. This being the case, all exceptions must be specifically authorized. Article XX provides for general exceptions to protect human health, public morals, and the environment. Article XXI authorizes exceptions to protect national security. Other discriminatory measures such as anti-dumping and countervailing duties and retaliatory measures against contracting parties that fail to meet their obligations are also expressly allowed. Preferential treatment, while in principle a violation of the MFN standard, is allowed to partners in a free trade area or a customs union as specifically provided for by article XXIV. From time to time, other preferential arrangements have been allowed by waiver action taken by the CONTRACTING PARTIES to the GATT under article XXV.5—the most notable example being the approval and subsequent renewal of the Generalized System of Preferences (GSP) granted to developing countries in 1971. Another example of particular importance to Canada was the approval of the Canada-US Auto Pact by waiver in 1966.

After the adoption of the Anti-Dumping Code in 1968 and even more so after the adoption of a series of complementary agreements at the end of the Tokyo Round of Multilateral Trade Negotiations in 1979, the MFN principle was under great pressure, since these agreements applied only between signatories of the specific agreement and granted no rights to non-signatories. This amounted, in essence, to a regime of conditional MFN treatment within the scope of matters covered by these agreements. Some commentators and delegations expressed the fear that this created the danger of divided and, ultimately, of weakened GATT obligations. Fortunately, this threat to the integrity of the MFN principle has been lifted by the GATT 1994, which has done much to bring unity and coherence to the law of the WTO by requiring all WTO members to subscribe to all the rules of annexes 1, 2, and 3.

2. *National Treatment*

The second means of guaranteeing non-discriminatory treatment of imports is the NT standard. Article III.4 of the GATT states in part:

> The products of the territory of any contracting party imported into the territory of any other contracting party shall be accorded treatment no less favourable than that accorded to like products of national origin in respect to all laws, regulations and requirements affecting their internal sale, offering for sale, purchase, transportation, distribution or use … .

This article requires that imported goods be treated as if they were domestic products; any form of discrimination against them is prohibited. The point of comparison here is the treatment that the importing state affords its own products and no longer, as is the case with respect to the MFN standard, the products of a third country. The NT standard thus reflects the most advantageous position possible for the imported product. This principle has been applied and interpreted by many dispute settlement panels.[37] Perhaps the broadest formulation of the principle is to be found in the panel report on the sale and distribution of beer by Canadian liquor monopolies, where the panel ruled that the principle requires the availability of "competitive opportunities at least equal to those awarded to domestic products."[38] Recent panel reports have thus moved beyond a

37 National treatment was an issue notably in the following cases: *Italian Discrimination against Imported Agricultural Machinery*, BISD, 7th Supp. 60 (1958); *EEC—Measures on Animal Feed Proteins*, BISD, 25th Supp. 65 (1989); *Canada—Administration of the Foreign Investment Review Act*, BISD, 30th Supp. 137 (1984); and *United States—Taxes on Petroleum and Certain Imported Substances*. See also the GATT, Analytical Index at 148 on panel rulings on art. III: 4.

38 See, for example, *Canada—Imports, Distribution and Sale of Certain Alcoholic Drinks by Provincial Marketing Agencies*, *supra*, note 23 at 78f. citing *United States—Section 337 of the Tariff Act of 1930*, BISD, 36th Supp. 345 (1989).

purely formal standard of comparison to a more substantively based approach to the determination of national treatment.

As with MFN treatment, any exception must be specifically authorized. Thus, article III.8(a) exempts from the NT standard purchases made by governmental agencies of products for governmental purposes.

3. Non-Discrimination

Together, the MFN and the NT principles amount to a principle of non-discrimination, which is of the essence of the commitment that WTO members must make to each other.

4. Transparency

Closely related to the above principles is the principle of transparency. Non-discrimination requires that the laws, regulations, and practices of WTO members be open and transparent in order that all may be assured that the system of multilateral trade rules is in fact operating. This principle is of the essence of a number of agreements in annex 1A and is constantly stressed in WTO debates.

5. Dispute Settlement[39]

The GATT 1994 makes the commitment to compulsory dispute settlement almost a general principle of the WTO. The Understanding on Dispute Settlement of Annex 3 further refines the panel process by making it virtually compulsory when a WTO member invokes it, by making the process applicable to virtually all the law of the GATT 1994 and by adding an appeal procedure from panel reports that gives binding rulings on points of law. This amounts to a commitment that is close to a presumption of a right to compulsory dispute settlement applicable in all cases except those where dispute settlement is specifically excluded.

6. The Commitment to Tariffs and the Prohibition of Quotas

The preferred trade barrier of the WTO is the tariff. In principle, all other barriers are prohibited or must be justified. It follows that quotas—restriction of the number, volume, value, or origin of foreign products—are prohibited. Thus, article XI.1 states:

> No prohibitions or restrictions other than duties, taxes or other charges, whether made effective through quotas, import or export licenses or other measures, shall be instituted or maintained by any contracting party on the importation of any product of the territory of any other contracting party or on the exportation or sale for export of any product destined for the territory of any other contracting party.

This article serves as a restraint on the imposition of new quotas and also has served as the basis for pressure brought by GATT contracting parties on those who continued to maintain quotas through the 1950s and 1960s pursuant to their grandfathered rights

39 For a full discussion of the WTO dispute settlement procedures, see chapter 15, *infra*.

under the Protocol of Provisional Application.[40] Quotas made directly or indirectly through the technique of import licensing became harder to maintain in 1979 as a result of the adoption of the first Agreement on Import Licensing Procedures,[41] subsequently renewed and expanded by the GATT 1994 Annex 1A. The GATT 1994 has also made significant progress towards the disciplining of use of quotas in the Agreement on Textiles and Clothing.[42] The Agreement on Agriculture[43] requires that all WTO members transform their agricultural quotas, formerly justified under article XI.2(c) into tariff rate quotas.[44]

7. *Exceptions and Waivers of Obligations*

Articles XX and XXI provide for a number of exceptions to the application of the general rules of the GATT 1994. Article XX allows for a range of exceptions subject to the proviso that "such measures are not applied in a manner which would constitute a means of arbitrary or unjustifiable discrimination … ." Subject to this limitation, non-conforming national measures may be adopted that are necessary to protect public morals and human health, national treasures, or are necessary to secure compliance with laws or regulations. Article XX(g) allows measures "relating to the conservation of exhaustible natural resources if such measures are made effective in conjunction with restrictions on domestic production or consumption." This provision is applicable to trade in natural resources such as fisheries products and, in the absence of a more specific reference to environmental concerns, is likely to be invoked in this context, in conjunction with the reference to human and plant health in article XX(b). During the Uruguay Round, some delegations were in favour of adding an explicit reference to the environment. These concerns were heightened by the two dispute settlement panels arising out of Mexican and European Communities (EC) complaints against the application of the US Marine Mammals Protection Act,[45] where the issue of measure taken for

---

40 This grandfather right has been eliminated by the GATT 1994.

41 BISD, 26th Supp. 154 (1978-79).

42 Annex 1A.

43 Annex 1a.

44 Canada and its principal trading partners undertook this process in 1995. Canadian implementation of this obligation was the object of the first dispute under chapter 20 of the North American Free Trade Agreement. See *In the Matter of Tariffs Applied by Canada to Certain US-Origin Agricultural Products*, Final Report of the Panel, 2 December 1996, CDA-95-2008-1.

45 *United States—Restrictions on Imports of Tuna*, GATT Doc. DS 21/R, BISD, 39th Supp. 155 (1991), reprinted in 30 *ILM* 1594 (1991); *United States—Restrictions on Imports of Tuna*, GATT Doc. DS 29/R, June 1994, 33 *ILM* 839 (1994) (*EC v. United States/Tuna II*); see also *United States—Prohibition of Imports of Tuna and Tuna Products from Canada*, BISD, 29th Supp. 99 (1982); for a fuller treatment of the tuna-dolphin panel rulings and the possibility of invoking art. XX (b) in relation to environmental protection, see Charnovitz, "The Environment vs. Trade Rules: Defogging the Debate" (1993), 23 *Environmental Law* 475; Trebilcock and Howse, *The Regulation of International Trade* (London:

(The footnote is continued on the next page.)

environmental protection was argued but not clearly decided.[46] Similar concerns have been expressed subsequently that trade remedies included in international environmental agreements such as the Montreal Protocol on the Protection of the Ozone Layer might be deemed to be in violation of the GATT and might not be saved by article XX.2.[47] Further, the potential application of this article to trade in water between Canada and the United States was the subject of intense speculation in Canada during the negotiation of the Canada-US Free Trade Agreement in 1987-88.[48]

Perhaps the leading panel report on the application of article XX is that arising out of the complaint against the application by the United States of section 337 of the Tariff Act.[49] In this report, the panel held that non-conforming measures to enforce patent rights could not be adopted where the original measures were themselves in violation of the GATT 1947.[50]

Article XXI is designed to allow WTO members to protect their essential security interests by taking non-conforming measures in time of peace or war, or to implement UN obligations.

A further means of providing exceptions to the rules of the GATT has been the recourse to "waivers" of general obligations by virtue of article XXV.5. The practice of

---

45 Continued ...
Routledge, 1995), 344-50; Petersmann, "International Trade Law and International Environmental Law. Prevention and Settlement of International Environmental Disputes in GATT" (1993), 27 *J of World Trade* 43; Petersmann, *International and European Trade and Environmental Law after the Uruguay Round* (Boston: Kluwer Law International, 1995), 29-35. Trebilcock and Howse, "The Fair Trade—Free Trade Debate: Trade, Labor, and the Environment" (1996), 16 *Int'l. Rev. of Law & Economics* 6 consider the systemic threat to the liberal trading order that unilateral trade measures to impose higher environmental or labour standards may pose.

46 See Petersmann (1993), 27 *J of World Trade* 43, at 60 (discussing *Tuna I*), *supra*, note 45.

47 This fear is echoed in a recent Canadian contribution: Weir, "The GATT and the Unmaking of International Environmental Law" (1996), 6 *Dal. J Leg. Stud.* 1-30 and in McDonald, "Greening the GATT: Harmonizing Free Trade and Environmental Protection in the New World Order" (1993), 23 *Environmental Law* 397, at 450-62; Ward, "Trade and Environment in the Round—And After" (1994), 6 *J of Env'l L* 262, at 279 *et seq.* Walker, *Environmental Protection Versus Trade Liberalization: Finding the Balance* (Brussels: PU de FUSL, 1993), at 108 *et seq.*; Trebilcock and Howse, *The Regulation of International Trade*, *supra*, note 45, at 360 *et seq.* The compatibility of Trade-Related Environmental Measures under Multilateral Environmental Agreements with GATT-WTO obligations has become the focus of the WTO's newly created Committee on Trade and Environment, see Petersmann (1993), 27 *J of World Trade* 43, at 69, *supra*, note 45, citing Report on the GATT Symposium on Trade, Environment and Sustainable Development, GATT Doc. TE 008, of 28 July 1994; Papers presented at the GATT Symposium on Trade, Environment and Sustainable Development, GATT Doc. TE 009, 28 July 1994.

48 See de Mestral and Leith (eds.), *Canadian Water Exports and Free Trade* (Ottawa: Rawson Academy of Aquatic Science, 1989).

49 *United States—Section 337 of the Tariff Act of 1930*, BISD, 36th Supp. 345 (1989).

50 *Ibid.*, at 392.

the GATT was to vote on the requests of contracting parties to be temporarily relieved from specific obligations. Such votes were taken by a two-thirds majority. Although it could be argued that waivers constituted a useful safety valve for contracting parties in difficult situations, some waivers had a devastating effect upon the rules of the GATT, particularly upon trade in agricultural commodities. The Understanding in respect of Obligations under Article XXIV of the GATT 1994 is designed to place a much greater burden on those WTO members seeking waivers from the WTO and places an automatic two-year limit on their duration. Thus, without abolishing waivers, WTO members have made them much harder to obtain and maintain.

B. Operation of the WTO Principles and GATT 1994 Agreements and Understandings Governing Trade in Goods

1. Introduction

The GATT contains the following articles regulating the administration of customs legislation: I, General Most-Favoured-Nation Treatment; II, Schedules of Concessions; III, National Treatment on Internal Taxation and Regulation; VII, Valuation for Customs Purposes; VIII, Fees and Formalities Connected with Importation and Exportation; IX, Marks of Origin; and X, Publication and Administration of Trade Regulations. These articles build on the principles of non-discrimination and transparency that run throughout the GATT and that are essential if the world is to enjoy a free and open international trading system. They are designed to stop WTO members from using different aspects of their customs administration as indirect or hidden barriers to trade. The scope of these basic articles of the GATT 1994 has been greatly expanded by the following multilateral trade agreements in respect of customs procedures:

- The Agreement on Customs Valuation;
- The Agreement on Preshipment Inspection;
- The Agreement on Rules of Origin; and
- The Agreement on Import Licensing Procedures.

Trade in textiles and agricultural goods is governed by certain articles of the GATT, but the law applicable to these goods has been greatly expanded and clarified by:

- The Agreement on Agriculture; and
- The Agreement on Textiles and Clothing.

Trade remedies in respect of dumping, subsidies, and safeguards are the object of articles VI and XIX of the GATT. These articles have been much expanded by:

- The Agreement on the Implementation of Article VI of the GATT 1994 (anti-dumping);
- The Agreement on Subsidies and Countervailing Measures; and
- The Agreement on Safeguards.

These agreements, all found in Annex 1A to the GATT 1994, together with a number of understandings on the interpretation of certain articles and a number of important ministerial decisions and declarations[51] now define the obligations of WTO members in respect of trade in goods.

2. Tariff Binding

The tariff, a tax on the value, weight, or volume of goods, is the only general barrier to the entry of foreign goods allowed by the GATT. The basic function of the GATT has always been to provide a forum for the negotiation and reduction of tariffs. Despite the gradual extension of the scope of GATT and its related codes, tariff reduction has remained at the heart of each of the eight negotiating rounds in which the contracting parties have participated since 1947.

In the early years, tariff reductions were negotiated on a bilateral or product-by-product basis between the principal supplier[52] and the principal buyer countries. Negotiations were—and between developed countries continue to be—on the basis of reciprocity. Thus, tariff reductions on one commodity offered by a WTO party had to be met by reductions of equivalent value offered in return by the other contracting party. As the scope of negotiations was expanded to cover most manufactured and semi-manufactured goods as well as certain primary products, it became impossible to manage negotiations on a product-by-product or a bilateral basis. By the 1960s, it became common for groups of countries to negotiate together with respect to increasingly broad sectors of products. In the most recent rounds of multilateral trade negotiations, it became the custom to seek to achieve reductions in percentage terms on broad categories of goods. Thus, the Tokyo Round of 1973-79 concluded with general commitments to reduce tariffs on industrial goods by 50 percent. The Uruguay Round also was completed on the basis of substantial percentage decreases or the outright elimination of tariffs in many areas.

Once agreement has been reached on new tariff levels, these tariffs are "bound" by virtue of article II.1.[53] The bound tariffs are incorporated in a schedule that sets out all the commitments made by each contracting party. The schedule forms part of the GATT by virtue of article II.7. In principle, the schedules can be changed only by agreement of the other WTO members. The modification of schedules is contemplated by article II as well as articles XXXVIII and XXXVIII bis. These articles create both procedural and substantive barriers to the renegotiation upward of bound tariffs. Unauthorized withdrawals or increases of tariffs can attract retaliation in the form of "compensatory adjustment" by way of the withdrawal or increase of tariffs having equivalent value to those lost. Where increased tariffs negotiated between WTO members have an adverse impact on other members, the latter must receive "adequate compensation," or if not, they may also be authorized to take retaliatory measures. For these reasons, tariffs have seldom been increased.

---

51 *The Results of the Uruguay Round of Multilateral Trade Agreements: The Legal Texts* (Geneva: WTO, 1994).

52 For purposes of modification or withdrawal of a concession, the principal supplier concept is now defined by the Understanding on the Interpretation of Article XXVII of the GATT 1994.

53 Tariff bindings must include "other duties or charges" levied on the bound items. See the Understanding on the Interpretation of Article II:1(b).

The present level of tariffs of industrialized countries on manufactured products, will average between 3 percent to 5 percent by the end of the phase-in period of the Uruguay Round, with many categories of goods being entirely exempt. Tariffs of developing countries are still on average much higher than those of developed countries, but WTO membership has had the same effect on them. For many developing countries, the decision to enter the GATT during the 1980s marked a decision to turn away from protectionism and protectionist import substitution policies toward acceptance of the premises of the liberal international trading order and thus reflected a significant shift of policy. The newly industrialized countries have made dramatic reductions in their tariffs in the 1980s. The countries of Central Europe have also made drastic reductions in their tariff levels since the conclusion of the Uruguay Round and have come much closer to full participation in the liberal international trading system. As the countries of the former USSR move their economies toward the market economy model, it will be necessary for them to establish tariffs and to negotiate tariff levels with other WTO members.

3. Customs Valuation

Article VII sets out the principle that valuation shall be based on the "actual value of the imported merchandise" and not on some arbitrary or fictitious estimate. When the actual value cannot be ascertained, the article requires recourse to the "nearest ascertainable equivalent of such value." The article also precludes the inclusion in the value for customs purposes of internal taxes from which the product was exempted by reason of export. The principles enshrined in this article have been expanded in the Agreement on Implementation of Article VII of the GATT 1994. First adopted in 1979,[54] this agreement imposes a new uniform standard of valuation, the "transaction value." Article 1 of the agreement, which lays down the basic rule, must be read with article 8, which provides for adjustments to be made to the price actually paid when this price does not include certain items that are considered to form part of the customs value. Articles 2 to 7 and Annex 1 set out alternative means of determining customs value when the transaction value cannot be ascertained. In such circumstances, the agreement requires that there be consultation between the customs administration and the importer in order to obtain all relevant information. The agreement establishes a technical committee to oversee its implementation and provides for dispute settlement between WTO members under the general procedure of Annex 2 to the GATT 1994. Special and differential treatment, limited in time, is envisaged to deal with the situation of developing countries.

4. Other Provisions on Customs Administration

Article VIII of the GATT requires that import and export fees be limited strictly to "the approximate cost of services." WTO members are also required to minimize and simplify export formalities. Article X requires that contracting parties promptly publish laws and regulations pertaining to customs valuation and classification or to other rates of

---

54 BISD, 26th Supp. 116 (1978-79).

duty or taxes applicable to imports. No such measure can be applied to imports until it has been duly published. WTO members are required by article X to establish judicial, arbitral, or administrative tribunals or procedures to provide "prompt review" of decisions pertaining to customs administration.

The Agreement on Preshipment Inspection and the Agreement on Import Licensing Procedures are both designed to bring greater transparency to the application of customs administration in these areas. Preshipment inspection systems used by developing countries can either simplify or complicate the process of exportation and importation and the goal of this agreement is to ensure that government agencies or private firms having the authority to issue preshipment certificates of conformity with national rules act in a manner designed to facilitate international trade. Similarly, import licensing procedures used by many countries, particularly in the developing world, to administer quotas and tariff rate quotas have the potential to greatly complicate the process of importation. The second agreement, based on the Tokyo Round code on the same subject, seeks to ensure that procedures are applied in a fair and transparent manner.

The Agreement on Rules of Origin has no analogue in the earlier Tokyo Round codes, although rules of origin have long been seen as a potential source of protective and manipulative behaviour by national customs administrations. This agreement seeks to bring some discipline to national rules of origin immediately by requiring the administrative determinations of origin to be based on a transparent classification system and that they not be used to pursue trade objectives. A process of harmonization is established whereby WTO members should develop common standards and definitions of origin to be based on the alternate criteria that goods originate in the country where the good is wholly obtained or the last country where substantial transformation has been carried out (article 3). This process is to culminate in a ministerial conference. A committee on rules of origin and a Technical Committee are established to conduct the work program as well as responding to problems that arise in the day-to-day administration of national rules of origin (Annex I). The agreement also seeks to ensure that preferential rules of origin implemented in regional or bilateral trade agreements are based on a positive and objective standard and are implemented in a transparent manner (Annex II). Thus, although the immediate impact of the agreement may not be great, the long-term potential for harmonization is considerable.

5. *Trade in Textiles*

One area of trade that has proven to be almost impervious to GATT discipline in developed countries (which are generally most anxious to impose it on others) is that of trade in textiles. Canada is quite typical in this regard, in that it has a large indigenous textile and clothing industry, which employs many people. In principle, this is an area where developing countries have a clear comparative advantage in labour, but no Canadian government has been willing to abolish the barriers to their products. As a result, Canada, the United States, the EC, and Japan have all maintained barriers, generally in the form of quotas, against less-developed country (LDC) textiles.

Originally, some of the quotas on textiles could be justified under the grandfathering provisions of article I and the Protocol of Provisional Application of the GATT

1947, but as the years went by, this basis became harder to maintain as new barriers had to be created. It also became harder for the developed countries to justify such a flagrant deviation from GATT rules and theory at the same time as they attempted to convince developing countries of the virtues of liberalization and the LDCs clamoured for greater access for their goods to the markets of the developed world. On the principle that if sin cannot be eradicated, it is preferable to legalize it as an exception to the general rule, the principal contracting parties to the GATT negotiated the Agreement on Trade in Textiles, which was replaced by the Multi-Fibre Arrangement (MFA)[55] in 1974. The MFA was subsequently extended on four occasions. The MFA was signed by a group of importing and a group of exporting states. The essence of the agreement was the negotiation and the management of a system of import quotas between the parties. Under the MFA, each exporter and importer established a network of quotas. These quotas could be adjusted on a yearly basis but only within a certain limit, thus giving producing states an acquired right to the quotas they had in previous years. The entry of new producing states was possible but inevitably caused disruption to the existing pattern of quotas.

The MFA was an example of managed trade. It was seen as being *sui generis* and not as a precedent for other fields, particularly since it was a clear infringement of the MFN and NT standards. For these reasons, the Tokyo Round unsuccessfully attempted to bring it closer to established GATT principles. The Uruguay Round has been more successful. The Agreement on Textiles and Clothing is designed to bring trade in textiles within the discipline of the WTO. The system of quotas existing under the MFA is not immediately abolished but WTO members are required to bring different categories of textiles and clothing within the GATT 1994 in a number of stages. The new agreement requires all member states to make a declaration listing all textile and clothing quotas existing at the entry into force of the agreement. Within 12 months, WTO members are then required to "integrate into GATT 1994"[56] products accounting for no less than 16 percent of their 1990 imports of textile and clothing goods listed in the annex to the agreement. The effect of this step is to remove the quotas from these products. The remaining 84 percent of products are to be integrated in three stages over a nine-year period. The agreement makes provision for a special safeguard procedure, which allows WTO members to reimpose quotas for up to three years.[57] The agreement also provides for the creation of a Textile Monitoring Board (TMB) to supervise implementation as well as provisions against circumvention. The agreement is under the jurisdiction of the Council for Trade in Goods, which must conduct a review after each stage of implementation, and is subject to the Dispute Settlement Understanding. The agreement terminates at the end of the phase-in periods and cannot be extended.[58]

The Agreement on Textiles and Clothing thus constitutes a significant step toward removing a major anomaly from the practice of the WTO. It also represents an important advantage for developing WTO members. However, given the tremendous obstacles in

---

55 BISD, 21st Supp. 3 (1975), as am.

56 Art. 2.6.

57 Art. 6.

58 Arts. 8 and 9.

the face of full implementation, skepticism has been expressed about the chances of complete implementation within the period envisaged.[59]

6. Trade in Agricultural Products

In principle, agricultural products have been subject to the GATT. However, as a result of recourse to waivers adopted under article XXV.5, contracting parties to the GATT 1947 did much to exclude the application of GATT in practice. The most notable example was the waiver granted to the United States in 1955, and renewed periodically until 1993, allowing the United States to maintain quotas on the importation of a wide range of agricultural commodities.[60] The United States had requested the waiver in order to protect the integrity of its agricultural price and income support programs and other GATT contracting parties took advantage of this situation to implement similar quotas. The Tokyo Round was not successful in bringing agricultural products back under the discipline of the GATT, but the Uruguay Round Agreement on Agriculture represents a major step toward expanding the coverage of the WTO in this most important area of international trade that had been protected from liberalization for too long.

The Agreement on Agriculture is a multifaceted document, premised on the assumption that it would be insufficient to deal with the foreign trade dimension of agricultural products without dealing with the domestic policies that are the cause of so many trade problems in this area. Thus the agreement requires commitments from WTO members limiting domestic support programs and export subsidies. In this area, it replaces the Agreement on Subsidies. The agreement also deals with quotas as well as requiring some modest tariff reductions.

The Agreement on Agriculture covers a wide range of products.[61] Domestic supports, which are often the cause of surpluses that are traded on the international market, are subject to a minimum reduction of 20 percent over a six-year period. This is calculated by reference to the aggregate measure of support during the period 1986-89.[62] Export subsidies are to be reduced by 21 percent in terms of volume of products subsidized and by 36 percent in terms of their cash value over the same six-year period. After the end of this period, subsidies are not to be expanded to replace the reductions. This, in effect, modifies article XVI of the GATT. Furthermore, a variety of non-tariff border measures, particularly import quotas, must all be converted into their tariff equivalents.[63] The ensuing tariffs are subject to a requirement that they be subsequently reduced by 36 percent overall and by 15 percent in each product category. This measure

59 See Howse and Trebilcock, *supra*, note 45, at 325.

60 *United States—Waiver Granted to the US in Connection with Import Restrictions Imposed Under s. 22 of the US Agricultural Adjustment Act*, BISD, 3rd Supp. 3 (1954-55). This waiver has been effectively lifted by the Agreement on Agriculture.

61 All products listed in HS chapters 1-24, see Agreement, Annex 1.

62 Agreement on Agriculture, arts. 1(a), 6, and Annex 3. Direct payments to farmers to reduce areas under cultivation are not subject to this requirement and are non-actionable under the Agreement on Subsidies.

63 In Canada, this has given rise to tariffs between 100 and 300 percent.

must be accompanied by steps that allow at least 3 percent, rising to 5 percent, of the domestic market to be supplied by foreign produce. This is an ambitious program for an area where, with a few exceptions, producers have long lived behind a high protective wall. Not surprisingly, it has been necessary to provide for special safeguard procedures to deal with potential hardship to producers.[64]

C. Non-Tariff Barriers

1. General Considerations

As tariff barriers came down through the decades following 1947, it became increasingly apparent that non-tariff barriers (NTBs) presented a major challenge to the liberal trading order. The Tokyo Round of Multilateral Trade Negotiations, which was launched in 1973, made NTBs a major theme; for the first time tariff barriers ceased to be the central issue of a GATT negotiation. The improvement of the rules disciplining non-tariff barriers continued to be a central theme of the Uruguay Round of Multilateral Trade Negotiations between 1986 and 1994. The GATT 1994 maintains the disciplines of the basic GATT articles and strengthens the substantive provisions of the various agreements found in Annex 1A, in particular the:

- Agreement on the Implementation of Article VI of the GATT 1994 (anti-dumping);
- Agreement on Subsidies and Countervailing Measures;
- Agreement on Safeguards; and
- Agreement on Technical Barriers to Trade.

Also relevant to the discussion of NTBs are the Understanding on the Interpretation of Article XVII of the GATT 1994 and the Agreement on Government Procurement.[65]

Several articles of the GATT address the problems posed by NTBs: IV, Films; V, Freedom of Transit; VI, Anti-Dumping and Countervailing Duties; VIII, Fees and Formalities; XV, Exchange Arrangements; XVI, Subsidies; XVII, State Trading Enterprises; as well as articles XI to XIV on quotas. These articles were taken somewhat at random from the then uncompleted text of the Constitution of the International Trade Organization and added to part II of the GATT in order to provide certain minimum standards, but as the years passed they became increasingly incomplete and outdated. For this reason, the choice before the Tokyo Round and Uruguay Round negotiators was between major amendments to the GATT or the negotiation of other subsidiary agreements. Due to the difficulty in amending the GATT and due to the complexity of implementing such amendments in certain countries, such as the United States, it was decided to choose the second option.

2. Elimination of Quotas

Article XI of the GATT 1994 prohibits the recourse to quantitative restrictions on imports and exports, subject to certain exceptions. Over the years, quotas have given rise to

---

64 The hardship to consumers is not an issue upon which this agreement dwells at great length.

65 This agreement is one of the four plurilateral trade agreements that bind only those WTO members that assume its obligations. Canada and 39 other states were parties in 1996.

numerous disputes within the GATT. In recent years, Canada has been the object of several successful complaints of violation of this article. For example, the domestic sourcing requirements of the FIRA, the Canadian landing requirements of the BC Fisheries Regulations, and the quotas imposed on the importation of ice cream and yogurt were all declared to be in violation of article XI.[66] It is interesting to note that while the quota disputes in the first two decades of the GATT dealt with more traditional forms of quotas, in recent years, article XI has been used successfully to attack export quotas as well as import quotas with respect to natural resources as well as manufactured articles. Members have also successfully attacked barriers having the equivalent effect of quotas.

The text of article XI does provide certain exceptions to the prohibition against quotas. Article XI.2 allows the imposition of quotas on exports of food to relieve a domestic food shortage. Import and export restrictions are also permitted when necessary for the implementation of standards and regulations for the classification or marketing of goods in international trade. The most significant single exception, which has had a profound impact on trade in agricultural commodities, is found in article XI.2(c):

> Import restrictions on any agricultural or fisheries product, imported in any form, necessary to the enforcement of governmental measures which operate:
>
> (i) to restrict the quantities of the like domestic product permitted to be marketed or produced … .

This provision has been the basis for Canadian quotas restricting the entry of foreign eggs, poultry, milk, and milk products, etc., which have been subject to Canadian marketing board schemes. During the Uruguay Round,[67] the Canadian delegation attempted to seek a modification of this language to ensure that marketing board schemes and the products covered by them would remain exempt from attacks similar to the US complaint against Canadian quotas on yogurt and ice cream.[68] This effort was not successful. Instead, the GATT 1994 Agreement on Agriculture requires that WTO members abandon the use of quotas and replace them with tariff rates. Canada and other WTO members complied during the course of 1995. Quotas are permitted, at least for the next decade, by the Agreement on Textiles and Clothing.[69]

Quotas will continue to be used to enforce safeguard measures. Article XII allows the imposition of temporary quotas to restrain imports during a balance of payments crisis. This provision was frequently invoked by European contracting parties until the late 1960s. Canada and the United States have also used the article—the last time in

66 See *Canada—Administration of the Foreign Investment Review Act*, BISD, 30th Supp. 140 (1982-83); *Canada—Measures Affecting Exports of Unprocessed Salmon and Herring*, BISD, 35th Supp. 98 (1989); *Canada—Restrictions on Import of Ice Cream and Yoghurt*, BISD, 36th Supp. 68 (1989).

67 The Canadian Delegation to the Uruguay Round proposed new language to clarify art. XI.2(c) in order to ensure that quotas imposed to reinforce agricultural schemes would remain effective under more precise and verifiable rules. See *Canadian Proposal on GATT Article XI*, GATT Doc. MTN.GNG/NG5/W/159, 19 March 1990.

68 *Restrictions on Import of Ice Cream and Yoghurt*, *supra*, note 66.

69 GATT 1994.

1972. Developing countries continue to have recourse to the article. Article XIII provides that the quotas must be applied on a non-discriminatory basis.

A further means of providing exceptions to the rule prohibiting quotas has been the recourse to waivers of general obligations by virtue of article XXV:5. The Understanding in respect of Waiver and Obligations under the GATT 1994 is designed to place a much greater burden on those WTO members seeking waivers from the WTO and places an automatic two-year limit on their duration.

3. State Trading Enterprises

Article XVII dealing with state trading was designed to inhibit the use of state trading organizations as disguised quotas. State trading enterprises are under a general obligation to deal in a non-discriminatory manner in import and export transactions. This article was invoked against Canada in the EC complaint on *Import, Distribution and Sale of Alcoholic Drinks by Canadian Provincial Marketing Agencies* in 1988.[70] The Understanding on the Interpretation of Article XVII of the GATT 1994 was adopted to bring a greater degree of transparency to the policies of state trading enterprises and to reinforce the obligation of article XVII that these enterprises should respect the general principles of non-discrimination.

4. Anti-Dumping Duties

Article VI of the GATT sets out the principle that anti-dumping duties may only be levied when dumping of imports causes or threatens material injury to the production of like goods by the domestic industry or when it materially retards the establishment of a domestic industry. The article also requires the anti-dumping duty not to exceed the margin of dumping. The Agreement on the Implementation of Article VI of the GATT 1994, which builds on the Anti-Dumping Codes of 1968 and 1979, contains extensive provisions fleshing out these principles and defining the administrative process by which anti-dumping duties may be levied. It allows the offering of price undertakings by the importer of the allegedly dumped goods in order to avoid the imposition of anti-dumping duties. It also provides that findings of dumping and injury must be periodically reviewed and that anti-dumping duties be removed when the original conditions no longer exist. Efforts to include provisions on harmonized anti-circumvention measures were unsuccessful.[71] The agreement does provide for dispute settlement under the general WTO procedure, but article 17.6 of the agreement contains specific guidance for a dispute settlement panel where the issue turns upon the standard of review applied by a domestic administrative tribunal.[72]

---

70 *Supra*, note 22.

71 But they remain on the WTO agenda under the Decision on Anti-Circumvention. The alleged problems of circumvention were highlighted by the panel report on *EEC—Regulation of Imports of Parts and Components*, BISD, 37th Supp. 132 (1990).

72 As indicated by the Decision on Review of Art. 17.6 of the Understanding on Art. VI of the GATT 1994, this issue was one of considerable controversy in the Uruguay Round. Further changes can be expected.

The 1968 and 1979 codes and the 1994 agreement have succeeded in bringing a measure of uniformity to the rules governing the imposition of anti-dumping duties in signatory countries. This is particularly true for the rules in the United States, the EU and Canada, which are responsible for initiating the vast majority of anti-dumping actions. However, the agreement has by no means alleviated many of the problems between these three jurisdictions and the results of the Uruguay Round were disappointing to those seeking fundamental change and greater discipline. The standard of injury continues to be a source of concern and actually appears to have been further relaxed. The EU and Canada consider that it remains too easy for American manufacturers to launch complaints and that the cost of defending an anti-dumping action in the United States is a non-tariff barrier in itself. Difficulties with US anti-dumping laws were a major issue during the Canada-US Free Trade negotiations in 1987-88 resulting in the inclusion of special dispute settlement provisions in articles 1906 and 1907 of the Free Trade Agreement (FTA). Similar provisions are to be found in the NAFTA. The possibility of replacing anti-dumping legislation *inter se* by the laws governing competition was seriously discussed between Canada and the United States during the FTA and NAFTA negotiations. This remains an option for both countries but, as of 1996, its realization had proved elusive.

5. Subsidies

Trade distortions created by subsidies to producers or transporters became a major source of contention in the 1970s, particularly between Canada and the United States, but also with the trading partners of the EC and with many developing countries. The most dramatic complaints involved agricultural commodities but they extended to the full range of manufactured products. For this reason, subsidies were a major theme in the Tokyo Round and the Uruguay Round of Multilateral Trade Negotiations.

Article VII of the GATT sets out the principle that countervailing duties, defined as duties levied to offset government subsidies to production, shall not exceed the amount of the subsidy. Furthermore, countervailing duties are only to be levied when subsidies have or will likely have the effect of causing material injury to an established domestic industry or threaten to retard the establishment of such an industry. Article XVI creates a general duty to inform other contracting parties of the existence of any domestic subsidy that has the effect of increasing exports and to discuss this with any interested contracting party. With respect to export subsidies, contracting parties "should seek to avoid the use of subsidies on the export of primary products." If an export subsidy is maintained on the export of a primary product, "... such subsidy shall not be applied in a manner which results in that contracting party having more than an equitable share of world export trade in that product ... ." These rules were applied in several cases,[73] but they

73 *France—Assistance to Exports of Wheat and Wheat Flour*, BISD, 7th Supp. 46 (1959). More recently, the Committee on Subsidies and Countervailing Measures has handed down a number of panel reports on the 1979 Subsidies Codes. Panel Report *United States—Countervailing Duties on Non-Rubber Footwear from Brazil*, GATT Doc. Restricted SCM/94 of 4 October 1989; *United States—Imposition of*

(The footnote is continued on the next page.)

are very soft rules to deal with an extremely hard subject. Furthermore, they provide very little discipline for subsidies on manufactures, and in the light of the waivers granted in the early years of the GATT for the maintenance of agricultural quotas to reinforce agricultural price supports, no discipline for subsidies on primary products.

Attempts were made within the GATT in the 1960s to reach agreement on a definition of prohibited subsidies. An Illustrative List of Export Subsidies was adopted in 1960. The problem was increasingly urgent in the 1970s as US legislation became increasingly rigid, leaving the US administration little or no choice but to levy countervailing duties, without any requirement that material injury to domestic production be proven. The 1979 Subsidies Code that arose from the Tokyo Round constituted a marked advance over the text of the GATT but, for a variety of reasons, it failed to resolve a number of fundamental issues. Many problems remained, not the least being the almost intractable problems posed by agricultural subsidies as well as the general issue of defining which subsidies were prohibited and which were permitted. Subsidies were, therefore, a major theme of the Uruguay Round.

The Agreement on Subsidies and Countervailing Duties, like the 1979 Subsidies Code, seeks to regulate both domestic proceedings against alleged subsidies and interstate conduct concerning subsidies. The new agreement retains the general principles flowing from the basic GATT text and reflects much of the 1979 Subsidies Code. Thus, subsidy inquiries must be conducted in an impartial manner; they must take all relevant factors into account, including the policies of the complaining industry; and they must cease when no subsidy or no injury is found or when the importer offers price undertakings. The countervailing duty must not exceed the subsidy. However, in many respects, the Agreement on Subsidies constitutes a radical advance over the 1979 Subsidies Code. The agreement does much to clarify the law by bringing into sharper focus the disctinction between prohibited and permissible subsidies. Unfortunately, there still remains considerable ambiguity over the treatment of subsidies that fall in the grey area between the two categories.

Article 1 of the agreement defines a subsidy broadly as a "financial contribution by a government" whereby a "benefit" is conferred through the transfer of goods, services, or funds or by forgoing revenue. A subsidy is prohibited, under part II, or actionable, under part III, where it is "specific." Specificity is defined by article 2 as being "specific to an enterprise or industry or group of enterprises or industries" whether *de jure* or *de facto*.

Prohibited subsidies are those that are contingent in law or in fact upon export performance or contingent on the use of domestic goods over imported goods, and include those in the illustrative list in Annex I to the agreement. After bilateral consultations, WTO members can bring complaints against prohibited subsidies to the Dispute Settlement Body (DSB), which issues a ruling. The DSB can enlist the help of the

---

73 Continued ...

Countervailing Duties on Imports of Fresh and Chilled Atlantic Salmon From Norway, GATT Doc. Restricted SCM/153 of 4 December 1992; and *Brazil—Imposition of Provisional and Definitve Countervailing Duties on Milk Powder and Certain Types of Milk From the European Economic Community*, GATT Doc. Restricted SCM/179/Corr. 1 of 31 January 1994.

Permanent Group of Experts in its inquiry. Should the panel report or the decision of the appellate body not be followed within 60 days, the DSB may authorize the complaining WTO Member to take "appropriate countermeasures."

Part IV lists subsidies that are non-actionable. The purpose of this part is to clear the air with respect to these categories of subsidies in order to ensure that they are not the object of countervailing duty investigations. The principal category of non-actionable subsidies are subsidies that are not specific. In this way, the concept of specificity is used to exclude certain subsidies from the ambit of the agreement as well as to include others. In addition, the following specific subsidies are listed as being non-actionable: assistance for the research activities of firms and higher education institutions in defined circumstances; assistance to disadvantaged regions in defined circumstances; and assistance to existing enterprises to meet new environmental requirements in defined circumstances.[74] Non-specific subsidies and specific subsidies in the three listed categories are not to be the object of countervailing duty investigations. However, article 9.1 permits a WTO member whose domestic industry is suffering "serious adverse effects as a result of those subsidies" to request consultations concerning the problem and, ultimately, the complaining member may be authorized to take "appropriate countermeasures" by the Committee on Subsidies and Countervailing Duties if the offending member refuses to make the changes that are recommended by the committee.

The third category of subsidies governed by the agreement are actionable subsidies. Part III of the agreement requires that no WTO member should cause "adverse effects to the interests of other Members" by the granting of specific subsidies not exempted by part IV. Adverse effects are defined as "injury to the domestic industry of another Member," "nullification or impairment" of benefits under the GATT 1994, or "serious prejudice" to the interests of another member.[75] The concept of serious prejudice, drawn from article XVI of the GATT 1994, is further defined in article 6. It is deemed to exist in certain circumstances;[76] and it includes the threat of serious injury and the displacement of the complaining member's goods from the markets of a third country. Agricultural subsidies are covered by the Agreement on Agriculture and are thus removed from the application of this agreement,[77] as are subsidies on aircraft production.[78]

Actionable subsidies give rise either to interstate disputes before the DSB under the Understanding on Dispute Settlement,[79] or to domestic countervailing duty procedures. The latter are the object of the extensive provisions of part V of the Agreement on Subsidies and Countervailing Duties.[80] These articles build upon the comparable articles

74 It is interesting to note the fairly close resemblance between these categories and the practice of the Commission of the EC under art. 93 of the EC Treaty, with respect to state aids.

75 Art. 5.

76 These are 5 percent *ad valorem* subsidization of the product, subsidies covering operating losses, and direct forgiveness of debt.

77 Art. 7.1.

78 See art. 6, footnotes 15 and 16.

79 See art. 7.

80 Arts. 10-23.

of the 1979 Subsidies Code and deal with the following aspects of the conduct of countervailing (CV) procedures: institution of the investigation; admissible evidence; consultations between WTO members; the calculation of the amount of a subsidy in terms of the benefit to the recipient; the determination of injury; the definition of the domestic industry for the purposes of opening a complaint procedure and defining injury; the granting of provisional measures; undertakings in lieu of CV duties; the levying of CV duties; limiting retroactivity of CV duties; limiting the duration and requiring review of CV duties; requiring public notice and justification of CV duties; and the requirement that judicial review be available for CV decisions.

Much was achieved in the Agreement on Subsidies and Countervailing Duties; it is clearly a great advance over the previous 1979 Subsidy Code. However, the agreement is not entirely satisfactory. The definitions of subsidy and specificity are somewhat elastic,[81] and, for all its detail and the laudable attempt to discipline CV duty procedures, the very existence of a CV regime is an invitation to protectionists and rent seekers and arguably constitutes a non-tariff barrier in its own right.[82]

6. Gray Area Measures

Throughout the years of the Tokyo and the Uruguay Round negotiations, governments became increasingly concerned with the impact of so-called gray area measures. The term covers a multitude of sins and peccadillos; it is used to designate those practices that developed over the years either as a means of bending GATT rules, particularly the ban on quotas, or as a way of dealing with situations that were not obviously regulated by specific GATT articles. In the latter sense, they reflect the problems caused by the failure of GATT contracting parties to update and modernize a text that had originally been conceived as an interim and short-term measure. But, in the former sense, gray area measures reflect the dangers posed by inadequate GATT discipline and the consequent emergence of covert non-tariff barriers coupled with the spectre of managed trade. However, it was also argued by those called upon to defend gray area measures that they did not violate the GATT because they were consensual arrangements and were not imposed unilaterally. At worst, it was suggested, gray area measures violated only the spirit but not the letter of the GATT.

The original gray area measure was the Agreement on Trade in Textiles, subsequently the MFA[83] and now the Agreement on Textiles and Clothing. This arrangement

---

81 As the Government of Canada discovered when the United States amended its legislation to define Canadian stumpage dues as subsidies in 1995 in order to reopen the vexed softwood lumber dispute for a third time.

82 Trebilcock, Chandler, and Howse, *Trade and Transition: A Comparative Analysis of Adjustment Policies* (London: Routledge, 1990), at 211-15.

83 Arrangement Regarding International Trade in Textiles, BISD, 21st Supp. 3 (1973-74), renewed and am. 1977, 1981, and 1986. Protocol Extending the Arrangement Regarding International Trade in Textiles, BISD, 24th Supp. 5 (1976); Protocol Extending the Arrangement Regarding International Trade in Textiles, BISD, 28th Supp. 3 (1981); and Protocol Extending the Arrangement Regarding International Trade in Textiles, BISD, 33rd Supp. 7-15 (1986).

at least had the advantage of bringing the problem out into the open, but it offered the dangerous precedent of exporting states formally consenting to the imposition of quotas by importing states. During the Uruguay Round, this problem was recognized and, as described above, an important step was taken to eliminate this form of non-tariff barrier by bringing it within the discipline of WTO rules and procedures. The full implementation of the Agreement on Textiles and Clothing will not be completed until well after the year 2000.

On a number of occasions, beginning in the 1970s, the United States, Canada, and the EC dealt with trading problems in areas such as steel, automobile imports,[84] and footwear by inviting exporters to restrain their exports "voluntarily." The invitation sometimes was addressed solely to private firms but on many occasions negotiations were conducted at the governmental level and agreements, of varying degrees of formality, were exacted by importing governments. Often these so-called voluntary agreements were backed up by quotas or the threat of anti-dumping measures if they were not respected. Voluntary restraint agreements were sometimes public but usually they remained confidential. It was thus difficult to assess their full impact but some calculations suggested that voluntary restraint agreements affected up to 15 percent of world trade into the OECD countries in 1990. It was thus imperative that the Uruguay Round deal with them.

The first line of attack on gray area measures is the Agreement on Textiles and Clothing, the second is to be found in the Agreement on Safeguards, analyzed below. This agreement is based on the premise that a viable system of safeguards should eliminate the temptation to negotiate voluntary restraints, and it requires that all voluntary restraints be declared to the WTO and eliminated within four years of the entry into force of the GATT 1994.[85] This ambitious program is overseen by the Committee on Safeguards and the Trade Policy Review Mechanism of the WTO. Concerns have been expressed about the enforceability of this commitment.[86]

7. *Safeguards*

Article XIX of the GATT envisages the possibility of situations arising where the domestic industry is suddenly and irresistibly threatened, not by unfair trade practices, but by completely fair trade. In such circumstances, the GATT 1947, drawing upon previous bilateral treaty practice, allowed for the imposition of temporary safeguard measures. Such measures could be imposed only by contracting parties:

> 1(a) If, as a result of unforeseen developments and of the effect of the obligations incurred by a contracting party under this Agreement, including tariff concessions, any product is being imported into the territory of that contracting party in such increased quantities and under such conditions as to cause or threaten serious injury to domestic producers ... .

---

84 See Wong, "The Japanese Automotive Voluntary Export Restraint Agreements and International Law" (1985), 23 *Can. Ybk. Int'l. L* 297.

85 Agreement on Safeguards arts. 11.1 and 2.

86 See, generally, Trebilcock and Howse, *The Regulation on International Trade*, *supra*, note 45, at 176.

In such circumstances, states were permitted to withdraw or modify the concessions "to the extent and for such time as may be necessary to prevent or remedy such injury." Such measures had to be imposed on an MFN basis. In principle, they could be imposed only with the prior approval of the other contracting parties but in practice, this approval was sought *post facto* and very little control was exercised over the undue continuation of safeguard measures. Exporting countries that were affected by safeguard measures could request compensation in the form of tariff reductions by the importing country or, if such accommodation could not be reached, the exporting country might take retaliatory measures. Such measures were, in turn, subject to the discipline of the GATT.

The perceived ineffectiveness of the safeguards regime was an object of concern in both the Tokyo and Uruguay Rounds of Multilateral Trade Negotiations. It had been variously argued that both a stricter and a more lenient safeguards regime would be conducive to greater compliance with the article and would lead to fewer attempts to circumvent other GATT provisions by resorting to gray area measures or new forms of retaliation. The Tokyo Round studied the issue of safeguards, but it proved impossible to reach agreement. Safeguards were again a major item on the agenda of the Uruguay Round. The Agreement on Safeguards that emerged is one of many significant achievements of the round. Rather than attempt to revise the text of article XIX of the GATT 1947, it was decided to develop a much more detailed agreement whose purpose would be both to regulate the imposition of safeguard measures but also, as set out above, to use a revised safeguards regime to eliminate the temptation to resort to voluntary restraints.

The Agreement on Safeguards that forms part of the GATT 1994 builds upon the principles of article XIX, expands them, and gives them a broader purpose in international trade law. The agreement sets a much more stringent standard for administrative proceedings leading to the adoption of safeguard measures and requires that safeguard measures only be imposed if increased imports, as a result of trade concessions, are the cause or threaten to cause serious injury to the production of like or competitive products by the domestic industry. Safeguard measures must be applied irrespective of the source; they must be periodically reviewed and must not remain in force more than eight years. WTO members imposing safeguards must compensate other members in order to maintain a "substantially equivalent level of concessions and other obligations."[87] By virtue of article 11, WTO members agreed to phase out all safeguard measures and all voluntary restraints and similar import and export measures within four years of entry into force of the GATT 1994. Compliance with the agreement is reviewed by a committee on safeguards and is subject to the general Understanding on Dispute Settlement.

The agreement is thus an ambitious step but it is not without risks. On the positive side is the attempt to discipline safeguard proceedings and to eliminate voluntary restraints. On the potentially negative side is the likelihood that safeguard measures will be more extensively used and may become non-tariff barriers in their own right. In addition, it is not clear that there are sufficient incentives for WTO members to abandon

87 Agreement on Safeguards, art. 8.1.

voluntary restraints or to refrain from reimposing them in the future. In this regard, the discipline appears to be very weak.[88]

8. Technical Standards

Technical standards concerning the safety, condition, description, or packaging of products are vital means in the hands of governments and industry of ensuring public welfare and facilitating trade. They are widely used in the industries of all modern industrial states and the legitimacy is seldom in question. However, it is true that meeting differing or conflicting standards is an added cost to doing business, particularly international business where the foreign producer seldom participates in the formulation of the standard. From time to time, it is even alleged that standards are used deliberately by governments to keep out foreign goods. In order to address the issues, a "Standards Code" was adopted in 1979 and ratified by some 40 states after the Tokyo Round. The extension of this code and its general application was an objective of the Uruguay Round that succeeded in negotiating two agreements: the Agreement on Technical Barriers to Trade and the Agreement on the Application of Sanitary and Phytosanitary Measures.

The basic obligation of the agreement on Technical Barriers to Trade is to grant national treatment and MFN treatment in applying national standards to foreign goods.[89] Second, the agreement contains a number of provisions designed to ensure that standards are not designed to be and do not act as "unnecessary obstacles to international trade." Article 2.2 states that technical standards "shall not be more trade restrictive than necessary to fulfill a legitimate objective." Legitimate objectives include national security, prevention of deceptive practices, and protection of public health and the environment. When a technical standard is designed to deal with these objectives, there is a rebuttable presumption that it is not an unnecessary obstacle to trade. Where relevant international standards exist "Members shall use them."[90] This is one of a number of strong incentives in the text for WTO members to use international standards unless they would be "ineffective and inappropriate."[91] WTO members are also required by article 5 to ensure that their domestic conformity assessment procedures are available to foreign products on a non-discriminatory basis and are not designed or applied with the effect of creating unnecessary obstacles to trade. "Wherever possible," WTO members should accept the results of foreign conformity assessments.[92] Inquiry points must be created to provide answers to all reasonable inquiries from foreign traders. In addition, various provisions seek to ensure that local and non-governmental bodies also act in a manner

---

88 The proposed resolution of the softwood lumber dispute between Canada and the United States in March 1996 on the basis of an export restraint agreement and subsequently an export tax did not bode well. See, generally, Howse and Trebilcock, *The Regulation on International Trade*, *supra*, note 45, at 176 and 420 for suggestions as to further future reforms of the GATT-WTO safeguards regime.

89 Agreement on Technical Barriers to Trade, art. 2.1.

90 *Ibid.*, art. 2.4.

91 *Ibid.*, art. 2.4.

92 *Ibid.*, art. 6.1.

compatible with the agreement. Article 12 provides for special and differential treatment of developing countries.

The Agreement on Technical Barriers to Trade is a document of considerable weight and it is one aspect of the GATT 1994 that has caused considerable concern to consumer protection and environmental groups.[93] Experience with the somewhat weaker 1979 code does not bear out these fears. However, interpretation of the agreement based solely on the promotion of trade, regardless of social and environmental consequences, will not enhance public acceptance of the GATT 1994.

IV. OTHER DISCIPLINES

A. Establishment of Free Trade Areas and Customs Unions

Under a system premised on MFN treatment, any derogation must be expressly authorized. The formation of a customs union, of a free trade area, or of any other type of preferential arrangement would violate the GATT were it not for the existence of article XXIV, which expressly authorizes the creation of free trade areas or customs unions. The drafters of the GATT 1947 did not expect that this article would be invoked frequently, but in fact there have been many attempts to form regional trading associations over the history of the GATT.[94] The most remarkable example is the European Economic Community (EEC), founded in 1957, but there are many other early examples including the European Free Trade Association (EFTA), the East African Economic Community (EAEC), the Latin American Free Trade Association (LAFTA), the Canada-US Auto Pact, as well as a host of association agreements concluded by the EC with neighbouring states, only some of which led to EC membership. During the decade of the 1980s and even more in the present decade, we have witnessed the emergence of numerous new regional or bilateral trading agreements. The original motivation for many of these arrangements may have been the fear that the GATT was being replaced by regional trading blocs, but the movement has continued after the unexpectedly successful completion of the Uruguay Round of Multilateral Trade negotiations and the emergence of the WTO. Thus, we have seen the emergence of the Canada-US Free Trade Agreement in 1988, followed by the NAFTA in 1995; the Andean Pact of northern Latin American states has been revamped; the 1991 MERCOSUR agreement now links the southern Latin American states in a very successful customs union; Mexico has built up a number of bilateral arrangements with its southern neighbours; Europe has witnessed the emergence of the "Visigrad Agreement" among the states of Central Europe; and the Baltic states have concluded a number of bilateral and regional trading arrangements. The EU has concluded the European Economic Space Agreement in 1992 with its EFTA neighbours, some of whom subsequently joined the EU, as well as a number of

93 See Dunne, "Fears over Gattzilla the Trade Monster," *Financial Times*, 30 January 1992, at 3 and, with a reproduction of a "Gattzilla Monster" pamphlet; McDonald, *supra*, note 47, at 399-400.

94 WTO Secretariat, *Regionalism and the World Trading System* (Geneva: WTO, 1995). Howse and Trebilcock, *supra*, *The Regulation of International Trade*, note 45, at 92 report that more than 80 regional trade agreements were notified to the GATT between 1947 and 1990.

"Europe Agreements" with Central European states, and a customs union with Turkey in 1995. In 1995, states of the Asia-Pacific region concluded a much-enhanced Asia Pacific Economic Committee (APEC) Agreement. Many more bilateral agreements exist.[95] Other multilateral trade and aid initiatives, such as the Lomé Agreements of the EC, or the Caribbean Basin Initiative of the United States, reflect the same phenomenon. Some of these associations have been more successful than others; many of the earlier agreements have fallen by the wayside. What is clear is that regionalism and bilateralism remain important and dynamic aspects of international trade law.[96]

Over the years, GATT contracting parties have shown great tolerance concerning the nature and variety of bilateral and regional preferential arrangements. Article XXIV.12 has been interpreted very flexibly and no such agreement has ever been condemned by the GATT or the WTO. Some view this as laxity; however, in policy terms, there is no incompatibility provided that, with respect to a customs union or a free trade area or an interim agreement leading to the formation of such a union or area, the basic condition of article XXIV is met. This condition is set out in the following terms for a customs union:[97]

> ... the duties and other regulations of commerce imposed at the institution of any such union or interim agreement in respect of trade with contracting parties not parties to such union or interim agreement shall not on the whole be higher or more restrictive than the general incidence of the duties and regulations of commerce applicable in the constituent territories prior to the formation of such union or the adoption of such interim agreement as the case may be.

In economic terms, the requirement is that the new union or free trade area must be trade-creative and that, in the aggregate, the new barriers are no higher and preferably lower than those that existed before. This is precisely the objective of the GATT in overall terms and is thus compatible. The danger that many have feared is that customs unions and free trade areas will emerge as giant and powerful trading blocs, too large to discipline and capable of a considerable degree of self-sufficiency in the event of a trade conflict. There have been times when it appeared that this fear had been realized in the EU. Similarly, the EU and Japan are nervous at the emergence of a North American trading bloc. On balance, WTO members, like the contracting parties of the GATT, have always deemed it preferable to run this risk rather than attempt to stop a phenomenon that has so many positive advantages.

B. Plurilateral Agreements

Annex 4 to the GATT 1994 contains four agreements that are binding only on the states that agree to be bound. They deal with trade in three commodities that have caused particularly difficult problems for the international community—beef, dairy products,

95 See chapters 3 and 4.

96 In the four years between 1990 and 1994 alone, more than 30 agreements were notified to the GATT, see WTO, *supra*, note 94, at 25.

97 Art. XXIV.5(a). As to a free-trade area, see art. XXIV.5(b).

and civil aircraft, as well as the important issue of the rules governing government procurement.

C. Government Procurement

1. Historical Background

The need to establish an agreed international framework of rights and obligations with respect to laws, regulations, and practices regarding government procurement had been recognized for a long time. A first attempt to regulate this area was made in the OECD, but without success. Progress was achieved at the regional level, in the framework of the EFTA and of the then EEC. However, nothing was accomplished at the international level until the issue emerged at the Tokyo Round of negotiations late in 1976 and resulted in the preparation and adoption by a certain number of countries, including Canada and the United States, of an Agreement on Government Procurement.[98]

Liberalization of government procurement was a new field of activity for GATT, as article III:8(a) of the GATT stipulates that the non-discrimination obligation in respect of foreign suppliers and producers does not apply to the procurement by government agencies of products purchased for governmental purposes. In the course of the negotiations, it gradually became clear that not all government purchases could be opened to international competition. The ability of some countries to subscribe to certain obligations was limited due to their structure. Furthermore, certain sectors were the responsibility of the private economy or of the state, according to the country concerned. Finally, at the time of concluding the Tokyo Round in 1979, the EC could not accept an agreement with broader coverage than that existing within the community.

The impact of the 1979 code was very limited. But participants in the Uruguay Round were able to make progress on government procurement, since the EC had just adopted important measures designed to diminish intra-community barriers and Canada and the United States had taken somewhat more modest steps with the adoption of chapter 13 of the FTA in 1988, subsequently expanded under NAFTA in 1994.[99] The Agreement on Government Procurement was amended by protocol in 1988[100] in negotiations that took place in parallel with the Uruguay Round. Subsequently, an amended version of the agreement was included among the four plurilateral trade agreements of Annex 4 to the GATT 1994; this agreement entered into force on January 1, 1996. The agreement is thus not binding on all WTO members, but it has been ratified by Canada, the United States, the EC, and a significant number of other states[101] and is thus of considerable importance for Canada.

---

98 BISD, 26th Supp. 33 (1978-79), as am. by Protocol in 1987, BISD, 34th Supp. 12 (1986-87) also called the Government Procurement Code and GATT, *Practical Guide to the Agreement on Government Procurement* (am. 1988).

99 NAFTA, pt. IV, chapter 10.

100 Protocol Amending the Agreement on Government Procurement, BISD, 34th Supp. 12 (1988).

101 Thirty-nine states have ratified.

2. *Objectives and Scope*

The main objective of the agreement is to ensure increased international competition, thus permitting the more effective use of resources. To this end, it lays down the principles of non-discrimination and of national treatment[102] for the products and supplies of those countries who are parties to the agreement in respect of legislation, procedures, and practices regarding government procurement.

As regards coverage, the government entities bound by the Agreement have been fixed by negotiation, and a list of them is annexed to it. Virtually all federal government entities are covered; for the first time, sub-national entities such as Canadian provinces were required to make at least limited commitments. the agreement applies to all products purchased by the entities covered. As regards civil defence purchases, an exhaustive list of the products covered is annexed. The agreement relates to contracts for the supply of goods of a value not less than 130,000 Special Drawing Rights (SDR). It also covers service and construction contracts. The parties to the agreement agree to undertake further negotiations periodically with a view to broadening and improving it on the basis of mutual reciprocity.

3. *Tendering Procedures*

Apart from the lists of entities covered, most of the provisions of the agreement are devoted to tendering procedures.[103] Transparency is particularly important in those procedures, so that non-discrimination in respect of foreign suppliers can be implemented and monitored. Moreover, parties to the agreement must furnish a list of the publications carrying official information on government procurement.[104] However, exceptions are provided for the protection of essential security interests.[105]

4. *Developing Countries*

The agreement makes provision for more favourable treatment for developing countries, recognizing that government procurement is still more important for them than for industrialized countries, in the light of their financial and industrial development needs.[106] It allows exemptions from certain obligations under the agreement, subject to negotiation. In addition, the Committee on Government Procurement can grant temporary exemptions from the rules on national treatment to certain entities of developing countries. Finally, industrialized countries are called upon to give technical assistance to developing countries and to extend the benefits of the agreement to least-developed countries not parties to it.

---

102 Art. III.

103 Arts. VII-XV.

104 Appendix II.

105 Art. XXIII.

106 Art. V.

5. Consultations and Dispute Settlement

The Committee on Government Procurement oversees implementation of the agreement. Parties to the agreement are required to establish domestic bid challenge procedures and they are required to submit disputes concerning the application and interpretation of the agreement to the general WTO dispute settlement procedure.[107]

6. Implementation of the Agreement by Canada

The Department of Supply and Services, which acts as the acquisition agency for goods and related services for all Canadian government departments, is responsible for the application of the provisions of the agreement. Procedures have been adopted for the purpose of ensuring that foreign suppliers receive the same treatment as domestic suppliers of the goods and related services covered by the agreement.[108] In order to provide a consistent approach to the establishment and use of the monetary threshold, its value in Canadian funds is established in advance of each calendar year.[109] As of 1996, provincial governments had not accepted significant commitments.[110]

V. THE GENERAL AGREEMENT ON TRADE IN SERVICES

The increasing integration of the world economy has inevitably led to the extension of the GATT to trade in services. Services now represent more than 20 percent of international trade and, for many developed countries, they represent the most dynamic sectors of the modern knowledge-based economy. Legal protection of services and the removal of barriers to their free movement has become a matter of pressing concern. In Europe, the free movement of services has been a principle of the EC since its inception in 1957 and, more recently in North America, the FTA and NAFTA both reflect similar liberalization. Even developing countries, whose representatives were initially very skeptical about the advantages of service liberalization, have gradually come to realize that they share a community of interest with the developed world. While the United States attempted to initiate negotiations on trade in services during the Tokyo Round without success, it was in the Uruguay Round that it was possible to conclude the GATS.[111]

The GATS is both a success and a disappointment: a success because it puts services squarely within the concerns of the WTO and thus, will gradually lead to the erosion of the many barriers to trade in services; a disappointment, because it has proved difficult to make rapid progress on a number of important issues. For this reason, the initial impact of the agreement on trade in services is modest.

---

107 Art. XXI.

108 RSC 1985, c. S-25, as am. See also Procedures for Implementing the GATT Agreement on Government Procurement, 123 *Can. Gaz.*, pt. I, 21 January 1989, at 263.

109 *Ibid.*

110 The provinces were largely exempted from the agreement in Canada's schedule.

111 GATT 1994, Annex 1B.

The GATS is made up of three main elements. The first, involving parts I, II and V, set out the general framework of the agreement. The second deals with the establishment of schedules of commitments flowing from parts III and IV. The third element of the GATS is made up by the sectoral annexes, which deal with the elimination of barriers to specific services.

Part I of the GATS governs the coverage of the agreement. It covers four means of supplying a service:

— trade from the territory of one member into the territory of any other member;
— trade in the territory of one member to the service consumer of any other member;
— trade by a service supplier of one member, through commercial presence in the territory of any other member; and
— trade by a service supplier of one member, through presence of natural persons of a member in the territory of any other member.

The GATS covers measures taken by central, regional, and local governments as well as non-governmental bodies exercising governmental powers.

Part II requires WTO members to accord unconditional MFN treatment to services and service suppliers in respect of any measure covered by the GATS. This is immediately qualified by article II.2, which stipulates that all members may maintain inconsistent measures provided that they are listed in the Annex. The result of this approach is that MFN treatment applies to any foreign service or foreign service supplier that they agree to allow into their territory. Part II requires all domestic regulatory requirements to be applied in a transparent manner. Article V of the GATS allows WTO members to make more generous concessions in the context of regional economic integration agreements on very much the same terms as required for goods. Article V also encourages WTO members to recognize educational qualifications, licences, or certifications of other members through systems of harmonization of such standards, and requires that recognition of standards, once implemented, shall not constitute a means of discrimination between them. Monopolies and exclusive service suppliers are permissible but they must not violate the general MFN principle or act in a manner contrary to commitments in the schedules or annexes.[112] No special regime of safeguards is established, but WTO members are committed to further negotiations on the subject,[113] as well as to negotiations on the impact of subsidies on services.[114] Obligations are subject to a right to protect the balance of payments,[115] government procurement systems,[116] as well as to articles XIV and XIV bis, which allow for both general and national security exceptions, comparable to those of articles XX and XXI of the GATT 1994. Finally, article XI requires that members shall not restrict payments and transfers relating to services covered by their specific commitments.

112 GATS, art. VII.

113 GATS, art. X.

114 GATS, art. XV.

115 GATS, art. XII.

116 GATS, art. XIII.

Part III of the GATS commits WTO members to engaging in a process of negotiating specific commitments relating to the modes of supply and the sectors identified in article II. This commitment is essentially an agreement to negotiate. For developing countries, it involved only the requirement to schedule one commitment. Canada and its major trading partners made more extensive commitments and began a long-term process of negotiations, which will doubtless extend through future negotiating rounds.[117] The most significant consequence of including a service or supplier on a schedule of commitments is that this involves a commitment to national treatment of that service or supplier in the future. Thus, national treatment—the second pillar of WTO law—is also included in the GATS, albeit on a more restricted basis than MFN treatment.

Four sectoral annexes were appended to the GATS to deal with financial services, basic telecommunications, mobility of service providers, and air transportation. The issues concerning financial services and basic telecommunications were not fully resolved at the close of the Uruguay Round in 1993 and it was decided to proceed immediately with further negotiations.[118]

Part V of the GATS creates a Council for Trade in Services, which is charged with surveillance of the schedules and exceptions, development of the annexes, and an impressive program of future negotiations. By virtue of article XXIII, interpretation and application of the GATS is subject to the general WTO dispute settlement procedure.

VI. AGREEMENT ON TRADE-RELATED ASPECTS OF INTELLECTUAL PROPERTY RIGHTS

International trade in the contemporary knowledge-based environment is heavily reliant on protection for intellectual property. It was not surprising, therefore, that those states participating in the Uruguay Round, which were the principal source of intellectual property, should wish to raise the standard of protection in all states enjoying the benefits of the GATT. The United States was the first to make such a demand and the strongest in expressing its dissatisfaction with lax standards of protection in certain countries, but similar concerns were felt in many quarters and the United States gradually won over a sufficient number of supporters.[119] Many developing countries were hesitant and remain unhappy with the text that emerged from the Uruguay Round. There are serious theoretical arguments that uniform standards and high levels of intellectual

117 Canadian provinces were required to make commitments by January 1, 1996, but were unable to meet this deadline.

118 As of June 1996, neither negotiation had fully succeeded since by the deadlines of June 1995, for financial services, and May 1996, for basic telecommunications, the United States had rejected the agreements as drafted, arguing that neither guaranteed a sufficient degree of market liberalization, and did not become a party to the Protocol on Financial Services. See chapter 9, *infra*. The December 1996 Ministerial Meeting of the WTO decided to continue these negotiations.

119 The United States was not successful in convincing Canada in the FTA negotiations but did succeed in winning over Canada and Mexico in the NAFTA, chapter 17, thus laying the groundwork for the Uruguay Round.

property protection will inhibit rather than enhance international trade.[120] In a number of developing countries, there is concern about the implications of patenting the genetic codes of natural organisms and in many countries there is no consensus about the legitimacy of patenting new life forms. However, the concerns of a number of developed countries raised by unauthorized reproduction of audio and video material as well as pharmaceutical patent violations won the day, and the resulting Agreement on Trade-Related Aspects of Intellectual Property Rights (TRIPS) is one of the major innovations of the Uruguay Round.

The TRIPS Agreement involves both commitments as to the standard of treatment of intellectual property, which are defined in the agreement itself, as well as a range of commitments to abide by the requirements of the major intellectual probate conventions already in existence.[121] It is divided into seven parts dealing with the following issues: (1) general principles governing the standard of treatment of intellectual property rights including the relationship of the TRIPS Agreement and the Berne and Paris conventions; (2) specific commitments with respect to the recognition and treatment of different types of intellectual property rights; (3) commitments with respect to domestic enforcement of these rights; (4) commitments with respect to the acquisition and maintenance of intellectual property rights under domestic law; (5) dispute settlement; (6) transitional arrangements; and (7) institutional arrangements.

Subject to certain exceptions,[122] the TRIPS Agreement requires that national treatment and MFN treatment shall be accorded to the nationals of other WTO members with respect to the protection of intellectual property. Articles 7 and 8 of the TRIPS Agreement contain statements of general principles seeking to reconcile the interests of all states in promoting and protecting technological development with other national interests, such as public health and economic development. In both parts I and II, there are a series of very specific legal commitments to protect intellectual property rights defined in the text or defined by means of direct reference to various intellectual property conventions. Thus, article 2 requires WTO members to abide by specific articles of the Paris Convention; similarly, article 9, in part II requires WTO members to comply with the first 21 articles of the Berne Convention and makes a virtual amendment to the latter convention in requiring that computer programs shall be protected as literary works. Where part II does incorporate various conventions, it contains substantive obligations concerning copyright, trademarks, geographical indications, industrial designs, patents, and topographies of integrated circuits. Of particular importance in Canada and many other countries is the requirement guaranteeing patent protection for a period of 20 years

---

120 See Trebilcock and Howse, *The Regulation of International Trade*, *supra*, note 45, at 252-54.

121 The Paris Convention for the Protection of Industrial Property, adopted at Stockholm 14 July 1967; the Berne Convention for the Protection of Literary and Artistic Works, adopted at Paris 24 July 1971; the International Convention for the Protection of Performers, Producers of Phonograms and Broadcasting Organizations, adopted at Rome 26 October 1961; and the Treaty on Intellectual Property in Respect of Integrated Circuits, adopted at Washington 26 May 1989.

122 For example, those permittted by the Paris and Berne conventions or those negotiated on a bilateral basis before the entry into force of the GATT 1994 such as the US-Japan semi-conductor agreements: Japan-US: Arrangement concerning Trade in semiconductor Products, 11 June 1992 (1992), 31 *ILM* 1074.

from the date of filing. This required a controversial change to Canada's drug patent protection. Similarly, the rules on geographical indications required Canada to protect "appellations d'origine" for the first time. Article 40 deals with the relationship of contractual licences and competition legislation, an area of particular concern to the EU due to the very strict interpretation of articles 85 and 86 of the EC Treaty.

Part III of the TRIPS Agreement contains extensive provisions requiring the enforcement of intellectual property rights by civil, administrative, and criminal procedures. These rules, while not being self-executing, nevertheless have considerable impact on the domestic enforcement systems of WTO members. Among the remedies envisaged are border measures initiated by states or private citizens to restrict the importation of goods produced in violation of intellectual property rights. The TRIPS Agreement also provides for the application of the general WTO dispute settlement procedures between WTO members, but article 64 defers full implementation of this principle until five years after the entry into force of the GATT 1994. The agreement also provides for deferred implementation by developing countries and countries in the process of moving from a centrally planned to a market economy. A council is created to implement the TRIPS Agreement. By virtue of article 70, the agreement does not give rise to rights or obligations in respect of acts that occurred before the entry into force of the GATT 1994. Unlike most of the GATT 1994, reservations are permitted to the TRIPS Agreement but only with the consent of other WTO members. Article 73 provides for security exceptions on a narrow range of matters.

The TRIPS Agreement is thus an ambitious and far-reaching document. It has had a significant impact upon domestic law and the administration of intellectual property rights by many WTO members. It remains controversial in many parts of the world, including Canada, and well may prove to have been one of the most constraining parts of the GATT 1994.

VII. AGREEMENT ON TRADE-RELATED INVESTMENT MEASURES

Foreign direct investment is arguably an even more significant driving force behind economic growth than trade in goods and services. As the GATT has expanded its reach beyond trade in goods, it has become necessary to address the issues posed by other barriers to trade, including those that are the result of foreign investment controls. Foreign investment controls often take the form of commitments enacted by the host country from the investor as to levels and the form of investment, methods of production, sourcing of components of production, disposition of the goods produced, and restrictions on the repatriation of profits and capital. These are not matters expressly covered by the GATT 1947. However, it can be argued that they violate articles III.4, national treatment; XI, the ban on quotas; XV, IMF exchange requirements; and XVI, subsidies.[123] The fact that the GATT had implications for at least some foreign investment controls was revealed by the FIRA panel report,[124] where it was held that local sourcing requirements denied national treatment to foreign goods in Canada.

---

123 See Trebilcock and Howse, *The Regulation of International Trade, supra*, note 45, at 287.

124 *Canada—Administration of the Foreign Investment Review Act (FIRA)*, BISD, 30th Supp. 140 (1984).

The issue of extending GATT disciplines to investment controls was controversial during the Uruguay Round and there was no agreement to make extensive new commitments. However, the Trade-Related Investment Measures (TRIMS) Agreement reflects a recognition of the problems that exist and a willingness at least to codify the principles of the FIRA panel. The essence of this short agreement is to require all WTO members not to apply TRIMS "in a manner incompatible with" article III or article XI of the General Agreement. This commitment is accompanied by a brief illustrative list of incompatible programs including local content and sourcing requirements and import and export restrictions. Article 4 maintains existing exceptions in favour of developing countries and a seven-year phase-in of other obligations for them.

The TRIMS Agreement is thus a very modest beginning. However, it reflects recognition of a wider issue and heralds major negotiations on foreign investment protection in the future.

VIII. THE GATT AS APPLIED TO LESS-DEVELOPED COUNTRIES

There were few LDCs among the original contracting parties to the GATT but their number has increased slowly over the years to the point that the 1996 membership of the WTO of over 120 has placed them in the very great majority. Numbers do not necessarily give power in the WTO, which is presently dominated by the three economic giants: the United States, the EU, and Japan. But the concerns of the LDCs cannot and should not be ignored. This fact has long been recognized within the GATT and subsequently, the WTO.

Major amendments to the text of the GATT since 1947, including part IV on Trade and Development adopted in 1965, have dealt with the obligations of LDCs.[125] LDCs viewed the GATT as a rich man's club through the first three decades of its existence, prefering the forum of the UN Conference on Trade and Development (UNCTAD). However, this view changed during the 1980s, which witnessed the entry of many more LDCs, including the last major developing countries, such as Mexico, and the granting of observer status to others, such as China. The concerns of the LDCs were very much a part of the Tokyo Round. These concerns focused mainly on attenuating the effect of GATT rules upon LDCs.

A major issue throughout the years has been the extent to which the LDCs should be subject to the full discipline of the GATT rules. The general trend of the changes made over the first 25 years was to lessen the obligations of the LDCs. Thus, the 1955 amendments to article XVIII, Governmental Assistance to Economic Development, were designed to protect infant industries and the balance of payments of LDCs by granting them greater latitude with respect to the application of the generally applicable GATT rules. The most significant change in principle was made in 1965 with the adoption of part IV on Trade and Development. The new article XXXVI.8 states that: "The developed contracting parties do not expect reciprocity for commitments made by them in trade negotiations to reduce or remove tariffs or other barriers to the trade of less-

125 BISD, 3rd Supp. 170 (1954-55) and BISD, 13th Supp. 1 (1964-65).

developed contracting parties." A further major step was taken in 1971 with the adoption, by way of a waiver, of the Generalized System of Preferences (the GSP), by which the developed contracting parties agreed to grant preferential treatment on a range of exports of developing countries.[126] The GSP has subsequently been renewed. A number of the Tokyo Round codes, particularly the anti-dumping, subsidies, and government procurement codes, contained provisions that stated that developing country signatories are not under as stringent an obligation to respect the codes as the developed signatories.

By the inception of the Uruguay Round, the economic and political climate had undergone profound change and many LDCs, in joining the GATT, were seeking to give guarantees that they would play by the international rules rather than seek broad exceptions. The result is that the GATT 1994 texts, while often reserving special mention to LDCs, are much less inclined to give them blanket exemptions from the application of WTO standards. Rather, many of the GATT 1994 texts provide for extended phase-in periods rather than complete exceptions. Only the least-developed countries, whose presence on the international scene remains sadly marginal, are granted the kind of broad exceptions that were present in the Tokyo Round texts. The Uruguay Round was the first in which the LDCs played a major part and they can be expected to play a much more significant role in future multilateral trade negotiations.

IX. THE FUTURE OF THE GATT-WTO

When the Uruguay Round began in 1986, the GATT had become an extraordinarily complex economic, institutional, and legal phenomenon with a large membership. The tariff schedules had grown to immense lengths. The basic text was completed by a large number of subsidiary agreements. The GATT was under pressure to expand its scope from tariff and non-tariff barriers on goods, to trade in services, intellectual property, and trade-related investment measures. Agricultural and textile trade appeared to be virtually exempt from the normal disciplines of the GATT. Basic principles of the GATT—such as the MFN principle—were also under pressure both from LDCs wishing exemptions and from the array of subsidiary agreements, the benefits of which were only extended to signatories. The original GATT text was increasingly in need of modernization and the absence of a well-established institutional basis seemed ever more apparent. The fear that large trading blocs would decide that they were better served by managed trade than by a single multilateral system was constantly in the minds of GATT negotiators. To complete the complex picture, some of the states calling most strongly for reaffirmation of GATT disciplines and for the adoption of new rules in new areas were among the worst offenders against GATT rules in key areas such as agriculture.

Contrary to the expectations of many, the GATT 1994 was adopted at Marrakesh, and the WTO rose from the ashes of the GATT. The WTO has a reinforced membership, a stronger, broader text, whose principles are guaranteed by a unified dispute settlement system and that are grounded in a new institutional framework. The new institution began its work with an ambitious program designed to consolidate the GATT 1994 and

---

126 Generalized System of Preferences: BISD, 18th Supp. 24 (1970-71).

to develop a new international trade agenda that will take the WTO into issues raised by the environment, labour standards, competition policy, investment protection, and many others. The institutional framework and the dispute settlement system appear to be working and, while the challenges to the WTO are even greater than they were in earlier years, there is reason for modest optimism that the WTO rules and structure are capable of dealing with their challenges.[127]

X. SELECTED BIBLIOGRAPHY

A. Books

Abbot, *Law and Policy of Regional Integration: The NAFTA and Western Hemispheric Integration in the World Trade Organization* (1995).

Dennin, *Law and Practice of the World Trade Organization* (1995).

Hilf and Jacobs (eds.), *The European Community and GATT* (1986).

Hudec, *Enforcing International Trade Law. GATT Dispute Settlement in the 1980s* (1991).

Hudec, *The GATT Legal System and World Trade Diplomacy* (2nd ed., 1990).

Jackson, *Restructuring the GATT* (1990).

Jackson, *The Uruguay Round, World Trade Organization and the Problem of Regulating International Economic Behaviour* (Ottawa: Centre for Trade Policy and Law, 1995).

Jackson, *World Trade and the Law of the GATT* (1969).

Jackson, *The World Trading System: Law and Policy of International Economic Relations* (1989).

Long, *Law and Its Limitations in the GATT Multilateral Trade System* (1985).

Milne, *Canada-United States Free Trade: A Bibliography* (5th ed., 1989).

McGovern, *International Trade Regulation: GATT, the United States and the European Economic Community* (2nd ed., 1986).

Pescatore et al. (eds.), *Handbook of WTO/GATT Dispute Settlement* (1991).

Petersmann, *Constitutional Functions and Constitutional Problems of International Economic Law. International and Domestic Foreign Trade Law and Foreign Trade Policy in the U.S., the European Community and Switzerland* (1991).

Petersmann and Hilf (eds.), *The New GATT Round of Multilateral Trade Negotiations: Legal and Economic Problems* (1988).

---

127 The WTO held its first meeting of trade ministers at Singapore in December 1996. This meeting adopted an ambitious work program for the organization.

Simmonds and Hill, *Law and Practice under the GATT* (1989).

Stone, *Canada, the GATT and the International Trade System* (2nd ed., 1991).

Trebilcock and Howse, *The Regulation of International Trade* (1995).

Wolfhard, *The Mote in GATT's Eye: Intellectual Property Rights and International Trade in the Uruguay Round* (Ontario Centre for International Business, pub. no. 20, 1990).

B. Articles

Belley, "Les marchés publics: étude des obligations internationales du Canada; du GATT à l'ALÉNA" (1995), 36 *Cahiers* 503.

Berger, "Preferential Trade Treatment for Less Developed Countries: Implications of the Tokyo Round" (1979), 20 *Harv. Int'l. LJ* 540.

Bliss, "GATT Dispute Settlement Reform in the Uruguay Round: Problems and Prospects" (1987), 23 *Stan. J Int'l. L* 31.

Burchill, "Commentary on Some Treaties Signed by Canada in 1979" (1980), 18 *Can. YB Int'l. L* 384.

Castel, "The Uruguay Round and the Improvements to the GATT Dispute Settlement Rules and Procedures" (1989), 38 *Int'l. & Comp. LQ* 834.

Farless, "GATT and the Tokyo Round: Legal Implications of the New Trade Agreement" (1981), 11 *Calif. Western Int'l. J* 302.

Fisher, "The Most Favoured Nation Clause in GATT: A Need for Reevaluation?" (1967), *19 Stan. L Rev.* 841.

Graham, "Reforming the International Trading System: The Tokyo Round Negotiations in the Final Stage" (1979), 12 *Cornell Int'l. LJ* 1.

Grzybowski, "Socialist Countries in GATT" (1980), 28 *Am. J Comp. L* 539.

Haight, "Customs Unions and Free-Trade Areas under GATT: A Reappraisal" (1972), 6 *J World Trade L* 391.

Hudec, "GATT Dispute Settlement After the Tokyo Round: An Unfinished Business" (1980), 13 *Cornell Int'l. LJ* 145.

Jackson, "Governmental Disputes in International Trade Relations: A Proposal in the Context of GATT" (1979), 13 *J World Trade L* 1.

Macdonald, "Canadian Industrial Policy Objectives and Article III of GATT: National Ambitions and International Obligations" (1982), 6 *Can. Bus. LJ* 385.

McRae and Thomas, "The GATT and Multilateral Treaty Making: The Tokyo Round" (1983), 77 *Am. J Int'l. L* 51.

Meier, "The Tokyo Round of Multilateral Trade Negotiations and the Developing Countries" (1980), 13 *Cornell Int'l. LJ* 239.

Roessler, "The GATT Declaration on Trade Measures Taken for Balance-of-Payments Purposes: A Commentary" (1980), 12 *Case W Res. J Int'l. L* 383.

Thomas, "Litigation Process Under the GATT Dispute Settlement System: Lessons for the W.T.O." (1996), 30 JWT 53.

Waincymer, "Revitalising GATT Article XXIII. Issues in the Context of the Uruguay Round" (1988), 12.1 *World Competition* 5.

C. GATT Publications

Basic Instruments and Selected Documents [BISD].

FOCUS, GATT Newsletter.

GATT, *Analytical Index: Guide to GATT Law and Practice* (2 vols.) (Geneva: WTO, updated 6th ed., 1995).

GATT, *International Trade News Bulletin*, monthly.

GATT, *The Tokyo Round of Multilateral Trade Negotiations: Report by the Director-General.* Geneva, 1979 (Copies of GATT documents in print may be obtained from the GATT Secretariat: Centre William Rappard/154 rue de Lausanne/1211 Geneva 21/ Switzerland).

General Agreement on Tariffs and Trade (Organization), *Analytical Index: Guide to GATT Law and Practice* (Geneva: Contracting Parties to the General Agreement on Tariffs and Trade, 1994).

World Trade Organization, *Trade and the Environment* (Geneva: Information & Media Relations Division of the WTO, 1995).

WTO Secretariat, *Regionalism and the World Trading System* (Geneva: WTO, 1995).

CHAPTER TWO

The North American Free Trade Agreement

I. GENERAL OBJECTIVES AND SCOPE

A. Regional Economic Integration

The North American Free Trade Agreement (NAFTA), which entered into force between Canada, the United States and Mexico on January 1, 1994[1] is one of a large number of agreements that exist today to promote regional economic integration.[2] As volumes of international trade have increased year by year, many states have felt the need to remove trade barriers at a faster rate than is possible under the GATT-WTO system in order to facilitate trade with their major trading partners. Regional trade agreements allow neighbouring states to offer economies of scale to domestic producers and foreign investors by expanding the size of the regional market. They thus serve to attract foreign investors into the regional market as well as to increase the capacity of domestic producers to enter world markets. Another important function of these agreements is to serve as a vehicle for positive integration such as the harmonization of legislation and the adoption of common domestic regulatory standards.

Regional economic integration agreements are concluded among two or more states. In recent years, by far the most numerous bilateral agreements have been those concluded by the European Community (now incorporated into the European Union (EU)) with

1 North American Free Trade Agreement Implementation Act, SC 1993, c. 44. The NAFTA is reprinted in (1993), 32 *ILM* 296.

2 Between 1948 and 1994, 109 agreements were notified to the GATT: see WTO Secretariat, *Regionalism and the World Trading System* (Geneva: WTO, 1995), at 27.

neighbouring states, often with a view to eventual entry into the EU.[3] Other notable bilateral agreements include the Australia-New Zealand Free Trade Agreement of 1983,[4] and bilaterals between Israel and the United States and Canada.[5] Mexico has also concluded a number of bilateral agreements with its southern neighbours.[6] More common still are the regional agreements now found in every part of the world. The most notable of all is the EU, first established by six European states in 1957[7] and subsequently expanded to 15 members united by a supranational structure, to include a monetary union by 1999.[8] The

3 The EU has a host of bilateral agreements. Many bilaterals with Mediterranean countries are designed to remove certain barriers. The European Economic Area Agreement of 1992 provides a basis for very close economic association with the remaining European Free Trade Agreement (EFTA) members (with the exception of Switzerland, which declined to join). The "Europe Agreements" with the states of the Baltic and Central Europe may well pave the way to eventual entry into the EU, as is the case of the 1995 customs union with Turkey. In 1996, the EC Commission announced the beginning of a process of negotiation leading to removal of trade barriers with NAFTA countries. See Communication from the Commission to the Council on EU-Canada relations (1/2-1996), 29 *EU Bull.* 110, pt. 1.4.137 and Council Conclusions on EU-Canada relations, (3-1996), 29 *EU Bull.* 86, pt. 1.4.75. See also Joint Declaration on EU-Canada Relations, 17 December 1996.

4 (1983), 22 *ILM* 945.

5 US-Israel Free Trade Agreement (1985), 24 *ILM* 653; Canada-Israel Free Trade Agreement, DFAIT, News Release no. 135, 31 July 1996.

6 Notably with Chile, Bolivia, Costa Rica, and a trilateral agreement with Colombia and Venezuela, see Tratodo de Libre Comercio entre los Estados Unidos Mexicanos y la República de Bolivia, Diario Oficial de la Fédéración (DO), 28 December 1994; Tratado de Libre Comercio entre los Estados Unidos Mexicanos y la República de Costa Rica, DO, 21 June 1994; and Tratado de Libre Comercio entre los Estados Unidos Mexicanos y las República de Colombia y Venezuela, DO, 16 December 1994. It is currently negotiating further bilateral and multilateral agreements with Nicaragua and Guatemala, Honduras, and El Salvador, see G.E. Del Toro, Foreign Direct Investment in Mexico and the 1994 Crisis: A Legal Perspective (Montreal: McGill University, LLM thesis, 1996), at 52 *et seq.*

7 Based on the already existing Benelux Agreement of Belgium, Luxembourg, and Holland of 1944, operational since 1947, see Protocol to the Belgo-Luxembourg-Netherlands Customs Convention, signed at Brussels, on 22 December 1947, 32 UNTS 143 (no. 496) and the European Coal and Steel Community, 261 UNTS 142 (no. 3229); see Treaty establishing the European Economic Community, 298 UNTS 11; the amended version following the coming into force of the Maastricht Treaty (OJ C 191 of 29 July 1992) is reprinted as the Treaty establishing the European Community, [1992] CMLR 573.

8 See Title VI, EC Treaty on Economic and Monetary Union (EMU), in particular, art. 105 establishing the European system of Central Banks and the European Central Bank. Art. 109j (4) provides for the Third Stage of EMU—i.e., the introduction of a Europe-wide single currency—to come into force on 1 January 1999 if no other date has been agreed to prior to the end of 1997. The convergence criteria are laid down in a rather abstract fashion in art. 109j (1) and are fleshed out more concretely in a supplementary protocol to the Treaty on European Union. The Madrid European Council adopted a concrete scenario for the changeover to a single currency in December 1995, see Madrid European Council. Conclusions of the Presidency. Annex 1 (12-1995), 28 *EU Bull.* 9, at 24.

EU is the only full-fledged supranational union in existence, although the MERCOSUR Agreement[9] creates a customs union between Brazil, Argentina, Uruguay, and Paraguay and, since 1996, Peru and Chile, which could eventually develop along similar lines. Most regional agreements are free trade areas where member states agree to remove a variety of trade barriers reflecting local concerns and political constraints. The first important contemporary free trade agreements were the Benelux Agreement of 1947, which became basis for the EC, followed by the European Free Trade Area (EFTA) signed in 1960. These have been followed by a succession of agreements in Latin America,[10] the Caribbean,[11] Africa,[12] and Asia.[13] The demise of the USSR and the East Bloc has been followed by the formation of a large number of new agreements in Central Europe[14] and among the states of the former Soviet Union.[15] In 1996, no fewer than 20 regional trade agreements had been notified to the World Trade Organization (WTO). Between 1990 and 1996, an equal number had been concluded in Latin America alone. In many important respects, these regional economic integration agreements represent one of the most significant features of contemporary international relations.

The political and economic motivation for each agreement differs according to local circumstances, but it is hard to escape the conclusion that these agreements correspond to a widely felt common need, while continuing to reflect differing responses to the

9 See Treaty Establishing a Common Market Between the Argentine Republic, the Federal Republic of Brazil, the Republic of Paraguay and the Eastern Republic of Uruguay (the "Treaty of Asunción") (1991), 30 *ILM* 1034; Argentina-Brazial-Paraguay-Uruguay: Additional Protocol to the Treaty of Asunción on the Institutional Structure of MERCOSUR (Protocol of Rio Plata) (1995), 34 *ILM* 1244.

10 The Latin American Free Trade Association (LAFTA)—for documents see (1965), 4 *ILM* 682 & 761; (1966), 5 *ILM* 125; (1968), 7 *ILM* 747 and 851—was replaced by the Treaty of Montevideo establishing the Latin American Integration Association (LAIA) between Argentina, Bolivia, Brazil, Chili, Colombia, Ecuador, Mexico, Paraguay, Peru, Uruguay, and Venezuela, see (1981), 20 *ILM* 672.

11 Treaty establishing the Caribbean Community, done at Port of Spain, 4 July 1973 (1973), 12 *ILM* 1033; see also Caribbean Free Trade Association Agreement, signed 30 April 1968 (1968), 7 *ILM* 935.

12 See Economic Community of West African States (ECOWAS). Revised Treaty (1996), 35 *ILM* 660; Treaty Establishing the Common Market for Eastern and Southern Africa, done 5 November 1993 (1994), 33 *ILM* 1067; see also the Treaty establishing the Central African Economic and Customs Union (between Cameroon, the Central African Republic, Chad, Congo (Brazzaville), and Gabon, signed 8 December 1964 (1965), 4 *ILM* 699 and the articles of association of the Economic Community of West Africa (Dahomey, Ghana, Ivory Coast, Liberia, Mali, Mauritania, Niger, Nigeria, Senegal, Sierra Leone, Togo, and Upper Volta) (1967), 6 *ILM* 776.

13 Asia Pacific Economic Cooperation Forum (APEC). Declaration of Common Resolve, 15 November 1994 (1995), 34 *ILM* 758; Agreement on the Preferential Tariff. Scheme for the ASEA Free Trade Area, 28 January 1992 (1992), 31 *ILM* 513; Framework Agreement on Enhancing ASEAN Economic Cooperation, 28 January 1992 (1992), 31 *ILM* 506, and Singapore Declaration of 1992, 28 January 1992 (1992), 31 *ILM* 498.

14 Central European Free Trade Area, 21 December 1992 (1995), 34 *ILM* 3.

15 Commonwealth of Independent States. Treaty on Creation of Economic Union, 24 September 1993 (1995), 34 *ILM* 1298.

pressures of the world economy. It is also significant that this phenomenon is widespread: no longer is it restricted to the developed world. Developing countries find themselves drawn into such arrangements, both, *inter se*, as in Africa and Latin America, but also with developed countries as in the NAFTA. Even the states of Asia, long reluctant to commit themselves to legally binding structures, accepted a potentially tighter structure for the Asia Pacific Economic Committee (APEC).[16]

B. Regional Economic Integration Agreements and the WTO

Regional economic agreements can reinforce or weaken the principles of multilateralism enshrined in the WTO. The drafters of the GATT 1947 were aware of this danger and made provision for it in article XXIV.12, but they did not expect that the phenomenon would assume the proportions that it has. Article XXIV.12 permits customs unions or free trade agreements or arrangements that are designed to lead ultimately to these objectives, provided that the arrangement in the aggregate is trade creative rather than trade restrictive and that regional agreements do not serve to divert trade to the region which would otherwise be conducted internationally. It was assumed by the drafters of the GATT 1947 that, in principle, any further trade liberalization, beyond that required by the General Agreement, was compatible with the objectives of the multilateral trading order. This principle is still widely accepted, although economists are increasingly aware of the difficulty of making the call required by article XXIV.12, and there is increasing evidence that some regional agreements, or parts of some regional agreements, may well be diverting trade within the region rather than increasing international trade in the aggregate.[17] As a result, it can be expected that the WTO scrutiny of these agreements will become more rigorous in future years.

C. History of the Conclusion of NAFTA

In 1988, the Canada-United States Free Trade Agreement (FTA) entered into force, after a vigorous national debate and a general election in Canada largely centred on the agreement. The Conservative government of Prime Minister Mulroney had sought the FTA through negotiations beginning in 1985. This was the first comprehensive free trade agreement ever to enter into force with the United States and many Canadians had misgivings about its potential to put an end to Canadian economic self-affirmation as well as its apparent denial of Canada's long-standing commitment to the multilateral trading order.[18] In the United States, the FTA had not elicited any great public political controversy, although passage through the Senate had been very close.[19]

The situation became even more complex when Mexico approached the United States with a view to negotiating a free trade agreement similar to the FTA. Mexico desired a free trade arrangement that would give it assured access to the markets of the

16 See, generally, Trebilcock and Howse, *The Regulation of Internationals Trade* (1995).

17 See Trebilcock and Howse, *ibid.*, chapter 4; see also chapter 1 of this book, section V.A.

18 See chapter 2 of the first edition of this book.

19 The tied vote was broken by the chair.

United States. In seeking a free trade arrangement, the Government of Mexico was also seeking to consolidate its policy of economic liberalization reflected in its adhesion to the GATT in 1986. By signing a free trade agreement, Mexico hoped to be able to attract and keep more foreign investment as well as hasten the restructuring of its economy. In the United States, the Republican administration of President Bush was favourably disposed to the Mexican request and agreed to enter into an agreement. Such an agreement corresponded with its economic philosophy and, like the FTA, allowed the United States to negotiate agreements on issues like trade in services, foreign investment, and intellectual property protection that could serve as models for the ongoing Uruguay Round negotiations. However, the Bush administration was rapidly caught up in political controversy with those who feared that free trade with a major developing country would hasten the process of loss of manufacturing jobs to low-wage countries. The concerns arising from the globalization of the world economy felt by many Americans, their labour unions, and political representatives, thus found a voice in hostility to the negotiation of NAFTA.

In Canada, the federal government was not eager to embark on new negotiations at a moment when a recession, which many blamed on the FTA, was beginning to cause massive manufacturing job losses. But in the end, the government concluded that it had no other option but to insist on a place at the negotiating table in order to ensure that the advantages of the FTA not be lost, if possible to reinforce the FTA, and especially to avoid a situation in which the sole access to all three markets in North America would be through the United States.

All three countries participated fully in the negotiating process that was announced on February 5, 1991. Each country had its own separate objectives but they were united by the desire to succeed in a very short time. In this they were assisted by the existence of the FTA, which became the frame of reference. The negotiations became a process of adapting the FTA to Mexico and negotiating consequential trade concessions with Mexico, as well as returning to those matters where FTA negotiations had been incomplete or unsuccessful, such as services or intellectual property. Negotiations were concluded in September 1992 and the text was signed by the three governments in their respective capitals between December 8 and 17, 1992.[20] By that time, the NAFTA had become caught up in the political controversy of the 1992 US federal elections and candidate Clinton, in response to criticisms of NAFTA, particularly from the labour and environmental movements, had committed himself to refusing to implement the agreement as president unless new provisions were negotiated dealing with the protection of the environment and labour standards. President Clinton made good on his commitments and called for new negotiations on these issues as well as safeguards. The Mexican and Canadian governments reluctantly agreed in March 1993 but refused to reopen the NAFTA itself. The result was the adoption of the two "side agreements" on labour and environmental cooperation in September 1993.[21] In Canada, the passion of the FTA

20 See (1993), 32 *ILM* 289.

21 North American Agreement on Environmental Cooperation, 14 September 1993 (1993), 32 *ILM* 1480; North American Agreement on Labor Cooperation, 14 September 1993 (1993), 32 *ILM* 1499.

debate was rekindled in the October 1993 federal elections in which the Liberal party of Prime Minister Chrétien was elected with a mandate to renegotiate at least certain aspects of NAFTA. Discussions took place with President Clinton in November 1993, which resulted in a commitment by the United States to review the anti-dumping and subsidies legislation, as well as a statement on December 3, 1993 by all three heads of state, that the NAFTA had no application to water resources.[22] The Mexican ratification process was not without domestic political controversy,[23] but the formal process of ratification proceeded without incident.[24] The NAFTA thus entered into force as planned on January 1, 1994.

D. Structure and Interpretation of NAFTA

The NAFTA is primarily concerned with the removal of specific barriers to trade in goods and services across the borders of the three parties. Its first thrust is thus what is termed negative integration—the removal of barriers. But NAFTA goes beyond this, into what is termed positive integration, to the promotion of common forms of regulation in order to facilitate integration within the domestic economies of the three parties.[25] Positive integration is the hallmark of more advanced forms of economic integration agreements. It is most easily undertaken within a supranational structure, such as that of the EC. Without a common supranational legislative structure it is much more difficult to achieve harmonized rules and standards, since each step toward harmonization must be negotiated and agreed upon by the states involved and must take the form of an amendment to the treaty itself or to its annexes, rather than allowing for legislation under the treaty. This is true of the NAFTA, which is an extremely long, detailed, and complex set of commitments by the three parties. The advantage of this form of drafting is that all the agreement is in one text. The disadvantage of this form is that it results in a text where detail often takes precedence over general principle.

The structure of the NAFTA is fundamentally that of the GATT. This is revealed both in the style of drafting of the NAFTA, which is often very close to that of the GATT 1994, but also in the similarity of underlying concepts and principles between the two agreements. It would not be too much to assert that the logic of the GATT is the logic of the NAFTA and that to understand one is to understand the other. This was clearly the intention of the drafters and is stated at many points throughout the text.[26]

The NAFTA is built around several major and interrelated blocks of chapters. The most significant is found in part two, which is devoted to trade in goods and is made up

22 See Paterson and Band, *International Trade and Investment Law in Canada* (2nd ed., 1995), at 3-7.

23 The Chiapas uprising beginning on 1 January 1994, although not directly caused by the NAFTA, heralded the difficulties inherent in managing a free trade arrangement between countries of very disparate economic levels.

24 This process required constitutional change, as well as legislative and executive action.

25 Hart, *What's Next? Canada, the Global Economy and the New Trade Law Policy* (Ottawa: Centre for Trade Policy and Law, 1994).

26 Preamble, chapters 1, 2, 3, etc.

of several general and a number of more specific chapters. This part is complemented by part three dealing with technical barriers to trade. The second major block is found in part five, which deals with investment and service issues. Parts four and six, which deal with government procurement and intellectual property protection, modify both the major parts. Finally, several general chapters apply to the whole of the agreement: these cover the statement of objectives, general definitions, institutions and dispute settlement, exceptions, and final clauses. Throughout the NAFTA, both within each chapter and modifying the whole text, are many annexes. These annexes amount to roughly half the text and are essential to a complete understanding of the agreement. Annexes are used for a wide variety of purposes. The most significant annexes are those at the end of the text that set out the non-conforming legislation of the three parties that continues to apply despite divergence from the principles of the NAFTA. Specific references are required for derogations from NAFTA, rather than references to general categories of laws that had been the method adopted in the FTA. The lists of non-conforming laws were only completed in 1996, two years after the entry into force of the agreement, in order to allow states and provinces the time to prepare lists of their non-conforming laws. This system has the advantage over the FTA of providing much greater certainty as to inapplicable laws and of facilitating their removal in the future. Annexes are also used throughout the text to provide greater specificity and to allow for more detailed treatment of issues than might be possible in the main body of a chapter, or to allow for the adoption of additional regulations as they are negotiated in the future. Finally, annexes are regularly used throughout the text to set out detailed definitions of situations or concepts.

Interpretation of NAFTA involves both very close adherence to an extremely detailed text and reference to a number of general principles and presumptions. The first and most basic principle is that of the primacy of the text itself as between the parties.[27] The second and equally important principle is that of compatibility with the GATT. Reference is made regularly to the GATT either by way of affirmations of compatibility,[28] by requiring an interpretation compatible with the GATT,[29] or by incorporating GATT definitions or concepts.[30] Reference to the GATT extends to the Interpretative Notes to the GATT, as they were at the adoption of the NAFTA, and to successor agreements, which now requires reference to the full corpus of law under the GATT 1994.[31] Certain provisions affirm GATT rules but restrict their application between the parties.[32] Certain NAFTA rules are more restrictive than the GATT and, in such cases, the NAFTA text sets out the more restrictive rule.[33] NAFTA parties are committed to

---

27 Art. 103:2.

28 Art. 103:1.

29 Art. 309:1.

30 Arts. 201:1 and 603:1.

31 Art. 301:1.

32 Art. 315:1.

33 Art. 314.

continued cooperation within the GATT-WTO structures.[34] The presumption of compatibility with the GATT 1994 is thus central to understanding the NAFTA.

Several other presumptions also assist in interpreting the NAFTA. First is the presumption that national treatment is the general standard of treatment. In this, the NAFTA clearly goes beyond the GATT 1994 where national treatment (NT) still does not fully displace most-favoured-nation (MFN) treatment. With the NAFTA, unless the contrary is specified, national treatment is the operative standard. A second presumption of great significance with respect to goods is that tariffs will be completely eliminated at the end of the phase-in period. Again, in those areas where this will not happen such as agriculture and textiles, the contrary is clearly stated. A third presumption of very considerable importance is that the whole agreement is subject to compulsory dispute settlement. This presumption is subject to a limited number of clearly framed exceptions;[35] if not otherwise stated, the general procedure of chapter 20 is applicable. A further presumption of the whole agreement is that NAFTA applies to governments and is not directly applicable to private parties.[36] Each party has taken the necessary legislative measures to ensure full implementation.[37] Finally, it can also be presumed that the entire agreement is applicable to state and provincial governments,[38] although this principle is subject to very broad exceptions.

The NAFTA makes frequent reference to other international conventions. In some circumstances this is done in order to incorporate the convention by reference, in others it is in order to give priority to the referenced convention.[39] Some NAFTA articles also refer more generally to international standards developed by competent regional and multilateral organizations.[40]

E. NAFTA and the GATT

As set out above, the NAFTA is built upon a matrix of GATT law. This law includes not only the GATT as it was in 1994, but also the results of the Uruguay Round as they have entered into force after January 1, 1995. The two texts deal with similar issues and the NAFTA parties are bound to respect the GATT 1994. The normal rule of treaty interpretation is that the subsequent treaty prevails. This rule may be useful in assisting to

34 Art. 317.

35 See section V.B of this chapter and chapter 19 on GATT-WTO 1994 dispute settlement.

36 Art. 2021.

37 North American Free Trade Agreement Implementation Act, 8 December 1993, PL 101-182, 19 USCS § 3301; Decreto que reforma, adiciona y deroga disposiciones de diversas leyes relacionadas con El Tratodo de libre Comercio de América del Norte, DO of 22 December 1993; see also Mexico: Foreign Investment Act of 1993 (27 December 1993) (1994), 33 *ILM* 207.

38 NAFTA, art. 105.

39 NAFTA, Annex 608.2:2 and art. 104:1 (shielding trade obligations arising under certain international environmental agreements such as the Montreal Protocol or CITES from NAFTA).

40 *In the Matter of Tariffs Applied by Canada to Certain US-Origin Agricultural Goods*, Report of the Panel, 2 December 1996, CDA-95-2008-1.

understand the relationship between the two agreements. Indeed, in some instances, the NAFTA specifically makes provision for the future GATT 1994, but it is clearly not sufficient to say that GATT supersedes NAFTA because the very purpose of the NAFTA is to create a special preferential relationship between the three parties, which is not always exactly that of the GATT 1994. Context is relevant to understanding the relationship and is often assisted by specific provisions concerning future GATT law, as with safeguards and subsidies, where the new Uruguay Round agreements expand and clarify GATT law that is applied as part of the law of the NAFTA. Other cases are more complex, as revealed by the 1996 dispute initiated by the United States against Canada concerning Canadian tariffication of agricultural quotas, which had previously been maintained by virtue of GATT article XI.2(c), and which were transposed from tariffs into quotas pursuant to the WTO Agreement on Agriculture.[41]

F. NAFTA and the FTA

In virtually every respect, the NAFTA supersedes the FTA as between Canada and the United States, but this does not mean that the FTA has been completely replaced. The FTA has not been abrogated; it remains in force and would become the operative treaty again as between Canada and the United States should the NAFTA be abrogated. In certain cases, such as agriculture,[42] wines and spirits[43] and safeguards,[44] the FTA remains in operation or is incorporated by reference. As between the United States and Canada, there is very great continuity between the two agreements, their institutions, and basic principles. However, the trilateral relationship with Mexico is entirely new and in some respects different from that between the two original partners.

G. NAFTA and Canadian Law

As a treaty, the NAFTA has no legal force in Canadian law unless implemented by the Parliament of Canada or the provincial legislatures. In Canada, this required mainly federal legislation since most provincial measures were limited to administrative changes.[45] The Government of Canada is committed vis-à-vis the other parties to ensure full implementation of the agreement, including implementation by the provinces, and it can be assumed that the federal government would take the position that it is fully authorized to implement all parts of the NAFTA, on the grounds that the matters covered by the NAFTA relate to international trade.[46] It should be noted that the two side agreements on labour and environmental cooperation are not drafted on this assumption and

41 NAFTA, art. 713:5.

42 NAFTA, Annex 702.1.

43 NAFTA, Annex 312.2.

44 NAFTA, Annex 801.1.

45 As provincial commitments in respect of government procurement and services become more extensive, further legislative measures can be expected.

46 For discussion of jurisdiction in respect of agreements in the field of international trade, see chapter 1, *supra*.

specifically require that the Canadian provinces indicate their willingness to be bound both by the substance of the agreements and by their dispute settlement procedures.[47]

Although the influence is more indirect than direct, it would be wrong to assert that NAFTA has no direct impact upon Canadian law. In an important sense it has had a profound effect in that it is the source of many changes to laws and regulations. Beyond this, the NAFTA has become a significant element of business planning for all Canadian firms doing business in the United States and Mexico, and Canadian lawyers are regularly called upon to advise on the impact of the agreement. Furthermore, although article 2021 prohibits any of the parties from providing for private rights of action against other parties to enforce the agreement, various elements of the dispute settlement procedures, including articles 1116-37, 1717-18, and 2022 speak to private dispute settlement. In addition, article 2020 appears to envisage situations where courts and administrative tribunals charged with implementing certain rules of the NAFTA will need authoritative guidance from the NAFTA Commission.[48]

II. TRADE IN GOODS

A. General Principles

The chapters on trade in goods are made up of both general principles and very specific rules reflecting a series of compromises on different aspects of the negotiations. The general principles are applicable to all chapters unless overridden by some more specific rule.

The central principle of the NAFTA is that of national treatment of all goods originating in the territory of the other parties. NT is "in accordance with article III of the GATT," which is incorporated into the agreement.[49] Thus, the full body of GATT law defining national treatment is applicable and has in fact been invoked regularly by dispute settlement panels.[50] This national treatment requirement applies not only to the three federal governments but equally to state and provincial governments. The latter are required to accord treatment no less favourable than that which they accord to any "directly competitive or substitutable goods."[51] The obligation in respect of states and provinces is thus stated in an even stronger manner than is the case under the GATT

47 See art. 41 of the North American Agreement on Environmental Cooperation (NAAEC) and its Annex 41, limiting Canada's obligation in regard to provincial implementation of the agreement to provinces specifically listed in a declaration, as well as the Canadian Intergovernmental Agreement Regarding the North American Environmental Cooperation Agreement, specifying the procedure for provinces' participation in the enforcement and implementation of the NAAEC. The corresponding provisions in the Labour side agreement are art. 46 and Annex 46.

48 A similar provision exists in the FTA. As of 1996, neither provision had been invoked.

49 NAFTA, art. 301:1.

50 In *Re Canada's Landing Requirements for Salmon and Herring*, Canada-US Binational Panel Final Report, 16 October 1989, 12 ITRD 1027; *Lobster from Canada*, US-Canada Binational Panel Final Report, 24 May 1990: See chapter 1, *supra*, note 37, for GATT panel rulings on national treatment.

51 NAFTA, art. 301:2.

1994. Exceptions to the principle and generally to articles 301 and 309 are set out in Annex 301.3 for each of the parties. Canadian and American exceptions are limited in scope and reflect traditional protectionist policies in respect of fisheries and the merchant marine. Mexican exceptions, as might be expected for a country that only joined the GATT in 1986, are much more extensive and specific.

B. Tariff Treatment

Tariff treatment is the central and most immediately effective part of the NAFTA. It is governed by several general principles and detailed tariff schedules of each of the parties. The general principles are equally applicable to each of the parties; however, given that NAFTA is a free trade area and not a customs union, that each party had different economic policy concerns, and that Mexico is a developing country that only recently joined the GATT, the schedules of each party vary considerably in detail.

The first general principle is that no party may increase existing customs duties or create new customs duties. The NAFTA operates as a standstill on the establishment of any further tariff barriers. Second, the parties are committed to reducing their tariffs *inter se* on a progressive scale as set out in Annex 302.2, with the ultimate goal of very broad elimination. Each item in the customs tariff schedules is rated in one of four staging categories, the first requiring elimination of all duties upon entry into force of the NAFTA. Duties on items in staging category B must be revised by January 1. Duties on all of the items in category C must be eliminated by January 1, 2003, while all items in category C+ must be eliminated by January 1, 2008. Category D lists items that bore no duty in 1994; these must continue to remain duty-free. Provision is also made for accelerating duty reduction in article 302.3. This authority has been exercised at the behest of several industries.

The GATT allows the establishment of duty drawback and referral schemes and the parties have all made extensive use of this authority. However, the continued use of such schemes within the context of a free trade area, where transparency, equal treatment, and equal access are fundamental values, would allow a party to obtain an unfair advantage over the others. For this reason, articles 303 and 304 place restrictions on the use of schemes whose purpose is to encourage the subsequent re-export or incorporation of imported goods into a product destined for export or the substitution of the imported good by a domestic good that is subsequently exported. The ban is not total, unlike the FTA, but duties representing the difference between duties paid on entry to another party and the duty otherwise payable on direct entry to the party in question may not be refunded.[52] The parties are prohibited by article 304 from extending or creating any new waiver schemes whose purpose is the imposition of a performance requirement. The use of waiver schemes in force before NAFTA is regulated by Annexes 304.1 and 304.2. Mexico enjoys a fairly broad latitude until 2001; Canada is permitted to grant waivers pursuant to the rules governing the automotive sector; and Canada and the United States may use waivers permitted by the FTA until 1998.

52 NAFTA, art. 303.1.

C. Rules of Origin

In a free trade area, member states retain separate and different customs tariffs. This gives them greater autonomy than they would enjoy in a customs union but it is potentially divisive since it provides an incentive for importers to enter goods through the lowest tariff territory. In order to avoid this phenomenon, the parties have adopted rules of origin to define which goods may claim the advantages of NAFTA when they move across a NAFTA border. The FTA contained rules of origin and the experience with these rules assisted negotiators in avoiding certain problems that had emerged.[53] The NAFTA rules of origin set out in chapter 4[54] are more detailed and product specific than the FTA rules and it is claimed that the method of calculation is less ambiguous and more closely tied to standard accounting principles.[55]

Article 401 sets out four basic types of goods that qualify for treatment as goods originating in the NAFTA area:

1. goods wholly obtained or produced entirely in the territory of a NAFTA party;
2. non-originating goods that have undergone a change of their tariff status as a result of production occurring entirely in the NAFTA area;
3. goods wholly produced in the territory of one or more NAFTA parties from originating materials; or
4. goods made up of originating and non-originating materials produced in the NAFTA area, provided that the regional value of the final product is not less than 60 percent, when calculated according to the transaction value method, or not less than 50 percent when calculated by the net cost method.

Regional value and net cost-value methods of calculation are defined in article 403.[56] The method the most favourable to the exporter or producer can normally be used at their discretion. This rule and the percentage rates are subject to exceptions in certain cases, principally with respect to footwear, where the rate is 55 percent, and automobiles, where the percentage rises to 62.5 percent.[57] The situation is even more complex with respect to textiles and clothing where the rules of origin are a function of quotas on categories of goods and take into account the respective origins of fibres, threads, cloth, and place of manufacture of the garment. Automobiles are subject to special rules for calculating regional value content set out in article 403.

---

53 One major practical difficulty concerned the value to be ascribed to different components of a complex product. Another resulted in the convening of a dispute settlement panel under chapter 18 of the FTA: *Non-Mortgage Interest under Article 304*, Final Report, 8 June 1992; USA-92-1807-01.

54 Implemented in Canada by the NAFTA Rules of Origin Regulations, SOR/94-14, *Can. Gaz.* pt. II:60; SOR/95-23, *Can. Gaz.* pt. II:68; and SOR/95-328, *Can. Gaz.* pt. II:2214.

55 Paterson and Band, *supra*, note 22, at 3-27.

56 See Johnson, "What is a North American Good? The NAFTA Rules of Origin," C.D. Howe Commentary no. 40 (1993), and Johnson, *The North American Free Trade Agreement* (1994), chapter 3.

57 See Eden and Appel Molot, "The NAFTA's Automotive Provisions: The Next Step in Managed Trade," C.D. Howe Commentary, no. 53 (1993).

Chapter 4 contains a number of other rules. Article 404 permits the accumulation of the costs of several producers in different NAFTA territories. Article 405 provides that goods shall be automatically considered originating goods if the value of non-originating goods used in their production is less than 7 percent of the transaction value or total cost of the goods. Article 406 provides some necessary flexibility in the treatment of fungible goods. Spare parts, accessories, indirect materials, and packaging are covered by articles 407 to 410. Further treatment or production outside a NAFTA country can lead to the loss of NAFTA origin status under article 411.

Rules of origin are potentially the most serious barrier to trade liberalization at both the international and regional levels. It is no coincidence that the most managed products, such as textiles and automobiles, are subject to complex and restrictive rules of origin. These rules of origin have the greatest potential for trade diversion and are thus at the heart of criticisms levelled at regional trading arrangements like NAFTA. These rules are complex, their administration is costly, and compliance with their requirements by North American producers often involves the development of detailed accounting procedures to ensure adequate evidence if challenged by public authorities or competitors. However, until the unlikely time that NAFTA becomes a customs union, rules of origin will remain a necessary evil.

D. Non-Tariff Measures

Chapter 3 contains a number of provisions designed to restrain non-tariff barriers between the parties. Article 309.1 incorporates existing and future GATT prohibitions on import and export quotas. Particular reference is made to the prohibition of export price requirements, and import price requirements are equally proscribed, except in conjunction with anti-dumping and countervailing duty proceedings.

Article 315 creates an important discipline on the use of export restrictions by the parties. This article allows them to maintain GATT-compatible export restrictions, but only so long as the other parties continue to receive the same proportion of the total supply of goods as they received in the previous 36-month period. They are thus committed to reducing exports only so far as they restrict domestic supply of the same goods. They also prohibit export prices higher than domestic prices and agree "not to disrupt normal channels of supply."

Article 309 also deals with the politically vexed issue of trade restrictions maintained by a party against other states: goods to and from the embargoed state cannot escape restrictions by transiting the territory of another party. A number of other restrictions are also permitted: Mexico is allowed to maintain export taxes on basic foodstuffs.[58] Customs user fees, used by Mexico and the United States, are not to be increased and are to be phased out by June 1999. So long as the three parties maintain different tariff schedules and, in particular, so long as the terms of entry of Canadian and Mexican goods into the United States differ—a situation that will last at least until 2009—it is appropriate to maintain rules on the national origin of the goods as between

---

58 NAFTA, Annex 314.

NAFTA parties. But, in order to ensure that these rules are not used to impede trade between the parties they are committed by article 311 to creating uniform rules of origin for marking purposes.[59] They also accept "any reasonable method of marking" goods in force in the other party, including use of French and Spanish.

E. Special Cases

1. Trade in Automobiles

In 1965, Canada and the United States signed the Auto Pact,[60] a bilateral trade agreement designed to avoid trade frictions by managing the trade in automobiles and automotive products between them. At the time, the United States sought to restrict Canadian use of duty remission schemes that restricted the freedom of manoeuvre of the American companies that dominated the market. Canada was seeking to ensure that a greater proportion of North American automotive production remained in Canada. Governments and companies had an interest in an arrangement that allowed duty-free production and trade in order to achieve full economies of scale, rather than requiring the manufacture of a complete line of products in both countries.[61] Over the years, the Auto Pact has been the source of very substantial employment and a large proportion of Canada's international trade. Canada sought to preserve these benefits as the FTA and subsequent NAFTA negotiations took both countries toward more liberal trading rules in other sectors of the economy. However, the US government had become increasingly concerned that foreign automobile manufacturers located in Canada were taking undue advantage of autopact status to the detriment of potential production in the United States. Similarly, while Mexico was prepared to move away from its very restrictive rules on foreign investment and the foreign production of automobiles in Mexico, this could only happen gradually and had to be a carefully managed process. The result is Annex 300-A, which governs trade and investment in the automotive sector among the three countries.

As between Canada and the United States, the principal provisions of Annex 300-A relate to the rules of origin. The net-cost method must be used for the calculation of North American content and the rate rises to 62.5 percent for cars. Second, the number of non-big-three producers eligible to claim autopact status is capped and Canada is required to phase out certain duty remission schemes. Some of the advantages to Canada of the FTA scheme in attracting foreign producers to Canada appear to have been lost. The United States is committed to accepting Canadian and Mexican content as qualifying for domestic status under the Corporate Average Fuel Economy Standards. Much of Annex 300-A is taken up with Mexican commitments to liberalize its rules on domestic

---

59 Determination of Country of Origin for purposes of Marking Goods (NAFTA Countries) Regulations, SOR/94-23, *Can. Gaz.* pt. II:471; SOR/95-146, *Can. Gaz.* pt. II:692; SOR/95-348, *Can. Gaz.* pt. II:2109; and SOR/95-447, *Can. Gaz.* pt. II:2699.

60 Agreement concerning Automotive Products between the Government of Canada and the Government of the United States, Can. TS 1966, no. 14.

61 See the first edition of this book for a more complete description of the working of the Auto Pact.

production by foreigners and the importation of automobiles, trucks, and buses. In particular, the Mexican Auto Decree will be phased out by 2004. As a first step, Mexico has eliminated the requirement that vehicle imports be limited to a fixed number of domestic sales of cars produced in Mexico. The Mexican domestic content requirement of 36 percent will be gradually reduced to 29 percent. The market for used vehicles will be fully liberalized between the parties by 2009.

The overall result is a situation where the structure of a free trade arrangement, including high domestic content requirements, protects domestic producers and domestic employment. It is hard to believe that there has not been significant trade diversion in automobiles and even more in auto parts in this sector of North American trade.[62]

2. Trade in Textiles and Apparel Goods

Textiles and clothing remain among the most highly regulated commodities in international trade. The NAFTA takes some modest steps to removing barriers, but trade in this area remains subject to an extraordinarily complex set of rules. Annex 300-B, which regulates the sector, is 60 pages long. It is composed of different commitments between the three parties. These commitments include tariffs, tariff-rate quotas, rules of origin, quotas, and different products and the component elements of these products. As between Canada and the United States, tariff levels are to be phased out in 10 years according to chapter 3. The rate of tariff reduction agreed to by Mexico is more gradual but still significant. Trade in different categories of textiles and apparel is subject to quotas backed up by rules of origin that reflect as much the desire of the parties to protect domestic production as to liberalize trade. If anything, the Mexican commitments are less restrictive than those of Canada and the United States. The annex provides for two sets of special safeguard actions, one for originating goods and the second for non-originating goods. Such safeguards can take the form of tariff increases, but only once within the phase-in period, and with respect to non-originating goods they can also take the form of quota changes.

3. Wine and Spirits

Chapter 8 of the FTA contained a series of commitments to eliminate certain discriminatory practices with respect to access of American wine and spirits to the Canadian market.[63] These provisions are carried forward by Annex 312.2. As between Canada and Mexico, the same annex invokes the general rules of article 301, with some significant reservations. Beer is governed exclusively by the GATT 1994.

---

62 See also Johnson, *supra*, note 56, at 133 and 148 for an assessment of the Auto Pact's effects on Canada's domestic economy.

63 See Murray, "The Evolving Role of the Provinces in Canadian Trade Policy" in Brown and Smith (eds.), *Canadian Federalism: Meeting Global Economic Challenges?* (Kingston, Ont.: Institute for Intergovernmental Relations, 1991) 81, at 97 and footnote 49.

4. Natural Resources

Trade and investment in energy resources was a central concern for the United States in negotiating the FTA and led to the drafting of chapter 8 of that agreement. The same considerations led to the inclusion of chapter 6 in the NAFTA, dealing with energy and basic petrochemicals. If anything, sensitivities in Mexico were even greater than had been the case in Canada, since foreign ownership of energy resources is prohibited under Mexican constitutional law, and Mexico insisted in retaining this principle in the NAFTA. As a result, Mexico was able to relieve itself of most of the obligations of this chapter by taking major exceptions in respect of petroleum (and natural gas).

Chapter 6 is largely a repetition of the FTA, chapter 8, as well as the principles of the NAFTA, chapter 3. It mandates GATT standards in respect of trade in coal, oil, natural gas, uranium, and electricity, although the latter is arguably not covered by the GATT.[64] Export taxes and quotas are prohibited, and article 605 reproduces the controversial proportional sharing of reductions in exports found in the NAFTA, article 315, and in the FTA. This provision had been among the most controversial aspects of the FTA and its removal was deemed non-negotiable by the United States when questioned by the newly elected government of Prime Minister Chrétien in late 1993. The Prime Minister had to be content with making and interpretative statement that the article implies only a duty to refrain from adopting regulatory measures that would make the maintenance of a proportional share of exports impossible.[65] Article 606 is stronger than the parallel FTA, article 905, in that it provides more protection against discriminatory regulatory actions of US states. In the case of an international energy emergency, the Agreement on an International Energy Program (IEP), to which all NAFTA parties are party, is to prevail over the NAFTA.[66]

5. Agricultural Goods

Chapter 7 of the NAFTA is not always easy to understand. It is essentially a carrying forward of the FTA, chapter 7, combined with a set of three bilateral commitments among the parties. Its provisions are limited to the point that it does not even grant North American origin status to products originating in more than one NAFTA territory. Between Canada and the United States, it does little more than carry forward the provisions of the FTA and does not take liberalization much further than the GATT. However, as between Mexico and the two other parties, there is a considerable degree of liberalization with respect to market access in both directions. The somewhat complex drafting of the chapter is due both to the inherent difficulties in abandoning the intricate regulatory structure of trade in agricultural goods and the equally important fact that the Uruguay Round of Multilateral Trade Negotiations were continuing throughout the

64 Paterson and Band, *supra*, note 22, at 3-33.

65 Government of Canada, Declaration of the Government of Canada on Energy and the NAFTA, 2 December 1993.

66 NAFTA, Annex 608.2(2).

NAFTA negotiations, and Canada, at least, preferred to deal with major issues of principle concerning the protection of supply management in the Uruguay Round negotiations.[67] The chapters does bear the mark of the Uruguay Round negotiations in that it provides for the tariffication of some quotas to promote market access.

The parties did agree in common to rather vague provisions on market access and the removal of trade distortions. Progress was made on subsidies in that, as well as incorporating the disciplines on export subsidies of the FTA, the parties agreed in article 705 to work toward multilateral elimination of export subsidies and to regular consultations on the effect of agricultural subsidies. A special agricultural safeguard procedure is permitted under article 703.

As between Canada and Mexico, chapter 7 provides for a considerable degree of market access for "qualifying" goods—i.e., those of specifically Mexican origin—but excludes dairy, poultry, and egg goods from this right of access, thus protecting Canada's supply management schemes. This objective is further reinforced by Annex 703.2-B.6, which anticipates the changes to be brought about by the Agreement on Agriculture. The Mexico-US provisions on market access go even further—except with respect to sugar—in that they provide for full waiver of GATT article XI:2(c) rights. The rules governing market access of US agricultural goods to Canada are more restrictively framed: they essentially incorporate the provisions of articles 701, 702, 704-7, 710, and 711 of the FTA.[68] Canada made no commitment to abandon or tariffy its supply management quotas under GATT, article XI:2(c) and the United States did not agree in NAFTA to abandon its right to use section 22 of the Agricultural Adjustment Act against Canada. Unlike the Canada-Mexico provisions, there is no provision expressly contemplating the adjustment of this chapter, which entered into force in 1994, to the Agreement on Agriculture in 1995.[69]

The ambiguity about Canada's right to implement tariffs under the Agreement on Agriculture led to the first dispute under chapter 20 of NAFTA, since the United States took the position that Canada's action in converting its supply management quotas to tariffs in 1995 violated the prior NAFTA, chapter 3 commitments not to increase and to phase out tariffs. The NAFTA arbitral panel ruled in Canada's favour, both on the ground that the negotiations on agricultural products between Canada and the United States were to be resolved in the GATT Uruguay Round, not the NAFTA negotiations, and on the ground that the NAFTA carried forward article 710 of the FTA, which specifically envisaged the application of future GATT rules on agricultural products.[70]

---

67 Canada fought a long and difficult defence of its art. XI:2 rights and would have preferred the Agreement on Agriculture to have allowed for maintenance of quotas rather than requiring their tariffication.

68 FTA, art. 710 was deemed to be taken over by the new, and possibly more restrictive, provisions on phytosanitary standards. See section G, Standards, *infra*.

69 Although it should be noted that this may be the intention of the interpretative note to art. 302.1. Art. 302.1 prohibits increasing tariffs, while the note interprets this as not prohibiting tariff increases negotiated under the GATT.

70 *In the Matter of Tariffs Applied by Canada to Certain US-Origin Agricultural Goods*, Report of the Panel, 2 December 1996, CDA-95-2008-1.

F. Safeguard Remedies

The extent of the market access commitments of the NAFTA as well as the inclusion of a major developing country made it inevitable that there would be provisions on safeguards in the NAFTA. This has occurred. The danger with this is that these safeguard remedies to the point that, like Anti-Dumping and Countervailing (AD/CV) duty procedures, they become non-tariff barriers in their own right. It is not clear that this danger has been avoided in the NAFTA given the presence of additional safeguards for agricultural and textile goods. The recent increase in safeguard proceedings under various parts of the GATT 1994 also gives cause for concern. Fortunately, the NAFTA is drafted in a manner that indicates that the parties were sensitive to the dangers of new procedures and were prepared to be more restrictive in their approach than is the case under the WTO.

Chapter 8 envisages three safeguard procedures: two bilateral and the third relating to actions at the multilateral level. As between Canada and the United States, the provisions of article 1101 of the FTA are followed. This procedure restricts actions to situations where imports resulting from tariff reductions are actually causing serious injury. The NAFTA procedure applicable against Mexico is similar except that it can also be invoked in the face of a threat of serious injury. In both cases, the action is available only once against a particular commodity during the phase-in period; the imports must be the sole cause of serious injury; and the safeguard measure must be limited to three years' duration. After the end of the phase-in period, a party may take safeguard actions only with the consent of the other party. Multilateral safeguard proceedings under the WTO are permitted but they are applicable to other parties only when the imports in question from a party amount to a "substantial share" of total imports—i.e., when the party is among the top five suppliers, and when the imports from a party "contribute importantly" to the serious injury. These conditions constitute a significant protection for Canadian goods in the face of US safeguard actions, given the volume of trade between the two countries. A further advantage of the NAFTA safeguards over the FTA system is found in Annexes 803.3 and 805, which specify new procedural requirements to make NAFTA safeguard proceedings more transparent and fair to the importer.

By virtue of article 804, no proposed safeguard measure is subject to chapter 20 dispute settlement, although the interpretation and application of chapter 8 in general are no excluded.

G. Standards

Canada and the United States had already accepted tighter disciplines in chapters 6 and 7 of the FTA than those provided by the GATT[71] and it was to be expected that they would wish to see Mexico bound to similar disciplines. During the negotiation of the NAFTA, the parties were also involved in the renegotiation and expansion of the comparable provisions in the Uruguay Round negotiations. Chapter 9 on technical barriers to trade and chapter 7, section B, on sanitary and phytosanitary measures bear the imprint

71 Agreement on Technical Barriers to Trade, GATT, BISD, 26th Supp. 8.

of the multilateral trade negotiations, although they differ in some respects. It should be noted that these chapters, while primarily focused upon goods, are relevant to certain services.[72]

Chapter 9 applies to all "standards-related measures" of a party, a term that covers general standards, technical regulations, and conformity assessment procedures, except those covered by chapter 7, section B, on sanitary and phytosanitary standards and technical specifications for government procurement, covered by chapter 10. Unlike the FTA, the NAFTA technical standards provisions apply to state or provincial governments as well as to non-governmental standardizing bodies. However, the parties are required only to "seek to ensure observance" of the provisions by these bodies, a formulation that is less forceful than the obligations of article 105 and the comparable article 3 of the GATT 1994 Agreement on Technical Barriers to Trade. The basic standard of treatment under this chapter is national treatment in respect of standards for goods and service providers.[73]

Like the GATT and FTA texts, the NAFTA seeks to strike a balance between affirming the right of parties to adopt high standards, especially for consumer and environmental protection,[74] and the facilitation of trade by the promotion of common standards and the mutual recognition of national standards and standards testing bodies. Thus, article 904 begins by affirming the right of the parties "in accordance with this Agreement" to adopt standards and measures to enforce these standards, including the right to prohibit the entry of non-conforming goods and services. These standards may be set at the level that the party "considers appropriate." The counterpart to these rights is that standards shall apply to goods and services of other parties in a non-discriminatory manner and that standards shall not create "unnecessary obstacles" to trade. Standards meet this requirement when "the demonstrable purpose of the measure is to achieve a legitimate objective." By virtue of article 905, the parties agree to use relevant international standards as the basis for their measures, unless such standards are "ineffective or inappropriate" and agree that such conformity shall create a presumption of non-discrimination. Article 906 contains a best efforts commitment to make the respective national standards compatible and to accept each others' technical standards as equivalent where the other party demonstrates that its regulations fulfill the objectives of the importing party. Each party is also to accept "where possible" the conformity assessments of the other party. Risk and conformity assessments are within the sovereignty of each state but the parties agree to avoid discrimination and they recognize that it is to their mutual advantage to have compatible conformity assessment procedures. Inquiry points are to be created by each party to provide information on standards. This chapter also provides for the

---

72 Annex 913.5 refers to road transportation and telecommunications.

73 The GATT text is addressed to goods.

74 The NAFTA is more respectful of national jurisdiction over environmental protection than the GATT 1994 taking into account all relevant provisions and the Side Agreement on Environmental Protection. See Johnson, *supra*, note 56, at 252-70 and Johnson and Beaulieu, *The Environment and NAFTA. Understanding and Implementing the New Continental Law* (1996), at 117 *et seq.*

creation of a number of committees to undertake consultations to promote the conformity of standards and testing procedures.

Sanitary and phytosanitary standards—measures related to animal and plant life and health[75]—are dealt with separately in chapter 7, section B, on agriculture. By virtue of the exclusions in article 710, this section constitutes a self-contained code, overriding articles 301, 309, and 2102. States and provinces are bound by article 105 and non-governmental entities are covered as a result of article 712. The balance of rights and duties and the methods of achieving this balance are close to those set out in chapter 9. Among the points to be noted is the latitude for parties to choose high levels of environmental protection: in doing this, a party is not required to chose the "least trade-restrictive" approach as it would under the GATT 1994.[76] Also to be noted is the change in wording on the issue of equivalence as between the NAFTA, article 714, and the FTA, article 708.[77]

H. Government Procurement

As with other parts of the NAFTA, the objective of the parties in negotiating chapter 10 on government procurement was to take the process further than appeared possible in the Uruguay Round of Multilateral Trade Negotiations. In this case, Mexico was not a party to the GATT Agreement on Government Procurement.[78] With the addition of Mexico and with the increased scope of the NAFTA provisions, the covered North American government procurement market was worth $78 billion in 1995, as opposed to $20 billion under the FTA. The potential market, if all were opened, would exceed $1 trillion.[79]

The structure and principles of chapter 10 are close to those of the GATT Agreement on Government Procurement. Whether or not the chapter applies depends on four variables: (1) characterization of the transaction as a procurement, (2) purchase by a designated governmental entity of (3) covered goods and services, (4) whose worth is over a designated threshold. Federal entities of the United States and Canada are listed in the annexes and cover a wide range of government departments and other governmental bodies. Mexico made commitments on a temporary basis, pending a more complete list of central government entities. States and provinces are covered in principle, including local governments, unlike the FTA, but parties were allowed a grace period of two

75 Johnson, *supra*, note 56, at 235 notes that some matters like measures to prevent the spread of AIDS through the blood supply present difficult problems of categorization.

76 Compare NAFTA, art. 705.5 with the GATT Agreement on the Application of Sanitary and Phytosanitary Measures, art. 5.6.

77 Considered in the panel report *In the Matter of Puerto Rico Regulations on the import, distribution and sale of UHT milk from Québec*, USA-92-1807-02-1992.

78 GATT, BISD, 26th Supp. 33. An amended version of this agreement subsequently became one of the four Plurilateral Agreements of the GATT 1994 and, hence, Mexico was not obliged to conform to it.

79 Paterson and Band, *supra*, note 22, at 3-52. This figure is to be compared with a maximum of $10 billion under the 1979 GATT Agreement on Government Procurement.

years[80] to list their commitments. In principle, all goods and services are covered unless excepted. Exceptions include small and minority businesses in the United States and Canada. Research and development and health and social services as well as shipbuilding and repair were excluded by Canada and a broader set of exceptions was taken by Mexico, including some with respect to the Mexican petroleum monopoly Pemex. The general threshold value for the purchase of goods and services by federal government entities is $50,000 US for contracts for goods and $6.5 million for construction services; however, it drops to $25,000 between the United States and Canada. For governmental enterprises, the threshold is $250,000 for contracts for goods and $8 million for construction services.[81]

Chapter 10 covers the same categories of tendering procedures as the GATT Agreement on Government Procurement. In each case, the procedures are subject to a variety of disciplines designed to ensure that nationals of other parties have an opportunity to submit bids. Article 1017 requires the creation of a national bid challenge procedure by each party, open to the nationals of all parties. In Canada, this procedure is under the jurisdiction of the the Canadian International Trade Tribunal (CITT).[82] The procedure has been regularly used but more by Canadians than Americans or Mexicans. Negotiations on extension of obligations in respect of government procurement must begin again by the end of 1998.[83]

III. SERVICES AND INVESTMENTS

A. Introduction

The issues covered by part 5 on investments and services and part 6 on intellectual property represent some of the principal innovations of the NAFTA. They reflect a willingness of the parties to submit to trade disciplines not only in respect of goods and non-tariff barriers but also in order to deal with trade in services, as well as investments and related issues such as competition policy and the protection of intellectual property. The FTA had already taken important steps in the direction of services and the Uruguay Round was addressing the same issues during the period of the NAFTA negotiations. In some respects, the NAFTA represented a model of what the GATT could achieve but it is equally true that the Uruguay Round had a significant impact on the wording of these chapters. In other respects, these chapters can be seen, like those on trade in goods, as the efforts of the parties to take the process of trade liberalization further in the regional context than was possible in the multilateral framework.

---

80 Subsequently extended.

81 The thresholds applicable to state and provincial governments was to be negotiated together with their commitments but as of 1996 had not been announced.

82 See Canadian International Trade Tribunal Act, RSC 1985, c. 47 (4th Supp.), as am. by the North American Free Trade Agreement Implementation Act, SC 1993, c. 44, ss. 30.1, 30.11 to 30.19; and Canadian International Trade Tribunal Rules, SOR/93-601, *Can. Gaz.* pt. II:4541; SOR/95-13 and *Can. Gaz.* pt. II:28.

83 NAFTA, art. 1024. This deadline may be difficult to meet given the delays in obtaining state and provincial commitments in 1996.

B. Trade in Services

The FTA contained a fairly modest chapter on trade in services, covered designated services, and contained broad exceptions to its application. The GATS, although ambitious in scope for a new multilateral instrument, also contains significant limitations on its application. The basic standard of the GATS is MFN treatment; NT is considerably limited. Further, to receive the full benefit of the GATS, services need to be specifically included in schedules. Chapter 12 of NAFTA succeeds in expanding coverage, in principle, to all services and makes NT the basic standard between the parties. It is complemented by important chapters on financial services and telecommunications and a number of annexes dealing with specific professional services.[84] It should be noted that chapters 12 to 14 apply both to central governments and state and provincial governments: this is an important consideration, given the jurisdiction of states and provinces over the regulation of professional services and related powers in relation to consumer protection. These broad provisions are somewhat tempered by the right to take extensive exceptions and the two-year delay for states and provinces to specify their exceptions.[85]

C. Investments

Part 5 of the NAFTA, which focuses on the various aspects of trade in services, begins with a chapter on investments. This reflects two major concerns. First, the United States wished to maintain and extend to Mexico the provisions on investment protection since these provisions had greatly facilitated political acceptance of the FTA in those states where the Canadian National Energy Program was still remembered. The hope of restraining future discrimination against foreign investment was even stronger as concerned Mexico, given the troubled history of American foreign investment in Mexico and Mexico's traditional support of the Calvo Clause. The Government of Mexico also needed a strong chapter on investment as a guarantee to foreign investors of the continuance of domestic liberalization policies adopted since joining the GATT in 1986. Second, chapter 11 on investments in fact addresses a key aspect of trade in services: the right to enter and maintain a permanent presence in another territory, or as it is known in the law of the European Community, the right of establishment. This chapter is thus central to the NAFTA disciplines on trade in services.

Chapter 11 applies to both federal, state and provincial governments by virtue of article 105. Article 1102.3 specifically defines national treatment by states or provinces to mean the treatment that the state or province would accord its nationals in like circumstances. Chapter 11 covers measures relating to (1) investors of another party, (2) investments of such investors, and (3) all investments insofar as they are covered by article 1106 on performance requirements and article 1114 on environmental measures. Parties are allowed a broad right to make exceptions, provided that they are specifically listed in Annex III. The chapter does not apply to measures covered by chapter 14 on

84 See chapter 9 for a full discussion. See also Trebilcock and Howse, *supra*, note 16, chapter 9 and Johnson, *supra*, note 56, chapters 7 and 8.

85 This deadline was not respected and by agreement was extended beyond 1996.

financial services and, more generally, it is stated that in the event of inconsistency between chapter 11 and another chapter, the latter, more specific chapter will prevail. A final paragraph of article 1101 states that nothing in the chapter shall be interpreted to prevent the parties from performing functions in relation to public security, health, welfare, and education "in a manner that is not inconsistent with this Chapter."

The concept of an "investor" is broadly defined to include a national, a government, a state enterprise, or an enterprise incorporated in a party. These three categories are based on nationality. However, all corporations formed under the laws of a party are classed as investors, regardless of the nationality of those who control the corporation, subject to the proviso that this status can be denied to foreign-controlled corporations of countries with which the party does not have diplomatic relations or when the corporation does not have substantial business activities in the territory where it is incorporated.[86] "Investments" are defined to include equity securities, debt securities under certain conditions, real estate, and other tangible and intangible property.

The parties guarantee the more favourable of national and MFN treatment to each other in respect of "... the establishment, acquisition, management, conduct, operation and sale or other disposition of investments."[87] There is also a general guarantee of treatment according to the minimum standard required by international law and a guarantee of non-discriminatory treatment in respect of compensation arising from armed or civil conflict. Article 1106 incorporates the FTA list of prohibited performance requirements[88] while greatly expanding and refining that list. Parties are prohibited from investment rules limiting senior management positions in corporations to nationals although they can require that the majority of a corporate board or committee be composed of nationals.[89] Article 1110 contains rules that reflect acceptance by Canada and Mexico to abide by the traditional rules of public international law regarding compensation for the expropriation of alien property. Article 1109 provides for a very broad right of investors to remit profits, dividends, fees, and other amounts derived from investments.

Investment rules governing NT and MFN treatment are subject to a very broad right to take exceptions in Annexes I and III.[90] However, the rules on financial transfers and the protections in case of expropriation are not subject to these rights of exception.

Chapter 11 also reflects the concern of the parties to do more in the NAFTA to guarantee environmental protection than was possible in the Uruguay Round. Article 1114 contains the proviso that the parties should not be prevented from setting investment rules whose object is the protection of the environment. Second, the parties recognize that it is inappropriate to relax environmental standards in order to attract investments and they are committed to avoiding such practices.

---

86 NAFTA, arts. 113 and 1139. See Johnson, *supra*, note 56, at 284.

87 NAFTA, arts. 1103 and 1104.

88 With the exception of the FTA prohibition on substituting local for imported goods and services. See Johnson, *supra*, note 56, at 287.

89 NAFTA, art. 1107.

90 States and provinces were given a further two-year grace period. This deadline was not met and was extended.

Section B deals with the settlement of investment disputes. This section is noteworthy for making room in dispute settlement proceedings for private parties and for choosing several different dispute settlement techniques in order to do so.[91]

D. Competition Policy

Chapter 15 represents a modest introduction to a very large issue. A fundamental element of any liberal economic order is respect for free competition and the prevention of acts or situations that compromise that order. Domestic constitutions and legislation reflect this truth and provide the means for protecting competition in the marketplace. The Treaty of Rome, whose founders envisaged a common market for all member states, made provision for the protection of competition in articles 85 and 86 of the treaty. Protection of competition is a great deal more difficult in an international context where governments perceive themselves to be the agents for the advantage only of their own citizens. For this reason it has always been much harder to formulate commitments to protect competition in the international marketplace. As the degree of economic integration has progressed between GATT contracting parties, culminating in the extension of the GATT 1994 to many new areas, pressure has increased to take the GATT in this direction. This was not possible in the Uruguay Round; however, competition is clearly part of the "new international trade agenda" of WTO members.

The NAFTA parties have used their regional relationship to move competition policy forward faster between themselves than was possible in the Uruguay Round. Chapter 15 is a very modest beginning. The obligations of article 1501 involve a commitment to adopt and maintain measures to proscribe anti-competitive business conduct and to cooperate in the enforcement of these laws. This article contains one of the rare exceptions to the compulsory dispute settlement provisions. Articles 1502 and 1503 contain more extensive commitments than the FTA[92] to ensure that both monopolies and state enterprises act in a manner compatible with the NAFTA—including chapters 11 and 14—when they exercise regulatory functions and in accordance with commercial considerations when acting in the market. Government procurement, when undertaken through the instrumentality of monopolies and state enterprises, is covered by chapter 10. Failure to respect articles 1502 and 1503 in respect of a NAFTA private investor could give rise to dispute settlement under chapter 11.

Chapter 15 is thus the beginning of work between the parties. This work may have its first impact on the anti-competitive dimensions of anti-dumping legislation should the parties decide to liberalize these laws. There is greater scope for cooperative enforcement of competition laws and the development of common standards in this area. A working group on trade and competition is created by article 1504 to undertake this work.[93]

---

91 See chapter 20 for a more detailed discussion.

92 FTA, art. 2010, which covers only monopolies.

93 By 1996, little had been accomplished by the parties in this area under NAFTA.

E. Temporary Entry for Business Persons

The free movement of persons for business and other reasons is one of the fundamental freedoms guaranteed by states to their citizens. The Treaty of Rome sought to guarantee freedom of movement first to workers and, since 1987, the Single European Act provides for the freedom of movement of persons as part of the "internal market" concept.[94] Free movement of persons is much more difficult to achieve in the international context, whether it be regional or multilateral. States are jealous of their immigration laws and continue to exercise strict control over the entry of foreigners into their territory. Many states fear the influx of foreigners; these fears are present in developed states but are by no means limited to them. For these reasons, neither the WTO nor NAFTA reflect any desire to promote the mobility of workers. Indeed, NAFTA was justified in the United States as a means of strengthening the Mexican economy and promoting job creation in Mexico, thereby discouraging the illegal immigration into the United States of unskilled and semi-skilled workers and their families. For this reason, the NAFTA does not grant any right of movement of persons and all migration remains subject to domestic immigration legislation.

However, the modern service economy requires a greater degree of personal mobility than was the case in the past. This is particularly the case for professionals but there is also a need for greater mobility of technical service personnel specially trained to maintain complex equipment or to train indigenous workers in its operation. The NAFTA reflects this reality more extensively than the GATT 1994 both in the annexes to chapter 12 dealing with professional services and in chapter 16. This latter chapter, which carries forward provisions similar to those in the FTA,[95] is designed to facilitate the temporary entry of business persons in order for them to perform services that they are authorized to undertake in another party's territory. The chapter therefore speaks to immigration rules and formalities at border points and in airports and other points of entry. Annex 1603 of this chapter, like its FTA predecessor, has had an appreciable impact on relaxing border restrictions on the movement of professional and service personnel. However, it must be emphasized that no right of individual movement is given and the rights involved only relate to temporary entry. To emphasize this, Annex 1603-D.4 allows parties to set numerical limits on the temporary entry of professional persons.[96] A further indication of the limited nature of these rights is found in article

---

94 See now art. 7a of the EC Treaty, as am. by the Treaty of European Union, formerly art. 8a of the EEC-Treaty as inserted into the Treaty by the Single European Act, OJ 1987 L 169, pp. 1 *et seq*. In addition, the Treaty on European Union has created a new Union citizenship in art. 8, which comprises under art. 8a the right "to move and reside freely within the territory of the Member States," subject only to conditions provided for in the Treaty. The abolition of border controls could only be achieved by way of further bilateral and multilateral agreements among the continental member states (except Denmark), notably the Schengen Accord of 14 June 1985, applied since 1 December 1993 following a resolution of the Schengen Ministerial Committee of 30 June 1993.

95 FTA, chapter 15.

96 The United States has limited the annual entry of Mexican professionals to 5,000.

1606, which limits chapter 20 dispute settlement procedures to general complaints and excludes cases involving the refusal of entry to an individual, and in article 1607, which further restricts the obligations of this chapter.

IV. INTELLECTUAL PROPERTY

The objectives of chapter 17 on the protection of intellectual property are similar to those of the Uruguay Round Agreement on the Trade Related Aspects of Intellectual Property Rights (TRIPS)[97] and the two texts are often very close. In fact, much of the NAFTA chapter was drafted before the completion of the TRIPS Agreement. A first attempt to negotiate intellectual property issues was undertaken by Canada and the United States but failed due to differences concerning the protection of pharmaceutical patents.[98] The FTA negotiations did, however, serve to provide a model for the Uruguay Round and, in the end, the NAFTA text came into force a year before the TRIPS Agreement.

In the case of chapter 17, it is difficult to argue that the NAFTA text constitutes an extension of the multilateral agreement. There are some differences: chapter 17 is based on one standard only, NT; the drafting with respect to restrictions on trademark use is different in article 1708.10 and the TRIPS, article 20; Mexico is not allowed the same latitude with respect to implementation and exceptions that are possible under the TRIPS Agreement; and article 1707 contains specific commitments on protection of encrypted program-carrying signals and article 1711 contains more specific commitments with respect to trade secrets. But, broadly speaking, the structure, coverage, and principles of the two texts are very close. Like the TRIPS Agreement, chapter 17 is a mixture of substantive commitments as to intellectual property protection concerning copyright, patents, trademarks, sound recordings, encrypted signals, integrated circuits, trade secrets, industrial designs, and geographical indications, as well as the obligation to implement all or parts of five major intellectual property conventions.[99] While these conventions may not be formally incorporated by reference,[100] the parties must accede to them if they have not already done so. Similarly, the parties are committed by articles 1714 to 1721 to maintaining effective regulatory procedures, civil remedies, criminal penalties, and border enforcement procedures against counterfeit goods. These provisions, while not directly part of Canadian law, will surely have significant impact on future legislation.

---

97 Discussed in chapter 1, section VI. See also chapter 6, section VIII.

98 Paterson and Band, *supra*, note 22, at 3-86. The duration of pharmaceutical patent protection remained controversial and the change to a 20-year period in Canada resulted from the GATT 1994 TRIPS Agreement and not chapter 17.

99 The Paris Convention for the Protection of Industrial Property, 1967; the Berne Convention for the Protection of Literary and Artistic Works, 1971; the Geneva Convention for the Protection of Producers of Phonograms against Unauthorized Duplication of their Phonograms, 1971; the International Convention for the Protection of New Varieties of Plants 1971 or 1991 (UPOV Convention); and the Treaty on Intellectual Property in Respect of Integrated Circuits, 1991.

100 Paterson and Band, *supra*, note 22, at 435; this implies that the NAFTA is the prevailing document in case of divergence between texts.

As with the TRIPS Agreement, chapter 17 serves to highlight the very great significance that intellectual property rights have come to assume in international trade. This area of the law, generally left to a small number of initiates, is all pervasive in North American society, and the commitments made will have a great impact in the future.

V. INSTITUTIONAL ARRANGEMENTS AND DISPUTE SETTLEMENT

A. Institutional Arrangements

The institutions created by the NAFTA are modest but important. The central institution is the Free Trade Commission formed of the cabinet-level representatives responsible for international trade in their respective governments. The Commission must meet at least once a year and has been meeting at least three times a year. Its functions are to supervise the implementation of the agreement, to ensure its further development, and to resolve disputes that arise from time to time between the parties. The Commission supervises the work of the many working groups and joint committees of the NAFTA[101] and is empowered to create others as necessary. The Commission is essentially a meeting of the parties. It has no legal existence at domestic or international law separate from the parties and does not conduct negotiations with non-party states on behalf of the parties.

The Commission is assisted by a secretariat whose principal functions are threefold: to organize the meetings of the Commission, to provide administrative support to dispute settlement panels, and to support the work of the NAFTA working groups and committees.[102] Each party is required to set up a permanent office of the Secretariat and designate an official as Secretary of the national section. The national secretaries and their staffs perform all the functions required in their respective countries. There is no separate North American office.[103] The Secretariat has no mandate to act independently of the instructions of the parties. It has no corporate personality. The NAFTA is silent on the status of the Secretariat's archives but it can be presumed that documents enjoy certain protection under domestic and international law. National secretaries play a discrete but helpful role in furthering the work of the NAFTA; but, they are strictly the servants of the parties and have no public mandate or profile.

The work of the many communities and working groups of the NAFTA should not be ignored. They have the potential to serve as the locus for future development of the principles and the rules of the free trade agreement. Useful joint work has already been accomplished on customs procedures and, if the parties encourage it, the committees and working groups may emerge as the true common institutions of the NAFTA. As of 1996, they had not begun to realize their potential.

---

101 Thirty-eight working groups and joint committees were envisaged in the original text.

102 NAFTA, art. 2002.

103 Staff numbers range from 5 to 20 persons.

B. Dispute Settlement Under the NAFTA

1. Introduction

Like the FTA before it, the NAFTA is committed to the principle of compulsory dispute settlement, and there are even fewer exceptions to this principle than in the FTA. Also, like the FTA, the NAFTA experiments with different dispute settlement techniques and displays a willingness of the parties to adopt the different dispute settlement techniques best adapted to the problems posed by the issue in question. The NAFTA reproduces the two general procedures of the FTA—chapters 18 and 19—but it also innovates in significant ways in other chapters, particularly in respect of investments and financial services. The NAFTA dispute settlement system continues to be essentially international and intergovernmental, but it continues the FTA chapter 19 process, which provides access for private parties to AD/CV procedures and it provides a special procedure for private foreign investors to challenge governmental decisions in chapter 11. It also requires that domestic procedures be available to private parties to intellectual property and government procurement procedures.

The NAFTA does not set out the only applicable dispute settlement procedure. The two side agreements on environmental and labour cooperation contain their own similar but distinct procedures. In a variety of areas, recourse to the GATT 1994 procedure may be a preferred alternative since many matters are covered by both agreements.[104] For Canada and the United States, at least during the early years, there were disputes to complete under chapter 19 of the FTA and potentially some disputes that might have been taken under the FTA, chapter 20.[105] The NAFTA incorporates the dispute settlement procedures of the International Convention on the Settlement of Investment Disputes of the World Bank, or alternatively the UN Commission on International Trade Law (UNCITRAL) Arbitration Rules, to deal with investment disputes, completely removing these disputes from the purview of chapter 20. Where NAFTA gives priority to other conventions, this priority can extend to their dispute settlement procedures.

It must be stressed that in the minds of the drafters of this agreement, dispute avoidance through committees and working groups was also an important principle of the NAFTA. Such institutional arrangements are designed to reduce the likelihood that matters will have to be taken to formal dispute settlement.

2. Where To Find Provisions on Dispute Settlement Under the NAFTA

In order to facilitate an understanding of the complex set of provisions on dispute settlement, which are found throughout the NAFTA text and elsewhere, the following six categories can be distinguished:

104 In May 1996, the United States asked for the creation of a WTO panel to address their complaint concerning the taxation of printed matter.

105 This is not spent.

1. NAFTA
   Chapter 1, Objectives (articles 102.e, 103, and 104).
   Chapter 2, General definitions, function of the Commission.
   Chapter 5, Customs procedures (relationship of articles 513 and 2007—working group takes place of dispute settlement consultations).
   Chapter 6, Energy (article 607—national security exclusions).
   Chapter 7, Agriculture (article 723—2007 consultations).
   Chapter 8, Emergency action (article 804—exclusion from chapter 20).
   Chapter 9, Standards (articles 903—affirmation of other agreements, and 914—consultations).
   Chapter 10, Government procurement (article 1005—denial of benefits, and 1018—exceptions).
   Chapter 11, Investment (articles 1113 to 1139—special procedure).
   Chapter 13, Telecommunications (article 1307—exclusion from chapter 20).
   Chapter 14, Financial services (articles 1413—consultations, 1414—dispute settlement, and 1415—investment disputes in financial services).
   Chapter 15, Competition policy (article 1501—exclusion from dispute settlement).
   Chapter 16, Temporary entry (articles 1606—dispute settlement, and 1607—other chapters).
   Chapter 17, Intellectual property (articles 1701—other conventions, 1715—civil and administrative procedure, and 1717—criminal procedure).
   Chapter 19, Review of anti-dumping and countervailing duty procedures.
   Chapter 20, Institutional issues, general dispute settlement procedure, and dispute avoidance through working groups.
   Chapter 21, Exceptions.
2. NAFTA side agreements.
3. GATT 1994 and related agreements providing for dispute settlement.
4. The Canada-US FTA.
5. Other dispute settlement procedures incorporated by reference, ICSID, UNCITRAL Arbitration Rules, domestic tribunals (article 2020); alternative dispute resolution procedures (article 2022).
6. Other dispute settlement procedures having priority (environmental agreements; International Energy Agreement).

3. Chapter 19: Anti-Dumping and Countervailing Duty Procedures

Readers are referred to chapter 15.

4. Chapter 20: The General Procedure

Readers are referred to chapter 20.

VI. EXCEPTIONS

The NAFTA is in fact replete with derogations. There are numerous special regimes, exceptions, and derogations set out in the text and in the various annexes with respect to trade in goods and services. Chapter 21 sets out broader exceptions of a general nature, applicable to the whole agreement. This chapter carries forward, sometimes explicitly, the principles of the FTA, chapter 20, and incorporates the principles of the GATT 1994, articles XX and XXI.

Article 2101 has the effect of adding environmental protection to the protection of human, animal, or plant life as values justifying exceptional measures. This reflects the more environmentally friendly dimension of the NAFTA as compared with the Uruguay Round texts where this change was not made. The article also protects non-discriminatory measures designed to secure compliance with laws and regulations, provided that the original measures are in compliance with the NAFTA. What is curious and perhaps unfortunate is the broad exclusion of services, investments, and intellectual property from the benefit of the former exception, and investments and intellectual property from the latter.

Article 2102 sets out the general exception for national security, which parallels but is not identical to article XXI of the GATT 1994. The extent of the exception is largely self-defining, in that it allows a party to take measures that "it considers necessary for the protection of its essential security interests." This appears to vest wide discretion in the parties, although the stated purposes of the article relate essentially to military, nuclear and economic security and the enforcement of UN sanctions,[106] and it can certainly be argued that exceptional measures must be limited to the attainment of these purposes. It should be noted that this article does not apply to energy and government procurement, where articles 607 and 1108 specifically govern.

Article 2103 gives primacy to tax conventions over the NAFTA and generally creates the presumption that the NAFTA does not deal with tax issues. However, the article does seek to establish a limited principle of non-discrimination with respect to the application of taxes. Article 2104, like the GATT 1994, provides for the right to take measures to protect the balance of payments of a party, but attempts to limit the negative impact of these measures on trade between the parties. Such measures must be consistent with the rules of the International Monetary Fund (IMF).

Article 2106 carries forward the FTA exception for measures adopted in respect of cultural industries. This provision applies between Canada and the United States, and, as a result of the last sentence of Annex 2106, between Canada and Mexico. Mexico did not seek this exemption vis-à-vis the United States, although some of the measures covered by the Mexican annexes deal with cultural issues. The actual definition of "cultural industries" is slightly broader than that of the FTA: it includes books, magazines, periodicals, newspapers, film and video recordings, music in any form, and different forms of radiocommunication. The effect of this provision is to protect cultural industries from Canadian commitments with respect to non-discriminatory trade in goods, services, and especially investments.[107] The degree of protection actually afforded

106 It is not clear whether this covers the adoption of trade measures that violate the rights of other parties under international law, as is arguably the case with certain parts of the Helms Burton Act.

107 Johnson, *supra*, note 56, at 463.

is questionable, however, in that there is still an obligation to compensate the other party suffering from a diminution of its potential trading opportunities.

VII. COOPERATION RESPECTING LABOUR STANDARDS AND THE ENVIRONMENT

A. NAFTA and Non-Trade Issues

The NAFTA is a free trade agreement but it involves a degree of economic integration that is sufficiently advanced as to have elicited significant political reaction in all three countries. This reaction did not simply take the form of concern for the economic implications of free trade—the NAFTA like the FTA before it raised concerns with respect to a range of non-trade issues. The most immediate response related to the impact on employment in industries vulnerable to competition; this was accompanied by a concern for the possibility that employment would be shifted to the least-cost territory—the Southern United States with the FTA and Mexico for NAFTA. Similarly, environmentalists expressed the concern that free trade could have a detrimental impact on the environment if it was accompanied by policies or gave in to economic forces that put the imperative to trade before social and environmental concerns. The same concerns were voiced with respect to the Uruguay Round of Multilateral Trade Negotiations.

One response to these concerns was to include provisions in the NAFTA that were more clearly designed to respect environmental concerns and a number of articles of the NAFTA are distinctly more environmentally friendly than the GATT 1994.[108] This did not satisfy environmentalists and they brought pressure to bear during the 1992 presidential campaign in the United States. They succeeded in obtaining commitments from the future President Clinton that the environmental aspects of the NAFTA would be strengthened. Critics in the labour movement and candidate Ross Perot preferred to call for the complete abandonment of NAFTA and it proved more difficult to address their concerns, since the NAFTA was not designed to deal with labour issues. The solution found by President Clinton after his election was not to renegotiate the NAFTA, which Canada and Mexico strongly opposed, but to invite them to negotiate new "side agreements" on environmental cooperation and the protection of labour standards. These agreements respond only partially to the concerns expressed. Both are strictly international and intergovernmental in nature, like the NAFTA. Neither agreement requires the establishment of common North American environmental and labour standards, although the potential is there for a more North American approach to common problems. Neither agreement creates autonomous administrative organs to act as the conscience of the parties on environmental and labour issues, although both contain innovative solutions. Any call for supranational institutions was firmly rejected in favour of interstate cooperation. But this is not to say that the two agreements are without value or future potential. Both agreements represent a modest acceptance by the parties that some non-trade issues require common solutions and that they cannot be severed from the free trade agenda.

---

108 NAFTA, arts. 104, 1114, 2101, etc.

B. The North American Agreement on Environmental Cooperation (NAAEC)

This agreement is both ambitious and modest in its objectives. Ambitious because the parties commit themselves to maintaining high levels of environmental protection[109] and agree to allow challenges by private groups in cases where they fail to enforce their legislation adequately; modest because the commitment to common solutions to common continental problems is weak and because the dispute settlement procedures are restricted to a fairly narrow range of issues.

The obligations of the parties are essentially to maintain high levels of environmental protection, to ensure effective enforcement of these laws, and to provide appropriate private remedies and equitable and open procedures.[110] These articles are partially reinforced by the dispute settlement procedures of part V of the NAAEC. The reinforcement is only partial in that the commitment to submit to compulsory dispute settlement, on the model of the general provisions of the NAFTA, chapter 20, arises only with respect to an allegation of a "persistent failure" to "effectively enforce its environmental laws." Furthermore, this persistent failure must relate to a situation concerning the production of goods or services that are traded between the parties or that compete in the territory of the party subject to the complaint with goods and services of the complainant.[111] A special roster is kept of individuals willing to serve as panellists. The panellists must have knowledge of environmental law or other relevant knowledge. The panel process procedure is similar to that of the NAFTA, chapter 20. The panel report is submitted to the NAAEC Council and the parties then "may agree on a mutually satisfactory action plan, which normally shall conform to the determinations and recommendations of the panel."[112] Should this not happen or should there be a complaint that the losing party is not implementing the action plan, the panel can be reconvened and can reconfirm the plan and impose a monetary penalty for non-compliance. Should this penalty not be paid, the complaining party may suspend equivalent benefits.[113] Canada, which had objected to the introduction of trade sanctions into the NAAEC, committed itself to requiring that the monetary penalty could be collected by an action before the Federal Court of Canada.[114] It must also be noted that the obligations of the NAAEC only arise against those Canadian provinces that agree to be bound.[115]

The most innovative aspect of the NAAEC is to be found in its institutional arrangements. The basic system parallels the NAFTA, in that the agreement is supervised by a Commission for Environmental Cooperation composed of a council and a secretariat. The Council, which is composed of cabinet-level representatives, in Canada's case the federal Minister of the Environment, is charged with the oversight of the agreement and

109 NAAEC, art. 3.

110 NAAEC, arts. 3, 5, 6, and 7.

111 NAACE, art. 24.

112 NAAEC, art. 33.

113 NAAEC, art. 34:4.

114 NAAEC, art. 36A.

115 NAAEC, Annex 41.

the Secretariat and with the development of recommendations concerning a very wide range of environmental problems common to the parties. The Council is to encourage effective enforcement of environmental laws and cooperation between the parties. In this, it has a broad mandate to improve cooperation and especially to develop recommendations with respect to projects having significant transboundary effects. It is required to maintain close links with non-governmental organizations.[116]

The Secretariat is headed by an executive director who appoints the staff, made up of environmental and legal experts, prepares the work program, and directs its activities.[117] The Secretariat is required to act on the instructions of the Council and shall not seek or receive instructions from any government authority external to the Council, although this does not preclude maintaining relations with various NAFTA bodies. The Secretariat is thus a more autonomous institution than the NAFTA Secretariat. Articles 13 and 14 of the NAAEC illustrate this fact. Article 13 empowers the Secretariat to undertake studies either at the behest of the Council or on its own initiative "... on any matter within the scope of the annual programme." These studies are submitted to the Council. Article 14 is the core provision of the NAAEC: it empowers the Secretariat to receive submissions from non-governmental organizations or persons which assert that a Party "... is failing to effectively enforce its environmental laws." This authority can be the beginning of a process leading to a dispute, but it is designed in a much more positive spirit. It is really designed to gather information on environmental problems of common concern to the parties, with a view to understanding and resolving them. The Secretariat exercises discretion, within the guidelines of article 14, as to the propriety of responding to a submission and must advise the petitioner of its decision within 30 days. When the Secretariat agrees to act on the submission, it must first seek a response from the party in question. If the Secretariat considers that the submission warrants further study, after receiving the response of the party, it can then proceed to prepare a factual record on the basis of information received from the party, interested non-governmental bodies, independent experts, or its Joint Public Advisory Committee. The factual record must be presented to the Council, which may make it public or remit it to the Joint Public Advisory Committee.

The Secretariat chose to use its powers rather cautiously during the first years of its existence but it has acted under both articles 13 and 14 on a number of occasions. The first public act of the Secretariat was a study, including a much publicized visit to the site in 1995, of an incident involving the sudden death of 20,000 water birds in a Mexican reservoir. The Secretariat has received a number of submissions[118] and has prepared factual records in several cases.[119] The first two submissions involved legislative changes

---

116 NAAEC, art. 10.

117 The Secretariat is located in Canada.

118 The presentation of submissions is governed by procedures issued in 1995 after extensive consultations with the parties.

119 As of June 1996: *Biodiversity Legal Foundation et al.*, SEM-95-001; *Sierra Club et al.*, SEM-95- 002; *Comite para la Proteccion de los Recursos Naturales, A.C. et al.*, SEM-96-001; and *Mr. Aage Tottrup, P Eng*, SEM-96-002.

in the United States, in one case limiting the capacity of the federal environmental and forestry officials to act by cutting their budget or in the second case restricting private rights of action. In both cases, the Secretariat concluded that it was not dealing with a failure to enforce environmental laws on the ground that the application of a new legal regime could not be characterized as a failure to enforce the old, more generous, regime. The third submission, involving allegations that Mexican authorities had failed to enforce existing environmental legislation in allowing the construction of a major new harbour terminal at Cozumel, which threatened the local coral reefs, met with greater success. The Secretariat took up this complaint and prepared a factual record confirming the concerns of the submission.

The NAAEC can thus be seen as both a clear advance over the relative silence of the GATT 1994 on environmental issues and equally as an improvement over the text of the NAFTA. Whether the modest but real powers of the Commission will be used to develop a truly continental consciousness of common environmental problems and whether it will promote the adoption of common solutions has yet to be determined.[120]

C. The North American Agreement on Labour Cooperation (NAALC)

The NAALC is drafted in very much the same manner as the NAAEC. The parties maintain their right to adopt domestic labour standards but commit themselves to ensuring that their laws and regulations "... provide for high labour standards." They are also committed to effective enforcement, private remedies, and procedural guarantees of these standards. Dispute settlement is also based on the NAFTA model. However, like the NAACE, it is restricted in scope and is subject to even more procedural hurdles.

Like the NAACE, the most original aspects of the NAALC are to be found in the administrative structures and powers of the Commission. The Commission for Labour Cooperation is composed of a council, made up of cabinet-level representatives, which oversees the agreement, and of a secretariat, led by an executive director.[121] The Secretariat may prepare studies for which it is responsible to the Council. A major difference from the NAACE is that each party must establish a national advisory office (NAO) at the federal level. The NAO is the focal point for questions or complaints that may be received concerning the application of labour standards in the territory of another party. As such, it serves as the first stage of the complaints and dispute settlement process, but it is also empowered to take up the study of a broader range of issues than those susceptible to formal dispute settlement. Article 21 states that the NAO may request "consultations" with the other NAOs "... in relation to the other Party's labour law." The United States has chosen to grant its NAO investigative powers including the authority to receive complaints and hold public hearings with all concerned groups, including

120 See, generally, Johnson and Beaulieu, *The Environment and NAFTA: Understanding and Implementing the New Environmental Law* (1996).

121 The Secretariat is located in the United States.

nationals of another party.[122] The agreement also provides for the creation of an Evaluation Committee of Experts, a second institution not found in the NAACE. The basic function of these committees is to take up issues at the behest of the Council when they are not resolved by the NAO.

Dispute settlement is both similar and more complex than under the NAACE. The NAALC is similar, in that disputes must focus on the allegation that there has been a persistent failure by a party to enforce its own labour standards in relation to three categories: occupational safety and health, child labour, and minimum wage standards. The NAALC is different in that a matter must first be raised before a NAO and subsequently before an evaluation committee of experts before a party can initiate consultations leading to the constitution of an arbitral panel to study the dispute. The panel is formed from a roster of persons having specialized knowledge of labour issues. The dispute shall normally be resolved by the adoption and implementation of an action plan by the party declared in violation of the agreement. In the event of refusal, the consequences are similar to the NAACE.

The capacity of the NAALC to respond to the concerns raised by labour unions and the general public with respect to employment and labour standards is even more questionable than that of the NAACE for environmental issues. However, the agreement has already begun to produce certain results. The Ministers of Labour meet at least once a year and have taken up a number of thorny issues. Second, the procedures of the US NAO[123] have put the insufficiencies of Mexican labour law and its interpretation by Mexican authorities into dramatic focus in several cases. The first two complaints were made to the US NAO on February 14, 1994 by the United Brotherhood of Teamsters and the United Electrical, Radio and Machine Workers Union, claiming that General Electric Co. and Honeywell Inc. had violated Mexican labour laws and workers rights in the firings of some 100 workers. Both complaints resulted from specific labour conflicts where the unions believed that there had been a denial of the right of free association. The companies argued that the NAO had no authority to sit in judgment in such cases, that the NAO could not act as an appellate body from Mexican governmental decisions, and stressed that the role of the NAO was to establish facts concerning the enforcement of Mexican law. The NAO found no failure to respect freedom of association in both cases because the workers had accepted offers of compensation that, in law, precluded their right to pursue the lengthy and complex reinstatement procedures. These reports

---

122 US Department of Labor, "Revised Notice of Establishment of US National Administrative Office and Procedural Guidelines," 59 Fed. Reg. 16660 (7 April 1994). As of September 1996, Canada and Mexico had chosen not to adopt a process of public hearing and maintained NAOs in their respective Departments of Labour.

123 US Department of Labor, Notice of Hearing on Submissions 940001 and 040002, 59 Fed. Reg. 38492 (28 July 1994); Notice of Hearing on Submission 940003, 59 Fed. Reg. 52992 (20 October 1994); and Notice of Submission 940004, 59 Fed. Reg. 54094 (10 November 1995). See, generally, R. Herstein, "The Labour Cooperation Agreement among Mexico, Canada and the United States: Its Negotiation and Prospects" (1995), 3 *US-Mexico LJ* 121.

were criticized for ignoring the systemic difficulties under which Mexican workers labour and for ignoring the fact that the Mexican government exercises wide discretionary powers and is able to control most unions. However, the reports did establish that NAO consultations could cover a wide range of labour matters and helped to established the parameters for what is a rare occurrence, the administrative organ of one state inquiring into very specific events in another state.

The third complaint was filed in August 1994; it alleged that there had been a persistent failure to enforce Mexican labour laws in a situation involving a Sony subsidiary, Magneticos de Mexico, which it was alleged restricted union activities of workers and forced workers to work longer hours than allowed by the law. The NAO declined to consider the hours of work issue, on the grounds that local remedies had not been pursued. However, in this case, the NAO did not accept that the fact that most workers had signed releases and had accepted compensation should preclude it from inquiring into whether the dismissals masked a campaign to prevent the registration of an independent union and hence restrict freedom of association. The NAO consulted with its Mexican counterpart and held a public hearing as a result of which the NAO issued a report finding that: "... it appears plausible that the workers discharges occurred for the causes alleged, namely for participation in union organizing activities."[124] The NAO recommended ministerial consultations, which were subsequently held in April 1995 and which resulted in the establishment of a work program for each country to improve procedures for union certification and the constitution of a commission of independent experts to study union registration. This time the ministerial process has been the object of criticism since it did nothing specific to reinstate the workers or ensure registration of their independent union. In the ensuing months, the workers were subject to continued opposition from the company and their second attempt at registration of an independent union was also frustrated.

It is unlikely that the NAALC will provoke rapid change in the situation of Mexican workers; indeed, there is cause for pessimism, but there can be little doubt that the NAO process is a source of embarrassment to the Mexican government and assists those seeking a more just labour relations climate and a more open and democratic political process in that country.

VIII. THE FUTURE OF THE NAFTA

A. Enlargement of the NAFTA

One possible future for NAFTA is the expansion of the number of NAFTA members. All NAFTA parties had expressed willingness to contemplate a free trade zone for all of North and South America at the December 1994 Miami Summit of the Americas. Subsequently, the Canadian and the US governments had declared themselves willing to contemplate extension of NAFTA to Chile, but the denial of fast track negotiating authority by the US Congress in 1995 and 1996 precluded this at least until after the

124 US National Administrative Office, Public Report of Review, NAO Submission 940003 (US Department of Labor, 11 April 1995), at 27.

November 1996 elections. This left Canada to continue bilateral negotiations with Chile for a separate agreement, including environmental and labour questions, designed to be compatible with the NAFTA. Formally, adhesion of a new NAFTA party requires the consent of all the existing parties, and would have to include the specific terms of entry. Canada and Mexico have taken the position that Chile must adhere both to NAFTA and to the side agreements.[125]

Expansion of NAFTA seemed to be a logical step in 1995 but the political climate changed rapidly in the United States and, to a lesser extent, in Canada and Mexico. In 1996 the emergence of a patchwork of bilateral agreements or of loose understandings between North and South American trading blocs seemed the more probable outcome for the rest of the decade.

B. Deepening of the NAFTA

Another possible future for NAFTA may be the deepening or expansion of its substantive rules. This has already happened with respect to tariff cuts and customs procedures where agreements were reached to facilitate customs procedures through joint consultations and unilateral tariff reductions were made in some areas at the behest of industrial groups. The many joint committees established by the NAFTA also have the potential for development and renewal of NAFTA in such areas as standards. This was the purpose of their creation, since the format of a free trade area did not permit the establishment of a common supranational organization. The role for the secretariats of the NAFTA and of the side agreements could be expanded if the parties so desire, but there appears to be no disposition to do this. Currently, it appears that parts of the NAFTA most likely to develop relate to services and government procurement. In the latter case, states and provinces were required to make their own commitments two years after 1994.[126] Second, it is clear from the chapters on services that further negotiations are required to deepen and complete the original commitments. Further negotiations between the parties are to be expected on a range of services, beginning with professional services, financial services, and telecommunications.

The process of development and change will probably be slow, but it is clear that the NAFTA and the side agreements are not static documents. They are difficult to change, since formal change to these complex texts requires unanimous consent of all the parties, but it can be expected that the pressures for change will overcome the many difficulties that lie ahead.

---

125 This raises legal as well as political difficulties in the United States, since the NAFTA was concluded under the "fast track" trade agreement process and the side agreements are ordinary executive agreements. See Ackerman and Golove, "Is NAFTA Constitutional?" (1995), 108 *Harv. L Rev.* 799. Chile agreed to environmental commitments in its 17 December 1996 Free Trade Agreement with Canada. See chapter 3, *infra*.

126 This had not yet been done at time of publication in 1997.

IX. SELECTED BIBLIOGRAPHY

A. Books

Appleton, *Navigating NAFTA: A Concise User's Guide* (1994).

Baker and McKenzie, *NAFTA Handbook: A Practical Guide for Doing Business Under NAFTA* (1994).

Bernier, *Accord de libre-échange entre le Canada et les États-Unis annoté/Free Trade Agreement Between Canada and the United States Annotated* (1990) (looseleaf).

Boddez and Trebilcock, *Unfinished Business: Reforming Trade Remedy Laws in North America* (1993).

Canadian Bar Association Ontario, *Working with NAFTA: Maximizing the Benefits* (1994).

Department of Foreign Affairs, *North American Free Trade Agreement, Canadian Statement on Implementaion* (1994) extract of *Canada Gazette*, pt. I, January 1994.

Government of Canada, *The NAFTA Manual* (1993).

Holbein and Musch, *North American Free Trade Agreements* (1992).

Johnson, *The North American Free Trade Agreement. A Comprehensive Guide* (1995).

Johnson and Beaulieu, *The Environment and NAFTA* (1996).

Johnson and Schacter, *The Free Trade Agreement: A Comprehensive Guide* (1988).

Lipsey, *The NAFTA: What's In, What's Out, What's Next* (C.D. Howe Institue, 1994).

Paterson and Band, *International Trade and Investment Law in Canada* (2nd ed., 1995).

Steger, *A Concise Guide to the Canada-United States Free Trade Agreement* (1988).

Trebilcock and Howse, *The Regulation of International Trade* (1995).

B. Articles

Abbott, "Integration Without Institutions: the NAFTA Mutation of the EC Model and the Future of the GATT Regime" (1992), 40 *Am. J Comp. L* 917.

Ackerman and Golove, "Is NAFTA Constitutional?" (1995), 108 *Harv. L Rev.* 799.

Bernier and Malépart, "Les dispositions de l'Accord de libre-échange nord-américain relatives à la propriété intellectuelle et la clause d'exemption culturelle" (1994), 6 *Cahiers Prop. Intell.* 139.

Charnovitz, "NAFTA: An Analysis of Its Environmental Provisions" (1993), 23 *Env. L Reporter* 10067.

Glossop, "NAFTA and Competition Policy" (1994), 15 *Eur. Competition L Rev.* 191.

Gonzalez, "An Analysis of the Legal Implications of the Intellectual Property Provisions of the NAFTA" (1993), 34 *Harv. Int'l LJ* 305.

Grijalva and P.T. Brewer, "Monitoring and Managing North American Free Trade: The Administrative Bodies of the NAFTA" (1994), 2 *San Diego Justice J* 1.

Howse, "NAFTA and the Constitution: Does 'Labour Conventions' Really Matter any More?" (1994), 5 *Const. Forum* 54.

Huerta and Lujambio, "NAFTA: Recent Constitutional Amendments, Sovereignty Today, and the Future of Federalism in Mexico" (1994), 5 *Const. Forum* 63.

Jackson, "Reflections on the Implications of NAFTA for the World Trading System" (1992), 30 *Colum. J Transnat'l L* 501.

Lucas, "Natural Resources Trade Under NAFTA: The Interface with International Environmental Treaties" (1994), 12 *J Energy & Natural Resources L* 175.

Murphy, "Exporting Goods and Services Under the North American Free Trade Agreement" (1994), 6 *Int'l. Q* 1.

Saunders, "NAFTA and North American Agreement on Environmental Cooperation: A New Model for International Collaboration on Trade and the Environment" (1994), 5 *Colorado J Int'l. Env. L & Pol'y.* 273.

Schoenbaum, "NAFTA: Good for Jobs, for the Environment and for America" (1993), 23 *Georgia J Int'l. & Comp. L* 461.

Simpson, "North American Free Trade Agreement: Rules of Origin" (1994), 211 *NYLJ* 3.

Steward, "The NAFTA: Trade, Competition, Environmental Protection" (1993), 1 *US-Mexico LJ* 751.

Swenarchuk, "An Update on Trinational NAFTA Monitoring of Environmental Issues" (1994), 19 *Intervenor* 7.

Thomas and Tereposky, "The NAFTA and the Side Agreement on Environmental Co-operation" (1993), 27 *J World Trade* 5.

Wechter, "NAFTA: A Complement to GATT or a Setback to Global Free Trade?" (1993), 66 *Southern Calif. L Rev.* 264.

CHAPTER THREE

Canada's Bilateral and Regional Trading Arrangements

I. INTRODUCTION

As set out in chapters 1 and 2, the essence of Canada's international economic commitments is to be found in the General Agreement on Tariffs and Trade 1994 (GATT 1994), which binds members of the World Trade Organization (WTO) and the North American Free Trade Agreement (NAFTA). Multilateral and regional trading arrangements have thus largely replaced the network of bilateral treaties of friendship, navigation, and commerce (FCN), which characterized Canada's trading relationships with the United States and Europe until after the World War II. The strengthening of the multilateral trading order of the General Agreement on Tariffs and Trade (GATT) during the decades after 1947 removed the necessity of seeking bilateral guarantees of access to Canada's most important markets. Bilateral agreements served largely to deal with matters not covered by the GATT, such as immigration, investment protection, competition law, and scientific, technical, and cultural cooperation, to cement relations with countries that were not party to the GATT, or as a means of drawing neighbouring states into larger regional trading relationships.

The decades after the signing of the GATT, particularly the 1970s and 1990s, also witnessed a new phenomenon, the emergence of regional trading arrangements. The purpose of such regional arrangements was to cement particularly close economic and sometimes political relationships and to move economic integration further than was required by the GATT. Despite the success of the Uruguay Round of Multilateral Trade Negotiations in replacing the GATT by the WTO, regional trading arrangements continue to be a very significant feature of international trade law. Their function in the contemporary globalized economy is to provide closer economic integration than required by the WTO, to guarantee access to a larger single regional market, and to attract and keep foreign investment.

For the reasons set out above, Canada participates in a number of bilateral relationships and is party to two important regional trading arrangements, the NAFTA and the Asia Pacific Economic Cooperation Forum (APEC). Canada must also deal with many other economic groupings, particularly the European Union (EU) and with a host of bilateral relationships existing between other states. This brief chapter is designed to explain the principal regional and bilateral economic agreements to which Canada is a party.

II. REGIONAL AGREEMENTS TO WHICH CANADA IS A PARTY

The central regional agreement to which Canada is a party is the NAFTA. This is arguably the most complex and comprehensive free trade agreement in the world today. It superseded the Canada-US Free Trade Agreement (FTA), which covers many of the same issues, often in a similar and sometimes in an identical manner. Should the NAFTA cease to be in force between Canada and the United States, the FTA would revive between both countries.

For a full discussion of the NAFTA, readers are referred to chapter 2 of this book.

In 1989, Canada joined 17 other states bordering on the Pacific Ocean in the APEC forum. The APEC is a very different type of agreement from NAFTA; indeed, some would deny it the same status as the NAFTA, given the very heavy stress placed by the APEC on general and voluntary goals instead of explicit legal commitments. In this, the APEC reflects the philosophy of the great majority of its Oriental members who profess to be motivated more by moral than by legal commitments. The membership of the APEC comprises 18 states[1] of the Asia-Pacific region who came together in 1989 to promote open trade, investment, and economic cooperation. A small secretariat was established in Singapore but is given a very limited mandate. At the APEC meeting in Seattle in 1993, a major decision was taken to give greater focus and definition to APEC's objectives by committing members to achieving completely free and open trade and investment in the region for developed members by 2010 and 2020 for developing members. This goal was further clarified by decisions at the Bogor meeting in 1994 and the Osaka meeting in 1995[2] to begin negotiations on the elimination of regional barriers to trade and investment. Two standing committees on trade and investment and economics were established, as well as a business advisory council and 10 working groups dealing with key sectors of economic activity.[3]

APEC's objectives are extremely ambitious; they cover one of the most dynamic

1 Australia, Brunei, Canada, Chile, PRC, Hong Kong (to rejoin China in 1997), Indonesia, Japan, Republic of Korea, Malaysia, Mexico, New Zealand, Papua New Guinea, Philippines, Singapore, Chinese Taipei, Thailand, and the United States.

2 See the Asia-Pacific Economic Cooperation Forum (APEC) Declaration of Common Resolve, 15 November 1994 (1995), 34 *ILM* 758.

3 Information furnished by the Department of Foreign Affairs and International Trade (DFAIT).

spheres of the global economy. For Canada, APEC represents a means of staking out a position in the Asia-Pacific region and participating in its high economic growth. It also represents a means of dealing directly with a group of countries whose approach to economic development and trade commitments are very different from those traditionally followed by Canada in the WTO or in NAFTA. To realize its potential as a force for economic integration, APEC's goals will have to be translated into actions by member states. This has yet to be done but the potential cannot be denied and the Government of Canada has wisely decided to commit itself to APEC.

III. BILATERAL AGREEMENTS TO WHICH CANADA IS A PARTY

Canada is party to very few bilateral trade agreements today; at the end of the 20th century, regional and multilateral agreements are the essential means of promoting its trade interests. Bilateral trade agreements serve as a means to cement a special relationship, as is the case with the Canada-Israel Trade Agreement of 1996[4] and the framework agreement concluded with the European Community (EC) in 1976. Negotiations began in 1996 for the adoption of a new framework for trade relations between Canada and the EC.[5] The first agreement removes a variety of tariff and non-tariff barriers; the latter agreement is essentially a commitment to maintain close cooperation with Canada's second trading partner. Both agreements mirror agreements previously negotiated by the United States with the same parties.[6] Bilateral agreements can also fulfill the traditional function of structuring trade relations with countries not parties to the WTO/GATT 1994. Perhaps surprisingly, Canada does not presently have formal trade agreements with the principal non member of the WTO, the People's Republic of Chinca (PRC), although it does maintain close diplomatic relations and has signed several investment promotion agreements.[7] Otherwise, bilateral agreements serve to deal with matters not adequately covered by the GATT-WTO 1994 or NAFTA, such as investment protection[8] and cooperation in enforcement of competition legislation[9] or scientific or technical

---

4 Canada-Israel Free Trade Agreement, DFAIT, News Release no. 135, 31 July 1996. See also News Release no. 260, 27 December 1996, text furnished by DFAIT.

5 See Council conclusions on EU-Canada relations (3-1996), 29 *EU Bull.* 86, pt. 1.4.75. The EU Council wishes the new agreement to follow up on the existing Framework EC-Canada Cooperation Agreement, OJ L 260, 24 September 1976. See also Report of the European Community-Canada Joint Cooperation Committee, *15 Years of Cooperation* (Brussels: July 1991). See Canada-EU Political Declaration and Action Plan, 17 December 1996, text furnished by DFAIT.

6 See the US-Israel Free Trade Agreement (1985), 24 *ILM* 653; as for US-EU relations see the Transatlantic Agenda, adopted at the EU-US Summit following the Transatlantic Declaration (12-1995), 28 *EU Bull.*, pt. 1.4.104, reproduced as Annex 10 to conclusions of the Madrid European Council (12-1994), 28 *EU Bull.* 37, pt. I.71.

7 Team Canada Agreements (1996).

8 See Chronique de droit économique, Investissement (1991), 29 *Can. Ybk Int'l. L* 439 and subsequent volumes.

cooperation.[10]

One exceptional case is that of the Canada-United States Auto Pact of 1965 (Auto Pact).[11] This agreement is still in force, although it has largely been subsumed under chapter 3, Annex 300-A of the NAFTA. This agreement committed both parties to allowing the free movement of automobiles and autoparts across the border, thus allowing North American automobile producers to take advantage of economies of scale. Due to the stringent conditions set by the Auto Pact, it is better characterized as an managed sectoral trade agreement than a genuine free trade agreement. Many of the safeguards of the original Auto Pact appear to be limited by commitments in NAFTA but it remains in force as between Canada and the United States.

A further motive for concluding bilateral agreements is the future expansion of regional trading alliances. A case in point is the 17 December 1996 free trade agreement with Chile.[12] Canada has an interest in promoting trade with the increasingly dynamic economy of Chile as well as an interest in protecting Canadian investments in that country, but Canada is also committed to seeking the expansion of NAFTA towards the South since the December 1994 Miami Summit of the Americas. This objective was shared by the Government of the United States but not necessarily by the United States Congress, which plays an important role in defining the international economic policy of the United States. Canada has negotiated this bilateral treaty in a manner that makes it compatible with eventual Chilean adhesion to the NAFTA. The treaty is closely modelled upon the NAFTA and form and substance. It includes parallel agreements on environmental and labour cooperation that follow the NAFTA side agreements.[13] An innovative feature of this bilateral agreement is the gradual elimination of anti-dumping duties on trade between the two countries.

IV. SELECTED BIBLIOGRAPHY

A. Books

Abbot, *Law and Policy of Regional Integration: The NAFTA and Western Hemispheric Integration in the World Trade Organization* (1995).

Christensen, *Canada and the EU: A Relationship in Focus* (Ottawa, Delegation of the European Commission, 1995).

---

9 See, for instance, Canada-United States: Agreement Regarding the Application of their Competition and Deceptive Marketing Practices Laws, 13 August 1995 (1996), 35 *ILM* 309.

10 See, for instance, the Agreement on Scientific and Technical Cooperation between the European Community and Canada, Council Decision concluding the Agreement, OJL 74, 22 March 1996.

11 Agreement Concerning Automotive Products between Canada and the United States, signed on 16 January 1965, Can. TS no. 14.

12 DFAIT, News Release no. 211, 18 November 1996.

13 Canada-Chile Bilateral Trade Agreement, arts. M01-07, text furnished by DFAIT.

European Community-Canada Joint Cooperation Committee, *15 Years of Cooperation* (Brussels, 1991).

Hufbauer, *Western Hemisphere Economic Integration* (1994).

Trebilcock and Howse, *The Regulation of International Trade* (1995).

WTO Secretariat, *Regionalism and the World Trading System* (Geneva, WTO, 1995).

B. Articles

Ohmae, "The Rise of the Region State" (1993), 72 *Foreign Affairs* 78.

CHAPTER FOUR

Canada's Relations with the European Community and Other Regional Trading Groups

I. INTRODUCTION

Regional trading groups are arguably one of the most significant features of contemporary international relations. This is true despite the successful negotiation of the GATT 1994, the establishment of the WTO, and the adhesion of over 120 states. The multilateral system is the foundation of modern international trade law, but it does not appear to be sufficient. Many states, including all the most important trading nations, have found it expedient to commit themselves to regional trading agreements. The most important common purpose is the removal of further trade barriers that the GATT 1994 still permits. A second objective is the creation of large regional markets that allow regional producers to benefit from economies of scale by producing for the regional market. A third objective is the attraction to foreign investors of large regional markets. There are risks in the existence of regional trading agreements. They can promote international trade diversion rather than trade expansion and they run the risk of encouraging managed trade between blocs. However, at the present time, the manifest advantages appear to outweigh the risks.[1]

1 Roessler, "The Relationship between Regional Integration Agreements and the Multilateral Trade Order" in Anderson and Blackhurst (eds.), *Regional Integration and the Global Trading System* (Geneva: Harvester Wheatsheaf, 1993).

Canada's participation in two such regional agreements, the NAFTA and the APEC forum, have been described in chapters 2 and 3, respectively. This chapter sets out briefly the principal regional trading groups that exist in other parts of the world with which the government of Canada and Canadian business must deal.

II. EUROPE

The European Community (EC),[2] which now comprises 15 member states, is the most successful and ambitious regional economic agreement of modern times and has become the most powerful trading bloc in the world. Originally created in 1957 as a common market based on the free movement of goods, services, workers, capital, and payments, the EC has evolved through various treaty amendments into an economic union, to which will be added a monetary union by 1999, if the timetable of the Maastricht Treaty can be met. The EC is part of the broader political and intergovernmental European Union (EU). The EC, unlike the EU, is a supranational union, in the sense that EC law is superior to the domestic law of member states. Much EC law is automatically part of the domestic legal order of member states, by virtue of the principles of direct effect and direct application.[3] The rest of EC law must be incorporated into domestic law, although in some areas such as environmental protection, member states may adopt higher standards of protection than those required by the EC.[4] The EC was originally restricted to the achievement of the four freedoms of movement and the maintenance of a competitive market. Today, its mandate runs to consumer and environmental protection, research, communications networks, transportation systems, deregulation of many monopolies, etc. To achieve its mandate the Council of the EC, in conjunction with the Commission and the Parliament is invested with broad legislative powers. The exercise of these new powers is subject to the principle of subsidiarity.

The EC has international legal personality and is empowered exclusively to represent member states in trade negotiations with other states in respect of international trade in goods.[5] Canada must therefore deal with the EC Commission rather than member states to negotiate a wide range of trade issues. In 1976, Canada and the EC negotiated a very general "Framework Agreement,"[6] which attempted without success to redirect Canadian trade toward the EC and away from dependence on the United States. In 1996, in the wake of similar negotiations between the EC and the United States,

---

2 The EC, founded in 1957 as the European Economic Community, is the "first pillar" of the European Union (EU) established in 1992 by the Maastricht Treaty of European Union, OJ C 191 of 27 July 1992; reprinted also in (1992), 31 *ILM* 247.

3 See also the effect of Regulations in art. 189.

4 See, *e.g.*, art. 100a(4) and 103t EU Treaty.

5 But as yet not services. See Opinion 1/94, [1995] 1 *CMLR* 205 (holding that Community had not yet acquired exclusive competence to negotiate vis-à-vis third countries over services withint the framework of the Uruguay Round).

6 Framework EC-Canada Cooperation Agreement, OJL 260, 24 September 1976; see also Can. TS 1976, no. 35.

Canada undertook "framework" negotiations on a new bilateral trade agreement designed to promote trade and to resolve disputes.[7] At various times during 1995 and 1996, the Canadian Ministers of International Trade suggested that it might be opportune to conclude a more extensive agreement between the EC and NAFTA.

The European Free Trade Area (EFTA) was established in 1960 by a number of European states, led by the United Kingdom, which at the time did not wish to subscribe to the principles of a supranational customs union. EFTA members did much to remove trade barriers among themselves with respect to goods and some services, but the EFTA gradually declined as nine of its members joined the EC. At present there are only four remaining members: Norway, Iceland, Lichtenstein, and Switzerland. The first three members are now linked to the EC by the European Economic Area Agreement,[8] a complex agreement that commits EFTA members to adopt most EC legislation implementing the single market concept. The EFTA is thus much reduced in importance.

As the most powerful economic group in the world, the EU has exercised a powerful attraction on both its neighbours and other regional groups around the world. Canada has twice sought to conclude economic agreements with the EC.[9] The United States and Mexico also negotiated agreements in 1996 and negotiations were undertaken with the MERCOSUR customs union of southern Latin America.[10]

Apart from its formal link to the EFTA, the EC has concluded many bilateral agreements with neighbouring states. Some of these agreements, such as those with the states neighbouring the Mediterranean, date back many years.[11] Some agreements, particularly the "Europe Agreements"[12] with Poland, Hungary, and the Czech and Slovak Republics (etc.) (and soon the Baltic states)[13] envisage membership in the EC at some indeterminate

---

7 Canada-EU Political Declaration and Action Plan, 17 December 1996, text furnished by the Department of Foreign Affairs and International Trade.

8 Agreement on the European Economic Area, OJ 1994 L1, at 3-523. Decision on the conclusion of the Agreement, OJ 1994 L7, at 3-1.

9 First under the Framework Cooperation Agreement cited, *supra*, in note 6 and more recently when renegotiating that agreement.

10 The negotiations with MERCOSUR were successfully concluded before the convening of the December 1995 Madrid European Council, see Conclusions of the Madrid European Council (12-1995), 28 *EU Bull.* 9.

11 *E.g.*, the association agreement with Turkey (1963), OJ 1964 L3681; Malta (1971), OJ L61, at 2; and Cyprus (1973), OJ L133, at 2.

12 See only (1992), OJ L 114 (Poland); L 115 (CSFR); L 116 (Hungary), and (1993), OJ 189 (Slovenia). The Agreement with Slovenia has as yet to be transformed into a full-fledged "Europe Agreement," see the Conclusions of the Madrid European Council (12-1995), 28 *EU Bull.* 9, at 19, pt. I.28. See also *ibid.*, at pt. I.29 and *Commission Report on the Current State of and Perspectives for Cooperation in the Baltic Sea Region*, COM(95) 609 for the EU's current and future cooperation with the Baltic States.

13 The "Draft Europe Agreements" with the Baltic States received parliamentary assent at the end of 1995, see OJ C 323 of 4 December 1995. In 1995, all three of the Baltic states formally requested membership in the EU (in addition to Romania, Bulgaria, and Slovakia). The council has adopted Decisions commencing accession procedures under art. O of the EU Treaty with regard to Romania, Slovakia, Latvia, and Estonia; see *European Commission General Report on the Activities of the European Union 1995* (1996), pt. 825 *et seq.*

future date and provide for closer economic ties in the interim. A recent agreement with Turkey, which has long sought EC membership, created a customs union between the two parties.[14] The EC therefore exercises a powerful influence on its immediate neighbours as well as upon the rest of the world. The EC maintains trade and aid links with 70 developing states through the fourth Lomé Agreement, which expires in 1999.[15]

The states of Central Europe have made significant efforts both to promote regional economic integration as well as seeking closer ties to the EC. The Baltic states have signed a network of bilateral agreements among themselves as well as with the EC, the Scandinavian states, and a number of EFTA states.[16] Poland, Hungary, and the Czech and Slovak Republics created the Central European Free Trade Agreement (CEFTA) in 1992.[17] This agreement is capable of producing important results but its initial years have been marred by difficulties between the Czech and Slovak Republics and a fundamental ambivalence of its members as to whether they prefer to concentrate on building a regional free trade area or on joining the EC at the earliest opportunity. The future of the CEFTA is thus unsure. The economic future of Romania and Bulgaria, which signed Europe agreements with the EC in 1993 but which are not party to the CEFTA is even less clear.

Of the states of the former Yugoslavia, only Slovenia has succeeded in developing a network of treaties with the EC and some of the CEFTA states.[18] The precise nature of the links between the states of the former USSR is even harder to determine. It appears to vary from something close to associate statehood with respect to Belarus, or monetary union for some to virtually complete severing of economic and political relations. Various attempts have been made to promote a former USSR-wide customs union or free trade area.[19] It is difficult to determine how meaningful these attempts have been but it is probable that they will be pursued in future years.

III. ASIA-PACIFIC REGION

The Asia-Pacific region has witnessed the formation of a number of free trade agreements. This process has accelerated in recent years. In 1965, Australia and New Zealand concluded a free trade agreement, which has been greatly intensified through amendments

---

14 In fact, the Association Agreement with Turkey goes as far back as 1963, see OJ 1964, at 3687. The European Parliament, however, recently gave its assent to a Proposal for a Council Decision that would permit the introduction of a customs union within the framework of the EC-Turkey Association Council, see Madrid European Council (12-1995), 28 *EU Bull.* 9, at 20, pt. I. 33 and European Commission, *General Report on the Activities of the European Union 1995* (1996), pt. 844.

15 Lomé IV Convention, OJ 1991 L 229. This agreement has recently been amended following the mid-term review, see Madrid European Council (12-1995), 28 *EU Bull.* 9, at 20, pt. I. 43.

16 See *Regionalism and the World Trading System* (Geneva: WTO, 1995), at 32.

17 Central European Free Trade Area, 21 December 1992 (1995), 34 *ILM* 3 (also known as the Visigrad Agreement).

18 *Regionalism*, *supra*, note 16, at p. 87.

19 See, *e.g.*, Commonwealth of Independent States. Treaty on Creation of Economic Union, 24 September 1993 (1995), 34 *ILM* 1298.

in 1977, 1990, and 1992.[20] As a result, the two countries have eliminated barriers, even on agricultural goods, and on a wide range of services. The agreement is also notable for allowing considerable population mobility and for eliminating anti-dumping and countervailing measures. In 1981, Australia and New Zealand signed the South Pacific Regional Trade and Economic Agreement (SPARTECA) providing for preferential and non-reciprocal access to their markets to the goods of a number of Pacific island states.[21]

Among the most successful free trade agreements in the Asia-Pacific region is the ASEAN Preferential Trading Arrangement signed in 1965 by Indonesia, Malaysia, Singapore, Thailand, the Philippines, and subsequently Brunei. This agreement has been revised on a number of occasions, most recently in 1996;[22] it has clearly contributed to the remarkable economic performance of several "Asian Tigers." The most ambitious agreement in the Asia-Pacific region is the APEC Forum, discussed in chapter 3. This agreement involves a remarkably heterogeneous group of states on three continents. It has ambitious goals of removing all trade barriers between member states by 2010 for developed members and 2020 for developing members. It is also remarkable in that, at the insistence of the Asian members, the means chosen to attain these goals reflect Asian values and Asian methods of moral rather than legal commitment, coupled with increasingly complex intergovernmental and private sector consultative institutions. Given the dynamism of this region it would be most unwise to discount the possibility that APEC will achieve its objectives.

IV. LATIN AMERICA AND THE CARIBBEAN

Latin America has witnessed the formation of many regional economic integration agreements as well as many bilateral agreements. Most of the agreements signed in the decades of the 1960s and 1970s have not been successful. However, there has been a process of renewal and formation of new agreements during the present decade which is almost without precedent in Latin American history. Mexico performed an extraordinary volte face in approaching the United States to form the free trade area, which became the NAFTA. Mexico has continued to develop a network of bilateral and regional agreements with Central America, Chile, Columbia, and Venezuela throughout the decade.

The Latin American Free Trade Area (LAFTA), which dates from 1960, was originally based on policies of regional import-substitution and achieved only limited success. It was replaced in 1980 by the Latin American Integration Association (LAIA), which provides for limited preferential trading rights between Argentina, Bolivia, Brazil, Chile, Colombia, Ecuador, Mexico, Paraguay, Peru, Uruguay, and Venezuela. In 1969, the Andean Group was formed of the Andean members of the LAFTA. It was renewed by the Cartagena Treaty of 1987 and is now in force between Bolivia, Peru, Colombia,

20 Australia-New Zealand Free Trade Agreement (1966), 5 *ILM* 305. See also the Australia-New Zealand Agreement of 1983 (1983), 22 *ILM* 945.

21 Australia and New Zealand plus island states of the South Pacific, 1981; see *Regionalism, supra*, note 16, at 88.

22 ASEAN, Bangkok Declaration, reprinted in (1996), 35 *ILM* 1063.

Ecuador, and Venezuela, but the results in terms of tangible trade liberalization have been disappointing. The most dynamic regional group of the decade has clearly been the Southern Common Market (MERCOSUR), formed in 1991 by Brazil, Argentina, Paraguay, and Uruguay.[23] The MERCOSUR rapidly achieved its most important objective of creating a customs union by eliminating duties on 90 percent of domestic trade. The last 10 percent proved much harder to achieve. However important progress was made in 1995[24] to consolidate the customs union by establishing common institutions and by signing association agreements with Peru and Chile in 1996.[25] The institutions remain intergovernmental in character and it is not yet clear that Brazil is prepared to make the necessary sacrifices of its autonomy to create a genuine common market. Nevertheless the MERCOSUR is a remarkable agreement and in many ways provides an alternative pole of attraction away from the NAFTA for those who envisage a Latin American free trade area or hemispheric free trade.

The Caribbean Free Trade Agreement (CARIFTA) first signed in 1968 provides for a common external tariff and free movement of goods, services, and workers. Despite many difficulties, it has been an important force in promoting the economies of the region and in negotiating preferential access to the markets of North America.[26]

V. MIDDLE EAST

The political tensions of the Middle East have militated against the formation of durable economic integration agreements in this region. Only the Unified Economic Agreement among the States of the Gulf Co-operation Council, signed in 1981, has survived and that with difficulty. Other attempts at regional economic integration promoted by the Arab League or at the bilateral level have not withstood the test of time. Two states of the region have maintained strong ties outside the region. Israel has signed trade agreements with the United States, the EC, and Canada and Turkey is party to a customs union with the EU.[27]

VI. AFRICA

Africa has witnessed the signature of a number of regional trading arrangements. Many have not survived long.[28] Some such as the East African Common Market have been

---

23 Treaty Establishing a Common Market Between the Argentine Republic, The Federal Republic of Brazil, the Republic of Paraguay, and the Eastern Republic of Uruguay (Treaty of Asunción) (1991), 30 *ILM* 1034.

24 See Additional Protocol to the Treaty of Asunción on the Insitutional Structure of Mercosur (Protocol of Rio Plata) (1995), 34 *ILM* 1244.

25 Information made available by the DFAIT.

26 CARIFTA: Caribbean Free Trade Association Agreement (1968), 7 *ILM* 935 and the CARICOM: Treaty Establishing the Caribbean Community (1973), 12 *ILM* 1033.

27 European Community-Israel Trade Agreement (1975), 14 *ILM* 1104 and the Resolution to Establish the Arab Common Market (1964), 3 *ILM* 1102.

28 Economic Community of Eastern Africa (1966), 5 *ILM* 633. But see now the Treaty Establishing the Common Market for Eastern and Southern Africa (1994), 33 *ILM* 1067.

dissolved to reappear in the larger, looser form of the Preferential Trade Area for Eastern and Southern African States, formed in 1981. Similar agreements were signed among the French-speaking and English-speaking states of West Africa and now exist as the Economic Community of West Africa (ECOWAS),[29] and the Central African Economic and Customs Union (UDEAC).[30] The extreme fragility of the economies of these countries has made regional free trade a difficult goal to achieve.

VII. CONCLUSIONS

Regional economic integration agreements are very much part of the international economic environment within which Canadians do business. Canada is party to two major regional agreements and a much greater number of bilateral agreements. They constitute both an advantage and a threat; an advantage, in that they foster trade and economic growth and attract investment. The threat comes from the danger of exclusion of non-members from such regions and the danger that trade will be diverted from the most rational international exchange toward less than optimum regional trade—in essence, regional protectionism. The balance to be struck between regionalism and multilateralism is the WTO's greatest challenge today. Regionalism genuinely based on the same principles as the GATT 1994 will reinforce multilateralism, but regional arrangements designed to exclude outsiders or to manage trade with other regions could seriously weaken the achievements of the GATT 1994.

VIII. SELECTED BIBLIOGRAPHY

Abbot, *Law and Policy of Regional Integration: The NAFTA and Western Hemispheric Integration in the World Trade Organization* (1995).

Trebilcock and Howse, *The Regulation of International Trade* (1995).

WTO Secretariat, *Regionalism and the World Trading System* (Geneva: WTO, 1995).

29 Economic Community of West Africa, articles of association (1967), 6 *ILM* 776; Economic Community of West African States (ECOWAS), Revised Treaty, reprinted in (1996), 35 *ILM* 660.

30 Central African Economic and Customs Union (1965), 4 *ILM* 699. Treaty Establishing the African Economic Community (1991), 30 *ILM* 1241.

PART III

The National Framework: International and National Legal Considerations

INTRODUCTION

This part of the book is concerned with the private law aspects of the exportation and importation of goods or services from one country to another. Chapter 5 deals with export and import transactions founded on the contract of sale. Chapter 6 is devoted to agreements for the transfer of technology. Chapter 7 addresses the problem of insuring the goods that are the object of such transactions. The transportation of such goods is the object of chapter 8. Chapter 9 is concerned with the exportation and importation of services and chapter 10 with construction and long-term contracts including procurement. Methods of payment and financing of these transactions are analyzed in chapter 11.

The International Sale of Goods

I. INTRODUCTION

Export transactions usually involve the exportation of goods and services. When goods are exported, these transactions are based on the contract for the international sale of goods that has as its object the exportation of goods from Canada. A Canadian firm that sells most of its goods on the domestic market usually sells the rest directly to customers abroad. If the firm relies almost exclusively on the foreign market to sell its goods, it often carries out individual export sales through a network of representaçãves abroad who may be its own or independent distributors or agents, branch offices, or even subsidiaries. Joint ventures may be used if required by circumstances. Export merchants, such as export houses, also resort to the contract for the international sale of goods, whether they act as principal or agent for a foreign buyer, provided the goods leave Canada as a result of this contract.[1]

It is important to emphasize that this chapter does not deal with the domestic sale of goods that may be preparatory to their ultimate exportation. It is concerned with the selling or reselling of goods to a buyer abroad. In other words, the contract of sale must have as its objective the exportation of goods from Canada.

The contract for the international sale of goods evidenced by an invoice is the focus of the export transaction. It is always supported by several other related contracts because of the complexity of the transaction and the number of parties involved, especially the contract of carriage by sea, air, rail or road under which the goods are exported evidenced by a bill of lading (see chapter 8, *infra*) and the contract of insurance by which they are insured, evidenced by a document of insurance (see chapter 7, *infra*). These documents are usually delivered to the buyer, or an agent thereof, because they play an important role in the performance of the contract. If payment for the goods exported is made under a banker's letter of credit, further contracts are required between the banks involved and the buyer and seller, respectively (see chapter 11, *infra*).

International transactions do not differ in their fundamentals from domestic transactions, but they do give rise to particular considerations that relate largely to the fact that the parties are located in different countries. Distance, difficulties of communication, and the absence of the trust between the parties that may come from a long-standing commercial relationship, among other factors, create special problems for the transport of the goods and the related questions of their ownership, the responsibility to pay for them, and the risk associated with them while they are in transit, all of which may involve an interaction between the legal systems of the various states involved. Shipping, financing, and insurance documents reflect the practices that have grown over the centuries to deal with these problems.

Today, there is an important evolution in both practice and documentation to take account of more rapid transportation both at sea and in the air and communication by means of computers (paperless transactions using electronic data interchange (EDI)) and other modern forms of doing business that are altering many of the traditional legal rules that have governed shipping and payment modalities for a long period of time. This book cannot review all such changes, partly because of space considerations, partly because we are still uncertain as to what are the precise legal consequences of the use of new documents in multimodal transport ("through bills," for example) or electronic funds transfers in banking transactions. Where possible, we will alert attention to new

1 See, with respect to agency, *infra*, section IV.

developments but the reader should bear in mind that this is an area that presently is in a state of rapid evolution.[2]

A simple sale is one for cash. It is completed by the delivery of the chattel and the payment of the price. The usual international transaction is considerably more complex and usually involves several factors, such as the following: (1) the goods are in the possession of a third party, a shipper or warehouseman, who may be in neither the seller's nor the buyer's country; (2) documents may be exchanged in substitution for the goods, and different documents have distinct legal characteristics varying from a document of title (the bill of lading) or another document, such as an air waybill, or a warehouseman's receipt (which give a right to possession rather than title); or (3) financing arrangements may replace immediate payment upon receipt of the goods or the agreed-upon documents. These latter arrangements will usually involve a bank, because the seller will often want to replace the unknown credit of an unfamiliar buyer with the guarantee of a reliable financial institution, either foreign or domestic (the role of documentary credits).

In the result, some commercial documents, particularly the bill of lading, have developed specific legal characteristics to meet the needs of buyer, seller, and bank. Also, financing arrangements involving documentary credits for making payments in export transactions have now evolved into highly sophisticated mechanisms ("back-to-back" credits, "red-line" credits, and "stand-by" credits). This is an important part of the business of international banking.

Growing out of the law merchant that evolved in Western Europe and more recently throughout the world, trade practice has guaranteed that certain terminology and practices are fairly uniform between trading nations. This process has been furthered by the work of international institutions such as the International Chamber of Commerce (ICC), which has developed its Incoterms over the years to ensure terminological conformity for such terms as cost, insurance, and freight (CIF) and free on board (FOB), wherever they may be used. Also from the ICC are the Uniform Customs and Practices for Documentary Credits (UCP) that, where applicable, ensure a uniform determination of the reciprocal rights and duties of the drawer, beneficiary, and bank or banks participating in a letter of credit. It is one of the major objectives of the UN Commission on International Trade Law (UNCITRAL), which has focused much of its attention on the elaboration of uniform rules applying to international transactions using a series of diverse mechanisms, such as international conventions and model laws, to try to ensure a common approach by national jurisdictions to these issues. This is not an easy process, because it is often difficult to obtain a consensus on legal approaches between the common law and civil law systems (the 1980 Vienna Convention on the International Sale of Goods (CISG, the object of section III.A, *infra*) does not deal with the issue of the "passing of the property" for this reason). Recognizing the specific concerns of the developing countries, which seek a recognition of precepts of a New International Economic Order (NIEO) reflected

---

2 For a recent survey of the issues involved in the automation of international trade and payments, see, e.g., Toh See Kiat, *Paperless International Trade: Law of Telematic Data Interchange* (1992).

in the rules adopted, also can create difficulties in finding a satisfactory universal solution to these issues.

It is suggested that, for the international legal practitioner, familiarity with the work of UNCITRAL is as significant as the reports of law reform commissions in our domestic legal system. They are an important source for reviewing developments and detecting future trends in this area.

Other international institutions also play significant roles—for example, the International Institute for the Unification of Private Law (UNIDROIT) located in Rome,[3] not to mention hundreds of specialized trade organizations that contribute to the establishment of recognized trade practices and uniform documentation in their particular trade or industry.[4]

The major purpose of this chapter is to review the rules applicable to different types of international sale of goods wherein the seller's and buyer's rights and obligations in relation to payment, risk, insurance, and shipping charges crystallize at different transportation points, depending upon the nature of the agreement. As mentioned above, these are now fairly well-established concepts with uniform consequences in most jurisdictions and are embodied in such trade terms as FOB, CIF, free alongside ship (FAS), etc. The FOB and CIF trade terms have the longest historical usage and probably remain the most-used concepts, at least in maritime transport situations (they may also, of course, be employed in domestic situations). However, these trade terms had to be revised to take into account changes in transportation techniques and new developments in EDI. See section II.B.1 dealing with the Incoterms 1990.

Since export transactions extend over several legal units, they raise problems of private international law, principally the law applicable to any dispute that may arise between the parties to the contracts for the international sale of goods and the jurisdiction of the court that will adjudicate the issue. That court may have to apply a law that is not its own. Thus, it is of utmost importance for the parties to the contract to know, if possible, in advance, which law governs its various aspects, especially where the law prevailing at the place where the buyer resides or where the contract was made is different from that of the place where the goods are to be shipped. This question is discussed in section V, *infra*.

Still another issue is that of the possible existence of a *lex mercatoria*, or common general principles of international commercial law that may be applied to a contract,

---

3 See, in particular, the UNIDROIT's 1994 Principles of International Commercial Contracts, discussed in section III.C.

4 For a general overview of the various agreements and organizations relevant to international economic and commercial law, see Colas (ed.), *Global Economic Cooperation: A Guide to Agreements and Organizations* (1994). Note that the UNCITRAL has published a *Register of Texts of Conventions and Other Instruments Concerning International Trade Law* (see, e.g., Convention on Contracts for the International Sale of Goods (1980)). The International Chamber of Commerce has also published rules that ease the flow of commerce (e.g., Incoterms (International Rules for the Interpretation of Trade Terms) (1990 rev.), Uniform Customs and Practices for Documentary Credits (1993 rev.)(UCP500)). The US-UCC is also of great interest to Canada since most Canadian exports are to the United States.

thus obviating the necessity to have all rights and obligations between the parties established by reference to one legal system by virtue of private international law rules. The *lex mercatoria* is dealt with in section VI, *infra*.

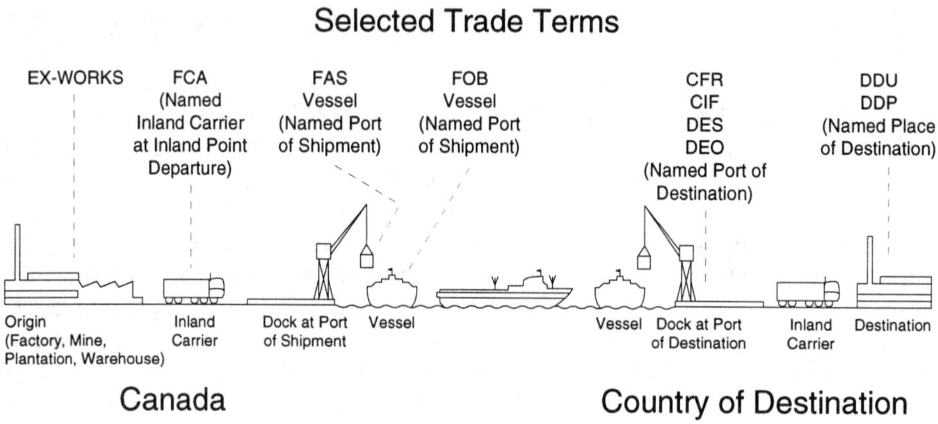

II. INTERNATIONAL TRADE TERMS

A. Introduction

Ideally, the manufacturer-exporter would like to be discharged of any responsibility with respect to the goods once they leave the factory, and to be paid immediately by the buyer-importer in exchange for the receipt of the goods given by the transportation company. On the other hand, the buyer-importer would like to incur no responsibility for the goods until they are delivered at their place of destination, and to be able to postpone payment until they have been inspected and accepted. Between the exporter's place of business and that of the importer, there exists a variety of points (for example, alongside the vessel, over the vessel's rail) at which the risks involved in an export transaction (for example, risk of destruction or damage in transit, delays in delivery, risk of non-payment, or devaluation of currency) can be shifted and payment demanded. These risks are allocated by the exporter and importer through their contract of sale using special price-delivery trade terms, such as "ex works," "ex dock," "alongside the vessel," FAS, FOB, CIF, etc.[5]

The choice of the correct price-delivery trade term by the parties to the contract for the international sale of goods determines many legal questions with respect to, *inter alia*, title to the goods, time and place of delivery, time and place of payment, time and place of the importer's right of inspection, and risks of loss of, or damage to, the goods in transit. Usually, the exporter sets the terms in the printed form of the contract of sale.

Where the buyer-importer conducts business in a foreign country through a branch office, a subsidiary, or overseas buyers, the goods are purchased in that country by the appointed representative and exported to the country of the importer. The buyer-importer

---

5 See, in general, Schmitthoff, *The Law and Practice of International Trade* (9th ed, 1990), at 9 *et seq.*

collects the goods at the seller-exporter's works. The purchase price is due on delivery of the goods, unless other arrangements have been made. Since the contract is both concluded and performed in the same country, it is normally governed by the law of that country. The transaction, whether ex mill, ex mine, ex warehouse, etc., is an export sale only in the sense that it contemplates an ultimate transfer of the goods to a foreign destination. Basically, it is a domestic sale. The buyer-importer has purchased goods abroad for the purpose of shipping them home. This is also the case where the representative of the buyer-importer does not want to collect the goods at the seller-exporter's works and requires the latter to load them onto an inland carrier and to pay the freight to the point of exportation. The price-delivery term quoted may thus be FOB (named inland carrier at named inland point of departure) or FOB (named inland carrier at named inland point of departure) *freight prepaid to* (named inland point of departure).

If, on the other hand, the buyer-importer enters into a destination or arrival contract, the seller-exporter must place the goods on board a ship bound for the country of destination and bear the risks of the voyage. The seller-exporter, now shipper, is liable if the goods do not arrive at their destination. The buyer-importer has no insurable interest in the goods. Usually, destination contracts take the form ex dock (named port of importation).

A seller-exporter who does not wish to assume the responsibilities peculiar to international trade may agree only to enter into a shipment contract whereby the goods are placed on board or alongside the vessel (in a lighter or on the wharf) and, in some cases, to arrange shipping space. Here, the buyer-importer must pay the purchase price and assume responsibility for the incidental charges of putting the goods on board and for the risks of the voyage. Such contracts are generally designated as FAS vessel (named port of shipment), FOB vessel (named port of shipment), CIF or cost and freight (CFR). Although this type of shipment contract also contemplates an eventual export by the buyer-importer, it is still an ordinary contract of sale because it fixes the place of performance in the country of export. The price-delivery term FAS vessel (named port of shipment) is one of several FOB terms. If improperly used, it can give rise to a dispute concerning the liability of the seller-exporter or the buyer-importer. Therefore, it is important for the price-delivery term FOB to be followed by a very precise designation and not merely a port.

When the price-delivery term FOB vessel is used, the seller assumes further responsibilities—namely, the undertaking to place the goods on board a vessel that has been named by the buyer and that stands at the agreed port of shipment. The buyer is the exporter. In most cases, the buyer is represented by a forwarding agent in the country of export who will attend to the various details that may affect the export process in order to complete the transaction. The seller will turn the mate's receipt for the goods over to the buyer's forwarding agent so that a bill of lading can be procured on the buyer's behalf. Since the place of delivery of the goods is on board the vessel, the seller expects payment upon presentment of the receipt for the goods to the buyer's agent.

In most international transactions, however, the seller exports the goods to the country of importation and for this purpose uses the CIF or CFR price-delivery term or some variants of the FOB price-delivery term. In each of these three cases, the seller usually secures the space on a selected vessel and places the goods on board. Once this is done, the seller (now exporter) receives a bill of lading, normally made out to order.

The exporter parts with this bill for value only, which is given by the importer or the importer's bank. Once the bill of lading is in possession of the importer, the goods can be dealt with long before they arrive in the country of import. Usually, the exporter arranges with the importer for payment of the goods upon presentation of the various documents representing the export transaction, including the bill of lading, to a bank in the exporter's country. The exporter's bank airmails the documents to the importer's bank, which reimburses it. Thus, the exporter is paid against the symbolic delivery of the goods.

Until the goods arrive at the port of destination and delivery is taken, the importer bears the risk of loss or damage to them without having physical possession of such goods. To cover this risk, the importer takes out a policy of marine insurance in addition to the liabilities assumed by the carrier under the bill of lading. Upon arrival of the goods, the importer usually takes delivery before reimbursing the bank that paid for the goods. To protect itself, this bank delivers the bill of lading to the importer under a trust receipt that operates as a security interest in the goods or their proceeds.

The question as to who provides the insurance for the benefit of the importer is determined by the price-delivery term. If the price-delivery term is CIF, the seller-exporter arranges for insurance for the benefit of the importer. If the price-delivery term is CFR, insurance is arranged by the importer.

Where an FOB vessel price-delivery term is used, but the seller undertakes to perform certain obligations (additional services), such as the booking of shipping space, procuring the bill of lading or an export licence, or even arranging insurance, the borderline between the FOB vessel and CIF price-delivery terms is difficult to discern. In a CIF sale, the seller is also the shipper as principal and not as agent for the buyer. In an FOB sale with additional services, is the seller acting as principal or as agent for the buyer when securing shipping space or insurance? If the seller is acting as principal, there is no difference between the CIF price-delivery term and this type of FOB price-delivery term. If the seller is acting as agent for the buyer, fluctuations in freight or insurance rates are at the buyer's risk. A seller who is not willing to assume the obligations to make shipping arrangements or to bear the risk of these fluctuations must contract FOB price-delivery terms with additional services at the buyer's risk.

International shipments of goods by rail (for example, free carrier (FCA), or free on rail (FOR)) and by air follow more or less the same rules. However, since the period of risk and inaccessibility of the goods on shipment by air is much shorter than in the case of carriage of goods by sea or by rail, the concept of symbolic delivery of goods by transfer of documents has not been applied to them. For instance, the air consignment note (air waybill) is not a document of title that can be transferred free of personal defences.

B. Uniform Trade Terms

Although FOB, FAS, CIF, etc., price-delivery trade terms have been the most widely used instruments of the export trade for almost two centuries,[6] they have not exactly the same meaning in every country of the world. To ensure a measure of uniformity concerning the

6 For a history of the origin of FOB and CIF terms, see D.M. Sassoon, "The Origin of FOB and CIF Terms and the Factors Influencing Their Choice," [1967] *J Bus. L* 32.

connotations of these terms, private international trade associations have formulated detailed definitions of the rights and obligations of the parties under each term. The two most important sets of definitions are: (1) the Incoterms 1990, and (2) the Uniform Commercial Code (UCC).

Standardized printed forms for the contract of international sale of goods prepared by trade associations also dominate the field. An exporter who wishes to avoid a misunderstanding with a foreign buyer concerning a given price-delivery term may either refer to a particular set of trade terms as governing the contract of sale or attempt to describe in the contract all the obligations of both the seller and the buyer. Otherwise, the proper law of the contract determines the meaning of the price-delivery term, unless resort can be had to the *lex mercatoria.*

1. Incoterms

In 1936, the ICC published a set of international rules for the interpretation of trade terms. These rules, known as the Incoterms 1936, were amended in 1953, 1967, 1976, 1980, and 1990 to keep up with the current practice of a majority of the business people engaged in international trade. The purpose of the Incoterms is "to provide a set of international rules for the interpretation of the most commonly used trade terms in foreign trade"[7] contracts, for the optional use of business people who prefer the certainty of uniform international rules to the uncertainties of the varied interpretations of the same terms in different countries. These rules define, in a simple and safe manner, the respective responsibilities of the buyer and seller, thus reducing any possibility of misunderstanding and subsequent dispute.[8]

Parties may adopt the Incoterms as the general basis of their contract and also specify particular variations of them or additions to them such as may be suited to the particular trade or the circumstances of the time or their particular convenience.[9] Although the Incoterms govern only if the parties expressly so provide, because of their wide acceptance in international commerce, they may influence the interpretation given to undefined terms by a court applying domestic law and may even develop over time into customary international usage with the force of law.

The Incoterms 1990 are practical rules, primarily designed to define the method of delivery of the goods sold. They are also concerned with cost distribution,[10] because the purchase price will depend upon the incidental charges included therein. Thus, a seller when quoting FOB will ask for a lower price than when quoting CIF since, in the latter case, the purchase price includes insurance and freight. Risk distribution is less important because it is normally regarded as a matter of insurance. In general, the Incoterms

---

7 Incoterms 1990, introduction, para. 1.

8 *Ibid.*, foreword, at 5.

9 *Ibid.*, introduction, para. 6. E.g., individual contracts may add to the basic trade term as FOB *stowed* and C & F or CIF *landed.*

10 Note that efforts have been made to simplify the cost distribution by preparing cost units for each trade term. These cost units incorporate all actual costs occurring in a particular traffic system. See, e.g., the Combiterms system used by freight forwarders.

1990 deal with such issues as transfer of risk, arranging carriage and insurance, export and import licences, nature and type of documents, and checking operations and certificates of the quality of the goods. It should be noted that the position of the respective contracting parties cannot be fully understood merely by an analysis of the chosen trade term. The contract as a whole with all its terms and conditions, including the applicable domestic law, must be considered.

The 1990 revision adapts the terms to the use of EDI when the parties to a contract of sale have to provide various documents, especially a bill of lading that may be used for the purpose of selling the goods while in transit. Thus, the terms ensure that when using EDI, the buyer has the same legal position as he or she would have obtained if he or she had received a more traditional bill of lading from the seller.

The 1990 revision also takes into account new transportation techniques such as the unitization of cargo in containers, multimodal transport and roll on-roll off (ro-ro) traffic with road vehicles, and railway wagons in "short sea" maritime transport. The term FCA now covers all types of transport irrespective of the mode and combination of different modes.[11]

The Incoterms 1990 begin with the E term, which contains the seller's minimum obligation (ex works). It is followed by the F terms whereby the seller must deliver the goods to a carrier appointed by the buyer (FCA, FAS, and FOB). The F terms indicate shipment contracts as the seller fulfills the contract in the country of shipment or dispatch. Next are the C terms, where the seller must contract for carriage without assuming the risk of loss of or damage to the goods or additional costs after shipment and dispatch (CFR, CIF, carriage paid to (CPT), and carriage and insurance paid to (CIP)). The C terms also indicate shipment contracts. Thus, unlike the E, F, and D terms, the C terms contain two critical points, one for the division of costs and another for the division of risks. Also, a buyer paying for the goods under a C term should ensure that the seller, upon payment, is prevented from disposing of the goods by new instructions to the carrier. Finally, the D terms contain the seller's maximum obligations, since he or she must bear all risks and costs in bringing the goods to the agreed place or point of destination (delivered ex ship (DES), delivered ex quay (DEQ), delivered duty unpaid (DDU), and delivered duty paid (DDP)). The D terms indicate arrival contracts.

The Incoterms conform with the 1978 UN Convention on the Carriage of Goods by Sea (the Hamburg Rules)[12] and the 1980 UN Convention on International Multimodal Transport of Goods.[13] The 1980 UN Convention on Contracts for the International Sale of Goods does not deal with the interpretation of the trade terms, although it adopts the general principle that delivery occurs and the risk passes when the goods are handed over to the first carrier for transmission to the buyer.[14]

---

11 Incoterms 1990, introduction, para. 5.

12 See chapter 8, *infra*, art. 4: The critical point is when the goods are handed to the first carrier.

13 Art. 14.

14 See CISG, arts. 31 and 67. See also art. 8, para. 2, which allows resort to the Incoterms for the interpretation of any particular trade term chosen in the contract of sale as "usage of which the parties knew or ought to have known and which in international trade is widely known to, and regularly observed by, parties to contracts of the type involved in the particular trade concerned." The CISG is discussed in section III.A, *infra*.

INCOTERMS 1990

Group E Departure	EXW	Ex Works
Group F Main Carriage Unpaid	FCA FAS FOB	Free Carrier Free Alongside Ship Free On Board
Group C Main Carriage Paid	CFR CIF CPT CIP	Cost and Freight Cost, Insurance, and Freight Carriage Paid To Carriage and Insurance Paid To
Group D Arrival	DAF DES DEQ DDU DDP	Delivered At Frontier Delivered Ex Ship Delivered Ex Quay Delivered Duty Unpaid Delivered Duty Paid

MODE OF TRANSPORT AND THE APPROPRIATE INCOTERMS 1990

Any Mode of Transport Including Multimodal	EXW FCA CPT CIP DAF DDU DDP	Ex Works (… named place) Free Carrier (… named place) Carriage Paid To (… named place of destination) Carriage and Insurance Paid To (… named place of destination) Delivered At Frontier (… named place) Delivered Duty Unpaid (… named place of destination) Delivered Duty Paid (… named place of destination)
Air Transport	FCA	Free Carrier (… named place)
Rail Transport	FCA	Free Carrier (… named place)
Sea and Inland Waterway Transport	FAS FOB CFR CIF DES DEQ	Free Alongside Ship (… named port of shipment) Free On Board (… named port of shipment) Cost And Freight (… named port of destination) Cost, Insurance, and Freight (… named port of destination) Delivered Ex Ship (… named port of destination) Delivered Ex Quay (… named port of destination)

The Incoterms relate only to trade terms used in the contract of sale. They do not deal with similar terms that may be used in contracts of carriage. Since the risk for loss of or damage to the goods, as well as the obligation to bear the costs relating to them pass to the buyer when the seller has fulfilled his or her obligation to deliver the goods, all Incoterms stipulate that such passing of risks and costs may occur even before delivery if the buyer does not take delivery as agreed or fails to give such instructions as the seller may require in order to fulfill his or her obligation to deliver the goods. In other words, the buyer cannot delay the passing of the risks and costs. However, this premature passing of risks and costs is conditional upon the goods having been identified or set aside for the buyer.

Ex Works, Ex Warehouse, Ex Store (EXW)

The seller's only responsibility is to make the goods available to the buyer at the former's works, warehouse, or store. The buyer bears the full cost and risks involved in bringing the goods from there to the desired destination. Thus, this term represents the minimum obligation of the seller.

The Incoterms 1990 describe the obligations of the parties as follows:

A. The seller must:

A1. Provision of goods in conformity with the contract
Provide the goods and the commercial invoice, or its equivalent electronic message, in conformity with the contract of sale and any other evidence of conformity that may be required by the contract.

A2. Licences, authorizations and formalities
Render the buyer, at the latter's request, risk and expense, every assistance in obtaining any export licence or other official authorization necessary for the exportation of the goods.

A3. Contract of carriage and insurance

a) Contract of carriage
No obligation.

b) Contract of insurance
No obligation.

A4. Delivery
Place the goods at the disposal of the buyer at the named place of delivery on the date or within the period stipulated or, if no such place or time is stipulated, at the usual place and time for delivery of such goods.

A5. Transfer of risks
Subject to the provisions of B.5., bear all risks of loss of or damage to the goods until such time as they have been placed at the disposal of the buyer in accordance with A.4.

A6. Division of costs
Subject to the provisions of B.6., pay all costs relating to the goods until such time as they have been placed at the disposal of the buyer in accordance with A.4.

A7. Notice to the buyer
Give the buyer sufficient notice as to when and where the goods will be placed at his disposal.

A8. Proof of delivery, transport document or equivalent electronic message
No obligation.

A9. Checking—packaging—marking
Pay the costs of those checking operations (such as checking quality, measuring, weighing, counting) which are necessary for the purpose of placing the goods at the disposal of the buyer.

Provide at his own expense packaging (unless it is usual for the particular trade to make the goods of the contract description available unpacked) which is required for the transport of the goods, to the extent that the circumstances relating to the transport (*e.g.* modalities, destination) are made known to the seller before the contract of sale is concluded. Packaging is to be marked appropriately.

A10. Other obligations
Render the buyer at the latter's request, risk and expense, every assistance in obtaining any documents or equivalent electronic messages issued or transmitted in the country of delivery and/or of origin which the buyer may require for the exportation and/or importation of the goods and, where necessary, for their transit through another country.

Provide the buyer, upon request, with the necessary information for procuring insurance.

B. The buyer must:

B1. Payment of the price
Pay the price as provided in the contract of sale.

B2. Licences, authorizations and formalities
Obtain at his own risk and expense any export and import licence or other official authorization and carry out all customs formalities for the exportation and importation of the goods and, where necessary, for their transit through another country.

B3. Contract of carriage
No obligation.

B4. Taking delivery
Take delivery of the goods as soon as they have been placed at his disposal in accordance with A.4.

B5. Transfer of risks
Bear all risks of loss of or damage to the goods from the time they have been placed at his disposal in accordance with A.4. Should he fail to give notice in accordance with B.7., bear all risks of loss of or damage to the goods from the agreed date or the expiry date of any period fixed for taking delivery provided, however, that the goods have been duly appropriated to the contract, that is to say clearly set aside or otherwise identified as the contract goods.

B6. Division of costs
Pay all costs relating to the goods from the time they have been placed at his disposal in accordance with A.4.

Pay any additional costs incurred by failing either to take delivery of the goods when they have been placed at his disposal, or to give appropriate notice in accordance with B.7. provided, however, that the goods have been duly appropriated to the contract, that is to say clearly set aside or otherwise identified as the contract goods.

Pay all duties, taxes and other official charges as well as the costs of carrying out customs formalities payable upon exportation and importation of the goods and, where necessary, for their transit through another country.

Reimburse all costs and charges incurred by the seller in rendering assistance in accordance with A.2.

B7. Notice to the seller
Whenever he is entitled to determine the time within a stipulated period and/or the place of taking delivery, give the seller sufficient notice thereof.

B8. Proof of delivery, transport document or equivalent electronic message
Provide the seller with appropriate evidence of having taken delivery.

B9. Inspection of goods
Pay, unless otherwise agreed, the costs of pre-shipment inspection (including inspection mandated by the authorities of the country of exportation).

B10. Other obligations
Pay all costs and charges incurred in obtaining the documents or equivalent electronic messages mentioned in A.10. and reimburse those incurred by the seller in rendering his assistance in accordance therewith.

The purchase price must be paid on delivery unless other arrangements are made.

Free Carrier (... Named Place) (FCA)

Today, in maritime transport, the ship's rail as a critical point for the division of functions, costs, and risks between a seller and a buyer is no longer suitable in the light of new liner trade and cargo handling techniques, especially when goods are prepared in units before shipment on flats, or in pallets or containers, or when different modes of transport are combined by the multimodal transport operator. It is inappropriate that, in these cases, the seller who delivers the goods to cargo terminals before the arrival of the ship must assume the risk of loss of or damage to the goods until they are placed on board the ship, even though he or she has no control over them. To remedy this situation, the Incoterms 1990 use the term free carrier (... named place) (FCA) to cover unitization of cargo in container, multimodal transport, and ro-ro traffic by trailers and ferries. The main characteristic of this term is that the risks and other legal incidents pass from the seller to the buyer when the first carrier takes charge of the goods. This is when delivery takes place.

The Incoterms 1990 provide as follows:

"Free Carrier" means that the seller fulfils his obligation to deliver when he has handed over the goods, cleared for export, into the charge of the carrier named by the buyer at the named place or point. If no precise point is indicated by the buyer, the seller may choose within the place or range stipulated where the carrier shall take the goods into his charge. When, according to commercial practice, the seller's assistance is required in making the contract with the carrier (such as in rail or air transport) the seller may act at the buyer's risk and expense.

This term may be used for any mode of transport, including multimodal transport.

"Carrier" means any person who, in a contract of carriage, undertakes to perform or to procure the performance of carriage by rail, road, sea, air, inland waterway or by a combination of such modes. If the buyer instructs the seller to deliver the cargo to a person, *e.g.* a freight forwarder who is not a "carrier," the seller is deemed to have fulfilled his obligation to deliver the goods when they are in the custody of that person.

"Transport terminal" means a railway terminal, a freight station, a container terminal or yard, a multi-purpose cargo terminal or any similar receiving point.

"Container" includes any equipment used to unitise cargo, *e.g.* all types of containers and/or flats, whether ISO accepted or not, trailers, swap bodies, ro-ro equipment, igloos, and applies to all modes of transport.

A. The seller must:

A1. Provision of goods in conformity with the contract

Provide the goods and the commercial invoice, or its equivalent electronic message, in conformity with the contract of sale and any other evidence of conformity which may be required by the contract.

A2. Licences, authorizations and formalities

Obtain at his own risk and expense any export licence or other official authorization and carry out all customs formalities necessary for the exportation of the goods.

A3. Contract of carriage and insurance

a) Contract of carriage

No obligation. However, if requested by the buyer or if it is commercial practice and the buyer does not give an instruction to the contrary in due time, the seller may contract for carriage on usual terms at the buyer's risk and expense. The seller may decline to make the contract and, if he does, shall promptly notify the buyer accordingly.

b) Contract of insurance

No obligation.

A4. Delivery

Deliver the goods into the custody of the carrier or another person (*e.g.* a freight forwarder) named by the buyer, or chosen by the seller in accordance with A.3.a), at the named place or point (*e.g.* transport terminal or other receiving point) on the date or within the period agreed for delivery and in the manner agreed or customary at such point. If no specific point has been agreed, and if there are several points available, the seller may select the point at the place of delivery which best suits his purpose. Failing precise instructions from the buyer, the seller may deliver the goods to the carrier in such a manner as the transport mode of that carrier and the quantity and/or nature of the goods may require.

Delivery to the carrier is completed:

i) In the case of *rail transport*, when the goods constitute a wagon load (or a container load carried by rail), the seller has to load the wagon or container in the appropriate manner. Delivery is completed when the loaded wagon or container is taken over by the railway or by another person acting on its behalf.

When the goods do not constitute a wagon or container load, delivery is completed when the seller has handed over the goods at the railway receiving point or loaded them into a vehicle provided by the railway.

ii) In the case of *road transport*, when loading takes place at the seller's premises, delivery is completed when the goods have been loaded on the vehicle provided by the buyer.

When the goods are delivered to the carrier's premises, delivery is completed when they have been handed over to the road carrier or to another person acting on his behalf.

iii) In the case of transport by *inland waterway*, when loading takes place at the seller's premises, delivery is completed when the goods have been loaded on the carrying vessel provided by the buyer.

When the goods are delivered to the carrier's premises, delivery is completed when they have been handed over to the inland waterway carrier or to another person acting on his behalf.

iv) In the case of *sea transport*, when the goods constitute a full container load (FCL), delivery is completed when the loaded container is taken over by the sea carrier. When the container has been carried to an operator of a transport terminal acting on behalf of the carrier, the goods shall be deemed to have been taken over when the container has entered into the premises of that terminal.

When the goods are less than a container load (LCL), or are not to be containerized, the seller has to carry them to the transport terminal. Delivery is completed when the goods have been handed over to the sea carrier or to another person acting on his behalf.

v) In the case of *air transport*, delivery is completed when the goods have been handed over to the air carrier or to another person acting on his behalf.

vi) In the case of *unnamed transport*, delivery is completed when the goods have been handed over to the carrier or to another person acting on his behalf.

vii) In the case of *multimodal transport*, delivery is completed when the goods have been handed over as specified in i)-vi), as the case may be.

A5. Transfer of risks

Subject to the provisions of B.5., bear all risks of loss of or damage to the goods until such time as they have been delivered in accordance with A.4.

A6. Division of costs

Subject to the provisions of B.6.

—pay all costs relating to the goods until such time as they have been delivered to the carrier in accordance with A.4.;

—pay the costs of customs formalities as well as all duties, taxes, and other official charges payable upon exportation.

A7. Notice to the buyer

Give the buyer sufficient notice that the goods have been delivered into the custody of the carrier. Should the carrier fail to take the goods into his charge at the time agreed, the seller must notify the buyer accordingly.

A8. Proof of delivery, transport document or equivalent electronic message

Provide the buyer at the seller's expense, if customary, with the usual document in proof of delivery of the goods in accordance with A.4.

Unless the document referred to in the preceding paragraph is the transport document, render the buyer at the latter's request, risk and expense, every assistance in obtaining a transport document for the contract of carriage (for example, a negotiable bill of lading, a non-negotiable sea waybill, an inland waterway document, an air waybill, a railway consignment note, a road consignment note, or a multimodal transport document).

When the seller and the buyer have agreed to communicate electronically, the document referred to in the preceding paragraph may be replaced by an equivalent electronic data interchange (EDI) message.

A9. Checking—packaging—marking

Pay the costs of those checking operations (such as checking quality, measuring, weighing, counting) which are necessary for the purpose of delivering the goods to the carrier.

Provide, at his own expense, packaging (unless it is usual for the particular trade to send the goods of the contract description unpacked) which is required for the transport of the goods, to the extent that the circumstances relating to the transport (*e.g.* modalities, destination) are made known to the seller before the contract of sale is concluded. Packaging is to be marked appropriately.

A10. Other obligations

Render the buyer, at the latter's request, risk and expense, every assistance in obtaining any documents or equivalent electronic messages (other than those mentioned in A.8.) issued or transmitted in the country of delivery and/or of origin which the buyer may require for the importation of the goods and, where necessary, for their transit through another country. Provide the buyer, upon request, with the necessary information for procuring insurance.

B. The buyer must:

B1. Payment of the price

Pay the price as provided in the contract of sale.

B2. Licences, authorizations and formalities

Obtain at his own risk and expense any import licence or other official authorization and carry out all customs formalities for the importation of the goods and, where necessary, for their transit through another country.

B3. Contract of carriage

Contract, at his own expense, for the carriage of the goods from the named place, except as provided for in A.3.a).

B4. Taking delivery

Take delivery of the goods in accordance with A.4.

B5. Transfer of risks

Bear all risks of loss of or damage to the goods from the time they have been delivered in accordance with A.4.

Should he fail to give notice in accordance with B.7., or should the carrier named by him fail to take the goods into his charge, bear all risks of loss of or damage to the goods from the agreed date or the expiry date of any period stipulated for delivery provided, however, that the goods have been duly appropriated to the contract, that is to say, clearly set aside or otherwise identified as the contract goods.

B6. Division of costs
Pay all costs relating to the goods from the time when they have been delivered in accordance with A.4.

Pay any additional costs incurred, either because he fails to name the carrier, or the carrier named by him fails to take the goods into his charge at the agreed time, or because he has failed to give appropriate notice in accordance with B.7. provided, however, that the goods have been duly appropriated to the contract, that is to say, clearly set aside or otherwise identified as the contract goods.

Pay all duties, taxes and other official charges as well as the costs of carrying out customs formalities payable upon importation of the goods and, where necessary, for their transit through another country.

B7. Notice to the seller
Give the seller sufficient notice of the name of the carrier and, where necessary, specify the mode of transport, as well as the date or period for delivering the goods to him and, as the case may be, the point within the place where the goods should be delivered to the carrier.

B8. Proof of delivery, transport document or equivalent electronic message
Accept the proof of delivery in accordance with A.8.

B9. Inspection of goods
Pay, unless otherwise agreed, the costs of pre-shipment inspection except when mandated by the authorities of the country of exportation.

B10. Other obligations
Pay all costs and charges incurred in obtaining the documents or equivalent electronic messages mentioned in A.10. and reimburse those incurred by the seller in rendering his assistance in accordance therewith and in contracting for carriage in accordance with A.3.a).

Give the seller appropriate instructions whenever the seller's assistance in contracting for carriage is required in accordance with A.3.a).

Free Alongside Ship (Named Port of Shipment) (FAS)

The seller must deliver the goods alongside the vessel so that they can be loaded on board by the vessel's tackle or by some other means at the expense of the buyer.

The Incoterms 1990 state that:

A. The seller must:

A1. Provision of goods in conformity with the contract
Provide the goods and the commercial invoice, or its equivalent electronic message, in conformity with the contract of sale and any other evidence of conformity which may be required by the contract.

A2. Licences, authorizations and formalities
Render the buyer, at the latter's request, risk and expense, every assistance in obtaining any export licence or other official authorization necessary for the exportation of the goods.

A3. Contract of carriage and insurance

a) Contract of carriage
No obligation.

b) Contract of insurance
No obligation.

A4. Delivery
Deliver the goods alongside the named vessel at the loading place named by the buyer at the named port of shipment on the date or within the period stipulated and in the manner customary at the port.

A5. Transfer of risks
Subject to the provisions of B.5., bear all risks of loss of or damage to the goods until such time as they have been delivered in accordance with A.4.

A6. Division of costs
Subject to the provisions of B.6., pay all costs relating to the goods until such time as they have been delivered in accordance with A.4.

A7. Notice to the buyer
Give the buyer sufficient notice that the goods have been delivered alongside the named vessel.

A8. Proof of delivery, transport document or equivalent electronic message
Provide the buyer, at the seller's expense, with the usual document in proof of delivery of the goods in accordance with A.4.

Unless the document referred to in the preceding paragraph is the transport document, render the buyer, at the latter's request, risk and expense, every assistance in obtaining a transport document (for example, a negotiable bill of lading, a non-negotiable sea waybill, an inland waterway document).

When the seller and the buyer have agreed to communicate electronically, the document referred to in the preceding paragraphs may be replaced by an equivalent electronic data interchange (EDI) message.

A9. Checking—packaging—marking
Pay the costs of those checking operations (such as checking quality, measuring, weighing, counting) which are necessary for the purpose of placing the goods at the disposal of the buyer.

Provide at his own expense packaging (unless it is usual for the particular trade to ship the goods of the contract description unpacked) which is required for the transport of the goods, to the extent that the circumstances relating to the transport (*e.g.* modalities, destination) are made known to the seller before the contract of sale is concluded. Packaging is to be marked appropriately.

A10. Other obligations
Render the buyer, at the latter's request, risk and expense, every assistance in obtaining any documents or equivalent electronic messages (other than those mentioned in A.8.) issued or transmitted in the country of shipment and/or of origin which the buyer may require for the exportation and/or importation of the goods and, where necessary, for their transit through another country.

Provide the buyer, upon request, with the necessary information for procuring insurance.

B. The buyer must:

B1. Payment of the price
Pay the price as provided in the contract of sale.

B2. Licences, authorizations and formalities
Obtain at his own risk and expense any export and import licence or other official authorization and carry out all customs formalities for the exportation and importation of the goods and, where necessary, for their transit through another country.

B3. Contract of carriage
Contract at his own expense for the carriage of the goods from the named port of shipment.

B4. Taking delivery
Take delivery of the goods in accordance with A.4.

B5. Transfer of risks
Bear all risks of loss of or damage to the goods from the time they have been delivered in accordance with A.4.

Should he fail to fulfil his obligations in accordance with B.2., bear all additional risks of loss of or damage to the goods incurred thereby and should he fail to give notice in accordance with B.7., or should the vessel named by him fail to arrive on time, or be unable to take the goods, or close for cargo earlier than the stipulated time, bear all risks of loss of or damage to the goods from the agreed date or the expiry date of the period stipulated for delivery provided, however, that the goods have been duly appropriated to the contract, that is to say, clearly set aside or otherwise identified as the contract goods.

B6. Division of costs
Pay all costs relating to the goods from the time they have been delivered in accordance with A.4.

Pay any additional costs incurred, either because the vessel named by him has failed to arrive on time, or will be unable to take the goods, or will close for cargo earlier than the stipulated time, or because the buyer has failed to fulfil his obligations in accordance with B.2., or to give appropriate notice in accordance with B.7. provided, however, that the goods have been duly appropriated to the contract, that is to say, clearly set aside or otherwise identified as the contract goods.

Pay all duties, taxes and other official charges as well as the costs of carrying out customs formalities payable upon exportation and importation of the goods and, where necessary, for their transit through another country.

Pay all costs and charges incurred by the seller in rendering assistance in accordance with A.2.

B7. Notice to the seller
Give the seller sufficient notice of the vessel name, loading place and required delivery time.

B8. Proof of delivery, transport document or equivalent electronic message
Accept the proof of delivery in accordance with A.8.

B9. Inspection of goods
Pay, unless otherwise agreed, the costs of pre-shipment inspection (including inspection mandated by the authorities of the country of exportation).

B10. Other obligations
Pay all costs and charges incurred in obtaining the documents or equivalent electronic messages mentioned in A.10. and reimburse those incurred by the seller in rendering his assistance in accordance therewith.

Free on Board (Named Port of Shipment) (FOB)

Here, the seller must place the goods on board a ship that has been named by the buyer and that is berthed at the agreed port of shipment. The buyer is only responsible for the charges incurred after the goods have been delivered over the ship's rail. It is also at this time that the buyer takes the risk of loss or damage to the goods and that the property passes to him or her unless such passing has been postponed by express or implied stipulation.

According to the Incoterms 1990:

A. The seller must:

A1. Provision of goods in conformity with the contract
Provide the goods and the commercial invoice, or its equivalent electronic message, in conformity with the contract of sale and any other evidence of conformity which may be required by the contract.

A2. Licences, authorizations and formalities
Obtain, at his own risk and expense, any export licence or other official authorization and carry out all customs formalities necessary for the exportation of the goods.

A3. Contract of carriage and insurance

a) Contract of carriage
No obligation.

b) Contract of insurance
No obligation.

A4. Delivery
Deliver the goods on board the vessel named by the buyer at the named port of shipment on the date or within the period stipulated and in the manner customary at the port.

A5. Transfer of risks
Subject to the provisions of B.5., bear all risks of loss of or damage to the goods until such time as they have passed the ship's rail at the named port of shipment.

A6. Division of costs
Subject to the provisions of B.6.

—pay all costs relating to the goods until such time as they have passed the ship's rail at the named port of shipment;

—pay the costs of customs formalities necessary for exportation as well as all duties, taxes and other official charges payable upon exportation.

A7. Notice to the buyer
Give the buyer sufficient notice that the goods have been delivered on board.

A8. Proof of delivery, transport document or equivalent electronic message
Provide the buyer at the seller's expense with the usual document in proof of delivery in accordance with A.4.

Unless the document referred to in the preceding paragraph is the transport document, render the buyer, at the latter's request, risk and expense, every assistance in obtaining a transport document for the contract of carriage (for example, a negotiable bill of lading, a non-negotiable sea waybill, an inland waterway document, or a multimodal transport document).

Where the seller and the buyer have agreed to communicate electronically, the document referred to in the preceding paragraph may be replaced by an equivalent electronic data interchange (EDI) message.

A9. Checking—packaging—marking
Pay the costs of those checking operations (such as checking quality, measuring, weighing, counting) which are necessary for the purpose of delivering the goods in accordance with A.4.

Provide, at his own expense, packaging (unless it is usual for the particular trade to ship the goods of the contract description unpacked) which is required for the transport of the goods, to the extent that the circumstances relating to the transport (*e.g.* modalities, destination) are made known to the seller before the contract of sale is concluded. Packaging is to be marked appropriately.

A10. Other obligations
Render the buyer at the latter's request, risk and expense, every assistance in obtaining any documents or equivalent electronic messages (other than those mentioned in A.8.) issued or transmitted in the country of shipment and/or of origin which the buyer may require for the importation of the goods and, where necessary, for their transit through another country. Provide the buyer, upon request, with the necessary information for procuring insurance.

B. The buyer must:

B1. Payment of the price
Pay the price as provided in the contract of sale.

B2. Licences, authorizations and formalities
Obtain, at his own risk and expense, any import licence or other official authorization and carry out all customs formalities for the importation of the goods and, where necessary, for their transit through another country.

B3. Contract of carriage
Contract, at his own expense, for the carriage of the goods from the named port of shipment.

B4. Taking delivery
Take delivery of the goods in accordance with A.4.

B5. Transfer of risks
Bear all risks of loss of or damage to the goods from the time they have passed the ship's rail at the named port of shipment.

Should he fail to give notice in accordance with B.7., or should the vessel named by him fail to arrive on time, or be unable to take the goods, or close for cargo earlier than the stipulated time, bear all risks of loss of or damage to the goods from the agreed date or the expiry date of the period stipulated for delivery provided, however, that the goods have been duly appropriated to the contract, that is to say, clearly set aside or otherwise identified as the contract goods.

B6. Division of costs
Pay all costs relating to the goods from the time they have passed the ship's rail at the named port of shipment.

Pay any additional costs incurred, either because the vessel named by him has failed to arrive on time, or is unable to take the goods, or will close for cargo earlier than the stipulated date, or because the buyer has failed to give appropriate notice in accordance with B.7. provided, however, that the goods have been duly appropriated to the contract, that is to say, clearly set aside or otherwise identified as the contract goods.

Pay all duties, taxes and other official charges as well as the costs of carrying out customs formalities payable upon importation of the goods and, where necessary, for their transit through another country.

B7. Notice to the seller
Give the seller sufficient notice of the vessel name, loading point and required delivery time.

B8. Proof of delivery, transport document or equivalent electronic message
Accept the proof of delivery in accordance with A.8.

B9. Inspection of goods
Pay, unless otherwise agreed, the costs of pre-shipment inspection except when mandated by the authorities of the country of export.

B10. Other obligations
Pay all costs and charges incurred in obtaining the documents or equivalent electronic messages mentioned in A.10. and reimburse those incurred by the seller in rendering his assistance in accordance therewith.

In principle, the buyer must arrange the freight and marine insurance cover.

The parties may use any of the following types of FOB term: the classic FOB term, the FOB term with additional services, and the FOB term (buyer contracting with carrier).[15] Each involves different obligations. This flexibility enables the FOB term to be used in international transactions of different character. The three types of FOB term have been described by the English Court of Appeal:[16]

In the first, or classic type, the buyer nominates the ship and the seller puts the goods on board for account of the buyer, procuring a bill of lading. The seller is then a party to the contract of carriage and if he has taken the bill of lading to his order, the only contract of carriage to which the buyer can become a party is that contained in the bill of lading which is endorsed to him by the seller. The second is a variant of the first, in that the seller arranges for the ship to come on the berth, but the legal incidents are the same. The third is where the seller puts the goods on board,

---

15 See *Pyrene Co. Ltd. v. Scindia Steam Navigation Co.*, [1954] 2 QB 402, at 424, [1954] 2 WLR 1005, [1954] 2 All ER 158.

16 See *The El Amria and El Minia*, [1982] 2 Lloyd's Rep. 28, at 32.

takes a mate's receipt and gives this to the buyer or his agent who then takes a bill of lading. In this latter type, the buyer is a party to the contract of carriage *ab initio*.

Cost, Insurance, and Freight (Named Port of Destination) (CIF)

This is the most frequently used type of term for the export of goods. It enables the seller to discharge his or her obligations with regard to delivery by tendering to the buyer or to a banker nominated in the contract a bill of lading covering the goods against payment of the purchase price. The seller must also procure and pay for marine insurance on minimum coverage against the buyer's risk of loss of or damage to the goods during the carriage.

The CIF export transaction is complicated by the fact that it involves three contracts: the contract of sale, the contract of carriage by sea, and the contract of marine insurance. In general, the on-board bill of lading is the only acceptable document to be presented by the seller to the buyer under the terms CFR and CIF to enable the latter to obtain delivery of the goods from the carrier at destination or to sell the goods in transit by surrendering the paper document to his or her buyer. The several originals in which the bill of lading is issued must all be surrendered before the buyer or a bank acting upon his or her instructions pays the seller. The bill must also indicate that the goods, as far as could be ascertained by the carrier, were received in good order and condition.[17] Although these various functions of the bill of lading are difficult to replace by EDI procedures, the Incoterms 1990 have tried to take these new procedures into proper account. Perhaps the answer is to use non-negotiable documents, such as a freight receipt or a sea waybill, when the buyer is not planning to sell the goods in transit.

According to the Incoterms 1990, the obligations of the seller and of the buyer are as follows:

A. The seller must:

A1. Provision of goods in conformity with the contract
Provide the goods and the commercial invoice, or its equivalent electronic message, in conformity with the contract of sale and any other evidence of conformity which may be required by the contract.

A2. Licences, authorizations and formalities
Obtain, at his own risk and expense, any export licence or other official authorization and carry out all customs formalities necessary for the exportation of the goods.

---

17 This means that the bill is clean. It is unclean if it bears superimposed clauses expressly declaring a defective condition of the goods or packaging. The following clauses do not convert a clean into an unclean bill of lading: (1) clauses that do not expressly state that the goods or packaging are unsatisfactory, "second-hand cases," "used drums," etc.; (2) clauses that emphasize the carrier's non-liability for risks arising through the nature of the goods or the packaging; and (3) clauses that disclaim on the part of the carrier knowledge of contents, weight, measurement, quality, or technical specification of the goods.

A3. Contract of carriage and insurance

a) Contract of carriage

Contract, on usual terms at his own expense, for the carriage of the goods to the named port of destination by the usual route in a seagoing vessel (or inland waterway vessel as appropriate) of the type normally used for the transport of goods of the contract description.

b) Contract of insurance

Obtain, at his own expense, cargo insurance as agreed in the contract, that the buyer, or any other person having an insurable interest in the goods, shall be entitled to claim directly from the insurer and provide the buyer with the insurance policy or other evidence of insurance cover.

The insurance shall be contracted with underwriters or an insurance company of good repute and, failing express agreement to the contrary, be in accordance with minimum cover of the Institute Cargo Clauses (Institute of London Underwriters) or any similar set of clauses. The duration of insurance cover shall be in accordance with B.5. and B.4. When required by the buyer, the seller shall provide, at the buyer's expense, war, strikes, riots and civil commotion risk insurances if procurable. The minimum insurance shall cover the price provided in the contract plus ten per cent (*e.g.* 110%) and shall be provided in the currency of the contract.

A4. Delivery

Deliver the goods on board the vessel at the port of shipment on the date or within the period stipulated.

A5. Transfer of risks

Subject to the provisions of B.5., bear all risks of loss of or damage to the goods until such time as they have passed the ship's rail at the port of shipment.

A6. Division of costs

Subject to the provisions of B.6.

—pay all costs relating to the goods until they have been delivered in accordance with A.4. as well as the freight and all other costs resulting from A.3., including costs of loading the goods on board and any charges for unloading at the port of discharge which may be levied by regular shipping lines when contracting for carriage;

—pay the costs of customs formalities necessary for exportation as well as all duties, taxes and other official charges payable upon exportation.

A7. Notice to the buyer

Give the buyer sufficient notice that the goods have been delivered on board the vessel as well as any other notice required in order to allow the buyer to take measures which are normally necessary to enable him to take the goods.

A8. Proof of delivery, transport document or equivalent electronic message

Unless otherwise agreed, at his own expense provide the buyer without delay with the usual transport document for the agreed port of destination.

This document (for example, a negotiable bill of lading, a non-negotiable sea waybill or an inland waterway document) must cover the contract goods, be dated within the period agreed for shipment, enable the buyer to claim the goods from the carrier at destination and, unless otherwise agreed, enable the buyer to sell the goods in transit by the transfer of the document to a subsequent buyer (the negotiable bill of lading) or by notification to the carrier.

When such a transport document is issued in several originals, a full set of originals must be presented to the buyer. If the transport document contains a reference to a charter party, the seller must also provide a copy of this latter document.

Where the seller and the buyer have agreed to communicate electronically, the document referred to in the preceding paragraphs may be replaced by an equivalent electronic data interchange (EDI) message.

A9. Checking—packaging—marking
Pay the costs of those checking operations (such as checking quality, measuring, weighing, counting) which are necessary for the purpose of delivering the goods in accordance with A.4.

Provide, at his own expense, packaging (unless it is usual for the particular trade to ship the goods of the contract description unpacked) which is required for the transport of the goods arranged by him. Packaging is to be marked appropriately.

A10. Other obligations
Render the buyer, at the latter's request, risk and expense, every assistance in obtaining any documents or equivalent electronic messages (other than those mentioned in A.8.) issued or transmitted in the country of shipment and/or of origin which the buyer may require for the importation of the goods and, where necessary, for their transit through another country.

B. The buyer must:

B1. Payment of the Price
Pay the price as provided in the contract of sale.

B2. Licences, authorizations and formalities
Obtain, at his own risk and expense, any import licence or other official authorization and carry out all customs formalities for the importation of the goods and, where necessary, for their transit through another country.

B3. Contract of carriage
No obligation.

B4. Taking delivery
Accept delivery of the goods when they have been delivered in accordance with A.4. and receive them from the carrier at the named port of destination.

B5. Transfer of risks
Bear all risks of loss of or damage to the goods from the time they have passed the ship's rail at the port of shipment.

Should he fail to give notice in accordance with B.7., bear all risks of loss of or damage to the goods from the agreed date or the expiry date of the period fixed for shipment provided, however, that the goods have been duly appropriated to the contract, that is to say, clearly set aside or otherwise identified as the contract goods.

B6. Division of costs
Subject to the provisions of A.3., pay all costs relating to the goods from the time they have been delivered in accordance with A.4. and, unless such costs and charges have been levied by regular shipping lines when contracting for carriage, pay all costs and charges relating to the goods whilst

in transit until their arrival at the port of destination, as well as unloading costs including lighterage and wharfage charges.

Should he fail to give notice in accordance with B.7., pay the additional costs thereby incurred for the goods from the agreed date or the expiry date of the period fixed for shipment provided, however, that the goods have been duly appropriated to the contract, that is to say, clearly set aside or otherwise identified as the contract goods.

Pay all duties, taxes and other official charges as well as the costs of carrying out customs formalities payable upon importation of the goods and, where necessary, for their transit through another country.

B7. Notice to the seller

Whenever he is entitled to determine the time for shipping the goods and/or the port of destination, give the seller sufficient notice thereof.

B8. Proof of delivery, transport document or equivalent electronic message

Accept the transport document in accordance with A.8. if it is in conformity with the contract.

B9. Inspection of goods

Pay, unless otherwise agreed, the costs of pre-shipment inspection except when mandated by the authorities of the country of exportation.

B10. Other obligations

Pay all costs and charges incurred in obtaining the documents or equivalent electronic messages mentioned in A.10. and reimburse those incurred by the seller in rendering his assistance in accordance therewith.

Provide the seller, upon request, with the necessary information for procuring insurance.

Payment of the price for the goods becomes due when the documents are tendered, unless the parties have agreed otherwise. The property in the goods usually passes when the bill of lading is delivered to the buyer or to the bank if payment is arranged under a letter of credit. After payment for the documents, the buyer may dispose of the goods subject to the condition subsequent that they shall revest to the seller if upon examination they are found not to be in accordance with the terms of the contract.

In a CIF contract, the right to reject the documents if they disclose a defect arises when they are tendered, and the right to reject the goods arises when they are landed and when, after examination, they are not found to be in conformity with the contract.[18] Although by taking up the defective documents and paying for them, the bank or buyer is precluded afterward from complaining, this does not mean that the buyer has lost the right to reject the goods after their arrival. A CIF buyer to whom the bill of lading has not been transferred and, thus, who is not the owner of the goods or has no possessory title to them but bears the risk on their shipment, cannot bring an action in negligence against the carrier if the goods are damaged.[19]

18 *Kwei Tek Chao v. British Traders and Shippers Ltd.*, [1954] 2 QB 459, at 481.

19 See for example, *Leigh and Sullivan Ltd. v. Aliakmon Shipping Co. Ltd.*, [1986] AC 785 (HL). (This case involved a C & F contract, but the rule is equally applicable to a CIF contract.)

If the goods are lost after shipment, the seller is still entitled to tender the shipping documents to the buyer and to claim the purchase price.[20] The buyer's remedy is a claim against the carrier or the insurer.

Cost and Freight (Named Port of Destination) (CFR)

This term is not used frequently. It means that the seller only has to arrange the carriage of the goods to the named port of destination at his or her expense, but not at his or her risk. In all other respects, the obligations of the parties are the same as under a CIF contract.

The term CIP (named place of destination) is a variant of the CIF term, whereas the term CPT (named place of destination) is a variant of the CFR term. The Incoterms define the rights and duties of the parties who use either of these terms.

Delivered at Frontier (Named Place) (DAF)

This term, generally used when goods are carried by rail or road, means that the seller's obligations are fulfilled when the goods have arrived at the place of delivery cleared for export at the frontier of the country named in the contract of sale.

Delivered Ex Ship (Named Port of Destination) (DES)

Here, the seller must pay the freight and the buyer must pay the purchase price when actual delivery of the goods is made at the stipulated port of delivery. The goods are not at the buyer's risks during the voyage.

Delivered Ex Quay (Duty Paid) (Named Port of Destination) (DEQ)

This term means that the seller must make the goods available to the buyer on the quay or wharf at the destination named in the contract of sale cleared for importation. Again, the seller has to bear the full costs and risks involved in bringing the goods there, including duties, taxes, and other charges of delivering the goods thereto.

Delivered Duty Unpaid (Named Place of Destination) (DDU)

The seller, when making the goods available at the named place of destination, has to bear the costs and risks involved in bringing the goods thereto, excluding duties, taxes, and other official charges payable upon importation, as well as the costs and risks of carrying out customs formalities.

Delivered Duty Paid (Named Place of Destination) (DDP)[21]

The goods must be placed at the seller's risk and expense, including import duties and inland carriage, at the buyer's disposal at the named place of destination. Payment is

---

20 *C. Groom Ltd. v. Barber*, [1915] 1 KB 316, at 324.

21 Also *franco domicile*, or free delivery.

made against actual delivery of the goods. This term is the most favourable which the buyer can obtain. It denotes the seller's maximum obligation.

2. *Uniform Commercial Code*

Most commercial transactions in the United States are governed by local state laws, not by federal law. The inconvenience of having different laws in each of the states led to the preparation during the 1950s of the first UCC by the American Law Institute and the National Conference of Commissioners on Uniform State Laws. The code, which has been amended several times, deals with sales, commercial paper, bank notes and collections, letters of credit, bulk transfers, bills of lading, and other documents of title. It is in force in all US states, except Louisiana, which, however, has adopted the section dealing with sales. Thus, notwithstanding local state jurisdiction, a uniform US commercial law has been created.

The code does not provide binding trade term definitions. In each case, the definition applies "unless otherwise agreed." For instance:[22]

Ss. 2319. FOB and FAS Terms

(1) Unless otherwise agreed, the term FOB (which means "free on board") at a named place, even though used only in connection with the stated price, is a delivery term under which

(a) When the term is FOB the place of shipment, the seller must, at that place, ship the goods in the manner provided in this division (Section 2504) and bear the expense and risk of putting them into the possession of the carrier; or

(b) When the term is FOB the place of destination, the seller must, at his own expense and risk transport the goods to that place and there tender delivery of them in the manner provided in this division (Section 2503);

(c) When under either (a) or (b) the term is also FOB vessel, car or other vehicle, the seller must, in addition, at his own expense and risk load the goods on board. If the term is FOB vessel, the buyer must name the vessel and, in an appropriate case, the seller must comply with the provisions of this division on the form of bill of lading (Section 2323).

(2) Unless otherwise agreed, the term FAS vessel (which means "free alongside") at a named port, even though used only in connection with the stated price, is a delivery term under which the seller must

(a) At his own expense and risk, deliver the goods alongside the vessel in the manner usual in that port or on a dock designated and provided by the buyer; and

(b) Obtain and tender a receipt for the goods in exchange for which the carrier is under a duty to issue a bill of lading.

(3) Unless otherwise agreed in any case falling within subdivision (1)(a) or (c) or subdivision (2), the buyer must seasonably give any needed instructions for making delivery, including, when the term is FAS or FOB, the loading berth of the vessel and in an appropriate case its name and sailing date. The seller may treat the failure of needed instructions as a failure of co-operation

---

22 See West's Annotated California Code, Commercial, vol. 23A. S. 2319 reproduces s. 2-319 of the 1962 official text of the UCC.

under this division (Section 2311). He may also, at his option, move the goods in any reasonable manner preparatory to delivery or shipment.

(4) Under the term FOB vessel or FAS, unless otherwise agreed, the buyer must make payment against tender of the required documents and the seller may not tender nor the buyer demand delivery of the goods in substitution for the documents.

Ss. 2320.[23] CIF and C & F Terms.

(1) The term CIF means that the price includes, in a lump sum, the cost of the goods and the insurance and freight to the named destination. The term C & F or CF means that the price also includes cost and freight to the named destination.

(2) Unless otherwise agreed and even though used only in connection with the stated price and destination, the term CIF destination or its equivalent requires the seller, at his own expense and risk, to

(a) Put the goods into the possession of a carrier at the port for shipment and obtain a negotiable bill or bills of lading covering the entire transportation to the named destination; and

(b) Load the goods and obtain a receipt from the carrier (which may be contained in the bill of lading) showing that the freight has been paid or provided for; and

(c) Obtain a policy or certificate of insurance, including any war risk insurance, of a kind and on terms then current at the port of shipment in the usual amount, in the currency of the contract, shown to cover the same goods covered by the bill of lading and providing for payment of loss to the order of the buyer or for the account of whom it may concern; but the seller may add to the price the amount of the premium for any such war risk insurance; and

(d) Prepare an invoice of the goods and procure any other documents required to effect shipment or to comply with the contract; and

(e) Forward and tender with commercial promptness all the documents in due form and with any indorsement necessary to perfect the buyer's rights.

(3) Unless otherwise agreed, the term C & F or its equivalent has the same effect and imposes upon the seller the same obligations and risks as a CIF term except the obligation as to insurance.

(4) Under the term CIF or C & F, unless otherwise agreed, the buyer must make payment against tender of the required documents and the seller may not tender nor the buyer demand delivery of the goods in substitution for the documents.

It is important to note that variations exist in each of the terms between the UCC and the Incoterms 1990.[24]

3. *Standard Contracts*

Individual firms and trade associations have developed standardized printed forms for contracts for the international sale of goods. Such contracts contain a large number of

---

23 S. 2320 reproduces s. 2-320 of the 1962 official text of the UCC.

24 In the United States, the American Foreign Trade Definitions 1941 are still used, but the Incoterms 1990 are gaining ground.

detailed rules defining the obligations of the parties. They remove the uncertainty and insecurity arising from differences in national legal systems and contribute indirectly to the unification of international trade law. They have a wider impact than standardized trade term definitions, which deal primarily with the price-delivery clause of the contract for the international sale of goods.

Most firms modify their contract forms periodically in the light of experience, market conditions, changing levels of competition, and changes in law and in public controls. In some cases, a party that has an overwhelming bargaining position may be able to dictate highly favourable contract terms.

III. THE UNIFICATION OF THE LAW OF INTERNATIONAL SALE OF GOODS

Many efforts have been made to promote greater uniformity in the laws of states relating to the international sale of goods. The most notable have been those of the Hague Conference on Private International Law in 1964 and, more recently, UNCITRAL. Using work already done by the League of Nations and by UNIDROIT, the Hague Conference adopted, in 1964, two conventions relating to a uniform law on the international sale of goods.[25] The first, the Uniform Law on the International Sale of Goods,[26] sets forth the basic obligations of the parties to such contracts: delivery of the goods, their conformity with the contract, payment of the price, excuses for non-performance, remedies for breach, and risk of loss. The second, the Uniform Law on the Formation of Contracts for the International Sale of Goods,[27] prescribes rules on offer and acceptance, revocation of offers, counter-offers, and related questions. Despite their excellence, these conventions did not succeed in attracting the necessary ratifications.[28] Beginning in 1966, the UNCITRAL, with a mandate to promote the harmonization and unification of international trade law, undertook the review and further study of the Hague conventions with a view to drafting a new convention that could command broader support.

A. The 1980 UN Convention on Contracts for the International Sale of Goods

1. Introduction

By the final act of the UN Conference on Contracts for the International Sale of Goods, the UN Convention on Contracts for the International Sale of Goods (CISG), was adopted at Vienna on April 11, 1980.[29] This convention supersedes, for those parties signatory to it, the two 1964 Hague conventions.[30]

---

25 Proceedings of the Hague Conference on the Unification of Private International Law, 1964 (1964), 3 *ILM* 864.

26 834 UNTS 107.

27 834 UNTS 169.

28 E.g., only two of the nine states that ratified the conventions, Gabon and Israel, were non-European.

29 UN Doc. A/Conf. 97/18.

30 Art. 99(3).

The CISG entered into force on May 1, 1988, following the requisite 10th ratification.[31] Canada and all of the provinces and territories have implemented the CISG.[32]

The CISG represents a significant, positive development in the harmonization and unification of international trade rules. It provides a neutral set of concisely codified, uniform norms to govern certain aspects of international sale of goods transactions. By removing some of the artificial legal barriers to the flow of international commerce, such norms promote clarity and certainty, and foster trust in international sales relationships. The CISG protects the reasonable expectations of the parties and calls upon both the parties to an international sales contract to act cooperatively in order to facilitate the performance of the contract.[33] The rules enshrined in the CISG are a blend of common and civil law concepts.

In addition to its contribution of uniform substantive norms, the CISG brings several significant private international law advantages to the law of international sales contracts. First, the CISG's presumptive application focuses the parties' attention on the issue of the governing law in a pre-emptive manner, avoiding the problematic situation where the parties fail to address choice of law issues until difficulties have arisen between them.[34] Second, because it is neutral and distinct from the law of the forum and the laws of the seller and buyer, it eradicates any perceptions of power disequilibria between the parties based on choice of law.[35] Third, resort to the CISG eliminates the need to prove and apply foreign law in domestic courts.

The CISG is intended as the cornerstone initiative for the unification of international sales law, to be supplemented by other flanking international agreements in related fields, including the 1974 Convention on the Limitation Period in the International Sale of Goods, with the 1980 amending protocol,[36] the 1983 UN Convention on Agency

---

31 The CISG became effective one year after the 10th ratification had been deposited: art. 99(1).

32 See art. 93 of the convention concerning the application of the convention to "federal states," such as Canada. Canada acceded to the CISG on 23 April 1991. The implementing legislation received assent on 1 February 1991 and the CISG entered into force on 1 May 1992: International Sale of Goods Contracts Convention Act, SC 1991, c. 13. For provincial and territorial legislation, see: Alta., pt. II and sched. II of the International Conventions Implementation Act, SA 1990, c. I-6.8; International Sale of Goods Act: Ont., RSO 1990, c. I-10; BC, SBC 1990, c. 20; PEI, RSPEI 1988, c. I-6; NS, SNS 1988, c. 13; NWT, RSNWT 1988, c. I-7; NB, SNB 1989, c. I-12.21; Man., SM 1989, c. 18; Nfld., RSN 1990, c. I-16; Que., SQ 1991, c. 68; Sask., SS 1990-91, c. I-10.3; and Yukon, SY 1992, c. 7.

33 See, e.g., art. 54, requiring the buyer to take steps necessary for payment to be made, and art. 32 requiring provision of information by the seller on request by the buyer regarding insurance.

34 See, e.g., Ziegel, "Canada Prepares to adopt the International Sales Convention" (1991), 18 *Can. Bus. L J* 1, 9.

35 See, e.g., Lavers, "CISG: To Use or Not To Use?" (1993), 21 *Int. Bus. Lawyer* 10, at 14.

36 Section III.B, *infra*. Convention on the Limitation Period in the International Sale of Goods, 14 June 1974 (UN doc. A./CONF.63/15) and (1974), 13 *ILM* 953; and Protocol Amending the Convention on the Limitation Period in the International Sale of Goods, 10 April 1980 (UN doc. A./CONF.97/18) and (1980), 19 *ILM* 696.

in the International Sale of Goods,[37] and the 1985 Hague Convention on the Law Applicable to Contracts for the International Sale of Goods.[38]

The CISG adopts most concepts of the two uniform laws of 1964, but it has refined them and made them more precise. The convention is divided into four parts: part I contains general provisions delineating the convention's sphere of application; part IV contains final provisions relating to the convention's entry into force and ratification. The CISG's substantive rules are set out in part II (formation of the contract)[39] and part III (sale of goods).[40]

2. *Interpretation*

In order for a truly uniform set of international rules to prevail and develop, signatories must also undertake to interpret the rules in a uniform manner. The CISG furnishes guidelines concerning its interpretation and application for arbitrators and national courts.[41] In interpreting the convention, "regard is to be had to its international character and the need to promote uniformity in its application and the observance of good faith in international trade."[42] Until a body of adequate international jurisprudence and scholarly writing has emerged, reference may be had to the CISG's extensive legislative and drafting history for aid in construction and interpretation of the CISG.[43] The Vienna Convention on the Law of Treaties also offers interpretive guidelines for the CISG.[44]

---

37 The UN Convention on the Agency in the International Sale of Goods is discussed in section IV.B, *infra*.

38 See section IV.D.2, *infra*, for a brief account of the 1985 Hague Convention on the Law Applicable to Contracts for the International Sale of Goods.

39 Based on the 1964 Uniform Law on the Formation of Contracts for the International Sale of Goods.

40 Based on the 1964 Uniform Law on International Sale of Goods. By virtue of art. 92, a state may elect, through a declaration at the time of signature, ratification, acceptance, accession, or approval, not to implement pt. II or pt. III of the convention. Neither Canada nor any of the provinces or territories have deposited such a reservation.

41 UNCITRAL has undertaken to compile relevant national jurisprudence through a network of national correspondents and to publish cases and case digests relating to the CISG and its interpretation. See, e.g., UN doc. A/CN.9/SER.C/ABSTRACTS/1.

42 Art. 7(1).

43 See, e.g., *Fothergill v. Monarch Airlines*, [1981] AC 251, in which the House of Lords upheld the use of extrinsic aids, including *travaux preparatoires*, for interpretation of international treaties where the text of the treaty is ambiguous. Comprehensive accounts of the convention's drafting history can be found in Honnold, *Uniform Law for International Sales under the 1980 United Nations Convention* (2nd ed., 1991) and Kritzer, *Guide to Practical Applications of the United Nations Convention on Contracts for the International Sale of Goods* (1989).

44 See arts. 31 to 33 of the Vienna Convention on the Law of Treaties, opened for signature 23 May 1969 (1969), 8 *ILM* 697, entered into force 27 January 1980. In accordance with art. 31(1), signatories are obligated to interpret a treaty in good faith in accordance with the ordinary meaning of the terms in context and in light of its object and purpose.

The need to promote uniformity in the application of the CISG requires that any interpretive gaps should be filled where possible within the scheme of the convention itself prior to resort to national laws. Questions concerning matters governed by the convention that are not expressly settled in it are to be settled in conformity with the general principles on which it is based or, in the absence of such principles, in conformity with the law applicable by virtue of the rules of private international law.[45] An explicit designation by the parties of the law applicable for the purposes of interpretation may therefore be useful.

The intent of the parties is to be inferred from relevant circumstances, including negotiations, practices established between the parties, usages, and subsequent conduct.[46]

3. *Sphere of Application*

Absent express contractual language to the contrary, the convention applies automatically to certain international contracts for the sale of goods,[47] that is, to contracts between parties whose places of business are in different contracting states[48] or when the rules of private international law lead to the application of the law of a contracting state.[49] Neither the nationality of the parties nor the civil or commercial character of the parties or of the contract are to be taken into consideration in determining the application of the convention.[50] Where a party has more than one place of business, the place of business is that which has the closest relationship (for example, the most substantial connection) to the contract and its performance.[51] The term "party" in article 10 is presumably broad enough to include a multinational enterprise. However, the "place of business" may be difficult to determine where a contract involves a parent company and a partially held subsidiary or branch in another jurisdiction, or in situations involving agency,[52] joint

45 Art. 7.

46 Art. 8(3).

47 The CISG applies only to contracts formed and concluded after its entry into force in the pertinent signatories (art. 100).

48 Art. 1(1)(a).

49 Art. 1(1)(b). Any state may declare at the time of its accession to the convention that it will not be bound by this subparagraph (art. 95). While British Columbia originally deposited such a reservation (see SBC 1990, c. 20, s. 2), this was withdrawn on 31 July 1993, with the result that no reservation is presently in effect with respect to Canada or any of its provinces or territories. Note also that parties from two non-signatory states could opt to be governed by the convention by using conflicts rules to point to the law of a contracting state. If this is not their intent, parties in non-signatory states should expressly exclude the convention's application.

50 Art. 1(2).

51 Art. 10(a). This "closest relationship" is measured with regard to the circumstances known or contemplated by the parties at or before the contract is concluded.

52 On international efforts to unify the law on agency in international sales contracts, see the 1983 UN Convention on Agency in the International Sale of Goods, intended to supplement the CISG. Canada has not yet acceded to this convention. The convention is discussed in section IV.B, *infra*.

venture, or other similar consortia arrangements.[53] Where complex multinational corporate or commercial arrangements are concerned, it is prudent for the parties to specify explicitly where the performance of the contract will occur and which law or laws are applicable to the transaction.

The CISG preserves the supremacy of the contract and the autonomy of the parties to define their own contractual relations. The parties to a contract to which the convention would otherwise apply are free to exclude its application, in whole or in part, by expressly providing in the contract that the local domestic law of a particular jurisdiction applies to it or that the CISG does not apply to it.[54] Parties who are familiar with a particular system of law relating to international sales may continue to choose that law to govern their contractual relations. This means that a full revision of standard form contracts relating to international sales of goods may not be necessary to conform to the convention.[55] Parties may also exclude particular provisions of the convention by specifying that other inconsistent rules, such as, for example, certain ICC Incoterms, will govern a particular aspect of the contract.[56] As validity of usage is excluded from the convention's scope,[57] national law will govern such validity issues. Regardless of their choice, the parties should strive to define precisely the scope of application of the convention to their agreement, rather than leave this to be implied after a dispute has arisen.

States with the same or closely related sale laws may make joint or reciprocal declarations that the convention is not to apply to contracts concluded between parties having their place of business in those states.[58]

The CISG applies only to sales contracts,[59] and it does not even then purport to provide a comprehensive international sales code.[60] Certain types of sale are excluded

53 See, e.g., Honnold, *supra*, note 43, at 77-78.

54 Art. 6. For example, the Ontario implementing legislation states: "Parties to a contract to which the Convention would otherwise apply may exclude its application by expressly providing in the contract that the local domestic law of Ontario or another jurisdiction applies to it or that the Convention does not apply to it" (RSO 1990, c. I-10, s. 6). Mere reference to the "law of Ontario" as the governing law would refer to the CISG as the applicable law of international sales.

55 See, e.g., Hellner, "The Vienna Convention and Standard Form Contracts" (1986), *International Sale of Goods Dubrovnic Lectures* 335; Farnsworth, "Review of Standard Forms or Terms under the Vienna Convention" (1988), 21 *Cornell Int. LJ* 439; and Crawford, "Drafting Considerations under the 1980 United Nations Convention on Contracts for the International Sale of Goods" (1988), 8 *JLC* 187.

56 Art. 6, and see art. 9 regarding trade usages.

57 See art. 4.

58 Art. 94.

59 The CISG does not affect related areas such as contracts for international carriage of goods, insurance, or modes of payment and security for payment. But see art. 32 (shipping arrangements and obligations concerning acquisition of insurance), art. 33 (time for delivery), and art. 34 (documents relating to the goods).

60 Note that the CISG omits any reference to certain aspects of international sales contracts, such as the rights of the unpaid seller against the goods, which form a substantial portion of much domestic sales legislation. See, i.e., pt. IV (ss. 37 to 46), Ont. Sale of Goods Act, RSO 1990, c. S-1.

outright from its sphere of application.[61] Contracts in which the party ordering goods to be manufactured undertakes to supply a substantial part of the materials for the manufacturing process are excluded from the scope of the convention, as are contracts in which the preponderant part of the obligations of the party furnishing the goods consists in the supply of labour or other services.[62]

Very importantly, the convention governs only certain features of contracts for the international sale of goods:[63] (1) the formation of the contract of sale; and (2) the rights and obligations of the seller and the buyer arising from such a contract. It is not concerned with the validity[64] of the contract or any of its provisions, or of any usage, or the effect that the contract may have on the property in the goods sold.[65] Nor does it regulate product liability.[66] The CISG also does not touch upon the forum for the settlement of disputes arising from the contract.

Since the convention does not govern the validity and certain other elements of the contract of sale, these questions will continue to be governed by state laws to be determined by ordinary private international law rules. Thus, every international sale contract will be subjected to at least two sets of rules.

4. Formation of the contract

Part II of the convention contains provisions concerning the formation of the contract (arts. 14 to 24). This part provides detailed rules governing offer and acceptance, codifying a combination of common and civil law concepts. Contrary to common law rules, the CISG provides that a contract and its modifications need not be in writing[67] and are not subject to further requirements concerning form.[68] A contract may be proved by any means, including witnesses. Although the risk of liability arising from an unintended oral contract is limited by the requirement that an oral offer must be accepted immediately,[69]

61 Art. 2. This includes sales of goods bought for personal use; by auction; on execution; of stocks, shares, investment securities, negotiable instruments, and money; of ships, vessels, hovercraft, or aircraft; and of electricity.

62 Art. 3.

63 The terms "sale" and "goods" remain undefined in the CISG.

64 The precise scope of the term "validity" remains unclear. The breadth of the concept is significant because it will determine whether particular issues fall to be settled under or outside the CISG.

65 Art. 4. However, certain aspects of title and intellectual property in the sale transaction are touched upon. See arts. 41 and 42.

66 Art. 5.

67 By virtue of arts. 12 and 96 of the CISG, states may deposit a reservation barring contracts or modifications to contracts to be made otherwise than in writing. Where one party has its place of business in a state that has deposited a reservation, all offers, acceptances, and modifications must be in writing.

68 Art. 11. This contrasts with the stipulation in s. 5 of the Ont. Sale of Goods Act that a contract for the sale of goods worth more than $40 is invalid unless evidenced in writing and signed by the party to be bound.

69 Art. 18(2).

in the interest of clarity and precision, it is still advisable that all components of a contract, including modifications, be in writing. The contract may contain an express stipulation to this effect.[70]

a. Offer

A proposal for the conclusion of a contract must be made to one or more specific persons and must be sufficiently definite to indicate an intention to be bound in case of acceptance. An offer is "sufficiently definite" if it indicates the goods and provides for the determination of the quantity and price, expressly or by implication.[71]

An offer is irrevocable if it so indicates by stating a fixed time for its acceptance or otherwise, or where it is reasonable for the offeree to rely on it as irrevocable and the offeree has acted in reliance upon it.[72] An offer, including an irrevocable offer, can be withdrawn only if the withdrawal reaches the offeree prior to or simultaneously with the offer.[73]

An offer becomes effective when it reaches[74] the other party,[75] rather than when it is sent. This stipulation promotes certainty by ensuring a common understanding of when a contract is concluded. It contrasts with the less precise common law "post box" rule.

A rejection terminates an offer, including an irrevocable offer.[76] This rule allows the offeror certainty and freedom to contract with another party promptly after the rejection without having to be concerned about any lingering obligation to the former offeree. The rejection may be either implicit or explicit and is effective when it reaches the offeror.

b. Acceptance

In contrast to the common law, there is no explicit requirement of legal consideration in the CISG. A contract is concluded when acceptance of an offer becomes effective.[77] Acceptance must be through a statement or conduct indicating assent; in accordance with the requirements of fair dealing, silence or inactivity does not in itself connote acceptance.[78] Nevertheless, the performance of a particular act without notice by the

70 See art. 29 concerning potential for inclusion of requirement for modifications and terminations to be in writing.

71 Art. 14(1). See also art. 55 concerning validly concluded contracts that make no reference to price. It provides that absent contrary provisions, the parties are deemed to have referred to the price ordinarily charged for similar goods in similar circumstances at the time that the contract was concluded.

72 Art. 16(2).

73 Art. 15(2). The same rule applies to the permissible timing for withdrawal of an acceptance (art. 22).

74 See art. 24 for the meaning of "reaches."

75 Art. 15(1). The same rule applies to the acceptance: art. 18(2).

76 Art. 17.

77 Art. 23.

78 Art. 18(1); see, e.g., Honnold, *supra*, note 43, at 219.

offeree may amount to acceptance where the offer, trade usage, or practices developed by the parties permits.[79]

An acceptance becomes effective when it reaches the offeror.[80] This must be within the time fixed, or within a reasonable period. The reasonableness of the time for acceptance is dependent upon the mode of communication. An oral offer must be accepted immediately, unless the circumstances indicate otherwise.[81]

While an offer lapses if acceptance is late, the offeror can preserve the effectiveness of a late acceptance by promptly giving notice to that effect.[82] Under the CISG, the late acceptance thus does not become a counter-offer. An acceptance that is late because of transmission delays remains effective unless it is defeated by a prompt statement or action by the offeror.

c. Battle of the Forms

The ordinary common law rule for the formation of a contract requires that the acceptance mirror the offer. The CISG alters this rule slightly: for a contract to exist under the CISG, the acceptance must essentially, though not completely, mirror the terms of the offer. This alteration adds an interesting wrinkle to the so-called problem of the "battle of the forms," or the determination of which party's general conditions apply to the contract.[83] Under the CISG, a reply to an offer that materially alters the offer constitutes a counter-offer rather than an acceptance.[84] However, a reply to an offer containing additional or different terms that do not materially alter the terms of the offer is an acceptance, unless the offeror promptly objects orally or in writing to the additional terms.

Additional or different terms relating, *inter alia*, to price, payment, quality and quantity of goods, place and time of delivery, extent of one party's liability to the other, or the settlement of disputes are deemed to alter materially the terms of the offer.[85]

The CISG's more flexible approach to the exchange of contractual terms allowing small modifications means that the often standard-form fine print in an extensive and continuing exchange of documents involved in an international sales transaction must

79 Art. 18(3).

80 Art. 18(2). As mentioned, art. 24 defines the term "reaches."

81 Art. 20 gives further guidance on the interpretation of the offeror's statements concerning the delineation of the time period for acceptance: a period of time for an acceptance fixed by letter begins to run from the date shown on the letter; where it is fixed by phone or other instantaneous means, it runs from the time it reaches the offeree.

82 Art. 21(1).

83 See, e.g., Hellner, *supra*, note 55; Vergne, "The Battle of the Forms under the 1980 United Nations Convention on Contracts for the International Sale of Goods" (1985), 33 *Am.J Comp. L* 233; and Moccia, "The United Nations Convention on Contracts for the International Sale of Goods and the Battle of the Forms" (1989-90), 13 *Fordham Int. LJ* 649.

84 Art. 19(1).

85 Art. 19(3).

therefore be carefully reviewed. If they encounter difficulties later, the parties may not wish to dispute that a contract was in fact concluded between them by arguing that there had been no *consensus ad idem* due to the exchange of disparate terms. However, if the parties wish to uphold their contract, it may be difficult to discern precisely which general conditions apply to the transaction.

Conduct indicating agreement as to added terms is deemed to be assent under the CISG,[86] and such terms will survive to govern the transaction. The chronological sequence of exchanged terms is thus significant. The CISG[87] appears to favour the party who fires the "last shot" to which the other party assents in the battle of the forms.[88] This is ordinarily the seller's confirmation of the buyer's purchase order. However, in a situation where the parties are engaged in performance contemporaneously with an ongoing exchange of terms, this "last shot" approach may be unhelpful or insufficient.[89] The only way for one party to be absolutely certain that its standard terms will prevail is to secure a signed confirmation or acceptance of the general printed conditions from the other party,[90] or, in the last resort, to make the entire transaction conditional upon the other party's acquiescence to all of the first party's standard terms.

As with other issues of interpretation under the convention, a "battle of the forms" question should be settled with a view to the CISG's international character and intent to promote uniformity,[91] with reference to the general principles underlying the CISG and with regard to the parties' prior relationship and trade usages. It may be only through consideration of the parties' intent and subsequent conduct that the true terms governing the contract can be discerned. Alternatively, the issue may be settled by domestic law where the CISG is deemed to be silent or where the question is one of contractual validity.[92]

5. *Sale of Goods*

If a contract has been formed in accordance with CISG, part II or other governing law as selected by the parties, the provisions of CISG, part III (articles 25 to 88) govern the obligations of the seller and buyer in the transaction. Part III consists of five sub-parts: (1) general provisions (articles 25 to 29), (2) obligations of the seller (articles 30 to 52), (3) obligations of the buyer (articles 53 to 65), (4) passing of risk (articles 66 to 70), and (5) common provisions for the buyer and seller (articles 71 to 88).

---

86 Art. 18(3).

87 Art. 19(1).

88 See, e.g., Bianca and Bonnell, *Commentary on the International Sales Law: The 1980 Vienna Sales Convention* (1987), at 179; Honnold, *supra*, note 43, at 225-39; and Kritzer, *supra*, note 43, at 182-84; see also Lord Denning's judgment in *Butler Machine Tool Co. v. Ex-cell-o Corp.*, [1979] 1 All ER 956 (CA) for a discussion of "battle of the forms" at common law.

89 See, e.g., Hellner, *supra*, note 55, at 341-42.

90 See, e.g., Schmitthoff, *Schmitthoff's Export Trade: The Law and Practice of International Trade* (9th ed., 1990), at 99-100.

91 Art. 7(1).

92 Art. 4.

a. Basic Obligations

The CISG details obligations of the seller (articles 30 to 52) and the buyer (articles 53 to 65), and their common obligations (articles 71 to 88), in an international sales contract, which the parties are free to exclude, expand upon, or modify. Consistent with the common law approach to sales law, under the CISG, the duties of the seller are more extensive and onerous than those of the buyer. It is the basic duty of the seller to deliver the goods, hand over relevant documentation, and transfer the property in the goods.[93] The buyer's basic obligations are simply to make payment and take delivery of the goods in accordance with the CISG and the contract.[94]

b. Obligations of the Seller

The principal obligation of the seller is to deliver goods that are of the quality, quantity, and description required by the contract, and contained or packaged in accordance with the contract.[95] Note that in this connection, the CISG emphasis is on the importance of the contract and its terms. The CISG does not make reference to the term "warranty," but combines the concepts of express and implied warranties and conditions as to fitness and quality found in most domestic sales legislation.[96] Unless otherwise provided for in the contract, and unless the buyer knew or could not have been unaware of the non-conformity at the time of conclusion of the contract,[97] the CISG enumerates specific requirements for conformity of the goods with the contract: they must be fit for the purposes for which they would ordinarily be used;[98] they must be fit for the particular purpose expressly or impliedly made known to the seller at the time the contract was concluded, except if the buyer did not rely, or relied unreasonably upon, the seller's skill and judgment;[99] they must have the qualities that the seller held out to the buyer as a sample or model;[100] and they must be packaged in the manner usual for such goods or, where a usual manner is not established, in a manner adequate to preserve and protect the goods.[101] The seller's liability for these guarantees may endure beyond the time of passage of risk in the goods.[102]

---

93 Art. 30.

94 Art. 53.

95 Art. 35(1).

96 Most domestic sales legislation contains provisions concerning express warranties and implied warranties of merchantability and fitness for a particular purpose: see, i.e., Ont. Sale of Goods Act, s. 15(1) and (2).

97 Art. 35(3).

98 Art. 35(2)(a).

99 Art. 35(2)(b).

100 Art. 35(2)(c).

101 Art. 35(2)(d).

102 Art. 36.

The seller also makes certain guarantees with respect to third-party claims to title and industrial or intellectual property.[103] The buyer is barred from relying on these qualities where he or she knew or could not have been unaware of the non-conformity of the goods at the time the contract was concluded.[104]

c. Buyer's Examination of the Goods

The buyer is under an obligation to inspect the goods within as short a time as is practicable[105] and to notify the seller of any non-conformity within a reasonable time after he or she has discovered or should have discovered it.[106] If notice is not given within two years of delivery of the goods,[107] the buyer loses the right to rely on non-conformity of the goods and may lose the right to recover compensatory damages in respect of the non-conformity. The parties are free to exclude or modify this provision through, for example, by the insertion of a contractual guarantee period to override the forfeiture of this right.

d. Obligations of the Buyer

i. PAYMENT The CISG mandates that the buyer take the requisite steps and comply with the requisite formalities under the contract and any laws or regulations to enable payment to be made.[108] While this article envisages the necessity for the buyer to make certain arrangements for the issuance of a letter of credit or for governmental authorization for the transmission of the funds to the seller, it is unclear whether this provision obliges the buyer to undertake definitively the securing of a letter of credit.[109] Where the intent of the parties is to impose upon the buyer an obligation to obtain a letter of credit, the parties should therefore include an express provision to this effect in the contract.

The CISG also contains provisions concerning the place[110] and time[111] for payment of the contract price, absent contrary contractual provisions or practices of the parties.[112] The buyer must pay the purchase price on the date fixed by the contract and the convention without further request or reminder from the seller.[113]

---

103 See arts. 41 and 42: compare Ont. Sale of Goods Act, s. 13(b) and (c). For a recent discussion of industrial or intellectual property claims under s. 42 of the CISG, see A.M. Shinn, "Liabilities under Article 42 of the UN Convention on the International Sale of Goods" (1993), 2 *Minn. J Global Trade* 115.

104 Art. 35(3); see also arts. 43 and 44.

105 Art. 38(1).

106 Art. 39(1).

107 Art. 39(2).

108 Art. 54.

109 For conflicting views on this point, see Kritzer, *supra*, note 43, at 389 and Honnold, *supra*, note 43, at 407.

110 Art. 57.

111 Arts. 58 and 59.

112 See arts. 6 and 9(1) regarding trade usages and practices.

113 Art. 59.

ii. TAKING DELIVERY In addition to making payment, the buyer's second major obligation under an international sales contract is to take delivery of the goods. This obligation presupposes that the buyer will conduct himself or herself cooperatively and do everything that could reasonably be expected of him or her in order to enable the seller to make the delivery.[114] This might include aiding with the arrangements for carriage of the goods, securing necessary licences or documents, or ensuring that the necessary infrastructure will be ready to take delivery of the goods where these elements fall within the responsibility of the buyer under the terms of the contract or under applicable trade usages, such as the ICC Incoterms. The obligation to take delivery presumes that the buyer will physically remove the goods from the carrier's possession, thereby terminating any possible liability on the part of the carrier for the cargo.

e. Passage of Risk

Of particular interest is the CISG rule that in a contract of sale involving the carriage of goods, unless otherwise provided by the parties, delivery includes the handing over of the goods to the first carrier for transmission to the buyer.[115] The risk passes to the buyer at that time, unless the goods are to be delivered at a particular place.[116] If the goods are sold in transit, the risk passes to the buyer from the time of the conclusion of the contract.[117] These rules contrast with common law rules[118] focusing on passage of title and should be compared with the Incoterms 1990 for FOB or CIF sales.[119]

f. Consequences of Breach and Remedies Available

The consequences and remedies available under the CISG upon breach are not dependent upon the nature of the provision breached but, rather, upon the gravity of the breach and the consequent harm caused to the aggrieved party. Thus, unlike the common law, the CISG makes no *prima facie* distinction between a breach of condition and a breach of warranty. A breach is either fundamental or non-fundamental. The CISG also addresses the issues of anticipatory breach and breach in the context of installment contracts.

i. FUNDAMENTAL BREACH Under the CISG, a fundamental breach is a breach that substantially deprives the innocent party of what he or she is entitled to expect under the contract. The breaching party bears the onus of establishing that he, she, or a reasonable person in the same circumstances could not have foreseen such a result.[120] It is unclear

---

114 Art. 60.

115 Art. 31(a).

116 Art. 67(1).

117 Art. 68.

118 As codified, e.g., in the Ont. Sale of Goods Act, s. 21.

119 Note that the Incoterms prevail over the Convention rules only when specific reference is made to them by the parties (art. 6) or if such terms are adopted by the parties as usages or customs under art. 9.

120 Art. 25. See also art. 49 (avoidance by the buyer); art. 64 (avoidance by the seller); art. 46(2) (requirement to deliver substitute goods); art. 51(2) (avoidance of whole contract based on fundamentally defective performance of part of contract); art. 72 (anticipatory breach); and art. 73 (installment contracts).

whether such foresight is to be measured at the time of the conclusion of the contract or at some other point.[121]

A fundamental breach of a contractual term allows the innocent party, on written or oral notice,[122] to terminate (avoid) the contract, thereby releasing both parties from the performance of their obligations.[123] Such avoidance is subject to the right of the aggrieved party to sue for any damages due and does not affect any provision of the contract for dispute settlement or any other contractual term governing the parties' rights and obligations upon termination. The non-breaching party may choose not to avoid the contract, and to seek another remedy.

With certain limitations, a seller's fundamental breach entitles the buyer to choose to terminate (avoid) the contract on notice, demand delivery of substitute goods, demand specific performance, or to reject the goods. A seller may also terminate (avoid) the contract upon fundamental breach by the buyer on notice, and require return of the goods, if already delivered. Restitution is available for any partial or whole performance of the contract.

ii. NON-FUNDAMENTAL BREACH By negative definition, a non-fundamental breach under the CISG is any breach that does not substantially deprive the aggrieved party of his or her legitimate contractual expectation. Where a breach is non-fundamental, the CISG generally entitles the aggrieved party to specific performance[124] and damages.[125]

The remedy of contractual avoidance is only available under the CISG in circumstances of fundamental breach, or where the breaching party fails to perform his or her obligations within an additional time period fixed by the innocent party. Where performance fails to take place within an additional time period as specified by the innocent party, avoidance of the contract by the innocent party is justified, whether or not the breach is actually fundamental.

iii. ANTICIPATORY BREACH A party may suspend performance of his or her obligations if, after the conclusion of the contract, it becomes apparent that the other party will not perform a substantial part of his or her obligations as a result of (1) a serious deficiency in his or her ability to perform, or his or her creditworthiness, or (2) his or her conduct in performing or preparing to perform the contract.[126]

iv. BREACH AND INSTALLMENT CONTRACTS The rights of an aggrieved party arising from the breach of an installment contract turn upon the gravity of the breach: if the

---

121 See Honnold, *supra*, note 43, at 257.

122 Art. 26. Clarity would seem to demand a written notice or confirmation of avoidance. Art. 27 covers the situation of delay or error in communicating notice of avoidance.

123 See arts. 81 to 84 on avoidance. This is distinct from a party's right to suspend performance of its obligations in circumstances of anticipatory breach under art. 71(1).

124 See arts. 28, 46, and 62.

125 Art. 74.

126 Art. 71(1).

failure of a party to perform any of his or her obligations with respect to any installment constitutes a fundamental breach,[127] the innocent party can declare the contract avoided with respect to that particular installment.[128] Further, where the innocent party believes that a fundamental breach will occur with respect to future installments, that party may, within a reasonable time, declare the contract avoided for the future.[129]

v. BUYER'S REMEDIES IN CASE OF BREACH BY SELLER If only part of the goods are delivered, or if only part of the goods delivered conform to the contract, the buyer faces a range of choices of action with respect to the goods, such as specific performance, allowing an additional period for performance, or proportionate reduction in purchase price[130] (or, where the breach is fundamental, avoidance of the entire contract on notice). Where the seller delivers the goods early, the buyer can accept or refuse to take delivery.[131] Where the seller delivers an excess quantity of goods, the buyer may refuse delivery of the excess or may accept and pay the contract rate for the excess.[132]

Where a seller is late in performing, the buyer may elect to permit the seller a further reasonable time period to perform[133] or, if the lateness constitutes a fundamental breach, to avoid the contract on notice.[134]

The seller may cure a breach prior to[135] or after[136] the date set for delivery by replacing or repairing non-conforming goods. The effect of such curing is to forestall any "substantial" harm to the buyer, thereby rendering a potentially grave breach non-fundamental.

vi. SELLER'S REMEDIES IN CASE OF BREACH BY BUYER Where the buyer is late in performing his or her obligations, the seller may compel specific performance[137] or fix an additional period of time for the buyer's performance.[138] If the buyer fails to perform within this additional specified period, the seller may declare the contract avoided.[139] In addition, if any deviation of the buyer from any of his or her obligations constitutes a fundamental breach, the seller may avoid the contract.[140]

---

127 See art. 25.

128 Art. 73(1).

129 Art. 73(2).

130 Art. 50. This price reduction remedy is a civil law concept: common law lawyers may wish to exclude its application.

131 Art. 52.

132 Art. 52(2).

133 Art. 47.

134 Art. 49.

135 Art. 37.

136 Art. 48. The seller must remedy the breach at his own expense, without unreasonable delay and without causing the buyer unreasonable inconvenience or uncertainty. The buyer is still entitled to claim damages.

137 Art. 62.

138 Art. 63(1).

139 Art. 64(1)(b). The breach in these circumstances need not be fundamental.

140 Art. 64(1)(a).

vii. SPECIFIC PERFORMANCE Specific performance, the right of one party to require the other to fulfill its contractual obligations in certain circumstances, is a remedy central to the CISG.[141] The buyer enjoys a qualified right to demand specific performance where he or she has not pursued an inconsistent remedy[142] (1) where the seller delivers defective goods, the buyer may require the delivery of substitute goods,[143] and (2) where it is not unreasonable in the circumstances, the buyer may demand that the seller repair the goods.[144] On the other hand, where the buyer fails to fulfill his or her contractual obligations, the seller enjoys an unqualified right to require that the buyer pay the purchase price, take delivery, or perform his or her other obligations.[145]

Specific performance may be onerous, inefficient, and costly to the performing party. Whereas specific performance is a remedy engrained in civil law systems, at common law, damages were traditionally considered the more appropriate remedy, unless the goods in question were unique or not readily attainable elsewhere. The CISG's provisions on specific performance represent a compromise between civil and common law positions. The right to demand specific performance may be modified by provisions requiring the party in the better position to dispose of unwanted or perishing goods[146] and by the requirement that the non-breaching party mitigate its damages.[147] In addition, the CISG provides the possibility to limit the availability of specific performance by deferring to domestic law: a court may refrain from granting specific performance in circumstances where the domestic law of the forum would not require it.[148] In exercising its discretion under this provision, a court should nevertheless keep in mind the contract's international character and the harmonizing or unifying intent of the CISG.[149]

viii. DAMAGES The breaching party is responsible for objectively foreseeable consequential damages,[150] including lost profits. This is in addition to the right to recover the difference between the contract price and the current price of the goods at the time of avoidance.[151] The CISG may thus lead to greater recovery in damages than would be available at common law or under certain provincial sales statutes.[152]

---

141 See Arts. 28, 46, and 62.

142 I.e., he or she has not elected to avoid the contract under art. 81(1). This would release both parties from their respective contractual obligations.

143 Only where the defect amounts to a fundamental breach: art. 46(2).

144 Art. 46(3). This right is not recognized at common law.

145 Art. 62.

146 Arts. 85 to 88.

147 Art. 77. See Honnold, *supra*, note 43, at 270.

148 Art. 28.

149 See Honnold, *ibid.*, at 366 and Kastely, "Right to Require Performance" (1988), 63 *Wash. L Rev.* 607, at 635-36.

150 Art. 74.

151 Art. 76.

152 See, i.e., Ont. Sale of Goods Act, ss. 48(3), 49(2), (3), and 52.

The CISG codifies the aggrieved party's duty to mitigate consequential damages in a reasonable manner.[153] The seller is permitted to resell the goods when the buyer wrongfully refuses to accept or pay for the goods; the buyer may compensate for the seller's non-delivery by buying comparable goods elsewhere to aid in establishing the amount of damage suffered.[154]

A party's right to recover interest on sums in arrears is without prejudice to the right to claim damages.[155] The CISG offers no guidance concerning the determination of a rate of interest.

g. Frustration and Force Majeure

Frustration refers to the impossibility of performance of a contract, due to a change of circumstances that makes performance physically or legally impossible or excessively onerous, or that fundamentally alters the nature of the transaction so that it no longer reflects the underlying commercial basis or the intention of the parties at the time they concluded their original contract. For frustration of a contract to occur, the supervening event must ordinarily be extreme, not within the control of the parties, and not reasonably foreseeable.

The CISG contains a *force majeure* provision clarifying when a contract may be deemed to be frustrated. The convention excuses the non-performance by a party of its obligations under a contract when the non-performance is due to an unforeseen or unexpected impediment beyond its control.[156] This may include the failure of a third party to perform.[157] While the aggrieved party retains the right to avoid the contract where other CISG provisions permit, there is no right to recover damages due to the excused non-performance,[158] unless the non-performing party fails to give notice of the frustration within a reasonable time.[159]

The CISG frustration provisions are unified and comprehensive. They are considerably less complex than frustration provisions contained in certain domestic sales legislation.[160] Not limited to a specific catalogue of events, they would presumably operate to defeat an international sales contract in many circumstances, including an act of God, the outbreak of war, insurrection, or hostilities, changes in the administrative or legal requirements for importing or exporting goods, civil disturbances, lock-outs, or strikes, and an unreasonable increase in the cost of labour or other inputs.

---

153 Art. 77.

154 Art. 75.

155 Art. 78.

156 Art. 79(1).

157 Art. 79(2).

158 Art. 79(5).

159 Art. 79(4).

160 See, i.e., Ont. Sale of Goods Act, ss. 12(4) (impossibility of fulfillment of condition or warranty), and 7 and 8 (destruction of ascertained goods).

The CISG contains relatively detailed provisions concerning the rights and duties of the parties as to the preservation of the goods[161] that may operate to pre-empt or limit potential frustration of the contract on these grounds.

B. The 1980 UN Convention on the Limitation Period in the International Sale of Goods

This convention, which was signed in 1974, must be read in conjunction with the protocol amending it, which was adopted by the UN Conference at Vienna on April 11, 1980, the same day that the Convention on Contracts for the International Sale of Goods (CISG) was approved.[162] The 1980 Protocol aligns the provisions of the 1974 convention with those of the 1980 CISG. It replaces conflicting national laws by a four-year time limit within which the buyer or the seller may press claims based on a contract for the international sale of goods.[163] It provides uniform rules establishing when a claim accrues and when the limitation period commences or ceases. The buyer and the seller must have their places of business in different states for the convention to apply. Certain sales, types of goods, and claims are excluded from the reach of the convention that specifies when the limitation period begins or ceases. Extensions of the limitation period may be granted in certain circumstances,[164] but cannot exceed 10 years from the date when that period began.[165]

The 1974 Convention and its protocol entered into force on August 1, 1988. The United States implemented them as of December 1, 1994. Canada has not yet adopted the convention.

C. The 1994 UNIDROIT Principles of International Commercial Contracts

In 1994, UNIDROIT published its international statement of general and uniform principles of international commercial contracts.[166] Not restricted to trade in goods, the principles may also be applicable to international commercial transactions in other areas such as services and investment. The principles are not a unification of international sales law per se, but, rather, an enunciation of common or uniform substantive norms to regulate international contracts. In addition to general provisions, such as those concerning freedom of contract and duties of good faith and fair dealing, the principles cover contractual formation, validity, interpretation, content, performance (including hardship), and non-performance (including termination, damages, and exemption clauses).

---

161 Arts. 85 to 88.

162 (1974), 13 *ILM* 952 and (1980), 19 *ILM* 696.

163 Art. 8.

164 Arts. 19 to 22.

165 Art. 23.

166 For the text of the principles and commentary, see UNIDROIT, *Principles of International Commercial Contracts* (1994). For an analysis and overview, see, e.g., Bonell, "Unification of Law by non-legislative means: the UNIDROIT Draft Principles of International Commercial Contracts" (1992), 40 *Am. J Comp. L* 617.

The parties may choose the principles as the "law" applicable to their transaction.[167] However, parties wishing expressly to choose the principles as the rules governing their contract would be wise to couple such a reference with an international arbitration agreement. Otherwise, mere reference to the principles may have the effect of simply incorporating them into the contract, leaving the governing law to be determined through private international law rules.

In addition to their potential to serve as guidelines for drafting international commercial contracts, the principles may also play a role in the interpretation or supplementing of existing international instruments, such as the CISG.[168]

IV. THE UNIFICATION OF THE LAW OF AGENCY IN THE INTERNATIONAL SALE OF GOODS

In international sales transactions involving agency, the seller handles certain elements of the transaction with the buyer through the intermediary of the sales agent. A sales agent is a person or entity that enjoys the actual (or ostensible) authority to represent the seller, or principal, in relation to third parties in a foreign market. The scope of the sales agent's authority may range from the capacity merely to introduce third persons to the principal, to promote and negotiate contracts on the principal's behalf, to the capacity definitively to conclude such contracts. The agent may act in its own name or in the name of the principal. An agent is ordinarily self-employed and remunerated on commission based on sales he or she initiates or concludes. Not an employee of the principal, the agent does not usually receive a regular salary or enjoy the protection and benefits extended to employees working abroad. For this reason, any protection or special arrangements for the benefit of the agent, as indeed for the principal, must generally be inserted explicitly into the agency contract.

An agency contract embraces two main relationships: (1) the "internal relationship" between the principal and the agent, including their mutual rights and duties, and remuneration, etc., and (2) the "external relationship" between the principal-agent and the third party, resembling in many respects an ordinary bipartite contract for the international sale of goods.

National laws fail to take into account the special concerns of international agency transactions, and these laws vary considerably among jurisdictions. Conflicts of law issues and substantive legal difficulties inevitably arise in both the internal and external aspects of the agency relationship in the international sale of goods, when the parties involved have their places of business in different jurisdictions. Such difficulties may threaten the security of both the internal and external aspects of the commercial agency relationship.

---

167 Note that the principles may also become the applicable law of the contract by operation of private international law rules, and in accordance with international choice of law conventions, such as the 1994 OAS Inter-American Convention on the Law Applicable to International Contracts (art. 9(2)). See discussion of this convention, *infra*, section V.D.3.

168 See, e.g., art. 1(4) of the principles, which states: "the Principles may be used to interpret or supplement instruments of international uniform law."

For example, one problematic area within the internal agency relationship that reflects wide divergences among jurisdictions is the sales agent's entitlement to an indemnity upon the expiration or termination of the contract not due to the agent's default. While certain countries recognize the agent's right to compensation for goodwill created by the agent but enjoyed by the principal after the contract ends,[169] other jurisdictions classify this as compensation for the loss to the agent in terms of forgone commission.[170]

There have been two significant international legislative attempts to unify or harmonize aspects of the substantive law of agency in international sales contracts:[171] (1) the 1986 EC Directive on Self-Employed Commercial Agents[172] dealing with the "internal" agency relationship, and (2) the 1983 UN Convention of Agency in the International Sale of Goods, focusing mainly on the "external" facets of the agency relationship. In addition, the ICC has released a model agency contract offering a contractual standard for the "internal" agency relationship. The 1978 Hague Convention on the Law Applicable to Agency deals with international conflict of laws issues concerning agency.

A. 1986 EC Directive on Self-Employed Commercial Agents

The EC Directive applies to self-employed agents with the authority to negotiate and conclude contracts for the sale or purchase of goods on the principal's behalf. It regulates certain internal aspects of the agency relationship between principal and agent, requiring each to act dutifully and in good faith.[173] While the directive harmonizes the national laws of the EU member states to some extent, it covers only certain elements of the agency contract: rights and obligations of the agent and principal; remuneration, including commission; and conclusion and termination of the agency contract. Other aspects are left to be governed by the different national laws. In addition, the directive allows for alternative choices by the member states in implementing some of its provisions. For example, with respect to the goodwill indemnity, member states may choose between article 17.1 (goodwill indemnity) or 17.2 (compensation for damage suffered as a result of the termination of the agency relationship) in their national implementing legislation. Alternative choices are also available with respect to the agent's eligibility for commission on repeat orders.[174] The directive also permits the maintenance of national derogations that favour the agent.

---

169 I.e., German, Austrian, Swiss, Italian, and Dutch law recognize such a right. See Schmitthoff, *supra*, note 90, at 310-11.

170 This is the case, e.g., in French law. Still other domestic laws do not recognize such a concept at all. See, e.g., *ibid.*, at 310-11.

171 There exist, in addition, international efforts to unify the conflicts of law rules relating to international agency contracts: see, e.g., the Hague Convention on the Law Applicable to Agency (1978). See discussion, *infra*.

172 Resolution 86/653 of 18 December 1986 on the coordination of the laws of the member states relating to self-employed commercial agents.

173 Arts. 3(1) and 4(1).

174 Art. 7 of the directive states that member states must include in their legislation a provision to the effect that the commercial agent shall be entitled to commission on transactions concluded during the period

(The footnote is continued on the next page.)

B. The 1983 UN Convention on Agency in the International Sale of Goods

The UN Convention on Agency in the International Sale of Goods (CAISG) was adopted in Geneva on February 17, 1983.[175] It will come into force when ratified or acceded to by 10 states.[176] Based on a 1974 draft UNIDROIT Convention, it is intended to complement the CISG by establishing uniform rules relating to certain aspects of the relatively common but complex practice of agency in the international purchase and sale of goods.[177] Like the CISG, the CAISG preserves the sanctity of contract and the autonomy of the parties: its acceptability was largely predicated on the fact that is open to the principal or the agent on the principal's behalf to agree with the third party to exclude or derogate from the convention.[178]

The CAISG applies to certain agency relationships[179] where an agent has authority[180] or ostensible authority[181] on behalf of the principal to conclude[182] a contract for the sale of goods[183] with a third party,[184] and the principal and third party have their places of business in different states.[185] The agent must have his or her place of business in a contracting state,[186] or private international law rules must point to the application

---

174 Continued ...
covered by the agency contract *either* where he is entrusted with a specific geographical area or group of customers *or* where he has an exclusive right to a specific geographical area or group of customers, and where the transaction has been entered into with a customer belonging to that area or group.

175 For proceedings of the conference adopting the convention, see UNIDROIT, *Uniform Law Review* (1983, I-II).

176 Art. 33.

177 See, generally, Bonnell, "The 1983 Geneva Convention on Agency in the International Sale of Goods" (1984), 32 *Am. J Comp. L* 717.

178 Art. 5, subject to art. 11. Art. 7 provides that the principal-agent and the third party may be bound by any agreed usage or practice.

179 Art. 3 lists exclusions from the convention's sphere of application.

180 Authority may be express or implied (art. 9(1)).

181 Art. 14(2) on ostensible authority provides that the principal may not invoke against a third party the agent's lack of authority where the conduct of the principal causes the third party reasonably and in good faith to believe that the agent enjoys authority to act on the principal's behalf and the agent is acting within the scope of that authority.

182 I.e., as opposed to authority merely to negotiate or promote contracts, or to introduce interested third parties to the principal.

183 Dealing only with agency in contracts for the purchase and sale of goods, the convention leaves untouched agency contracts for leasing, transportation, insurance, services, banking, etc.

184 Art. 1(1).

185 Art. 2(1). The agent's place of business is therefore not a relevant consideration in this clause. This correlates with the CISG so that, in theory, in an international sale transaction, the CISG would govern the contract itself while the CAISG would govern the effect of the acts of the agent in connection with the conclusion of the sale contract. See Bonnell, *supra.* note 177, at 727.

186 Art. 2(1)(a).

of the laws of a contracting state.[187] In these circumstances, the CAISG governs not only the conclusion of the contract by the agent, but also any act undertaken by him or her for the purpose of concluding the contract or in relation to its performance.[188] The CAISG applies, regardless of whether the agent acts in his or her own name or in the name of the principal.[189]

The convention's scope is essentially limited to the "external relations" between the agent or the principal on the one hand and the third party on the other,[190] leaving most aspects of the very difficult area of "internal relations" between agent and principal to continue to be governed by the applicable national law. The CAISG provides uniform norms for the establishment and scope of the authority of the agent,[191] the legal effect of acts carried out by the agent,[192] and termination of the agent's authority.[193] The CAISG is a blend of civil and common law agency principles in the international sale of goods. However, the scope of the convention is limited, and reference to national laws will still be necessary for many aspects of the agency relationship. As of January 1, 1995, Canada had not yet ratified the convention.

C. ICC Model Agency Contract (1993)

In addition to multilateral legislative measures to promote uniformity in agency contracts for the international sale of goods, the ICC has consolidated international commercial custom and current practice in this area through the design of its model agency contract.[194] The ICC model agency contract deals only with the internal agency relationship between the agent and the principal, and imposes upon the parties the duty to carry out their obligations in accordance with good faith and fair dealing.[195] The scope of application of the model agency contract is limited to international agency agreements by self-employed commercial agents (as opposed to employed agents or agents that could be classified as employees) for the sale (as opposed to the purchase) of goods. In order to avoid the difficulties caused by differing national laws, the model contract is governed by the terms of the contract itself and by the neutral regime of the *lex mercatoria*,[196] unless the parties choose to be governed by a particular national law.[197] International arbitration is the preferred mode of dispute settlement for disputes arising under

187 Art. 2(1)(b).

188 Art. 1(2).

189 Art. 1(4).

190 Art. 1(3).

191 Arts. 9 to 11.

192 Arts. 12 to 14.

193 Arts. 17 to 20.

194 For analysis of the model contract, see Bortollotti et al., *The ICC Agency Model Contract: A Commentary* (Deventer: Kluwer, 1993).

195 Art. 2(1).

196 Art. 23.2.A.

197 Art. 23.2.B.

the model agency contract, since national courts may not be willing to apply the general rules of the *lex mercatoria*, unless the principles coincide with concepts expressly recognized in the domestic laws of the forum. The ICC model agency contract proposes alternatives in certain problematic areas, such as the goodwill indemnity,[198] where national laws were so divergent that a single codification of the principle was impossible. While it necessarily requires adaptations to tailor it to the specific needs of the parties in a particular situation, the ICC model agency contract may provide an instructive base from which to begin the drafting process for an international agency contract.

D. The 1978 Hague Convention on the Law Applicable to Agency

The 1978 Hague Convention on the Law Applicable to Agency furnishes uniform rules establishing the governing law for both the internal (principal-agent)[199] and external (principal-agent/third party)[200] aspects of international agency relationships.[201] It applies where an agent has authority or ostensible authority to receive and communicate offers or negotiate on behalf of the principal in relation to third parties.

The convention preserves party autonomy: the parties may choose the law that will govern aspects of their internal relationship.[202] Where the parties do not choose explicitly, the applicable law is the law of the state of the agent's place of business or habitual residence at the time the relationship is established.[203] With regard to the external agency relationship, the existence and scope of the agent's authority and the effect of the agent's activities fall to be governed by the internal law of the place where the agent had his or her place of business at the time of performance, or, in certain circumstances, by the law of the place of performance. The laws chosen by the parties cannot be applied where this would be manifestly incompatible with public policy.[204]

The Hague Agency Convention required three ratifications to enter into force.[205] As of July 1995, it had been ratified by the Netherlands, France, Argentina, and Portugal.

---

198 Art. 21.

199 Pt. II, arts. 5 to 10. The law applicable to the internal relationship governs the formation and validity of the agency relationship, the obligations of the parties, the terms of performance, the consequences of non-performance, and the termination of obligations.

200 Pt. III, arts. 11 to 15. The law applicable to the external relationship governs the existence and scope of the agent's authority, as well as the effect of the agent's activities.

201 See, generally, H.L.E. Verhagen, *Agency in Private International Law: The Hague Convention on the Law Applicable to Agency* (1995).

202 Art. 5.

203 Art. 6.

204 Art. 17.

205 Art. 26.

V. PRIVATE INTERNATIONAL LAW ISSUES: THE LAW APPLICABLE TO THE CONTRACT FOR THE INTERNATIONAL SALE OF GOODS

A. Introduction

The determination of the law applicable to a contract of sale is a basic issue when the contracting parties are resident in different jurisdictions, and the contract is made in one jurisdiction and must be performed in another. Important rights, for example that of an unpaid vendor to exercise a right of "stoppage in transitu," will vary from jurisdiction to jurisdiction. Furthermore, the transaction may have several different components so that a different law may be applicable to the sale aspects as opposed to the financial arrangements, such as a letter of credit, resulting in what French doctrine refers to as *dépeçage*. Private international law notions have been further complicated in recent years by the evolution, fostered particularly by certain European continental doctrine, of a concept of *lex mercatoria*, or common general principles of international commercial law that may be applied to a contract, thus obviating the necessity to have all rights and obligations between the parties established by reference to a particular legal system.

Most systems recognize a fair degree of latitude enabling parties to select the applicable law to their transaction in the absence of fraud or other public policy impediments and, if possible, such a selection is usually the best advice counsel can offer his or her client. The choice of law need not be that of the parties or be directly related to the place of the transaction; the choice of English law in maritime contracts, such as charter parties or marine insurance, or the choice of certain provisions of the Swiss Code of Obligations as a "neutral" system are examples that one sees frequently in practice. Choice of a given legal system to govern the transaction may even be accompanied by a choice of exclusive jurisdiction conferred upon the courts of one country. However, it must be recognized that while this may be good advice, it is just not possible to follow it in many cases because of the nature of the contract, because the parties cannot agree to the choice of a specific law or, occasionally, because there are mandatory provisions that apply in different jurisdictions.

A sensitivity to private international law issues is thus a prerequisite to understanding international sales transactions, and it is this expertise that the practitioner can offer his or her client because this is an area of clearly legal rather than business concern.

B. Canadian Rules

1. Introduction

When the provisions of the CISG are not applicable, either because the contract or the issue is outside its sphere of application or because the parties have contracted out of its provisions, it is necessary to ascertain the law governing the various aspects of that contract.

Canadian private international law rules will be applied by the Canadian court where the action involving the contract is pending. These rules have adopted the doctrine of the proper law of the contract that governs most contractual issues.

The proper law may be determined in three ways: (1) by express selection by the parties; (2) by inferred selection from the circumstances, or, failing either of these; (3) by judicial determination of the system of law with which the transaction has the closest and most real connection.

2. Express Choice of the Proper Law

Where the parties expressly stipulate that a contract shall be governed by a particular law, that law will be the proper law of the contract.[206] This freedom of choice is subject to some limitations. The selection must be *bona fide*[207] and legal,[208] and there must be no reason for avoiding the choice on the ground of public policy.[209] It is assumed that where a law is expressly chosen to evade the provisions of the system of law with which the transaction, objectively, is most closely and really connected, that choice will be disregarded.[210]

If the express choice of law is meaningless, then the court will disregard it and determine the proper law according to the inferred or implied intentions of the parties.[211]

3. Inferred Choice of Law

If there is no express choice of the proper law, the court will consider whether it can ascertain that there was an inferred or implied choice of law by the parties. If the parties agree that arbitration shall take place in a particular legal unit, the court will usually,[212]

---

206 E.g., *Vita Food Products Inc. v. Unus Shipping Co. Ltd.*, [1939] AC 277, at 289, 290, and 292, [1939] 1 All ER 513, at 521, 522 (PC); *Drew Brown Ltd. v. The Ship "Orient Trader" and Owners*, [1974] SCR 1286, 34 DLR (3d) 339; *Syncrude Can. Ltd. v. Hunter Engineering Co.* (1985), 68 BCLR 367 (CA); and *Amin Rasheed Shipping Corp. v. Kuwait Insurance Co.*, [1984] 1 AC 50, at 61-62 and 72-73, [1983] 2 All ER 884, [1983] 3 WWR 241 (HL).

207 E.g., *Nike Infomatic Systems Ltd. v. Avac Systems Ltd.*, [1980] 1 WWR 528, 105 DLR (3d) 455, 16 BCLR 139, 8 BLR 196 (SC).

208 However, this begs the question by what law the legality is to be tested.

209 E.g., *Vita Food Products Inc. v. Unus Shipping Co. Ltd.*, *supra*, note 206, at 290 (AC) and 521 (ER) and *Greenshields Inc. v. Johnston*, [1981] 3 WWR 313, 119 DLR (3d) 714, aff'd. 131 DLR (3d) 234, 35 AR 487 (CA).

210 E.g., *Mynott v. Barnard* (1939), 62 CLR 68, at 80 (Aust. HC) and *Kay's Leasing Corp. Pty. Ltd. v. Fletcher*, 116 CLR 124, at 143, 144, [1965] ALR 673, at 682, 683 (Aust. HC). Where a statute in the forum expresses a policy applicable to the case before the court, that statute may have to be applied irrespective of the proper law, whether or not expressly chosen by the parties. In *Re Maritime Heating Co. Ltd.* (1969), 2 DLR (3d) 471 (NB CA), the law expressly selected was also most substantially connected.

211 *Compagnie Tunisienne de Navigation SA v. Compagnie D'Armement Maritime SA*, [1969] 3 All ER 589, [1969] 1 WLR 1338 (CA), rev'd. on a different interpretation of the clause in question, [1971] AC 572, [1970] 3 All ER 71 (HL).

212 E.g., *Hamlyn & Co. v. Talisker Distillery*, [1894] AC 202 (HL); *Vita Foods Products Inc. v. Unus Shipping Co. Ltd.*, note 206, at 290 (AC) and 521 (ER); and *Sayers v. International Drilling Co. NV*, [1971] 3 All ER 163, at 168, [1971] 1 WLR 1176, at 1182, 1183 (CA).

although not always,[213] conclude that the parties have impliedly chosen the law of the legal unit of arbitration as the proper law. Similarly, if the parties agree that the courts of a particular legal unit shall have jurisdiction over the contract, there is a strong inference that the law of that legal unit is to be the proper law.[214] Other factors from which the courts have been prepared to infer the intentions of the parties[215] with regard to the proper law are the legal terminology in which the contract is drafted, the form of the documents involved in the transaction, the currency in which payment is to be made, the use of a particular language, a connection with a preceding transaction, the nature and location of the subject matter of the contract, the residence but rarely the nationality of the parties, the head office of a corporation party to the contract, or the fact that one of the parties is a government. The proper law cannot be determined retrospectively by an event that, at the time the contract was made, was merely an uncertain event in the future.

4. Inference from Validity of the Contract

There is a body of authority in support of the proposition that where a contract is or any terms of it are void or invalid under one system of law, but good under another, the parties must be taken to have intended to contract with reference to that law by which the agreement would be valid.[216] This should not, however, be regarded as an irrebuttable presumption, but only as a pointer toward the intention of the parties.[217]

5. No Express or Inferred Choice of Law

Where the parties have not expressed a choice with regard to the proper law and no such choice can be inferred, the proper law of their contract is the system of law with which the transaction has the closest and most real connection.[218] In such a case, the court does not seek to find some presumed or fictitious intention of the parties but, rather, holds the contract to be governed by the system of law with which it is most closely and really connected, for that is what is presumed that reasonable businessmen would have decided.[219]

In determining with what system of law the transaction is most closely and really connected, the court should look at all the circumstances.[220] While firm rules cannot be

---

213 *Compagnie D'Armement Maritime SA v. Compagnie Tunisienne de Navigation SA*, [1971] AC 572, [1970] 3 All ER 71 (HL).

214 E.g., *Hamlyn & Co. v. Talisker Distillery, supra*, note 212, at 212 and 213 (HL).

215 The intention must be that of both parties and not of one of them.

216 E.g., *Sharn Importing Ltd. v. Babchuk*, 21 DLR (3d) 349, [1971] 4 WWR 517 (BC).

217 E.g., *Etler v. Kertesz*, [1960] OR 672 (CA).

218 E.g., *Imperial Life Assurance Co. of Canada v. Colmenares*, [1967] SCR 443, 62 DLR (2d) 138 and *United Nations v. Atlantic Seaways Corp.*, [1979] 2 FC 541, 28 NR 207, at 221, 99 DLR (3d) 609 (CA).

219 *Mount Albert Borough Council v. Australasian Temperance & General Mutual Life Assurance Society Ltd.*, [1938] AC 224, at 240, [1937] 4 All ER 206, at 214 (PC) and *The "Assunzione"*, [1954] P 150, at 176, 179, 186, [1954] 1 All ER 278, at 290, 291, 292, and 295 (CA).

220 E.g., *Imperial Life Assurance Co. v. Colmenares, supra*, note 218, at 468 (SCR) and *Dallas Oilfield Contractors Ltd. v. Syroteuk*, [1980] 3 WWR 119 (Sask. DC).

laid down,[221] it is clear that the court will look at such factors as the place of contracting, the place of performance, the place of residence or business of the parties, and the nature and subject matter of the contract.

When the place of contracting is the same as the place of performance, the court may find it practically impossible to apply any other law to the contract. In that case, it seems obvious that the state or province where these two events have occurred is most interested in having its system of law applied to issues arising under the contract.[222]

6. *Time*

The intention of the parties or the connection of the transaction with a legal unit or system of law must be determined at the time when the contract was made. The subsequent conduct of the parties cannot be used as an aid to the interpretation of the contract, unless the parties have agreed to vary the original contract or have entered into a new contract collateral to it, or their later conduct will amount to an estoppel.

7. *Determination of the Proper Law by Statute*

Some statutes provide a general choice of law rule that must be applied when determining the proper law. Other statutes limit the scope of their own application and provide choice of law rules for contractual issues covered by them, but leave unaffected the determination of the proper law in relation to issues outside the ambit of the statute.

For instance, the Bills of Exchange Act[223] contains specific choice of law rules applicable to negotiable instruments that eliminate the doctrine of the proper law. The Carriage by Air Act[224] gives effect to the 1929 Warsaw Convention Relating to the Unification of Certain Rules Relating to International Air Carriage, as amended by the Hague Protocol 1955. The convention declares that it applies to a contract for the "international"[225] carriage by air of persons, luggage, and goods, irrespective of any other law applicable by virtue of common law rules of private international law.[226]

With respect to contracts of maritime carriage entered into before May 6, 1993, the former Carriage of Goods by Water Act,[227] embodying the Hague Rules, regulates the liabilities and rights of a carrier by sea, under contracts evidenced by bills of lading. The Act restricts the scope of ordinary private international law rules by requiring the courts,

---

221 *Jacobs v. Crédit Lyonnais* (1884), 12 QBD 589, at 601 (CA).

222 E.g., *Rosencrantz v. Union Contractors Ltd. and Thornton* (1960), 31 WWR 597, 23 DLR (2d) 473 (BC); *Re Modern Fashions Ltd.* (1970), 8 DLR (3d) 590 (Man. QB); *Block Bros. Realty Ltd. v. Mollard and Detra Holdings Ltd.*, 122 DLR (3d) 323, 27 BCLR 17, [1981] 4 WWR 65 (CA); and *Jorges Carpet Mills Inc. v. Bondar*, [1981] 4 WWR 470 (Alta. QB).

223 RSC 1985, c. B-4, as am., ss. 159-63. See chapter 8, *infra*.

224 RSC 1985, c. C-26.

225 See the Act, s. 2(2) and the convention, art. 1(1). See chapter 8, *infra*. For a definition, see the Hague Protocol, art. 1(a).

226 Where the convention is silent on a particular question, the private international law rules of the forum are applicable.

227 RSC 1985, c. C-27.

in certain circumstances, to apply the provisions of the statute irrespective of the proper law of the contract or of the nationality of the vessel. Thus, the rules relating to bills of lading, have effect in relation to, and in connection with, the carriage of goods from any port in Canada to any other port in or outside Canada.[228] However, if a cargo is shipped from a port of a country other than Canada, which has adopted the Hague Rules, the Act does not apply and the parties may contract out of the rules by selecting, as the proper law of the contract, a system of law other than that of the port of shipment.[229]

Concerning contracts for carriage of goods by sea entered into after May 6, 1993, the Hague-Visby Rules[230] apply by virtue of the 1993 Carriage of Goods by Water Act.[231] These rules similarly restrict the ordinary conflict of law rules in certain circumstances. Courts must apply them in relation to the carriage of goods under a bill of lading issued in a contracting state, or covering transport from any port in Canada to any other port within[232] or outside Canada. They must similarly be applied where the contract provides that the rules, or the laws of a state giving effect to the rules, are to govern the contract.[233]

A federal or provincial statute that does not contain a general or a specific choice of law rule will be applicable only if it is part of the proper law of the contract or if it can be construed or interpreted so as to apply to the contract in question irrespective of the proper law.

8. *Scope of the Proper Law*

a. Splitting of the Contract

While most contractual issues are governed by the proper law, the parties can agree that different contractual issues may be governed by different laws.[234] There is no authority against the court deciding that the objectively ascertained proper law shall vary according to the contractual issue involved.[235] However, the court will not do this readily or without good reason.[236]

---

228 S. 2.

229 *Vita Food Products Inc. v. Unus Shipping Co., supra*, note 206, distinguished in *Dominion Glass Co. Ltd. v. Ship "Anglo Indian"*, [1944] SCR 409.

230 Annexed as sched. 1 to the 1993 Carriage of Goods by Water Act, SC 1993, c. 21.

231 SC 1993, c. 21.

232 An exception to the application of the rules to carriage of goods between two ports in Canada is where the contract of carriage is not evidenced by a bill of lading and stipulates that the rules will not apply (see s. 7(1)(b) and 7(4) of the 1993 Carriage of Goods by Water Act).

233 See art. X of the Hague-Visby Rules.

234 *Hamlyn & Co. v. Talisker Distillery, supra*, note 212.

235 *Re Helbert Wagg & Co. Ltd.'s Claim*, [1956] Ch. 323, at 340, [1956] 1 All ER 129, at 135 and *Re United Railways of The Havana and Regla Warehouses Ltd.*, [1960] Ch. 52, at 92, [1959] 1 All ER 214, at 234 (CA), aff'd. (sub nom. *Tomkinson v. First Pennsylvania Banking and Trust Co.*) [1961] AC 1007, [1960] 2 All ER 332 (HL).

236 *Montreal Trust Co. v. Stanrock Uranium Mines Ltd.*, [1966] 1 OR 258, 53 DLR (2d) 594 (HC) and *Kahler v. Midland Bank Ltd.*, [1950] AC 24, at 42, [1949] 2 All ER 621, at 633 (HL); but see

(The footnote is continued on the next page.)

Apart from express or implied agreement to the contrary,[237] the obligations of both parties will be governed by the same proper law.[238]

b. Renvoi

The proper law of the contract means the domestic rules of that legal system and not its rules of private international law. The doctrine of *renvoi*, simple or double,[239] has no place in the law of contract.[240]

c. Place of Contracting

The place of contracting, if relevant as a connecting factor in determining the proper law, must be ascertained in accordance with the domestic rules of the *lex fori*.[241]

d. Incorporation by Reference

Express selection of the proper law of the contract that will govern the contract as a whole must be distinguished from the incorporation into the contract of specific provisions of some foreign legal system to govern some particular issue,[242] such as the obligation to make a ship seaworthy,[243] the validity of an exemption clause,[244] or even the validity of a choice of law clause.[245]

---

236 Continued ...

Chamberlain v. Napier (1880), 15 Ch. D. 614; *British South Africa Co. v. De Beers Consolidated Mines Ltd.*, [1910] 1 Ch. 354, at 383, aff'd. [1910] 2 Ch. 502 (CA), rev'd. on another point, [1912] AC 52 (HL) and *Sayers v. International Drilling Co. NV, supra*, note 212, at 166 and 167 (All ER), and 1180 and 1181 (WLR).

237 *Re Helbert Wagg & Co. Ltd.'s Claim, supra*, note 235.

238 *Zivnostenska Banka National Corp. v. Frankman*, [1950] AC 57, at 83, [1949] 2 All ER 671, at 683 (HL) and *Montreal Trust Co. v. Stanrock Uranium Mines Ltd., supra*, note 236, at 267, 268, and 270 (OR), and 603 and 606 (DLR).

239 See, in general, on *renvoi*, Castel, *Canadian Conflict of Laws* (3rd ed., 1993), c. 4.

240 *Amin Rasheed Shipping Corp. v. Kuwait Insurance Co., supra*, note 206, at 246 (WWR), per Lord Diplock (HL); *Re United Railways of The Havana and Regla Warehouses Ltd., supra*, note 235, at 96, 97, and 115 (Ch.) and 246 (All ER); and *Rosencrantz v. Union Contractors Ltd. and Thornton*, supra, note 222, at 602 (WWR) and 478 (DLR), not following *Vita Food Products Inc. v. Unus Shipping Co. Ltd., supra*, note 206, at 292 (AC) and 522 (All ER).

241 E.g., *Re Modern Fashions Ltd., supra*, note 222. For a contract deemed to be made in Ontario, see the Insurance Act, RSO 1990, c. I.8, as am.

242 *Re Suse and Sibeth, ex parte Dever* (1887), 18 QBD 660 (CA); *G.E. Dobell & Co. v. Rossmore SS Co. Ltd.*, [1895] 2 QB 408 (CA); *Canada Ltd. v. Hunter Eng. Co.* (1984), 27 BLR 59 (BC SC); and *Travelers Can. v. MacDonald* (1984), 48 OR (2d) 714, 8 CCLI 314, 14 DLR (4th) 88 (CA).

243 *G.E. Dobell & Co. v. Rossmore SS Co. Ltd., ibid.*, and *Adamastos Shipping Co. Ltd. v. Anglo-Saxon Petroleum Co. Ltd.*, [1959] AC 133, [1958] 1 All ER 725 (HL).

244 *Stafford Allen & Sons Ltd. v. Pacific Steam Navigation Co.*, [1956] 2 All ER 716, [1956] 1 WLR 629 (CA).

245 *Ocean SS Co. Ltd. v. Queensland State Wheat Board*, [1941] 1 KB 402, [1941] 1 All ER 158 (CA).

The importance of the distinction between selection of the proper law and incorporation of a provision of foreign law into a contract by reference is most apparent where there is a change in the foreign law between the date of the contract and that of the proceedings. The proper law is normally the one in force in the legal unit in question from time to time, and effect will be given to any changes in that law before performance of the contract falls due,[246] such as where the requirement of legal tender is varied,[247] a debtor's obligations are varied by a moratorium,[248] there are changes in exchange control legislation,[249] where a gold value clause[250] is declared void retrospectively, or even where the sovereignty of a country changes.[251] However, where the provisions of a foreign law are incorporated, they constitute terms of the contract as at the date of incorporation and are unaffected by subsequent changes, as where a statute, whose terms have been incorporated into a contract, has been repealed or amended.[252]

9. *Illegality of the Contract and Public Policy*

A contract that by its proper law is void for illegality will not be enforced in Canada.[253] In England, there is a substantial weight of authority in support of the proposition that a contract illegal by the law of the country where it is to be performed will not be enforced.[254]

Whatever their proper law, contracts are illegal in Canada if illegal under a federal or provincial statute having extra-territorial effect, such as exchange control legislation,[255] or if contrary to Canadian ideas of public policy or morality. Although it is clear that a Canadian court will not enforce foreign penal or revenue laws,[256] it will also not

---

246 *Re Chesterman's Trusts; Mott v. Browning*, [1923] 2 Ch. 466, at 478 (CA); *Kahler v. Midland Bank Ltd.*, *supra*, note 236, at 56 (AC), and 641 and 642 (All ER); *Jabbour v. Custodian of Absentee's Property of State of Israel*, [1954] 1 All ER 145, at 157, [1954] 1 WLR 139, at 157 (QB); *Re Helbert Wagg & Co. Ltd.'s Claim*, *supra*, note 235, at 342 (Ch.) and 135 (All ER); and *Rossano v. Manufacturers' Life Insurance Co.*, [1963] 2 QB 352, at 362, [1962] 2 All ER 214, at 219.

247 *Re Chesterman's Trusts; Mott v. Browning*, *ibid.*

248 *Re Helbert Wagg & Co. Ltd.'s Claim*, *supra*, note 235.

249 *De Beéche v. The South American Stores Ltd. and Chilian Stores Ltd.*, [1935] AC 148 (HL), *Kahler v. Midland Bank Ltd.*, *supra*, note 236; and *Zivnostenska Banka National Corp. v. Frankman*, *supra*, note 238.

250 *R v. International Trustee for the Protection of Bondholders AG*, [1937] AC 500, [1937] 2 All ER 164 (HL).

251 *Jabbour v. Custodian of Absentee's Property of State of Israel*, *supra*, note 246, and see *Banco de Bilbao v. Sancha*, [1938] 2 KB 176, at 195, [1938] 2 All ER 253, at 260 (CA).

252 *Vita Food Products Inc. v. Unus Shipping Co. Ltd.*, *supra*, note 206, at 286 (AC) and 519 (All ER), and *Heath Steel Mills v. Schroder* (1963), 37 DLR (2d) 367 (NS).

253 E.g., *Etler v. Kertesz*, *supra*, note 217.

254 E.g., *Ralli Bros. v. Compania Naviera Sota y Aznar*, [1920] 2 KB 287 (CA).

255 *Bossevain v. Weil*, [1950] AC 327 (HL); *United City Merchants (Investments) Ltd. v. Royal Bank of Canada*, [1983] 1 AC 168 (HL).

256 Castel, *supra*, note 239.

enforce a contract whose object is to violate such penal or revenue laws[257] or exchange control legislation.[258] On the other hand, a contract void under its proper law for infringement of foreign exchange control legislation may be upheld as valid in Canada if that legislation is regarded as discriminatory.[259]

C. Conflict Avoidance

Several methods may be used to pre-select the governing law in order to avoid choice of law problems with respect to the contract for the international sale of goods, none of which is completely reliable. The most common is to insert an express stipulation in the contract to insure that any tribunal will apply the pre-selected law. For instance: "This agreement shall be construed and the legal relations between the parties determined in accordance with the laws of the province of Ontario." It is better to select the law of the place of performance of the contract as the controlling law if this is practical, since most controversies arise with respect to performance.

The second method is to tailor the transaction to ensure that under generally accepted principles of private international law, any tribunal seized with a controversy will apply the pre-selected law. Thus, all legal acts, contacts, and interests must be grouped in the state whose law has been pre-selected as applicable to the transaction. However, there are practical limitations upon the extent to which a transaction can be shaped in order to insure the application of a particular law. This approach is not necessary if the relevant private international rules allow the parties almost unlimited free choice of the applicable law. Another method is to combine a choice of law clause with a choice of forum clause calling for the exclusive jurisdiction of an arbitration tribunal or a state court.

A clause localizing disputes surrounding the transaction in the tribunals of the pre-selected state or province may not always be effective because it can be defeated by the doctrine of *forum non conveniens* or by local public policy. A choice of forum clause should also include an express consent to service of process and submission to the jurisdiction of the tribunal selected.

The ideal method of conflict avoidance is by international unification of the substantive laws or private international law rules applicable to the contract for the international sale of goods.

D. International Conventions on Conflict Avoidance

Three significant conventions endeavouring to harmonize private international law rules concerning international contracts for the sale of goods bear mention here: (1) the 1980 European Community Convention on the Law Applicable to Contractual Obligations (the Rome Convention), (2) the 1985 Hague Convention on the Law Applicable to

---

257 *Regazzoni v. K.C. Sethia (1944) Ltd.*, [1958] AC 301, at 322, 328, and 329 (HL).

258 *Etler v. Kertesz*, *supra*, note 217.

259 *Kahler v. Midland Bank Ltd.*, *supra*, note 236, at 26 (AC).

Contracts for the International Sale of Goods, and (3) the 1994 OAS Inter-American Convention on the Law Applicable to Contractual Obligations.

1. The 1980 European Community Convention on the Law Applicable to Contractual Obligations (the Rome Convention)

The European Community Convention[260] on the law applicable to contractual obligations (the Rome Convention) recognizes the principle of party autonomy[261] subject to the application of certain mandatory norms.[262] In the absence of express choice or choice discernible with reasonable certitude from the parties' intent, the law of the country with which the contract is most closely connected shall govern.[263] This is the Anglo-American approach. However, the Rome Convention attempts to be more specific in determining what constitutes the closest connection[264] and, thus, capitulates to "legal impressionism."[265] It is submitted that such an approach does not lend itself to codification.

---

260 *Official Journal of the European Communities*, OJ no. L 266, 9 October 1980 (1980), 29 *ILM* 1492. Opened for signature on 19 June 1980. Entered into force on April 1, 1991, [1991] OJC 51/1. See *Report on Convention* by Giuliano and Lagarde, *Official Journal of European Communities*, OJC 282, vol. 23, 31 October 1980. See also D.F. Cavers, "The Common Market's Draft Conflicts Convention on Obligations: Some Protective Aspects" (1975), 48 *South Cal. L Rev.* 603; Nadelmann, "Impressionism and Unification of Law: The EEC Draft Convention on the Law Applicable to Contractual and Non-Contractual Obligations" (1976), 24 *Am. J Comp. L* 1, Draft (1963), 21 *Am. J Comp. L 587;* in French (1973), 62 *Rev. Crit.* 209; Lipstein (ed.), *Harmonisation of Private International Law by the EEC* (1978); Lando (ed.), *European Private International Law of Obligations* (1975); North, [1980] *JBL* 382; and North (ed.), *Contract, Conflicts* (1982); Collins (1976), 25 *Int'l. & Comp. LQ* 35. More recently, see Plender, *The European Contracts Convention: the Rome Convention on the choice of law for contracts* (1991); and Kaye, *The New Private International Law of Contract in the European Community* (1993).

261 Art. 3. See, e.g., Hogan, "Contracting out of the Rome Convention" (1992), 108 *LQR* 12.

262 Art. 7; also, under art. 3(3), the parties cannot avoid mandatory rules by choosing the law of a country other than that which has the only substantial connection to the contract. Arts. 5 and 6 also contain important restrictions. On party autonomy and limitations thereto, see Rinze, "The Scope of Party autonomy under the 1980 Rome Convention on the Law Applicable to Contractual Obligations," [1994] *JBL* 412.

263 Art. 4(1).

264 Art. 4(2) to (5). Where no express choice of law is made, the convention contains a general *prima facie* presumption in favour of the application of the law of the principal place of business of the party making the "characteristic performance." This will ordinarily mean that the law of the seller's place of business will prevail, with explicit exceptions for real estate contracts (usually, law of the place where the real estate is situated), consumer contracts (usually, law of the consumer's residence), employment contracts (usually, law of place where work performed or employee resides), and transportation of goods (combination of elements).

265 See Nadelmann (1976), 24 *Am. J Comp. L* 1, at 12.

The Rome Convention limits the parties' choice of law to the laws of particular countries,[266] and would not permit designation of, for example, the *lex mercatoria* or UNIDROIT's 1994 Principles of International Commercial Contracts as the governing law.

The Rome Convention is not limited to regulating conflicts of law between EC member states, but is also applicable to conflict situations involving a member state and a non-member state. It would therefore apply, for example, to contracts between parties from Canada and the United Kingdom.

2. 1985 Hague Convention on the Law Applicable to Contracts for the International Sale of Goods

In October 1985, the Hague Conference on Private International Law adopted a Convention on the Law Applicable to Contracts for the International Sale of Goods. This convention superseded the 1955 Hague Convention on the Law Applicable to the International Sale of Goods, taking into account the provisions of the 1980 CISG.

The Hague Convention provides uniform rules for the determination of the law applicable to contracts of sale of goods between parties having their places of business in different states and in all other cases involving a choice between the laws of different states.[267] The convention preserves party autonomy: the applicable law is that chosen by the parties.[268] In the absence of choice, the contract is governed by the law of the state where the seller has his or her place of business at the time of conclusion of the contract, subject to exceptions in favour of the law of the state where the buyer at the time of conclusion of the contract has his or her place of business if certain conditions are met, or by the law most closely connected with the contract.[269] The convention also deals with formalities[270] and the scope of the applicable law.[271] It permits dépaçage, but only by express stipulation.[272] In relation to inspection of the goods, regard is to be had to the law of the state in which the inspection takes place.[273] The convention, which rejects *renvoi*,[274] declares that the application of the designated law may be refused only where such application would be manifestly incompatible with public policy.[275]

---

266 See wording of art. 1(1).

267 Art. 1. For limitations as to the scope of the Convention see arts. 2, 4, and 5. Art. 14 deals with the case where a party has more than one place of business and art. 6 allows for the application of a law that is not that of one of the contracting states.

268 Art. 7.

269 Art. 8. For other exceptions, see arts. 9 and 10.

270 Art. 11.

271 Art. 12.

272 Art. 7(1).

273 Art. 13.

274 Art. 15.

275 Art. 18.

It is unclear whether the convention limits the parties' choice of law to laws of countries, or whether it is open to the parties to designate an autonomous system of norms, such as the *lex mercatoria* or UNIDROIT's Principles of International Commercial Contracts, to govern their contract.[276]

3. The 1994 OAS Inter-American Convention on the Law Applicable to International Contracts

The 1994 Organization of American States Inter-American Convention on the Law Applicable to International Contracts (OAS Convention) was adopted at the Fifth Inter-American Specialized Conference on Private International Law in Mexico City on March 18, 1994 by 17 Latin American countries, the United States, and Canada.[277] Modelled on the EC's 1980 Rome Convention, the OAS Convention preserves party autonomy: the contract is to be governed by the law chosen by the parties[278] subject to considerations of public policy[279] and mandatory norms.[280] The choice of law may be express or inferred from the parties' intent as evidenced in the contract.[281]

Where the parties fail to choose a governing law effectively, the applicable law is that of the state with the "closest ties" to the contract. Avoiding the "legal impressionism" that plagues the EC's 1980 Rome Convention, the OAS Convention merely decrees that the court is to take into account all objective and subjective factors in making the determination of the applicable law.[282] And, in marked departure from the 1980 Rome Convention, the OAS Convention allows the court in addition to take into account "the general principles of international commercial law recognized by international organizations," which would presumably include such international norms as UNIDROIT's Principles of International Commercial Conduct. This is a welcome development in international conflicts of law relating to international sales.

Canada has not yet ratified the convention.

E. Proof of Foreign Law

It should be noted that in principle Canadian courts do not ascertain the applicable foreign law *ex officio*. It must be proved to their satisfaction by expert witnesses or other admissible evidence. If a party fails to adduce such evidence, the courts must apply their own domestic law. Thus, in Canada, a party should plead foreign law only if it is to his or her advantage.[283]

---

276 See wording of art. 15.

277 (1994), 33 *ILM* 732. See, generally, F.K. Juenger, "The Inter-American Convention on the Law Applicable to International Contracts: Some Highlights and Comparisons" (1994), 42 *Am. J Comp. L* 381.

278 Art. 7(1).

279 Art. 18.

280 Art. 11.

281 Art. 7(1).

282 Art. 9(2).

283 On the proof of foreign law see Castel, *supra*, note 239, at 147 *et seq*.

VI. THE LEX MERCATORIA

The parties to a contract for the international sale of goods may decide to subject it to the customs or usages of international trade or the rules of law that are common to all or most of the states engaged in international trade or to those that are connected with the contract, instead of agreeing to have it governed by the domestic law of a particular country. Clauses to this effect are often inserted in contracts between a government or government enterprise and a private enterprise since neither party wishes to submit to the laws of the other, especially if such laws are unfit for contracts for the international sale of goods. Generally accepted principles and customary rules elaborated in the framework of international trade without reference to a particular system of law constitute a *lex mercatoria,* whose elements include the rules of public international law on treaties; uniform laws such as the CISG; general principles of law recognized by the commercial nations of the world, such as the rule *pacta sunt servanda*; the resolutions, recommendations, and codes of conduct adopted by international organizations, including UNCITRAL and UNIDROIT;[284] the customs and usages of international trade, for example, the Incoterms 1990 and the UCP; as well as standard form contracts that have gained universal acceptance.

In continental Europe and in the common law countries, including Canada, it is not yet settled whether the parties to a contract may agree to have it governed by this *lex mercatoria.*[285] For example, in *Amin Rasheed Shipping Corp. v. Kuwait Insurance Co., the Al Wahab*, Lord Diplock stated:[286]

> My Lords, contracts are incapable of existing in a legal vacuum. They are mere pieces of paper devoid of all legal effect unless they were made by reference to some system of private law which defines the obligations assumed by the parties to the contract by their use of particular forms of words and prescribes the remedies enforceable in a court of justice for failure to perform any of those obligations; and this must be so however widespread geographically the use of a contract employing a particular form of words to express the obligations assumed by the parties may be.

This statement lends support to those who oppose the existence of a *lex mercatoria* on the ground that it does not derive its binding force from any state authority and furthermore does not constitute a substantial legal system.[287]

This view has been rejected by the supporters of the *lex mercatoria,* who claim that it is sufficient for its existence to be recognized as an autonomous norm system by the business community and by state authorities.[288]

---

284 In particular, the UNIDROIT Principles for International Commercial Contracts (1994).

285 For a recent article refuting the existence of a new *lex mercatoria* and arguing that the *lex mercatoria* can only constitute guiding principles rather than a governing law, see Wilkinson, "The New *Lex Mercatoria*: Reality or Academic Fantasy?" (1995), 12 *J Int. Arb.* 103.

286 [1984] 1 AC 50, [1983] 2 All ER 884, [1983] 3 WLR 241, at 249.

287 Mann, "Lex facit arbitrum," International Arbitration. Liber Amicorum for Martin Domke (1967), at 157.

288 See Lando, "The Lex Mercatoria in International Commercial Arbitration" (1985), 34 *Int'l. & Comp. LQ* 747, at 752. See also Strenger, "La Notion de Lex Mercatoria en Droit du Commerce International"

(The footnote is continued on the next page.)

VII. SELECTED BIBLIOGRAPHY

A. Books

Bianca and Bonell, *Commentary on the International Sales Law: The 1980 Vienna Sales Convention* (1987).

Boggiano, *International Standard Contracts* (1990).

Colas, *Global Economic Cooperation: A Guide to Agreements and Organizations* (1994).

Day, *The Law of International Trade* (1981).

Delaume, *Law and Practice of Transnational Contracts* (1988).

Ernst, *International Commodity Agreements: The System of Controlling the International Commodity Market* (1982).

Guest (ed.), *Benjamin's Sale of Goods* (2nd ed., 1981), 855-954.

Honnold, *Uniform Law for International Sales under the 1980 United Nations Convention*, 2nd ed.(1991).

International Chamber of Commerce, *Guide to Incoterms* (1991).

International Chamber of Commerce, *Incoterms* 1990.

Kennedy, *Contracts of Sale: CIF* (1959).

Klotz, *International Sales Agreements: An Annotated Drafting and Negotiating Guide* (1997).

Kritzer, *Guide to Practical Applications of the United Nations Convention on Contracts for the International Sale of Goods* (1989).

Magraw and Kathrein (eds.), *The Convention for the International Sale of Goods: A Handbook of Basic Materials* (1990).

Sarcevic (ed.), *International Contracts and Conflict of Laws* (1990).

Sassoon, *CIF and FOB Contracts* (1984).

Schmitthoff, *Schmitthoff's Export Trade: The Law and Practice of International Trade* (9th ed., 1990).

1st Conference on International Trade Law, Proceedings of the Conference on the New Rules Governing the International Sale of Goods (1987).

---

288 Continued ...

(1991), 227 *Receuil des Cours* 210 and Gaillard, "Trente ans de *lex mercatoria*: Pour une application sélective de la méthode des principes généraux de droit" (1995), 122 *Journal de Droit International* 5. Notably, the ICC has opted to have its 1993 model agency contract governed only by the *lex mercatoria* in order to avoid the difficulties caused by the lack of uniformity between different national laws. See, e.g., Bortolotti (ed.), *The ICC Model Agency Contract: A Commentary* (1993).

B. Articles

Berman, "Excuse for Non Performance in the Light of Contract Practices in International Trade" (1963), 3 *Colum. L Rev.* 1413.

Berman and Kaufman, "The Law of International Commercial Transactions (Lex Mercatoria)" (1978), 19 *Harv. Int'l. LJ* 221.

Bonnell, "Unification of Law by Non-Legislative Means: The UNIDROIT Draft Principles for International Commercial Contracts" (1992), 40 *Am. J Comp. L* 617.

Caproni, "The Exporting Process: Some Considerations for Practitioners" (1978), 8 *Ga. J Int'l. & Comp. L* 408.

Honnold, "The 1964 Hague Conventions and Uniform Laws on the International Sale of Goods" (1964), 13 *Am. J Comp. L* 451.

Juenger, "The Inter-American Convention on the Law Applicable to International Contracts: Some Highlights and Comparisons" (1994), 42 *Am. J Comp. L* 381.

Lavers, "The CISG: To Use or Not To Use?" (1993), 21:1 *Int. Bus. Lawyer 10.*

Reczei, "The Area of Operation of the International Sales Conventions" (1981), 29 *Am. J Comp. L* 513.

Rinze, "The Scope of Party Autonomy Under the 1980 Rome Convention on the Law Applicable to Contractual Obligations" (1994), *JBL* 412.

Schlechtreim, "From the Hague to Vienna: Progress in the Unification of International Sales Contracts?" in Horn and Schmitthoff (eds.), *The Transnational Law of International Commercial Transactions* (1982), 125.

Schmitthoff, "The Unification or Harmonisation of Law by Means of Standard Contracts and General Conditions" (1968), 17 *Int'l. & Comp. LQ* 551.

Strenger, "La notion de *Lex Mercatoria* en Droit de Commerce International" (1991), 227 *Receuil des Cours* 209.

Uniform International Sale of Goods Act, 1985 Uniform Law Conference of Canada, 172.

Winship, "Working in Canada with the UN Convention for the International Sale of Goods" (1994).

Winship, "Bibliography of Commentaries on the United Nations Sales Convention" (1987), 21 *Int. Lawyer* 585, supplements in (1988), 22 *Int. Lawyer* 605 and (1990), *Int. Lawyer* 307.

Winship, "The Convention on the Limitation Period in the International Sale of Goods: The United States Adopts UNCITRAL's Firstborn" (1994), 28 *Int. Lawyer* 1071.

Ziegel, "Canada and the Vienna Sales Convention" (1987), 12 *Can. Bus. LJ* 366.

Ziegel, "Canada Prepares to Adopt the International Sales Convention" (1991), 18 *Can. Bus. LJ* 1.

CHAPTER SIX

Agreements for the Transfer of Technology

I. INTRODUCTION

Today, business enterprises are increasingly research-oriented and the most advanced countries tend to develop and export technological know-how, follow-up services, and a variety of other intangible products in which the principal ingredient is intellectual property.

A business enterprise considering operations in overseas markets can choose from a number of operational strategies, ranging from the formation of a wholly owned foreign subsidiary to the conclusion of a contractual arrangement with an existing foreign firm, depending upon the type of marketing and manufacturing envisaged and also on how much capital the firm wishes to invest in ownership of foreign operations. Many of these strategies involve agreements for the transfer of the enterprise's technology, whatever the legal nature of this technology. These agreements cover many aspects of technology and take many forms.

II. SUBJECT MATTER

An agreement for the transfer of technology deals with the transmission of knowledge with or without the concurrent transfer of goods and services. Such knowledge may or may not be subject to legal protection.

Technology as a form of knowledge involves intangible property rights. Its subject matter is varied. For instance, it includes technology as a form of hardware and software, databases, methodologies, concepts, formulas, models, and designs involving or using suck knowledge, or it relates to a particular stage of development by the supplier of a scientific discovery. It may also relate to the particular stage of the technology that the recipient needs for its project. It is concerned with information of scientific or commercial value and is designed to change the recipient's operations in order to improve its products, increase the volume of production, lower costs and, more generally, advance its interests.

In general, the transfer of technology covers categories of intellectual property rights protected to various degrees, such as know-how, show-how, trade secrets, patents, trade-marks, copyright, and industrial designs.

A. Know-How

Know-how is the knowledge and experience that is generally the subject-matter of show-how. It may be common knowledge that is not confidential, not secret, and not patentable, or a secret manner or process of using common knowledge. Secret know-how may be patentable technology. In practice, it is protected as a trade secret or by strict corporate security and confidentiality. Proprietary know-how, such as trade secrets and secret processes, may be assigned. It cannot technically be licensed because the knowledge, being unknown, cannot be infringed. In a typical agreement for the transfer of technology, the supplier agrees to provide the recipient with the know-how for designing, manufacturing, applying, testing, maintaining, and repairing the product including associated patents, trade-marks, or copyrights that is the subject matter of the agreement.

B. Show-How

Show-how refers to the supply of instruction, teaching, and supervision services that assist (1) in the use of common knowledge readily available to the public (that is, knowledge that is not secret, not confidential, and not patentable) but not easily usable without special assistance, or (2) in the transfer of confidential information that is not common knowledge, such as trade secrets, or (3) in the use of a patent or other statutory rights. It often forms an integral part of a know-how or patent transfer. Show-how is not a statutory proprietary right. It can only be protected by contractual provisions or by rights arising from the special relationship between the parties. In a typical agreement for the transfer of technology, the supplier agrees to train the recipient's personnel to become familiar with the know-how associated with the product that is the subject matter of the agreement and to provide ongoing technical expertise, management, advice, and assistance, if required.

C. Trade Secrets

"A trade secret may consist of any formula, pattern, device or compilation of information which is used in one's business, and which gives him an opportunity to obtain an advantage over competitors who do not know or use it."[1]

The common law of Canada protects trade secrets against improper acquisition or disclosure provided the formula, pattern, device, or compilation of information possesses

---

1 *Restatement of the Law of Torts* (1939), s. 757, comment b (US).

a quality of secrecy, has been communicated to the recipient in circumstances giving rise to a duty of confidence (for example, contractual relationship between the owner of the trade secret and the recipient or, in the absence of a contract, where there exists a relationship of trust and confidence between the parties), and proof is made of an unauthorized use or disclosure of the information to the detriment of the owner of the trade secret. Trade secrets are not protected against independent discovery by third parties by legitimate means. Thus, the law of trade secrets gives them limited legal protection. As noted above, show-how and know-how may fall into the category of trade secrets.

Some trade secrets may be patentable but there is the danger that the disclosure requirement for a patent, where there is a subsequent decision of invalidity will result in the loss of the quality of secrecy. A trade secret that has become the subject of an issued patent loses its trade secret status to the extent of the specifications in the patent. Since trade secrets are proprietary rights, they may be sold and assigned or licensed.

D. Patents

Where technology is patented, the holder of the patent has the right to prevent or exclude others from making, using, and selling the invention involving such technology in the territory of the country where the patent is granted for a definite period of time. In order to obtain a patent, the applicant must disclose the underlying technology by illustrating and describing the physical embodiments of the invention. It is not necessary to disclose technical or engineering details that continue to be protected as trade secrets or know-how. Patents may be sold and assigned or licensed.

E. Trade-Marks and Service Marks

A trade-mark distinguishes the products or services of one business from another. It protects the brand image of products and services and is a symbol of the origin and quality of such products or services. A trade-mark may be a design, a word, or a combination of both.

Trade-marks are protected by law. They give the owner the right to exclude others from the use of the same trade-mark for the same products or services, or of marks that will create confusion with protected trade-marks. Trade-marks are granted for a limited period of time, but that period may be extended by renewal. Trade-marks may be sold and assigned or licensed. Generally, the licensing of a trade-mark is not directly concerned with the transfer of technology. However, on occasion, the supplier of technology may structure such transfer as part of the licence of a trade-mark.

F. Copyright and Industrial Design

Copyright—which prevents the copying of original artistic, dramatic, musical, or literary works, but not ideas, information, or data—and industrial design rights—which protect ornamental or aesthetic designs for articles of commerce, but not functional designs—are not the main object of a transfer of technology agreement.

G. Integrated Circuit Topography

Integrated circuit topographies may be the object of an agreement for the transfer of technology. Thus, section 7(2) of the Integrated Circuit Topography Act[2] states:

> (2) A topography, whether registered or unregistered and either as to the whole interest therein or as to any portion thereof, may constitute the subject-matter of a licence.

III. TYPES OF SUPPLIER OF TECHNOLOGY

Most types of supplier of technology are product manufacturers who provide not only the machinery and information but also the training and consulting services as part of their continuing support.

Other suppliers are technology licensors who only license the technology without any other services, technical assistance suppliers who provide skilled technicians and other personnel, and consultants who help to implement technology on a short-term basis.

IV. TRANSFER OF TECHNOLOGY TO DEVELOPING COUNTRIES

A. General

The nature and scope of the legal problems that arise in transfers of technology to developing countries depend in large part on the form or methods adopted to transfer such technology and the economic and legal systems prevailing in recipient countries, which differ widely. Although some countries still adhere to a centralized economy, the majority have a mixed economy where the government or a government-owned entity may be the recipient or joint venture partner, or where a governmental licence or approval is required. Others are free enterprise countries, where the government is involved only if its guarantees or concessions are desired.

Developing countries are almost entirely buyers and only very rarely sellers of technology. They are far more dependent on external sources of new technical knowledge than developed countries. Thus, from a policy point of view, developing countries believe that science, technology, and knowledge are part of the common heritage of humankind and must be made available to all with as few restrictions as possible. They also want to generate their own technology or at least adapt the technology available on a commercial basis after a serious selection process. Since transnational corporations dominate technology, developing countries are of the opinion that the government must intervene to set equitable rules for the transfer of such technology. On the other hand, developed countries feel that the transfer of technology should be made through the private sector and that the government should only intervene in cases of abuse. Since high value must be attached to the entrepreneurial spirit, cooperation should be based on expectations of mutual benefit, especially because knowledge and technological advancement are perceived by developed countries as the result of investment in research and development that, as such, must be protected and well remunerated.

---

2 SC 1990, c. 37, as am.

In a market economy, new technology would not be produced if its actual price were zero—that is, if the innovator or inventor had to make it instantly available to all for free. Innovations are made because they will generate profits in the future. If the innovator or inventor lets a competitor use the innovations, the price charged includes the future profits that are forgone by allowing an imitation on the market. A licensing agreement is a good example of this approach.

In practice, companies in developing countries, as elsewhere, buy technology directly through commercial agreements from developed country companies that use the processes in their own production, and indirectly, by the technology embodied in the products of machinery makers, engineering design firms, and the like.

Companies acquiring technology in developing countries frequently face serious obstacles in their commercial dealings with technology suppliers in developed countries. They arise in part from the imperfections of the market for technology, the scarcity of financial resources, high cost of technology, difficulties in arriving at a fair price, inadequate legal framework for technology transfer transactions, and the relative lack of experience and skill of companies in developing countries in conducting legal arrangements for the acquisition of technology. The attitudes of governments in both developed and developing countries may also impair the transfer of technology. The generally accepted rule is that all agreements for the transfer of technology from one country to another must be examined and submitted for the approval of the competent authority of the recipient country that must appraise the effective contribution of the goods incorporating the technology.

B. International Code of Conduct on the Transfer of Technology

The importance of technology transfers to developing countries has received increased attention since May 1972, when the third UN Conference on Trade and Development (UNCTAD) in Santiago, Chile called for a study of "possible bases for new international legislation" in the area.[3] Since then, under the UNCTAD auspices, much work has been done on the preparation of an international code of conduct on the transfer of technology.

A major issue to be resolved is whether the code should be a legally binding instrument, as the developing countries would prefer, or a non-binding set of guidelines, as the developed countries advocate. A further significant point of disagreement is the coverage of the code—whether it should apply to transfers of technology within a country between a branch of a foreign enterprise and a local firm, as argued by the developing countries, or whether transfers within national boundaries should be regulated by national legislation, rather than an international code, as argued by the developed countries.

Developing countries are concerned to receive maximum access to current technology with minimum restrictions on its use by their domestic enterprises. They are particularly wary of provisions such as grant-backs of improvements or tied procurement clauses that perpetuate their dependence on the developed world. Developed countries tend to emphasize the role of industrial property rights as an encouragement to invention and technological innovation. They warn that if owners of patents, trade-marks, and

3 Resolution 39 (III), UN doc. TD/180, vol. I, at 108.

know-how do not receive an equitable return for transferring their technologies to developing countries, the flow of knowledge may be substantially reduced and the developing countries' dependence accentuated.

The draft code, as at the close of the 6th session of the conference on June 5, 1985,[4] lists a number of provisions considered objectionable in technology transfer agreements, including grant-backs of improvements, resale price-fixing, export restrictions, tied procurement clauses, local research restrictions, restrictions on the use of local personnel, clauses prohibiting the acquiring party from challenging the validity of a patent, clauses prohibiting the use of competing technologies, and obligations or restrictions that continue after the expiration of the particular industrial property right. During the negotiation of a technology transfer agreement, both parties are to observe certain "fair and honest business practices," which include disclosure by the acquiring party of relevant legislation and official local economic and social development objectives, and disclosure by the supplying party of any known attacks on the validity of its industrial property right, as well as any serious health, safety, and environmental risks associated with the technology. The agreement, when negotiated, is to contain certain guarantees from each side, including appropriate guarantees of confidentiality and quality control on the part of the acquiring party, as well as warranties of validity of the industrial property right, of accurate description of the technology, and of suitability for production of the agreed goods and services on the part of the supplying party.

Since 1985, a number of governments have reiterated the importance they attach to the adoption of an international code of conduct on the transfer of technology. However, the developed market-economy countries have been of the view that the time was not opportune for completing the negotiations on such a code. The secretary general of the UNCTAD still pursues bringing the on-going consultations to a successful end. The Restrictive Business Practices Code adopted by the UN General Assembly on December 5, 1980 covers the antitrust aspects of agreements for the transfer of technology.[5]

V. CHOOSING A PARTICULAR METHOD OF TRANSFER

A. Concerns of the Supplier of the Technology

Many concerns play an important role in the supplier's decision to use one method rather than another to transfer technology. Some of these concerns relate to the laws in force in the markets where the technology is to be acquired and used (for example, licensing restrictions, restrictions on equity or local assets ownership by aliens, local government standards for the technology, tariff duties, customs laws and regulations, antitrust laws, tax liability laws, patent, trade-mark, copyright and industrial design protection, and risk of loss by expropriation or confiscation). Other concerns relate to marketing; for example, what is the supplier's position in the market for the product of the technology with respect to a particular use of this product or the territory where it will be sold? Are there any competitors? Will there be changes in the market structure

4 Draft International Code of Conduct on the Transfer of Technology (TD/Code TOT/47, 20 June 1985).

5 UN doc. TD/RBP/Conf./10, section (D)(3)(1980).

and in the owner's position in that market for the product in the near future? What type of distribution for the product is the best in that market? Will the supplier have full control over management, use of technology, quality control, and flow of products? Will the supplier retain the local market and receive all the profits? From the point of view of the technology itself, the supplier may be concerned about the stage of development that its technology has reached, the availability of an educated and trained local labour force, whether it is unionized, the availability of local raw materials and manufactured components, the need for capital and its local availability, whether a credible and responsible local recipient can be found, whether the technology and the product are culturally and socially acceptable in the country of intended use, how long it will take to implement the technology, whether substantial disclosure of technology will take place, and so on.

B. Concerns of the Governments Whose Nationals are the Suppliers or Recipients of Technology

Governments, particularly those of developing countries, are generally most interested in the transfer of technology. The concerns of governments whose nationals are supplying technology usually relate to the potential loss of employment opportunities, security matters and the control of what is transferred, the conditions of the transfer, and the loss of its nationals' competitive advantage in the foreign markets.

As mentioned above, the governments of recipient countries would like to receive maximum access to the latest technology with few restrictions on its use by their nationals at a minimum cost, since large payments could have an adverse effect on their currency. They are concerned with the social cost of the technology, the severity of the owner's restrictions inserted in the transfer agreement, and the loss of local research and development. Other concerns are whether economic value is received and whether the transfer of technology is in conformity with national objectives. Local legislation often reflects these concerns by providing for the control of transfers of technology, which may take the form of government participation in the negotiations of the agreement for the transfer of technology or subsequent review and registration.

VI. METHODS FOR THE TRANSFER OF TECHNOLOGY

A. General

Several methods can be used to transfer technology. The transfer may be minimal where the owner of the technology manufactures and sells the product that uses such technology, or quite extensive where the owner of the technology assigns it to the recipient.

Some of the major legal problems that arise in connection with the transfer of technology are the effective protection of the technology proposed to be transferred, its adequate remuneration, and the effective use of the technology from the point of view of both the supplier and the recipient.

B. Selecting the Parties

Ideally, a transfer of technology should involve parties of similar size who are complementary and willing to cooperate to achieve common economic objectives. There should be no direct competition between them or affiliated organizations. Each party should investigate the other thoroughly before entering into negotiations for the transfer of technology. For instance, the supplier should determine whether the intended recipient has the ability to use the technology, an adequate sales organization and market share, as well as a good reputation. The recipient should ascertain the inherent value of the technology, the reputation of the supplier, its technology and products, the availability of support from the supplier, and whether past transfers of technology by the supplier have been successful and have not resulted in litigation.

C. Planning for the Transfer of Technology

At the outset, it is important that both the technology supplier and the recipient develop a plan for the transfer in which the management quantifies their respective contribution and determines the methods to be followed.

An objective to sell technology is easy to achieve since it implies a type of transaction that can be fully completed, whereas a transfer of technology by way of licence or joint venture is more complicated and durable. Generally, the supplier of technology desires to maximize the immediate earning capacity of the technology by having it applied subject to a set of controls to protect its future earning capacity. On the other hand, the recipient wishes to use the technology subject to a minimum of restrictive conditions in order to obtain a satisfactory return on the investment.

When assessing the method to be used, it is necessary to consider the degree of interaction and cooperation that may be required between the technology supplier and the recipient as well as the degree of control that the supplier and the recipient wish to have over the use of the technology.

D. Some Specific Methods

1. Sale of Product

When the owner of the technology manufactures at home or abroad (through a branch plant, subsidiary or affiliate, or through an independent foreign contractor), a product that makes use of such technology and sells or distributes it directly through its own organization or indirectly through independent distributors or representatives, the transfer of technology is minimal, since the owner of the technology has full control over such technology and retains it except to the extent to which the independent foreign contractor gains access to it.

The owner of the technology retains the local market and has access to all the benefits but assumes all the risks.

2. Franchising

In the case of franchising, the proprietary rights are rented, as in licensing except that patent rights are rarely involved. The franchisor maintains greater control over the day-to-day operations of the franchisee's business.

3. Assignment of Technology

In some situations, for instance, where licensing is not permitted, the owner of the technology will transfer, by assignment to the recipient, the full legal ownership or an undivided ownership interest in all or part of that technology without limitation. In such a case, the assignor does not retain a legal interest to the assigned technology rights.

4. Turnkey Project

In a turnkey project, the owner of the technology provides for the recipient the initial planning, design and start-up operations of the project in the foreign market. The owner of the technology has full control over the technology until the project is operative in that market and the recipient takes over. However, substantial disclosure of technology takes place especially when the agreement setting up the project provides for long-term technical assistance. It also means loss of the local market and a heavy initial financial involvement by the owner of the technology.

5. Joint Venture

A decision to transfer technology by way of a joint venture presupposes that the parties have a common goal that can only be achieved by joining forces and that each potential partner has a valuable contribution to make in achieving this goal. Some of the reasons for entering into a joint venture are as follows:

- —An opportunity to apply a piece of technology in combination with another piece of technology available from the other party.
- —The integration of technical personnel from different companies to achieve a certain mix of complementary skills which are required for a specific goal.
- —An opportunity for penetration of a market with which one party has no familiarity.
- —An opportunity to draw on financial resources not otherwise available.
- —An association with a company in a specific geographical area because local culture dictates a local association.
- —An association among suppliers because the client wants it.
- —An association because the government wants it. This is often the case with developing countries.

Joint ventures may be unincorporated or incorporated. A joint venture is unincorporated when the supplier of the technology and the recipient only wish to establish an association for a particular purpose. The recipient demands full and direct access to each of the parties that undertakes joint and several liability for the contract performance. Each of the joint venturers makes its contribution separately without the need for integration among them to produce the goal of the joint venture. An example of this type of joint venture is an engineering construction consortium. The unincorporated joint venture is set up by the engineering company and the construction company to execute a specific turnkey project.

A joint venture may be incorporated as a limited liability company. This is particularly recommended when one party provides the technology and the other the capital or when the joint venturers are from different countries.

Some of the advantages of a joint venture whether or not it is incorporated are as follows:

- The investment by the co-venturers limits the risks.
- The supplier of the technology retains the local market without establishing competitors.
- The supplier has good control over the use of the technology and the products.
- A synergetic effect is possible.
- The local environment is more accessible to the supplier if the location of operations is in the country of one of the co-venturers.
- Local governments are generally more favourable to joint ventures.

However, there are also some disadvantages to using a joint venture:

- It generally requires substantial disclosure of the technology.
- Often some direct financial involvement is needed.
- Conflicts over managerial control and direction may occur.
- The unbundling of technology is difficult where the supplier is a co-venturer.
- There is always the risk of loss by expropriation or confiscation.
- Profits have to be divided in some defined proportion.

The legal effects of incorporating or not incorporating a joint venture depend upon the relevant applicable law, which should be expressly selected in the joint venture agreement.

6. *Licensing*

a. General

In principle, a licence is a consent whereby the owner of a right grants permission to another to invade that right free from legal recourse. It does not grant a right to use, only a waiver. In other words, a licence, as such, transfers no property in the technology. This definition seems to indicate that only technology protected by statute, for example, a patent, can be licensed. In practice, this is not the case since know-how or trade secrets that are not protected by statute may be the subject matter of a licence. Joint ventures and turnkey projects often involve one or more licensing agreements or clauses.

A licence is a satisfactory tool when each party has its own objectives that can be achieved without a continuous and direct dependence on the other party on a day-to-day basis.

In a licensing agreement, the licensee will usually pay royalties for the use of the technology based on sales or production. There will be an obligation of confidentiality on the licensee and there may be a requirement to maintain certain quality control standards. As part of the transfer of the technology, the licensor often undertakes to train the personnel of the licensee, either on site in the licensee's operations or through a posting at the licensor's head operations. Clauses concerning export and resale restrictions are common to prevent the licensee competing in the licensor's own markets. For reasons of market power and quality control, the licensor may want a "tied procurement" clause, making it the sole source of supply for the licensee. Under patent and know-how agreements, the licensor will be particularly interested in having a grant-back clause under which it receives any improvements in the technology made by the licensee. The licensor may also want a "non-attack" clause to prohibit the licensee from contesting the validity of the patents should a dispute arise.

A licensing agreement needs some flexibility in its provisions, because, generally, it is intended to last for a period of several years. On termination of the agreement, the licensee loses its rights to use the patents and trade-marks of the licensor, but retains the benefits of technological knowledge and trained personnel. Depending on the circumstances, the licensor may want to restrict competition from the licensee past the termination of the licensed use.

A licensing agreement is almost always in writing and may contain an express choice of law clause. The frequency of inclusion of an arbitration clause in a licensing agreement is greater than the frequency of inclusion of an express choice of law clause. Resort to an arbitration clause may well reflect uncertainty concerning the appropriate law or laws to be chosen as applicable, and concerning the effectiveness of an express clause designating the applicable law.[6] The concentration of patent rights, as well as accumulated know-how, in the hands of large, sometimes transnational industrial enterprises has contributed broadly to the practice of designating the law of the licensor's place of business. However, recent legal writings and developments in international organizations tend toward an increasing insistence on the law of the licensee's place of business as the applicable law. Some countries have supported the adoption of a mandatorily applicable code governing the transfer of technology to be part of the national laws of countries customarily receiving, rather than providing, technological information. The effect would be to restrict the autonomy of the parties in choosing the law applicable to their agreement, making the agreement void or unenforceable (either directly or through refusal of registration) if it designates a law other than that of the country where the technology is to be used, as being applicable. This approach requires that an agreement involving the use of a technology in several countries must be submitted, with regard to its validity and interpretation as well as to its performance, separately to the laws of each of these countries.

It should be noted that before a licensing agreement is made, the potential licensee will want to study the technology offered by its owner. This requires the licensor to disclose, at least in part, that which is the subject matter of the licence, including secret know-how and other confidential material. In such a case, the licensor may prepare two documents: the option itself, which consists of the draft licensing agreement ready for acceptance, although minor additions may be left to further negotiations, and an option agreement that stipulates the details governing the option, its duration, form of acceptance, confidentiality in case the option should not be accepted, the obligations of the optionee to return all drawings, etc., and a provision restraining the optionee from making use of what has been learned. A separate price may be agreed upon for the

---

6 See Draft International Code of Conduct for the Transfer of Technology as of 5 June 1985, UN doc. TD/Code TOT/47, c. 9. The 1994 WTO Agreement on Trade-Related Aspects of Intellectual Property Rights (TRIPS) does not contain choice of law provisions.

option, often called disclosure payment, which will be deducted from the royalties when the option results in an agreement on the licence. The option and option agreement may also be accompanied by a secrecy agreement that covers exclusively the know-how and other pertinent confidential material disclosed to the potential licensee.

Industrial property legislation often differs from jurisdiction to jurisdiction and drafters of international licensing agreements should be careful to comply with all relevant laws and regulations. Requirements for maintaining an industrial property right in a particular jurisdiction vary widely, from use and production obligations to an obligation to pay an annual fee. Since the licensing of industrial property rights can constitute a form of market domination, many countries regulate licensing through their competition laws. Since the technologies covered by industrial property rights can be significant to a country's industrial strategy, some countries regulate the terms under which such technologies can be licensed to operations in their territories. In international licensing, as in other areas of international business law, comprehensive foreign legal advice is essential.

Licensing usually brings in a lesser return to the licensor than does manufacturing and selling directly the product of the technology. It establishes a potential competitor and results in a loss of markets. The licensor also has minimal involvement in direct management of the licensee's quality control and marketing. However, licensing provides many benefits to the supplier of the technology. For instance, it enables the supplier to obtain the benefit of the licensee's marketing strength; it relieves the supplier from the need to provide capital for further development or for building a local plant; and it gives the supplier an immediate financial return on its research and development. The supplier may also receive in return other technology by grant back from the licensee relating to its existing or future technology. Finally, licensing also eliminates the possibility of the supplier becoming subject to local government acquisition.

b. Checklist of Issues To Be Covered in a Licensing Agreement[7]

A. Introductory Aspects

B. Preamble: Whereas Clauses; Recitals

C. Definitions of Key Words and Expressions

D. Scope of the Licence or Agreement
   1. Identification and Description of the Basic Technology
   2. Scope of the Licence or Agreement in General
   3. Field of Use or Activity
   4. Specification of the Territory of Manufacture and of Sale
   5. Exclusivity and Non-Exclusivity of the Territory
   6. Acquisition or Use of Competing Technology

E. Special Aspects Concerning Patents
   1. Refusal or Invalidation of the Patent
   2. Maintenance in Force of the Patent
   3. Working of the Patented Invention

7 This checklist is taken from *Licensing Guide for Developing Countries* (1977), at 8 to 11.

F. Technological Advances: Improvements and Developments within the Scope of the Licence or Agreement
   1. In General
   2. The Concept of a Technological Advance and the Definition of Improvement and Development
   3. Factors in, and Terms and Conditions of, the Availability of Improvements and Developments
   4. New Technology
   5. Research and Development

G. Know-How; Technical Information
   1. Disclosure of Information and Expertise as a Requirement of Patentability or of Industrial Design Protection: Supply of Technical Information under the Industrial Property Licence or the Technology Transfer Agreement
   2. Legal Means for Preventing Communication, Disclosure, or Use of Valuable Information and Expertise
   3. Disclosure of Know-How
   4. Guarantee of Know-How

H. Technical Services and Assistance
   1. In General
   2. Training
   3. Design and Engineering Services
   4. Technological Services
   5. Marketing and Commercial Services
   6. Management Services
   7. Planning, Research and Development Services

I. The Supply of Capital Goods, Intermediate Goods, Spare Parts, Components, or Raw Materials
   1. Technology Suppliers as a Source of Supply of Capital Goods
   2. Machinery Suppliers and Plant Constructors as a Source of Technology
   3. Link between the Technology To Be Supplied and Particular Capital Goods, Intermediate Goods, Spare Parts, Components, or Raw Materials
   4. Supply of Items at Competitive Prices
   5. Exclusion of Items from Definition of Net Selling Price
   6. Provision of Drawings, Designs or Specifications
   7. Legal Effect of Provisions Allowing or Requiring the Licensee or Technology Recipient to Acquire Items of a Specified Origin or from a Specified Source

J. The Production Phase
   1. In General
   2. Sub-Contracting
   3. Standard of Quality of the Product
   4. Quality Controls
   5. Need to Impart Know-How as to the Quality of the Product
   6. Volume of Production

K. Special Aspects Concerning Trade-Marks
   1. In General
   2. Problems Similar to Those Arising in Connection with Patents
   3. Devices for Conferring Rights to Use the Trade-Mark
   4. Form and Method of Use of the Trade-Mark
   5. Associated and Combined Trade-Marks
   6. Use of Foreign Trade-Marks
   7. Quality Control

L. Other Aspects Concerning the Marketing Phase
   1. Patent Marking and Indications of Manufacture under a Licence
   2. Product Labelling and Promotional Activities
   3. Distribution Channels
   4. Price and Other Resale Terms
   5. Import of the Product Manufactured Abroad by the Licensor or Technology Supplier or by Third Persons

M. Management Services

N. Compensation; Consideration; Price; Remuneration; Royalties; Fees
   1. In General
   2. Concepts and Terminology
   3. Direct Monetary Compensation: Lump-Sum Payment; Royalties; Fees
      a. Lump-Sum Payment
      b. Royalties
         (1) Production
         (2) Sales
            (a) Gross Selling Price
            (b) Net Selling Price
            (c) Fair Market Price
            (d) Time of Sale and Remittance
         (3) Profits
         (4) Minimum Royalties
         (5) Decreasing Royalties
         (6) Maximum Royalties
         (7) Choice of the Basis for Calculating Royalties
      c. Lump-Sum Payment Compared with Royalties
      d. Lump-Sum Payment and Royalties Combined
      e. Payment of Royalties "Free of Tax" or "Net of Taxes"
      f. Fees for Technical Services and Assistance
         (1) Fees for Technical Services and Assistance Related to the Patent or Trade-Mark Licence or to the Technical Know-How Agreement
            (a) In General
            (b) Cost of Training
            (c) Technical Experts Provided by the Licensor or Technology Supplier
            (d) Technical Services Concerning Capital Goods Needed in the Industrial Plant of the Licensee or Technology Recipient

(2) Fees for Management, Planning, Research and Development Services

4. Indirect and Non-Monetary Compensation or Expense
    a. Income from Related Operations
    b. Dividends and Value Increase and Financial Participation, Capitalization of the Lump-Sum Payment or the Royalties
    c. Cost Shifting or Sharing Measures
    d. Feed-Back of Technical Information: Rights in Technology Advances
    e. Acquisition of Market Data
    f. Cost Reductions and Savings to the Licensee or Technology Recipient
5. Maximum Amount of the Price or Cost of the Industrial Property Rights or the Technology
6. Separate Pricing of the Different Elements of the Technology

O. Settlement of Payment
1. Reporting
2. Maintenance, Inspection, and Review of Records
3. Designation of the Currency of the Obligation and of Payment
    a. Currency of the Obligation
    b. Currency of Payment
    c. Rate of Exchange
4. Foreign Exchange Controls
5. Designation of Instrumentalities for Remittance and Receipt of Payment
6. Effect of New or Changed Laws on Payment
7. Taxation

P. Most-Favourable Terms and Conditions
1. In General
2. Application of Laws against Unfair Competition or Controlling Restrictive Business Practices
3. Scope and Application of the Most-Favourable Terms and Conditions Provision
4. Merits of a Most-Favourable Terms and Conditions Provision

Q. Rights of Related Enterprises; Transfer and Assignment; Sub-Licensing; Sub-Contracting
1. Mutuality of Interests and Consent to Relations with Third Persons
2. Assignment of Rights and Delegation of Duties by the Licensor or Technology Supplier
3. Sub-Licensing by the Licensee or Technology Recipient
4. Sub-Contracting by the Licensee or Technology Recipient
5. Types of Provisions in the Licence or Agreement

R. Injury or Damage to Third Persons or Their Property; Insurance
1. Injury to Third Persons or Damage to Their Property
2. Insurance

S. Default; Changed Conditions or Events; Waiver; Remedies
1. Agreed Remedial Measures for Specified Types of Defaults

W. Modification or Amendment

X. Notices

Y. Execution
   1. Contents of the Execution Clause
   2. Location of the Execution Clause in the Licence or Agreement
   3. Principal Problems in Execution
      a. Authority to Sign
      b. Date of Signature and Effective Date of the Licence or Agreement

Z. Appendices, Annexes, Schedules

VII. COMMON ELEMENTS OF AGREEMENTS FOR THE TRANSFER OF TECHNOLOGY

Agreements for the transfer of technology are rarely standardized since they are drafted to reflect various possible combinations of know-how, show-how, and statutory rights limited only by the parties' experience and bargaining strength. Policies developed by some companies, as reflected in standard provisions or in form agreements, are only used as a basis for negotiations.

Regardless of the type of agreement for the transfer of technology used by the parties, such agreement must cover the following areas: (1) the rights to the technology generally available to the recipient and to the owner-supplier. These rights can be bundled or unbundled and transferred or shared on a separate basis; (2) the qualifications, limitations, and restrictions placed on these rights (for example, territory, time period, and exclusive basis); (3) the obligations assumed by the owner-supplier (for example, technical documentation, consulting services, warranties and representations, and monitoring and prosecuting infringements by third parties of the granted rights); (4) the obligations assumed by the recipient (for example, the obligation to exploit commercially the rights, the extent of reporting to the owner, and secrecy and non-disclosure arrangements for know-how and show-how); (5) the termination of the rights; (6) compensation that varies depending upon the type of technology and the structure of the agreement (for example, a lump-sum paid either up front on the initial transfer of the technology or in installments); costs and fees for information, technical assistance, and other professional services, including management or consulting fees; royalties for the use of intangible property or rights based on the number of units produced or sold, or on the value of such units; rentals for the use of tangible property such as industrial, commercial, or scientific equipment; ongoing or lump-sum payments for updates of technology or improvements; and (7) exclusion and disclaimer of liability provisions by the owner of the technology.

Where the supplier and the recipient reside or carry on business in different countries, it is advisable to include clauses dealing with the currency of payment, the formula for calculating the rate of exchange, the law applicable to the agreement, and the court or arbitration institution that will have exclusive jurisdiction to hear disputes should they arise.

VIII. CANADIAN LEGISLATION

A. Federal Laws

A number of federal laws are applicable to a transfer of technology governed by Canadian law.

1. Patent Act

The Patent Act provides for the assignment of a patent issued for an invention.[8] It also provides that the attorney general of Canada or any interested person may, at any time after the expiration of three years from the date of the grant of a patent, apply to the commissioner of patents alleging, in the case of that patent, that there has been an abuse of the exclusive rights thereunder, and asking for relief. The exclusive rights under a patent are deemed to have been abused in any of the following circumstances:[9]

> 65.(2)(c) if the demand for the patented article in Canada is not being met to an adequate extent and on reasonable terms;
>
> (d) if, by reason of the refusal of the patentee to grant a licence or licences on reasonable terms, the trade or industry of Canada or the trade of any person or class of persons trading in Canada, or the establishment of any new trade or industry in Canada, is prejudiced, and it is in the public interest that a licence or licences should be granted;
>
> (e) if any trade or industry in Canada, or any person or class of persons engaged therein, is unfairly prejudiced by the conditions attached by the patentee, whether before or after the passing of this Act, to the purchase, hire, licence or use of the patented article or to the using or working of the patented process; or
>
> (f) if it is shown that the existence of the patent, being a patent for an invention relating to a process involving the use of materials not protected by the patent or for an invention relating to a substance produced by such a process, has been utilized by the patentee so as unfairly to prejudice in Canada the manufacture, use or sale of any materials …

If a case of abuse of the exclusive rights under a patent has been established, the commissioner may exercise any of the following powers as he or she may deem expedient in the circumstances:[10]

> 66.(1)(a) he may order the grant to the applicant of a licence on such terms as the Commissioner may think expedient, including a term precluding the licensee from importing into Canada any goods the importation of which, if made by persons other than the patentee or persons claiming under him, would be an infringement of the patent, and in that case the patentee and all licensees for the time being shall be deemed to have mutually covenanted against that importation;
>
> (c) if the Commissioner is satisfied that the exclusive rights have been abused in the circumstances specified in paragraph 65(2)(f), he may order the grant of licences to the applicant and to such of his customers, and containing such terms, as the Commissioner may think expedient;

---

8 RSC 1985, c. P-4, as am., s. 50.

9 *Ibid.*, s. 65.

10 *Ibid.*, s. 66.

(d) if the Commissioner is satisfied that the objects of this section and section 65 cannot be attained by the exercise of any of the foregoing powers, the Commissioner shall order the patent to be revoked, either forthwith or after such reasonable interval as may be specified in the order, unless in the meantime such conditions as may be specified in the order with a view to attaining the objects of this section and section 65 are fulfilled, and the Commissioner may, on reasonable cause shown in any case, by subsequent order extend the interval so specified, but the Commissioner shall not make an order for revocation which is at variance with any treaty, convention, arrangement, or engagement with any other country to which Canada is a party; or

(e) if the Commissioner is of opinion that the objects of this section and section 65 will be best attained by not making an order under the provisions of this section, he may make an order refusing the application and dispose of any question as to costs thereon as he thinks just.

2. Trade-marks Act, Industrial Design Act, Integrated Circuit Topography Act, and Copyright Act

These statutes deal with registration,[11] assignments,[12] and transfer of these intellectual property rights,[13] and therefore may be applicable to agreements for the transfer of technology.

3. Competition Act and Restrictive Business Practices[14]

Both the Patent Act and the Competition Act have a common objective—to encourage innovation. The Patent Act seeks to encourage innovation by rewarding inventors with the exclusive use of their inventions and the Competition Act seeks to encourage innovation by preventing artificial restrictions of competition. The Patent Act contains provisions designed to prevent some abuses of the monopoly rights conferred, for example, by requiring the timely working of the patents. These provisions are designed to avoid the conflict that could develop between the Patent Act and the Competition Act since, under the former, a limited monopoly is granted to the patentee and, under the latter, abuse of dominant position and other exclusionary practices are prohibited. The Competition Act is primarily concerned with restrictive business practices arising from licensing agreements. The patentee must not expand his or her monopoly beyond its legal boundaries and thus illegally restrain competition. For example, cross-licensing agreements and pooling arrangements of competing inventions, under certain circumstances, may lead to a reduction of the flow of inventions and create, in the international field, non-tariff barriers, especially where patent power is concentrated in the hands of a small number of enterprises. Outright sales or assignments of patents are unlikely to violate the Competition Act. Violations of the Competition Act occur when the licensor of a patent seeks to restrain the activities of the licensee in order to obtain an optimum return

11 E.g., Trade-marks Act, RSC 1985, c. T-13, as am., s. 50 (registered users).

12 E.g., Industrial Design Act, RSC 1985, c. I-9, as am., s. 13 and Copyright Act, RSC 1985, c. C-42, as am., s. 13(4).

13 E.g., Trade-marks Act, RSC 1985, c. T-13, as am., s. 48.

14 RSC 1985 (2nd Supp.), c. 19, as am.

on the licensed patent. The most common forms of restraints that pose risks under the Competition Act are tie ins,[15] tie-outs,[16] post-expiration royalties,[17] mandatory package licensing,[18] total sales royalties,[19] non-diminishing royalties,[20] grant-backs,[21] veto powers clauses,[22] quantity or volume restrictions,[23] field of use restrictions,[24] territorial restrictions,[25] and resale restrictions.[26] Thus, when drafting a licensing agreement, the parties should determine whether any restraint imposed upon the licensee is designed to prevent, limit, or lessen unduly competition[27] or is within the scope of the lawful main purpose of the licence and necessary to effect that purpose since the Patent Act allows certain restraints that would otherwise be illegal. To be lawful, the restraint should be within the technical scope of the patent and the duration of the restraint should not extend beyond the life of the patent. In other words, the restraint should be reasonably within the reward that the patentee, by the grant of the patent, is entitled to secure. It should be mentioned that the Competition Act could apply to the use of technology outside the territorial limits of Canada where this use has adverse effects on competition in Canada.[28] Therefore, an international technology transfer may be subject to Canadian law as well as the law of the country where the technology is used. In addition to general

---

15 Where the transferring party extends his or her technology rights beyond their legal scope by forcing the purchase of products and services not protected by a legitimate technology right.

16 Where the technology transferor restricts the transferee's freedom to buy a competitor's product or sell competitive products or services.

17 The payment of royalties beyond the life of the technology rights.

18 The patentee requires a licensee to pay for additional licences in order to get the licences he or she desires.

19 The royalty for the transferred technology is paid on the basis of the sale or use of products or services encompassed by the transferred technology rights.

20 It involves the payment of a level royalty throughout the term of the technology licence, even though some of the technology or patents within the package may expire during the term of the licence.

21 The transferee of the technology agrees to grant to the transferor, in whole or in part, rights to technology developed by the transferee.

22 Either the transferor or the transferee is restrained from granting further licences to the technology without the express permission of the other party.

23 The transferor sets the minimum or maximum number of products that can be manufactured using the transferred technology.

24 The transferor limits the product line or industrial use to which his or her technology can be applied.

25 The transferor restricts the geographical territory in which the transferee can use the technology or market the products made or performed by the technology.

26 The transferor restricts the sale or use of goods made with technology after the transferee has parted with title to the goods.

27 Competition Act, ss. 32 and 45(1)(c) and (d). See also ss. 50 (illegal trade practices, price discrimination), 52 (misleading advertising), 61 (price maintenance), 77 (exclusive dealing, tied selling, and market restriction), 78-79 (abuse of dominant position), and 80 (delivered pricing).

28 Competition Act, *ibid.* See *infra*, chapter 16 and Castel, *Extraterritoriality in International Trade* (1988), at 32 to 36.

penal and civil remedies, the Competition Act[29] contains special remedies applicable to the abuse of patents, trade-marks, and copyrights:[30]

32.(1) In any case where use has been made of the exclusive rights and privileges conferred by one or more patents for invention, by one or more trade-marks, by a copyright or by a registered integrated circuit topography, so as to

(a) limit unduly the facilities for transporting, producing, manufacturing, supplying, storing or dealing in any article or commodity that may be a subject of trade or commerce,

(b) restrain or injure, unduly, trade or commerce in relation to any such article or commodity,

(c) prevent, limit or lessen, unduly, the manufacture or production of any such article or commodity or unreasonably enhance the price thereof, or

(d) prevent or lessen, unduly, competition in the production, manufacture, purchase, barter, sale, transportation or supply of any such article or commodity,

the Federal Court may make one or more of the orders referred to in subsection (2) in the circumstances described in that subsection.

(2) The Federal Court, on an information exhibited by the Attorney-General of Canada, may, for the purpose of preventing any use in the manner defined in subsection (1) of the exclusive rights and privileges conferred by any patents for invention, trade-marks, copyrights or registered integrated circuit topographies relating to or affecting the manufacture, use or sale of any article or commodity that may be a subject of trade or commerce, make one or more of the following orders:

(a) declaring void, in whole or in part, any agreement, arrangement or licence relating to that use;

(b) restraining any person from carrying out or exercising any or all of the terms or provisions of the agreement, arrangement or licence;

(c) directing the grant of licences under any such patent, copyright or registered integrated circuit topography to such persons and on such terms and conditions as the court may deem proper or, if the grant and other remedies under this section would appear insufficient to prevent that use, revoking the patent;

(d) directing that the registration of a trade-mark in the register of trade-marks or the registration of an integrated circuit topography in the register of topographies be expunged or amended; and

(e) directing that such other acts be done or omitted as the Court may deem necessary to prevent any such use.

(3) No order shall be made under this section that is at variance with any treaty, convention, arrangement or engagement with any other country respecting patents, trade-marks, copyrights or integrated circuit topographies to which Canada is a party.

---

29 RSC 1985 (2nd Supp.), c. 19, as am. For an analysis, see I.R. Feltham, "The Interface Between Intellectual Property Law and Competition in Canada" (1987), 12 *Can.-US LJ* 149.

30 Note that s. 79(5), which prohibits the abuse of dominant position, provides that: "For the purpose of this section, an act engaged in pursuance only to the exercise of any right or enjoyment of any interest derived under the Copyright Act, Industrial Design Act, Integrated Circuit Topography Act, Patent Act, Trade-marks Act, or any other Act of Parliament pertaining to intellectual or industrial property is not an anti-competitive act."

Although the courts have not regularly applied the legislative provisions in this field, the Restrictive Trade Practices Commission[31] and the director of investigation and research have delivered opinions on certain restrictions relating to patents or licences, in reports published after inquiries were carried out in certain industrial sectors in Canada.

Even if patents have been used in a manner contrary to anticombines legislation, the patent rights remain in effect and may be used as a basis for an action for patent infringement.[32]

4. *Miscellaneous Federal Laws*

The Investment Canada Act,[33] the Corporations and Labour Union Returns Act,[34] and the Export and Import Permits Act[35] may be applicable to the transfer of technology.

B. Provincial Laws

Subject to the possible application of the relevant provisions found in federal laws referred to in the preceding subsection, an agreement for the transfer of technology is governed mostly by the law of contract, which is a subject matter within the legislative competence of the provinces. From a private international law point of view, it is advisable to insert a choice of law clause in the agreement and to comply with the requirements of the law thus selected. Choice of law clauses are given effect in all provinces provided the choice is *bona fide* and legal.[36] However, the patent or trade-mark that is the object of the agreement is governed by the law of the place where it has been granted with respect to validity, interpretation, and effects. In general, the agreement must be clear and unambiguous and contain certain essential provisions. It may cover rights that are wider or narrower than the applicable statutory protection given to a patent or a trade-mark. Any right, for example, the right to use, to manufacture, to obtain improvements, etc., must be specifically mentioned.

If the supplier of the technology has expressly warranted the validity of the patent, it is recommended to insert in the agreement a provision preventing the recipient from attacking the validity of the patent during the existence and after the termination of the agreement.

C. International Conventions for the Protection of Intellectual Property

1. *General*

Numerous international conventions governing different aspects of industrial and intellectual property have been concluded over the past 115 years. Canada is a party to many

31 Now the Competition Tribunal.

32 *Philco Products v. Thermionics*, [1943] SCR 396, [1943] 3 DLR 449, 3 Fox Pat. C 92, leave to app. to PC granted 29 November 1943.

33 SC 1985, c. 20, RSC 1985 (1st Supp.), c. 28, as am.

34 RSC 1985, c. C-43, as am.

35 RSC 1985, c. E-19, as am.

36 In general, see Castel, *Canadian Conflict of Laws* (3rd ed., 1994), para. 427.

of these conventions, which have implications for the transfer of technology. These international conventions are under the auspices of the World Intellectual Property Organization (WIPO).

In the area of international industrial property protection, Canada is a member of the union created at Paris in 1883. The basis of this union is that foreign applicants for patents and other industrial property are treated as if they were nationals. The main instrument of the Union is the Paris Convention for the Protection of Industrial Property (the Paris Convention) of March 20, 1883, revised at Brussels in 1900, Washington in 1911, the Hague in 1925, London in 1934, Lisbon in 1958, and Stockholm in 1967.[37] Canada now adheres to the 1967 Stockholm text. As of January 1, 1996, 136 states were parties to the Paris Convention.[38]

Under the Paris Convention, Canada must extend the same industrial property protection to nationals of other contracting states as it grants to its own nationals. Canada is further obligated not to let any foreign declarations of invalidity affect the validity of Canadian industrial property rights, not to issue compulsory patent licences to remedy any practices that Canada considers "abuses" until three years have elapsed from the time of patent issuance, and not to provide for revocation of patents because the patentee is supplying the domestic market with imports. Perhaps the most important provision of the convention is that contained in article 4, whereby a person who has duly filed an industrial property application in a member country is given a right of priority of twelve months (patents) and six months (trade-marks)[39] for filing corresponding applications in other convention countries. This means that such an application filed in any member country within this period cannot be invalidated by any action done in the interval.

Canada is also a party to the Patent Co-operation Treaty (PCT), which was signed at a diplomatic conference in Washington on June 19, 1970, amended in 1979, and modified in 1984. Under the treaty, a single application counts as a filing in all the designated participating countries and provision is made for one international novelty search to replace or supplement national novelty searches.[40] The treaty is open to all states party to the Paris Convention. As of January 1, 1996, 86 states were parties to the PCT.[41]

The field of literary and artistic works is governed by the Berne Convention on the Protection of Literary and Artistic Works (the Berne Convention) signed in 1886 and revised in Paris in 1896 and Berlin in 1908, completed at Berne in 1914, revised at Rome in 1928, in Brussels in 1948, in Stockholm in 1967, and in Paris in 1971. Canada

---

37 Stockholm Text: (1970), 21 UST 1583, TIAS 6923; 7 *Int'l. Leg. Mat.* 981 (1968); and World Intellectual Property Organization (WIPO), Paris Convention for the Protection of Industrial Property, Official English Text (Geneva, 1978).

38 See WIPO, *World Intellectual Property Organization: General Information* (1996).

39 Note that a new trade-mark law treaty was concluded under the auspices of WIPO in 1994, aiming to simplify and harmonize procedures for trade-mark registration in signatory countries. The treaty was not yet in force on 1 January 1996, and Canada was not among the 50 signatories on that date.

40 WIPO, *Industrial Property*, vol. 18 (January 1979), at 15; text (1970), 9 *Int'l. Leg. Mat.* 978, signed by Canada and referred to in Patent Act, RSC 1985, c. P-4, as am., s. 12(1)(i).

41 See WIPO, *supra*, note 38.

adheres to the 1928 text. If Bill C-32 amending the Copyright Act is passed, Canada proposes to adhere to the 1971 text as well as to the Rome Convention of 1961 for the Protection of Performers, Producers of Phonograms and Broadcasting Organisations. While the Convention does not explicitly refer to computer software as covered subject matter, both the North American Free Trade Agreement (NAFTA)[42] and the WTO Agreement on Trade-Related Aspects of Intellectual Property (TRIPS)[43] stipulate that computer programs qualify as literary works within the meaning of the convention and must be accorded the same level of protection, thus confirming the convention's relevance for the transfer of software technology. Under the Berne Convention, Canada must extend national treatment (NT) in the protection of works originating in one of the contracting states. This protection must be automatic (that is, not dependent upon compliance with any registration or formality), as well as independent (that is, not dependent upon the existence of protection in the work's country of origin). With certain exceptions, the protection amounts to an exclusive right of authorization concerning, *inter alia*, adaptations, arrangements and reproductions of the work. The duration of the protection must generally be 50 years after the death of the author. Developing countries benefit from special provisions permitting restricted non-exclusive and non-transferable licences concerning the translation and reproduction of works. As of January 11, 1996, there were 117 states party to the Berne Convention.[44]

Chapter 17 of the NAFTA and the WTO TRIPS refer to and expand upon the obligations contained in the Paris and Berne conventions. Members of the WTO, even if they are not parties to the Paris and Berne conventions, must comply with the substantive provisions of these conventions, by virtue of the WTO-TRIPS Agreement.[45]

Intellectual property relevant to the transfer of technology also includes layout designs (topographies) of integrated circuits and undisclosed information (trade secrets). Numerous other international conventions governing specific aspects of intellectual property are referred to in NAFTA and the TRIPS Agreement.[46] The most relevant of these for the transfer of technology is the 1989 Treaty on Intellectual Property in Respect of Integrated Circuits.[47] Providing for the protection of the layout design (topographies) of integrated circuits for a maximum period of 10 years, this convention may affect the transfer of technology in the area of microelectronics and computer microchips.

The WIPO is an umbrella organization that administers the Paris and Berne conventions, as well as other international conventions dealing with intellectual property. The

---

42 Art. 1705(1).

43 Art. 10.

44 See WIPO, *supra*, note 38.

45 See WTO-TRIPS Agreement, arts. 2.1 and 9.1.

46 These other conventions are: the Geneva Convention for the Producers of Phonograms Against Unauthorized Duplication of their Phonograms (1971); the Rome Convention for the Protection of Performers, Producers of Phonograms and Broadcasting Organisations (1961); the International Convention for the Protection of New Varieties of Plants, 1978 in force in Canada CTS 1991, no. 5; and the International Convention for the Protection of New Varieties of Plants, 1991, not yet in force in Canada.

47 See Integrated Circuits Topography Act, SC 1990, c. 37 (c. I-14.6), as am.

convention establishing WIPO was concluded in Stockholm on July 14, 1967 and entered into force in 1970. WIPO became a specialized agency of the United Nations in 1974. It is located in Geneva. It aims to promote the worldwide protection of intellectual property and to ensure administrative cooperation among the intellectual property unions created by the Paris, Berne, and other conventions. The dispute settlement and enforcement mechanisms available within the system administered by WIPO have generally not been considered effective. Although both the Paris and Berne conventions contain the possibility for disputes among signatories to be taken to the International Court of Justice, this has never occurred. A new convention on WIPO dispute settlement is now under negotiation.

In December 1995, WIPO and the WTO concluded an agreement, which entered into force on January 1, 1996[48] providing for cooperation between the international bureau of WIPO and the WTO Secretariat concerning technical assistance to developing countries and notification and compilation of intellectual property laws of WTO members.

2. *The NAFTA, the WTO, and Trade-Related Aspects of Intellectual Property Rights*

It is clear that a close relationship exists between technology, intellectual property rights, and trade. The use of technology often requires access to secret know-how belonging to the entity that developed it. A transfer of technology therefore frequently requires cooperation between the producer of the technology and the enterprise in the host country that wishes to acquire it. Such cooperation on the part of the supplier of the technology is much more likely to exist where the host country provides an adequate regime for the protection of intellectual property rights. Only then can the supplier be assured that the secret know-how that it imparts will be protected. Where technology cannot be readily copied, even compulsory licensing will not lead to the transfer of technology without cooperation from the producer of the technology.

If intellectual property rights are not protected adequately, the flow of trade will be distorted and impeded. In the past, the WIPO was widely considered not to possess adequate or effective enforcement capabilities and had not acted decisively in this respect. The United States asked its trading partners—both regionally within the NAFTA and multilaterally within the GATT-WTO—to adopt a stronger regime for intellectual property protection backed by discipline and enforcement measures. Such a regime would lead to greater technology transfers from developed to developing countries and create incentives for more direct foreign investment. However, the regime could not be so strict as to constitute a non-tariff barrier or a weapon of protectionism to control imports.[49]

---

48 See Agreement between the World Intellectual Property Organization and the World Trade Organization, 1995 (Geneva: WIPO, 1996).

49 E.g., a domestic patent owner can prevent importation of products that infringe his or her patent and also the importation of products manufactured by a foreign licensee or a foreign owner of a corresponding patent if the owner of that patent is different from the owner of the domestic patent. Prior to the establishment of the WTO and the entry into force of the TRIPS Agreement, unfair substantive and

(The footnote is continued on the next page.)

While several different types of intellectual property rights could have an impact upon the transfer of technology, those most relevant to such transfers are patents and trade secrets. Of less significance, but still relevant, are trade-marks, industrial design, copyright (as it affects technology transfer of software), and the protection of integrated circuits (as it affects the microelectronics and semi-conductor industry). The following paragraphs therefore focus upon the provisions of NAFTA, chapter 17 and the TRIPS Agreement dealing with patents and trade secrets, and touch upon the provisions of these agreements relating to trade-marks, industrial design, copyright of computer programs, and the protection of integrated circuit layouts.

a. The NAFTA

Although Canada and the United States had originally attempted to negotiate substantive provisions governing the protection of intellectual property rights in the Canada-United States Free Trade Agreement (FTA), the inclusion of such provisions was blocked by a disagreement concerning pharmaceutical patents. In the end, FTA, article 2004 required Canada and the United States to cooperate to improve intellectual property protection in the context of the General Agreement on Tariffs and Trade (GATT) Uruguay Round negotiations. As such cooperation overlapped with the negotiation of NAFTA, in many areas, NAFTA, chapter 17 on the protection of intellectual property is substantively identical to the WTO-TRIPS Agreement, described below.

The NAFTA regime for the protection of intellectual property establishes minimum standards among the signatories in the main categories of intellectual property, bolstered by rules on enforcement. NAFTA countries are to provide adequate and effective protection of intellectual property rights to nationals of other parties.[50] In the areas relevant to the transfer of technology, these minimum standards consist of certain provisions of NAFTA, chapter 17 and the Paris Convention for the Protection of Industrial Property, and the Berne Convention for the Protection of Literary and Artistic Works.[51] The obligations of these international conventions are referred to but not directly incorporated into the NAFTA, chapter 17.[52] More extensive protection is also permitted, as long as it is not inconsistent with the provisions of chapter 17.[53]

---

49 Continued ...

procedural rules in national legislation dealing with intellectual property were subject to the GATT principles of minimum standard protection (art. XI), national treatment (art. III), and most-favoured national treatment (arts. I and XIII). See also GATT, *United States—Imports of Certain Automotive Spring Assemblies*, BISD, 30th Supp. 107 (1984), which involved s. 337 of the US Tariff Act of 1930 (19 USC, s. 1337).

50 Art. 1701.

51 Note that the Berne Convention is relevant in this context because it covers computer software, by virtue of NAFTA, art. 1701(2).

52 In the event of a conflict between the NAFTA and the rules of these conventions, see, generally, NAFTA, art. 103(2). It states that, in the event of any inconsistency between the NAFTA and other international agreements to which the NAFTA parties are signatories, the NAFTA will prevail to the extent of the inconsistency.

53 Art. 1702.

Without prejudice to the provisions in the WIPO conventions concerning the acquisition and maintenance of intellectual property rights, the NAFTA, chapter 17 NT obligation[54] requires Canada to extend to nationals of other NAFTA signatories treatment that is no less favourable than the treatment accorded to Canadian nationals with regard to the protection and enforcement of intellectual property rights. Derogation from national treatment is permitted concerning judicial and administrative procedures for the enforcement of intellectual property rights, as long as such derogation is (1) consistent with the enumerated international conventions, (2) necessary to secure compliance with measures, that themselves are consistent with obligations in chapter 17, and (3) not applied in a manner that would constitute a disguised restriction on trade. "Nationals of a party" are defined in terms of the pertinent international conventions, or, if an intellectual property right is not the subject of one of those conventions (for example, trade secrets), are at least individuals who are citizens or permanent residents of a NAFTA country.[55]

Acknowledging the possibility for conflict between intellectual property protection and competition policy, NAFTA, article 1704 allows the NAFTA states to specify licensing practices or conditions constituting an abuse of intellectual property rights having an adverse effect on competition and to adopt appropriate measures to prevent or control such practices or conditions.

The treatment of patents in the domestic law of the NAFTA signatories is governed by the Paris Convention and by the NAFTA, article 1709. The NAFTA parties must provide a system for patent protection making patents available for inventions (whether products or processes) in all fields of technology, provided that such inventions are new, result from an innovative step, and are capable of industrial application. Certain exclusions from patentability exist concerning *ordre public*, morality, and other factors. The minimum term of patent protection is 20 years from the date of filing. Product patents confer on the owner the right to prevent unauthorized use, and use, sale or import of the product. Process patents[56] confer on the owner the right to prevent other persons from using the process and from using, selling, or importing without authorization at least the product obtained directly from that process. Limited exceptions to exclusive patent rights are permitted as long as they do not unreasonably conflict with a normal exploitation of the patent and do not unreasonably prejudice the legitimate interests of the patent owner. Patents must be available and patent rights enjoyable without discrimination as to the field of technology, the territory of the party where the invention was made, and whether products are imported or locally produced. Patent owners must be able to assign and transfer by succession their patents and to conclude licensing agreements. A special rule deals with agricultural or pharmaceutical chemical patents.

Revocation of a patent may occur only in certain limited circumstances: where grounds exist that would have justified a refusal to grant the patent originally or where the grant of a compulsory licence has not remedied the lack of exploitation of the patent.

---

54 Art. 1703.

55 See also NAFTA, art. 201.

56 Note that NAFTA, art. 1709(11) provides special rules concerning the burden of proof in infringement proceedings involving process patents.

Compulsory licensing, allowing the use of a patent without the owner's consent, is permitted subject to certain conditions.[57] These conditions are more rigorous than those set out in the Paris Convention.[58] Except in circumstances of national emergency, extreme urgency, or public non-commercial use, the proposed user must have made efforts to obtain authorization from the right holder on reasonable commercial terms and conditions, efforts that have not been successful within a reasonable period of time. A licence must be limited in scope and duration to the purpose for which it was authorized. Use is non-exclusive and essentially non-assignable and must be authorized predominantly for the supply of the domestic market. These conditions do not apply where the use is permitted to remedy a practice determined by a judicial or administrative process to be anticompetitive.

In all cases, the right holder is to receive adequate compensation, taking into account the economic value of the authorization. Any decision relating to the remuneration and the legal validity of any decision relating to the authorization must be subject to review or appeal by a distinct higher domestic authority. Termination may occur when the circumstances leading to the licence cease to exist and are unlikely to recur. A NAFTA party may not authorize the use of the subject matter of a patent to permit the exploitation of another patent except as a remedy for an adjudicated violation of domestic laws regarding anticompetitive practices.

In respect of trade secrets,[59] the domestic law of the NAFTA parties must furnish the legal means for any person to prevent trade secrets from being disclosed to, acquired by, or used by others without the consent of the person lawfully in control of the information in a manner contrary to honest commercial practices.[60] To qualify for protection, such information must be secret and therefore have actual or potential commercial value and the person lawfully in control of the information must have taken reasonable steps under the circumstances to keep it secret. A party may require that, to qualify for protection, a trade secret must be evidenced in certain materials. The duration of protection must be unlimited. The NAFTA parties are precluded from discouraging or impeding the voluntary licensing of trade secrets. Special rules deal with pharmaceutical or agricultural chemical products.

Minimum standards for trade-marks are provided by the Paris Convention and NAFTA, article 1708. The NAFTA parties must provide a trade-mark registration system with certain minimum elements. The nature of the goods or services to which a trade-mark is to be applied shall in no case form an obstacle to registration. Initial registration must be for at least 10 years, with subsequent indefinite renewal for terms of no fewer than 10 years. Use of the trade-mark must be required for the maintenance of registration. Owners of a registered trade-mark enjoy certain rights, including the right to prevent

57 See NAFTA, art. 1709 (10); in Canada, see ss. 19 to 19.3 of the Patent Act, *supra*, note 8.

58 See Paris Convention, art. 5.

59 Art. 1711.

60 Art. 1721 defines "in a manner contrary to honest commercial practices" as "at least practices such as breach of contract, breach of confidence and inducement to breach, and includes the acquisition of undisclosed information by other persons who knew, or were grossly negligent in failing to know, that such practices were involved in the acquisition."

unauthorized commercial use of identical or similar signs where this would result in a likelihood of confusion. The NAFTA signatories may determine conditions for the licensing and assignment of trade-marks, although compulsory licensing is prohibited.

The term of protection of independently created industrial designs that are new or original must be at least 10 years.[61] The protection, which may be subject to certain limited exceptions, must afford the owner of a protected industrial design the means to prevent others from commercially making or selling without consent articles bearing or embodying a design that is a copy, or substantially a copy, of the protected design. In particular, requirements for securing protection for textile designs must not unreasonably impair the opportunity to seek and obtain such protection.

With respect to copyright, which also applies to computer programs, NAFTA, article 1705 furnishes minimum standards for protection in conjunction with the Berne Convention. Authors' and successors' rights must be protected in accordance with the Berne Convention, including the right to authorize importation of unauthorized copies of the work, and sale or rental. The minimum period of protection is 50 years from the year of the first authorized publication or of making, where not based on the life of a natural person.[62]

Layout designs (topographies) of semi-conductor integrated circuits are governed by NAFTA, article 1710 and the articles 2 to 7, 12, and 16(3) of the Treaty on Intellectual Property in Respect of Integrated Circuits. Compulsory licensing in this domain is expressly prohibited by article 1710(5). The domestic law of the NAFTA parties must make it unlawful for any person, knowingly, without the right holder's authorization to import, sell, or commercially distribute a protected layout design and an integrated circuit in which a protected layout design is incorporated. Where registration is a prerequisite for protection, the minimum term for protection must be 10 years from the application or first worldwide commercial exploitation. Where no registration is required, the minimum term must be 10 years from first worldwide commercial exploitation. Nevertheless, protection may lapse 15 years from the creation of the layout design. Mexico must implement these disciplines by January 1, 1998.

NAFTA articles 1714 to 1718 stipulate legal procedural and remedial requirements which must be available under the domestic law of the NAFTA parties for the enforcement of intellectual property rights. These must include expeditious remedies to prevent infringements and remedies to deter further infringements. Intellectual property right enforcement procedures must be fair and equitable, not unnecessarily complicated or costly, and not entailing unreasonable time-limits or unwarranted delays. Judicial review of final domestic administrative decisions must be available. Following the general provisions of article 1714, article 1715 governs specific procedural and remedial aspects of civil and administrative procedures, and article 1716 covers provisional measures. With respect to trade-mark counterfeiting and copyright piracy, criminal procedures and remedies,[63] and the enforcement of intellectual property rights at the border are also addressed.[64]

---

61 Art. 1713.

62 Art.1705(4).

63 Art. 1717.

64 Art. 1718.

b. The WTO-TRIPS Agreement

Acknowledging that the transfer of technology was a critical factor in future economic growth, the contracting parties of the GATT acceded to the US request to design a stronger multilateral regime for intellectual property protection and agreed to discuss intellectual property rights as a trade problem requiring multilateral resolution. Thus, the agenda of the Uruguay Round, adopted in September 1986, included the trade-related aspects of intellectual property rights:[65]

In April 1989, at its mid-term review, the trade negotiations committee decided that negotiations should encompass the following issues:[66]

(a) the applicability of the basic principles of the GATT and of relevant international intellectual property agreements or conventions;

(b) the provision of adequate standards and principles concerning the availability, scope and use of trade-related intellectual property rights;

(c) the provision of effective and appropriate means for the enforcement of trade-related intellectual property rights, taking into account differences in national legal systems;

(d) the provision of effective and expeditious procedures for the multilateral prevention and settlement of disputes between governments, including the applicability of GATT procedures;

(e) transitional arrangements aiming at the fullest participation in the results of the negotiations.

The result of these negotiations is the TRIPS Agreement, the most extensive and comprehensive multilateral agreement for the protection and enforcement of intellectual property rights ever to be concluded. Alongside trade in goods and services, the TRIPS Agreement has therefore become an essential component of the multilateral trading system. Subject to the transition provisions it contains, the TRIPS Agreement, constituting Annex 1C to the Agreement Establishing the World Trade Organization (the WTO Agreement), became effective with the entry into force of the WTO Agreement and the establishment of the WTO on January 1, 1995. As a component of the WTO single undertaking, it is binding upon all WTO members, and disputes arising under it are governed by the integrated dispute settlement mechanism set forth in the Understanding

65 Punta del Este Declaration, BISD, 33rd Supp. 19, at 25-26 (1987):

> In order to reduce the distortions and impediments to international trade, and taking into account the need to promote effective and adequate protection of intellectual property rights, and to ensure that measures and procedures to enforce intellectual property rights do not themselves become barriers to legitimate trade, the negotiations shall aim to clarify GATT provisions and elaborate as appropriate new rules and disciplines.
>
> Negotiations shall aim to develop a multilateral framework of principles, rules and disciplines dealing with international trade in counterfeit goods, taking into account work already undertaken in the GATT.
>
> These negotiations shall be without prejudice to other complementary initiatives that may be taken in the [World Intellectual Property Organization] and elsewhere to deal with these matters.

66 GATT Secretariat, Mid-Term Meeting, GATT doc. MTN. TNC/11 (MIN) (1989), at 21.

on Rules and Procedures Governing the Settlement of Disputes (DSU).[67] Supplementing existing international intellectual property right conventions, the TRIPS Agreement establishes minimum substantive standards of protection for the main kinds of intellectual property rights. Because it builds upon the foundations provided by the pre-existing international conventions, it is often referred to as a "Paris- and Berne-plus" agreement. The TRIPS Agreement also contains far-reaching requirements for the procedures and remedies that must be in place within the domestic legal systems of WTO members for the enforcement of intellectual property rights. The detail and scope of these requirements is a noteworthy achievement in international law.

The TRIPS Agreement establishes minimum standards. As long as these minimum standards are satisfied, WTO members are free to regulate intellectual property rights as they wish. Members are also free to implement stronger intellectual property right protection, either unilaterally or in implementation of regional agreements, such as the NAFTA, as long as this is not inconsistent with the TRIPS Agreement.[68] The TRIPS Agreement, therefore, does not mandate harmonization of the domestic intellectual property laws of WTO members.

The TRIPS Agreement aims "to reduce distortions and impediments to international trade, ... taking into account the need to promote effective and adequate protection of intellectual property rights, and to ensure that measures and procedures to enforce intellectual property rights do not themselves become barriers to legitimate trade."[69] It recognizes "the underlying public policy objectives of national systems for the protection of intellectual property, including developmental and technological objectives," in addition to "the special needs of the least developed country Members in respect of maximum flexibility in the domestic implementation of laws and regulations in order to enable them to create a sound and viable technological base." Article 7 sets forth the objectives of the agreement:

> The protection and enforcement of intellectual property rights should contribute to the promotion of technological innovation and to the transfer and dissemination of technology, to the mutual advantage of producers and users of technological knowledge and in a manner conducive to social and economic welfare and to a balance of rights and obligations.

Article 8, "Principles," acknowledges the right of WTO members to adopt measures necessary to promote the public interest in sectors of vital importance to their socio-economic and technological development. In addition, it recognizes that appropriate measures may be needed to prevent the abuse of intellectual property rights by right

---

67 See chapter 19, *infra*. Note that the provisions on retaliation in art. 22 of the DSU make it possible for WTO members to suspend concessions in relation to another member in a sector of the WTO that differs from the sector forming the subject matter of a dispute settlement report (the principle of cross-retaliation). Thus, e.g., a WTO member could be authorized to suspend concessions relating to services following the failure to comply with a panel or appellate body ruling on the inconsistency of a measure under the TRIPS Agreement.

68 Art. 1.1.

69 See the preamble to the TRIPS Agreement.

holders or the resort to practices that unreasonably restrain trade or adversely affect the international transfer of technology. Any such measures must be consistent with the agreement. These provisions are significant for developing countries because of their particular emphasis upon the transfer and spread of technology.

The fundamental NT and most-favoured-nation (MFN) requirements are contained in part I of the agreement. Supplementing these, part II of the agreement sets out the protected subject matter, minimum substantive standards, and the term of protection with respect to each of the major categories of intellectual property rights.

The basic TRIPS-NT provision requires WTO members to accord nationals of other members treatment no less favourable than the treatment it accords to its own nationals. This is subject to exceptions already contained in the relevant existing international conventions. Judicial and administrative procedures are also excepted where necessary to secure compliance with laws and regulations that are not inconsistent with the agreement and where not applied in a manner that would constitute a disguised restriction on trade.

The term "nationals" includes natural or legal persons who are domiciled in or have a real and effective industrial or commercial establishment in the territory of a member.[70] The determination of eligible nationals is in accordance with the criteria for eligibility contained in the existing international convention that is relevant to the intellectual property right in question.[71] The concept is applied to all WTO members, regardless of whether they are actually signatories of these conventions.

Members of the WTO, even if they are not parties to the Paris and Berne conventions, must comply with the substantive provisions of these conventions, by virtue of the TRIPS Agreement.[72] This is the case, for example, for India and Pakistan in respect of the Paris Convention and for Colombia and Indonesia in respect of the Berne Convention.[73]

The TRIPS Agreement MFN obligation requires non-discrimination as between nationals of other WTO members. Exemptions exist, *inter alia*, for international agreements related to intellectual property protection that entered into force prior to the WTO Agreement under certain enumerated conditions.

Patent protection must generally be available in all WTO members for inventions in all fields of technology, provided that they are new, involve an inventive step, and are capable of industrial application.[74] Exceptions to patentability may exist where necessary

70 See TRIPS Agreement, art. 1.3, note 1.

71 E.g., with respect to patents, see the Paris Convention, arts. 2 and 3.

72 See TRIPS Agreement, arts. 2.1 and 9.1. WTO members must comply with arts. 1 to 12 and art. 19 of the Paris Convention (1967): art. 2.1. They must also comply with arts. 1 to 21 of the Berne Convention (1971) with the exception of article 6 bis on moral rights: art. 9.1. They must extend the existing obligations they have with each other under the Paris Convention, the Berne Convention, and the Treaty on Intellectual Property in Respect of Integrated Circuits: art. 2.2.

73 See WIPO, *supra*, note 38. Note that WTO members that are not party to the Berne Convention are not bound by the convention's provisions on moral rights (TRIPS Agreement, art. 9.1).

74 S. 2(1) of the Patent Act was amended by adding the definition of "country" that includes any member of the WTO. This permits patent applications by WTO members. See the World Trade Organization Agreement Implementation Act, SC 1994, c. 44, s. 141.

to protect *ordre public* or morality, as well as in certain specified domains.[75] Discrimination on the basis of place of invention, place of production, or field of technology is prohibited. The term of protection must be at least 20 years from the filing date. Product patents must confer upon the owner the exclusive rights[76] to prevent unauthorized making, use, offering for sale, sale, or importation of the product for these purposes. Process patents[77] must confer upon the patent owner the exclusive right to prevent the unauthorized use of the process and the unauthorized use, offering for sale, sale, or importation for these purposes at least of the product obtained directly by that process. Patent owners must also enjoy the exclusive right to assign, or transfer by succession, the patent and to conclude licensing contracts. WTO members must make available judicial review for any decision to revoke or forfeit a patent.[78]

As under the NAFTA, compulsory licensing and unauthorized use is permitted subject to certain conditions.[79] Except in circumstances of national emergency, extreme urgency or public non-commercial use, the proposed user must have made efforts to obtain authorization from the right holder on reasonable commercial terms—efforts that have not been successful within a reasonable period of time. The use must be limited in scope and duration to the purpose for which it was authorized. Use is non-exclusive and essentially non-assignable and must be authorized predominantly for the supply of the domestic market. These conditions do not apply where the use is permitted to remedy a practice determined after judicial or administrative practice to be anticompetitive. In all cases, the right holder is to receive adequate remuneration, taking into account the economic value of the authorization. Any decision relating to the remuneration and the legal validity of any decision relating to the authorization must be subject to review or appeal by a distinct higher domestic authority. Termination may occur when the circumstances leading to the authorization cease to exist and are unlikely to recur. The TRIPS Agreement contains special conditions, which differ from the NAFTA, relating to the situation where use is authorized to permit the exploitation of a patent (the second patent) that cannot be exploited without infringing another patent (the first patent): (1) the invention claimed in the second patent must involve an important technical advance of considerable economic significance in relation to the invention claimed in the first patent; (2) the owner of the first patent must be entitled to a cross-licence on reasonable terms to use the invention claimed in the second patent; and (3) the use authorized in respect of the first patent must be non-assignable, except with the assignment of the second patent.

With respect to undisclosed information, which includes trade secrets and know-how, WTO members must extend protection to information that is secret, that therefore

---

75 Any country excluding plant varieties from patent protection must introduce an effective *sui generis* system of protection.

76 Art. 28.

77 Note that, like NAFTA, art. 1709(11), art. 34 of the TRIPS Agreement provides special rules concerning the burden of proof in infringement proceedings involving process patents.

78 See TRIPS Agreement, art. 31 and NAFTA, art. 1709(10).

79 Art. 31.

has commercial value, and that has been subject to reasonable steps to keep it secret.[80] Natural and legal persons must enjoy the possibility of preventing information lawfully within their control from being disclosed to, acquired by, or used by others without their consent in a manner contrary to honest commercial practices. Members' approval processes for the marketing of pharmaceutical and agricultural chemical products using new chemical entities are subject to certain special conditions.[81]

In the area of trade-marks, any sign capable of distinguishing the goods or services of one undertaking from those of other undertakings must be eligible for registration as a trade-mark, as long as it is visibly perceptible.[82] Registrability may be made dependent on use.[83] The nature of the goods or services to which a trade-mark is to be applied shall not form an obstacle to registration.[84] The registered trade-mark owner must enjoy the exclusive right to bar the unauthorized commercial use of identical or similar signs for goods or services that are identical or similar to those in respect of which the trade-mark is registered, where such use would result in a likelihood of confusion.[85] Likelihood of confusion is presumed in the case of use of an identical sign for identical goods or services. Any exceptions to trade-mark rights must take account of the legitimate interests of the trade-mark owner and third parties.[86] Registration must be for a term of no fewer than seven years and must be indefinitely renewable.[87] Compulsory licensing is prohibited. WTO members may otherwise determine conditions for the licensing and assignment of trade-marks, provided that the registered trade-mark owner has the right to assign a trade-mark with or without the transfer of the business to which the trade-mark belongs.[88]

Independently created industrial designs that are new or original must enjoy a minimum total term of protection of at least 10 years.[89] Special requirements for the protection of new designs in the textile sector exist: any cost, examination, or publication must not unreasonably impair the opportunity to seek and obtain such protection.[90]

Like the NAFTA, the TRIPS Agreement clarifies that computer programs are to be protected as literary works under the copyright obligations of the Berne Convention.[91] With certain exceptions, members must provide authors and their successors the right to

80 Art. 39.

81 Art. 39.3.

82 Art. 15.1.

83 Art. 15.3.

84 Art. 15.4.

85 Art. 16.1.

86 Art. 17.

87 Art. 18.

88 Art. 21.

89 S. 29 of the Industrial Design Act was amended to allow applications from WTO members. See World Trade Organization Agreement Implementation Act, *supra*, note 38, s. 118(2).

90 Arts. 25 and 26.

91 Art. 10.

authorize or prohibit commercial rental.[92] The minimum period of protection, when based on other than the life of a natural person, is 50 years from the year of first authorized publication or of making.[93] Limitations or exceptions must be confined to special cases that do not conflict with a normal exploitation of the work.

The WTO members must provide the protection to layout designs of integrated circuits contained in the Treaty on Intellectual Property in Respect of Integrated Circuits, bolstered by certain additional requirements. These additional requirements involve the term of protection (which must be 10 years rather than 8 years), the treatment of articles incorporating an unlawfully reproduced layout design, the handling of innocent infractions, and compulsory licensing or other unauthorized use.[94]

The TRIPS Agreement generally does not cover procedures for the acquisition and maintenance of intellectual property rights, leaving these areas to be governed by the relevant international conventions.[95] Nevertheless, part IV of the agreement contains some general provisions relating to these issues aiming to ensure that procedural difficulties do not jeopardize the protection mandated by the agreement.

The TRIPS Agreement contains extensive requirements concerning domestic intellectual property right enforcement machinery. While it requires that effective enforcement is available to intellectual property right holders, this must also be applied to avoid the creation of barriers to legitimate trade and to provide for safeguards against their abuse.[96] Because the TRIPS Agreement formed the basis for much of NAFTA, chapter 17, many of the provisions of the two agreements on domestic enforcement are similar or identical. Thus, as under the NAFTA, the WTO members must ensure that enforcement procedures are available under their domestic law to permit effective action against intellectual property right infringement, including expeditious remedies to prevent infringements and remedies that constitute a deterrent to further infringements. Such procedures must be fair and equitable, and must not be unnecessarily complicated or costly, or entail unreasonable time limits or unwarranted delays. Judicial review of final domestic administrative decisions must be available. Specific requirements concerning civil and administrative procedures and remedies are provided, including minimum criteria for fair and equitable proceedings, evidence, injunctions, damages, and other remedies to create an effective deterrent to infringement. Prompt and effective provisional measures must be available. Special requirements relating to border measures, as well as to criminal procedures, are also mandated in relation to trade-mark counterfeiting and copyright piracy.

---

92 Art. 11.

93 TRIPS Agreement, art. 13; similar to NAFTA, art. 1705(4).

94 See TRIPS Agreement, arts. 35 to 38. In Canada, the Integrated Circuits Topography Act, *supra*, note 47, was amended to make it binding upon the federal and provincial Crown, to allow for the filing of applications by "a national of a WTO Member" and to allow for public non-commercial use by federal and provincial governments of registered topographies under certain conditions.

95 See TRIPS Agreement, art. 5, which exempts procedures provided in multilateral agreements concluded under the auspices of WIPO from the NT and MFN requirements in this area.

96 See pt. III, arts. 41 to 64.

Certain TRIPS commitments—the obligation not to provide a lesser degree of consistency with TRIPs disciplines during the transitional period[97] and the requirement to provide a "mail-box" mechanism for the filing of patent applications relating to agricultural and pharmaceutical chemical products[98]—have been applied since the agreement's entry into force on January 1, 1995. With respect to other obligations, the TRIPS Agreement allows transition periods, which depend on the level of economic development of a WTO member. Subject to the general NT and MFN obligations, industrialized WTO members had one year (to January 1, 1996) to bring their laws into compliance; and developing country members and certain other members in economic transition are entitled to an additional four years. Moreover, developing country members who do not currently extend product patent protection to agricultural or pharmaceutical chemical products may delay the application of the provisions on patents in these areas of technology up to January 1, 2005. Nevertheless, such developing countries are still bound by the "mail-box" requirement to provide a mechanism for the filing of patent applications in these areas of technology from January 1, 1995. Developed country members are to provide technical and financial cooperation on request in favour of developing and less-developed country (LDC) members.[99]

Within the WTO, the council for TRIPS, composed of all WTO members, bears the responsibility for administering the agreement. It monitors the operation of and WTO members' compliance with the agreement.[100] As mentioned above, disputes among WTO members concerning their obligations under the TRIPS Agreement are now subject to the integrated dispute settlement system set out in the WTO-DSU.

The International Bureau of WIPO and the WTO Secretariat concluded an agreement, which entered into force on January 1, 1996,[101] providing for cooperation concerning technical assistance to developing countries and notification and compilation of the intellectual property laws of WTO members.

IX TAX TREATMENT OF AGREEMENTS FOR THE TRANSFERS OF TECHNOLOGY

The domestic tax treatment of a transfer of technology depends upon the rights in such technology that are the subject matter of the transfer, the form of the transfer, and the manner in which it is paid for by the recipient of such technology.[102]

In the case of most forms of property, the manner in which it is exploited determines the appropriate tax treatment for the parties. However, since technology is unique property in that it is so divisible, it makes the determination of the proper tax results very difficult in a particular case. Depending upon the manner in which the technology is exploited, the owner may receive a lump sum payment on an outright sale or transfer

97. Art. 65.5.

98 Art. 70.8.

99 Art. 67.

100 Art. 68.

101 See, *supra*, note 48.

102 In general, see Brown, *Tax Aspects of the Transfer of Technology: The Asia-Pacific Rim* (1990).

or fees or royalties in the case of a licence. Sales of technology, however, may also be made for royalties based upon the use or profits derived from the use of such technology. Similarly, a licensee of technology may pay for such licence by a lump-sum payment that is unrelated to use.

Since the domestic tax treatment may differ depending upon the form of payment, it is important to take this into consideration when drafting an agreement for the transfer of technology. If the owner assigns a patent outright or grants an exclusive licence for a lump-sum payment, this will ordinarily give rise to a capital receipt. If the payment received on the assignment or the licensing is a royalty based on production from the exploitation of the patent, this royalty will likely be an income receipt. In addition to the domestic tax treatment of a transfer of technology, international considerations may become relevant when the recipient is a resident of a foreign country. The owner of the technology must then cope with two tax systems and the resulting double taxation. Adding to the complexity, a relevant bilateral tax convention may have an impact on the transfer and on the final tax liability of the supplier of technology. When a country is a net importer of technology, its primary focus is generally on the tax treatment of the payments made to the non-resident owner or licensor of the technology transferred. A withholding tax will be levied by the recipient country, which is often based on gross income rather than net income, although its rate may be reduced by a bilateral tax convention, or a foreign tax credit may be available in the country of the supplier if there is sufficient foreign income. The allocation of the transfer payment to the various components of the transfer agreement often presents a serious challenge for the suppliers of technology. Developing countries usually prefer to view all technology transfer payments as a whole without allocating and to withhold on that basis under the royalty provisions of the tax conventions. It is easier and does not pose a threat of lost revenue. This approach enables these countries to reduce the cost of acquiring technology.

X. SELECTED BIBLIOGRAPHY

A. Books

Arnold, McCarthy, *Domestic and International Licensing of Technology* (1980).

Brookhart, Leach, and Tobor (eds.), *Current International Legal Aspects of Licensing and Intellectual Property* (1980).

Brown, *Tax Aspects of the Transfer of Technology: The Asia-Pacific Rim* (1990).

Business International Corporation, *International Licensing* (1977).

Business International Corporation, *International Licensing Management* (1988).

Business International Corporation, *Investing, Licensing and Trading Conditions Abroad* (1991-).

Canadian Technology Acquisition Workshop (1993).

Constructive Change: Managing International Technology Transfers (1995).

Dobkin et al., *International Joint Ventures* (2nd ed., 1988).

Eckstrom, *Licensing in Foreign and Domestic Operations*, 3 vols. (1972).

Foreign Investment, Technology and Economic Growth (1991).

Goldscheider, *Licensing in Foreign and Domestic Operations: Forms* (1978-79), 2 vols. (looseleaf).

Goudreau (ed.), *Exploring Our Technology: International Protection and Transfer of Industrial Innovation* (1995).

Kasto, *International Law of Technology* (1992).

Katzarov (ed.), *Katzarov's Manual on Industrial Property* (9th ed., 16th rev., 1996).

Lacasse and Perret, *Joint Venturing Abroad* (1989).

Law Society of Upper Canada, *Patent Law: Licensing of Patents and Know-How* (1975).

Mason, *Standard Clauses in a Licensing Agreement* (1970).

Meller (ed.), *International Patent Litigation* (1996 update).

Nanyenya-Takirambudde, *Technology Transfer and International Law* (1980).

OECD, *Technology and the Economy* (OECD, 1992).

Office of Industrial Innovation, *Supplying or Acquiring Technology: A Canadian Business Guide to Structuring and Negotiating Technology Transfer Agreements* (Ottawa: Technology Transfer Services, 1986).

Okolie, *Legal Aspects of the International Transfer of Technology to Developing Countries* (1975).

Organized by the Centre for Trade Policy and Law and Faculties of Law and Administration of University of Ottawa, *Exploring our Technology* (Ottawa: Canadian Exporter's Assn., 1993).

Pollzien and Langen, *International Licensing Agreements* (2nd ed., 1973).

Rouach, Klatzmann, *Les Transferts de Technologie* (1993).

Tang, *Canada-US Approach to International Technology Transfer* (1992).

Taylor, *Transfer of Technology: A Bibliography of Materials in the English Language* (1985).

Technology Transfer in International Business (1991).

Transfer of International Technology: Europe, Japan and the US in the 20th Century (1993).

UNCTAD, *Handbook on the Acquisition of Technology by Developing Countries* (1978).

Vuillermoz, *Filière des Contrats Internationaux de Transfert de Technologie* (1992).

World Intellectual Property Organization, *Industrial Property Law and Treaties* (1976); *Licensing Guide for Developing Countries* (1977); *General Information* (1996).

B. Articles

Arnold and Others, "The Interface between Intellectual Property Law and Competition Law in the North America Context" (1987), 12 *Can.-US LJ* 121.

Branda, "When Worlds Collide: Client/Server Systems in Information Technology" (1994), *58 Business Q* 89.

Bronckers, "The Impact of TRIPs: Intellectual Property Protection in Developing Countries" (1994), 31 *CMLR* 1245.

Brown, "1995 Canada-US Protocol: Scope of New Royalty Provisions" (1995), 43 *Can. Tax J* 592.

"Canada-United States Economic Ties: The Technology Context. Conference Proceedings" (1986), 11 *Can.-US LJ* 1.

Clark, "Intellectual Property and Transfer of Technology" (1993), *Meredith Memorial Lect.* 113.

Cottier, "The Prospects for Intellectual Property in GATT" (1991), 28 *CMLR* 383.

Dobkin, "Negotiating an International Technology Joint Venture" (1985-86), 1 *Conn. J Int'l. L* 81.

Feltham, "The Interface Between Intellectual Property Law and Competition Law in Canada" (1987), 12 *Can.-US LJ* 149.

Geller, "Intellectual Property in the Global Marketplace: Impact of TRIPs Dispute Settlement?" (1995), 29 *Int. Lawyer* 99.

Goekjian, "Legal Problems of Transferring Technology to the Third World" (1977), 25 *Am. J Comp. L* 565.

"High Technology Import and Export: A Symposium" (1986), 20 *Int'l. Law.* 1127.

Jeffries, "Regulation of Transfer of Technology, An Evaluation of the UNCTAD Code of Conduct" (1977), 18 *Harvard Int'l. LJ* 309.

Kiang, "Technology Transfer to People's Republic of China: A Canadian Lawyer's Perspective" (1992), 12 *CIPR* 119.

Mendes da Costa, "Canadian Patent Law under GATT: What's Coming Next?" (1995), 11 *CIPR* 61.

Murray, *Computer Software: Canadian and Cross Border Issues* (1993), *Conference Report Can. Tax Foundation* 27:1.

Primak, "Technology Licensing in Canada" (1979), 38 CPR (2d) 33.

Ramsay, "Drafting Confidentiality Agreements in Canada" (1988), 4 *Intel. Prop. J* 157.

Reichman, "Universal Minimum Standards of Intellectual Property Protection under the TRIPS Component of the WTO Agreement" (1995), 29 *Int. Lawyer* 99.

Richards, "Trade Related Intellectual Property Issues (TRIPS)" (1990), 72 *Pat. Trademark Office Soc.* 906.

Roffe, "UNCTAD: Code of Conduct for the Transfer of Technology" (1980), 14 *J World Trade L* 160.

Slough, "Problems in International Licensing of Industrial and Intellectual Property" (1979), 2 *Can.-US LJ* 209.

"Symposium: Toward a Theory of Technology Licensing" (1988), 25 *Stan. J Int'l. L* 194.

Thomson, "High Technology Export Control Regimes in Canada and the US: Origins Current Operation and Anticipated Changes" (1994), 9 *I.P.J.* 19.

"Transfers of Technology in the International Marketplace: a Symposium" (1984), 7 *BC Int'l. & Comp. L Rev.* 235.

C. United Nations Documents

Ad Hoc Working Group on the Interrelationship Between Investment and Technology Transfer, *Compendium of Documents and Reports Relating to the Work of UNCTAD* (New York: United Nations, 1995).

Draft International Code of Conduct on the Transfer of Technology as of 4 November 1983 (quoted as TD/CODE TOT/41).

The Role of the Patent System in the Transfer of Technology to Developing Countries: A Report by the UN Department of Economic and Social Affairs, the UNCTAD Secretariat and the World Intellectual Property Organization. TD/B/AC.11/19/Rev. 1 (1975).

UN Center on Transnational Corporations, *Joint Ventures as a Form of International Economic Co-operation* (1988).

CHAPTER SEVEN

Insurance

I. INTRODUCTION

This chapter contains a brief survey only of insurance of goods against losses incident to their transportation mostly by sea or by air from the warehouse of the seller to that of the overseas buyer, since many excellent studies have been published on this topic, a selected list of which is found in section IV.

Insurance by the Export Development Corporation (EDC) providing cover to the exporter against both commercial and political risks inherent in export sales of goods, services, or technology is analyzed in chapter 18, *infra*.

Because of the diversity of domestic laws and private international law rules on product liability, manufacturers of a finished product or of a component part, producers of a natural product, suppliers of a product or a service or technology and other persons involved in the commercial chain of preparation or distribution across borders of such product, service or technology, including their agents or employees, should be insured against the risk of product liability. Insurance cover may be obtained in a separate product liability policy or it may be added by amendment to a general public liability policy. Self-insurance is only used by very large manufacturers. General principles of private international law and of insurance law apply to product liability insurance.

II. MARINE INSURANCE

A. Sources

Marine insurance is first and foremost a contract of maritime law, not an application of insurance law to the maritime area since it preceded other forms of insurance by several centuries. In Canada, in 1983, the Supreme Court[1] decided that although strictly speaking marine insurance is a matter forming part of "property and civil rights in the province,"[2] it has nonetheless been assigned to Parliament as part of "navigation and shipping,"[3] except as regards that part of this power that remains within provincial jurisdiction.[4] The Federal Court has concurrent jurisdiction over maritime law.[5]

Despite this federal competence, only provincial legislation regulated marine insurance in Canada until 1993. Five common law provinces enacted statutes specifically dealing with marine insurance,[6] based on the UK Marine Insurance Act 1906,[7] which codified the common law existing at that date.[8] The Quebec Civil Code also covers

1 *Triglav v. Terrasses Jewellers Inc. et al.*, [1983] 1 SCR 283.

2 Constitution Act, 1867, s. 92(13).

3 *Ibid.*, s. 91(10). See also s. 91(13).

4 *Ibid.*, s. 92(10).

5 See s. 22(2)(r) of the Federal Court Act, RSC 1985, c. F-7.

6 BC, Insurance (Marine) Act RSBC 1979, c. 203; Man., Marine Insurance Act, RSM 1987, c. M40; NB., Marine Insurance Act, RSNB, 1973, c. M-1; NS, Insurance Act, RSNS 1989, c. 231 (pt. IX, Marine Insurance, ss. 227 to 316); and Ont., Marine Insurance Act, RSO 1990, c. M.2 (hereinafter referred to as the Ont. Act).

7 6 Edw. 7, c. 41 (UK).

8 It is suggested that this common law is part of Canadian maritime law.

marine insurance.[9] In the other common law provinces and territories, marine insurance contracts are part of the legislation dealing with insurance generally.[10]

The 1983 Supreme Court decision enabled Parliament to adopt a new federal Marine Insurance Act, which entered into force in 1993.[11] It, too, is based on the 1906 UK Marine Insurance Act.

The rules of Canadian maritime law and the common law including the law merchant, save insofar as they are inconsistent with the statutory provisions, continue to apply to contracts of marine insurance.[12]

B. Importance, Definition, and Scope

Marine insurance is essential in order to take full advantage of the credit system of finance of an export transaction. It provides a security given against loss or damage since it is a contract whereby the insurer undertakes to indemnify the insured, in the manner and to the extent agreed in the contract, against marine losses incident to the transportation of the goods to their destination,[13] including losses arising from incidental air or land peril, and losses incidental to the building, repair, or launch of a ship.[14]

By agreement of the parties, marine insurance may therefore be extended to cover goods from the time they leave the warehouse at the point of shipment until they are delivered at the destination named in the policy. This coverage, which includes transportation on land, on inland waters, and in the air during part of the voyage, is provided for in a warehouse-to-warehouse clause or a marine extension or extended-cover clause.[15]

9 Civil Code, 1991 and Marine Insurance, arts. 2505 to 2628.

10 Alta., Insurance Act, RSA 1980, c. I-5; PEI, Insurance Act, RSPEI, 1988, c. I-4; Sask., Insurance Act, RSS 1978, c. S-26; and NWT, Insurance Act, RSNWT 1988, c. I-4. Two provincial statutes specifically exclude contracts of marine insurance from their application: the Yukon Insurance Act, RSY 1986, c. 91 (s. 45(c)) and the Nfld. Insurance Contracts Act, RSN 1990, c. I-12 (s. 3(c)).

11 SC 1993, c. 22 (hereinafter referred to as the Can. Act). Note that the new federal Marine Insurance Act entered into force on 6 May 1993, the same date that the Hague-Visby Rules concerning the maritime transport of cargo became effective in Canada by virtue of the Carriage of Goods by Water Act, SC 1993, c. 21.

12 Can. Act, s. 4 and Ont. Act, s. 90.

13 Can. Act, s. 2(1) refers to the transportation process as a "marine adventure," meaning "any situation where insurable property is exposed to maritime perils," including (1) the earning or acquisition of any freight, commission, profit or other pecuniary benefit, or the security for any advance, loan or disbursement, is endangered by the exposure of insurable property to maritime perils; and (2) any liability to a third party may be incurred by the owner of, or other person interested in or responsible for, insurable property, by reason of maritime perils. S. 2(1) of the federal Act defines "maritime perils" as "the perils consequent on or incidental to navigation, including perils of the seas, fire, war perils, acts of pirates or thieves, captures, seizures, restraints, detainments of princes and peoples, jettisons, barratry and all other perils of a like kind and, in respect of a marine policy, any peril designated by the policy." An annex to the federal statute contains principles of construction for marine policies pertaining to certain of the terms used in this definition.

14 See, e.g., Can. Act, s. 6(1) and Ont. Act, s. 2.

15 Can. Act, s. 6(1) and Ont. Act, s. 3(1).

Under the terms of a deviation clause, goods are held covered, in case the ship is diverted from its ordinary or planned course, although this coverage, while automatic, calls for an additional premium under certain circumstances.

The importance of marine insurance arises from the fact that, unlike common carriers, such as railways, which are liable for loss or damage in connection with goods they have accepted as freight, the liability of ocean shipping companies is strictly limited. As indicated in the next chapter, it arises mainly from loss or damage caused by negligence in loading, in stowage, or delivery of cargo. The carrier is obliged to provide a seaworthy ship, with officers and crew chosen with reasonable care. However, it is not responsible for their errors or omissions. The bill of lading covers possible liabilities completely, and the result is that the shipping company is exempt from responsibility for by far the greater part of the mischances that are likely to befall goods in their transit from one country to another. The risk is not normally borne by the owner of the goods, but is shifted to the insurance company. If reliance is placed on a documentary bill of exchange offered for discount, banks must obtain an insurance policy or a certificate of insurance under an open policy, or other acceptable evidence to the effect that insurance has been covered by the drawee of the bill of exchange. Thus, insurance policies or certificates, like bills of lading, should be made out to order of shippers or drawers, and endorsed by them, so that the loss, if any, may be collected by the holder of the policy or certificate. In cases where bills of lading are made out to order of the bank, insurance policies or certificates should have the loss made payable to the bank.

As indicated in the preceding chapter, the terms of the contract of sale will indicate whether the buyer or the seller must pay the cost of marine insurance, and, sometimes, the amount of insurance required. For instance, the Incoterms 1990 provide that in a cost, insurance, and freight (CIF) contract, the seller must:

> A.3.(b) Obtain at his own expense cargo insurance as agreed in the contract, that the buyer, or any other person having an insurable interest in the goods, shall be entitled to claim directly from the insurer and provide the buyer with the insurance policy or other evidence of insurance cover.
>
> The insurance shall be contracted with underwriters or an insurance company of good repute and failing express agreement to the contrary, be in accordance with minimum cover of the Institute Cargo Clauses (Institute of London Underwriters) or any similar set of clauses. The duration of insurance cover shall be in accordance with B.5. and B.4.[16] When required by the buyer, the seller shall provide at the buyer's expense war, strikes, riots and civil commotion risk insurances if procurable. The minimum insurance shall cover the price provided in the contract plus ten per cent (i.e. 110%) and shall be provided in the currency of the contract.

Where the transaction involves a letter of credit expressly incorporating the Uniform Customs and Practice for Documentary Credits (UCP500),[17] unless otherwise stipulated in the credit,

---

16 B4 deals with taking delivery by the buyer and B5 deals with the transfer of risks.

17 The ICC Uniform Customs and Practice for Documentary Credits (1993 rev.), doc. 500, art. 34(f)(ii). See chapter 11, *infra*.

the minimum amount for which the insurance document must indicate the insurance cover to have been effected is the CIF (cost, insurance and freight (… "named port of destination")) or CIP (carriage and insurance paid to (… "named port of destination")) value of the goods, as the case may be, but only when the CIF or CIP value can be determined by the documents on their face. Otherwise, banks will accept as such minimum amount 110% of the amount for which payment, acceptance or negotiation is requested under the Credit, or 110% of the gross amount of the invoice, whichever is greater.

C. Risks Covered

It is advisable for the parties to the contract of sale to mention specifically which risks are to be covered by the insurance policy as well as the value of the insurance coverage that the seller has to obtain. If goods are to be shipped on deck, care should be exercised that proper coverage is obtained as such goods are normally insured free of claims for damage arising from exposure to the elements. While pilferage is not covered in certain policies, it can be written in and, in general, exceptional risks not provided for in any particular policy may be included by special arrangement. Policies can be obtained to guard against practically any eventuality that may arise. The insurer is entitled to insure for at least an amount covering the invoice price of his goods plus freight and other charges. The marine insurance policy or certificate forms part of the shipping documents.

D. Types of Policy

Marine insurance policies fall into different categories, such as valued,[18] unvalued,[19] voyage,[20] time,[21] mixed (combined),[22] floating,[23] and open cover.

Most of the cargo insurance written today for recurring shipments is under an open cover policy, which is a contract between the insurance company and the shipper by which the insurance company binds itself to protect by insurance, in accordance with the policy conditions, all shipments made by the insured. The protection extends automatically from the moment the shipment leaves the factory, store, or warehouse at the initial

18 Can. Act, s. 30(2): "a marine policy is a valued policy if it specifies the agreed value of the subject-matter insured"; see also Ont. Act, s. 28(2).

19 Can. Act, s. 30(3): "a marine policy is an unvalued policy if it does not specify the value of the subject-matter insured and, subject to the limit of the sum insured, leaves the value to be determined in accordance with section 19"; see also Ont. Act, s. 29. Unvalued policies are rarely used in the export trade.

20 Can. Act, s. 29(2): "A marine policy is a voyage policy if the contract insures the subject-matter 'at and from,' or 'from,' one place to another place or other places"; see also Ont. Act, s. 26.

21 Can. Act, s. 29(3): "A marine policy is a time policy if the contract insures the subject-matter for a definite period"; see also Ont. Act, s. 26.

22 A contract may be both a voyage and time policy: Can. Act, s. 30(3); see also Ont. Act, s. 26.

23 Can. Act, s. 31 and Ont. Act, s. 30. It is a policy that describes the insurance in general terms and leaves the name of the ship or ships and other particulars to be defined by subsequent declaration. The insured receives a formal policy document.

shipping point in the interior, until delivery at the factory, store, or warehouse at destination. The consideration for such insurance is that the insured shall, as soon as practicable after they have knowledge thereof, report all their shipments to the insurance company and, at the end of each month, pay the premiums on shipments reported in accordance with the schedule of rates attached to the policy.

Where individual shipments are of small value, it may be easier to take out a blanket policy that exempts the insured from advising the insurer of these shipments and provides for the payment of a lump-sum premium to cover them instead of a premium at several rates.

Where an open cover policy is used, the insurance company furnishes the insured with a supply of certificates to be used and countersigned by them as needed, thus obviating any delay. No formal policy is issued to the insured, unless they require it.

The certificate contains particulars of the shipment, its value, destination, and markings. Usually, but not always, two certificates go with the documents; one copy goes to the underwriters and one is a file copy. It should be noted that the English courts have decided that when a policy of insurance is called for under a letter of credit or a contract of sale, a certificate of insurance cannot properly be substituted.[24] In order to avoid trouble, it is advisable, unless the buyers lack confidence in the probity of the sellers, to allow the latter the choice of furnishing either a policy of insurance or a certificate issued under an open policy.[25] This problem is resolved in transactions involving a letter of credit governed by the UCP500, which makes clear that, "[i]f a Credit specifically calls for an insurance certificate or a declaration under an open cover, banks will accept, in lieu thereof, an insurance policy."[26]

E. Marine Insurance Brokers

Normally, an exporter who requires marine insurance will use the services of a qualified marine insurance broker, who acts as the agent of the insured although he or she is paid by the insurer.[27]

Whether acting for one or the other, the agent must use reasonable care in carrying out his or her duties.[28]

---

24 See discussion in C.M. Schmitthoff, *Schmitthoff's Export Trade* (9th ed., 1990), at 39-40.

25 Note that a broker's cover notes are merely advice sent by brokers to the insured that insurance cover has been obtained. Letters of insurance addressed by the insured seller to the buyer to confirm the taking out of insurance have no status in law.

26 UCP500, art. 34(d).

27 *Amin Rasheed Corp. v. Kuwait Insurance*, [1982] 1 WLR 961, at 967. Note that if the insurer is a company, the employee of that company authorized to bind the company on insurance risks is known as the underwriter.

28 See, e.g., *Fine's Flowers Ltd. et al. v. General Accident Assurance Co. of Canada et al.* (1978), 17 OR (2d) 529, at 538, per Wilson JA, 81 DLR (3d) 139, 2 BLR 257 (CA) and *Norlympia Seafoods Ltd. et al. v. Dale & Co. Ltd.*, [1983] ILR 1-1688 (BCSC).

F. The Contract of Insurance

General principles of insurance law apply to marine insurance contracts.

1. Insurable Interest

The insured must have an insurable interest in the goods insured at the time of the loss, though he or she need not be interested when the insurance is effected. Where the goods are insured "lost or not lost," the insured may recover, even though he or she may not have acquired his or her interest until after the loss, unless at the time of effecting the contract of insurance the insured was aware of the loss and the insurer was not.[29]

In the absence of an insurable interest, the contract is deemed to be a gaming or wagering contract that is void.[30] Whether the seller or the buyer of goods has an interest if a loss occurs while the goods are in the course of transit depends upon the moment when the property in the goods sold passes from the buyer to the seller. For example, under a free on board (FOB) contract of sale, the seller has an insurable interest until the goods are delivered on board ship. Thereafter, the buyer acquires an insurable interest and effects insurance. However, an insurable interest is not confined to a strict legal right of property. Any interest that would be recognized by a court of law or equity is an insurable interest. Possession of the goods insured or the right to immediate possession constitutes an insurable interest. While the policy must specify the subject matter insured with reasonable certainty, the nature and extent of the interest of the insured in the goods insured need not be specified in the policy.[31]

A mortgagee, consignee, or other person having an interest in the goods insured may insure them on behalf and for the benefit of other persons interested as well as for his or her own benefit.[32]

Where the insured assigns or otherwise parts with his or her interest in the subject matter insured, he or she does not thereby transfer to the assignee his or her rights under the contract of insurance unless there is an express or implied agreement with the assignee to that effect.[33]

2. Insurable Value

The Marine Insurance Acts contain rules for ascertaining the insurable value of the goods insured in the case of an unvalued policy.[34]

---

29 Can. Act, ss. 7 to 18, especially s. 7, and Ont. Act, ss. 5 to 16, especially s. 7(1).

30 Can. Act, s. 18 and Ont. Act, s. 5.

31 Can. Act, s. 28(1) and Ont. Act, s. 27(2).

32 Can. Act, s. 16(2) and Ont. Act, s. 15(2).

33 Can. Act, s. 17 and Ont. Act, s. 16. The provisions of this section do not apply in respect of a transmission of interest by operation of law. See also Can. Act, ss. 51 and 52 and Ont. Act, which deal with the assignment of insurance policies.

34 Can. Act, s. 19, outlines the methodology for calculation of the insurable value on a ship, freight, goods, or any other subject matter. As to the measure of indemnity, see Can. Act, ss. 66 to 80. See also Ont. Act, s. 17 (measure of indemnity, ss. 68 to 72).

3. Disclosure and Representation

A contract of marine insurance is a contract based upon the utmost good faith, and if the utmost good faith is not observed by either party, the contract may be avoided by the other party.[35] Thus, the insured must disclose to the insurer, before the contract is concluded, every material circumstance that is known to the insured, and the insured is deemed to know every circumstance that in the ordinary course of business ought to be known by him or her. If the insured fails to make such disclosure, the insurer may avoid the contract.[36]

Every circumstance is material that would influence the judgment of a prudent insurer in fixing the premium or determining whether the risk should be taken.[37]

In the absence of inquiry, some circumstances need not be disclosed—for example, any circumstance that is known[38] or presumed to be known by the insurer.[39] Whether a particular circumstance that is not disclosed is material or not is, in each case, a question of fact.[40]

The Marine Insurance Acts also deal with what must be disclosed by an agent of the insured who is effecting the insurance.[41] Every material representation made by the insured or his or her agent to the insurer during the negotiations for the contract, and before the contract is concluded must be true. If it be untrue the insurer may avoid the contract.[42] Whether a particular representation is material or not is in each case a question of fact.[43]

The contract of marine insurance is deemed to be concluded when the proposal of the insured is accepted by the insurer, whether the policy is then issued or not. For the purpose of showing when the proposal was accepted, reference may be made to the slip or covering note or other customary memorandum of the contract.[44] On numerous occasions, the courts have had to decide what type of information an exporter of goods has to

35 Can. Act, s. 20 and Ont. Act, s. 18.

36 Can. Act, s. 21 and Ont. Act, s. 19(1). For a recent case on this issue, see *Neepawa Yacht Ltd. v. Laurentian P & C Insurance Co.* (28 December 1994, BC SC) (prior material losses not disclosed either through inattention or lack of candour on the part of the agent tainted the insurance policy and allowed avoidance of the claim).

37 Can. Act, s. 21(3) and Ont. Act, s. 19(2).

38 Can. Act, s. 21(5)(b).

39 Ont. Act, s. 19(3)(b).

40 Can. Act, s. 21(4) and Ont. Act, s. 19(4).

41 Can. Act, s. 21(2) and Ont. Act, s. 20.

42 Can. Act, s. 21(7) and Ont. Act, s. 21(1). See, e.g., *Biggin v. British Marine Mutual Insurance Assn.* (1992), 14 CCLI (3d) 66 (Nfld. SC) (non-intentional misstatement of purchase price by agent was an innocent misrepresentation that did not avoid the insurance contract).

43 Can. Act, s. 21(4) and Ont. Act, s. 21(7).

44 Can. Act, s. 23 and Ont. Act, s. 22. Once the insured and the broker have agreed upon the terms and conditions of the proposed cover, a memorandum or slip will be prepared by the broker and submitted to the insurer. Initialling of the memorandum or the slip by the insurer creates a binding contract.

give to the insurer, especially with respect to dangerous goods. Upon payment of an additional premium, the insured may wish to include a held covered clause in the contract of insurance. Such clause covers a material innocent misdescription of the goods in the policy that would have enabled the insurer to avoid the contract on the ground of misrepresentation.

4. The Policy

The contract of marine insurance is inadmissible in evidence unless it is embodied in a marine policy in accordance with the Marine Insurance Acts.[45] The policy may be executed and issued either at the time when the contract is concluded or afterward.[46]

A marine policy must contain some pertinent information such as the name of the insured, the subject matter insured, the risk insured against, the voyage or period (or both) covered, etc.[47] The policy must be signed by or on behalf of the insurer.[48]

The words of the policy must make sense to those most likely to read and rely upon them.[49]

5. The Premium

The premium[50] is payable to the insurer when the policy is issued unless another arrangement is agreed upon by the parties or required by trade custom.[51] In principle, it is the broker who is responsible solely and directly to the insurer for the payment of the premium.[52] Unless otherwise agreed, the broker has, as against the insured, a lien upon the policy for the amount of the premium and his or her charges in respect of effecting the policy.[53]

6. Warranties or Conditions

The sections on warranties found in the federal and provincial Marine Insurance Acts deal with promissory warranties by which the insured undertakes that some particular thing shall or shall not be done, or that some condition shall be fulfilled, or whereby he or she affirms or negatives the existence of a particular state of facts.[54] Such warranties

45 Can. Act, s. 25(1).

46 Can. Act, s. 25(2) and Ont. Act, s. 23. As to the form of the policy, see Ont. Act, s. 31.

47 Can. Act, s. 26 and Ont. Act, s. 24.

48 Can. Act, s. 27 and Ont. Act, s. 25(1).

49 See, e.g., *Burrard Towing Co. v. Reed Stenhouse Ltd.* (1994), 29 CCLI (2d) 29.

50 Note that Can. Act., s. 47 stipulates that the premium must be "reasonable." The Ont. Act contains no corresponding qualification.

51 Can. Act, ss. 47 to 50 and Ont. Act, ss. 53 to 55. See also Ont. Act, s. 32(2), with respect to additional premium. As to the return of premium in certain cases, see Can. Act, ss. 82 to 85 and Ont Act., ss. 83 to 85.

52 Can. Act., s. 49(1)(a).

53 Can. Act, s. 49(1)(b) and Ont. Act, s. 54(2).

54 I.e., Can. Act, s. 32(1).

are express or implied.[55] They are conditions that must be complied with exactly, whether they be material to the risk or not.[56] If they are not so complied with, then, subject to an express provision in the policy, the insurer is discharged from liability as from the date of the breach of warranty, but without prejudice to any liability incurred by him or her before that date.[57] A breach of warranty is not excused only because the breach was remedied and the warranty complied with before any loss was incurred.[58]

G. Institute Clauses

The schedule to the provincial Marine Insurance Acts in force in Canada contains a form of marine insurance policy that may be used by the insured.[59] It is the Lloyd's S. & G.[60] Policy dating back to 1779. Clauses, which in Europe are usually the Institute of London Underwriters Clauses, may be added to this form.

As a result of strong criticism of this policy by the United Nations Conference on Trade and Development (UNCTAD), the Technical Clauses Committee of the Institute of London Underwriters prepared a new policy and five sets of clauses to be used with it. They were introduced on January 1, 1982 with a transitional period until March 31, 1983 after which the old ones were withdrawn from the London market.[61] They are known as the Lloyd's Marine Policy, the Institute Cargo Clauses A, B, and C, the Institute War Clauses (Cargo) and the Institute Strike Clauses (Cargo). On October 1, 1983 new Institute Time Clauses (Hulls) were also introduced to the marine insurance market.

The Lloyd's Marine Policy no longer contains the terms of insurance. It is only a schedule that lists the policy number; the name of the insured; the vessel; the voyage or period of insurance; the subject matter insured; the agreed value, if any; the amount insured; the premium, clauses, and endorsements to be attached and forming part of the policy; and special conditions and warranties.

Institute Cargo Clauses A cover all risks of loss of or damage to the subject matter insured with some exclusions—for example, loss or damage attributable to willful misconduct of the insured. Institute Cargo Clauses B and C cover specific perils, again

---

55 Can. Act, s. 32(2) and ss. 33 to 39 and Ont. Act, s. 34(2) and ss. 36 to 42.

56 Can. Act, s. 39(1). In *Century Ins. Co. of Canada v. Case Existological Laboratories Ltd.*, [1983] 2 SCR 47, the court held that the use of the term "warranted" in a marine insurance policy is not conclusive of the existence of a warranty.

57 Can. Act, s. 39(2) and Ont. Act, s. 34. As to when a breach of warranty is excused, see Can. Act, s. 39(4) and Ont. Act, s. 35. Promissory warranties must not be confused with exceptive warranties, e.g., warranted free of loss or damage caused by war, which means that the risk of war is not covered.

58 Can. Act, s. 39(5).

59 Ont. Act, s. 31(1). This is not included in the federal legislation.

60 Ship and Goods.

61 For an analysis, see S. Mankabady, "The New Lloyd's Policy and Cargo Clauses" (1982), 13 *J of Maritime Law and Commerce* 527 and A.L. Parks, "Recent Developments in Marine Insurance Law" (1983), 14 *J of Maritime Law and Commerce* 159.

subject to a list of exclusions. All clauses cover general average and salvage charges as well as pre-shipment and post-shipment risks.[62] Since war and strike risks are excluded, the insured who requires this coverage must ask for the addition of the Institute War Clauses (Cargo) and the Institute Strikes Clauses (Cargo). As for the old "sue and labour clause" found in the original Lloyd's S. & G., it has been replaced by the "duty of the insured clause" to avert or minimize loss that is recoverable.[63]

H. UNCTAD Model Clauses

The UNCTAD endorsed its Model Clauses on Marine Cargo Insurance in 1987,[64] to serve as a non-mandatory international model. The model clauses provide for three alternative types of cover (1) all risks, (2) intermediate, and (3) restricted.

The all risks cover provides coverage for all risks of physical loss of or damage to the insured cargo.[65] The intermediate cover provides coverage for physical loss of or damage to the cargo caused by an enumerated list of events.[66] The restricted cover provides even more limited coverage.[67] All three types of cover are subject to enumerated general exclusions.

The general exclusions are extensive. They include any loss, damage, or liability resulting from, *inter alia*, war, civil war, political sabotage, strikes, lockouts, civil commotions, riots, and any personal act or omission of the insured done with the intent to cause such loss or damage, or recklessly and with knowledge that such loss or damage would probably result.

The model clauses for all three forms of cover further include provisions concerning general average and salvage, sue and labour, forwarding charges, period of coverage, measure of indemnity, and insurable interest.

---

62 See Duration (transit clause).

63 Institute Cargo Clauses A, cls. 16 and 17.

64 UNCTAD, *Model Clauses on Marine, Hull and Cargo Insurance* (1989). The UNCTAD Working Group on International Shipping Legislation adopted the Model Clauses on Marine Cargo Insurance in 1984. The UNCTAD Trade and Development Board endorsed them in 1987 (see TD/B1042, TD/B/C.4/287, TD/B/C.4/ISL/50).

65 This insurance also covers loss of or damage to the insured cargo caused by any act of any governmental authority to prevent or minimize pollution resulting from damage to the carrying vessel, provided such act of governmental authority has not resulted from want of due diligence by the assured.

66 These include sinking of the cargo vessel; collision, explosion, or fire; general averaging sacrifice; jettison; earthquake and similar natural calamities; leakage; discharge at a port of distress; and total loss of a package overboard.

67 Restricted cover does not embrace loss of or damage to the cargo due to natural calamities, or the total loss of a package overboard.

I. Losses and Their Settlement

1. General

The insurer is liable for any loss proximately[68] caused by a peril insured against.[69] No liability exists for any loss attributable to the willful misconduct of the insured.[70] Unless the policy otherwise provides, the insurer is not liable for loss caused by delay, or resulting from ordinary wear and tear, ordinary leakage and breakage, inherent vice or nature of the subject matter insured, or for any loss proximately caused by rats or vermin, or for any injury to machinery not proximately caused by maritime perils.[71]

A loss may be either total or partial (which includes particular average or general average).[72]

2. Actual or Constructive Total Loss

A total loss may be either an actual total loss or a constructive total loss.[73] An actual total loss occurs where the subject matter insured is destroyed or so damaged as to cease to be a thing of the kind insured, or where the insured is irretrievably deprived thereof.[74] Unless a policy otherwise provides, there is a constructive total loss where the subject matter insured is reasonably abandoned on account of its actual total loss appearing to be unavoidable, or because it could not be preserved from actual total loss without an expenditure that would exceed its value when the expenditure had been incurred.[75] For example, constructive total loss occurs where the insured is deprived of the possession of the goods by a peril insured against and it is unlikely that they can be recovered or the cost of recovering them would exceed their value when recovered at all, or still where the cost of repairing the damage and forwarding the goods to their destination would exceed their value on arrival.[76] Where there is a constructive total loss, the insured may either treat the loss as a partial loss or abandon the subject matter insured to the insurer and treat the loss as if it were an actual total loss.[77] Where the insured elects to abandon the subject matter insured to the insurer, notice must be given to the insurer with reasonable diligence; otherwise the loss can only be treated as a partial loss.[78]

---

68 See *Canada Rice Mills Ltd. v. Union Marine & General Insurance Co.*, [1941] DLR 1 (PC).

69 Ont. Act, s. 56(1).

70 In *Century Ins. Co. of Canada v. Case Existological Laboratories Ltd.*, [1983] 2 SCR 47, the negligence of the master and crew, which caused the vessel to sink, was held to be a peril of the seas and the proximate cause of loss.

71 Can. Act, s. 53(2) and Ont. Act, s. 56(2).

72 Can. Act, s. 54 and Ont. Act, s. 57(1).

73 Can. Act, s. 55(1) and Ont. Act, s. 57(2).

74 Can. Act, s. 56(1) and Ont. Act, s. 58(1).

75 Can. Act, s. 57 and Ont. Act, s. 61.

76 Can. Act, s. 57(2) and Ont. Act, s. 61(2).

77 Can. Act, s. 57(3) and Ont. Act, s. 62. See also *Rumsey v. Providence Washington Insurance Co.* (1880), 13 NSR 393 (CA).

78 Can. Act, s. 58(2) and Ont. Act, s. 63(1).

While policies may be extended to cover many more risks than are found in the printed form, conversely, policies may be restricted to exclude certain losses (for example, free from particular average policies).

3. Settlement of Losses

a. Average

In marine insurance policies, the word "average" is customarily used to signify partial loss or damage. There are two kinds of average: general average and particular average.

b. General Average

General average is peculiar to maritime adventures. It is the loss arising out of a voluntary and reasonable sacrifice made of any part of the cargo or any part of the ship to endeavour to prevent the loss of the whole, and made for the benefit of all persons at interest.[79] The voluntary sacrificing may take the form of jettisoning part of the cargo or cutting away part of the ship, such as the masts, to prevent foundering, or it could be the water damage caused to goods in fighting a common peril, such as a fire in the hold of a vessel.

A general average act also includes a voluntary and reasonable expenditure incurred at a time of peril in order to preserve the property.[80]

The persons at interest would be the various owners of the cargo and the owners of the ship itself, together with the operators of the ship who are interested to the extent of the freight earned. Where the freight or any part of it is prepaid, this amount will be included in the value of the goods. If the voluntary sacrifice saves the ship, the value of the jettisoned cargo, or whatever the case may be, becomes a charge *pro rata* against the entire value of the ship, freight, and cargo.

The Canadian Marine Insurance Act provides that:[81]

> 3) Subject to the conditions imposed by maritime law, a person who incurs a general average loss is entitled to receive from the other interested persons a rateable contribution, known as a general average contribution, in respect of the loss.
>
> 4) Subject to any express provision in the marine policy,
>
> (a) an insured who incurs a general average expenditure may recover from the insurer in respect of the proportion of the loss falling on the insured;
>
> (b) an insured who incurs a general average sacrifice may recover from the insurer in respect of the whole loss, without having enforced the insured's right to contribution from other persons.
>
> 5) Subject to any express provision in the marine policy, an insured who has paid, or is liable to pay, a general average contribution in respect of the subject-matter insured, may recover the contribution from the insurer.

---

79 Can. Act, ss. 65(1) and (2), and Ont. Act, ss. 67(1) and (2).

80 Can. Act, s. 65(2).

81 Can. Act, s. 65(3) to (7); see also Ont. Act, ss. 67(4) to (7). For Canadian cases dealing with general average, see R.M. Fernandes, *Marine Insurance Law of Canada* (1987), at 112 *et seq*.

6) Subject to any express provision in the marine policy, an insurer is not liable for a general average loss or a general average contribution unless the loss was incurred for the purpose of averting, or in connection with the avoidance of, a peril insured against.

7) Where any ship, freight, and goods, or any two of them are owned by the same insured, the liability of the insurer for a general average loss or a general average contribution shall be determined as if they were owned by different persons.

The adjustment of claims resulting from a general average loss is determined by general average adjusters. The preparation of such an adjustment, in the case of a large steamer loaded with miscellaneous cargo and possibly owned by hundreds of different shippers or consignees, is a task involving tremendous detail.[82] The adjusters may demand security for the payment of charges before they will permit goods to be released. In the case of uninsured goods, the owner would be required to make a cash deposit sufficient to cover the estimated charges. As marine insurance covers the risk of general average, the adjusters would usually be willing to accept the guarantee of the underwriters for claims against insured property.[83]

c. Particular Average

Particular average is a partial loss or damage that is not a general average loss.[84] It is a partial loss suffered by a particular shipment. Particular average claims arise from accidental causes, such as stranding, collision, fire, water damage, and so forth and, of course, have no connection with a jettisoning or similar operation. Marine insurance often does not cover partial losses except in certain circumstances and, in this case, the policy is said to be free of particular average (FPA).[85]

---

82 The York-Antwerp Rules 1974 contain standard rules for the adjustment of general average. Although they do not have the force of law, they are frequently adopted by the parties. They are to be found in Fernandes, *Marine Insurance Law of Canada*, *ibid.*, at 173.

83 Note that s. 64 of the Can. Act provides:

> (1) Salvage charges are charges recoverable under maritime law by a salvor independently of any contract, but do not include expenses incurred for services in the nature of salvage rendered by the insured or the insured's agent, or any person hired by the insured or the insured's agent, for the purpose of averting a loss by a peril insured against.
>
> (2) Subject to any express provision in the marine policy, salvage charges incurred for the purpose of averting a loss by a peril insured against may be recovered from the insurer as a loss by such peril.

S. 66 of the Ont. Act contains a similar provision.

84 Can. Act, s. 63(1) and Ont. Act, s. 65(1).

85 Can. Act, s. 77:

> (1) Where the subject-matter insured under a marine policy is warranted free from particular average, the insured cannot recover for a loss of part of the subject-matter, other than a loss incurred by a general average sacrifice, unless the contract evidenced by the

(The footnote is continued on the following page.)

Alternatively, the insurance may cover partial losses that amount to more than a stated percentage of the value of the shipment. This is similar in many ways to automobile collision insurance that is usually written with a stipulated deductible amount for which the insured is responsible. However, in a marine policy, claims are paid in full if they amount to or exceed the stated percentage. Sometimes an all risk policy is written with a fixed amount deductible in order to minimize petty loss claims.

FPA—Free of Particular Average

The form of clause commonly used in marine insurance policies reads "Free of Particular Average unless the vessel be stranded, sunk, burnt, on fire or in collision." This indicates that the insurance does not cover partial losses, unless caused by one of the marine perils mentioned.

WA or WPA—With Average—With Particular Average

The clause commonly used reads: "With Average if amounting to 3 per cent or the vessel be stranded, sunk, burnt, on fire or in collision." In this case, partial losses are paid if the damage amounts to 3 per cent or more of the insured value of each package. If any of the marine perils mentioned are encountered, all losses, partial or otherwise, are fully covered. In placing marine insurance, an exporter should give due consideration to the type of goods involved when deciding whether to carry the risk of partial loss. In a large percentage of cases, the exporter will wish all risk coverage. However, even policies that contain an all risk clause may exclude certain specific risks. The exclusion of coverage for damage caused by inherent vice (or the nature of the goods being insured) is most

---

85 Continued ...

policy is apportionable, in which case the insured may recover for a total loss of any apportionable part.

(2) Where the subject-matter insured under a marine policy is warranted free from particular average, either wholly or under a specified percentage, the insurer is nevertheless liable for salvage charges and, if the policy contains a sue and labour clause, for particular charges and other expenses properly incurred under the clause for the purpose of averting a loss by a peril insured against.

(3) Unless the policy otherwise provides, where the subject-matter insured under a marine policy is warranted free from particular average under a specified percentage, a general average loss cannot be added to a particular average loss in order to attain that percentage.

(4) Where the subject-matter insured under a marine policy is warranted free from particular average under a specified percentage, for the purpose of determining whether that percentage has been attained, only the actual loss incurred in respect of the subject-matter may be considered, and no particular charges or expenses incurred in establishing the loss may be included.

See also Ont. Act, s. 77. See also Can. Act., s. 64(3) and Ont. Act, s. 65 (2), concerning the treatment of expenses that are not salvage charges.

reasonable. However, some underwriters will cover even this damage in their all risk policies. Typical examples of inherent vice would be, fruit rotting, meat becoming putrid, wine souring, or internal rotting of potatoes.

A marine insurance policy provides protection against perils of the seas. If a vessel springs a leak as the result of an accidental occurrence, the damage caused would, of course, be a charge against the underwriters. However, when a leak occurred because of the unseaworthy state of the ship when it sailed or from wear and tear or natural decay, underwriters for many years declined liability. Today, the seaworthiness of the vessel, as between the insured and the underwriters, is admitted so as not to prejudice an innocent insured for any wrongful act or misconduct of the shipowner or ship operators. Since the basic marine rates are established on the assumption that the cargo will be carried in an approved vessel meeting the requirements of the Institute Classification Clause (for example, not over 20 years old—occasionally amended to not over 25 years old—and not under 1,000 tons net), the basic marine rates would be subject to increase if a vessel is operated out of usual trade for which it was built. Additional premiums levied for over-age, low tonnage, or out of usual trade are called "vessel penalties." Such rates are established and promulgated by a special committee composed of marine underwriters from several insurance companies. These vessel penalties are obligatory and not competitive.

As already noted, all risks of war are excluded from a marine policy as is also damage caused by rioters, strikers, and locked-out workers. These risks may be covered by an endorsement on the policy at a very reasonable rate.

Exporters should note that in certain circumstances insurance cover on goods going to some countries must be effected with the foreign importer insurance company if the insurable risk is for the account of such importer.

J. Measure of Indemnity

The measure of indemnity is the sum recoverable by the insured in respect of a loss on a policy by which he or she is insured. In the case of an unvalued policy, it is the full extent of the insurable value and in the case of a valued policy the full extent of the value fixed by the policy.[86] Thus, in principle, where there is a total loss of the goods insured, if the policy is a valued policy, the measure of indemnity is the sum fixed by the policy; if the policy is an unvalued policy, the measure of indemnity is the insurable value of the goods insured.

In the case of partial loss of the goods or movables, the measure of indemnity is, subject to any express provision in the policy, as follows:[87]

> (a) where part of the goods or movables insured by an unvalued policy is totally lost, the insurable value of the part lost, ascertained as in case of total loss.
>
> (b) where part of the goods or movables insured by a valued policy is totally lost, that proportion of the value of the goods or movables specified by the policy that the insurable value of the part lost bears to the insurable value of all the goods or movables, ascertained as in the case of an unvalued policy.

---

86 Can. Act, s. 66 and Ont. Act, s. 68.

87 Can. Act, s. 70 and Ont. Act, s. 72.

(c) where the whole or any part of the goods or movables insured has been delivered damaged at its destination, that proportion of the insurable value of all the goods or movables in the case of an unvalued valued policy, or the value of all the goods and movables specified by the policy in the case of a valued policy, that the difference between the gross value[88] in their damaged condition at the destination bears to the gross value of all the goods or movables in a sound condition at the destination.

Where different species of property are insured under a single valuation, the valuation must be apportioned over the different species in proportion to their respective insurable values, as in the case of an unvalued policy. The insured value of any part of a species is such proportion of the total insured value as the insurable value of the part bears to the insurable value of the whole, ascertained in both cases as provided by the Marine Insurance Acts.[89] Where a valuation has to be apportioned and particulars of the prime cost of each separate species, quality, or description of the goods cannot be ascertained, the division of the valuation may be made over the net arrived sound values of the different species, qualities, or descriptions of goods.[90]

K. The Insurer's Right of Subrogation

Where the insurer pays for a total loss, he or she thereupon becomes entitled to take over the interest of the insured in whatever may remain of the subject matter so paid for, and he or she is thereby subrogated to all the rights and remedies of the insured in and in respect of that subject matter as from the time of the casualty causing the loss.[91] In case of payment for a partial loss, the insurer acquires no title to the subject matter insured or such part of it as may remain, but he or she is thereupon subrogated to all rights and remedies of the insured in and in respect of the subject matter insured as from the time of the casualty causing the loss insofar as the insured has been indemnified for the loss.[92] The purpose of subrogation is to prevent the insured from recovering more than once for the same loss. The Marine Insurance Acts also deal with the right of contribution where the insured is overinsured by double insurance[93] and the case where the insured is underinsured.[94]

88 In these provisions, "gross value" means the wholesale price, or if there is no such price, the estimated value with, in either case, freight, landing charges, and duty paid beforehand. In the case of goods or merchandise customarily sold in bond, the bonded price is the gross value. "Gross proceeds" means the gross value of the goods in their damaged condition—that is, the actual price obtained at a sale where all charges on sale are paid by the sellers.

89 Can. Act, s. 71(2) and Ont. Act, s. 73(1).

90 Can. Act, s. 71(2) and Ont. Act, s. 73(2).

91 Can. Act, s. 81(1) and Ont. Act, s. 80(1).

92 Can. Act, s. 81(2) and Ont. Act, s. 80(2).

93 Can. Act., ss. 86 and 87, and Ont. Act, s. 81.

94 Can. Act, s. 88 and Ont. Act, s. 82.

III. AIR CARGO INSURANCE

A. Marine Clauses

Cargo sent by air may be insured in the marine market under special Institute Cargo Clauses (Air) for use with Lloyd's Marine Policy form. They cover all risks of loss of or damage to the goods insured subject to a number of exceptions, including exceptions for war and strikes. These two risks can be covered by the Institute War Clauses (Air Cargo) and Institute Strike Clauses (Air Cargo).

B. Air Waybill Cover

The occasional shipper of cargo by air may wish to apply for insurance via the air carrier waybill in order to be covered by the air carrier's own policy. This type of insurance, if offered by the carrier, is rarely used by the professional shipper who prefers to use the Institute Cargo Clauses (Air). Declaring value for carriage by air as a form of insurance if the value of the cargo exceeds the limits set under the applicable international conventions,[95] only has the effect of raising the air carrier's liability to the declared value. Additional charges must be paid by the shipper.

IV. SELECTED BIBLIOGRAPHY

A. Books

Arnould, *The Law of Marine Insurance and Average* (Mustill and Gilman, 16th ed., 1981).

Chalmers, *Marine Insurance* (9th ed., 1983).

Fernandes, *Marine Insurance Law of Canada* (1987).

Ivamy, *Marine Insurance* (4th ed., 1985).

Margo, *Aviation Insurance* (2nd ed., 1989).

Parks, *The Law of Marine Insurance and Average* (1988).

Schmitthoff, *Schmitthoff's Export Trade: The Law and Practice of International Trade* (9th ed., 1990).

UNCTAD, *Legal and Documentary Aspects of the Marine Insurance Contract* (1982).

UNCTAD, *Model Clauses on Marine, Hull and Cargo Insurance* (1989).

Witherby (ed.), *Reference Book of Marine Insurance Clauses* (56th ed., 1984).

Wells, *Introduction to Aviation Insurance* (1986).

---

95 See Carriage by Air Act, RSC 1985, c. C-26, implementing the 1928 Warsaw Convention (CTS 1947 no. 15, 137 LNTS 13), as am., by the 1955 Hague Protocol (CTS 1964 no. 29, 478 UNTS 371).

B. Articles

Fernandes, "Current Issues in Transportation Law and Insurance" (1993), 2 *Uberrimae Fides* 10.

Mankabady, "The New Lloyd's Policy and Cargo Clauses" (1982), 13 *J of Maritime Law and Commerce* 527.

Perkins, "Marine Insurance: The Legal Relationship Between the Underwriter and the Broker in Canada," [1986] *Meredith Memorial Lectures* 361.

Tetley, "The Buenos Aires Maru: Has the Whole Nature of Canadian Maritime Law Been Changed?" (1988), 10 *Sup. Ct. LR* 399.

CHAPTER EIGHT

The Transportation of Goods

I. INTRODUCTION

This chapter covers the international transportation of goods that are the subject of an export or import transaction from the point of departure to the point of destination whether by sea, air, or land or by a combination of these modes of transport.

When the goods are carried by only one mode of transport, the international transportation is unimodal. The contract of transport is usually evidenced by a document particular to the mode of transport used (for example, an ocean bill of lading, an ocean waybill, an air waybill, or an air, rail, or road consignment note).[1] This document, which is issued by the carrier at the point of departure, contains the terms of the contract of transport including liability for loss of, or damage to, the goods while in charge of the carrier. It may also refer to any international convention or national law that regulates that mode of transport.

Canada is a party to only one unimodal international transport convention, the 1929 Warsaw Convention, as amended, concerning air transport.[2] With respect to sea transport, although Canada has not ratified the 1924 Brussels Convention (the Hague Rules), its revisions (the Hague-Visby Rules), or the more recent 1978 UN Convention on the Carriage of Goods by Sea (the Hamburg Rules), Canada has incorporated their provisions in its domestic legislation.[3]

---

1 The bill of lading, etc., is not the contract of affreightment between the shipper and the carrier.

2 See section IV, *infra*, Convention for the Unification of Certain Rules Relating to International Carriage by Air, 137 LNTS 13, as am., at the Hague in 1955, 478 UNTS 371.

3 See section II, *infra*, International Convention for the Unification of Certain Rules Relating to Bills of Lading, 120 LNTS 157 (the Hague Rules); the Visby Protocol 23 February 1968 (the Hague-Visby Rules)

(The footnote is continued on the next page.)

When goods are carried by several modes of transport, the international transportation is multimodal or combined. The goods, often in packed containers, go from the point of departure to the point of destination by successive use of more than one mode of transport. This through movement of goods implies either the issue of a series of separate single-mode transport documents or their replacement by a through start-to-finish transport document usually called a combined or multimodal transport document.

Canada is not a party to the 1980 UN Convention on International Multimodal Transport of Goods.[4] Thus, in general, it is customary to use standard multimodal transport documents elaborated by international organizations that state that they are issued subject to the 1992 UN Conference on Trade and Development (UNCTAD)-International Chamber of Commerce (ICC) Rules for Multimodal Transport Documents,[5] or individual combined transport documents that either refer to the UNCTAD-ICC Rules expressly or incorporate their provisions.

Besides dealing with the carriage of goods by sea, air, and land, this chapter addresses the special legal problems raised by new transportation techniques, especially containerization and automation of the functions of bills of lading and other trading documents through the use of electronic data interchange (EDI).

In addition to a discussion of the 1991 UN Convention on Liability of Operators of Transport Terminals in International Trade,[6] this chapter also devotes a special section to international freight forwarders, shipping agents, and customs brokers.[7]

II. CARRIAGE OF GOODS BY SEA

A. Sources

The Federal Court of Canada enjoys concurrent original jurisdiction over Canadian maritime and admiralty law by virtue of the Federal Court Act.[8] The Supreme Court of Canada has recently defined maritime law as a uniform and cohesive body of federal law[9] that should be interpreted within the modern context of commerce and shipping.[10] Although the demarcation line between federal and provincial competence regarding

---

3 Continued …

and the Protocol amending the International Convention for the Unification of Certain Rules relating to Bills of Lading of 21 December 1989 (the SDR Protocol). The UN Convention on the Carriage of Goods by Sea (The Hamburg Rules) (1978), 17 *ILM* 608, promoted by UNCITRAL, was adopted with a view to abolishing the Hague-Visby Rules. For the status of these international instruments under current Canadian domestic legislation (Carriage of Goods by Water Act, SC 1993, c. 21) see section II.F, *infra.*

4 (1980), 19 *ILM* 938. See section III, *infra.*

5 ICC doc. 481, which came into effect on 1 January 1992. These newer rules are phasing out the 1975 ICC Uniform Rules for a Combined Transport Document, ICC doc. 298.

6 See *infra*, section VII.

7 See *infra*, section VI.

8 RSC 1985, c. F-7, ss. 2, and 22(1) and (2).

9 *ITO-Terminal Operators v. Miida Electronics Inc.*, [1986] 1 SCR 752; *Chartwell Shipping Ltd. v. Quebec Paper Company*, [1989] 2 SCR 683; and *Whitbread v. Whalley*, [1990] 3 SCR 1273.

10 *Monk. Corp. v. Island Fertilizers Ltd.* [1991] 1 SCR 779.

negligence in maritime carriage remains to be definitively settled, contracts of carriage by sea and the discharge of cargo fall within the scope of maritime law, as does any claim for loss or damage to goods relating to the carriage of goods on a ship under a through bill of lading.[11]

The two major pieces of federal legislation relating to contracts of international carriage of goods by sea are the Bills of Lading Act[12] and the Carriage of Goods by Water Act.[13]

B. Bills of Lading and Charterparties

An exporter of goods, usually called the shipper, may ship them by sea in two ways: in the case of small shipments, as part of the ship's general cargo under a contract of carriage by sea, also called contract of affreightment, evidenced by an ocean bill of lading;[14] and, in the case of a large shipment, by hiring the whole ship under a charterparty. In other words, the bill of lading is a contract pertaining to the goods and the charterparty is a contract pertaining to the ship.

Today, there are three basic types of a charterparty: (1) a charterparty by demise that involves the lease of the ship; (2) a voyage charterparty when the ship is chartered for a certain voyage or voyages; and (3) a time charterparty when the ship is chartered for a certain period of time. In the case of a charterparty by demise, the charterer, who is the person entitled to the use of the ship, has it in his or her possession and control. This is not the case with respect to a voyage or time charterparty, which usually confers on the charterer simply the right to have his or her goods carried by a particular vessel. Charterparties by demise are used mostly in the oil tanker trade.

Most goods involved in export transactions that must be carried by sea are covered by ocean bills of lading.

There are many types of bills of lading. The most common are shipped (or on board) bills, whereby the shipowner acknowledges that the goods are loaded on board the ship; received for shipment (or alongside) bills, whereby the shipowner acknowledges that the goods are delivered into its custody; freight prepaid or freight collect bills; clean or claused bills, depending upon the condition of the goods received by the shipowner;

---

11 S. 22(2)(f) of the Federal Court Act, RSC 1985, c. F-7; see, e.g., *ITO-Terminal Operators* v *Miida Electronics Inc.*, [1986] 1 SCR 752 and *Anglophoto Ltd. v. The Ikaros*, [1973] FC 483. But see *Marley Co. v. Cast North America (1983) Inc.*: [1995] FCTD, 31 March 1995. In *New Term Ltd. v. Ship M.Y.S. Budyonnogo* (1992), 54 FTR 215 (TD), an action for negligence for harm to nearby cars caused by paint being used to spray paint a ship in the harbour was held to be sufficiently connected to shipping to fall within the Federal Court's s. 22 jurisdiction.

12 RSC 1985, c. B-5.

13 SC 1993, c. 21.

14 The remuneration paid to the shipowner is called the freight. Freight rates for shipments in liner vessels are often fixed by shipping conferences. As to their validity in Canada, see Shipping Conferences Exemption Act 1987, RSC 1985, c. 17 (3rd Supp.). See also Convention on a Code of Conduct for Liner Conferences signed at Geneva on 6 April 1974 and entered into force on 6 October 1983 (1974), 1 *ILM* 910. Canada is not yet a party to this convention. In general, see J. Lawrence, "The UNCTAD Liner Code: A Preliminary Examination of the Implications of the Code of Conduct for Liner Conferences" (1985), 16 *JMLC* 181.

non-negotiable (or straight) bills; negotiable bills that, if made out to bearer, are transferable by delivery and, if made out to a particular person or his or her order, are transferable by endorsement and delivery; charterparty bills that incorporate by reference some of the terms of the charterparty; through bills, when the goods must be carried by several land or ocean or other carriers that enable the shipper to deal with only the carrier who signs the through bill; container bills, which cover the multimodal transport of goods in a container; non-negotiable liner waybills, data freight receipts, or shipping certificates; and house bills and combined transport bills issued by freight forwarders. Some of these bills of lading are dealt with in this and other sections of this chapter.

C. The Ocean Bill of Lading

Once the exporter delivers the goods to a ship pursuant to a free on board (FOB) or cost, insurance, and freight (CIF) contract (or other transaction) as described in chapter 5, he or she will receive a bill of lading as evidence of the contract of carriage. The parties to the bill of lading are the shipper (usually the seller or owner-exporter), the carrier (the shipowner or charterer), and the consignee or order (usually the buyer-importer). These basic arrangements may be subject to many variations, most of which result from the introduction of modern technology and involve containerization and multimodal transport by a combination of land and sea transport. In the latter case, the original bill of lading issued will be a multimodal or combined bill of lading rather than an ocean bill but, insofar as the ocean part of the voyage is concerned, the comments in this section are relevant. Multimodal or combined bills are described in section III, below. Further complications may arise where the ship is under charterparty.

The usual course of the transaction is for the seller, exporter, or shipper to deliver the goods to the port for shipment. A bill of lading cannot be issued at that time and, depending on the custom of the port, a warehouseman's receipt may be issued for the goods by the port authorities or other agent of the carrier or, if the goods are delivered directly to the ship, a mate's receipt setting out the quantity of the goods and their condition on delivery. Where agents are used to store the goods or lightermen employed to get the goods to the ship (or at the delivery end), this raises the questions of the liability of such persons in the case of damage to the goods and whether they are covered by the terms of the bill of lading.

Of the various documents issued at this early stage, the mate's receipt is probably the most important because it results from the goods having been checked upon delivery. Their condition, quantity, etc., is noted on the receipt. It thus may be "clean" or "claused" (containing notations of damage or defects in quantity). In law, its consequences are twofold: it is evidence of the delivery of the goods to the carrier that are henceforth held at the carrier's risk subject to the same terms and conditions as the bill of lading (whether that is expressly stated in the receipt or not); and, it is *prima facie* evidence of the ownership of the goods, entitling the carrier to issue the bill of lading to the named person, absent notice to the contrary.[15]

15 For a description of the process of issuing a mate's receipt, see Schmitthoff, *Schmitthoff's Export Trade. The Law and Practice of International Trade* (9th ed., 1990), at 541 *et seq.*

Carriers' standard form bills of lading are readily available and the shipper usually provides one of these in draft form to the former's agent; if the quantity of the goods and their condition correspond to the draft, it is then completed and returned, signed, to the shipper. The shipper guarantees the accuracy of the information supplied.[16] If there are no problems, it will be a "clean" bill of lading; otherwise it will be "claused" or "unclean." Banks operating under letters of credit usually require clean documents of transport.[17] The master of the ship must be careful not to issue a clean or even ambiguous bill if he or she has noticed defects; even an exculpatory clause in the bill will not save the carrier from liability in such a case.[18] Sometimes this problem may be cured by the shipper providing the carrier with an indemnity in return for issuing a clean bill; such an indemnity is only valid, however, when the problem is relatively minor, such as one that would not entitle the buyer to refuse to accept delivery of the goods; otherwise, the shipper and carrier would be entering into an agreement to defraud the consignee and any banks providing financing based on the bill. In this latter case, the indemnity is invalid and illegal, and the proper course of action is for the exporter to obtain the buyer's agreement to amend the terms of the underlying contract and the terms of the credit.[19]

The bill of lading is usually issued in duplicate originals in the United Kingdom, in triplicate in Canada, and, in some jurisdictions, in quadruplicate. In the case of export financing, a bill of lading is included in the set of documents delivered to the advising (confirming) bank and forwarded to the issuing bank. Otherwise, it is forwarded directly to the consignee or agent, air, or other rapid mail. In the past, it arrived well before the goods themselves and, since its delivery is assimilated to the delivery of the goods, delivery of the bill will, in the standard FOB or CIF contract, satisfy the seller's obligation of delivery. Today, the goods may arrive before the original bill in which case the goods may be delivered to the consignee against his or her (or a bank's) guarantee, a practice that is changing the use of the bill as a document of title.[20]

The bill is not always issued by the shipowner; a charterer may also issue bills. In the case of a dispute over liability for the carriage of goods, conflicting provisions in the

---

16 "Hague-Visby Rules" relating to bills of lading, sched. I to the Carriage of Goods by Water Act, SC 1993, c. 21 (the Hague-Visby Rules), art. III.5. The Hague-Visby Rules are applicable to contracts of maritime carriage entered into after 6 May 1993. This article is the same as the provision in the former "Rules Relating to Bills of Lading" Schedule to the Carriage of Goods by Water Act, RSC 1985, c. C-27 (the Hague Rules), applicable to contracts of maritime carriage entered into before 6 May 1993.

17 Art. 32 of the Uniform Customs and Practice for Documentary Credits (1993 rev.), ICC doc. 500 (UCP500).

18 *The Skarp*, [1935] P 134, and see discussion of this issue and the issue of estoppel in Schmitthoff, *supra*, note 15, at 587.

19 *Brown, Jenkinson & Co. Ltd. v. Percy Dalton (London) Ltd.*, [1957] 2 QB 621 (CA), per Pearce LJ at 639 and Schmitthoff, *ibid.*, at 594-95.

20 See discussion below; J. Ramberg, "The Multimodal Transport Document" in Schmitthoff and Goode (eds.), *International Carriage of Goods: Some Legal Problems and Possible Solutions*, Centre for Commercial Law Studies (1988), at 7.

bill and the charterparty may give rise to problems. Thus, in *Union Industrielle et Maritime v. Petrosul International Ltd.*,[21] the owner of a ship brought an action against the shipper for damage caused to the ship by the loading of sulphur mixed with chlorine. The underlying contract of sale provided for arbitration in Vancouver. The bill of lading provided that the terms of the charterparty, including its arbitration clause (which provided for arbitration in Paris before the Chambre Arbitrale Maritime, and the application of French law), were incorporated into the bill, while it also contained a clause to the effect that it was governed by Canadian law and that the Federal Court had exclusive jurisdiction. In the circumstances, the Federal Court refused the shipowner's application for a declaration that the Paris arbitration clause was applicable.

In Canada, it has been held that where there is no demise of the vessel to a time-charterer and no specific undertaking by the charterer to the shipper, and a bill of lading is issued by the master on behalf of the owner, the latter remains liable to the shipper as carrier for any damages due to the former for failure to perform the contract of carriage.[22]

The question of the extent to which the terms of a charterparty are incorporated into a bill of lading was examined by Sir John Donaldson MR in *The Varenna*[23] and has been considered in other English cases as well. It is clear from these authorities that any such incorporation must be specifically referred to in the bill: it may not be presumed from the terms of the charterparty (to which shipper and consignee are stranger) however relevant these may be to the terms of the shipment. The Uniform Customs and Practice for Documentary Credits (1993 rev.), ICC doc. 500 (UCP500) contain a special provision on charterparty bills of lading.[24]

D. The Legal Characteristics of the Bill

A bill of lading serves three purposes: (1) it is a receipt to the shipper from the carrier acknowledging that goods described in the bill have been received for shipment in a named ship to a named port; (2) it is also "evidence" of the terms and conditions of the contract of carriage between the shipper and the carrier; and (3) it is a document of title to the goods described in the bill enabling the consignee of the goods to dispose of them, usually by endorsement and delivery of the bill (in the case of a negotiable bill). It is this last characteristic that distinguishes bills of lading from other forms of transport documents and that has made them such an indispensable tool in international trade since their origins in the 16th century.

The bill's characteristic as a document of title derives largely from mercantile custom. Its contract of carriage aspect, the reciprocal rights and obligations of the shipper, consignee, and carrier have been codified in two principal pieces of federal legislation:

---

21 (1984), 26 BLR 309 (FC TD), also considered in the subsection on bills as documents of title, *infra*.

22 *Aris Steamship v. Associated Metals & Minerals Corporation*, [1980] 2 SCR 322.

23 *Skips A/S Nordheim v. Syrian Petroleum Co. Ltd. The Varenna*, [1984] QB 599 (CA). See also Schmitthoff, *supra*, note 15, at 560 and Tetley, *Marine Cargo Claims* (3rd ed., 1988), c. 2.

24 Art. 25. See chapter 11, *infra*.

the Bills of Lading Act and the Carriage of Goods by Water Act.[25] In some cases, provincial legislation may also be applicable (although not to ocean bills).[26]

E. The Contract of Carriage

The contract of carriage is a hybrid of common law rules of contract and a series of statutory dispositions of international origin. The latter seek to establish a fair balance between the rights of the owner of the goods and the carrier.

The Bills of Lading Act,[27] which applies to railway bills, interprovincial trucking bills, and ocean bills provides that a consignee or endorsee of a bill to whom the property in the goods has passed possesses all the rights and liabilities as if the bill had been made with him or her originally. These rights are without prejudice to any right of stoppage *in transitu* and certain rights of the parties to the underlying contract or the bill, principally the rights of an unpaid vendor in Quebec. The consignee is further protected by a provision that the bill is "conclusive" evidence of the shipment as described within it, unless such person had actual notice that the goods were not on board when receiving the bill. This provision is somewhat different from the Hague Rules (and Hague-Visby Rules), which provide that the bill is *prima facie* evidence of the receipt of the goods by the carrier,[28] a matter considered in *"The Ermua"*.[29]

As has been noted above, the bill is really only evidence of a contract of carriage that has already been entered into between the shipper and the carrier. Usually, it has been partially performed (the goods have been stowed aboard) prior to its issue. It is presumed that the parties have acceded to its terms but, as in the case of other standard form contracts, it is possible for them to vary the non-mandatory terms and conditions by their agreement or conduct.

Re Ardennes[30] is a good example of this latter proposition. In that case, a shipper of mandarin oranges orally agreed with the captain of the Ardennes that it was to proceed directly to England from Spain. The shipper wished to benefit from the prices that promptly delivered mandarins would get on the English market and avoid the imposition of an import duty that was to be imposed shortly after the ship's scheduled arrival. In fact, the ship put in at Antwerp on the way and arrived after the date for the imposition of the import duty and after prices on the English market had fallen, because of the arrival of a considerable quantity of other mandarin oranges.

---

25 Bills of Lading Act, RSC 1985, c. B-5 and Carriage of Goods by Water Act, SC 1993, c. 21 (replacing Carriage of Goods by Water Act, RSC 1985, c. C-27).

26 The Mercantile Law Amendment Act, RSO 1990, c. M-10, ss. 1 and 7.

27 RSC 1985, c. B-5.

28 Note that the Visby revision to the Hague Rules, art. III.4 contain the added stipulation that "proof to the contrary shall not be admissible when the bill of lading has been transferred to a third party acting in good faith."

29 *Coutinho, Caro & Co. (Canada) Ltd. v. Owners of the Vessel "Ermua" et al.* (1981), 121 DLR (3d) 571, [1982] 1 FC 252 (CA).

30 *Re Ardennes*, [1951] 1 KB 55; See also *Cormorant Bulk-Carriers Inc. v. Canficorp (Overseas Products) Ltd.* (1984), 54 NR 66 (FCA).

In its defence to an action in damages, the carrier relied on the "deviation clause" in the bill, a normal clause in all bills authorizing the carrier to proceed by any reasonable route and to carry the goods directly or indirectly to the port of destination.[31] The court held, however, that that contract of carriage had been entered into prior to the issue of the bill and that the contract contained an express warranty that overruled any inconsistent terms of the bill. The carrier was thus liable for the damages that resulted from the failure to take the promised direct route to London. In this case, the damages amounted to the difference in the price of mandarins on the date of delivery vis-à-vis the anticipated arrival date, and the amount of the duty.

It is interesting to note that the shipper brought the action. If the property had passed to a consignee (the usual case in a FOB or CIF sale), a Canadian court would have had to interpret the wording of section 2 of the former Act, which referred to "the contract contained in the bill of lading," as extending to such collateral arrangements, in order for such a person to be successful in his or her action against the carrier.[32]

F. Liability of the Carrier

The second key piece of legislation governing bills of lading is the 1993 Carriage of Goods by Water Act.[33] The primary purpose of this legislation is to replace the original 1924 Hague Rules, a set of internationally developed rules that seek to balance the interests of the carrier and the cargo owner, by incorporating into Canadian law the Hague-Visby Rules. These rules, which are a product of two important revisions to the Hague Rules, are included in schedule I of the 1993 Act. The secondary purpose of the 1993 Act is to provide a mechanism for the eventual replacement of the Hague-Visby Rules in Canadian law by the Hamburg Rules, in schedule II of the 1993 Act.

Thus, in Canada, three potential sets of rules may apply to a contract of carriage by sea: (1) contracts of carriage entered into before May 6, 1993 are governed by the Hague Rules; (2) contracts of carriage entered into after that date (and before the entry into force of the Hamburg Rules) are governed by the Hague-Visby Rules: and (3) maritime carriage contracts entered into after the entry into force of the Hamburg Rules (if and when they actually enter into effect) will fall to be governed by those rules.[34] The

31 The right of deviation is also specifically authorized by the Hague and Hague-Visby Rules, art. IV.4.

32 A purchaser of goods who is not a consignee of the bill has no action under it: *Canadian National Railway Company v. Frozen Foods Limited* (1972), 3 Nfld. & PEIR 327 (Nfld. CA).

33 SC 1993, c. 21, repealing former eponymous legislation (RSC 1985, c. C-27).

34 The date of the introduction of the Hamburg Rules into Canadian law is subject to certain modalities: while the Hamburg Rules technically "have the force of law in Canada" (s. 8(1)), they are not immediately applicable. They will replace the Hague-Visby Rules and apply to contracts of carriage by sea only after pt. II of the Carriage of Goods by Water Act has entered into effect (s. 8(2)). Ss. 4 and 5 of the 1993 Act outline the procedure for the future entry into force of pt. II of the Act: the Minister of Transport must, on or before 31 December 1999 and thereafter every five years, consider whether the Hamburg Rules should replace the Hague-Visby Rules and report the results of this consideration to

(The footnote is continued on the next page.)

central object of the three sets of international rules is to allocate risk and liability between the shipper and the carrier. Because the three sets of rules differ markedly, it is extremely important to know which is applicable to a given bill of lading.

Many bills of lading (and even waybills) contain what has come to be referred to as the "clause paramount"—a clause expressly incorporating the Hague Rules into the bill. In Canada, the former Carriage of Goods by Water Act required such a clause for shipments originating in Canada;[35] inbound bills could also contain this clause even when not required by law, as in the case of the United Kingdom, which adopted the Hague-Visby Rules in 1971.[36] In such a case, the Hague Rules were incorporated as a matter of contract rather than law; their terms would prevail over wider exculpatory language contained elsewhere in the bill.[37] By virtue of the 1993 Carriage of Goods by Water Act, the Hague-Visby Rules apply in Canada as a matter of law to goods under bills of lading issued in Canada or another contracting state or goods originating from a contracting state[38]—that is, essentially all inbound and outbound cargo, thereby removing the need for such a contractual "clause paramount."

This section will examine the main provisions of the Hague Rules, trace the Visby revisions and additions, and then outline the changes that will eventually be introduced by the application of the Hamburg Rules. Keep in mind that as far as Canada is concerned, the Hague Rules apply only to certain contracts for the carriage of goods by sea that were entered into before May 6, 1993. However, with certain significant revisions, they form the basis for the Hague-Visby Rules that are now in force in Canada by virtue of the current legislation. In addition, some countries, most notably the United States, continue to apply the Hague Rules. This section is designed to give a summary review of the basic applicable principles, and alert the student and practitioner to certain recurring problems of which he or she should be aware.

1. The Hague Rules

The Hague Rules, 1924, relating to bills of lading, arose out of a series of diplomatic conferences held in Brussels in the 1920s. Uniformization of the conditions applicable

---

34 Continued ...

Parliament. A parliamentary committee will review the report and present its findings, including its view on the advisability of adopting the Hamburg Rules to the House of Commons. It is therefore still unclear exactly when the Hamburg Rules will begin to apply to Canadian contracts of carriage as a result of this procedure.

35 Carriage of Goods by Water Act, RSC 1985, c. C-27, s. 4.

36 Schmitthoff, *supra*, note 15, at 567.

37 *Anglo-Saxon Petroleum Co. Ltd. v. Adamastos Shipping Co. Ltd.*, [1957] 2 QB 233 (CA), per Lord Denning, at 266 and Schmitthoff, *ibid.*, at 568.

38 See art. X of the Hague-Visby Rules, in sched. I to SC 1991, c. 21. Note that, by virtue of s. 7(2)(b) of the Carriage of Goods by Water Act, the Hague-Visby Rules also apply to the carriage of goods from one place in Canada to another place in Canada, whether directly or by way of a place outside Canada, except where the transport is not covered by a bill of lading and the parties contract out of the application of the Rules.

to bills of lading had become by then essential: a complex matrix of differing mandatory legal provisions and shipowners' standard form contracts had a serious impact on the usefulness of the bill of lading as a universally acceptable instrument of international commerce. The Hague Rules impose upon the carrier certain mandatory obligations regarding the issuance of a bill in a particular form and the exercise of due diligence to make the ship seaworthy and to care for the cargo. They also provide for certain exemptions for the carriers and a limitation on their liabilities in case of a breach of their obligations.

The former Carriage of Goods by Water Act,[39] implementing the Hague Rules, applied to bills of lading relating to the carriage of goods by water "from any port in Canada to any other port whether in or outside Canada."[40]

The Hague Rules cover four basic elements: (1) the duty of the carrier to issue a bill of lading; (2) the description of the goods in the bill; (3) the responsibility of the carrier to care for the goods; and (4) the monetary limits to its liability.[41]

The carrier must issue a bill of lading that identifies the goods delivered, their quantity, weight or number of packages, and their apparent condition.[42] In so doing, it is entitled to rely on the guarantee of accuracy of information provided by the shipper,[43] but this does not protect it from claims by a consignee. The inaccuracy of the description of the goods has led to considerable litigation between disappointed purchasers and carriers. A statement that the goods have been received in "apparent good order and condition" constitutes a "clean" bill; a carrier is justified in issuing such a bill upon an inspection that is reasonable in accordance with the circumstances of loading.[44] If any deficiencies would have appeared from such an inspection, the carrier is estopped from subsequently alleging that the goods were not so received, even if the cause of damage was a peril excepted by the Hague Rules, such as "insufficiency of packing."[45] While the Hague Rules provide that the carrier must state the number of packages or the

---

39 RSC 1985, c. C-27.

40 1985 Carriage of Goods by Water Act, s. 2. For the present scope of the Hague-Visby Rules, see s. 7 of the 1993 Act and art. X of the Hague-Visby Rules. When pt. II of the 1993 Act enters into effect, the Hamburg Rules will have an even broader scope: see s. 8 of the 1993 Act and art. 2 of the Hamburg Rules.

41 For Canadian law relating to the liability of a carrier under a contract for the carriage of goods by sea under the Hague Rules, see, generally, Tetley, *Marine Cargo Claims*, *supra*, note 23.

42 Hague Rules and Hague-Visby Rules, art. III.3.

43 However, see art. 16 of the Hamburg Rules, imposing upon the carrier a positive duty to state explicitly in the bill of lading a reservation concerning inadequacies, grounds of suspicion, or lack of reasonable means of verifying information.

44 *Re National Petroleum Co., The "Athelviscount"* (1934), 39 Comm. Cas. 227.

45 *Silver v. Ocean Steamship Co. Ltd.*, [1930] 1 KB 416 (CA); but see *Franco-Steel v. Fednav Ltd.* (1990), 37 FTR 184 (TD), where the judge allowed evidence of pre-shipment condition of cargo because inspection at time of loading had only verified the condition of the packaging rather than the cargo inside it. Because the plaintiff's loading was potentially insufficient or improper, the carrier was not held liable.

quantity or the weight of the goods received and that such a description in the bill is *prima facie* evidence of the receipt of such goods, if the carrier has complied with the rules by providing the required information, its liability for the description may be attenuated by a superimposed clause of the type "weight, quantity, or quality unknown," which is found in many bills of lading.[46] The "small print" of such clauses has, in some cases, caused them to be ignored by the courts.[47] The bill must also indicate whether cargo is shipped on deck because this requires the specific agreement of the shipper; otherwise the carrier will be liable for any loss to the goods.[48] Because it is the master who signs the bill, the carrier's liability sometimes turns on the master's actual or ostensible authority when so acting.[49]

Insofar as the carrier's duty to care for the goods in transit and deliver them in good condition is concerned, the rules impose certain obligations on the carrier and then provide it with a series of specific protections and immunities, some of which relate to the dangers of a sea voyage (errors of navigation, management of the ship, fire, and saving or attempting to save life or property at sea), some of which are found in traditional *force majeure* clauses (acts of God, riots, and "fait du prince"), and some of which relate to the goods themselves (inherent vices or defects). To the latter may be added the per package limitation, the right of deviation, special rules for inflammable or dangerous cargo, and limitation periods for making claims or initiating actions.

Two primary obligations on the carrier are set out in article III of the Hague Rules, one relating to the ship, the other to the goods. Insofar as the ship is concerned, the carrier is to exercise due diligence to make the ship seaworthy, before and at the beginning of the voyage. This obligation includes the proper crew, equipment, and supply of the ship to receive and preserve safely the goods during transportation. The goods themselves must be properly loaded, stowed, cared for, and discharged. Deck carriage, for example, without the consent of the shipper constitutes a fundamental breach of the contract that prevents the carrier from relying on any limitations in the bill or the rules.[50]

Contrasting those general obligations are the series of immunities and exemptions referred to above that are contained in article IV of the Hague Rules. Some of these exemptions are straightforward; others have given rise to problems of interpretation and application. For example, the cargo owner is of the opinion that the loss is due to a failure to observe the requirements of article III, whereas the carrier seeks to show that the loss falls within the limitations of article IV with respect to the general duty to make the ship seaworthy.

---

46 *Coutinho, Caro & Co. (Canada) Ltd. v. Owners of the Vessel "Ermua" et al.* (1981), 121 DLR (3d) 571, [1982] 1 FC 252 (CA) and the cases cited by Tetley, *supra*, note 23, at 280. On the issue of *prima facie* evidence, see *Produits Alimentaires Grandma Ltée v. Zim Israel Navigation Co.* (1987), 8 FTR 191, aff'd. (1988), 86 NR 39, 17 FTR 159 (CA).

47 Tetley, *ibid.*, at 87.

48 *Svenska Traktor Aktiebolaget v. Maritime Agencies (Southampton) Ltd.*, [1953] 2 QB 295 (QB).

49 Schmitthoff, *supra*, note 15, at 588 and 589.

50 Tetley, *supra*, note 23, at 655.

Article IV.1 provides that neither the ship nor the carrier shall be liable for loss or damage caused by unseaworthiness existing before the voyage, unless it is caused by want of due diligence as required by article III. The burden of proof is on the carrier to establish the exercise of due diligence. This provision has given rise to many cases of "unseaworthiness" in which the courts have been required to determine whether that condition was the responsibility of the carrier or a condition that arose after the sailing and so could be said to be a risk of the voyage. Similarly, the provision in article IV.2(a) exempting the carrier from liability for errors made in the navigation or in the management of the ship has given rise to many cases seeking to distinguish the latter factor from the general duty to exercise care for the cargo.[51]

Maxine Footwear Co. Ltd. v. Canadian Government Merchant Marine Ltd.[52] is a good illustration of the disagreements that arise among judges when applying these criteria. In that case, a fire was started on a ship by independent contractors who came aboard to thaw ice that had formed on some pipes passing through the ship into the scuppers. This took place before the ship had sailed from Halifax and before the goods had been entirely stowed. The trial judge found as a fact that the officer who had ordered and supervised the thawing had been negligent. The trial judge was of the view that the carrier had exercised its duty to make the ship seaworthy, that for these goods at least, the voyage had started, and that article IV protected the carrier in two respects: the fire arose from negligence in the management of the ship (article IV.2(a)) and, in any event, there was, in these circumstances, no actual fault or privity of the carrier (article IV.2(b)). The Supreme Court of Canada was of the view that article III applied; although the voyage had not yet started, the carrier had exercised due diligence. Cartwright J dissented and was of the view that the carrier was responsible for the acts of its servants in failing to make the vessel seaworthy. The Privy Council concurred in this view, emphasizing that the obligation in article III is an "overriding obligation" that, if not fulfilled, does not allow subsequent recourse to the immunities provided for in article IV. In so doing, the Privy Council rejected the previously developed "doctrine of stages" (which was more properly applicable to the absolute liability of a common carrier and not to the due diligence obligation in the rules) and held that a voyage begins, for the purpose of article IV, not when the goods commence to be loaded, but when the ship sails.

From other authorities, it is clear that a carrier is liable under article III for acts of its servants or even independent contractors employed by it. "Seaworthiness" extends to the fitness of the ship to receive cargo and its general condition, including the supply of proper navigational charts,[53] although there are significant differences between the various national authorities regarding the required level of sophistication of charts and other forms of navigational aids required to make the vessel seaworthy.[54] Clearly, there is also an obligation to have an experienced and competent crew who are knowledgeable about

51 Tetley, *ibid.*, c. 16.

52 [1959] AC 589, [1959] 2 All ER 740 (PC).

53 Schmitthoff, *supra*, note 15, at 595.

54 Tetley, *supra*, note 23, at 383-85.

the ship.[55] The question whether the carrier has exercised due diligence is a matter of fact. It is not an absolute test but, rather, one that seeks to ascertain whether an intelligent and efficient attempt has been made to insure that the ship is seaworthy. An element of unseaworthiness that escapes such reasonable inspection will not, therefore, result in liability.[56]

The duty to stow the cargo properly has also been extensively interpreted, although here again fine distinctions may be drawn between a failure to stow the cargo properly and an error of "management" of the ship once the voyage has begun, which is then protected by article IV.2(b).[57]

While the immunities provided in article IV seem extensive, the burden of proof for bringing oneself within them is on the carrier and the majority are covered by the standard marine insurance policy.

In addition to the limitations contained in the rules, one must bear in mind that the bill itself may contain other limitations on the carrier's risks that are quite acceptable if they do not offend any mandatory provisions of the rules. One such familiar limitation is the "tackle to tackle" clause limiting the liability of the carrier to the period when the goods are actually within its control. In such cases, the terms of the bill will be very important; in one case, for example, the carrier was liable even though the goods had not crossed the ship's rail because the bill provided that the carrier was responsible for loading.[58]

Other important limitations contained in the rules are the right to reasonable deviation,[59] limitation periods for the bringing of actions and the per package limitation established by article IV.5. The latter has given rise to many problems in the definition of what is a package or unit for the purposes of the rule, particularly since the advent of containerization. This aspect of the question is considered below in section III dealing with container transport. It was also generally accepted that the $500 limit established by the former 1985 Canadian legislation is low. The Hague-Visby Rules have extended this to 666.67 units of account special drawing rights (SDR) per unit,[60] and the Hamburg Rules even further.[61] Thus, it may be very important to know which national law governs the bill since different regimes have incorporated different monetary limits and even different concepts of what is a package or unit for the purpose of the rules. This aspect is also considered below in the section on private international law considerations.

---

55 *Ibid.*, at 385.

56 *The Zarembo*, 136 F2d 320 (2nd Cir., 1943) and Tetley, *ibid.*, at 389.

57 Compare *Gosse Millerd, Ltd. v. Canadian Government Merchant Marine Ltd.*, [1929] AC 223, 32 Lloyd's LR 91 (HL) (goods damaged because deck hatches left open is not management of the ship so as to afford protection under art. IV.2(a)) and *International Packers London Ltd. v. Ocean Steam Ship Co. Ltd.*, [1955] 2 Lloyds LR 218 (QB) (water damage through inadequate fixing of hatches, management of the ship, affording protection under art. IV.2(a)).

58 *Pyrene Co., Ltd. v. Scindia Steam Navigation Co., Ltd.*, [1954] 2 All ER 158, [1954] 2 WLR 1005, [1954] 2 QB 402 (QB).

59 On deviation generally, see Tetley, *supra*, note 23, c. 35.

60 Art. 5(a).

61 I.e., to 835 units of account (SDR) per package or unit: art. 6(1)(a).

The date of the bill may also be important under the terms of the underlying contract; if it is not properly stated it may initiate the terms of the credit arranged for the transaction.[62]

2. The Hague-Visby Rules

The Hague Rules underwent modifications in response to both technological developments that have changed the way in which cargo is handled (that is, containerization and multimodal transport). These changes produced the perception in some quarters that the liability provisions of the rules were too biased in favour of carriers.

The first change to the rules resulted from the Brussels Protocol of 1968, known as Hague-Visby Rules.[63] The Hague-Visby Rules were adopted by the United Kingdom in 1971,[64] and several other important shipping states,[65] with the notable exception of the United States.[66] As already mentioned, Canada incorporated them into its domestic law in 1993.[67]

The primary difference introduced by the Visby revisions to the Hague Rules is that the per package limitation was raised to 666.67 units of account per package or unit, or two units of account per kilogram of gross weight, whichever is higher.[68] The Hague-Visby Rules[69] extend these limits of liability, as well as other defences available to the

---

62 *United City Merchants (Investments) Ltd. v. Royal Bank of Canada (The "American Accord")*, [1982] 2 WLR 1039, [1982] 2 All ER 720 (HL).

63 Tetley, *supra*, note 23, at 1132 *et seq*. The Hague-Visby Rules were further amended by the Brussels Protocol of 21 December 1979 relating to SDRs. See, i.e., Tetley, *ibid*., at 1139 *et seq*.

64 Carriage of Goods by Sea Act 1971, Stats. UK 1971, c. 19.

65 See list in Schmitthoff, *supra*, note 15, at 563.

66 For an interesting examination of the grounds for US non-acceptance of the Visby revisions, see Allan I. Mendelsohn, "Why the US did not ratify the Visby Amendments" (1992), 23 *JMLC* 29 to 53. Even though the United States has not yet ratified the Visby amendments, US courts have on occasion applied the higher limits contained in the Visby Rules: see, i.e., *Daval Steel Products v. M/V Acadia Forest*, 683 Fed. Supp. 444 (SDNY 1988); *Francosteel Corp. v. M/V Deppe Europe* (1990), AMC 2967 (SDNY, 1990); *INA v. The Atlantic Coroner*, 704 F Supp. 528 (SDNY, 1989); and *Associated Metals & Minerals Corp. v. The Arktis Sky* (1991) AMC 1499 (SDNY). But see *Sunds Fibrator Inc. v. The Atlantic Star* (1986) AMC 368 (SDNY, 1983) and *INA v. The Sealand Developer* (1990) AMC 2967 (SDNY 1989), in which the court refused to apply Visby provisions. See also W. Tetley, "Acceptance of Higher Visby Limits by US Courts" (1992), 23 *JMLC* 55 to 71.

67 SC 1993, c. 21, pt. I and sched. I. For a thorough examination of the Hague-Visby Rules, see H.M. Kindred et al., *The Future of Canadian Carriage of Goods by Water Law*, Dalhousie Ocean Studies Program, Halifax (1982) and Kindred, "Goodbye to the Hague Rules: Will the New Carriage of Goods by Water Act Make a Difference?" (1994-95), 24 *CBLJ* 404.

68 Protocol to amend the International Convention for Unification of Certain Rules of Law Relating to Bills of Lading (the Brussels Protocol of 1968), art. 2. This provision also implicitly applies the monetary limit of liability to bulk cargoes.

69 See art. IV bis (2) to (4).

carrier, to servants and agents of the carrier (but not independent contractors), thus enshrining the "Himalaya clause."[70] The Hague-Visby Rules provide that the carrier is not entitled to the limitation on liability where the damage was caused intentionally or recklessly with knowledge that damage would probably result.[71] As well, the Hague-Visby Rules acknowledge the recent trend toward transport containerization by stipulating that where goods are consolidated into a container or pallet for transport, unless the bill of lading enumerates the constituent packages or units, the container or pallet is regarded as the package or unit.[72]

Other provisions of the Hague Rules were also amended,[73] notably article X of the convention dealing with the scope of application of the Rules, one result of which is to apply them to inbound as well as outbound cargo "whatever may be the nationality of the ship, the carrier, the shipper, the consignee, or any other interested person." The Hague-Visby Rules also apply to carriage of goods between two places in Canada,[74] except where the contract of carriage is not covered by a bill of lading and additionally stipulates that the rules do not apply.[75]

The Hague-Visby Rules have been criticized for several reasons, the most important being a lack of clarity in the scope of their application and, from the perspective of non-ship-owning states, a continuation of the perceived unfair distribution of the risks of sea carriage. Too, the increase in the per package liability limitation has been viewed as inadequate.[76]

3. The Hamburg Rules

As a result of their inadequacies, the Hague-Visby Rules were extensively revised in a UN Commission on International Trade Law (UNCITRAL)-inspired set of rules contained in the Hamburg Rules.[77] These rules entered into force on November 1, 1992 when the requisite number of 20 states had ratified or acceded to them.[78]

---

70 See section II.F.4, *infra.* This overcomes the difficulty presented in *Midland Silicones Ltd. v. Scruttons Ltd.*, [1962] AC 446 (HL), where the House of Lords held that the Hague Rules did not apply to third parties.

71 See art. IV.5(e) and *Ontario Bus Industries Inc. v. Calumet*, [1992] 1 FC 251 (TD).

72 Art. IV.5(c).

73 See e.g., modifications to art. III.4 (no evidence admissible to contradict bill of lading as *prima facie* evidence of carrier's receipt of the goods when bill of lading transferred to third party acting in good faith), art. III.6 (time for notice), and art. III.bis (actions for indemnity).

74 Carriage of Goods by Water Act, SC 1993, c. 21, s. 7(2)(b).

75 *Ibid.*, art. 7(4).

76 See, e.g., Kindred, *supra*, note 67, at 407-8 and 416.

77 (1978), 17 *ILM* 603; Tetley, *supra*, note 23, at 1143 *et seq.*; Mankabady (ed.), *The Hamburg Rules on the Carriage of Goods by Sea* (1978); Moore, "The Hamburg Rules" (1978), 10 *JMLC* 1, at 11; Werth, "The Hamburg Rules Revisited—A Look at the US Options" (1990), 22 *JMLC* 50, at 70 to 73; Waldron, The Hamburg Rules—A Boondoggle for Lawyers?", [1991] *JLC* 305, at 318; and Sweeney, "UNCITRAL and the Hamburg Rules" (1991), 22 *JMLC* 511.

78 See art. 30 of the convention. The Hamburg Rules have largely been supported by developing countries. At 1 September 1994, 24 states had ratified the convention; an additional 24 states, including the United States, have signed the convention.

As mentioned, Canada is not a signatory to the convention, but has incorporated the Hamburg Rules into its domestic law and established the mechanism for their future application in part II and schedule II to the Carriage of Goods by Water Act,[79] to potentially enter into force at a later date.[80]

The changes introduced by the Hague-Visby modifications were considered insufficient to address the major problem of the Hague Rules—that is, their undue favouring of carriers' interests. However, the introduction of additional changes in the liability regime in the form of the Hamburg Rules also raises concern as to the potential economic and commercial costs of the new arrangements on the shipping industry.[81] There is hesitation to discard the jurisprudence and commercial practice that have evolved around the Hague and Hague-Visby rules.[82]

The advantages of the Hamburg Rules over the Hague-Visby Rules have been described as their greater comprehensiveness, their clarity, their promotion of greater certainty, and their fairer distribution of the risks of sea carriage between carrier and shipper.[83]

They are more comprehensive in several respects. Taking into account the recent diversification in shipping documentation, they extend beyond bills of lading to encompass waybills and other contracts of carriage[84] except charterparties.[85] The parties may also agree to incorporate the rules into the contract of carriage. The Hamburg Rules clearly extend to inbound as well as outbound goods.[86] The "tackle to tackle" limitation by carriers now must extend to port to port.[87] With regard to the issue of multiple or successive carriers, unaddressed in the Hague Rules, the Hamburg Rules apply to both

79 SC 1993, c. 21.

80 See discussion of the procedure for the application of sched. II, *supra*.

81 On the anticipated effects of the Hamburg Rules, see the UNCTAD, *The Economic and Commercial Implications of the Entry into Force of the Hamburg Rules and the Multimodal Transport Convention* (1991).

82 See, e.g., Moore, "The Hamburg Rules" (1978), 10 *JMLC* 1, at 11; Werth, Hamburg Rules Revisited (1990), 22 *JMLC* 50, at 70 to 73; Waldron, "The Hamburg Rules ... ," [1991] *JBL* 305, at 318; and Honnold, "Ocean Carriers and Cargo; Clarity and Fairness—Hague or Hamburg?" (1993), 24 *JMLC* 75.

83 Kindred et al., *supra*, note 67; Bauer, "Conflicting Liability Regimes: Hague-Visby v. Hamburg Rules—A Case by Case Analysis" (1993), 24 *JMLC* 53; and Honnold, *ibid.*, at 75.

84 Art. 1(6) defines a "contract of carriage by sea" as any contract whereby the carrier undertakes against payment of freight to carry goods by sea from one port to another, as long as the port of loading or discharge is in a contracting state; or the bill of lading or other contract of carriage is issued in a contracting state or provides that the convention's provisions or the laws of a state implementing the convention are to govern the contract (art. 2). The Hague Rules applied only to bills of lading and other documents of title (art. 1(b)).

85 Art. 2(3).

86 Art. 2(1).

87 Art. 4(1) defines the period of responsibility of the carrier as the period during which the carrier is in charge of the goods at the port of loading, during the carriage, and at the port of discharge. Exceptions are outlined in art. 4(2).

the "actual" carrier and the "contractual" carrier[88] and both may be liable to the shipper jointly and severally.[89] Deck cargo[90] and delays in delivery are covered.[91] In addition, the Hamburg Rules cover letters of guarantee,[92] jurisdictional issues,[93] and arbitration.[94]

Some of the above factors also contribute to greater clarity. The clear liability of the named contracting carrier and the actual carrier reduces present problems of identifying the person responsible for the loss and the extension to waybills alleviates the present situation where the Hague Rules are sometimes incorporated by reference into waybills, sometimes not. The "shipping unit" replaces the per unit or package for the purposes of the monetary limitation. If the unit is identified as parcels of goods, even if containerized, then each parcel is the unit; if a container is supplied by the shipper and no reference is made to the number of parcels in it, that is the unit. The carrier's limitations are clearly extended to employees and agents, thereby eliminating the uncertainty and the need for Himalaya clauses. This latter extension will not, however, eliminate the problem of stevedores, warehousemen, and other independent contractors, and there remain other obscurities to which the new rules may even contribute.[95]

The principal function of the Hague, Hague-Visby, and Hamburg Rules is to allocate the risks associated with the carriage of goods by sea. The Hague Rules were drafted based upon the conditions of ocean transport prevailing in the early part of the 20th century. Changes in cargo handling, navigation, and ship construction, to name a few factors, have rendered them obsolete and have forced our courts to wrestle with statutory provisions that have become ill-suited to present conditions.[96] The Hamburg Rules seek, therefore, to distribute the risks more "fairly," given modern conditions of transport. Fairness or reasonableness are not precise concepts, however, and the rules may be criticized in the degree to which they achieve this goal in their specific provisions. Fairness is also a subjective concept: the Hague Rules were perceived as unfair by third world countries who are large cargo importers and exporters, yet who own few of the carriers. From their perspective, new rules were needed to impose more duties on the carriers. To some extent, of course, any higher standard of care imposed on carriers just shifts the cost of insuring the risks that in turn will be reflected in rates. It is nonetheless important to achieve a set of internationally accepted standards to facilitate the free movement of goods.

---

88 Art. 10.

89 Art. 10(4). Art. 11 excuses the contracting carrier from liability only where a contract of carriage explicitly provides that a specified part of the carriage is to be performed by a named person.

90 Art. 9.

91 Art. 5(1) and (2).

92 Art. 17.

93 Art. 21.

94 Art. 22.

95 Kindred et al., *supra*, note 67, at 299 *et seq.*

96 Per Friendly CJ in *Leather's Best, Inc. v. S.S. Mormaclynx*, 451 F2d 800 (2nd Cir., 1971), cited by Collier J, in *J.A. Johnston Company Ltd. v. The Ship "Tindefjell"*, [1973] FC 1003, at 1009 (TD).

The Hamburg Rules extend the concept of the carrier's duty of care in several ways. They do away with the specific duties (and immunity from liability in the case of navigational error or deviation) of the carrier, regarding the duty to ensure the seaworthiness of the vessel before and at the beginning of the transit.[97] Rather, the liability of the carrier under the Hamburg Rules is based on the "principle of presumed fault or neglect" with the burden of proof ordinarily resting on the carrier.[98] Thus, the Hamburg Rules introduce a novel, unified "basis of liability" that stipulates that the carrier is liable for loss resulting from loss of or damage to the goods, as well as from delay in delivery, if the occurrence that caused the loss, damage, or delay took place while the goods were in its charge, unless the carrier proves that it, its servants, or agents took all the measures that could reasonably be required to avoid the occurrence and its consequences.[99]

This responsibility is extended to the whole of the period in which the goods are in the carrier's charge (article 4(1)). The list of excepted perils in the Hague Rules, except for the case of fire, is abolished, and the carrier will have to show that it exercised reasonable care throughout. This standard will, presumably, still afford it a defence against claims resulting from the acts of others, quarantines, riots, inherent vices of the goods, etc., which are contained in the Hague and Hague-Visby Rules, article IV exceptions, provided that reasonable measures have been taken against them. In case of fire, the carrier is no longer given a blanket protection; if the claimant can prove default in its prevention or elimination, the carrier will be liable.[100] Similarly, the traditional exemption from vicarious liability for the carelessness of the master or crew in the navigation and management of the ship is eliminated in favour of a reasonable standard of care on their part. Deck cargo, formerly exempted, is brought within the general standards (recognizing the new form of container carriage) and absolute liability is imposed in the case of cargo carried on deck without the owner's knowledge.[101]

When one combines these changes with the increased per unit limits,[102] a shifting of the burden of proof in some cases to the carrier, and extended time limits for bringing suits, the result will be a fairer distribution of the risks of the carriage transaction.[103]

---

97 See Hague Rules, Arts. 111(1) and (2).

98 See "Common Understanding Adopted by the UN Conference on Carriage of Goods by Sea" annexed to the Hamburg Rules.

99 Art. 5(1).

100 Art. 5(4).

101 Art. 9.

102 As mentioned, the original Hague Rules provided in art. IV:5 that loss or damage would be limited to "100 pounds per package or unit"; the Hague-Visby revisions increased this to the equivalent of "Frcs. 10,000 per package or unit or Frcs. 30 per kilo of gross weight, whichever is higher." The 1979 SDR Protocol limited the amount to "666.67 units of account per package or unit, or 2 units of account per kilogramme … whichever is higher" (units of account were IMF-determined SDRs). The Hamburg Rules also use SDRs: the limit is "835 units of account per package or other shipping unit, or 2.5 units of account per kilogramme … whichever is the higher" (art. 6(1)(a)).

103 Kindred, *supra*, note 67, at 321.

Uniformity of international regulation relating to contracts for the maritime carriage of goods remains an important objective, but will not be realized until all states adhere to the same international agreement. At the present time, a confusing matrix exists, created by the existence of three possible sets of applicable rules: the continued adherence of some states to the old Hague Rules, some to Hague-Visby, and some to the more recent regime of the Hamburg Rules. This matrix poses the problem of determining which limitation rules apply to a particular transaction of carriage. Although the Hamburg Convention has now entered into effect, it is not clear when it will be implemented into the domestic law of key states.

For these reasons the application of the Hamburg Rules in Canada is desirable, but it is yet to be seen when (or if) the provisions of part II of the new Carriage of Goods by Water Act will become effective, or whether we will continue to be satisfied with the much more limited reforms contained in the Hague-Visby Rules.

4. The "Himalaya" Clause

Clauses in bills of lading often seek to extend the immunities and privileges of the bills of lading to employees, servants, and even independent contractors. Some early cases developed a notion that the shipper had agreed to such a contract through the agency of the carrier even before the bill was issued.[104] These cases clearly raise the problem of third-party beneficiaries to contracts.[105] The Privy Council has recognized, however, the extension of such immunities, under a properly worded clause, to stevedores based upon the device of an implied contract between the shipper and the stevedores entered into through the agency of the carrier.[106] These clauses have come to be known as "Himalaya" clauses after an early case that gave rise to their use.[107] Their efficacy has recently been affirmed in Canada by the Supreme Court in a case that recognized that "the weight of opinion in commercial circles favours, at least in general terms, the adoption or recognition of the Himalaya clause."[108] In that case, such a clause was applied to limit the liability of warehousemen who were sued by the consignee for negligence in storing goods as agents of the carrier after the goods were unloaded from a vessel. The case also raised interesting questions regarding the jurisdiction of the Federal Court and the application of "admiralty law" to facts occurring after the goods left the ship. Because the goods in question were stolen shortly after they were deposited

104 *Pyrene Co., Ltd. v. Scindia Navigation Co. Ltd.*, [1954] 2 All ER 158, [1954] 2 WLR 1005, [1954] 2 QB 402 (QB).

105 *Greenwood Shopping Plaza Ltd. v. Beattie*, [1980] 2 SCR 228, (1980), lll DLR (3d) 257 and *Scruttons Ltd. v. Midland Silicones Ltd.*, [1962] AC 446 (HL).

106 *New Zealand Shipping Co. Inc. v. (A.M.) Satterthwaite & Co. Ltd. ("The Eurymedon")*, [1974] 1 All ER 1015 (PC) and *Port Jackson Stevedoring Pty. v. Salmond & Spraggon (Australia) Pty. ("The New York Star")*, [1980] 3 All ER 257 (PC).

107 *Alder v. Dickson (The "Himalaya")*, [1955] 1 QB 158 (CA).

108 *ITO-International Terminal Operators Ltd. v. Miida Electronics Inc. et al.*, [1986] 1 SCR 752, 28 DLR (4th) 641, at 663.

with the warehousemen, there remains a question in such cases (clearly not applicable to lightermen) about the exact point at which admiralty jurisdiction ceases and ordinary notions of bailment subject to provincial court jurisdiction commences. The case also raises the question of the appropriateness of extending the protection of the "tackle to tackle" clause to such persons.

Changes enshrined in the Hague-Visby Rules[109] have obviated the need for a contractual Himalaya clause by extending the maximum limits of liability, as well as other defences available to the carrier, to agents and servants of the carrier (but not to independent contractors, such as stevedores and warehousemen) except in cases of fundamental breach. The Hamburg Rules perpetuate the extension of the carrier's defences and limitations of liability to employees and agents.[110] They also extend the limitation of liability to independent contractors acting within the scope of their employment.

Under the Hague Rules, an insurer or surety has been held to be able to claim the protection of the limitation of liability clauses.[111] This protection will presumably be similarly extended under the Hague-Visby and Hamburg Rules.

5. *Interpretation of the Rules*

The first thing the jurist should bear in mind concerning any of the three sets of international rules for maritime carriage is their international character. The rules are the result of a series of international conferences. They have been adopted, with minor modifications, by many jurisdictions. It is important, therefore, that they should be interpreted and applied in a way which is sensitive to their special character. Lord MacMillan, in *Stag Line, Ltd. v. Foscolo Mango & Co., Ltd.*, with reference to the English Carriage of Goods by Sea Act[112] observed:[113]

> It is important to remember that the Act of 1924 was the outcome of an international conference and that the rules in the schedule have an international currency. As these rules must come under the consideration of foreign courts it is desirable in the interests of uniformity that their interpretation should not be rigidly controlled by domestic precedents of antecedent date, but rather that the language of the rules should be construed on broad principles of general acceptation.

This "international" approach to the interpretation of statutes that incorporate international rules is important if Canada's interests and requirements as a trading nation are to be advanced. Our courts are required to deal more and more with international instruments that, by way of statutory incorporation or otherwise, have a bearing on legal rights and obligations in Canada. There is a growing recognition that these must be approached with their international origin and the needs for international uniformity in

---

109 See art. IV bis.

110 Art. 7(2).

111 *Trenton Works Lavalin Inc. v. Panalpina Inc.*, 21 February 1995 (NSCA).

112 Stats. UK 1924, 14 & 15 Geo. 5, c. 22.

113 [1931] All ER 666, at 677 (HL), cited with approval by Lord Somervell of Harrow in *Maxine Footwear Co. Ltd. v. Canadian Government Merchant Marine*, [1959] AC 589, [1959] 2 All ER 740 (PC).

mind. The Hague Rules and their revisions have thus often been considered from the point of view of how they have been interpreted by US, British, and even continental courts. As a result, our courts have, in bills of lading cases, referred to continental as well as US and British cases when interpreting the meaning of the Hague Rules.[114]

As with the Hague Rules, this practice will and should continue in relation to the Hague-Visby and Hamburg Rules. This conceptual cross-fertilization should facilitate the uniform application of the Rules.

Canada is not a contracting party to the Hague, Hague-Visby, or Hamburg Rules and, therefore, was not bound to incorporate them into its domestic legislation. Since it has done so in any event, this is of no direct practical importance since they have mandatory statutory effect. In the case of other signatory states, the manner and degree to which they have been adopted will depend upon their constitutional framework and the laws they have passed to incorporate them.[115]

G. Private International Law Considerations

The introduction of new sets of rules has complicated an area where private international law problems had been extensively reduced through the acceptance of rules that were pretty well universally applied. Three possible international sets of rules may now apply to a bill of lading as well as contractual provisions that may differ in accordance with other mandatory provisions in force from jurisdiction to jurisdiction. Canadian law generally allows a free choice of law by the parties to an international contract, a principle that was originally recognized in a bill of lading case.[116]

The 1993 Carriage of Goods by Water Act, however, confirms that the Hague-Visby Rules apply as a matter of law to outbound cargo and cargo in relation to which the bill of lading was issued in a contracting state, including Canada (this overcomes the *Vita Food Products* dilemma) and resolves the issues surrounding the mandatory nature of the Hague Rules.[117] The Hamburg Rules, once applicable, will clearly apply as a matter of law to both inbound and outbound cargo.

With regard to contracts of maritime carriage entered into before May 6, 1993 still governed by the old Hague Rules, inbound cargo may or may not be subject to them, depending on the proper law of the bill of lading, whether by way of an express choice of law in the bill or otherwise. US law applies the Hague Rules to both inbound and

---

114 See, e.g., the judgment of Collier J in *J.A. Johnston Company Ltd. v. The Ship "Tindefjell"*, [1973] FC 1003 (TD).

115 Note that both s. 7(3) (concerning the Hague-Visby Rules) and s. 8(3) (concerning the Hamburg Rules) of the 1993 Carriage of Goods by Water Act stipulate that the expression "contracting state" in the rules includes Canada and any other state that, without being a contracting state, gives the force of law to the respective rules.

116 *Vita Food Products, Incorporated v. Unus Shipping Co., Ltd.*, [1939] AC 277, [1939] 2 DLR 1 (PC). See also J.-G. Castel, *Canadian Conflict of Laws* (3rd ed., 1993) and Tetley, "Vita Food Products Revisited: Which Parts of the Decision Are Good Law Today?" (1992), 37 *McGill LJ* 292.

117 SC 1993, c. 21, s. 7 and Hague-Visby Rules, art. X.

outbound cargo,[118] an attitude considered by some other states as legal imperialism. Since Canada now applies the Hague-Visby Rules and the United States continues to apply the Hague Rules, important differences may arise between our two countries, as cases such as *The "Tindefjell"* illustrate.[119] Bills of lading themselves may contain alternative provisions depending on which law applies and a court will have first to decide which is the applicable law to the bill of lading,[120] and then to decide which of those contractual clauses do not conflict with mandatory provisions of that law. Where terms are used in a bill that are appropriate for one legal system but not for another, problems of interpretation result. Where a mandatory legal provision does not apply, the proper approach is to ascertain the intention of the parties, as evidenced by the bill as a whole.[121] Where the Hague Rules are not applied as a matter of law but as a matter of contract they presumably lose their mandatory character and may be modified by other contractual provisions in the bill, subject to the clause paramount concept discussed above. Furthermore, our courts will not give effect to a choice of jurisdiction clause where the courts of the jurisdiction selected would limit the carrier's liability in a way not permitted by the Act and the rules.[122]

For these and other reasons, it is obvious that international shipping would be simplified by the adoption of a uniform and universal set of rules. It is to be hoped that the Canadian government advances this process by initiating the application of the Hamburg Rules to contracts of carriage through mobilization of part II of the 1993 Carriage of Goods by Water Act without delay.

H. The Bill of Lading as a Document of Title

It is this characteristic that, combined with its negotiability, makes the bill of lading uniquely useful in international trade, enabling the property in the goods to pass upon delivery or endorsement and delivery of the bill. Thus the goods may be disposed of or pledged to secure an advance while in transit.

In the case of a CIF (or FOB) contract, the buyer is usually obliged to pay the price upon tender of the bill (together with the other documents called for in the contract of

---

118 Carriage of Goods by Sea Act, 1936, 46 US Code, Appendix, s. 1312.

119 [1973] FC 1003 (TD). See section III, *infra*.

120 An interesting recent case concerning conflict of law issues arising from a bill of lading is *Ontario Bus Industries v. Federal Calumet (The)*, [1992] 1 FC 245 (TD). In this case, the bill of lading was ambiguous as to whether the Hague Rules, by virtue of German law where the bill of lading was issued, or the Hague-Visby Rules, by virtue of Belgian law where the goods were loaded, applied concerning the limitation of liability. Applying the conflict of law rules of the *lex fori*, the court held that the Hague-Visby Rules were the governing law. The court followed the *contra preferentum* principle, applying the Hague-Visby Rules, which favoured the plaintiff due to the additional clauses providing that the limitation of liability did not apply where damage was caused intentionally or recklessly and with knowledge that damage would probably result. This exclusion was not available under the Hague Rules.

121 Per Collier J, in *The "Tindefjell"*, [1973] FC 1003, at 1012 (TD).

122 *Agro Co. of Canada Ltd. v. The "Regal Scout"* (1983), 148 DLR (3d) 412 (FCTD).

sale). As stated in one leading case, "the bill of lading in law and in fact represents the goods" and delivery of the bill operates as a "symbolical delivery of the cargo" or as the key to the door of the warehouse containing them.[123]

While delivery of the bill transfers a right to possession, it does not always transfer the property in the goods, however, since the passing of property remains a matter of the intention of the parties as determined by the presumptions set out in the Sale of Goods Act.[124] Where, for example, the bill is transferred to an agent of the shipper to obtain delivery of the goods, this does not pass the property; nor would a transfer to a bank to serve as a pledge pass property, unless the advance is not repaid. Even the taking out of the bill in the name of the purchaser does not always result in passing the property.[125]

The carrier, however, may deliver the goods to the holder of the bill without any liability, unless it is aware of some defect in that person's right to receive them. In cases of doubt, the carrier will normally insist upon an indemnity of some kind being provided before delivery because otherwise the carrier is liable in conversion and the "tackle to tackle" clause will not protect it even if the delivery takes place after removal of the goods from the ship.[126] As a result, the holder of the bill of lading may be able to obtain delivery of the goods as against a true owner; even the latter cannot insist on obtaining the goods without the bill.[127]

Not all bills of lading are negotiable; by mercantile custom, a bill "to order" or "to order or assigns" is negotiable but a bill made out exclusively to a named consignee (a "straight" bill) is not.[128] Usually, bills indicate clearly how they are to be filled out so the shipper will indicate whether they are negotiable or not. While the assignee of the bill has the right to the delivery of the goods from the carrier, he or she has no higher ownership rights than the transferor. In this sense, the transferee is not in the same position as a holder in due course of a bill of exchange.

In US law, the general principle is that the holder of a negotiable document of title to goods is the owner of the document and the goods (vis-à-vis third parties without notice of any defect in such rights). And the negotiable bill of lading conveys similar rights in continental legal systems.[129]

Finally, there may be cases where persons take out a bill in their name exclusively for the purpose of protecting their ownership in the goods; in such a case, they are not a

---

123 *Biddell Brothers v. E. Clemens Horst Co.*, [1912] AC 18, [1911] 1 KB 934, at 957 (CA), per Kennedy LJ and see *Newfoundland and Labrador Hydro v. Day & Ross Ltd.* (1981), 31 Nfld. & PEIR 203, 87 APR 203 (Nfld. TD).

124 In Ontario, see Sale of Goods Act, RSO 1990, c. S-1, s. 19. Schmitthoff, *Schmitthoff's Export Trade: The Law and Practice of International Trade* (9th ed. 1990) at 590-91; see discussion in Ramberg, *supra*, note 20, at 3 *et seq*. See also Ontario International Sale of Goods Act, RSO 1990, c. I-10, discussed in chapter 5, *supra*.

125 *The Kronprinsessan Margareta*, [1921] 1 AC 486, at 517 (PC).

126 *Sze Hai Tong Bank v. Rambler Cycle Co. Ltd.*, [1959] AC 576 (PC).

127 *Trucks & Spares Ltd. v. Maritime Agencies (Southampton) Ltd.*, [1951] 2 All ER 982 (CA).

128 Baxter and Feltham, *Export Practice* (1964), at 1-12.

129 *Ibid.*

party to the contract of carriage and are not liable for damage to the ship caused by the cargo.[130]

I. Ocean Waybills

An ocean waybill "is a non-negotiable contract of carriage of goods by sea, dependent on the terms and conditions found in the waybill."[131] It is a modern substitute for a negotiable ocean bill of lading. Although an ocean waybill is a contract of carriage and a receipt, it is not a document of title. Thus, the waybill consignee cannot obtain delivery of the goods by merely presenting it. Proof must be made that the consignee is the person named in the waybill.

Ocean waybills were, with some exceptions, subject to the former Carriage of Goods by Waters Act.[132] The new Carriage of Goods by Water Act implementing the Hague-Visby Rules applies to "contracts of carriage," a term applying only to contracts of carriage covered by a bill of lading "or any similar document of title."[133] As the ocean waybill is not a document of title, it may fall outside the scope of the legislation and the convention.

The Comité Maritime International (CMI) has adopted a set of "Uniform Rules for Sea Waybills" that apply "when adopted by a contract of carriage which is not covered by a bill of lading or similar document of title, whether the contract be in writing or not."[134] The rules provide that a sea waybill is subject to any applicable international convention or national law that is or, if the contract of carriage had been covered by a bill of lading or similar document of title would have been, compulsorily applicable.[135] If incorporated into a sea waybill, the rules would therefore have the effect of subjecting the Canadian waybill to the Hague-Visby Rules. The rules contain provisions on agency;[136] description of the goods;[137] the right of control;[138] and delivery.[139]

III. CONTAINER TRANSPORT

A. Introduction

Containerization, whether used in unimodal or multimodal international transportation of goods, raises a number of legal problems.

130 *Union Industrielle et Maritime v. Petrosal International Ltd.* (1984), 26 BLR 309 (FC TD).

131 W. Tetley, *Marine Cargo Claims* (3rd ed., 1988), at 942.

132 See Tetley, *ibid.*, at 946, 952, and 10012. See also Kindred et al., *supra*, note 67, at 333 *et seq.*, "Carriage Under Waybills."

133 See art. 1(b) of the Hague-Visby Rules, in sched. 1 to the Carriage of Goods by Water Act, SC 1993, c. 21.

134 Art. 1(ii).

135 Art. 4(i).

136 Art. 3.

137 Art. 5.

138 Art. 6.

139 Art. 7.

Where the goods to be sent by the exporter-consignor fill a full container load, the carrier[140] usually sends the container to the exporter's place of business for loading. It is sealed by the carrier when picked up. The container will then be delivered to the buyer-consignee's place of business. This type of transport is called door-to-door container. Where the goods for export fill less than a full container load, they are taken to a container freight station for consolidation with the goods of other exporters in a groupage container. On arrival at the container freight station at the point of destination, the goods are separated and delivered to the various consignees.

The recipient of a full container load or a groupage container will issue a receipt to the exporter(s)-consignor(s) that may take the form of a container bill of lading, combined transport bill of lading, or any other form of receipt.

B. The Contract of Export Sale

The Incoterms 1990 deal with the unitization of cargo in containers and multimodal transport. The most suitable trade term is without doubt free carrier, named point (FCA).[141]

C. The Liability of the Carrier

Where the transport is unimodal, the liability of the carrier for loss, damage, or delay depends upon the mode of transport used.[142] In the case of multimodal transport, each successive carrier is subject to different rules concerning liability.

No single regime applies to the whole transport from the point of departure to the point of destination. Also, it is often difficult to ascertain at which stage of the carriage the goods were damaged or lost. With respect to the carriage of goods by sea, the former Carriage of Goods by Water Act, which incorporated the Hague Rules, declared, *inter alia*, that neither the carrier nor the ship would be liable for any loss or damage to the goods in an amount exceeding $500 per package unit, unless the nature and value of such goods had been declared by the shipper before shipment and inserted in the bill of lading.[143] This raised the question of whether a package or unit is the container or the packages inside. The answer depended upon the intention of the parties, which may be found on the face of the bill of lading since article III.3 required the carrier and shipper to describe the goods on that bill, and the shipper guaranteed to the carrier the accuracy of the description of such goods.[144]

In addition to raising the limitation threshold of liability, both the Hague-Visby Rules, in part I of the 1993 Carriage of Goods by Water Act (now in effect in Canada),

140 Note that carriers often lease containers.

141 See chapter 5, *supra*.

142 See sections II (sea transport), IV (air transport), and V (land transport). In general as to sea transport, see Tetley, *supra*, note 131, c. 30, at 639 *et seq*.

143 Art. IV.5.

144 Art. III.4. Contrast with art. 16 of the Hamburg Rules, which imposes on the carrier a duty to take reasonable measures to ascertain the accuracy of the bill of lading.

and the Hamburg Rules in part II of the 1993 Act (to come into effect in Canada at a later date) directly address the issue of containerization and packaging. The Visby revisions to the Hague Rules clarify the effect of consolidating cargo in containers and revised the monetary limit based on weight. According to article 5(c) of the Hague-Visby Rules, a container will be deemed a "package or unit" only where the number of packages or units consolidated inside are not enumerated on the bill of lading; if they are enumerated in the bill of lading, this number of packages or units will be the ones used. The Hamburg Rules contain a similar clarification.[145]

Even before the Hague-Visby clarifications entered into effect in Canada, Canadian courts had adopted the stance that "package" means each package inside the container if the number of packages is listed on the face of the bill of lading.[146] However, if on the face of the bill, only the container is mentioned, the container is the package.[147]

It should be noted that the carriage of containers on deck without a declaration to that effect on the bill of lading violated the Hague Rules, with the result that the carrier could not invoke any of the limitations of liability in the contract or in the Hague Rules.[148] The Hamburg Rules expressly provide that carriage on deck is permitted only where it is in accordance with an agreement with the shipper or with the "usage of a particular trade or is required by statutory rules or regulations."[149] Absent an express declaration in the bill of lading evidencing agreement concerning deck carriage, where the carrier fails to discharge the burden of proving that such an agreement was in fact reached, the carrier is liable for loss, damage, or delay. Deck carriage in contravention of an agreement to carry goods under deck leads to the loss of the right to limit responsibility under the Hamburg Rules.[150]

---

145 Art. 6(2)(a). See also increased content requirements in art. 5.

146 *Quebec Liquor Corp. v. Dart Europe* (1979), AMC 2382 (FC); *International Factory Sales Services v. The "Alexandr Serafimovich*, [1976] 1 FC 35 (TD); *Johnston Co. Ltd. v. The Ship Tindefjell et al.*, [1973] FC 1003 (TD); *Carling O'Keefe Breweries of Can. Ltd. v. C.N. Marine Inc.* (1986), 7 FTR 178 (TD); and *Consumers' Distributing Co. Ltd. v. Dart Containerline Co. Ltd.* (1980), 31 NR 181 (Fed. CA).

147 E.g., in *Trenton Works Lavalin Inc. v. Panalpina Inc.* (NS SC, 23 November 1993), involving the carriage of 285 railway cars, the court interpreted a "package" to be one railway car. The carrier's liability for damaging one railway car in transit was thus limited to $500 under the Hague Rules. While the trial judge held that the insurer could not benefit from the limitation of liability, on appeal (NS CA, 21 February 1995), the court held that the surety enjoyed the benefit of the limitation of liability clause contained in the underlying contract, and that the liability of the surety cannot exceed that of the principal.

148 See Tetley, *supra*, note 131, at 653 *et seq.*

149 Art. 9(1) of the Hamburg Rules, in sched. II to the Carriage of Goods by Water Act, SC 1993, c. 21.

150 Hamburg Rules, arts. 9(4) and 8.

D. The 1980 United Nations Convention on International Multimodal Transport of Goods[151]

This convention, which is not yet in force,[152] adopts a uniform system of liability[153] for the multimodal transport operator for international carriage involving at least two different modes of transport.[154] It was inspired by the Hamburg Rules. The convention covers any container, pallet, or similar article of transport or packaging if supplied by the consignor.[155] The carrier must be acting as principal, not as agent or on the consignor's behalf. In this circumstance, "[t]he responsibility of the multimodal transport operator for the goods under the Convention covers the period from the time he takes the goods in his charge to the time of their delivery."[156]

Article 16 deals with the basis of liability of the multimodal transport operator:

> 1. The multimodal transport operator shall be liable for loss resulting from loss of or damage to the goods, as well as from delay in delivery, if the occurrence which caused the loss, damage or delay in delivery took place while the goods were in his charge as defined in article 14, unless the multimodal transport operator proves that he, his servants or agents or any other person referred to in article 15 took all measures that could reasonably be required to avoid the occurrence and its consequences.
>
> 2. Delay in delivery occurs when the goods have not been delivered within the time expressly agreed upon or, in the absence of such agreement, within the time which it would be reasonable to require of a diligent multimodal transport operator, having regard to the circumstances of the case.
>
> 3. If the goods have not been delivered within 90 consecutive days following the date of delivery determined according to paragraph 2 of this article, the claimant may treat the goods as lost.

Liability may be limited to an amount not exceeding the greater of 920 SDR per package or shipping unit or 2.75 SDR per kilogram of the goods lost or damaged.[157]

---

151 (1980), 19 *ILM* 938; G.F. FitzGerald, "The United Nations Convention on the International Multimodal Transport of Goods" (1980), 5 *Ann. Air & Sp. L* 51.

152 The convention requires adherence by 30 states before entry into force (art. 36). At 1 September 1993, it had seven ratifications (Chile, Malawi, Mexico, Morocco, Rwanda, Senegal, and Zambia) and two additional signatories (Norway and Venezuala).

153 The drafting of the convention was strongly influenced by the Hamburg Rules concerning the carriage of goods by sea.

154 Art. 30(4) of the convention stipulates that transport transactions covered by the Convention on the Carriage of International Carriage of Goods by Road of 19 May 1956 (CMR) and the International Convention concerning the Carriage of Goods by Rail of 25 February 1961 (CIM) (embodied in COTIF) are deemed not to be multimodal and are thus excluded from the convention's scope of application.

155 Art. 1.7.

156 Art. 14.1.

157 Art. 18.

However, the right to limitation of liability is lost where the cause of loss, damage, or delay was intentional or done recklessly with knowledge that it would probably result.[158]

The convention also provides that where a container, pallet, or similar article of transport is used to consolidate goods, the packages or other shipping units enumerated in the multimodal transport document as packed in such article of transport are deemed packages or shipping units. Otherwise, the goods in such article of transport are deemed one shipping unit.[159]

The UNCTAD and the ICC have jointly prepared a set of rules[160] governing multimodal transport that have been accepted by a large majority of multimodal operators around the world. The new UCP500, prepared by the ICC Banking Commission, take account of these UNCTAD-ICC Rules.[161]

E. Container Transport Documents

1. General

Many documents are used as container transport documents. The most relevant are the multimodal transport document and the container bill of lading.

2. UNCTAD-ICC Rules

Until the 1980 UN Convention on International Multimodal Transport of Goods enters into force and is widely applied, the 1992 UNCTAD-ICC Rules for Multimodal Transport Documents will be used predominantly. These rules are replacing the 1975 ICC Uniform Rules for a Combined Transport Document[162] in the transport industry.

The UNCTAD-ICC Rules are based on the Hague and Hague-Visby rules. They are minimum standard rules and not standard conditions,[163] and do not apply automatically: they must be incorporated into the contract between the exporter-consignor and the multimodal transport operator (MTO). Some of the rules can be used as such in the multimodal transport document; others must be adapted to put them in the form of contractual conditions. When incorporated into a contract of carriage, the rules supersede any additional terms of the multimodal transport contract that are in contradiction to them, except insofar as they increase the responsibility or obligations of the MTO.[164]

---

158 Art. 21.

159 Art. 18.2(a). The formula for limitation of liability in art. 18.1 is the higher of 920 SDRs per package or 2.75 SDRs per kilogram of goods lost or damaged.

160 See UNCTAD-ICC Rules for Multimodal Transport Documents (1992), ICC doc. 481.

161 See art. 26(a) of the UCP500.

162 ICC doc. 298.

163 The ICC recommends that an MTO wishing to use the rules as a basis for a multimodal transport contract supplement the rules with provisions on optional stowage, routing, freight and charges, liens, both-to-blame collision, general average, jurisdiction, and governing law. Such additions may only be made to the extent they are not contrary to the rules.

164 R. 1.2.

The FIATA Multimodal Transport Bill of Lading, relied upon by the Canadian International Freight Forwarders Association (CIFFA), is based upon the UNCTAD-ICC Rules.

The rules provide for the issue of the multimodal transport document in either negotiable form, in which case it must be surrendered at destination before the goods may be delivered, or in non-negotiable form, in which case delivery is made to a consignee without the need to surrender any document.[165] The multimodal transport document covers the entire voyage from the place at which the goods are taken in charge in one country to the place of delivery in another country. It is a through start-to-finish transport document, which replaces the separate unimodal transport documents used when several modes of carriage are involved. It is issued by the MTO, who either provides the transport or at least part of it, or has merely arranged for the provision of the transport. In both cases, the MTO acts as principal vis-à-vis the consignor. The responsibility of the MTO for the goods covers the period from the time the MTO has taken the goods in his or her charge to the time of the delivery of the goods.[166]

The rules outline the liability of the MTO concerning the loss of or damage to the goods, and for delay, while the goods are in his or her charge.[167] Consistent with the Hague-Visby Rules, the UNCTAD-ICC Rules provide exemptions from liability for nautical fault and fire.[168] As under the Hague-Visby regime, these defences are subject to the requirement that, when the loss or damage has resulted from unseaworthiness of the vessel, the MTO can prove due diligence concerning seaworthiness at the start of the voyage. There is a limitation of liability of 666.67 SDR per package or unit[169] or 2 SDR per kilogram, whichever is higher.[170] Where the contract does not include carriage of goods by sea, the limit is 8.33 SDR per kilogram.[171] Since the rules do not possess the force of law, they are subject to the limits of compensation prescribed in international conventions or national laws applicable during any particular stage of the multimodal transport.[172] The MTO is also liable with respect to consequential loss.[173] The rules on liability and limitations of liability also apply to servants, agents, and other persons employed by the MTO concerning claims grounded in either tort of contract.

Expressly envisaging the use of EDI, the rules define a multimodal transport document as "a document evidencing a multimodal transport contract and which can be replaced by electronic data interchange meassages insofar as permitted by applicable law."[174]

---

165 R. 2.6.

166 R. 4.1.

167 R. 5.1.

168 R. 5.4.

169 As under the Hague-Visby Rules, where a container is loaded with more than one package or unit, the container constitutes the unit unless the packages of other shipping units are enumerated in the multimodal transport document (r. 6.2).

170 R. 6.1.

171 R. 6.3.

172 R. 6.4.

173 R. 6.5.

174 R. 2.6.

3. Container Bill of Lading

The container bill of lading is a bill of lading subject to the Hague-Visby Rules (or, potentially, the Hamburg Rules) contained in the Carriage of Goods by Water Act with respect to the portion of carriage by sea or to the Warsaw Convention, as amended, for the portion of carriage by air. When the stage where the loss of or damage to the goods cannot be ascertained, the liability of the carrier is determined by agreement of the parties.[175] Canadian carriers use their own in-house multimodal transport bill of lading that covers containers, also subject to relevant international conventions and Canadian legislation.

When issuing a clean container bill of lading, the carrier does not comment on the order and condition of the goods at shipment, unless it actually packed the container.

IV. CARRIAGE OF GOODS BY AIR

A. Sources

Federal legislative jurisdiction exists over aeronautics by virtue of the Constitution Act, 1867.[176] It is based on section 91, which confers upon Parliament the power to make laws for the peace, order, and good government of Canada.[177] Pursuant to this power, Parliament has enacted the Aeronautics Act,[178] the Canada Transportation Act 1996,[179] and the Carriage by Air Act.[180] This last piece of legislation gives effect to the Warsaw Convention of October 12, 1929,[181] as amended by the Hague Protocol of September 28, 1955,[182] which provides for the unification of certain rules relating to international carriage by air.[183]

---

175 This is known as the network liability system. The standard clause reads as follows:

> When the goods have been damaged or lost during through transportation and it cannot be established in whose custody the goods were when the damage or loss occurred, the damage or loss shall be deemed to have occurred during the carriage by water and the Hague Rules as defined above shall apply.

176 (1867), 30 & 31 Vict., c. 3, as am. (UK).

177 See *Johannesson v. West St. Paul*, [1952] 1 SCR 292 and Hogg, *Constitutional Law of Canada* (3rd ed., 1992).

178 RSC 1985, c. A-2, as am., esp. ss. 4 to 6 and 8(1)(e).

179 SC 1996, c. 10, as am., esp. ss. 55-86.

180 RSC 1985, c. C-26. Other Canadian statutes relating to aeronautics are not directly relevant to our topic.

181 CTS 1947, no. 15, 137 LNTS 13.

182 CTS 1964, no. 29, 478 UNTS 371. Canada is not a party to the 1961 Guadalajara Convention, 500 UNTS 31 (which entered into force on 1 May 1964), dealing with the unification of certain rules relating to international carriage performed by a person other than the contracting carrier, or the 1971 Guatemala City Protocol, ICAO doc. 8932 (not yet in force); the Montreal Protocol no. 4 of 1975, ICAO doc. 9148 is not in force in Canada.

183 Other international civil aviation conventions and agreements that are in force in Canada are not relevant to our topic. Note that passengers on a journey to, from or with an agreed stopping place in the

(The footnote is continued on the next page.)

The words "navigation and shipping" and "aeronautics" in the Federal Court Act[184] give jurisdiction to the Federal Court to entertain a claim arising out of a contract for the carriage of goods by air.

B. Application of the Warsaw-Hague Convention

The convention as amended by the Hague Protocol applies to all "international carriage of cargo performed by aircraft for reward as well as gratuitous carriage by aircraft performed by an air transport undertaking." "International carriage" is defined as "any carriage in which, according to the agreement between the parties, the place of departure and the place of destination[185] ... are situated either within the territories of two High Contracting Parties, or within the territory of a single High Contracting Party, if there is an agreed stopping place within the territory of another State, even if that State is not a High Contracting Party."[186]

When the place of departure is in the territory of a state party to the original convention and the place of destination is in the territory of a state party to the amended convention, only the original convention applies.

C. Document of Carriage: Air Waybill

Every carrier of cargo has the right to require the consignor to make out and hand over to it a document, called an "air waybill," and every consignor has the right to require the carrier to accept this document. The absence, irregularity, or loss of this document does not affect the existence or the validity of the contract of carriage, which is nonetheless governed by the convention except with respect to limits of liability applicable to cargo.[187] The air waybill must contain an indication of the places of departure and destination. If these places are within the territory of a single high contracting party, and one or more agreed stopping places are within the territory of another state, there must be an indication of at least one such stopping place. The air waybill must also contain a notice to the consignor to the effect that, if the carriage involves an ultimate destination or stop in a country other than the country of departure, the convention may be applicable;

---

183 Continued ...

United States are governed by the Montreal Agreement of 13 May 1966, which contains a higher limitation of liability than under the Warsaw Convention, as am. by the Hague Protocol: (1966), 44 Civil Aeronautics Board Reports 819. The United States is not a party to the Hague Protocol.

184 RSC 1985, c. F-7, ss. 22(1) and 23. *Bensol Customs Brokers Ltd. v. Air Canada* (1980), 99 DLR (3d) 623, [1979] 2 FC 575 (CA).

185 Regardless of breaks, transhipment, or numbers of consecutive contracts or successive carriers.

186 Art. 1(1) and (2). Note that s. 2(3) of the Carriage by Air Act, RSC 1985, c. C-26, provides that the Governor in Council may, by proclamations published in the *Canada Gazette*, certify who are the high contracting parties to the convention and such proclamations are conclusive evidence of the matter so certified.

187 Art. 5.

and that it governs and, in most cases, limits the liability of carriers in respect of loss of or damage to cargo.[188]

If with the consent of the carrier, "cargo is loaded on board the aircraft without an air waybill having been made out or does not include the notice to the consignor required with respect to the application of the Convention and the limits of liability, the carrier is not entitled to avail itself of such limits."[189]

Although, in practice, air waybills are not negotiable, nothing in the convention prevents the issue of a negotiable air waybill.[190]

The air waybill is *prima facie* evidence of the conclusion of the contract, of the receipt of the cargo, and of the conditions of carriage.[191]

The consignor has the right to dispose of the cargo prior to delivery to the consignee[192] and the consignee is entitled on arrival of the cargo at the place of destination to require the carrier to hand over the air waybill to him or her and to deliver the cargo to him or her on payment of the charges due and on complying with the conditions of carriage set out in the air waybill.[193]

D. Liability of the Carrier

The carrier is liable for damage sustained in the event of the destruction or loss of or damage to any cargo, if the occurrence that caused the damage so sustained took place during the carriage by air. Carriage by air comprises the period during which the cargo is in the charge of the air carrier, whether in an aerodrome or on board an aircraft, or, in the case of a landing outside an aerodrome, in any place whatsoever. This period does not extend to any carriage by land, by sea, or by river performed outside an aerodrome. If, however, such a carriage takes place in the performance of a contract for carriage by air, for the purpose of loading, delivery, or transhipment, any damage is presumed, subject to proof to the contrary, to have been the result of an event that took place during the carriage by air.[194] The carrier is also liable for damage occasioned by delay in the carriage by air of cargo.[195]

The air carrier is not liable if it proves that all necessary measures to avoid the damage were taken or that it was impossible to have taken such measures.[196]

---

188 Art. 8.

189 Art. 9.

190 Art. 15. Due to the speed of air transport, it would be pointless to issue a negotiable air waybill.

191 Art. 11.

192 Art. 12.

193 Art. 13.

194 Art. 18.

195 Art. 19.

196 Art. 20. Contributory negligence of the consignor may exonerate the carrier partly or wholly from its liability: art. 21.

In the carriage of cargo, the liability of the carrier is limited to a sum of 250 francs[197] per kilogram, unless the consignor has made, at the time when the package was handed over to the carrier, a special declaration of interest in delivery at destination and has paid a supplementary sum if required. In that case, the carrier will be liable to pay a sum not exceeding the declared sum, unless it is proved that that sum is greater than the consignor's actual interest in delivery at destination.[198] In the case of loss, damage, or delay of part of the cargo or of any object contained therein, the weight to be taken into consideration in determining the amount to which the carrier's liability is limited shall be only the total weight of the package or packages concerned. Nevertheless, when the loss, damage, or delay of a part of the cargo, or of an object contained therein affects the value of other packages covered by the same air waybill, the total weight of such package or packages shall also be taken into consideration in determining the limits of liability.[199]

Any provision tending to relieve the carrier of liability or to fix a lower limit than that which is laid down in the convention is null and void but does not cause the nullity of the whole contract.[200]

Provisions governing loss or damage from the inherent defect, quality, or vice of the cargo carried are not null and void.[201]

The limits of liability do not apply if it is proved that the damage resulted from an act or omission of the carrier, its servants, or agents, done with intent to cause damage or recklessly and with knowledge that damage would probably result; provided that in the case of such an act or omission of a servant or agent, it is also proved that he or she was acting within the scope of his or her employment.[202]

---

197 This refers to a currency unit consisting of 65.5 milligrams of gold of millesimal fitness nine hundred. Conversion of the sums into national currencies other than gold shall, in the case of judicial proceedings, be made according to the gold value of such currencies at the date of judgment: art. 22(5). The Carriage by Air Act, RSC 1985, c. C-26, in s. 2(6) also provides that "Any sum in francs mentioned in Article 22 of Schedule I shall, for the purpose of any action against a carrier, be converted into Canadian dollars at the rate of exchange prevailing on the date on which the amount of any damage to be paid by the carrier is ascertained by the court." Note that the Montreal protocols one, two, and three established the limit of liability in special drawing rights. These Protocols are not in force in Canada.

198 Art. 22(2)(a).

199 Art. 22(2)(b). Note that the limits prescribed do not include court costs or other expenses of litigation incurred by the plaintiff: art. 22(4). For a recent discussion of limits to liability, see Milde, "Warsaw System and Limits to Liability—Yet Another Crossroad?" (1993) *Ann. Air. & Space L* 201.

200 Art. 23(1).

201 Art. 23(2). In *AG Canada v. Flying Tiger Air Line, Inc.* (1987), 61 OR (2d) 673 (HC), the inclusion in a contract for the shipment of live calves of a provision excluding liability for death, injury, or escape was ineffective; live cargo did not necessarily have "defect, quality or vice."

202 Art. 25. See also *Swiss Bank Corporation v. Air Canada* (1981), 129 DLR (3d) 85, [1982] 1 FC 756 (TD), upheld generally by the FCA (sub. nom. *Air Canada v. Swiss Bank Corp.*) [1988] 1 FC 71 (CA);

(The footnote is continued on the next page.)

Servants and agents of the carrier enjoy the benefits of the same limits of liability of the carrier if they acted in the course of their employment. The aggregate of the amounts recoverable from the carrier, its servants and agents, in that case, cannot exceed the limits set by the convention.[203]

E. Actions

The persons who have rights of action are the consignor, the consignee, and the owner[204] of the damaged, lost, or delayed goods. In the absence of fraud by the carrier, these rights of action are only exercisable with respect to damage if the person entitled to delivery has complained in writing to the carrier; receipt of goods by the consignee without complaint constitutes a rebuttable presumption that the goods have been delivered in good condition. Such complaint must be made forthwith after the discovery of the damage and not later than 14 days from the date of receipt of the cargo. In the case of delay, the complaint must be made at the latest within 21 days from the date on which the cargo has been placed at the consignee's disposal.[205] Since the convention does not define the carrier, it is assumed that the carriers who may be sued are the contracting carrier, the successive carrier, and the actual carrier.[206]

The action for damages must be brought, at the option of the plaintiff, in the territory of one of the high contracting parties, either before the court having jurisdiction where the carrier is ordinarily resident, or has its principal place of business, or has an establishment by which the contract has been made, or before the court having jurisdiction at the place of destination.[207] Choice of law and of jurisdiction clauses are null and void. However, for the carriage of cargo, arbitration clauses are permissible, provided

202 Continued …

and *Prudential Assurance Co. v. Canada*, [1993] 2 FC 293 (CA), where the FCA held that although the loss was unintentional, the defendant was aware that misdelivery of the goods to an unauthorized person was likely to cause loss.

203 Art. 25 A.

204 Regarding the owner's standing to bring a claim, see, i.e., *George Straith v. Air Canada* (BC SC, 20 September 1991) and *Gatewhite Ltd. v. Iberia Lineas Areas de Espana SA* (1988), [1989] 1 All ER 944.

205 Art. 26(2).

206 Note that art. 30(1) and (3) provides that in the case of carriage to be performed by various successive carriers and falling within the definition of art. 1(3), each carrier who accepts cargo is subjected to the rules set out in the convention and is deemed to be one of the contracting parties to the contract of carriage insofar as the contract deals with that part of the carriage, which is performed under its supervision. Thus, the consignor has a right of action against the first carrier, the consignee has a right of action against the last carrier, and each may take action against the carrier who performed the carriage during which the destruction, loss, damage, or delay took place. The carriers are jointly and severally liable to the consignor or consignee. See *Connaught Laboratories Ltd. v. Air Canada* (1978), 23 OR (2d) 176, 94 DLR (3d) 586 (HC).

207 Art. 28 and see also *Carriage by Air Act*, RSC 1985, c. C-26, s. 3.

arbitration takes place within one of the jurisdictions where a judicial action is allowed by the convention to take place.[208]

The right to damages is extinguished if an action is not brought within two years from the date of arrival at the destination, or from the date on which the aircraft ought to have arrived, or from the date on which the carriage stopped.[209]

F. Combined Carriage

In the case of combined carriage performed partly by air and partly by any other mode of transport, the provisions of the convention as amended apply only to the carriage by air, provided it falls within the scope of the convention. The parties can always insert in the document of air carriage conditions relating to other modes of carriage.[210]

G. IATA Universal Air Waybill

Over the years, the members and non-members of the International Air Transport Association (IATA) have used a common form of air waybill and conditions of contract for interline and online carriage known as the Universal IATA Air Waybill. This document provides a receipt to the shipper for the shipment at the time of delivery to the carrier, indicates the rates and charges for the carriage, makes possible the carriage of the shipment over more than one air carrier on the same document, provides a means of settlement of charges between carriers, sets forth the conditions of contract, complies with the requirements of the Warsaw convention, as amended, and uses to advantage data processing and document transmission.[211]

V. CARRIAGE OF GOODS BY LAND COVERED BY BILLS OF LADING

A. International Conventions

Canada is not party to any international convention concerning unimodal or multimodal carriage of goods by rail or by road such as the Convention concerning International Carriage by Rail of May 8, 1980 (COTIF),[212] the Convention on the Contract for

---

208 Art. 32, referring to art. 28.

209 Art. 29.

210 Art. 31.

211 This description is taken from W.E. Murnigham, "The Development of the IATA Air Waybill" in *Meredith Memorial Lectures* (1982), at 163.

212 This convention embodies the International Convention concerning the Carriage of Goods by Rail of February 25, 1961 (CIM). COTIF entered into force 1 May 1985. The convention provides for a single transport document permitting direct international transportation of passengers, baggage, and goods. All railways involved in the carriage of goods are collectively responsible for loss or damage of goods in transit. As of 1 September 1994, the convention had 39 ratifications.

International Carriage of Goods by Road of May 19, 1956 (CMR),[213] and the UN Convention on International Multimodal Transport of Goods of May 24, 1980.[214]

B. Canadian Sources

Section 92(10)(a) read with section 91(29) of the Constitution Act 1867[215] confers on the federal Parliament the power to make laws in relation to railways and other works and undertakings extending beyond the limits of any province. For our purposes, this power finds its expression in the Railway Act[216] and the National Transportation Act 1987,[217] together with the relevant regulations adopted pursuant thereto.[218]

With respect to the regulation of extra-provincial motor carriers, the federal Parliament enacted the Motor Vehicle Transport Act, 1987,[219] which provides that if a motor carrier wishes to operate an extra-provincial truck undertaking in a province it must obtain a licence from the provincial transport board if one is required for the operation of a local truck undertaking. When licensing an extra-provincial motor carrier, the provincial transport board must do so on the like terms and conditions and in the like manner as if the extra-provincial truck undertaking were a local truck undertaking. By this legislation, Parliament has delegated some of its regulatory power to the provinces.[220] For instance, in Ontario the extra-provincial carriage of goods by truck is governed by the Truck Transportation Act[221] and the regulations made thereunder that cover bills of lading.[222]

C. Liability of Carrier for Loss of or Damage to the Goods

At common law, the common carrier is almost an insurer of the cargo against loss, unless it can be established that the loss falls within a few classes of exemptions. Thus, in *George C. Anspach Co. v. Canadian National Railway Co.*,[223] the court remarked that:

---

213 399 UNTS 189. The convention entered into force on 2 July 1961. Its additional protocol (Geneva) entered into force 28 December 1980. See, i.e., M.A. Clarke, *International Carriage of Goods by Road: CMR* (2nd ed., 1991).

214 For an analysis, see G.F. FitzGerald, "The United Nations Convention on the International Multimodal Transport of Goods" (1980), 5 *Ann. Air & Sp. L* 51. See also section III.D, *supra*.

215 (1867), 30 & 31 Vict., c. 3, as am. See also in RSC 1985, app. II, no. 5. McNairn, "Transportation, Communication and the Constitution. The Scope of Federal Jurisdiction" (1969), 47 *Can. Bar Rev.* 355.

216 RSC 1985, c. R-3, as am.

217 SC 1987, c. 34, RSC 1985 (3rd Supp), c. 28.

218 See Railway Traffic Liability Regulations, SOR-91/488. The impact analysis statement relating to these regulations is found in *Can. Gaz.* pt. I, vol. 124, no. 28, 14 July 1990, at 2584.

219 SC 1987, c. 35, RSC 1985 (3rd Supp), c. 29, ss. 7 and 8.

220 For a discussion, see *Coughlin v. Ontario Highway Transport Board*, [1968] SCR 569, 68 DLR (2d) 384.

221 RSO 1990, c. T.22, as am.

222 RRO 1990, regs. 1086 to 1089, as am.

223 [1950] OR 317, at 330 (HC).

It is acknowledged in all common law jurisdictions that the duty of the common carrier is to transport goods safely from the place of shipment to the place of delivery, except where the loss or damage to the goods is caused by an act of God, the public enemy, or natural shrinkage.

In the absence of statutory restrictions, a common carrier may by contract limit its liability at common law, even when the loss is the result of its own negligence.

Section 137 of the Canada Transportation Act 1996[224] provides:

(1) A railway company shall not limit or restrict its liability to a shipper for the movement of traffic except by means of a written agreement signed by the shipper or by an association or other body representative of shippers.

(2) If there is no agreement, the railway company's liability is limited or restricted to the extent provided in any terms and conditions that the [Canada Transport] Agency may

(a) on the application of the company, specify for the traffic; or

(b) prescribe by regulation, if none are specified for the traffic.

A Multimodal (Combined) Transport Through Bill of Lading[225] may be issued to deal with the documentation and liability structure of multimodal transport when goods are exported overseas, especially in containers. Such bills of lading are used more often by shipping companies and freight forwarders than by railway companies. In multimodal transit, it is customary for the through bill of lading to contain provisions that incorporate limitations in the bills of lading issued by successive carriers. Conversely, these bills of lading may contain provisions that attract the operation of the exculpatory provisions of the through bill of lading. Since as far as the cargo claimant is concerned there is only one bill of lading, the connecting carriers are always subject to its conditions. The terms and conditions of a multimodal bill of lading and a unimodal bill of lading covering one phase of that multimodal carriage will determine which set of terms and conditions prevails.[226]

It is customary to issue a through bill of lading when carriage is divided in separate stages to be performed by other land or sea carriers to the ultimate destination. The shipper who takes out a through bill of lading need not contract with the various carriers who have to carry the goods at the consecutive stages of the journey. He or she deals with the carrier who signs the through bill of lading. A single document is used from the inland place of shipment through the different modes of transport to the final place of delivery without the need to resort to a series of individual carriage documents that would otherwise be necessary for a door-to-door shipment.

With respect to the extra-provincial carriage of goods by road, all provinces have adopted regulations making mandatory the issuance of a bill of lading in inland transit by road that must include certain prescribed provisions. For example, the regulations

---

224 SC 1996, c. 10, as am.

225 For multimodal (combined) transport and container transport see section III, *supra*.

226 See *Dopplemayr Lifts Ltd. v. Hapag-Lloyd Aktiengesellschaft*, [1982] 2 FC 772 (TD); *Lufty Ltd. v. Canadian Pacific Railway*, [1973] FC 1115 (TD) and *Bombardier v. Canadian Pacific Ltd.*, *supra*, note 228.

made pursuant to the Ontario Truck Transportation Act[227] deal with the general freight carrier's liability in the following terms for shipments originating in that province:

1. Liability of Carrier
The carrier of the goods herein described is liable for any loss of or damage to goods accepted by the carrier or the carrier's agent except as hereinafter provided.

5. Exceptions from Liability
The carrier shall not be liable for loss, damage or delay to any of the goods described in the bill of lading caused by an act of God, the Queen's or public enemies, riots, strikes, a defect or inherent vice in the goods, an act or default of the consignor, owner or consignee, authority of law, quarantine or difference in weights of grain, seed or other commodities caused by natural shrinkage.

9. Valuation
Subject to Article 10, the amount of any loss or damage for which the carrier is liable, whether or not the loss or damage results from negligence, shall be the lesser of,

i. the value of the goods at the place and time of shipment, including the freight and other charges if paid, and

ii. $4.41 per kilogram computed on the total weight of the shipment.

11. Consignor's Risk

i. If it is agreed that the goods are carried at the risk of the consignor, such agreement covers only such risks as are necessarily incidental to the carriage and the agreement does not relieve the carrier from liability for any loss or damage or delay that results from the negligence of the carrier or the carrier's agents or employees.

ii. The burden of proving absence of negligence shall be on the carrier.

The regulations also cover the liability of successive carriers under a through bill of lading:

2. Liability of Originating and Delivering Carriers
Where a shipment is accepted for carriage by more than one carrier, the carrier who issues the bill of lading (hereinafter called the originating carrier) and the carrier who assumes responsibility for delivery to the consignee (hereinafter called the delivering carrier), in addition to any other liability hereunder, are liable for any loss of or damage to the goods while they are in the custody of any other carrier to whom the goods are delivered and from which liability the other carrier is not relieved.

As in the case of carriage by rail, there is one contract arrangement whose terms bind the shipper, the consignee, and all the carriers involved in the performance of the contract represented by the bill of lading issued by the truck carrier of origin for the through transit. Both the originating and delivering carriers are responsible for claims relating to loss of or damage to the cargo and it does not matter to the claimant on whose line the loss occurred. The issuance of bills of lading by intermediate carriers has no effect on the relationship between the cargo owner and the originating and delivering carriers.

---

227 RSO 1990, c. T.22, as am., RRO 1990, reg. 1086, sched., ss. 1 and 5. For an excellent survey of Canadian Law, see J.S. McNeil, *Motor Carriers Cargo Claims* (2nd ed., 1989).

Section 3 of the Ontario regulations deals with recovery from connecting carriers:

3.(i) The originating carrier or the delivering carrier, as the case may be, is entitled to recover from any other carrier to whom the goods are delivered the amount that the originating carrier or delivering carrier, as the case may be, is required to pay for the loss of or damage to the goods while they were in the custody of such other carrier.

(ii) If there is concealed damage and the goods were interlined between carriers so that it is not clear as to who had custody of the goods when they were damaged, the originating carrier or delivering carrier, as the case may be, is entitled to recover from each of the interlined carriers an amount prorated on the basis of each carrier's revenue for carriage of the damaged goods.

VI. INTERNATIONAL FREIGHT FORWARDERS, SHIPPING AGENTS, AND CUSTOMS BROKERS

A. International Freight Forwarders

The main function of international freight forwarders is to undertake to forward goods by one or more modes of transportation on behalf of shippers or cargo owners who are small exporters and do not possess their own export organization or shipping department. They may act as agents or as principals or both.[228]

Traditionally, international freight forwarders are considered to act as agents for the shippers or owners of the goods to make arrangements for their carriage to their destination. When acting in that capacity, their primary responsibility is to take reasonable care in choosing carriers for the transportation of these goods. The shipper or owner of the goods contracts with the carrier. As agents, most international freight forwarders operate with compensation paid them by the ocean carriers, in the form of booking commissions and fees assessed to the shippers based on the extent of the services performed.

With the advent of door-to-door delivery linking multiple modes of transportation and often involving the assembling and consolidation of goods in containers, international freight forwarders began to act as non-vessel-vehicle-owning multimodal transport operators—that is, as principals in direct competition with the package of transport services offered by multimodal carriers.

With one exception,[229] no specific Canadian legislation covers the liability of international freight forwarders as principals. However, when dealing with their clients, international freight forwarders developed their own in-house bills of lading, which provided little protection to the shippers or owners of the goods. For this reason, in-house bills of lading soon fell in disrepute. They have now been replaced by the FIATA[230] Multimodal Transport Bill of Lading approved by the ICC, and issued subject

228 For a discussion of the issue of international freight forwarder as principal (i.e., carrier) or agent, see, i.e., *Bertex Fashions v. Cargonaut Canada Inc.* (29 May 1995 FCTD); see also P.F.M. Jones, Meredith Memorial Lectures, "The Forwarder—Principal or Agent—A Carrier or Not" (1986) and Tetley, *Marine Cargo Claims* (3rd ed., 1988), esp. at 694-95.

229 Ontario, see *infra*.

230 Fédération Internationale des Associations des Transitaires et Assimilés.

to the UNCTAD-ICC Rules for Multimodal Transport Documents.[231] The FIATA Multimodal Transport Bill of Lading is used by most international freight forwarders all over the world and especially by the members of the CIFFA.[232] For example, in clause 2.1(a), by the issuance of the Multimodal Transport Bill of Lading, the international freight forwarder undertakes to perform and/or, in his or her own name, to procure the performance of the entire transport from the place at which the goods were taken in charge to the place designated for delivery on the bill of lading. This language indicates that the international freight forwarder acts as principal.

Clause 6 deals with the extent of liability of the international freight forwarder:[233]

6.1 The responsibility of the Freight Forwarder for the goods under these conditions covers the period from the time the Freight Forwarder has taken the goods in his charge to the time of their delivery.

6.2 The Freight Forwarder shall be liable for loss of or damage to the goods as well as for delay in delivery if the occurrence which caused the loss, damage or delay in delivery took place while the goods were in his charge … , unless the Freight Forwarder proves that no fault or neglect of his own, his servants or agents or any other person referred to in Clause 2.2[234] has caused or contributed to such loss, damage or delay. However, the Freight Forwarder shall only be liable for loss following from delay in delivery if the Consignor has made a declaration of interest in timely delivery which has been accepted by the Freight Forwarder and stated in this FBL.

6.3 Arrival times are not guaranteed by the Freight Forwarder. However, delay in delivery occurs when the goods have not been delivered within the time expressly agreed upon or, in the absence of such agreement, within the time which would be reasonable to require of a diligent Freight Forwarder, having regard to the circumstances of the case.

6.4 If the goods have not been delivered within ninety consecutive days following such date of delivery as determined in Clause 6.3, the claimant may, in the absence of evidence to the contrary, treat the goods as lost.

6.5 When the Freight Forwarder establishes that, in the circumstances of the case, the loss or damage could be attributed to one or more causes or events, specified in a-e of the present clause, it shall be presumed that it was so caused, always provided, however, that the claimant shall be entitled to prove that the loss or damage was not, in fact, caused wholly or partly by one or more of such causes or events:

---

231 ICC doc. 481.

232 A few international freight forwarders still use in-house bills of lading.

233 For a survey of Canadian law on the liability of freight forwarders, see D. Saul and M.L. Madras, "Canadian Law Governing the liability of the Freight Forwarder and Its Carriers" (1978), 6 *Int'l. Bus. Lawyer* 435.

234 Cl. 2.2 states: "Subject to the conditions of this FBL, the Freight Forwarder shall be responsible for the acts and omissions of his servants or agents acting within the scope of their employment, or any other person of whose services he makes use for the performance of the contract evidenced by this FBL, as if such acts and omissions were his own."

a) an act or omission of the Merchant, or person other than the Freight Forwarder acting on behalf of the Merchant or from whom the Freight Forwarder took the goods in charge;

b) insufficiency or defective condition of packaging or marks and/or numbers;

c) handling, loading, stowage or unloading of the goods by the Merchant or any person acting on behalf of the Merchant;

d) inherent vice of the goods;

e) strike, lockout, stoppage or restraint of labour.

6.6 *Defences for carriage by sea or inland waterways.* Notwithstanding Clauses 6.2, 6.3 and 6.4, the Freight Forwarder shall not be liable for loss, damage or delay in delivery with respect to goods carried by sea or inland waterways when such loss, damage or delay during such damage has been caused by:

a) act, neglect or default of the master, mariner, pilot or the servants of the carrier in the navigation or in the management of the ship;

b) fire, unless caused by the actual fault or privity of the carrier, however, always provided that whenever loss or damage has resulted from unseaworthiness of the ship, the Freight Forwarder can prove that due diligence has been exercised to make the ship seaworthy at the commencement of the voyage.

The conditions state that actions against the freight forwarder may be instituted only in the jurisdiction of the place of business of the freight forwarder, and are governed by the law of that jurisdiction (clause 19).

The conditions governing the FIATA Multimodal Transport Bill of Lading also contain limitations of the freight forwarder's liability.[235] Subject to certain conditions, the freight forwarder's liability for the goods is not to exceed the higher of 666.67 SDR per package or unit or two SDR per kilogram, unless the special quality of the goods has been declared and a value stated in the bill of lading.[236] The container or pallet is deemed to be the package or unit, unless the bill of lading itemizes the contents of the container or pallet. Where the loss or damage to the goods occurs during a particular phase in the transport, and another applicable international convention or mandatory national law would have provided another limitation of liability had a separate contract been concluded for that phase of transport, then liability is to be determined with reference to that convention or mandatory law.[237] The freight forwarder forfeits the limitation of liability if the loss or delay resulted from a personal act or omission done intentionally, or recklessly with knowledge that such loss or delay would probably result.[238]

The conditions governing the FIATA Multimodal Transport Bill of Lading apply even if only one mode of transport is used[239] and only take effect to the extent that they

235 Cl. 8.

236 Where the transport does not include carriage of goods by sea or inland waterway, the freight forwarder's liability is limited to 8.33 SDR per kilogram (cl. 8.5).

237 Cl. 8.6(a).

238 Cl. 8.9.

239 See cl. 1.

are not contrary to the mandatory provisions of international conventions or national law applicable to the contract.[240] The Hague Rules, or for those countries like Canada where they are already in effect, the Hague-Visby Rules, apply to carriage of goods by sea.[241]

An international freight forwarder who acts as principal enters into a contract of services with the shipper or owner of the goods.

The CIFFA Standard Trading Conditions[242] deal, *inter alia*, with the position of an international freight forwarder when providing services as an agent or as a principal, as well as limitations of liability:[243]

Company as an Agent

27. Clauses 28 to 30 below inclusive apply where and to the extent that the Company[244] in accordance with these conditions is acting as agent on behalf of the Customer.

28. The Company shall be entitled and the Customer[245] hereby expressly authorises the Company, except insofar as has been otherwise specifically agreed between the Company and the Customer, to enter into contracts on behalf of the Customer,

(i) for the carriage of goods by any route or means or person;

(ii) for the storage, packing, trans-shipment, loading, unloading or handling of the goods by any person or at any place, and for any length of time;

(iii) for the carriage or storage of goods in or on transport units or with other goods of whatever nature; and

(iv) to do such acts as may in the opinion of the Company be reasonably necessary in the performance of its obligations in the interests of the Customer.

29. The Company shall be entitled to perform any of its obligations herein by itself or by its parent, subsidiary or associated companies or by any other person, firm or company. In the absence of agreement to the contrary any contract to which these Conditions[246] apply is made by the Company on its own behalf and also as agent for and on behalf of any such parent, subsidiary or associated company, and such company shall be entitled to the benefit of these Conditions.

30. Where there is a choice of rates according to the extent or degree of the liability assumed by carriers, warehouseman or others, no declaration of value where optional will be made except under special arrangements; nor shall the Company be under any liability to the Customer by reason of having entered into any contract on behalf of the Customer whereby the extent or degree of the liability assumed by a carrier, warehouseman or other party is in any respect excluded

240 Cl. 7.1.

241 Cl. 7.2.

242 May 1986, as am., 1988.

243 Limitation of liability according to CIFFA, para. 35 would not be available to the carrier in cases of fundamental breach. For recent judicial treatment of the application of the limitation of liability provisions in CIFFA, para. 35, see,i.e., *Crompton Sage Enterprises Inc. v. Lep International Inc.* (BC SC, 14 February 1994).

244 It is the CIFFA member trading under these conditions.

245 Means any person at whose request or on whose behalf the company undertakes any business, or provides advice, information, or services.

246 The entire undertakings, terms, conditions, and clauses embodied herein.

or limited save where such contract is entered into contrary to specific instructions given by the Customer and accepted by the Company.

Company Contracting as Principal

31. Clauses 32 to 33 inclusive apply where and to the extent that the Company in accordance with these Conditions is contracting as principal save and except where an "FBL"[247] is issued pursuant to Clause 3(C).

32. The Company is not a common carrier and deals on the basis of these Conditions alone. The Company reserves to itself a reasonable liberty as to the means, route and procedure to be followed in the handling, storage and transportation of goods.

33.(A) When and to the extent that the Company has contracted as principal for the performance of any services, the Company undertakes to perform and/or in its own name to procure the performance of those services, and subject always to the totality of these Conditions accepts liability for loss of or damage to goods taken into its charge occurring between the time when the Company takes the goods into its charge and the time when the Company is entitled to call upon the Customer, consignee or owner to take delivery of the goods.

(B) The Company shall be deemed to have taken the goods into its charge when they have been received by the Company or have been released or handed over by the Customer or any person acting on behalf of the Customer to any person acting on behalf of the Company in accordance with any directions of the Company for the performance of the Customer's instructions.

Limitations of Liability

34.(A)(i) the Company shall be liable for loss of or damage to the goods occurring between the time when the Company takes the goods into its charge and the time of delivery.

(ii) the Company shall, however, be relieved of liability for any loss or damage if such loss or damage was caused by:

(a) an act or omission of the Customer, owner, or person acting on their behalf, other than the Company;

(b) insufficiency or defective condition of the packaging or marks and/or numbers, save where the Company has undertaken to carry out the packing, application of marks or labelling or numbering of the goods;

(c) handling, loading, stowage or unloading of the goods by the Customer, owner or any person acting on their behalf;

(d) inherent vice of the goods;

(e) strike, lockout, stoppage or restraint of labour, the consequences of which the Company could not avoid by the exercise of reasonable diligence;

(f) any cause or event which the Company could not avoid and the consequences whereof they could not prevent by the exercise of reasonable diligence;

(g) a nuclear incident if the operator of a nuclear installation or a person acting for him is liable for this damage under an applicable international convention or national law governing liability in respect of nuclear energy.

---

247 FBL means a bill of lading or a waybill covering the carriage of goods, and includes the FIATA Multimodal Transport Bill of Lading.

(iii) the burden of proving that the loss or damage was due to one or more of the above causes or events shall rest upon the Company.

(B) In any case where, in accordance with these Conditions, the Company is liable to pay compensation in respect of loss or damage to goods, and it is known where such loss or damage occurred, the extent and the amount of the liability in respect of such loss or damage shall be determined by the provisions contained in any applicable convention or law, which provisions

(i) cannot be departed from by private contract to the detriment of the claimant; and

(ii) would have applied if the claimant had made a separate and direct contract with the actual provider of the particular service in respect of that service or that part of any operation where the loss or damage occurred and had received as evidence thereof any particular document which must be issued in order to make such convention or law applicable.

35.(A) When the Company is liable for compensation in respect of loss of or damage to the goods, such compensation shall be calculated by reference to the value of such goods at the place and time they are delivered to the Consignee in accordance with the contract or should have been so delivered.

(B) The value of the goods shall be fixed according to the current commodity exchange price, or if there be no such price, according to the current market price, or, if there be no commodity exchange price or current market price, by reference to the normal value of goods of the same kind and quality.

(C) Compensation shall not, however, exceed 2 SDR (SDR = Special Drawing Right) units per kilo of gross weight of the goods lost or damaged. Under special arrangements, the Company may accept liability in excess of the limits set out in Sub-clause (A) and (B) above upon the Customer agreeing to pay the Company's additional charges for accepting such increased liability. Details of the Company's additional charges will be provided upon request.

(D)(i) in no circumstances whatsoever shall the Company be liable to the Customer or owner for consequential loss or loss of market however caused.

(ii) without prejudice to any other conditions herein or other defences which may be open to the Company, in no circumstances whatsoever shall the Company be liable to the Customer or owner for delay or deviation however caused in a sum in excess of twice the Company's own charges in respect to the relevant transaction.

In the case of all other claims;

(a) the value of the goods the subject of the relevant transaction between the Company and the Customer, or

(b) a sum at the rate of two SDR's per kilo of gross weight of the goods the subject of the said transaction, or

(c) 75,000 SDR's in respect of any one transaction whichever shall be the least.

Warsaw Convention

36. If the Company acts as principal in respect of a carriage of goods by air, the following notice is hereby given: if the carriage involves an ultimate destination or stop in a country other than the country of departure, the Warsaw Convention may be applicable and the convention governs and in most cases limits the liability of carriers in respect of loss of or damage to cargo. Agreed stopping places are those places (other than the places of departure and destination) shown under requested routing and/or those places shown in carriers' timetables as scheduled stopping places for the route. The address of the first carrier is the airport of departure.

As principals, international freight forwarders incorporate their profit margin within the rate quoted to the shippers or owners of the goods.

It should be noted that when, as principals, they act as carriers, the minimum limits on liability below which they cannot contract and the time limits restricting court action set by the Carriage by Air Act[248] and the Carriage of Goods by Water Act[249] are applicable to them. This is not the case when they act as transportation contractors.

With respect to international freight forwarders involved in the transportation of cargo by road, Ontario is the only province that requires them to be licensed, unless they act on behalf of the consignor or consignee for a fixed pre-arranged fee.[250]

International freight forwarders using other methods of transportation—for example, rail or ocean facilities—are not subject to the Ontario legislation.

When a dispute involving an international freight forwarder as principal cannot be resolved by application of the provisions of the relevant international conventions or statutory provisions applying to the particular mode of transport, the CIFFA Standard Trading Conditions, or the terms of the contract, resort to the common law concept of bailment may be necessary. The international freight forwarder as the carrier who has possession of the owner's goods with the latter's consent is the bailee whose duty is to take reasonable care to keep the goods safe. This rule applies to the sub-bailee who takes charge of the goods with the consent of their owner.

B. Shipping Agents

Generally speaking, shipping agents are persons whose services are engaged for the purpose of facilitating the movement of cargo across international borders. They are also known as transportation brokers, load brokers, and forwarding agents. An inquiry into the precise nature of an agent's undertaking will determine whether he or she has assumed the character of an international freight forwarder as agent or principal.

C. Customs Brokers

Customs brokers or agents are only engaged to perform the service of making entry of the cargo on behalf of its owner or importer.[251]

D. Carnet Canada

A document of which exporters should be aware is the Carnet Canada.

The ATA (Admission Temporaire-Temporary Admission) carnet is an internationally recognized customs document used by business and industry to facilitate the importation of goods, such as commercial samples, into the territories of other contracting parties. It is designed to assist businesses by permitting them to make customs arrangements in

---

248 RSC 1985, c. C-26, implementing the Warsaw Convention, as am. See section III, *supra*.

249 SC 1993, c. 21, implementing the Hague-Visby Rules. See section II, *supra*.

250 Truck Transportation Act, RSO 1990, c. T.22, s. 3(8). They are called "intermediaries."

251 See Customs Act, RSC 1985, c. 1 (2nd Supp.), ss. 9 and 10.

advance for trips to other countries, to make those arrangements quickly and at a predetermined cost prior to departure from Canada, using a single carnet for goods that will pass through the customs of several countries, and to use a single carnet for several business trips during the course of the one-year validity period.

The TIR (Transit International Routier-International Highway Transit) carnet is another internationally known customs document designed to facilitate the trans-border movement of goods in sealed, approved road vehicles, or containers from a country of export to a country of destination, either direct or through one or more intermediate member countries.

A carnet eliminates the necessity of regular customs inspection and resealing of loads in each of the member countries through which the container or vehicle passes en route to its destination. In addition, the carnet incorporates an international financial guarantee for the payment of duties, taxes, other charges, and penalties to a specified maximum $50,000, which removes the necessity of posting performance bonds with the various customs administrations encountered during the journey.[252]

VII. OPERATORS OF TRANSPORT TERMINALS

The UN Convention on Liability of Operators of Transport Terminals in International Trade[253] (OTT Convention) contains rules governing the limits of liability that operators[254] of transport terminals who perform transport-related services[255] in relation to goods involved in international carriage[256] may seek in case of loss of or damage to the goods, or delay in handing them over before and after such carriage. The convention thus endeavours to establish uniform norms governing liability[257] and limits of

252 Carnets are generally sold and administered by the chamber of commerce in each of the contracting countries. Businesses in Canada should contact Carnet Canada, Canadian Chamber of Commerce, 55 Metcalfe Street, Ottawa, ON K1P 6N4.

253 UNCITRAL draft (1989), 20 *ILM* 1503 (1991). The final text of the convention was adopted in Vienna on 19 April 1991. The final Act is found in Official Records, UN Conference on the Liability of Operators of Transport Terminals in International Trade, A/CONF.152/14 (1993). For a thorough examination of the convention, see Larsen et al., "The Treaty on Terminal Operator Liability" (1994), 25 *JMLC* 339. For discussion of the earlier work done by the UNCITRAL Working Groups and of the draft convention, see Larsen et al., "The Uniform Rules on the Liability of Operators of Transport Terminals" (1989), 20 *JMLC* 21 and, by the same authors (1990), 21 *JMLC* 449.

254 The convention avoids using the term "warehouseman" or "stevedore" for a terminal operator. In addition, a person is not an operator whenever considered a carrier under applicable legislation.

255 These include storage, warehousing, loading, unloading, stowage, trimming, dunnaging, and lashing (art. 1(b)).

256 "International carriage" is defined in art. 1(c) as "any carriage in which the place of departure and the place of destination are identified as being in two different states when the goods are taken in charge by the operator."

257 The operator bears the onus of proving that it and its servants or agents took all reasonable measures to avoid the loss or damage to the goods (art. 5).

liability[258] during the time period when the transported goods are not subject to other relevant modal transport conventions. The harmonization of such limits should make it easier to predict insurance needs and facilitate recourse actions. The convention provides deadlines for notification of loss or damage[259] and provides for a limitation period of two years.[260]

The OTT Convention does not modify any rights or duties that may arise under other international carriage conventions[261] that have been adopted or given legal effect by states. Therefore, for example, the convention would perpetuate the limitation of liability available by virtue of Himalaya clauses under the Hague Rules to stevedores clearly identified in the bill of lading as subcontracting agents or employees of the maritime carrier.[262]

The OTT Convention contains innovative provisions on the use of EDI in bills of lading.[263]

The convention will enter into force upon ratification by five states.[264] Until this convention is adopted by Canada, existing federal and provincial laws governing the liability of operators of transport terminals in international trade make no mention of the limits of liability to which they are subjected when performing their transport related services. This matter is usually left to contract.

VIII. AUTOMATION AND THE USE OF EDI IN INTERNATIONAL BILLS OF LADING AND OTHER TRADING DOCUMENTS

A. Automation of the Functions of Bills of Lading

As noted above, traditionally, a bill of lading serves three main functions: (1) it is a receipt to the shipper or consignor for the goods transported by the carrier; (2) it is evidence of the terms and conditions of the contract of carriage; and (3) it is a transferable document of title to the goods described in the bill.[265] The elimination of the bill of

---

258 Liability resulting from loss of or damage to the goods may be limited to amount not exceeding SDR 8.33 per kilogram (art. 6) or SDR 2.75 where goods are transported by sea or inland waterway. Liability limits may be altered where the operator agrees (art 6.4).

259 Art. 11.

260 Art. 12.

261 Art. 15.

262 See, i.e., Larsen et al., *supra*, note 253, at 341 *et seq*.

263 Art. 4. See discussion below.

264 As of 1 September 1994, the convention had no ratifications, but had been signed by five states: the United States, France, Mexico, Philipinnes, and Spain.

265 See, e.g., Kindred, "Trading Internationally by Electronic Bills of Lading" (1992), 7 *BFLR* 265, at 268. See also Toh See Kiat, *Paperless International Trade* (1992), at 1, who describes the functions of paper in international trade generally as (1) a carrier of information and instructions; (2) a carrier of authentication symbols and devices; (3) a carrier of evidence; (4) a carrier of legally significant symbols; and (5) an entity with formal legal functions.

lading as a paper document and the preservation of its functions by a system of automated or EDI and processing pose significant legal problems that have not yet been entirely solved.[266]

In the first place, electronic data transmission and processing must take account of the bill of lading as a receipt for the goods. This may be difficult in Canada where most legal requirements are still concerned with paper transactions only. Also, it is obvious that delivery cannot be made to depend upon the physical presentation of a computer system.

Second, and this is also true with respect to the other two functions of a bill of lading, a distinction must be made between negotiable and non-negotiable bills of lading. When a bill of lading is not negotiable, there is no need to present any documents to the carrier in order to receive the goods. The carrier delivers them to the named consignee. In such a case, there are few legal obstacles to replacing the bill and the information and rights it contains by data transmission and processing. However, such a system is only useful and effective between the carrier, the shipper, and the consignee. When the bill of lading is negotiable and is used as a security for a letter of credit, complex procedural requirements must be met that, in the present state of the law, are difficult to replace by electronic data transmission and processing.

If a negotiable bill of lading is transmitted through the network and printed out at several different terminals, can each of the printouts be considered an original and therefore negotiable or are they all copies? This could also be the case where the bill is transmitted by telefax. How will the data be authenticated in the face of national legislation requiring a "signature" to give value to a bill of lading as a negotiable instrument of title?

As evidence of the contract of carriage, an automated carriage transaction is more practical than a documentary bill of lading, provided it can be authenticated and be considered as proof of the contract of carriage. Again, signature is important. In other words, how can an electronically-made and -recorded contract of carriage be proved?[267]

---

266 See, e.g., Elliott, "The Changing Face of Documentation in the Carriage of Goods"; Kindred, "When Bits Replace Bills, What Shall the Law Byte On? Legal Consequences of Automating Carriage Documentation" in Sharpe and Spicer (eds.), *New Directions in Maritime Law 1984* (1985), at 193 and 207, respectively; Mapp, "Documentary Problems of Intermodal Transport" (1978), 12 *J World Trade L* 514; Henriksen, *The Legal Aspects of Paperless Trade and Transport* (1982); Hawkland, "Documentary Transactions: New Solutions to Old Problems" (1986), 18 *Uniform Commercial Code LJ* 291; Groenfors, "The Paperless Transfer of Transport Information and Legal Functions" in Schmitthoff and Goode (eds.), *International Carriage of Goods: Some Legal Problems* (1988); Chandler, "The Electronic Transmission of Bills of Lading" (1989), 20 *JMLC* 571; Merges and Reynolds, "Toward a Computerized System for Negotiating Ocean Bills of Lading" (1986), 6 *JLC* 23; and Walden and Savage, "The Legal Problems of Paperless Transactions," [1989] *JBL* 102.

267 Legal problems may arise with respect to the discovery of electronic carriage data since present rules are geared to discovery of *documents*; the admissibility of computer data files and printouts especially if documentary proof is required, and their probative force. In this connection see s. 30 of the Canada Evidence Act, RSC 1985, c. C-5.

In Canada, there is no need for the signature to be an original handwritten one. It may be made by any kind of instrument. Thus, the question of signature should not be a significant barrier to a system of data transmission and processing. Electronic signatures could be used unless the law prescribes the form of authentication for the carriage data to be transmitted in terms of documentary procedures.[268]

B. Treatment of Automation and EDI in International Agreements and Conventions Concerning the Carriage of Goods

In light of rapid technological advancement, international uniform rules and multilateral conventions on maritime and multimodal transport of goods have evolved in their treatment of the increasing automation and computerization of bills of lading,[269] and have accommodated to some extent the use of EDI.

The UCP500 allows the use of documents produced by reprographic, automated, and computerized systems, and for electronic signatures.[270] This rule would apply to cargo data under a letter of credit.[271] The ICC-Incoterms 1990 have been revised to render them fully compatible with new developments in electronic data interchange.[272] The 1992 UNCTAD-ICC Rules for Multimodal Transport Documents expressly embrace EDI by stating that multimodal transport document means "a document evidencing a

268 See, e.g., Carriage of Goods by Water Act, SC 1993, c. C-21.

269 See, e.g., Gliniecki and Ogada. "The Legal Acceptance of Electronic Documents, Writings, Signatures and Notices in International Transportation Conventions: A Challenge in the Age of Global Electronic Commerce" (1992), 13 *Northwestern J of Int'l. Law and Bus.* 117.

270 ICC doc. 500 (1993 rev.). See art. 20(b): "Unless otherwise stipulated in the credit, banks will also accept as an original(s) document(s) produced or appearing to have been produced: i. by reprographic, automated or computerized systems ... provided it is marked as original and, where necessary, appears to be signed"; and "[a] document may be signed by handwriting, by facsimile signature, by stamp, by symbol or by any other mechanical or electronic method of authentication." See also art. 11, which enables the banks to issue and pay credits by teletransmission.

271 Art. 4.

272 ICC doc. 460. See chapter 5, *supra*. With respect to the standardization of the *methods* of trade data communication by electronic data interchange, see the Uniform Rules of Conduct for Interchange of Trade Data by Teletransmission sponsored by the ICC and the UN Economic Commission of Europe (publication no. 452). These rules are intended to facilitate the interchange of trade data effected by transmission through the establishment of agreed rules of conduct by parties engaged in such transmission. The rules are voluntary and apply only if the parties adopt them by virtue of a trade data interchange application protocol. For other rules applicable to computer transfer of commercial or administrative transactions using an agreed standard to structure and format data pertaining to that transaction, see the 1988 UN Rules for Electronic Data Interchange for Administration, Commerce and Transport (UN-EDIFACT), a product of the UN Commission on the Facilitation of International Trade. All of these rules do not deal with the standardization of the *substantive* contents of communications by electronic data interchange, as to which see the Trade Data Elements Directory (UNTDED) supplemented

(The footnote is continued on the next page.)

multimodal transport contract and which can be replaced by electronic data interchange messages insofar as permitted by applicable law."[273]

While the Hague and Hague-Visby Rules are silent as to the permissible format of bills of lading, the Hamburg Rules (as well as the 1980 Multimodal Transport Convention that was largely modelled on the Hamburg Rules) contain recognition of the possibility of using electronic bills of lading. For example, article 1(8) of the Hamburg Rules provides that "writing" includes, *inter alia*, telegram and telex, thereby permitting other, possibly electronic, forms of writing. In addition, article 14 of the Hamburg Rules expressly recognizes the possibility for an electronically-generated signature,[274] as long as this is not inconsistent with the law of the country where the bill of lading was issued. Thus, where local law requires a handwritten signature, this requirement will override the convention.

The OTT Convention contains even more innovative rules concerning electronic bills of lading. Under this agreement, any "notice" or "request" is allowed when "made in a form which provides a record of the information contained therein,"[275] a requirement that could be satisfied electronically. As well, a computer record would satisfy the condition in article 4(3) of the convention that the customer's document or receipt and the terminal operator's documents be issued in any form generating a permanent record. The provision also explicitly permits replacement of these documents by EDI messages[276] where agreed by the parties. A signature may be handwritten, by facsimile or "an equivalent authentication effected by other means." The OTT Convention thus omits the reservation in article 14(3) of the Hamburg Rules concerning inconsistency with the law of the country of issuance of the bill of lading.

The wider use of an electronic equivalent to a bill of lading that fulfills all its traditional functions depends in great part upon the removal of the remaining legal obstacles found in Canadian law and in the applicable international conventions. It is important to recall that these developments are not an isolated occurrence; they are flanked by accompanying measures in the field of trade payments, such as electronic funds transfer and collections systems.[277]

---

272 Continued ...

by a Trade Data Interchange Directory (UNTDID) produced by the International Organization for Standardisation (1985, ISO 7372), and Beer, "Informatics in International Trade: Harmonization of Standards for Telecommunicated Messages" (1985), 19 *J World Trade L* 570. See also, generally, Thompsen & Wheble, *Trading with EDI* (1989).

273 R. 2.6.

274 "The signature on the bill of lading may be in handwriting, printed in facsimile, perforated, stamped, in symbols, or made by any other mechanical or electronic means."

275 Art. 1(e) and (f).

276 Art. 4(3).

277 An example is SWIFT. See, e.g., Rowe, *Electronic Trade Payments* (1987).

C. CMI Uniform Rules for Electronic Bills of Lading

Several attempts have been made to regulate the exchange of information through electronic bills of lading, including Seadocs[278] and CARDIS.[279] More recently, the CMI Rules for Electronic Bills of Lading, adopted by the CMI in June 1990, offer a uniform regime regulating electronic bills of lading limited to certain aspects of an international shipping transaction.[280] The CMI Rules apply only when the parties to a transaction agree.[281] They operate in conjunction with the procedural rules in the Uniform Rules for Interchange of Trade Data by Teletransmission 1987 (UNCID), where the latter are not in conflict.[282] In the absence of other agreed arrangements by the parties, EDI should conform with UN-EDIFACT standards.[283] Significantly, by agreeing to use the CMI Rules, the parties make certain commitments as to formality requirements: they agree that the electronic data is equivalent to any writing and signature requirement under national law or custom, and waive any defence that the contract is not in writing.[284] Nevertheless, the option to issue or receive a paper document remains open at any time prior to delivery of the goods.[285] However, it is unclear whether parties are permitted to waive statutory writing requirements in this manner when it would be contrary to local law or custom.

The CMI Rules offer a mechanism for the effective transmission of the three principal functions of a bill of lading to electronic format. In brief, first, article 5 of the CMI Rules permit incorporation of the carrier's standard terms and conditions of carriage into the contract, fulfilling the evidentiary and contractual functions of a paper bill of lading.

Second, the CMI Rules provide that the carrier will send a "receipt message" to the shipper on receipt of the goods from the shipper.[286] The receipt message contains details

---

278 "Seadocs," or the Seaborne Trade Documentation System. Launched in the mid-1980s, it aimed first to establish a central depositary of shipping documentation to record all transactions concerning a specific shipment, and then envisaged a second phase where electronic data would replace paper within the registry. It never progressed past the first phase. See, e.g., Merges and Reynolds, "Toward a Computerised System for Negotiating Ocean Bills of Lading" (1986), 23 *JLC* 23; Albert, "The Seadocs Registry" (1986), 14 *Int'l Bus. Lawyer* 430; and Toh See Kiat, *supra*, note 265, at 178-79.

279 CARDIS, or Cargo Data Interchange System, aimed to integrate all shipping industry users in one port onto one electronic data system, but was stalled by the non-standardization in electronic data interchange.

280 The CMI Rules for Electronic Bills of Lading are discussed, for instance, in Kindred, "Trading Internationally by Electronic Bills of Lading" (1991-92), 7 *BFLR* 265; Kozolchyk, "Evolution and Preset State of the Ocean Bill of Lading from a Banking Law Perspective" (1992), 23 *JMLC* 161; Toh See Kiat, *supra*, note 265; and Roberts, "Electronic Bills of Lading" in Wilde (ed.), *International Transactions* (1993), at 85 *et seq.*

281 Art. 1.

282 Art 3(a).

283 Art. 3(b).

284 Art. 11.

285 Art. 10.

286 Art. 4(a).

such as the name of the shipper,[287] a description of the goods and the date and place of their receipt,[288] and the carrier's terms and conditions of carriage.[289] This information "has the same force and effect as if the receipt message were contained in a paper bill of lading."[290] In addition, the receipt message will contain the "private key."[291] The private key—the cornerstone of the CMI Rules and its device to answer concerns about privacy, security, and fraud—is a security code in any technically appropriate form, such as a combination of numbers and letters, that the parties agree upon to ensure the authenticity and integrity of the transmission.[292] Once the shipper confirms the receipt message, the shipper becomes a holder—the one entity with the capacity to claim delivery of the goods, nominate a consignee, assign the right of control and transfer, and instruct the carrier on any subject concerning the goods "as if he or she were the holder of a paper bill of lading."[293]

Third, the private key mechanism fulfills the bill of lading's negotiability function concerning the transfer of title in the goods, by providing that the transfer of the "Right of Control and Transfer" has the same effects as the transfer of such rights under a paper bill of lading.[294]

The CMI Rules appear largely compatible with the 1993 revision of the UCP500.[295] In addition, the CMI Rules permit the Hague Rules, Hague-Visby Rules, or other compulsorily applicable international conventions to take precedence over them and over the carrier's standard trading conditions and thus to govern EDI transactions in a more predictable and certain fashion. The CMI has also adopted uniform rules on sea waybills that apply, whether or not the contract of carriage is in writing, thus embracing EDI.

IX. SELECTED BIBLIOGRAPHY

A. Books

Arroyo and Ignacio, *International Maritime Conventions* (1991).

Astle, *Shipping and the Law* (1980).

CMI, "Uniformity of the Laws of Carriage of Goods by Sea in the 1990's—Problems of the Hague-Visby Rules and Possible Solutions," Report of the International Sub-Committee to the CMI (1990), UNIF-17-111-90.

Colas (ed.), *Global Economic Co-operation: A Guide to Agreements and Organizations* (1994).

287 Art. 4(b)(i).

288 Art. 4(b)(ii) and (iii).

289 Art. 4(b)(iv).

290 Art. 4(d).

291 Art. 4(b)(v).

292 Arts. 2(f) and 8.

293 Art. 7(a).

294 Art. 7(d).

295 See, e.g., Dolan and Van Huizen, "The UCP: A Final Report" (1993), 9 *BFLR* 173, at 193 *et seq.*

Glass, *Introduction to the Carriage of Goods* (1989).

Gorton and Ihre, *A Practical Guide to Contracts of Affreightment and Hybrid Contracts* (1990).

Henriksen, *The Legal Aspect of Paper-less Trade and Transport* (1982).

Hill, *Freight Forwarders* (1972).

International Chamber of Commerce, *Clean Transport Documents* (1989).

International Chamber of Commerce, *Guide to a Combined Transport Document* (1991).

International Chamber of Commerce, *Rules for a Combined Transport Document* (1991).

Ivamy, *Modern Bills of Lading* (1987).

Kindred, *Freight Forwarders' Legal Liability for the Multimodal Movement of Goods* (1987).

Kindred et al., *The Future of Canadian Carriage of Goods by Water Law* (1982).

Mankabady (ed.), *The Hamburg Rules on the Carriage of Goods by Sea* (1978).

McNeil, *Motor Carrier Cargo Claims* (2nd ed., 1989).

Mocatta, Mustill, and Boyd, *Scrutton on Charterparties and Bills of Lading* (19th ed., 1984).

Naveau, *International Air Transport in a Changing World* (1989).

Ritter, *The Legal Facilitation of International Electronic Commerce: Current Initiatives and Future Directions* (1992).

Rowe, *Electronic Trade Payments: A Practical Guide to Electronic Banking and International Trade* (1987).

Schmitthoff and Goode, *International Carriage of Goods: Some Legal Problems* (1988).

See Kiat, *Paperless International Trade: Law of Telematic Data Interchange* (1992).

Stevens, *Shipping Practice* (1977).

Tetley, *Marine Cargo Claims* (3rd ed., 1988).

UNCTAD, *Multimodal Transport and Containerization* (1984).

UNCTAD, *The Economic and Commercial Implications of the Entry into Force of the Hamburg Rules and the Multimodal Transport Convention* (1991).

UNCTAD-ICC, *Rules for Multimodal Transport Documents* (1992).

Wilde (ed.), *International Transactions* (1993).

Wilson, *Carriage of Goods by Sea* (1988).

B. Articles

Angus, "Legal Implications of "The Container Revolution" in International Carriage of Goods" (1968), 14 *McGill LJ* 395.

Bauer, "Conflicting Liability Regimes: Hague-Visby v. Hamburg Rules—A Case by Case Analysis" (1993), 24 *JMLC* 53.

Bell, "Damages Arising from Domestic or International Air Carriage of Passengers, Baggage and Cargo" (1987), 8 *Advocates' Q* 276.

Chandler, "The Electronic Transmission of Bills of Lading" (1989), 20 *JMLC* 71.

Davenport, "Limits on the Hague Rules" (1989), 105 *LQ Rev.* 521.

Di Baggio, "Carriage of Goods by Sea Act—Package Limitation—Fair Opportunity to Declare Higher Values" (1987), 18 *JMLC* 293.

FitzGerald, "The United Nations Convention on the International Multimodal Transport of Goods" (1980), 5 *Ann. of Air & Space L* 51.

Gliniecki and Ogada. "The Legal Acceptance of Electronic Documents, Writings Signatures and Notices in International Transportation Conventions: A Challenge in the Age of Global Electronic Commerce" (1992), 13 *Northwestern J of Int. Law and Bus.* 117.

Goldie, "Effect of Hamburg Rules on Shipowner's Liability Insurance" (1993), 24 *JMLC* 111.

Honnold, "Ocean Carriers and Cargo; Clarity and Fairness—Hague or Hamburg?" (1993), 24 *JMLC* 75.

Kindred, "Goodbye to the Hague Rules: Will the New Carriage of Goods by Water Act Make Any Difference?" (1994-95), 24 *CBLJ* 404.

Kindred, "Trading Internationally by Electronic Bills of Lading" (1992), 7 *BFLR* 265.

Lloyd, "The Bill of Lading: Do We Really Need It?", [1989] *Lloyds Mar. & Comm. LQ* 47.

Mankabady, "The Multimodal Transport of Goods Convention: A Challenge to Unimodal Transport Conventions" (1983), 32 *Int'l. & Comp. LQ* 120.

McCune, "Delivery of Cargo Carried Under Straight Bills of Lading: The Ocean Carrier's Rights and Obligations" (1985), 17 *UCCLJ* 344.

Mendelsohn, "Why the US Did Not Ratify the Visby Amendments" (1992), 23 *JMLC* 29 to 53.

Merges and Reynolds, "Toward a Computerized System for Negotiating Ocean Bills of Lading" (1986), 6 *JLC* 23.

Milde, "Warsaw System and Limits to Liability—Yet Another Crossroad?" (1993), *Ann. Air. & Space L* 201.

Powles, "The Himalaya Clause—A Confirmation of Practice," [1985] *JBL* 64.

Pratter, Jonathan. "Selected Bibliography on the Law of Carriage of Goods by Sea, 1975-1992" (1993), 24 *JMLC* 191.

Reynolds, "Authority to Sign Bill of Lading," [1986] *JBL* 220.

Saul and Madras, "Canadian Law Governing the Liability of the Freight Forwarder and Its Carriers" (1978), 6 *Int'l. Bus. Lawyer* 435.

Schmitthoff, "Letter of Credit; Bill of Lading Marked 'Received for Shipment' and 'Shipped'," [1986] *JBL* 323.

Scowcroft, "Recent Developments Concerning the Package Limitation" (1989), 20 *JMLC* 403.

Sturley, "Changing Liability Rules and Marine Insurance—Conflicting Empirical Arguments About Hague, Visby and Hamburg in a Vacuum of Empirical Evidence" (1993), 24 *JMLC* 119.

Sweeney, "The UNCITRAL Draft Convention on Carriage of Goods by Sea (Part I)" (1975), 7 *JMLC* 69, (pt. II) (1976), 7 *JMLC* 327.

Sweeney, "UNCITRAL and the Hamburg Rules" (1991), 22 *JMLC* 511.

Tetley, "Acceptance of Higher Visby Liability Limits by US Courts" (1992), 23 *JMLC* 55 to 71.

Tetley, "Canadian Comments on the Proposed UNCITRAL Rules: An Analysis of the Proposed UNCITRAL Text (1977-78), 9 *JMLC* 251.

Tetley, "The Hamburg Rules—A Commentary," [1979] *Lloyd's Mar. & Comm. LQ* 1

Tetley, "Waybills, the Modern Contract of Carriage of Goods by Sea" in *New Developments in the Law of Export Sales* (1982), at 176.

Tetley, "Who May Claim or Sue for Cargo Loss or Damage?" (1986), 17 *JMLC* 153.

Waldron, "The Hamburg Rules—A Boondoggle for Lawyers?", [1991] *JBL* 235.

Wei Jia Ju, "UN Multimodal Transport Convention" (1981), 15 *J World Trade L* 283.

Werth, "The Hamburg Rules Revisited—A Look at US Options" (1991), 22 *JMLC* 59.

Zawitoski, "Limitation of Liability for Stevedores and Terminal Operators Under the Carrier's Bill of Lading and COGSA" (1985), 16 *JMLC* 337.

CHAPTER NINE

International Regulation of Trade in Services

I. INTRODUCTION

Since the first edition of this book appeared, two significant developments have continued the liberalization of the transborder trade in services through the establishment of multilateral disciplines. The first was the signing by Canada, the United States, and Mexico of the North American Free Trade Agreement (NAFTA), which extended and refined the rules set out in the Free Trade Agreement (FTA) between Canada and the United States (and which were described in the previous edition). The second was the negotiation, as a result of the Uruguay Round, of a General Agreement on Trade in Services (GATS). As a result of these agreements, disciplines affecting trade in services have both been deepened and widened and now apply to North Americans, both at the regional and global level. There is clearly a linkage between developments at the regional and global levels. The extensive integration in the area of services achieved by the European Union (EU) and the more limited success of the FTA drove the Uruguay Round multilateral negotiations, while the elaboration of the NAFTA rules drew heavily on the experience of the first six years of the GATS negotiation.[1]

1 Hoekman and Sauvé, *Liberalizing Trade in Services* (1994), at 21.

Services are now an important part of every modern economy. It is estimated that services industries represent approximately 70 percent of the gross domestic product of the United States, and the proportion is similiar in other developed countries, including Canada.[2] In less-developed countries (LDCs), they are not as important, but are growing. These proportions are reflected in world trade, where it is estimated that commercial services account for about 22 percent of global trade for a value of more than US$1 trillion. Furthermore, trade in services is growing more rapidly than trade in goods and now exceeds the combined trade in agricultural commodities, petroleum, and petroleum products and minerals.[3] There is as well a complex and important inter-relationship between the manufacturing and service sectors. Service transactions are commingled with the production and the trade of goods to such an extent that it is difficult to talk of liberalizing one without the other.[4]

The United States is the world's most important exporter of services, although its proportion of total world service trade has diminished since the 1970s.[5] US initiatives to liberalize world service trade therefore have been significant. Congress placed trade in services on a par with trade in goods in the Trade and Tariff Act of 1984 by enabling the president to take remedial action under section 301 against "unfair" trade practices in the services area. This power was extended in the Omnibus Trade and Competition Act of 1988 with the use of "Super 301," which envisaged a broad range of "unfair" trade practices, including those in the services area.[6] The GATS achievements at the Uruguay Round and the NAFTA reflect US preoccupation with the liberalization of trade rules applicable to services.[7]

Crafting a regime of international disciplines to apply to trade in services gives rise to many complex problems that differ substantially from those that had to be addressed when liberalizing trade in goods. In the first place, it is difficult to draft rules that apply to services when economists generally have difficulty in agreeing on their economic

2 Grubel and Walker, *Service Industry Growth* (1989), at 4, 67 to 69 and Finlayson, "Directions for Canadian Trade Policy: A Private Sector View" (1993), 1 *Can. Foreign Pol.* 113, at 117.

3 Hoekman and Sauvé, *supra*, note 1, at 4; Enderwick, *Multinational Service Firms* (1989), at 219; see, generally, Sims and Rivers, "The International Trade in Services Agenda" in Series on Trade, The Institute for Research on Public Policy, Victoria (1987), at 24.

4 Hufbauer and Schott, *Trading for Growth: The Next Round of Trade Negotiations* (1985), at 66 and Department of External Affairs, Canada, *The Canada-US Free Trade Agreement Synopsis* (1988), at 42.

5 Sims and Rivers *supra*, note 3, at 10 and 17; it is estimated by Statistics Canada that Canada's foreign trade was, in 1993, 16 percent comprising services, imports generally exceeding exports: Lee, "Services: The Continuing Agenda" in *Trade, Investment and Competition*, mimeograph (Ottawa: Centre for Trade Policy and Law, 1994), at 58.

6 Omnibus Trade and Competitiveness Act 1988, Pub. L 100-418. Pub. L 102 specifically mandates the president to pursue the liberalization of trade in services as part of the Uruguay Round negotations.

7 Hufbauer and Schott, *supra*, note 4; Finger and Olechowsky (eds.), *The Uruguay Round: A Handbook on Multilateral Trade Negotiations* (1987); and Cloney, "Impetus in the United States for the Liberalization of International Trade in Services" (1989), 19 *Ga. J Int'l. and Comp. L* 314.

characteristics.[8] Services are unlike goods in that they are processes and depend upon the skills of the service provider. Supply of services is thus not finite in the same way as that of goods. Since they depend upon the skill of the service provider, their free supply of services is often dependent on the free movement of the provider or the consumer, thus relating the guarantee of their free supply to sensitive immigration issues and the right to work in another jurisdiction. Where supply of the service requires a local establishment, rules relating to the right of establishment or investment (FDI) also must be considered, including the right to repatriate the profits from such transactions. In many cases, states themselves may own the service providers or provide for the establishment of regulated local monopolies.

Technological developments constantly change the way in which services are furnished, thus blurring the distinction originally made between "traded" and "non-traded" services.[9] For example, large projects requiring foreign architectural or engineering services at one time required a significant local establishment by the foreign service providers; this need has been somewhat reduced by fax and computer telecommunications, thus rendering them what were once clearly non-traded services more like traded services. And advances in information technology may permit service providers, like goods manufacturers, to split their operations among different jurisdictions, thus allowing service providers to take advantage of lower wage rates, more readily available language skills, or favourable fiscal policies.[10] Canadian lawyers today may provide advice by telephone or fax to foreign clients (trade in the service), visit their foreign clients (temporary presence), or establish offices abroad (right of establishment). Different regulatory measures apply to these three types of service now familiar to the legal profession.

The drafting of international rules to liberalize trade in services faces several natural barriers that differ in nature and degree from those applicable to goods. Many services are subject to fairly intense domestic regulatory regimes that, while constituting non-tariff barriers (NTBs) to free trade in such services, respond to a variety of perfectly legitimate concerns of the enacting state. Financial services, for example, are regulated with a view to protecting the savings of citizens and, ultimately, the financial integrity of the state itself. Communications may be regulated with a view to ensuring the protection of a certain cultural identity or even of national security. These types of services go to the heart of the social infrastructure of a nation, and this has often been the basis for

---

8 For different analyses of the trade in services issue, see, generally, Feketekuty, *International Trade in Services* (1988); Nicolaides, "The Usefulness of a Broad Perspective on Services: Comment on D. Nayyar's Article: 'Some Reflections on the Uruguay Round and Trade in Services' " (1989), 23 *J of World Trade* 65; Nayyar, "Some Reflections on the Uruguay Round and Trade in Services" (1988), 22 *J of World Trade* 35; and Holmstrom, "The Provision of Services in a Market Economy" in Inman (ed.), *Managing the Service Economy: Prospects and Problems* (1985).

9 Hoekman and Sauvé, *supra*, note 1, at 4.

10 Hoekman and Sauvé, *ibid.*, at 5; in Canada, New Brunswick has, e.g., aggressively sought to position itself as a provider of bilingual services in various areas by stressing certain natural endowment factors together with state aid.

strenuous opposition to the opening of domestic markets to foreign, "culturally different" service providers.[11] Legal, accounting, engineering, medical, and other services are regulated in order to ensure the professional competence of the service providers. Transborder data flow raises issues of privacy and the free flow of information. Such factors have given rise to a complex web of domestic regulatory measures which, while having a protectionist effect, respond to the perfectly legitimate national concern of protecting the consumer. In the case of a federal state, such regulation may emanate from different levels of government. The latter is particularly true of Canada, where there is extensive provincial legislation governing services, and of the United States, where such important areas as banking and insurance are subject to extensive controls by the states.

Of course, the process of domestic deregulation in many states has made the international penetration of domestic markets easier, and one sees a certain correlation between the processes of international and domestic liberalization in this important sector. One may talk of "a convergence of approaches to regulation and deregulation in a wide range of countries" that will facilitate the multilateral approach to this issue.[12] One must constantly bear in mind, however, that the type of non-tariff barriers that must be dealt with in this area differs significantly from those that apply to goods.[13]

On the international plane, some services for a long time have been provided internationally, and, as a result, there has grown a series of sectoral regimes providing international "disciplines." Civil aviation and international air transport are governed by the International Civil Aviation Organization (ICAO) and the International Air Transport Association (IATA), and telecommunications are covered by the International Telecommunication Union (ITU), to name two examples. International organizations, such as the Organisation for Economic Co-operation and Development (OECD) and the UN Conference on Trade and Development (UNCTAD) concern themselves with the movement of invisibles, as well as certain underlying issues, such as capital flows and restrictive business practices, which have an impact on the free flow of services.

An OECD Code on Services has been in existence since 1951 and has been amended some 50 times. It includes sectoral consideration for the banking, tourism, and insurance sectors.[14] The OECD Committee on Capital Movements and Invisible Transactions monitors the application of these provisions and may make non-binding recommendations to the member states, many of which retain reservations in respect to certain sectors, often in the area of audiovisual, maritime transport, and insurance services.[15]

Thus, there has existed for some time a web of international bilateral and multilateral arrangements, some accompanied by institutional structures, established by way of

11 Radwanski, *Ontario Study of the Service Sector*, Ministry of Treasury and Economics, Ontario (1986), at 89 and Nusbaumer, *The Service Economy: Lever to Growth* (1987), at 74.

12 Trebilcock and Howse, *The Regulation of International Trade* (1995), at 247.

13 Hoekman and Sauvé, *supra*, note 1, at 7.

14 OECD, Code of Liberalisation of Current Invisible Operations (November 1990) and OECD, *Liberalisation of Capital Movements and Financial Services in the OECD Area* (1990).

15 Trebilcock and Howse, *supra*, note 12, at 224 and 237.

conventions, codes or other forms of agreement among governments and non-governmental agencies, which have had an impact on this area. However, many of these arrangements do not necessarily have as their object the liberalization of trade in services, in the sense of access to markets but, rather, deal with the elaboration and guarantee of technical standards. Some, such as the IATA and the maritime conferences, may even have as their purpose the protection or "cartelization" of markets.

In the case of services, protective measures cannot take the same form as in the case of goods. Tariffs or border restrictions seldom apply to services. Other types of impediments to the free flow of services have been identified as being of principal concern, such as restrictions on local ownership and the right of establishment, currency controls, restrictions on the free movement of service providers and consumers, impediments to technology transfers, controls on transborder data flow, limits on the scope of business activities in certain sectors by government procurement policies, and the use of a name by a firm.[16] From the international perspective, it is the effect of such national rules that discriminate on the basis of nationality and residence that must be addressed.

How can international rules be drafted to promote trade in services that will satisfy very different national perspectives and concerns about these issues? Are concepts of national treatment (NT), "reciprocity," most-favoured-nation (MFN) or conditional MFN, "transparency," and others that have been developed for trade in goods applicable to trade in services? What "rules of origin" should apply? Are there dumping and subsidization problems and, if so, how could contingent protection measures, including safeguards, that can be applied to goods as they cross borders, be applied to non-traded services that are created and delivered within the jurisdiction?[17] To what extent should developing countries be allowed to protect their infant service industries? How will an objective evaluation of the appropriateness of domestic regulations be ensured? Are the General Agreement on Tariffs and Trade (GATT)-type institutions generally (and dispute resolution mechanisms in particular) satisfactory for the interpretation, application, and enforcement of such rules?[18]

Because of these factors, any agreement that was able to satisfy the very different perspectives of the GATT members was difficult to achieve. As noted above, there is some debate among experts as to what actually constitutes a service. This difficulty in defining what constitutes a service that should be the subject matter of international rules was reflected in the positions taken by the various parties. The developing countries, for example, having a comparative advantage in wage rates, maintained that labour is a service like others; the United States, on the other hand, took the position that labour

---

16 Noyelle and Dutka, *International Trade in Business Services* (1988), at 53; and see the "Illustrative List—Barriers to Services Trade" (1989), 19 *Ga. J Int'l. and Comp. L* 458.

17 Jackson, "Constructing a Constitution for Trade in Services" (1988), 11 *World Economy* 201.

18 For a test of the appropriateness of a domestic service regulation, see the OECD proposal: OECD/TC, 1987 (2): 12, cited in Stevers and Wilkinson, "Appropriate Regulation for Communication and Information Services" in Robinson, Sauvant, and Govitrikar (eds.), *Electronic Highways for World Trade* (1989), at 157.

is an input to other services or manufactured goods and that liberalization measures should be restricted to those services that are finished products, such as financial services. Thus, the debate, as often occurs in this type of negotiation, centred on the appropriateness of liberalizing trade in those areas where the proponent had a comparative advantage and the various trade-offs reflected the relative bargaining strengths of the negotiating parties.[19]

These differences between the parties gave rise to concerns that any agreement achieved would be narrow in scope and weak in obligations. Indeed, the difficulties in achieving concrete liberalizing measures were foreseen in the Punta Del Este Declaration of 1986, which provides that any framework for services shall "respect the policy objectives of national laws and regulations applying to services."

The inclusion of the issue of the liberalization of trade in services in the Punta Del Este Declaration had been foreshadowed by various developments in previous GATT negotiations. The Havana Charter itself had covered certain services, for example, telecommunications. These were not carried over into the GATT although it does contain some specific articles dealing with services in a limited way: article 111.10 and article IV (films), and article V (traffic in transit) are examples. The Tokyo Round produced four codes that addressed, albeit incidentally, issues of trade in services: (1) the Government Procurement Code, (2) the Standards Code, (3) the Subsidies Code, (4) and the Customs Valuation Code. The Government Procurement Code extends to services incidental to the supply of products, provided that the value of services does not exceed that of the goods supplied under the contract. The Standards Code addresses the question of discrimination in the results of foreign testing laboratories. The Subsidies Code deals with certain subsidized services—primarily financial—associated with the export of goods. The Customs Valuation Code covers some services, such as transport, insurance, and commercial banking, that may be included for the purpose of valuation.

Thus, while the concern that liberalization measures for the trade in goods would be linked to concessions in respect of services made some countries such as India and Brazil resist the inclusion of services in the Uruguay Round, given the importance of the subject and the determination of the United States, it was inevitable that services would be a part of the negotiations. The differences over how services would be treated were satisfied by including them in part 11 of the Punta Del Este Declaration and by providing for their negotiations in a separate framework.[20]

A World Bank paper has suggested that several issues must be considered to determine to what degree the GATS and regional agreements have actually achieved liberalization in the trade in services. These issues are (1) the rules and disciplines that have been developed including NT, MFN, the right of non-establishment, mutual recognition of training and certification procedures, and non-discriminatory market access restrictions; (2) the degree to which the agreements cover services, whether sectorally or in the

19 Trebilcock and Howse, *supra*, note 12, at 217.

20 In the words of Jackson, a separate agreement for trade in services was essential. Any suggestion that the GATT could simply be amended to include services was "not feasible," Jackson, *supra*, note 17, at 189.

nature of the disciplines applied; (3) how government policies that distort free movement, such as subsidies and government procurement, are dealt with; (4) the dispute resolution mechanism; (5) rules of origin; and (6) safeguards.[21]

Clearly these criteria owe much to the notions developed in relation to trade in goods, but their application is, as will be developed hereunder, somewhat different.

II. GENERAL AGREEMENT ON TRADE IN SERVICES

The negotiations for the NAFTA were concluded prior to those for the GATS, and, therefore, it is logical to describe first its provisions and then turn to the GATS. However, the NAFTA and GATS negotiations overlapped to a large degree, and the thinking developed in the GATS process had a considerable impact on the NAFTA, such that it may be said that the provisions of the latter, however much they may differ from those in the GATS, often find their genesis in the experience of the GATS negotiations.

It may also be said that the GATS negotiations were influenced by experience acquired in regional arrangements, such as the FTA or the EU, or even in the broader multilateral context of the OECD, but the specific nature of these other agreements made it impossible simply to transfer their features into the GATS.[22] Indeed, largely for the reasons set out above, the GATS negotiations were much more complex than foreseen at the outset, and, until the very end, there was a very large risk of failure. As it is, part IV in the agreement recognizes that it creates, in a large sense, a framework for continuing negotiations and provides some future obligations and rules that will govern that process, an implicit recognition that there are many areas that are as yet incomplete.[23]

In addition, it is clear that satisfactory conclusions could not be achieved both for certain generally applicable rules or in the case of some sectors. Thus, government procurement practices are carved out of the market access, NT, and MFN obligations, with the provision that subsequent negotiations relating thereto will take place within two years after the establishment of the WTO.[24] Agreement could not be reached on how safeguards might be regulated, and this will require further negotiations.[25] The same approach was taken toward the development of rules that will apply to the subsidization of the export of services. This has been left to subsequent negotiations that must consider "the appropriateness of countervailing procedures" but for which no timetable has been specified.[26]

Given the fact that domestic regimes do not presently provide for contingent protection such as countervail or anti-dumping duties in the case of subsidized services, little

---

21 Hoekman and Sauvé, *supra*, note 1, at 2.

22 Lee, *supra*, note 5, at 41.

23 General Agreement on Trade in Services, art. XIX.1 provides for a new general round of negotiations to be launched within five years of the agreement's entry into force.

24 Art. XIII.

25 Art. X.

26 Art. XV and see Lee, *supra*, note 5, at 51.

attention has been paid to this area to date.[27] The fact that consultations may be entered into when a member considers that it is adversely affected by a subsidy of another member may introduce some moderating influence in this area.

Insofar as certain specific sectors are concerned, financial services proved to be a difficult sector and therefore required more limited treatment, as discussed below. The transportation sector proved similarly difficult. Air transportation is already governed by the "Chicago Convention," Convention on International Civil Aviation, and ICAO;[28] maritime transportation raises politically sensitive issues both internationally and domestically in the United States (the Jones Act[29]) and raises issues relating to the appropriate share of maritime services among developing and developed nations.[30] Telecommunications also had to be dealt with in special annexes. All three of these sectors were "withdrawn" by the United States during the negotiations, because, in their view, insufficient concessions were forthcoming from other members.

Finally, it might be said that the very structure of the agreement recognizes the inchoate nature of the obligations reached, in that important obligations[31] will only apply to those sectors covered in each national schedule and to the extent provided therein.[32] Each national schedule may subsequently be modified and re-negotiated, albeit subject to some international disciplines.

The institutional framework of the GATS reflects both its specific requirements and its place within the overall WTO system. Part V, which deals with institutions, provides for the establishment of a council for trade in services, which can also establish sub-bodies, such as a financial services committee, to respond to the particular requirements of given sectors. Dispute resolution, on the other hand, is incorporated into the general system for the resolution of disputes in the World Trade Organization (WTO). This is a significant and important recognition by members of the need for the relatively binding dispute settlement procedures established in the Understanding on Rules and Procedures

---

27 The EU has made some attempts in this area in respect of "unfair pricing practices in maritime transport" in a regulation that combines both anti-dumping and anti-subsidy notions: Behboodi, *Industrial Subsidies and Friction in World Trade* (1994), at 102 *et seq.*

28 (1951), CTS no. 7. See also a Supplementary Exchange of Notes (1971), CTS no. 17.

29 Merchant Marine Act, 1920, 46 USC, s. 861 (1988).

30 Final Act of the United Nations Conference on the Carriage of Goods by Sea, see UN doc. A/CONF. 89/13, 30 March 1977 and (1978), 17 *ILM* 603; Castel, de Mestral, and Graham, *International Business Transactions and Economic Relations: Cases, Notes, and Materials on the Law as it Applies to Canada* (1986), at 582; *Towards a New International Economic Order: A Final Report by a Commonwealth Experts' Group* (1977), at 74-5; the Director-General for Development and International Economic Co-operation, *Towards the New International Economic Order* (New York: United Nations, 1982); and Finlayson, *The End of the South? Developing Countries and International Trade Regimes in the 1990s* (1990).

31 Art. 16 (market access) and art. 17 (NT).

32 While the GATS-MFN obligation (art. 2) is not commitment specific, although members are able to claim sector-specific exemptions (e.g., Canada has taken MFN exemptions for air and maritime transport, film, video, and television programming co-production and the United States did the same for financial services).

Governing the Settlement of Disputes.[33] Given the degree to which service issues touch on sensitive issues of domestic regulation, this may raise some significant political problems about the application of the rules by third-party tribunals, particularly in the formative stages of the agreement.[34] Furthermore, the incorporation of the "unfortunately ambiguous" notion of nullification and impairment into the agreement may well inhibit the inclusion of certain services or the making of additional commitments in respect thereof, particularly insofar as extensive domestic regulatory regimes are concerned.[35]

Subject to the observations below, the system created seeks to be all encompassing. Thus, the general obligations and disciplines contained in part II apply across the board to all items covered by the agreement. The two most important of these disciplines are the MFN principle and transparency rules. In this sense, the GATS goes beyond the FTA, for example, where the sectoral annexes had to be consulted to get a real sense of the application of the rules. Here, too, however, while coverage under article I extends to all services, except services supplied in the exercise of a governmental authority, the extent to which the general obligations will apply is largely determined by the obligations accepted in the national commitments.

Measures affecting trade in services that are covered by the agreement are defined to include measures established by all levels of government or by organizations exercising powers delegated by government. Members are obliged to "take such reasonable measures as may be available to it to ensure ... observance ..." by sub-national levels of government and non-governmental bodies.[36] While this obligation to include provinces and states is not as firm as that contained in the NAFTA, in Canada, it certainly raises the issue of the provinces' participation in the agreement and the extent to which the constitutional authority of the federal government might be invoked to require provincial compliance with the agreement in what constitutes extensive areas of provincial jurisdiction over services.[37] It also raises the issue of the extent to which other members

33 Final Act Embodying the Results of the Uruguay Round of Multilateral Trade Negotiations, Annex 2: Understanding on Rules and Procedures Governing the Settlement of Disputes in (1994), 33 *ILM* 1226. For an analysis see, chapter 19, *infra.*

34 Lee, *supra*, note 5, at 43.

35 Art. XXIII.3. On nullification and impairment see discussion *infra*. Jackson described the notion as "an unfortunately ambiguous phrase" in *Restructuring the GATT System* (1991), at 62.

36 Art. I.3.

37 For a discussion of the Canadian treaty-making power, see Kindred et al. (eds.), *International Law, Chiefly as Interpreted and Applied in Canada* (5th ed., 1993), at 161-74; Bernier, "La Constitution canadienne et la réglementation des relations économiques internationales au sortir du 'Tokyo Round'" (1979), 20 *C de D* 673; Howse, "The Labour Conventions Doctrine in an Era of Global Interdependence: Rethinking the Constitutional Dimensions of Canada's Economic Relations" (1990), 16 *Can. Bus. LJ* 160; and Hogg, *Constitutional Law of Canada*, vol. 1 (3rd ed., 1992), c. 20 on the trade and commerce power. Two provinces have adopted legislative measures that relate to possible changes to their legislation arising out of international trade agreements. Alberta has adopted the International Trade and Investment Agreements Implementation Act, SA 1995, c. I-6.9, which sets out a framework

(The footnote is continued on the next page.)

might argue that their rights under the agreement have been nullified and impaired by a provincial or local measure by virtue of the federal government's possible failure to ensure compliance by a province or a provincially regulated non-governmental body. As will be seen from the discussion below, however, this problem could only arise in respect of the market access and NT obligations where Canada's national schedule has made commitments in respect of such a service and it is clear that no commitments have been made to date without the collaboration of the provinces in respect of areas within their jurisdiction.

Given the resistance by many developing countries to the very notion of a services agreement, it is interesting to note that there is no equivalent to part IV of the GATT, which sets out a special regime for developing countries. Of course, it has been argued that special consideration for the need of developing countries never really furthered their interests,[38] and this agreement may reflect an evolution away from the principles expressed in the New International Economic Order.[39] However, the needs of developing countries are addressed in specific articles. They are given greater flexibility insofar as future liberalization is concerned[40] and the system of national schedules allows considerable flexibility for countries at different levels of development. Article IV is directed to the issue of their increasing participation in the system. It includes a provision that service suppliers in developing countries are to have access to "contact points" established in developed countries to provide them with information about services, supply regulation, and technology.[41] Technical assistance at the multilateral level is also to be provided.[42] The role of subsidies in the development programs of developing countries is to be taken into account during negotiations on this issue[43] And so it may be said that throughout its provisions the agreement recognizes the special needs of developing countries without creating a special regime for them.

---

37 Continued …

whereby the province may adopt the legislative and regulatory measures necessary to conform to international trade and investment obligations. Quebec has enacted An Act Respecting the Implementation of International Trade Agreements, LQ 1996, c. 6.

38 See, generally, Nicolaides, "Preferences for Developing Countries: A Critique" (1985), 19 *JWTL* 373; Balassa, "Liberalizing Trade Between Developed and Developing Countries" in Balassa, *New Directions in the World Economy* (1989), at 17; and Chakravarthi, *Recolonization: GATT, the Uruguay Round and the Third World* (1990).

39 As the recent meeting of the Non-Aligned Movement in Cartegena illustrated, however, the principles of the NIEO still form an important part of the political discourse of many developing countries. See *Report of Chairman of the Non-Aligned Movement on the Activities of the Movement (Sept. 1992-Oct. 1995)* (1995).

40 Art. XIX.2.

41 Arts. IV and XXV.1.

42 Art. XXV.2.

43 Art. XV.1.

A. The Agreement

The most that a textbook of this nature can do for the reader is to provide a summary of the contents of the agreement with some brief comments on its more salient features.[44] Structurally, it is broken down into six parts to which are added several sectoral and thematic annexes. The six parts are (1) scope and definition; (2) general obligations and disciplines; (3) specific commitments; (4) progressive liberalization; (5) institutional provisions; and (6) final provisions. The annexes deal with limits on the exemptions permitted to article II (the MFN obligation), the movement of national persons supplying services under the agreement, financial services (two annexes), telecommunications and basic telecommunications (two annexes), air transport services, and a framework for negotiations on maritime transport services.[45]

Part I, scope and definition, provides that the agreement applies to measures taken by members, affecting trade in services. Trade in services consists of the supply of a service that is either cross-border, by virtue of consumption abroad, a commercial presence, including the establishment of a juridical person, or through the presence of a natural person.[46] As noted above, these measures are defined to include those taken by sub-national levels of government or agencies exercising governmentally delegated powers. On the other hand, services supplied by governmental authority—that is, "any service supplied neither on a commercial basis, nor in competition with one or more service suppliers"—are not governed by the agreement, but the competition reservation could have quite a limiting effect on this exemption as the process of government downsizing and privatization leads to the delivery of many government services in conjunction with private service. Part I is supplemented by definitions set out in article XXVIII that deal with such issues as the notion of commercial presence and "natural" and "juridical persons" of members. These latter definitions are important since any member may deny the benefits of the agreement to services supplied from the territory of a non-member. In the case of juridical persons of another member, this has always been a difficult area in trade agreements involving complex notions of the localization of the ownership and control of corporations.[47]

Part II, general obligations and disciplines, sets out the basic principles that apply to trade in services. The two most important of these are the MFN principle and transparency. The MFN principle is treatment "no less favourable" than that accorded to "like services and service suppliers" of any other country. This principle is subject to the exemptions that are filed by each Member in a "Final List of MFN Exemptions."[48] The

---

44 Descriptions and comments on the agreement may also be found in Trebilcock and Howse, *supra*, note 12; Lee, *supra*, note 5; and Weiss, "The General Agreement on Trade in Services 1994" (1995), 32 *CML Rev.* 1177.

45 The annexes form an integral part of the Agreement: art. XXIX.

46 Art. I.

47 Kindred et al. (eds.), *supra*, note 5, at 399-412; see, e.g., art. 1416 of the NAFTA for a definition of "financial institution of another party."

48 E.g., Canada, Final List of Article II (MFN) Exemptions, GATS/EL/16, 15 April 1994.

scope and extent of such exemptions is, in turn, governed by the annex on article II exceptions, that provides, *inter alia*, that all exemptions of a duration of more than five years shall be reviewed by the council at the end of that period in order to determine whether the conditions requiring them still exist. These are, of course, subject to the negotiations for further trade liberalizing rounds provided for in part IV. It may be said that the permitted exemptions are much less extensive than it was originally feared would be the case and that the MFN principle was accepted to a degree that one would have thought unlikely until right up to the final stages of the negotiations.[49]

The transparency provisions are important, ensuring as they do that information about regulations will be accessible through "inquiry points" established by each country. For countries where regulatory regimes are very opaque, this may, in itself, represent an important step. Even in more open countries like Canada and the United States, this may encourage a more accessible system even for nationals. While there is no need for consultation or advance notice in relation to changes in a given domestic regulatory framework the council must be notified of such changes, at least annually, to the council.[50]

As noted above, this part also contains a provision for facilitated access by developing countries to the markets of developed countries.[51] Part II also contains the equivalent of article XXIV of the GATT for free trade agreements, or other forms of regional economic integration that are subject to review by the council and may not result in a raising of the level of barriers to trade in services.[52] Furthermore, the role of labour markets integration agreements is addressed.[53] The role of domestic regulation is recognized, and where specific commitments have been made, regulations must be administered in a reasonable, objective, and impartial manner. This is the case for the application of standards, qualifications, and licensing requirements. They are subject to a proportionality test to ensure that their protectionist effect does not exceed their legitimate purpose. The council is given the authority to establish disciplines in this area.[54] Insofar as the recognition of foreign qualifications are concerned, the agreement provides that where a country does recognize foreign qualifications, it shall afford other members equality of access to such recognition procedures and shall not discriminate among countries in the application of such standards.[55] Finally, the need for multilateral

49 Lee, *supra*, note 5, at 69.

50 Art. III.3.

51 Art. VI.

52 Art. V.

53 Art. V. bis.

54 Art. VI.

55 Art. VII. The recognition of qualifications of other member states within the EU, to take one example, has taken many years and is the subject matter of many European directives and member country implementing laws. This work may be of some value to other countries. See Part IV: The Free Movement of Persons and Freedom to Provide Services (chapters 8, 9, and 10) at 161-223 in Wyatt and Dashwod, *The Substantive Law of the EEC* (1987); Smit and Herzog, *The Law of the European Economic*

(The footnote is continued on the next page.)

criteria is recognized as well as the role that non-governmental organizations play in establishing such common international standards.[56]

Competition rules are envisaged in two circumstances: first, monopolies are restricted from extending their monopoly power outside of the area of their monopoly, a problem addressed in the NAFTA in the area of enhanced telecommunication services.[57] Furthermore, if a new monopoly is set up where commitments have been made, notice must be given to the council and re-negotiation is required.[58] Consultations are also required in respect of "certain business practices" that may restrict trade in services even if they are not of the kind specifically dealt with in article VIII.

Restrictions on payments or transfers relating to transactions that are the subject of specific commitments and balance of payments issues are treated largely as they are under the GATT. Rights and obligations of members under the International Monetary Fund (IMF) are safeguarded; measures taken are not to be discriminatory, are to be reported to the council, and are the subject of consultations with the Committee on Balance of Payments Restrictions of the WTO.[59]

General exceptions also are similiar to those contained in the GATT. The usual list had to be varied to recognize the differences for services and a number of complex and controversial tax issues had to be included.[60] Reference is made to the protection of public morals and public order;[61] human, animal, or plant life or health; and consumer interests that, in this case, include the protection of privacy and the confidentiality of records.[62] The security exception basically replicates GATT, article XXI.[63] There is no general exception for services having a cultural dimension, unlike Annex 2106 of the

---

55 Continued ...
Community: A Commentary on the EEC Treaty, Vol. 2 (1984), at 624-36; Lasok and Bridge, *Law and Institutions of the European Communities* (4th ed. 1987), at 408; and Weiss, *supra*, note 44. So, too, Canada and the United States have successfully negotiated provisions for architects at the time of the FTA and are working on these for accountants and lawyers with Mexico (foreign legal consultants) (NAFTA, Annex 1210.5). These, ideally, might be extended to the GATS members where appropriate.

56 Art. VII.5.

57 Art. VIII and NAFTA, art. 1305.

58 Art. VIII.4.

59 Arts. XI and XII.

60 Art. XIV.

61 Public order ("ordre public"), a term that gives some difficulty because of the differences in treatment in common law and civil law systems, may only be invoked in the case of a "genuine and sufficiently serious threat is posed to one of the fundamental interests of society." See Husserl, "Public Policy and Order Public" (1938-1939), 25 *Virginia L Rev.* 37; and Lloyd, "Public Policy, A Comparative Study in English and French Law" (1953).

62 Boehmer and Palmer, "The 1992 EC Data Protection Proposal: An Examination of Its Implications for US Business and Privacy Law" (1993), 31 *Am. Bus. LJ* 265.

63 Art. XIV bis.

NAFTA, and this may have interesting consequences for US-Canada relations as discussed below in the section on the NAFTA.[64]

As already noted, the appropriateness of the application of countervailing duties to subsidies on the export of a service is reserved for further negotiations,[65] as is the issue of safeguard measures,[66] and the government procurement of services.[67]

Obligations relating to market access and NT are set out in part III, which also sets out the means whereby specific national commitments and "additional commitments" may be made in respect of each sector. Members agree to specific commitments in respect of any given sector by entering them in their national schedules, the contents of which were negotiated over the negotiating period for the agreement. The schedules outline the sectors to which part III will apply and contain any reservations that circumscribe the right to market access and NT conferred. It may thus be said that the way that this system works and the way the negotiation of mutually acceptable concessions was pursued is so similar to the approach to tariffs under the GATT that what we have here is the "tariffication" of obligations in respect of the transborder supply of services.

The market access obligation[68] is to provide to each GATS member no less favourable access than that set out in the schedule. In this sense, it is the equivalent to article II of the GATT. The article also lists measures that a member may not adopt, either in respect of a regional subdivision or its entire territory, unless otherwise specified in its schedule. This list covers a great many of the types of restrictions found in many national systems, including limitations on the number of service providers, quotas, the type of juridical entity that may provide the service, limits on foreign shareholdings, or the "total value of individual or aggregate foreign investment."[69]

It is clear then that the commitments to open a sector are very extensive indeed and would affect many areas that, in Canada, are presently subject to federal and provincial restrictions on foreign participation, whether for prudential, consumer protection, or cultural policy reasons. For example, limits on foreign participation are extensive in the insurance, banking, and broadcasting fields.[70] The nature of the undertakings set out in

---

64 However, Canada has not listed several sectors that are typically referred to as cultural industries in its schedule of commitments. Further, Canada has taken MFN exemptions in certain sensitive cultural industries sectors, e.g., film, video, and television programming.

65 Art. XV.

66 Art. X.

67 Art. XIII.

68 Art. XVI.

69 Art. XVI.2.

70 The Investment Canada Act of 1985 regulates foreign investment in Canada, RSC 1985, c. 28 (1st Supp.), as am. The Act requires that all direct acquisitions of businesses with assets exceeding $5 million and indirect acquisitions exceeding $50 million be subject to review. Culturally sensitive sectors, such as broadcasting, are subject to review regardless of size. Foreign investors are required to submit business plans indicating that their ownership will yield a net benefit to Canada. The Bank Act, RSC 1991, c. 46, as am., limited foreign ownership of Canadian banks to 25 percent total ownership. The Act also required all

(The footnote is continued on the next page.)

the schedules are thus very carefully considered and, in the case of Canada, care was taken to ensure that no commitment was made in a schedule that affects provincial jurisdiction, unless the provinces affected were in agreement.[71]

The definition of NT in article XVII codifies the liberal interpretation that successive GATT panels have given to article III of the GATT, in that it provides for equality of competitive opportunity. As a result, the obligation to provide treatment no less favourable than that accorded to national service suppliers is not met if a local measure provides for formal equality, but the "conditions of competition," which result from the provision, favour the local supplier over the foreign one. There are many provisions that are, on their face, origin-neutral but that may impose an additional burden on the foreign service provider, and these must now be addressed. Indeed, one such example, provided by the Secretariat to the group of negotiations on services during the multilateral trade negotiations[72] is where a measure stipulates that prior residency is required for the issuing of a licence to provide a service.[73]

As is obvious from this discussion, the notion of national schedules is key to the way in which the agreement works and to understanding the scope of the obligations of each member. The general obligations discussed above may have application to services generally, but it is the market access and NT obligations that are key to obtaining a place in any given national market place. They will only prevail insofar as the schedules determine. In this sense, the agreement works very much like the Government Procurement Code for which we must consult that country's list of entities in order to understand the extent to which it applies to any one country.[74] Each national schedule contains four columns: the first describes the sector or sub-sector covered; the second, limitations on market access; the third, limitations on national treatment; and the fourth, additional commitments. The schedule in turn is broken into two parts, the first covering "horizontal commitments," the second, "sector-specific commitments."

For example, to understand Canada's obligations in respect of engineering services, one must consult the schedule, which provides that there are different limitations on

---

70 Continued …

non-US subsidiaries to receive ministerial approval to open more than one branch. The GATS eliminates these restrictions. The Canadian implementing legislation (World Trade Organization Implementation Act, SC 1994, c. 47) required consequential amendments to another 21 federal statutes.

71 It is worth signalling the difference between the GATS and the NAFTA in this respect. Under GATS the market access provisions, in order to apply, require the specific commitment as set out in the Schedule. Under NAFTA, all provisions apply generally unless specifically reserved against.

72 MTN.GNS/W/164, 3 September 1993.

73 The Secretariat explains that although the measure does not formally distinguish service suppliers on the basis of national origin, it *de facto* offers less favourable treatment to foreign service suppliers because they are less likely to be able to meet a prior residency requirement than "like" service suppliers of national origin.

74 Final Act Embodying the Results of the Uruguay Round of Multilateral Trade Negotiations, Annex 4: Agreement on Government Procurement.

market access, which vary from province to province. Limitations on NT, while far less extensive, also exist. Saskatchewan requires local residency, for example.[75]

The schedule also contains an additional commitments column for those not covered by access or NT obligations. Such commitments relate to regulatory regimes governing qualifications, standards, or licensing requirements. Few such commitments have been undertaken to date, but Canada has, for example, made some with respect to foreign legal consultants.[76]

In view of the importance of commitments made in the schedules, the parties have prepared a manual[77] on scheduling that, while not formally a part of the GATS, serves as a guide on how to schedule commitments. As such, it may have some interpretive value in the case of a dispute.

Part IV sets out the obligations of members to achieve progressively higher levels of liberalization. To this end, members are obliged to enter into successive rounds of negotiations to ensure effective market access. Recognition is given to the need for flexibility in the case of the obligations of individual developing countries that should reflect their "development situation." The Council for Trade in Services is to carry out an assessment of trade in services and establish negotiating guidelines and procedures.[78] It also provides for the contents of the schedules[79] and sets out the means and conditions (including time frames) and the basis for compensatory adjustments, of modifying the schedules.[80]

Part V, which deals with the institutional framework, has largely been dealt with above. It is clear that the Council for Trade in Services will have an extensive role to play in the future, both through its dispute resolution role and through the fact that the agreement requires completion in so many areas. Throughout the agreement, one finds requirements for the members to notify the council or for future action by the council. This reflects the fact that the agreement is not complete in many respects, but also that one of its most important features is that it provides the principles and an institutional framework for the resolution of many remaining issues. It is not certain whether this rather embryonic and skeletal institutional structure will suffice to address the politically sensitive and complex issues at stake in services trade.[81]

---

75 Canada, Schedule of Specific Commitments, GATS/SC/16, 15 April 1994 at 21 *et seq.*

76 *Ibid.*, at 17 *et seq.* and 72 *et seq.*

77 Scheduling of Initial Commitment in Trade and Services: Explanatory note, MTN.GNF/W/164, 3 September 1993; *Scheduling of Initial Commitments in Trade and Services: Explanatory Note*, MTN.GNF/W/164/Add.1, 30 November 1993.

78 Art. XIX.

79 Art. XX.

80 Art. XXI.

81 Compare, e.g., the much more complete institutional framework of the EU.

B. The Unfinished Agenda

1. Financial Services

It is clear that there remains a substantial unfinished agenda in the overall framework governing trade in services. In three very important areas—financial services, basic telecommunications, and maritime transport—the lack of progress was particularly significant. In the end, the United States effectively took these three sectors "off the table," largely because it perceived other countries as being far from making the level of concessions that it had expected.[82]

In respect of financial services, the United States has clearly served notice that if other countries do not come on board, it will maintain its exemption and proceed with bilateral and regional arrangements. The establishment of international rules in this area has always been difficult. The financial services sector is complex and involves very different considerations depending on whether one is speaking of banking, fiduciary, or insurance institutions, for example. Consumer and depositor protection has involved intense levels of regulation that have in turn responded to substantial financial obligations incurred by the state as in the case of bank failures in Canada or the savings and loan scandals in the United States. The integrity of the financial services sector has an impact on the financial health of the economy and the security of the state itself and therefore the role of foreign institutions has always been carefully monitored.[83] The annex on financial services, subject to a proviso limiting the use of colourable measures, clearly reflects these preoccupation's when it provides:[84]

> Notwithstanding any other provisions of the Agreement, a Member shall not be prevented from taking measures for prudential reasons, including for the protection of investors, depositors, policy holders or persons to whom a fiduciary duty is owed by a financial service supplier, or to ensure the integrity and stability of the financial system.

Furthermore, economists question the degree to which free trade in financial services leads to financial market integration, as well as the macro-economic and structural effects that might result from such integration.[85]

That is to not to say that there is no international rules governing this sector. The Cooke Formula established by the Bank for International Settlements set standards for bank solvency that were extensively applied during the late 1980s.[86] The OECD has

---

82 Trebilcock and Howse, *supra*, note 12, at 241; For financial services, the United States opted out of the MFN obligation entirely.

83 González-Hermosillo and Suavé, "Financial Services and NAFTA: Implications for Canadian Financial Institutions" (Toronto: C.D. Howe Institute, 5 and 6 December 1992).

84 Annex on Financial Services, art. 2(a).

85 González-Hermosillo, *supra*, note 83, at 1, 7 *et seq*.

86 The Cooke Formula is named for Peter Cooke, the Chairman of the Basle Committee. The Basle Committee developed the Basle Accord on Capital Adequacy, which established guidelines for stricter rules for bank liquidity. See Kapstein, *Supervising International Banks: Origins and Implications of the Basle Accord*, Essays in International Finance no. 185 (1991).

established codes that relate to transborder financial services, as noted above in the introduction of this chapter.

The EU, which has a higher degree of integration than most regional organizations, has established rules allowing for bank mobility and cross-border investment based on the principles of mutual recognition, home country rule, and a degree of regulatory harmonization that is changing the nature of European financial markets.[87] In North America, the NAFTA made substantial progress beyond that achieved in the FTA.[88] All this has had some impact on domestic regulatory régimes, as in Canada, for example, where the limits on the foreign ownership of Canadian Schedule I banks, and the threshold limits on the participation of foreign banks in the market place generally have been altered, first vis-à-vis the United States in the FTA and NAFTA implementing legislation[89] and, subsequently, in the WTO implementing legislation.[90]

In the GATS, commitments in respect of the financial services sector were dealt with in a separate "understanding" that, while not formally a part of the GATS, does form a part of the final Act.[91] The understanding sets out a series of limitations on the concepts of market access commitments with respect to "cross border" and "consumption abroad" as found in paragraphs 2(a) and 2(b) of article I of the GATS and deals as well with the degree of the commitments in respect of a "commercial presence" and the "presence of natural persons." Members have subscribed to these commitments in their individual schedules that determine the degree to which they will be bound. As such, it is an alternative to the framework set out in part III of the GATS. While some of the language creates less than firm obligations ("endeavour to remove" certain non-discriminatory regulatory measures inhibiting market access by non-nationals), there are important provisions ensuring access to regulatory bodies and clearing agencies on a non-discriminatory basis.

There is also a second protocol in addition to the two financial services annexes. Each signatory's general obligations are set out in two annexes to that protocol, the first providing a list of Article II (MFN) exemptions, the second consisting of a schedule of specific commitments in respect of financial services.[92] Canada's first schedule sets out certain reservations, for example, that address inconsistencies with article II necessitated by certain NAFTA obligations. The second sets out federal and provincial limits on

---

87 Arts. 67 to 73 concern freedom of movement of capital in the EU, see Smit and Herzog, *supra*, note 55; Lasok and Bridge, *supra*, note 55, at 408; and Trebilcock and Howse, *supra*, note 12, at 237.

88 On the unsatisfactory nature of the financial services agreement in the FTA, see Castel, de Mestral, and Graham, *The Canadian Law and Practice of International Trade* (1st ed., 1987), c. 6.

89 Canada-United States Free Trade Agreement Implementation Act, SC 1988, c. 65, ss. 47 to 49 and North American Free Trade Agreement Implementation Act, SC 1993, c. 44, s. 28.

90 World Trade Organization Implementation Act, SC 1994, c. 47, s. 24, amends s. 422.1 of the Bank Act, SC 1991, c. 46, as am., and s. 25 repeals s. 422.3 of the Bank Act; Second Protocol to the General Agreement on Trade in Services, Schedule of Specific Commitments, supp. I, rev., at 12.

91 Understanding on Commitments in Financial Services in (1994), 23 *ILM* 1260-63.

92 Second Protocol to the General Agreement on Trade in Services, WTO (Geneva, 6 October 1995).

market access and on NT for the provision of services in the fields of insurance, banking, trust institutions, mortgage brokers, cooperatives, securities dealers, and brokers.[93] It contains no additional commitments.

While this framework has been said to represent a "very extensive degree of liberalization,"[94] it is certainly open to serious criticisms concerning its scope and application. The second protocol, for example, is applicable only to its signatory states and, therefore, may be said to establish an important precedent for the abandonment of the principle of universality in favor of a plurilateral system such as that which was reflected in some of the GATT codes.

Its obligations are set out in different instruments and are often vague. They would be difficult to interpret and apply in the case of a dispute. The arrangement is to prevail until the first of November 1997 and it will be interesting to see to what extent states take up the challenge to extend its scope and application, particularly where it will require the participation of many sub-levels of government, such as the states of the United States and the Canadian provinces. In sum, it provides, at best, the basis for future negotiations.

2. Telecommunications

The GATS contains an annex on enhanced telecommunications, the terms of which are very similiar to those in chapter 13 of the NAFTA and will therefore be considered in the part of this chapter dealing with the NAFTA. Access to a party's basic telecommunications transport networks is to be on "non-discriminatory and reasonable terms"[95] but, as in the other parts of the agreement, the real extent of a party's commitments, particularly in respect of enhanced and value-added services, will depend on the commitments made in the schedules to the annex.

In addition to the annex, a "Decision on the Negotiations on Basic Telecommunications" sets out a framework for the conduct of future negotiations respecting the progressive liberalization of trade in this area. A limited number of states indicated an intention to pursue these negotiations, which gave rise to serious concerns about the issue of "free riders," particularly by the Americans. These were originally to be completed by spring 1996 but were extended for another year. At the ministerial summit in Singapore in December 1996, ministers reaffirmed their commitment to arrive at a multilateral agreement based on the GATT principles covering basic telecommunications services by early 1997. The International Chamber of Commerce (ICC) has emphasized the need to reach a "broad-coverage multilateral agreement based on substantial market-opening commitments" but it remains to be seen whether obstacles to such an agreement can be overcome, even in the course of the extended time frame, particularly one that will extend universally and beyond a limited number of like-minded states. As a result, the telecommunications sector is presently open to the same

93 *Ibid.*; Canada, List of Article II (MFN) Exemptions; Supplement 1, Revision, at 1.

94 Trebilcock and Howse, *supra*, note 12, at 243.

95 Art. V.

criticism as those levelled at the financial sector insofar as the limited nature of the scope and application of its provisions is concerned.

Until there has been more experience with the system established by the agreement, it is perhaps premature to say to what extent the negotiations were successful. Whether the glass is half full or half empty will depend a great deal on the perspective of the observer. The limited success in certain sectors, such as transportation, financial services, and telecommunications may be considered negative. The way the system works may permit the evolution of a system in which groups of countries, usually at the same level of development, will adhere to certain agreements, thus creating sub-sets of sectoral free trade arrangements between a limited number of countries and opening the way to the same sort of criticisms that were levelled at the "code" system of the GATT.[96]

But the establishment of a framework for future negotiations with generally accepted principles is a good beginning for many important sectors. In many ways, too, the agreement may be said to be an investment agreement because it covers many areas common to investment and the provision of services. Even the movement of persons is touched upon in some areas where general obligations would extend to labour mobility, as evidenced by Canada's MFN exemption in respect of services incidental to agriculture (respecting the temporary entry of agricultural workers from countries with which Canada has specific memoranda of understanding).[97] It is clear, however, that the movement of professional, technical, and managerial personnel across national boundaries is crucial to modern business practices in many sectors. Thus the Understanding on Commitments in Financial Services addresses the right of temporary entry of senior management, operations specialists and technical specialists (such as computer services personnel) in the financial services sector.[98] But the annex is fairly weak and the agreement has ben criticized by the ICC for a failure to achieve any substantive liberalization in this area.

When one considers the complexity of these issues and the lack of consensus on many of them, one is forced to conclude that the achievement of universally binding rules as extensive as those in the GATS is indeed remarkable. Regional arrangements such as the EU and the NAFTA demonstrate that the solution to issues of transborder investment, transborder movement of service providers, mutual recognition of qualifications, and other similiar features of the international supply of services requires time and innovative legal procedures if success is to be achieved. They also demonstrate that solutions are possible over time and that one cannot be too ambitious at the beginning.[99]

---

96 E.g., The Telecommunications Agreement. See Trebilcock and Howse, *supra*, note 12, at 246.

97 *Supra*, note 48, at 5.

98 Art. IX.

99 Consider, e.g., the trade barriers remaining between the various Canadian provinces in many areas. See The Canadian Chamber of Commerce, *The Agreement on Internal Trade and Interprovincial Trade Flows: Building a Strong United Canada* (1996).

III. THE NORTH AMERICAN FREE TRADE AGREEMENT

As noted above, while the NAFTA came into effect prior to the Uruguay Round Agreements, including the GATS, the NAFTA negotiations on services were able to build upon the considerable consensus that had already been reached in the ongoing multilateral negotiations on trade in services. The NAFTA provisions, therefore, built upon both the GATS negotiations and the ground-breaking services provisions embodied in the FTA.[100]

Although the NAFTA obligations and language parallel, to a large extent, the language and scope of the GATS, there is an important difference between the NAFTA and GATS approaches. In the GATS, only the MFN and transparency provisions apply generally and market access and NT obligations apply only to sectors in which a country has made specific commitments. In contrast, the NAFTA services provisions apply generally, unless a country specifically exempts measures or sectors from the application of the NAFTA obligations. Thus, while parties are required to "opt in" to the market access provisions in the GATS, the NAFTA provisions apply unless a party expressly "opts out" of the provisions.[101] As a theoretical matter, the NAFTA approach represents a more expansive or liberalizing perspective although in practice, the end result of the two approaches may be very similar, particularly as the states and provinces have expressed blanket reservations for all present legislation, thus effectively grandfathering any existing inconsistencies with the NAFTA obligations.

Services are addressed in the NAFTA in a general chapter (chapter 12) and specific chapters on telecommunications (chapter 13) and financial services (chapter 14). These chapters are all included in part V of the agreement which also addresses investment (chapter 11), regulation of anti-competitive practices (chapter 15), and free movement of business persons (chapter 16). Similar to the GATS, disputes concerning the application of the provisions in the services chapters fall within the general dispute resolution provisions of the agreement, as provided for in chapter 20. Chapter 11 establishes additional procedures for disputes between investors and a party, while chapter 14 provides for the appointment of expert panelists for the adjudication of disputes in relation to financial services.

Like the GATS, the NAFTA provisions apply to measures taken by all levels of government, including state and provincial and local governments. The effect of the agreement on areas of provincial or state jurisdiction is, however, limited by the ability to "reserve" existing non-conforming measures from application of many of the NAFTA services obligations.[102] The federal governments of the parties have all taken significant

---

100 The services provisions of the FTA are discussed in the previous edition of this book.

101 The GATS and NAFTA approaches are sometimes referred to as "positive" and "negative" approaches to coverage. See, e.g., Stockfish and Fracassi, "International Trade in Services: A New Frontier for Commercial Lawyers" (1995), 1 *Can. Int. Lawyer* 153.

102 Note that existing non-conforming measures by local governments are automatically reserved; there is no requirement to list these measures in order to reserve them (art. 1206:1(a)(iii)). See also Stockfish and Fracassi, *ibid.*, at 157.

reservations and, as noted above, the provinces and states have taken blanket reservations for all existing non-conforming measures.

General principles governing cross-border trade in services are set out in chapter 12 of the agreement. Subject to permissible reservations set out by a party and the exceptions set out in chapter 21 of the NAFTA, all of the provisions in chapter 12 apply to all types of services, excluding financial services (covered by chapter 14) and certain air services.

Chapter 21 of the agreement sets out a number of general exemptions that apply to the services provisions. These include measures necessary to ensure compliance with laws not inconsistent with the agreement and certain measures in relation to national security, taxation, and balance of payments difficulties. Of particular importance, however, to the issue of trade in services is the exemption for cultural industries. This exemption is unique to the NAFTA; it is not contained in the GATS, although the requirement to list sectors and services covered by the NT and market access obligations in the GATS makes a cultural industries exemption much less important.

Annex 2106 of the agreement incorporates by reference the cultural industries exemption in the Canada-US/FTA. As between Canada and either the United States or Mexico, any measure applying to cultural industries and any measure of equivalent commercial effect taken in response, are governed exclusively by the terms of the FTA. FTA, article 2005.1 exempts cultural industries, with some minor exceptions, from the provisions of the FTA. That is not to say, as recent events have demonstrated, that all acts taken in protecting cultural industries are without consequence. Article 2005.2 of the FTA provides that a party may take measures of equivalent commercial effect in response to actions that would be inconsistent with the FTA were it not for the exemption in favour of cultural industries contained in article 2005.1. In fact, few, if any, cultural services are "covered services" under the FTA and hence the circumstances in which a measure relating to the provision of services by cultural industries would breach the FTA in the absence of the cultural industries exemption are very limited. The situation is, however, quite different under the NAFTA, where all measures affecting the provision of services by cultural industries would be subject to the NAFTA but for the incorporation of the FTA cultural industries exemption. The official Canadian position is that only measures that breach the FTA give rise to the right to invoke measures of equivalent commercial effect; measures that breach only the NAFTA, but not the FTA, would not trigger the right to retaliate in article 2005.2.[103] It is not clear, however, that the United States concurs with this interpretation of the scope of the cultural industries exemption.[104]

The United States has often recognized, in international forums, the proposition that measures that are intended to reflect "the traditions and cultures" of countries constitute

103 *Can. Gaz.* pt. 1, 1 January 1994, at 218-19.

104 Note, though, that even under the Canadian interpretation, the United States is not precluded from invoking trade sanctions in respect of cultural or other industries, such as basic telecommunications services, that are not covered by the NAFTA.

the elaboration of legitimate domestic policies that must be exempt from trade liberalization obligations. The US perspective is rooted, as well, however, in its position as the world's most important exporter of "cultural" products: films and television programs. For the United States, culture and the entertainment industry are difficult to distinguish and they naturally regard with suspicion safeguards that other countries assert are cultural rather than economic in nature.

Since the NAFTA came into force, cultural issues have played a very significant role in trade disputes between Canada and the United States. The United States has threatened to take retaliatory measures over the last year in response to three separate measures taken by Canada in respect of cultural industries: the decision by the Canadian Radio-television and Telecommunications Commission (CRTC) to remove Country Music Television (CMT) from the list of foreign specialty television services eligible for distribution in Canada; the suggestion by the CRTC that it would ban distribution of US programming that did not comply with Canadian violence rating requirements; and the United States requested the WTO to adjudicate the dispute. By proceeding in this manner, the United States avoided issues relating to the cultural industries exemption in the NAFTA. A preliminary ruling has been rendered in favour of certain positions adopted by the United States. While the decision is not yet public and is still subject to appeal, reports suggest that it was based upon the premise that this case is one involving trade in products, not services.

These events evidence that cultural services and the cultural industries exemption is and will continue to give rise to problems of interpretation and application, and cultural industries can be expected to be a continuing and growing source of trade friction between the United States and Canada.

As in the GATS, both government subsidies and government procurement are expressly excluded from the scope of chapter 12.[105] Government procurement of services is, though, addressed in a separate chapter of the agreement. The provisions in chapter 10 cover the procurement of services and construction services by listed federal entities and enterprises that exceed specific dollar thresholds, and each country has excluded certain services from the application of the chapter as described therein. Like the GATS, chapter 12 applies to measures relating to cross-border trade in services, which is defined as the provision of a service from one NAFTA country into another NAFTA country, within a NAFTA country by a person of another NAFTA country, or within a NAFTA country by a person of that country to a person of another NAFTA country. Unlike the GATS, however, it does not cover investment in a service provider or the provision of services by an investor.[106] Treatment of investments and investors is dealt with solely under the investment provision contained in chapter 11 of the NAFTA.

Also like the GATS, the agreement applies to natural persons who are citizens or permanent residents of the parties and to enterprises constituted under the laws of a party. Article 1211 clarifies the extent to which a NAFTA country may deny the benefits

105 Art. 1201.2.

106 The provision of services by an investment like a business enterprise is regulated under chapter 11 (Investment) of the NAFTA.

of chapter 12 to corporations that are owned and controlled by nationals of a non-party. Specifically, a party may deny benefits to a service provider owned or controlled by nationals of a non-party if (1) the denying party does not maintain diplomatic relations with the non-party; (2) the denying party adopts or maintains measures with respect to the non-party that prohibit transactions with the service provider or that would be circumvented if the benefits of chapter 12 were extended to the service provider; or (3) subject to prior notification and consultation requirements, the party establishes that the service provider has no substantial business activities in the territory of any party.

The key obligation in chapter 12 is to provide the better of NT and MFN treatment to service providers of another party.[107] The imposition of any requirement to establish or maintain a commercial presence as a condition for cross-border provision of a service is also prohibited.[108] As indicated above, these obligations apply generally. Parties are permitted, however, to "reserve" existing non-conforming measures and sectors or activities from the obligations relating to NT, MFN treatment, and establishment of a commercial presence, where these reservations are listed in annexes to the agreement.[109] Existing non-conforming measures that are maintained by a party at the federal or state or provincial level must be set out in Annex I to the agreement. Measures listed in Annex I may be continued or amended, as long as the amendment does not decrease the conformity of the measure. In addition, in Annex II to the agreement, parties may list sectors or activities that are exempted from application of the provisions dealing with NT, MFN treatment, or the prohibition on requiring a commercial presence. All countries have taken important reservations under Annexes I and II. Canada, for example, has taken reservations for the energy, telecommunications, and transportation sectors, as well as in other areas. In addition, as noted earlier, the provinces have all taken a blanket exemption for all existing non-conforming measures.

Quantitative restrictions on the number or activities of service providers are not prohibited, but again must be listed in Annex V of the agreement and the parties are to meet at least once every two years to attempt to negotiate liberalization of these restrictions.[110]

Finally, article 1210 of the NAFTA delimits obligations in respect of licensing and certification that mirror the requirements in the GATS. Each party has agreed to endeav-

---

107 Arts. 1202, 1203, and 1204. The NT obligation in chapter 12 does not specifically extend to "equal competitive opportunities" as in the GATS. This issue of "equal competitive opportunities" is raised in the NAFTA only in the context of the requirement, in chapter 14, to accord NT to providers of financial services.

108 Art. 1205.

109 Art. 1206. Existing non-conforming measures by local governments are not required to be listed specifically in the annex. For a detailed review of reservations by the federal governments of the Parties, see Johnson, *The North American Free Trade Agreement: A Comprehensive Guide* (1994), at 297-323.

110 Art. 1207. As a practical matter, the quantitative measures that have been reserved by the federal governments of the parties are quite limited. Canada, for example, has listed only six restrictions (relating to postal services, radio frequency licences, electricity transmission, oil and gas transportation, importation of alcoholic beverages, and interprovincial bus services).

our to ensure that licensing and certification procedures are based on objective and transparent criteria, are not more burdensome than necessary to ensure quality, and do not constitute a disguised restriction on the cross-border provision of a service.[111] In addition, there is agreement that where a party recognizes the licences or certifications of another party or non-party, the party shall afford another party the opportunity to demonstrate that its licences and certifications should also be recognized, but there is no requirement to accord such recognition.[112] Parties are also required to eliminate any citizenship or permanent residency requirements in respect of licensing of professional service providers by January 1, 1996 or face reciprocal requirements from another party,[113] and the parties are to consult periodically on the removal of citizenship requirements for other types of service providers.[114] A separate annex to the chapter sets out requirements relating to the processing of applications and the delineation of standards for professional service providers, for consultations regarding standards and procedures for licensing of foreign legal consultants, and for temporary licensing of professional engineers,[115] separate agreements for which are presently under negotiation.

The investment provisions found in chapter 11 complement the obligations in respect of services, since all investments incidental to the provision of a service and/or in a service provider benefit from the measures in this chapter. Parties are required to accord investors of another party, and investments of investors or a non-party, the better of NT and MFN treatment,[116] and to ensure that treatment of investments by investors of another party complies with international law.[117] The imposition of investment-related performance requirements (such as local content, import substitution, technology transfer, and balance of trade requirements) on investments of an investor of either a party or a non-party is prohibited, as is conditioning the conferral of subsidies in respect of an investment on certain performance requirements (such as local content or balance of payment restrictions).[118] The NAFTA also prohibits the imposition of citizenship requirements on senior management positions (although a party may require that a majority of directors be of a particular nationality as long as the requirement does not materially impair the ability of an investor to control its investment)[119] and restrictions on transfers or the repatriation of profits and the like from investments.[120] Finally, any expropriation of an investment must be conducted in accordance with the rules of international law; it

111 Art. 1210.1.

112 Art. 1210.2.

113 Art. 1210.3.

114 Art. 1210.4.

115 Annex 1210:5. See Castel, "Les Prestations transfrontières de services juridiques en vertu de l'Accord de Libre Echange Nord-Américain" (1994), 1 *CP du N* 77.

116 Arts. 1102, 1103, and 1104.

117 Art. 1105.

118 Art. 1106.

119 Art. 1107.

120 Art. 1109.

must be for a public purpose, be accomplished with due process, and be accompanied by fair and adequate compensation.[121]

As in the case of the services chapter, existing non-conforming measures and sectors or activities may be exempted from the key obligations in the investment chapter, if a party lists these reservations in Annexes I and II to the agreement.[122]

The investment chapter contains its own dispute resolution provisions, which permit investors, on their own behalf or on behalf of an investment, to submit claims arising under the chapter to arbitration under the International Centre for the Settlement of Investment Disputes (ICSID) Convention, the additional Facility Rules of ICSID, or the UN Commission on International Trade Law (UNCITRAL) arbitration rules (provided certain conditions precedent are satisfied).[123] These provisions are significant, since they provide for third party, rather than government to government, resolution of disputes.

Issues related to competition law and the designation of monopolies or state enterprises are also dealt with in a separate chapter of the agreement (chapter 15). Parties are subject to a general obligation to proscribe anti-competitive business conduct and to cooperate to further effective enforcement of competition laws.[124] As in the GATS, while the designation of monopolies is not prohibited, parties are to give notice of any intention to designate a monopoly and must endeavour to minimize any nullification or impairment of benefits resulting from the designation of a monopoly. In addition to the requirement to ensure that a monopoly does not use its monopoly to acquire an anti-competitive advantage in non-monopoly markets (a requirement that is also addressed specifically in the chapter on telecommunications), parties must ensure that a government-designated monopoly acts, subject to certain limitations, "solely in accordance with commercial market considerations in its purchase or sale of the monopoly good or service" and does not discriminate, in the purchase or sale of the monopoly good or service, against investors or service providers of another party.

The temporary entry of service providers from one country to another is dealt with in chapter 16. While the obligations in this chapter are somewhat more extensive than those contained in the GATS Annex on the movement of natural persons, the NAFTA commitments remain limited. Annex 1603 enumerates certain classes of persons whose free entry into the territory of another NAFTA party is permitted provided the person is carrying out functions in seven listed areas. Clearly these obligations are nowhere near as comprehensive as those contained in the European Communities Treaty and subsequent legislative enactments and further work in this area is required.

As in the GATS, the importance and unique requirements of the telecommunications and financial services sectors are recognized in the NAFTA. While the GATS addresses the specific requirements of these sectors in various separate documents, telecommunications and financial services are each addressed in separate chapters of the NAFTA.

---

121 Art. 1110.

122 Art. 1108. Specifically, parties may take reservations in respect of the obligations concerning national treatment, MFN treatment, performance requirements, and senior management and boards of directors.

123 Arts. 1115-38.

124 Art. 1501. See chapter 16, *infra*.

Chapter 13 of the NAFTA delineates rules that apply to the telecommunications sector. The general provisions in relation to investment and services in chapters 11 and 12 of NAFTA continue to apply to this sector, except to the extent of any inconsistency between chapter 13 and chapters 11 and 12, in which case the requirements of chapter 13 prevail.[125] The provisions of this chapter parallel (with minor differences) the provisions in the GATS Annex on telecommunications. In broad terms, parties are required to ensure reasonable and non-discriminatory access to telecommunications facilities and services.[126] Unlike the GATS, however, which limits this commitment to access by service providers in sectors in which a member has made specific commitments, this obligation applies generally. Parties are also required to ensure that any licensing of enhanced or value-added service providers is transparent, non-discriminatory, and expeditious.[127] In addition, the chapter addresses issues related to the approval of telecommunications equipment,[128] competitive provision of enhanced services by monopoly providers of basic telecommunications transport services,[129] and the publication (or transparency) of conditions of access and use of telecommunications facilities and services.[130] As in the GATS, there is no requirement to permit competitive provision of basic telecommunications services, and measures relating to cable or broadcast distribution of programs are specifically excluded from the scope of the chapter.[131]

Financial services are accorded discrete treatment in chapter 14 of the NAFTA; the general provisions in chapters 11 and 12 do not apply to financial services, except to the extent that they are explicitly incorporated by reference in chapter 14.[132] The NAFTA provisions dealing with financial services are much more expansive than the provisions contained in the GATS. It is for this reason that Canada was not particularly concerned by the impasse at the negotiations on financial services pursuant to the GATS. As in the NAFTA investment and services chapters, parties are required to accord NT and MFN treatment to investors and financial institutions of another party.[133] NT extends to the requirement to accord equal competitive opportunities, a concept of national treatment that is embodied in the GATS.[134] Parties are also prohibited from imposing citizenship

125 Art. 1307.

126 Art. 1302.

127 Art. 1303.

128 Art. 1303.

129 Art. 1305.

130 Art. 1306.

131 Art. 1301. For a more detailed overview of the treatment of telecommunications in the NAFTA and the various negotiating stances of the parties, see Shefrin, "The North American Free Trade Agreement: Telecommunications in Perspective" (1993), 7 *Telecommunications Policy* 14.

132 Arts. 1101.3 and 1201.2(a).

133 Arts. 1405 and 1406. In the case of MFN treatment, parties are entitled to recognize prudential measures taken by other parties on a unilateral basis. In these circumstances, however, the party must provide any other party with the opportunity to demonstrate that its prudential measures should be granted similar recognition.

134 Arts. 1405.5 and 1405.6.

requirements on senior management or from requiring that more than a simple majority of the board of directors of a financial institution be composed of nationals.[135] The provisions in chapter 11 dealing with transfers and expropriation are incorporated by reference in chapter 14.[136]

On the issue of the establishment of financial institutions, the agreement recognizes that investors should be able to choose the juridical form of financial institutions, to provide a range of financial services, to expand geographically throughout the territory of a party, and to be uninhibited by ownership requirements specific to foreign financial institutions. Market access provisions are to be reviewed, in light of these principles, when the United States lifts territorial restrictions on financial institutions.[137]

Finally, parties are precluded from imposing new measures restricting cross-border trade in financial services. Furthermore, a party must permit nationals to purchase financial services from cross-border financial service providers, although a party is not required, by this provision, to permit these service providers to do or solicit business in its territory.[138]

As in the investment and services chapters, parties are permitted to exclude nonconforming measures (existing or new) from the application of many of the financial services obligations, where the measures are listed in an annex to the agreement.[139] Article 1410 also explicitly provides that nothing in the chapter precludes the adoption of prudential measures by a party or the conferral of monopoly rights to provide financial services.

IV. CONCLUSION

It is clear that dealing with the transborder trade in services raises issues that are of a different order of magnitude than those that apply to trade in goods. As a result, the international mechanisms necessary to achieve integration in this area are, as yet, much less developed than those that deal with trade in goods. As is the case of goods, achieving concensus at a multilateral level is obviously a much more complicated task than on a regional basis where states have a greater chance of being at similar levels of development and of sharing similiar economic concepts. As a result, regional agreements tend to be more sophisticated than the GATS.

Furthermore, achieving true market access for cross-border services requires a certain degree of approximation of domestic legislation and ultimately some degree of harmonization or mutual recognition of standards of service providers. It is not surprising, therefore, that great achievements in this field have been made in the EU where there exists an institutional framework for enacting rules that are binding on the member states and may be interpreted and applied by a court having broad jurisdictional powers.

---

135 Art. 1408.

136 Art. 1401.2.

137 Art. 1403.

138 Art. 1404.

139 Art. 1409 and Annex VII.

Thus, an examination of the case of services causes us to consider whether the institutional frameworks of the NAFTA and the WTO are sufficiently developed to enable much further significant progress.

When one examines the international institutional framework one must also take into account the means whereby international rules are transformed into the domestic legal system. Canada, the United States, and Mexico are all federal states, each one of which has its own form of constitutional constraints on the way in which international trade agreements may become effective on its territory. We can be certain that the creation of an effective system for the cross-border free trade in services between these countries, as well as at the level of the GATS, will raise complex legal issues requiring cooperation between the various federal governments and their provinces, states, and territories. For many, then, this is a new and challenging area of law that will require new skills by lawyers and policy makers alike at all levels of government in the member states.

V. SELECTED BIBLIOGRAPHY

A. Books

Appleton, *Navigating NAFTA: A Concise User's Guide to the North American Free Trade Agreement* (1994).

Daniels, *Services in the World Economy* (1993).

Grubel and Walker, *Service Industry Growth* (The Fraser Institute, 1989).

Hoekman and Sauvé, *Liberalizing Trade in Services* ((The World Bank, 1984).

Lee, "Services: The Continuing Agenda" in *Trade, Investment & Competition* (Ottawa: Centre for Trade Policy and Law, 1994) (mimeograph).

Melvin, *Trade in Services: A Theoretical Analysis* (Halifax Institute for Research on Public Policy, 1989).

Messerlin and Sauvant (eds.), *The Uruguay Round: Services in the World Economy* (The World Bank and The United Nations Centre for Transnational Corporations, 1990).

OECD, Trade in Services and Developing Countries (OECD).

Trebilcock and Howse, *The Regulation of International Trade* (1995).

Walter, *Liberalization of Trade in Financial Services* (1988).

B. Articles

Bernier, "La Constitution canadienne et la réglementation des relations economiques internationales au sortir du 'Tokyo Round' " (1979), 20 *C de D 673.*

Broadman, "GATS: The Uruguay Round Accord on International Trade and Investment in Services" (1974), 17 *The World Economy* 281 and "International Trade and Investment in Services: A Comparative Analysis of the NAFTA" (1993), 27 *Int'l. Lawyer* 623.

Hoekman, "Market Access Through Multilateral Agreement: From Goods to Services" (1992), 15 *The World Economy* 707.

Jackson, "Constructing a Constitution for Trade in Services" (1988), 11 *The World Economy* 187.

Stockfish and Fracassi, "International Trade in Services: A New Frontier for Commercial Lawyers" (1995), 1 *Canadian International Lawyer* 153.

Trachtman, "Trade in Financial Services Under GATS, NAFTA, and the EC: A Regulatory Jurisdiction Analysis" (1995), 34 *Column. J Transnat'l. L* 37.

Weiss, "The General Agreement on Trade in Services 1994" (1995), 32 *CML Rev.* 1177.

CHAPTER TEN

International Construction Contracts

I. INTRODUCTION

International contracts for construction differ from other international contracts for the sale or supply of goods or services in several important respects. For example, the subject matter of the contract, which could be the construction of a power plant or other industrial facility, may be intricate and highly technical. As well, the nature, scope, and expense of the project means that governments or government agencies are usually the "employer" party to the contract. Furthermore, the long-term nature of the project means that the employer and the contractor enter into a legal contractual relationship that may span several years. These elements mean that terms and concepts customarily used in contracts for the sale of goods or services may not be appropriate to deal with particular problems and issues that can arise in long-term construction contracts.

Long-term contracts are not confined to the domain of international construction projects. They are also essential for other international economic and commercial transactions, such as loan agreements, project financing, and intellectual property agreements concerning the licensing of technology, know-how, or show-how.[1] This chapter focuses upon the international construction contract, although some of the issues and concerns it identifies may also be relevant in the context of other long-term international contracts. Such long-term contracts are particularly susceptible to changes in circumstances, raising the issue of the need to insert special contractual provisions dealing with variation, adaptation, price or scheduling adjustment, or even more extensive renegotiation of the allocation of contractual rights and responsibilities, in order to accommodate new or unforeseen developments.

Due to their long-term character and the substantial amounts of money they involve, construction projects may yield significant economic benefits to the local economy of the place of construction, in terms of the services, materials, and labour they demand. This factor has often caused governments to distort competition in the process of selecting construction contractors by expressly or implicitly favouring domestic tenderers and therefore making the selection of a contractor on a basis other than the quality and price of bids. In addition, governments have imposed requirements upon foreign tenderers to utilize local materials and labour in the performance of their construction contracts. Since 1979, Canada has been a signatory to international agreements, both regional (that is, in the Canada-US Free Trade Agreement (FTA) and the North American Free Trade Agreement (NAFTA)) and multilateral (that is, in the General Agreement on Tariffs and Trade-World Trade Organization (GATT-WTO) framework), which aim to ensure that the government procurement practices and policies of signatories are fair, open, and transparent to foreign tenderers. These international agreements have consistently strengthened non-discriminatory international trade law disciplines dealing with government procurement policies and practices of signatories. Following a brief introduction to procurement methods in section II, these international agreements, as well as the UN

1 For an overview of the nature of long-term contracts in international trade, see Horn (ed.), *Adaptation and Renegotiation of Contracts in International Trade and Finance* (1985). In that volume, see, in particular, Horn, "The Concepts of Adaptation and Re-Negotiation in the Law of Transnational Commercial Contracts" 3, at 3 to 5.

Commission on International Trade Law (UNCITRAL) Model Law on Procurement are addressed in section III, below. International procurement financing is covered in section IV. Section V highlights some of the particular concerns associated with the long-term nature, cost, and technical complexity of international construction contracts.

II. PROCUREMENT

There are two basic approaches to international procurement. The first, direct negotiation of the contract by the procuring entity with a particular contractor, does not involve a prior competitive bidding process. The second, calling for competitive tenders from a range of interested contractors and then selecting the most competitive bid, generally fosters greater efficiency through competition in the form of lower cost and higher quality results. It is this second method, international procurement through competitive tendering, that is addressed in the rest of this chapter.

Tendering may be open, selective, or limited. In open tendering, all eligible interested suppliers are invited to submit a bid. In selective tendering, a limited number of contractors, usually selected through a pre-qualification procedure, are invited to submit tenders. Procuring entities often maintain permanent lists of qualified suppliers, although there is no uniform method for the pre-qualification of suppliers. Some entities simply require that any interested contractor that can demonstrate its technical expertise and ability in a certain industry through submission of a company background, annual reports, and an outline of project experience may register itself with the entity. In limited tendering, the procuring entity contacts suppliers individually.

The tendering process generally consists of the following stages: the pre qualification procedure, invitation to tender, the submission of the tender (including the tender guarantee), the opening and examination of tenders, and the selection of the winning tender.

III. INTERNATIONAL AGREEMENTS ON GOVERNMENT PROCUREMENT AND UNCITRAL MODEL LAW

A. Procurement Under the FTA and NAFTA

1. Canada-US Free Trade Agreement, Chapter 13

Incorporating and building upon the principles in the 1979 GATT Tokyo Round Agreement on Government Procurement (discussed below), chapter 13 of the Canada-US FTA aimed to liberalize and promote fairness and transparency in federal government procurement practices between the United States and Canada. It applied only to goods, and services incidental to the delivery of goods. Construction contracts were therefore excluded from its scope. The FTA introduced a national treatment (NT) requirement for certain Canadian goods in the United States. It also required the establishment in Canada and the United States of a domestic review mechanism for government procurement procedures.[2] In Canada, the establishment of the procurement review board satisfied this requirement.

2 See FTA, art. 1305.

2. *North American Free Trade Agreement, Chapter 10*

Building on chapter 13 of the FTA and mirroring many of the obligations in the WTO Agreement on Government Procurement, NAFTA, chapter 10 extended most of the benefits available under chapter 13 of the FTA to Mexico.[3] It also considerably broadened the FTA's coverage to encompass construction and services contracts.[4] The threshold for goods procurement involving Mexico is $50,000; the FTA threshold of $25,000 still applies as between Canada and the United States. For construction procurement, the NAFTA established thresholds of $6.5 million for federal government entities[5] and US$8 million for "government enterprises."[6] Rules for the valuation of contracts are provided.[7] As under the FTA and the GATT and WTO Agreements on Government Procurement, fairness, transparency, and non-discrimination among suppliers of signatory countries are the core components of the agreement.

The NAFTA procurement chapter applies to identified construction services procured by covered entities,[8] with certain exceptions. Canada has excluded dredging contracts and contracts tendered by or on behalf of the Department of Transport. The US Schedule states explicitly that, in accordance with chapter 10, "buy national requirements on articles, supplies and materials acquired for use in construction contracts covered by this Chapter shall not apply to goods of Canada and Mexico." Mexico is allowed additional time to comply with the obligations under the agreement with respect to non-energy construction, time limits for tendering, and the provision of additional information.[9]

The NAFTA non-discrimination requirements, in the form of NT and most-favoured-nation (MFN) obligations, apply to procurement measures covered by chapter 10. A NAFTA party must accord to the goods of other parties, and to suppliers and service suppliers of other parties treatment no less favourable than the most favourable treatment accorded to its own or another party's goods and suppliers.[10] No discrimination is permitted against locally established suppliers based on degree of foreign affiliation or ownership, or on the basis that goods and services offered are those of another party.[11]

Covered entities are precluded from considering or imposing offsets, defined as conditions imposed or considered by an entity prior to or in the course of its procurement process that encourage local development or improve a party's balance of payments

---

3 Mexico is not yet a signatory of the WTO Agreement on Government Procurement.

4 Art. 1001.1(b).

5 Federal government entities are listed in Annex 1001.1a-1.

6 Government enterprises are listed in Annex 1001.1a-2.

7 Art. 1001.1(c).

8 See Annex 1001.1b-3; app.ix 1001.1b-3-A contains the Common Classification System, Construction Work Codes, based on the United Nations Central Product Classification (CPC) Division 51.

9 Annex 1001.2a

10 Art. 1003.1.

11 Art. 1003.2.

accounts by means of requirements of local content, licensing of technology, investment, counter-trade or similar requirements.[12] In addition, technical specifications in the procurement process are not to create unnecessary obstacles to trade.[13]

As under the WTO Agreement on Government Procurement, the NAFTA provisions on tendering procedures are based on non-discrimination and transparency. The process for the qualification of suppliers is subject to a specific NT provision.[14] Except with regard to limited tenders, all covered entities must publish an invitation containing certain information notifying all potential suppliers concerning eligible procurements.[15] Further provisions regulate time limits in the tendering process[16] and contents of tender documentation.[17]

Selective tendering is permitted, subject to certain conditions.[18] Limited tendering procedures may be used in certain circumstances, including situations of extreme emergency, provided such procedures are not used with a view to avoiding maximum possible competition or in a manner that would constitute a means of discrimination between suppliers of the other parties or protection of domestic suppliers.[19] Negotiations with suppliers may only be held in certain limited circumstances,[20] such as where it is not evident that one tender is clearly the most advantageous, and must be non-discriminatory as among suppliers.

Norms concerning the submission, receipt, and opening of tenders, and the awarding of contracts emphasize fairness and openness.[21] Specific criteria for the awarding of the contract stipulate that "unless the entity decides in the public interest not to award the contract, the entity shall make the award to the supplier that has been determined to be fully capable of undertaking the contract and whose tender is either the lowest-priced tender or the tender determined to be the most advantageous in terms of the specific evaluation criteria set out in the notices or tender documentation."[22] Unsuccessful tenderers must be informed of the decision. Within 72 days of awarding the contract, the entity must publish certain information concerning the award and the winning supplier.

A bid-challenge mechanism must be available in the domestic systems of the NAFTA parties where unsuccessful bidders can challenge any aspect of the procurement procedures and the awarding of the contract. In Canada, the bid-challenge functions of

12 Art. 1006.

13 Art. 1007.

14 Art. 1009.

15 Art. 1010.

16 Art. 1012.

17 Art. 1013.

18 Arts. 1010.6 and 1011. Note that art. 1011(4) requires that an entity furnish, upon request, reasons to any supplier that is not invited to submit a tender.

19 Art. 1016.

20 Art. 1014.

21 Art. 1015.

22 Art. 1015.4(b).

the procurement review board were transferred under the NAFTA to the Canadian International Trade Tribunal (CITT).[23]

Two general exceptions exist to NAFTA, chapter 10 obligations.[24] Nothing in chapter 10 prevents a NAFTA country from taking action or not disclosing information that it considers necessary for the protection of its essential security interests concerning military procurements. In addition, no NAFTA country is prevented from taking measures necessary to protect public morals or human animal or plant life or health.

Further negotiations on the liberalization of government procurement practices between NAFTA signatories are to begin no later than 1998. The NAFTA parties have also undertaken to obtain commitments, on a voluntary and reciprocal basis, to accept the principles in Chapter 10 from sub-national (state and provincial government) entities.[25] Both NAFTA, chapter 10 and the WTO Agreement on Government Procurement will apply to certain procurements between Canada and the United States. The NAFTA parties agreed to increase their obligations and coverage under chapter 10 to be at least commensurate with the obligations under the WTO Agreement on Government Procurement.

B. Government Procurement Under the GATT and WTO

1. The GATT Tokyo Round Agreement on Government Procurement

Prior to the Uruguay Round of Multilateral Trade Negotiations, international construction contracts were not subject to international trade law discipline under the GATT. Indeed, the original GATT exempted government procurement policies entirely from the GATT non-discriminatory NT requirement.[26]

During the Tokyo Round of Multilateral Trade Negotiations (1973-79), the Agreement on Government Procurement was negotiated and concluded, entering into force for the signatories (including Canada and the United States) on January 1, 1981.[27] The scope of the Tokyo Round Agreement was narrow, applying only to goods (and services incidental to supply of the goods and worth less than 50 percent of the value of the goods). It excluded construction and service contracts; contracts with a value under the special drawing right (SDR) 130,000 threshold, and contracts listed in article viii (that is, relating to defence, and health and safety). In addition, only those federal government agencies specifically enumerated in the annex to the agreement fell to be governed by its provisions. Sub-national (that is, provincial, state, and municipal) governments were not included in this annex.

---

23 See ss. 30.1 to 30.19 of the Canadian International Trade Tribunal Act, RSC 1985, c. 47 (4th Supp.), inserted by the North American Free Trade Agreement Implementation Act, SC 1993, c. 44. See also the North American Free Trade Agreement Procurement Inquiry Regulations, SOR/93-602.

24 Art. 1018.

25 Art. 1024.4

26 See GATT, art. III.8.a.

27 See Agreement on Government Procurement, BISD 26th Supp. 33 (1979). An Amending Protocol entered into force on 14 February 1988.

The Tokyo Round Agreement on Government Procurement established a legal framework that sought to liberalize the government procurement legislation, regulations, practices, and procedures of the signatories and render them more transparent and fair to foreign suppliers. The agreement required NT in eligible public procurement, and contained rules to ensure fairness, transparency and non-discrimination in the tendering process. In addition to enumerating appropriate tendering methods, the agreement also outlined disciplines for qualification of suppliers and criteria for awarding contracts. These rules permitted open, selective and, in restricted circumstances, single tendering procedures. A 1988 amendment prohibited differential treatment for locally established suppliers from other locally established suppliers on the basis of degree of foreign affiliation or ownership, or on the basis of the country of production of the good in question, where that country is a signatory. The agreement also contained provisions on notification, consultation, surveillance, dispute settlement and enforcement, and established a committee on government procurement to monitor the operation of the agreement.

2. The WTO Agreement on Government Procurement

As noted in chapter 1, the WTO Agreement on Government Procurement was signed on April 15, 1994, and entered into force on January 1, 1996.[28] Extensive multilateral regulation of government procurement policies was not acceptable to all WTO members. Therefore, the WTO Agreement on Government Procurement is binding only upon its signatories,[29] rather than upon the entire WTO membership.[30] It is administered by the WTO Secretariat.[31]

While its signatories still remain relatively few in number, the WTO Government Procurement Agreement considerably revised and expanded upon the Tokyo Round Agreement. Significantly, the coverage of the agreement was extended to include construction and service contracts.[32] In addition, procurement by sub-central (provincial,

---

28 As the Tokyo Round Agreement on Government Procurement has not yet been terminated as of 1 September 1996, the two agreements are co-existing for the time being.

29 The following were the original signatories: Canada, the United States, Japan, the European Union (12), the five European Free Trade Association (EFTA) countries (Austria, Sweden, Finland, Norway, and Switzerland; on 1 January 1995, Austria, Sweden, and Finland acceded to the EU), Israel and South Korea. Aruba (through the Kingdom of the Netherlands) and Liechtenstein have since acceded, and further accession negotiations are underway with other states, such as Hong Kong, Singapore, and Chinese Taipei. Five WTO members have observer status: Australia, Colombia, Iceland, Singapore, and Turkey. Three non-WTO members have observer status: China, Taipei, and Latvia. Note that the Ministerial Decision on Accession to the Agreement on Government Procurement, adopted by the Trade Negotiations Committee on 15 December 1993 at Marrakesh, aims to facilitate accession to the agreement.

30 The agreement is binding only upon its signatories by virtue of its inclusion as a Plurilateral Trade Agreement in Annex 4 to the Agreement Establishing the World Trade Organization (the WTO Agreement). It does not form part of the WTO single undertaking, which includes the Multilateral Trade Agreements contained in Annexes 1 to 3 of the WTO Agreement.

31 Art. XXIV.13.

32 See art. 1.

state, and municipal) governments within the territories of most signatories, with the exception of Canada, is now covered. For Canada, the agreement offers access to the federal-level[33] services and construction markets of the European Union (EU), Japan, and the other signatories, estimated to be worth approximately US$50 billion per year.[34] The threshold figures for Canada for the period January 1, 1996 to December 31, 1997 are SDR 5,000,000 (C$9,900,000) for construction and SDR 130,000 (C$259,500) for goods and services.[35] To be covered, a construction contract must be among the services listed in Canada's Annex 5 to the WTO Government Procurement Agreement. Annex 5 includes all of the services covered by the United Nations Central Product Classification (CPC) Division 51, with the exception of dredging contracts, and contracts tendered by the Department of Transport. These exceptions allow flexibility for Canada concerning strategic industrial development in the areas of high-technology communications, transportation-related construction, dredging, and other services.[36] Exceptions specific to other signatories also exist.

The fundamental principle of the WTO Agreement on Government Procurement is non-discrimination, based on NT and MFN obligations. Thus, governments of the signatories must treat goods and services from other parties, and suppliers of such goods and services, no less favourably than they treat their own domestic goods, services, and suppliers or than they accord to goods, services and suppliers of any other signatory for contracts covered by the agreement.[37] No discrimination with respect to laws, regulations, or procedures is permitted against locally established suppliers based on the extent of foreign affiliation or ownership or of the country of production of the good or service being supplied, as long as it is a signatory of the agreement.[38] In addition, signatories must ensure that the purpose and effect of technical specifications is not to impose unnecessary obstacles to trade.[39] To this end, technical specifications in tender documentation should comply with international standards where appropriate.[40]

The principle of non-discrimination permeates the agreement's provisions on tendering and bid-challenge procedures. These extensive procedural provisions aim to ensure

33 While other signatories undertook to have the agreement apply to sub-central governmental entities, such as provincial and state governments, Canada limited its original commitments to the federal government level. However, Canada proposed the coverage of entities in the provinces, and undertook consultations with the provinces to this effect. Further discussions were held with other signatories in order to assess Canada's balance of commitments. See *Canadian Statement on Implementation, Agreement Establishing the World Trade Organization, Can. Gaz.* pt. I, 31 December 1994 ("*Canadian Statement of Implementation*"), at 4950.

34 See *Canadian Statement on Implementation*, at 4949.

35 Art. 2 contains rules for the valuation of contracts.

36 *Canadian Statement of Implementation*, at 4949-50.

37 See art. III.

38 Art. III:2.

39 Art. VI.

40 Art. VI.2.

that covered procurement practices in signatory states are open, fair, transparent,[41] and predictable. Open competitive tendering is the preferred procurement method. Selective tendering is also permitted. The use of limited tendering is restricted to certain very narrow circumstances,[42] such as in cases of extreme urgency, or in the purchase of construction services that were not specified in the initial contract but that have since become necessary[43] or are repeat construction services. Such tendering processes are not to be used in a discriminatory manner or to avoid maximum possible competition and must be as competitive as possible. Under the open procurement procedure, qualification of suppliers must be non-discriminatory[44] and covered contracting entities must advertise all of their eligible procurements exceeding the threshold value in specific journals, listed in appendix ii to the agreement.[45] The WTO Government Procurement Agreement stipulates the required content of such notices.[46] The notice must indicate whether the tendering procedure will be open, selective, or limited; the nature and quantity of supplies required; the date for delivery or completion; any economic and technical requirements; information required from suppliers; and the deadline for tenders to be received by the procuring entity.

Tendering documentation provided to suppliers must contain all the information necessary to permit them to submit responsive tenders, including certain specified information.[47] Unless an entity decides in the public interest not to issue the contract, the contract must be awarded to the lowest-priced tender or to the one that is most economically advantageous having regard to the specific evaluation criteria set out in the tender documentation.[48] Imposing, seeking, or considering offset requirements, such as the necessity for foreign tenderers to use domestic content, technology licensing, investment requirements, counter-trade, or similar requirements is not permitted.[49]

Within 72 days of the awarding of the contract, a post-award notice must be published in the appropriate publication, containing information on the winning tenderer. Unsuccessful tenderers may receive information on the characteristics and relative advantages of the successful bid.[50]

The WTO Government Procurement Agreement establishes mandatory bid-challenge procedures[51] requiring each party to provide an impartial, non-discriminatory,

41 See, in particular, art. XVII.

42 Art. XV.

43 Art. XV.f. The total value of contracts awarded for the additional construction services may not exceed 50 percent of the amount of the main contract.

44 Art. VIII.

45 In Canada, this is the *Can. Gaz.*

46 Art. IX.6.

47 Art. XII.

48 Art. XIII.4.

49 See art. XVI. Offsets were permitted under the GATT-Tokyo Round Agreement on Government Procurement (art. V.15.b).

50 Art. XVIII.

51 Art. XX.

timely, transparent, and effective mechanism where foreign suppliers can challenge alleged breaches of the agreement, including bid procedures and contract awards. Interim measures to correct breaches of the agreement and preserve commercial opportunities must be available, as must measures to correct a breach of the agreement. Compensation "may be limited to costs for tender preparation or protest."[52] In Canada, the CITT conducts this bid-challenge function.[53]

The disciplines under the agreement are subject to exceptions with respect to, *inter alia*, signatories' essential security interests; measures necessary for the protection of public morals, human, animal, or plant life or health; and intellectual property.

Signatory countries may resort to consultation and dispute settlement under the WTO Dispute Settlement Understanding (DSU)[54] if they deem their rights under the agreement to be nullified or impaired.[55] As a plurilateral agreement in Annex 4 of the WTO Agreement, the WTO Agreement on Government Procurement would not automatically be subject to the dispute settlement rules and procedures outlined in the DSU. Nevertheless, subject to the special or additional provisions set out in article XXII.2-7, the DSU applies to disputes arising under the agreement as a result of article XXII.1 of the agreement.[56]

A committee on government procurement was established to administer and monitor the operation of the agreement. To facilitate the committee's surveillance task, the agreement mandates that each signatory compiles annual statistics on the procurement contracts awarded.

The implementation of the WTO Agreement on Government Procurement in Canada required changes to the Financial Administration Act to permit the government to issue directives or regulations regarding Crown corporations to ensure compliance with Canada's obligations.[57] Amendments were made to the definition of "potential supplier" in the Canadian International Trade Tribunal Act to accommodate the requirements for the bid-challenge mechanism.[58] Certain changes were also made to the CITT regulations.[59] Because the Canadian procurement procedures already complied with the requirements of NAFTA, chapter 10, Canadian implementation of the WTO Agreement on Government Procurement did not require extensive statutory or regulatory amendments.

52 Art. XX.7.c.

53 *Canadian Statement of Implementation*, at 4949-50.

54 See, generally, the chapter on WTO Dispute Settlement, chapter 19, *infra*.

55 Art. XXII.1, except as otherwise provided in art. XXII.2-7.

56 Art. XXII:2-7 has been notified to the WTO Dispute Settlement Body as special or additional rules governing the settlement of disputes, in accordance with Appendix II to the DSU.

57 RSC, c. F-11, s. 89.2, added by the Act to Implement the Agreement Establishing the World Trade Organization (the WTO Agreement Implementation Act), SC 1994, c. 44, s. 116.

58 RSC 1985, c. 47 (4th Supp.), s. 30.1.

59 See *Canadian Statement on Implementation*, at 4949-50.

C. The UNCITRAL Model Law on Procurement

The UNCITRAL Model Law on Procurement of Goods, Construction and Services[60] (the model law) was adopted by UNCITRAL on June 15, 1994. It is intended to serve as a model to countries for the evaluation and modernization of their procurement laws and practices, and for the establishment of procurement legislation in countries where no such legislation is in place.[61] Targeting in particular developing countries that often lack financial resources for public procurement, the model law aims to ensure that government purchasing practices operate as transparently, efficiently, and effectively as possible. It also aims to reduce obstacles to international trade by decreasing disparities among, and uncertainties concerning, national procurement regimes. It aspires to promote the participation in procurement proceedings by suppliers and contractors wherever possible, regardless of their nationality.

Open competitive tendering is the favoured procurement method. With respect to procurement of construction, a procuring entity may only use another method of procurement (for example, two-stage tendering, request for proposals or competitive negotiation, restricted tendering, request for quotations, or single-source procurement) in certain limited circumstances. The model law also covers tendering proceedings and provides for a bid-challenge mechanism permitting suppliers and contractors suffering loss or injury due to the failure of the procuring entity to abide by its legal obligations to request review of the procurement decision. The model law excludes defence or security-related contracts as well as those expressly excluded by national legislation or regulations. Certain individual procurements may also be excluded from its scope. Corruptive practices are addressed through the requirement to reject a tender or other offer if the contractor or supplier gives or agrees to give any present or former officer or employee of the procuring entity any gratuity or inducement with respect to any act, decision, or procedure in the procurement proceedings.

The model law is a framework law that may be supplemented by administrative and procedural regulations. It has no legal force until enacted in a country's domestic legal regime.

IV. PROCUREMENT FINANCING FROM INTERNATIONAL INSTITUTIONS AND AGENCIES

The substantial sums of money frequently involved in international procurement contracts often make it necessary for procuring entities to seek financing for certain projects, particularly those in developing countries, from international agencies. Two of the principal international agencies involved in funding international procurement contracts are the International Bank for Reconstruction and Development (IBRD or World Bank) and the International Development Association (IDA).

60 (1995), 34 *ILM* 718. This model law expands upon and does not supersede the earlier UNCITRAL Model Law on Procurement of Goods and Construction adopted on 16 July 1993 (1994), 33 *ILM* 445.

61 See commentary in (1994), 33 *ILM* 445.

The World Bank issues guidelines concerning procurement under IBRD loans and IDA credits.[62] These guidelines outline procurement procedures and arrangements for projects financed in part by the World Bank or the IDA. In general, these agencies extend loans for specific projects. The legal relationship between the borrower (that is, the employer in the construction project) and the bank (that is, either the World Bank or the IDA) is governed by the loan agreement. The guidelines apply to procurement of goods and works for the project, to the extent provided for in the loan agreement. The rights and obligations of the borrower and the suppliers of goods and works for the project are governed by the tender and contract documents, rather than by the loan agreement or the guidelines. The guidelines provide for an internationally competitive tendering procedure in most circumstances, although a margin of preference for local contractors is permitted in certain situations.

Financing is also available through the UN Development Program, the International Finance Corporation (IFC) and regional development banks (the Inter-American Development Bank, the African Development Bank, the Asian Development Bank, the Caribbean Development Bank, and the European Bank for Reconstruction and Development). Because Canada is a member of these regional development banks, Canadian contractors may bid for contracts financed by them. Often pre-registration with the development bank is required. Canadian contractors registered with the Canadian International Development Agency (CIDA) may also bid for contracts financed by that agency.[63]

V. THE INTERNATIONAL CONSTRUCTION CONTRACT

A. UNCITRAL Legal Guide

The 1987 UNCITRAL *Legal Guide on Drawing Up International Contracts for the Construction of Industrial Works* provides extensive and detailed guidance for drafting international construction contracts, covering both matters that arise prior to the time when the contract is drawn up, and specific provisions to be included in the contract. The guide contains instructive recommendations concerning the manner in which certain issues in the contract may best be resolved.

B. FIDIC Standard Form Contract and Tender Documents

The Fédération Internationale des Ingénieurs-Conseils (FIDIC) issues the Conditions of Contract for Works of Civil Engineering Construction,[64] the standard form contract used most frequently in internationally financed civil engineering construction projects conducted in developing countries. The World Bank frequently uses the FIDIC Conditions as a basis for its contracts.

The FIDIC Conditions consist of two parts. Part I contains general conditions, intended to be of universal application. Part II contains provisions of particular application,

---

62 The most recent edition is the 4th ed., published in 1992.

63 See Raworth, *Legal Guide to International Business Transactions* (1991), 133-34.

64 The 4th edition of these conditions of contract was published in 1987, and is still widely used. The 5th edition is scheduled for publication in 1997.

which are to be tailored by the parties to the specific transaction. Certain clauses in part I must be supplemented by elements found in part II. This is the case, for example, with respect to language and applicable law.

The FIDIC Conditions set out the general obligations of the employer (the procurer of the civil engineering works concerned), the contractor (the person whose tender has been accepted by the employer), and the engineer (technical expert appointed by the employer), as well as the subcontractor and the engineer's representative. The construction project is referred to as the "works." The FIDIC Conditions state that unless otherwise provided, the legal priority of documents is the contract agreement (if completed), the letter of acceptance, the tender, part II of the conditions, and part I of the conditions, followed by any other document forming part of the contract. After setting out the general obligations of the various parties involved, part I of the FIDIC Conditions contains provisions on labour; materials; plant and workmanship (including inspection); suspension of work; commencement of the works and delays; defects liability; alterations; additions and omissions; procedure for claims; contractor's equipment; temporary works and materials; measurement; provisional sums; nominated subcontractors; certificates and payment; remedies; special risk; payment in event of release from performance; default of the employer; changes in cost and legislation; and currency and rates of exchange.

Part I of the FIDIC Conditions also contains standard forms of both the tender and the agreement recommended by the FIDIC contract. The tender form requires the contractor to stipulate the price, and the number of days it will consider itself bound by the tender. Unless and until a formal agreement is concluded, the tender and written acceptance constitute a binding contract. The appendix to the tender contains the time frames for the entire work (that is, periods for commencement, completion, and maintenance of the work, as well as the time period for payment upon acceptable completion), as well as financial details (for example, the amounts of the performance guarantee and liquidated damages).[65] The standard form agreement incorporates by reference into the contract: the letter of acceptance; the tender; the Conditions of Contract (parts I and II); the specification; the drawings; and the bill of quantities.

With respect to dispute settlement, the FIDIC Conditions confer upon the consulting engineer the authority to resolve disputes between owners and operators arising out of the contract or of the conduct of the project, whether during or after the completion of construction.[66] If either the employer or the contractor is dissatisfied with the decision of the engineer, or if the engineer fails to give notice of his decision within a set period,

65 See also Schmitthoff, *Schmitthoff's Export Trade: The Law and Practice of International Trade* (9th ed., 1990), at 739.

66 See FIDIC Conditions, s. 67.1. This authority may be curtailed in future editions of the conditions, see Lyon, "The Role of the Consulting Engineer in Developing Country Construction under the FIDIC Form Contract" (1994), 26 *Law and Pol. in Int'l. Bus.* 273, 274. See also, e.g., Hochuli, "Role of the Engineer under FIDIC Standard Contracts" (December 1991), 19 *Int. Bus. Lawyer* 542 and Ludlow and Rees, "Engineer's Role under FIDIC Standard Conditions of Contract" (1992), 20 *Int. Bus. Lawyer* 525.

or if either party fails to comply with the engineer's decision, the dispute may be submitted to arbitration.[67]

The engineer further bears the responsibility for issuing certificates of satisfactory completion of certain phases or of the whole project; and for issuing orders, for example, with respect to alterations, additions, and omissions of the project.

C. Particular Contractual Considerations

1. Financing

The financial import of international construction contracts has resulted in parties frequently resorting to contract guarantees such as tender guarantees, performance guarantees, and demand guarantees.[68]

In the tendering phase, a tender guarantee may be required to support a contractor's bid. The conditions of tender may stipulate that the tender security be in the form of a cash deposit, bank draft, irrevocable letter of credit, guarantee, or bond.[69] The tender security of the winning tenderer will ordinarily be discharged upon signing the construction contract and the furnishing of the requisite performance security. The function of a tender guarantee is generally to confirm the contractor's interest in the project and to protect the employer against a breach by the tenderer of its tendering obligations.[70] Thus, the conditions of tender may dictate that a tender guarantee is forfeited where a tenderer withdraws his bid during the period of tender validity, or where a winning tenderer fails to sign the construction contract or to furnish the requisite performance guarantee within a specified time period.

With respect to the contractual phase, in many states, contractors are required to provide unconditional performance bonds in the form of first demand bank guarantees and letter of credit security. Such performance guarantees may deny any obligation on the part of the employer to certify that the contractor has failed to fulfill the terms of the contract. In the past, employers or project owners have called on the guarantee without any regard for the actual value of the deficiencies in contract performance forming the basis of the call. In recent years, there has been a trend toward balancing more appropriately the rights and obligations of the employer and the contractor in financing arrangements. An attempt has been made to limit the opportunity for abusive, arbitrary, or improper calls on performance or demand guarantees through modification of unconditional performance guarantees and letter of credit security.[71]

---

67 See FIDIC Conditions, ss. 67.2 to 67.4.

68 See ICC Uniform Rules for Contract Guarantees (URCG) (doc. no. 325, 1978) and Uniform Rules for Demand Guarantees (doc. no. 458, 1992). See also the UNCITRAL Draft Convention on International Guaranty Letters. These are discussed in the chapter 11, *infra*, on payment and financing.

69 See the URCG and URDG, *ibid.*

70 Schmitthoff, *supra*, note 65, at 742.

71 See discussion on guarantees in section V of chapter 11, *infra*. See also Myers, Marsten and Rubino-Sammartano, ""Illustrative Forms of Performance Guarantee and Counter Guarantee Security for Inter-

(The footnote is continued on the next page.)

2. Contract Pricing, Payment, and Currency

The three most common methods of contract pricing in international construction contracts are (1) the lump-sum method, (2) the cost-reimbursable method, and (3) the unit-price method.[72] The lump-sum method requires the employer to pay a particular amount that remains constant although the actual cost of construction may be different than anticipated at the time the contract was concluded. The contract may permit price adjustment or revision. The cost-reimbursable method requires the employer to pay all of the reasonable construction costs, along with an agreed fee. The amount may be capped at a certain threshold. The unit-price method allows the parties to agree upon a price for each unit of construction, and to calculate the total contract price on the basis of total units actually used. This third approach may be preferable where the parties are unable to agree on a lump-sum amount at the outset, but is of limited use and therefore may need to be supplemented by other pricing methods in respect of those aspects of the construction project that are not readily divisible into units.

The method of payment of the contract will depend upon the specific nature of the construction project and upon the preferences of the parties. Because of the long-term nature of the construction project, the payment conditions in international construction contracts frequently contemplate the payment by installments of specified percentages of the price at successive phases of construction, depending upon the progress of the construction. An advance payment may be made to the contractor to cover the costs incurred in the initial stages of the construction and to cover any risk of loss that may occur during this time.[73]

Many international construction contracts provide for the withholding by the employer of a portion of the contract price during a specified period after completion of the project. Often referred to as "retention money," this sum protects the employer by allowing him to ensure that the contract has been complied with and that the completed facility operates satisfactorily.

The currency of payment in international construction contracts is also an important element for consideration by a lawyer drawing up such a contract. Exchange rate risk is

---

71 Continued ...

national Construction Contracts" (1992), 20 *Int'l. Bus. Lawyer* 243. These forms were prepared by the Committee on International Construction Contracts, in the business law section of the International Bar Association to provide a basis to assist international construction project participants in implementing performance guarantee security. The illustrative forms consist of the following: Performance Guarantee with Schedules A to D [Schedule A—Certificate Confirming that Contractor Has Not Objected to Employer's Demand for Payment; Schedule B—Certificate Confirming Contractor's Objection; Referral to ICC Pre-Arbitral Referee; and Provision of Counter-Guarantee for Repayment to Contractor; Schedule C—Certificate Confirming Pre-Arbitral Referee's Decision; Schedule D—Counter Guarantee]; Agreement Regarding Provisional Dispute Resolution with Respect to the Performance Guarantee; and Summary Checklist.

72 UNCITRAL, *UNCITRAL Legal Guide on Drawing up International Contracts for the Construction of Industrial Works* (1987) (the *UNCITRAL Legal Guide*), at 76 *et seq.*

73 See, e.g., *UNCITRAL Legal Guide, ibid.*, at 93-94.

always present when dealing with foreign currencies. It is not necessary for payment of the contract price to be made in the currency in which the contract is denominated. Rather, a distinction may be drawn between the currency of account and the currency of payment. The contract price may be stipulated in the currency of account, while payment may be made to the contractor (and any subcontractor) in the currency of payment. A currency clause may be inserted into the contract providing for the linkage of the exchange rate of the currency of payment and the currency of account. To avoid confusion, the exchange rate should be stipulated as of a certain date. Where the rate of exchange has fluctuated, the price to be paid may be adapted so that the amount in terms of the currency of account remains constant. Where the employer has received a loan for the construction of the project, the employer may wish to pay the contract price in the currency in which the loan was granted.[74]

Alternatively, rather than basing the contract price upon a national currency, the parties may also wish to denominate the contract price in a unit-of-account, composed of a weighted basket of currencies. The unit of account of the International Monetary Fund (IMF), the SDR, is one option available to the parties.

3. Allocation of Contractual Responsibilities Between Employer, Contractors, and Subcontractors

The appropriate balance of contractual rights and obligations between the employer and the contractor vary depending upon the nature of the project. For example, the employer or a consulting engineer appointed by the employer may be responsible for initial engineering and design requirements and for supervising the contractor in the construction of the project and subsequent start-up of the facility. Another possibility, the turnkey contract, ordinarily gives the contractor control over the entire project, and the responsibility to hand over a full operational facility to the employer. In both of these cases, the contractor will usually bear the responsibility for subcontractors, although the arrangement may be such that the employer participates in the selection of the subcontractor, or pays the subcontractors directly. The right of the contractor to subcontract should be expressly provided for in the contract. Particularly where the employer supplies the design of technology for the project, the employer may wish to limit the contractor's right to subcontract in the interests of protecting the confidentiality of the design or technology.[75] The contract may explicitly specify those contractual obligations that can and cannot be subcontracted. A further option is for the employer to contract directly with multiple contractors that each bears responsibility for a particular portion of the project. In this case, there is usually no need for subcontractors. Finally, in so-called "fast track" contracting, the employer contracts separately and directly with contractors for consecutive phases of the project. This approach may be associated with difficulties in coordinating among the various contractors concerning the successive phases of the work.[76]

---

74 *Ibid.*, at 84.

75 *Ibid.*, at 131.

76 Schmitthoff, *supra*, note 65, at 745.

4. *Inspection and Acceptance*

Because of the long-term nature of the construction contract and the complex nature of the construction work underlying the contract, it is advisable that the contract provide for periodic inspection and acceptance by the employer of the contractor's work during the construction process, as well as for inspection and final acceptance upon completion of construction.

With respect to inspection and acceptance during the construction, the contract may therefore entitle the employer periodically to inspect the progress of the construction on site. In order to facilitate such inspection and to help the employer to keep abreast of the progress of the construction project, the contract may also require the contractor to maintain thorough records of the construction process and to furnish these to the employer upon request. Such inspection generally serves to satisfy the employer that construction is progressing in conformity with the schedule and other conditions specified in the contract. It is prudent for the employer to provide in the contract that failure on the employer's part to identify a defect or omission in the construction through such an inspection does not preclude him from later raising a claim to remedy a defect.[77]

Concerning completion of the construction and final acceptance, it is advisable that the contract identify precisely when the project is deemed to be completed by the parties, as well as the legal effects of completion and of acceptance of this completion by the employer. The contract should also deal with the timing, conditions, and legal effects of take-over of the facility by the employer. The transfer of risk of loss or damage may occur either on the date of acceptance or the date of take-over, depending upon the terms of the contract.[78]

The contractor may be required under the contract to demonstrate completion of construction by successfully conducting specified completion tests. The construction may then be deemed formally completed upon termination of these tests. The employer may be under an obligation to take over the facility upon successful demonstration of completion. Often, however, the legal relationship between the parties does not terminate with the completion of the construction. The contract may contemplate a trial operation period or a transition period. During this period, depending upon the contractual provisions and the nature of the project, the contractor may have certain obligations with respect to maintenance of the facility, and with respect to training and the transfer of technology (know-how and show-how) concerning the operation and maintenance of the works following the project's start-up phase. For example, in the case of "build, own and transfer" (BOT) projects, the constructing contractor customarily continues to operate and manage the constructed work after completion during a defined period (which can be relatively lengthy), during which training, along with other necessary transitional preparations, occurs.

Acceptance by the employer of the completion of the construction may also be linked with the conduct of performance tests. Such tests serve to demonstrate that the

77 See *UNCITRAL Legal Guide*, *supra*, note 72, at 141.

78 *Ibid.*, at 146-57.

facility satisfies technical contractual specifications. Depending upon the nature of the construction project and the requirements of the parties, the contract may stipulate that performance tests must be performed before acceptance occurs, or after completion of construction, or within a certain time after a period of trial operation.[79]

5. Variation and Adaptation

Depending on the nature of the transaction and the particular contract involved, there are several ways in which parties may treat the issue of variation or adaptation of contractual terms. For example, parties may not attempt to anticipate events, and leave specific areas in the contract to be fleshed out through a specified process when the need arises. In addition, they may predict certain changes in circumstances and insert variation or adaptation clauses into the contract. They may also envisage the occurrence of certain events inherent in the construction project, which could include changes of an economic, financial, legal, or technological nature, that render contractual performance onerous or impossible for one party through the allocation of risk or through the inclusion of "hardship" or "special risks" clauses in the contract.[80]

Circumstances may arise requiring an alteration in the construction differing from the obligations in the original contract documents. It is advisable for contracts to contain an obligation on the part of the contractor to accept and implement variations ordered by the employer. Thus, the employer may enjoy the right to direct the contractor to alter, change, modify, or omit any of the work under the contract. Such variations may include changes in the scope of construction or in construction services required under the project specifications.[81] Where the contractor deems that such a directed variation involves a change in the contract price, the contract may require notification of this in writing to the employer before work on the variation begins. The contract may dictate that the parties must come to an agreement concerning any change in the price before the variation proceeds. Some contracts oblige the contractor to implement the variation order by the employer only where the contractor does not object to it on reasonable grounds. Certain contracts may also allow the contractor to submit to the employer written proposals for variations or modifications in the construction. The purchaser may not be under any obligation to accept such proposals except where the proposals are necessary to remedy defects that have arisen in the work.

"Hardship" clauses usually deal with the situation where the parties desire, or are forced by their situation, to continue their contractual relationship. Such clauses obligate the parties to negotiate an adaptation of the contract in the event of certain changes in

79 *Ibid.*

80 See Horn, "The Concepts of Adaptation and Renegotiation in the Law of Transnational Commercial Contracts" in Horn (ed.), *Adaptation and Re-Negotiation of Contracts in International Trade and Finance* (1985), at 3 to 5 and Bockstiegel, "Hardship, Force Majeure and Special Risks Clauses in International Contracts in Horn (ed.), *ibid.*, at 159 *et seq.* See also ICC, *Force Majeure and Hardship* (doc. no. 421, 1985).

81 See *UNCITRAL Legal Guide*, *supra*, note 72, at 249.

circumstances. Adaptations could take the form of an adjustment in price, timetable, etc. Hardship clauses should be reinforced by an arbitration clause, in case the parties are unable to come to an agreement concerning the adaptation of the contract within a specified period of time.[82] A hardship clauses could also be reinforced by a clause allowing termination of the contract by either party on notice. While hardship clauses have the benefit of providing a framework within which to adapt the contract, they may also make the contract unstable precisely because of this possibility of renegotiation.[83] A precise definition of what will constitute hardship is crucial, and the parties may wish to include a list of specific events in this regard.

"Special risks" clauses usually identify explicitly particular changes in circumstances anticipated by the parties. These may include changes to the tax treatment of the project forming the subject matter of the contract, and changes to the domestic legislation of the country where the construction project is being conducted. These clauses set out the obligations of the parties if such events do occur.

Finally, *force majeure*—in the form of natural disasters, war, or political or economic upheaval—may make contractual performance impossible and necessitate either termination or substantial adaptation of the terms of the contract. In any of these situations, an obligation to renegotiate or otherwise adapt the contract may be expressly inserted into the contract.[84]

6. *Liquidated Damage Clauses*

International construction contracts customarily contain a liquidated damage clause providing for the employer to receive an agreed sum of money in the event that the contractor fails to perform certain specified obligations under the contract, usually in situations where the contractor does not meet time deadlines specified for the completion of the project. Less frequently, such a clause may also be included in respect of a failure to perform on the part of the employer. The sum of money agreed upon should represent a reasonable approximation of the actual loss that is likely to result from the failure to perform. Punitive damages are not valid in many jurisdictions and may therefore be set aside. Nevertheless, the sum should be large enough to provide an incentive for timely performance by the contractor. A precise definition of when the project will be considered completed is important, so that it is clear that failure to meet this definition will trigger payment of the liquidated damages.[85]

---

82 Schmitthoff, *supra*, note 65, at 752.

83 *UNCITRAL Legal Guide*, *supra*, note 72, at 243.

84 Horn has argued that *force majeure* or the international law concept of *rebus sic stantibus* and the duty to negotiate complex long-term contracts in good faith are recognized as "internationally accepted concepts." He bases this argument, *inter alia*, on the articulation of the *force majeure* concept in art. 62 of the Vienna Convention on the Law of Treaties (in public international law) and in art. 79 of the UN Convention on Contracts for the International Sale of Goods (in private international law). See Horn, "Changes in Circumstances and the Revision of Contracts in some European Laws and in International Law" in Horn (ed.), *Adaptation and Re-negotiation of Contracts in International Trade and Finance* (1985), at 25-27.

85 See *UNCITRAL Legal Guide*, *supra*, note 72, at 219-22.

Liquidated damages may not be recoverable where the failure to perform is due to acts or omissions of the other party, or to events beyond the contractor's control. Such events may be specifically identified in an "exemption clause,"[86] a clause exempting a party that fails to perform a contractual obligation from the legal consequences flowing from this failure.

A contract may also provide for bonus payments to the contractor for early completion of the works.

7. *Resolution of International Construction Disputes*

The complex and technical nature of international construction projects, coupled with their long-term duration, renders them particularly vulnerable to the emergence of disputes among the often multiple parties with an interest in the project. Often the parties include governmental agencies, which may heighten the complexity of a dispute. Disputes may arise concerning the issue of whether a party has failed to perform its obligations under the contract, and the effects flowing from this failure; questions may also emerge relating to whether the events stipulated in "variation," "hardship," or "special risks" clauses have actually occurred.[87] The facts forming the subject-matter of disputes under an international construction contract may disappear or ultimately be absorbed into the completed structure, making the later establishment of facts and the reconstruction of evidence through documentary evidence and witnesses difficult and costly.[88] These factors make the early and prompt settlement of international construction disputes a priority. Furthermore, alternative dispute resolution techniques, including conciliation, mediation, and arbitration may, for these reasons, be especially preferential to lengthy, costly, and more formal international construction litigation. Arbitration has the advantage of neutrality, because it does not occur in a domestic court of any of the parties to the dispute. It also benefits from the expertise and specialized competence of the arbitrators. The 1958 UN Convention on the Recognition and Enforcement of Arbitral Awards promotes the enforcement of arbitral awards in the territories of its signatories.[89]

Many international construction contracts provide for early recourse to a pre-arbitral authority—an engineer or other authority with technical expertise—in order to facilitate prompt settlement of disputes. The FIDIC Conditions, for example, provide for the possibility of calling upon the project consulting engineer to resolve disputes that arise relating to the construction contract or project. Also, through the ICC, the parties may appoint a neutral third person, the arbitral referee, to assist them in promptly defusing a

86 *Ibid.*, at 220.

87 *Ibid.*, at 307.

88 Schwartz, "Resolution of International Construction Disputes" (1995), 23 *Int. Bus. Lawyer* 149. Schwartz points out, however, that settling a dispute while the construction project is in progress may not be possible because of the lack of resources and expertise to be devoted to the dispute settlement process during this period.

89 See chapter 21, *infra*, on the settlement of international trade disputes by arbitration.

dispute that has arisen between them concerning the performance of the contract.[90] The ICC arbitral referee enjoys the authority to issue interlocutory rulings and orders relating to, *inter alia*, factual matters, evidence, and the preservation of property. While the decisions of a referee do not have the status of an arbitral award and may therefore encounter difficulties concerning enforcement, the fact that the referee has been appointed by consensus between the parties usually means that parties will respect the decision. Reference to the engineer under a FIDIC contract, or to the ICC arbitral referee, do not preclude subsequent resort to arbitration.

To avoid any uncertainty in this regard, the parties may wish, to the extent permitted under the law applicable to the proceedings, to specify the relationship between referee and arbitral and judicial or arbitral proceedings. Thus, the parties may stipulate that matters falling within the referee's scope of authority must be submitted first to him, and that arbitration or judicial proceedings cannot be launched until a specified period of time after submission of the dispute to the referee has lapsed.[91]

Where the parties do not agree to settle their disputes through arbitration, it may be advisable for them to reduce uncertainties concerning judicial proceedings by expressly selecting a particular court in a particular jurisdiction to settle disputes between them. This can be achieved through an exclusive jurisdiction clause.

8. Applicable Law

Many legal systems permit parties to a contract to expressly designate the law that will govern their contract. It is advisable that parties make an express choice of applicable substantive law in order to avoid any uncertainty. This does not necessarily have to be the law of the place of construction; it may be the law of the contractor's country or the law of a third country.[92]

It is not necessary for the entire contract to be governed by the same law, although the express choice by the parties of a single system of substantive law is a simpler approach.

Many aspects of the international construction contract will inevitably be affected by the mandatory legal rules in the domestic law of the place where the construction is carried out, for example, in areas such as safety requirements, and environmental, health, and labour laws, as well as import, export, and foreign exchange restrictions. However, foreign laws may also be relevant to part or all of the elements in the transaction. In the absence of an express choice by the parties, or where the law chosen by the parties is inappropriate, a court or arbitral tribunal must determine the proper law of the contract by identifying the law with the most substantial connection to the contract. This law may frequently be the law of the place of construction, since this is usually the law of the place where the contract is concluded as well as performed. In determining the

90 See ICC pub. no. 480 (1990).

91 *UNCITRAL Legal Guide*, *supra*, note 72, at 311.

92 See Westring, "Construction and Management Contracts" in Horn and Schmitthoff (eds.), *The Transnational Law of International Commercial Transactions* (1982), at 181-82.

proper law of a contract, or any part thereof, courts may also consider the currency of payment of the contract, and the law of any government agency that is a party to the contract. With respect to the latter element, courts tend to refer the contract to the laws of the country of that government agency.[93]

In projects involving multiple contractors and/or subcontractors, it may be preferable for the employer to choose as applicable law the law governing the contracts concluded with all contractors, a law that ideally will be the same as the law governing contracts concluded with subcontractors and suppliers.[94]

Parties should be aware of the possibility that the UN Convention on Contracts for the International Sale of Goods (CISG)[95] may apply to govern aspects of the contract. The CISG applies to contracts for the sale of goods when the parties have their places of business in different states, or when private international law rules lead to the application of the law of a signatory state.[96] Contracts for the supply of goods to be manufactured or produced are deemed to be sales contracts, with the exception of (1) contracts in which the preponderant part of the obligations of the contractor consists in the supply of labour or other services, and (2) contracts for the supply of goods to be manufactured or produced where the buyer undertakes to supply a substantial part of the materials necessary for such manufacture or production.[97] Where uncertainty exists as to whether their international construction contract will fall within the scope of the CISG, the parties may wish to expressly provide for or exclude its application. Finally, if the CISG is applicable, the parties may adapt its provisions to suit the particular requirements of their transaction.[98]

VI. SELECTED BIBLIOGRAPHY

A. Books

Arrowsmith, *Government Procurement and Judicial Review* (1988).

Canada, *Selling to Government: A Guide to Government Procurement in Canada* (1989).

Canada (Minister of Supply and Services), *The Canada-US Free Trade Agreement and Government Procurement: An Assessment* (1989).

Clough, *Construction Contracting* (1969).

Hoekman and Mavroidis, *The WTO Agreement on Government Procurement: Expanding Discipline, Declining Membership.* Centre for Economic Policy Research (1995) (discussion paper).

93 *Ibid.*

94 *UNCITRAL Legal Guide*, *supra*, note 72, at 299.

95 See chapter 5, *supra*.

96 CISG, art. 1.

97 CISG, art. 3.

98 See *UNCITRAL Legal Guide*, *supra*, note 72, at 303-4.

Horn (ed.), *Adaptation and Renegotiation of Contracts in International Trade and Finance* (1985).

IBRD, *Procurement and Cofinancing: Methods and Procedures* (1988).

Johnson, *The North American Free Trade Agreement* (1994).

Paterson and Band, *International Trade and Investment Law in Canada* (1994).

Schmitthoff, *Schmitthoff's Export Trade: The Law and Practice of International Trade* (9th ed., 1990).

Trebilcock and Howse, *The Regulation of International Trade* (1995).

UNCITRAL, *Legal Guide on Drawing up International Contracts for the Construction of Industrial Works* (1987).

UNCTAD, *Collusive Tendering* (1985).

Westring, *International Procurement: A Training Manual* (1985).

B. Articles

Blank and Marceau, "The History of the Government Procurement Negotiations since 1945" (1996), 5 *Public Procurement L Rev.* 77.

De Graaf and King, "Towards a More Global Government Procurement Market: The Expansion of the GATT Government Procurement Agreement in the Context of the Uruguay Round" (1995), 29 *Int. Lawyer* 435.

Hochuli, "Role of the Engineer under FIDIC Standard Contracts" (1991), 19 *Int. Bus. Lawyer* 542.

Ludlow and Rees, "Engineer's Role under FIDIC Standard Conditions of Contract" (1992), 20 *Int. Bus. Lawyer* 525.

Lyon, "The Role of the Consulting Engineer in Developing Country Construction under the FIDIC Form Contract" (1994), 26 *Law and Policy in Int. Bus.* 273.

Myers, Martin, and Rubino-Sammartano et al., "Illustrative Forms of Performance Guarantee and Counter Guarantee Security for International Construction Projects" (1992), 20 *Int. Bus. Lawyer* 243.

Reich, "Government Procurement and Bid-Challenging After the Free Trade Agreement" (1991), 18 *Can. Bus. LJ* 195.

Schwartz, "Resolution of International Construction Disputes" (1995), 23 *Int. Bus. Lawyer* 149.

Stein, "Construction Financing and BOT Projects" (1995), 23 *Int. Bus. Lawyer* 173.

Stone and Hughes, "Ease of Entry into Foreign Construction Markets: Hurdles for US Contractors in the Middle East, South-East Asia and Eastern Europe" (1994), 22 *Int. Bus. Lawyer* 169.

Westring, "Construction and Management Contracts" in Horn and Schmitthoff (eds.), *The Transnational Law of International Commercial Transactions* (1982), at 175.

C. Legal Instruments, Guidelines, Uniform Rules, and Standard Form Contracts

FIDIC, *Conditions of Contract (International) for Works of Civil Engineering Construction* (4th ed., 1987).

GATT, *Agreement on Government Procurement* (1979).

GATT, *Agreement on Government Procurement*, in Annex 4 to the *Agreement Establishing the World Trade Organization* (1994).

GATT, *Practical Guide to the GATT Agreement on Government Procurement* (1985).

IBRD, *Guidelines for Procurement under IBRD Loans and IDA Credits* (4th ed., 1992).

ICC, *Uniform Rules for Contract Guarantees*, 1978 (doc. no. 325).

ICC, *Uniform Rules for Demand Guarantees*, 1991 (doc. no. 458).

UNCITRAL, *Draft Convention on International Guaranty Letters* (1993).

UNCITRAL, *Model Law on Procurement of Goods, Construction and Services* (1994).

CHAPTER ELEVEN

Payment and Financing

I. INTRODUCTION

In a contract for the international sale of goods, the parties when selecting a particular method of payment must agree upon the time, mode, place, and currency of payment. In most cases the parties will use a method of payment that calls for the intervention of banks in the payment process, such as a collection arrangement (see section III, *infra*) or payment under a letter of credit (see section IV, *infra*). On rare occasions, the buyer may remit the purchase price for the goods to the seller on open account (for example, cash with order, sight payment, cash against documents, or cash on delivery). Another method of payment is for the seller-exporter to draw a bill of exchange (also called draft) on the buyer that the seller can negotiate immediately (see section II, next). These last two methods of payment do not necessarily involve the intervention of a bank. Each method of payment involves some risks for the buyer or the seller. When the parties fail to provide for the method of payment, the custom prevailing in the particular trade usually determines how the price is to be paid and on which terms. The proper law of the contract of sale could also be used.

It should be noted that the terms of a financing package can make a significant difference to the overall cost of an export deal. Thus, when competing with a foreign supplier of manufactured goods or services, a Canadian supplier of like goods for sale to a buyer in a third country may only be able to conclude a sale on the basis of better financing terms, provided the seller can convert the receivable into cash. In assessing the competitiveness of financing terms, at least the following factors should be taken into consideration: the cost, for example, the interest rate; the currency favoured by the buyer; the term or duration of the financing that may be extended; the timing of payments; and the nature and cost of perfecting the security.

The financing or credit to be made available by or for a Canadian exporter may be a supplier credit payment mechanism, whereby the Canadian seller of the goods or services provides the buyer with terms for the payment of the purchase price, or a buyer credit payment mechanism, whereby the buyer obtains directly from a third-party financial institution, a loan or credit facility to pay for the goods or services in accordance with the payment terms stipulated in the contract of sale. In either case, the buyer is liable on the credit. A buyer-credit payment mechanism is less risky for the supplier because it is unlikely that the financial institution will not honour its obligation to the seller under an irrevocable letter of credit. In the case of a supplier-credit payment mechanism, the seller having parted with the title to and possession of the goods in exchange for the buyer's promise to make payments over a period of years is exposed to commercial (for example, insolvency of the buyer) as well as political (for example, moratorium on foreign exchange) risks. Fortunately, the Export Development Corporation (EDC) provides government export assistance with respect to the payment terms and the risks involved for the Canadian seller who exports goods or services abroad (see chapter 18, *infra*).

Major international banks also offer a variety of loan packages and lines of credit to finance export and import transactions. Non-recourse finance, international factoring, financial leasing, and forfaiting are also used to finance exports (see section VI, *infra*).

II. PAYMENT BY BILLS OF EXCHANGE

A. General

A bill of exchange[1] whose primary function is to secure the payment of money plays a very important role in international commercial transactions. In documentary international sales, payment usually involves the presentation of a draft in the form of a bill of exchange, although more modern methods of payment are now current.

---

1 "A bill of exchange is an unconditional order in writing, addressed by one person to another, signed by the person giving it, requiring the person to whom it is addressed to pay, on demand or at a fixed or determinable future time, a sum certain in money to or to the order of a specified person, or to bearer": s. 16(1) of Canadian Bills of Exchange Act, RSC 1985, c. B-4, as am. A bill is sometimes called a draft, and an accepted bill, an acceptance. The person to whom a bill is addressed is called the drawee, and, if the drawee signifies assent to the order in due form, then the drawee is called the acceptor. In Canada a bill of exchange may be drawn under three different terms: demand, sight and term. For instance, a cheque is a prime example of a demand bill: "A cheque is a bill of exchange drawn on a bank, payable on demand.": *ibid.*, s. 165(1). Payment is to be made on first presentation. In a sight bill, the drawee must signify acceptance of the drawing within two business days of presentation. Acceptance consists of the drawee writing across the face of the bill "Accepted, the date, payable at ..." and affixing his or her signature. In a term bill, a fixed or determinable future date is incorporated into the draft, such as "thirty days after sight" or "90 days after bill of lading date" or a specific future date. "A promissory note is an unconditional promise in writing made by one person to another, signed by the maker, engaging to pay, on demand or at a fixed or determinable future time, a sum certain in money, to, or to the order of, a specified person, or to bearer.": *ibid.*, s. 176(1). See *Canadian Imperial Bank of Commerce*

(The footnote is continued on the next page.)

The bill of exchange has for a long time served as the principal method of payment in a documentary sale, cost, insurance, and freight (CIF), free on board (FOB), or their variants. The exporter-seller (drawer) draws a draft, usually on the importer-purchaser or a bank designated for that purpose (drawee); it may be addressed to any third party but this assumes a debtor-creditor relationship between that party and the importer purchaser. The drawee is instructed to pay a certain sum of money to a specific person called the payee (who may be the exporter-seller), or to the order of that person, either on the presentation of the draft (a sight draft), or at a specified time in the future that may be expressed as a specific date or a number of days after sight (a time draft). In the case of a time draft, it is the acceptance by the drawee (or possibly another party, such as a bank) who writes "accepted" and the date and signs the draft on its face, that fixes the liability of that person.

Meanwhile, the payee may have transferred the draft to another person by endorsement and delivery if the draft is payable to order or by mere delivery if it is payable to bearer. Thus, a draft may have passed through several hands and been endorsed by different persons located in different jurisdictions, who have incurred liability as endorsers or holders or holders in due course. This transfer through various jurisdictions raises issues of private international law, which are discussed in section C, *infra*.

B. UN Convention

The law applicable to bills of exchange is far from uniform, giving rise to a host of difficulties when these negotiable instruments cross national borders and become subject to the rules of different legal systems. Although in 1930 and 1931, a serious effort was made by way of international conventions to unify the law of bills of exchange, promissory notes, and cheques, including the rules concerning stamp duties and certain conflicts of laws, Canada, England, and the United States[2] did not adopt these conventions.[3]

---

1 Continued …

v. Morgan, [1993] 7 WWR 171, 10 BLR (2d) 72 (Alta. QB) for a case in which a bank plan note did not meet the requirements of the definition of a promissory note contained in this provision.

In Canada, under sight or term drawings, a period of three days called "grace" is to be included when calculating the maturity date. Therefore, a sight draft accepted on 2 December, would be payable on 5 December. If the due date is a legal holiday, payment would be on the next business day. If no grace is to be allowed, the draft should incorporate a phrase to the effect, such as "Days of grace waived," or "No grace period."

When documents are forwarded in two separate mailings, two drafts are issued marked "First of Exchange (second unpaid)" and "Second of Exchange (first unpaid)." On presentation and acceptance of one, the other will be considered a duplicate and not required to be paid. In this latter instance, the seller has taken steps to ensure the buyer obtains a full set of documents in the event one set is lost or delayed.

2 See Uniform Commercial Code, Commercial Paper, art. III (1962).

3 Convention Providing a Uniform Law for Bills of Exchange and Promissory Notes, Geneva, 7 June 1930 (1933-34), 143 LNTS 257; Convention on the Stamp Laws in connection with Bills of Exchange and Promissory Notes, Geneva, 7 June 1930 (1933-34), 143 LNTS 337; Convention for the Settlement

(The footnote is continued on the next page.)

More recently, the United Nations General Assembly (UNGA) approved the Convention on International Bills of Exchange and International Promissory Notes, which had been prepared by the UN Commission on International Trade (UNCITRAL).[4] The convention preserves party autonomy and is optional in nature. It makes available a comprehensive single legal regime to govern the financing of international trade transactions, thereby offering the possibility of overcoming discrepancies and deficiencies among the various national rules.

The convention applies to certain bills of exchange[5] and promissory notes[6] only.[7] It creates a new type of negotiable instrument for use exclusively in international transactions that is capable of commercial acceptance and of free circulation in international commerce. This instrument is subject to the convention if it circulates internationally[8]

---

3 Continued ...
of Certain Conflicts of Laws in connection with Bills of Exchange and Promissory Notes, Geneva, 7 June 1930 (1933-34), 143 LNTS 317; Convention Providing a Uniform Law for Cheques, Geneva, 19 March 1931 (1933-34), 143 LNTS 355; Convention on the Stamp Laws in connection with Cheques, Geneva, 19 March 1931 (1933-34), 143 LNTS 7; and Convention for the Settlement of Certain Conflicts of Laws in Connection with Cheques, Geneva, 19 March 1931 (1933-34), 143 LNTS 407.

4 1988 United Nations Convention on International Bills of Exchange and International Promissory Notes, adopted by UNGA on 9 December 1988, Resolution 43/165. For the text and commentary see (1989), 28 *Int'l. Leg. Mat.* 170.

5 The convention defines a bill of exchange as a written instrument—payable on demand or at a definitive time and dated and signed by the drawer—containing an unconditional order whereby the drawer directs the drawee to pay a definite sum of money to the payee or to his or her order. In contrast to most national rules, note that the convention's requirement of a definite sum of money does not exclude the possibility of floating and negotiable rates of interest. See art. 8(6) and (7) and Herrmann, "International Bills of Exchange and Promissory Notes: Legal Problems and Disparities Overcome by New United Nations Convention" in Horn (ed.), *The Law of International Trade Finance* (1989) 259, at 270.

6 The definition of a promissory note is a written instrument—payable on demand, or at a definite time, and dated and signed by the maker—containing an unconditional promise that the maker undertakes to pay a definite sum of money to the payee or to his order (art. 3(2)). See note above concerning the possibility of floating and negotiable rates of interest.

7 Art. 1(3). International checks do not fall within the scope of the convention.

8 Art. 2:

> (1) An international bill of exchange is a bill of exchange which specifies at least two of the following places and indicates that any two so specified are situated in different States:
>
> (a) The place where the bill is drawn;
>
> (b) The place indicated next to the signature of the drawer;
>
> (c) The place indicated next to the name of the drawee;
>
> (d) The place indicated next to the name of the payee;
>
> (e) The place of payment:
>
> provided that either the place where the bill is drawn or the place of payment is specified on the bill and that such place is situated in a Contracting State.

(The footnote is continued on the next page.)

and the parties have chosen the convention as its governing law.[9] In such a case, the instrument will continue to be governed by the same substantive legal regime as it circulates in international commerce among contracting states.

If the parties have not chosen the convention as the proper law of the international instrument, the proper law will be determined by ordinary private international law rules. With respect to non-contracting states, the instrument may be governed by the convention if it is its proper law by virtue of the private international law rules of these states.

The convention allows instruments to be payable by installments, and to contain an acceleration clause.[10] It provides for a uniform limitation period of four years for the exercise of all rights of action arising from the instrument. The only exception is for recourse actions, where each party has only one year from the date of his or her payment.[11]

In addition to delineating its scope of application, the convention provides rules on interpretation (chapter II); transfer of instruments (chapter III); rights and liabilities of a holder[12] and a protected holder, the signatories, which include the drawer,[13] the maker, the drawee, and the acceptor, the endorser, the transferor by endorsement or mere delivery,

---

8 Continued …

> (2) An international promissory note is a promissory note which specifies at least two of the following places and indicates that any two so specified are situated in different States:
>
> (a) The place where the note is made;
>
> (b) The place indicated next to the signature of the maker;
>
> (c) The place indicated next to the name of the payee;
>
> (d) The place of payment:
>
> provided that the place of payment is specified on the note and that such place is situated in a Contracting State.

Note that once these conditions are satisfied, the convention continues to apply where the instrument circulates within the territory of a contracting state.

9 Art. 1. In order for the convention to apply, both the heading and body of the instrument's text must include the words "International Bill of Exchange (UNCITRAL Convention)" or "International Promissory Note (UNCITRAL Convention)," as appropriate.

10 See art. 7(b) and (c).

11 Art. 84(2).

12 The convention does not use the terminology of "holder in due course," but distinguishes between a "holder" and a "protected holder." A holder is presumed to be a protected holder unless the contrary is proved (art. 32). A protected holder is a holder without knowledge of a defence upon or a claim to the instrument, and who was *bona fide* when he or she acquired it (art. 29). Nevertheless, certain defences may be raised against a protected holder (art. 30). An ordinary holder may still enjoy a certain degree of protection since certain claims and defences based on the underlying agreement are limited to the situation where the holder had knowledge of them or obtained the instrument by fraud or theft (art. 28).

13 Note that the convention facilitates the practice of forfaiting (see section VI.D, *infra*), by expressly permitting the drawer to exclude or limit his or her liability for payment as long as another party, such as the acceptor or guarantor, becomes liable for payment.

and the guarantor (chapter IV); presentment, dishonour through non-acceptance or non-payment, and recourse (chapter V); and discharge (chapter VI) and lost instruments (chapter VII).

The convention, which has been signed by Canada, has not yet entered into force.

C. Private International Law Issues

1. General

Issues of private international law arise quite frequently in this area of human activity, because often a bill of exchange may be drawn in Canada, accepted in a foreign country, endorsed in another and dishonoured in yet another.

To understand the rules adopted in Canada, it must be kept in mind that a negotiable instrument is a document that contains several contracts dependent on one original contract. For example, in the case of a bill of exchange drawn by A on B to the order of C and endorsed by C in favour of D, the original contract is between A the drawer and C, the payee. The other contracts are made by acceptors and endorsers.

Should the whole bill of exchange, including all the supervening contracts, especially the position of each contracting party, be determined by a single law or by several laws? In Canada, Parliament has favoured the view that the different contracts are independent contracts, each governed by its proper law.

Whether an instrument for securing the payment of money is "negotiable" depends upon the law of the jurisdiction where the alleged transfer by way of "negotiation" takes place,[14] that is the jurisdiction in which the instrument is situated at the time of delivery. This rule stems from the fact that, for choice of law purposes, negotiable instruments are tangible movables. Thus, a foreign instrument may be regarded as negotiable in the country of its origin but not negotiable for the purpose of its transfer in Canada.[15]

2. The Bills of Exchange Act

The Bills of Exchange Act[16] contains specific choice of law provisions applicable to bills and notes drawn in one country and negotiated, accepted, or payable in another, that cover formal validity, interpretation, the duties of the holder, the rate of exchange, and the due date of payment.[17]

The Act also contains a few provisions of the domestic law of Canada that are of practical importance in cases involving legally relevant foreign elements. They are concerned with the

---

14 *Alcock v. Smith*, [1892] 1 Ch. 238 (CA) and *Picker v. London & County Banking Co.* (1887), 18 QBD 515.

15 In Canada, "negotiable" means that "(1) property in the instrument, and all rights under it, pass by endorsement and delivery or by mere delivery to the holder and (2) the holder for value who receives the instrument *bona fide* has a perfectly good title to it, however defective may be the title of the transferor or of the transferor's predecessors in title, and whatever personal defences may be available against these persons"; Falconbridge, *Banking and Bills of Exchange* (7th ed., 1969), at 642 and Bills of Exchange Act, RSC 1985, c. B-4, as am., s. 59. But see s. 191, rights of holder of consumer bill or note.

16 RSC 1985, c. B-4, as am.

17 Ss. 159-163.

production of a notarial copy of protest in a foreign country,[18] the protest of foreign bills and notes,[19] the rights of the holder of a bill governed by the law of Canada but dishonoured abroad,[20] and the distinction between inland bills and foreign bills and notes.[21]

In the absence of statutory provisions on a particular question, the Act provides that "the rules of the common law of England, including the law merchant, save in so far as they are inconsistent with the express provisions of this Act, apply to bills of exchange, promissory notes and cheques."[22] However, if the question is outside the law of bills of exchange and promissory notes in a strict sense, this provision does not apply and resort must be had to the choice of law rules of the *lex fori*.

3. Foreign Bills

Section 24 of the Act draws a distinction between inland bills and foreign bills. (1) "An inland bill is a bill that is, or on the face of it purports to be (a) both drawn and payable within Canada; or (b) drawn within Canada on a person resident in Canada. (2) Any other bill is a foreign bill."[23] According to section 177(1), "A note that is, or on the face of it purports to be, both made and payable within Canada, is an inland note. (2) Any other note is a foreign note." To determine whether a bill or note is inland or foreign, Canada is considered as one country.

The distinction between inland and foreign bills or notes is important not only from the point of view of the duties of the holder, but also with regard to the interpretation of the endorsement abroad of an instrument governed by the law of Canada. Thus, according to section 111:

> (1) Where a foreign bill appearing on the face of it to be such has been dishonoured by non-acceptance it must be duly protested for non-acceptance.
>
> (2) Where a foreign bill that has not been previously dishonoured by non-acceptance is dishonoured by non-payment, it must be duly protested for non-payment.
>
> (3) Where a foreign bill has been accepted only as to part it must be protested as to the balance.
>
> (4) Where a foreign bill is not protested as required by this section the drawer and endorsers are discharged.

On the other hand, section 187 provides that "Where a foreign note is dishonoured, protest thereof is unnecessary, except for the preservation of the liabilities of endorsers."

---

18 S. 11.

19 Ss. 111 and 187.

20 S. 135.

21 Ss. 24, 177.

22 S. 9.

23 S. 24(1) does not include a bill of exchange drawn on a foreign agency of a Canadian bank since a bank carrying on business in a foreign country is resident in that country for the purpose of cheques drawn on its foreign agency: *Canada Life Assurance Co. v. Canadian Imperial Bank of Commerce*, [1979] 2 SCR 669, 98 DLR (3d) 670, 27 NR 227.

Unless the contrary appears on the face of the bill indicating that it is a foreign bill, the holder may treat it as an inland bill, although it does not purport to be both drawn and payable within Canada, or drawn within Canada upon some person resident therein.

4. Formal Validity

According to section 159(1) of the Bills of Exchange Act, the formal validity of a bill, drawn in one country and negotiated, accepted, or payable in another, is determined by the law of the place of issue, and the formal validity of each supervening contract, such as acceptance, or endorsement or acceptance under protest, is determined by the law of the place where such contract is made.

The "place of issue" is not always the place where the bill is written out or signed by the drawer since issue is defined in the Act as "the first delivery of a bill or note, complete in form, to a person who takes it as a holder."[24] Thus, the place of issue is where the first delivery is made.[25] "The place where the contract was made" is also the place of delivery.

The *lex loci contractus* exclusively governs all questions of form, such as, for example, whether an endorsement is made in due form[26] or whether the bill is unconditional.[27] The rule can be justified in the case of bills and notes that are often transferred from one holder to another since in most cases, the subsequent holder would be unable to ascertain the circumstances in which they were originally signed and issued or transferred to earlier holders.

There are two exceptions to the imperative application of the *lex loci contractus* dictated by business considerations. The first is that in no case does the omission to stamp a bill issued out of Canada in accordance with the foreign law prevailing at the place of issue invalidate the bill, even if that is the effect of the foreign law.[28]

The second exception[29] deals with the case of a bill issued out of Canada that is formally valid according to the law of Canada, though not according to the law of the place of issue. For the purpose of enforcing payment[30] thereof, such bill may be treated

---

24 S. 2.

25 *Chapman v. Cottrell* (1865), 3 H & C 865. See also *O'Donovan v. Dussault* (1973), 35 DLR (3d) 280 (Alta. CA).

26 *Koechlin et Cie v. Kestenbaum Bros.*, [1927] 1 KB 889 (CA).

27 *Guaranty Trust Co. of New York v. Hannay & Co.*, [1918] 2 KB 623 (CA).

28 S. 159(2). Where a bill is issued out of Canada, it is not invalid by reason only that it is not stamped in accordance with the law of the place of issue.

29 S. 159(3). Where a bill, issued outside of Canada, conforms with respect to requisites in form to the law of Canada, it may, for the purpose of enforcing payment thereof, be treated as valid as between all persons who negotiate, hold, or become parties to it in Canada.

30 As to what is meant by an action for enforcing payment, see *Guaranty Trust Co. of New York v. Hannay and Co., supra*, note 27. Bailache J was of the opinion that the expression enforcing payment does not include the obtaining of a declaration that the holder of a bill who has been paid is entitled to retain the money, and that as the action was brought by the plaintiffs for the purpose not of obtaining payment, but of preventing the defendants from getting the money back the proviso did not apply.

as valid as between all persons who negotiate, hold, or become parties to it in Canada. The purpose of this exception is to protect the Canadian holder of a bill by removing impediments to negotiability. The holder relying on section 159(3) must prove that both he or she and the person against whom he or she is seeking to enforce payment became parties to the bill in Canada.

5. Capacity

There is no provision in the Act dealing with the law applicable to the capacity of the parties to conclude any of the several contracts involved in a bill of exchange. General choice of law rules must be applied.[31]

6. Interpretation of Drawing, Acceptance, and Endorsement

The interpretation of each contract contained in a bill of exchange or note is governed by its own *lex loci contractus*.[32] The "place where such contract is made," such as in section 159, is the place of delivery.

However, when an inland bill[33] is endorsed in a foreign country, the endorsement with regard to the payer[34] is interpreted according to the law of Canada.[35] This is a concession to the proper law doctrine that favours the purchaser of an inland bill. Thus, payment must be made to an endorsee of an inland bill if the endorsement is valid under the Act, although void by the law of the place of endorsement. Payment must also be made to an endorsee of a foreign bill on an endorsement valid by the law of the place of endorsement although void under the Act.

7. Intrinsic Validity and Effect

Whether the word "interpretation" in section 160 also includes the intrinsic validity and effect of the drawing, endorsement, or acceptance of a bill or note is debatable. If "interpretation" only covers matters of construction, as it should, the law applicable to the intrinsic validity and effect of a bill must be determined by the ordinary choice of law rules of each province.

---

31 *Bondholders Securities Corp. v. Manville*, [1933] 3 WWR 1, [1933] 4 DLR 699 (Sask. CA). However, in that case the *lex loci contractus* was also the proper law of the contract.

32 S. 160. *Canada Life Assurance Co. v. Canadian Imperial Bank of Commerce*, *supra*, note 23. Note that in *Rooney v. Dawson* (1959), 15 DLR (2d) 102 (BC CA), which involved a cheque drawn on a Montana bank, but made and delivered in British Columbia, it was held that when a foreign bill is completed by delivery within the jurisdiction and later dishonoured, an action on the bill is an action on a "breach of an obligation within the jurisdiction." *Sanders v. St. Helens Smelting Co. Ltd.* (1906), 39 NSR 370 (interpretation of the acceptance whether qualified or general). See also *North-Western National Bank v. Jarvis* (1884), 2 Man. R 53 (*lex loci contractus*) (pre-Act decision).

33 For the definition of an inland bill, see s. 24.

34 The acceptor of a bill or the maker of a note. The exception does not apply to a dispute between two holders of a bill endorsed in a foreign country. See *Alcock v. Smith*, [1892] 1 Ch. 238 (CA).

35 S. 160. This would seem to include the legal effect of the endorsement.

If, on the other hand, the word "interpretation" in section 160 includes intrinsic validity and effect, it means that the *lex loci contractus* applies to matters that normally should be governed by the *lex loci solutionis* as the law that appears most substantially connected with each of the contracts in a bill.

Where a bill is accepted in one country and made payable in another, it would seem to be logical and practical to say that the obligation of the acceptor ought to be governed by the law of the place of payment. To include intrinsic validity and effect within the scope of section 160 is self-defeating since it leads to the *lex loci contractus*.

Section 160 deals with interpretation *stricto sensu* and applies the *lex loci contractus*. With respect to intrinsic validity and effect, the ordinary rules of private international law in the field of contracts are applicable[36] independent of the Act.

Section 160 cannot be construed as including something that in its natural sense it does not include, even if it is contrary to principle. Unfortunately, some courts in Canada[37] have held that the word "interpretation" in section 160 includes the obligations of the parties as deduced from such interpretation, or the legal effect of each of the contracts embodied in a bill.

8. *Discharge*

The Act does not contain choice of law rules dealing with the validity and effect of a discharge from liability under a bill or note. General principles applicable to contracts must be used. Each contract is discharged in accordance with its proper law.[38]

9. *Transfer*

No specific choice of law rules applicable to the transfer abroad of a negotiable instrument appear in the Act. The choice of the relevant rule depends upon the characterization of the problem. If the validity of the transfer is characterized as a matter of form or interpretation, it is governed by sections 159 and 160 of the Act; if it is a matter of the transfer of a chattel, the *lex situs* is applicable; or if it is considered as involving an assignment of a contractual right, the proper law of the contract is the relevant law.

The correct approach seems to be that sections 159 and 160 are not concerned with the subject of transfer of a negotiable instrument because the Act deals with the law of contract and not the law of property. Thus, the question of which law governs the passing of property in a negotiable instrument whether an inland bill or a foreign bill is to be considered as a matter of the transfer of a chattel governed by general choice of

---

36 For a case involving a note made without consideration and applying the *lex loci contractus*, see *Allen v. Hay*, 64 SCR 76, 69 DLR 193, [1922] 3 WWR 366.

37 See *London & Brazilian Bank v. Maguire* (1895), QR 8 SC 358, where interpretation was held to include legal effect. The liability of the endorser was governed by the law of the country where the endorsement took place and not by the law of the place of payment or by the law of the endorser's domicile. See also *Canada Life Assurance Co. v. Canadian Imperial Bank of Commerce*, [1979] 2 SCR 669, 98 DLR (3d) 670, 27 NR 227. S. 160 applies to the legal effect of an endorsement.

38 *International Harvester Co. of Canada v. Zarbok*, [1918] 3 WWR 38, 11 Sask. LR 354 (KB).

law rules. The principles applicable to the transfer of property in a tangible movable are relevant. The *lex rei sitae*, which here is the same as the *lex loci actus*, governs the validity of the transfer. This is the law of the place where the instrument is situated at the time of the transfer.

The holder is entitled to the instrument if each prior transfer is valid by its own *lex rei sitae* at the material time. The *lex rei sitae* at the time of transfer will also determine whether the holder is a holder in due course or entitled to take free from equities attaching to the instrument or defects of title of prior parties.

10. Duties of Holder: Presentment, Protest, and Notice of Dishonour

Section 161, which deals with the determination of the law applicable to the problems that arise upon the dishonour of a bill that has circulated in a number of countries, provides:

> The duties of the holder with respect to presentment for acceptance or payment and the necessity for or sufficiency of a protest[39] or notice of dishonour, are determined by the law of the place where the act is done or the bill is dishonoured.[40]

11. Currency—Rate of Exchange

It is provided in section 162 that:

> Where a bill is drawn out of but payable in Canada, and the sum payable is not expressed in the currency of Canada, the amount shall, in the absence of some express stipulation, be calculated according to the rate of exchange for sight drafts at the place of payment on the day the bill is payable.

This test does not give rise to difficulties of interpretation.[41]

---

39 When a drawee refuses to accept a bill or does not provide payment at maturity, it may be necessary to protest the item in order to protect the holder's rights against previous endorsers and the drawers, and in order to preserve legal action against the party or company concerned. Bills should normally be protested at the place where they are dishonoured and normally on the day the bill is dishonoured or shortly thereafter. The act of protesting usually consists of having a notary visit the customary address of the drawee, present the bill, and draw up a document over his or her signature stating the reason given, if any, for non-acceptance or non-payment, or stating that the drawee could not be found. A copy of the bill must be included in this notarial document. However, since the necessity to protest bills and the legal effect of this action varies from country to country, exporters should acquaint themselves with the practice in countries to which they export and be in contact with local attorneys or notaries to seek their advice on local custom.

40 *Provincial Bank v. Bellefleur*, [1936] 1 DLR 795 (NB) and *Sparks v. Hamilton* (1920), 47 OLR 55. The specified place of payment of the note governs the duty to protest and the manner of presenting for payment. Compare *Hanson v. Collette* (1931), 5 MPR 363 (NB) as to sufficiency of notice of dishonour.

41 In *Newaygo Co. Ltd. v. Russell* (1921), 21 OWN 47, aff'd. 22 OWN 366 (CA), the plaintiff sued on a promissory note made payable in Wisconsin, US. It was held that he was entitled to judgment for as

(The footnote is continued on the next page.)

12. *Due Date of a Bill*

According to section 163: "Where a bill is drawn in one country and is payable in another country, the due date thereof is determined according to the law of the place where it is payable." The due date of a bill or note is determined by the *lex loci solutionis* with regard to all parties who became liable thereon.[42] This is a concession to the "single law" theory.

13. *Damages for Dishonour*

The Bills of Exchange Act does not contain any choice of law rules for the determination of the measure of damages recoverable for the breach of any of the contracts contained in a bill of exchange. General principles of private international law governing the measure of damages are applicable. The law most substantially connected with each of the contracts embodied in a bill of exchange applies to the measure of damages, which is considered a matter of substantive law. This is usually the law of the place of payment of each obligation.

In the domestic law of Canada, it is provided in sections 133 and 134 of the Act that where a bill is dishonoured, its holder may recover from any party liable on the bill; the drawer who has been compelled to pay the bill may recover from the acceptor; and an endorser who has been compelled to pay the bill may recover from the acceptor or from the drawer or from a prior endorser:

> 133. ...
> (a) the amount of the bill;
> (b) interest thereon from the time of presentment for payment, if the bill is payable on demand, and from the maturity of the bill in any other case; and
> (c) the expenses of noting and protesting.[43]

In the case of a bill that has been dishonoured abroad, in addition to these damages the holder may, according to section 135, "recover from the drawer or any endorser, and the drawer or an endorser who has been compelled to pay the bill may recover from any party liable to him, the amount of the re-exchange with interest thereon until the time of payment."

The re-exchange is "the amount of a sight bill drawn at the time and place of dishonour at the then rate of exchange on the place where the drawer or endorser sought

---

41 Continued ...
much Canadian money as, if remitted in Wisconsin at the due date would produce there the amount due. See *First National Bank of Oregon (1st Interstate Bank of Oregon, NA) v. A.H. Watson Ranching, Ltd.* (1984), 34 Alta. LR (2d) 110 (QB) (amount owing calculated using exchange rate at date holder of note demanded payment in full).

42 See *Rouquette v. Overmann* (1875), LR 10 QB 525, at 535-38 and *Re Francke & Rasch*, [1918] 1 Ch. 470.

43 S. 134. A foreign drawer of a bill drawn abroad and accepted and dishonoured in Canada can also recover the re-exchange that he had to pay under the foreign law to the holder. See *Re Billespie Ex p. Robarts* (1887), 18 QBD 286.

to be charged resides, sufficient to realize at the place of dishonour the amount of the dishonoured bill and expenses consequent on its dishonour."[44]

14. Interest

Since it is doubtful whether section 160 can be applied to the determination of the liability to pay interest and the rate thereof in the case of dishonour of a bill of exchange in one country and accepted and endorsed in another, it is generally held that this is a matter governed by the proper law of the contract. The law of the place of payment of each obligation usually prevails in this field.[45]

III. CREDIT TRANSFERS AND COLLECTION ARRANGEMENTS

A. UNCITRAL Model Law on International Credit Transfers

The increasing frequency of international trade payments made by credit transfer, in both electronic and paper-based form, gave rise to a need for uniform legal treatment and provided impetus for the designing of the UNCITRAL Model Law on International Credit Transfers, adopted on May 15, 1992.[46]

The model law applies to international credit transfers. A credit transfer is a series of operations, beginning with the sender's unconditional payment order to a receiving bank to place fixed or determinable funds at the disposal of a beneficiary.[47] Upon acceptance by the receiving bank, the sender becomes obligated to pay the receiving bank for the payment order. The receiving bank then issues a payment order to the beneficiary's bank or an intermediary bank. On acceptance, the beneficiary's bank must place the funds at the beneficiary's disposal or otherwise apply the credit in accordance with the payment order and the governing law. A credit transfer is international and thus within the scope of the model law when the sending and receiving banks are in different states.[48]

Concerning conflicts of law, the model law recommends that those jurisdictions that enact it should add a provision that, except for questions concerning the sender's authority and, in the absence of agreement by the parties, the law of the state of the receiving

---

44 Falconbridge, *Essays on the Conflict of Laws* (2nd ed., 1954), at 368.

45 *R. v. Grand Trunk Ry. Co.* (1890), 2 Ex. CR 132. Note that in *Livesley v. Horst Co.*, [1925] 1 DLR 159, [1924] SCR 605, Duff J said *obiter*, at 609: "As a rule the place of payment under each of the contracts embodied in the bill will be the place where the contracting party has become a party to the bill." See also *Rooney v. Dawson* (1959), 15 DLR (2d) 102 (BC CA). In *Hochberger v. Rittenberg* (1917), 54 SCR 480, it was held that the liability of the endorser of a promissory note is governed by the law of the place where the note is drawn up and made payable. In *Wallace v. Souther* (1879), 2 SCR 598, that rate of interest on a note was said to be governed by the law of the place of payment.

46 UNCITRAL, ref. V.93-91299 February 1994-3,000 UN 1994. For a general description of the model law, see Colas (ed.), *Global Economic Cooperation: A Guide to Agreements and Organizations* (1994), at 397. See also UNCITRAL, *Guide to Electronic Funds Transfers* (1987).

47 Art. 2(a).

48 Art. 1(1).

bank governs.[49] This does not apply to the relationship between the beneficiary and his or her bank.

Acknowledging the increased automation of international credit transfers, the model law permits the use of electronic data interchange (EDI).[50]

Canada has not yet implemented the model law.

B. Collection Arrangements

1. General

Where payment for the goods does not take place in the seller's country, the seller will ask his or her bank or some other person to arrange for collecting such payment overseas. The banking practice relating to foreign collection arrangements is standardized by the International Chamber of Commerce (ICC) Uniform Rules for Collection (1992 rev.) (the URC522), which must be specifically referred to by the parties in their contract (see section 3, *infra*). Using the services of a bank is important because the seller-exporter and buyer-importer by definition live in different countries and the export transaction requires currency conversion. Also, it is usually accompanied by the transmission of the documents, bill of lading, insurance certificate or policy, invoice, import or export clearances, etc., that are necessary to complete delivery. Indeed, several banks may be involved and they may substitute their credit for that of the purchaser through the use of a letter of credit (discussed in section IV, *infra*). Collection processed through banks protects the seller, who is assured that the documents will not be released until the collection instructions have been observed. However, the bank processing the collection documents is not responsible for examining them, except to ascertain that the indicated copies are included and that any negotiable documents are in good form. The international departments of banks are specialized in furnishing these services. Often their advantage lies in having branches or agencies in the place of business of both the buyer and the seller.

In the usual transaction, where the seller-exporter draws a draft on the buyer-importer, the seller-exporter will transfer it to his or her own bank, which will then forward it to a bank in the country of the buyer-importer in a CIF sale for collection. A draft accompanied by commercial documents is referred to as a "documentary draft," as contrasted with a "clean draft," one unaccompanied by commercial documents. The exchange of the documents of title representing the goods and the payment of the price are normally effected at the place at which the buyer carries on business.

---

49 Art. Y.

50 See art. 5(2).

2. Royal Bank of Canada Practice

Royal Bank of Canada
Foreign Collections
(Excerpts)

TYPES OF COLLECTIONS

Clean Collections—Any form of financial document such as bill of exchange (draft, cheque or promissory note), payment receipt or other similar instrument for obtaining the payment of money.

Documentary Collections—Commercial documents such as invoices, shipping documents or documents of title, etc., which may or may not be accompanied by financial documents.

PARTIES TO A COLLECTION & DEFINITION OF SOME DOCUMENTS

Principal—The customer entrusting the operation of collection to his bank. In a documentary collection the principal may be the drawer but in a cheque collection it would be the payee or last endorser.

Remitting Bank—The bank to which the principal has entrusted the operation of collection.

Collecting Bank—Any bank, other than the remitting bank, involved in processing the collection order.

Presenting Bank—The collecting bank making presentation to the drawee.

Collection Order—The instructions issued by the remitting bank which lists the documents enclosed and provides the terms and conditions under which the collection is to be paid and the documents released.

RISK IS AN IMPORTANT CONSIDERATION

The seller accepts all risks and expenses of the collection in an export transaction. The seller may use the services of his bank and a bank in the country of the buyer but they act only on the instructions set out in the collection order. Bank charges may be shared or borne by either party, according to previous agreement.

Credit Risk—Since there are inherent risks in using the collection method, the seller should always ensure, prior to the shipment of goods, that the buyer is of good reputation and financial standing. For instance, a buyer could refuse goods after shipment in the hope of negotiating a price reduction. Failure by the buyer to take up goods promptly upon arrival at the final destination could result in substantial demurrage and insurance costs, as well as damage to those goods of a perishable nature. The risk may be greater when the collection is on a term basis and the documents are released against an accepted draft. If the draft is unpaid at maturity, the seller may not be able to recover the shipment.

Foreign Exchange Risk—If payment is to be effected in the buyer's local currency, the seller must understand the risk of conversion to his own currency. When settlement is to be in the currency of the seller and the buyer may have local currency available, exchange regulations in the importing country may be so restrictive that the exchange allotment may not be authorized for some time after

Figure 1—Foreign Documentary Collections
Usually seven steps are involved when collections are used to finance foreign sales transactions

the shipment arrives at its destination. Moreover, the political stability of the importing country is also a risk factor which could cause delayed payment. The Royal Bank of Canada, through its International Centres and correspondents throughout the world, can assist in these situations by obtaining credit reports on the buyer and providing advice on the currency exchange.

DOCUMENTATION

It is important to realize that in a collection, the banks involved have no way of knowing if the goods are properly described. The bank's examination actually consists of ensuring that the specified number of forms are included and that they are in good order. So, the seller should take steps to ensure the description is as agreed on the purchase order or agreement; that all copies of documents are provided; and that negotiable documents such as drafts, bills of lading and insurance policies are correctly endorsed. Care in preparing and processing documents can save sellers considerable delay in receiving settlements and the additional expense of providing copies.

The buyer, when examining the documents presented should ensure they are in order before acceptance. Provided the buyer and seller understand their mutual requirements and settlement is prompt, the collection procedure will work to the benefit of both parties. A misunderstanding which causes delayed settlement can result in lost sales or reduced profits.

PROTEST

In many countries the protesting of bills entails heavy charges and is also resented by the drawee. To avoid confusion, definite instructions should be given to the collecting bank regarding protest and these instructions should be meticulously followed by the presenting bank for acceptance and payment.

It sometimes occurs that banks refuse to handle items subject to protest. It is possible, for instance, that in rural areas or small towns where no branch bank is located or no practising notary is available, that bills may be very difficult to protest in the event of non-acceptance or non-payment.

Please note that unless specifically requested in the collection letter, the bill of exchange will not be protested.

AN IMPORT COLLECTION

Assuming both buyer and seller are satisfied that each party will comply to the terms of their contract, the steps described below represent an import transaction having shipping terms C.I.F. (Cost, Insurance, Freight) Montreal, and settlement 60 days sight.

The seller prepares the shipment, arranges for the ship to be loaded, and has the necessary documentation prepared. The seller then presents the draft, supporting documents and instructions relating to the collection to his bank. The remitting bank completes their collection order and forwards it, together with the necessary documents, to the collecting bank, in this example, The Royal Bank's Quebec International Centre. On receipt, the collection order is examined for specific instructions and to ensure that the supporting documents are as stated. The importer is then advised that the documents are available for examination and acceptance through a Royal Bank branch which acts as the presenting bank.

The buyer, after checking and approving the documents, accepts the draft. The presenting bank authorizes the release and completes any required endorsements on the documents. The maturity date of the draft is calculated and advised to the remitting bank and also to the buyer who must arrange to honour the drawing on maturity.

When the cargo arrives, the buyer uses the documents to process the entry through customs and to obtain release of the shipment from the carrier. Finally, on maturity, the draft is charged to the account of the buyer and the proceeds are remitted in keeping with the instructions in the collection order, with advice to the remitting bank.

A variety of documents are required for each shipment from one country to another. The documents illustrated on the following pages, covering a shipment from Japan to Canada, show how each document provides a common description of the shipment in relation to the other documents.

Figure 4—Commercial Invoice: These invoices describe the shipment in full. Note the cost includes freight and insurance premium and the ship and destination is clearly described, together with the marks and number of pieces shipped.

Figure 5—Bill of Lading: This document includes marks and number of pieces, and is similar to the commercial invoice. The Bill of Lading is marked "Freight Prepaid" and "on Board" and consigned to the order of Shipper. In order for the buyer to control the shipment, all three original Bills of Lading must be available, endorsed by the shipper. Any one of the originals will clear the shipment. The two remaining become void.

Figure 6—Customs Invoice: Since January 1985 Canada Customs no longer requires that the customs invoice be certified or signed. Providing there is sufficient information included in the commercial invoice Canada Customs will accept that document in lieu of the customs invoice. Your customs broker can provide information which may reduce the number of documents your supplier must prepare.

Figure 7—Marine Insurance Policy: Coverage is "all Risks" for 110% of the invoice value. The effective date of the policy should be prior to or coincide with the date the goods were loaded on board the vessel. The description of the goods is similar to that on the commercial invoice. The shipper must endorse the reverse of the document to place it in negotiable form so that the buyer may collect on any claims. Naturally, the terms of insurance coverage should be settled between the buyer and seller before the shipment is made.

Figure 8—Financial Documents: The documents shown in figures 4 to 8 inclusive will be released to the buyer after the draft has been accepted. As indicated, payment will be due 60 days after acceptance date, 3 days grace.

MISSING DOCUMENTS
(On An Import Collection)

In a documentary collection it is general practice to package the documents in two sets and forward them in consecutive mailings. For any number of reasons, there are times when the collection does not arrive before the carrier is prepared to unload the shipment. As delays in unloading can cause additional expense to the buyer, an alternative means must be available to acquire control of the goods.

The marine carrier expects to receive a properly endorsed negotiable bill of lading before the shipment will be released. However, there is an alternative. A guarantee form, such as that shown in figure 9, signed by the consignee and a guarantor, such as a bank, will permit release of the shipment, on the understanding that an original bill of lading will be presented at a later date. When a bank indemnifies the carrier for a missing bill of lading, it becomes responsible to the shipper for claims arising from the shipment, and the bank therefore requests a suitable indemnity, as shown in figure 10. In the following examples, the drawee has agreed to pay the bill of exchange on presentation and to arrange return of the guarantee by substituting it with an original bill of lading. In some cases, the bank may require additional security.

It follows, the buyer must be prepared to accept the documents in the missing collection when presented. In many cases, the seller or shipper will mail extra copies of the documents relative to the collection, with the exception of a negotiable bill of lading, direct to the buyer. If these documents are not received, the buyer may obtain a customs release for the shipment by completing a "Sight Entry." A customs broker will provide advice and assistance in processing the shipment through customs.

AN EXPORT COLLECTION

In this example the "Canadian Exporter" has agreed to sell to "European Buyer" on a FOB (Free On Board) Toronto basis, with settlement at sight. The Canadian Exporter arranges loading on

Figure 4 — Commercial Invoice

COMMERCIAL INVOICE

① Shipper / Exporter KATAR INDUSTRIES CO., LTD. C.P.O. 5673 TOKYO, JAPAN	⑧ No. & date of invoice JC 1689 JAN. 12. ⑨ No. & date of L/C ORDER G 996 SEPT. 23. ⑩ L/C issuing bank
② For Account & Risk of Messrs. VODAN IMPORTS LTD. 1233 ANYSTREET MONTREAL, QUE. H5M 2S3	⑪ Remarks:
③ Notify party VODAN IMPORTS LTD. 1233 ANYSTREET MONTREAL, QUE. H5M 2S3	
④ Port of loading: TOKYO, JAPAN ⑤ Final destination: MONTREAL	
⑥ Carrier: PACIFIC ARROW V-7W ⑦ Sailing on or about: JAN. 20.	

⑫ Marks and number of PKGS	⑬ Description of goods	⑭ Quantity/Unit	⑮ Unit-price	⑯ Amount
			C.I.F. Montreal, P.Q.	
JC 1689 VODAN MONTREAL VIA VANCOUVER C/NO. 1 MADE IN JAPAN	VALVE PARTS (PIPE FITTING)			
	BACK SEATS DWG. #572-004 3"x150 & 300 LBS. STAINLESS STEEL TYPE 410	1,300 PCS.	@Can$2.00	Can$ 2,600.00
	BACK SEATS DWG. #572-004 4"x150 & 300 LBS. STAINLESS STEEL TYPE 410	1,150 PCS.	@Can$2.50	Can$ 2,875.00
	BACK SEATS DWG. #572-004 6"x300 LBS. & 8"x150 LBS.STAINLESS STEEL TYPE 410	1,600 PCS.	@Can$3.00	Can$ 4,800.00
TOTAL:	ONE (1) CASE ONLY	4,050 PCS.		Can$10,275.00

KATAR INDUSTRIES CO., LTD.

DIRECTOR

Figure 5 — Bill of Lading

BILL OF LADING

BILL OF LADING NUMBER: ACT 7

Pacific Line

SHIPPER

KATAR INDUSTRIES CO.LTD
C.P.O. 5673
TOKYO, JAPAN

CONSIGNEE

TO ORDER OF SHIPPER

NOTIFY ADDRESS (WITHOUT LIABILITY TO CARRIER)

VODAN IMPORTS LTD.
1233 ANYSTREET
MONTREAL, QUEBEC
H5M 2S3

PRE-CARRIAGE BY	PLACE OF RECEIPT		
OCEAN VESSEL	**PORT OF LOADING**	**ORIGIN OF SHIPMENT**	
PACIFIC ARROW 7W	TOKYO	TOKYO	
PORT OF DISCHARGE	**PLACE OF DELIVERY**	**FREIGHT PAYABLE AT**	
VANCOUVER	MONTREAL	TOKYO	

MARKS & NUMBERS	CONTAINER No.	No. OF PKGS., DESCRIPTION OF GOODS	WEIGHT	MEASURE
JC 1689 VODAN MONTREAL VIA VANCOUVER C/NO. 1 MADE IN JAPAN	PAC 1234	1 CASE VALVE PARTS (PIPE FITTING) "FREIGHT PREPAID"	GROSS 735 kg NET 700 kg	0.538M3

NO. OF PKGS. IN WORDS: ONE CASE ONLY

SHIPPED on board the ocean vessel or substitute, or if to be pre-carried **RECEIVED** for pre-carriage to port of loading and for shipment on board ocean vessel or substitute, in apparent good order and condition at the date hereof, unless otherwise stated herein, the goods or packages or containers of merchandise, as may be specified above, all particulars thereof being as stated by the Shipper but unknown to the Carrier, for carriage to port of discharge and also, if applicable, for on-carriage to port or place of delivery by Pacific Line or substitute carrier(s) by land or water.

In accepting this Bill of Lading the Merchant accepts and agrees to all its stipulations, exceptions and conditions, on both pages, whether written, printed, stamped or otherwise incorporated.

IN WITNESS whereof three (3) Original Bills of Lading (unless otherwise stated here) all of this tenor and date have been signed one of which being accomplished the other(s) to be void.

DATED JAN 20 TOKYO

SIGNATURE

ORIGINAL

A Signature

For and on behalf of the Carrier.

Figure 6 — Customs Invoice

Revenue Canada Customs and Excise — Revenu Canada Douanes et Accise

CANADA CUSTOMS INVOICE
FACTURE DES DOUANES CANADIENNES

Page of / de

1. Vendor (Name and Address)/*Vendeur (Nom et adresse)*

Katar Industries Co. Ltd.
C.P.O. 5673
Tokyo, Japan

2. Date of Direct Shipment to Canada/*Date d'expedition directe vers le Canada*

Jan. 20

3. Other References (Include Purchaser's Order No.)
Autres références (Inclure le no de commande de l'acheteur)

G 996 Sept. 23

4. Consignee (Name and Address)/*Destinataire (Nom et adresse)*

Vodan Imports Ltd.
1233 Anystreet
Montreal, Que.

5. Purchaser's Name and Address (If other than Consignee)
Nom et adresse de l'acheteur (S'il diffère du destinataire)

6. Country of Transhipment/*Pays de transbordement*

Canada

7. Country of Origin of Goods
Pays d'origine des marchandises

Japan

IF SHIPMENT INCLUDES GOODS OF DIFFERENT ORIGINS ENTER ORIGINS AGAINST ITEMS IN 12
S'IL EXPEDITION COMPREND DES MARCHANDISES D'ORIGINES DIFFERENTES PRECISER LEUR PROVENANCE EN 12

8. Transportation: Give Mode and Place of Direct Shipment To Canada
Transport: Préciser mode et point d'expédition directe vers le Canada

Tokyo to Vancouver, B.C. per "Pacific Arrow V-7W"
Vancouver to Montreal by rail

9. Conditions of Sale and Terms of Payment
(i.e. Sale, Consignment Shipment, Leased Goods, etc.)
Conditions de vente et modalites de paiement
(p. ex. vente, expédition en consignation, location de marchandises, etc.)

Sale - CIF Montreal, Que.
Collection 60 days sight

10. Currency of Settlement/*Devises du paiement*

CAD

11. No. of Pkgs / *Nbre de colis*	12. Specification of Commodities (Kind of Packages, Marks and Numbers General Description and Characteristics, i.e. Grade, Quality) / *Désignation des articles (Nature des colis, marques et numéros, description générale et caractéristiques, p. ex. classe, qualité)*	13. Quantity (State Unit) / *Quantité (Préciser l'unité)*	Selling Price/*Prix de vente* — 14. Unit Price / *Prix unitaire*	15. Total
1 case	JC 1689 / Vodan, Mtl / Via, Vancouver — Valve Parts (pipe fitting) / Back Seats DWG / Stainless Steel Type 410			
	# 572-004 3"x150 & 300 lbs	1300	C$ 2.00	C$ 2,600.00
	# 572-004 4"x150 & 300 lbs	1150	C$ 2.50	C$ 2,875.00
	# 572-004 6"x300 lbs x 8" x 150 lbs	1600	C$ 3.00	C$ 4,800.00

18. If any of fields 1 to 17 are included on an attached commercial invoice, check this box ☐
Si tout renseignement relativement aux zones 1 à 17 figure sur une ou des factures commerciales ci-attachées, cocher cette case

Commercial Invoice No /*Nº de la facture commerciale* JC 1689

16. Total Weight/*Poids Total* — Net: 700 kg — Gross/*Brut*: 735 kg

17. Invoice Total / *Total de la facture*: C$10,275.00

19. Exporter's Name and Address (If other than Vendor)
Nom et adresse de l'exportateur (S'il diffère du vendeur)

20. Originator (Name and Address)/*Expéditeur d'origine (Nom et adresse)*

R. Rondon, Director
c/o Katar Industries Co. Ltd.
Tokyo, Japan

21. Departmental Ruling (If applicable)/*Décision du Ministère (S'il y a lieu)*

22. If fields 23 to 25 are not applicable, check this box ☐
Si les zones 23 à 25 sont sans objet, cocher cette case

23. If included in field 17 indicate amount:
Si compris dans le total à la zone 17, préciser:

(i) Transportation charges, expenses and insurance from the place of direct shipment to Canada
Les frais de transport, dépenses et assurances à partir du point d'expédition directe vers le Canada
C$ 3,150.00

(ii) Costs for construction, erection and assembly incurred after importation into Canada
Les coûts de construction, d'érection et d'assemblage après importation au Canada

(iii) Export packing
Le coût de l'emballage d'exportation
C$ 150.00

24. If not included in field 17 indicate amount:
Si non compris dans le total à la zone 17, préciser:

(i) Transportation charges, expenses and insurance to the place of direct shipment to Canada
Les frais de transport, dépenses et assurances jusqu'au point d'expédition directe vers le Canada

(ii) Amounts for commissions other than buying commissions
Les commissions autres que celles versées pour l'achat

(iii) Export packing
Le coût de l'emballage d'exportation

25. Check (If applicable):
Cocher (S'il y a lieu):

(i) Royalty payments or subsequent proceeds are paid or payable by the purchaser
Des redevances ou produits ont été ou seront versés par l'acheteur ☐

(ii) The purchaser has supplied goods or services for use in the production of these goods
L'acheteur a fourni des marchandises ou des services pour la production des marchandises ☐

Figure 7 — Marine Insurance Policy

The Marine Insurance Company, Limited

TOKYO, JAPAN

Original

Assured(s), etc.

Katar Industries Co., Ltd.

Invoice No. JC 1689

No. Y6/13456

Amount insured

Can. $11,303

Claim, if any, payable at/in

CONDITIONS:

Against All Risks.

by ATKINS, SWEENEY & CO.
625 DOMINION SQUARE
MONTREAL, CANADA
H3C 4G2

Local Vessel or Conveyance | From (interior port or place of loading)

Ship or Vessel called the	at and from	Sailing on or about
Pacific Arrow	Tokyo	Jan. 20.
arrived at/transhipped at	thence to	
Vancouver	Montreal by connecting conveyance	

Goods and Merchandises

1 Case (4,050 Pcs.)

of

Valve Parts

(Pipe Fitting)

-In container on deck allowed-

Including risks of War, Strikes, Riots and Civil Commotions.

Subject to the following Clauses printed on the back hereof:

Institute Cargo Clauses.

Institute War Clauses.

Institute Strikes, Riots and Civil Commotions Clauses.

Institute Theft, Pilferage and Non-Delivery (Insured Value) Clause (Applicable when this Policy covers these risks).

Institute Replacement Clause (Applying to Machinery).

Duty Clause (Applicable when Duty is separately insured under this Policy).

Label Clause (Applying to Labelled Goods).

Co-Insurance Clause (Applicable in case of Co-Insurance)

Marks and Numbers as per Invoice No. specified above or otherwise specified herein.

Place and Date signed in	No. of Policies issued
Yokohama, Jan. 17.	Two

The said Goods and Merchandises are and shall be valued at the same as the Amount insured.

Code Nos.		
700600	7701	670
359 C		

as arranged

In Witness whereof, I the Undersigned of THE MARINE INSURANCE COMPANY, LIMITED,

In case of loss or damage, please refer to the "IMPORTANT" clause printed on the back hereof and act accordingly.

Notice to holders of policies: No claim for loss by theft &/or pilferage shall be paid hereunder unless notice of survey has been given to the Agents stated in this Policy within 10 days of expiry of this insurance.

For THE MARINE INSURANCE COMPANY, LIMITED

A Signature

AUTHORIZED SIGNATORY

Figure 8 — Financial Document — Draft or Bill of Exchange

No JC-1689

Bill of Exchange TOKYO, JAPAN JAN. 27,

For CAN$10,275.00

At 60 days after sight of this **FIRST** Bill of Exchange (Second of the same tenor and date being unpaid) pay to A Japanese Bank or order the sum of

CANADA DOLLAR TEN THOUSAND TWO HUNDRED AND SEVENTY-FIVE ONLY.

Value received and charge the same to account of VODAN IMPORTS LTD. 1233 ANYSTREET MONTREAL, QUE. H5M 2S3

Drawn under INVOICE JC-1689

L/C No. ______ dated ______

To VODAN IMPORTS LTD.
1233 ANYSTREET
MONTREAL, QUE. H5M 2S3

KATAR INDUSTRIES LTD.

DIRECTOR

Figure 9 — Guarantee for Delivery of Goods

The Shipping Company

Montreal
Agents for: NYZ LINES INC.

GUARANTEE FOR DELIVERY OF GOODS WITHOUT PRODUCTION OF ORIGINAL BILL OF LADING

In consideration of your delivering to us or to our order the following goods:

40 cases Glassware   Marks
"RTL-Montreal   Container No. 127892
15290/1-40"

Shipped by Messrs. Glassexport on or about September 25.

in the M/S S V.B. MYERS Voy. 27B B L 243-9786 From HAMBURG

and consigned to us or order, the Bills of Lading for which have not arrived.

We hereby undertake to hold you and each of you harmless and keep you and each of you indemnified against all claims which may be made upon you and each of you or any of you under said Bills of Lading or any one of the set of which it forms part, and against all loss, costs, damages and expenses which you or any of you may suffer or be put to by reason of the delivery of the said goods to us. And if any proceedings be commenced with respect to the said goods, from time to time to provide you with sufficient funds to defend the same, and if called upon to do so any time whilst the goods are in our possession to redeliver the same to you. The undersigned consignees undertake to produce the Bills of Lading for the above goods duly endorsed as soon as these documents have arrived.

In case the vessel or any property belonging to you should be arrested for any claim in connection with the delivery of the goods in question to us, we undertake to provide bail to get the vessel or other arrested property released and to indemnify you for any loss and expenses caused you by the arrest whether same is justified or not.

DATED AT MONTREAL, QUE. THIS 3RD DAY OF OCTOBER 19

WITNESS	SIGNATURE OF CONSIGNEE
....	LYK TRADING LTD.
WITNESS	GUARANTEE OR TRUST CO.
....	THE ROYAL BANK OF CANADA 360 ST. JAMES ST. BRANCH MONTREAL, QUE.

Figure 10 — Guarantee re Bill of Lading

Guarantee re Bill of Lading

FORM 836 (6-86)

To THE ROYAL BANK OF CANADA

In consideration of The Royal Bank of Canada (the "Bank") becoming a party to a guarantee, a copy of which is attached hereto,

Dated October 3,

In favour of THE SHIPPING COMPANY
(Name of Transport Company)

Covering delivery of the following goods without bill of lading 243-9786 Sept. 25.

Brief description of transport documents, goods and approximate value.

40 cases Glassware - Marks "RTL-MONTREAL 15290/1-40"
CONTAINER NO. 127892 SHIPPED FROM HAMBURG TO MONTREAL
PER "V.B. MYERS" VOY 27B VALUE CAN. $12,000.00

the undersigned agree(s) to hold the Bank harmless and indemnify it against any and all claims, demands, actions, suits and proceedings of whatsoever nature upon or in respect of or in any manner arising out of the said guarantee which are made, brought or prosecuted against the Bank and against all losses, costs, charges, damages and expenses which the Bank may incur by reason of any such claim, demand, action, suit or proceeding. The undersigned agree(s) to do all things which may be required in order to obtain delivery of the bill(s) of lading covering the aforesaid goods including, but without in any way limiting the generality of the foregoing, the payment of any bills of exchange, and to deliver such bill(s) of lading to the Bank upon receipt thereof. The obligations hereunder of the undersigned, if more than one, shall be joint and several.

The undersigned will not require the Bank to refuse payment of any bills of exchange or other demand for payment arising in connection with the aforesaid bill(s) of lading for any reason, and further covenants that the indemnity contained in this agreement shall apply to any such payments.

This agreement shall be binding upon the undersigned absolutely and unconditionally upon delivery to the Bank notwithstanding that it is not executed by any other person by whom it was to have been signed.

This agreement shall be binding upon the undersigned and the heirs, executors, administrators, successors and assigns of the undersigned and shall enure to the benefit of the Bank and its successors and assigns.

Applicable to the province of Quebec only.

The undersigned has expressly requested that this document be drawn up in the English language. Le(s) soussigné(s) a(ont) expressément demandé que ce document soit rédigé en langue anglaise.

Dated at MONTREAL this 3RD day of OCTOBER 19____

Witness:

LYK TRADING LTD.

Figure 11 — Collection Instructions

FORM 1496 (5-87)

THE ROYAL BANK OF CANADA

BRANCH	DATE
(1) LOCAL BRANCH	OCTOBER 24

TO THE MANAGER

We enclose for collection the bills of exchange and documents described as follows.

DOCUMENTARY BILLS

DATE	TERM OR DUE DATE	DRAWEE NAME AND ADDRESS	CURR	AMOUNT
OCT 23	At Sight (2)	European Importer Any City Europe (3)	CAN.	$1,000.00 (4)

	DRAFTS	BILLS OF LADING ORIGINAL	BILLS OF LADING N/N	COMMERCIAL INVOICES	CUSTOMS INVOICES	CONSULAR INVOICES	INSURANCE CERTIFICATE	INSPECTION CERTIFICATE	CERTIFICATE OF ORIGIN	PACKING LIST	MISCELLANEOUS
DOCUMENTS [X] (5) OR CLEAN BILLS [ ]	2	3	2	3		3				3	

CARGO	CARRIER OR VESSEL	BILL OF LADING NUMBER
20 Cases Roofing Shingles FOB Toronto Oct.22	ORION	#4

FOLLOW INSTRUCTIONS MARKED "X"

(6) DOCUMENTS [X] DELIVER AGAINST PAYMENT [ ] DELIVER AGAINST ACCEPTANCE [ ] DELIVER AGAINST TRUST RECEIPT [ ] HOLD FOR ARRIVAL OF GOODS

PROTEST (7) [X] NO PROTEST [ ] PROTEST NON PAYMENT [ ] PROTEST NON ACCEPTANCE

CHARGES (8) [ ] ALL CHARGES FOR ACCOUNT OF PRINCIPAL [X] ALL CHARGES FOR ACCOUNT OF DRAWEE INCLUDING ROYAL BANK CHARGES [ ] DO NOT WAIVE CHARGES [ ] WAIVE CHARGES IF REFUSED BY DRAWEE [ ] CHARGES IN COUNTRY OF DRAWEE FOR ACCOUNT OF DRAWEE

INTEREST [ ] FOR ANY DELAY IN PAYMENT COLLECT INTEREST AT ______% PER ANNUM UNTIL APPROXIMATE DATE OF ARRIVAL OF FUNDS AT DESTINATION [ ] DO NOT WAIVE INTEREST

(9)

DISCOUNT [ ] ALLOW DISCOUNT OF ______% IF PAY BY ______

FATE (10) [ ] ADVISE ACCEPTANCE [ ] BY CABLE [ ] BY AIRMAIL | [ ] ADVISE NON ACCEPTANCE [ ] BY CABLE [ ] BY AIRMAIL | [X] ADVISE NON PAYMENT [X] BY CABLE [ ] BY AIRMAIL

PERMIT PROCEEDS BY (11) [X] AIRMAIL [ ] CABLE [ ] ______

IN CASE OF NEED (12) [ ] REFER TO ______ [ ] WHO MAY ASSIST IN HAVING DRAFT HONOURED AS DRAWN [ ] WHOSE INSTRUCTIONS MAY BE ACCEPTED IN EVERY RESPECT

LOCAL CURRENCY (13) [ ] IN EVENT COVER IS NOT IMMEDIATELY OBTAINABLE, A PROVISIONAL DEPOSIT IN LOCAL CURRENCY MAY BE ACCEPTED UNDER DRAWEES WRITTEN OBLIGATION TO ASSUME ALL EXCHANGE RISKS. DO NOT SURRENDER DRAFT UNTIL FINAL SETTLEMENT FOR FACE AMOUNT IS OBTAINED

DISPOSITION OF FUNDS (14) [ ] CREDIT OUR ACCOUNT NO 123 456 7 [ ] MAIL DRAFT DIRECT TO US [ ] CONVERT FOREIGN CURRENCY AT (DELETE ONE) CURRENT RATE / FUTURE RATE ______

SPECIAL INSTRUCTIONS

Please forward documents in two sets.
Drawee's bank is Overseas Bank, Any City, Europe.
(15)

THIS COLLECTION IS SUBJECT TO THE UNIFORM RULES FOR COLLECTIONS (1978 REVISION) INTERNATIONAL CHAMBER OF COMMERCE, PUBLICATION NO. 322 AND SUBSEQUENT REVISIONS.

PRINCIPAL'S NAME AND SIGNATURE: CANADIAN EXPORTER (16)

INVOICE NO. (IF APPLICABLE): 753

Figure 12 — Direct Collection Order and Draft

OUTGOING COLLECTION ORDER — FORM 14087 (8-84)

THE ROYAL BANK OF CANADA

INTERNATIONAL TRADE CENTRE — ONTARIO
COLLECTIONS • 180 WELLINGTON ST.
TORONTO, ONTARIO, CANADA M5J 1J1

OUR NUMBER: TD 228087
DATE: June 12

MAIL TO:
A BANK IN NEW ZEALAND
AUCKLAND, NEW ZEALAND

DRAWEE NAME AND ADDRESS: BUYER'S NAME AND ADDRESS

TERM OR DUE DATE: 30 DAYS SIGHT

We enclose for collection and remittance after final payment only. Please account direct to the above-named branch of The Royal Bank of Canada quoting our number.

DOCUMENTS [X] OR CLEAN BILLS [ ]

	Drafts	Bills of Lading: Original	Bills of Lading: N.N.	Commercial Invoices	Customs Invoices	Canada Air Invoices	Insurance Certificate	Certificate of Origin	Packing List			
First Mail	1	2/3	1	3	4		1		2			
Second Mail	1	1/3	1	1	1		1		1			

CARGO: 10CTNS ELECTRONIC PARTS - ORDER B-17
CARRIER OR VESSEL: PACIFIC
BILL OF LADING NUMBER: BL 3456

FOLLOW INSTRUCTIONS MARKED "X"

CURRENCY: CAD
AMOUNT: 30,000.00

DOCUMENTS: [ ] DELIVER AGAINST PAYMENT ONLY [X] DELIVER AGAINST ACCEPTANCE [ ] DELIVER AGAINST TRUST RECEIPT [X] HOLD FOR ARRIVAL OF GOODS

PROTEST: [X] NO PROTEST [ ] PROTEST NON PAYMENT [ ] PROTEST NON ACCEPTANCE

CHARGES: [ ] ALL CHARGES FOR ACCOUNT OF PRINCIPAL [X] ALL CHARGES FOR ACCOUNT OF DRAWEE INCLUDING ROYAL BANK CHARGES CAD 37.50
[X] DO NOT WAIVE CHARGES — PLUS AIRMAIL CHARGES
[ ] WAIVE CHARGES IF REFUSED BY DRAWEE [ ] CHARGES IN COUNTRY OF DRAWEE FOR ACCOUNT OF DRAWEE

INTEREST: [X] FOR ANY DELAY IN PAYMENT COLLECT INTEREST AT 18 % PER ANNUM UNTIL APPROXIMATE DATE OF ARRIVAL OF FUNDS AT DESTINATION [X] DO NOT WAIVE INTEREST [ ] ________

DISCOUNT: [ ] ALLOW DISCOUNT OF ____ % IF PAID BY ________

FATE: [X] ADVISE ACCEPTANCE [X] ADVISE NON ACCEPTANCE [X] ADVISE NON PAYMENT
[X] BY CABLE [ ] BY AIRMAIL [X] BY CABLE [ ] BY AIRMAIL [X] BY CABLE [ ] BY AIRMAIL

REMIT PROCEEDS BY: [ ] AIRMAIL [X] CABLE [ ] ________

WHERE ACCOUNTS ARE CONDUCTED BY EITHER BANK IN THE CURRENCY OF COLLECTION, CREDIT OUR ACCOUNT OR AUTHORIZE US TO DEBIT YOUR ACCOUNT. WHEN PAYMENT IS EFFECTED THROUGH A THIRD BANK A DIRECT ADVICE MUST BE SENT TO THE REMITTING BANK.

IN CASE OF NEED: [X] REFER TO YOUR AGENT'S NAME AND ADDRESS, IF APPLICABLE
[X] WHO MAY ASSIST IN HAVING DRAFT HONOURED AS DRAWN [ ] WHOSE INSTRUCTIONS MAY BE ACCEPTED IN EVERY RESPECT

LOCAL CURRENCY: [X] IN EVENT COVER IS NOT IMMEDIATELY OBTAINABLE A PROVISIONAL DEPOSIT IN LOCAL CURRENCY MAY BE ACCEPTED UNDER DRAWEES WRITTEN OBLIGATION TO ASSUME ALL EXCHANGE RISKS. DO NOT SURRENDER DRAFT UNTIL FINAL SETTLEMENT FOR FACE AMOUNT IS OBTAINED.

SPECIAL INSTRUCTIONS:

ORIGINAL COLLECTION ORDER

THIS COLLECTION IS SUBJECT TO THE UNIFORM RULES FOR COLLECTIONS (1978 REVISION) INTERNATIONAL CHAMBER OF COMMERCE, PUBLICATION NO. 322.

PRINCIPAL: CANADIAN EXPORTER
CE 546

2 — ORIGINAL COLLECTION ORDER

THE ROYAL BANK OF CANADA
TD 228087

TORONTO, ONTARIO JUNE 12 19____

30 DAYS AFTER SIGHT OF THIS FIRST OF EXCHANGE (SECOND UNPAID)

PAY TO THE ORDER OF THE ROYAL BANK OF CANADA THE SUM OF
-----THIRTY THOUSAND 00/100 CANADIAN DOLLARS $ 30,000.00

VALUE RECEIVED

To BUYER'S NAME
AND ADDRESS

CANADIAN EXPORTER

COLLECTING BANK'S REFERENCE

Figure 13 — Direct Collection Disposition Instructions

DISPOSITION INSTRUCTIONS

REMOVE ONLY PARTS 2, 3, 9 AND 10 AND DISPOSE AS FOLLOWS:

PART 2 – FORWARD TO COLLECTING BANK BY REGISTERED AIRMAIL TOGETHER WITH ORIGINAL DOCUMENTS.
PART 3 – FORWARD TO COLLECTING BANK BY AIRMAIL 2 DAYS LATER. IF NO DUPLICATE DOCUMENTS, DESTROY.
PARTS 9 & 10 – RETAIN AS YOUR RECORD.

DELIVER REMAINDER OF SET TO ROYAL BANK BRANCH OR INTERNATIONAL TRADE CENTRE.

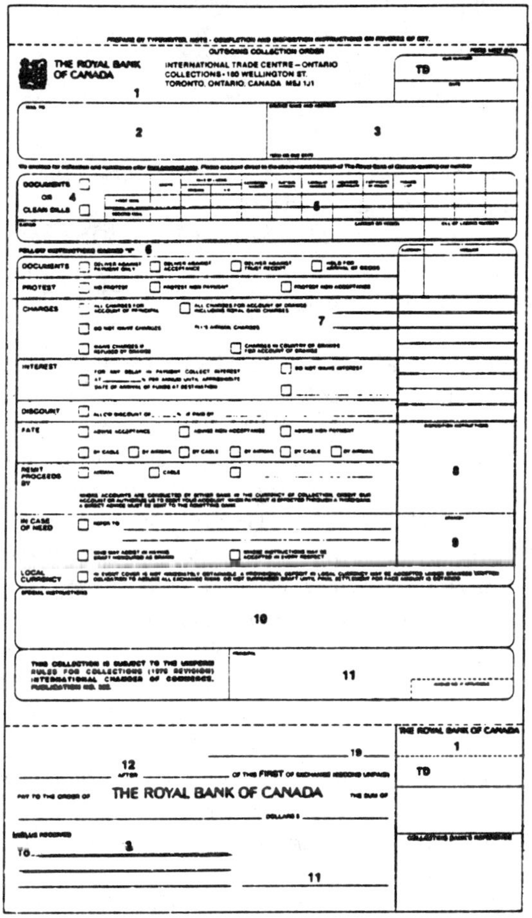

1. ADDRESS OR ROYAL BANK INTERNATIONAL TRADE CENTRE. OBTAIN FROM YOUR BRANCH IF NOT PREPRINTED.
2. NAME AND ADDRESS OF THE CORRESPONDENT BANK OR ROYAL BANK BRANCH TO RECEIVE THE COLLECTION.
3. DRAWEE'S (YOUR CUSTOMER'S) NAME AND ADDRESS.
4. INDICATE IF DOCUMENTARY COLLECTION OR CLEAN BILL (NO DOCUMENTS).
5. ENUMERATE DOCUMENTS FORWARDED WITH FIRST MAIL (ORIGINAL) AND SECOND MAIL (DUPLICATE) ON THE SEPARATE LINES INDICATED.
6. COMPLETE THIS SECTION BY MARKING WITH AN "X" THE APPLICABLE ITEMS AND ENTERING REQUESTED INFORMATION.
7. INDICATE CHARGES (OBTAIN FROM YOUR BRANCH) AND AIRMAIL CHARGES ON SEPARATE LINES.
8. INDICATE ACCOUNT TO BE CREDITED WITH PROCEEDS AND ANY OTHER DISPOSITION INSTRUCTIONS.
9. ROYAL BANK BRANCH WHERE YOU CONDUCT YOUR ACCOUNT.
10. COLLECTION INSTRUCTIONS NOT PROVIDED ELSEWHERE.
11. YOUR COMPANY'S NAME AND AUTHORIZED SIGNATURE.
12. INDICATE TERM EG. "ON DEMAND" AFTER "DATE"; "30 DAYS" AFTER (A SPECIFIC DATE).

board, prepares the documentation and, if the buyer is arranging insurance, may be required to state the name of the vessel and on board date by telex. For protection, the seller should consider insurance coverage on the shipment from the factory up to the loading on board date. The seller prepares the draft and presents the required documents together with collection instructions to our local branch. These instructions are numbered in accordance with their entry in specimen Figure 11 which should provide the following information:

1. Name of local branch and date.
2. Date of draft and term or due date.
3. Name & address of drawee.
4. Currency and amount of draft.
5. Enumerate the documents relating to the collection. Drafts in duplicate should be provided if collection is to be forwarded in two shipments.
6. State if documents are to be released on payment or acceptance and if the collection may be held until goods arrive in port.
7. Protest instructions. Always mark no protest, unless the principal is prepared to absorb the expense of protest.
8. Instructions relating to Canadian and Foreign bank charges and whether the buyer or seller is to be responsible for their payment.
9. Interest charges to be added to late payment, or discount charges to be deducted if early payment is provided. Please note the collecting bank may waive interest charges if the drawee refuses them unless instructions clearly state interest is not to be waived.
10. State if fate of collection is to be advised by the collecting bank by airmail or cable.
11. State if proceeds are to be forwarded by the collecting bank either by airmail or cable.
12. If the seller has an agent with specified authority in the country of the buyer, the collecting bank should be advised if it is to refer the collection for assistance.
13. Due to exchange regulations in the country of the buyer, it may be necessary to authorize the collecting bank to accept a local currency deposit until payment is officially authorized in the currency of the collection. Please note the exchange risk is to be borne by the buyer and the related documentation is to be released in order to obtain exchange control approval.
14. State account to be credited on receipt in Canada. If the collection is in foreign currency you may authorize the branch to convert at the current rate or at a rate previously arranged.
15. In the space reserved for special instructions, insert additional information necessary to the collection, not covered above.
16. The "Canadian Exporter" affixes name and signature and if desired a cross reference number such as that of the invoice. The International Centre uses its own reference number when processing the collection.

DIRECT COLLECTION SYSTEM

For export customers, where volume warrants, the Royal Bank offers an alternative method of collection. The collection order is completed in the office of the seller, or by the freight forwarder or customs broker, and the documentary collection is forwarded direct to the collecting bank. Copies of the collection order will later be presented to our International Centre staff, who follow the collection process until final settlement is obtained. Delays in delivering the documents to our International Centre and their preparation of the collection order is eliminated. There is a common reference number printed on the form which can be used by the seller, together with the remitting and collecting banks. We have found that this procedure enables payment to be received about five days earlier than with the regular system. Refer to Figures 12 and 13 for examples of a completed direct collection, together with the incorporated instructions.

3. ICC Uniform Rules for Collection

In 1956, the ICC published its Uniform Rules for Collection of Commercial Paper. They were revised in 1967, 1978, and 1995. The 1995 revision, called Uniform Rules for Collections (URC522), came into force on January 1, 1996.[51] It retains the structure of the 1978 rules. The URC522 apply only if expressly incorporated by the parties into the text of their collection order.

All financial[52] and commercial[53] documents sent for clean[54] or documentary[55] collection by banks must be accompanied by a collection order giving complete and precise instructions,[56] because banks are only permitted to act upon these instructions and in accordance with these rules, unless otherwise expressly agreed by the parties or unless contrary to the provisions of a national law or regulation that cannot be departed from. Unless otherwise authorized in the collection order, banks will ignore all instructions other than those from the party who charged them with the collection operation.

In the case of exports of goods, the collecting bank involved in processing the collection order will present to the buyer the financial documents accompanied by commercial documents. Banks must verify that the documents received appear to be as listed in the collection order and must immediately advise the party from whom the collection order was received of any documents missing. They have no further obligation to examine the documents.[57] The documents and the collection order may be sent to the collecting bank directly or through another bank as intermediary,[58] for example, the remitting bank—that is, the bank to which the principal, in general the seller, has entrusted the operation of collection.[59]

Banks assume no responsibility for the authenticity, genuineness, or legal effect of any document, or for the quality, quantity, or condition of any goods to which the

51 ICC doc. 522.

52 Art. 2(b)(i). Financial documents means bills of exchange, promissory notes, cheques, payment receipts, or other similar instruments used for obtaining the payment of money.

53 Art. 2(b)(ii). Commercial documents means invoices, shipping documents, documents of title, or other similar documents, or any other documents whatsoever, not being financial documents.

54 Art. 2(c). Clean collection means collection of financial documents not accompanied by commercial documents.

55 Art. 2(d). Documentary collection means collection of financial documents accompanied by commercial documents or commercial documents not accompanied by financial documents.

56 Art. 4(a)(i).

57 Art. 12(a).

58 Art. 5(e).

59 Art. 3(a)(iii).

documents relate.[60] The presenting bank[61] is responsible for seeing that the form of the acceptance of a bill of exchange appears to be complete and correct, but is not responsible for the genuineness of any signature nor for the authority of any signatory to sign the acceptance.[62] Similarly, the presenting bank assumes no responsibility as to the authenticity of any signature or for the authority of any signatory to sign a promissory note, receipt, or other instrument.[63]

The collection order should give specific instructions regarding protest in the advent of non-acceptance or non-payment. In the absence of such specific instructions, the banks concerned with the collection have no obligation to have the documents protested.[64] The presenting bank will only release the documents to the drawee[65] after full payment has been received.[66]

The URC522 also contain provisions dealing with the powers of the principal's representative in case of need in the event of non-acceptance and or non-payment of the collection order,[67] and the protection of the goods to which a documentary collection relates.[68] Miscellaneous articles are devoted to payment without delay;[69] currency of payment;[70] the payment of interest, charges, and expenses by the drawee or the principal;[71] and *force majeure*.[72]

IV. LETTERS OF CREDIT

A. Introduction

The efficient operation of international trade is largely dependent upon the use of letters of credit to guarantee international payments and finance exports. They have been described as "the life blood of international commerce."[73] It has been said that between the

60 Art. 13.

61 Defined in art. 3(a)(iv), the presenting bank is the collecting bank making presentation to the drawee.

62 Art. 22.

63 Art. 23.

64 Art. 24.

65 The drawee is the person to whom presentation is to be made according to the collection order.

66 See Art. 19.

67 Art. 25.

68 Art. 10. Banks are under no obligation to take any measure with respect to the goods to which a documentary collection relates, even if specific instructions have been given to that effect (art. 10(b)). Any action taken by a bank for the protection of the goods, whether or not taken on instructions received, is taken with no liability concerning the state of the goods.

69 Art. 16.

70 Arts. 17 and 18.

71 Arts. 20 and 21.

72 Art. 15.

73 Per Griffiths LJ in *Power Curber International Ltd. v. Bank of Kuwait S.A.K.*, [1981] 1 WLR 1233, at 1243, [1981] 3 All ER 607, at 614 (CA). See also per Donaldson LJ in *Intraco Ltd. v. Notis Shipping Corporation of Liberia. The Bhoja Trader*, [1981] 2 Lloyds Rep. 256, at 257.

issuing bank and the beneficiary of the credit: "A letter of credit is like a bill of exchange given for the price of goods. It ranks as cash and must be honoured."[74] The letter of credit itself is, however, not the means by which payment is effected; that is usually done by way of cash, an electronic funds transfer or a bill of exchange. The issuing or confirming bank, however, in the terms of the ICC's Uniform Customs and Practice for Documentary Credits (UCP)[75] undertakes to pay or to accept, or to be responsible for their acceptance at maturity, or to purchase or negotiate without recourse to drawers and/or *bona fide* holders, drafts drawn by the beneficiary.[76] The use of a letter of credit in a documentary credit transaction substitutes the credit of a bank for that of the buyer, distancing the beneficiary from the risk of non-performance of the underlying contract. This alleviates the concern of the seller that he or she be paid and also answers the buyer's concern that the goods be delivered once payment has been made.[77]

Banking practice, confirmed by judicial decisions in both common and civil law jurisdictions and the almost universal reference to the UCP, has resulted in an instrument that is generally well understood in international banking circles. Indeed, the rules governing its use may be said to form a part of the *lex mercatoria* or the uniform law of international trade.[78]

B. Types and Characteristics of Letters of Credit

The form of a letter of credit to some extent depends upon the function it performs. The basic categories of letters of credit used in international trade are "documentary" or "stand-by."

The documentary letter of credit is used for the purpose of effecting payment for goods or services. It facilitates the financing of the operation by bridging the period between shipment and payment; this is the real function of the documentary credit.[79] It is usually provided by a bank to the seller of the goods (the beneficiary). The payment by the bank is "triggered" by the presentation of certain specified documents by the seller, his or her agent, or assignee. These documents may serve as security for the bank until payment by the buyer.

---

74 Per Lord Denning, in *Power Curber International Ltd. v. Bank of Kuwait*, [1981] 1 WLR 1233, at 1241, [1981] 3 All ER 607, at 612.

75 (1993), pub. no. 500 (UCP500).

76 Arts. 2 and 9 of the UCP500.

77 For a general description of the operation of the letter of credit in an international transaction see ICC, *Guide to Documentary Credit Operations* (1985), pub. no. 415, Sarna, *Letters of Credit: The Law and Current Practice* (3rd ed., 1989), c. 1, s. 2. See also bibliography at the end of this chapter.

78 Berman and Kaufman, "The Law of International Commercial Transactions (*Lex Mercatoria*)" (1978), 19 *Harv. Int'l. LJ* 221, at 246. Note that the current UCP500 (1993 rev.) stipulates that it does not codify trade usage or custom but merely provides guidelines for banking practice that must be incorporated by reference into the letter of credit in order for them to govern (see art. 1 of the UCP500).

79 Per Lord Wright in *T.D. Bailey, Son & Co. v. Ross T. Smyth & Co. Ltd.* (1940), 56 TLR 825, at 828.

The stand-by letter of credit, on the other hand, is not primarily intended to effect payment. It is given as a guarantee, usually by the seller, either to secure performance or as a bid bond and, therefore, if the transaction proceeds successfully, will not be called upon.

The essence of the functioning of the letter of credit, in both situations, is its autonomy from the underlying contracts,[80] establishing relationships between the participating banks themselves and their customers, which are distinct from those that exist between the seller and the buyer. However, as the letter of credit is a means of performance of that underlying contract, it is independent in many aspects, and yet related in others to it. In this section, we will explore those independent yet related transactions that make up the credit with the hope that the analysis will illustrate the basic characteristics of the letter of credit. For more sophisticated refinements, the reader is referred to the extensive literature found in the bibliography at the end of this chapter.

Put simply, the "commercial documentary letter of credit is an undertaking by a bank to honour the seller's draft upon compliance with the conditions specified in the credit."[81]

These specified conditions respond to the many needs of an individual transaction, perhaps requiring advances prior to delivery ("packing credits"), transferability, or even divisibility of the credit.[82] Any one of those operations will require a different set of documents and require a specific set of instructions to the banker.

As a result of the many uses to which it may be put, it has been observed that "a commercial letter of credit may better be described than defined, and described by reference to the course of business effected by it."[83] Perhaps it may most simply be said to act as a conditional guarantee of payment by a bank in favour of its customer.

The courts have recognized the danger of trying to impose too rigorous a definition of such a credit, noting that no particular form for it is prescribed and preferring to leave it free from any comprehensive definition so that it may grow and change "in accordance with the development of legitimate business practice."[84]

The definition of what constitutes a documentary credit[85] and the terms by which such transactions are regulated have largely been codified by the UCP, last revised in

---

80 The autonomy of the letter of credit from the underlying transaction it secures is evident in, e.g., *Bank of Nova Scotia v. Angelica-Whitewear Ltd.*, [1987] 1 SCR 59. The UCP underlines the concept in arts. 3 and 4.

81 Bermann and Kaufman, *supra*, note 78, at 247.

82 For a description of different forms of documentary credit operations, see ICC, *Guide to Documentary Credit Operations* (1985).

83 A. Davis, *The Law Relating to Commercial Letters of Credit* (3rd ed., 1963), at 13.

84 *Moss v. Old Colony Trust Co.*, 140 NE 803, at 807 (Mass. 1923).

85 Art. 2 of the UCP500 (1993 rev.) states that "documentary credit(s)" and "standby letter(s) of credit" mean any arrangement,

> whereby a bank (the "Issuing Bank") acting at the request and on the instructions of a customer (the "Applicant") or on its own behalf,

(The footnote is continued on the next page.)

1993 with the collaboration of UNCITRAL.[86] These rules have virtual universal acceptance by all banks.[87]

Whereas previous revisions of the UCP have stated that the UCP applied to all documentary credits "unless otherwise expressly agreed,"[88] note that article 1 of the 1993 UCP500[89] stipulates that the UCP applies to all documentary credits only "where they are incorporated into the text of the credit." Rather than purporting to represent international trade custom, the UCP appear to be limited by this clause to a role more reminiscent of incorporated contractual terms. However, the exact legal status of the UCP—as terms that may simply be incorporated into the contract by explicit reference or as principles of international commercial custom—remains unclear. In 1989, Schmitthoff noted, "at present, the UCP cannot be accorded normative character, but they are a transnational trade usage of contractual nature, the transnational character being derived from their formulation by the ICC."[90] Whatever their exact legal status, the UCP cannot be expected to provide a comprehensive regulatory regime for letters of credit, because the ICC lacks surveillance and enforcement capability. There thus remains a need for supplementary national rules and enforcement.

In the United States, the UCP complement the provisions of article 5 of the Uniform Commercial Code (UCC) that governs letters of credit and in some jurisdictions may form a part of the "law" applicable to them. Otherwise, it may serve as evidence of a custom. This varies from state to state.[91] Under English and Canadian law, the UCP500 must be specifically incorporated by reference in the document, usually done by a notation to that effect on the face of the letter of credit itself. In other countries, standard conditions adopted by banking associations incorporate them by reference.[92] They also

---

85 Continued ...

> i) is to make a payment to or to the order of a third party (the "Beneficiary"), or is to accept and pay bills of exchange (Draft(s)) drawn by the Beneficiary, or
>
> ii) authorises another bank to effect such payment, or to accept and pay such bills of exchange (Draft(s)), or
>
> iii) authorises another bank to negotiate, against stipulated document(s), provided that the terms and conditions of the Credit are complied with.

Note that this definition now embraces two-party credits—i.e., the situation where a bank acts on its own behalf by securing its obligation with another of its own obligations.

86 The UCP was first introduced in 1933 and subsequently revised in 1951, 1962, 1974, 1983, and 1993. The 1993 rev. came into operation on 31 December 1993.

87 C. Schmitthoff, *Schmitthoff's Export Trade: The Law and Practice of International Trade* (9th ed., 1990), at 402.

88 See, e.g., UCP 1983, ICC doc. no. 400, art. 1.

89 ICC doc. no. 500.

90 See Schmitthoff, "International and Procedural Aspects of Letters of Credit" in Horn (ed.), *The Law of International Trade Finance* (1989) 227, at 229. See also, e.g., Dolan and van Huizen, "International Rules for Letters of Credit" (1993), 9 *BFLR* 173, at 175.

91 A.M. Squillante, "Letters of Credit: A Discourse" (1979), 84 *Com. LJ* 372, at 372-73.

92 C. Schmitthoff, *supra*, note 87, at 402.

govern the relations between the banks and SWIFT (the automated international transfer system) where that mode of payment is used.[93]

Two concepts are essential. Letters of credit may be "revocable" or "irrevocable," "confirmed" or "unconfirmed."

The concept of revocability requires no comment. It gives little protection to the exporter and for that reason is seldom acceptable. Note that in the absence of an indication concerning revocability or irrevocability, a credit is now deemed to be irrevocable.[94] In addition, a credit is irrevocable after a nominated bank has acted in reliance upon it.[95]

A credit is unconfirmed when the bank in the place of the beneficiary (the seller) acts only as an "advising" or "notifying bank," a sort of "conduit pipe" for the purpose of forwarding documents to the issuing (buyer's) bank; a credit is confirmed when the bank in the place of the beneficiary has a direct responsibility to the seller to honour drafts when presented to it with the accompanying documents. This makes confirmed credits more attractive to the seller-exporter. It also makes them more expensive.

Most international credits are confirmed and irrevocable. The result is that the usual case involves "four autonomous though inter-connected contractual relationships."[96] They are:

(a) the contract for the sale of goods between the buyer and the seller;

(b) the arrangement between the buyer and his or her bank whereby the latter issues the credit and agrees to pay the seller (or to accept or negotiate bills of exchange drawn by the seller) either through an advising or confirming bank upon receipt of specified documents;

(c) if payment is to be made through an advising bank, then the arrangement by the bank to accept the documents for transmittal; if payment is to be made through a confirming bank then the inter-bank contract whereby the confirming bank agrees to pay to the beneficiary upon receipt of the stipulated documents and the issuing bank agrees to reimburse the confirming bank upon receipt thereof;

(d) the arrangement between the seller and the named bank whereby it either undertakes to receive and transmit documents (unconfirmed) or to pay, without recourse, to the seller upon receipt of the appropriate documents (confirmed).

These are the basic relationships established in all transactions. To them may be added as many complexities as ingenious solicitors may devise. Quite often, for example, the beneficiary may have assigned his or her rights to receive payment as a means of financing the transaction and it is his or her assignee who obtains the documents for presentation to the confirming bank and the right to receive payment upon presentation.

---

93 *Ibid.*

94 UCP500, art. 6(c). See also observations hereinafter concerning the position in the United States under the UCC.

95 UCP500, art. 8(b).

96 *United City Merchants (Investments) Ltd. v. Royal Bank of Canada*, [1982] 2 WLR 1039, at 1045, [1963] AC 168, [1983] 2 All ER 720 (HL) (the *American Accord*). See also *Bank of Nova Scotia v. Angelica-Whitewear Ltd.*, [1987] 1 SCR 59, at 177.

Article 9(a) of the UCP500 sets out four means by which the seller may receive payment, by sight payment, by deferred payment, by acceptance, or by negotiation.

In the case of sight payment, the bank pays against delivery of documents whereas by deferred payment the bank pays at a later date, usually fixed as a date later in time to the occurrence of an event (such as the date of issuance of the bill of lading). Neither of these cases involves the use of a bill of exchange.

If the credit is an acceptance or negotiation credit, the bill of exchange is used. In the first case, the seller draws the bill on the issuing bank, the advising bank, or the buyer in the specified manner. Where the credit has been confirmed by the advising bank, it is obliged to accept the bill and thus becomes liable as an acceptor. In the second case, the advising bank only acts to negotiate a bill drawn on the buyer or the issuing bank and so accepts no liability except as an endorsee.[97]

Drafts may be sight or time drafts in accordance with the terms of the credit. Time drafts may be negotiated by the drawer-payee, subject to deductions for interest and commission, as a means of getting an advance payment.

The letter of credit itself is a thing in action[98] and may be assigned by the beneficiary prior to presenting the documents or the drafts as a way of obtaining an advance payment. The credit may also be "transferred" (if it so provides) so that another person steps into the shoes of the beneficiary (usually a supplier) and may take advantage of the credit provided that he or she complies with its terms.[99] The effectiveness of such an assignment may depend on whether the credit is expressly negotiable or transferable. In such a case, the assignee becomes a holder in due course with rights independent of the original beneficiary—a consequence that is most important in the case of fraud by the latter.[100]

The bank must carefully consider how it acts when dealing with the credit. If, for example, an advising bank acts like a confirming bank and accepts a bill of exchange in circumstances in which its only obligation was to negotiate the bill on to the issuing bank, it may find itself liable as the acceptor of the bill, even where it is subsequently informed by the issuing bank that documents are non-conforming. In such a case, it was held that a bank so acting had no recourse against the issuing bank or, in the absence of fraud by the beneficiary, any claim against him or her for recovery of the monies paid.[101]

---

97 An advising bank may advise a credit to a beneficiary without engagement or liability on its part. However, it must take reasonable care to check the apparent authenticity of the credit which it advises: UCP500, art. 7. In addition, see UCP500, art. 9 and Dolan and van Huizen, supra, *note 90*, at 189: the mere fact of rendering advice does not bind the advising bank to honour the beneficiary's draft. UCP500, art. 10(b)(ii) states that "negotiation" means the giving of value for Draft(s) and/or document(s) by the bank authorized to negotiate. Mere examination of the documents without giving of value does not constitute a negotiation.

98 Per Denning LJ in *Trans Trust S.P.R.L. v. Danubian Trading Co. Ltd.*, [1952] 2 QB 297, at 305.

99 Art. 48 of the UCP500. See section C *infra*.

100 The case law on assignability and its consequences is not entirely clear. J.F. Dolan, *The Law of Letters of Credit* (1984-), c. 10. See also *Singer & Friedlander v. Creditanstalt-Bankverein*, 17 Cg. 72/80 (Handelsgericht Wien 1980) referred to by S. Rolitsky, "Introduction to Letters of Credit" in W. Hancock (ed.), *Laws of International Trade* (1986), vol. 2, 702.11.

101 See *Michael Doyle and Associates v. Bank of Montreal*, [1984] 5 WWR 193 (BC CA).

Figure 2—Documentary Letter of Credit, Flow Chart

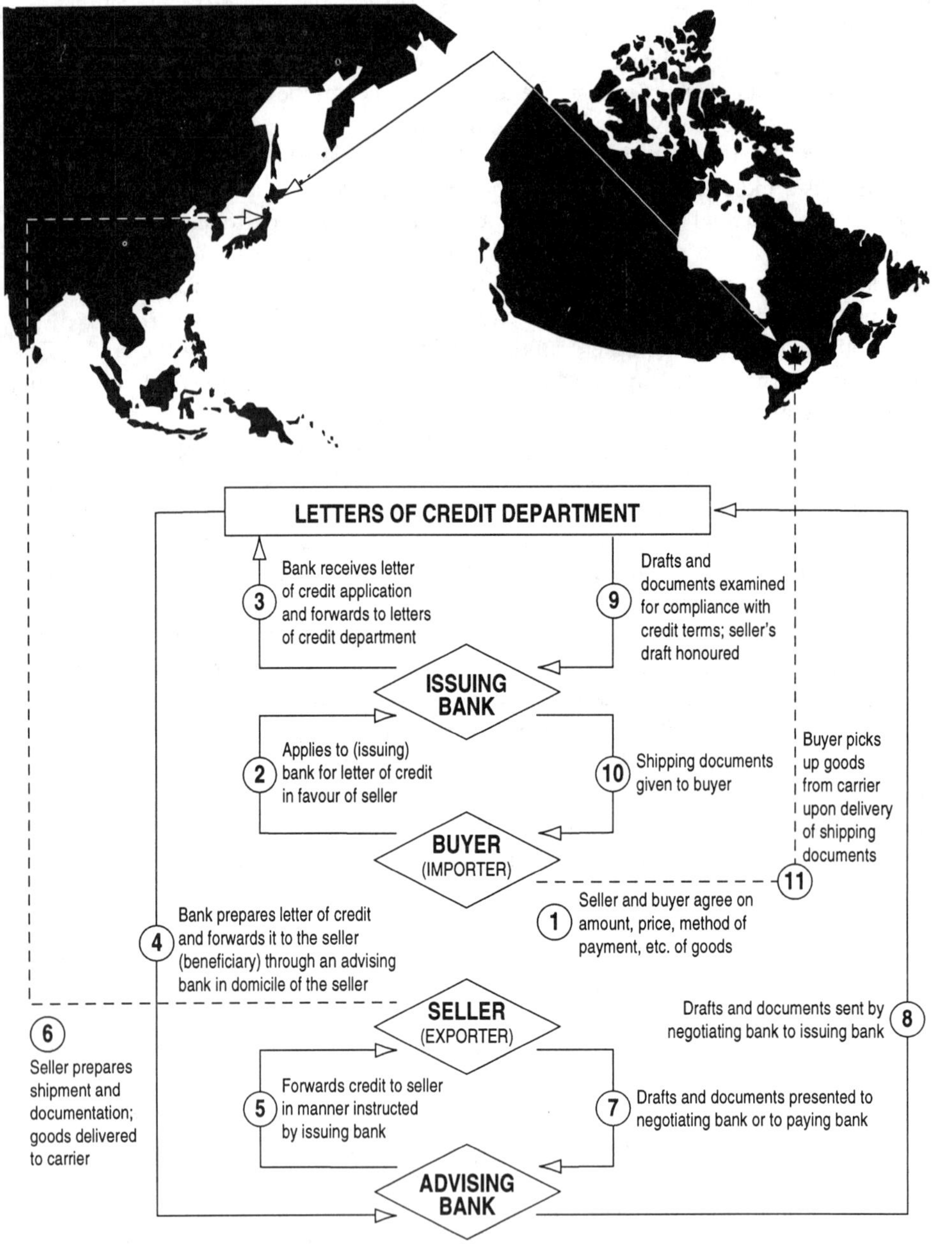

The nature of the relationship between the beneficiary of the letter of credit and the issuing bank (in the case of an unconfirmed credit) or the confirming bank (where the credit has been confirmed) has given rise to some theoretical and practical problems of a purely legal nature that relate to the position of a third-party beneficiary to a contract.[102] It is suggested that this is not a practical issue because no bank wishing to carry on business could refuse to honour its obligation for this technical legal reason. The debate has, in any event, been resolved in favour of a contractual relationship between the two, whatever theoretical discussions might exist about the nature of the consideration arising from the beneficiary to the bank.[103] No problem exists in civil code jurisdictions that recognize the binding contractual nature of a "stipulation pour autrui" and the confirming bank is recognized as owing a direct obligation to the seller as provided for in the UCP500.[104]

As a consequence of this contractual relationship, the seller's damages for the bank's failure to honour its obligations may exceed the amount of the credit where loss of profits or other damages are foreseeable.[105]

The credit expires on a date provided therein after which the advising bank will refuse to accept the documents presented by the seller. Articles 42 to 44 of the UCP500 provides some refinements to the concept of expiry.

C. Special Credits

1. Revolving Credit[106]

A revolving credit that may be revocable or irrevocable is one where under the terms and conditions thereof, the amount made available is automatically renewed or reinstated. Such credit is used when the buyer-importer is a regular customer of the seller-exporter.

A revolving credit may revolve in relation to time or value. If it revolves in relation to time it may be cumulative or non-cumulative. In the latter case, any sum not drawn during a period cannot be carried over to a subsequent period within the overall fixed period of the credit.

A credit that revolves in relation to value within an overall period of time is rarely used by a buyer-importer as it may involve the buyer and the issuing bank in an incalculable liability.

---

102 Gutteridge and Megrah, *The Law of Bankers' Commercial Credits* (6th ed., 1979), at 21 *et seq*. See also the observations of McIntyre J in *Greenwood Shopping Plaza v. Beattie et al.* (1980), 111 DLR (3d) 257 (SCC), the comment on "The Third Party Rule" in J. Swan and B. Reiter, "Developments in Contract Law: The 1979-80 Term" (1981), 2 *Supreme Court L Rev.* 125, at 133 and the discussion in chapter 8, *supra*, on the position of warehousemen and stevedores as third-party beneficiaries to "Himalaya clause" limitations in the bill of lading.

103 See *Urquhart Lindsay & Co. Ltd. v. Eastern Bank Ltd.*, [1922] 1 KB 318; Lord Diplock in the *American Accord, supra*, note 96, at 1045, refers specifically to the confirming bank's "contractual obligation" to the seller.

104 Art. 9(b). Sarna, *Letters of Credit: The Law and Current Practice* (3rd ed., 1989), c. 2, s. 3.

105 *Urquhart Lindsay & Co. Ltd. v. Eastern Bank Ltd.*, [1922] 1 KB 318.

106 ICC, *Guide to Documentary Credit Operations* (1985), at 32.

A revolving credit does not include a credit available by installments[107] or an evergreen clause in a letter of credit that automatically extends it for another fixed period.

2. *Red Clause Credit*[108]

A red clause credit is one that incorporates a special clause, originally written in red ink, that authorizes the advising or the confirming bank to make advances to the beneficiary before the presentation of documents. This type of credit provides the seller-exporter with funds prior to shipment. The buyer-importer as applicant for the credit is liable for repayment of the advances if the beneficiary fails to present the documents called for under the credit.

3. *Transferable Credit*[109]

A transferable credit is one that, at the request of the applicant, is irrevocable and allows the original beneficiary to transfer it to one or more other parties.[110] It is used when the first beneficiary does not supply the merchandise but acts as a middle person. The second beneficiary cannot transfer the credit to a third beneficiary. The transfer is effected at the request of the first beneficiary by the bank where the credit is available.

4. *Back-to-Back Credit*

In a back-to-back credit, the immediate seller of goods, as beneficiary of the confirmed credit issued by the bank at the request of the ultimate buyer, offers it as security when applying to the advising bank for the issuance of a second credit in favour of a supplier from whom the immediate seller must purchase the goods sold to the ultimate buyer. The immediate seller may also request his or her own bank to issue the second credit as a counter to the first one. This second credit is called a counter credit. The applicant for the second credit is responsible for reimbursing the bank for payments made under it, even if he or she is not paid under the first credit.[111]

Back-to-back credits are often used where a Canadian trader buys goods in one foreign country and sells them in another foreign country or where the same commodity (for example, oil) is sold and resold by several middle persons before being bought by the ultimate buyer.[112] The credit opened by the ultimate buyer in favour of the immediate seller is called the overriding credit.

107 As to which see art. 41 of the UCP.

108 ICC, *Guide to Documentary Credit Operations* (1985), at 33.

109 ICC, *Guide to Documentary Credit Operations* (1985), at 34.

110 Art. 48 of the UCP500.

111 ICC, *Guide to Documentary Credit Operations* (1985), at 35. For a case involving a back-to-back credit see *Bank of Nova Scotia v. Angelica Whitewear Ltd.*, [1987] 1 SCR 59, 36 DLR (4th) 161.

112 Called "string contracts."

D. The Autonomy of the Credit

The efficient operation of the system depends to no small degree upon the autonomy of the contractual relationships established among the various parties to the four contracts described above in section B. The banker's obligation is therefore to honour the terms of the documentary credit upon the receipt of the appropriate documents, whatever dispute might exist between the seller and buyer in respect of their underlying contract. The courts are swift to issue a summary judgment against a bank attempting to avoid its obligations under an irrevocable or confirmed letter of credit where the proper documents are tendered. This procedural strictness bolsters the effectiveness and stability of payment by letter of credit.[113]

The notion that the issuing bank's obligation to the beneficiary must at all times be independent of the underlying contract was developed early in the cases, and confirmed by Article 4 of the UCP500 that the confirming bank and the seller "deal in documents, and not in goods"[114] and that:

> [C]redits, by their nature, are separate transactions from the sales or other contract(s) on which they may be based and banks are in no way concerned with or bound by such contract(s), even if any reference whatsoever to such contract(s) is included in the credit. ...

If the documents are in order on their face as per the agreement between the parties that is reflected in the terms of the letter of credit, the confirming bank is obliged either to pay or to accept, or to be responsible for their acceptance at maturity, or to purchase or negotiate without recourse to drawers and/or *bona fide* holders, drafts drawn by the beneficiary on the issuing bank.[115] This feature has been affirmed as "the fundamental principle governing documentary letters of credit and the characteristic which gives them their international commercial utility and efficacy."[116]

The purpose of the rule was put by Lord Diplock in the *American Accord*:[117]

> The whole commercial purpose for which the system of confirmed irrevocable documentary credit has been developed in international trade is to give to the seller an assured right to be paid before he parts with the control of the goods that does not permit of any dispute with the buyer as to the performance of the contract of sale being used as a ground for non-payment or reduction or deferment of payment.

This obligation is subject to an exception limited to fraud or misrepresentation by the seller as to the documents, which will be considered below.

---

113 See, e.g., Schmitthoff, "International and Procedural Aspects of Letters of Credit" in Horn (ed), *The Law of International Trade Finance* (1989), 227, at 239-41.

114 *American Accord, supra*, note 96, at 1045.

115 This obligation to honour conforming documents is found in art. 9 of the UCP.

116 *Bank of Nova Scotia v. Angelica Whitewear, supra*, note 111, at 70 per Le Dain J.

117 *Supra*, note 96, at 1045; see also *Maurice O'Meara Co. v. National Park Bank of New York*, 146 NE 636, at 639 (1925, NY CA).

E. The Doctrine of Strict Compliance[118]

The bank is also under an obligation to ensure that the documents conform to the instructions contained in the credit;[119] if it fails to do so, it will have acted at its own risk. This duty is owed, not to the beneficiary of the credit, but to the customer who opened it (the buyer). The corollary of this rule is that if the documents are not in conformity with the instructions in the credit, the bank may, and usually will, refuse to accept them since it is otherwise acting at its own risk. A bank examining documents may obtain a waiver of the discrepancies from the customer.[120] The bank has a duty to examine the documents within a reasonable time, not to exceed seven banking days[121] and to give notice of defects within seven banking days.[122]

A short discussion of a few cases that have arisen will serve to illustrate how the concept of the autonomy of the credit and the doctrine of strict compliance have been applied in various circumstances where complex relationships have arisen in international transactions.

In the first place, the duty of strict compliance goes to the form of the documents rather than their substance or ultimate legal effect.[123] In *Gian Singh & Co. Ltd. v. Banque de l'Indochine*,[124] for example, the bank accepted a forged document. The court held that the bank had exercised due care in examining the documents and, in such a case, its customer had to bear this risk. On the other hand, even seemingly minor discrepancies in the documents can give rise to liability on behalf of the bank if it accepts them without its client's approval.[125] In the United States, a more flexible test of "substantial compliance" is put forward in some cases. This approach was rejected by Le Dain J in the *Angelica Whitewear* case,[126] although he did state that there exists "some latitude for minor variations or discrepancies that are not sufficiently material to justify a refusal of payment."[127] Even though the plaintiff in that case had acted on the contract and had taken delivery of the goods (thus ignoring the discrepancy itself), this fact could not excuse the bank for its failure to insist on strict compliance. To hold

---

118 For a fuller discussion of the doctrine see *Schmitthoff, supra*, note 87, at 406 *et seq.*

119 Art. 13 of the UCP500 states: "Banks must examine all documents stipulated in the credit with reasonable care, to ascertain whether or not they appear, on their face, to be in compliance with the terms and conditions of the credit ..." Compliance of the documents with the terms and conditions of the credit is "determined by international standard banking practice as reflected in these Articles." Banks are under no obligation to examine documents not stipulated in the credit.

120 Art. 14(c) of the UCP500 (1993 rev.).

121 UCP500, art. 13.

122 UCP500, art. 14.

123 Art. 15 of the UCP500.

124 [1974] 1 WLR 1234, [1974] 2 All ER 754 (PC).

125 *Banque de l'Indochine et de Suez S.A. v. J.H. Rayner Ltd.*, [1983] QB 711, at 729, [1983] 2 WLR 841, [1983] 1 All ER 1137.

126 *Angelica Whitewear, supra*, note 111.

127 *Ibid.*, at 96.

otherwise would be to ignore the concept of the autonomy of the credit and the client's expectation that the bank would reject non-conforming documents.

If the document is on its face what is called for in the letter of credit in light of an "intelligent" and informed reading by the bank, it appears immaterial that it does not bear the correct title or contain the correct terminology. In *Banco Nacional de Cuba v. Bank of Nova Scotia*,[128] the letter of credit required a quality certificate, but contained no further definition or specification of what constituted such a certificate. Simply because a document describing the characteristics, aspects, properties and attributes of the goods did not contain the terms "quality" or "certificate" did not mean that the document was not a quality certificate and thus in compliance with the terms of the letter of credit. The addition of the descriptive heading "quality certificate" by a bank employee responsible for verifying documentary compliance was not improper and did not alter or amend the document.[129]

However, in another case,[130] involving the issue of recourse by the advising bank against the beneficiary, the BC Court of Appeal upheld the trial judgment rejecting the bank's defence that it had accepted a promissory note under a mistake or other vitiating circumstances. The letter of credit in the case, which concerned a shipment of herring fillets from Vancouver to Rotterdam, required the seller to tender a health certificate tendered by the Canadian Department of Fisheries. The certificate actually tendered by the seller vouched for the quality but not the health of the fish. The Court of Appeal held that the defect in the certificate was patent, rather than latent. Under the circumstances, it was clear that the certificate was not a health certificate and that the bank was estopped from raising the defence of mistake given its prior acceptance of the certificate.

In considering the documents the banker is responsible for knowledge of banking practice but is not required to be familiar with merchant practice[131]—that is, trade terms or other specified knowledge outside of the normal course of business. In the well-known case of *J.H. Rayner & Co. v. Hambros Bank Ltd.*,[132] a confirmed documentary credit was to be provided "available by drafts on this bank at sight accompanied by the following documents—invoice, clean on board bills of lading in complete set issued to order … covering a shipment of about fourteen hundred Coromandel groundnuts in bags at … ." The plaintiff presented the defendant bank a draft accompanied by an invoice for bags of Coromandel groundnuts and three bills of lading in which the goods were described as "bags of machine-shelled groundnuts kernels." While evidence at trial established that "machine-shelled groundnuts kernels" were the same commodity as Coromandel groundnuts and would be "universally understood to be so in the trade in London," the Court of Appeal held that the bank had acted correctly in refusing a bill of lading that was not precisely in accordance with the terms of the credit.

---

128 (1988), 4 OR (3d) 100 (HC), aff'd. (1991), 4 OR (3d) 132 (CA).

129 Contrast with *Re Salomon & Co. v. Naudszuz* (1899), 81 LT 325, in which documents were obviously and materially altered.

130 *Michael Doyle and Associates Ltd. v. Bank of Montreal*, [1984] 5 WWR 193 (BC CA).

131 See *Angelica Whitewear, supra*, note 111.

132 [1943] 1 KB 37, [1942] 2 All ER 694 (CA).

On the other hand, it has been held that where a bank receives a set of documents that, when taken together, satisfies the descriptions set out in the request for credit, this will meet the requirement for strict compliance, even though the bill of lading itself is deficient in some particular.[133] In that case, the letter of credit specifically required a set of documents and the court was of the view that the performance of the bank's duties should be tested against the set of documents which it had received, and not in respect of one document taken in isolation. The bank was therefore liable for failure to honour the credit. Insofar as description is concerned, the commercial invoice is the most important document: in it, the description must correspond with the description in the credit. In other documents, the description must not be inconsistent with the description of the goods in the credit.[134]

Where the description of the goods in the commercial invoice corresponds with the description in the credit, but the description in the bill of lading is inconsistent with the description found in the commercial invoice and the credit, documents were held to be irregular on their face and not in accordance with the terms and conditions of the credit.[135] In this case, although the bank brought certain irregularities in the documentation to the client's attention (which the client approved), it did not point out that the bills of lading referred to the shipment as comprising "oranges and lemons" as opposed to the "oranges" specified in the letter of credit. The court held that the bank should not have accepted the document without the customer's prior approval of the irregularity and was responsible for the consequences.

The cases have established several principles that govern the bank's obligation to act in strict compliance with its instructions. Some important factors to bear in mind are the following:

1. The bank is obliged to ensure that documents conform to their instructions but the "fine print" of the documents does not concern them. Thus, the usual clause in a bill of lading providing that "weight, measure, rates, numbers, quality, contents and value if mentioned in the bill of lading are to be considered as unknown" does not render nugatory the description of the goods in the bill for the purposes of the bank's obligations.[136]
2. A bank may lose its rights to reject non-conforming documents if it does not act within a reasonable period.[137]

---

133 *Midland Bank Ltd. v. Seymour*, [1953] 2 Lloyd's Rep. 147.

134 Art. 37(c) of the UCP500.

135 *69971 Manitoba Ltd. v. National Bank of Canada* (27 March 27 1995) (Man. CA), referring for further consideration [1994] 5 WWR 658 (Man. QB), add. reasons to [1994] 4 WWR 46 (Man. QB); see also *69971 Manitoba Inc. v. National Bank of Canada*, [1992] 3 WWR 673 (Man. CA).

136 *Midland Bank v. Seymour*, [1953] 2 Lloyd's Rep. 147, at 151.

137 *Bank Melli Iran v. Barclays Bank (D.C.O.)*, [1951] 2 Lloyd's Rep. 367, [1951] 2 TLR 1057. Art. 13(b) of the UCP500 states that a bank must examine the documents and inform the customer whether it will take up or refuse the documents within a reasonable time, a maximum of seven days after receipt. While

(The footnote is continued on the next page.)

3. If the bank acts reasonably in the circumstances where there is an ambiguity in the documents it will be protected.[138]
4. A bank rejecting documents must indicate its reasons for doing so to enable the beneficiary to cure any defect prior to the expiry of the credit.[139]
5. Where the documents are non-conforming, the bank may still honour the credit upon the seller furnishing an indemnity or by making payment under reserve.[140]
6. Acknowledging the increased use of particular types of transport bills of lading, such as non-negotiable sea waybills, and combined transport bills of lading accompanying containerization and multimodal transport, articles 23 to 30 of the most recent UCP revision have extensively altered the treatment of transport documents in the context of documentary credits. The UCP500 now contain specific rules dealing with the nature of documentation required for different types of transport documents: marine-ocean bill of lading (article 23);[141] non-negotiable sea waybill (article 24); charter-party bill of lading (article 25);[142] multimodal transport document (article 26);[143] air transport document (article 27); road, rail, or inland waterway transport document (article 28); courier and post receipts (article 29); and transport documents issued by freight forwarders (article 30).[144] These provisions are important and should be closely studied: multimodal transport documentation may not fulfill the requirements for a marine-ocean bill of lading or for an air

---

137 Continued …
there is no preclusion rule under art. 13(b), note that art. 14(d) of the UCP500 sets a seven-day maximum period within which a bank must notify its refusal of the documents to the beneficiary or to the bank from which it received the documents. After this period, the bank is precluded from claiming that the documents are not in compliance with the credit.

138 *Commercial Banking Co. of Sydney Ltd. v. Jalsard Pty. Ltd.*, [1973] AC 279, per Lord Diplock, at 286 and Schmitthoff, *supra*, note 87, at 410.

139 Schmitthoff, *ibid.*, at 411.

140 Art. 14(c) of the UCP500.

141 This provision permits a bill of lading that includes some or all of the terms and conditions of the contract of carriage. Banks will not examine such terms and conditions.

142 The UCP400 (1983 rev.) did not permit a charter-party bill of lading, which does not require the identification of the carrier unless otherwise stipulated in the credit. Banks may thus accept a charter-party bill of lading with or without the name of the carrier.

143 Thus banks will now accept a multimodal transport covering the through movement of goods and their transfer from one mode to another. This reflects consistency with the FIATA Multimodal Transport Bill of Lading, based on the 1992 UNCTAD/ICC *Uniform Rules for Multimodal Transport Documents* (ICC doc. 481). See, e.g., ICC, *UCP500 and 400 Compared* (ICC doc. 511).

144 The provisions on freight forwarder documents do not endorse any particular model or association. Banks will accept any freight forwarder's transport documents provided that (1) it is authorized in the credit, or (2) it is issued and signed by the freight forwarder in accordance with the conditions of the UCP500 articles covering the specific type of transport documents required by the credit. See *UCP500 and 400 Compared* (ICC doc. 511).

transport document in all circumstances.[145] In addition, the UCP500 have special provisions on the requirements for insurance documents and types of cover.

7. The most recent UCP revision accommodates to some extent the replacement of bills of lading and other transport documentation by automated or electronic data transmission.[146]

F. The Interdependence of the Credit and the Underlying Contract

While the cases often emphasize the autonomy of the credit from the underlying contract, one must also bear in mind that, in some cases, there can exist circumstances where the credit transaction may influence the reciprocal rights and obligations of the parties to the underlying contract.

One such example is *W.J. Alan & Co. Ltd. v. El Nasr Export & Import Co.*,[147] where an irrevocable letter of credit was issued by a Spanish bank on behalf of its client specifying "shillings" for the purpose of a contract for the purchase of coffee from Kenya. This letter was confirmed by a Tanzanian bank. The letter of credit was accepted by the Kenyan sellers who then drew upon it at the time of shipment and delivery of documents and accepted payment in English shillings. Subsequently there was a devaluation of English sterling and the question arose as to whether the use of the letter of credit and acceptance of payment of the equivalent English sterling "estopped" the sellers from claiming the balance of the purchase price in Kenyan shillings.

The underlying contract had been made pursuant to the terms and conditions of the London Coffee Trade Federation, which included their standard form FOB contract with an arbitration clause. That contract provided that if payment was to be realized by means of a letter of credit it was to be "in strict conformity with the contract." In this case, the contract called for payment in Kenyan rather than English currency.

In holding that the vendor could not recover the balance of the price arising as a result of the subsequent devaluation, the Court of Appeal had to consider the nature of the letter of credit and whether its delivery was, by itself, "payment" or whether it was only a means of payment. It held that it was, when given, a "conditional payment," that when honoured became final.

The rationale behind this decision lay in an extensive analysis by the court of the doctrine of waiver that led to the conclusion that, since the Spanish buyers had paid in English sterling thinking that that was the full price, it would not be "equitable" to impose an additional cost upon them. Such a concept is closely connected with the

---

145 This is contrary to the situation permitted under art. 26 (b)(i) of the UCP400 (1983 rev.). See Dolan and Van Huizen, *supra*, note 90, at 187.

146 See the definition of "documents" in UCP500, arts. 20 and 21; UCP500, art. 11 appears to permit teletransmitted documents. See also the discussion of international transportation of goods and the automation of international cargo documents in chapter 8, *supra*; Dolan and Van Huizen, *supra*. note 90, at 186*ff.*, and Kozolchyk, "Evolution and Present State of the Ocean Bill of Lading from a Banking Law Perspective" (1992), 23 *J Mar. Law & Com.* 161.

147 [1972] 1 Lloyd's Rep. 313, [1972] 2 WLR 800, [1972] 2 All ER 127.

relationships established by the underlying contract and the effect of the letter of credit on the payment obligations of the buyer must be analyzed in this context.

For the beneficiary of the credit the lesson is clear: if the currency of the letter of credit does not conform to the contract, clear up any misunderstanding prior to obtaining payment. However, because the acceptance of the letter of credit is "conditional" payment only, an intervening event, such as the insolvency of the issuing bank, prior to honouring any draft will interfere with the effecting of that payment, leaving the buyer as primary obligor still liable to make payment under the sale contract.[148] That is not to say, of course, that the seller can "short circuit" the letter of credit and make a claim directly on the buyer in the ordinary case.

Another illustration of the way in which the terms of a letter of credit may affect performance of the underlying contract is the case of *Ficom S.A. v. Sociedad Cadex Limitada*,[149] another coffee case, this time from South America. The underlying contract of sale (a Coffee Trade Federation standard form) provided for payment by irrevocable letter of credit to be opened at a bank at the seller's place of business (Bolivia). In respect of quality, the contract provided that, in the absence of fraud, an adjustment would be made in the purchase price to reflect any difference; the buyer had no right to cancel the contract on that ground. The letter of credit, on the other hand, provided for the delivery of a certificate of quality. This, when provided, did not conform to the specified requirement. The advising bank refused to honour the letter of credit. On arbitration pursuant to the contract, the arbitrators found for the seller in accordance with the provisions of the underlying contract. On a stated case, Robert Goff J, found for the buyer on the ground that the parties had, by their conduct, substituted the terms of the letter of credit for the terms of the original contract that were inconsistent therewith.

In the result, it may be said that parties may vary their contractual terms by the language used in their letter of credit or, where the contract is silent or ambiguous, "may fill the contractual gap and so supplement the terms of the sale contract."[150]

The letter of credit then is a part of the transaction as a whole and its use may affect that operation. An opening of the credit may be a condition precedent to the formation of the contract.[151] Failure to open a credit as provided for in the contract or, in the absence of a specified date, within a reasonable time, may be a condition precedent to the formation of the contract, may constitute a breach of the contract, or even increase the amount of damages normally obtainable under the law applicable to the contract. Illegality of the contract in the place of the buyer and the issuing bank may not serve as defence to an action by the beneficiary against the buyer or the confirming bank.[152]

---

148 *E.D. & F. Man Ltd. v. Nigerian Sweets and Confectionary Co. Ltd.*, [1977] 2 Lloyd's Rep. 50, at 56. See also discussion of such cases as *Sales Continuation Ltd. v. Austin Taylor & Co. Ltd.*, [1967] 2 Lloyd's Rep. 403 in Gutteridge and Megrah, *supra*, note 102, at 35 *et seq.*

149 [1980] 2 Lloyd's Rep. 118.

150 *Ibid.*, at 131.

151 *Toprak Mahsulleri Ofisi v. Finagrain Compagnie Commerciale Agricole et Financière S.A.*, [1979] 2 Lloyd's Rep. 98 (CA) and *Diamond Cutting Works Federation Ltd. v. Triefus & Co. Ltd.*, [1956] 1 Lloyd's Rep. 216.

152 See Graham, "Letters of Credit Basic Considerations" in *Meredith Memorial Lectures* (1982), at 104.

Changes in legislation that affect the ability of one of the parties to perform the contract is clearly a risk of a foreign transaction. If Canadian buyers provide irrevocable letters of credit to their foreign sellers, intervening actions by Canadian authorities restricting the import of the goods because of quotas or for other reasons will probably not relieve them of their obligations under the letter of credit.[153]

The above discussion has been a very limited review of the basic considerations applying to the letter of credit. It has not considered many issues, such as the application for the credit and the nature of the documents involved (particularly insurance documents). The reader is referred to the text of the UCP and to the major works listed in the bibliography for greater detail.

G. Stand-By Letter of Credit

Many international transactions, particularly those involving the delivery of sophisticated and expensive equipment or large construction projects, require the seller to produce a guarantee, either of performance or delivery or, at the time of the bid, by way of a bid bond. In many countries (particularly in the Middle East) the institution of the North American surety company is unfamiliar or unknown and these transactions usually take the form of a guarantee given by an issuing bank in the place of business of the seller, confirmed by a bank in the country of the buyer. These are often referred to as a stand-by letter of credit, bank guarantees, or performance guarantees.

At first, the practice was for banks to issue a standard form confirmed irrevocable letter of credit; subsequent practice, except in the case of US banks, has tended more to the use of a "letter of guarantee," which is analogous in many respects to a letter of credit and is subject to the same legal principles.[154]

A "stand-by" credit, in whatever form, has many of the characteristics of a documentary letter of credit insofar as the liability of the banks, their relationship to their customers, and the rights of the beneficiary (in the case of confirmed irrevocable credit) are concerned. As a transaction, it is the mirror image of the usual documentary letter of credit. It is given as a guarantee by the seller and, thus, the issuing bank is that of the seller rather than the buyer and the confirming bank is in the country of, or is specified by, the buyer.

The standard form commercial letter of credit presents certain difficulties when used in a stand-by situation because the nature of the documents presented to trigger payment are very different. Its continuing popularity may arise from the fact that US banks, prohibited from engaging in the business of providing guarantees or engaging in the surety business, give their "guarantees" in the form of a traditional banking document.[155]

---

153 *Ibid.*, at 115.

154 See, e.g., *Edward Owen Engineering Ltd. v. Barclays Bank International Ltd.*, [1978] 1 All ER 976, [1978] QB 159, [1977] 3 WLR 764 (CA).

155 12 USC, art. 24, 7th power. *Wichita Eagle & Beacon Publishing Co. Inc. v. Pacific National Bank of San Francisco*, 493 F2d 1285 (9th Cir. 1934) and H. Harfield, "The National Bank Act and Foreign Trade Practices" (1948), 61 *Harv. L Rev.* 782, at 789.

While there may at one time have been similar concerns about the powers of Canadian chartered banks to provide such guarantees in a form other than that of a standard letter of credit, these were eliminated by the 1980 revisions to the Bank Act.[156]

Because of the different characteristics of this type of transaction, the ICC issued special Uniform Rules for Contract Guarantees (URCG),[157] that must be specifically incorporated by reference in the guarantee in order to be applicable. The URCG have proved unsatisfactory in several circumstances and are generally not referred to by banks. They obviously would not apply to a standard form letter of credit used in a stand-by situation that by its terms would refer to the UCP. To address certain inadequacies of the ICC-URCG, the ICC has also issued Uniform Rules for Demand Guarantees (URDG).[158] While stand-by letters of credit are technically within the definition of a demand guarantee, the URDG state that it is "expected that issuers of standby credits will continue to use the UCP, which are both more detailed and more appropriate to the particular requirements of standby credits" (at 2).[159] Nevertheless, it is possible if desired to incorporate the URDG into the credit or guarantee. These rules are sufficiently different from the UCP to require careful examination before use.

Payment of the credit may be triggered by simple demand of the purchaser (if it has sufficient bargaining power to insist upon such terms), a factor that has given rise to several contentious situations of fraud or "unjustified calls."[160] The UNCITRAL Draft Convention on International Guaranty Letters[161] when adopted, may remedy the problem of payment of stand-by letters of credit on demand. Acknowledging the utility in some situations of considering the underlying contractual obligations before paying on a stand-by letter of credit or guarantee, it provides for non-payment by the issuer where facts show the demand to be manifestly and clearly improper.

Bank guarantees, the ICC-URCG, the URDG, and the UNCITRAL Draft Convention on International Guaranty Letters are analyzed below in section V.

H. Fraud

The problem of fraud has arisen in cases of documentary and stand-by credits. Even in cases where the courts have refused to interfere with the payment by a bank to the beneficiary upon the application of a buyer disappointed by the seller's performance,

---

156 RSC 1985, c. B-1, s. 173(1)(g), as am.

157 ICC doc. 325 (1978).

158 ICC doc. 458 (1992).

159 Note that the current 1993 revision of the UCP must be explicitly incorporated by reference into the contract.

160 E.g., in *Harbottle v. National Westminster Bank*, [1977] 2 All. ER 862 (QB), the court noted that performance guarantees "are sometimes drawn upon, partly or wholly, without any apparent justification." This risk may be minimized by the inclusion in the credit of a requirement for an affidavit or certificate of non-performance, which would permit subsequent action on the underlying contract to determine whether non-performance actually occurred (see, e.g., Wilton-Siegel, "International Business Agreements: Security for Payment, Part II" (1992), 11 *Nat. Banking L Rev.* 1, at 7.

161 June 1993, doc. A/CN9/374.

express reservation has been made for the case of fraud.[162] The exception is also established in some applicable legislation, such as the UCC, which refers to an exception in the case of fraudulent or forged documents as well as where there is "fraud in the transaction."[163] Current transnational legal formulations of the ICC are largely silent on the issue of fraud. While they emphasize the autonomy of the credit, the ICC UCP500 (1993 revision) do not mention fraud, leaving national courts to determine the scope of the fraud exception. The unsuccessful ICC-URCG[164] made payment on the guarantee conditional upon proof of the principal's default, while the more recent ICC-URDG[165] require merely that the beneficiary submit a statement that default in the underlying transaction has occurred. The ICC-URDG then leave any further fraud-related issues to the discretion of national courts.[166]

Once it is accepted that the presence of fraud may prevent a banker from honouring the letter of credit, three subsidiary questions arise: is the exception limited in documentary cases to situations where the documents themselves are tainted by fraud or may it be extended to fraud in the transaction itself?[167] By whom need the fraud be committed? And what form of proof is required by the bank or, in the event of an injunction application, by the court, given that the request to restrain payment is usually based on evidence supplied exclusively by the "defrauded" party? Many disappointed buyers believe that they have been defrauded when they receive inferior quality goods; clearly, there must be a distinction between a contractual dispute over the quality of the goods and the case of fraud; otherwise, the concept of the autonomy of the credit is significantly eroded. These are generally difficult cases where the court must balance its duty to protect parties from the fraudulent conduct of others with a clear obligation to guarantee the integrity of the letter of credit system, on which the orderly conduct of much of international trade depends.

While the principle is equally applicable to documentary and stand-by credit cases, the circumstances of the latter cases make them particularly difficult. The fraudulent nature of documents may be ascertained, but how does one identify the fraud in a simple demand for payment when the terms of the stand-by credit are that it shall be honoured upon such a demand?

---

162 See, e.g., *Hamzeh Malas & Sons v. British Imex International Ltd.*, [1958] 2 QB 127, comment by Sellers LJ at 130, [1958] 2 WLR 100, [1958] 1 All ER 262 (CA).

163 Art. 5-114(2) of the UCC.

164 ICC doc. 325 (1978).

165 ICC doc. 458 (1992).

166 See, e.g., Dolan, "Commentary on Legislative Developments in Letter of Credit Law" (1993), 8 *BFLR* 52, and 63 to 65.

167 The Ontario Court of Appeal has held that an allegation that a transaction underlying a letter of credit is void *ab initio* due to fraud does not make it void until a final judgment of the court: *Ash v. Lloyd's Corp.* (1992), 9 OR (3d) 755 (CA), rev'g. in part (1991), 6 OR (3d) 235, 87 DLR (4th) 65 (Gen. Div.). Note that the motions court decision appealed from had incorrectly formulated the relationship between the fraud and the autonomy principle as follows: "where fraud is alleged, the autonomy principle no longer applies … ." See (1991), 87 DLR (4th) 65, at 69. For a case comment, see, e.g., Gellert, "Documentary Letters of Credit: Ash v. Lloyd's Corp." (1993), 9 *BFLR* 93.

In an early US case, *Sztejn v. Henry Schroeder Banking Corporation*,[168] a vendor in India shipped "rubbish" instead of bristles of a quality specified in the contract. The purchaser brought a motion to restrain payment on the irrevocable letter of credit that had been issued by the defendant bank in favour of the sellers and that had been drawn upon by them through an Indian advising bank that, in turn, had presented the necessary documents to the defendant bank for payment.

The court, while restating the importance of the independence of the letter of credit transaction from that of the underlying contract and while emphasizing that the issuing bank had no duty to go behind the documents or, indeed, could not be called upon to account if it honoured its credit upon their regular presentment, went on to distinguish this case from that of a classic dispute between a buyer and a seller as to the warranty of the fitness of the goods. Rather, the court was of the view that this was a case in which it had to assume that fraud had been proven and of which the bank had notice prior to honouring the credit. The Indian bank presenting the draft for payment could not be considered a holder in due course but rather "a mere agent for collection for the account of the seller charged with fraud."[169]

Subsequent US cases indicate that the fraud must be perpetrated by the beneficiary of the credit and be material and may extend to conduct beyond altering the documents themselves. Article 5 of the UCC codified these decisions giving a bank acting in good faith the option of not honouring a demand for payment in the event of "fraud, forgery or other defect not apparent on the face of the documents" unless the claim for payment is made by a holder in due course of the credit.[170] Exactly what constitutes "fraud" for this purpose remains somewhat subjective; some cases insisting on a notion of gross fraud, while others take a more liberal view.[171] It is submitted that the best view is that the fraud exception should be limited to those cases where:

> ... the wrongdoing of the beneficiary has so vitiated the entire transaction that the legitimate purposes of the independence of the issuer's obligation would no longer be served.[172]

In the United Kingdom, a narrow view of the fraud exception has been confirmed by the House of Lords in the *American Accord*,[173] a case that holds that it may only be extended to cases where the documents themselves have been tainted by fraud and in circumstances where the beneficiary has not been a party to the falsification of documents,

168 31 NYS (2d) 631 (1941, S Ct.).

169 *Ibid.*, at 635.

170 Art. 5-114(2) of the UCC.

171 Compare *Intraworld Industries Inc. v. Girard Trust Inc.*, 336 A2d 316 (SC Pa., 1975) (a narrow view of fraud) and *United Bank Ltd. v. Cambridge Sporting Goods Corp.*, 392 NYS 2d 265 (CA, 1976) (old, mildewed boxing gloves supplied instead of new ones constitutes fraud). See Harfield, "Code, Customs and Conscience in Letter-of-Credit Law" (1971), 4 *UCCLJ* 7.

172 *Intraworld Industries Inc. v. Girard Bank, ibid.*, at 324 (SC Pa., 1975).

173 *Supra*, note 96. To similar effect, see *Harbottle (R.D.) Mercantile Ltd. v. National Westminster Bank*, [1977] 2 All ER 862, [1977] 3 WLR 752, [1978] QB 146.

even where the "fraudulent" aspect of the document in question is known to the confirming bank when called upon to honour the credit.

In this case, a shipping document was altered by the agent of the shipper to show an earlier loading date. The beneficiary was unaware of the alteration when he presented the documents to obtain the credit and the House of Lords held, reversing the Court of Appeal, that the confirming bank could not, although aware of the misdescription, refuse to honour the credit.

This decision, while in some respects emphasizing the narrowness of the fraud exception, does raise several questions of significance to the relationship between the issuing and confirming banks and has been criticized for putting a bank in the position of having to accept a document that it knows to be false in some particulars, and thus causing unease in banking circles.[174] The case is, however, restricted to a fairly narrow point. Lord Diplock specifically said that it was the lack of knowledge on the part of the beneficiary that enabled him to collect on the letter of credit; if he had known of the alteration, he would have been a party to the misrepresentation and barred from making the claim.[175] Nor did the House of Lords express a view on what the position would have been had the bill of lading, which in this case was valid in all other respects except as to the stated date of sailing, been a complete nullity as a forgery.[176] Presumably in that latter case, a confirming bank would not be obliged to accept a useless document from however innocent a beneficiary as part of its agreement with the beneficiary that the documents are received by way of security for its advance.[177]

The narrowness of the fraud exception in the United Kingdom was recently also apparent in *Society of Lloyd's v. CIBC*.[178] Here, a notice of "possible" fraud was insufficient to release the bank from its obligation to pay out on a stand-by letter of credit.

The Canadian position on the fraud exception in documentary letter of credit cases has been authoritatively laid down by a judgment of Mr. Justice Le Dain in the *Angelica Whitewear* case,[179] already discussed under the doctrine of strict compliance. That case involved complex issues of back-to-back credits established by a Canadian buyer for the acquisition of goods in Hong Kong. The confirming bank had accepted documents pertaining to two shipments and had made payment to the seller in both cases. The Canadian buyer honoured the first payment but prior to the second payment received a shipment of the goods and ascertained that the invoice price had been inflated by some 20 percent. It so advised the bank, alleging fraud, but the bank insisted on making good

---

174 G.W. Smith, "Irrevocable Letters of Credit and Third Party Fraud: *The American Accord*" (1983), 24 *Va. J Int'l. L* 55.

175 *Supra*, note 96, at 1048.

176 *Ibid.*, at 1049.

177 On the bank's liability in regard to documents see art. 17 of the UCP. This case also dealt with the question of illegality of a part of the contract as an exchange control evasion: the "Bretton Woods Point."

178 [1993] 2 Lloyd's Rep. 579 (QB).

179 *Bank of Nova Scotia v. Angelica Whitewear Ltd.*, [1987] 1 SCR 59, 36 DLR (4th) 161, and cases cited therein.

on the call from the Shanghai bank, which had already advanced funds to the seller. The buyer thereupon refused to honour a promissory note that it had given the bank as security for the letter of credit. The Quebec Court of Appeal held that there was fraud of which the bank had been notified and that it therefore had to bear the risk of its advance to the Shanghai bank.

This aspect of the case was reversed in the Supreme Court of Canada. Mr. Justice Le Dain observed that:[180]

> The potential scope of the fraud exception must not be a means of creating serious uncertainty and lack of confidence in the operation of letter of credit transactions; at the same time the application of the principle of autonomy must not serve to encourage or facilitate fraud in such transactions.

Mr. Justice Le Dain canvassed the US and British cases and leaned more closely to the US view that the fraud exception need not be restricted to cases where there is fraud in the documents alone; fraud in the underlying transaction should also vitiate the letter of credit obligation where a beneficiary would be able to obtain the benefit of the credit in circumstances where he or she was a party to that fraud.

Mr. Justice Le Dain recognized the difficulty that a bank has in such cases, given its obligation to honour the credit, and reasoned that a customer would therefore be obliged to demonstrate to the bank an obvious or clear case of fraud. In this case, although the bank had some notice of previous dubious behaviour of the beneficiary, this did not put the bank on notice or impose on it any special obligation in respect of documentary transactions with that person.[181]

The case may thus be said to recognize a "liberal" scope to the fraud exception while limiting the exception to fraud by the beneficiary, protecting certain holders in due course of the beneficiary's draft,[182] and insisting on a degree of proof of fraud that recognizes the bank's obligation to treat the credit obligation autonomously from the underlying contract.[183] The importance of the degree of proof that a court will insist upon in an interlocutory application or require from a bank when its client alleges fraud is, then, a most important element of these cases and will be considered at the end of this section after a short consideration of fraud in stand-by credits.

---

180 *Ibid.*, at 72.

181 See, to the same effect, *Tukan Timber Ltd. v. Barclays Bank PLC*, [1987] 1 Lloyd's Rep. 171.

182 For a recent case addressing, *inter alia*, the issue of "holders in due course" in the context of the fraud exception, see *ATL Industries Inc. v. Han Eol Ind. Co.* (1995), 36 CPC 288 (Ont. Gen. Div.).

183 As has already been noted, the case also deals with the doctrine of strict compliance; the discrepancy in the documents rendered the bank liable. *Angelica Whitewear* has been followed in *Platinum Communications Systems Inc. v. IMAX Corporation and Bank of Nova Scotia* (1988), 31 BCLR (2d) 64. See McDorman, "International Letters of Credit" (1988), 2 *Rev. Int'l. Bus. L* 253. In an interesting situation involving a credit granted to back up a "cohabitation agreement," see *Rosen v. Pullen* (1982), 126 DLR (3d) 62 (Ont. HC), cited in *Yugocanada Inc. v. Terpstra Management Ltd.* (1990), 80 Nfld. & PEIR 345, 249 APR 345 (Nfld. TD), which involved a stand-by letter of credit.

In principle, the application of the fraud exception to stand-by letters of credit or analogous "bank guarantees," presents no different issues from those that arise in the documentary credit cases. Indeed, many judgments have emphasized the fact that the court is applying the normal law to such situations, both insofar as the autonomy of the bank's obligation is concerned and the strict burden of proof demanded of plaintiffs who seek to restrain their issuing banks from honouring the credit they have caused to be opened.

Some differences do arise from the nature of the instrument, however. The stand-by guarantee has traditionally been called upon "simple demand," with no requirement of proof of default on the part of the vendor or contractor whatever. There is thus absent even the "documentary" control in the commercial letter of credit cases and this aspect has certainly contributed to the problems that have arisen.

The classic case in English jurisprudence is *Edward Owen Engineering v. Barclays Bank*[184] where the Court of Appeal refused an injunction in circumstances where a Libyan buyer had called upon a guarantee given by the defendant bank on behalf of the plaintiff-seller (confirmed by a Libyan bank). The Libyan buyer was clearly in default under the contract because it had failed to open an irrevocable letter of credit for the purchase price of the goods that it was obliged to do under the contract and that was the counterpart to the plaintiff's credit.

The Court of Appeal refused to consider that a call in these circumstances amounted to fraud justifying an interference with the normal operation of the credit. Brown LJ observed that fraud had to be "clearly established." Lord Denning MR considered this form of bank guarantee a virtual blank cheque given to the buyer—the equivalent of a discount to the buyer that the supplier probably took into account when setting his price.[185]

This case and many of the principles enunciated in it were adopted in the Ontario case of *Aspen Planners Limited v. Commerce Masonry and Forming Ltd.*,[186] which emphasized the autonomy of the letter of credit from the underlying contract, although it should be said that in that case there was no room for the application of the fraud exception.

The Iranian revolution and the disruption of contracts in Iran that followed it provided considerable litigation in many jurisdictions in which courts had to deal with hard cases where calls were made on stand-by letters of credit or bank guarantees that generally had been given as performance guarantees, and where the Iranian buyer-beneficiary (often a ministry) was in default of its obligations under the contract and yet had made a call, usually through the state-owned Iranian confirming bank. It was obvious in these cases that the seller would have little hope of receiving anything in any action it might commence in Iran under Iranian law (whose law and courts were often specified in these contracts) and thus the independence of the relationship under the underlying transaction was put in a highly favourable light.

---

184 *Edward Owen Engineering Ltd. v. Barclays Bank International Ltd.*, [1978] 1 All ER 976, [1977] 3 WLR 764, [1978] QB 159 (CA).

185 *Ibid.*, at 984 and 982, respectively.

186 (1980), 25 OR (2d) 167, 7 BLR 102.

The US cases[187] fall generally into three categories. The first is where the courts were asked to require a bank to notify any demand received from an Iranian beneficiary and provide a delay during which the seller could seek to provide evidence of fraudulent conduct by the beneficiary. The courts were generally receptive to this approach because it did not prejudice the ultimate disposition of the issue of fraud.[188]

In the second category, more ambitious sellers sought an injunction restraining payment prior to any demand. These applications were generally refused because any irreparable harm was purely conjectural and fraud could not be presumed to exist by virtue only of the unsettled state of affairs in Iran.[189]

The third category involves cases where an injunction was sought after a demand had been made and in circumstances where the beneficiary was clearly in default under the underlying contract (usually in respect of payment). In these cases, the courts generally refused to grant an injunction. In *American Bell International v. Islamic Republic of Iran*,[190] for example, the New York court held that the plaintiff had rights under the contract that, while probably "futile" if sought to be exercised in Iran, could be exercised against Iran in the United States under the Foreign Sovereign Immunities Act.[191] The court was not prepared to find, in the absence of any document that was in itself fraudulent because of an omission or a misrepresentation, any "fraud in the transaction" as alleged by the plaintiff.[192] Of particular interest was the court's recognition of the responsibility of the issuing bank, the harm to its letter of credit system that might follow from an injunction, and the bank's exposure to seizure of its assets in Iran.[193]

Calls on stand-by credits have given rise to litigation in Canada with no consistent approach adopted by the courts. In one Ontario case, the court granted an interlocutory injunction restraining the Bank of Nova Scotia from honouring its guarantee given to the Bank Melli Iran that, at the former's request, had issued an unconditional guarantee payable on simple demand to the Iranian Ministry of War as a "delivery guarantee" under a contract for the delivery of vehicles to Iran.[194] The guarantee was expressly governed by the law of Iran. The court, in granting the injunction, observed that there was evidence before it that the vehicles had been delivered to Iran. A *prima facie* case of fraud had been established by the ministry calling upon the delivery of the guarantee in these circumstances. The court was of the view that the Bank Melli Iran was the mere agent of the Ministry of War and therefore was by law a party to the fraud. In the view of the court, the plaintiff would be unlikely to recover in any action in Iran. While recognizing the need to preserve the integrity of the international banking system and

---

187 See Becker, "Standby Letters of Credit and the Iranian Cases: Will the Independence of the Credit Survive?" (1981), 13 *UCCLJ* 335.

188 See *Stromberg-Carlson Corporation v. Bank Melli Iran*, 467 F Supp. 530 (SDNY 1979).

189 See *KMV International v. Chase Manhattan Bank, N.A.*, 606 F2d 10 (2d. Cir., 1979).

190 474 F Supp. 420 (SDNY, 1979).

191 *Ibid.*, at 423.

192 *Ibid.*, at 423-24.

193 *Ibid.*, at 426.

194 *CDN Research & Development Limited v. Bank of Nova Scotia et al.* (1980), 18 CPC 62 (Ont. HC).

the difficult position of the Bank of Nova Scotia, the court nonetheless was of the view that the plaintiff's likelihood of being defrauded "without any realistic hope of redress is a greater harm than that which is risked by the defendant."[195] Leave to appeal this decision was refused. A Quebec decision reached a similar result.[196]

In a subsequent case involving Iraq, however, the Ontario Divisional Court reversed a decision granting an injunction based partly on an interpretation of the applicability of the UCP to the credit.[197] The court did not consider the UCP applicable in these circumstances and, following *Edward Owen*, expressed the view that "a confirmed performance guarantee is like a promissory note on demand." On the issue of fraud, the court was not of the view that the plaintiff had established a clear *prima facie* case of fraud such as that which had existed in the *Iranian* cases. The court approved the test of a "strong *prima facie*" proof of fraud rather than that of "clear or established" fraud as set out in *Edward Owen*. Here, where the contract was subject to the law of Iraq and the jurisdiction of the Iraqi courts, "the element of unreliability and uncertainty of litigation in certain war-torn parts of the world," while a hardship on the defendant, could not be said to constitute fraud.

This case illustrates the importance of the burden of proof required of a court before granting such an injunction. While the Ontario Divisional Court did not adopt the position of the English Court of Appeal on the burden of proof, it did indicate that in a case of this nature a plaintiff will have to establish a "strong *prima facie*" case. The raising of a "substantial issue" on the authority of *Yule Inc. v. Atlantic Pizza Delight Franchise (1968) Ltd.*[198] is not sufficient. A more recent Ontario case[199] adhered to the "clear and obvious fraud" standard and held the fraud defence to be unsuccessful since neither the allegations nor the materials and documentation relied on were sufficient to constitute clear and obvious fraud established to the knowledge of the banks. In this case, the banks were obliged to conclude that they had an obligation to make payment on the letters of credit.

When considering the degree of proof that should be required by a bank before it refuses to honour a credit, Mr. Justice Le Dain in *Angelica Whitewear* emphasized the obligation of the bank to promptly honour drafts accompanied by apparently conforming documents and affirmed that it could only refuse to pay if proof of the fraud furnished by the person opening the credit was obvious or clear, which is the test set out by Lane LJ in *Edward Owen Engineering*.[200] It is submitted that the bank operates under constraints

---

195 *Ibid.*, at 66.

196 *B.G. Checko International Ltée. v. B.N.P. Canada Inc.* (1982), CS Qué., doc. no. JE 81-922.

197 *CDN Research & Development Limited v. Bank of Nova Scotia et al.* (1981), 32 OR (2d) 578, 122 DLR (3d) 485 (HC), rev'd. in part (1982), 39 OR (2d) 13, 136 DLR (3d) 656 (Div. Ct.).

198 (1977), 17 OR (2d) 505, 80 DLR (3d) 725, 35 CPR (2d) 273.

199 *Royal Bank of Canada v. Darlington* (19 April 1995).

200 [1978] QB 159, at 175. Other recent Canadian cases involving international letters of credit where the party alleging fraud failed to discharge the onus of proof include *Royal Bank of Canada v. Steyr-Forsttechnik GmbH* (10 February 1993) (BC SC) (beneficiary took advantage of a business situation but conduct did not amount to fraud) and *Banco Nacional de Cuba v. Bank of Nova Scotia, supra*, note 128 (so-called suspicious circumstances indicating that beneficiary eager to be paid did not approach the requisite level of clear and obvious fraud).

different from that of a court hearing an interlocutory injunction and that this is another way of phrasing the obligation already referred to as acting reasonably given the circumstances. The burden of proof on a person seeking to fix liability on a bank for payment with notice of fraud will be higher there than that required by our courts. This is a recognition of the bank's need to ensure the integrity of its international credit system.

Because of the problems that have arisen by "unjustifiable calls" on guarantees, the EDC has made available insurance to Canadian banks and other financial institutions to protect them from this form of risk.[201]

I. Choice of Law

Few letters of credit contain a specific choice of law clause. As a result, the system of law to be applied by the courts is that with which the credit has its closest and most real connection. This is called the proper law. As between the buyer and the issuing bank, the proper law is likely to be that of the country in which the bank carries on business and has issued the credit. As between the seller-beneficiary and the issuing or advising or confirming bank, the proper law is likely to be that of the advising or confirming bank where payment is to be made under the letter of credit. It is more difficult to determine the proper law applicable to the relationship between the issuing bank and the advising bank. We suggest that this law should be that of the advising or confirming bank since any controversy between the banks is most likely to relate to the credit issued in favour of the beneficiary.

While the UCP's uniform rules mean that letters of credit are treated similarly in most jurisdictions, the national law applied to the credit concerning matters not falling explicitly or implicitly within the scope of the UCP may, on occasion, lead to different results. The effect of illegality or exchange controls, the concept of frustration or fraud, or even the question of whether the documents presented satisfy the requirement of strict compliance may vary from jurisdiction to jurisdiction. In the *American Accord*, it was the law of England that determined the illegality point and the possibility of partial performance. It is reasonable to assume that if the law of Peru had applied, the entire payment obligation might have been void as part of a scheme to avoid Peruvian exchange control laws. In the case of a sale contract, the term "letter of credit" or "business credit" suggests an irrevocable credit under the UCC, now consistent with the presumption in the UCP500. In the case of stand-by credit by way of bank guarantees, some European jurisdictions apply rules that give rise to defences available in the case of a guarantee that they would not recognize if they characterized the operation as one of a commercial credit. These are only a few examples of how the proper law of the credit might affect it.

As has been pointed out above, there are distinct relationships that give rise to the overall operation of the letter of credit: that between the customer and the issuing bank, that between the beneficiary and the issuing or confirming bank, and that between the banks themselves. It is possible to consider that each of these relationships is governed

201 EDC Information Circular no. 80-1 (rev.), chapter 14, section III, *infra*.

by a different proper law that, due to the autonomy of the credit, may not be the same as the proper law of the underlying contract.

Perhaps because of these complex possibilities, the UCP500 provides no choice of law rules for documentary credits. The rules for bank guarantees foresee the application of the law of the place of the guarantor (or the issuing branch, if the bank has more than one place of business), in the absence of a specific choice of law by the parties.

Court decisions indicate that, at least in the case of documentary credits and in the absence of a specific choice of law clause, it is the law of the place of payment that governs the obligations of the issuing bank.[202] As a result, illegality under the latter's national law, or a restraining order issued by its courts, will not usually be an effective stop to a claim for payment by a beneficiary.

In the case of *Power Curber International Ltd. v. National Bank of Kuwait S.A.K.*,[203] the English Court of Appeal held that the proper law of the obligation of a Kuwait bank that, at the request of its client, had issued a letter of credit in favour of a North Carolina seller of goods who had been advised through a North Carolina bank acting on instructions from the Bank of America in Miami, was the law of North Carolina. Both Lord Denning and Lord Justice Griffiths were of the view that the law of North Carolina as the law of the place of performance was the proper law of the bank's obligation. Lord Denning went further and observed that letters of credit were unlike normal debts and that the *lex situs* of this debt was not the place of residence of the debtor but rather North Carolina as the place where the bank was obliged to pay upon presentation of the documents. Since letters of credit are like bills of exchange and do not allow any set off or counter-claim, the court refused to recognize an injunction issued by the Kuwait courts restraining the Kuwait bank from honouring the credit because of other obligations owed by the North Carolina seller to the Kuwait buyer. The Kuwait bank's restraining order was considered to be contrary to internationally accepted principles.

This case illustrates another matter that the practitioner must bear in mind: the flexibility provided for relief in modern commercial circumstances where business is carried on simultaneously in many jurisdictions. In *Power Curber*, the North Carolina seller could not recover from the local bank; it was not a confirming bank and had not been put in funds by the issuing bank. It therefore discontinued the action it had originally brought there and brought action in London where the issuing bank had a branch and assets.[204] Given the number of branches and agencies in London or New York, the opportunity for forum shopping in cases of this nature is substantial. There is also a lesson in this for Canadian banks. If our courts grant injunctions too liberally in fraud cases or in other circumstances that will not be recognized by other jurisdictions, the banks may well be obligated to make payment in another jurisdiction where they carry on business. This risk of double jeopardy should be borne in mind by our courts when considering the desirability of harmonizing our rules with those of our principal trading partners.

---

202 E.g., *Offshore International v. Banco Central (Offshore)*, [1976] 3 All ER 749.

203 *Supra*, note 73. For a recent case that similarly held that the law of the place of payment was the proper law, see: *Bank of Baroda v. The Uysya Bank Ltd.*, [1994] 2 Lloyd's Rep. 87.

204 English courts will accept jurisdiction under their rules in these circumstances.

With respect to choice of forum, it appears courts have also followed the approach of the place of performance or payment.[205]

V. GUARANTEES GIVEN BY BANKS, INSURANCE COMPANIES, OR OTHER THIRD PARTIES

A. General Principles

In this section, the word guarantee means a primary and independent undertaking by the guarantor, at the request of the principal, to pay a stipulated sum of money to a named or stipulated beneficiary if the conditions of the guarantee are satisfied.

Guarantees may be simple or first demand guarantees whereby the guarantor must pay claims upon the beneficiary's request or upon simple presentation of an agreed set of documents without independent evidence of the validity of such claims. Guarantees may also be conditional guarantees whereby the obligation of the guarantor depends upon the fulfillment of a condition or the happening of a certain event. Simple or first demand guarantees are most frequently used, although when procured by the seller, they involve the risk that the foreign buyer might make a claim that is wholly unjustified in the circumstances.

There are many types of guarantees, bonds, indemnities, and sureties or similar undertakings given by banks, insurance companies, and other third parties. The most commonly used are the tender guarantee (tender bond, bid bond) to provide an assurance of the intention of the party submitting the tender to sign the contract if the tender is accepted; the performance guarantee, which is used as a safeguard against the party to whom the contract is awarded failing to meet his or her obligations under such contract; the repayment guarantee, which protects the interest of the party awarding the contract in respect of the repayment of payments or advances made by him or her in the event of the principal not fulfilling the contract terms; the counter-guarantee, where the seller obtains a guarantee from his or her bank and that bank gives the guarantee to a bank in the buyer's country which then gives this buyer a counter-guarantee; and the super-guarantee, where the buyer obtains, besides the guarantee of the seller's bank, the guarantee of another better-known bank.

Bank guarantees that are issued in Canada by banks subject to the *Bank Act*,[206] may be procured by the buyer for the benefit of the seller if, for example, no letter of credit is issued in the seller's favour or no payment is made in the manner and at the time

---

205 See *Ash v. Lloyd's Corp.* (1992), 9 OR (3d) 755 (CA), rev'g. in part (1991), 6 OR (3d) 235 (Gen. Div.). Although the case deals with an exclusive jurisdiction clause, the court stated: "Even without the exclusive jurisdiction clauses, the contracts are to be performed in England, the alleged wrongful conduct was on the part of a large number of English residents who carry out the day-to-day functions under Lloyd's jurisdiction, and the overall picture is of an overwhelming affinity with England … ." See, however, *Can. Pioneer Petroleum v. F.D.I.C.* (1985), 25 BLR 1 (Sask. QB), where the court held that it had no jurisdiction to hear proceedings for injunctive relief against payment on a letter of credit even though it was the jurisdiction of payment.

206 SC 1991, c. 46, as am.

stipulated in the contract of sale. They may also be procured by the seller in order to protect the buyer against non performance.[207]

The bank enters into an absolute undertaking and must pay even if the principal objects, unless the demand made by the beneficiary is fraudulent and he or she knew of the fraud.

The law applicable to the guarantee is that determined by the private international law rules in force in the forum where the dispute between the guarantor and the beneficiary is pending.

B. ICC Uniform Rules for Contract Guarantees

In 1978, the International Chamber of Commerce (ICC) issued a set of URCG in order to secure "a uniformity of practice based upon an equitable balance between the interests of the parties concerned while observing the commercial purpose of the guarantee, that is, to ensure the availability of funds with an independent third party in the event of the beneficiary having a justified claim against the principal."[208]

Under the 1978 URCG, the beneficiary has to present a court judgment or arbitral award in order to obtain judgment under the guarantee. The rules do not provide for simple or first demand guarantees, which do not require the beneficiary to evidence their claim to payment under the guarantee, on the premise that international trade conducted on the basis of contract guarantees should develop in an atmosphere of confidence. Also excluded from the rules are the nature of the guarantee—that is, whether it is a primary and independent obligation or a secondary and accessory one—and the relationship between the principal and the guarantor. The application of the rules is voluntary.

The URCG apply to various types of guarantee (article 2): tender guarantees,[209] performance guarantees,[210] and repayment guarantees.[211]

---

207 See *Edward Owen Engineering Ltd. v. Barclays Bank International Ltd.*, [1978] QB 159, which involved a demand performance guarantee given by the seller.

208 (1978), pub. no. 325, at 8. The rules have been supplemented by ICC Uniform Rules for Demand Guarantees (1992), pub. no. 458.

209 I.e., an undertaking given by a bank, insurance company, or other party ("the guarantor") at the request of a tenderer ("the principal") or given on the instructions of a bank, insurance company, or other party so requested by the principal ("the instructing party") to a party inviting tenders ("the beneficiary") whereby the guarantor undertakes—in the event of default by the principal in the obligations resulting from the submission of the tender—to make payment to the beneficiary within the limits of a stated sum of money.

210 An undertaking given by a bank, insurance company, or other party ("the guarantor") at the request of a supplier of goods or services or other contractor ("the principal") or given on the instructions of a bank, insurance company, or other party so requested by the principal ("the instructing party") to a buyer or to an employer ("the beneficiary") whereby the guarantor undertakes—in the event of default by the principal in due performance of the terms of a contract between the principal and the beneficiary ("the contract")—to make payment to the beneficiary within the limits of a stated sum of money or, if the guarantee so provides, at the guarantor's option, to arrange for performance of the contract.

(Footnote 211 appears on the next page.)

The guarantor is liable to the beneficiary only in accordance with the terms and conditions specified in the guarantee and the rules, and up to an amount not exceeding that stated in the guarantee. This amount cannot be reduced by reason of any partial performance of the contract unless so specified in the guarantee. Finally, the guarantor may rely only on those defences that are based on the terms and conditions specified in the guarantee or are allowed under the rules.[212]

The URCG also deal with, *inter alia*, the last date by which a claim must be received by the guarantor,[213] the expiry of guarantees,[214] the return of guarantees,[215] amendments to contracts and guarantees,[216] how to submit a claim,[217] and the documentation required to support it.[218]

When a guarantee does not indicate the law by which it is to be governed, the applicable law is that of the country where the guarantor has its place of business. If the guarantor, for example, a bank, has more than one place of business, the applicable law is that of the country where the branch issued the guarantee.[219] This law will apply to matters that are not covered by the rules. The applicable law is not the one that governs the basic contract because it is not always possible to determine such law accurately and the obligation that characterizes the guarantee operation is that of the guarantor. Furthermore, in some countries, the guarantor can only issue guarantees according to its own national law.

Last, the URCG provide for the settlement of disputes between the guarantor and the beneficiary relating to the guarantee. In the absence of an arbitration clause or choice of jurisdiction clause, such disputes shall be settled exclusively by the competent court of the country where the guarantor's place of business is located or, if the guarantor has more than one place of business by the competent court of the country where its main place of business is located or, at the option of the beneficiary, by the competent court of the country where the branch that issued the guarantee is located.[220] The purpose of these provisions is to prevent the parties from being exposed to the jurisdiction of the courts of several countries.

---

211 An undertaking given by a bank, insurance company or other party ("the guarantor") at the request of a supplier of goods or services or other contractor ("the principal") or given on the instructions of a bank, insurance company or other party so requested by the principal ("the instructing party") to a buyer or to an employer ("the beneficiary") whereby the guarantor undertakes—in the event of default by the principal to repay in accordance with the terms and conditions of a contract between the principal and the beneficiary ("the contract") any sum or sums advanced or paid by the beneficiary to the principal and not otherwise repaid—to make payment to the beneficiary within the limits of stated sum of money.

212 Art. 3.

213 Art. 4.

214 Art. 5.

215 Art. 6.

216 Art. 7.

217 Art. 8.

218 Art. 9.

219 Art. 10.

220 Art. 11.

Because they do not apply to "demand guarantees," preferred by beneficiaries for their relative flexibility, the URCG have not been successful and have not enjoyed broad or general use.

C. ICC Uniform Rules for Demand Guarantees

Issued by the ICC in 1992, the URDG[221] supplement (but do not for the moment replace) the 1978 URCG. The URDG are intended to provide a uniform regime for the use of demand guarantees—that is, guarantees, bonds, and other written payment undertakings by a bank, insurance company, or other body or person, under which the duty of the guarantor or issuer to make payment arises on the presentation of a written demand and any other documents (for example, architect's or engineer's certificate, judgment, or arbitral award) specified in the guarantee, and is not conditional on actual default by the principal in the underlying transaction.[222] The URDG also apply to counter-guarantees.[223] Excluded from the scope of the rules are suretyship or conditional bonds or guarantees requiring the guarantor to pay only on actual default by the principal. In addition, the drafters of the URDG intended that issuers of stand-by letters of credit should continue to use the UCP, which they believe provide a more detailed and appropriate regulatory code.

The URDG deal with scope and application of the rules, definitions and general provisions, liabilities and responsibilities, demands, expiry provisions, and governing law and jurisdiction.

Under the URDG, the guarantor does not consider the issue of whether the principal and beneficiary have actually fulfilled their obligations in the underlying transaction. The guarantor's standard for examination of documents to ascertain whether they conform with the terms of the guarantee is one of "reasonable care."[224] The guarantor has a reasonable time to examine a demand under a guarantee and to decide whether to pay or refuse the demand.[225] Under the URDG, the guarantor and instructing party assume no liability and responsibility for the form, sufficiency, accuracy, genuineness, or legal

221 See, e.g., Goode, "The New International Chamber of Commerce Uniform Rules for Demand Guarantees," [1992] *LMCLQ* 190.

222 See Introduction to URDG, ICC pub no. 458. URDG, art. 2(a) contains the definition of a demand guarantee.

223 URDG, art. 2(c) defines "counter-guarantee" as "any guarantee, bond or other payment undertaking of the Instructing Party, however named or described, given in writing for the payment of money to the Guarantor on presentation in conformity with the terms of the undertaking of a written demand for payment and other documents specified in the counter-guarantee which appear on their face to be in accordance with the terms of the counter-guarantee. Counter-guarantees are by their nature separate transactions from the guarantees to which they relate and from any underlying contracts or tender conditions and Instructing Parties are in no way concerned or bound by such guarantees, contracts or tender conditions, despite the inclusion of a reference to them in the counter-guarantee."

224 URDG, art. 9.

225 *Ibid.*, art. 10.

effect of documents presented to them;[226] for consequences arising out of delay or loss in transit of messages, demands, or documents;[227] or for instructions they transmit that are not carried out.[228] These exemptions from liability do not exclude responsibility for failure to act in good faith and with reasonable care.[229]

The URDG are less onerous than the URCG on the beneficiary, because they do not require the presentation of a judgment or arbitral award, unless the guarantee so requires. Nevertheless, guarantees incorporating this requirement would still fall within the rules. URDG, article 20 requires a beneficiary's written demand or claim to be accompanied by the beneficiary's statement objectively outlining the manner in which the principal is in default. The beneficiary is free to exclude or modify this article, allowing parties the flexibility to structure their relationship to suit their needs. The issuer must notify the applicant of the demand immediately.[230]

The URDG balance the interests of the beneficiary and the principal: they provide the beneficiary with quick access to funds if the principal fails to fulfill his or her obligations in the underlying transaction, while also protecting the principal from abusive and unfair demands by allowing the principal to be informed in writing how he or she has allegedly breached his or her obligations.

The application of the URDG is voluntary: they must be explicitly incorporated into the guarantee in order to apply. The parties may explicitly exclude or modify their URDG obligations in order to tailor their agreement to suit their particular requirements.

A guarantor is liable to the beneficiary only in accordance with the terms specified in the guarantee and in the rules, and liability is limited to the amount of the guarantee.[231] URDG, article 8 allows reduction of the amount of the guarantee by specified amounts on specified dates upon tender of the requisite documents.

The URDG provisions on choice of law and choice of jurisdiction preserve party autonomy, allowing the parties to select their law and forum. In the absence of an express choice by the parties, however, the governing law is that of the place of business of the guarantor or instructing party or, where there is more than one place of business, of the branch that issued the guarantee or counter-guarantee.[232] As for choice of jurisdiction, failing an explicit stipulation in the guarantee or counter-guarantee, the forum for disputes between the guarantor and beneficiary concerning the guarantee or between the issuer and instructing party regarding the counter-guarantee are the courts of the place of business of the guarantor or instructing party. Where there is more than one place of business, the forum is the country of the branch that issued the guarantee or counter-guarantee.[233]

226 *Ibid.*, art. 11.

227 *Ibid.*, art. 12.

228 *Ibid.*, art. 14(b).

229 *Ibid.*, art. 15.

230 *Ibid.*, art. 21.

231 *Ibid.*, art. 16.

232 *Ibid.*, art. 27.

233 *Ibid.*, art. 28.

Under the URDG, the expressions "writing" and "written" include an authenticated teletransmission or tested EDI message equivalent.

D. UNCITRAL Draft Convention on International Guaranty Letters

The UNCITRAL Draft Convention aims to provide a uniform substantive regime governing international guarantee letters and stand-by letters of credit.[234] The Draft Convention attempts to harmonize with existing international legal rules concerning this domain, such as the UCP500 and the URDG of the ICC. It is still under negotiation.

The Draft Convention applies to international guarantee letters issued in contracting states. A guarantee letter is an independent undertaking given by a bank or other institution or person (the "issuer") to pay to another person (the "beneficiary") a certain or determinable amount of a specified currency, or unit of account, or other item of value (or to accept a bill of exchange for a specified amount) in conformity with the terms and conditions of the undertaking when so demanded according to the terms of the undertaking. Such an instrument is international where at least two of the issuers, beneficiary, and principal or instructing party are located in different states.

In addition to its scope of application, the Draft Convention also covers interpretation; effectiveness of guarantee letters; rights, obligations, and defences; provisional court measures; jurisdiction; and conflicts of law.

With respect to abusive calls against letters of credit, the Draft Convention recognizes the need to examine underlying contractual obligations in certain situations. The issuer need not make payment on the guarantee if it is shown facts that make the demand manifestly and clearly improper.[235] The convention enumerates a list of circumstances in which the issuer may refuse payment based on improper demand.

The parties may tailor the terms and conditions of guarantee letters, as long as they abide by the mandatory provisions of the Draft Convention. Unless the parties otherwise agree, "generally accepted international rules and usages of guarantee or standby letters of credit will be implied into the agreement."[236] The issuer must act in good faith and

---

234 For a description of the Draft Convention, see Bergsten, "A New Regime for International Independent Guaranties and Standby Letters of Credit: the UNCITRAL Draft Convention on Guaranty Letters" (1993), 27 *Int. Lawyer* 859 and Jones, "UNCITRAL Draft Convention on International Guaranty Letters" (1994), 22 *Int. Bus. Lawyer* 28. See also UNCITRAL reports: 12th sess. A/CN.9/316; 13th sess. A/CN.9/330; 14th sess. A/CN.9/342 and A/CN.9/WG.II/WP.68; 15th sess. A.CN.9/345 and A/CN.9/WG.II/WP.70; 16th sess. A/CN.9/358 and A/CN.9/WG.II/WP.73 and add. 1; 17th sess. A/CN.9/361 and A/CN.9/WG.II/WP.73 and add. 1; 18th sess. A/CN.9/372 and A/CN.9/WG.II/WP76 and add. 1; and 19th sess. A/CN.9/374 and corr. 1.

235 Another option considered by the UNCITRAL Working Group as a basis for non-payment read: "The issuer shall not make payment if, having due regard to the independent and documentary character of the undertaking, it is "clear and beyond doubt" to the issuer that the demand is improper." See Jones, "UNCITRAL Draft Convention on International Guaranty Letters" International Business Lawyer, *supra*, note 234.

236 Art. 12(1).

exercise reasonable care. As under the URDG, the Draft Convention excludes exemption from liability for bad faith or gross negligence.

The rules in the Draft Convention on preliminary injunctions, requiring the party seeking the injunction to demonstrate that the demand is manifestly improper, are necessarily limited, respecting the autonomy of national legal procedures.

Concerning choice of law and forum, the Draft Convention preserves party autonomy. In the absence of express choice by the parties, the law governing an independent guarantee is that of guarantor's place of business. Absent express choice by the parties, the forum for disputes between the issuer and beneficiary will be courts of state where guarantee letters were issued.

Permitting the use of electronic data interchange (EDI), the Draft Convention defines a "document" as any communication made in a form that provides "a complete record thereof."[237]

VI. MISCELLANEOUS METHODS OF FINANCING

In addition to the traditional international trade financing techniques discussed in sections II, III, and IV, banks and finance houses also make available to exporters and importers more modern and flexible financing procedures, such as non-recourse finance, factoring, financial leasing, and forfaiting.

A. Non-Recourse Finance

In a typical non-recourse finance transaction,[238] the finance house enters into two contracts, one with the exporter and one with the importer both involving the same export transaction. In the first contract, the finance house undertakes to pay the exporter at once the purchase price in full less any deposit given by the importer to the exporter. The payment is to be made on delivery of specified transport documents to the finance house. The contract stipulates that the finance house is not responsible for any claim arising out of or in connection with the export transaction whether made by the exporter against the importer or vice versa. It also provides for a particular and general lien in favour of the finance house. In the second contract, the importer undertakes, upon presentation of the transport documents, to pay the finance house the purchase price and the charges it has incurred, less the deposit given to the exporter. The other clauses are similar to those found in the first contract.

In this type of financing, the financial house accepts the financial risk of the transaction. It does not share it with the exporter. However, like the bank issuing a letter of credit, the finance house is not concerned with the goods that are the subject matter of the export transactions.

237 Art. 6.

238 See Schmitthoff, *supra*, note 87, at 466 *et seq*.

B. Factoring

Small- and medium-sized Canadian firms often resort to international factoring[239] to finance their exports and to collect foreign debts.[240] They sell the short-term debts (approved receivables) owed to them by the importer to a factor without recourse, in order to obtain cash immediately (in which case their value is usually discounted); regularly on a calculated average settlement date; or as the debts mature (pay as paid factoring); and to be protected against bad debts. If the factoring contract is with recourse, the factor has a claim against the exporter for indemnification should the importer fail to pay.

In Canada, part IX of the Bank Act provides that, with certain restrictions, a bank may acquire and carry out factoring activities through a "factoring Corporation."[241]

In general, where there are no factoring services available in the country of import, factoring is direct. Upon assignment of the claim for the price, the factor in the country of export deals directly with the importer. Otherwise, two factors are involved: a factor located in the country of export and a factor located in the country of import. Factoring is indirect. The factor located in the country of import makes a second assignment[242] to the factor located in the country of export who assesses the accounts receivable and the credit risk involved and, upon notification to the debtor of both assignments, collects these accounts and assumes the risk of default in payment. The factor located in the country of export pays the exporter on a non-recourse basis if it is so provided in the factoring contract, unless the exporter has acted fraudulently. No contractual relationship exists between the exporter and the factor located in the country of import. The two factors then settle their accounts.

The factoring contract, which is separate from the supply contract, is governed by its proper law. It is usually that of the place where the factor carries on business.

The factoring contract may or may not be disclosed to the importer. If it is disclosed, it amounts to a legal assignment of debt that must meet the requirements of the law applicable to it. An undisclosed factoring contract[243] constitutes an equitable assignment of the debt that may not be recognized as valid by the law applicable to it. To be on the safe side, it is better to notify in writing the assignment of the debt to the importer-debtor as soon as possible. In most legal systems, this notification gives the factor priority over other secured creditors of the debtor.

---

239 An international factor does not fall within the definition of "mercantile agent" in the *Factors Act*, RSO 1990, c. F.1, s. 1(1).

240 For a general overview of factoring, see, e.g., Jaeger, "Export Factoring and Forfaiting" in Horn (ed.), *The Law of International Trade Finance* (1989), at 277.

241 SC 1991, c. 46, ss. 464 *et seq*. A "factoring corporation" means a body corporate the activities of which are limited to acting as a factor in respect of accounts receivable, which activities include the raising of money for the purpose of acting as a factor and the lending of money while acting as such a factor.

242 The factoring contract may prohibit subsequent assignments.

243 E.g., invoice discounting on a recourse basis.

1. *The 1988 Convention on International Financing*[244]

The convention, prepared by the International Institute for the Unification of Private Law (UNIDROIT), was adopted by a Diplomatic Conference at Ottawa on May 28, 1988. It entered into force on May 1, 1995. Canada has not yet signed the convention.

The convention aims to facilitate and simplify factoring as a method of trade finance by providing a uniform substantive code to foster legal certainty and overcome differences and shortcomings in national legal systems. The convention is not comprehensive, and thus must still be supplemented in some areas by national laws. It applies to a factoring contract whether disclosed or not to the debtor whereby:[245]

(a) the supplier may or will assign to the factor receivables arising from contracts of sale of goods made between the supplier and its customers (debtors) other than those for the sale of goods bought primarily for their personal, family or household use;

(b) the factor is to perform at least two of the following functions:

—finance for the supplier, including loans and advance payments;
—maintenance of accounts (ledgering) relating to receivables;
—collection of receivables;
—protection against default in payment by debtors.

The receivables assigned to the factor must arise from a contract of sale of goods between a supplier and a debtor whose places of business are in different states and (1) those states and the state in which the factor has its place of business are contracting states, or (2) both the contract of sale of goods and the factoring contract are governed by the law of a contracting state.[246]

An assignment of receivables from the supplier to the factor is effective even though it is prohibited by agreement between the supplier and the debtor.[247]

The debtor has all the same defences and rights of set-off against the factor as it could have raised against the supplier.[248] In case of default by the supplier, the debtor's right of recovery from the factor is limited.[249]

Finally, it should be noted that the convention does not deal with questions of priority of competing claims to receivables.

C. Financial Leasing

1. *General Principles*

The long-term, cross-border leasing of capital goods, such as aircraft or heavy equipment, to a foreign lessee may be financed by banks and finance houses when the lessor

244 (1988), 27 *Int'l. Leg. Mat.* 923, at 943 and Goode, [1988] *JBL* 510. The Uniform Law Conference of Canada has prepared draft uniform legislation for implementing the convention: 1995 *Proceedings* 156.

245 Art. 1(2).

246 Art. 2(1).

247 Art. 6, but see art. 18.

248 Art. 9.

249 Art. 10.

does not wish to accept any financial risk. The owner of the goods, called the supplier, instead of acting as lessor sells them, usually for cash, to a bank or financial house called the creditor, who leases them to the lessee called the debtor. Two agreements are generally concluded: the supply agreement between the lessor-creditor and the supplier and the leasing agreement between the lessor-creditor and the lessee-debtor. The lessor-creditor who does not take delivery of the goods from the supplier is their legal owner and receives rental payments from the lessee-debtor.

Possession of the goods leased reverts to the lessor-creditor when the lease comes to an end unless the lessee-debtor has the option of acquiring the property in the leased goods.

The advantage of financial leasing is that the supplier of the goods is paid immediately.

In Canada, the Bank Act[250] provides that a bank may, subject to certain restrictions, acquire and carry out financial leasing operations through a subsidiary financial leasing corporation.

The agreements must be valid by their proper law.

2. *The 1988 Convention on International Financial Leasing*[251]

The convention was prepared by the International Institute for the Unification of Private Law (UNIDROIT) and adopted by a diplomatic conference at Ottawa on May 28, 1988. This convention entered into force on May 1, 1995, but Canada has not yet signed it.

Its main objective is to place liability to the lessee-debtor for loss caused by non-delivery, late delivery, or delivery of non-conforming equipment on the supplier and not on the lessor-creditor, who only has a financial interest in the lease, unless the loss is caused by the reliance of the lessee-debtor on the skill and judgment of the lessor-creditor or the lessor-debtor has intervened in the selection of the supplier or the equipment.[252] The lessor-creditor, as such, is not liable to third parties for death, personal injury, or damage to property caused by the equipment leased,[253] although it may be liable as owner.[254] Furthermore, the lessor-creditor is not responsible for a default by virtue of non-delivery, late delivery, or delivery of non-conforming equipment to the lessee-debtor, unless it is caused by an act or omission of the lessor-creditor.[255] The lessee must care for the equipment.[256] As for the supplier, its obligations under the supply contract are equally owed to both the lessor-creditor and the lessee-debtor, although it cannot be liable to both in respect of the same damage.[257]

---

250 SC 1991, c. 46, ss. 464 *et seq.*

251 (1988), 27 *Int'l. Leg. Mat.* 923, at 931 and Goode, [1988] *JBL* 347. The Uniform Law Conference of Canada has prepared draft uniform legislation for implementing the convention: 1995 *Proceedings* 160.

252 Art. 8(1)(a).

253 Art. 8(1)(b).

254 Art. 8(1)(c).

255 Art. 12(5).

256 Art. 9(1).

257 Art. 10.

The convention governs the supply agreement between the lessor-creditor and the supplier and the leasing agreement between the lessor-creditor and the lessee-debtor.[258] The convention also deals, *inter alia*, with the rights of the lessor-creditor and the lessee-debtor under the leasing agreement[259] and the lessee-debtor's insolvency.[260]

For the convention to apply to a financial leasing transaction,[261] the lessor-creditor and the lessee-debtor must have their place of business in different states, and these states and the state in which the supplier has its place of business must be contracting states, or both the supply agreement and the leasing agreement must be governed by the law of a contracting state.[262]

D. Forfaiting

Forfaiting is a financial technique often used by exporters to meet the credit demands of importers for long-term credit periods that free exporters from the risks attached to such credit.

The forfaiter, usually a bank, finance house, or discount company, purchases at discount from the creditor on a non-recourse basis, a debt expressed in a negotiable instrument that matures at a some future date. This technique enables the creditor to obtain immediate payment of a long-term debt or one payable in installments. The forfaiter assumes the exchange rate risk and faces the impossibility of acceleration of the due date for the negotiable instrument should the importer default.[263]

The forfaiter will only purchase the debt on a non-recourse basis if security is given by a third party, preferably a well-known bank, in the form of an aval stamped on the negotiable instrument signed by the avalising third party, or in the form of a separate bank guarantee, or stand-by letter of credit issued in the forfaiter's favour that the instrument will be paid at maturity.

In an export transaction, the negotiable instrument will be avalised by a bank in the importer's country or that bank will guarantee its performance.

The exporter will then negotiate the negotiable instrument to his or her own bank without recourse by that bank to him or her. The forfaiting arrangement agreed upon in

---

258 Art. 1.

259 Arts. 12 and 13.

260 Art. 7.

261 See art. 12, which describes its characteristics:

> (a) the lessee specifies the equipment and selects the supplier without relying primarily on the skill and judgment of the lessor; (b) the equipment is acquired by the lessor in connection with a leasing agreement which, to the knowledge of the supplier, either has been made or is to be made between the lessor and the lessee; and (c) the rentals payable under the leasing agreement and calculated so as to take into account in particular the amortization of the whole or a substantial part of the cost of the equipment.

262 Art. 3(1).

263 See Wilton-Siegel, "International Business Agreements: Security for Payment, Part II" (1992), 11 *NBLR* 1, at 4 and 5.

the export contract can only be carried out if the exporter has obtained the prior agreement of his or her bank that it will forfait the negotiable instrument and the importer also has obtained the prior agreement of his or her bank that it will avalise or guarantee such negotiable instrument.

In Canada, the avalizer is in the same legal position as an endorser.[264] In countries where the aval does not exist, a separate bank guarantee must be used, which puts the guarantor in the same position as the principal debtor.

The security supporting the negotiable instrument that is purchased by the forfaiter is autonomous. It does not depend upon the incidents concerning the underlying export transaction. However, the non-recourse clause does not protect the seller if he or she was involved in a fraud.

When the forfaiter renegotiates the negotiable instrument he or she has purchased, difficult legal problems may arise.

Since the aval is not known in all legal systems, it is important to include a choice of law clause in the contract between the exporter and the forfaiter as well as in the guarantee that the third party gives the forfaiter that calls for the application of a law that recognizes an aval, which operates as an irrevocable and unconditional guarantee, so that the avalising third party will be primarily liable for payment at maturity.

VII. SELECTED BIBLIOGRAPHY

A. Books

Baxter, *International Banking and Finance* (1989).

Cox and Mackenzie, *International and Factoring* (1986).

Davis, *The Documentary Credits Handbook* (1988).

Dolan, *The Law of Letters of Credit* (2nd ed., 1991).

Guild, *Forfaiting: An Alternative Approach to Export Trade Finance* (1985).

Gutteridge and Megrah, *The Law of Banker's Commercial Credits* (6th ed., 1979).

Hedley, *Bills of Exchange and Bankers' Documentary Credits* (1986).

Horn (ed.), *The Law of International Trade Finance* (1989).

Insight, *Letters of Credit* (1989).

International Chamber of Commerce, *Bills of Exchange* (1990).

International Chamber of Commerce, *Case Studies on Documentary Credits* (doc. 459, 1989).

International Chamber of Commerce, *Case Studies on Documentary Credits* (doc. 535, 1995)

---

264 S. 131 of the Bills of Exchange Act, RSC 1985, c. B-4 seems to recognize the aval. See *Gallagher v. Murphy*, [1929] 2 DLR 124, [1929] SCR 288.

International Chamber of Commerce, *Documentary Credits. Standard Documentary Credit Application Guidance Notes for Credit Applicants* (doc. 416A, 1986).

International Chamber of Commerce, *Documentary Credits, Standard Documentary Credit. Forms—Guidance Notes—Recommendations* (doc. 416, 1986).

International Chamber of Commmerce, *Documentary Credits—UCP 500 and 400 Compared* (doc. 511, 1993).

International Chamber of Commerce, *Funds Transfer in International Banking* (doc. 497, 1992).

International Chamber of Commerce, *Guide to Documentary Credit Operations* (doc. 415, 1985).

International Chamber of Commmerce, *Guide to Documentary Credit Operations for the UCP500* (doc. 515, 1995).

International Chamber of Commerce, *More Case Studies on Documentary Credits* (doc. 489, 1991).

Jack, *Documentary Credits* (2nd ed., 1993).

Kurkela, *Letters of Credit in International Trade Law: UCC, UCP and Law Merchant* (1984).

Meredith Memorial Lectures, *New Developments in the Law of Export Sales* (1982).

Mugasha, *Standby Letters of Credit in International Transactions* (1988).

Pierce, *Demand Guarantees in International Trade* (1993).

Rowe, *Electronic Trade Payments* (1987).

Rowc, *Letters of Credit* (1985).

Royal Bank of Canada, *Letters of Credit* (1985).

Royal Bank of Canada, *Foreign Collections* (1985).

Saligen, *Factoring. A Guide to Factoring Practice and Law* (1984).

Sarna, *Letters of Credit: The Law and Current Practice* (3rd ed., 1989).

Schmitthoff, *Schmitthoff's Export Trade. The Law and Practice of International Trade* (9th ed., 1990).

UNCITRAL, *Guide to Electronic Funds Transfers* (1987).

van Houtte, *The Law of International Trade* (1995).

Ventris, *Bankers' Documentary Credits* (2nd ed., 1983).

Wilde (ed.), *International Transactions: Trade and Investment, Law and Finance* (1993).

Wood, *Law and Practice of International Finance* (1980).

B. Articles

Arora, "The Duties of Issuing and Confirming Banks to Beneficiaries of Letters of Credit" (1984), 5 *Company L* 181.

Arora, "The Dilemma of an Issuing Bank: To Accept or Reject Documents Tendered Under a Letter of Credit," [1984] *Lloyds Mar. & Com. LQ* 81.

Bergsten, "A New Regime for International Independent Guaranties and Standby Letters of Credit: the UNCITRAL Draft Convention on Guaranty Letters" (1993), 27 *Int. Lawyer* 859.

Berman and Kaufman, "The Law of International Commercial Transactions (*Lex Mercatoria*)" (1978), 19 *Harv. Int'l. LJ* 221.

Brodie, "Payment Mechanisms Used in International Trade" in *Insight Letters of Credit* (1989).

Buckley, "The 1993 Revision of the Uniform Customs and Practice for Documentary Credits" (1995), 28 *Geo. Washington J of Int. L and Eco.* 265.

Deak, "Letters of Credit" (1981), 2 *NYLS J Int'l. & Comp. L* 229.

Dighe, "Letters of Credit, Strict Compliance and Autonomy: Robinson v. Ontario New Home Warranty Programme" (1995), 10 *BFLR* 275.

Dighe, "Standby Letters of Credit: Are They Insured Deposits?" (1986), *32 Wayne L Rev.* 1165.

Dolan, "Commentary on Legislative Developments in Letter of Credit Law: An Interim Report" (1993), 8 *BFLR* 53.

Dolan, "Documentary Credit Fundamentals: Comparative Aspects" (1989), *3 BFLR* 121.

Dolan, "Strict Compliance with Letters of Credit: Striking a Fair Balance" (1985), 102 *Banking LJ* 18.

Dolan and van Huizen, "International Rules for Letters of Credit—The UCP: A Final Report" (1993), 9 *BFLR* 173.

Ellinger, "Developments in Letter of Credit Law," [1990] *JBL* 58.

Ellinger, "Fraud in Documentary Transactions," [1981] *JBL* 258.

Ellinger, "The Autonomy of Letters of Credit After the American Accord" (1983), 11 *Australian Bus. L Rev.* 118.

Ellinger, "The Uniform Customs—Their Nature and the 1983 Revision," [1984] 3 *LMCLQ* 578.

Furman-Dann, "Confirming Bank Liability in Letter of Credit Transactions: Whose Bank Is It Anyway?" (1983), 51 *Fordham L Rev.* 1219.

Gellert, "Documentary Letters of Credit: Ash v. Lloyd's Corp." (1993), 8 *BFLR* 93.

Getz, "Enjoining the International Standby Letter of Credit: The Iranian Letter of Credit Cases" (1980), 21 *Harv. Int'l. LJ* 189.

Geva and Graham, "Standby Credits in Canada" (1984), 9 *Can. Bus. LJ* 180.

Goode, "Some Aspects of Factoring Law," [1982] *JBL* 240, 338, 410, and 527.

Goode, "The New International Chamber of Commerce Uniform Rules for Demand Guarantees," [1992] *LMCLQ* 190.

Goode, "Conclusion of the Leasing and Factoring Conventions," [1988] *JBL* 347, at 510.

Gozlan, "Rules Applicable to International Letters of Credit in Matters of Conflict of Laws: A Comparative Study" (1994), 13 *National Banking Law Review* 58 to 98; (1995), 14 *Nat. Banking L Rev. 3.*

Graham, "Letter of Credit, Basic Considerations," in McGill *Meredith Memorial Lectures* (1982), at 104.

Lalonde, "Documentary Letters of Credit: *B.N.S. v. Angelica-Whitewear*" (1987-88), 2 *BFLR* 377.

Lipton, "Uniform Rules of Standby Letter of Credit and Other First Demand Security Instruments in International Transactions" (1993), 10 *JIBL* 402.

Maduegbuna, "The Collection of Bills in International Trade" (1992), 8 *BFLR* 155.

McDorman, "International Letters of Credit" (1988), 2 *Rev. of Int'l. Bus. L* 253.

McLaughlin, "Letters of Credit: Basic Principles and Current Controversies" (1989), 17 *Australian Bus. L Rev.* 302.

McLaughlin, "Standby Letters of Credits and Guarantees: An Exercise in Cartography" (1993), 34 *William and Mary LR* 1139.

Merkin, "International Fraud and Documentary Credits" (1982), 4 *Liverpool L Rev.* 76.

O'Connor, "Payment and Financing Mechanisms" in *New Dimensions in Int'l. Trade Law* (1982).

Peters, "Standby Letters of Credit in Financing Transactions" (1994), 13 *NBL Rev.* 40 and 13 *NBLR* 49.

Reiss, "Banker's Acceptances and Priority Principles" (1986), 5 *NBLR* 26.

Richard, "Export Development Operation and Letters of Credit" (1988), 7 *NBLR* 224.

Schmitthoff, "Confirmed Documentary Credit: Issue Illegal but Confirmation Legal," [1980] *JBL* 129.

Schmitthoff, "Discrepancy of Documents in Letters of Credit Transactions," [1987] *JBL* 94.

Schmitthoff, "The Law Governing a Documentary Credit," [1982] *JBL* 55.

Schwank, "Electronic Documentary Credits and Guarantees: Emerging Legal Problems" (1980), 7 *IBL* 19.

Smith, "Fraud Affecting Letters of Credit: Minimizing the Importer's Risk" (1985), 1 *Trade LT* 2.

Smith, "Irrevocable Letters of Credit and Third Party Fraud: *The American Accord*" (1983-84), 24 *Va. J Int'l. L* 55.

Squillante, "Letter of Credit: A Discourse" (1979), 84 *Com. LJ* 372, 426, 474; (1980), 85 *Com. LJ* 48, 89, 145, 177, and 220.

Stack, "The Conflict of Laws in International Letters of Credit" (1983-84), 24 *Va. J Int'l. L* 171.

Tank, "Quasi-Strict Compliance of Documents" (1987), 18 . *of Miami Inter-Am. L Rev.* 535.

Van Houten, "Letters of Credit and Fraud: A Revisionist View" (1984), 62 *Can. Bar Rev.* 371.

Zeitler, "Letters of Credit: Problems with Non-Conforming Documents" (1987), 15 *Int'l. Bus. L* 250.

PART IV

Government Regulation of Export and Import Transactions

INTRODUCTION

Producers of goods in Canada for domestic consumption or for export should be thoroughly familiar with the type of protection that, in certain circumstances, is afforded by Canadian law against their foreign competitors. For instance, a Toronto firm making sweet biscuits for sale in Canada may be injured by the import of similar goods from the United States or from France that are sold in Canada at a low price because they are dumped or state subsidized goods. How can the Toronto firm protect itself against such dumped or subsidized foreign imports?

The North American Free Trade Agreement (NAFTA), which lowers tariffs and retains the traditional trade remedies on both sides of the border but provides for a new method of reviewing final anti-dumping and countervailing duty determinations, has brought to the fore the importance of knowing the obstacles that may stand in the way of the import of goods from another country.

Tariff protection and import relief available in Canada affect business decisions, especially those with respect to new investment.

Canadian producers have at their disposal a variety of means to lessen the effects of foreign competition that they perceive to be unfair. For example, they may resort to procedures leading to the imposition of anti-dumping or countervailing duties, argue that the imported goods do not meet Canadian standards, especially those that relate to safety, question the origin, tariff classification and tariff description of these goods, or point out that their import is or should be subject to a permit or a licence. They may try to convince the Canadian government to order their customs officers to work to rule. In some cases, they may be able to rely on federal or provincial purchase restrictions. If everything else fails, they may request a subsidy from the federal or provincial authorities in order to meet the low cost of the imported goods. However, when resorting to any one or more of these tactics, Canadian producers should be aware that their public image and their future relationship with their potential customers may suffer as resulting higher prices do not sit well with consumers.

In chapters 12 (canadian trade remedies), 13 (export controls), 14 (custom duties), 15 (subsidies and dumping), and 16 (restrictive business practices), tariff barriers and trade remedies will be examined in detail. Chapter 17 deals with the conduct of multinational corporations and chapter 18 with government measures to encourage the export of Canadian goods and services.

Canadian Trade Remedies

I. INTRODUCTION

The availability of adequate trade remedies is essential for the protection of Canadian suppliers of goods and services against essentially unfair foreign competition.

The Department of National Revenue administers and enforces, at points of entry, orders made pursuant to the Customs Tariff Act[1] (safeguard measures), the Special Import Measures Act[2] (anti-dumping and countervail) and the Export and Import Permits Act[3] (quantitative restrictions and safeguard measures). This Department is also responsible for investigating anti-dumping and countervail complaints and for making preliminary and final determinations of dumping and subsidizing. However, it is the Canadian International Trade Tribunal (CITT) that plays the most important role in the implementation of Canadian trade law and remedies.

II. THE CANADIAN INTERNATIONAL TRADE TRIBUNAL

The CITT,[4] an independent, quasi-judicial body reporting to Parliament through the Minister of Finance, became operational on January 1, 1989. It took over all the inquiry and appeal functions of the Canadian Import Tribunal (CIT), the Tariff Board, and the Textile and Clothing Board.

1 RSC 1985, c. 41 (3rd Supp.), as am.

2 RSC 1985, c. S-15, as am.

3 RSC 1985, c. E-19, as am.

4 RSC 1985, c. 47 (4th Supp.), as am., CITT Regs. SOR/93-600, 95-12, and 95-27.

The CITT is composed of not more than nine full-time members including a chairperson and two vice-chairpersons, all of whom serve terms of up to five years.[5] It has rules and procedures similar to those of a court of law,[6] but not quite as formal or strict. Thus, hearings must be conducted as informally and expeditiously as the circumstances and considerations of fairness permit.[7] Generally, hearings are open to the public and normally held in Ottawa, where the head office of the CITT is located but, when appropriate, may take place anywhere in Canada.[8] Subject to some exceptions,[9] three members constitute a quorum of the CITT.[10]

The principal officers of the CITT are the executive director, research, responsible for economic and financial analysis of firms, industries, and other parties involved in CITT inquiries; the secretary, responsible for administration, external and public relations, and the court registrar functions of the tribunal; and the general counsel, responsible for the provision of legal services to the CITT.[11]

The duties and functions of the CITT are to:[12]

(a) conduct inquiries and report on matters referred to the Tribunal for inquiry by the Governor in Council or the Minister under this Act:

(a.1) conduct mid-term reviews under section 19.02 [certain orders made pursuant to the Customs Tariff and the Export and Import Permits Act] and report on the reviews;

(b) consider complaints and extension requests filed with the Tribunal by domestic producers of like or directly competitive goods under this Act and, where appropriate, conduct inquiries into the complaints and extension requests and report on them;

(b.1) receive complaints, conduct inquiries and make determinations under sections 30.1 and 30.19 [Government procurement];

(c) hear, determine and deal with all appeals that, pursuant to any other Act of Parliament or regulations thereunder, may be made to the Tribunal, and all matters related thereto; and

(d) exercise and perform such other duties or functions that, pursuant to any other Act of Parliament or regulations thereunder, shall or may be exercised or performed by the Tribunal.

The judicial and advisory functions of the CITT may be summarized as follows:

A. Judicial Functions

The CITT acts as an administrative court with respect to:

1. Appeals by individuals and businesses wishing to contest Revenue Canada decisions on customs, federal sales and excise taxes, and related matters;[13]

---

5 S. 3.

6 S. 17. CITT Rules, SOR/91-499, am. SOR/93-599, 93-601, and 95-13.

7 S. 35.

8 Ss. 11.12.

9 Ss. 30.11(3), 38(2), and 39(2).

10 S. 13.

11 Ss. 14 and 15.

12 S. 16.

13 S. 16(c).

2. inquiries and findings on whether or not imported goods, which Revenue Canada has found to be subsidized or dumped, are causing "material injury" to Canadian production of such goods;[14] and
3. review of government procurement decisions.[15]

Decisions of the CITT can be appealed to the Federal Court of Canada and, where anti-dumping and countervailing duty cases involve US trade, to binational panels that are provided for under the North American Free Trade Agreement (NAFTA). They may also be the subject of a complaint brought before the World Trade Organization (WTO) Dispute Settlement Body.

B. Advisory Functions

The CITT acts almost as a standing commission of inquiry with respect to:

1. Import safeguard inquiries that include:
    a. government-directed import safeguard inquiries;[16]
    b. producer-directed import safeguard inquiries;[17]
    c. safeguard inquiries concerning the General Preferential Tariff Program and the Commonwealth Caribbean Program;[18] and
    d. safeguard inquiries under the NAFTA.[19]
2. General inquiries into any matter in relation to the economic, trade, or commercial interests of Canada with respect to any goods or services of any class thereof[20] and any tariff-related matters, including any matters concerning the international rights or obligations of Canada in connection therewith,[21] at the request of the Governor in Council.

---

14 S. 16(d).

15 Ss. 30.1 to 30.18.

16 S. 20.

17 Ss. 22 *et seq.*

18 S. 20 and Customs Tariff Act, 1985 (3rd Supp.), c. 41, as am., s. 42.

19 Ss. 19.01 and 20.01. Some of these matters are dealt with in chapter 14, *infra*.

20 S. 18.

21 S. 19.

TABLE OF MAJOR CANADIAN TRADE REMEDY LAWS APPLICABLE TO US AND FOREIGN GOODS[22]

Import Relief—Contingent Protection Over and Above Statutory Rates of Customs Duty

Legal Basis	Protection Against	Responsible Agency	Criteria for Violation	Remedies
• Anti-Dumping Duties SIMA, RSC 1985, c. S-15, as am. • GATT 1947, art. VI • GATT-WTO Anti-Dumping Code 1994 • North American Free Trade Agreement, c. 19 • Canadian International Trade Tribunal Act, RSC 1985, c. 47 (4th Supp.), as am.	Artificially low prices, injury of industry	Department of National Revenue for Customs and Excise and Canadian International Trade Tribunal (CITT)	Proof of dumping and material injury or retardation	Anti-dumping duties levied on goods
• Export and Import Permits Act, RSC 1985, c. E-19, as am., s. 5 • GATT 1947, arts. XVI, VI, and XXIII • GATT-WTO Subsidies Code 1994 • North American Free Trade Agreement, c. 19 • Canadian International Trade Tribunal Act, RSC 1985, c. 47 (4th Supp.), as am.	Subsidized imports, injury of industry	Department of National Revenue for Customs and Excise and CITT	Proof of prohibited subsidy and material injury or retardation	Countervailing duties levied on goods

(The table is continued on the next page.)

22 In general, see Boddez and Trebilcock, *Unfinished Business: Reforming Trade Remedy Laws in North America* (1993).

TABLE CONTINUED

Legal Basis	Protection Against	Responsible Agency	Criteria for Violation	Remedies
• Export and Import Permits Act, RSC 1985, c. E-19, as am., s. 5 • GATT 1947, art. XIX • GATT-WTO Agreement on Safeguards 1994 • Canadian International Trade Tribunal Act, RSC 1985, c. 47 (4th Supp.), as am.	Import in increased quantities of goods	Department of Foreign Affairs and CITT	Proof of serious injury or threat of serious injury	Quotas imposed on goods via Import Control List
• Customs Tariff, RSC 1985, c. 41 (3rd Supp.), as am., s. 59 • Canadian International Trade Tribunal Act, RSC 1985, c. 47 (4th Supp.), as am.	Breach of trade agreement or foreign acts, policies, and practices discriminating, etc., having adverse effects on trade in Canadian goods or services	Department of National Revenue for Customs and Excise, Department of Finance, and CITT	Proof of discrimination, etc., adverse effects on trade in Canadian goods	• Suspension or withdrawal of privileges • Surtax levied on goods • Inclusion of goods on Import Control List • Special rates of customs duty applied to goods

(The table is continued on the next page.)

TABLE CONTINUED

Legal Basis	Protection Against	Responsible Agency	Criteria for Violation	Remedies
• Customs Tariff, RSC 1985, c. 41 (3rd Supp.), as am., ss. 59.1, 60, 60.1, and 60.11 • GATT-WTO Agreement on Safeguards 1994 • GATT 1947, art. XIX • North American Free Trade Agreement, c. 8 • Canadian International Trade Tribunal Act, RSC 1985, c. 47 (4th Supp.), as am., ss. 19.1, 20, 23, and 26 • Export and Import Permits Act, RSC 1985, c. E-19, as am., s. 5	Import of increased quantities of goods	Department of National Revenue for Customs and Excise, Department of Finance, and CITT	Proof of serious injury or threat of injury to Canadian producers of like or directly competitive goods	• Surtax levied on goods • Other remedies
• Customs Tariff, RSC 1985, c. 41 (3rd Supp.), as am., ss. 42-45 • Canadian International Trade Tribunal Act, RSC 1985, c. 47 (4th Supp.), as am., s. 19 • GATT-WTO, part IV	Import of increased quantities of goods from countries entitled to the General Preferential Tariff (GPT)	Department of National Revenue for Customs and Excise, Department of Finance, and CITT	Proof of surge of imports causing injury or threat of injury to Canadian producers of like or directly competitive goods	• Tariff rate quotas imposed on goods • Goods in excess of quotas subject to tariff applicable in absence of GPT • Other remedies
• Competition Act, RSC 1985, c. 19 (2nd Supp.), as am., s. 31 • GATT-WTO, art. XIX	Prevention or substantial lessening of competition on an article facilitated by customs duties	Department of National Revenue for Customs and Excise	Proof of prevention or substantial lessening of competition	Reduction or removal of customs duties on goods

(The table is concluded on the next page.)

TABLE CONCLUDED

Legal Basis	Protection Against	Responsible Agency	Criteria for Violation	Remedies
• Copyright Act, RSC 1985, c. C-42, as am., ss. 44-45	Import of copies of works infringing copyright	Department of National Revenue for Customs and Excise	Proof that copies made out of Canada would infringe copyright if made in Canada	Import prohibited and inclusion in schedule VII to the Customs Tariff
Canadian International Trade Tribunal Act, RSC 1985, c. 47 (4th Supp.), as am., ss. 30.1-30.19 • North American Free Trade Agreement, c. 10 • GATT-WTO Agreement on Governmental Procurement 1994	Improper procurement process	Department of Government Services, Treasury Board, and CITT	Proof of seriousness of deficiency in procurement process (s. 30.15(3))	Various remedies (s. 30.15(2))

CHAPTER THIRTEEN

Export Controls and Their Extraterritorial Application*

I. EXPORT CONTROLS IN CANADA

A. History of Export Controls in Canada

The first export controls, in the modern sense, adopted by Canada are to be found in the Export Act[1] and the Customs Tariff Act, 1897.[2] Both of these statutes provided for the

* An earlier version of this chapter appears in a volume published by the ILA Committee on Extraterritoriality, Meeson, *The Extraterritorial Application of Export Control Laws* (1990).

1 SC 1897, c. 17.

2 SC 1897, c. 16.

regulation of the exportation of certain commodities, such as logs, for purely economic reasons. The first Canadian export controls adopted for reasons of military security were the Consolidating Orders respecting the Export of Commodities,[3] issued under the Customs Act and the War Measures Act in 1915. They prohibited the export of certain goods, including arms, either absolutely or to certain destinations. These orders generally exempted exports to the United Kingdom or British possessions.

The first comprehensive export control statute was the Export and Import Permits Act[4] (EIPA) of 1947. This Act set the pattern followed in subsequent legislation to the present time. The Act authorized the creation of lists of goods that could not be exported without specific authorization; these were first prepared at the time of its adoption,[5] as were regulations granting general exemption for goods of small value. In 1948, the Act was amended to allow the prohibition of all exports to specific countries.[6] The Act authorized the adoption of regulations requiring export permits relating to (1) arms and munitions, (2) ensuring adequate supply of the goods in Canada, and (3) implementing an intergovernmental arrangement or commitment. These categories have been expanded since 1947 but they have always remained the central categories. The breadth of the categories and the fact that the grant or refusal of a permit is entirely at the discretion of the government, which is not required to give reasons for its decisions, has the effect of giving the government a virtually limitless power to regulate exports.[7]

These powers were further strengthened in 1954 when a revised EIPA was adopted,[8] which characterized arms and munitions as those that might be "detrimental to the security of Canada" and "articles capable of being converted thereinto … or otherwise having a strategic nature." Short supply controls were qualified with the phrase "for defence or other needs." Until 1974, the Act was adopted for limited periods of three years; after that date, it became permanent.[9] During the subsequent years, the grounds for the imposition of export controls have been expanded to allow for more action based on economic or domestic regulatory grounds and to implement Canada's rights and obligations under multilateral and regional trade agreements.[10] The Act is a penal statute, and violators are subject to severe fines or imprisonment of up to five years.

The EIPA, like its more draconian counterpart, the US Export Administration Act,[11] is a creature of the Cold War. It has been used primarily over the years to buttress the

3 No. 200, *Extra Can. Gaz.*, 1 to 7, 28 April 1915, reprinted in Proclamations, Orders in Council and Documents Relating to the European War, 1st supp. 1914-15, at 353.

4 SC 1947, c. 17.

5 Export Permit Regulations, SOR/47-480 and 482, 14 May 1947 (1947), 81 *Can. Gaz.* pt. II:1111.

6 SC 1948, c. 16.

7 Attempts to challenge the export dimensions of the Act or specific decisions before the courts have failed.

8 SC 1953-54, c. 27.

9 SC 1974, c. 9, s. 3.

10 See now the consolidated version of the Export and Import Permits Act, RSC 1985, c. E-17, as am.

11 See Export Administration Act of 1979 Extension, PL 103-277; 108 Stat. 1407 and Export Administration Act of 1979, PL 96-72, 93 Stat. 503.

military and economic security of Canada, although it has also been used to reinforce domestic regulatory controls of agricultural production as well as to implement export prohibitions on a variety of products and substances, such as precious metals, raw materials, and other resource products. It has long been used to implement the controls over the export of nuclear fuels, required by the Nuclear Non-Proliferation Treaty[12] and more recently it has been used to implement controls over the export of environmentally unfriendly substances and wastes as required by a variety of international conventions.[13] Finally, the implementation of the Free Trade Agreement (FTA) and the North American Free Trade Agreement (NAFTA) also required amendments to the Act.[14]

The EIPA continues to be the central export control statute, but since 1992 a second statute, the Special Economic Measures Act,[15] has been available to the Government of Canada to deal with economic emergencies in a more flexible and modern fashion than is possible under the EIPA,[16] which contains no specific authority to restrict travel and service trade by Canadians, or the United Nations Act,[17] which requires the adoption of mandatory sanctions by the Security Council of the United Nations before regulations can be adopted in Canada. The Special Economic Measures Act allows the Government of Canada to respond to international situations requiring detailed limitations upon service transactions, financial operations, and travel by Canadian citizens and residents in a more flexible manner than is provided by the EIPA or in circumstances were there are no formal UN Security Council mandatory sanctions. This statute was used in 1992-94 to deal with the events in Haiti, following the ouster of the democratically elected President Aristide.

The EIPA envisages two forms of action: the first involves controls over specified goods (the export control list), and the second involves action against specified countries (the country control list). Both types of measures have been adopted by the Government of Canada over the years.

The export control list has been based essentially on the NATO Co-ordinating Committee for Multilateral Strategic Export Controls (COCOM) lists since the entry in force of that system. The Canadian list had been divided into 10 chapters until 1989 when a major policy and terminological revision was introduced with the purpose of modernizing the categories.[18] The new list is divided into five groups: industrial goods,

---

12 Treaty on the Non-Proliferation of Nuclear Weapons, CTS 1970, no.7.

13 Notably the Convention on International Trade in Endangered Species of Wild Fauna and Flora, 993 UNTS 243 and the Montreal Protocol on Substances That Deplete the Ozone Layer (1987), 26 *ILM* 289.

14 Canada-United States Free Trade Agreement Implementation Act, SC 1988, c. 65, ss. 116-23 and North American Free Trade Agreement Implementation Act, SC 1993, c. 44, ss. 146-54. The thrust of these amendments is to restrict the use of the Act against the United States and Mexico.

15 SC 1992, c. 17.

16 The difficulties in working with the EIPA in certain circumstances were revealed during the Gulf War emergency. See Lebouthillier and Morin, "Réflexions sur la validité des opérations entreprises contre l'Iraq en regard de la Charte des Nations Unies et du droit canadien" (1991), 29 *Can. Ybk. of Int'l. L* 142.

17 RSC 1985, c. U-2.

18 123 *Can. Gaz.* pt. II:2102, 13 April 1989.

munitions, atomic energy, technology, and miscellaneous. The export control list was further modified in 1990 as a result of the COCOM decision to relax controls on trade with the states of the former USSR.[19] In 1994, the COCOM was formally disbanded and plans were announced to replace it with a new system, probably with an expanded membership, better adapted to the post-Cold War era and to the new threats to political and economic security that are perceived to exist.[20] In the interim, previously existing controls in Canada and other COCOM countries have been kept in place, with some relaxation in content and administration.[21]

Since the end of World War II, Canadian export controls have also been adopted under other statutes. Of particular interest is the United Nations Act,[22] under which the Rhodesia Regulations and the United Nations Iraq Regulations[23] were issued. Canada has only resorted to a special statute once with the Iranian Economic Sanctions Act[24] of 1980. This Act remained in force for a very short period of time. Other statutes imposing various forms of export controls in very specific areas include the Cultural Property Export and Import Act,[25] the Atomic Energy Control Act,[26] the Act to Implement the International Convention on Biological and Chemical Weapons,[27] the National Energy Board Act,[28] the Gold Export Act,[29] the Canadian Wheat Board Act,[30] and other statutes

---

19 Export Control List, amendments, SOR/90-440, 124 no. 17; *Can. Gaz.* pt. II:3300, 27 July 1990; see also Lists of Agreements Reached in COCOM on Multilateral Strategic Export Controls (Industrial and Munitions Lists), 124 *Can. Gaz.* pt. I, supp. of 14 April 1990.

20 At the time of publication, this new system has not entered into force. When it does, considerable revision of the existing export control list can be envisaged. This change will probably be paralleled by a considerable simplification of the immensely complex and discretionary system of export controls existing in the United States.

21 A major development in this period has been the decision of the European Union (EU) to adopt controls on "dual-use goods" at the union level. See Council Regulation (EC) no. 3381/94 of 19 December 1994 setting up a community regime for the control of exports of dual use goods, OJ 1994 L 363, at 1-8 as amended by Council Regulation (EC) no. 837/95 of 10 April 1995, OJ 1995 L 90, at 1 (modifying date as of when Regulation would be applicable). See also Council Decision of 19 December 1994 on the joint action adopted by the council on the basis of article J.3 of the Treaty on European Union concerning the control of exports of dual use goods, OJ 1994 L 373, at 8 *et seq.*

22 RSC 1985, c. U-2.

23 Rhodesia: SOR/67-93, 101 *Can. Gaz.* pt. II:324, 8 March 1967, revised SOR/69-14, 103 *Can. Gaz.* pt. II:58, 8 January 1969 and Iraq: SOR/90-531, 124 *Can. Gaz.* pt. II:3629, 7 August 1990, as am., SOR/90-694, 124 *Can. Gaz.* pt. II:4509, 1 October 1990.

24 SC 1980-81-82-83, c. 39.

25 SC 1974-75-76, c. 50.

26 RSC 1985, c. A-16.

27 SC 1995, c. 25.

28 RSC 1985, c. N-7.

29 RSC 1970, c. G-5, repealed by SC 1980-81-82-83, c. 159.

30 RSC 1985, c. C-24.

dealing with the marketing of agricultural commodities, although the regulation of the export of such commodities has usually been effected under the EIPA.

Export controls are also used to enforce a variety of international conventions, particularly in recent years, international environmental agreements. The legislative basis for such controls may be found in specific legislation or in more general legislation dealing with environmental protection and natural resource management.

B. The Objectives of Canadian Export Control Legislation

Modern Canadian export control legislation has its origins in World War II and the subsequent Cold War. It has been aimed particularly at the East Bloc and at states fostering terrorism or engaged in domestic and international conflicts. In this, Canada's objectives probably differ little from those of many of its Organisation for Economic Co-operation and Development (OECD) partners. What sets Canada's legislation and its administration apart is the unique relationship with the United States. The Canadian and US economies are closely linked. Without any formal commitment to general economic integration, until January 1, 1989,[31] Canada has become the most important trading partner of the United States, with close to 80 percent of Canada's exports going to that country. Indeed, the degree of integration of the Canadian economy with that of the United States far exceeds that of most European Community (EC) member states.

The Government of Canada has therefore been particularly concerned to ensure that exports could come into Canada from the United States burdened by a minimum of US export controls. With respect to industrial goods, Canada has been successful, since, even before the FTA and NAFTA, virtually no restrictions were placed on such exports. The principal means of ensuring the unrestricted flow of industrial goods has been the adherence to the North Atlantic Treaty Organization (NATO)-COCOM system of multilateral controls and the special commitment outlined below to control the re-export of non-COCOM goods of US origin from Canada.[32] These rules have been administered by the export controls division of the Department of Foreign Affairs and International Trade (DFAIT).[33] Of necessity, the maintenance of a sound working relationship has entailed close cooperation between this office and the US Export Control Administration. On occasion, the relationship requires Canada to defer to the judgment of the United States as to the advisability of the re-export of a US origin product, even where Canada might be inclined to allow the export of a similar product of Canadian origin.

Despite the close cooperation that exists, a point of occasional friction is in respect of goods of US origin that have been integrated into a Canadian product. The Canadian Export Control List, item 5400,[34] and Canadian policy leave this determination solely up

---

31 Canada-United States Free Trade Agreement, SC 1988, c. 65, Schedule-Part A; superseded by the NAFTA, reprinted in (1993), 32 *ILM* 289.

32 See note 50, *infra*.

33 Until 1983, this office was a part of the Department of Industry, Trade and Commerce.

34 See *infra*, note 50. The adoption of the General Export Permit no. ex. 12—US Origin Goods, simplified the situation for Canadian exporters, see note 46, *infra*.

to the discretion of the Canadian authorities, on the basis of the principle that the manufacture of goods in Canada is a matter which is exclusively subject to Canadian sovereignty.

The export of arms from Canada to the United States is subject to US controls, but it has long been subject to bilateral commitments and understandings concerning defence production. These commitments go back to the Ogdensburg Agreement of 1940[35] and the Hyde Park Declaration of 1941,[36] and have been enshrined in subsequent joint defence production agreements.[37] The effect of the existing arrangements is to create a very high degree of integration of the Canadian and US defence production industries.

Enforcement of the Canadian export control system is committed to the DFAIT (formerly the Department of External Affairs) in Canada. This department is assisted by other departments of the Government of Canada. Bilateral cooperation in enforcement is ensured by cooperation at the working level. The system of domestic enforcement is completed by a bilateral agreement and an arrangement to ensure more effective implementation.[38]

Canada's objectives with respect to arms control and high technology result essentially from international and bilateral commitments. The more strictly domestic objectives flow from various statutes dealing with the production, processing, and consumption of foodstuffs and raw materials and reflect essentially economic concerns. It can be seen that potential issues of re-export and extraterritoriality relate more to the former categories than to the latter.

C. The Operation of Canadian Export Controls

The EIPA authorizes the establishment of an export control list and an area control list. The grounds for including items on the export control list are very broadly framed.[39] They include protecting the military security of Canada, ensuring secondary processing and short-supply controls of resources in Canada, implementating obligations under both an "intergovernmental arrangement and commitment,"[40] ensuring an adequate supply and distribution of an article in Canada, and enforcing controls on prohibited weapons under the Criminal Code.[41] The authority to place a country on the area control list depends entirely on the decision of the minister.[42] Given this broad discretion, it would seem

35 18 August 1940, CTS 1940, no. 14.

36 20 April 1941, CTS 1941, no. 14.

37 See CTS 1947, no. 43; Exchange of Notes of 12 April 1949, CTS 1949, no. 8; and Defence Production Sharing Agreement, 12 June 1961, CTS 1961, no. 5, extended by the Exchange of Notes, 25 June 1970, CTS 1970, no. 18.

38 Agreement between Canada and the USA Regarding Mutual Assistance and Cooperation between their Customs Administrations, 8 January 1985, CTS 1985, no. 23 and Treaty on Mutual Legal Assistance in Criminal Matters, 18 March 1985, reprinted in (1985), 24 *ILM* 1092.

39 EIPA, s. 3.

40 The word commmitment is used to cover informal and non-binding understandings between states.

41 EIPA, s. 4.1.

42 EIPA, s. 4.

extremely difficult to challenge the decision of the minister to place an item or a country on the respective lists. No such decision has ever been successfully challenged.[43]

The export of any goods is prohibited without a permit issued under the Act when the goods are on the export control list or are destined for a country on the area control list. This permit must accompany the goods at the time of export.

The export control list[44] is divided into eight broad categories:

Group 1 covers a range of so-called "dual-use" goods and technologies (advanced materials, software, telecommunications, information, navigation technology etc.) having both economic and strategic significance, formerly developed by the COCOM. The export of these goods requires a permit for all destinations except the United States.

Group 2 covers a range of military goods and technologies (arms, bombs, toxic agents, aircraft, vessels etc.) formerly developed by the COCOM. The export of these goods requires a permit for all destinations except the United States.

Group 3 covers atomic energy materials, including ores, facilities, related equipment and software. This list was formerly developed by the COCOM and all items require an export permit for all destinations. The Atomic Energy Control Act is also applicable to the export of these goods.[45]

Group 4 covers materials, data and technologies, many of which are dual-use goods, which must be controlled in order to meet Canada's obligations under the Nuclear Non-Proliferation Treaty (NPT). Policy concerning this list is made in the International Atomic Energy Agency as well as the Nuclear Suppliers Group, established to deal with non-parties to the NPT. An export licence for all destinations is required.

Group 5 covers a variety of goods (endangered species, albumin, logs, pulp, herring roe, prohibited weapons) whose export is controlled for social, economic and political reasons. This group also controls the export of US origin goods[46] and goods in transit to destinations other than the United States.

Group 6 covers the export of missile technology and missile parts and systems as required by Canada's participation in the Missile Technology Control Regime, established in 1987 to limit the spread of these weapons.

Group 7 covers biological and chemical weapons technology, agents and dual-use equipment, including biological testing and inspection equipment. Export of these items permitted without permit to NATO and other OECD countries.

Group 8 prohibits the export of chemicals used in the production of illicit drugs as agreed at the London G-7 Economic Summit in 1991.[47]

---

43 See *Teal Cedar Products (1977) Ltd. v. R.* (1988), 18 CER 214 (FCA).

44 EIPA, s. 3.

45 RSC 1985, c. A-16, s. 9.

46 See the export control list, SOR/89-202, 123 *Can. Gaz.* pt. II:2101, 26 April 1989, as am., by subsequent regulations (last am., SOR/96-175, 130 *Can. Gaz.* pt. II:1241, 17 April 1996) and General Export Permits no. ex. 12 for United States Origin Goods, SI/89-120, 123 Can. Gaz. pt. II:2484, 10 May 1989; SI/90-93, 124 *Can. Gaz.* pt. II:3113, 1 August 1990; SI/92-8, 126 *Can. Gaz.* pt. II:427, 29 January 1992; SI/92-170, 126 *Can. Gaz.* pt. II:3812, 23 September 1992.

47 See *Canada's Export Controls*, April 1995, DFAIT. See also *Annual Proceedings of the 19th Annual Conference of the Canadian Council on International Law* (1990), at 229-35.

Over the years, the items of particular interest have been those of the export control list dealing with the re-export of goods, particularly the re-export of goods of US origin. In 1949, the export control list was amended by adding group 9, "Goods Originating Outside Canada," which required an export permit for:

[a]ll goods originating outside Canada when tendered for export in the same condition as when imported, without further processing or manufacture in Canada, with the exception of:

a) goods in transit in bond …

b) goods consigned to the United States …[48]

These exceptions had the effect of facilitating re-export to the United States, while at the same time allowing Canada to control the re-export of goods from the United States. The exceptions were further clarified in 1953, with a view to strengthening the controls in Canada on the re-export of goods of US origin.[49] A further refinement adopted in 1973, was the splitting of group 9 into items 9001 and 9002, which had the effect of further highlighting the special treatment of goods of US origin by placing such goods in a special category.[50] This ensured that the US border would be largely open to the export of industrial goods to Canada without US export controls, while at the same time assuring US export control authorities that Canada would not become a back door for the illegal re-export of goods of US origin.

The relevant provision is now item 5400—US Origin Goods:

All goods that orignate in the United States, unless they are included elsewhere in this List, whether in bond or cleared by Canadian Customs, other than goods that have been further processed or

---

48 SOR/49-552 (1950), 84 *Can. Gaz.* pt. II:224, 25 January 1950.

49 SOR/52-275 (1952), 86 *Can. Gaz.* pt. II:588, 23 July 1952.

50 SOR/73-253 107 *Can. Gaz.* pt. II:1100, 14 May 1973:

Group 9—Goods Originating Outside Canada

9001 All goods originating in the United States, whether in bond or cleared by Canadian Customs, except any such goods that have been further processed or manufactured outside the United States, by combining them with other goods or otherwise, so as to result in a substantial change in value, form and use of the goods or in the production of new goods, unless the goods to be exported are listed in another Group in this List.

9002 All goods originating outside Canada, whether in bond or cleared by Canadian Customs, that are listed in another Group in this List, except any such goods that are in transit in bond on a through journey on a billing originating outside Canada which billing

(a) clearly indicates that the ultimate destination of the goods is a country other than Canada, and

(b) in the case of goods shipped from the United States, is accompanied by a copy of the United States Shipper's Export Declaration, certified by the exporter to be a true copy, which export declaration does not contain terms conflicting with those of the billing and is presented to the Canadian Collector of Customs.

This item is now numbered 5400 as a result of the 1988 revision: note 14, *supra*; General Export Permit no. ex. 12—U.S. Origin Goods, SI/89-120, 123 *Can. Gaz.* pt. II, 2484, as am.

manufactured outside the United States so as to result in substantial change in value, form or use of the goods or in the production of the goods.[51]

Since 1989, the export of US origin goods has been facilitated in most cases by the adoption of general permit no 12, which allows the export of such goods to a number of countries without a specific permit.[52]

General permits[53] may be issued in order to simplify the application of the EIPA and generally to facilitate the sending of goods having minimal value or a humanitarian purpose that would otherwise be covered by the export control list or the area control list. The export of goods covered by a general permit does not require a permit.[54]

The area control list[55] issued under the Act had been of equal significance. The area control list specifying countries has varied in length over the years. Until recently,[56] most or all of the former East Bloc countries have been on the list. During times of crisis, other territories, such as Rhodesia, or countries, such as Iran, have been on the area control list. Until the end of the apartheid regime in 1994, South Africa was included on the list. In recent years, the list has been restricted to states suspected of promoting international terrorism and states involved in domestic warfare having international repercussions, such as Afganistan, Angola, and the states of the former Yugoslavia.

The formalities for the issuance of an export permit are governed by the EIPA and the Export Permits Regulations.[57] The issuance of a permit by the export controls division of the DFAIT is at the sole discretion of the minister. No reasons are given for issuing or for refusing to issue a permit. The discretion of the minister to issue a permit on such terms and conditions as prescribed in the permit, or to refuse a permit is phrased

---

51 The Export Permits Regulations, s. 8 requires that all exports to destinations other than the United States must be accompanied by a declaration that "This export does not contain goods imported from the United States that have not been further processed or manufactured in Canada and the Export is in accordance with the Export and Import Permits Act and Regulations."

52 SI/89-120, 123 *Can. Gaz.* pt. II:2484, 10 May 1989, as am.

53 EIPA, s. 7(1.1) and Export Permits Regulations, s. 6.

54 The export controls division of the Department of Foreign Affairs and International Trade issues useful explanatory material on request. See also *Canadian Export Controls: An Exporter's Guide* (Canadian Exporters Association, 1989).

55 EIPA, s. 4; as of January 1996, the area control list covered Angola SOR/94-231; Boznia-Herzegovina SOR/92-476; Libya SOR/86-110; and Yugoslavia SOR/91-713. Yugoslavia and Bosnia-Herzegovina have been taken off the list again following the signing of the Dayton Accords, see Area Control List Regulation, SOR/96-94, 130 *Can. Gaz.* pt. II, 663 of 7 February 1996 (Yugoslavia) and SOR/96-223, 130 *Can. Gaz.* pt. II:1552 of 14 May 1996. The countries remaining on the list are Libya and Angola, at the time of publication.

56 SOR/89-201, 123 *Can. Gaz.* pt. II:2098, 13 April 1989.

57 Regulations Respecting Export Permits, CRC 1978, c. 602, as am., SOR/87-319, 121 *Can. Gaz.* pt. II:2245 26 June 1987 and SOR/95/34, 129 *Can. Gaz.* pt. II:128, 11 January 1995.

in such broad language that the possibility of judicial review of the exercise of this discretion is virtually nil.[58] There is no reported case of successful challenge.

Permits can be issued rapidly except where a decision must be referred to consultations with other governments,[59] in the case of highly sensitive items. In order to assist exporters who are engaged in the process of negotiating potential exports, officials of the export controls division are normally prepared to give preliminary, but non-binding, opinions in response to requests for information, whether or not a permit will be issued or refused in a specific case.

D. Legislation Regulating the Export of Cultural Property

The export of cultural property is regulated for two different purposes. The first is to ensure that Canada's cultural heritage is not exported to the detriment of the national interest.

The second is to ensure that Canada plays its role in the international effort to suppress the international trade in stolen cultural property pursuant to the UNESCO Convention on the Means of Prohibiting and Preventing the Illicit Import, Export and Transfer of Ownership of Cultural Property. The governing law is the Cultural Property Import and Export Act.[60] Obligations to return stolen cultural property arise between Canada and countries with which Canada has concluded a "cultural property agreement" pursuant to authority granted by section 37 of the Act.

Cultural property held in Canada may be denied an export permit if it is of a kind covered by the Canadian Cultural Property Export Control List and if it is determined by appropriate experts, pursuant to section 7 of the Act that the object in question "... is of outstanding significance by reason of its close association with Canadian history ..." and that "... its loss to Canada could significantly diminish the national heritage." Subsequent to such a determination, the Act allows for the appeal of a decision to refuse an export permit to the Cultural Property Review Board. Should the board uphold the decision to refuse an export permit, the Act provides for the subsidization of the purchase of the object by a Canadian cultural institution or the provision of an appropriate income tax credit to the owner who is willing to donate it to a cultural institution in Canada.[61]

---

58 Some authorities are of the view that no review of a decision denying an export permit lies under the Federal Court Act RSC 1985, c. F-7. See Paterson and Band, *International Trade and Investment Law of Canada* (2nd ed., 1994), at 6-30. Paterson cites the decision of the Federal Court of Appeal involving a ministerial directive to the Atomic Energy Control Board not to issue export licences in respect of sales of uranium oxide: *AGIP S.p.A. v. Canada (AECB)* (1978), 87 DLR (3d) 530, at 534-35.

59 Until 1994, this procedure was formalized within the COCOM. New consultative procedures are under negotiation at the present time. The decision to export certain categories of US origin goods is only taken after consultation with authorities of that country.

60 RSC 1985, c. F-7, as am. First adopted in 1975, the Act is administered by the Department of Canadian Heritage, pursuant to the Cultural Property Export Regulations, CRC, c. 449 and the Cultural Property Export Control List, CRC, c. 448.

61 See Williams, *The International Protection of Movable Cultural Property* (1978); Williams, "Protection of Cultural Property: The Canadian Approach" (1986), 20 *Arizona L Rev.* 737; and Paterson "The Legal Dynamics of Cultural Property Export Controls: Ortiz Revisited" (1995), *UBC L Rev.* (special issue) 241.

E. The Canadian Domestic Legislative Record with Respect to Extraterritoriality

In some respects, Canadian objectives with respect to export controls do not differ widely from those of the United States. Canada has an interest in preventing the re-export of controlled goods to certain countries for its own purposes and, in addition, has the very strong incentive to prove to the US authorities that it is not a back door for the illegal export of US origin goods. On the philosophical level, Canada has supported the functionalist view of the basis of the development of rules of international law and might be expected to accept the US argument that only extraterritorial measures are genuinely effective as a threat against would-be illegal re-exports. This section examines the Canadian legislative and regulatory record to determine the extent to which Canada has resorted to extraterritorial measures. Section II is devoted to the examination of the Canadian response to extraterritorial export controls, particularly those of the United States.

The central question to be determined relates to the EIPA. Has this Act, which has been the principal vehicle of Canadian export controls since 1947, ever been given extraterritorial application? This is most easily determined by examining the sections on offences. The principal sections are sections 13 and 15:

> 13. No person shall export or attempt to export any goods in an Export Control List or any goods on an Area Control List except under the authority and in accordance with an import permit issued under this Act.
>
> 15. Except with the authority in writing of the Minister, no person shall knowingly do anything in Canada that causes or assists or is intended to cause or assist any shipment, trans-shipment or diversion of any goods included in an Export Control List to be made, from Canada or any other place, to any country included in an Area Control List.

The essentially territorial character of these sections can be determined both from their wording and from general principles. The general principle applicable to Canadian statutes is that they apply only within the land territory of Canada, unless they are given extraterritorial effect.[62] In this case, it is clear from the text of the sections that the basic offence is exporting from Canada in violation of the Act. Section 15 only makes diversion an offence when it is aided or condoned by a person in Canada. For a person outside Canada, even a Canadian, to re-export goods of Canadian origin is not, in itself, an offence under the legislation. This logic is followed in section 20, which requires that where a permit is issued to a non-resident, the person in Canada who applies on his or her behalf remains responsible for, and can be punished for, any breach of the permit that occurs with his or her knowledge or consent, or where he or she fails to exercise due diligence to prevent the commission of the offence. The regulations issued under the Act naturally follow the same principle. The export control list applies to goods in material form, and group 4 of the list also includes "technical data, including technical drawings, photographic imagery, models, formulas, engineering designs and specifications, technical and operating manuals, whether in written form or on disk, tape, ROM or other

62 *Reference re Continental Shelf Offshore Newfoundland*, [1984] 1 SCR 86.

medium." Unlike US controls, the Canadian Export Control List does not apply to knowledge in the mind, which alleviates the necessity of attempting to control the movements and the statements of Canadians abroad.

It is clear, therefore, that Canada has refrained from giving extraterritorial application to its basic law in the area. The problem of diversion of sensitive goods and technology has been dealt with over the years through multilateral cooperation, particularly through the IC/DV system of additional documentation developed under COCOM. Pending the adoption of a new international system, Canada continues to apply the IC/DV documents to Canadian-controlled exports and enforces the system with respect to goods entering Canada under such documents. It should be noted that virtually all the items and countries on the export and area control lists are there as a result of COCOM or other international action. Consequently, Canada has chosen to deal with export controls almost exclusively on an international basis.[63]

Canada's legislative record reveals virtually no recourse to extraterritorial measures as a matter of general policy. However, there are limited examples in Canadian law, since 1945, of recourse to extraterritorial export controls.

The first example of Canadian extraterritorial export controls is that of the Rhodesia Regulations[64] issued in 1967, under the United Nations Act.[65] Recourse to the United Nations Act is only possible to implement Canada's obligations under the United Nations Charter to implement mandatory sanctions adopted by the security council. Section 31 of the Rhodesia Regulations stated:

> No person shall knowingly do anything, in Canada or in any other place, that causes or assists or is intended to cause or assist any shipment, trans-shipment or diversion of any goods specified … to be made from Canada, or any other place, to Rhodesia.

The Rhodesia Regulations applied to Canadian citizens and to Canadian corporations. These regulations clearly had extraterritorial effect in respect of Canadian nationals, but this was done at the behest of and pursuant to a decision of the UN Security Council. The United Nations Iraq Regulations[66] also have extraterritorial effect. However, this extraterritorial effect is limited to acts done abroad by Canadian citizens. These measures, which have extraterritorial effect, were also promulgated pursuant to mandatory sanctions adopted by the UN Security Council.

---

63 The only important exceptions are those items whose export is controlled to enforce agricultural marketing legislation or the very occasional short supply controls. On occasion, in recent years, Canada has used the EIPA to impose controls on exports to the United States to resolve a trade dispute between the two countries. See export control list, item 5304 "Specialty Steel Products." The most recent example is the Canada-US Softwood Lumber Agreement of 2 April 1996. DFAIT, news release, no. 157, 10 September 1996.

64 SOR/67-93, 101 *Can. Gaz.* pt. II:324, 8 March 1967, as am., SOR/69-14, 103 *Can. Gaz.* pt. II:58, 8 January 1969.

65 *Supra*, note 17.

66 *Ibid.*

A second somewhat analogous although much less stringent case is that of Canadian measures adopted to combat apartheid in South Africa and Namibia. In the wake of the Security Council's resolution 181[67] and subsequent resolutions 418, 473, and 558, Canada maintained an embargo on the export of arms and nuclear technology to South Africa under the EIPA, until these resolutions were revoked by the United Nations in 1994. This embargo was based on international action of a formally non-binding character. South Africa was one of two countries left on the area control list in 1989. Canada did not adopt comprehensive anti-apartheid legislation comparable to that of the United States,[68] but it did adopt a set of increasingly stringent policies designed to induce the Government of South Africa to abandon the policy of apartheid. Thus, in 1970, the Canadian government announced that it had contacted Canadian companies doing business in South Africa and had encouraged them "to act, within the bounds of South African law, as good corporate citizens in the Canadian sense in regard to the payment of salaries to their black workers."[69] On April 28, 1978, the Canadian government issued a Code of Conduct Concerning the Employment Practices of Canadian Companies Operating in South Africa.[70] This Code of Conduct was similar to that issued by the EC and certain member states such as the United Kingdom;[71] it involved a measure of extraterritoriality in that it passed judgment upon apartheid as it sought to change the behaviour of Canadian companies doing business in South Africa in a way that violated South African governmental policy. Compliance with the Code of Conduct was monitored by the voluntary submission of an annual report by concerned companies. Compliance with this voluntary requirement was not high. The justification given for these extraterritorial measures was the need to implement international human rights standards that had become binding on all states under international law, even if the UN resolutions were not, in themselves, formally mandatory. For this reason, the Government of Canada has argued that this rather cautious measure of extraterritoriality was justified under international law.[72]

Another instance of extraterritorial export controls is the Iranian Economic Sanctions Act of 1980.[73] This Act was adopted in response to the hostage taking at the US embassy in Teheran and was specifically restricted in operation to one year. The Act had extraterritorial application as evidenced by section 3, which provided for:

---

67 UN SCOR, UN doc. S/PV 5386 (1963).

68 See the Anti-Apartheid Act of 1986, 100 Stat. 1086, Comprehensive Anti-Apartheid Act of 1986, PL, 99-440, 100 Stat. 1086, 22 USCS §§5001 *et seq.*; reprinted in (1987), 26 *ILM* 77, 79, and 95.

69 House of Commons Debates, 1972-73, vol. IV, at 5503, 11 July 1973.

70 Communiqué no. 44, 28 April 1978, Department of Foreign Affairs and International Trade. See *Shell Canada Products Ltd. v. Vancouver (City)*, [1994] 1 SCR 231, in which the Supreme Court dealt with a municipal resolution refusing to do business with South Africa.

71 Cmnds. 5845 and 7233.

72 *Supra*, note 70.

73 SC 1980-81-82-83, c. 39.

(a) restricting or prohibiting the sale or supply by any person in Canada or by a Canadian outside Canada of goods or services to or destined for the Islamic Republic of Iran or any person situated therein;

Subsections (d) and (f) similarly restricted the ability of Canadians outside Canada to make loans or offer credit to Iran or persons in Iran in furtherance of commercial contracts. The Act remained in force for only six months due to the early resolution of the crisis. A few export permits were denied under the legislation, but it is not certain that the extraterritorial provisions were actually applied. The justification for these exceptional measures given by the Secretary of State for External Affairs was that, despite the USSR veto of the proposed mandatory sanctions resolution in the Security Council, the international community had condemned Iran for a flagrant breach of international law and that this justified the sanctions.[74]

In 1996, the Government of Canada has protested and has joined in international statements of protest against the extraterritorial aspects of the Cuban Liberty and Democratic Solidarity (the Helms-Burton) Act,[75] and the Iran and Libya Sanctions Act of 1966.[76]

In conclusion, it can be seen from the above that Canada has adopted a legislative policy that has avoided the extraterritorial application of its export controls, except where there existed authorization or a duty under international law, or where the measure commanded wide support as a means of promoting respect for fundamental humanitarian values.

II. THE CANADIAN RESPONSE TO THE EXTRATERRITORIAL APPLICATION OF EXPORT CONTROL LAWS BY OTHER STATES

A. Pressures to Which Canada Has Had To Respond

From time to time, the United States has adopted measures having extraterritorial effect that have applied directly to persons or companies in Canada or to business transactions taking place in Canada involving goods, know-how, or knowledge of US origin. In March 1996, the US Congress took a new step in adopting a prohibition on travel to the United States by persons having investments in Cuba or persons employed by companies having investments in Cuba, particularly investments in property that had been expropriated by the Castro régime.[77] These measures put private persons and companies in jeopardy of severe penalties in the United States. Difficult decisions have to be taken in the face of such measures about whether to comply quietly or to seek the diplomatic protection of the Government of Canada. There are no easy answers to the practical problems of those caught between the policies of the two governments. This section seeks to illustrate how the Government of Canada can be expected to respond in such situations.

---

74 House of Commons Debates, 1980-83, vol. III, at 2981, 16 July 1980, reprinted in de Mestral, "Canadian Practice in International Law, 1980" (1981), 19 *Can. Ybk. Int'l. L* 347, at 372.

75 PL 104-114, 110 Stat. 786.

76 DFAIT, news release, no. 137, 6 August 1996. See chapter 17, *infra*.

77 Cuban Liberty and Democratic Solidarity Act of 1996, *supra*, note 75.

The contexts in which Canada has had to respond to the extraterritorial application of foreign export control laws have been threefold. In the first instance there has been US unilateralism. The second case has involved incidents, often in the nature of international action against a particular state in which Canada participated, but where the United States chose to implement its own response, at least partially, in the form of extraterritorial measures and where Canada had to adopt a position in reaction to the US measures. The final context regards situations where international action involving extraterritorial measures was taken by a group of states, but Canada did not participate. In all of these situations the Government of Canada has had to respond, either by accepting or joining the measures, or by making clear its opposition and adopting an appropriate response in practical terms to ensure that the measures would not affect business activity in Canada.

The United States is not the only state adopting extraterritorial measures; in other contexts, particularly involving competition legislation, a number of states do so. Even with respect to export controls, as evident from Canadian practice, the United States is not alone in doing so. However, in practical terms, as far as export controls are concerned, in the three situations listed above, the only state that has attempted to apply its export controls to Canada is the United States.

The United States has used a variety of means of extraterritorial application of its export controls. The principal forms of extraterritorial application of export controls are those that apply to:

(a) nationals and permanent residents of the United States;
(b) corporate nationals on the basis of incorporation or business done in the United States;
(c) subsidiaries of US corporate nationals incorporated abroad;
(d) foreign but controlled corporations doing business abroad;
(e) companies producing goods abroad pursuant to a US-origin licensing agreement;
(f) goods produced abroad pursuant to (e);
(g) goods exported from the United States;
(h) "know-how" and other forms of knowledge leaving the United States;
(i) "submission clauses" in contracts involving the export of goods from the United States;
(j) certain forms of verification of performance of export licensing commitments in the territory of the importing state;
(k) sanctions, including denial of entry to the United States, against persons, companies and their employees having investments in Cuba.

Not only do the forms of extraterritorial application differ, but frequently the underlying justification will also differ. Many export controls are justified on the basis of the protection of national security, while others are justified as necessary to protect various aspects of the economic security of the United States; finally, some export controls are specifically adopted to promote foreign policy goals of the United States. These justifications may affect the assessment made by the Government of Canada of the legality of the measures at international law.

B. The Pattern of Response

The Canadian response to the extraterritorial application of export controls can take a variety of forms. The first response has been detailed above: it is to be found in the legislative practice of the Parliament and Government of Canada. A second response is to be found in the reaction of the Government of Canada to the actions of other states, especially that of the United States, when they have adopted extraterritorial measures as part of an internationally coordinated set of sanctions in which Canada participates. By refraining from adopting extraterritorial export controls in such situations, Canada sends a message about its own view of the propriety of extraterritoriality. A similar message can be read in the reaction of Canada to extraterritorial measures that are part of international action in which it does not participate. The most explicit message is to be found in the Canadian reaction to unilaterally adopted extraterritorial export controls by the United States.

As a result of the intensity of the Canada-US relationship, Canada has a particularly complex relationship with the United States with respect to extraterritorial export controls; so much so that Canada has developed a virtual pattern of responses to such US action. From 1945, through until the late 1960s, bilateral standing committees played a role in the discussion and resolution of problems raised by extraterritorial export controls. The first of these committees was the Joint Committee on Trade and Economic Affairs.[78] The second was the Canada-US Committee on Joint Defence first formed in 1947.[79] From time to time, these joint committees played a significant role, but frequently, during the first 30 years after World War II, Canada responded to a number of crises in its relations with the United States over extraterritoriality in an essentially *ad hoc* fashion. Thus, in 1957, when the United States sought, in one of the most publicized cases of its type, to block the sale to China of 1,000 Canadian-made vehicles by the Canadian subsidiary of the Ford Motor Company, the Government of Canada denied that the permission of the US government was needed for such a sale and maintained that the only law applicable to such matters was Canadian law.[80] As a result of this incident and the fear of others, the Canadian government sought to negotiate an arrangement with the US government. The July 9, 1958 Eisenhower-Diefenbaker joint communiqué[81] sought to address the differences between Canada and the United States on trade with China in general and extraterritorial export controls in particular, by committing both governments to looking for "appropriate procedures" to deal with the problem. The upshot was a vague understanding that Canadian companies might obtain *ad hoc* exemptions from US controls when the Canadian government intervened on their behalf and when the preponderant impact was upon the Canadian economy. This procedure was invoked successfully on a number of occasions in the immediately subsequent years.[82] However, the fragility of such *ad hoc* expedients was revealed by the difficulties following the imposition of stringent extraterritorial controls by the United States in

78 30 *US Dept. State Bull.* 511, 5 April 1954.

79 Exchange of Notes, 2 September 1958, CTS 1958, no. 22.

80 House of Commons Debates, 1958, vol. II, 18 July 1958, at 2090; see, generally, Corcoran, "The Trading With the Enemy Act and the Controlled Canadian Corporation" (1968), 14 *McGill LJ* 174.

81 39 US Dept. State Bull. 204, 4 August 1958.

82 Corcoran, *supra*, note 80, at 200.

1963.[83] Ten years after the adoption of these regulations, the Canadian government was forced to intervene in support of proposed exports from Canada by US subsidiaries in Canada. A well-publicized example was the proposed sale of locomotives by the MLW-Worthington Company to Cuba. The sale was blocked by the US government through the US parent until the Canadian government intervened.[84]

The pattern of intervention was essentially *ad hoc* during these years. This form of response had the effect of developing a pattern of consultation between the two states to the point that it could be argued there existed a duty of consultation on such matters. The second result was that the Government of Canada began to enunciate a position of principle, by parliamentary declaration and by diplomatic notes, which embraced not simply the specific case, but the general issue of extraterritoriality and the international legality of various techniques of extraterritorial application of laws adopted by the United States. Thus, with respect to the MWL-Worthington incident, a Canadian diplomatic note stated that "the *Cuban Assets Control Regulations* should not be given effect through the parent-subsidiary relationship ..."[85] This attempt to enunciate general principles also took the form of the promulgation of "codes of conduct" for foreign corporations doing business in Canada. The principal themes of these codes of conduct were the duty to respect Canadian law and to act as a good corporate citizen.[86]

As the number of incidents increased and as the ambit of the extraterritorial application intensified at the end of the Carter Presidency and more particularly during the first term of the Reagan Presidency, the Government of Canada maintained its policy of intervening on behalf of Canadian companies and of formulating its response in terms of general principles of international law. At this point, the Government of Canada went even further by adopting a policy of intervening even in cases where it was not immediately or directly affected, but where the US law or policy in question appeared to raise issues of general principle.[87]

The Government of Canada also sought to use multilateral forums such as the OECD to stimulate international discussion of the issue of extraterritoriality. This approach was pursued much less aggressively than the bilateral discussions, since the subject of extraterritoriality is inherently difficult to manage in the multilateral context where the interests of states are often highly divergent.

The final element of the Canadian response to extraterritorial export controls was the adoption of the Foreign Extraterritorial Measures Act.[88] This measure had originally

83 Cuban Assets Control Regulations, 31 CFR 515.

84 House of Commons Debates, 1974, vol. I, at 20, 14 February 1974.

85 Note of 13 February 1974, made public on 6 March 1974.

86 "New Principles of International Business Conduct" issued on 18 July 1975, chapter 17, *infra*. These principles replaced those originally issued in 1967 by the Minister of Industry Trade and Commerce.

87 The Bureau of Legal Affairs of the Department of Foreign Affairs and International Trade took the step of assigning a legal officer with exclusive responsibility for extraterritoriality.

88 RSC 1985, c. F-29, as am. in 1996, SC 1996, c. 28. See chapter 17, *infra*. See also Lussenburg, "The Collision of Canadian and US Sovereignty in the Area of Export Controls" (1994), 20 *Canada-US LJ* 145.

been proposed during the final years of the Liberal Government of Prime Minister Trudeau, whose years in government had been marked by the adoption of a number of nationalistic measures, but the Act was actually adopted in 1985, early in the administration of Prime Minister Mulroney's Conservative Government. The Act is similar to a number of other such laws adopted during the period in Europe. It authorizes the Government of Canada to order any "person in Canada" not to comply with the extraterritorial measures of a foreign government "involving business carried on in whole or in part in Canada." Such measures can include export controls.[89]

C. The Canadian Response to Specific Techniques of Extraterritorial Application of Export Controls

The Government of Canada has developed a comprehensive position on the extraterritorial reach of export controls as a result of the necessity of responding to a great variety of US measures since 1945. This position has been enunciated in a variety of forms just detailed in section B. This section briefly documents the Canadian position on different techniques of extraterritorial application of export controls, particularly as it appears from a number of recent diplomatic notes sent by the Government of Canada in response to specific incidents.

On a number of occasions, the Government of Canada has expressed the view that different forms of extraterritorial application of laws employed by the United States violate Canadian sovereignty and thus violate international law as it is understood in Canada. Similarly, the Government of Canada has expressed opinions upon the legitimacy of various justifications of the extraterritorial application of US laws advanced either by the US government or in the laws themselves.

The basic tenet of the Canadian position, reiterated on many occasions, is that Canadian law must govern business activity in Canada and, consequently, business transactions and persons doing business in Canada must defer to Canadian law. One of the strongest assertions of this principle was made in Parliament in 1958 in response to reports that the Ford Motor Company had refused permission to its Canadian subsidiary to export vehicles to China, in deference to US law and policy. The Canadian Minister of Finance stated:[90]

> ... the only law that is binding upon Canadians when in Canada or corporations that are doing business in Canada, to the extent to which they are doing business in Canada lawfully, is the law of Canada.

---

89 *Ibid.*, s. 5. The 1996 amendment, *ibid.*, provides, *inter alia*, for the establishment of a list of foreign acts which the attorney general deems to be in violation of international law. See *Hunt v. T&N plc*, [1993] 4 SCR 289, in which the Supreme Court deals with the interprovincial implications of blocking statutes. Commented by Wisner, "Uniformity, Diversity and Provincial Extraterritoriality: *Hunt v. T&N plc*," (1995), 40 *McGill LJ* 759.

90 House of Commons Debates, 1958, vol. II, 10 July 1958, at 2090, The Hon. D.M. Fleming, Minister of Finance.

Two decades later, the same principle was reiterated in a diplomatic note commenting upon proposed amendments to the US Export Administration Act:[91]

> The view that a foreign legislative body may impose obligations upon a Canadian person or corporation in respect of his or its activities in Canada or in a third country continues to be completely unacceptable to the Canadian government.

While the fundamental Canadian stance has always been firm, it has not been rigidly dogmatic and has sought to enunciate an international rule based on a realistic evaluation of the interests of other states. Canada cannot be described as having asserted a rigidly territorialist position. Thus, speaking in 1982, Canadian Ambassador Allan Gotlieb stated with respect to territoriality and nationality:[92]

> These concepts may provide useful first premises in determining jurisdiction, but they no longer provide—if ever they did—any basis for claims of absolute exclusiveness. On the other hand, I find equally unhelpful the assertion that any connection at all with a jurisdiction legitimises the application of its laws.

In the same year, the Embassy of Canada sent a note to the US Department of State concerning the assumption, inherent in the US legislation, that US investment in or control over a foreign company abroad gave the United States jurisdiction over it. The note stated:[93]

> The Government of Canada wishes to observe that such an assumption is incompatible with the principles of self-restraint and non-interference that underlie the international order.

In stating the Canadian position in this way in 1982, the Canadian government has chosen to found its arguments in more functionalist terms rather than was the case in earlier years. However, Canadian views of the legitimacy of specific forms and justifications of US extraterritorial export controls have changed very little.

The Government of Canada has always rejected the right of a foreign government to exercise jurisdiction in Canada through the medium of US nationals doing business in Canada. A memorandum of the legal bureau of the Department of Foreign Affairs and International Trade reasoned in 1974:[94]

> [I]t appears a state is prevented from requiring such acts from its citizens abroad as are forbidden to them by the municipal law of the state in which they reside and from ordering them not to

---

91 Note of the Embassy of Canada to the US Department of State, 15 May 1974. Files of the Canadian Department of Foreign Affairs and International Trade. Reproduced with the permission of the department.

92 "Canadian Ambassador Allan Gotlieb's Address to the American Society of International Law on Legal Aspects of International Investment, The Canada/US Experience, 22 April 1982," *US Import Weekly* 137, at 140, 5 May 1982.

93 Diplomatic note of the Canadian Embassy to the US Department of State, 7 July 1982. Reproduced with the permission of the Department of Foreign Affairs and International Trade.

94 Memorandum dated 20 October 1977 reprinted in Copithorne, "Canadian Practice in International Law During 1977 as Reflected Mainly in Public Correspondence and Statements of the Department of Foreing Affairs and International Trade" (1978), 16 *Can. Ybk. Int'l. L* 359, at 362-63.

commit such acts as they are bound to commit according to the municipal law of the state in which they reside.

The same approach has been adopted on a number of occasions with respect to the assertion of extraterritorial jurisdiction by the United States, on the basis of the corporate parent subsidiary relationship. Thus, in 1974, the Embassy of Canada to the United States stated in a note that:[95]

> The Canadian Government holds that the *Cuban Assets Control Regulations* of the USA should not be given effect in Canada through the parent-subsidiary relationship or in any other way … .

With respect to the foreign subsidiaries of Canadian corporations, the Government of Canada has stated that:[96]

> Under Canadian law, the government cannot force a mode of conduct on business operations of subsidiaries of Canadian corporations in Namibia. It is furthermore a principle of government policy not to interfere in the operations of Canadian corporations abroad.

In the context of Namibia, this position earned the government considerable domestic criticism.[97]

The same position has been adopted with respect to foreign companies controlled by US interests. In a note concerning proposed reporting requirements under US legislation, the Embassy of Canada to the United States stated in 1978:[98]

> The Canadian Government considers the US authorities are not entitled to exercise extraterritorial jurisdiction over Canadian companies solely on the basis that those companies are deemed to be controlled by US citizens. Such companies, as Canadian corporate citizens, cannot be regarded as US persons.

During the Siberian Pipeline controversy in 1982, the Government of Canada rejected the assumption of the United States that it was entitled to exercise jurisdiction over products produced outside the United States under a US licence. In a note to the US Department of State, the Embassy of Canada stated:[99]

> It is not apparent under what principle of international law the US asserts jurisdiction over the commercial and trading activities of foreign persons and entities when they have previously entered into private contractual arrangements with US persons that were in accordance with US law and US export policy of the day.

There does not appear to have been any diplomatic correspondence between Canada and the United States on the subject of the legitimacy of resorting to "submission

---

95 Note of 13 February 1974 sent by the Embassy of Canada to the US Department of State. Reprinted with the permission of the Department of Foreign Affairs and International Trade.

96 House of Commons Debates, 1974-75, vol. XII, at 12136, 25 March 1976.

97 Meret, "Canada and Namibia" (1979), 17 *Can. Ybk. Int'l. L* 314.

98 Note no. 49 of 27 January 1978. Reproduced by permission of the DFAIT.

99 Note of the Embassy of Canada to the US Department of State, 7 July 1982. Reproduced with the permission of the DFAIT.

clauses" in private contracts as a way of enforcing US export controls abroad by indirect means. However, it would appear that, if the imposition of a submission clause were to have the effect of violating Canadian sovereignty, the Government of Canada would protest and would certainly be empowered under the Foreign Extraterritorial Measures Act[100] to block the execution of the clause in Canada.

The right of the US government to impose conditions unilaterally, as opposed to acting pursuant to international agreement, has often been a source of contention between Canada and the United States. As a matter of course, Canada has faithfully enforced COCOM prohibitions on re-export of original products and of components and has furthermore imposed a unilateral control of the re-export of goods of US origin,[101] but difficulties have often arisen over components subject to non-COCOM US export controls. The Government of Canada has taken the position that such components can be exported if Canadian law and policy allow it, and that US controls cannot be enforced in Canada against them. Hence, the Embassy of Canada sent a note to the Department of State in 1977 stating that:[102]

> ... with respect to the transformation of US components in a Canadian product, it has long been the Canadian view that imported goods and services incorporated into Canadian products take on the identity in completed form of a Canadian product.

This position has even been taken with respect to defence equipment, much of which is subject to COCOM control and all of which is subject to Canadian export controls. The following statement was made in Parliament:[103]

> Defence equipment sold by Canada to the US is absorbed into the general inventory of the military services of that country and its ultimate disposition and destination is a matter for the authorities of the US to decide. The same principle applies to defence equipment which Canada purchases from the US.

From time to time, agents of the US government have attempted to enforce US export controls in Canada by writing to Canadian companies in Canada or by visiting Canadian companies in Canada. Such contacts, which do not have the express prior consent of the Government of Canada, are deemed to violate Canadian sovereignty and have been protested in the past. Thus, in a note sent in early 1983 the Embassy of Canada informed the Department of State that:[104]

> We cannot accept ... that US officials take steps in Canada in support of the application of US law to inhibit Canadian firms from pursuing express Canadian government policy of promoting

---

100 RSC 1985, c. F-29.

101 *Supra*, note 51.

102 Note no. 591, 21 November 1977. Reproduced with the permission of the DFAIT.

103 House of Commons Debates, 1971, vol. VI, at 5949, 19 May 1971.

104 Extract of a note of the DFAIT, reproduced with the permission of the Department of External Affairs. On 31 July 1978, the Embassy of Canada sent note no. 374 objecting to surveys under US anti-boycott legislation.

trade with Cuba in non-strategic goods ... if they [the steps] are indeed long-standing they should be discontinued.

The Government of Canada's policy with respect to the extraterritorial application of US export controls is viewed as having a bearing not only on governmental action, but also on private corporate conduct. Thus, the "New Principles of International Business Conduct" issued by the government on July 18, 1975 state, in principle 12, that foreign-controlled firms should:[105]

... give appropriate support to recognised national objectives and established government programs, while resisting any direct or indirect pressure from foreign governments or associated companies to act in a contrary manner.

D. Canadian Views as to the Avoidance of Conflict

The Government of Canada has sought both to defend its sovereignty and to promote the development of rules of international conduct that reflect the legitimate interests of all states. To this end, the Canadian position cannot be described as purely territorialist, even though Canada has been jealous of its sovereignty.

The basis of conflict-avoidance is cooperation. This was described by the Embassy of Canada in a note to the US Department of State, in 1983, in the following terms:[106]

The Government of Canada and the Government of the US have long cooperated with respect to export controls, following the 1942 *Hyde Park Agreement*. This is manifest in the treatment that is accorded each country in the administration of the export control laws of the other. Generally speaking, pursuant to the *Hyde Park Agreement*, US goods are exported to Canada without US export licences, and vice versa. To prevent the circumvention of US controls, Canada regulates the re-export of controlled US-origin goods. This system has benefitted both countries. It has helped to maintain bilateral trade flows free of the impediment of export licences, while still safeguarding mutual security objectives.

Beyond cooperation, the Government of Canada has, on occasion, argued that extraterritorial export controls would only be appropriate on a basis of reciprocity. This was urged in the same note to the Department of State in 1983:[107]

The Government of Canada believes that extraterritorial problems and conflicts of jurisdiction would be greatly limited if the United States would take due account of the principle of reciprocity and assert unilaterally its jurisdiction over conduct outside its territory only in circumstances where it would be prepared to recognise and accept, in similar circumstances and on the same basis, the same unilateral assertion of jurisdiction by another state over conduct within United States territory.

---

105 See chapter 17, *infra*. For a more detailed review of Canadian state practice, see de Mestral and Gruchalla-Wesierski, *Extraterritorial Application of Export Control Legislation: Canada and the USA* (1990).

106 Note no. 139 to the Department of State of 4 May 1983. Reproduced with the permission of the DFAIT.

107 *Ibid.*

In the final analysis, it would appear that the Canadian approach can best be described by the "principles of self-restraint and non-interference that underlie the international order."[108] These principles have been urged upon the United States by Canada on several occasions in diplomatic notes and within the OECD.[109]

Canadian export controls are imposed in a manner that seeks to respect the sovereignty of other states. Canadians and companies doing business in Canada can expect the Government of Canada to attempt to insulate them from the effects of foreign extraterritorial export controls whenever this is possible.

E. NAFTA and US Extraterritorial Measures

The issue of extraterritoriality is not covered explicitly by the NAFTA. Article 310.3 envisages the situation where a NAFTA party maintains an export or import embargo against a non-party and even provides that reqirements may be imposed against the possible circumvention of the boycott by re-routing the goods through the territory of another NAFTA party. Article 310.4 calls for consultations between parties to avoid disruption of trade patterns. Article 2102 allows the taking of exceptional measures to protect national security for a variety of purposes similar to, but not as extensive as those provided by article XX of the GATT. Article 1113 of the chapter on investments provides for the denial of benefits to investors of a party and the prevention of circumvention of such measures, when a NAFTA party adopts measures prohibiting transactions with a non-party. Article 1211 contains analogous provisions with respect to services. Finally, it is probable that the several grandfathering provisions with respect to these chapters are also relevant to the issue of exceptional measures, including some that involve potential extraterritoriality. However, these provisions are not without ambiguity and it is probable that their full impact on thc issuc of cxtraterritoriality must await further negotiations or a dispute settlement proceeding.[110]

F. Conclusion

The weight of export controls upon Canadian exporters was considerably lightened as a result of the end of the Cold War during 1989 and 1990.[111] However, the crisis provoked

---

108 *Supra*, note 93.

109 OECD, *International Investment and Multinational Enterprises* (rev. ed., 1984). See at 23-24 on "Conflicting Requirements," endorsed by ministers on 17 May 1984, para. 5. It is to be regretted that these discussions on questions of extraterritoriality have not been made public and that they do not appear to have been pursued in the field of export controls subsequent to 1984.

110 The Government of Canada called for discussion of the impact of the Cuban Liberty and Democratic Solidarity Act of 1996 (Helms-Burton Act) *supra*, note 75, on Canada's rights under the NAFTA in March 1996 immediately following enactment of the legislation and joined the EC challenge to this legislation of the WTO under the GATT 1994.

111 See measures cited, *supra*, note 19. The compatibility of the Helms-Burton Act with the NAFTA has not yet been tested.

by the Iraqi invasion of Kuwait in 1990 and the response of the UN Security Council, served to show that Canadian exporters could not expect the complete dismantling of the Canadian export control administration. The Cold War is over, but it has been replaced by the war against state-sponsored terrorism and it is clear that export controls are here to stay. Similarly, while much was done in 1989 and 1990 to lighten the burden of US extraterritorial export controls upon Canadians, there is no reason to believe that the Government of the United States has altered its view that it is authorized to adopt such extraterritorial measures.

III. SELECTED BIBLIOGRAPHY

A. Books

Castel, *Extraterritoriality in International Trade: Canada and United States of America Practices Compared* (1988).

de Mestral and Gruchalla-Wesierski, *Extraterritorial Application of Export Control Legislation: Canada and the USA* (1990).

Doxey, *Economic Sanctions and International Enforcement* (1980).

Meesson, *The Extraterritorial Application of Export Control Laws* (1990).

Morgan, *International Law and the Canadian Courts: Sovereign Immunity, Criminal Jurisdiction, Aliens' Rights and Taxation Powers* (1990).

Nincic et al. (eds.), *Dilemmas of Economic Coercion* (1983).

Tereposky, *Extraterritoriality in the 1990s* (Ottawa: Investment Canada, 1993).

B. Articles

Corcoran, "The Trading With the Enemy Act and the Controlled Canadian Corporation" (1968), 14 *McGill LJ* 174.

Dattu et al., "Seeking Redress of Customs Decisions" (1995), 14 *Nat. BL Rev.* 74.

Ellicott, "Sovereignty and the Regulation of International Business in the Export Control Area" (1994), 20 *Canada-US LJ* 133.

Hughes and Wright, "International Efforts to Secure the Return of Stolen or Illegally Exported Cultural Objects: Has UNIDROIT Found Global Solutions?" (1994), 32 *Can. Ybk. Int'l. L* 219.

Lauzon, G., "Extraterritorial Acts Good and Bad," [1995] *Can. Inter. Lawyer* 75.

Lussenburg, S.M., "The Collision of Canadian and US Sovereignty in the Area of Export Controls" (1994), 20 *Can-US LJ* 145.

Merrymen, "What Do Matisse, Van Gogh and Hitler Have in Common?" (1995), *UBC L Rev.* (special issue) 273.

Paterson, "The Legal Dynamics of Cultural Property Export Controls: Ortiz Revisited" (1995), *UBC L Rev.* (special issue) 241.

Thomson, "High Technology Export Control Regimes in Canada and the United States: Origins, Current Operation and Anticipated Changes" (1994), 9 *Intel. Property J* 19.

Trachtman, "Reflections on the Nature of the State: Sovereignty, Power and Responsibility" (1994), 20 *Canada-US LJ* 399.

Walden, "Canada's Cultural Property Export and Import Act: The Experience of Protecting Cultural Property" (1995), *UBC L Rev.* (special issue) 203.

CHAPTER FOURTEEN

Customs Duties and Other Import Controls

I. GENERAL PRINCIPLES GOVERNING CANADIAN IMPORT CONTROLS

Canadian law governing the importation of goods reflects the changing reality of Canadian society and the Canadian economy. During the early years of Confederation, Canadian industry was protected by a high tariff wall as a result of the National Policy of the government of Sir John A. MacDonald. Suggestions by the Liberal party, in the early part of this century, that the tariff wall be breached by a reciprocity treaty with the United States were not accepted. Canadian tariff protection remained high and even increased during the 1930s. Other protective measures included requirements for the withdrawal of trade concessions if "reciprocity" was not offered by Canada's trading partners. Tariff policy toward the British Empire and, subsequently, the Commonwealth was governed by the principles of Imperial and Commonwealth preference as developed at a series of conferences. The Imperial and Commonwealth Preference System tended to maintain strong trading links between Canada and the United Kingdom. Trading ties with other major trading partners were governed by bilateral treaties such as the Canada-France Trade Agreement 1933.[1] Treaties of friendship, commerce, and navigation (FCN) as they were called generally dealt extensively with the level of customs duties applicable to trade between both countries. They also dealt with other barriers that might be established against trade and the right of either party to impose temporary restrictions as safeguards against the sudden influx of foreign products.

For the first half of this century, Canadian legislation reflected domestic concerns, both in form and content, since there was no international constraint, apart from the necessity to implement a limited number of bilateral FCN treaties. This changed considerably in 1947 with the adoption of the General Agreement on Tariffs and Trade (GATT). Since then, Canadian legislation and policy governing imports have increasingly been subject to multilaterally agreed international standards. The situation today is that virtually no issue relating to the importation of goods and increasingly a range of services, as well as intellectual property rights and investments, is untouched by international treaties, agreements, and understandings.

Canadian laws governing the importation of goods and services, despite the antiquity of some of them,[2] have all been substantially revised since 1984. The Special Import Measures Act[3] was adopted in 1984 to implement the Anti-Dumping and Subsidies Codes,[4] negotiated in the Tokyo Round of Multilateral Trade Negotiations held under the aegis of the GATT. The Customs Act[5] underwent fundamental revision in 1986; these changes were designed to modernize one of the oldest of federal statutes and

1 SC 1932-33, c. 30.

2 SC 1904, c. 11, s. 19. The Customs Act is as old as Confederation. The first anti-dumping legislation was adopted in Canada in 1903. See Paterson and Band, *International Trade and Investment Law in Canada* (2nd ed., 1994), c. 5.

3 RSC 1985, c. S-15, as am.

4 See chapter 11, *supra*.

5 RSC 1985 (2nd Supp.), c. 1, as am. The Customs and Excise Offshore Application Act, RSC 1985, c. C-53, as am., extended the application of customs and tax legislation to the Canadian offshore and to all platforms operating there in 1984. It also applies to all future legislation.

to implement international rules such as the Tokyo Round Valuation Code.[6] The Canadian International Trade Tribunal Act[7] was adopted in 1988 to create new trade remedies and a new institution, the Canadian International Trade Tribunal (CITT), by merging the Canadian Import Tribunal with the Textile and Clothing Board and the Tariff Board, the latter being one of the oldest federal administrative tribunals. In 1993, the functions of the Government Procurement Review Board were transferred to the CITT.[8] The Customs Tariff Act[9] also underwent major revision in 1988 to modernize the previous legislation, to implement international agreements, and to create new remedies against imports. The Canada-US Free Trade Agreement Implementation Act,[10] which was also adopted in 1988, made substantial amendments to the Customs Tariff Act and to many rules governing trade between the two countries. Further major legislative changes to these and other statutes were made in 1993, with the adoption of the North American Free Trade Agreement Implementation Act,[11] and in 1994, on the conclusion of the Uruguay Round of International Trade Negotiations, and the subsequent adoption in Canada of the Act to Implement the Agreement Establishing the Word Trade Organization (WTO).[12]

As a result of these legislative developments, Canadian regulation of imports is very closely aligned to that existing in other related states. The differences are either matters of degree and shading, or result from different remedies that can be exercised by governments and private parties against imports over and above those that are generally agreed between GATT-WTO members and NAFTA parties. Some of these extraordinary remedies are matters of great controversy among states.

Apart from the statutes listed above, there is a wide range of other statutes that authorize the Government of Canada to regulate the entry of foreign products into Canada.[13]

---

6 See chapter 1, *supra*.

7 RSC 1985 (4th Supp.), c. 47, as am.

8 See ss. 16(b.1) and 30.11 of the Canadian International Trade Tribunal Act, RSC 1985, c. 47 (4th Supp.), as am., ss. 35 and 44 of North American Free Trade Agreement Implementation Act SC 1993, c. 44. See also the Canadian International Trade Tribunal Regulations, SOR/89-35, 123 *Can. Gaz.* pt. II:255, 18 January 1989, as am., by reg. SOR/93-600, 127 Can. Gaz. pt. II:4539, 29 December 1993, last am., by reg. SOR/96-229, 130 *Can. Gaz.* pt. II:1564, 15 May 1996; the Canadian International Trade Tribunal Rules, SOR/91-499, 125 *Can. Gaz.* pt. II:2912, 28 August 1991, as am., by reg. SOR/93-599, 127 *Can. Gaz.* pt. II:4534, 29 December 1993, SOR/93-601, 127 *Can. Gaz.* pt. II:4541, 29 December 1993 and SOR/95-13, 129 *Can. Gaz.* pt. II:28, 11 January 1995; and the Canadian International Trade Tribunal Procurement Inquiry Regulations, SOR/93-602, 127 *Can. Gaz.* pt. II:4547, 29 December 1993, last am., by SOR/96-30, 130 *Can. Gaz.* pt. II:470, 24 January 1996.

9 RSC 1985 (3rd Supp.), c. 41, as am.

10 SC 1988, c. 65.

11 SC 1993, c. 44.

12 SC 1994, c. 47.

13 Among the most important are the Export and Import Permits Act, RSC 1985, c. E-19, as am.; Energy Administration Act, RSC 1985, c. E-6, as am.; Excise Tax Act, RSC 1985, c. E-14 as am.; Atomic

(The footnote is continued on the next page.)

The Canadian system of import regulation is fundamentally designed in favour of the right of Canadians to make purchases abroad and to import into Canada. This reflects Canada's commitment to the liberal world trading order as embodied in the GATT-WTO. As required by the GATT 1994, the fundamental method of regulating imports is the customs tariff; any other barriers to imports—and a number do exist under Canadian law—are exceptions to the general rule. The administration of the Customs Tariff continues to be a central preoccupation of the law. However, the level of customs barriers has vastly diminished over the years, as a result of WTO commitments, and tariffs will be eliminated on imports from the United States and Mexico at the end of the NAFTA phasing-in period in 2008. For this reason, it is important to examine a range of other protective devices in this chapter, including customs duty remission, drawbacks, and discretionary removal of customs duties in certain circumstances by virtue of special statutory authority. Preferential tariffs under general or bilateral trade agreements are also reviewed. Safeguard actions, which until recently constituted a marginal phenomenon in Canadian law, have come to assume an increasingly important place. The range of extraordinary remedies, such as quotas, tariff quotas, or surcharges, against goods entering Canada as a result of normal or unusual circumstances is also reviewed. Also important to understand are those instances where Canadian legislation, as well as judicial and administrative interpretation, are biased in favour of Canadian producers of goods and services.

II. JURISDICTIONAL ISSUES

There has been no doubt since the decision in the case of *The Citizens' Insurance Co. v. Parsons*[14] that Parliament has exclusive jurisdiction over the setting of tariffs and the regulation of the movement of goods into Canada.[15] Conversely, it is also clear that the

---

13 Continued ...

Energy Control Act, RSC 1985, c. A-16; and the Criminal Code, RSC 1985, c. C-46, as am. Other statutes include the Agricultural Products Marketing Act, RSC 1985, c. A-6; Animal Disease and Protection Act, RSC 1985, c. A-11, as am.; Chemical Weapons Convention Implementation Act, SC 1995, c. 25; Canadian Environmental Protection Act, RSC 1985 (4th Supp.), c. 16, as am.; Canadian Wheat Board Act, RSC 1985, c. C-24; Copyright Act, RSC 1985, c. C-42, as am.; Explosives Act, RSC 1985, c. E-17, as am.; Feeds Act, RSC 1985, c. F-9, as am.; Financial Administration Act, RSC 1985, c. F-11, as am.; Fisheries Act, RSC 1985, c. F-14, as am.; Food and Drugs Act, RSC 1985, c. F-27, as am.; Foreign Extraterritorial Measures Act, RSC 1985, c. F-29; Hazardous Products Act, RSC 1985, c. H-3, as am.; Importation of Intoxicating Liquors Act, RSC 1985, c. I-3, as am.; Investment Canada Act, RSC 1985, c. 28 (1st Supp.) as am.; Livestock and Livestock Products Act, RSC 1985, c. L-9, as am.; Meat Import Act, RSC 1985, c. M-3, as am.; Patent Act, RSC, 1985, c. P-4, as am.; Pest Control Products Act, RSC 1985, c. P-9, as am.; Radiation Emitting Devices Act, RSC 1985, c. R-1; Seeds Act, RSC 1985, c. S-8, as am.; and Trade-Marks Act, RSC 1985, c. T-13, as am.

14 (1881), 7 App. Cas. 96.

15 See also *Gold Seal Ltd. v. Dominion Express Co.* (1921), 62 SCR 424 and *Caloil Inc. v. The A.G. Québec*, [1971] SCR 543.

provincial legislatures are not empowered to set tariffs on the importation of goods into a province,[16] although some restrictions on the free movement of goods into the provinces may be imposed under other heads of provincial jurisdiction.[17] The ambit of federal jurisdiction to implement international commercial treaties dealing with the treatment of imported goods has always been the object of some doubt as a result of the *Labour Conventions Reference*.[18] The recent decision of the Supreme Court of Canada in *General Motors v. City National Leasing*[19] has raised the possibility of a broader reading of the general trade and commerce power and possibly of the ambit of the power to regulate international trade.[20] Section 92A of the Constitution Act, 1982[21] can be read as confirming federal jurisdiction to regulate international trade, at least insofar as the international movement of goods is concerned.

The Constitution Act, 1867[22] grants Parliament very broad jurisdiction over the regulation of international capital movements and foreign investment. By virtue of section 95 of this Act, Parliament and the provincial legislatures enjoy concurrent jurisdiction over agriculture and immigration, subject to federal paramountcy. During the 1980s, the Government of Quebec, by virtue of an administrative agreement with the federal government, assumed broad responsibilities for the selection and reception of immigrants planning to settle in that province.

The most difficult area of concern is that of the regulation of the international movement of services. The Constitution Act, 1867 has been interpreted as granting broad discretion to the provincial legislatures to regulate labour standards and professional activities. This being so, it is generally accepted that professional persons coming into a Canadian province from abroad enjoy no immunity from provincial regulation of their professional status or activities.[23] The capacity of Parliament to require the provinces to afford any given standard of treatment to foreign professional services and service providers is a matter of considerable constitutional uncertainty. On June 1, 1995, the provincial governments bound themselves to a complex but legally very unconstraining Agreement on Internal Trade.[24]

---

16 *Murphy v. The CPR*, [1958] SCR 626.

17 See Bernier and Binette, *Les provinces canadiennes et le commerce international* (IRPP/CQRI, 1989). Provincial restrictions particularly affect purchases by government departments, Crown agencies, and public corporations such as school commissions and hospitals. As of 1 June 1995, an interprovincial Agreement on Internal Trade has been in force, but as yet it has done little to restrain protectionist policies of provincial governments.

18 [1937] AC 326.

19 [1989] 1 SCR 641.

20 Arguably, s. 92A of the Constitution Act, 1982 serves as an implicit confirmation of federal jurisdiction over international trade in all commodities.

21 Enacted as sched. B to the Canada Act, 1982 (UK) 1982, c. 11.

22 1867, 30 & 31 Vict., c. 3 (UK).

23 See Hogg, *Constitutional Law of Canada* (4th ed., 1996), at 474.

24 See, generally, Michael Trebilcock and Daniel Schwanen (eds.), *Getting There: An Assessment of the Agreement on Internal Trade* (Toronto: C.D. Howe Institute, 1995).

Recent proposals and consequent steps taken to remove the Government of Canada from certain areas where it exercised considerable influence by virtue of the federal spending power are not designed to restrict federal authority over international trade, but they do not remove the uncertainty regarding the outer limits of federal jurisdiction noted above.

Finally, it is to be noted that both the federal government, through the Department of Foreign Affairs and International Trade and related departments, and the provincial governments, through their departments of industry, trade, or international trade, provide important programs of assistance to importers. The federal functions are designed both to regulate customs and excise, foreign investment controls, as well as international trade, while the provincial role is generally directed to the facilitation of international trade and investment.

III. RULES GOVERNING CUSTOMS

A. Function and Relationship of the Customs and Tariff Acts

Two statutes govern the imposition and administration of customs duties: the Customs Act[25] and the Customs Tariff Act.[26] Important procedural matters are dealt with in the Canadian International Trade Tribunal Act.[27] The first two statutes are inextricably linked and, despite recent amendments, it is not always easy to explain why some matters are dealt with in one rather than in the other.

The logic of the division relates essentially to administration and status. The Customs Tariff Act sets the tariff that is to be levied on each category of imports; it governs the level of treatment to be accorded to the goods of broad categories of states and empowers the federal government to determine the category into which each state is classed. The Customs Tariff Act thus has an important public international law dimension. It also provides for a number of other methods of taxing or regulating the flow of imports into Canada apart from the tariff. These procedures are largely but not exclusively governed by the WTO, again reflecting the international dimensions of the Act. The Customs Tariff Act is completed by seven schedules: I—description of goods; II—goods incorporated into other goods; III—tariff treatment by country; IV—goods subject to drawback for home consumption; V—goods subject to drawback when used for certain purposes; VI—machinery and equipment; and VII—prohibited goods.

The Customs Act deals with the administration of the customs system—the tariff and other remedies instituted by the Customs Tariff Act. The Customs Act empowers the Minister of National Revenue (Customs and Excise) to enforce the customs system at the Canadian border or at other appropriate points in Canada or on the Canadian offshore. The Act also empowers the Minister and the Department of National Revenue (Customs and Excise) to adopt a wide variety of regulations governing the classification, determination of origin, and the valuation of imported goods, as well as the formalities

---

25 RSC 1985 (2nd Supp.), c. 1, as am.

26 RSC 1985 (3rd Supp.), c. 41, as am.

27 RSC 1985 (4th Supp.), c. 47, as am.

for the declaration of their origin and value. Included in the Customs Act are the rules on the valuation of goods for customs purposes. Also included are the rules governing the procedures for appeal from departmental decisions on such matters as the origin, valuation, and classification of goods—first to the higher echelons of the Department of National Revenue (Customs and Excise), then to the CITT and ultimately, on questions of law, to the Federal Court of Canada. These remedies are governed by the Canadian International Trade Tribunal Act[28] and the Federal Court Act,[29] respectively.

B. Customs Tariff Status

The Customs Tariff Act authorizes the Government of Canada to determine the status of countries for customs purposes. This is essentially a political and public choice that is made by the government on the basis of its discretion or its international commitments. These commitments flow largely from the GATT 1994, arrangements made under the aegis of the WTO, such as the Generalized System of Preferences for developing countries, traditional commitments to countries of the British Commonwealth of Nations, commitments flowing from bilateral FCN treaties or from special bilateral treaties such as the Canada-US Free Trade Agreement (FTA) and subsequently the North American Free Trade Agreement (NAFTA). Section 13(2)(b) of the Customs Tariff Act lists a number of potential tariff treatments that may be ascribed to a state: most-favoured-nation (MFN) (GATT or special bilateral agreements); United States, Mexico, and Mexico-US (NAFTA); British preferential (Commonwealth); general preferential tariff (commitments approved by the GATT benefitting developing countries); and "other tariff treatment" (particularly the special commitments made to the Commonwealth Caribbean countries, to the less developed countries (LDCs), and to New Zealand and Australia). Subject to some exceptions, where more than one tariff treatment is indicated for a country in schedule III, the treatment that applies to such country is the treatment that is most favourable to it.[30]

The decision as to tariff status has immediate practical and private implications for individual importers, since each status implies a different range of tariffs. If no particular status can be claimed, the rate of duty is 35 percent of the declared value.[31] The MFN tariff, which is enjoyed by WTO members, is normally well below at an average of 4 to 5 percent on industrial goods, and a very large number of items now bear no duty at all. The rates applicable to Commonwealth goods, or goods enjoying the other preferential rates, are lower than the MFN rate in respect of particular ranges of goods. These preferential rates cover particular ranges of goods and not necessarily the whole tariff schedule. The exception to this rule relates to the US, Mexican, and US-Mexican tariffs

28 *Ibid.*, and Canadian International Trade Tribunal Rules, SOR/91-499, 125 *Can. Gaz.* pt. II:2912, 28 August 1991; SOR/93-599, 127 *Can. Gaz.* pt. II:4534, 29 December 1993; SOR/93-601, 127 *Can. Gaz.* pt. II:4541, 29 December 1993; and SOR/95-13, 12 *Can. Gaz.* pt. II:28, 11 January 1995.

29 RSC 1985, c. F-7, as am., and rules.

30 Customs Tariff Act, s. 21(2).

31 *Ibid.*, s. 46.

under the NAFTA, which covers the whole Customs Tariff and which will reduce tariffs on goods from Mexico and the United States to "0" percent by January 1, 2008.

The status enjoyed by a country governs the tariff treatment of its exports to Canada. MFN status confers a very considerable financial advantage over the general tariff, as does the NAFTA tariff over the MFN tariff. The various special preferential rates also confer benefits over the MFN rate with respect to particular categories of goods from certain groups of states. Tariff status is authoritatively indicated by the listings in schedule III to the Customs Tariff Act.

Sections 22 to 58 of the Customs Tariff Act govern the grant of these different levels of treatment by the Government of Canada. The Act authorizes the Government of Canada to extend the benefits of MFN, British preferential tariff, general preferential tariff, or Commonwealth Caribbean preferential treatment as a matter of discretion. General preferential tariff and Caribbean preferences can be withdrawn on the same basis. However, withdrawal of MFN or of British preferential tariff is only permitted if authorized by a resolution of both Houses of Parliament within 180 days of the order withdrawing the benefits.[32] Preferential treatment under the NAFTA flows from the Canada-US Free Trade Agreement Implementation Act,[33] and, subsequently, the North American Free Trade Agreement Implementation Act, which has largely superseded the former Act.[34] Adjustments of the US tariff in certain circumstances are permitted[35] but the two Acts do not envisage wholesale withdrawal of US, Mexican, or US-Mexican tariff status, except insofar as the NAFTA itself provides for its own termination.[36]

Tariff status under Canadian law is thus a matter of some complexity given the mix of special bilateral and multilateral relationships in which Canada finds itself.

C. Rules of Origin

The grant of tariff status to a state has the consequence that importers must prove the origin of the goods that they import in order to enjoy the benefits of this status. There is one general rule of origin in the Customs Tariff Act that states:

> 13.(1) Subject to any regulations made under subsection (2), for the purposes of this Act, goods originate in a country if the whole of the value of the goods is produced in that country.

The difficulty with this rule is that a great many products are composite items made from components manufactured in many different countries and assembled and finished in others. It is necessary to refer to the many regulations that the Governor in Council is

---

32 *Ibid.*, s. 32(1).

33 SC 1988, c. 65, s. 82. The Act includes a complete revision of the Customs Act, sched. I, setting out the US tariff.

34 SC 1993, c. 44.

35 See Order Respecting the Suspension of Privileges Granted Under the Free Trade Agreement, SOR/89-54, 123 *Can. Gaz.* pt. II:787.

36 See chapter 2, *supra*.

authorized to make to assist in designating the country of origin.[37] These regulations deal with both the documentation required for proof of origin on entry of the goods into Canada, and the rules established to assist in determining the origin of goods composed of parts from different sources.

The fundamental principle that is enshrined in these rules of origin regulations is that a minimum percentage of the costs of production of the goods must have been incurred in the country of origin and that the goods must have been finished in a country that is a beneficiary of the status claimed. The rules allow for an accumulation of these criteria among more than one country enjoying the status claimed. The percentage for the MFN and British preferential tariff is 50 percent; the rule for the general preferential tariff and Caribbean tariffs is 60 percent, while the LDCs are granted the more favourable rate of 40 percent. Chapter 3 of the FTA and subsequently chapter 4 of the NAFTA set out detailed rules concerning the goods that may qualify for US, Mexican, and US-Mexican tariff status. The basic rule under the agreement is that the goods must incorporate at least 50 percent US value, as defined by the chapter, to qualify for US tariff status. Special considerations apply to automotive parts under chapter 3 of the NAFTA and the Canada-US Auto Pact of 1965,[38] and under regulations made pursuant to both agreements.[39] Of particular importance are the Marking of Imported Goods Regulations,[40] which require that all foreign goods be marked with their country of origin. Marking regulations issued pursuant to the NAFTA are necessary to distinguish between Mexican and US origin goods, since they bear different rates of duty during the phase-in period of the NAFTA.

Since the basic principle of the Act is not always easy to implement, and the regulations contain a wide variety of highly specific but uncoordinated rules, Canadian importers are often left to make difficult choices. The most widely used approach in case of doubt is to declare the country of origin to be the country where the goods assumed their final form.[41]

---

37 See, *inter alia*, the Regulations Respecting the Proof of Origin Requirements, etc., SOR/88-83, 122 *Can. Gaz.* pt. II:850; Most Favoured Nation Tariff and British Preferential Tariff Rules of Origin Regulations, SOR/78-215, as am., SOR/88-76, 122 *Can. Gaz.* pt. II:812; SOR/89-52, 123 *Can. Gaz.* pt. II:800; GPT and Least Developed Countries Rules of Origin Regulations, CRC vol. V, c. 528, as am.; and Caribbean Rules of Origin Regulations, SOR/89-52, 123 *Can. Gaz.* pt. II:802. See also the relevant D memos issued by the Department of National Revenue: D11-4-3 (MFN and BP); D11-4-4 (GPT and Least Developed); and D11-4-5 (Caribbean). See also Rules of Origins necessitated by the recent trade agreements to which Canada is a party NAFTA Rules of Origin Regulations, SOR/94-14, 128 *Can. Gaz.* pt. II:60, 12 January 1994, as am.

38 CTS 1966, no. 14.

39 See, *inter alia*, Automotive Parts Tariff Reduction Order 1966, CRC vol. V, c. 512, 3565; Automotive Parts Tariff Removal Order, 1988, SOR/89-36, 123 *Can. Gaz.* pt. II:262, 18 January 1989 and Automotive Goods Rules of Origin Regulations SOR/93-610, 127 *Can. Gaz.* pt. II:4585, 29 December 1993.

40 SOR/85-837, 119 *Can. Gaz.* pt. II:3786, 18 September 1985; revised by Marking of Imported Goods Regulations, SOR/94-10, 128 *Can. Gaz.* pt. II:46, 12 January 1994.

41 Recent CITT decisions include *Provincial Wallcovering Limited and the Deputy Minister of National Revenue for Customs and Excise*, [1994] CITT no. 96 (QL) and *Kelsea Sales & Importing Ltd. and the Deputy Minister of National Revenue for Customs and Excise*, [1994] CITT no. 90 (QL).

D. Valuation for Customs Purposes

Valuation of imported goods for customs purposes is governed by sections 44 to 57 of the Customs Act. These articles were first adopted in 1984 pursuant to Canadian ratification of the GATT Valuation Code of 1979. Subsequently, these sections have been amended pursuant to the FTA of 1988, the NAFTA of 1993, and the Agreement Establishing the WTO of 1995.[42] These rules constitute a radical simplification of the law that prevailed in Canada previous to 1984.[43] The earlier system was premised upon the requirement of establishing the "fair market value" of the goods. This rule, however reasonable its original intention, gave rise to foreign charges that Canadian law was uncertain, discretionary, and open to manipulation for protective purposes. The new standard of "transaction value" has the advantage of being both more neutral in scope and of being widely accepted by WTO members. The law of customs valuation thus underwent a major change in 1984; much earlier case law is no longer relevant, although cases dealing with certain related matters, such as trade levels and related parties, etc., are still accepted as authoritative.

The basic rule of customs valuation is set out in section 48 of the Customs Act:

> 48.(1) Subject to subsections (6) and (7), the value for duty of goods is the transaction value of the goods if the goods are sold for export to a purchaser in Canada and the price paid or payable for the goods can be determined ...[44]

As the term implies, the transaction value rule makes the declared value represented by invoices or other documents of sale the *prima facie* basis for valuation. The importer is presumed to be telling the truth as to the value of the goods and the Department of National Revenue will normally assess customs duty on this basis.

The Act describes the transaction value of the goods as "the primary basis of valuation." However, this is subject to a number of qualifications and conditions allowed by the GATT Valuation Code. While the transaction value is the primary basis of valuation, it is only the first in a series of five established by section 48 of the Customs Act, each one being applicable if the conditions necessary for the previous option are not present. The four supplementary bases of valuation set out in section 48(2) are:

(a) the transaction value of identical goods;
(b) the transaction value of similar goods;
(c) the deductive value of the goods; and
(d) the computed value of the goods.

---

42 Canada-US Free Trade Implementation Act, SC 1988, c. 65, ss. 70 and 71; North-American Free Trade Implementation Act, SC 1993, c.44, ss. 88 to 90; and World Trade Organization Implementation Act, SC 1995, c.47, s. 71.

43 For a full and careful review of the old and the new systems, see Irish, *Customs Valuation in Canada* (1985).

44 It should be noted that this section constitutes a considerable redrafting of the previous s. 48(1) of the Customs Act. See Act to amend the Customs Act, SC 1995, c. 41.

Transaction value is established according to section 48 of the Act. Use of the transaction value method is subject to certain requirements. In particular, the Act requires that there be no restrictions respecting the disposition of the goods by the importer; or that the price paid for the goods not include a component relating to a condition or consideration for which a value cannot be determined. Thus, the transaction value cannot be used for barter transactions. A further condition is that no proceeds from subsequent sales should accrue to the seller, unless the price has been adjusted in consequence. In principle, the seller and buyer should not be related to each other. However, non-arm's-length values are permitted if it can be shown that (1) the relationship did not influence the price paid, and (2) the importer of the goods demonstrates that the transaction price closely approximates comparable transaction prices described in section 48(3). The Customs Act is much more liberal in its approach to non-arm's-length sales than was the previous legislation.[45]

By virtue of section 48(5)(a) of the Customs Act, the transaction value declared must be adjusted by adding a number of items. The principal adjustments listed in the Act are commissions and brokerage fees paid by the buyer to a non-agent;[46] packing costs and charges;[47] and assists, which include (1) goods incorporated into the imports, (2) goods used but not consumed in the production of imports, (3) materials consumed in the production of imports, and (4) know-how. Other adjustments added to the declared value are royalties and licence fees,[48] proceeds of a subsequent sale accruing to the exporter, export duties and taxes paid in the country of export,[49] and costs of transportation to the port of exportation.[50] By virtue of section 48(5)(b), the transaction

---

45 On customs valuation, see the D memorandum series D-13-4 *et seq*. See, in particular, memorandum D-13-4-5, Related Persons.

46 In this regard, the Tariff Board decision in the *Magnasonic* case is still relevant in determining whether fees were paid to an agent: *Magnasonic Canada Ltd. v. DMNR*, app. no. 1330, 29 August 1978, 112 *Can. Gaz.* pt. I:7264. Leading recent decisions of the CITT dealing with adjustments for buying and selling commissions are *Chaps-Ralph Lauren, Division of 131384 Canada Inc. and Modes Alto Regal and the Deputy Minister of National Revenue for Customs and Excise*, [1995] CITT no. 79 (QL); *Mexx Canada Inc. and the Deputy Minister of National Revenue for Customs and Excise*, [1995] CITT no. 10 (QL); and *Radio Shack, Division of InterTAN Canada Ltd. and the Deputy Minister of National Revenue for Customs and Excise*, [1993] CITT no. 107 (QL).

47 See, regarding packing, the *Koyo Seiko* decision of the Tariff Board, *DMNR v. Koyo Seiko Co. Ltd.*, app. 1025, 29 April 1974, 5 TBR 458.

48 *Reebok Canada Inc. and the Deputy Minister of National Revenue for Customs and Excise*, [1993] CITT no. 100 (QL) (on appeal to the FCTD) and *Polygram Inc. and the Deputy Minister of National Revenue for Customs and Excise*, [1992] CITT no. 57 (QL).

49 See memorandum D13-4-7.

50 See *Monark Import-Export Inc. v. DMNR* (1990), 2 TCT 2191; *Consulac Architectural Products Ltd. and the Deputy Minister of National Revenue for Customs and Excise*, [1993] CITT no. 59 (QL); and *Western International Forest Products, Inc. and the Deputy Minister of National Revenue for Customs and Excise*, [1991] CITT no. 14 (QL).

value is adjusted downward by deducting the following items: transportation costs from the port of export; reasonable charges incurred for the purpose of construction, erection, or maintenance of the goods after importation; and duties or charges paid to import the goods. The Act also requires that rebates or other decreases in the price paid or payable after the goods are imported must be disregarded.[51] With respect to transportation costs, it is to be noted that Canada chose to exclude inland transportation costs from the calculation of export value.

Where the transaction value cannot be ascertained, the Customs Act requires that the four other methods of valuation be used each in turn. The first alternative, the transaction value of identical goods, is set out in section 49. If the required conditions are not present, the transaction value of similar goods, as defined by section 50, must be used. The third alternative is the deductive value method. This is established, in accordance with section 51, by gathering price and quantity data about sales of similar or identical goods sold in Canada at the same or substantially the same time as the import transaction, and at the same trade level as the importer. Under section 52 of the Act, the computed value is to be used after the deductive value method or, at the option of the importer, it may be used before the deductive value method. The computed value method is essentially a cost-plus method.

In the final analysis, where the value for duty cannot be calculated under sections 48 to 52, section 53 of the Customs Act provides the "residual method," which involves resort to all five methods by the Department of National Revenue, using information available in Canada. This is a largely discretionary power, but it confers a much narrower discretion than that existing under previous Canadian legislation.[52]

Since 1989, the Department of National Revenue has sought to interpret section 48 of the Customs Act as requiring for valuation purposes that there be a sale to persons in Canada.[53] The department has taken this position in its rulings and before the CITT in the case of *Harbour Sales (Windsor) Ltd. v. Deputy Minister of National Revenue*.[54] The CITT rejected the position, as did the Federal Court of Canada.[55] On June 13, 1995, the Minister of Finance tabled a notice of ways and means, subsequently Bill C-102, proposing

51 *Quadra Chemicals Ltd. and the Deputy Minister of National Revenue for Customs and Excise*, [1994] CITT no. 113 (QL) and *Nordic Laboratories Inc. and the Deputy Minister of National Revenue for Customs and Excise*, [1992] CITT no. 87 (QL).

52 See Irish, *supra*, note 43. See also the Valuation for Duty Regulations, SOR/86-792, 120 *Can. Gaz.* pt. II, 3130 and *Peter Kanis Jr. and the Deputy Minister of National Revenue for Customs and Excise*, [1993] CITT no. 60 (QL), leave to app. denied (1993), 66 FTR 284.

53 Memorandum D13-4-2, Customs Valuation: Sold for Export to Canada (Customs Act, s. 48), 21 August 1989.

54 4 November 1994, app. no. AP-93-322 (CITT).

55 Leave to app. denied 2 February 1995, per Noel J, 95-T-5 (FC TD). A further decision of note distinguishing *Harbour Sales* on its facts is *JewelWay International Canada, Inc. and Canada (DMNR)*, [1996] CITT no. 26 (QL) applies Harbour Sales but distinguishes on the basis that Canadian subsidiary is an agent of the US parent.

that section 48(1) of the Customs Act be amended to require that sales be to a purchaser in Canada. The effect of this amendment is to move the transaction a step up the transaction chain and thus result in the payment of a higher rate of duty. Arguably, this amendment is neither in conformity with the WTO Valuation Code nor with the NAFTA.[56]

E. Customs Classification

Schedule I of the Customs Tariff Act is a document covering almost 1,000 pages and listing many thousands of categories of goods. The present classification system is based on the Harmonized Commodity Description and Coding System, established by the Customs Cooperation Council based in Brussels. Canada was a party to the council from the early 1950s and has always used parts of the harmonized system. However, it was only in anticipation of the necessity of having a common classification system for the FTA that Canada and the United States both adopted the complete system. In Canada's case, this was done in 1987. The Customs Cooperation Council meets regularly to update its system, to discuss problems that arise and to give opinions on the interpretation of the nomenclature. Section 11 of the Customs Tariff Act states that schedule I can be interpreted in the light of the Compendium of Classification Opinions to the Harmonized Commodity Description and Coding System, and the Explanatory Notes as amended from time to time and published by the Brussels Cooperation Council.

The existence of all these categories often results in overlap. Given the fact that different tariff items carry different rates of duty, importers may have a strong financial interest in classifying their goods under one heading rather than under another. The problems are almost infinite. Perhaps the most celebrated case in Canadian law is one that occurred under the Excise Act and involved the vexed question of whether a peanut should be classified as a fruit or a vegetable. The Exchequer Court of Canada, in its wisdom, determined that a peanut for the purposes of the Act was neither; rather, it was a peanut.[57] Another classic case involved the question of whether a power shovel having a dipper capacity of two and one-half cubic yards was the equivalent of a power shovel made in Canada having the dipper capacity of two cubic yards or less.[58] In a more recent case, the Supreme Court was called upon to decide whether the synthetic drug oxytetracycline was a "derivative" of the naturally produced drug tetracycline. The court decided this case by invoking the normal and non-technical meaning of the word "derivative."[59] Customs classification raises questions of considerable difficulty frequently involving very considerable sums of money.

The harmonized system is designed to simplify the process of classification. It establishes 31 sections into which all items must be classified. Sections are subdivided into chapters that are further subdivided into sub-chapters according to a standard pattern.

---

56 SC 1995, c. 41.

57 *Planters Peanuts v. MNR*, [1951] Ex. CR 122.

58 *Dominion Engineering Works v. DMNR*, [1958] SCR 652.

59 *Pfizer Co. Ltd. v. DMNR*, [1977] SCR 456.

These three elements of the classification correspond to three double-digit numbers that must be used in each national classification. Each state may add two double-digit classes to specify further sub-categories of items. The latter sub-items can be numbered as the national customs administration considers appropriate. This uniformity of classification, numbering, and subdivision constitutes a considerable advance over the previous Customs Tariff Act but it has by no means removed all potential problems.

Schedule I of the Customs Tariff Act contains a short list of rules of interpretation. Among them are the following:

(a) a reference in a heading to an article includes reference to that article in the incomplete or unfinished state unless the contrary is specified;

(b) a reference to a material in a heading shall include reference to mixtures and combinations of the substance unless the contrary is stated;

(c) the heading which provides the most specific description shall be preferred to headings providing a more general description;

(d) mixtures or composite goods which cannot be classified according to rule (c) shall be classified as if they consisted of the material which gives them their essential character;

(e) goods which cannot be classified under (a)-(d) shall be classified under the heading appropriate to the goods to which they are most akin;

(f) where a Canadian and an international term are present in the nomenclature the commonly accepted meaning of the international term shall take precedence.

These general rules are completed throughout the schedule by supplementary notes to sections and chapters, as well as by interpretive provisions within individual descriptions.

The primary onus is on the importer to declare the classification of the goods. This can be rejected by the department and, in the event of continued disagreement, an appeal can be taken to the CITT, which assumed the functions of the Tariff Board in 1988. The Department of National Revenue has issued a host of D memoranda dealing with different aspects of the interpretation of tariff items listed in schedules I and II. The Governor in Council from time to time has issued regulations for the purpose of interpreting and implementing the classification system.[60] Since its creation before World War II, the tariff board, now replaced by the CITT, has issued thousands of decisions on tariff classification. The methods of interpretation used by the Department of National Revenue, the CITT, and the courts are quite varied. Particular emphasis is laid on grammatical, textual, and historical interpretation of the bilingual text. Teleological or economic analysis is generally avoided but occasionally finds its way into the reasoning. Recourse to the harmonized system is now fully authorized and while, in principle, a statute still has precedence over a treaty, the Customs Tariff Act itself provides for use of the harmonized system[61] in

---

60 See, e.g., Chemical and Plastics Tariff Interpretation Rules, CRC, vol. V, c. 518, r. 3577.

61 Recent CITT decisions dealing with the harmonized system are *Stochem Inc. and the Deputy Minister of National Revenue for Customs and Excise*, [1990] CITT no. 2 (QL), which discusses use of HS/EN pre-1988 amendment and post, as well as the "declaratory" nature of the amendment; *Thinkway Trading Corp. v. Canada (DMNR)*, [1996] CITT no. 23 (QL) and *Centennial Optical Ltd. v. Canada (DMNR)*, [1996] CITT no. 36 (QL).

aid of interpretation of the schedules. From time to time, the board and tribunal have considered parliamentary statements and commercial standards developed by commercial associations.

It may be argued that, in principle, the findings of the Deputy Minister of National Revenue (Customs and Excise) or of the CITT on questions of classification are questions of fact. Three points can be made in response. First, the distinction between matters of fact and law in administrative law has grown increasingly tenuous over the years. Second, since there is a right of appeal to the CITT on matters of classification, a characterization as a matter of fact is no bar to a hearing before the tribunal. Third, over the years, the courts have shown considerable willingness to review controversial decisions of the tariff board on matters of classification. On the other hand, it must be noted that recently, the Supreme Court of Canada, in a case involving subsidization, has refused to review a controversial decision of the International Trade Tribunal, where it was argued by a dissent in that tribunal[62] and the Federal Court of Appeal[63] that the decisions failed to conform to the requirements of the GATT Subsidies Code concerning countervailable subsidies. The Supreme Court of Canada rejected the appeal on the ground that the discretion of an administrative tribunal, such as the CITT, should not be interfered with except in the case of a manifestly unreasonable decision involving an error of law.[64] This difference in approach can be ascribed to the different statutory basis for review of fundings of fact in dumping and subsidies matters.

Finally, it must be noted that many of the decisions of the tariff board and of the courts rendered before the adoption of the new legislation in 1988 are no longer binding. However, those that deal with general matters or aspects of the law that have not been changed may still be relied upon. The CITT has only recently begun its work in the field of tariff classification in 1988, so its own case law on tariff classification is not abundant.[65] It has rendered some 150 decisions in this area. Notable among them are *Unisys Canada Inc. v. DMNR (C & E)*,[66] which deals with the classification of university computers used both for research and administration; *Gilmour Sports Ltd. v. DMNR (C & E)*,[67] which decided that "snow boards" were more properly classified as "snow skis" than as "other sports equipment"; *San Francisco Gifts Ltd. v. DMNR (C & E)*,[68] which determined that rollerblades were better classified as "roller skates" than as "other articles and equipment for general exercise"; and *Calavo Foods Inc. v. DMNR (C & E)*,[69] classifying guacamole as a "mixture of fruit" rather than as a "mixed condiment."

62 [1987] CITT no. 4 (QL).

63 [1989] 2 FC 517, 58 DLR (4th) 642.

64 *American Farm Bureau Association v. Canadian Import Tribunal*, [1990] 2 SCR 1324, (1991), 114 NR 81, 3 TCT 5303, 74 DLR (4th) 449 discussed in chapter 15, section III.K and III.U, *infra*.

65 See, e.g., *Reginald Bradley v. DMNR* (1990), 3 TCT 2188, which involved the classification of auto parts, and *Nova Aqua Sea Ltd. v. DMNR* (1990), 3 TCT 2233, which dealt with component parts of a fish farm.

66 [1992] CITT no. 101 (QL).

67 [1993] CITT no. 132 (QL).

68 [1994] CITT no. 54 (QL).

69 [1995] CITT no. 66 (QL).

F. Administration of the Customs System and Appeals from Decisions

Sections 11 to 43 of the Customs Act govern the administration of the customs system by the Department of National Revenue (Customs and Excise). Goods must be declared at the point of entry into Canada in the manner set out in the Act and regulations.[70] Information required must be fully provided. Duty is payable on the goods upon their declaration. Failure to declare goods or failure to supply appropriate information can leave the importer liable to serious penalties as well as lead to seizure of the goods and the vehicles used to transport them into Canada. Customs duties are debts owing to the Crown and follow the goods into the hands of third parties.

It is to be expected that in the near future the process of declaration of commercial goods will be done through electronic data-processing techniques, and that physical inspection at the border or in customs warehouses will be limited to *post facto* spot checks. The simplification of customs formalities was called for in the FTA[71] and has been pursued under the NAFTA.[72]

If the declaration of origin, value, or classification is not accepted by the customs officer receiving the declaration, it may be re-appraised within 30 days. Sections 57 to 66 of the Customs Act provide for a process of re-appraisal and appeal within the department, ultimately to the deputy minister. According to section 67(1) of the Customs Act: "A person who deems himself aggrieved by a decision of the Deputy Minister pursuant to section 63 or 64 may appeal from the decision to the Canadian International Trade Tribunal … ." Appeals are not restricted to questions of law. Section 67(3) empowers the Tribunal to make "such order, finding or declaration as the nature of the matter may require … ."[73] By virtue of section 68, such order, finding or declaration may be appealed by the appellant, the Deputy Minister or an intervenor, but appeals lie on "a question of law" to the Federal Court of Canada.[74] Ultimately, an appeal from a final decision of the Federal Court of Appeal can be taken by leave to the Supreme Court of Canada.

IV. REDUCTION, REMISSION, OR REBATE OF CUSTOMS DUTIES

A. Reduction or Removal of Customs Duties

Customs duties constitute a tax. Constitutional principle requires that they can only be established or raised by specific legislative action. However, the Governor in Council is

---

70 Customs Act, 1986, SC 1986, c. 1; RSC 1985, c. 1 (2nd Supp), s. 11; see also Reporting of Imported Goods Regulations, SOR/86-878, 120 *Can. Gaz.* pt. II:3715, 3 September 1986, as am.

71 See art. 406, Annex 406.D.

72 NAFTA, c. 5.

73 Canadian International Trade Tribunal Act, RSC 1985 (4th Supp.), c. 47, as am., ss. 18 to 24. On the jurisdiction of the CITT, see *Wilson Machine Co. Limited and the Deputy Minister of National Revenue for Customs and Excise*, [1992] CITT NO. 80 (QL), holding that CITT jurisdiction does not extend to considerations of equity.

74 The jurisdiction of the Federal Court is set out in s. 28(1)(e) of the Federal Court Act RSC, 1985, c. I-7. RSC 1985, c. F-11, as am., s. 23. The requirement to obtain leave of the Federal Court was removed by s. 20(c) of the Act to amend the Customs Act, SC 1995, c. 41.

authorized by section 62 of the Customs Tariff Act to reduce or to remove duties applicable to the goods of any country "... by way of compensation for concessions granted ..." by that country; as otherwise required by Canada's international obligations; or to reduce temporary surcharges set pursuant to section 60. Section 68 also authorizes certain very specific reductions of customs duties.[75] The Competition Act[76] authorizes the Governor in Council to reduce duties on goods where the duties are contributing to the lessening of competition in respect of certain goods.

B. Remission of Customs Duties

The Financial Administration Act[77] gives broad discretion to the Governor in Council, on recommendation of the Treasury Board, to remit customs duties. Such remission may be total or partial, conditional or unconditional. It has been used in very specific cases to relieve temporary difficulties of importers or manufacturers, often in consideration of specific undertakings. The power is totally discretionary and can lead to violations of Canada's international obligations.

The Customs Tariff Act also provides for various forms of duty remission covering a variety of circumstances, in particular, (1) goods of a class or kind not made in Canada, (2) goods imported and subsequently exported, (3) goods consumed in the process of processing of goods subsequently re-exported, (4) certain machinery and equipment not available in Canada, and (5) automotive machinery and equipment. Thus, section 12 of that Act and the corresponding provisions in the Schedules allow for lower rates of duty to be levied on certain items provided that they are not of "a class or kind made in Canada." The definition of class or kind not made in Canada has been the object of a number of decisions[78] and is the object of a regulation that fixes the minimum percentage of Canadian production to be 10 percent.[79]

Sections 80 to 87 make provision for the remission or reduction of duty upon goods that are brought into Canada and then subsequently re-exported, notably when the goods have been used in the manufacture of goods subsequently exported from Canada. These provisions are designed to encourage the establishment of production facilities in

---

75 Chemicals, plastics, and goods used in the manufacture of goods that are not otherwise available from Canadian production. Concessionary rates are set out in sched. II of the customs tariff.

76 RSC 1985, c. C-34, as am., s. 31.

77 See, *inter alia*, the following orders dealing with duty remission: Customs Duty on Certain Products Remission Order 1986, SI/86-83, 120 *Can. Gaz.* pt. II:2403, 11 June 1986 and Automotive Machinery and Equipment Remission Order, 1990, SI/90-85, 124 *Can. Gaz.* pt. II:3067, 18 July 1990.

78 *DMNR (Customs & Excise) v. St John Shipbuilding and Drydock Co.* (1965), 3 TBR 180 (SCC); see also *Electric Mobility (Canada) Corp. and the Deputy Minister of National Revenue for Customs and Excise*, [1994] CITT no. 2 (QL).

79 Substantial Quantity of Goods Percentage Order, 1987, SOR/88-81,122 *Can. Gaz.* pt. II:843, 20 January 1988 and XVth Commonwealth Games Remission Order, SOR/94-480, 128 *Can. Gaz.* pt. II:2735, 23 June 1994. For an example of a remission order, see, *inter alia*, Non-alcoholic Wine Remission Order, 1990, SOR/90-610, 124 *Can. Gaz.* pt. II:4064.

Canada and are thus often the object of specific programs or arrangements with particular manufacturers.[80] Sections 73 to 79 of the Customs Tariff Act empower the Minister of Finance to make lists of machinery not produced in Canada and to remit duties normally payable. This power is the basis of the Machinery Duty Remission Program, which exists to allow Canadian manufacturers to have access to advanced equipment not available from Canadian production, but allows the imposition of duties when such production occurs.[81] The program applies only to "goods not available from production in Canada" at the time of their importation into Canada.[82] Duty remission is also possible for the temporary entry of machinery to be used in a particular project.

Special provisions have long existed with respect to the provision of machinery and equipment used in the manufacture of parts and accessories used as original equipment for motor vehicles or in the manufacture of tooling for the production of these parts and accessories.[83] The use of similar powers by the Canadian government in earlier years led to protests from the US government and the conclusion of the Canada-US Auto Pact[84] in 1965.

C. Duty Drawbacks

Sections 66 to 72 of the Customs Tariff Act grant broad discretion to the Minister of Finance to establish duty drawback schemes for the purpose of encouraging the establishment of industrial production in Canada. Goods subject to drawback for home consumption or for other specified purposes are set out in schedules IV and V. Unlike remission, which affects the amount of duty payable at the point of entry to Canada, the drawback entitles the manufacturer to receive back a percentage of the duty paid if certain specified conditions are met.[85] Drawback schemes exist under the Customs Tariff Act to encourage the manufacture in Canada of goods instead of their acquisition abroad (home consumption drawbacks)[86] and to encourage the importation of

---

80 See, *inter alia*, Temporary Importation Regulations, SOR 89-427, 123 *Can. Gaz.* pt. II:3928, 13 September 1989, as am., by subsequent regulations and as interpreted by National Revenue memorandum D8-1-1; and Machinery and Equipment Parts Remission Order, 1988, SOR/88-82, 122 *Can. Gaz.* pt. II:844, 20 January 1988. For inward procession remissions, see National Revenue memorandum D7-3-1.

81 See National Revenue Memoranda D8-5-1 and D8-5-2. Goods covered are listed in sched. VI of the customs tariff.

82 See *Bristol-Meyers Canda Inc. v. MNR* (1993), 3 TTR 244 (FCA).

83 Customs Tariff Act, RSC 1885, c. 41 (3rd Supp.), as am., ss. 79.1 to 79.5.

84 CTS 1965, no. 14, now subsumed under NAFTA, Annex 300A.

85 See, *inter alia*, Customs Drawbacks on Toy Skins, SOR/88-76,122 *Can. Gaz.* pt. II:814, 20 January 1988; Canadian Manufactured Tires and Tubes (Exported Vehicles) Drawback Regulations, SOR/86-992, 120 *Can. Gaz.* pt. II:4230, 1 October 1986, revoked by reg. SOR/96-41, 130 *Can. Gaz.* pt. II:504, 1 January 1996; Duty Free Shop Regulations, SOR/86-1072, 120 *Can. Gaz.* pt. II:4758, 26 November 1986, last am. by reg. SOR/96-153, 103 *Can. Gaz.* pt. II:1153, 3 April 1996.

86 See National Revenue memorandum D7-2-1.

goods to be used in the manufacture of goods in Canada that are subsequently exported (export drawbacks).[87]

D. Implications of the Canada-US Free Trade Agreement and the North American Free Trade Agreement

Under the FTA, Canada committed itself in 1988 to limit the use of discretionary tariff reduction, remission, and drawback schemes and to abandon them in bilateral trade by June 30, 1998. This was done on the assumption that such preferential schemes were incompatible with the principles of non-discrimination, national treatment (NT), and free trade enshrined in the agreement.[88] Thus, most of the powers authorizing the creation of specific or general duty rebate or remission schemes have been severely restricted with respect to goods destined for the United States and, subsequently, Mexico. This is particularly true of automotive parts and products.[89] The FTA required the complete elimination of duty rebate and remission schemes. However, in a re-appraisal of this policy, the drafters of the NAFTA provided for the waiver or reduction of duty in an amount equal to the lesser of the duty paid or owed in one NAFTA country and the duty paid to another NAFTA country on the exportation of the goods.[90] Both parties have also reaffirmed their commitment not to use quotas and have agreed not to impose export taxes on bilateral trade.[91]

V. SPECIAL MEASURES

A. Recourses

1. Balance of Payments Action and Other Remedies

The Customs Tariff Act has long provided for several exceptional remedies that allow the government to take measures affecting imports in retaliation against foreign governmental practices or to deal with a domestic balance of payments crisis. The balance of payments action has a clear basis in the GATT; other measures taken unilaterally by states have always been a threat to the integrity of the GATT-WTO system. For this reason, it has been an objective of the GATT-WTO or of regional economic arrangements, such as the FTA or the NAFTA, to place additional disciplines on recourse to

---

87 See Customs Tariff Act, RSC 1985 (3rd Supp.), c. C-41, as am., s. 82; Canadian Manufactured Goods Exported Regulations SOR/86-877, 120 *Can. Gaz.* pt. II:3726, 3 September 1986, and Goods Imported and Exported Regulations, SOR/86-795, 120 *Can. Gaz.* pt. II:3142, 6 August 1986, revoked by Regulation SOR/96-41, 130 *Can. Gaz.* pt. II:504, 1 January 1996; and National Revenue memorandum D7-3-4. For the concept of consumption in Canada, see *CAE Metal Abrasives Division of CAE Enterprises v. DMNR (Customs & Excise)* (1985), 9 CER 159 (FCA).

88 FTA, arts. 404 and 405.

89 See NAFTA, c. 3.

90 NAFTA, art. 303(2)(d), implemented by the Customs Tariff Act, s. 83.02.

91 FTA, arts. 407 and 408.

such measures. Over the years, this has been done and constraints have been placed on WTO members through a series of increasingly specific agreements, culminating in the GATT 1994 and the NAFTA. However, as a result of this action, Canadian legislation now contains more, albeit limited, special remedies against imports than was the case a decade ago.

The Customs Tariff Act, the Export and Import Permits Act, and the Canadian International Trade Tribunal Act, in particular, provide a range of special remedies against imports. Due to the restraints accepted by the Government of Canada in various trade agreements, some of these measures can only be used against certain states, such as non-WTO or non-NAFTA parties. Others must only be used after a formal inquiry by the CITT. Some remedies may be initiated at the behest of the affected industry while others may be imposed directly by the government on the recommendation of the Minister of Finance, and some are subject to the scrutiny of Parliament.

2. *Balance of Payments Surcharge*

One of the most long-standing remedies contemplated by article XII of the GATT is the right to levy a temporary and non-discriminatory surcharge on imports to remedy a balance of payments crisis. This remedy is set out in section 61 of the Customs Tariff Act. It is initiated by the Minister of Finance, who is under no duty to seek the opinion of the CITT.

3. *Trade Retaliation*

Section 59 of the Customs Tariff Act also provides for a broad right of the Governor in Council to take a variety of measures, including the withdrawal of privileges under a trade agreement, the imposition of a surtax, the imposition of quotas under the Export and Import Permits Act, or the imposition of tariff quotas. This provision reflects earlier legislation and authorizes action that would not necessarily be compatible with the GATT 1994. It does not formally require recourse to a hearing by the CITT before the Governor in Council may act, but to do so without such a hearing for NAFTA parties or WTO members, would involve violation of these agreements.

4. *Safeguard Measures*

When legitimate imports cause or threaten serious injury to domestic production, safeguard procedures may be invoked. They constitute a right of response to fair trade practices contemplated in certain circumstances by article XIX of the GATT and, since 1994, by the agreement on safeguards, as well as by a number of other special agreements on safeguards with respect to trade in particular goods and services to be found in the GATT 1994. The remedies which are envisaged in sections 59.1, 60, and 60.1 to 60.5 of the Customs Tariff Act and sections 20 and 26 of the Canadian International Trade Tribunal Act amount to a safety valve for difficulties created for Canadian producers by commitments made under the GATT-WTO 1994, the FTA, and, subsequently, the NAFTA, the general preferential tariff, the Caribbean initiatives, and any other new trade or aid agreements. They may be initiated either by the Minister of Finance or by Canadian producers and in almost all cases they require reference of the allegations to the CITT for a full hearing and a recommendation as to the necessity of governmental action. If the CITT recommends a response, the Minister of Finance is authorized to impose a variety of remedies according to the circumstances, the type of goods, or the origin of the goods. The principal remedy contemplated by the legislation is a temporary surtax, but other remedies include temporary roll-backs of duty reductions and the re-imposition of duties and quotas under the Export and Import Permits Act. In the case of agricultural commodities and television picture tubes, the legislation does not require reference of the complaint to the CITT.[92]

As well as introducing a variety of remedies, the extensive legislative changes resulting from implementation of the NAFTA in 1994 and the GATT 1994 in 1995,[93] now contemplate two standards of injury justifying the imposition of safeguard measures. Section 60(1), which applies generally to goods from all countries, contemplates the necessity of a report by the Minister of Finance or of a CITT finding that:

> ... goods of any kind, that are imported from any country, are being imported into Canada under such conditions as to cause or threaten serious injury to Canadian producers of like or directly competitive products ...

Where an order is based on the report of the Minister of Finance, the measures must be approved by both Houses of Parliament within 180 days or referred to the CITT for an injury determination, in which case it remains in force for three years. To implement the FTA, this section can only apply to US origin goods when there is a "surge" of the imported goods entering Canada from the United States.

Section 59.1 implements a similar procedure as contemplated by the NAFTA.[94] It further limits the right of the Minister of Finance to act unilaterally to circumstances that are deemed "critical" or that relate to perishable agricultural products.[95] The section also requires that safeguard measures only be taken against NAFTA origin goods when the imports of such goods are "substantial" in comparison to the total quantity of goods of the same kind imported from other countries, and when the volume of NAFTA origin goods "contributes importantly to serious injury or the threat thereof ... ."

Sections 60.1 to 60.5 implement special safeguard rules applicable to US and Mexican origin goods as required by the NAFTA, particularly with respect to agricultural goods, including fresh fruit and vegetables, textiles, and television picture tubes. The general test is even more restrictive than other safeguard rules since they can only be invoked when the imported goods are "being imported into Canada in such increased quantities and under such conditions as to alone constitute a principal cause of serious injury" as a general rule. Textiles are subject to the requirement that they must be causing "serious damage" ... "in absolute terms or relative to the domestic market for the goods ... ." The remedies concerning imports of certain agricultural goods pursuant to these sections can be applied without referral to the CITT.

---

92 See ss. 60.4 and 5 of the Customs Tariff Act.

93 *Supra*, notes 11 and 12.

94 Section 59.1 (1) refers to "goods" rather than "products."

95 Section 59.1(1) and (1.1).

Safeguard remedies are completely separate and distinct from anti-dumping and countervailing duty proceedings, however, some commentators[96] have noted that the injury determination process is conducted by the same body, the CITT, and the process of analysis is not entirely dissimilar.

5. Other Remedies

The Canadian International Trade Tribunal Act would seem to provide an independent safeguard remedy against goods.[97] This Act also applies to services—a matter of increasing significance as the GATT Agreement on Services contemplates the possibility of safeguard actions against foreign service providers. The Export and Import Permits Act also provides a legislative basis for the imposition of quotas on imports. Use of this power without taking into account Canada's international commitments would certainly lead to serious difficulties with our trading partners.[98]

6. CITT Procedures

The procedures for a safeguard complaint follow a set pattern in conformity with the law and the practice of the CITT.

The tribunal undertakes inquiries both at the behest of the Minister of Finance and at the behest of private parties.[99] The recommendation by the tribunal is not in itself binding. It is forwarded to the minister, who is empowered by the legislation to impose the range of remedies reviewed above.

B. Prohibitions and Other Restrictions

The Customs Tariff Act prohibits the importation of certain goods into Canada,[100] for example, offensive weapons as defined in the Criminal Code.[101] A wide variety of other federal statutes provide for the prohibition or the regulation of the importation of goods and services into Canada.[102]

The FTA and subsequently the NAFTA allow the imposition of import and export control measures to protect essential security and legitimate national interests.[103] These measures are also justified under the GATT.[104]

---

96 See Paterson and Band, at 6-41.

97 See s. 23 of the Canadian International Trade Tribunal Act, RSC 1985, c. 47 (4th Supp.).

98 See chapters 1 and 2, *supra*.

99 See *Uncoated Biaxially Oriented Polypropylene (BOPP) Film of a Thickness of 0.025 More or Less (Petition for Safeguard Action by Mobil Chemical Canada Ltd.)*, 10 March 1989, which involved the general preferential tariff (1989), 2 TCT 1075.

100 Sched. VII, item 9965.

101 RSC 1985, c. C-46, as am., s. 2.

102 *Supra*, note 13.

103 FTA, arts. 1201 and 2003; NAFTA, arts. 2101-2102.

104 GATT 1947, arts. XX and XXI.

C. Implications of the North American Free Trade Agreement

The NAFTA, like the FTA before it, contains serious limitations on the right of the Government of Canada to employ these extraordinary remedies against goods of US and Mexican origin. Chapter 8, dealing with emergency action, restricts the right to use safeguard procedures during the 10-year transition period to a maximum of three years and requires that such action may only be taken once during that period against any particular product. After the end of the transition period, emergency measures shall only be taken by Canada with the consent of the United States and vice versa. As noted above, it is also agreed under chapter 8 that global safeguard measures taken by Canada shall not apply to another NAFTA party, unless exports are the principal cause contributing seriously to the injury. No such action shall be taken by either party against the other without prior notification and subject to a right to compensation in the form of concessions having substantially equivalent trade effects.

VI. QUOTAS AND VOLUNTARY RESTRAINTS

GATT, article XI has always prohibited the use of quantitative restrictions in international trade, and Canada has generally been prepared to respect this ban. A similar prohibition is to be found in article 407 of the FTA and in article 309 of the NAFTA. The GATT 1994 has greatly widened the scope of the discipline placed upon the use of quotas and, in the case of quotas used to protect supply management systems, these quotas have been converted into tariff quotas. However, Canada has not relinquished the use of quotas. The main vehicle for imposing import quotas is the Export and Import Permits Act.[105] The Act empowers the Governor in Council to establish lists of imports, whose importation is prohibited without a permit from the federal export import permits office. Authority to include goods on the import control list or to authorize or to refuse permission to import such products is very broad and has seldom been challenged with success.[106] This Act is used in support of policies established under other Acts, in particular, federal and provincial legislation designed to regulate the production and supply of agricultural commodities.[107] In 1989, Canadian quotas on the importation of yogurt and ice cream were the subject of a GATT panel report.[108] The quotas were held to violate certain aspects of the GATT.

---

105 RSC 1985, c. E-19, as am. See also Import Permit Regulations, SOR/79-5, 113 *Can. Gaz.* pt. II:8 , 10 January 1979, last am. by reg. SOR/96-49, 130 *Can. Gaz.* pt. II:538, 1 January 1996.

106 The discretion is not absolutely unlimited, however; see *Maple Lodge Farms v. Government of Canada*, [1982] 2 SCR 2 and *Dantex Woollen Co. v. Min. of Industry, Trade and Commerce*, [1979] 2 FC 585.

107 See also legislation listed *supra*, note 13. The Act is also used to ensure the integrity of provincial agricultural marketing legislation enacted to coordinate with the federal Agricultural Products Marketing Act, *supra*, note 13.

108 *Restrictions on the Importation of Ice Cream and Yoghurt*, GATT Doc. L/6568, 27 September 1989, BISD, 36th Supp. 68.

Canada has long used quotas to implement the Multi-Fibre Arrangement (MFA),[109] which establishes a complex system of allocations of the right of textile producers to export, subject to the right of consuming countries to restrict the entry of products in excess of these allocations. With the adoption of the GATT 1994, the MFA has been subsumed under the GATT Agreement on Textiles, which requires that all such quota arrangements on textiles be made subject to the disciplines of the GATT over a 10-year phase-in period. In principle, many textile quotas will have disappeared by 2009 and trade-in textiles should then be governed by non-discriminatory tariff duties. The FTA and the NAFTA also allow for the use of quotas or tariff quotas to control trade in textiles between the two countries.[110]

A more difficult issue to document is the use of "voluntary export restraints" (VERS) by Canada. During the decades of the 1970s and 1980s, the United States and the European Communities (EC) are known to have pressed some foreign producers, particularly Japan and the "Asian Tigers," to restrain their exports of some products, such as automobiles, under threat of various forms of retaliation, including the imposition of quotas. The Government of Canada was relatively discreet as to whether it was using the same tactic to protect Canadian industries in time of difficulty. It was reported that the Japanese government made commitments to Canada not to re-direct automobile exports to Canada during the period in the 1980s when the Japanese had publicly made voluntary export commitments to the United States. Since the practice become sufficiently widespread to be denounced by many states at the GATT, it can be assumed that Canada did not have entirely clean hands in the matter.[111] In principle, all voluntary restraints are in process of being phased out pursuant to the GATT Agreement on Safeguards that forms part of the GATT 1994 and that requires that all WTO members abandon existing voluntary restraints and respect a standstill on the creation of any new VERS. When this period is over, VERS should, in principle, be a thing of the past.

---

109 See, generally, the import control list issued under the Export and Import Permits Act. See also Import Certification Regulations, CRC vol. VI, c. 603, 4115; Import Permit Regulations, SOR/79-5, 113 *Can. Gaz.* pt. II:8; and General Permit, Textiles, SOR/82-235, 116 *Can. Gaz.* pt. II:870.

110 See FTA, Annex 301.2, section XI and NAFTA, Annex 300B.

111 See Wong, "The Japanese Automotive Voluntary Export Restraint Agreements and International Law" (1985), 23 *Can. Ybk. Int'l. L* 297.

Import Safeguard Complaints by Domestic Producers

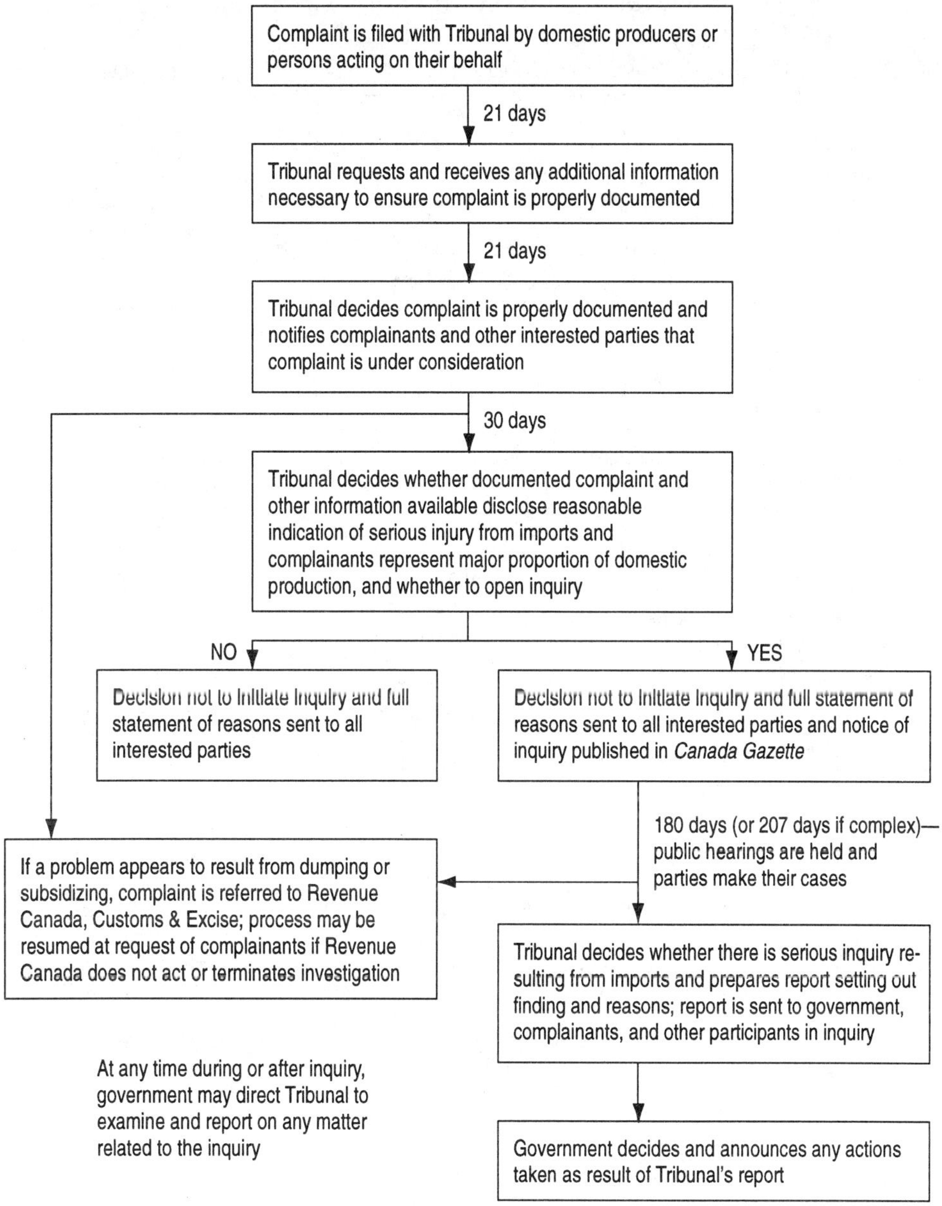

Import Safeguard Complaints Concerning the General Preferential Tariff (GPT) or CARIBCAN

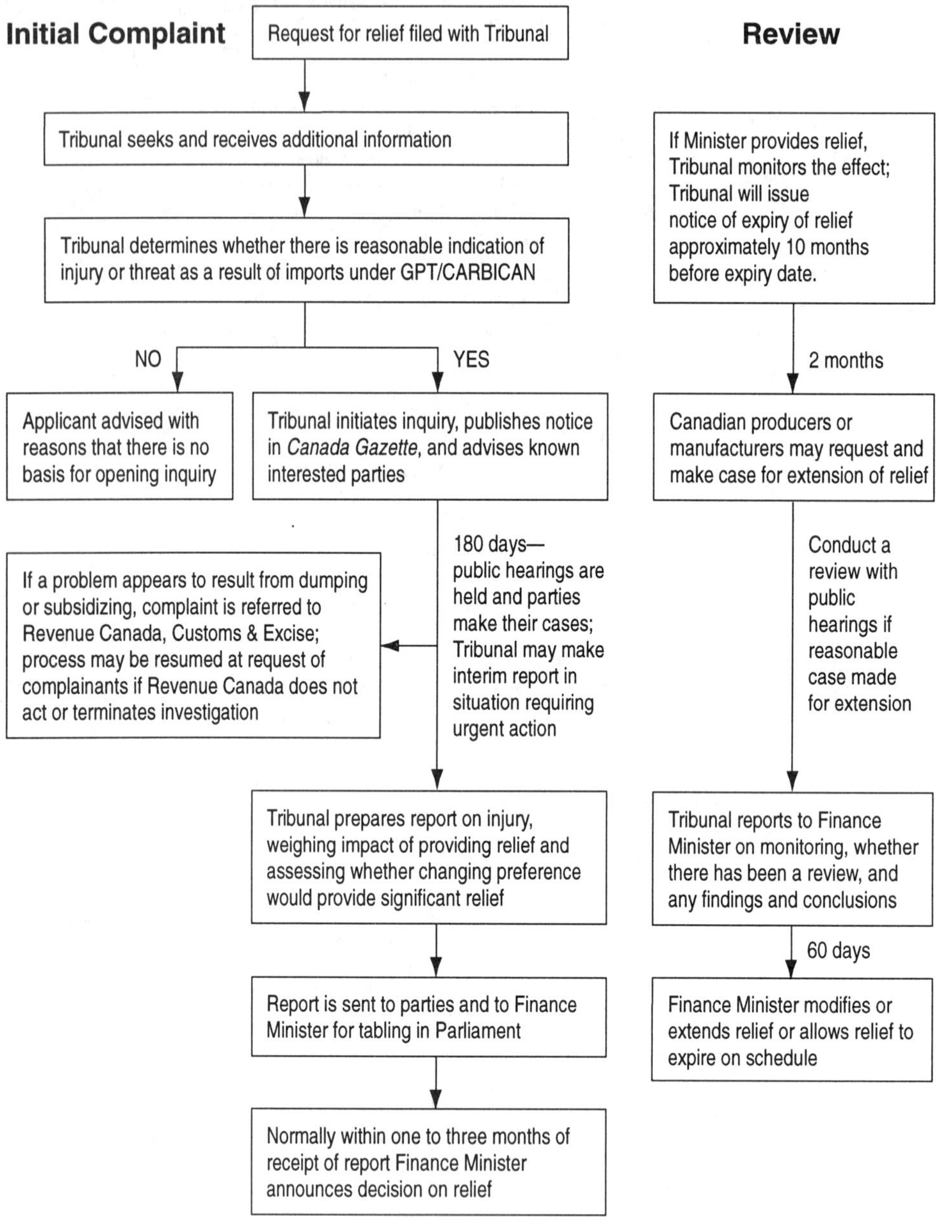

VII. SELECTED BIBLIOGRAPHY

A. Books

de Lotbinière Panet (ed.), *National Trade and Tariff Service* (1990).

Gottlieb and Pearson (eds.), *International Trade Law of Canada* (1992).

Irish, *Customs Valuation in Canada* (1985).

Irish, *The Harmonized System and Tariff Classification in Canada* (McGill University thesis, DCL, 1992).

Paterson and Band, *International Trade and Investment Law in Canada* (2nd ed., 1995).

Prabhu, *The Annotated Customs Act* (1988).

Trebilcock and Howse, *The Regulation of International Trade* (1995).

B. Articles

Adamcyk, "A Survey of Tariff Classification—Ironing out the Creases" (1982), 7 *Can. Bus. LJ* 101.

Akin, "The Customs Valuation Agreement in the New GATT and Its Effect on Valuation of Imports into Canada" (1979-80), 4 *Can. Bus. LJ* 316.

Behrendt, "Technical Analysis of the Customs Valuation Agreement" (1980), 12 *Law & Pol. Int'l. Bus.* 159.

Dattu et al., "Seeking Redress of Customs Decision" (1995), 14 *Nat. BL Rev.* 74.

Irish, "Interpretation and Naming: the Harmonized System in Canadian Customs Tariff Law" (1993), 31 *Can. Ybk. of Int'l. L* 89.

Irish, "Machinery and Remission: Transparency and the Role of Law" (1994), 23 *Can. Bus. LJ* 161.

Sherman, "Reflections on the New Customs Valuation Code" (1980), 12 *Law & Pol. Int'l. Bus.* 119.

Slayton and Quinn, "The GATT and the Deep Structure of Customs Administration," in Quinn and Slayton (eds.), *Non-Tariff Barriers After the Tokyo Round* (1982).

Zacher, "The Insurer's Duty to Indemnify for Loss of Illegally-Imported Goods" (1994), 5 *Can. Ins. L Rev.* 293.

CHAPTER FIFTEEN

Subsidies and Dumping

I. INTRODUCTION

Canadian producers of goods identical to or closely resembling imported goods are sometimes concerned that such imported goods may have received production or export subsidies or are being dumped on the Canadian market.

Since subsidizing and dumping are considered unfair trade practices that distort prices or profits, disrupt markets, and injure producers of competitive goods in the country of import, these practices have been regulated by special federal legislation[1] based on articles XVI and VI of the General Agreement on Tariffs and Trade (GATT), the Agreement on Implementation of Article VI of the GATT 1994,[2] and the 1994 Agreement on Subsidies and Countervailing Measures.[3]

The Canada-US Free Trade Agreement (FTA), and subsequently the North American Free Trade Agreement (NAFTA), do not alter the substantive law on subsidies and anti-dumping in Canada, but provide for certain procedural reforms. The most significant of these reforms is dispute settlement through binational panel review where subsidies and dumping of goods originating in or exported from the United States or Mexico are involved. These arrangements have been implemented into Canadian domestic law through the Special Import Measures Act (SIMA). More recently, the Canada-Chile Free Trade Agreement signed on December 17, 1996 bars the application of the domestic

---

1 Special Import Measures Act (SIMA), RSC 1985, c. S-15, as am., RSC 1985, c. 23 (1st Supp.); RSC 1985, c. 1 (2nd Supp.); RSC 1985, c. 47 (4th Supp.); SC 1988, c. 65; SC 1994, c. 44; and SC 1994, c. 47 and Special Import Measures Regulations, SOR/84-927, as am., SOR/89-63, SOR/89-578, SOR/90-662, SOR/92-236, SOR/92-590, SOR/94-20, SOR/95-26. See also Interest Rate for Customs Purposes Regulations, SOR/86-1121, as am., SOR/88-72, SOR/89-53, and SOR/92-517.

2 Called the 1994 Anti-dumping Code, replacing the Agreement on Implementation of Art. VI of the GATT, BISD, 26th Supp. 171 (1978-79) (called the Revised Anti-dumping Code).

3 Called the 1994 Subsidies Code, replacing the Agreement on the Interpretation and Application of Arts. VI, XVI, and XXIII of the GATT, BISD, 26th Supp. 56 (1978-79) (called the Subsidies and Countervailing Measures Code).

anti-dumping laws of the parties to the goods of the other party, subject to certain transitional provisions. In addition, the Agreement establishes a Committee on Trade Remedies to consult with a view to eliminating the need for domestic countervailing duty measures between them, and to facilitate Chile's full accession to the NAFTA.

II. TRADE IN GOODS: GATT-WTO AND THE CODES

On April 15, 1994 in Marrakesh, over 120 countries signed the Final Act Embodying the Results of the Uruguay Round of Multilateral Trade Negotiations and the Agreement Establishing the World Trade Organization (the WTO Agreement). The World Trade Organization (WTO) was established to administer the revised GATT 1994 and "to provide a common institutional framework for the conduct of trade relations among its Members."[4] The WTO Agreement and its integral annexes represent a "single undertaking approach" to trade obligations, imposing uniformity and consistency in international trade law. Thus, WTO members have agreed to abide by all of the obligations found in all of the agreements in annexes 1, 2, and 3. Included in Annex 1A of the WTO Agreement, containing the Multilateral Agreements on Trade in Goods, are (1) the Agreement on Implementation of Article VI of the General Agreement on Tariffs and Trade 1994 (the 1994 Anti-Dumping Code), and (2) the Agreement on Subsidies and Countervailing Measures (the 1994 Subsidies Code). All members are bound by the new codes. These arrangements supersede the 1979 Tokyo Round Codes on Subsidies and Countervailing Measures[5] and on Anti-dumping, which were binding only upon their relatively limited number of signatories.[6] They represent a far more comprehensive and effective approach to regulating anti-dumping and countervailing practices, ensuring greater certainty, fairness, and transparency to the parties. In addition, subsidies and anti-dumping disputes now fall under the aegis of the WTO Dispute Settlement Understanding (DSU).[7] Along with introducing an appellate body to review panel reports, the DSU provides a more consistent and rule-oriented dispute settlement process, involving greater automaticity in the establishment of panels and the adoption of panel and appellate reports, strict time limits for each step, and more robust surveillance procedures to ensure the implementation of panel and appellate rulings.[8]

---

4 WTO Agreement, art. II.1. See *supra*, chapter 1.

5 Agreement on Interpretation and Application of Arts. VI, XVI and XXIII of the GATT, BISD, 26th Supp. 56 (1978-79) (the 1979 Subsidies Code).

6 Agreement on Implementation of Art. VI of the GATT, BISD, 26th Supp. 171 (1978-79) (the Revised Anti-dumping Code or the 1979 Anti-dumping Code).

7 Annex 2 to the WTO Agreement, "Understanding on Rules and Procedures Governing the Settlement of Disputes." Note that a separate "Declaration on Dispute Settlement Pursuant to the Agreement on Implementation of Art. VI of the GATT 1994 or Part V of the Agreement on Subsidies and Countervailing Measures" annexed to the WTO Agreement recognizes "the need for the consistent resolution of disputes arising from anti-dumping and countervailing duty measures."

8 The WTO-DSU is further discussed in chapter 19. Note that app. 2 to the DSU, entitled "Special or Additional Rules and Procedures Contained in the Covered Agreements," lists arts. 17.4 to 17.7 of the

(The footnote is continued on the next page.)

A. Subsidies

In general, a subsidy is a financial contribution or other form of support by a state or quasi-state agency conferring a benefit upon an industry or company. The original GATT, article XVI imposed two obligations upon GATT contracting parties granting subsidies: (1) notification to the contracting parties of any subsidy they maintained or granted that had the effect of increasing exports or decreasing imports, and (2) consultation with any contracting party alleging injury with a view to the possibility of limiting the subsidization. It did not provide any precise definition of what constituted a subsidy. While internal subsidies and production subsidies were not prohibited, export subsidies on products other than primary products were prohibited under paragraph 4. Export subsidies on primary products that "contracting parties should seek to avoid" could "not be applied in a manner which result[ed] in that contracting party having more than an equitable share of world export trade in the product."

GATT, articles XXII and XXIII dispute settlement provisions were generally applicable to disputes relating to subsidies and dumping arising between the contracting parties.

The Agreement on Interpretation and Application of Articles VI, XVI, and XXIII of the GATT (the 1979 Subsidies Code) was negotiated during the Tokyo Round of Multilateral Trade Negotiations, entering into force for the signatories on January 1, 1980. The 1979 Subsidies Code's preamble recognized "that subsidies are used by governments to promote important objectives of national policy," but "also that subsidies may have harmful effects on trade and production." It expressed the signatories' aim of elaborating rules for the regulation of subsidies and countervailing measures "in order to provide greater uniformity and certainty" in the implementation of GATT, articles VI, XVI, and XXIII; to ensure that the use of subsidies did not adversely affect or prejudice the interests of any signatory, and that countervailing duties did not unjustifiably impede international trade; and to provide for rapid, effective, and equitable dispute resolution so that relief was available to producers adversely affected by the application of subsidies.

Supervised by a committee consisting of representatives of its signatories, the 1979 Subsidies Code interpreted and developed the GATT provisions and outlined procedural standards for the conduct of subsidy investigations. It introduced innovations concerning (1) internal subsidies which the signatories could not use in such a manner as to cause serious prejudice;[9] (2) an illustrative list of export subsidies on products other than primary products presumed to have adverse effect;[10] (3) the concept of displacement of exports in another signatory in the case of export subsidies on primary products;[11] and

---

8 Continued …

1994 Anti-dumping Code and arts. 4.2 to 4.12, 7.2 to 7.10, 8.5, 24.4, 27.7, footnote 35, and Annex V of the 1994 Subsidies Code. DSU, art. 1.2 states that to the extent that the DSU and the special or additional rules set forth in app. 2 are inconsistent, the latter will prevail.

9 1979 Subsidies Code, *supra*, note 5, art. 11.

10 Annex to the 1979 Subsidies Code, *ibid.*

11 1979 Subsidies Code, *ibid.*, art. 10.

(4) the determination of injury based upon an objective examination of the volume of subsidized imports and their effect on domestic prices, and of the impact of those imports on domestic producers.[12]

The 1979 Subsidies Code emphasized the importance of transparency[13] and contained special provisions for consultations, conciliation, and dispute settlement.[14] A signatory could request consultations if it believed another signatory was granting subsidies inconsistent with the code or it believed its benefits under the GATT were nullified, impaired, or its interests seriously prejudiced. Where the consultations did not resolve the dispute, the parties could request the establishment of a panel to examine the issue and release a report. However, since either party could block the adoption of the report by the committee administering the Code, the mechanism was of limited effectiveness. Under the previous fragmented GATT dispute settlement system, dispute settlement concerning subsidies was also available under articles VI and XVI of the GATT 1947. Such disputes were dealt with by the GATT CONTRACTING PARTIES. The availability of dispute settlement procedures under both the 1979 Subsidies Code and the GATT 1947 caused confusion, and led to the possibility of forum-shopping.

The 1994 Subsidies Code expands, elaborates upon, and significantly modifies the provisions of the 1979 Subsidies Code. The new code offers a more comprehensive approach to the regulation of subsidies and countervailing measures, providing more stringent procedural and substantive parameters for the conduct of members' subsidies investigations and regulation of countervailing duties procedures. Remedying the problem of forum-shopping that plagued the pre-WTO regime, the 1994 Subsidies Code integrates subsidies disputes into the uniform WTO dispute settlement procedures under the DSU. In addition, the 1994 Subsidies Code establishes a Committee on Subsidies and Countervailing Measures, composed of representatives from each of the members, to monitor the operation of the agreement.[15] This committee appoints a permanent group of experts (PGE),[16] composed of five highly qualified and independent individuals, who assist the dispute settlement panel,[17] may be consulted by any member, and give advisory opinions on any current or proposed subsidy of a member.[18]

The 1994 Subsidies Code provides more detailed standards for the conduct of countervailing duty investigations by domestic authorities, based on transparency, procedural fairness, and specific time deadlines.[19]

A major accomplishment of the Uruguay Round Subsidies negotiations was the insertion in the 1994 Subsidies Code of a detailed and internationally agreed-upon definition of

---

12 *Ibid.*, art. 6.

13 *Ibid.*, art. 7.

14 *Ibid.*, arts. 12-13 and 17-18.

15 1994 Subsidies Code, *supra*, note 3, art. 24.1.

16 *Ibid.*, art. 24.3.

17 *Ibid.*, arts. 24.3 and 4.5.

18 *Ibid.*, art. 24.4.

19 *Ibid.*, art. 22.

"subsidy,"[20] as well as criteria for determining whether a subsidy is specific[21] and therefore actionable and/or countervailable. While the 1979 Subsidies Code prohibited *de facto* export subsidies,[22] the 1994 Subsidies Code extends this prohibition to embrace subsidies contingent upon export performance.[23] The annexed list of prohibited export subsidies practices reflects this evolution. Subsidies contingent upon the use of domestic goods are also prohibited. The 1994 Subsidies Code allows countries three years from its entry into force to bring inconsistent practices into conformity with the agreement.

The 1994 Subsidies Code imposes control upon members' subsidization practices in two ways:[24] (1) multilateral disciplinary proceedings, and (2) unilateral countervailing duty proceedings. The 1994 Subsidies Code divides subsidies into three categories, which determine their treatment:

(i) prohibited subsidies[25] which are deemed to be specific[26] and are actionable even when no adverse effect is attached to them. They include subsidies contingent upon export performance, or upon the use of domestic over imported goods.[27] Where a member has reason to believe another member is granting such a subsidy, it may request consultations with the subsidizing country. Where no mutually acceptable solution is reached within 30 days (or longer if extended by mutual agreement), either member may refer the dispute to the WTO's Dispute Settlement Body "DSB" for the establishment of a panel. The provisions of the WTO DSU and Articles 4.2-4.12 of the 1994 Subsidies Code[28] govern the dispute from that time on.[29]

---

20 *Ibid.*, art. 1.1.

21 *Ibid.*, art. 2. The concept of specificity is further discussed in the context of the SIMA, *infra*, at III.B.2; essentially, a subsidy is specific where it is explicitly limited to certain enterprises. Where a subsidy is granted pursuant to objective legislative or regulatory criteria mandating automatic eligibility (i.e., permitting no discretion on the part of the granting authority) a subsidy is not specific, subject to certain additional considerations.

22 1979 Subsidies Code, *supra*, note 5, art. 9.

23 See art. 3.1(a) of the 1994 Subsidies Code, *supra*, note 3.

24 Note 35 under art. 10 of the 1994 Subsidies Code, *ibid.* explains that the provisions of pt. II (prohibited subsidies) or III (actionable subsidies) of the code may be invoked in parallel with the provisions of pt. V (countervailing measures), but only one form of relief will be available to remedy the effects of a particular subsidy on the domestic market (i.e., either a countervailing duty under pt. V or a retaliatory measure under pt. II or III). Pts. III and V are not to be invoked in relation to non-actionable subsidies under pt. IV of the code.

25 Sometimes referred to as "red light" subsidies. See 1994 Subsidies Code, pt. II, *supra*, note 3, arts. 3 and 4.

26 1994 Subsidies Code, *ibid.*, art. 2.3.

27 With the exception of those provided for in the 1994 WTO Agreement on Agriculture, art. 13 of this agreement exempts certain domestic support measures and export subsidies from the 1994 Subsidies Code.

28 See DSU, app. 2 and art. 1.2 on the relationship between the DSU provisions and the special or additional rules listed in app. 2, which include arts. 4.2 to 4.12 of the 1994 Subsidies Code, *ibid.*

29 Under the DSU and the special rules in arts. 4.2 to 4.12 of the 1994 Subsidies Code, *supra*, note 3, the panel must issue its report within 90 days. Where the panel determines that the subsidy under consideration is a

(The footnote is continued on the next page.)

(ii) permissible subsidies which are actionable under multilateral proceedings and countervailable unilaterally if they cause adverse trade effects.[30] Article 5 of the 1994 Code enumerates three types of adverse effects: injury to another Member's domestic industry; nullification or impairment of benefits accruing indirectly or directly to another Member under GATT 1994; and serious prejudice[31] to another Member's interests. Where a Member has reason to believe that another Member is applying a subsidy having adverse effects upon it, it may request consultations with the subsidizing country (Article 7). If no mutually acceptable solution is achieved within 60 days (or a longer period established by mutual agreement), either country may refer the dispute to the DSB for the establishment of a panel. The WTO DSU provisions and Articles 7.2-7.10 of the 1994 Subsidies Code then apply.[32]

(iii) subsidies which are non-actionable and non-countervailable if they qualify under criteria which limit their distorting potential.[33] In order to be non-actionable, these subsidies must be notified in advance to the Committee on Subsidies and Countervailing Measures (the "Committee").[34] Notification to the Committee precludes any resort to multilateral proceedings before a WTO panel. However, other avenues for review of the measure are available. A Member may request review of the subsidy by the WTO Secretariat to determine whether the measure satisfies the non-actionable criteria. The Secretariat will report its findings to the Committee. A Member may then request that the Committee review the Secretariat's findings on fulfillment of the conditions for non-actionability. Where a Member is dissatisfied with the Committee review, it may request that the matter be submitted to binding arbitration.[35] Further, even if a notified measure is consistent with the non-actionable criteria, a Member that has reason to believe it has suffered serious adverse effects may request consultations and, where no mutually acceptable solution has been reached within 60 days, subsequent review (within 120 days) by the Committee.[36]

---

29 Continued ...

prohibited subsidy, it will recommend that the subsidizing party withdraw it within a certain time period. Within 30 days of its issuance, the report may be adopted or appealed to the appellate body. Where no appeal is taken, the DSB must adopt the report, unless there is a consensus against its adoption. The appellate body normally has 30 days and no more than 60 days to issue a report, which the DSB must adopt within 20 days of its issuance, in the absence of consensus against adoption. Where a party fails to withdraw a condemned measures, the DSB may authorize retaliatory action.

30 Sometimes referred to as "yellow light" subsidies, 1994 Subsidies Code, *ibid.*, pt. III, arts. 5 to 7.

31 1994 Subsidies Code, *ibid.*, art. 6 contains a detailed definition of "serious prejudice."

32 Under the DSU, the panel must issue its report within 120 days, and where neither party appeals the report, the DSB must adopt it in the absence of consensus against adoption. Where an appeal is made to the appellate body, the appellate body must issue its report within 60 days (and definitely no later than 90 days). The DSB must then adopt the appellate body's report, in the absence of consensus against its adoption. Where a panel or appellate body report determines that the subsidy causes adverse effect to the complainant, it may recommend that the measure be withdrawn. If the subsidizing country has not complied within six months, the DSB may authorize the complainant to implement certain retaliatory measures.

33 Sometimes referred to as "green light" subsidies. See 1994 Subsidies Code, *supra*, note 3, pt. IV, arts. 8 and 9.

34 Established under 1994 Subsidies Code, *ibid.*, art. 24.

35 See 1994 Subsidies Code, *ibid.*, art. 8.5 and DSU, art. 25.

36 1994 Subsidies Code, *ibid.*, art. 9.

Countervailing duties may only be imposed pursuant to investigations initiated and conducted in accordance with GATT 1994 article VI and the provisions of part V of the 1994 Subsidies Code. A member may invoke a unilateral countervailing duty proceeding where a written application by or on behalf of a domestic industry contains sufficient information alleging the existence of a subsidy causing injury.[37] An investigation must be terminated immediately where the amount of subsidy is *de minimis*—that is, less than 1 percent of the value of the imports[38]—or where the actual or potential volume of subsidized imports is negligible. Part V of the Subsidies Code contains detailed provisions concerning initiation and subsequent investigation by domestic authorities of allegations that another member's subsidies are causing injury;[39] evidentiary requirements;[40] consultations with the members whose products may be subject to investigation;[41] calculation of the amount of a subsidy in terms of the benefit to the recipient;[42] determination of injury;[43] definition of domestic industry, including regional industry;[44] provisional measures;[45] undertakings;[46] imposition and collection of countervailing duties;[47] retroactivity of countervailing duties;[48] duration and review of countervailing duties and undertakings;[49] transparency requirements;[50] and judicial review.[51]

37 *Ibid.*, art. 11.4 provides that an application for initiation of an investigation "... shall be considered to have been made 'by or on behalf of the domestic industry' if it is supported by those domestic producers whose collective output constitutes more than 50 percent of the total production of the like product produced by that portion of the domestic industry expressing either support for or opposition to the application. However, no investigation shall be initiated when domestic producers expressly supporting the application account for less than 25 percent of total production of the like product produced by the domestic industry."

38 *Ibid.*, art. 11.9. For products from developing country members, the *de minimis* threshold is 2 percent of the value of the imports, or 4 percent of the total value of the imports of the like products of the importing member, unless imports from developing country members collectively represent more than 9 percent of the total imports of the like product in the importing member (see also 1994 Subsidies Code, art. 27.10).

39 *Ibid.*, art. 11.

40 *Ibid.*, art. 12.

41 *Ibid.*, art. 13.

42 *Ibid.*, art. 14.

43 *Ibid.*, art. 15.

44 *Ibid.*, art. 16.

45 *Ibid.*, art. 17.

46 *Ibid.*, art. 18.

47 *Ibid.*, art. 19.

48 *Ibid.*, art. 20.

49 *Ibid.*, art. 21.

50 *Ibid.*, art. 22.

51 *Ibid.*, art. 23.

A countervailing duty is to be terminated not later than five years from the date of its imposition, unless a review by domestic authorities determines that the expiry of the duty "would be likely to lead to continuation or recurrence of subsidization and injury."[52]

B. Dumping

Dumping occurs when goods are sold by an exporter in a foreign market at prices that are lower than those charged for the same or similar goods sold in the internal market of the exporter. Thus, goods are dumped when their normal value exceeds their export price. The amount by which the normal value exceeds the export price of the goods is referred to as the "margin of dumping."

The original GATT, article VI condemned dumping and set out the conditions to be fulfilled before a contracting party could impose an anti-dumping or countervailing duty. The imposition of an anti-dumping or countervailing duty was only justified where the dumping or subsidization caused or threatened to cause material injury to an established domestic industry in the territory of a contracting party or materially retarded the establishment of a domestic industry.[53] The GATT, article XXIII dispute settlement process was also applicable to anti-dumping disputes arising between the contracting parties.

The Agreement on Implementation of Article VI, negotiated during the Kennedy Round of multilateral trade negotiations, represented the first attempt to flesh out and interpret the GATT 1947's anti-dumping provisions. It was finalized on June 30, 1967 and entered into force on July 1, 1968.[54] Among other things, it stipulated that in order for anti-dumping measures to be imposed, dumping had to be the "principal cause" of material injury.[55]

Revisions to the 1967 Agreement were proposed during the Tokyo Round and the resulting Agreement on Implementation of Article VI took effect on January 1, 1979, replacing the 1967 Code.[56] The 1979 Agreement recognized the legitimacy of anti-dumping duties where material injury to or retardation of domestic industry occurred. To justify the imposition of anti-dumping measures, rather than requiring that dumping be the "principal cause" of injury, it required a finding that dumping was demonstrably causing injury. It made explicit in the preamble the signatories' desire to secure equitable and open procedures as the basis for dumping investigations and effective dispute resolution. It outlined general procedures and minimum standards for the conduct of national anti-dumping authorities during dumping investigations "in order to provide greater uniformity and certainty" in the application of article VI. Stressing the importance of transparency, it also contained special provisions for consultations, conciliation, and dispute settlement.[57] The 1979 Code established a Committee on Anti-Dumping

52 *Ibid.*, art. 21.3.

53 GATT 1947, art. VI(a).

54 The "Kennedy Code," BISD, 15th Supp. 24 (1968).

55 Kennedy Code, *ibid.*, art. 3.

56 By virtue of art. 16.5 of the 1979 Anti-dumping Code *supra*, note 6.

57 *Ibid.*, art. 15.

Practices, with all signatories as members.[58] In the fragmented pre-WTO dispute settlement system, an Anti-dumping Code signatory could choose to bring a dumping dispute either before the Anti-dumping Committee under the 1979 Anti-dumping Code, or before the GATT 1947 CONTRACTING PARTIES under article VI of GATT 1947, raising the possibility of forum-shopping.

The 1994 Anti-dumping Code continues and elaborates upon the detailed rules in the 1979 Revised Anti-dumping Code concerning the determination of normal value, export price, and the conduct of anti-dumping investigations. As well, anti-dumping disputes are now dealt with through the more effective and binding integrated dispute settlement procedures outlined in the DSU, except where otherwise provided.[59] The new code is monitored by a Committee on Anti-dumping Practices, composed of representatives of all WTO members.[60]

The provisions concerning determination of injury are essentially unaltered from the 1979 Code except that now, for example, the size of the margin of dumping can be considered to determine whether dumping is causing injury;[61] sales below cost are explicitly excluded from calculation of normal value under certain circumstances;[62] export prices to third countries should be the basis for normal value when home market sales are less than 5 percent of the sales to the importing country; there are more precise rules on the method for calculating the constructed normal value and there are additional provisions relating to currency conversion and weighted averages in the comparison of normal value and export price.[63] Several factors are listed in the new Code for consideration in determining whether a threat of injury exists.[64] The 1994 Code requires as a rule that an individual margin of dumping be established for each identified exporter and producer unless the number of exporters, producers, importers, or product types is so large as to make this impracticable.[65] It also expressly condones the practice of "cumulation,"

---

58 *Ibid.*, art. 14.

59 See the Agreement on Implementation of Article VI of the GATT 1994 (the 1994 Anti-dumping Code), art. 17. In particular, arts. 17.2 to 17.7 are listed as special or additional rules in app. 2 to the DSU, and therefore prevail over DSU provisions to the extent of any inconsistency. See DSU, art. 1.2.

60 1994 Anti-dumping Code, *ibid.*, art. 16.

61 *Ibid.*, art. 3.4. On reforms introduced by the 1994 Anti-Dumping Code, see, e.g., Lorentzen, "Overview of Major Changes Contained in the Uruguay Round Anti-dumping and Subsidies Agreements," Practicing Law Institute: The Commerce Department Speaks on International Trade and Investment, October 1994.

62 1994 Anti-dumping Code, *ibid.*, arts. 2.2.1.1 and 2.2.2. Below-cost sales are deemed "substantial" at the level of 20 percent of total sales.

63 *Ibid.*, arts. 2.4.1 to 2.4.2, and 2.6.

64 *Ibid.*, art. 3.7: (i) a significant rate of increase of dumped imports in the domestic market indicating the likelihood of substantially increased importation; (ii) capacity of the foreign exporter to dump; (iii) potential for depressing effect on domestic prices and increase in demand for further imports; (iv) exporter inventories.

65 *Ibid.*, art. 6.10.

whereby injury is determined through a collective assessment of the impact of imports from multiple countries under investigation.[66]

The 1994 Code provides additional rules concerning the application of provisional measures, which may not be imposed earlier than 60 days after an investigation has been initiated.[67]

Like the 1994 Subsidies Code, the 1994 Anti-dumping Code introduces a new threshold for standing that must be met before domestic authorities may commence a dumping investigation.[68] An investigation must be terminated immediately where the authorities determine that the margin of dumping is *de minimis*[69] or the potential or actual volume of dumped imports is negligible.[70] Also, the 1994 Anti-dumping Code requires a review of injury and dumping at least each five years after an anti-dumping order is issued. The anti-dumping order must be terminated where there is evidence that injurious dumping would not be likely to continue or resume if the order is rescinded.[71]

Annexes to the new Code outline procedures for on-the-spot investigations carried out on the territory of other members;[72] and for the use of best information available where parties refuse to provide information necessary to an investigation.[73]

III. THE SPECIAL IMPORT MEASURES ACT (SIMA)

A. Introduction

One of Canada's primary instruments of trade policy, the SIMA, regulates the imposition of both countervailing and anti-dumping duties. The SIMA has been revised to implement the 1994 Uruguay Round Subsidies and Anti-dumping Codes. The SIMA revised and replaced the Anti-dumping Act.[74] When enacted, it set up a new Canadian

---

66 *Ibid.*, art. 3.3.

67 *Ibid.*, art. 7.

68 1994 Anti-dumping Code, art. 5.4: "The application shall be considered to have been made 'by or on behalf' of the domestic industry" if it is supported by those domestic producers whose collective output constitutes more than 50 percent of the total production of the like product produced by that portion of the domestic industry expressing either support for or opposition to the application. However, no investigation may be initiated when the domestic producers expressly supporting the application account for less than 25 percent of the total production of the like product produced by the domestic industry.

69 I.e., less than 2 percent of the export price.

70 I.e., less than 3 percent of imports of the importing member's imports of like products, unless the imports of several countries collectively account for more than 7 percent of the importing member's imports of like products.

71 1994 Anti-dumping Code, *supra*, note 2, art. 11.3.

72 See Annex 1 to the 1994 Anti-dumping Code, *ibid.*: "Procedures for on-the-spot investigations pursuant to paragraph 7 of Art. 6."

73 Annex II of the 1994 Anti-dumping Code, *ibid.*: "Best Information Available in Terms of Paragraph 8 of Art. 6."

74 RSC 1970, c. A-15.

Import Tribunal, which took the place of the Anti-dumping Tribunal. In 1988, Parliament created the Canadian International Trade Tribunal (CITT), which took over the functions of the Canadian Import Tribunal and was also entrusted with other responsibilities with respect to Canada's international trade.[75]

The SIMA continues the previous pattern of shared responsibilities between the Deputy Minister of National Revenue, who investigates the existence of subsidization or dumping, and the CITT, which determines the issues of material injury and retardation, established by former legislation.

B. Definitions of Subsidized Goods, Subsidy, and Dumping

1. Subsidized Goods

Under the SIMA, "subsidized goods" are[76] (1) goods (or components or inputs of goods) in respect of the production, manufacture, growth, processing, purchase, distribution, transportation, sale, export, or import of which a subsidy has been or will be paid, granted, authorized, or otherwise provided, directly or indirectly, by a foreign government, and (2) goods (or components or inputs of goods) that are disposed of at a loss by a foreign government.

2. Subsidy

The SIMA defines subsidy as,

> (a) a financial contribution by a foreign government[77] that confers a benefit to persons engaged in the production, manufacture, growth, processing, purchase, distribution, transportation, sale, export or import of goods;[78] or
>
> (b) any form of income or price support within the meaning of Article XVI of the GATT 1994, that confers a benefit.

In accordance with the 1994 Subsidies Code,[79] the SIMA[80] clarifies that subsidy is defined as a financial contribution by a foreign government or public body (or nongovernmental body or funding mechanism with an analogous mandate) where there is a

---

75 RSC 1985, c. 47 (4th Supp.), as am., SC 1988, c. 65; SC 1993, c. 44; SC 1994, c. 13; and SC 1994, c. 47, referred to as the CITT or the tribunal.

76 SIMA, RSC 1985, c. S-15, as am., RSC 1985, c. 23 (1st Supp.); RSC 1985, c. 1 (2nd Supp.); RSC 1985, c. 47 (4th Supp.); SC 1988, c. 65; SC 1994, c. 44; SC 1994, c. 47, s. 2(1)(definitions).

77 See SIMA, *ibid.*, s. 2(1.6) and the 1994 Subsidies Code, art. 1.

78 This does not include the amount of any duty or internal tax imposed on goods by the government of the country of origin or country of export from which the goods, because of the exportation from the country of export or the country of origin, have been exempted or have been or will be relieved by means of refund or drawback.

79 1994 Subsidies Code, *supra*, note 3, art. 1.

80 SIMA, *supra*, note 76, s. 2(1.6). See also Special Import Measures Regulations, SOR/84-927, as am., SOR/89-63, SOR/89-578, SOR/90-662, SOR/92-236, SOR/92-590, SOR/94-20, and SOR/95-26, pt. II, rr. 26 to 36.

benefit conferred by the direct[81] or contingent[82] transfer of funds or liabilities; government revenue due or owing is exempted, forgiven, or not collected; or the government provides goods or services, other than general governmental infrastructure, or purchases goods.

In order to be countervailable under the 1994 Subsidies Code[83] and under the SIMA, a subsidy must be "specific." A subsidy is specific where it is limited, pursuant to a legislative, regulatory, administrative, or other public instrument, to a particular enterprise or certain enterprises,[84] or where it is a prohibited subsidy.[85] A subsidy that is limited to certain enterprises located within a designated geographical region is also specific.[86] A subsidy is not specific where the criteria are objective, set out in a legislative, regulatory, or administrative instrument, or other public document, and applied in a non-preferential and non-exclusive manner.[87]

The deputy minister retains some discretion under the SIMA concerning the specificity of a subsidy. Even if a subsidy is not limited to a particular enterprise, the deputy minister may determine that specificity exists where[88] (1) there is exclusive use of the subsidy by a limited number of enterprises, (2) there is predominant use of the subsidy by a particular enterprise, (3) disproportionately large amounts of the subsidy are granted to a limited number of enterprises, and (4) the manner in which discretion is exercised by the granting authority indicates that the subsidy is not generally available. In making this determination, account is taken of the extent of diversification of economic activities within the jurisdiction of the granting authority, as well as of the length of time during which the subsidy program has been in operation.

Certain subsidies are non-actionable[89] even if they may be specific. These include subsidies for (1) industrial research assistance, (2) pre-competitive development assistance; (3) assistance to disadvantaged regions, (4) assistance for the adaptation of existing facilities to new environmental standards, (5) assistance for research activities conducted by institutions of higher education and research establishments, and (6) domestic support for an agricultural product listed in Annex 1 of the WTO Agreement on Agriculture.

---

81 I.e., grants, loans, or equity infusion.

82 I.e., loan guarantees.

83 See art. 2 of the 1994 Subsidies Code, *supra*, note 3.

84 See, e.g., *Fresh, Chilled or Frozen Pork from Canada* (1991), 6 TTR 52 decided under the Canada-US FTA.

85 In accordance with art. 3 of the 1994 Subsidies Code, *supra*, note 3, SIMA, s. 2(1) defines "prohibited subsidy" as an export subsidy or as a subsidy contingent on the use of local goods.

86 1994 Subsidies Code, *ibid.*, art. 2.2.

87 SIMA, *supra*, note 76, art. 2(7.1). 1994 Subsidies Code, *ibid.*, art. 2.1(b).

88 See SIMA, *ibid.*, s. 2(7.3) and 1994 Subsidies Code, *ibid.*, art. 2.1(c).

89 See the definition of "non-actionable subsidy" in SIMA, *ibid.*,s. 2(1), which is based on art. 8 in pt. IV of the 1994 Subsidies Code, *ibid.* See also Special Import Measures Regulations, *supra*, note 80, pt. I.2, r. 25.3.

The deputy minister may not initiate an investigation relating to a subsidy that has been notified as being non-actionable[90] to the WTO Subsidies Committee in accordance with article 8.3 of the 1994 Subsidies Code, unless there is a determination or redetermination that the subsidy is not, or is no longer, non-actionable as a result of review by the committee,[91] or by a binding arbitration body.[92] Where the deputy minister believes that a subsidy not notified to the committee is in fact a non-actionable subsidy or that a subsidy determined by the committee or an arbitration body to be non-actionable may in fact be actionable due to substantial modification in its nature, the deputy minister must notify the the Deputy Minister of Finance and the complainant.[93] On receipt of this notification, the Deputy Minister of Finance must notify the Deputy Minister of International Trade and any other interested person.[94]

Under the SIMA, the "amount of subsidy" is to be determined in accordance with section 30.4.[95] Where no manner of determining an amount of subsidy has been prescribed or the deputy minister believes that sufficient information has not been provided or is not otherwise available to enable the determination of the amount of subsidy, it may be determined by ministerial specification.[96] An amount of subsidy will not include any amount attributable to a non-actionable subsidy.[97]

The following is the illustrative list of export subsidies found in the annex to the 1994 Subsidies Code:

ILLUSTRATIVE LIST OF EXPORT SUBSIDIES 1994[98]

(a) The provision by governments of direct subsidies to a firm or an industry contingent upon export performance.

(b) Currency retention schemes or any similar practices which involve a bonus on exports.

(c) Internal transport and freight charges on export shipments, provided or mandated by governments, on terms more favorable than for domestic shipments.

(d) The provision by governments or their agencies either directly or indirectly through government-mandated schemes, of imported or domestic products or services for use in the production of exported goods, on terms or conditions more favorable than for provision of like or directly competitive products or services for use in the production of goods for domestic consumption, if (in the

90 See SIMA, *supra*, note 76, ss. 31.1 (1) to (3).

91 1994 Subsidies Code, *supra*, note 3, art. 8.4.

92 1994 Subsidies Code, *ibid.*, art. 8.5.

93 SIMA, *supra*, note 76, s. 31.1(4).

94 *Ibid.*, s. 31.1(5).

95 See also Special Import Measures Regulations, *supra*, note 80, pt. II, rr. 26 to 36.

96 SIMA, *supra*, note 76, s. 30.4(2).

97 *Ibid.*, s. 30.4(3).

98 Annex 1 to the 1994 Subsidies Code. Other annexes include: guidelines on consumption of inputs in the production process; guidelines on the determination of substitution drawback systems as export subsidies; calculation of the total *ad valorem* subsidization for the purpose of determining serious prejudice; procedures for developing information concerning serious prejudice; procedures for on-the-spot investigations in the territory of other members; and criteria for developing country members.

case of products) such terms or conditions are more favorable than those commercially available[99] on world markets to their exporters.

(e) The full or partial exemption remission, or deferral specifically related to exports, of direct taxes[100] or social welfare charges paid or payable by industrial or commercial enterprises.[101]

(f) The allowance of special deductions directly related to exports or export performance, over and above those granted in respect to production for domestic consumption, in the calculation of the base on which the direct taxes are charged.

(g) The exemption or remission, in respect of the production and distribution of exported products, of indirect taxes[102] in excess of those levied in respect of the production and distribution of like products when sold for domestic consumption.

(h) The exemption, remission or deferral of prior-stage cumulative indirect taxes[103] on goods or services used in the production of exported products in excess of the exemption, remission or deferral of like prior-stage cumulative indirect taxes on goods or services used in the production of like products when sold for domestic consumption; provided, however, that prior-stage cumulative indirect taxes may be exempted, remitted, or deferred on like products when sold for domestic consumption, if the prior-stage cumulative indirect taxes are levied on inputs that are

---

99 The term "commercially available" means that the choice between domestic and imported products is unrestricted and depends only on commercial considerations.

100 For the purpose of this agreement: the term "direct taxes" shall mean taxes on wages, profits, interests, rents, royalties, and all other forms of income, and taxes on the ownership of real property; the term "import charges" shall mean tariffs, duties, and other fiscal charges not elsewhere enumerated in this note that are levied on imports; the term "indirect taxes" shall mean sales, excise, turnover, value added, franchise, stamp, transfer, inventory, and equipment taxes, border taxes, and all taxes other than direct taxes and import charges; "prior-stage" indirect taxes are those levied on goods or services used directly or indirectly in making the product; "cumulative" indirect taxes are multi-staged taxes levied where there is no mechanism for subsequent crediting of the tax if the goods or services subject to tax at one stage of production are used in a succeeding stage of production; "remission" of taxes includes the refund or rebate of taxes; and "remission or drawback" includes the full or partial exemption or deferral of import charges.

101 The members recognize that deferral need not amount to an export subsidy where, for example, appropriate interest charges are collected. The members reaffirm the principle that prices for goods in transactions between exporting enterprises and foreign buyers under their or under the same control should for tax purposes be the prices that would be charged between independent enterprises acting at arm's length. Any member may draw the attention of another member to the administrative or other practices that may contravene this principle and that result in a significant saving of direct taxes in export transactions. In such circumstances, the members shall normally attempt to resolve their differences using the facilities of existing bilateral tax treaties or other specific international mechanisms, without prejudice to the rights and obligations of members under the GATT 1994, including the right of consultation created in the preceding sentence. Paragraph (e) is not intended to limit a member from taking measures to avoid the double taxation of foreign-source income earned by its enterprises or the enterprises of another member.

102 See definition, *supra*, note 100.

103 See definition, *supra*, note 100.

consumed in the production of the exported product (making normal allowance for waste).[104] This item shall be interpreted in accordance with the guidelines on consumption of inputs in the production process contained in Annex II.

(i) The remission or drawback of import charges[105] in excess of those levied on imported inputs that are consumed in the production of the exported product (making normal allowance for waste); provided however, that in particular cases a firm may use a quantity of home market inputs equal to, and having the same quality and characteristics as, the imported inputs as a substitute for them in order to benefit from this provision if the import and the corresponding export operations both occur within a reasonable time period, not to exceed two years. This item shall be interpreted in accordance with the guidelines on consumption of inputs in the production process contained in Annex II and the guidelines in the determination of substitution drawback systems as export subsidies contained in Annex III.

(j) The provision by governments (or special institutions controlled by governments) of export credit guarantee or insurance programmed, of insurance or guarantee programmed against increases in the cost of exported products or of exchange risk programmed, at premium rates which are inadequate to cover the long-term operating costs and losses of the programmed.

(k) The grant by governments (or special institutions controlled by and/or acting under the authority of governments) of export credits at rates below those which they actually have to pay for the funds so employed (or would have to pay if they borrowed on international capital markets in order to obtain funds of the same maturity and other credit terms and denominated in the same currency as the export credit), or the payment by them of all or part of the costs incurred by exporters or financial institutions in obtaining credits, in so far as they are used to secure a material advantage in the field of export credit terms; provided, however, that if a Member is a party to an international undertaking on official export credits to which at least twelve original Members to this Agreement are parties as of 1 January 1979 (or a successor undertaking which has been adopted by those original Members), or if in practice a Member applies the interest rates provisions of the relevant undertaking, and export credit practice which is in conformity with those provisions shall not be considered an export subsidy prohibited by this Agreement.

(l) Any other charge on the public account constituting an export subsidy in the sense of Article XVI of GATT 1994.

3. *Dumping*

As mentioned, dumping is defined as the practice of price discrimination that occurs when goods are sold by an exporter in a foreign market at prices lower than those charged for the same or similar goods sold in the internal market of the exporter. Thus, "dumped" in relation to goods signifies "that the normal value of the goods exceeds the export price thereof."[106] The amount by which the normal value exceeds the export price of the goods is referred to as the "margin of dumping."[107] Dumping also occurs in

104 Para. (h) does not apply to value-added tax systems and border-tax adjustment in lieu thereof; the problem of the excessive remission of value-added taxes is exclusively covered by para. (g).

105 See definition, *supra*, note 100.

106 SIMA, *supra*, note 76, s. 2(1) (definitions).

107 *Ibid.*, s. 2(1) (definitions).

the context of international predatory pricing, where goods are sold for export at prices lower than their full or total cost in order to drive domestic producers out of the market.

The SIMA's anti-dumping provisions are intended to offset the effects of an exporter's unfair discriminatory pricing and unfair trade practices. The imposition of anti-dumping duties compensates for international price discrimination by exporters where injury occurs to Canadian producers of like goods. The imposition of anti-dumping duties therefore protects Canadian industry from unfair foreign competition.

From an economic point of view, the imposition of anti-dumping duties helps Canadian industry by insulating it from foreign competition, although it imposes severe costs on Canadian consumers. The anti-competitive and distortive impact of anti-dumping duties and practices becomes particularly anomalous within a free trade area, such as that created by the NAFTA, where the possibility of regulating dumping and predatory pricing through general competition law principles has been extensively explored.[108] As economic intergation within a free trade area increases and the area begins more and more to resemble a unified market, the rationale for maintaining anti-dumping or countervailing duty laws erodes. For example, while the Treaty of Rome does contain provisions against state aids,[109] there are presently no anti-dumping or countervailing duty laws within the European Union (EU); the Rome Treaty does, however, contain stringent competition provisions.[110] Within the Canadian domestic market, geographic price discrimination, and predatory pricing are prohibited by sections 50(1)(b) and (c) of the Competition Act.[111]

C. Transactions That May Be Investigated

A subsidy or anti-dumping duty investigation examines the sale of goods by a foreign exporter to an importer in Canada. The SIMA defines "sale" to include "leasing and renting, an agreement to sell, lease or rent and an irrevocable tender."[112] This definition is crafted to meet the needs of Canadian producers of capital goods equipment. The mere submission of an irrevocable tender,[113] even prior to acceptance by a customer, can form the basis of a complaint and investigation. Where only one of numerous foreign

---

108 NAFTA, art. 1504 provides for the establishment of a working group on trade and competition law, composed of representatives of the three parties. Within five years of the coming into effect of the NAFTA, the working group will report and make recommendations on "relevant issues concerning the relationship between competition law and policies and trade in the free trade area." This working group will carry on the task of the working group established under the Canada-US FTA to consider possible convergence of anti-dumping and competition law.

109 See art. 92 of the Treaty of Rome.

110 See arts. 85 and 86 of the Treaty of Rome.

111 RSC 1985, c. C-34.

112 SIMA, *supra*, note 76, s. 2(1) (definitions). See also *Hydraulic Turbines*, [1990] CITT no. 30 (19 June 1990).

113 In *Rail-Car Axles and Rail-Car and Certain Locomotive Axles* (1985), 10 CER 51, a single non-binding offering of goods at low prices did not fall within the definition of sale.

producers is successful on a project for which all submitted tenders, all may be investigated and be found guilty of dumping or subsidization and causing injury. This factor constitutes a difficulty for a foreign tenderer to win a contract in Canada, for as soon as a Canadian producer files a dumping or subsidization complaint while the tender is under consideration, a Canadian customer is likely to reject the tender for fear that, if the complaint is justified, he or she will have to pay the anti-dumping or countervailing duties imposed.

D. Rules for Establishing Normal Value, Export Price, Margin of Dumping, and Amount of Subsidy

The SIMA contains detailed provisions concerning the determination of normal value, export price, margin of dumping, and amount of subsidy for the guidance of the deputy minister in determining the existence and extent of dumping or subsidization.[114]

1. Normal Value

The margin of dumping in relation to any goods is the amount by which the normal value of the goods exceeds the export price.[115] The determination of normal value and export price is therefore of prime significance as the deputy minister must terminate the investigation if the margin of dumping is "insignificant"[116]—that is, if the margin of dumping is less than 2 percent of the export price of the goods.[117]

The normal value of goods is ordinarily the comparable price, in the ordinary course of trade, for the like product when destined for consumption in the exporting country.[118] This is referred to as the home market method of calculation of normal value. Where the home market price is difficult to determine or where the level of home market sales is insufficient,[119] the 1994 Anti-dumping Code allows normal value to be determined by either the cost of production in the country of origin (constructed cost method of calculation of normal value) or by reference to comparable sales to a third country (third country method of calculation of normal value).[120]

Home Market Method of Calculation of Normal Value. The home market price is deemed to be the preponderant price charged for like goods in the home market during a period of 60 days selected by the deputy minister. Where there is no preponderant price, the deputy minister uses the weighted average of the prices throughout the 60-day period. If the number of home market sales to calculate normal value is insufficient, the deputy minister may use the third country method of calculation of normal value or the constructed cost method of calculation of normal value. Once the home market price is

114 See also Special Import Measures Regulations, *supra*, note 80.

115 SIMA, *supra*, note 76, s. 2(1) (definitions).

116 *Ibid.*, s. 35(1)(a)(ii).

117 SIMA, *supra*, note 76, s. 2(1) (definitions). See article 5.8 of the 1994 Anti-dumping Code, *supra*, note 2.

118 See GATT 1994, art. VI(1) and 1994 Anti-dumping Code, *ibid.*, art. 2.1.

119 I.e., less than 5 percent of the sales to the importing country.

120 1994 Anti-dumping Code, *supra*, note 2, art. 2.2.

calculated, it is adjusted to take into account quantitative and qualitative differences, differences in the terms of sale, the tax treatment of the imports, but not advertising or promotion costs.[121] The home market method, by relying on the difference between the exporter's home market price and the export market price, penalizes international price discrimination.

Constructed Cost Method of Calculation of Normal Value. According to this method, the deputy minister examines all costs including production, administration, selling, and overhead incurred by the exporter, plus a reasonable profit margin based on profits made in the home market.[122] Sales below cost are not to be taken into account in calculating normal value.[123] The constructed cost method, by relying on the extent to which the exporter's export price is lower than its constructed cost, penalizes international predatory pricing.

Third Country Method of Calculation of Normal Value. Using this method, the deputy minister determines the normal value on the basis of the price of the like product in export sales to an appropriate third country in the relevant period. The deputy minister must select an export market that is comparable, often a difficult task given the range of economic and market variables.

a. Basic Rules

SIMA section 15 sets out the basic rules for the determination of the normal value of goods. Subject to SIMA sections 19 and 20,[124] the normal value of the goods is the price of like goods when they are sold by the exporter to: (1) unrelated purchasers at a similar trade level to the importer; (2) in similar quantities; (3) in the ordinary course of trade for use in the country of export; (4) during a period of 60 days or longer at the discretion of the deputy minister; and (5) at the place from which the goods were shipped to Canada. The value is then to be "adjusted in the prescribed manner and circumstances to reflect the differences in terms and conditions of sale, in taxation, and other differences relating to price comparability between the goods sold to the importer and the like goods sold by the exporter."[125]

b. Additional Rules

Where sales in the country of export fail to satisfy all of the criteria in section 15, SIMA section 16 provides additional and alternative rules in order to calculate normal value.

---

121 SIMA, *supra*, note 76, s. 15 and Special Import Measures Regulations, *supra*, note 80, rr. 3 to 10.

122 SIMA, *ibid.*, s. 19 and Special Import Measures Regulations, *ibid.*, r. 11. According to 1994 Anti-dumping Code, *ibid.*, art. 2.2, profits are to be based on above-cost sales of the product under investigation by the same producer, or, if this information is not available, average profits on all sales of either (1) the same product made by other producers, or (2) different products made by the same producer.

123 1994 Anti-dumping Code, *ibid.*, art. 2.2.

124 See *infra*.

125 For the basic adjustments to be made to the price of like goods in the context of determining normal value and export price, see Special Import Measures Regulations, *supra*, note 80, rr. 3 to 10.

For example, where there were insufficient sales of like goods made by the exporter at the place of direct shipment to Canada, sales made by the exporter at one or at the nearest of several other places in the country of export may be included in sales of like goods.[126] In addition, if there were insufficient sales to arm's-length purchasers at the same trade level as the importer, then sales made to those at the trade level nearest and subsequent to the importer may be referred to.[127] Also, where there were insufficient sales of like goods in the country of export because sales were solely or primarily for export or made to related purchasers, another vendor or vendors may be substituted for the exporter and their sales used in determining normal value.[128] Not to be taken into account in the calculation of normal value under section 15 are the sales to a purchaser where the vendor did not, at the same time, sell goods to other unrelated purchasers at the same level,[129] and sales of a substantial quantity[130] of like goods within a period of not less than six months that are made below cost.[131] Twenty percent of total sales is the threshold at which below-cost sales are viewed as "substantial."

c. Price of Like Goods

Once sufficient and suitable sales of like goods upon which to base normal value have been pinpointed under SIMA sections 15 and 16, SIMA section 17 focuses on the selling price of the like goods. It stipulates that the preponderant price,[132] or, in the absence of a preponderant price, the weighted average price of all relevant sales of like goods by the exporter during the relevant period, should be used for determination of normal value.[133]

d. Goods Deemed To Be Like Goods

SIMA section 18 applies where goods imported into Canada and the goods being used as the basis for normal value determination are like goods except for a trade-mark appearing on the goods remaining in the country of export that does not appear on the goods imported into Canada. Where the deputy minister is of the opinion that the goods are being imported into Canada without the trade-mark for the purpose of avoiding normal value determination under section 15, and that the trade-mark will be applied after their importation into Canada, then the goods are deemed to be like goods.

e. Where Normal Value Cannot Be Determined: Alternative Methods
for Calculating Normal Value

When the basic rules in SIMA sections 15 and 16 concerning the home market method of determining normal value cannot be used because of an insufficient number of qualifying

---

126 SIMA, *supra*, note 76, s. 16(1)(a).

127 *Ibid.*, s. 16(1)(b).

128 *Ibid.*, s. 16(1)(c).

129 *Ibid.*, s. 16(2)(a).

130 *Ibid.*, s. 16(2)(b) and the 1994 Anti-dumping Code, art. 2.2.1.

131 *Ibid.*, s. 16(2)(b) and 1994 Anti-dumping Code, *ibid.*, art. 2.2.1.

132 *Ibid.*, s. 17(a).

133 *Ibid.*, s. 17(b).

sales, SIMA section 19 provides two alternative methods that the deputy minister may select to determine normal value: (1) the third country method and (2) the constructed cost method. These alternate methods are envisaged in the 1994 Anti-dumping Code, article 2.2.

i. THIRD COUNTRY METHOD[134] This method involves the determination of normal value based on the price of the like product in export sales to an appropriate third country in the relevant period. The deputy minister must be satisfied that such price "fairly reflects the market value of the goods at the time of the sale of the goods to the importer in Canada." Because of the difficulty of establishing this and the danger that an exporter dumping goods in Canada is also dumping goods in other markets, this method is seldom used.

ii. CONSTRUCTED COST METHOD[135] This method calculates normal value with reference to the cost of production of the actual goods in the country of origin, plus a reasonable amount for administrative, selling, and all other costs, and for profits. The cost of production includes all costs attributable to the production of the goods, including material, labour, overhead, design, and engineering.[136] Where home market profits cannot be calculated, a weighted average of profit margins of other producers in the country in question will provide the standard.[137] All administrative, selling, and general costs attributable directly and indirectly to the goods are to be included in determining normal value, limited only by the requirement that they be reasonable.

f. Normal Value Where Export Monopoly

SIMA section 20 applies to the determination of normal value of goods directly exported to Canada from countries where, according to the deputy minister, the government has a monopoly or substantial monopoly of its export trade, the government substantially determines domestic prices, and there is sufficient reason to believe that they are not substantially the same as they would be if determined in a competitive market.

Under these conditions, SIMA section 20 provides three methods for determining normal value: (1) the domestic selling price of like goods in a surrogate (open market) country designated by the deputy minister;[138] (2) the constructed costs of the goods in the surrogate country based on the aggregate of the cost of production of like goods, a reasonable amount for administrative, selling, and other costs, and for profits;[139] and, where neither (1) nor (2) are feasible due to insufficiency of information, (3) the importer's

---

134 *Ibid.*, s. 19(a).

135 *Ibid.*, s. 19(b) and Special Import Measures Regulations, *supra*, note 80, rr. 11 to 12.

136 Special Import Measures Regulations, *supra*, note 80, rr. 11(a) and 12.

137 *Ibid.*, r. 11 sets the normal rules to determine profits; rr. 12 and 13 contain additional provisions relating to the determination of profits.

138 *Ibid.*, s. 20(c)(i) and Special Import Measures Regulations, *ibid.*, rr. 3, 10, and 14 to 17.

139 *Ibid.*, s. 20(c)(ii) and Special Import Measures Regulations, *ibid.*, rr. 4 to 6, 9, 11, and 14 to 17.

selling price in Canada of like goods from a third country, adjusted to reflect differences relating to price comparability.[140]

g. Credit Sales of Like Goods

Where any sale of like goods was made on credit terms other than cash discounts, the price is deemed to be the present value of the payments of principal and interest reasonably attributable to the like goods, calculated by reference to a specified discount rate.[141]

h. Purchasers To Be Regarded as One

By virtue of SIMA section 22, for the purpose of normal value determination under SIMA section 15, two or more purchasers who are associated with each other during the relevant investigation period are to be regarded as a single purchaser.

i. Where Exporter Provides Benefit on Resale in Country of Export

SIMA section 23 deals with direct or indirect benefits provided to persons in the exporter's domestic market who repurchase the like goods from the exporter's domestic customers. Where the normal value of goods sold to an importer in Canada is required to be determined by reference to the price of like goods sold by the exporter in the domestic market, such benefits on resale—which may be in the form of rebate, service, other goods, or otherwise—must be factored into the determination of normal value of like goods in the country of export. Once established, the value of the benefit is deducted from the normal value as ordinarily calculated.

j. Costs During Start-Up Period

In any calculation of the normal value of goods involving an investigation period that includes a start-up period of production, SIMA section 23.1 now stipulates that the cost of production, and the administrative, selling, and all other costs attributable to the goods for the start-up period must be determined in the prescribed manner.[142]

---

140 *Ibid.*, s. 20(d) and Special Import Measures Regulations, *ibid.*, r. 16.

141 *Ibid.*, s. 21. Special Import Measures Regulations, *ibid.*, r. 18 outlines five additional methods to determine the discount rate. Where credit terms for export sales are different from those relating to domestic sales, reference should be had to Special Import Measures Regulations, *ibid.*, r. 5(d)m, which provides for adjustments to the price of the like goods.

142 See Special Import Measures Regulations, *supra*, note 80, rr. 11(a) and (c), 12, and 13.1. The regulations define "start-up period of production" as the period that begins on the date that (1) new production facilities are first used for commercial production, or (2) commercial production first commences of a product that is new or substantially different from products previously produced, and ends on the date that the level of production is no longer limited to a significant degree owing to technical difficulties related to the use of new production facilities or the production of a new or substantially different product.

2. *Export Price*

a. Basic Rule

SIMA section 24 furnishes the basic rule for determining the export price of the goods, which is the lesser of the exporter's selling price and the importer's purchase price. Both of these selling and purchase prices are adjusted by deducting (1) costs, charges and expenses incurred in preparing the goods for shipment to Canada that are additional to those generally incurred on sales for use in the country of export; (2) Canadian duties or taxes paid by or on behalf of the exporter; and (3) all other costs, charges, and expenses relating to the export and shipment of the goods to Canada. The deduction of these costs and charges excludes delivery costs from the export price, thereby bringing it, for the purposes of comparison, to the same point that is used for determining normal value. While the 1994 Anti-dumping Code[143] provides that a fair comparison of export price and normal value is normally to be made at the ex-factory level, the SIMA does not contain this provision. Only where the factory is also the place of direct shipment to Canada will the values be calculated at the ex-factory level under the SIMA.

b. Additional Rules

Where there is no exporter's sale price, no price at which the importer has purchased or agreed to purchase the goods, or the deputy minister believes that the export price is unreliable because the sale occurred between associated persons or involved a compensatory arrangement, SIMA section 25 contains additional rules for export price determination. These additional rules are envisaged in article 2.3 of the 1994 Anti-dumping Code, which stipulates that, under these conditions, the export price may be constructed on the basis of the price at which the imported products are first resold to an independent buyer, or, if the products are not resold to an independent buyer, or not resold in the condition as imported, "on such reasonable basis as the authorities may determine." Article 2.4 of the 1994 Code states that, in making these calculations, allowances for profits and for costs, including duties and taxes incurred between importation and resale, should be made.

Thus, where there is no export price or the export price is unreliable, and where goods are sold in the same condition as imported, SIMA section 25(1)(c) dictates that the export price is the price for which the goods were sold to unassociated purchasers in Canada by the importer, adjusted by deducting (1) all costs including Canadian duties, (2) an amount for profit,[144] and (3) all costs, charges, and expenses incurred by the exporter, importer or any other person in preparing the goods for shipment to Canada, or arising from their exportation from the place of shipment.

Where there is no export price or the export price is unreliable, and where the imported goods are to be assembled, packaged, or further manufactured, or incorporated

143 1994 Anti-dumping Code, *supra*, note 2, art. 2.4.

144 Special Import Measures Regulations, *supra*, note 80, rr. 20 to 22 outline the manner in which to calculate the amount for profit for the purposes of SIMA, s. 25. Under r. 22(c), profits are deemed to be 7.4 percent of the sale price if they cannot be otherwise calculated.

into other goods in the course of manufacture or production in Canada, SIMA section 25(1)(d) states that the export price is the price for which the goods were sold to unassociated persons in Canada by the importer, adjusted by deducting (1) an amount for profit;[145] (2) the administrative, selling, and all other costs incurred in selling the goods; (3) the costs attributable to the assembly, packaging, or further manufacture of the goods; and (4) all costs, charges, and expenses incurred in preparing the goods for shipment, or arising from their exportation from the place of shipment, including duty and taxes.

SIMA sections 25(1)(c)(i) and 25(1)(d)(v) both envisage the deduction of duties in calculating the export price. This includes the deduction of duties imposed by the operation of the SIMA itself. This factor forces the importer to pass on to the purchaser in Canada any anti-dumping duty imposed on the goods, by raising the sale price in an amount equal to the anti-dumping duty. If the importer fails to increase the sale price, the margin of dumping will grow, causing greater anti-dumping duties to be imposed on subsequent imports. Consequently, no deduction for the SIMA anti-dumping duties should occur before the importer has been notified and given the opportunity to adjust the sale price in Canada accordingly. In addition, no deduction for the SIMA duties is to be made where the export price, without making such a deduction, is equal to or greater than the normal value of the goods.[146]

Finally, where there is no export price or the export price is unreliable, in cases not falling under SIMA sections 25(1)(c) and (d), SIMA section 25(1)(e) mandates resort to ministerial specification for the determination of export price.

c. Export Price Where Agreement Affects Anti-Dumping Duty

Where the only reason for considering the export price calculated under the basic SIMA section 24 rule to be unreliable is that the manufacturer, producer, vendor, or exporter has undertaken to pay, for or on behalf of the importer or purchaser, all or part of any anti-dumping duty imposed on the goods, SIMA section 26 specifics that this situation is not a compensatory arrangement falling under SIMA section 25(1)(b)(ii). Rather, SIMA section 26 states that the export price in such circumstances should be calculated under section 24, with the exception that the amount of the anti-dumping duty paid on importer's or purchaser's behalf is to be deducted from the export price. This arrangement ensures that the importer cannot avoid paying the anti-dumping duty.

d. Credit Sales of Goods to Importers in Canada

SIMA section 27, relating to export price, corresponds to SIMA section 21, requiring that normal value determination be based on the present value of credit sales. Section 27 provides that for any sale of goods referred to in sections 24 and 25 that is based on credit or extended financing terms other than cash discounts, the sale price is deemed to

---

145 *Ibid.*, rr. 21 and 22 outline the method of calculation of the amount for profit.

146 SIMA, *supra*, note 76, s. 25(2).

be the present value of principal and interest payments reasonably attributable to the goods, calculated with reference to a prescribed discount rate.[147]

e. Where Exporter Provides Benefit on Resale in Canada

SIMA section 28, relating to export price, corresponds to SIMA section 23 concerning benefits provided on the resale of goods in the determination of normal value. SIMA section 28 provides that where an exporter of goods sold to an importer in Canada agrees with the importer to provide direct or indirect benefits (in the form of rebate, service, other goods, or otherwise) to those who repurchase the goods from the importer, this benefit must be factored into the determination of export price.

3. Normal Value and Export Price in Certain Cases

SIMA sections 29 and 30 contain special rules with respect to normal value and export price for the following circumstances: where information has not been furnished or is not available; for consignment shipments; and where goods are exported to Canada through another country or shipped indirectly to Canada.

a. Ministerial Specification

i. WHERE INFORMATION NOT FURNISHED OR NOT AVAILABLE SIMA section 29(1) states that where the deputy minister is of the opinion that sufficient information has not been furnished or is not available for the determination of normal value and export price under sections 15 to 28, then these will be set by ministerial specification.[148]

ii. CONSIGNMENT SHIPMENTS SIMA section 29(2) deals with shipments on consignment to Canada where there is no known purchaser. Under these circumstances, the normal value and export price will be determined by ministerial specification. There is no known purchaser when the goods have not been sold to a purchaser in Canada or when the identity of the purchaser(s) to whom goods have been sold is unknown.

b. Goods Exported to Canada Through Another Country

The SIMA defines the "country of export" as the country from which goods were shipped directly to Canada or the country from which the goods would be shipped

---

147 Where the discount rate cannot be calculated by reference to SIMA, *ibid.*, s. 27, Special Import Measures Regulations, *supra*, note 80, r. 23 provides five additional methods for determination of the discount rate for export price purposes. Special Import Measures Regulations, *ibid.*, r. 24 applies when the export price determination is under SIMA, *ibid.*, s. 25.

148 See, e.g., *Wilson Machine Co. v. Deputy Minister of National Revenue (Customs & Excise)* (1992), 9 TTR 151 (CITT). The deputy minister has a duty to disclose a ministerial specification to affected parties. This a requirement of the principles of natural justice and procedural fairness: *Toshiba International Corp. v. Canada (Deputy Minister of National Revenue, Customs and Excise—MNR)* (28 June 1994, FC TD). In this case, the non-disclosure deprived Toshiba of the opportunity to address the issues raised by the specification or to challenge its legality.

directly to Canada under normal trade conditions.[149] However, where the goods are shipped to Canada through an intermediate country, additional rules are needed to determine which is the country of export. Consistent with article 2.5 of the 1994 Anti-dumping Code, SIMA section 30(1) states that where goods are exported to Canada from one country but pass through another country, the normal value and export price of the goods is to be determined as if the goods were shipped directly to Canada from the initial country of export provided that[150] (1) the bill of lading indicates Canada to be the ultimate destination of the goods; (2) the goods have not passed through or remained in any other country except for the purpose of transshipment; and (3) the bill of lading is filed with the deputy minister.

c. Goods Shipped Indirectly to Canada

SIMA section 30(2) provides that where goods are shipped indirectly to Canada from the country of origin through another country, the intermediate country may become the country of export. The deputy minister must then select the higher of the two normal values of the country of export and the country of origin and use this in determining the margin of dumping.

The CITT in determining injury has no jurisdiction to review methods and procedures of the deputy minister in arriving at normal values, export prices, and thus margins of dumping.[151]

4. Margin of Dumping

In accordance with the 1994 Anti-dumping Code,[152] SIMA section 30.1(1) provides that the margin of dumping during the investigation stage in relation to goods from a particular country is the weighted average of the margins of dumping determined pursuant to one of several methods outlined in SIMA section 30.2.[153] Normally, the margin of dumping in relation to goods from a particular exporter is zero, or the amount determined by

---

149 SIMA, *supra*, note 76, s. 2(1) (definitions).

150 See Special Import Measures Regulations, *supra*, note 80, r. 25.

151 *Drywall screws from South Korea* (1987), 13 CER 305 and *12 Gauge Shotshells* (1984) 9 CER 8. In *Fresh, Whole Delicious, Red Delicious and Golden Delicious Apples from the United States* (RR-93-002) (CITT, 7 February 1994), the CITT noted that it had "no jurisdiction" to review the deputy minister's determination of normal values. However, the issue under tribunal review was whether dumping was likely to resume, not whether normal values should remain in place. The tribunal then stated that normal values, and by extension the manner in which they are established, were "but one of the factors" that the tribunal had to consider in determining the likelihood that dumping would resume if the finding of material injury were rescinded.

152 1994 Anti-dumping Code, art. 2.4.2.

153 See also Special Import Measures Regulations, *supra*, note 142, r. 25.1 concerning the adjustment of the export price where the sale of goods to an importer in Canada takes place over a period in which there is a sustained movement in the rate of exchange resulting in an appreciation of the foreign currency in terms of the Canadian dollar.

deducting the weighted average export price from the weighted average normal value, whichever is greater.[154] However, where the deputy minister finds significant variations in the prices of goods among (1) purchasers, (2) regions of Canada, or (3) time periods, the deputy minister may determine the margin of dumping from that exporter to be the weighted average of selected individual export transactions of the exporter.[155]

Where the deputy minister believes that it would be impracticable to determine a margin of dumping in relation to all goods under consideration, the determination may be based instead upon the largest percentage of goods from each of the countries whose goods are under investigation that can reasonably be investigated or statistically valid samples of the goods from each country.[156]

5. *Amount of Subsidy*

The amount of subsidy is the amount of financial benefit conferred by a government or associated agency upon an enterprise or industry.[157] Subject to public interest considerations,[158] a countervailing duty in the amount of subsidy will be imposed where imports of subsidized goods have caused, are causing, or will cause injury.

Under the SIMA, as mentioned, the "amount of subsidy" is to be determined in accordance with section 30.4.[159] Where no manner of determining an amount of subsidy has been prescribed or the deputy minister believes that sufficient information has not been provided or is not otherwise available to enable the determination of the amount of subsidy, it may be determined by ministerial specification.[160] An amount of subsidy will not include any amount attributable to a non-actionable subsidy.[161]

E. Associated Persons

The SIMA contains a broad definition of associated persons that makes it possible to reject export prices as well as domestic sales in determining normal value when the exporter and importer are related. Under the Act, associated persons are:[162]

(a) persons related to each other; or

(b) persons not related to each other, but not dealing with each other at arm's length. It is a question of fact whether persons not related with each other are dealing at arm's length.[163]

---

154 SIMA, *supra*, note 76, s. 30.2(1).

155 *Ibid.*, s. 30.2(2).

156 *Ibid.*, s. 30.03(1). See also s. 30.03(3) and Special Import Measures Regulations, *supra*, note 80, pt. I.1, r. 25.2 concerning the calculation of the margin of dumping in relation to goods not included in the percentage sample under SIMA, s. 30.03(1).

157 See the 1994 Subsidies Code, art. 1.1.

158 See section R, Public Interest Inquiries, *infra*.

159 See also Special Import Measures Regulations, *supra*, note 80, pt. II, rr. 26 to 36.

160 SIMA, *supra*, note 76, s. 30.4(2).

161 *Ibid.*, s. 30.4(3).

162 *Ibid.*, s. 2(2).

163 *Ibid.*, s. 2(4).

Persons are related to each other if:[164]

(a) they are individuals connected to each other by a blood relationship, marriage or adoption within the meaning of s. 251(6) of the *Income Tax Act*;

(b) one is an officer or director of the other;

(c) each such person is an officer or director of the same two corporations, associations, partnerships or other organizations;

(d) they are partners;

(e) one is the employer of the other;

(f) they directly or indirectly control or are controlled by the same person;

(g) one directly or indirectly controls or is controlled by the other;

(h) any other person directly or indirectly owns, holds or controls 5% or more of the outstanding voting stock or shares of each such person; or

(i) one directly or indirectly owns, holds or controls 5% or more of the outstanding voting stock or shares of the other.

Where the exporter and importer are associated or related, the export price is determined under SIMA section 24 where this meets the threshold of reliability. Otherwise, under SIMA section 25, the export price will be determined by working backward from the resale price in Canada and deducting (1) all costs incurred on or after the importation of the goods including costs of sale, (2) all costs from the point of direct shipment to Canada, and (3) an amount for profits, reflecting the value of the profit that would be made on the sale of the goods by the importer in the ordinary course of trade. This is the amount for profit generally reflected on sales of like goods, or, failing that, of goods of the same general category by vendors in Canada at the same or substantially the same trade level as the importer to purchasers in Canada who are not related to the vendor. If this amount cannot be determined, it is an amount equal to 7.4 percent of the price at which the goods were sold to the importer.[165]

F. Remedies Available

Where dumping or subsidization has caused, is causing, or is threatening to cause material injury to the production in Canada of like goods, or has caused or is causing material retardation of the establishment in Canada of the production of like goods, a duty is to be imposed on the imported goods. In the case of dumped goods, the duty is an anti-dumping duty and is equal to the margin of dumping of the imported goods. Where subsidized goods are involved, the duty is a countervailing duty equal to the amount of subsidy of the imported goods.[166] It is for this reason that the determination of normal value and export price of the foreign goods sold in Canada is crucial in order to establish the margin of dumping or amount of subsidy.

---

164 *Ibid.*, s. 2(3).

165 Special Import Measures Regulations, *supra*, note 80, rr. 20 and 22.

166 SIMA, *supra*, note 76, ss. 3 to 7. Where an undertaking has been given in respect of dumped or subsidized goods under ss. 3 and 4, no duty is imposed (SIMA, s. 7.1).

Persons representing a major proportion of domestic producers of like goods[167] with reason to believe they have been injured or are threatened by imported dumped or subsidized goods must send a properly documented complaint[168] to the deputy minister of National Revenue, who will investigate it. The deputy minister may commence an anti-dumping or subsidization investigation on his or her own initiative[169] or may initiate an investigation upon receiving notice to that effect from the CITT.[170]

Where two or more anti-dumping investigations, two or more subsidy investigations, or one or more dumping investigations and one or more subsidies investigations concern the same or like goods, the investigations may be joined and carried on as one investigation at any time before the making of a preliminary determination.[171]

G. Procedure and Timing Prior to a Finding of Injury or Retardation by the CITT

Procedures under the SIMA involve two distinct stages of proceedings: first, the determination of subsidy or dumping by the deputy minister[172] involving commencement and

---

167 See definition of "domestic industry" in SIMA, *ibid.*, s. 2(1) and "major proportion" standing requirement in SIMA, s. 31(2); art. 16.1 of the 1994 Subsidies Code; and art. 4.1 of the 1994 Anti-dumping Code. An investigation may only be initiated as a result of a complaint supported by producers of 25 percent of the total domestic production of the like goods.

168 SIMA, *ibid.*, s. 31(1); s. 2(1): "properly documented," in relation to a complaint respecting the dumping or subsidizing of goods, means that

(a) the complaint

(i) alleges that the goods have been or are being dumped or subsidized, specifies the goods and alleges that the dumping or subsidizing has caused injury or retardation or is threatening to cause injury,

(ii) states in reasonable detail the facts on which the allegations referred to in subparagraph (i) are based, and

(iii) makes such other representations as the complainant deems relevant to the complaint, and

(b) the complainant provides

(i) such information as is available to the complainant to prove the facts referred to in subparagraph (a)(ii),

(ii) such information as is prescribed, and

(iii) such other information as the Deputy Minister may reasonably require.

The complainant bears the onus.

169 *Ibid.*, s. 31(1).

170 Canadian International Trade Tribunal Act, RSC 1985, c.47 (4th Supp.), as am., ss. 26(4) and 28(1).

171 SIMA, *supra*, note 76, s. 10 and Special Import Measures Regulations, *supra*, note 80, rr. 38 and 39. Notice of the joining of investigations must be given in writing to the importer, exporter, complainant, and government of the country of export. Special Import Measures Regulations, *ibid.*, r. 40.

172 *Ibid.*, ss. 31(1) to 41.2.

conduct of an investigation,[173] preliminary determination,[174] and final determination;[175] and second, the inquiry and determination of material injury or retardation by the CITT.[176] It is only after both subsidy or dumping and material injury or retardation therefrom have been established that countervailing or anti-dumping duties may be levied definitively. These duties are added to the regular duties of custom. When dumping and countervailing proceedings have been joined, it is possible to find both dumping and subsidization at the same time. The importer will be assessed an anti-dumping duty and a countervailing duty. If part or all of the margin of dumping is attributable to an export subsidy, the amount of anti-dumping duty is reduced accordingly.[177]

1. Commencement[178]

The commencement of an investigation is dependent upon the deputy minister, but there are several avenues available for immediately challenging a refusal by the deputy minister to commence an investigation.

Within 21 days of the receipt of a written complaint concerning the dumping or subsidizing of goods, the deputy minister must decide whether the complaint is properly documented. The deputy minister will therefore either inform the complainant and the government of the country of export that the complaint is properly documented, or, where the complaint is not properly documented, inform the complainant that additional information is required in order for the complaint to be properly documented.[179]

When such additional information is received, the deputy minister is deemed to have received a "new" complaint and has a further 21-day period in which to evaluate whether the complaint is now properly documented.[180]

A written complaint filed with the CITT by domestic producers concerning the import of goods in increased quantities and under such conditions as to cause or threaten serious injury to domestic producers of like or directly competitive goods[181] will be referred to the deputy minister when the injury or threat of injury alleged in the complaint appears to be caused by the dumping or subsidizing of the imported goods.[182]

Where a complaint is properly documented, the deputy minister has a further 30 days in which to evaluate the complaint. Where there is evidence that the goods have been dumped or subsidized and there is a reasonable indication that the dumping or

---

173 *Ibid.*, ss. 31(1) to 37.

174 *Ibid.*, ss. 38 to 40.

175 *Ibid.*, ss. 41(1) to 41.2.

176 *Ibid.*, ss. 42 to 47.

177 *Ibid.*, s. 10.

178 *Ibid.*, ss. 31(1) to 31(3).

179 *Ibid.*, s. 32(1).

180 *Ibid.*, s. 32(2).

181 Canadian International Trade Tribunal Act, s. 23(1). See "Global Emergency Measures" under ss. 59.1ff. of the Customs Tariff Act, RSC 1985, c. 41 (3rd Supp.), as am.

182 Canadian International Trade Tribunal Act, ss. 26(4) and 28(1).

subsidy has caused injury or retardation or is threatening to cause injury,[183] the deputy minister must initiate an investigation.

The deputy minister may decide to reject a properly documented complaint where, for example, it is not supported by a sufficient proportion of the domestic industry; where he or she does not believe that evidence of dumping or subsidizing exists; or where he or she does not believe a reasonable indication of injury resulting from the dumping or subsidy is present. In this case, the deputy minister must give written, reasoned notice to the complainant and to the government of the country of export.[184] This written notice must be issued within 30 days of advising the complainant that the complaint was properly documented. Where a complaint is rejected only on the basis of lack of evidence of injury or retardation or threat of injury, the deputy minister (on the date on which he or she gives notice to the complainant of intention not to initiate an investigation) or the complainant may, within 30 days, refer the issue of injury to the CITT.[185] The CITT must release its decision within 30 days on the basis of information in the possession of the deputy minister.[186] Where the CITT then finds that the evidence reasonably indicates that material injury has been caused, the deputy minister must initiate an investigation.

Notice of the initiation of an investigation must be given to the complainant, exporters, importers, and relevant foreign government and published in the *Canada Gazette*.[187] Within 30 days of the initiation of the investigation by the deputy minister, exporters, importers, or governments of the country of export may immediately challenge the deputy minister's finding of injury by referring to the CITT the issue of whether the evidence discloses a reasonable indication of injury, retardation, or threat of injury caused by dumping or subsidization.[188] The CITT must render its opinion within 30 days solely on the basis of material in the possession of the deputy minister.[189] Where the CITT determines, pursuant to such a reference, that the evidence does not disclose a reasonable indication of injury, the investigation must be terminated.[190] If, on the other hand, the CITT decides that the evidence does indeed disclose a reasonable indication of injury, retardation, or threat of injury, the deputy minister is obliged to continue the investigation.[191]

The deputy minister must terminate the investigation at any time prior to making a preliminary determination if he or she is satisfied that there is insufficient evidence of

183 SIMA, *supra*, note 76, s. 31(1).

184 *Ibid.*, s. 33(1).

185 *Ibid.*, s. 33(2).

186 *Ibid.*, s. 37.

187 *Ibid.*, ss. 34(1)(a)(i) and (ii).

188 *Ibid.*, s. 34(1)(b).

189 *Ibid.*, s. 37(a). In *Hot-Rolled Carbon Steel* (1992), 10 TTR 344 (CITT), the tribunal determined, on the basis of the information that was before the deputy minister, that such information reasonably indicated a causal link between material injury and dumped imports.

190 *Ibid.*, s. 36.

191 *Ibid.*, s. 34(2).

dumping or subsidizing; that the margin of dumping or amount of subsidy is insignificant; that the volume of dumped or subsidized goods is negligible; or that the evidence fails to disclose a reasonable indication of injury, retardation, or threat of injury.[192] Otherwise, where an undertaking is not accepted and the investigation suspended,[193] the deputy minister must make a preliminary determination of dumping or subsidizing between 59 and 90 days after initiation of the investigation.[194] This brief period makes it difficult to conduct a proper preliminary investigation and may lead to arbitrary decisions. In exceptional circumstances, involving, for example, unusually complex or novel issues, a large variety of goods or persons, or difficulty obtaining satisfactory evidence, the time may be extended to 135 days.[195]

The preliminary determination process is purely administrative, does not affect the substantive rights and interests of any party, and may not trigger the requirements of natural justice.[196] It appears, however, that the deputy minister is under a common law duty of fairness and a duty to consider relevant information submitted in the investigation. In *Shaw Industries, Inc. v. Canada (MNR)*,[197] the Federal Court, Trial Division held that the considerations leading to a preliminary determination were essentially matters within the deputy minister's discretion and the Court would only intervene in the presence of the clearest evidence that discretion was exercised or was to be exercised without regard to relevant factors or with regard to irrelevant factors. In that case, the Court held that no evidence existed that the deputy minister breached a duty of fairness or a duty to disregard relevant information. In a related case,[198] the same court stated that the "yet to be articulated rights" of the parties were a strong factor that disinclined the Court from looking behind the preliminary determination. Similarly, in *Hyundai Motor Co.*, the court held that the decision to initiate an investigation was a threshold decision and an administrative act in respect of which the deputy minister could fix his own procedure. At that point, no rights or interests of the person being investigated were being determined. Accordingly, the proceedings did not give rise to a right to a fair hearing under section 2(e) of the Bill of Rights. Similarly, reference to the tribunal is not determinative of anything. It only seeks an expression of opinion by the tribunal, and thus no substantive rights and obligations are affected until the deputy minister makes a preliminary determination and the tribunal conducts its inquiry on the issue of injury.[199]

---

192 *Ibid.*, s. 35(1).

193 SIMA, *supra*, note 76, s. 49(1).

194 *Ibid.*, s. 38(1).

195 *Ibid.*, s. 39(1).

196 *Sabre Int. Ltd. and MNR*, [1974] 2 FC 704 (CA) (need not be made on a judicial or quasi-judicial basis). See also *Hyundai Motor Co. et al. and A.G. Can. et al.* (1987), 14 CER 248, 14 FTR 316, [1988] 1 FC 333 (TD).

197 10 January 1993 (FCTD).

198 *Shaw Industries, Inc. v. Canada (MNR)* (17 March 1992) (FCTD).

199 See *Ronald A. Chisholm Ltd. v. Dep. MNR Customs & Excise* (1986), 5 FTR 1 (TD).

2. *Provisional Duties*

Provisional duties are imposed on goods where the deputy minister makes a preliminary determination of dumping or subsidizing and considers that a provisional duty is necessary to prevent injury, retardation, or threat of injury.[200] They are imposed for the duration of the provisional period, which lasts from the date of the preliminary determination by the deputy minister until either the deputy minister terminates the investigation or the CITT makes a finding.[201] The amount of the provisional duty is equal to the estimated margin of dumping or amount of subsidy on the goods. Alternatively, an importer may post security.[202]

Provisional duties are also imposed where a binational panel has reviewed a CITT finding of no injury and has sent it back to the CITT for reconsideration.[203] Provisional duties are then due retroactively from the date of the preliminary determination of dumping or subsidization, with liability for the duties terminating on the day the CITT either confirms its original finding or rescinds it and makes a new finding.

3. *Undertakings*

In the course of an investigation, the deputy minister may accept an undertaking with respect to dumped or subsidized goods.[204] An undertaking is a binding written commitment given by an exporter or foreign government to the deputy minister concerning goods under investigation, guaranteeing price revision, or the elimination or reduction of the dumping, subsidy, or injury being caused to the domestic industry.[205] The SIMA provisions on undertakings are based upon article 8 of the 1994 Anti-dumping Code and upon article 18 of the 1994 Subsidies Code. Undertakings are a quicker and cheaper alternative to a full-fledged investigation by the deputy minister and a final determination by the CITT concerning the existence or non-existence of injury.

The deputy minister may only accept an undertaking with respect to dumped or subsidized goods after having made a preliminary determination.[206] The former SIMA provision stated that the deputy minister could only accept an undertaking *prior* to making a preliminary determination. This revision brings the SIMA in line with the WTO codes[207] and is fairer to exporters and foreign governments. As a result of the revision, they now enjoy the opportunity of knowing whether they are dumping or subsidizing and to make an informed decision about whether to provide an undertaking,

---

200 SIMA, *supra*, note 76, s. 8. See 1994 Anti-dumping Code, art. 7; 1994 Subsidies Code, art. 17. See also *Wirth Ltd. v. Deputy MNR Customs and Excise* (1990), 3 TCT 2012.

201 The CITT has a maximum of 120 days to make a finding.

202 SIMA, *supra*, note 76.

203 *Ibid.*, s. 8(1.1).

204 *Ibid.*, s. 49(1). See also *Boneless manufacturing beef* (1986), 12 CER 62 (CITT).

205 *Ibid.*, s. 2(1) (definitions).

206 *Ibid.*, s. 49(2)(b).

207 Art. 18.2 of the 1994 Subsidies Code and art. 8.2 of the 1994 Anti-dumping Code.

or to face the extensive expense and time requirements of a full investigation and a possible finding of injury or retardation.

The deputy minister may not accept an undertaking where he or she believes that (1) observance of the undertaking will cause the price at which the goods are sold to importers in Canada to increase by more than the estimated margin of dumping or amount of subsidy,[208] or (2) it would not be practicable to administer the undertaking, given the number of exporters or countries or the complexity of the goods subject to investigation.[209] These prohibitions give wide discretion to the deputy minister, which the WTO codes seem to condone in allowing non-acceptance of undertakings where acceptance would be impractical for "reasons of general policy."[210] This is an acknowledgment of the difficulties inherent in monitoring and enforcing undertakings, a prime reason why the deputy minister has not accepted many undertakings in the past.

Upon acceptance of an undertaking by the deputy minister, the investigation and tribunal inquiry must be suspended,[211] unless the undertaking is accompanied by a request from the exporter or foreign government for the deputy minister to complete the investigation[212] and a request is made to the tribunal to complete its inquiry.[213] Acceptance of the undertaking has the effect of suspending the collection of provisional duties, whether or not a request for the investigation to continue accompanies the undertaking.[214]

An accepted undertaking suspends the operation of any time limit under the Act; time starts running again when the undertaking is terminated.[215]

The deputy minister may only accept an undertaking where it accounts for all or substantially all of the goods exported to Canada.[216] Revenue Canada interprets this to mean 85 percent or more of the volume of dumped or subsidized goods, a virtually impossible level to reach where numerous exporters are involved. Furthermore, since a concerted undertaking by a group of exporters could violate the provisions of the

---

208 SIMA, *supra*, note 76, s. 49(2)(a).

209 *Ibid.*, s. 49(2)(c). The deputy minister prefers to avoid undertakings on the ground that they are too difficult to monitor. This explains why undertakings are not commonly used to resolve unfair trade cases in Canada.

210 See art. 18.3 of the 1994 Subsidies Code, *supra*, note 3 and art. 8.3 of the 1994 Anti-dumping Code.

211 SIMA, *supra*, note 76, ss. 50(a)(iii) and 50(b). The deputy minister may not terminate a dumping inquiry in respect of goods from non-undertaking countries merely because he or she has accepted price undertakings from certain other countries: *Re Carbon Steel Welded Pipe* (1992), 7 TTR 323 (CITT). See SIMA, *ibid.*, s. 35(1).

212 *Ibid.*, s. 49(3)(a).

213 *Ibid.*, s. 49(3)(b).

214 *Ibid.*, s. 50(a)(ii).

215 *Ibid.*, s. 50.1.

216 *Ibid.*, s. 2(1), definition of "undertaking." See, e.g., *Revenue Canada, Statement of Reasons re: Preliminary Determination of Dumping in Respect of Certain Stainless Steel Welded Pipe Originating from Taiwan* (8 May 1991) for an example of the Deputy Minister refusing to accept an undertaking on the basis that it did not meet the "all or substantially all" requirement.

Competition Act,[217] exporters or governments must give the undertaking individually. This restriction is not found in the WTO codes.

The deputy minister must terminate an undertaking and resume the investigation upon receipt of a request to that effect from directly interested parties. These include an importer or exporter of the goods, the complainant, or, where subsidized goods are involved, the government of the exporting country. The request must be received within 30 days after the date of notice of acceptance of the undertaking.[218] This provision ensures that all parties involved are satisfied that acceptance of the undertaking is an appropriate manner in which to stop the dumping or subsidizing. If not, each directly interested party enjoys a veto power of termination within 30 days of its acceptance.

The deputy minister must also terminate an undertaking and resume the investigation where he or she: (1) is satisfied that the undertaking is being or has been violated;[219] or (2) would not have accepted the undertaking given new information or circumstances that only came to light after it was accepted.[220]

The deputy minister must terminate an undertaking where (1) there has been a determination that no dumping or subsidization exists, that the margin of dumping or amount of subsidy is insignificant, or that the actual or potential volume of goods involved is negligible;[221] (2) there is an order or finding that dumping or subsidization has caused no injury, retardation, or threat of injury; or (3) the tribunal has rescinded an order or finding concerning the goods.

Except where the CITT has made an order or finding under SIMA section 43(1) of dumping or subsidization causing injury or retardation that has not been rescinded, the deputy minister must terminate an undertaking where the original conditions for having accepted the undertaking under section 49 no longer exist.[222] Such a termination also stops all proceedings under the Act, unless the deputy minister has accepted two or more undertakings with respect to the goods in question.[223] Where an undertaking is not terminated, the deputy minister must review it within five years of its acceptance and before the expiration of each subsequent period, and may renew it for up to five further years where it continues to serve its intended purpose.[224] Where an undertaking

217 SC 1986, c. 26; RSC 1985, c. 19 (2nd Supp.), as am.

218 SIMA, *supra*, note 76, s. 51.

219 *Ibid.*, s. 52(1)(a). Where only one of several exporters is in violation of the undertaking, termination of all the undertakings may not be necessary. Factors to be considered include the percentage of market share which the exporter accounts for; the proportionate percentage of imported product sold by the exporter; the size and trade level of the exporter's Canadian purchasers; the extent of decline in the level of representation of exporters (i.e., below the notional 85 percent threshold set by the department).

220 *Ibid.*, s. 52(1)(b) and (c).

221 *Ibid.*, s. 52(1.1)(a).

222 *Ibid.*, s. 52(1.2).

223 *Ibid.*, s. 52(1.3).

224 *Ibid.*, s. 53(1).

is not renewed, it expires,[225] ending all proceedings under the Act, unless the deputy minister has accepted two or more undertakings with respect to the goods.[226]

The decision to renew or not to renew an undertaking is a decision subject to review by the Federal Court of Appeal or, in the case of goods from the United States or NAFTA, to a binational dispute settlement panel.[227]

An undertaking may be amended at any time,[228] although a decision to renew or not to renew an undertaking and allow it to expire would take precedence over any amendment.[229]

4. Access to Information

Consistent with the emphasis on transparency and openness in the 1994 Anti-dumping[230] and Subsidies[231] Codes, the SIMA allows every party directly involved in the proceedings the right of access to any information provided to the deputy minister, unless the person providing the information has designated it as confidential.[232] In that case, along with a statement explaining why the information should be kept confidential, the person must supply a non-confidential edited version or non-confidential summary of the information in sufficient detail to convey a reasonable understanding of the material.[233] In the alternative, the person may submit a statement that such a non-confidential edited version or summary cannot be made or would disclose facts that the person has proper reasons for wishing to keep confidential.[234] The deputy minister may question whether the designation is warranted and compel the person to take corrective action.[235] Counsel for any party to the proceedings may obtain access to information designated confidential on giving certain undertakings,[236] usually where non-confidential information is insufficient in order to ensure equitable treatment of the parties. Similar provisions exist for information provided to the CITT for the purposes of any proceedings before it.[237] In the absence of a valid undertaking, counsel is not entitled

---

225 *Ibid.*, s. 53(2).

226 *Ibid.*, s. 53(3).

227 *Ibid.*, ss. 77.01, 77.1, and 96.1.

228 *Ibid.*, s. 54.

229 *Ibid.*, s. 53.

230 1994 Anti-dumping Code, *supra*, note 2, art. 6.

231 1994 Subsidies Code, *supra*, note 3, art. 12.

232 SIMA, *supra*, note 76, ss. 82 to 88. See also the Access to Information Act, RSC 1985, c. A-1, particularly s. 20, which provides that disclosure of commercial information is prohibited where it would cause undue financial prejudice to the party requesting the confidentiality.

233 SIMA, *supra*, note 76, s. 85(1).

234 *Ibid.*, s. 85(1)(b).

235 *Ibid.*, ss. 86 and 87.

236 *Ibid.*, s. 84(3). See also Customs Act, RSC 1985 (2nd Supp.), c. 1, as am., s. 108(1)(b) concerning requests for disclosure of confidential information.

237 Canadian International Trade Tribunal Act, RSC 1985, c. 47 (4th Supp.), as am., ss. 43 to 49, especially ss. 45, 46, and 49(b).

access to confidential information or permitted to attend *in camera* sessions of the CITT.[238] In-house counsel may not be permitted access to confidential material or to attend *in camera* sessions in any case, due to the increased risk of disclosure of sensitive and confidential information to business competitors.[239] Any person interested in the importation of goods into Canada may obtain from the deputy minister the name of the importer of the goods.[240] "Person interested" means any person (or their representative) engaged in the production, purchase, sale, export, or import of any goods that are the subject of an investigation, or of goods that are like goods.[241]

The SIMA also provides authority for the deputy minister to require any person to furnish evidence where the deputy minister is of the opinion that the person is able to provide evidence relevant to the investigation. Evidence under SIMA section 78 is subject to different treatment and, where the person supplying the evidence designates it as confidential, the deputy minister may not question this designation or require the person to take remedial measures.[242]

5. *Injury Inquiry*

The CITT will inquire into the question of material injury or retardation after it has received notice of the preliminary determination of dumping or subsidizing from the deputy minister.[243] For this purpose, the CITT begins the inquiry process by issuing a notice of commencement of inquiry, which is sent to all interested parties, including members of the industry concerned and governments of the exporting countries that may be involved.[244] All notices and findings of the tribunal are published in the *Canada Gazette*. The notice of commencement of inquiry sets out the subject matter of the inquiry, the procedures for filing submissions and counsel's undertakings, the treatment of confidential information, and the date and location of the public hearing.

Questionnaires are sent to producers, importers, and any other parties, including exporters, possessing information relevant to the inquiry.

Parties proposing to participate in the hearing process must file a notice of appearance with the tribunal within one month of the commencement of the inquiry. Parties may conduct their own cases before the CITT, or be represented by legal or other counsel. After filing of counsels' undertakings concerning maintenance of confidentiality, and of the parties' preliminary briefs and completed questionnaires, the tribunal staff then prepares a pre-hearing report containing all of the factual information available at

---

238 See *Electrohome Ltd. et al. v. MNR*, [1986] 1 FTR 212, 11 CER 31 (TD), for an example of a case where the deputy minister refused to disclose confidential information.

239 See, e.g., *Polypropylene* (1983), ADT-3B-79.

240 SIMA, *supra*, note 76, s. 95.

241 Special Import Measure Regulations, *supra*, note 80, rr. 41 and 42.

242 SIMA, *supra*, note 202, s. 88.

243 *Ibid.*, s. 42(1).

244 See Canadian International Trade Tribunal Regulations, SOR/93-600, as am., SOR/95-12, SOR/95-27, rr. 54 and 55.

the time. Once adopted and approved by the tribunal, this becomes its report. All the material received, including the staff report, is segregated into public and confidential books. A copy of the non-confidential book is made available to each party who filed a notice of appearance. Only independent counsel who signed and filed with the tribunal a written undertaking of non-disclosure may obtain a copy of the confidential book. Within a week of receiving the books, the complainant must file its case, including written statements of evidence of witnesses being called. Parties opposed in interest, such as importers and exporters, are provided with this material, and have a week to file their submissions, which are made available to the complainant.

At that time, the deputy minister's final determination is ordinarily received and made available to the parties.[245] The CITT then has about one month to conduct the public hearing, review the evidence, and render an order or finding. The CITT must issue its finding within 120 days of receiving notice of the preliminary determination.[246] A statement of reasons must follow within 15 days.[247]

The procedure is informal. The tribunal may summon before it, by subpoena, any person and require that person to give evidence on oath or affirmation and to produce the documents.[248] The sole issue before the tribunal is injury. It is not concerned with dumping or subsidizing, which has already been determined by Revenue Canada. The complainant's case is usually challenged by importers, and sometimes exporters, who present contrary evidence. After cross-examination, each side has an opportunity to respond to the other's case and summarize its own. Upon completion of the hearing, the tribunal staff prepares post-hearing notes that comment on the evidence elicited in the course of the hearing and are made available to the members of the tribunal who heard the case. These members will meet to discuss the case, review the relevant evidence, and make their finding. The finding, which need not be unanimous, together with the statement of reasons must be forwarded by registered mail to all interested parties, participants, and governments concerned, including the deputy minister.

It should be noted that the SIMA enables the tribunal to advise the deputy minister where evidence in an injury inquiry indicates that dumping or subsidizing from other similar goods may be occurring and causing injury.[249] The deputy minister may then cause an investigation with respect to the dumping or subsidizing of such goods to be initiated.

---

245 See SIMA, *supra*, note 76, s. 41, which provides that within 90 days of issuing a preliminary determination, the deputy minister, if satisfied that the evidence of dumping or subsidizing is conclusive, must issue a final determination that more accurately reflects the margin of dumping or amount of subsidy.

246 *Ibid.*, s. 43(1).

247 *Ibid.*, s. 43(2).

248 Canadian International Trade Tribunal Rules, SOR/91-499, as am., SOR/93-599, SOR/93-601, and SOR/95-13, r. 20.

249 SIMA, *supra*, note 76, s. 46. See *Drywall Screws from Taiwan* (1986), CER 16 and *Drywall Screws from South Korea* (1987), 13 CER 305. Both cases deal with former s. 46 of SIMA, which provided that the tribunal could direct the deputy minister to initiate such an investigation.

6. *Final Determination*

Where the deputy minister has made a preliminary determination of dumping or subsidization, he or she must, within a further 90 days, make a final determination of dumping or subsidization or terminate the investigation.[250] Thus, where the deputy minister finds that the goods to which the preliminary determination relates have been dumped or subsidized, that the margin of dumping or amount of subsidy is not insignificant, and that the actual or potential volume of dumped or subsidized goods is not negligible, he or she must make a final determination of dumping or subsidization. This final determination must be more precise than a preliminary determination, specifying (as opposed to estimating) the goods to which it applies and the applicable margin of dumping or amount of subsidy.[251] In the case of subsidized goods, the final determination must identify whether the whole or any part of the subsidy on the goods is a prohibited subsidy and specify the amount of the prohibited subsidy.[252]

Where the final determination finds no injury, the investigation will be terminated[253] and the provisional duty refunded[254] with interest.[255] A final determination is reviewable by the Federal Court of Appeal or by a binational panel under the FTA or the NAFTA, implying that it must be made in accordance with the principles of natural justice and fairness.

H. Concept of Injury

The SIMA outlines the basic criteria for a finding of injury.[256] After having received notice of the preliminary determination, the tribunal must carry out an inquiry and make a finding about whether the imports found to have been dumped or subsidized have caused, are causing, or are likely to cause injury to Canadian producers; have caused or are causing retardation to the establishment of the domestic production of like goods; or would have caused injury or retardation had provisional duties not been imposed.[257]

The tribunal must determine, in the case of dumped goods subject to a preliminary determination, that a considerable importation of like goods were dumped, causing injury (or having the potential to cause injury had anti-dumping measures not been taken), or that the importer was or should have been aware that the exporter was dumping and that the dumping would cause injury. In addition, with respect to either dumped goods subject to a preliminary determination or goods that have been specified as subject to a prohibited subsidy,[258] the Tribunal must determine whether injury was caused by reason of the

---

250 *Ibid.*, s. 41(1).

251 *Ibid.*, s. 41(1)(iii) and (iv).

252 *Ibid.*, s. 41(1)(iv)(C).

253 *Ibid.*, s. 41(1)(b).

254 *Ibid.*, s. 8(2)(a)(i).

255 *Ibid.*, s. 8(3).

256 *Ibid.*, s. 42(1) and (2). See also ss. 3 to 6.

257 *Ibid.*, ss. 42 and 43.

258 *Ibid.*, under s. 41(1)(a)(iv)(C).

fact that the dumped or subsidized goods (1) constitute a massive importation into Canada; or (2) form part of a series of importations into Canada, which in the aggregate are massive and have occurred within a relatively short time; and an anti-dumping or countervailing duty is necessary in order to prevent recurrence of the injury.

Where the tribunal receives notice of the termination of an undertaking, it must resume the investigation with respect to the subject goods as to whether dumping or subsidizing has caused injury or retardation.[259]

Under the SIMA, "injury" means material injury to a domestic industry.[260] The determination of injury must be related to the class of goods established by the deputy minister to which the preliminary determination applies. Although the tribunal cannot broaden this class of goods, its injury finding may contain some adjustments or exemptions. After receiving notice of the deputy minister's final determination, and not later than 120 days after receipt of notice of the preliminary determination, the Tribunal must make an order or finding with respect to the goods, and declare to what goods, including from what supplier and from what country of export, the order or finding applies.[261] A copy of the reasons for the order or finding must follow within 15 days.[262]

Where an inquiry deals with goods of more than one NAFTA country, or with goods of one or more NAFTA countries and goods of one or more other countries, the tribunal must make a separate finding with respect to the goods of each NAFTA country.[263]

Before anti-dumping or countervailing duties can be imposed definitively on imported goods after a preliminary or final determination of dumping or subsidizing, the tribunal must find that injury or retardation exists, that the injury or retardation is material, and that there is a causal connection between the material injury or retardation and the dumping or subsidizing.

The SIMA and the Special Import Measures Regulations provide little guidance for determining when injury becomes material.[264] Canada's international obligations under the 1994 Anti-dumping and Subsidies Codes provide that a determination of injury is to be based on positive evidence and involve an objective examination of both (1) the

259 *Ibid.*, s. 42(2). The tribunal's powers in s. 42(2)(a) and (b) are to be read conjunctively, i.e., the tribunal may conduct an injury inquiry both as to whether dumping has caused, is causing, or is likely to cause material injury and whether dumping would have caused material injury during any period after an undertaking had it not been accepted: *Re Carbon Steel Welded Pipe* (1992), 7 TTR 323 (CITT).

260 SIMA, *supra*, note 76, s. 2(1) (definitions).

261 *Ibid.*, s. 43(1).

262 *Ibid.*, s. 43(2).

263 *Ibid.*, s. 43(1.01). This is to implement the NAFTA. See *Polyphase Induction Motors originating in or exported from Brazil etc. and the United States of America* (1989), 2 TCT 1097 dealing with the treatment of US goods under the pre-NAFTA, FTA, and SIMA, ss. 43(1.1) and 76(4.2). See also SIMA, *ibid.*, s. 76(4.11).

264 How does one distinguish material injury from serious injury? See GATT 1994, art. XIX and *Customs Tariff Act*, SC 1987, c. 49, as am., s. 60(1). Differences are of degree. Generally, it is necessary to show that the imports cause or threaten injury that is more than just material before a finding of serious injury can be made. Serious injury may be equated with survival of the industry.

volume of the dumped or subsidized goods and the effect of the dumped or subsidized imports on prices in the domestic market for like goods, and (2) the consequent impact of these imports on the domestic producers of such products.[265] "Injury" is defined in the international instruments to mean material injury to a domestic industry, threat of material injury to a domestic industry or material retardation of the establishment of such an industry. The question of when injury becomes material is therefore one of judgment to be exercised by the tribunal. Generally speaking, the tribunal considers material injury to be essentially a question of important harm.[266]

The 1994 Subsidies Code[267] and 1994 Anti-dumping Code[268] provide that the examination of the impact of subsidized imports on the domestic industry must include an evaluation of all relevant economic factors affecting the industry, including actual and potential decline in output, sales, market share, profits, productivity, return on investments, or use of capacity; factors affecting domestic prices; and actual and potential negative effects on cash flow, inventories, employment, wages, growth, ability to raise capital, or investments. This list is not exhaustive, nor can one or several of these features give decisive guidance. In its inquiry, the tribunal will therefore consider all or some of the following indicators of material injury: loss of orders;[269] market share and profit; unused capacity; loss of employment; price deterioration or suppression;[270] margin erosion; cancelled or postponed expansion; high inventories; higher distribution costs; reduced research and development activity;[271] declining land values; and instances of bankruptcy.[272]

---

265 See 1994 Anti-dumping Code, *supra*, note 210, art. 3.1 and the 1994 Agreement on Subsidies and Countervailing Measures (the 1994 Subsidies Code), art. 15.1.

266 In *Acrylonitrile-Butadiene-Styrene Resins in Powder or Pellet form from Korea* (1986), 12 CER 238 (ADT), a member of the Tribunal remarked that material injury has always been considered to be something less than serious, but something more than *de minimis*.

267 1994 Subsidies Code, art. 15.4.

268 1994 Anti-dumping Code, art. 3.4.

269 *Nickel and Nickel Alloy Pipe and Tubing (Review)* (1985), 9 CER 185.

270 See, e.g., *Chemically Presensitized Aluminum Offset Printing Plates from Japan and the UK (Review)* (1987), 15 CER 69; *Re Drywall Screws from France* (1988) 15 CER 311; *Photo Albums (Review)* (1987), 15 CER 129; *Re Sour (Tart) Cherries from the United States*, [1989] 1 TST 1004, 18 CER 318, 2 TCT 1025; *Re Pocket Albums* (1988), 16 CER 165; *Women's Leather and Non-Leather Boots and Shoes* (1990), 3 TCT 2150 (injury finding partially rescinded, RR-94-003, [1995] CITT, no. 27, 2 May 1995); and *Photo Albums with Self-Adhesive Leaves from Indonesia* (1991), 4 TCT 3053. In *Cars (Hyundai)* (1988), 16 CER 185, price suppression was not primarily attributable to dumped imports. See also *Fabric-Covered Padded Wooden Clothes Hangars from Taiwan* (1991), 4 TCT 3083.

271 See, e.g., *Tetanus Immune Globulin (Human) Originating in the USA.*, ADT-3-74; 1994 Anti-dumping Code, *supra*, note 2, art. 3.4; and 1994 Subsidies Code, *supra*, note 3, art. 15.4. As to non-price factors, see *Surgical Adhesive Tapes and Plasters* (1985) 10 CER 174 and *Polyphase Induction Motors* (1985) 10 CER 69 (cumulative effect of dumping and subsidizing).

272 Re *Fresh, Whole, Delicious, Red Delicious and Golden Delicious Apples from the United States*, [1989] 1 TST 1013, 18 CER 332, 2 TCT 1031 (finding of injury rescinded, RR-93-002, [1994] CITT no. 22 (7 February 1994)).

The Rules of Procedure of the tribunal contain a summary of the evidence that the tribunal may direct a party to provide in considering any issue of injury or retardation:[273]

(a) the actual and potential volume of the dumped or subsidized goods imported into Canada and the effect of the dumped or subsidized goods on the prices of like goods in the domestic market, including

(i) whether there has been a significant increase in the importation into Canada of the dumped or subsidized goods, either absolutely or relative to the production or consumption in Canada of like goods,

(ii) whether the prices of the dumped or subsidized goods imported into Canada have significantly undercut the prices of like goods produced and sold in Canada, and

(iii) whether the effect of the importation into Canada of the dumped or subsidized goods has been

(A) to depress significantly the prices of like goods produced and sold in Canada, or

(B) to limit to a significant degree increases in the prices of like goods produced and sold in Canada; and

(b) the impact of the dumped or subsidized goods on the production of like goods in Canada and all relevant economic factors and indices that have a bearing on the industry that comprises or includes the like goods, including, without limiting the generality of the foregoing,

(i) actual and potential decline in output, sales, market share, profits, productivity, return on investments and utilization of production capacity,

(ii) factors affecting domestic prices, and

(iii) actual and potential negative effects on cash flow, inventories, employment, wages, industry growth, ability to raise capital or investments and, in the case of subsidization of agricultural product, whether there has been an increase in the financial burden on a federal or provincial government agricultural support program in Canada; and

(c) any other matters relevant to the inquiry.

I. Likelihood of Future Injury[274]

Where past and present injury is found by the CITT, it is likely to continue into the future unless the dumping or subsidization is terminated.[275] Where the evidence discloses no past or present harm to domestic industry due to dumping or subsidization, it may be more difficult to establish the likelihood or threat of injury in the future. The tribunal must find indicators that justify a likelihood finding.[276] Both the WTO Agreements and

---

273 CITT Rules, r. 61.

274 SIMA, *supra*, note 260, s. 42(1)(a)(i).

275 See, e.g., *Re Fresh, Whole, Red Delicious and Golden Delicious Apples from the United States*, *supra*, note 272, and see *Black granite memorials of all sizes and shapes and black granite slabs in thicknesses equal to or greater than three inches, originating in or exported from India*, NQ-93-006 (20 July 1994) (CITT).

276 See, e.g., *Colour Television Sets from United States, Japan, Taiwan and Singapore (Hitachi)*, ADT- 4-75 (29 October 1975); and *Japanese Generators*, ADT-11-79 (29 February 1980). For more recent examples

(The footnote is continued on the next page.)

the SIMA acknowledge circumstances where the imposition of anti-dumping or countervailing duties may be necessary to counter future injury. Where an action is based on threat or likelihood of injury, the contemplated injury due to dumping or subsidizing must be clearly foreseen and imminent, not based upon allegation, conjecture, or remote possibility.[277] Evidence must be substantial.[278] A finding of future injury is more likely where the domestic industry is already in a weakened position, and is therefore more susceptible to suffer harm from import competition. Possibility of future injury involves consideration, among other things, of the trends in volume and pricing of imports; and the production capacity and inventory levels of foreign suppliers.[279]

In *Hydraulic Turbines for Electric Power Generation, not including bulb type turbines originating in the USSR*,[280] the tribunal found that the continuance of dumping by the then USSR would deny markets in Canada to Canadian producers leading to material injury in reduced usage of capacity and profitability.[281] In *12-gauge shotshells*,[282] anti-dumping measures were imposed because future dumping would have serious negative consequences for the domestic industry's profitability and employment and would also adversely affect planned investment for the manufacture of certain components used in the production of the subject goods. In *Boneless Manufacturing Beef Originating in or Exported from the EEC*,[283] the tribunal held that, despite the fact that subsidized imports had not caused and were not causing harm to domestic producers, they were likely to cause injury. The element of causation was not strictly the subsidized imports or the subsidies, but rather the threat of retaliation by the United States if there was a diversion into that country of Canadian beef as a result of the subsidized imports.

---

276 Continued ...
of CITT determinations that dumped imports had not caused, were not causing, but were likely to cause material injury to the production in Canada of like goods, see *Flat Wooden Toothpicks* (1992), 8 TTR 153 (CITT) and *12-gauge shotshells originating in or exported from the Czech Republic and the Republic of Hungary* (22 June 1994) (CITT).

277 See SIMA, *supra*, note 260, s. 2(1.5); art. 3.7 of the Agreement on Implementation of Article VI of the GATT 1994 (the 1994 Anti-dumping Code); art. 15.7 of the 1994 Subsidies Code, *supra*, note 265. One example given in the GATT codes is that there is convincing reason to believe that there will be, in the near future, substantially increased importation of the product at dumped or subsidized prices. See also art. 3.6 of the 1979 Anti-dumping Code and Recommendation of 21 October 1985 BISD (32nd Supp.) 182.

278 *Fresh, Chilled or Frozen Pork from Canada* (1991), 6 TTR 25 (Canada-US Free Trade Panel), aff'd. (1991), 6 TTR 238 (ECC).

279 See art. 3.7 of the 1994 Anti-dumping Agreement and art. 15.7 of the 1994 Subsidies Agreement.

280 (27 July 1976) ADT-4-76. There was no finding of past and present material injury. Compare *Polyphase Induction Motors*, *supra*, note 271, where a finding of likelihood of material injury was made. In the *Dry Pasta Case* (1986), 13 CER 288 (ADT), the tribunal held that in the absence of any import penetration that could be attributable to low pricing or to greater promotional expense arising from a subsidy, subsidized imports are not likely to cause material injury in the future.

281 Finding as to likelihood of material injury rescinded (1990), 3 TCT 2208 (CITT).

282 *Supra*, note 276.

283 (1986), 12 CER 62. See also *Oil and Gas Well Casing* (1986), 11 CER 213.

The tribunal may consider submissions concerning retardation as more appropriately dealt with under the issue of likelihood of future injury. In *Solder joint pressure pipe fittings*,[284] the CITT held that the likelihood of future injury to domestic production of the subject goods was limited to a time period of 18 months. Production was clearly foreseen and imminent within this time frame because the required production equipment was in place, and there remained few inputs to purchase. However, beyond the 18-month time frame, the tribunal determined that no likelihood of future injury existed: production plans were uncertain and at an early stage of development, with no formal commitments having been made.

Where it is clear that the dumped or subsidized goods have penetrated the Canadian market substantially over a short period of time, the tribunal will find likelihood of future injury.[285] Propensity to dump in a related product area creates a presumption of likelihood of future injury with respect to a product that is closely related and involves the same exporters and importers. The shifting of production from one country to another by the previously guilty exporter may also be taken as evidence of likelihood of future injury.[286]

J. Retardation

Retardation is an additional form of injury noted under the WTO Agreements[287] and the SIMA.[288] Retardation in the context of SIMA means material retardation of the establishment of an industry in Canada.[289] The CITT may find retardation where domestic production of like goods does not yet exist, but its establishment is impeded or hampered by dumping or subsidization.[290] Substantiation of retardation allegations requires provision by the potential Canadian producer of documents relating to definite plans for establishment of the industry, such as the purchase of a factory or equipment, or cancellation or postponement of a proposed project. The establishment of an industry must be

---

284 NQ-93-001 (18 October 1993) (CITT).

285 *Drywall Screws from Taiwan* and *Drywall Screws from South Korea, supra*, note 249.

286 *Photo Albums with Self-Adhesive Leaves* (1986), 11 CER 75. In *Alpine Ski Poles (Review)* (1987), 13 CER 179, the tribunal refused to rescind an order because the propensity to dump the subject goods from France and Italy was still present. For a case where no propensity to dump the subject goods was shown since earlier findings, see *Synthetic Baler Twine Review* (1987), 15 CER 65. As to future injury caused by future dumping, see also *Japan Electrical Manufacturers Association v. The Anti-Dumping Tribunal*, [1982] 2 FC 816 (CA).

287 See footnote 9 in art. 3 of the 1994 Anti-dumping Code and footnote 45 in art. 15 of the 1994 Subsidies Code.

288 SIMA, *supra*, note 76, s. 42(1).

289 *Ibid.*, s. 2(1) (definitions). See *Bicycle Tires and Tubes*, ADT-4-72 (1972) (retardation); *Stainless Steel Sheet*, ADT-17-1982 (1982) (no retardation); and *Tetanus Immune Globulin*, ADT-3-74 (no retardation).

290 In *Solder Joint Pressure Pipe Fittings from the United States*, NQ-93-007 (18 October 1993), the tribunal considered submissions concerning the question of retardation to be more appropriately dealt under consideration of future injury.

definitely contemplated,[291] and the complainant must have made a "substantial commitment" to its establishment.[292] Plans to improve production and develop new product offerings must be definite and committed. Even proof of rapid emergence and past entrepreneurial drive and achievement may not suffice to demonstrate the degree of firmness of the alleged development plans needed for the tribunal to find retardation.[293] Among the factors that the tribunal will consider in the context of retardation are commercial feasibility of the proposed plans or project, possible cost of production, modernization of existing facilities; the timing of the confirmation and cancellation of the plans, and the timing of the commencement of the importations and of the dumping or subsidizing of goods. Threat of retardation is not mentioned under the SIMA.[294]

K. Causal Connection[295]

Dumping or subsidizing must be the cause of material injury, retardation, or threat of injury. Thus, a determination of material injury must be based on positive findings and not mere unsubstantiated allegations or hypothetical possibilities. The 1994 Subsidies Code states:[296]

> It must be demonstrated that the subsidized imports are, through the effects of subsidies, causing injury within the meaning of this Agreement. The demonstration of a causal relationship between the subsidized imports and the injury to the domestic injury shall be based on an examination of all relevant evidence before the authorities. The authorities shall also examine any known factors other than the subsidized imports which at the same time are injuring the domestic industry, and the injuries caused by these other factors must not be attributed to the subsidized imports.

Relevant factors in this respect include the volumes and prices of non-subsidized imports of the particular product, contraction in demand, or change in the patterns of consumption or general economic conditions, such as recession, trade restrictive practices of and competition between the foreign and domestic producers, developments in technology, and the export performance and productivity of the domestic industry.

---

291 See *Plywood Concrete Forming Panels* (1985), 12 CER 35.

292 *Preformed fiberglass pipe insulation with a vapor barrier from the United States of America*, NQ-93-002 [1993] (19 November 1993). In that case, because the complainant owned and operated a manufacturing plant which was producing like goods, the tribunal held that, on the basis that there existed a domestic industry producing like goods, the claim of retardation must fail.

293 *Aluminum coil stock and steel head and bottom rails, for use in the production of horizontal venetian blinds, originating in or exported from Sweden*, NQ-91-004, [1992] CITT no. 15, 8 TTR 32 (7 February 1992).

294 See *Re Stainless Steel Strip* (1983), 5 CER 285.

295 SIMA, *supra*, note 76, s. 42(1)(i). See L.L. Herman, "Injury findings by the Canadian Import Tribunal: the decisive elements" (1987), 1 *Rev. of Int. Bus.* 373.

296 1994 Subsidies Code, *supra*, note 265, art. 15.5. A similar provision in the context of dumping is found in art. 3.5 of the 1994 Anti-dumping Code, *supra*, note 277.

In *Subsidized Grain Corn*,[297] the tribunal found that material injury had been suffered by Canadian grain corn growers as a result of the low US and world prices and that there was an increased financial burden on federal and provincial agricultural support programs.[298] The majority was of the opinion that the issue with respect to causation was not whether imports had taken place, but whether they would have increased substantially in the absence of a price response by the domestic producers to the subsidized US grain corn. The openness of the Canadian market would have resulted in a much higher level of imports had Canadian grain corn farmers not decreased their prices substantially, which resulted in material injury to them. The dissent expressed the view that causality can only be established in relation to actual subsidized imports and not potential imports. By supporting the broad interpretation of section 42(1) favoured by the majority of the tribunal and the Federal Court of Appeal, the Supreme Court of Canada has given the green light to Canadian producers, who will be able to bring actions against foreign subsidized goods, even though they have not been exported to Canada.[299]

The SIMA does not identify the requisite degree of causality between dumping or subsidizing and injury, although it is clear that dumping need not be the sole or exclusive cause of injury. The tribunal does not appear to have a uniform causation standard and has held, for example, that dumping is a "significant,"[300] and "direct"[301] cause, and simply "a cause" of injury.[302]

Where the injury suffered by the complainant is attributable to a number of major factors of which the dumped or subsidized imports are but one, the tribunal may find that such injury is not sufficient to constitute material injury. However, the fact that a domestic producer initiated price declines does not lead to the conclusion that any injury to it is self-inflicted.[303]

The SIMA does not pinpoint a methodology for the tribunal to follow in determining whether a causal link exists. The binational panel in *Flat Hot-Rolled Carbon Steel Sheet*[304] held that it was not an error *per se* for the tribunal to have used a bifurcated causality test, first determining whether the domestic industry had suffered material injury, and then considering whether there was a causal link between that injury and the

---

297 (1987), 14 CER 1, aff'd. by majority of FCA in *National Corn Growers Association and Canadian Import Tribunal* (1989), 18 CER 268, 2 TCT 4053, [1989] 2 FC 517, 58 DLR (4th) 642, 92 NR 264 (no error in law). The majority of the FCA chose to ignore arts. 2, 4, and 6 of the Subsidies Code, which required that the subsidized imports be the cause of the injury.

298 See SIMA, *supra*, note 260, s. 2(1) (definition of injury).

299 Aff'd. by unanimous SCC (8 November 1990) (1990), 3 TCT 5303, 74 DLR (4th) 449 (sub nom. *American Farm Bureau Federation et al. v. Canadian Import Tribunal*).

300 *Wide Flange Steel Shapes* (1986), 9 CER 175, at 184.

301 *Drywall Screws from Taiwan* (1987), 12 CER 16, at 24.

302 *Machine Tufted Carpeting* (1992) 8 TTR 96 (CITT). See also the binational panel decision in *Flat Hot-Rolled Carbon Steel Sheet* (18 May 1994).

303 *Charcoal Briquets* (1985), 10 CER 40.

304 18 May 1994.

dumped imports. An alternative approach discussed in the case was a determination first of whether the dumped imports have caused injury, and, if so, whether the injury caused was material.

A finding of injury must be made in respect of each class of goods in issue.[305]

L. Production in Canada of Like Goods

The "like goods" concept is fundamental to the SIMA. Under section 42(1) of the SIMA, the tribunal must inquire into whether the dumping of goods is causing material injury to the "production in Canada of like goods." Therefore, as part of its task in determining material injury to production in Canada, the tribunal must determine what the like goods are. If production in Canada of like goods does not exist, the tribunal must make a negative injury determination. The description of the class of goods that the deputy minister chooses to use in his or her preliminary determination affects the determination of the industry.[306] In *Steam Trap Controls*, decided before the SIMA,[307] the tribunal was of the opinion that the question whether goods are like goods must be determined by market considerations. Do they compete directly with each other? Do they target the same consumers? Do they fulfill the same needs? Do they have the same end use functionally? Can they be substituted for one another? More recently, the tribunal based its finding of like goods on similarity of uses, substitution, and other characteristics.[308]

Section 2(1) of SIMA now defines "like goods"[309] in relation to other goods, as:

> (a) goods that are identical in all respects to the other goods, or
>
> (b) in the absence of any goods described in paragraph (a), goods the uses and other characteristics of which closely resemble those of the other goods.

Where goods attract the same buyers and compete with the goods in question, they may be deemed to be like goods.[310] Often goods that are similar are deemed not to be like goods. In *Cauliflower*, the tribunal held that cauliflower grown for the fresh market and cauliflower grown for processing were not "like goods" because they were not identical in all respects within the meaning of SIMA section 2(1)(a). Concerning their uses and characteristics, the tribunal held that the different varieties used in the two markets do not share similar physical characteristics, the purchasers of these products

305 *Noury Chemical Corporation and Minerals and Chemicals Ltd. v. Pennwalt of Canada Ltd.* (1982), 4 CER 53 (FCA).

306 See *Mitsui & Co. Ltd. et al. v. W.W. Buchanan*, [1972] FC 944 (CA).

307 ADT-10-76 (9176). See also *Sarco Canada Ltd. v. The Anti-Dumping Tribunal*, [1979] 1 FC 247 (CA) applied in *Madison Industrial Equipment Ltd. v. Dep. MNR Customs and Excise* (1991), 4 TCT 3131.

308 *Machine Tufted Carpeting*, *supra*, note 302, holding that there were three sub-categories of machine tufted carpeting, namely residential, commercial, and artificial grass.

309 The counterpart of the SIMA term "like good" in the WTO Anti-dumping and Subsidies Codes is "like product," which is a product which is identical, or has characteristics closely resembling those of the product under consideration (see 1994 Anti-dumping Code, *supra*, 277, art. 2.6).

310 *Hyundai*, *supra*, note 270.

distinguish between them in that buyers in the two markets prefer different varieties, and these varieties only compete with each other in limited circumstances. Therefore, the tribunal was of the view that the uses and characteristics of cauliflower grown for the fresh market and cauliflower grown for processing do not closely resemble each other and are not "like goods" under section 2(1)(b).[311]

In the *Boneless Manufacturing Beef Originating in or Exported from the EEC* case, which involved subsidizing,[312] the tribunal found that "like goods" were produced in Canada because the domestic product produced by the complainants "closely resembled" the imported subsidized beef. Furthermore, the tribunal was of the opinion that since the production process for boneless manufacturing beef consists of a single, continuous line starting with one raw material, the cow, which yields only one commercially significant end product—namely, the chunks of boneless manufacturing beef—the industry concerned included the complainants (Canadian Cattlemen's Association), cow producers, and feed lot operators even though they did not act as slaughterers, boners, etc., or packing houses. Even though the slaughterers, the boners, the dairy industry, and the packing houses contributed in varying degree to the goods in question, they should not be isolated into separate industries. In other words, producers of agricultural products can be treated as part of the industry producing a processed product. The tribunal adopted the single line of production test but rejected the second branch of the US International Trade Commission test, which requires the existence of a substantial degree of economic integration between the growers and the processors for them to be part of the same industry. This interpretation was the object of a complaint to the GATT by the European Communities (EC) under the 1979 Code on Subsidies and Countervailing Measures and led to the establishment of a panel. In its report, the panel agreed with the EC that the Canadian Cattelmen's Association could not be considered under the code to be producers of the like product and, therefore, they had no standing to file the petition as they were not part of the domestic industry for the purpose of a determination of injury. The panel ruled that:[313]

> (i) the term "producer" in Article 6:5 of the Code could not be interpreted to include the cattle producers represented by CCA as "producers" of manufacturing beef;
>
> (ii) the cattle producers represented by CCA could not, therefore, be considered as part of the "domestic industry" for the purpose of the Article 2:1 requirements defining standing to complain and the Article 6 requirements governing the determination of material injury and
>
> (iii) accordingly, the imposition of countervailing duties based on a petition of the CCA, and also based on a determination of threat of injury to the cattle producers represented by the CCA, was not in conformity with Canada's obligations under the Code.
>
> The Panel suggests, therefore, that the Committee recommend that Canada terminate the outstanding countervailing duty order on manufacturing beef from the EEC, and that it refund any duties collected under that order.

---

311 *Fresh Cauliflower Originating in or Exported from the United States of America*, NQ-92-003, [1993] CITT no. 14 (19 January 1993).

312 (1986), 12 CER 62.

313 SCM/85, 13 October 1987, 20 to 22, para. 5.17. The panel's reasons, cited in the following paragraphs, appear at paras. 5.13-5.14.

In support of these rulings, the panel gave the following reasons:

... both the text and the negotiating history of the relevant Code provisions made it impossible to accept Canada's contention that governments intended the concept of "domestic industry" to be interpreted with sufficient flexibility to permit treating input suppliers as "producers" of the like product when economic circumstances warranted. The Panel therefore found that Canada's interpretation of the term "producer" in this case was inconsistent with the relevant Code provisions. The only way such an interpretation could be adopted would be to amend the Code through negotiation.

5.14 The Panel did not agree that adherence to the narrow definition of "domestic industry" in Article 6:5 and 6:6 would cause outcomes to vary according to the degree of vertical integration which happened to exist at a particular time or in a particular country. The definition of "domestic industry" involves two criteria, neither of which depends on vertical integration as such. First, there must be a determination of which product or range of products constitutes the "like product." If the production process for that "like product" happens to be subdivided into two or more separate stages, that fact will not mean that each stage must be considered a separate "domestic industry"; as long as the products at the various stages are enough "like" each other to be considered different forms of the same "like product," the separate production stages will all be part of the same "domestic industry." The second criterion—whether the production process for the "like product" can be separately identified—is likewise independent of vertical integration. If the process of production for one "like product" can be separately identified, it will be treated as a separate industry whether or not it is owned in common with parallel, earlier or subsequent production lines. The only case in which the fact of common ownership will affect the definition of industry will be the case in which common ownership results in such a complete integration of production processes that it is impossible to analyze each one separately.

What level or degree of operation is required before an activity qualifies as production in Canada has been determined by the tribunal on a number of occasions. For instance in the *Sultana Raisins* case,[314] packaging was not considered as production. If the product is unchanged, a change of packaging, together with a change in the quantity offered to the consumer does not constitute production. Something more is required to qualify as "the production in Canada of like goods." In *(Cars) Hyundai*,[315] the tribunal excluded domestic production for export from consideration.

M. Major Proportion of the Production of Goods in Canada

It is important to establish whether producers alleging material injury represent a major proportion of the goods in issue. The definition of "domestic industry" in article 4.1 of the 1994 Anti-dumping Code and article 16.1 of the 1994 Subsidies Code has been integrated directly into SIMA section 2(1), which provides that the term means the domestic producers as a whole of the like goods or whose collective production of the

---

314 ADT-1-77 (1977), compare *Surgical Adhesive Tapes and Plasters* (1985), 10 CER 174, where the tribunal found Canadian production to exist citing *R. v. York Marble Tile and Terazzo Ltd.*, [1968] SCR 140.

315 *Supra*, note 270.

like goods constitutes a major proportion of the total domestic production of the like goods except that, where a domestic producer is related to an exporter or importer of dumped or subsidized goods, "domestic industry" may be interpreted as meaning the rest of those domestic producers. Thus, where one or more of the domestic producers joining in the complaint are related to exporters and importers of the dumped or subsidized goods or are themselves importers of these goods, they must be excluded from the domestic industry for the purpose of a dumping or subsidization finding of injury.[316]

An investigation may not be initiated in the first place unless the complaint is supported by "a major proportion of the total Canadian production." This means domestic producers whose production represents more than half of the total production of like goods by those domestic producers who express either support for or opposition to the complaint and the production of the domestic producers who support the complaint represents 25 percent or more of the total production of like goods by the domestic industry.[317] The term "major proportion" does not mean that 50 percent or more of the industry are in support of the complaint; rather, it means "significant proportion,"[318] which would seem to fall in the 25 to 50 percent range. In *Boneless Manufacturing Beef*, under an earlier version of the SIMA, the complainants who represented 44 percent of the Canadian industry producing low-grade beef were considered to be a major proportion of the Canadian industry.[319]

The SIMA and the 1994 WTO codes also allow the division of a domestic market into isolated or regional markets where certain conditions are satisfied.

---

316 See, e.g., *Aluminum coil stock and steel head and bottom rails (Sweden), supra*, note 293 and *Gasoline Powered Chainsaws* (1987), 14 CER 171. The power to exclude domestic producers is discretionary, and such an exclusion will not be granted where the effect would be to deny the existence of a domestic industry: *Re Women's Footwear*, RR-94-003, [1995] CITT no. 27 (2 May 1995); *Certain Solder Joint Pressure Pipe Fittings*, NQ-93-001 (18 October 1993). Canadian subsidiaries may obtain anti-dumping or subsidization protection against foreign parent corporations if they can establish that an adversarial relationship with the parent exists and that their parent is engaged in injurious dumping or is the recipient of an injurious subsidy.

317 SIMA, *supra*, note 76, s. 31(2). See 1994 Anti-dumping Code, *supra*, note 2, art. 5.4 and 1994 Subsidies Code, *supra*, note 3, art. 11.4. When a complainant's production does not represent a major proportion of Canadian production, an investigation will not be initiated on the grounds that there is no evidence of injury caused to Canadian production. However, if other producers submit complaints, a reconsideration of whether to initiate an investigation would occur.

318 *Chain Saws*, ADT-5-76 (1976). See also *Brunswick International (Canada) Ltd. v. Anti-dumping Tribunal* (1979), 108 DLR (3d) 216) (FCA); *Japan Electrical Manufacturers' Association v. Anti-Dumping Tribunal* (1986), 32 DLR (4th) 222 (FCA), relying upon *McCulloch v. Anti-dumping Tribunal*, [1979] 1 FC 222, at 225 (CA).

319 *Supra*, note 312.

N. Regional Market

The tribunal and its predecessors have had numerous opportunities to consider the regional market issue.[320] An isolated or regional market is one in which the supply and demand is independent from the supply and demand for the same product in other regions of the territory. This independence translates into little or no movement of goods across the regional boundary.[321]

In *Solid Urea*, the CIT pointed out that the absence of movement across the regional boundary could be caused by multiple factors, such as natural or geographical impediments, governmental, regulatory, economic, competitive, structural or physical barriers, or the intrinsic physical characteristics of a product. It also pointed out that the analysis should not be limited to a static consideration of the situation, but should take into account the dynamic effects of forces that tended to encourage or discourage transfrontier movement of goods over time.

The concept of domestic injury based on regional markets outlined in the 1994 WTO Anti-dumping and Subsidies Codes[322] has been integrated directly into the SIMA.[323] SIMA section 2(1.1) states:

> 2(1.1) In exceptional circumstances, the territory of Canada may, for the production of any goods, be divided into two or more regional markets and the domestic producers of like goods in any of those markets may be considered to be a separate domestic industry where (a) the producers in the market sell all or almost all of their production of like goods in the market; and (b) the demand in the market is not to any substantial degree supplied by producers of like goods located elsewhere in Canada.

The tribunal may only find that dumping or subsidizing has caused injury, retardation, or is threatening to cause injury where there is a concentration of those goods in the regional market; and the dumping or subsidizing of those goods has caused injury, retardation, or is threatening to cause injury to the producers of all or almost all of the production of like goods in the regional market.[324]

---

320 See, e.g., *Beer (Review)*, RR-94-001, [1994] CITT no. 151 (2 December 1994), rescinding (1991), 4 TCT 3353, NQ-91-002 (2 October 1991) (CITT); *Fresh Cauliflower Originating in or Exported from the United States of America*, NQ-92-003 (19 January 1993) (CITT); *Fresh Iceberg (Head) Lettuce Originating in or Exported from the United States of America* (1992), 10 TTR 310 (CITT); *Recreational Vehicle Entrance Doors* (1988), 16 CER 174 (CIT-12-87); *Fertilizer Blending Equipment* (1987), 14 CER 290 (CIT-3-87) (15 October 1987); and *Whole Potatoes* (1984), 7 CER 284 (ADT-4-84) (4 June 1984). See also *Re Solid Urea* (1988), 15 CER 277, aff'd. (1988) 2 TCT 4042 (FCA); *Re Hot-Rolled Steel Reinforcing Bars* (1988), 15 CER 253; *Re Phenol* (1988), 15 CER 228; and *Re Delicious Apples* (1988), 18 CER 332.

321 See *Solid Urea, ibid.*, at 287 and 289 (CIT), aff'd. in *C-I-L v. Canada* (1988), 2 TCT 4042 (CIT), 18 CER 267 (FCA); see also *Hot Rolled Carbon Steel Concrete Reinforcing Bars, ibid.*

322 See art. 4.1(ii) of the 1994 Anti-dumping Code and art. 16.2 of the 1994 Subsidies Code.

323 See SIMA, *supra*, note 76, ss. 2(1.1) and 42(5).

324 *Ibid.*, s. 42(5).

Under the SIMA and the WTO codes, four criteria must therefore be satisfied for a finding of injurious dumping or subsidization to regional industry, which will occur only in "exceptional circumstances":

1. *The regional producers must sell all or almost all of their production of the product within the market.* With respect to the requirement that the regional producers sell "all or almost all" of their production of the product within the market, the tribunal appears to have adopted 80 to 90 percent as the rough threshold level. In *Lettuce*,[325] the tribunal held that 88 percent represented "all or almost all"; in *Yellow onions*,[326] 90 percent satisfied the criterion; and in *Carbon Steel Reinforcing Bars*,[327] 80 percent was apparently sufficient.[328]

The *Beer* case provides an interesting example of the tribunal's treatment of this aspect of the regional market issue. In 1991, the CITT,[329] and subsequently the FTA binational panel,[330] found that British Columbia met the requirements for a regional market for beer under the identical article 4(1)(ii) of the former GATT Anti-dumping Code. In December 1994, the CITT[331] rescinded its original 1991 finding of material injury in a regional market, a result subsequently upheld by a binational panel (November 15, 1995). In the period from April 1, 1990 to March 31, 1991, BC producers sold 95 to 100 percent of their production of packaged beer in British Columbia. However, in 1992 and 1993, such sales accounted for only 76 and 78 percent of production, respectively. This fell below the acceptable threshold for a regional market.

2. *The demand in that market must not be to a substantial degree supplied by producers of the product located elsewhere in Canada.* The criterion that the demand in the market not be satisfied "to any substantial degree" by producers of like goods located elsewhere in Canada appears to have a threshold of approximately 20 percent. In *Solid Urea*,[332] where the sole producer in the alleged regional market made no sales outside that market, the CIT found that a regional market did not exist, on the ground that there was an 11.5 percent inflow of solid urea into the market from other provinces. In *Whole Potatoes*,[333] the tribunal's finding that less than 5 percent of the regional

325 *Supra*, note 320.

326 NQ CIT-1-87.

327 *Supra*, note 320.

328 In *Reinforcing Bars*, *supra*, note 320, the CIT noted that BC producers sold 80 percent or more of their production in British Columbia. However, as the CIT had already concluded that there was not an isolated market on the basis of the inflow of goods from other provinces into British Columbia, it did not decide whether BC producers sold "all or almost all" of their production in the province. See (1989), 15 CER 253, at 262.

329 NQ-91-002 (2 October 1991). See (1991), 7 TTR 255, 8 TTR 5.

330 See CDA-91-1904-02 (26 August 1992) and (1995), 10 TTR 110.

331 See RR-94-001 (2 December 1994) (CITT).

332 *Supra*, note 320, at 288.

333 *Supra*, note 320.

market's needs were met by extra-provincial suppliers was held to be not substantial, and consistent with finding a regional market. In *Reinforcing Bars*, the CIT found that an isolated market did not exist, on the basis that between 20 to 27 percent of the BC market for the goods in question was supplied by production from other provinces.[334]

In the *Beer* case, with respect to sales of packaged beer in British Columbia by producers located in other provinces, from 1987-90, less than 1 percent of the BC market was supplied by beer produced in other provinces. However, the evidence adduced in this proceeding indicates that the situation had changed considerably by 1992 and 1993. Given the consistent and increasing pattern of a significant movement of packaged beer both into and out of British Columbia—that is, the first two elements in the regional market analysis attributable chiefly to the conclusion of the interprovincial and international agreements relating to trade in beer[335]—the tribunal found that there was no longer a regional industry in packaged beer in the province.

A binational panel affirmed this finding.[336]

3. *Dumped imports must be concentrated in the isolated regional market (the "concentration test").*[337] The requirement that there be a "concentration of dumped imports" in the regional market will be automatically satisfied where all of the dumped goods are sold and consumed within the market. However, where exporters dumping in the regional market are also selling the goods elsewhere in Canada, this criterion is evaluated in accordance with comparisons of the volume of dumped imports within the regional market to the total regional market volume (the "density test"); the volume of imports into the regional market to the volume of imports into the rest of Canada (the "penetration" or "distribution test");[338] or the regional market's share of the imports to the regional market's share of total consumption in Canada.

4. *The dumped imports must be causing injury to all or almost all of the production within the market.* The requirement that the dumped imports must be causing injury to "all or almost all" of the production within the isolated market contrasts with the ordinary

---

334 *Supra*, note 320, at 261.

335 The 1991 Intergovernmental Agreement between the federal and provincial governments; two agreements between Canada and the United States, which relate to trade in packaged beer, an agreement in principle concluded on 25 April 1992, and the MOU concluded on 5 August 1993; and the 18 July 1994, Agreement on Internal Trade between the federal and provincial governments, which will come into force on 1 July 1995. Chapter 10 of that agreement obligates the provinces to eliminate measures that operate as obstacles to interprovincial trade in alcoholic beverages, including beer.

336 15 November 1995.

337 In *Recreational Vehicle Entrance Doors, supra*, note 320, the tribunal noted that this "concentration test" could be measured by a "density test" or a "penetration (distribution) test." See also *Solid Urea supra*, note 320 and *Beer* (1991), 4 TCT 3353 (CIT).

338 This test was applied in, e.g., *Recreational Vehicle Entrance Doors, ibid.*; *Solid Urea, supra*, note 320; and *Beer, ibid.* In *Beer*, the regional market's level of 20 to 37 percent of the total subject markets in Canada were considered adequate to satisfy the distribution test (finding subsequently rescinded in *Beer*, RR-94-001, [1994] CITT no. 151 (2 December1994).

test requiring injury only to a "major proportion" of the production in the national market. In *Fertilizer Blending Equipment*,[339] although the complainant supplied 75 percent of the regional industry's production of the subject goods, this did not meet the "all or almost all" test. The outcome in this case may have been different if other regional producers had supported the complainant. It therefore appears that the minimum threshold for the "all or almost all" requirement is 80 percent, and may approach 90 percent. For example, in *Beer*,[340] sales of beer in the regional market by the complainants accounted for 99 percent of the total sales of like goods made by all regional producers.

O. Cumulative Impact

In accordance with the 1994 Anti-dumping and Subsidies Codes,[341] the SIMA has now been revised to provide expressly for the possibility of assessment of cumulative effect where imports into Canada from more than one country are simultaneously subject to an investigation[342] if (1) the margin of dumping or the amount of the subsidy in relation to the goods from each of those countries is not insignificant[343] and the volume of the goods from each of those countries is not negligible,[344] and (2) an assessment of the cumulative effect would be appropriate taking into account the conditions of competition between the imported goods from any of the countries, or between the imported goods and like goods of domestic producers.[345] Resort to cumulative assessment by the tribunal in evaluating injury and causation is discretionary rather than mandatory.

Cumulation refers to the analysis of the aggregate effect that all imports subject to the investigation have on the competing domestic industry, rather than analysis through

339 *Supra*, note 320.

340 *Supra* note 337.

341 See art. 3.3 of the 1994 Anti-dumping Code and art. 15.3 of the 1994 Subsidies Code.

342 SIMA, *supra*, note 323, s. 43(3).

343 *Ibid.*, s. 2(1) defines "insignificant" in relation to a margin of dumping as less than 2 percent of the export price of the goods; and in relation to an amount of subsidy, as less than 1 percent of the export price of the goods.

344 *Ibid.*, s. 2(1) contains the following definition of "negligible": "Negligible" means, in respect of the volume of dumped goods of a country,

> (a) less than 3 percent of the total volume of goods that are released into Canada from all countries and that are of the same description as the dumped goods, except that
>
> (b) where the total volume of dumped goods of three or more countries, each of whose exports of dumped good into Canada is less than 3 percent of the total volume of goods referred to in paragraph (a), is more than 7 percent of the total volume of goods referred to in paragraph (a), the volume of dumped goods of any of those countries is not negligible.

345 In making this cumulative assessment, SIMA, *ibid.*, s. 42(4) stipulates that the tribunal is to take into account the provisions of art. 27.12 of the 1994 Subsidies Agreement. Although the ordinary *de minimis* level for a subsidy is 1 percent *ad valorem* (1994 Subsidies Code, *supra*, note 341, art. 11.9), art. 27.12 of the 1994 Subsidies Code mandates that the provisions of arts. 27.10 and 27.11 will apply to the determination of *de minimis* with regard to countervailing duty investigations of products originating in

(The footnote is continued on the next page.)

segregation of the separate impact of imports from each separate source.[346] Cumulation is also at issue when complaints against both dumping and subsidizing are before the CITT: the tribunal ordinarily considers dumping and subsidization determinations as requiring a single inquiry and analyzes the cumulative impact of both on domestic production.[347]

The issue of cumulation relates directly to the question of exclusions. Where the preliminary determination involves imports from a number of countries, representatives of some of these countries may ask for an exemption from a finding of injury when the volume of exports to Canada from these goods is so minuscule or the margin of dumping so low as not to cause a problem for the Canadian industry. The policy followed by the tribunal was articulated in *Wide Flange Shapes*:[348]

> It is not at all unusual for the preliminary determination of dumping to encompass a number of dumping countries with great variations between them in volumes exported, in the degree of dumping found and in the margins of dumping determined. Where the ratio of dumped to undumped goods and the margins of dumping in each individual case are considered significant, as is usually the case, the Tribunal considers the effect en masse of the dumped goods, regardless of origin. Thus, if a country is named as one of five and its exports are small in volume but all or most of which are dumped at a substantial margin, then, in the absence of other overriding factors, the Tribunal would not be inclined to exclude that country from an injury finding. The Tribunal has, on a number of occasions, qualified its findings to provide for exclusions from an affirmative finding of injury, but in all such cases the margin of dumping has been considered too small to have any discernible market effect.

It is thus within the tribunal's discretion to grant exclusions.[349] The onus is on the person requesting the exclusion to establish that it is warranted,[350] which is usually only

---

345 Continued …

a developing country. The *de minimis* level (below which an investigation must be terminated) under these circumstances is 2 percent *ad valorem* (and 3 percent for those developing countries that have eliminated export subsidies prior to the termination of the eight-year transition period from the date of entry into force of the WTO Agreement); or when the volume of the subsidized imports represents less than 4 percent of the total imports of like product in the importing member.

346 See, e.g., *Hot-rolled Carbon Steel Plate*, Binational Panel Memorandum opinion and order, NQ-92-007 (20 December 1994).

347 See *Polyphase Induction Motors* (finding rescinded) (1989), 1 TTR 58.

348 ADT-9-83 (1983).

349 *Preformed Fiberglass Pipe Insulation with a Vapor Barrier*, NQ-93-002, [1993] CITT no. 137 (19 November 1993); *Hitachi Limited v. The Anti-dumping Tribunal*, [1979] 1 SCR 93; *Sacilor Acieries v. The Anti-dumping Tribunal* (1985), 9 CER 210 (FCA); *Aluminum coil stock and steel head and bottom rails (Sweden)*, *supra*, note 316. See also the binational panel decision, *Certain Dumped Integral Horsepower Induction Motors, One Horsepower (1 HP) to Two Hundred Horsepower (200 HP) Inclusive, with Exceptions, Originating in or Exported from the United States of America*, (1991) 4 TCT 7065.

350 See *Preformed Fiberglass Pipe Insulation with a Vapor Barrier*, *ibid.*, and *Hot-Rolled Carbon Steel Plate and High-Strength Low-Alloy Plate*, NQ-92-007 (21 May 1993).

in exceptional circumstances.[351] The CITT has held that it is only after the cumulative effect of the dumped goods from all subject countries has been analyzed that the tribunal may contemplate exclusions for any particular country.[352]

Thus, even when dumped imports from certain sources are small and "cannot be found to have contributed significantly to the plight of the domestic producers when considered separately," it may be their cumulative impact combined with all other imports that is to be assessed in considering the question of material injury.[353] The tribunal may decide against granting exclusions where the requesting parties all export significant quantities of the subject goods to Canada; the margins of dumping and the percentage of the subject goods dumped by each of the companies are high; and the companies' collective actions result in declines in domestic prices for the subject goods and cause material injury to the domestic industry.[354]

Under the former SIMA and 1979 GATT Anti-dumping and Subsidies Codes, cumulative assessment (and the exclusion of subject goods from the determination only on *de minimis* grounds) was neither prohibited nor mandated. Former SIMA sections 42 and 43 contained no reference to cumulation or to exclusion. It was merely a permitted administrative practice that the tribunal could apply as appropriate to reflect the facts of each particular case.[355] There was therefore in the past no requirement that the CITT cumulate, nor that "cumulation" had to occur in accordance with a particular methodology.

Cases under the previous SIMA and GATT arrangements reveal no consistent past administrative practice concerning cumulation.[356] A consistent administrative practice of granting exclusions only where *de minimis* grounds exist has also been lacking.[357]

---

351 *Aluminum coil stock and steel head and bottom rails (Sweden), supra*, note 316.

352 *Polyphase Induction, supra*, note 347, at 77; *Cold-rolled steel sheet originating in or exported from the Federal Republic of Germany, France, Italy, the United Kingdom and the United States of America*, NQ-92-009 [1993] (29 July 1993) (CITT); and *Hot-Rolled Carbon Steel Plate and High-Strength Low-Alloy Plate, supra*, note 350, "Dissenting Opinion of Member Fraleigh," at 28.

353 *Cold-rolled steel sheet, ibid.* and *Carbon and Alloy Plates Originating in or Exported from Belgium, Brazil, Czechoslovakia, the Federal Republic of Germany, France, the Republic of South Africa, the Republic of Korea, Romania, Spain and the United Kingdom* (1983), 6 CER 21, at 33-34 (ADT).

354 *Preformed Fiberglass Pipe Insulation with a Vapor Barrier, supra*, note 349.

355 See the binational panel decision in *Hot-rolled Carbon Steel Plate, supra*, note 346.

356 See the binational panel decision in *Hot-rolled carbon steel plate, ibid.* Cumulation occurred, e.g., in: *Polyphase Induction Motors, supra*, note 347; *Bars, Plates and Forgings* (CIT 1985); *Cold-rolled steel sheet, supra*, note 352; *Carbon and Alloy Plates, supra*, note 353; and *Stainless Steel, Nickel and Nickel-Alloy Pipe and Tubing* (ADT, 1984). Cumulation did not occur in, for example: *Hot-rolled carbon steel plate*, NQ-92-007 (20 December 1994); *Wide Flange Shapes, supra*, note 348; *Citric Acid* (ADT 1980); *Rail-Car Axles* (CIT 1985); *Methyl Ethyl Ketone* (ADT 1980); *Alpine Ski Poles* (ADT 1984); and *Merkuria Foreign Trade Corp. v. The Anti-Dumping Tribunal* (1980), 2 CER 142 (FCA).

357 *Hot rolled Carbon Steel Plate, supra*, note 346. See, e.g., *Synthetic Baler Twine Originating in or Exported from Portugal, Italy, the United Kingdom, the Netherlands and the Federal Republic of Germany*, ADT-8-81 (23 February 1988), at 10-12 (exclusion based on finding that price was not a

(The footnote is continued on the next page.)

With respect to goods from a NAFTA country, the SIMA[358] requires a separate order or finding with respect to the goods of each NAFTA country where an inquiry involves goods of more than one NAFTA country or of one or more NAFTA countries and goods of another or other countries. This provision raises the question whether the tribunal may include goods from the NAFTA countries in calculating cumulative effects. The proper interpretation would seem to leave the matter of cumulation within the discretion of the tribunal, since the NAFTA does not contemplate a change in the domestic substantive anti-dumping and countervailing duty law of the signatories.[359]

P. Component Parts

When the preliminary determination of dumping or subsidizing by the deputy minister includes components or parts as well as the finished product, it is not necessary to assess the impact of each component part on the domestic production of each like part.[360] The tribunal has regularly found that a finished product and its principal components represent a single class of like goods.[361] It would be an exorbitant task for the domestic producers to give evidence of material injury to the production of components. The usual criteria for establishing material injury, such as loss of market share, reduced profitability, diminished employment, idle capacity, etc., lose their relevance when components are considered independently of the finished product. Nevertheless, an injury inquiry may consider the impact of dumping on component parts. For instance, in *12-gauge shotshells*,[362] one of the

---

357 Continued ...
motivating factor in decision to buy) and *Chemically Pre-sensitized Aluminum Offset Printing Plates Originating in or Exported from Japan and the United Kingdom*, CIT-4-87 (27 October 1987), at 12 (exclusion based on finding that factors such as customer satisfaction played more significant role than price in decision to buy). *Wide Flange Steel Shapes* noted that product exclusions had been based on *de minimis* conditions in the past, but it also stated that the Tribunal has the discretion to grant exclusions whenever presented "with other overriding factors."

358 SIMA, *supra*, note 323, s. 43(1.01). The operation of SIMA, *ibid.*, s. 43(1.1) providing for a separate order or finding for goods from the United States in accordance with the provisions of the Canada-US FTA is suspended as long as s. 43(1.01) is in force.

359 See NAFTA, arts. 1901.3 and 1902.1. See *Polyphase Induction Motors* (1989), 2 TCT 1097 (finding rescinded) and *Integral horsepower induction motors and polyphase induction motors*, RR-93-004, [1994] CITT no. 105 (30 June 1994).

360 In *Re Y.K.K. Zipper Co. of Canada Ltd.* (Slide Fasteners), ADT-1-74 (1974), aff'd. [1975] FC 68 (CA) components were not treated separately because the dumped components were assembled in a finished product.

361 See, e.g., *Black Granite*, NQ-93-006, [1994] CITT no. 116 (20 July 1994); *Photo Albums with Self-Adhesive Leaves from Indonesia, Thailand and the Philippines*, NQ-90-003 (17 January 1991) (CITT); *Single Row Tapered Roller Bearings from Japan*, NQ-91-007 (24 July 1992) (CITT); and *Bicycles and Frames Originating in or Exported from Taiwan and the People's Republic of China*, NQ-92-002 (29 December 1992) (CITT).

362 *Supra*, note 276; 22 June 1994 (CITT).

reasons for the imposition of anti-dumping duties for future dumping was that planned investment for future manufacture of certain components of the subject goods would be adversely affected. In *Aluminum coil stock and steel head and bottom rails from Sweden*,[363] the tribunal held that the components (aluminum coil stock and steel rails) were so intimately related that they were part of the same product class because they were of little commercial use if they were not used together. A separate inquiry into material injury is not required in respect of each and every component identified, unless there is production in Canada of the major components of the finished product.[364]

Q. Injury Order or Finding

The CITT has 120 days in which to conduct the inquiry and to make an order or finding.[365] An additional 15 days are allowed to issue the statement of reasons. While the tribunal is conducting its inquiry, the deputy minister will continue to investigate the dumping or subsidizing in order to make a final determination within 90 days from the date of the preliminary determination. If the final determination discloses no dumping or subsidy or only negligible levels, the investigation is terminated and so is the inquiry by the tribunal. In general, the hearing before the tribunal follows the final determination by the deputy minister. If the tribunal does not find material injury or retardation, the proceedings are terminated and the provisional duties collected are refunded with interest; otherwise, these duties are confirmed with respect to past, present, and future material injury. A finding restricted to likelihood of future material injury calls for the imposition of duties to imports made after the decision of the tribunal and all provisional duties must be refunded with interest. The tribunal must declare to what goods, including where applicable, from what supplier, and from what country of export the order or finding applies.[366]

Under certain conditions, duties may be applied on a retroactive basis.[367] The SIMA provides for the application of a retroactive anti-dumping duty equal to the margin of dumping for the 90-day period prior to the preliminary determination,[368] where the CITT finds that injury has been caused by a massive importation of dumped goods or finds a series of importations of dumped goods that are massive in the aggregate and that have occurred within a relatively short time.[369]

363 (1992), 8 TTR 32 (CITT).

364 *Bicycles and component parts*, ADT-11-77 (1977).

365 SIMA, *supra*, note 76, s. 43(1).

366 *Ibid.*, s. 43(1).

367 *Ibid.*, ss. 5 and 6. See the 1994 Subsidies Code, *supra*, note 3, art. 20 and the 1994 Anti-dumping Code, *supra*, note 2, art. 10. See also *Photo Albums with Self-Adhesive Leaves from Indonesia* (1991), 4 TCT 3053.

368 *Ibid.*, s. 5. This will only apply in relation to goods that were not released prior to the initiation of an investigation under SIMA, *ibid.*, s. 31.

369 See *Wooden Clothespins from China* (20 October 1984) (CITT) for an example of injury findings involving massive importations. And see *Rubber hockey pucks* (1986), 11 CER 142 and *Re pocket albums* (1988), 16 CER 165 for examples of cases where no massive importation was found.

To trigger the application of the retroactive anti-dumping duty, the CITT must find that the dumping has caused past injury, would have caused it had provisional duties not been applied, or that the importer "was or should have been aware that the exporter was practicing dumping and that the dumping would cause injury."[370]

The SIMA also gives authority for the retroactive imposition of a countervailing duty in the amount of subsidy on the imported goods that constitutes a prohibited subsidy.[371] This will only apply in relation to goods that were not released prior to the initiation of an investigation under section 31; and in relation to goods that the deputy minister has made a specification under SIMA section 41(1)(a)(iv)(C) that all or part of the subsidy is a prohibited subsidy. In accordance with article 3 of the 1994 Subsidies Code, SIMA section 2(1) defines "prohibited subsidy" as a subsidy that is prohibited by virtue of being (1) an export subsidy, or (2) a subsidy or portion of a subsidy that is contingent, in whole or in part, on the use of goods that are produced or that originate in the country of export. The CITT must find that injury has been caused by a massive importation of goods or a series of importations that are massive in the aggregate and that have occurred within a relatively short time, and that imposition of a duty is necessary in order to prevent recurrence of injury.

Neither SIMA nor the 1994 Anti-dumping or Subsidies Codes offer detailed guidance as to what constitutes "massive importations" or a "relatively short time" in relation to the retroactive imposition of anti-dumping or countervailing duties, so the CITT must determine these on a fact-driven basis in each case. Elements indicating the existence of a massive importation include the relative percentage of dumped or subsidized importation in relation to the nature and size of the domestic market and the domestic industry, and the length of the industry's business cycle and its relationship with the time period within which the ostensibly massive importation occurred.

It should also be noted that a retroactive imposition of duty is possible where an undertaking is accepted by the deputy minister and then is subsequently terminated.[372]

R. Public Interest Inquiries

In order to safeguard the interests of consumers, intermediate producers, and the public, the SIMA[373] provides for the examination of public interest considerations during a CITT inquiry into injury caused by unfair foreign competition. In the event of a finding

---

370 SIMA, *supra*, note 76, s. 5(a)(i)(B), and art. 10.6 of the 1994 Anti-dumping Code. See, e.g., *Stainless steel fittings*, ADT-7-79 (1979) (finding) and *12-Hydroxystearic acid*, ADT-3-82 (1982) (no finding). Retroactive duties were imposed in, e.g.: *Drywall screws from Taiwan* (1986), 12 CER 16 and *Drywall screws from South Korea* (1987), 13 CER 305.

371 *Ibid.*, s. 6.

372 *Ibid.*, s. 4.

373 *Ibid.*, s. 45. See also Canadian International Trade Tribunal Rules, rr. 62 and 63. The CITT has issued "Guidelines for Public Interest Investigations" (February 1995) elaborating on these rules. The guidelines are available from the Secretary of the CITT.

of material injury,[374] where the CITT is of the opinion that the imposition of the full amount of anti-dumping or countervailing duty, in whole or in part, might or would not serve the interests of the Canadian public, it must report its findings and the reasons for its opinion to the Minister of Finance. The Minister of Finance then has the responsibility to act appropriately on the basis of the report, but is not bound by the CITT's findings. The Minister of Finance may elect to take no action or may accommodate public interest concerns through reduction of duty, either by exempting goods from SIMA's application,[375] or by remitting all or part of the duty under the Financial Administration Act.[376]

The CITT must afford any "person interested" the opportunity to appear and make submissions concerning the issue of whether the imposition of an anti-dumping or countervailing duty is in the public interest and whether the tribunal should submit a report to the Minister of Finance to that effect. The expression "person interested"[377] includes persons involved in the production, purchase, sale, export, or import of the goods under investigation or of like goods produced in Canada; persons or entities required by federal or provincial legislation to appear; and users of any like goods, including consumer interest groups in Canada. Under the Competition Act,[378] the director of investigation and research has the authority to intervene and make submissions to the CITT.[379]

The CITT has no discretionary authority to impose a duty constituting less than the full margin of dumping where a finding of injury is made.[380] This lack of authority is contrary to the spirit of article 9(1) of the 1994 Anti-dumping Code, which stipulates that the imposition of a duty should be permissive and the "the duty be less than the margin if such lesser duty would be adequate to remove the injury to the domestic industry."[381]

---

374 Obviously, where the tribunal makes a finding that the dumping or subsidizing has not caused, is not causing and will not cause injury, there is no reason to pursue the public interest inquiry. See, e.g., *Tomato paste in containers larger than 100 fluid ounces from the US* (30 March 1993) (CITT).

375 Under SIMA, *supra*, note 76, s. 14.

376 RSC 1985, c. F-11, as am.

377 See Special Import Measures Regulations, *supra*, note 80, r. 41.

378 RSC 1985, c. C-34, s. 125, as am.

379 See *Refined Sugar from the United States of America* (1984), 7 CER 30 and *Cars (Hyundai) from Korea* (1988), 16 CER 185, where the CITT accepted the Director's submission in finding no material injury. In *Beer from the United States of America* (1991), 7 TTR 255, 8 TTR 5, the CITT made a finding of material injury but, on the basis of the director's submissions, recommended that the full amount of anti-dumping duties not be charged. *In Preformed fiberglass pipe insulation from the United States of America*, *supra*, note 349, the CITT found material injury and refused the director's application for reduction of duties on the basis of public interest.

380 SIMA, *supra*, note 375, s. 3, subject to the proviso in SIMA, *ibid.*, s. 7.1 concerning the situation where an undertaking in respect of the goods has been accepted and not terminated.

381 Art. 19.3 of the 1994 Subsidies Code provides the corresponding provision concerning countervailing duties.

The tribunal has stated that the SIMA, in its entirety, was enacted by Parliament in the public interest, and the primary object of the SIMA is to protect Canadian producers from injury caused by unfair foreign competition in the form of dumped or subsidized imports.[382] The tribunal will make a public interest report to the Minister of Finance only where it is satisfied that there is a sufficiently compelling public interest issue to warrant a departure from the primary object of the SIMA. Where no interested persons make representations, or the representations fail to satisfy the high threshold set for establishing a threat to the public interest that outweighs the SIMA's primary object, the tribunal will impose the full amount of the duty and decline to submit a report to the Minister of Finance.[383]

Public interest is ordinarily considered solely with respect to the imposition of duties,[384] not in connection with the determination of injury.[385] In general, the CITT must be persuaded that compelling and "exceptional circumstances" in the public interest outweigh the necessity of protecting Canadian production from injurious subsidizing or dumping.

In *Grain Corn*, the tribunal remarked that such exceptional circumstances could arise "when the relief provided producers causes a substantial and possibly unnecessary burden to users (downstream producers) and consumers of the product."[386]

In *Beer*,[387] the CITT noted that the public interest included the protection of employment and investment in the subject industry as well as in upstream and associated service industries. Emphasizing that an anti-dumping duty should only be imposed to remove the material injury, the CITT determined that it would not be necessary nor in

382 See, e.g., *Preformed fiberglass pipe insulation from the US*, PB-93-001, [1994] CITT no. 27 (28 January 1994).

383 See, e.g., *Preformed fiberglass pipe insulation from the US*, *ibid.*; *Assembled or unassembled bicycles from Taiwan and China*, PB-92-001 (27 January 1993) (CITT); *Machine tufted carpeting originating in or exported from the US* (21 April 1992)(CITT) (no report to Minister of Finance). In *Yellow onions*, *supra*, note 236 and *Women's footwear* (CITT 89-003) where, despite the CITT's request, no public interest submissions were made, the CITT decided not to hold a public interest inquiry.

384 This appears to be more restrictive than what is envisaged in art. 6.12 of the 1994 Anti-dumping Code, which states: "The authorities shall provide opportunities for industrial users of the product under investigation, and for representative consumer organizations in cases where the product is commonly sold at the retail level, to provide information which is relevant to the investigation regarding *dumping, injury and causality*" (emphasis added). Art. 12.10 of the 1994 Subsidies Code contains a similar provision relating to the public interest in subsidies inquiries. However, see *Bicycles* (CITT, 92-002) where no separate inquiry into the public interest held. Rather, the public interest was examined as a component of the general injury inquiry.

385 E.g., in *Grain Corn* and *Beer*, separate hearings into the public interest issue were held six and two months, respectively, after the release of the CITT's injury finding. See, e.g., Marceau, *Anti-Dumping and Anti-Trust Issues in Free Trade Areas* (1994), 147-49.

386 Report on Public Interest: *Grain Corn* (CIT, 1987), at 2.

387 25 November 1991.

the public interest to impose the full amount of anti-dumping duties on certain beer imports into British Columbia, stating:

> ... anti-dumping duties at levels higher than necessary to remove material injury are excessive. Duties that are excessive penalize certain products and exporters by raising prices unnecessarily high and, perhaps, excluding them from the market altogether. In our view this is not in the public interest. Not only does it provide an unnecessary benefit for the BC industry, but it also means higher prices and less choice for consumers.

The tribunal is not charged with "a broad responsibility for trading off benefits to one group against injury to others ... ."[388] Nor does the tribunal conceive of itself as an "advisor to the Minister of Finance on the distribution of wealth and income between different private interests."[389] The CITT will not make a recommendation to remove or decrease a duty where such an action would impose *any* injury at all on the domestic producers.

The fact that the imposition of the full anti-dumping or countervailing duties would have the effect of raising prices for the subject goods in the Canadian market has been held to be not a sufficient reason to initiate public interest hearings[390] or to submit a public interest report to the Minister of Finance. Such price increases have been labelled "a natural consequence of the regulatory scheme established by Parliament under SIMA."[391] The tribunal has also held that difficulty in marketing the subject goods competitively after imposition of the full duty, necessitating reconsideration of sourcing and market strategies, is not a matter that warrants a public interest report to the Minister of Finance.[392] Price increases or other effects of the duty must cause an "undue," or "substantial" and "unnecessary" burden on the interested party, even to the extent of exclusion from the market, to warrant a CITT report to the Minister of Finance.

The CITT *Guidelines for Public Interest Investigations*[393] outline the procedural steps and approximate time deadlines in a public interest inquiry as follows:

> i) The notice of commencement of inquiry issued under SIMA section 42 and published in the *Canada Gazette* must indicate that interested persons will be able to make public interest representations in the event of a material injury finding and the date by which interested persons should notify the tribunal of their intention to make such representations;
>
> ii) Four weeks after issuing the notice of commencement of inquiry, the Tribunal will give notice to all persons who have notified it of their intention to make representations and to all parties to the SIMA section 42 inquiry that certain people have notified their desire to make public

---

388 Report, *supra*, note 386, at 4.

389 *Ibid.*

390 *Ibid.*, at 2. See also *Subsidized Grain Corn from the US* (1990), 3 TCT 2113, in which the issue referred to the CITT was whether there was a reasonable indication of a material change of circumstances to warrant a second inquiry into the public interest issue. The CITT held that there was not.

391 See *Preformed Fiberglass Pipe Insulation*, *supra*, note 382.

392 *Machine-tufted Carpeting* (21 April 1992) (CITT).

393 See *supra*, note 373.

interest representations, that those people should file their representations by a specific date (within four weeks of the finding) in the event of a material injury finding, and that responses should be filed within 6 weeks of the finding;

iii) If there is a finding of material injury, on the date of the finding, the Tribunal will inform those people having notified their wish to make representations and all parties to the inquiry of the deadlines for representations and responses as well as an envisaged date for the Tribunal's decision on whether to conduct a further investigation;

iv) Public interest representations, containing sufficient information for the Tribunal to form an opinion as to whether a compelling public interest exists, should be filed with the Tribunal within four weeks of the finding;

v) Responses to public interest representations, containing sufficient information for the Tribunal to form an opinion as to whether a compelling public interest exists, should be filed within six weeks of the finding;

vi) Nine weeks after the finding, the Tribunal decides whether there is a public interest concern meriting further investigation. If so, the Tribunal will issue a notice and schedule of procedures;

vii) Twenty weeks after the finding, the tribunal will decide whether to recommend reduction or elimination of duties in the public interest. If it finds no compelling public interest, it will issue a brief, reasoned, report. If it decides that the public interest warrants a reduction or elimination of duties, it will issue a report to the Minister of Finance, with reasons and recommendations as to the amount by which duties should be reduced. The report will be published in the *Canada Gazette*.

S. Collection of Duty and Definition of Importer

Where duty is payable in respect of any goods imported into Canada, it must be paid by the importer of such goods.[394] The SIMA defines an "importer" in relation to goods as "the person who is in reality the importer of the goods."[395] The importer in Canada liable to pay duty under SIMA will ordinarily be resident in Canada for the purpose of conducting business. Factors indicative of a business being resident in Canada are permanent business facilities, offices, or permanent employees in Canada. Factors to be considered in determining the identity of the importer are: the initiation of the purchase order and acceptance of the order, and where the goods are sent—that is, directly to the user or to an intermediary or agent and then to the user.[396]

Where there is doubt about the identity of the actual importer, the deputy minister may, and at the request of any person interested in the importation of the goods, must, seek a decision from the CITT "as to which of two or more persons is, for the purposes of the Act, the importer in Canada of goods imported or to be imported into Canada on which duty is payable or has been paid or will be payable if the goods are imported."[397]

---

394 SIMA, *supra*, note 76, s. 11(1).

395 *Ibid.*, s. 2(1) (definitions).

396 See *Photo albums from the PRC* (11 June 1986); *Artificial graphite electrodes from the USA* (4 November 1986) and *Stainless steel pipe from the USA* (30 December 1988 and 15 December 1989).

397 SIMA, *supra*, note 76, s. 89(1).

A request for a ruling must state which of the two or more persons the deputy minister believes is the importer; whether the goods involved are subject to a preliminary determination and ongoing investigation; and provide the CITT with information the deputy minister deems useful.[398] The deputy minister must also give notice of the request for a ruling to such persons as the tribunal may require.[399]

The tribunal must make its ruling as to who is the importer without delay upon receiving the request.[400] If the goods in question were subject to an investigation following a preliminary determination, the CITT will not make its ruling until after it makes an order or finding in the investigation, or until the investigation has been otherwise terminated.[401]

Where, after a finding of injury, the CITT determines that the true importer is a person other than the person specified by the deputy minister, the deputy minister must reconsider and then confirm, rescind, or amend any final determination of dumping of subsidization.[402] The CITT may on its own initiative or at the request of the deputy minister or other interested person reconsider any order or finding.[403] The order or finding of the CITT is reviewable by the Federal Court of Appeal[404] or by a NAFTA binational panel.[405]

Where a duty payable under SIMA is not paid within 30 days after the demand for payment is made, the minister may require "any person in Canada to whom the goods are sold" to pay the duty.[406] This would include the ultimate consumer.

T. Timing and Chart

In general, the whole process from the time a properly documented complaint is made to the time when the decision of the CITT results in a final order or finding lasts a maximum of about seven months.

U. Re-determination, Review, and Appeal

1. Expedited Review

Under the SIMA, it is now possible for an exporter to whom an order or finding of dumping or subsidization causing injury applies and who is therefore liable to pay anti-dumping or countervailing duties to request an expedited review by the deputy minister of normal value, export price, or amount of subsidy. The exporter must not be associated with any other exporter of goods from the country impugned in the order or finding,

---

398 *Ibid.*, s. 89(2).

399 *Ibid.*, s. 89(2)(d).

400 *Ibid.*, s. 90(a) and (b).

401 *Ibid.*, s. 90(c).

402 *Ibid.*, s. 91(d).

403 *Ibid.*, s. 91(3).

404 *Ibid.*, s. 96.1(1)(g).

405 *Ibid.*, s. 96.2.

406 *Ibid.*, s. 81(1).

Chart of Canadian Anti-Dumping and Countervailing Process Pursuant to the Special Import Measures Act, Canada (SIMA)

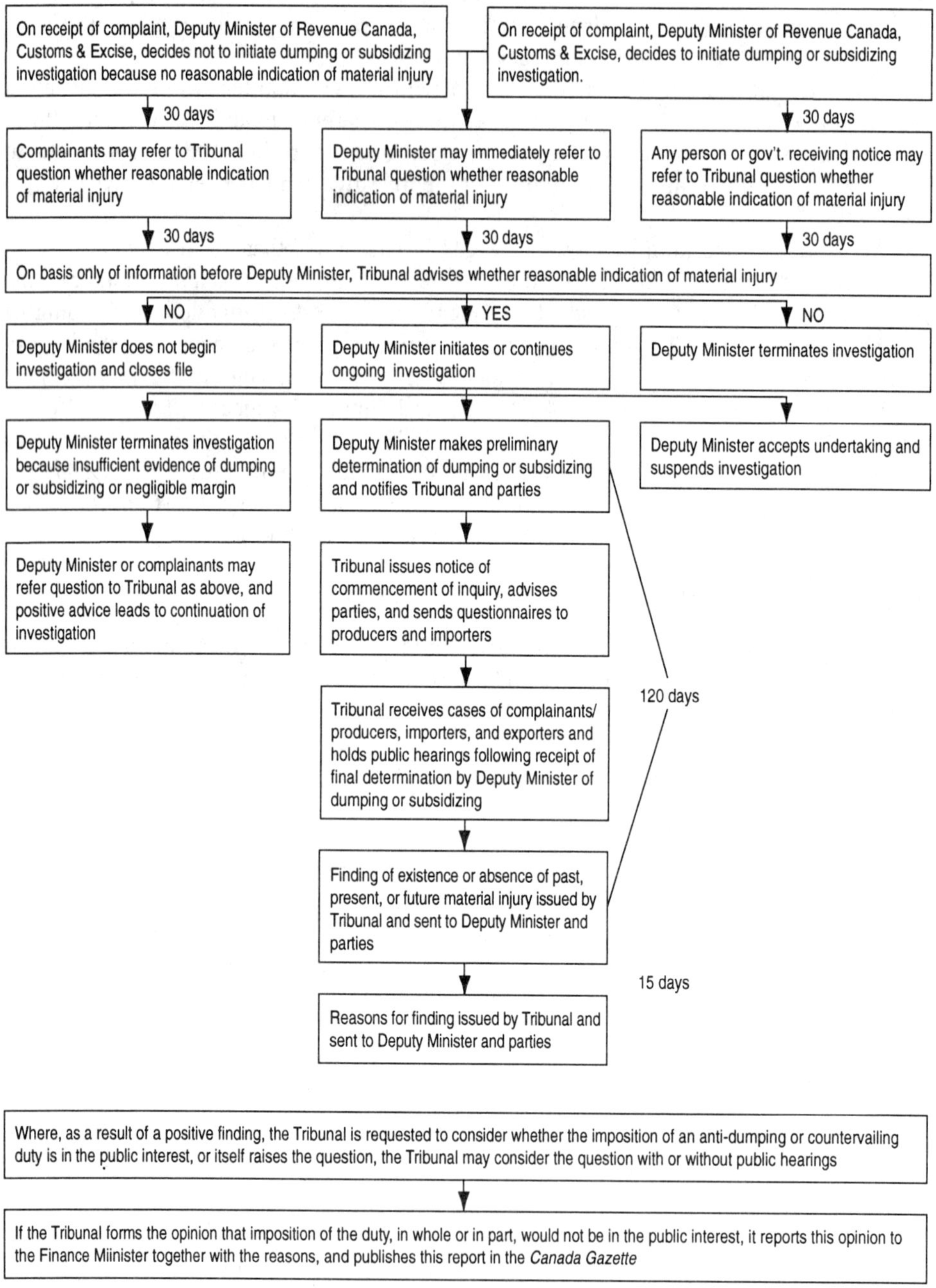

must not have been given notice of the investigation[407] or of the preliminary or final determinations,[408] and must not have been requested to give information. The deputy minister must initiate and conduct an expedited review on the receipt of a qualifying and properly documented request, and either confirm or amend the value, price, or amount. This confirmation or amendment is deemed to be a designated officer determination.[409]

2. *Designated Officer Determination*

When a final determination of dumping or subsidizing under SIMA section 41(1) has been made by the deputy minister with respect to any goods and the CITT has made an order or finding of injury described in SIMA sections 4 to 6 with respect to the goods to which the final determination applies,[410] a designated officer must determine, within six months of the order or finding, whether the goods are the same as those described in the order or finding, and the amount of anti-dumping or countervailing duty to be paid.[411] This designated officer determination, which constitutes the final assessment of duty on goods imported during the "provisional" period preceding a CITT finding of injury, is applicable only to goods released[412] (i) during the provisional period between the dates of the preliminary determination and the acceptance of an undertaking in respect of the goods; (2) during the retroactive period of 90 days preceding the date of preliminary determination where a massive importation of dumped[413] or subsidized[414] goods is involved; (3) between the dates of termination of an undertaking under SIMA section 52 and the date of the CITT finding; or (4) during the periods described in SIMA section 4(1)(b) or 2(c).[415]

---

407 *Ibid.*, s. 34(1)(i)(a).

408 *Ibid.*, ss. 38(3)(a) and 41(3).

409 *Ibid.*, s. 56(1).

410 In *Sunezco International Inc. v. Canada (Deputy Minister of National Revenue, Customs and Excise MNR)* (6 May 1994) (FCA), the Court dismissed as moot an application for judicial review of a final determination of dumping made by the deputy minister. A CITT inquiry, commenced after the determination, found that no material injury was being caused or likely to be caused to the production in Canada of like goods. Sunezco had sought a dismissal with reasons indicating that the effect of s. 47 was to eliminate any evidentiary value that a final determination of dumping might have in subsequent cases or an adjournment *sine die*.

411 SIMA, *supra*, note 76, s. 55(1).

412 *Ibid.*, s. 55(2).

413 *Ibid.*, s. 5(b).

414 *Ibid.*, s. 6(b).

415 I.e., between the date of the preliminary determination and the date of the CITT finding (SIMA, *ibid.*, s. 4(1)(b)); or during the retroactive period, beginning up to 90 days preceding the date of notice of termination of an undertaking under SIMA, *ibid.*, s. 52(1)(a) and (e) ending on the date of the CITT finding (SIMA, *ibid.*, s. 4(2)(c)(i)), or beginning on the date of notice of termination of an undertaking under SIMA, *ibid.*, s. 52(1)(b), (c), and (e) and the date of the CITT order or finding (SIMA, *ibid.*, s. 4(2)(c)(ii)).

A designated officer may also make a determination in respect of goods released following a CITT determination of injury, within 30 days after the release of the goods.[416]

Following a section 56 determination, the avenues for appeal and review are: to a designated officer (sections 56(1.01), (1.1), and 57); to the deputy minister (section 58); to the CITT (section 61); and to the Federal Court of Appeal (section 62)). Where the goods involved are from a NAFTA country, the government of that NAFTA country or the exporter, producer, or manufacturer may request a redetermination. The importer and the NAFTA party will then have the same routes of appeal as above, or they may choose to have the decision of the deputy minister or the CITT reviewed by a NAFTA chapter 19 binational panel.

An importer who has paid the duty may request a redetermination of that duty by the designated officer, or the officer may redetermine it on his or her own initiative.[417]

A determination or redetermination by a designated officer may be redetermined by the deputy minister at the request of the importer.[418] While the deputy minister is under a duty to conduct the re-determination in accordance with the principles of natural justice and procedural fairness, he or she is not obliged to give reasons in his or her re-determination.[419]

A person dissatisfied with a deputy minister's re-determination[420] may appeal to the CITT. In the case of goods from a NAFTA country or from the United States, an aggrieved party may request that a SIMA section 59(1) or 59(3) re-determination be reviewed by a binational panel rather than by the CITT.[421]

---

416 *Ibid.*, s. 56(1). This determination does not apply to duty assessed on goods released in the provisional period.

417 *Ibid.*, ss. 56(1.01)(a), 56(1.1)(a), and 57. See also *XYZ Dynamo Ltd. v. Dep. MNR Customs & Excise* (1991) 4 TCT 3153. Whether or not the importer has paid the duty, where the goods in question are goods of a NAFTA country, or goods of the United States, the government of that NAFTA country or the United States, or the producer, manufacturer, or exporter of the goods where they are of that NAFTA country or the United States, may make a request for re-determination (SIMA, *ibid.*, s. 56(1.01)(b) and 56(1.1)(b)).

418 *Ibid.*, ss. 58 and 59. The request for deputy minister redetermination must be made within 90 days of the determination (SIMA, *ibid.*, s. 55) or re-determination (SIMA, *ibid.*, s. 57). Subsequent appeals are then to the CITT (SIMA, *ibid.*, s. 61) and to the FCA (SIMA, *ibid.*, s. 62).

419 See *Toshiba International Corp. v. Canada (Deputy Minister of National Revenue, Customs and Excise—MNR)* (28 June 1994) (FCTD). Denault J held that, in the absence of a specific statute-imposed obligation to provide reasons, an insufficiency in the deputy minister's reasons could not provide grounds for review. However, Denault J held that a breach of the duties of natural justice and procedural fairness had occurred prior to the deputy minister's re-determination, in the non-disclosure of a ministerial specification that was issued nine days after Toshiba filed its request for re-determination.

420 SIMA, *supra*, note 76, s. 59.

421 See *ibid.*, ss. 96.1, 77.011, 77.012, 77.11, and 77.12.

3. *Exemption from Application of the Act*

The Governor in Council may, on the recommendation of the Minister of Finance, exempt any goods or class of goods from the application of the Special Import Measures Act.[422]

4. *Finality and Review of Decisions, Orders, and Findings by the Deputy Minister and the CITT*

a. CITT Review

Unless it has been reviewed and rescinded earlier, extended, or amended by the tribunal, an order or finding is valid for five years.[423] Normally, the tribunal will issue a notice of expiry approximately eight months prior to the date of expiry. In the notice, interested parties are asked to make submissions, giving the facts and reasons why a review should be held or why the finding should simply be allowed to lapse.[424] If a review gives rise to a decision to maintain an order or finding, anti-dumping or countervailing duties may be collected for a further five-year period, unless the finding is again reviewed. The tribunal may review its orders or findings on the question of injury on its own initiative, or at the request of the deputy minister, or any other person or foreign government.[425]

In a review, the tribunal follows procedures similar to those in the original injury inquiry. It issues a notice, obtains information by way of questionnaires, calls for submissions, and schedules a public hearing. The time limits are also similar to those in an injury inquiry.

The review deals with the same kind of injury criteria covered in an original inquiry and finding, focusing in particular on whether market circumstances have changed and whether there is continued subsidizing or a propensity to dump. The tribunal may rehear any matter in its review.[426]

Upon completion of a review, the tribunal must issue a decision with reasons, much as in the case of an injury inquiry. If the finding is rescinded, anti-dumping or

---

422 *Ibid.*, s. 14.

423 *Ibid.*, s. 76(5). Reviews of findings of material injury must be instituted within the five-year period: *Carbon and Alloy Steel Plates from Belgium* (1990), 3 TCT 2122. However, it is not necessary for the Tribunal to render its decision within this period: *Polyphase Induction Motors* (1991), 6 TTR 296 (Canada-US Free Trade Panel), aff'g. on other grounds (1990), 3 TCT 2362, 14 TTR 207 (CITT). The five-year limit is in accordance with Canada's international obligations under the 1994 Anti-dumping Code, art. 11.3 and the 1994 Subsidies Code, art. 21.3.

424 See pt. VI of the Canadian International Trade Tribunal Rules. See also CITT, *Guideline: Changes in the Tribunal's Practice in Proceedings Related to the Expiry of Orders and Findings and to Reviews under Section 76 of the Special Import Measures Act*. The Guideline deals chiefly with right of response to submissions, access to confidential information, and placing information from prior related proceedings on the record.

425 SIMA, *supra* note 76, s. 76(2). The review must be warranted: SIMA, s. 76(3) and *Plain Hardboard Sheets or Panels from the USSR and Poland* (1990), 3 TCT 2274.

426 *Ibid.*, s. 76(2).

countervailing duties are no longer levied on imports. The tribunal may also continue its original finding without amendment, or may amend or alter the original finding to exclude a certain product or a country from it. On numerous occasions, the tribunal has partially or wholly rescinded or continued its orders or findings.[427]

The inability of Canadian manufacturers to supply certain products is often raised by importers before the tribunal when it conducts a review of its earlier findings of injury in order to exclude such products from the findings.[428] Elements such as envisaged negative effects on producer prices, production and sales volumes, profit margins, and investment plans constitute risks of injury that the tribunal has decided to forestall by refusing to rescind an injury finding.[429] Reduced vulnerability of an industry to injury due to improved sales and financial performance and enhanced competitive ability brought about by modernization and rationalization, coupled with a demonstrated ability on the part of the exporters to compete in the domestic market at prices above the normal value of the goods, may lead the tribunal to rescind its original material injury finding.[430]

Where, due to economic or regulatory developments, a question arises concerning the continued existence of the domestic industry—whether regional or national—the tribunal will consider the propriety of a material injury finding in the context of a review. In *Certain butt welding pipe fittings originating in or exported from Japan*,[431] the tribunal rescinded its injury finding where the sole domestic producer no longer produced the goods that formed the subject of the order, and therefore no longer required protection.[432] In the case of a regional industry, the tribunal review will focus first upon the issue of whether a regional market still exists. If one is found, the tribunal will then proceed to a consideration of whether there is a continued threat of material injury.[433] In rescinding its original injury finding in *Beer*, the tribunal stated,[434] "[s]imply put, without a domestic industry, there can be no finding of material injury."

---

427 E.g., *Photo albums with self-adhesive leaves*, RR-94-006 (25 August 1995); *Women's leather and non-leather boots and shoes*, RR-94-003, [1995] CITT no. 27 (2 May 1995) (partial rescind); *Canned ham and canned pork-based luncheon meat*, RR-94-002 (21 March 1995) (continue without amendment); *Beer*, RR-94-001, [1994] CITT no. 151 (2 December 1994) (rescind); *Fresh, whole, delicious, red delicious and golden delicious apples from the USA*, RR-93-002, [1994] CITT no. 22 (7 February 1994) (rescind); *Paint brushes from China*, RR-93-003, [1994] CITT no. 16 (18 January 1994) (continue without amendment); *Yellow onions from the USA*, RR-91-004, [1992] CITT no. 60 (22 May 1992) (continue without amendment); *Integral horsepower induction motors and polyphase induction motors*, RR-93-004, [1994] CITT no. 105 (30 June 1994) (rescind); *Deep tillage sweeps*, RR-93-001, [1992] CITT no. 69 (23 November 1993) (continue without amendment); and *Brass replacement key blanks from Italy*, RR-91-005 CITT no. 69 (1 June 1992) (rescind).

428 *Re Brass Coated Carbon Steel Wire* (1989), 2 TCT 1229.

429 E.g., *Women's leather and non-leather boots and shoes*, *supra*, note 427.

430 See, e.g., *Certain carbon and alloy steel plates* [1990] CITT no. 17 (1 May 1990).

431 RR-92-002, [1992] CITT no. 139 (13 November 1992).

432 See also *Brass replacement key blanks from Italy*, *supra*, note 427.

433 See *Beer* and *Yellow onions*, *supra*, note 427.

434 *Ibid.* Finding aff'd. by binational panel 15 November 1995.

Any analysis of material injury in a regional industry case is predicated upon a finding that there is a regional industry: without a regional industry, there is nothing against which to consider the likely impact of dumped imports.

b. Bifurcated Appeal and Review: The Federal Court of Appeal and Dispute Settlement Under the NAFTA

Canada has implemented a bifurcated system for appeal and review of definitive decisions of the CITT and the deputy minister concerning dumping and subsidization, depending on whether the goods in question originate from a NAFTA or non-NAFTA country.

Where the goods involved are from a non-NAFTA country, decisions of the deputy minister and findings of the CITT are subject to review by the Federal Court of Appeal.[435]

In the case of goods from a NAFTA country—that is, Mexico—parties wishing to contest certain definitive decisions by the deputy minister or CITT may seek review of the decision by a binational panel.[436] Goods from the United States are treated under the binational panel review process that was established under the Canada-US FTA and continued under the NAFTA.[437]

i. REVIEW BY THE FEDERAL COURT OF APPEAL Except in cases involving goods from the United States or from a NAFTA country, SIMA section 96.1(1) provides that the Federal Court of Appeal has jurisdiction to review and set aside the following determinations and decisions of the deputy minister and orders or findings of the CITT and the deputy minister:[438]

> (a) a final determination of the deputy minister under paragraph 41(1)(a);
>
> (b) a decision of the Deputy Minister under paragraph 41(1)(b) to cause an investigation to be terminated;
>
> (c) a decision of the Deputy Minister under s. 53(1) to renew or not to renew an undertaking;
>
> (d) an order of the Tribunal under s. 76(3.1);
>
> (e) an order of the Tribunal under s. 76(4);
>
> (f) an order or finding of the Tribunal under s. 76(4.1) in respect of a review pursuant to 76(2.1); or
>
> (g) an order or finding of the Tribunal under s. 91(3).

The grounds for review are denial of natural justice; misapplication of jurisdiction, mistake of law or of fact; action, or failure to act, based on fraud or perjured evidence; and action in any other way contrary to law.[439]

---

435 See SIMA, *supra*, note 76, ss. 76 and 96.1.

436 *Ibid.*, ss. 77.01ff. and NAFTA , art. 1904.

437 *Ibid.*, ss. 77.1ff.

438 An order or finding made by the CITT not mentioned in the above list may nevertheless be reviewable under the provisions of the Federal Court Act, RSC 1985, c. F-7, as am.

439 These grounds are set out in s. 18.2(4) of the Federal Court Act. SIMA, *supra*, note 76, s. 96.1(2) states:

(The footnote is continued on the next page.)

Formerly, SIMA section 76(1) stated that subject to certain exceptions "every order or finding of the tribunal under this Act is final and conclusive." This constituted a statutory privative clause, circumscribing the scope of review, and requiring the Federal Court of Appeal to review the CITT's determination using the standard of "patent unreasonableness." Judicial review would only occur where the tribunal's decision could not be sustained by any reasonable interpretation of the facts or the law,[440] such as where the tribunal exceeded its jurisdiction by reason of its conclusions being patently unreasonable,[441] or interpreted its constitutive statute in a patently unreasonable manner.[442] For a decision to be "patently unreasonable," the Court must not merely find a decision is wrong, but that it is "clearly irrational."[443] If, however, the question at issue concerned a legislative provision limiting the tribunal's powers, a mere error would cause it to lose jurisdiction and subject the tribunal to judicial review.[444] In other words, the standard of review for CITT jurisdictional issues would be the correctness standard.[445]

---

439 Continued ...

(2) An application may be made under this section on the ground that the Deputy Minister, or the Tribunal, as the case may be,

(a) acted without jurisdiction, acted beyond the jurisdiction of the Deputy Minister or Tribunal or refused to exercise that jurisdiction;

(b) failed to observe a principle of natural justice, procedural fairness or other procedure that the Deputy Minister or the Tribunal was required by law to observe;

(c) erred in law in making a decision or an order, whether or not the error appears on the face of the record;

(d) based a decision or order on an erroneous finding of fact that the Deputy Minister or the Tribunal made in a perverse or capricious manner or without regard for the material before the Deputy Minister or the Tribunal;

(e) acted, or failed to act, by reason of fraud or perjured evidence; or

(f) acted in any other way that was contrary to law.

440 *Pezim v. BC (Superintendent of Brokers)*, [1994] 2 SCR 557; *National Corn Growers Assn. v. Canada (Import Tribunal)*, [1990] 2 SCR 1324, at 1367 and 1369, per Gonthier J; and *U.E.S. Local 298 v. Bibeault*, [1988] 2 SCR 1048.

441 *Bibeault, ibid.*; *American Farm Bureau Association et al. v. Canadian Import Tribunal*, [1990] 2 SCR 1324.

442 *American Farm Bureau Association, ibid.*

443 *Canada (Attorney-General) v. PSAC*, [1993] 1 SCR 941, per Cory J and *CUPE (Canadian Union of Public Employees, Local 963 v. New Brunswick Liquor Corp.*, [1979] 2 SCR 227, at 237. In *United Brotherhood of Carpenters and Joiners of America, Local 579 v. Bradco Construction Limited*, [1993] 2 SCR 316, at 340-41, the Court stated: "A patently unreasonable error is more easily defined by what it is not than by what it is. This court has said that a finding or decision of a tribunal is not patently unreasonable if there is any evidence capable of supporting the decision even though the reviewing court may not have reached the same conclusion." See also *CAIMAW v. Paccar*, [1989] 2 SCR 983.

444 *Bibeault*, *supra*, note 442.

445 See *Syndicat des Employés de Production du Québec et de l'Acadie v. Canada Labour Relations Board*, [1984] 2 SCR 412.

The NAFTA implementing legislation repealed the privative clause with respect to CITT final determinations. SIMA sections 76(1) and 96.1 now provide that, with the exception of appeals under SIMA section 61(3) and determinations respecting goods of the United States or a NAFTA country, the Federal Court of Appeal has jurisdiction to review CITT orders and findings according to the standard of review outlined in section 18.1(4) of the Federal Court Act. Despite the repeal of the privative clause, on questions of law or fact, a decision of the tribunal acting within its jurisdiction and expertise may still be subject to an extensive degree of curial deference.[446]

ii. DISPUTE SETTLEMENT UNDER THE NAFTA The Canada-US FTA, implemented on 1 January 1989, did not alter existing substantive anti-dumping and countervailing duty laws of the parties. Rather, it obliged Canada and the United States to develop, over a five- to seven-year period, mutually advantageous substitute rules applicable to government subsidies and private anti-competitive pricing practices such as dumping.[447] Until then, each party was to retain its domestic laws and reserve the right to apply them to goods imported from the territory of the other party.[448] Chapter 19 of the FTA-imposed notification and consultation requirements concerning legislative amendments to countervailing and anti-dumping laws, requiring in addition that such amendments be consistent with the GATT and the FTA. As well, FTA, chapter 19 provided for review by a binational panel of (1) legislative amendments appearing to be inconsistent with the GATT and FTA norms, and (2) final domestic administrative determinations of injury caused by subsidization or dumping.

Proposals under the aegis of the FTA to place the regulation of anti-competitive pricing practices under domestic competition laws and to negotiate a new regime for the regulation of subsidies were side-tracked by the NAFTA negotiations, and by the GATT Uruguay Round negotiations dealing with many similar substantive issues.

On ratification of NAFTA,[449] the operation of the Canada-US FTA binational dispute settlement mechanism was therefore basically maintained and extended to embrace Mexico. The provisions of the NAFTA, chapter 19 thus essentially replicate those of FTA, chapter 19, except they are seen more as permanent than transitional.[450] As under the FTA, each party reserves the right to apply its own anti-dumping and countervailing

446 *Dayco (Canada) v. NAAAIWU* (1993), 152 NR 1 (SCC), per La Forest J and *Bell Canada v. Canada (CRTC)*, [1989] 1 SCR 1722.

447 FTA, arts. 1906 and 1907. If the parties failed to produce a substitute set of rules within that time period, each had the right to terminate the FTA on six months' written notice.

448 FTA, art. 1902.1.

449 Implemented in Canada by the North American Free Trade Agreement Implementation Act, SC 1994, c. 44, effective 1 January 1994.

450 Under NAFTA, art. 1907.2, the parties must consult on developing a more effective anti-dumping and subsidies regime, but no time limit is imposed. A working group has been established to consider directions for potential evolution. For an analysis of the development of a more effective subsidy and anti-dumping regime see, e.g., Boddez and Trebilcock, *Unfinished Business: Reforming Trade Remedy Laws in North America* (1993).

duty laws.[451] Legislative changes to domestic anti-dumping and countervailing duty laws are subject to notice and consultation requirements and binational panel review. Canadian producers still enjoy the right to seek remedy from injury caused by dumped or subsidized imports from other NAFTA countries under the SIMA, but any domestic administrative decision is now subject to review by a binational panel.

A chapter 19 panel must be binational in nature. Where a dispute involves goods from both other NAFTA parties, two binational panels will be established. No procedure exists for the consolidation of similar panel actions, or for the participation or input of a party not directly involved in the bilateral dispute. A chapter 19 binational panel is composed of five members, a majority of which are lawyers in good standing, drawn chiefly from a roster of 75 candidates (that is, 25 from each NAFTA party) established at the date of entry into force of the NAFTA. Roster members are citizens of the NAFTA countries chosen on the basis of "good character, high standing and repute, and ... chosen strictly on the basis of objectivity, reliability, sound judgment and general familiarity with international trade law."[452]

aa. DISPUTES ARISING FROM AMENDMENTS TO DOMESTIC LEGISLATION Under the NAFTA, the investigative and administering authorities of the parties continue to enforce domestic anti-dumping and countervailing duty laws within their jurisdiction, and the legislatures may amend these laws.[453] In addition, legislative amendments apply to goods from another NAFTA party only where the amending statute expressly so provides.[454] This provision principally benefits Canada and Mexico by exempting them from the application of US unfair trade legislation, unless they are specifically named in the legislation.

However, emphasis on transparency and the development of consistent norms among the NAFTA parties is evident in the requirements: (1) that the amendments are consistent with the norms enshrined in the GATT Anti-dumping and Subsidies Codes and their successor agreements (that is, the 1994 Anti-dumping and Subsidies Codes) and with the object and purpose of the NAFTA;[455] (2) that the amending party provide

---

451 NAFTA, art. 1902. Note that under the FTA between Canada and Chile, signed on 17 December 1996, Canada and Chile have agreed not to apply their domestic anti-dumping laws to goods of the other party (art. M-01), subject to certain phase-in provisions (art. M-03). In addition, the Agreement establishes a Committee on Trade Remedies to, *inter alia*, consult with a view to defining subsidy disciplines further and eliminating the need for domestic countervailing duty measures on trade between them, and facilitates Chile's full accession to the NAFTA, and, in particular, chapter 19 (art. M-05).

452 See NAFTA, Annex 1901.2.

453 NAFTA, arts. 1902.1 and 1902.2.

454 NAFTA, art. 1902.2(a).

455 NAFTA, art. 1902.2(d) states that the "object and purpose" of NAFTA and of chapter 19 is "to establish fair and predictable conditions for the progressive liberalization of trade between the parties ... while maintaining effective and fair disciplines on unfair trade practices." This "object and purpose" is to be ascertained from NAFTA's provisions, preamble and objectives and the practices of the parties.

prior written notice of the proposed legislative amendment; and (3) that the amending party, if requested, consult with any party to which the amendment applies.

In addition, at the request of a party affected by an amendment, a binational panel[456] may review and issue a declaratory opinion with respect to such legislative changes and recommend modifications. These opinions may declare the changes to be contrary to the GATT or to the object and purpose of the NAFTA,[457] or to have the effect of overturning a prior binational panel decision *and* not be consistent with GATT or NAFTA norms.[458]

In the event a panel recommends modifications to existing or proposed legislation, the parties must begin consultation immediately in order to achieve a mutually satisfactory solution to the matter within 90 days of the issuance of the panel's final declaratory decision. Such a solution may include remedial legislation. Where remedial legislation fails to be introduced into law within nine months of the end of the 90-day period, and no other mutually accepted solution is reached, the party that requested the panel may take retaliatory action in the form of comparable legislative or executive action or may terminate the agreement with regard to the amending party on 60 days' written notice.

bb. DISPUTES ARISING FROM FINAL DETERMINATIONS BY DOMESTIC ADMINISTERING AUTHORITIES Like the FTA before it, the NAFTA provides for replacement of judicial review by domestic courts of final determinations concerning dumping, subsidization, and material injury. Instead, a binational panel determines whether the domestic substantive laws of the importing country were applied correctly and fairly.[459] Preliminary determinations are not eligible for review.[460] Even when such a review is possible, the administering authorities retain their jurisdiction where the parties or their governments do not request or initiate a panel review.[461] In accordance with NAFTA, chapter 19, the SIMA authorizes the establishment of a binational dispute settlement mechanism to operate bilaterally between the NAFTA countries that are parties to the dispute.

The NAFTA country governments may refer a final determination on anti-dumping or countervailing duties to a binational panel for review. Only the governments can require the establishment of a panel, but each government must do so at the request of a private party who would otherwise be entitled under domestic law of the importing country to commence domestic procedures for judicial review.[462] The referral of a

456 NAFTA, Annex 1903.2 details the binational panel procedure.

457 NAFTA, art. 1903.1(a).

458 NAFTA, art. 1903.1(b). It appears that even where a legislative change has the effect of overturning a prior binational panel decision, it could still be saved by being consistent with the norms dictated by the GATT or NAFTA.

459 NAFTA, art. 1904.

460 NAFTA, art. 1904.10 states that the agreement will not affect the parties' judicial review procedures with respect to determinations other than final determinations.

461 NAFTA, art. 1904.12.

462 NAFTA, art. 1904.5. A request for binational panel review must be made to the Canadian Secretary of the NAFTA Secretariat. When a request is properly made, the Minister of International Trade must

(The footnote is continued on the next page.)

determination to a binational panel under chapter 19 precludes judicial review by the Federal Court of Appeal.[463]

A binational dispute panel established pursuant to section 77.01 (for goods from a NAFTA country) or 77.1 (for goods from the United States) has the power to review the following definitive decisions of the deputy minister or of the CITT:[464]

(a) a final decision of the Deputy Minister under paragraph 41(1)(a);

(b) a decision of the Deputy Minister under paragraph 41(1)(b) to cause an investigation to be terminated;

(c) an order or finding of the CITT under s. 43(1);

(d) a decision of the Deputy Minister under s. 53(1) to renew or not to renew an undertaking;

(e) a redetermination of the Deputy Minister under s. 59(1);

(f) a redetermination of the Minister under s. 59(3);

(g) an order of the CITT under s. 76(3.1);

(h) an order of the CITT under s. 76(4);

(i) an order or finding of the CITT under s 76(4.1) respecting a review pursuant to s. 76(2.1);

(i.1) an order or finding of the CITT under paragraph 76.1(2)(b) or (c); or

(j) an order or finding of the CITT under s. 91(3).

A request for review to a panel must be made on grounds set out in section 18.1(4)[465] of the Federal Court Act, RSC 1985, c. F-7. This section provides that the tribunal's decision will be reviewed on the grounds that it (1) failed to observe a principle of natural justice; (2) acted beyond or refused to exercise its jurisdiction; (3) erred in law in making its decision or order; (4) based its decision or order on an erroneous finding of fact that is made in a perverse or capricious manner or without regard for the material before it; (5) acted or failed to act by reason of fraud or perjured evidence; or (6) acted in any other way contrary to law.

The binational panel applies[466] "... the standard of review set out in Article 1911 and the general legal principles that a court of the importing Party otherwise would apply to a review of a determination of the competent investigating authority." Under NAFTA,

---

462 Continued ...

invoke the binational panel process. A request may be made by a person entitled to make a request under the following Acts: Federal Court Act (the attorney general or any party directly affected by the decision or order); SIMA, *supra*, note 76, s. 96.1 (any person directly affected by the determination or decision); and, where a deputy minister re-determination is concerned, by a person entitled to file an appeal to the CITT under SIMA, s. 61 (any person aggrieved by a re-determination).

463 NAFTA, art. 1904.11.

464 See SIMA, *supra*, note 76, s. 77.01 and NAFTA, Annex 1911.

465 Formerly, under the FTA, the standard of review for a chapter 19 binational panel was detailed in s. 28 of the Federal Court Act that, at the time of implementation of the FTA, provided for review only where the tribunal (1) failed to observe a principle of natural justice or otherwise acted beyond or refused to exercise its jurisdiction; (2) erred in law; or (3) based its decision or order on an erroneous finding of fact that was made in a perverse or capricious manner or without regard for the material before it.

466 See NAFTA, art. 1904(3) and Annex 1911.

article 1911, "general legal principles" include principles such as standing, due process, rules of statutory construction, mootness, and exhaustion of administrative remedies.

In a dispute where Canada is the importing party, the panel determines on the basis of the same standard used by the Federal Court of Appeal whether existing laws were applied correctly. Panel decisions must be rendered within 315 days of the date on which the request for a panel was made.[467] No appeal is possible from a binational panel decision to the domestic courts of the NAFTA signatories.[468] A panel finding is thus final and binding. A panel may uphold a final determination or, where a panel determines that an administrative authority (that is, in Canada, the deputy minister or the CITT) erred, it can remand—that is, it may send the issue back to that authority to correct the error and make a new determination.

With regard to the scope of the standard of review, formerly, SIMA section 76(1) stated that subject to certain exceptions "every order or finding of the tribunal under this Act is final and conclusive." This, as already noted, constituted a statutory privative clause, circumscribing the scope of binational panel review by requiring the binational panel to review the CITT's determination using the standard of "patent unreasonableness"[469] for issues of fact and law within its jurisdiction.[470]

However, the enactment of the North American Free Trade Agreement Implementation Act[471] (the NAFTA Implementation Act), effective January 1, 1994 revised the SIMA by, *inter alia*, repealing the privative clause in the SIMA[472] concerning determinations involving the United States or Mexico. The combined effect of SIMA, articles 76(1), 77.011, and 77.11 is to make a definitive order or finding of the tribunal

467 NAFTA, art. 1904.

468 NAFTA, art. 1904.11. SIMA, *supra*, note 76, s. 77.02 states that an order or decision of a binational panel is final and binding and not subject to appeal, subject to the provisions of SIMA, *ibid.*, s. 77.015(4) (panel review of action taken by the appropriate domestic authority pursuant to a panel's order) and SIMA, *ibid.*, s. 77.019 (extraordinary challenge proceeding).

469 See the binational panel decisions in *Hot-rolled Carbon Steel Plate* (20 December 1994); *Beer* (1992), 5 TCT 8199; and *Integral horsepower induction motors* (1991), 4 TCT 7065. See also *Dayco (Canada) Ltd. v. CAW-Canada*, [1993] 2 SCR 230 and *National Corn Growers v. CITT*, *supra*, note 440, at 1370, per Gonthier J and the discussion *supra*, concerning the privative clause in the context of the scope of review of the FCA.

470 However, a breach of natural justice affecting the essential fairness of the hearing would have the result of invalidating the tribunal's decision: *Polyphase Induction Motors* (1991), 6 TTR 296 (Canada-US Free Trade Panel), aff'g. on other grounds (1990), 3 TCT 2362, 4 TTR 207 (CITT).

471 SC 1994, c. 44.

472 A binational panel has held that the privative clause in former s. 76(1) of SIMA, *supra*, note 76, gives rise to a substantive legal right, within the meaning of s. 43 of the Interpretation Act, RSC 1985, c. I-21, as it defines the scope of permissible review. See *Hot-Rolled Carbon Steel Plate*, *supra*, note 469. See also *Attorney General of Canada v. Langille*, [1982] 2 FC 208, at 209, where the Court of Appeal found that the right of appeal was a "substantive right and is not affected by the repeal of the provision authorizing it and the substitution of a new and narrower right of appeal." See also *Hot-Rolled Carbon Steel Sheet Products* (18 May 1994), CDA-93-1904-07.

fully subject to binational panel scrutiny. Errors of jurisdiction attract a "correctness" standard.[473] Absent a privative clause, the panel reviews the CITT's determination within its jurisdiction using a standard of "reasonableness."[474] Curial deference must nevertheless be given to decisions of a specialized administrative tribunal made within the scope of its expertise even in the absence a privative clause.[475] The establishment of the degree of curial deference to be accorded to a tribunal's decision is done through a pragmatic and functional determination of the tribunal's jurisdiction, as reflected in the wording of the enactment conferring its jurisdiction, the reason and purpose of the statute creating the tribunal and the relative expertise of the tribunal.[476] The binational panel in *Hot-Rolled Carbon Steel Sheet* reviewed the CITT's enabling legislation finding that the legislative language lead to the conclusion that "[The tribunal] ... is a specialized administrative body whose findings within its area of expertise are entitled to deference under Canadian law."

A panel's inquiry in a review of a determination on remand (DOR) is much narrower than the scope of its review of the panel's original determination. It is not open to the panel to revisit the original determination with respect to any issue not covered by the remand. Thus, the panel's inquiry in reviewing the DOR is limited to deciding whether the tribunal addressed the questions the panel directed to it, followed the panel's instructions and reached a result that is not patently unreasonable.[477]

The CITT has the right to appear before the binational panel and to make submissions about the appropriate standard of review and its interpretation of the law surrounding the standard of review.[478] The appearance of binational panel roster members before the CITT does not present a reasonable apprehension of bias and therefore does not contravene the principles of natural justice.[479]

---

473 E.g., in *Beer* (CDA-91-1904-02, 26 August 1992), the binational panel found that the tribunal had exceeded its jurisdiction under SIMA, *supra*, note 76, s. 42 by combining dumping and extraneous non-dumping factors in concluding that dumping was causing material injury. The panel applied the correctness standard and remanded.

474 *Bell Canada v. Canada (CRTC), supra*, note 446, at 1745-46; *Machine Tufted Carpeting*, CDA-92-1904-01 (19 May 1993), at 6 and 7; and *Hot-rolled carbon steel plate and high-strength low-alloy plate heat-treated or not* (binational panel, memorandum opinion and order, 20 December 1994).

475 *Bell Canada v. Canada (CRTC), ibid.* and *Dayco (Canada) Ltd. v. CAW-Canada, supra*, note 446.

476 See, e.g., *Pezim, Bibeault, Dayco, supra*, note 440 and *Domtar Inc. v. Quebec (Commission D'Appel en Matière de Lesions Professionnelles)*, [1993] 2 SCR 756.

477 *Machine-Tufted Carpeting* (21 April 1994). The decision left open whether the standard was "patent unreasonableness" or the more lenient "reasonableness." See also *Beer, supra*, note 473, and *Pork, supra*, note 84.

478 See r. 40 of the art. 1904 panel rules; and *Hot-Rolled Carbon Steel Plate, supra*, note 469 (20 December 1994). For participation of administrative agencies in the judicial review process generally, see *CAIMAW v. Paccar of Canada, Ltd.*, [1989] 2 SCR 983 and *British Columbia Government Employees Union v. Industrial Relations Council* (unreported) (24 May 1988) (BC CA).

479 *Hot-Rolled Carbon Steel Plate, ibid.* The appearance of roster members before the tribunal was a circumstance recognized and accepted by Canada and the United States in negotiating the FTA, and

(The footnote is continued on the next page.)

cc. EXTRAORDINARY CHALLENGE COMMITTEE The government of any NAFTA country[480] that was party to the final determination under panel review may invoke an extraordinary challenge proceeding[481] where it is alleged that a panelist was guilty of gross misconduct, bias, a serious conflict of interest, or otherwise materially violated the rules of conduct; that a panel seriously departed from a fundamental rule of procedure or that a panel manifestly exceeded its powers, authority, or jurisdiction; and that any of these actions materially affected the panel's decision and threatened the integrity of the binational review panel process.[482] The time frame for the Extraordinary Challenge Committee process is 90 days. The committee may allow the panel ruling to stand where the grounds for the challenge are not established,[483] or it may set aside the panel ruling and a new panel will be appointed to conduct a review of the definitive decision that was the subject of that order.[484] The committee may also refer a panel order back to the panel, in which case the panel must act consistently with the committee's decision.[485]

dd. SPECIAL COMMITTEE REVIEW PROCEDURE The NAFTA has also established a special committee review procedure, intended to safeguard the integrity of the binational panel system.[486] This procedure provides recourse where a party alleges that the application of another party's domestic law prevents the establishment of a panel, prevents the panel from rendering a final decision, prevents the implementation of a panel's decision (or denied binding force or effect), or results in a failure to provide opportunity for panel or judicial review. Where the special committee finds that the allegations are established, parties may consult to reach a "mutually agreeable solution," failing which the operation of article 1904 may be suspended at any time between 60

---

479 Continued ...

ratified by Parliament. A reasonable apprehension of bias cannot exist when it is the direct consequence of the statutory scheme at issue: *Brosseau v. Alberta Securities Commission* [1989] 1 SCR 301, at 315.

480 Private persons may not invoke the extraordinary challenge procedure.

481 NAFTA, art. 1904.13 and Annex 1904.13 set out the extraordinary challenge procedure. See also SIMA, *supra*, note 76, ss. 77.017 to 77.019 and 77.17 to 77.19.

482 For an analysis and critique of the binational panel system in general and of the ECC in particular in the aftermath of *Softwood Lumber from Canada*, ECC-94-1904-01 USA (3 August 1994) see Gastle and Castel, "Should the North American Free Trade Agreement Dispute Settlement Mechanism in Antidumping and Countervailing Duty Cases Be Reformed in the Light of *Softwood Lumber III*?" (1995), 26 *Law and Policy in Int'l. Business* 822.

483 See *Fresh, Chilled or Frozen Pork from Canada*, ECC-91-1904 USA, 4 TCT 7037; *Live Swine from Canada*, ECC-93-1904-01 USA, 5 TCT 8088; and *Softwood Lumber from Canada*, ECC-94-1904-01 USA, [1994] FTAD no. 8 (3 August 1994) decided under the Canada-US FTA.

484 SIMA, *supra*, note 76, ss. 77.019(4) and 77.19(4).

485 *Ibid.*, s. 77.019(5) and s. 77.19(5).

486 *Ibid.*, s. 77.023 and NAFTA, art. 1905.

and 90 days following an affirmative finding, or other retaliatory action may be taken by the aggrieved party.[487]

5. Request for Review by the Minister of Finance Pursuant to WTO Dispute Settlement Body Ruling

Where the WTO Dispute Settlement Body issues a recommendation or ruling, the Minister of Finance may request that the deputy minister or the CITT review a SIMA decision, determination, order, or finding.[488] As a result of this review, the deputy minister or the tribunal may elect to continue, with[489] or without[490] amendment, or rescind and replace[491] the SIMA decision, determination, order, or finding.

IV. TRADE IN SERVICES: THE GENERAL AGREEMENT ON TRADE IN SERVICES (GATS)

Constructing an international framework for the effective regulation of trade in services has proved exceedingly difficult, not in the least due to their mainly intangible or invisible nature and the diversity of practices that may fall under the rubric of services, including insurance, banking, construction, transportation, and telecommunications.

The 1994 General Agreement on Trade in Services (GATS),[492] Annex 1B to the WTO Agreement, establishes a general multilateral framework of principles and rules for international trade in services. It covers a supply of a service: from the territory of one member into the territory of another member; in the territory of one member to a consumer of another member; or by a supplier of one member through a commercial presence, or the presence of natural persons, in the territory of another member.

Most-favoured-nation (MFN)[493] and transparency represent the most significant universal mandatory commitments under the GATS.[494] Otherwise, because of the GATS

---

487 *Ibid.*, s. 77.028.

488 *Ibid.*, s. 76.1(1).

489 *Ibid.*, s. 76.1(2)(a).

490 *Ibid.*, s. 76.1(2)(b).

491 *Ibid.*, s. 76.1(2)(c).

492 Chapter 9, *supra*.

493 I.e., meaning that once a concession is extended to one WTO member, it must be extended in a non-discriminatory manner to all members.

494 Note that NT is not a mandatory requirement under the GATS, in contrast to the situation with respect to goods under the GATT 1994. GATS, art. XVII.1 states that the NT requirement is limited to the sectors included in a member's GATS schedule, and then "subject to any conditions and qualifications set out therein." Because of the particular characteristic of certain services which may require delivery through the establishment of a commercial presence within the territory of another member, a universal requirement of unconditional national treatment would have meant absolute free trade in services, a result that is simply not yet feasible. Market access obligations are also conditional under the GATS (art. XVI).

"positive list" schedule approach, WTO members may condition their GATS commitments according to their individual needs and priorities.[495]

A. Subsidies

The problem of subsidies in the services context has been acknowledged in the GATS, but much work remains to be done in this area. By virtue of GATS article XV, WTO members recognize that in certain circumstances, subsidies (governmental financial contributions conferring a benefit) may have a distortive effect on trade in services. WTO members have committed themselves to negotiations aimed at developing the necessary multilateral disciplines to avoid such trade distortion. The negotiations will also address the appropriateness of countervailing duty procedures.

Presently, any member considering that it is adversely affected by a subsidy of another member may request consultations with that member. Such a request must be accorded sympathetic consideration.[496] This provision is distinct from the general GATS institutional and dispute settlement provisions.[497]

B. Dumping

Dumping in the services context is problematic; many of the concepts readily applicable to goods do not transfer well to services.[498] For example, because dumping involves the comparison of sales and export prices, such prices must be determinable. Many service contracts, such as construction contracts, are long term. They are vulnerable to unforeseen circumstances and must frequently be adapted or re-negotiated to reflect new developments. This feature makes it difficult to ascertain the "sale price" of the service until the project is fully complete.

In addition, many services, particularly in the banking sector, involve fluctuating variables, such as interest rates. The value of such services may not be definitively ascertained until repayment, which could be uncertain or a long time in the future. The banking services sector provides its own unique set of problems because prices and interest rates are denominated in the various national currencies, often preventing worthwhile price comparisons and calculations.

The GATS contains no specific provision concerning discriminatory pricing or dumping of services, or the imposition of anti-dumping duties on services.

---

495 GATS, art. XX. The "positive list" approach allows WTO members to enumerate specifically only those practices and sectors that will be governed by the GATS in their GATS schedule. Service sectors that members choose to keep outside the GATS framework proceed essentially unregulated.

496 GATS, art. XV.2.

497 GATS, arts. XXII and XXIII.

498 For instructive analyses of antidumping in the services sector, see Kubo, "Can antidumping law apply to trade in services?" (1991), 12 *Mich. J Int. Law* 828; Sullivan, "Antidumping law and the dumping of services" (1992), 24 *NYU J of Int. Law and Politics* 1677; and Footer, "GATT and the Multilateral Regulation of Banking Services" (1993), 27 *Int. Lawyer* 343, 365-66.

At the time that the GATS was being negotiated, it was generally felt that a provision relating to the dumping of services was not necessary. Because WTO members retain the power to condition and structure their individual GATS commitments in their GATS schedule, subject to the general obligations of MFN and transparency, the present GATS offers an ample range of instruments to shield a domestic economy from the rigours of competition in the area of services. Members may condition and limit their market access and national treatment (NT) obligations. In addition, several related GATS provisions could be used to combat discriminatory pricing practices or dumping. These include the provisions on monopolies and exclusive service providers (GATS, article VIII), business practices (GATS, article IX), and safeguards (GATS, article X). However, as the GATS evolves, and as progressive liberalization limits the permissible schedule conditions and exclusions, it will be necessary to revisit the issue of dumping and services under the aegis of the WTO.

C. SIMA: Does It Apply to Trade in Services?

It appears that the current version of the SIMA, the Canadian domestic legislation relating to the imposition of anti-dumping and countervailing duties, does not apply to trade in services.

The SIMA defines subsidy[499] as a financial contribution by a foreign government that confers a benefit to persons engaged in the production, sale, etc., of *goods*; or, any form of income or price support within the meaning of article XVI of the GATT 1994 that confers a benefit. The GATT 1994 deals exclusively with goods.

The SIMA also specifies that dumped in relation to goods means that normal value exceeds export price.[500]

Neither of these SIMA definitions seem to encompass services. However, under the SIMA certain services are indirectly taken into consideration with respect to the determination of normal value and export price of goods. This is the case, for example, with respect to delivery costs[501] and design or engineering costs.[502]

V. SELECTED BIBLIOGRAPHY

A. Books

Anti-dumping Tribunal, *Annual Reports*.

Bierwagen, *GATT Article VI and the Protectionist Bias in Anti-Dumping Laws* (1990).

Boddez and Trebilcock, *Unfinished Business: Reforming Trade Remedy Laws in North America* (1993).

Canadian Import Tribunal, *Annual Reports*.

---

499 SIMA, *supra*, note 76, s. 2(1).

500 *Ibid.*, s. 2(1).

501 Special Import Measures Regulations, *supra*, note 80, rr. 7 and 8.

502 *Ibid.*, rr. 11 and 12.

Canadian Import Tribunal, *Report on Public Interest: Grain Corn* (1987).

Canadian International Trade Tribunal, *Annual Reports*, 1990- .

Canadian International Trade Tribunal, *Bulletin*, 1989- .

Finger, *Anti-Dumping* (1993).

GATT, Analytical Index (1994).

Hines, "Scope for Procedural Protectionism Under the Special Import Measures Act," *Report of the Policy Forum on Special Import Measures Legislation* (John Deutsch Institute, 1984).

Hutton and Trebilcock, *An Empirical Study of the Application of Canadian Anti-Dumping Laws: A Search for Normative Rationales* (Ontario Centre for International Business, pub. no. 21, 1989).

Jackson, *The World Trading System* (1989).

Kaye, Plaia Jr., Hertzberg, *International Trade Practice* (1981-).

Marceau, *Anti-Dumping and Anti-Trust Issues in Free Trade Areas* (1994).

Martin, "The Capital Goods Sector Bias of the Special Import Measures Act," *Report of the Policy Forum on Special Import Measures Legislation* (John Deutsch Institute, 1984).

McAnsh, "SIMA Viewed from the Perspective of a Domestic Capital Goods Manufacturer," *Report of the Policy Forum on Special Import Measures Legislation* (John Deutsch Institute, 1984).

McCartin, "Red, Yellow or Green: GATT 1994's Traffic Light Subsidies Categories," Practicing Law Institute: The Commerce Department Speaks on International Trade and Investment, October 1994.

Paterson and Band, *International Trade and International Investment Law in Canada* (1994).

Quinn, "Anti-Dumping Legislation as Procedural Discrimination," *Report of the Policy Forum on Special Import Measures Legislation* (John Deutsch Institute, 1984).

Rugman and Anderson, *Administered Protection in America* (1987).

Schoenbaum, *Anti-Dumping and Countervailing Duties and the GATT: An Evaluation and a Proposal for a Unified Remedy for Unfair International Trade* (The Dean Rusk Center for International and Comparative Law, 1987).

Stegemann, *Raising the Deterrence Level* (Kingston: Institute for Economic Research, Queen's University, 1982).

Sub-Committee on Import Policy, *Report on the Special Import Measures Act*, House of Commons, 1st Sess., 32nd Parl., issue no. 31, 9 June 1982.

Trebilcock and Howse, *The Regulation of International Trade* (1995).

Trebilcock and York (eds.), *Fair Exchange: Reforming Trade Remedy Laws* (1990).

B. Articles

Bierwagen and Heilbronner, "Input, Downstream, Upstream, Secondary, Diversionary and Components or Subassembly Dumping" (1988), 22 *J of World Trade* 27.

Buchanan, "Anti-Dumping Law and the Special Import Measures Act" (1985), 11 *Can. Bus. LJ* 2.

Denton, "(Why) Should Nations Utilise Anti-dumping Measures" (1989), 10 *Michigan J of Int'l. Law* 224.

"For No One's Benefit: Canada's Use of Foreign Aid to Subsidize Exports" (1988), 46 *U of T Fac. L Rev.* 303.

Gastle and Castel, "Should the North American Free Trade Agreement Dispute Settlement Mechanism in Antidumping and Countervailing Duty Cases Be Reformed in the Light of *Softwood Lumber III*?" (1995), 26 *Law and Policy in Int'l. Business* 822.

Gottlieb, Steger, and Pearson, "Current and Possible Future International Rules Relating to Trade Adjustment Policies—Subsidies, Safeguards, Trade Adjustment Assistance: A View from Canada" (1988), 14 *Can.-US LJ* 127.

Herman, "Injury Findings by the Canadian Import Tribunal: The Decisive Elements" (1987), 1 *Rev. Int'l. Bus. L* 373.

Horlick and Clarke, "The 1994 WTO Subsidies Agreement." Practicing Law Institute: The Commerce Department speaks on International Trade and Investment, October 1994.

Horlick and Shea, "The World Trade Organization Antidumping Agreement" (1995), 29 *J of World Trade* 5.

Latimer, "Trade Laws: A Canadian Perspective" (1985), 10 *Can.-US LJ* 157.

Lorentzen, "Overview of Major Changes Contained in the Uruguay Round Antidumping and Subsidies Agreements," Practicing Law Institute: The Commerce Department Speaks on International Trade and Investment, October 1994.

Magnus, "The Canadian Antidumping System" in Jackson and Vermulst (eds.), *Antidumping Law and Practice: A Comparative Study* (1989), at 167.

Matsumo and Finlayson, "Dumping and Anti-Dumping: Growing Problems of World Trade" (1990), 24 *J of World Trade* 5.

Musgrove, "Special Import Measures Act, Regional Markets and Contingency Protection" (1988), 14 *Can. Bus. LJ* 423.

Palmeter and Spak, "Resolving Antidumping and Countervailing Duty Disputes: Defining GATT's Role in an Era of Increasing Conflict" (1993), 24 *Law and Pol. in Int. Bus.* 1145.

Rugman and Porteous, "Canadian and US Unfair Trade Laws: A Comparison of Their Legal and Administrative Structures" (1989), 16 *Can. Bus. J* 1.

Rugman and Porteous, "The Softwood Lumber Decision of 1986: Broadening the Nature of US Administered Protection" (1988), 2 *Rev. Int'l. Bus. L* 35.

Skogstad, "The Application of Canada and US Trade Remedy Laws" (1988), 31 *Can. Pub. Admin.* 539.

Terry, "Sovereignty, Subsidies, and Countervailing Duties in the Context of the Canada-United States Trading Relationship" (1988), 46 *U of T Fac. L Rev.* 48.

Tougas, "Softwood Lumber from Canada: Natural Resources and the Search for a Definition of Countervailable Domestic Subsidy" (1988-89), 24 *Gonz. L Rev.* 135.

Walker, "Chapter Nineteen of the NAFTA: Binational Panels as the Trade Courts of Last Resort" (1993), 27 *Int. Law.* 707.

CHAPTER SIXTEEN

The International Dimension of Enforcing the Competition Act

I. INTRODUCTION

Although most states devoted to a free market economy agree that restrictive business practices that are unreasonable and misallocate scarce resources should be discouraged unless they are specifically approved and supervised by competent government authorities, lack of agreement exists as to how this objective can be achieved. To what extent may a state hold individuals or companies responsible for activities or their harmful consequences within or without its territory? In other words, what are the minimum contacts adequate to support the imposition of economic regulation? Also, to what extent should recognition be given to foreign laws dealing with restrictive business practices?

Many connecting factors could serve as a basis for a satisfactory legislative hold on restrictive business practices. For example, the citizenship, domicile, or residence of a person or corporation, or the initiation and execution of activity within the state, or the impact of foreign activity within the state, singly or together, may provide a sufficient basis for the extraterritorial application of economic regulation. Private international law techniques could be used by analogy in order to develop bilateral rules of choice of law applicable to the regulation of competition.

Since foreign commerce is not spatially contained, a state must be able to exercise jurisdiction over restrictive business practices when they take place beyond its boundaries, especially where their direct and substantial effect on its commerce can be shown. The reach of the jurisdiction is very important when the activities of transnational enterprises are examined. The laws regulating competition cannot be confined solely to those foreign trade activities that take place within the territory of the regulating state.

Where restrictive business practices affect two states, both may be prepared to assert jurisdiction. This raises the question of the limits of such jurisdiction when several states are involved. Should one state defer to the other to avoid any overlap and occasional conflict? Such conflict may also occur where the acts or conduct abroad that are sought to be prohibited are consistent with and in furtherance of the law or economic policy of the foreign state involved. In such a case, the maintenance of an amicable diplomatic relationship with that foreign state may require abstention based upon the recognition that not every state has the same economic laws. Generally speaking, where the policy interests of and the legal contacts with the foreign state are greater than those of the domestic state in deterring anticompetitive conduct, no extraterritorial enforcement should take place.

Until recently, the world picture presented a great diversity of attitudes toward activities affecting competition on the part of states dedicated to a system of private enterprise in a free market economy. Today, however, most industrialized states have adopted broad legislation[1] that is designed to reach foreign as well as domestic acts in

---

1 Laws regulating competition or "antitrust laws," as they are called in the United States, are laws designed to promote and preserve free and open competition as the rules of trade in a system of private enterprise in a free market economy. In general, they deal with conspiracies, restrictive trade practices, and mergers and monopolies affecting competition, and constitute rules for proper conduct in the marketplace. This chapter is based on parts of Castel, *Extraterritoriality in International Trade. Canada and United States of America Practices Compared* (1988).

restraint of trade. Also, many enforcement authorities are making a concerted effort to harmonize their activities. To be effective, the enforcement of the laws regulating competition should be directed to the whole arrangement including foreign participants; yet, in extending the reach of such laws, states should be concerned with the legitimate claims or interests of other states, as well as the interests or concerns of private individuals or companies.

This chapter contains an analysis of the relevant provisions of the Canadian Competition Act[2] that may be applied extraterritorially and Canadian responses to the extraterritorial application of similar foreign legislation since both Canadian and foreign laws prohibiting restrictive business practices affect the export and import of Canadian and foreign goods. It also examines methods of cooperation in this field of the law.

II. THE COMPETITION ACT[3]

A. Overview

The competition policy of Canada is expressed in the Competition Act whose purpose "is to maintain and encourage competition in Canada in order to promote the efficiency and adaptability of the Canadian economy, in order to expand opportunities for Canadian participation in world markets while at the same time recognizing the role of foreign competition in Canada, in order to ensure that small- and medium-sized enterprises have an equitable opportunity to participate in the Canadian economy and in order to provide consumers with competitive prices and product choices."[4] To this end, the Act seeks to eliminate certain practices in restraint of trade and to overcome the negative effects of concentration that tend to prevent the economic resources of Canada from being used most effectively to the advantage of all. The Competition Act contains, *inter alia*, civil law provisions applicable to mergers and to abuse of dominant position and criminal law provisions applicable to conspiracies in restraint of trade. Pre-notification of certain transactions is required. A private right of action for damages is given to victims of anticompetitive conduct. Enforcement is in the hands of independent agencies: the director of investigation and research (the Director) who administers the Bureau of Competition Policy (the Bureau) investigates anticompetitive conduct; the Competition Tribunal, an independent quasi-judicial agency with authority to review certain anti-competitive practices; and the courts.[5]

2 RSC 1985 (2nd Supp.), c. 19, as am. This Act, which amends and renames the Combines Investigation Act, RSC 1985, c. C-34, is discussed throughout as amended and cited as the Competition Act.

3 *Ibid.* See, generally, Goldman and Bodrug, *Competition Law of Canada* (1995).

4 *Ibid.*, s. 1.1.

5 In June 1995, the director proposed a number of amendments to the Competition Act, *supra*, note 2. At the time of writing, these amendments had not been enacted, however, the director proposed improving the notification process applicable to large merger transactions; providing a non-criminal adjudicative alternative for misleading advertising and an array of potential remedies; reviewing the concept of "ordinary selling price" under the misleading advertising provisions; shifting the treatment of price

(The footnote is continued on the next page.)

Some activities are partially exempted from the legislation—for example, certain agreements between members of shipping conferences[6] and conspiracies, contributions, and agreements or arrangements to restrain or injure competition relating only to the export of products from Canada.[7] There is no exemption for activities that have resulted in or are likely to result in a reduction or limitation of the real value of exports of a product or have restricted or are likely to restrict any person from entering into or expanding the business of exporting products from Canada or have prevented or lessened or are likely to prevent or lessen competition unduly in the supply of services facilitating the export of products from Canada.[8] These conditions make it difficult for an export consortium to benefit from the exemption.[9] Limiting competition in a foreign market is not relevant.

It should also be mentioned that whenever it appears that competition in respect of any article has been prevented or lessened substantially as a result of an inquiry under the Competition Act, a judgment of a court or a decision of the Competition Tribunal, and the prevention or lessening of competition is facilitated by duties of custom imposed on the article, or on any like article, the Governor in Council, by order, may remove or reduce any such duties of custom.[10]

B. Merger Review

1. Overview

For the purposes of the Competition Act, a "merger" is defined broadly to include any form of an acquisition of control over or a "significant interest" in the whole or a part of a business. The Director considers that the merger provisions may apply not only to

---

5 Continued ...

discrimination and promotional allowances from a criminal prohibition to civil review before the tribunal; allowing private parties to file applications before the tribunal in respect of some civil reviewable matters; and expanding the scope of prohibition orders to allow them to include terms that are prescriptive in nature. See Industry Canada, *Bureau of Competition Policy Discussion Paper: Competition Act Amendments* (June 1995). See also Industry Canada, Competition Bureau Statement, *Remarks of George N. Addy, Director of Investigation and Research to the Canadian Institute* (10 May 1996).

6 Shipping Conference Exemption Act, 1987, RSC 1985 (3rd Supp.), c. 17, ss. 4 and 5.

7 Competition Act, *supra*, note 2, s. 45(5).

8 *Ibid.*, ss. 45(6)(a) to (c). What about an industry agreement to restrict exports by a voluntary quota in order to preserve an export market in a country that imposes sanctions if a certain level of imports is exceeded?

9 Note that the Energy Supplies Emergency Act, RSC 1985, c. E-9, s. 33, as am., provides that where there is a shortage of energy, cooperative arrangements among oil companies or other energy suppliers may be totally exempted from the Competition Act, *ibid.*, for a 24-month period, upon application to the National Energy Board for an order to that effect. The National Energy Board may grant such a request only after consulting with the Minister of Industry, who is responsible to Cabinet for the administration of the Competition Act. A similar procedure could be used to exempt the investors of an export consortium.

10 Competition Act, *ibid.*, s. 31.

share and asset acquisitions, but also to contracts that give a person the ability to influence materially another business. Asset transactions that may fall within the scope of the Act's merger provisions include purchases or leases of a brand name or intellectual property rights.[11] If he or she determines that a merger is likely to prevent or lessen competition substantially, the Director may apply to the tribunal for an order to dissolve or enjoin a merger at any time within three years of the substantial completion of the merger.

Certain large mergers may be subject to pre-closing notification and waiting period requirements under part IX of the Competition Act that are similar to the requirements of the Hart-Scott-Rodino Antitrust Improvements Act of 1976[12] in the United States, but whether or not a merger exceeds the compulsory pre-closing notification criteria, all mergers of all sizes are subject to the substantive merger provisions of the Act.[13]

In defining relevant product and geographic markets, the merger guidelines adopt a "hypothetical monopolist" approach that is broadly similar to that described in the 1992 US Horizontal Merger Guidelines.[14] The merger guidelines do not make use of the Herfindahl-Hirschman Index, and the Competition Act specifically provides that the tribunal may not rely solely on market shares.[15] However, the merger guidelines do state that the director is not likely to challenge a merger on the basis of concerns regarding the unilateral market power of the parties to the transaction if the post-merger market share will be less than 35 percent. Similarly, the Director is not likely to challenge a merger on the basis of concerns relating to the interdependent exercise of market power where the four largest firms would have less than 65 percent of the market or where, notwithstanding this fact, the merged entity would have less than a 10 percent share.[16] These are not fixed rules. A merger below these thresholds could be challenged and many mergers with market shares above these thresholds are not challenged. In its first contested merger case, the tribunal declined to dissolve a merger that resulted in a 60 percent market share in the rendering business in southern Ontario.[17] Both the Director and the Tribunal will tolerate market share thresholds that are clearly much higher than levels that would likely be challenged in the United States.

Another distinguishing feature of Canadian merger enforcement compared to that in the United States is that the Director's focus, at least to date, has been on the likelihood of the merged entity being able to exercise unilateral market power, rather than an

11 Director of Investigation and Research, "Merger Enforcement Guidelines," *Info. Bulletin no. 5* (1991) (hereinafter merger guidelines), at pt. I.

12 Pub. L 94-435, 30 September 1976, 90 Stat. 1383 (15 USCA, ss. 1 note, 8 note, 12, 15c to 15g, 16, 18a, 26, 66, and 1311 to 1314; 18 USCA, s. 1505; and 28 USCA, s. 1407).

13 For a discussion of the pre-merger notification provisions of the Goldman and Bodrug, see *supra*, note 3, at §10.09.

14 62 *Antitrust & Trade Reg. Rep. (BNA Special Supp.) no. 1559* (2 April 1992).

15 Competition Act, *supra*, note 2, s. 92(2).

16 Merger guidelines, *supra*, note 11, s. 4.2.1.

17 *Director of Investigation and Research v. Hillsdown Holdings (Can.) Ltd.* (1992), 41 CPR (3d) 289.

assessment of the likelihood of interdependent conduct.[18] The Canadian de-emphasis of market share and the risk of interdependent conduct reflects a recognition of the relatively concentrated markets in Canada and the need for Canadian firms to achieve internationally competitive economies of scale.

The Competition Act contains a list of factors that the Tribunal may take into account in assessing a merger, including the impact of foreign competitors, barriers to entry (including tariffs and regulatory control over entry), the degree of effective competition remaining, whether the merger will result in the removal of a vigorous and effective competitor, and the nature and extent of change and innovation in a relevant market. Of these factors, foreign competition and the level of barriers to entry appear to have the greatest influence on the Director's decision whether to challenge a merger.[19]

To date, the Director does not appear to have applied an incipiency standard to seek any remedies where there are some speculative concerns about the possible exercise of market power by the merged entity. In some cases, however, the Director has advised parties to a merger that the bureau intends to monitor the merged entity and the relevant industry under both the merger and abuse of dominance provisions of the Competition Act.

The Act expressly recognizes the "failing firm" factor and the merger guidelines suggest that if one of the parties to a merger is likely to either fail or exit the market if the proposed merger does not proceed, then any lessening of competition would occur in any event and cannot be attributed to the merger.[20] By extending the "failing firm" defence to exiting firms, the Canadian guidelines may provide a somewhat broader "failing firm" defence than the US guidelines, although it may be difficult for a firm that is not failing to satisfy the director that there are no competitively preferable purchasers willing to pay more than the net liquidation value of the firm, or that the firm is not likely to remain in the market if the merger is not permitted to proceed.

2. *Efficiency Exception*

In the context of mergers, the Competition Act would appear to give greater weight to efficiencies than in the United States, although whether this will be the case in practice has been cast in doubt by the tribunal. Pursuant to section 96 of the Act, the Tribunal may not make an order under the merger provisions if it finds that (1) the gains in efficiency likely to be brought about by the merger will be greater than and will offset the effects of any prevention or lessening of competition that are likely to result from the merger, (2) the claimed efficiency gains would not likely be attained if the order were

---

18 Merger guidelines, *supra*, note 11, at s. 2.2. However, the tribunal has identified "enhanced ability for tacit collusion" as one of the issues which should be the focus of attention in any merger case: *Director of Investigation and Research v. Imperial Oil Ltd.* (26 January 1990), CT./89-3, no. 390 (Comp. Trib.), at 54 (unreported).

19 See Khemani and Shapiro, "An Empirical Analysis of Canadian Merger Policy" (1993), 41 *J of Industrial Economics* 161, at table II.

20 Merger guidelines, *supra*, note 11, ss. 4.1 and 4.4.1.

made, and (3) the alleged efficiency gains would not be brought about by reason only of a redistribution of income. In addition, the Act directs the Tribunal to consider whether such efficiency gains will result in a significant increase in the real value of exports or a significant substitution of domestic products for imported products. Conflicting views have been expressed about how any such increase in exports or substitution of imports is to be taken into account.[21] A full panel of the Tribunal is yet to rule on this issue.

In *Hillsdown*, both the Director and the acquiror took the position that section 96 directs the tribunal to balance the gains in efficiency likely to arise from a merger against the misallocation of resources or loss to society as a whole resulting from the increased prices (the "deadweight loss") that the merged firm is able to impose as a result of the merger (that is, the "total welfare" approach). In the Director's view, there is no need to establish that the efficiency gains will be passed on to the consumer. The chair of the Tribunal suggested in *obiter dicta*, however, that section 96 could be read to permit it to take into account a much broader range of effects, including wealth transfers.[22]

The Tribunal also reviewed "the various purposes served by competition law in relation to efficiency gains" and commented that:

> … one traditional purpose has been to protect the consumer from being charged supra-competitive prices. While one can argue that this is insignificant from the point of view of loss to the economy as a whole, … there is a powerful political argument for preventing such accretions of wealth at the consumer's expense. Another purpose which has traditionally been seen as served by competition law is to encourage the dispersal of power and the distribution of wealth … . A third objective of competition law is seen as that of protecting the small firm against more powerful rivals … . These objectives can run counter to the fourth objective which is that of furthering the efficiency of the economy as a whole.[23]

Against this background, the Tribunal questioned whether it was appropriate to give precedence to the efficiency objective in the purpose clause over the provision of "competitive prices" and "equitable opportunities for small and medium sized enterprises."[24]

Finally, the Tribunal raised "as a question" whether wealth transfers are always neutral and posed the following two examples: (1) a merger of two drug companies where the relevant product is a life-saving drug, and (2) a merger resulting in a dominant firm that charges supra-competitive prices resulting in all the wealth transfer leaving Canada. These examples suggest that the Tribunal may be willing to consider a very broad range of possible negative effects of a merger that must be demonstrated to be offset by efficiency gains in order for section 96 to apply.

Furthermore, it has been suggested that the combined effect of the deadweight loss and the neutral wealth transfer resulting from a price increase typically far exceeds any efficiencies which may be brought about by a merger.[25] Thus, the approach of the

---

21 See Goldman and Bodrug, *supra*, note 3, at §10.05.

22 *Hillsdown*, *supra*, note 17, at 343.

23 *Ibid.*, at 338-39.

24 *Ibid.*, at 343.

25 Fisher and Lande, "Efficiency Considerations in Merger Enforcement" (1983), 71 *Cal. LR* 1580, at 1644-45.

Tribunal in the *Hillsdown* case could leave the efficiency exception as a largely academic possibility.[26] Nevertheless, the Director continues to apply the approach set forth in the merger guidelines[27] and the subsequent Director has identified the efficiency exception in the Canadian legislation as one of the factors that lead to different decisions by the Canadian Bureau and the European Commission in the de Havilland case that the director decided not to challenge, on the basis that it was not likely to substantially lessen competition in Canada, while the EC blocked the transaction on the basis that it would create a dominant position in the world market for commuter aircraft.[28]

3. Strategic Alliances

While acknowledging that it is difficult to define a "strategic alliance" because of the myriad inter-firm cooperative agreements that are possible, the Director has publicly stated that most do not raise issues under the Competition Act.[29] However, the Director has also indicated that they may be analyzed under the criminal conspiracy provisions or the civil merger review provisions of the Competition Act. The Director further stated that the greater the market power collectively held by the parties to the alliance, the more likely is behaviour that is potentially injurious to competition and the greater the likelihood of an inquiry under the conspiracy provisions of the Competition Act.[30]

III. EXTRATERRITORIAL REACH: JURISDICTION TO PRESCRIBE

The penal provisions of the Competition Act and the Criminal Code,[31] as criminal legislation, are limited by the general principle that "no person shall be convicted for an offence committed outside Canada." However, the Competition Act attaches civil and penal consequences to conduct, acts, or agreements outside Canada that have adverse effects within Canada. Thus, legal action can take place against enterprises operating in Canada for agreements that they have entered into abroad if they affect competition in Canada. The nationality of persons or enterprises engaged in the prohibited conduct is

---

26 For an alternative perspective on the analysis of efficiencies of merger cases in Canada, see Warner, "Efficiencies and Merger Review in Canada, the European Community and the United States: Implications for Harmonization/Convergence" (1994), 26 *Vanderbilt J. Transnat'l. L* 1059.

27 Wetston, QC, Director of Investigation and Research, "Decisions and Developments: Competition Law and Policy," *Remarks delivered to the Canadian Institute*, Speech no. S-10728/92-07 5 (8 June 1992).

28 Addy, "International Coordination of Competition Policies," *Paper delivered to the HWWA-Institute Fur Wirtschaftsforschung—Hamburg* (9 to 11 October 1991).

29 Industry Canada, *Strategic Alliances Under the Competition Act* (1995), at vi.

30 *Ibid.*

31 RSC 1985, c. C-46, as am., s. 6(2). The code also deals with conspiracies in restraint of trade: s. 466. For an early study, see Feltham, "Extraterritorial Application of Antitrust Legislation as Viewed from the Standpoint of Commonwealth States" in Wilson (ed.), *International and Comparative Law of the Commonwealth* (1968), at 130, esp. at 139. Hunter, "Extraterritoriality and Anti-Trust Considerations: The Canadian Perspective" in Fray and Radebaugh (eds.), *Regulation of Foreign Direct Investment in Canada and the United States* (1983), at 77.

irrelevant.[32] This was recognized in 1965 by the Canadian Restrictive Trade Practices Commission, now replaced by the Competition Tribunal, which, in an opinion on shipping conferences practices, stated that:[33]

The Commission considers that where any overt act which takes place in Canada flows from an agreement which is contrary to the public policy, public interest or public order of Canada, such agreement comes within the Canadian jurisdiction even if it was not made in Canada. In such circumstances, even if the agreement does not violate the law of the country where it was made, it is within the purview of the Canadian courts.

An agreement or conspiracy entered into abroad is also within the scope of the legislation if an overt act in pursuance of the common design is done in Canada.[34] During the first years of existence of the Combines Investigation Act,[35] enforcement action was concerned mainly with the activities of Canadian enterprises within Canada that had no international implications. This situation has changed rapidly in recent years since many subsidiaries of foreign parents, mostly transnational enterprises based in the United States, are now doing business in Canada to the extent that Canada is often described as a "branch plant economy." It has been argued that non-tariff barriers to trade arising from the anticompetitive activities of these transnational enterprises may have had detrimental effects on Canada's economy. As a result of multilateral and bilateral trade liberalization, certain monopolistic or oligopolistic practices and international cartel behaviour have become more detectible. Since Canada is heavily dependent on foreign trade, particularly for the development of new markets in order to supplement the small number of Canadian customers, it was felt that a more vigorous enforcement of the Combines Investigation Act was needed and that its territorial scope should be broadened. Thus, in 1976,[36] the Act was amended by adding to it section 46(1), which provides that:

46(1) Any corporation, wherever incorporated, that carries on business in Canada and that implements in whole or in part in Canada, a directive, instruction, intimation of policy or other communication to the corporation or any person from a person in a country other than Canada who is in a position to direct or influence the policies of the corporation, which communication is for the purpose of giving effect to a conspiracy, combination, agreement or arrangement entered

32 See, generally, for a discussion of Canadian judicial recognition of the "effects" jurisdictional doctrine, Goldman et al., "International Mergers and the Canadian Competition Act" (1992), *Fordham Corporate Law Institute* 217, and 231-34.

33 *Restrictive Trade Practices, A Report in the Matter of an Inquiry Under the Combines Investigation Act in Connection with the Transportation of Commodities by Water from and to Ports in Eastern Canada* (Ottawa: 17 June 1965), at 98. The only connection with Canada was the use of Canadian ports.

34 See *R. v. Campbell*, [1964] 2 OR 487 (CA), affd. without written reasons [1966] 4 CCC 333n, 58 DLR (2d) 673n (SCC) (international resale price maintenance); *R. v. Burrows* (1968), 54 CPR 95 (BC SC). See also possibly Criminal Code, *supra*, note 31, s. 465(3) and (4).

35 *Supra*, note 2.

36 *Ibid.*, s. 32, added by SC 1974-75-76, c. 76, now RSC 1985, c. C-34, s. 46.

into outside Canada that, if entered into in Canada, would have been in violation of section 45,[37] is, whether or not any director or officer of the corporation in Canada has knowledge of the conspiracy, combination, agreement or arrangement, guilty of an indictable offence and is liable on conviction to a fine in the discretion of the court.

(2) No proceedings may be commenced under this section against a particular corporation where an application has been made by the director under section 41 for an order against that corporation or any other person based on the same or substantially the same facts as would be alleged in proceedings under this section.

This section, which is addressed to corporations, only covers foreign directives to Canadian affiliates.

The Competition Tribunal may prohibit the implementation, in whole or in part, of a decision made or about to be made by a person in Canada or a Canadian corporation as a result of a foreign law or a foreign directive, instruction, intimation of policy, or other communication to that person or corporation for the purpose of giving effect to that foreign law, etc., that, if implemented, would or would likely have an adverse effect upon competition in Canada, the efficiency of trade or industry in Canada, and the foreign trade of Canada, or would otherwise restrain or injure trade or commerce in Canada without compensating advantages.[38] The Competition Tribunal may also prohibit the implementation of decisions made or about to be made by a person in Canada or a Canadian corporation as a result of a directive, instruction, intimation of policy or other communication to that person or corporation or to any other person, from a person in a foreign country who is in a position to direct or influence the policies of that person or corporation, where the communication is for the purpose of giving effect to a conspiracy, combination, agreement, or arrangement entered into outside Canada that, if entered into in Canada, would have been in violation of section 45.[39] Such procedure cannot be used against a corporation when proceedings have been commenced against it under section 46(1).

These provisions do not violate international law because they are legitimate exercises of jurisdiction to prescribe based on the effects doctrine.

Section 49 of the Competition Act, which prohibits certain agreements between banks, does not apply to agreements with respect to a deposit or loan made or payable outside Canada,[40] or with respect to the amount of any charge for a service or the kind of service provided to a customer outside Canada, payable or performed outside Canada, or payable or performed in Canada on behalf of a person who is outside Canada,[41] or

---

37 *Ibid.*, 45 gives a list of the offences in relation to competition.

38 Competition Act, *supra*, note 2, s. 41(1)(a).

39 *Ibid.*, s. 41(1)(b). Note that since both ss. 46(1) and 41 refer to offences covered by section 45, one could argue that ss. 41 and 46(1) do not apply to affiliated companies in the light of s. 45(8) which exempts them from s. 45(1). For a definition of affiliated companies for the purpose of the Act, see ss. 2(2) and (3). See also s. 61(7).

40 *Ibid.*, 49(2)(a).

41 *Ibid.*, 49(2)(f).

with respect to the persons or classes of persons to whom a loan or other service will be made or provided outside Canada.[42]

Finally, it should be reiterated that, according to section 93, in determining whether or not a merger or proposed merger prevents or lessens, or is likely to prevent or lessen, competition substantially, the tribunal may have regard to the following factors: "the extent to which foreign products or foreign competitors provide or are likely to provide effective competition to the business of the parties to the merger or proposed merger"; and "any barriers to entry into a market, including: (i) tariff and non-tariff barriers to international trade, (ii) interprovincial barriers to trade, and (iii) regulatory control over entry, and any effect of the merger or proposed merger on such barriers."

Before the 1976 amendments, inquiries have shown some of the difficulties faced by Canada when dealing with restrictive business practices by multinational enterprises. For instance, the *Report of the Royal Commission on Farm Machinery*[43] documented the existence of a multiple price system on farm tractors operated by manufacturers in Europe. The Canadian market was supplied by exports direct from the UK manufacturing plants to Canadian distributors, including subsidiaries of the manufacturing companies. The price level in Canada was such that a Canadian purchaser could obtain tractors in the United Kingdom from domestic dealers, import them into Canada, and place them at the point of use considerably cheaper than by purchasing them from the Canadian distribution network. When attempts were made to organize a purchasing arrangement from UK domestic dealers through a farmers' cooperative, the manufacturers enforced a condition against their UK dealers that prohibited them from selling to any person for export. The study identified restrictive practices in the United Kingdom that helped achieve that result. Despite the fact that one of the companies, Massey Ferguson, was Canadian based, there proved to be little that could be done to protect Canadian farmers from the effects of those arrangements.

In the *Erco* case,[44] a wholly owned subsidiary of a British company was the only Canadian producer of red phosphorus. The parent firm was in an international cartel. Erco was not a signatory to the agreement, but it was *de facto* a part of it because of the parent company's control over its foreign trade. The fact that Erco was only indirectly involved made it unlikely that a prosecution under the Combines Investigation Act would have succeeded.

Today, however, sections 41 and 46 can be used in cases where a company in Canada is involved by foreign directive in the implementation of collusive arrangements entered into outside Canada that, if entered into in Canada, would be contrary to section 45.

Importers of foreign articles may be liable for false advertising by virtue of section 52(2), which provides that ordinarily misleading representations on or accompanying an article are deemed to be made to the public by the person who caused the representation

42 *Ibid.*, 49(2)(g).

43 (1971) and Royal Commission on Farm Machinery, *Special Report on Prices of Tractors and Combines in Canada and Other Countries* (1969).

44 Restrictive Trade Practices Commission, *Report on Trade Practices in the Phosphorus Products and Sodium Chlorate Industries* (1966).

to be made, unless that person is outside Canada. In the latter case, the representations are deemed to be made by the person who imported the article into Canada.

Finally, section 84 provides that where a foreign supplier refuses to sell to a Canadian person and sells instead to a second person in Canada, the Competition Tribunal may order (1) that the second person in Canada supply the Canadian buyer who has been refused supplies by the foreign supplier, and/or (2) that the second person cease dealing with the foreign supplier. The remedies apply not only to outright refusal to sell, but also to any form of discrimination between buyers. The tribunal may make the order only in circumstances where it finds that the refusal to sell or discrimination was initiated by or resulted from "the exertion of buying power outside Canada by another person." This section is intended to cover the situation where a transnational enterprise abroad uses its buying power outside Canada to persuade a foreign supplier to switch its business in Canada away from a Canadian company, with whose service it is satisfied, to a Canadian subsidiary of the transnational enterprise.

It should be noted that the Competition Act is not directed at conduct within or without Canada, which only has anticompetitive effects outside its borders as long as the Canadian domestic market is not affected.

Section 466 of the Criminal Code, which deals with conspiracies in restraint of trade, has not been applied to conspiracies abroad to do or to procure any unlawful act in restraint of trade in Canada, nor has it been applied to a conspiracy in Canada to do or to procure any such act in a foreign country.[45] It is doubtful whether sections 465(3) and (4), which deal with conspiracies, in or out of Canada, to commit an indictable offence, can be made applicable to section 466 since section 465(1) states: "Except where otherwise expressly provided by law, the following provisions apply in respect of conspiracy … ."

IV. EXTRATERRITORIAL REACH: JURISDICTION TO ADJUDICATE AND TO ENFORCE

Canada exercises jurisdiction to adjudicate—that is, to subject persons or enterprises to the process of its courts or administrative tribunals, in order to give effect to the relevant provisions of the Competition Act and the Criminal Code. This is also the case with respect to jurisdiction to enforce for the purpose of inducing or compelling compliance or punishing individuals or enterprises for non-compliance with these provisions. Well-established statutory or common law rules of private international law dealing with the international jurisdiction of courts[46] and of criminal procedure are applied by Canadian courts.[47] Not all of these rules may be acceptable on the international level, even in cases where Canada has jurisdiction to prescribe. It is with respect to the investigation abroad of alleged violations of the Competition Act that Canadian procedures must be examined.

---

45 The application of this section is territorially restricted by s. 5(2).

46 See Castel, *Canadian Conflict of Laws* (3rd ed., 1994), c. 12, esp. paras. 116, 117, and 119-23.

47 See Williams and Castel, *Canadian Criminal Law: International and Transnational Aspects* (1983), cc. 7, 8, and 24.

The investigation of alleged violations of the Act is the responsibility of the director of investigation and research. After he or she has decided to launch a formal inquiry, he or she may exercise certain special powers, such as entering premises, examining witnesses under oath, requiring sworn returns of written information, etc.; however, he or she cannot exercise any investigative powers before obtaining the approval of a superior court judge or a Federal Court judge. Eventually, the inquiry may lead to legal action. The Competition Act does not limit any of the formal powers that the director of investigation and research may exercise to the national territory of Canada. Although the Act does not require that the director seek the permission of a foreign government to exercise such powers, their exercise must be preceded by notification and consultation as provided by the Organisation for Economic Co-operation and Development (OECD) and bilateral antitrust cooperation arrangements to which Canada has subscribed.[48]

The director may request information from foreign nationals or legal persons located outside Canada informally or may request sworn returns of written information, but there is no legal compulsion to answer the notice for written return. However, on the *ex parte* application of the director, a judge may order the attendance of persons not resident but present in Canada for oral examination as witnesses under oath,[49] but if they are not in Canada they cannot be compelled to attend.

Foreign natural or legal persons who are not incorporated in Canada, either federally or provincially, but who have an agent or representative in Canada, can be compelled to answer written returns and the agent, of course, can be required to attend and give evidence under oath. The judge may also order the production of records located in Canada that are in the possession of the agent or representative.[50] The Competition Act allows the judge to order a company in Canada to produce records that are in the possession of an affiliate of such company whether the affiliate is located in Canada or abroad[51] and are relevant to the inquiry.

The powers of the director are exercised under the Competition Act at the inquiry stage. Once a legal action has begun, the courts may resort to other means of compulsion by virtue of the Criminal Code or provincial legislation. Canadian courts will not ordinarily make orders that require someone to compel another person in a foreign state to break the laws of that state.[52] However, they are not prevented from compelling a witness *in* Canada by the fact that giving the evidence sought may constitute a crime in another state.[53]

---

48 See *infra*, section VIII.

49 Competition Act, *supra*, note 2, s. 11(1)(a).

50 *Ibid.*, s. 11(1)(b).

51 *Ibid.*, s. 11(2). For a definition of an affiliated company, see s. 2(2) and (3).

52 *Frischke v. Royal Bank of Canada* (1977), 17 OR (2d) 388 (CA). Note also that a Canadian court will not pierce the corporate veil and compel a Canadian bank to produce documents held by its foreign subsidiary: *Bowlen v. The Queen*, [1978] 1 FC 798 (TD) (tax case).

53 *Spencer v. R.* (1983), 145 DLR (3d) 344, 2 CCC (3d) 526, setting aside (1982), 8 WCB 111, aff'd. by SCC: [1985] 2 SCR 278.

Where the person abroad whose testimony is sought or who is requested to produce documents, agrees to do so without resort by the Canadian authorities to legal compulsion, such evidence will likely be taken according to Canadian procedures. However, the government of the state concerned must consent to these procedures after prior notification and consultation.

Where the person does not agree voluntarily to comply with the request to give evidence, either oral or documentary, the Canadian government will retain counsel in the foreign state and seek the foreign court's authority to issue and enforce subpoenas and take evidence. In such cases, the evidence will be taken according to that foreign state's rules of evidence and procedure.

Failure to obtain information from foreign private persons has occurred primarily as a result of the foreign resident's decision not to provide evidence voluntarily. Canada has been reluctant to use proceedings in foreign courts to secure evidence where foreign residents have withheld cooperation.

During the period from 1968 to 1972,[54] Canadian authorities discussed with US officials the possibility of obtaining evidence from a US company in relation to a Canadian inquiry into sugar. Since it was concluded that it was unlikely that the company would be willing to have its officers testify voluntarily in the Canadian inquiry, the company was not approached for evidence.

Another unsuccessful attempt to secure evidence from private foreign persons occurred during the farm machinery inquiry and involved persons resident in the United Kingdom who refused to provide evidence on a voluntary basis. No further action was taken. It must be emphasized that the possible methods for taking evidence abroad are limited by the requirements of the foreign state for taking evidence in its territory as well as Canadian federal and provincial statutes.

The rules of practice, the Evidence Acts of the various Canadian provinces,[55] and the Canada Evidence Act[56] may also apply to the taking of evidence abroad. Three methods are possible: the first is the taking of evidence by a person appointed and authorized by a court in Canada.[57] This method cannot be used in a state where the

---

54 See app. I of the OECD *Report on the Operation of the 1967 Council Recommendations Concerning Co-operation Between Member Countries on Restrictive Business Practices Affecting International Trade* (C(67) 53 Final) during the period 1967-75 and Annex I of Restrictive Business Practices of Multinational Enterprises, *Report of the Committee of Experts on Restrictive Business Practices* (OECD 1977).

55 See Castel, *supra*, note 46, para. 72. E.g., Ontario Evidence Act, RSO 1990, c. E.23, s. 60(1), as am., s. 176(2). Note that, under Federal Court Rules, CRC 1978, c. 663, rr. 448, 451, and 453-56, discovery may lie against a foreign subsidiary of a Canadian corporation. See also r. 464 (production of documents from a non-party).

56 RSC 1985, c. C-5, ss. 43 to 51.

57 See the Criminal Code, *supra*, note 31, ss. 709-14; *R. v. K.C. Irving Ltd. et al.* (1974), 16 CCC (2d) 49; and *R. v. Atlantic Sugar Ltd., and S.L.S.R. Holdings Co.* (1975), 26 CPR (2d) 14, aff'd. 115 DLR (3d) 21, 54 CCC (2d) 373, 53 CPR (2d) 1, [1980] 2 SCR 644, which rev'd. (1978), 41 CCC (2d) 209, 91 DLR (3d) 618, 41 CPR (2d) 5 (Que. CA); see also Reschenthaler and Stanbury, "Price Fixing, Market

(The footnote is continued on the next page.)

procedure is not authorized and its use would normally be confined to cases where the person is willing to testify voluntarily.

The second method consists of the taking of evidence by the courts of the state of execution pursuant to letters of request by a Canadian court to the foreign court of competent jurisdiction.

The third method involves the taking of evidence by an examiner appointed and authorized by the courts of the state of execution, pursuant to letters of request by a Canadian court.[58] The choice of the appropriate method depends upon the practice followed by the state of execution and any relevant international convention. Despite the possibility of using rogatory commissions to secure evidence from residents of foreign states, the evidence of such persons can, for practical purposes, be obtained only if they agree to give it voluntarily because the expected value of the testimony in the inquiry is frequently less than the cost of retaining foreign counsel and making application by letters of request to a foreign court.

Foreign laws on confidentiality may limit the information that Canadian authorities may obtain abroad from private persons or public authorities.

V. RECOGNITION AND ENFORCEMENT OF FOREIGN COMPETITION LAWS, JUDGMENTS, DIRECTIVES, AND DECREES

A. Recognition of Foreign Competition Laws and Directives

Canadian courts will not recognize and apply foreign competition laws that are of a penal nature.[59] In principle, there is no reason why Canadian courts should refuse to apply foreign laws regulating competition that provide a civil remedy to an aggrieved party. However, at the present time, no special choice of law rules have been adopted by the courts to deal with competition cases.

As already noted above, where the Competition Tribunal finds that a decision has been or is about to be made by a person in Canada or a Canadian corporation as a result of a foreign law or a directive from a foreign government or a person for the purpose of giving effect to that foreign law or directive, and the decision would, if implemented, adversely affect competition in Canada or adversely affect Canada's domestic and foreign trade, the tribunal may, by order, direct that no measures be taken in Canada to implement the foreign law or directive.[60]

---

57 Continued ...
Sharing and the Public Interest: The Atlantic Sugar Case" (1981), 2 *Can. Comp. Pol.* 1; McFetridge and Wong, "Agreements to Lessen Competition after Atlantic Sugar: A Comment" (1981), 5 *Can. Bus. LJ* 329; Engelhart, (1981), 6 *Can. Bus. LJ* 104.

58 Unlike the United States, Canada is not yet a party to the Convention on the Taking of Evidence Abroad in Civil or Commercial Matters, Done at the Hague March 18, 1970, TIAS 7444; 23 UST 2555 so Canada cannot benefit from or be compelled to abide by the agreed procedures for facilitating letters of request.

59 Castel, *supra*, note 46, para. 91.

60 Competition Act, RSC 1985 (2nd Supp.), c. 19, as am., s. 41(1)(a).

On occasion, Canada has cooperated with foreign states in the enforcement of their laws regulating competition, although neither the Competition Act nor the Criminal Code provides for specific administrative or judicial assistance to a foreign enforcement authority wishing to request information directly from persons or companies located in Canada.[61]

Foreign authorities may conduct inquiries in Canada, including the search of public records and the voluntary giving of evidence either on affidavit or by deposition, without involving the Canadian legal system or courts. However, in such a case, the conduct of the hearing must receive prior consent from the Canadian government. Voluntary "in person" interviews by foreign officials with private persons in the form of conversations are not illegal, but the Canadian government expects that this would be preceded by notification and consultation. Canadian officials also retain the right to attend such interviews.

If the foreign authorities are seeking evidence in the form of testimony of a witness before a rogatory commission or similar body, Canadian authorities would expect that the same notification and consultation standards are met as apply to other means for seeking information from private persons in Canada. Provided that neither the person whose testimony is sought nor the Crown in right of Canada or a province object to the gathering of such evidence, it is not necessary for the foreign commissioners to satisfy any further formal requirements.

The compulsory taking of evidence of Canadian residents or citizens in criminal and civil matters and the compulsory service of documents in Canada require that the foreign authorities retain Canadian counsel to obtain a court order and a provincial government official (for example, sheriff or bailiff) to serve the order. Rules of evidence are governed by the law of the province in which the evidence will be taken. While rules of civil procedure vary from province to province, there is considerable uniformity, particularly among the common law provinces.[62]

The issues of notification and consultation is discussed in more detail in section VIII, below.

B. Recognition and Enforcement of Foreign Judgments and Decrees

Ordinary rules of Canadian private international law apply to the recognition and enforcement of foreign judgments and orders, provided they are not of a penal nature[63] or

---

61 However, in 1995, the director proposed amending the Competition Act, *ibid.*, to provide for such assistance to foreign antitrust authorities; see, *supra*, note 5.

62 See, in general, Castel, *supra*, note 46, paras. 72-73.

63 Castel, *ibid.*, para. 91 and *Huntington v. Attrill*, [1893] AC 150 (HL). In *McIntyre Porcupine Mines Ltd. v. Hammond* (1975), 119 DLR (3d) 139 (Ont. HC), the court refused to enforce a foreign judgment based on the US Securities Exchange Act, 1934 (2nd Sess.), c. 404. Note that s. 9(1) of the MLACMA, RSC 1985, c. 30 (4th Supp.), provides for the enforcement of fines imposed by a foreign court of criminal jurisdiction. The fines are recoverable in civil proceedings instituted in Canada by the foreign state.

contrary to the public policy[64] of the forum. However, section 82 of the Competition Act provides that:

Where, on application by the Director, the Tribunal finds that

(a) a judgment, decree, order or other process given, made or issued by or out of a court of other body in a country other than Canada can be implemented in whole or in part by persons in Canada, by companies incorporated by or pursuant to an Act of Parliament or of the legislature of a province, or by measures taken in Canada, and

(b) the implementation in whole or in part of the judgment, decree, order or other process in Canada, would

(i) adversely affect competition in Canada,

(ii) adversely affect the efficiency of trade or industry in Canada without bringing about or increasing in Canada competition that would restore or improve that efficiency,

(iii) adversely affect the foreign trade of Canada without compensating advantages, or

(iv) otherwise restrain or injure trade or commerce in Canada without compensating advantages,

the Tribunal may, by order, direct that

(c) no measures be taken in Canada to implement the judgment, decree, order or process or

(d) no measures be taken in Canada to implement the judgment, decree, order or process except in such manner as the Tribunal prescribes for the purpose of avoiding an effect referred to in sub-paragraphs (b)(i) to (iv).

The Foreign Extraterritorial Measures Act[65] also contains some provisions designed to block the effects in Canada of foreign judgments in the regulation of competition matters.

VI. CANADIAN RESPONSES TO ASSERTIONS BY STATES OF EXTRATERRITORIAL JURISDICTION IN THE REGULATION OF COMPETITION

In the past, Canada has adopted defensive measures in response to the extraterritorial application of foreign laws regulating competition especially the US antitrust laws.[66] As early as 1947, as a result of an investigation by the US Department of Justice of the practices of the pulp and paper industry in the provinces of Quebec and Ontario[67] and their effects on consumers within the United States, the legislature of Ontario passed a law that prohibits the removal of business records from the province pursuant to an

64 *Re Westinghouse Electric Corpn. and Duquesne Light Co.* (1977), 16 OR (2d) 273, 78 DLR (3d) 3 (HC).

65 RSC 1985, c. F-29, ss. 5 and 8.

66 For an analysis of the extraterritorial application of the US antitrust laws, see J.-G. Castel, *supra*, note 1, at 49 *et. seq.*

67 See *Re Grand Jury Subpoena Duces Tecum Addressed to Canadian Intl. Paper Co.*, 72 F Supp. 1013 (SDNY 1974).

order or subpoena of a legislative or judicial authority outside the province.[68] Similar legislation was adopted by Quebec 10 years later.[69] The normal furnishing of records to the head office of a foreign parent corporation is not prohibited.

In response to the specific problems encountered in the *Westinghouse* litigation, the Canadian government adopted the Uranium Information Security Regulations,[70] which prohibited a person from releasing any written matter or documentation with respect to the period of January 1, 1972 to December 31, 1975 unless required to do so by Canadian law or by the Minister of Energy, Mines, and Resources. The regulations also prohibited the giving of oral evidence that might have revealed the contents of any communications to which the regulations applied.[71] The object of the regulations was to prevent the disclosure of documents that would have shown that the acts of the Canadian defendants had been carried out in accordance with Canadian law and government policy.

The validity of these regulations that was challenged by some of the parties to the *Westinghouse* litigation was upheld by the Supreme Court of Canada.[72] In a report published by the Canadian government in 1972, it was pointed out that Canada had experienced the impact of the extraterritorial extension of US antitrust laws by US courts in three basic ways:[73]

(i) The United States courts have asserted direct jurisdiction over persons and firms in Canada, actually having made such persons defendants in antitrust suits.

(ii) The United States courts have attempted to secure evidence which was held in the files of Canadian companies.

---

68 Business Records Protection Act, RSO 1990, c. B.19 and *Re Inter-City Truck Lines Inc. and AGUS* (1982), 133 DLR (3d) 134 (Ont. HC).

69 Business Concerns Records Act, LRQ 1977, c. D-12 and *Asbestos Corp. v. Eagle-Picher Industries Inc.*, [1984] CA 151. See also Groffier, "La Communication de documents économiques à l'étranger" (1984), 44 *R du B* 736. The constitutionality of this rather broad blocking statute was addressed in *Hunt v. Lac D'Amiante du Quebec*, [1993] 4 SCR 289; however, while calling into question the use of blocking statutes in an increasingly integrated world, the Court simply "read down" the statute as not applying to other provinces.

70 SOR/76-644, PC 1976-2368, 21 September 1976, CRC 1978, vol. III, c. 366, pursuant to the Atomic Energy Control Act, RSC 1985, c. A-16.

71 SOR/77-836, CRC 1978, vol. III, c. 366.

72 *Gulf-Oil Corp. v. Gulf Canada Ltd.*, [1980] 2 SCR 39, 111 DLR (3d) 74, 31 NR 451 and Rankin, "The Supreme Court of Canada and the International Uranium Cartel: Gulf Oil and Canadian Sovereignty" (1981), 2 *Supreme Court LR* 411. See also in *Re Westinghouse Elec. Corp. & Dusquesne Light Co.* (1977), 16 OR (2d) 273 (HC), where the court stated that the enforcement of letters of request is based on international comity that will not be exercised in violation of the public policy of the state to which the request is made. In the United Kingdom, see *Rio Tinto Zinc Corp. v. Westinghouse Elec. Corp.*, [1978] 1 All ER 434 (HL).

73 *Foreign Direct Investment in Canada* (1972), at 270. See also *Foreign Ownership and the Structure of Canadian Industry* (January 1968) and the *Report of the Economic Council of Canada, Interim Report on Competition Policy* (1969).

(iii) The decrees following a conviction of a Canadian or United States defendant have directed that specific corrective measures be taken in Canada or that the offensive behaviour cease.

Although US courts have paid little attention to Canadian policy, there are only a few cases in which US decrees affected Canadian activities and their economic impact has probably been beneficial in terms of increasing Canadian industrial efficiency. Nevertheless in 1976, the Combines Investigation Act was amended for the purpose of restricting the extraterritorial application of foreign antitrust laws to Canada. That legislation, as noted previously, enables the Competition Tribunal to forbid the implementation in Canada of a foreign judgment, decree, order, or process that would adversely affect, *inter alia*, the domestic or foreign trade of Canada.[74]

The tribunal also has the power to prohibit the implementation in Canada of any law, directive, instruction, intimation, policy, or other communication from a foreign government or agency, or from a person in a foreign state who is in a position to direct or influence the policies of a Canadian person or corporation when the implementation of such law, directive, etc., would adversely affect, *inter alia*, the domestic or foreign trade of Canada.[75]

The *Westinghouse* case prompted the Canadian Parliament to pass the Foreign Extraterritorial Measures Act,[76] which provides that:

> [W]here a foreign tribunal has given a judgment in proceedings instituted under an antitrust law and, in the opinion of the Attorney General of Canada, the recognition or enforcement of the judgment in Canada has adversely affected or is likely to adversely affect significant Canadian interests in relation to international trade or commerce involving a business carried on in whole or in part in Canada or otherwise has infringed or is likely to infringe Canadian sovereignty, the Attorney General of Canada may: (a) in the case of any judgment, by order, declare that the judgment shall not be recognized or enforcable in any manner in Canada; or (b) in the case of a judgment for a specified amount of money, by order, declare that, for the purposes of the recognition and enforcement of the judgment in Canada, the amount of the judgment shall be deemed to be reduced to such amount as is specified in the order.[77]

This provision is aimed at treble damages awards made under US antitrust laws.

Where a judgment in respect of which an order has been made by the attorney general of Canada, has been given against a party who is a Canadian citizen, a resident of Canada, a corporation incorporated by or under a law of Canada, a province, or a person carrying on business in Canada, that party may, in Canada, sue for and recover from a person in whose favour the judgment was given, any amount obtained from that party by that person under the judgment or any amount that is in excess of the amount to which that judgment is deemed to be reduced.[78]

---

74 RSC 1985 (2nd Supp.), c. 19, as am., s. 82.

75 Competition Act, *ibid.*, s. 41.

76 RSC 1985, c. F-29, as am. See Graham, "The Foreign Extraterritorial Measures Act" (1986), 11 *Can. Bus. LJ* 410.

77 *Ibid.*, 8(1).

78 *Ibid.*, 9(1).

A court that renders a Canadian judgment in favour of such party may, in addition to any other means of enforcing it, order the seizure and sale of any property, including shares of any corporation incorporated by or under a law of Canada or a province in which the person against whom the Canadian judgment is rendered has a direct or indirect beneficial interest, regardless of whether the share certificates are located inside or outside Canada.[79]

Section 3(1) of the Foreign Extraterritorial Measures Act also provides in part that:[80]

Where in the opinion of the Attorney General of Canada, a foreign tribunal has exercised, is exercising or is proposing or likely to exercise jurisdiction or powers of a kind or in a manner that has adversely affected or is likely to adversely affect significant Canadian interests in relation to international trade or commerce involving a business carried on in whole or in part in Canada or that otherwise has infringed or is likely to infringe Canadian sovereignty, or jurisdiction or powers that is or are related to the enforcement of a foreign trade law [as for instance in the case of a foreign antitrust action] … , the Attorney General may by order prohibit or restrict:

(a) the production before or the disclosure of identification to, or for the purposes of, a foreign tribunal, of records that, at any time while the order is in force, are in Canada or are in possession or under the control of a Canadian citizen or a person resident in Canada;

(b) the doing of any act in Canada, in relation to records that at any time while the order is in force are in Canada or are in the possession or under the control of a Canadian citizen or a person resident in Canada, that will, or is likely to, result in the records, or information as to the contents of the records or from which the records might be identified, being produced before or disclosed or identified to or for the purposes of a foreign tribunal; and

(c) the giving by a person, at a time when he is a Canadian citizen or a resident of Canada, of information before, or for the purposes of, a foreign tribunal in relation to the contents or identification of, records that, at any time while the order is in force, are or were in Canada or under the control of a Canadian citizen or a person resident in Canada.

The order may be directed to a particular person or to a class of persons. It may relate to a particular foreign tribunal or to a class of foreign tribunals and to a particular record or to a class of records:

Where production before, or disclosure or identification to, or for the purposes of, a foreign tribunal of a record, and the giving by a person of information before, or for the purposes of, a foreign tribunal in relation to, or in relation to the contents or identification of, a record is prohibited or restricted by an order of the [Attorney General], a tribunal in Canada shall not, for the purposes of proceedings before the foreign tribunal, (a) where the order is in the nature of a prohibition, receive the record or information; or (b) where the order is in the nature of a restriction, receive the record or information if, as a result of so doing, the order may be contravened.[81]

Finally, it should be mentioned that the Official Secrets Act blocks the disclosure of information covered by its provisions.[82]

---

79 *Ibid.*, 9(2).

80 See also, *ibid.*, s. 5, which deals with measures by a foreign state or foreign tribunal.

81 *Ibid.*, 3(2).

82 RSC 1985, c. O-5.

VII. EXAMPLES OF EXTRATERRITORIAL ASSERTIONS OF JURISDICTION BY CANADA

The relatively few statements of policy concerning the extraterritorial application of antitrust laws that have been made over the years on behalf of the bureau have reflected tension between the official position of the Government of Canada and the growing recognition by antitrust authorities that effective enforcement of competition laws may require at least some extraterritorial reach.[83] Until recently, Canada had a long history of opposing the extraterritorial application of the US antitrust laws to conduct occurring in Canada or involving Canadian parties.[84]

However, in recent years there has been growing judicial recognition in Canada that the federal Parliament is "expressly permitted by [the Canadian] Constitution to legislate with internationally extraterritorial effect."[85] This trend is also reflected in recent enforcement actions by the bureau and, arguably, decisions of the Canadian Competition Tribunal. For example, the bureau has reviewed proposed mergers to be effected by way of share acquisitions where shares were held and traded outside Canada, and in which Canadian markets were affected only through a Canadian subsidiary.[86] More recently, a Japanese company, its Canadian subsidiary, and a US subsidiary of another Japanese company pleaded guilty and were fined a total of C$1.7 million for price fixing and price maintenance conspiracies in Canada.[87] In another case, the tribunal, arguably, asserted extraterritorial jurisdiction by accepting "the director's submission that the use of a monopoly position (created by [a] United States patent) to obtain a competitive advantage of a dominant firm in another market is an anti-competitive act."[88]

---

83 E.g., compare Hunter, "Extraterritoriality and Antitrust Considerations: The Canadian Perspective" in Fry and Radebaugh (eds.), *Regulation of Foreign Direct Investment in Canada and the United States* (1983) to address by Addy, "Address to International Coordination of Competition Policies," HWWA-Institut für Wirtschaftsforschung-Hamburg (9 to 11 October 1991).

84 See *Continental Ore Co. v. Union Carbide*, 370 US 690 (1962); *United States v. General Electric Company*, 1962 Trade Cases (CCH) §§70,342 at 70,361, 70,428, at 76,718 and 70,546, at 77,195; and *Zenith Radio Corp. v. Hazeltine Research, Inc.*, 395 US 100 (1969). See also Warner, "Note on *Hunt v. Lac D'Amiante du Québec*," 88 *Am. J Int'l. L* 532 (1994).

85 *Hunt v. Lac D'Amiante du Québec*, *supra*, note 69, at 328. See also *R. v. Libman*, [1985] 2 SCR 178; *R. v. Rowbotham and Roblin* (1992), 60 OAC 75, aff'd. [1993] 4 SCR 834; and, generally, Brief of the Government of Canada as Amicus Curiae in Support of Certain Petitioners, *Hartford Fire Insurance Co. v. California*, 113 S Ct. 2891 (1993).

86 See the discussion of the Schneider/Square D merger in C.S. Goldman et al., "International Mergers and the Canadian Competition Act," [1992] *Fordham Corporate Law Institute* 217.

87 Second fine levied under the Competition Act *supra*, note 74, in joint Canada-US investigation, News Release Bureau of Competition Policy, NR-11546/94-18, 5 August 1994 and fine levied under the Competition Act in joint Canada-US investigation, news release, Director of Investigation and Research (12 July 1994).

88 *Director of Investigation and Research v. NutraSweet Co.* (1990), 32 CPR (3d) 1, at 46 (Comp. Trib.).

VIII. INTERNATIONAL COOPERATION

With the increased economic integration on a North American and global level, and with the reduction of tariff and other non-tariff barriers to trade, certain private anticompetitive behaviour has become more apparent. As the director recently stated, "[t]here are no territorial limits to cartel discussions around boardrooms."[89] Hence, antitrust enforcement is increasingly moving from an issue of contention to an issue of cooperation. This section discusses the most significant international agreements involving Canada with respect to cooperation in enforcement of competition policy. These include treaties of mutual legal assistance, memoranda of understanding, the North American Free Trade Agreement (NAFTA), the OECD, and the World Trade Organization (WTO).

A. Mutual Legal Assistance

In 1988, Parliament passed the Mutual Legal Assistance in Criminal Matters Act (the MLACMA).[90] The MLACMA provides that the government may enter into a treaty with another nation for reciprocal assistance in the investigation and enforcement of criminal matters. To be considered as a treaty under the MLACMA, a treaty must contain provisions respecting the following: the right of Canada, for reasons of security, sovereignty, or public interest, to refuse to give effect to a request; the restriction of assistance to acts that, if committed in Canada, would be indictable offences; the confidentiality of information sent by Canada to a foreign state pursuant to a request for legal assistance; the information that must be set out in requests presented by foreign states; and the type of assistance available under part I of the MLACMA.[91]

Part I provides that the Minister of Justice may not give effect to a request unless the treaty provides for assistance with respect to the subject matter of the request.[92] The Minister of Justice may approve a request for the foreign state to enforce a fine imposed by its own criminal courts and empowers Canadian courts to enforce the fine that is recoverable in a civil suit brought by the foreign state.[93] Part I also provides for assistance with respect to search and seizure, the use of evidence abroad, and the transfer of detained persons to the foreign state.[94] The general framework of the MLACMA requires the foreign antitrust authority to request the assistance of the Minister of Justice, who then approves the application by such authority to a Canadian court for a search warrant, and the minister agrees to provide support for that application. Part II provides for the admissabiliy in Canada of evidence obtained abroad pursuant to a treaty.

---

89 See Addy, *supra*, note 5, at 9.

90 RSC 1985 (4th Supp.), c. 30, as am.

91 *Ibid.*, s. 2(2).

92 *Ibid.*, s. 8.

93 *Ibid.*, s. 9(1), however, the proceeding may not be instituted more than five years after the fine was imposed; *ibid.*, s. 9(2).

94 *Ibid.*, ss. 1016, 17 to 23, and 24 to 29.

In 1990, the Canada-US Treaty on mutual legal assistance in criminal matters, which was signed in 1985, came into force.[95] For Canada, article I defines an "offence" as an offence created by a law of Parliament that may be prosecuted upon indictment, or an offence created by the legislature of a province specified in the annex. The annex lists consumer protection as a covered category of offence. Article II sets forth the scope of application such that the parties shall provide, in accordance with the provisions of this treaty, mutual legal assistance in all matters relating to the investigation, prosecution, and suppression of offences. Assistance shall include examining objects and sites, exchanging information and objects, locating or identifying persons, serving documents, taking the evidence of persons, providing documents and records, transferring persons in custody, and executing requests for searches and seizures.[96]

Assistance shall be provided without regard to whether the conduct under investigation or prosecution in the requesting state constitutes an offence or may be prosecuted by the requested state.[97] This treaty is intended solely for mutual legal assistance between the parties and shall not give a right to a private party.[98] Article IV provides that a party seeking to obtain documents, records, or other articles known to be located in the territory of the other party shall request assistance pursuant to the provisions of this treaty.[99] Where denial of a request or delay in its execution may jeopardize the successful completion of an investigation or prosecution, the parties shall promptly consult, at the instance of either party, to consider alternative means of assistance.[100]

Article V limits compliance where the request is not made in conformity with the provisions of this treaty, or execution of the request is contrary to its public interest, as determined by its central authority.[101] The requested state may postpone assistance if execution of the request would interfere with an ongoing investigation or prosecution in the requested state.

Article I also provides for certain limitations on the use of information obtained pursuant to the treaty, such as the following: the central authority of the requested state may require, after consultation with the central authority of the requesting state, that information or evidence furnished be kept confidential, or be disclosed or used only subject to terms and conditions it may specify; the requesting state shall not disclose or use information or evidence furnished for purposes other than those stated in the request without the prior consent of the central authority of the requested state. However, information or evidence made public in the requesting state may be used for any purpose.

Unlike the memoranda of understanding discussed below, mutual legal assistance treaties are especially important because they have the force of law.

---

95 (1985), 24 *Int'l. Leg. Mat.* 1092.

96 *Ibid.*, art. II(2).

97 *Ibid.*, art. II(3).

98 *Ibid.*, art. II(4).

99 *Ibid.*, art. IV(1).

100 *Ibid.*, art. IV(2).

101 *Ibid.*, art. V(1).

B. Memoranda of Understanding

1. The 1984 Memorandum of Understanding

In 1959, Canada and the United States adopted an informal antitrust notification and consultation procedure. It was prompted by strong Canadian reaction in the late 1950s to a series of US antitrust actions collectively known as the *Canadian Radio Patents* cases.[102] In accordance with this procedure, Canada and the United States, when enforcing their antitrust laws, had to consult with each other if it appeared that the interests of the other state could be affected by such enforcement.

The primary object of the antitrust notification and consultation procedure was to avoid situations arising out of the enforcement of the restrictive business practices laws of one state that might have given rise to a misunderstanding in the other state, particularly in cases where it might have appeared to one state that such enforcement had extraterritorial effects or constituted an infringement of sovereignty. The normal procedure was for each state to notify the other upon or prior to the institution of an antitrust suit involving the interest of a national of the other state so that there could be consultation concerning the contemplated suit. In all cases, each government kept the other informed of significant developments in the litigation.

On November 3, 1969, after discussions in Washington, the Minister of Consumer and Corporate Affairs, and the US attorney general issued a joint communiqué confirming and extending the antitrust notification and consultation procedure of 1959.

While the purpose of the 1959 understanding was to defuse potential conflicts arising from antitrust proceedings, few investigations were resolved by recourse to the procedure of notification and consultation.[103] This situation led the prime minister of Canada and the president of the United States to discuss the negative impact on relations between the two states that results in certain situations from the extraterritorial application of the US antitrust laws in Canada. Pursuant to this discussion, the US attorney general met with Canadian officials in Ottawa on June 17, 1977 to consider ways to avoid or to alleviate this problem. At that time, it was agreed to establish a continuing consultative mechanism to provide for more extensive consultation and cooperation in antitrust matters. During a visit to Ottawa, on January 18, 1978, the US vice-president conveyed an offer by the United States to consult prior to seeking information in Canada related to antitrust investigations. Meetings were held by officials of the two governments to follow up those exchanges and, in 1979, Canada and the United States were close to agreement on the principles to be applied. However, it was not until March 9, 1984, that a "Memorandum of Understanding between the Government of Canada and the Government of the United States of America as to Notification, Consultation and Co-operation with Respect to the Application of National Antitrust Laws" was signed by

---

102 *United States v. General Elec. Co. and Westinghouse Elec. Corp.; N.V. Phillips*, [1962] Trade Cases, 70,342, 70,420, and 70,546 (USDC, SDNY, 1962).

103 Campbell, "The Canadian-United States Antitrust Notification and Consultation Procedure: A Study in Bilateral Conflict Resolution" (1978), 56 *Can. Bar Rev.* 459, at 494.

the two states (the 1984 MOU).[104] The understanding outlined arrangements for notification and consultation between the parties with respect to the application of their respective antitrust laws, with the purpose of avoiding or moderating conflicts of interests and policies. The understanding also established procedures for closer cooperation in order to enhance the substantial benefits that both derive from mutual assistance in the enforcement of their antitrust laws.

2. 1995 Cooperative Agreement

In August 1995, Canada and the United States updated and broadened the 1994 MOU by signing A Cooperative Enforcement Agreement Regarding the Application of Their Competition and Deceptive Marketing Practices Laws (the 1995 Cooperative Agreement).[105] The stated purpose of the 1995 Cooperative Agreement is to promote cooperation and coordination between the competition authorities of the parties, to avoid conflicts arising from the application of the parties' competition laws and to minimize the impact of differences on their respective important interests, and, in addition, to establish a framework for cooperation and coordination with respect to enforcement of deceptive marketing practices laws.

Article II sets forth when notification of enforcement activities is required. Each party shall, subject to article X(1), notify the other party in the manner provided by this article and article XII with respect to its enforcement activities that may affect important interests of the other party. Enforcement activities that may affect the important interests of the other party and therefore ordinarily require notification include those that:

(a) are relevant to enforcement activities of the other party;

(b) involve anticompetitive activities, other than mergers or acquisitions, carried out in whole or in part in the territory of the other party, except where the activities occurring in the territory of the other party are insubstantial;

(c) involve mergers or acquisitions in which—one or more of the parties to the transaction, or—a company controlling one or more of the parties to the transaction, is a company incorporated or organized under the laws of the other party or of one of its provinces or states;

(d) involve conduct believed to have been required, encouraged or approved by the other party;

(e) involve remedies that expressly require or prohibit conduct in the territory of the other party or are otherwise directed at conduct in the territory of the other party; or

(f) involve the seeking of information located in the territory of the other party, whether by personal visit by officials of a party to the territory of the other party or otherwise.

Notification pursuant to this article shall ordinarily be given as soon as a party's competition authorities become aware that notifiable circumstances are present, and when certain enumerated events occur.

---

104 (1984), 23 *Int'l. Leg. Mat.* 275 and Dyal, "The Canada-United States Memorandum of Understanding Regarding Application of National Antitrust Law: New Guidelines for Resolution of Multinational Antitrust Enforcement Disputes" (1984-85), 6 *Northwestern J of Int'l. L & Bus.* 1065.

105 (1995), 69 *Antitrust & Trade Reg. Rep.* 177.

In article III, the parties acknowledge that it is in their common interests to cooperate in the detection of anticompetitive activities and the enforcement of their competition laws to the extent compatible with their respective laws and important interests, and within their reasonably available resources. The parties further acknowledge that it is in their common interests to share information that will facilitate the effective application of their competition laws and promote a better understanding of each other's enforcement policies and activities. The parties will consider adopting such further arrangements as may be feasible and desirable to enhance cooperation in the enforcement of their competition laws. Each party's competition authorities will, to the extent compatible with that party's laws, enforcement policies, and other important interests:

> (a) assist the other party's competition authorities, upon request, in locating and securing evidence and witnesses, and in securing voluntary compliance with requests for information, in the requested party's territory;
>
> (b) inform the other party's competition authorities with respect to enforcement activities involving conduct that may also have an adverse effect on competition within the territory of the other party;
>
> (c) provide to the other party's competition authorities, upon request, such information within its possession as the requesting party's competition authorities may specify that is relevant to the requesting party's enforcement activities; and
>
> (d) provide the other party's competition authorities with any significant information that comes to their attention about anticompetitive activities that may be relevant to, or may warrant, enforcement activity by the other party's competition authorities.

Nothing in this agreement prevents the parties from seeking or providing assistance to one another pursuant to other agreements, treaties, arrangements, or practices between them.

Article IV provides for coordination with regard to related matters. Where both parties' competition authorities are pursuing enforcement activities with regard to related matters, they will consider coordination of their enforcement activities. In such matters, the parties may invoke such mutual assistance arrangements as may be in force from time to time. In considering whether particular enforcement activities should be coordinated, either in whole or in part, the parties' competition authorities shall take into account the following factors, among others:

> (a) the effect of such coordination on the ability of both Parties to achieve their respective enforcement objectives;
>
> (b) the relative abilities of the Parties' competition authorities to obtain information necessary to conduct the enforcement activities;
>
> (c) the extent to which either Party's competition authorities can secure effective relief against the anticompetitive activities involved;
>
> (d) the possible reduction of cost to the Parties and to the persons subject to enforcement activities; and
>
> (e) the potential advantages of coordinated remedies to the Parties and to the persons subject to the enforcement activities.

In any coordination arrangement, each party's competition authorities shall seek to conduct their enforcement activities consistently with the enforcement objectives of the other party's competition authorities. In the case of concurrent or coordinated enforcement activities, the competition authorities of each party shall consider, upon request by the competition authorities of the other party and where consistent with the requested party's enforcement interests, ascertaining whether persons that have provided confidential information in connection with those enforcement activities will consent to the sharing of such information between the parties' competition authorities. However, either party's competition authorities may at any time notify the other party's competition authorities that they intend to limit or terminate coordinated enforcement and pursue their enforcement activities independently and subject to the other provisions of this agreement.

Article V provides for cooperation regarding anticompetitive activities in one party that adversely affect the interests of the other party. The parties note that anticompetitive activities may occur within the territory of one party that, in addition to violating that party's competition laws, adversely affect important interests of the other party. The parties agree that it is in their common interests to seek relief against anticompetitive activities of this nature. If a party believes that anticompetitive activities carried out in the territory of the other party adversely affect its important interests, the first party may request that the other party's competition authorities initiate appropriate enforcement activities.

The request shall be as specific as possible about the nature of the anticompetitive activities and their effects on the interests of the party, and shall include an offer of such further information and other cooperation as the requesting party's competition authorities are able to provide. The requested party's competition authorities shall carefully consider whether to initiate enforcement activities, or to expand ongoing enforcement activities, with respect to the anticompetitive activities identified in the request. The requested party's competition authorities shall promptly inform the requesting party of its decision. If enforcement activities are initiated, the requested party's competition authorities shall advise the requesting party of their outcome and, to the extent possible, of significant interim developments. Nothing in article V limits the discretion of the requested party's competition authorities under its competition laws and enforcement policies about whether to undertake enforcement activities with respect to the anticompetitive activities identified in a request, or precludes the requesting party's competition authorities from undertaking enforcement activities with respect to such anticompetitive activities.

Article VI sets forth principles for the avoidance of conflicts. Within the framework of its own laws and to the extent compatible with its important interests, each party shall, having regard to the purpose of this agreement as set out in article I, give careful consideration to the other party's important interests throughout all phases of its enforcement activities, including decisions regarding the initiation of an investigation or proceeding, the scope of an investigation or proceeding, and the nature of the remedies or penalties sought in each case. When one party informs the other that a specific enforcement activity may affect the first party's important interests, the second party shall provide timely notice of developments of significance to those interests.

While important interests of a party may exist in the absence of official involvement by the party with the activity in question, it is recognized that such interests would normally be reflected in antecedent laws, decisions, or statements of policy by its competent authorities. A party's important interests may be affected at any stage of enforcement activity by the other party. The parties recognize the desirability of minimizing any adverse effects of their enforcement activities on each other's important interests, particularly in the choice of remedies. Typically, the potential for adverse impact on one party's important interests arising from enforcement activity by the other party is less at the investigative stage and greater at the stage at which conduct is prohibited or penalized, or at which other forms of remedial orders are imposed. Where it appears that one party's enforcement activities may adversely affect the important interests of the other party, each party shall, in assessing what measures it will take, consider all appropriate factors, which may include but are not limited to:

(i) the relative significance to the anticompetitive activities involved of conduct occurring within one party's territory as compared to conduct occurring within that of the other;

(ii) the relative significance and foreseeability of the effects of the anticompetitive activities on one party's important interests as compared to the effects on the other party's important interests;

(iii) the presence or absence of a purpose on the part of those engaged in the anticompetitive activities to affect consumers, suppliers or competitors within the enforcing party's territory;

(iv) the degree of conflict or consistency between the first party's enforcement activities (including remedies) and the other party's laws or other important interests;

(v) whether private persons, either natural or legal, will be placed under conflicting requirements by both parties;

(vi) the existence or absence of reasonable expectations that would be furthered or defeated by the enforcement activities;

(vii) the location of relevant assets;

(viii) the degree to which a remedy, in order to be effective, must be carried out within the other party's territory; and

(ix) the extent to which enforcement activities of the other party with respect to the same persons, including judgments or undertakings resulting from such activities, would be affected.

Article VIII provides that either party may request consultations regarding any matter relating to this agreement. Article IX further provides that officials of the parties' competition authorities shall meet at least twice a year to: exchange information on their current enforcement efforts and priorities in relation to their competition and deceptive marketing practices laws, exchange information on economic sectors of common interests, discuss policy changes that they are considering, and discuss other matters of mutual interest relating to the application of their competition and deceptive marketing practices laws and the operation of this agreement.

Article X addresses the issue of confidentiality of information. Notwithstanding any other provision of this agreement, neither party is required to communicate information to the other party if such communication is prohibited by the laws of the party possessing the information or would be incompatible with that party's important interests. Unless otherwise agreed by the parties, each party shall, to the fullest extent possible, maintain the confidentiality of any information communicated to it in confidence by the other party under this agreement. Each party shall oppose, to the fullest extent possible consistent with that party's laws, any application by a third party for disclosure of such confidential information.

The degree to which either party communicates information to the other pursuant to this agreement may be subject to and dependent upon the acceptability of the assurances given by the other party with respect to confidentiality and with respect to the purposes for which the information will be used. Notifications and consultations pursuant to articles II and VIII of this agreement and other communications between the parties in relation thereto shall be deemed to be confidential. A party may not, without the consent of the other party, communicate to its state or provincial authorities information received from the other party pursuant to notifications or consultations under this agreement. The party providing the information shall consider requests for consent sympathetically, taking into account the other party's reasons for seeking disclosure, the risk, if any, that disclosure would pose for its enforcement activities, and any other relevant considerations.

The notified party, after the notifying party's competition authorities have advised a person who is the subject of a notification of the enforcement activities referred to in the notification, may communicate the fact of the notification to, and consult with that person concerning the subject of the notification. Upon request, the notifying party shall promptly inform the notified party of the time at which the person has or will be advised of the enforcement activities in question.

In general, information communicated in confidence by a party's competition authorities to the competition authorities of the other party in the context of enforcement cooperation or coordination shall not be communicated to third parties or to other agencies of the receiving competition authorities' government, without the consent of the competition authorities that provided the information. A party's competition authorities may, however, communicate such information to the party's law enforcement officials for the purpose of competition law enforcement. Similarly, information communicated in confidence by a party's competition authorities to the competition authorities of the other party in the context of enforcement cooperation or coordination pursuant to articles III, IV, or V of this agreement shall not be used for purposes other than competition law enforcement, without the consent of the competition authorities that provided the information.

Nothing in this agreement shall require a party to take any action or to refrain from acting in a manner that is inconsistent with its existing laws, or require any change in the laws of the parties or of their respective provinces or states.[106]

The 1995 Cooperative Agreement was used in a case involving Canada Pipe Company Limited and US Pipe and Foundry Company. Canada Pipe pleaded guilty to conspiring with US Pipe to have the latter exit the Canadian market for ductile iron pipe. The director has stated that he received extensive cooperation from the US Department of Justice that enabled him to secure a record $2.5 million fine.[107] Another example of international cooperation pursuant to the 1995 Cooperative Agreement involves the

---

106 *Ibid.*, art. XI.

107 See Industry Canada, Competition Bureau Statement, *Remarks of George N. Addy, Director of Investigation and Research to the Canadian Institute* (10 May 1996), at 11.

thermal facsimile industry. In 1994, Kanzaki Specialty Papers Inc., a US company, pleaded guilty in the Federal Court of Canada to price fixing and was fined $950,000. Later that year, the court fined Mitsubishi Corporation, of Japan and its Canadian subsidiary, Mitsubishi Canada Limited, $950,000 after they entered guilty pleas to price fixing. In 1995, Rittenhouse Ribbons & Rolls Ltd. was fined $98,000 following a guilty plea to price maintenance. Concurrently, fines have also been imposed in the United States.[108]

In the director's proposed amendments to the Competition Act, explicit statutory authority to share confidential information is sought, although not that which has been voluntarily provided to him, by foreign competition authorities.[109] Such authority is required because reciprocal assistance is a condition of receiving confidential information from US antitrust authorities.[110]

C. 1994 North American Free Trade Agreement[111]

In chapter 15 of the NAFTA, the parties have agreed to adopt or maintain measures to proscribe anticompetitive business conduct and to consult periodically about the effectiveness of measures undertaken by each party. Furthermore, the parties have agreed to cooperate on issues of competition law enforcement with respect to mutual legal assistance, notification, consultation, and exchange of information relating to enforcement. However, the competition provisions are not subject to the dispute settlement provisions of the NAFTA.

NAFTA, chapter 15 expressly provides that the parties may designate a monopoly and may maintain or establish state enterprises. Article 1502:3 provides that:

> ... each party shall ensure, through regulatory control, administrative supervision or the application of other measures, that any privately-owned monopoly that it designates and any government monopoly that it maintains or designates:
>
> (a) acts in a manner that is not inconsistent with the party's obligations under this Agreement wherever such a monopoly exercises any regulatory, administrative or other governmental authority that the party has delegated to it in connection with the monopoly good or service, such as the power to grant import or export licenses, approve commercial transactions or impose quotas, fees or other charges;
>
> (b) except to comply with any terms of its designation that are not inconsistent with subparagraph (c) or (d), acts solely in accordance with commercial considerations in its purchase or sale of the monopoly good or service in the relevant market, including with regard to price, quality, availability, marketability, transportation and other terms and conditions of purchase or sale;

---

108 *Ibid.*

109 *Ibid.*

110 Pub. L 103-438, 2 November 1994, 108 Stat. 4597 (15 USCA, ss. 46, 57b-1, 1311, 1312, 6201, 6201n, and 6202 to 6212).

111 Chapter J of the 17 December 1996 Canada-Chile Free Trade Agreement contains a similar provision on competition policy, monopolies, and state enterprises.

(c) provides non-discriminatory treatment to investments of investors, to goods and to service providers of another party in its purchase or sale of the monopoly good or service in the relevant market; and

(d) does not use its monopoly position to engage, either directly or indirectly, including through its dealings with its parent, its subsidiary or other enterprise with common ownership, in anticompetitive practices in a non-monopolized market in its territory that adversely affect an investment of an investor of another party, including through the discriminatory provision of the monopoly good or service, cross-subsidization or predatory conduct.

However, paragraph 3 does not apply to procurement by governmental agencies of goods or services for governmental purposes and not with a view to commercial resale or with a view to use in the production of goods or the provision of services for commercial sale.

Article 1503 provides that nothing in this agreement shall be construed to prevent a party from maintaining or establishing a state enterprise. Each party shall ensure, through regulatory control, administrative supervision, or the application of other measures that any state enterprise that it maintains or establishes acts in a manner that is not inconsistent with the party's obligations under chapters 11 (investment) and 14 (financial services), wherever such enterprise exercises any regulatory, administrative, or other governmental authority that the party has delegated to it, such as the power to expropriate, grant licences, approve commercial transactions, or impose quotas, fees, or other charges. Each party shall ensure that any state enterprise that it maintains or establishes accords non-discriminatory treatment in the sale of its goods or services to investments in the party's territory of investors of another party.

For purposes of article 1503(3), "state enterprise" with respect to Canada means a Crown corporation within the meaning of the Financial Administration Act (Canada)[112] or a Crown corporation within the meaning of any comparable provincial law or equivalent entity that is incorporated under other applicable provincial law.

The parties also agreed to set up a working group on trade and competition with a five-year mandate to make recommendations on the relationship between competition laws and trade laws. Traditional trade law matters, such as subsidies and dumping, are not subjected to any discipline, but are subjected to a specialized dispute settlement provision that authorizes panels to determine whether each party correctly applied its own laws to a given case. As a condition of signing the NAFTA, the Canadian government insisted on the continuation of the work begun under article 1907 of the Canada-US Free Trade Agreement (FTA) with respect to developing more effective rules and disciplines concerning the use of government subsidies, and a substitute system of rules for dealing with unfair pricing and government subsidization. That working group was supposed to fulfill the unexpired mandate established under article 1907 and to terminate on December 31, 1995.[113] However, the working group has been continued informally.

112 RSC 1985, c. F-11, as am.

113 Office of the Prime Minister, *Prime Minister Announces NAFTA Improvements; Canada to Proceed with Agreement* (2 December 1993).

Article M-05 of the December 17, 1996 Canada-Chile Free Trade Agreement establishes a bilateral Committee on Trade Remedies to, *inter alia*:

(a) consult with a view to defining subsidy disciplines further and eliminating the need for domestic countervailing duty measures on trade between them;

(b) work together in multilateral fora, including the World Trade Organization, and in the context of negotiating Chile's full accession to the NAFTA and the establishment of a Free Trade Area of the Americas, with a view to improving trade remedy regimes to minimize their potential to impede trade;

(c) consult on opportunities for working together with other like-minded countries with a view to expanding agreement on the elimination of the application of anti-dumping measures within free trade areas; ... [and]

(e) meet annually, and on the request of either Party, to review the operation of this Chapter and other related matters including competition laws and policies.

In article M-06, the parties further agreed to meet to review this chapter and to determine whether any changes should be made to its provisions, not later than five years after the coming into force of the agreement.

Some suggestions have been made for expanding the scope of the NAFTA's competition coverage, but so far they have not been adopted.[114] They include identifying as a fundamental NAFTA goal the creation of a barrier-free North America and limit anticompetitive government acts that undermine that goal; creating formal mechanisms for mutual notification, consultation, and cooperation; adopting a "direct substantial and reasonably foreseeable" jurisdiction test; prohibiting "hard-core cartels"; harmonizing procedures; replacing anti-dumping laws with competition laws; and developing dispute settlement mechanisms for competition disputes.

D. Informal Multilateral Cooperation Under the Auspices of the Organisation for Economic Co-operation and Development[115]

The closest thing to an international agreement in respect of competition law matters remains the competition provisions of the OECD *Guidelines for Multinational Enterprises* set forth in the 1976 OECD *Declaration on International Investment and Multinational Enterprises*. These guidelines, of course, are not binding, but they do specify the matters that, if made mandatory, could form the basis of a limited agreement on substantive competition law matters.[116] For example, enterprises are advised to conform to the official competition rules of the countries in which they operate. Specifically, enterprises

114 American Bar Association Section of Antitrust Law, *Task Force Report on the Competition Dimension of NAFTA* (1994) and Canadian Bar Association National Competition Law Section, *Commentary on the Competition Dimension of the NAFTA* (1995).

115 See OECD Convention on the Organisation for Economic Co-operation and Development, 14 December 1960, TIAS no. 4891, 12 UST 1728. See also Kintner, Joelson, and Vaghi, "Groping for a Truly International Antitrust Law" (1973), 14 *Va. J Int'l. L* 75, at 94, and UN Set of Multilaterally Agreed Equitable Principles and Rules for the Control of Restrictive Business Practices (1980), 19 *Int'l. Leg. Mat.* 813.

116 OECD, *The OECD Guidelines for Multinational Enterprises* (1994).

are advised to refrain from taking actions that would adversely affect competition in a relevant market, by abusing market power or a dominant position with respect to anticompetitive acquisitions; predatory behaviour toward competitors; unreasonable refusals to deal; anticompetitive abuse of intellectual property rights; discriminatory pricing, including transfer pricing; and cartel behaviour. However, other enumerated provisions would probably be the subject of intense debate because some relate to vertical practices that, as discussed above, probably tend not to be anticompetitive in the absence of market power. Of course, to become operational, the Guidelines would require intense negotiations around such issues as binding and enforceable dispute settlement provisions.

Nonetheless, the Committee of Experts on Restrictive Business Practices of the OECD, has prepared several recommendations on cooperation between member states on restrictive business practices affecting international trade that have been adopted by the council of the OECD. The recommendation of September 25, 1979[117] provided for intergovernmental cooperation on a purely voluntary basis without impairment of sovereignty and in accordance with each state's laws and policies in the following areas: notification, exchange of information, coordination of action, consultation, and conciliation.

In 1984, at a ministerial meeting to review the 1976 Guidelines for Multinational Enterprises,[118] as amended in 1979, the ministers endorsed certain general considerations and practical approaches dealing with conflicting legal requirements.[119] Some are particularly relevant to conflicts of jurisdiction in the competition field:

> 27. In contemplating new legislation, action under existing legislation or other exercise of jurisdiction which may conflict with the legal requirements or established policies of another Member country and lead to conflicting requirements being imposed on multinational enterprises, the Member countries should:
>
> (i) Have regard to relevant principles of international law;
>
> (ii) Endeavour to avoid or minimize such conflicts and the problems to which they give rise by following an approach of moderation and restraint, respecting and accommodating the interests of other Member countries;
>
> (iii) Take fully into account the sovereignty and legitimate economic, law enforcement and other interests of other Member countries;
>
> (iv) Bear in mind the importance of permitting the observance of contractual obligations and the possible adverse impact of measures having a retroactive effect.

The practical approaches include, *inter alia*, cooperation pursued on a bilateral basis and prompt and sympathetic consideration to requests for notification and bilateral consultation on an *ad hoc* basis made by any member state that considers that its interests

---

117 C(79) 154 (Final). See also Recommendation of 5 October 1967 (C(67) 52 (Final)) and Recommendation of 3 July 1973 concerning a Consultation and Conciliation Procedure on Restrictive Business Practices Affecting International Trade (C(73) 99 (Final)).

118 Paras. 4 to 8 of these guidelines deal with competition.

119 Paras. 23 to 30 DOC C/MIN (84) 5 (Final). See also Recommendation for Co-operation between Member Countries in Areas of Potential Conflict between Competition and Trade Policies, adopted by Council of OECD on 23 October 1986 (1987), 26 *Int'l. Leg. Mat.* 857.

may be affected by any conflicting measure taken by another member state with which it does not have such bilateral arrangements.

In 1986, the OECD revised the 1979 Recommendation,[120] and more recently in 1995 revised it again.[121] Like the 1995 Cooperative Agreement, the 1995 Recommendation emphasizes coordination of investigations and assistance in an investigation or proceeding in a member country; strengthens the protections for confidentiality information; and specifies more detail to be included in merger investigations. The suggested steps for coordination are:[122]

(a) providing notice of applicable time periods and schedules for decision-making;

(b) sharing factual and analytical information and material, subject to national laws governing the confidentiality of information and the principles relating to confidential information set forth in the Recommendation;

(c) requesting, in appropriate circumstances, that the subjects of the investigation voluntarily permit the co-operating countries to share some or all of the information in their possession, to the extent permitted by national laws;

(d) co-ordinating discussions or negotiations regarding remedial actions, particularly when such remedies could require conduct or behaviour in the territory on more than one member country; and

(e) in those member countries in which advance notification of mergers is required or permitted, requesting that the notification include a statement identifying notifications also made or to be made to other countries.

The suggested steps for cooperation are:[123]

(a) assisting in obtaining information on a voluntary basis from within the assisting member's country;

(b) providing factual and analytical material from its files, subject to national laws governing the confidentiality of information and the principles relating to confidential information set forth in the Recommendation;

(c) employing on behalf of the requesting member country its authority to compel the production of information in the form of testimony or documents, where the national laws of the requested member country provides for such authority; and

(d) providing information in the public domain relating to the relevant conduct of practice. To facilitate the exchange of such information, member countries should consider collecting and maintaining data about the nature and sources of such public information to which other member countries could refer.

The recommendation suggests that when one member country learns of an anticompetitive practice occurring in the territory of second member that could violate

---

120 The Revised Recommendation Concerning Cooperation Between Member Countries on Restrictive Business Practices Affecting International Trade (C(86) 44 (Final)).

121 Revised Recommendation of the Council Concerning Co-Operation Between Member Countries on Anticompetitive Practices Affecting International Trade (C(95) 130 (Final).

122 *Ibid.*, s. 5.

123 *Ibid.*, s. 6.

the laws of the second member, the first should consider informing the second and providing as much information as practicable subject to the national law of the first country.

Furthermore, the recommendation suggests that:[124]

(a) member countries should use moderation and self-restraint and take into account the substantive and procedural rules in the foreign forum when exercising their investigatory powers with a view to obtaining information located abroad;

(b) before seeking information located abroad, member countries should consider whether adequate information is available within their own country; and

(c) any requests for information abroad should be framed in terms that are as specific as possible.

E. Possible Future Cooperation Under the Auspices of the World Trade Organization

In 1944, US President Franklin Roosevelt, among others, urged that measures to protect competition in world trade should be included in the foundation document of the International Trade Organization (ITO), the Havana Charter.[125] The draft Havana Charter would have obliged the members of the proposed ITO to take "appropriate" measures to prevent private commercial enterprises that had "effective control of trade" from "restrain[ing]competition, limit[ing] access to markets, or foster[ing] monopolistic control in international trade" where such conduct would "have harmful effects on production and trade and interfere with the achievement" of the Charter's objectives.[126] Harmful effects were presumed (although rebuttable) in the case of price fixing, allocation of markets, boycotts, suppression of technology, unauthorized extension of patent monopolies, and other specified conduct.[127] Under the Havana Charter, member countries could complain about prohibited restraints (where enterprises "possess effective control of trade among a number of countries in one or more products"). The ITO could then investigate and could demand information in the course of its investigation, it could recommend remedial action to government's of member nations[128] However, because of US Congressional concerns over sovereignty, the ITO never came into fruition, and the GATT text never included the competition language.[129]

More recently, traditional competition principles have been added to international trade agreements. article 9 of the Agreement on Trade-Related Investment Measures (TRIMS) does set forth a five-year time period for the Council for Trade in Goods to

124 *Ibid.*, s. 10.

125 Havana Charter for an ITO, UN doc. E/Conf. 2/78 (1948, reprinted in UN doc. ICITO/1/4 (1948)).

126 *Ibid.*, art. 46, c. V.

127 *Ibid.*, arts. 46(1) to (3).

128 *Ibid.*, art. 48.

129 Fox, "Competition Law and the Next Agenda for the WTO" in OECD, *New Dimensions of Market Access in a Globalising World Economy* (1995).

consider whether the TRIMS agreement should be "complemented with provisions on investment and competition policy."

Other important competition principles may be found in articles VIII and IX of the General Agreement on Trade in Services (GATS). These provisions relate specifically to monopolies and exclusive service suppliers and business practices of service suppliers. Article VIII provides that each member "shall ensure that such a supplier does not abuse its monopoly position" to act in a manner inconsistent with the GATS article II most favoured nation provision and other "specific commitments." In article IX, the members recognize that certain unspecified "other business practices of service suppliers ... may restrain competition, and thereby restrict trade in services." The members further agree to cooperate in eliminating such practices.

Furthermore, in article 40 of the Agreement on Trade Related Aspects of Intellectual Property Rights (TRIPS), the members agree that "some licensing practices or conditions pertaining to intellectual property rights which restrain competition may have adverse effects on trade and may impede the transfer and dissemination of technology." Article 40 lists as examples of such anticompetitive practices "exclusive grantback provisions, conditions preventing challenges to validity and coercive package licensing."

Most recently, in the Inter-Ministerial Meeting of the WTO held in Singapore in December 1996, the members formally recognized the importance of competition policy to the world trading order by agreeing:[130]

> to establish a working group to study issues raised by Members relating to the interaction between trade and competition policy, including anti-competitive practices, in order to identify areas that merit further consideration in the WTO framework.

IX. CONCLUSION

In the regulation of competition field, it must be recognized that anticompetitive impact upon the domestic market of a state constitutes a reasonable link that should be recognized by international law as a valid basis for that state to assert jurisdiction to prescribe with extraterritorial reach. On the other hand, if the effects of the foreign conduct do not result in substantial and direct restraints on competition in the domestic market of the regulating state, jurisdiction to prescribe is not justified.

A case could be made in favour of a balanced regime of unilateral extraterritorial enforcement where at least one of the defendants is a citizen of the enforcing state and also in the case of evasion of the competition laws of the territorial state by unscrupulous transnational enterprises. Strict territoriality is unworkable in this field of the law because it encourages shopping for a state free of legal restrictions. Also, it can affect adversely domestic consumers and competitors of enterprises acting anticompetitively abroad. Illegal conduct aimed at the territory from the outside, especially by foreigners, may be difficult to detect and to sanction by authorities whose information gathering and enforcement procedures are territorially limited.

---

130 WTO, Singapore Ministerial Declaration, adopted on 13 December 1996, WT/MIN(96)/DEC. A similar working group was also established to look at trade and investment issues.

Extraterritorial enforcement of the laws regulating competition has legitimate objectives, when it is applied with sensitivity to foreign sovereign interests, to deter the purely private anticompetitive conduct of the nationals of the regulating state not encouraged by foreign laws or policies in order to reach unambiguous violations of domestic law recognized by other states and causing direct and substantial harm to the domestic market.

To the extent that countries can cooperate in the investigation and enforcement of anticompetitive practices that have an international dimension, the legal concerns over extraterritoriality will recede in importance. In fact, the increased global and North American integration appears to be having that effect.

X. SELECTED BIBLIOGRAPHY

A. Books

American Bar Association Section of Antitrust Law, *Report of the Special Committee on International Antitrust* (1991).

American Bar Association Section of Antitrust Law, *Report of the Task Force of the ABA Section of Antitrust Law on the Competition Dimension of NAFTA* (1994).

Brewster, *Antitrust and American Business Abroad* (1st ed., 1958; 2nd ed., 1981), 2 vols. with J.R. Atwood.

Canadian Bar Association National Competition Law Section, *Commentary on the Competition Dimension of the NAFTA* (1995).

Castel, *Extraterritoriality in International Trade. Canada and United States of America Practices Compared* (1988).

Edwards and Bruchey, *Economic and Political Aspects of International Cartels* (1976).

Feltham, Salem, Mathieson, and Wonnacott, *Competition (Antitrust) and Anti-Dumping Laws in the Context of the Canada-US Free Trade Agreement. A Study for the Committee on Canada-United States Relations of the Canadian Chamber of Commerce and the Chamber of Commerce of the United States* (1991).

Global Forum on Competition and Trade Policy, *Harmonization of International Competition Law Enforcement* (1995).

Goldman and Bodrug, *Competition Law of Canada* (1995).

Industry Canada, *Merger Enforcement Guidelines* (1991).

Industry Canada, *Strategic Alliances Under the Competition Act* (1995).

OECD (European Productivity Agency), *Guide to Legislation on Restrictive Business Practices: Europe and North America*, 3 vols.

OECD, *Market Access After the Uruguay Round: Investment, Competition and Technology Perspectives* (1996).

OECD, *Merger Cases in the Real World: A Study of Merger Control Procedures* (1994).

OECD, *New Dimensions of Market Access in a Globalising World Economy* (1995).

OECD, *OECD Guidelines for Multinational Enterprises* (1994).

United States Department of Justice, Antitrust Division, *Antitrust Guide for International Operation*, 26 January 1977.

B. Articles and Papers

Baker, "Antitrust Conflicts Between Friends: Canada and the United States in the Mid-1970's" (1978), 11 *Cornell Int'l. LJ* 165.

Baker, "Extraterritorial Application of United States Antitrust Law: Problems for Canada—Recommendations for the United States and Canada" (1979), 2 *Can.-US LJ* 152.

Campbell, "The Canada-United States Antitrust Notification and Consultation Procedure, A Study in Bilateral Conflict Resolution" (1978), 56 *Can. Bar Rev.* 459.

"Cooperative Antitrust Enforcement Efforts Between Canada and the United States: Investigations, Information Sharing and Confidentiality in Criminal Proceedings," *ABA Section of Antitrust Law Unpublished Paper* (1995).

Davidson, "The Canadian Response to the Overseas Reach of United States Antitrust Law: Stage I and Stage II Amendments to the Combines Investigation Act" (1979), 2 *Can.-US LJ* 166.

Feltham, "The Extraterritorial Application of Domestic Law II: Antitrust Law, The Canadian Radio Patents Case, The Peat Moss Case" (1960), 1 *UBC L Rev.* 340.

Goldman et al., "International Mergers and the Canadian Competition Act," *Fordham Corporate Law Institute* (1992).

Goldman and Kisack, "Joint Sovereign Criminal Investigations: US and Foreign Governments—Can They Really Do That?—A Canadian Perspective," *ABA Section of Antitrust Law Unpublished Paper* (1995).

Griffin, "The Impact on Canada of the Extraterritorial Application of the US Antitrust Laws" (1988), 57 *Antitrust LJ* 435.

Grippando, "Declining to Exercise Extraterritorial Antitrust Jurisdiction on Grounds of International Comity" (1983), 23 *Va. J Int'l. L* 395.

Grover, "Canadian Antitrust Aspects of Competing in Foreign Markets" (1988), 14 *Can.-US LJ* 93.

Grover and Kwinter, "The New Competition Act" (1987), 66 *Can. Bar Rev.* 267.

Idot, "Les conflits de lois en droit de la concurrence" (1995), 122 *JDI* 32.

Kines, "Confidentiality, Conflicts and Comity: Problems and Solutions in the New Era of International Co-operation for the Purposes of Enhancing Competition Law Enforcement" (1996), 43 *Netherlands Int. L Rev.* 19.

Pappe, "The Canadian Competition Act: A Leap Forward" (1988), 22 *Int'l. Law* 1071.

"Recent Canadian Blocking Legislation: A Vehicle to Foster Extraterritorial Discovery Cooperation between the United States and Canada?" (1987), 10 *Fordham Int'l. LJ* 671.

Rosenthal, "Antitrust Implications of the Canada-United States Free Trade Agreement" (1988), 57 *Antitrust LJ* 399.

Warner, "Efficiencies and Merger Reviewing Canada, the European Community and the United States: Implications for Convergence and Harmomization" (1994), 26 *Vanderbilt J of Transnational L* 1059.

CHAPTER SEVENTEEN

Principles of International Business Conduct

I. INTRODUCTION

Individuals and business enterprises, whether Canadian or foreign, when engaged in the export or import of goods and services through branches, wholly owned subsidiaries, joint ventures, agents, or independent distributors, etc., must comply with various principles of business conduct found primarily in the laws and regulations of the states in which they operate. In other words, business enterprises, whatever their legal form, nationality, domicile, or residence, must be "good local corporate citizens." For example, they should not attempt to avoid the payment of local taxes or to circumvent exchange control legislation through transfer pricing. They should not follow foreign directives that are harmful to the host state. They should act in an ethical manner and not make illicit payments or offer bribes to a Canadian or foreign official to obtain a government contract or an import or export licence.

II. REGULATION OF THE CONDUCT OF INTERNATIONAL BUSINESS IN CANADA

A. Regulation of Foreign Direct Investment in Canada

The principal Canadian legislation restricting the ability of a non-Canadian to acquire a Canadian business is the Investment Canada Act (ICA).[1] This is currently the only such legislation of general application. Foreign ownership in specific industries, such as airlines, banks and other financial institutions, and broadcasting systems is regulated by other legislation in a manner similar to foreign ownership restrictions in many other countries.

1. The Investment Canada Act

In general, any investment by a non-Canadian to establish or acquire control of a business carried on in Canada is either notifiable or reviewable under the ICA. Establishments of new Canadian businesses are normally only notifiable. Whether an acquisition is notifiable or reviewable depends on the value of the assets of the Canadian business being acquired. The ICA applies whether or not the acquired business is currently controlled by Canadians and also applies where a Canadian business is acquired indirectly by virtue of the acquisition of a foreign corporation with a Canadian subsidiary. Whether a company is "Canadian" depends on the citizenship or residency of its ultimate controlling shareholders or, in some cases, the members of its board of directors.

Notification, when required, involves the filing of only very basic corporate information and does not represent an impediment to an acquisition. However, if an acquisi-

1 RSC 1985, c. 28 (1st Supp.), as am.

tion is subject to review under the ICA, the acquirer potentially may be required to divest or be prohibited from acquiring the Canadian business if the minister of the federal Cabinet responsible for the ICA is not satisfied that the acquisition is likely to be of "net benefit to Canada."[2]

Generally, acquisitions of Canadian businesses having assets of C$5 million or more or certain "indirect" acquisitions of Canadian businesses having assets of C$50 million or more are reviewable under the ICA. The ICA provides that for "World Trade Organization (WTO) investors" the asset thresholds must be adjusted annually for inflation so that the statutory review thresholds are maintained in real terms.[3] However, acquisitions of some types of "cultural businesses" may be subject to review under the ICA, regardless of the value of the assets involved. Even the establishment of new "cultural business" can be subjected to a review and, potentially, an order to divest. In fact, the special rules for WTO investors do not apply in respect of an investment to acquire control of a Canadian business that engages in the production of uranium and owns an interest in a producing uranium property in Canada; provides any financial service, excluding the underwriting and selling of insurance policies; provides any transportation service; or is a cultural business.

For these purposes, a "cultural business" includes the production, sale, or exhibition of books, compact discs, videos, movies, and similar products. The actual scope of this definition is much wider than might first appear because there is no *de minimis* exception to the determination of whether a business carries on any cultural activity. Thus, a convenience store that sells newspapers is likely to be considered a cultural business.

2. Special Rules for "NAFTA Investors" Under the North American Free Trade Agreement

Pursuant to the North American Free Trade Agreement (the NAFTA), there are two sets of review thresholds under the ICA: (1) the general thresholds (described above) that apply to all transactions before the NAFTA, and (2) the higher NAFTA thresholds applicable only to acquisitions by or from a "NAFTA investor."[4] Direct acquisitions of most Canadian businesses by or from a NAFTA investor implemented in 1994 are reviewable if the assets of the business exceed C$153 million. Indirect acquisitions of most Canadian businesses by or from a NAFTA investor are not reviewable at all, but will still be notifiable under the ICA.

---

2 Until 1993, the ICA was administered by an independent agency, Investment Canada, under the supervision of the responsible minister. Effective 25 July 1993, the ICA was administered by a director of investments in the Ministry of Industry, Science and Technology. See SC 1995, c. 1, ss. 45(1) and (2), 50(2), and 51.

3 ICA, s. 14.1 and SC 1994, c. 47, s. 133.

4 The definition of a "NAFTA investor" under the ICA is complex, but is generally similar to the definition of a "Canadian," discussed above, insofar as it relates to citizenship in a country (other than Canada) that is party to the NAFTA.

However, acquisitions of Canadian businesses engaged in (1) uranium mining, (2) certain cultural businesses, (3) certain financial services, and (4) transportation services are excluded from the FTA review thresholds and continue to be subject to the lower general review thresholds. Again, there is no *de minimis* exception to the determination of whether a business carries on any such activities, so that a corporation primarily engaged in some other type of business that also, for example, provides some trucking services is excluded from the higher NAFTA thresholds even if such services represent a very small part of the corporation's activities.

3. The Review Criterion—"Net Benefit to Canada"

If an acquisition is subject to review, the minister responsible for the ICA must be satisfied that the proposed acquisition is likely to be of "net benefit to Canada." The ICA requires the minister to take into account certain factors, including the effect of the acquisition on the level and nature of economic activity in Canada (including employment in Canada); the degree and significance of participation by Canadians in the Canadian business; the effect of the investment on productivity; industrial efficiency; technological development; product innovation and product variety in Canada, the effect of the acquisition on competition in Canada; the compatibility of the acquisition with national industrial, economic, and cultural policies and the contribution of the acquisition to Canada's ability to compete in world markets. However, the ICA does not suggest any weighting or hierarchy to these potentially conflicting factors and it would appear that the minister's decision is not subject to judicial review on the merits.[5]

In order to satisfy the "net benefit" criterion, the minister sometimes requires undertakings from the acquirer. Typical undertakings in the past have related to maintaining existing employees of the Canadian business, guaranteeing participation of Canadians as directors or in management, processing resource products in Canada, making capital expenditures or investing in research and development in Canada, transferring technology to Canada, and protecting the environment and supporting local communities.[6] In order to obtain approval of its acquisition of Woolco's retail stores in Canada, Wal-Mart Inc. provided the minister with an undertaking relating to the identification of the origin of goods on display in its stores and to "make commercially reasonable efforts to provide Canadian-based suppliers with a full and fair opportunity to supply Wal-Mart Canada."[7]

As a practical matter, it may be noted that Investment Canada has not, to date, instituted any formal process to block any acquisition or require divestiture. It would appear that all issues arising to date have been resolved by undertakings. However, it is not possible to measure the number of investments that may not have proceeded because

---

5 *Baril v. Minister of Regional Industrial Expansion*, [1986] 1 FC 328 (CA).

6 See, e.g., *Investment Canada approves Li Ka-shing's acquisition of Husky Oil Limited, Investment Canada News Release* (20 December 1991) and *Investment Canada Approves Bayer's acquisition of Nova/Polysar's Rubber Division, Investment Canada News Release* (21 September 1993).

7 "Wal-Mart Vows To Sell Canadian Talent, Goods," *The Toronto Star*, Wednesday, 3 August 1994.

of indications from Investment Canada that it would not have approved the transaction. In this regard, Investment Canada does not release information concerning its decision making to nearly the same extent as the director under the Competition Act. The ICA has also presented significant impediments to investment in the uranium industry and, until recently, the oil and gas industry in Canada. However, economic factors appear to have forced the federal government in March 1992 to abandon its oil and gas acquisitions policy (which had prohibited the sale of Canadian-controlled oil and gas assets valued in excess of $5 million unless the companies were in financial difficulty). The Minister of Energy, Mines and Resources Canada commented that "the policy imposed increased costs, uncertainty and delays on the industry" and noted that the change was intended to "allow Canadian and foreign oil and gas companies to rationalize their operations and improve their competitiveness in global markets."[8]

Notwithstanding a recent sale of a publishing business by a Crown corporation apparently in contravention of Investment Canada's guidelines for the publishing industry, in our experience Investment Canada is becoming more aggressive in enforcing the ICA with respect to both establishments and acquisitions of cultural businesses. We are aware of recent instances in which Investment Canada has requested undertakings from companies acquiring Canadian businesses that have limited "cultural" activities relative to their business as a whole—for example, to offer for sale or advertise cultural products of Canadian authors or artists. In July 1993, the federal government announced a policy to restrict significantly the ability of a foreign-owned publisher of magazines in Canada to establish new magazines in Canada.[9] Recent "anti-avoidance" amendments to the ICA may also signal more vigorous enforcement of the ICA with respect to cultural businesses.

B. Canadian Directives to Foreign Corporations and Their Subsidiaries and Affiliates

The ICA is the successor to the Foreign Investment Review Act (FIRA).[10] The FIRA was enacted as a consequence of 1960s concerns over the level of foreign ownership and control of Canadian industry.[11] The FIRA created a Foreign Investment Review Agency, which reviewed foreign investment whether effected through new establishment or acquisition. The agency referred such investment under a test of "significant benefit" to Canada, not the current "net benefit" test established in 1985 upon the creation of Investment Canada. However, in reviewing such investments, the agency considered the same statutory factors considered by Investment Canada, and now the director of investments in the Ministry of Industry, Science and Technology.

8 Energy Mines and Resources Canada, news release (25 March 1992).

9 Related business guidelines, July 1993 issued by the Minister of Industry, Science and Technology under the authority of s. 38 of the ICA and "Magazines Offered Canadian Shield," *Globe and Mail*, 20 July 1993.

10 SC 1973-1974, c. 56.

11 Warner, "Appendix: A History of United States-Canada Trade and Investment Relations" in Rugman, *Multinationals and Canada-United States Free Trade* (1990).

While FIRA was revised in 1985, other policies and guidelines enacted at the same time and with the same motive were not formally revised. An example of such policies are the following principles of good corporate behaviour that were recommended by the Canadian government in July 1975.[12] While these guidelines were never actively enforced, they may still be relevant since the rise of globalization and tariff and non-tariff barriers to trade have forced Canadian subsidiaries increasingly to negotiate with their foreign parents for world product mandates or otherwise to justify their existence.[13] The guidelines provide that foreign businesses must pursue policies that will foster their independence in decision making, their innovative and other entrepreneurial capabilities, their efficiency, and their identification with Canada and the aspirations of the Canadian people.

If following these guidelines, foreign-controlled firms in Canada would:

1. Pursue a high degree of autonomy in the exercise of decision-making and risk-taking functions, including innovative activity and the marketing of any resulting new products.
2. Develop as an integral part of the Canadian operation an autonomous capability for technological innovation, including research, development, engineering, industrial design and preproduction activities; and for production, marketing, purchasing and accounting.
3. Retain in Canada a sufficient share of earnings to give strong financial support to the growth and entrepreneurial potential of the Canadian operation, having in mind a fair return to shareholders on capital invested.
4. Strive for a full international mandate for innovation and market development, when it will enable the Canadian company to improve its efficiency by specialization of productive operations.
5. Aggressively pursue and develop market opportunities throughout international markets as well as in Canada.
6. Extend the processing in Canada of natural resource products to the maximum extent feasible on an economic basis.
7. Search out and develop economic sources of supply in Canada for domestically produced goods and for professional and other services.
8. Foster a Canadian outlook within management, as well as enlarged career opportunities within Canada, by promoting Canadians to senior and middle management positions, by assisting this process with an effective management training program, and by including a majority of Canadians on boards of directors of all Canadian companies, in accordance with the spirit of federal legislative initiatives.
9. Create a financial structure that provides opportunity for substantial equity participation in the Canadian enterprise by the Canadian public.
10. Pursue a pricing policy designed to ensure a fair and reasonable return to the company and to Canada for all goods and services sold abroad, including sales to parent companies and

---

12 (Ottawa: Supply and Services, 1975). See also Department of Trade and Commerce, *Foreign-Owned Subsidiaries in Canada* (1967), at 40-41: "Some Guiding Principles of Good Corporate Behaviour for Subsidiaries in Canada of Foreign Companies."

13 Morrison and Crookell, "Free Trade: The Impact on Canadian Subsidiary Strategy" in Radebaugh, *Investment in the North American Free Trade Area* (1991).

other affiliates. In respect of purchases from parent companies and affiliates abroad, pursue a price policy designed to ensure that the terms are at least as favourable as those offered by other suppliers.

11. Regularly publish information on the operations and financial position of the firm.

12. Give appropriate support to recognized national objectives and established government programs, while resisting any direct or indirect pressure from foreign governments or associated companies to act in a contrary manner.

13. Participate in Canadian social and cultural life and support those institutions that are concerned with the intellectual, social, and cultural advancement of the Canadian community.

14. Endeavour to ensure that access to foreign resources, including technology and know-how, is not associated with terms and conditions that restrain the firm from observing these principles.

Principles 4, 5, 7, 10, and 14 are particularly relevant to the export and import of Canadian and foreign goods and services.

C. Trade Law and the Regulation of International Business Conduct

The contracting parties to the GATT have addressed trade-related investment measures (TRIMS) squarely in a decision that arose out of a complaint by the United States against certain aspects of the then Canadian FIRA.[14] The FIRA provided that an independent review agency would consider certain factors in determining whether a proposed investment was or was likely to be of "significant benefit" to Canada.[15] Although the FIRA did not require that investors give written undertakings to demonstrate how an investment would satisfy this test, as the FIRA was administered such undertakings were routinely submitted.[16] The GATT dispute settlement panel (the FIRA panel) found, as a matter of fact, that:[17]

> Undertakings given by investors [dealt] with any aspect of the conduct of a business, *including employment, research and development*, participation of Canadian shareholders and managers, productivity improvements as well as practices with respect to purchasing, manufacturing and exports. (Italics added.)

The United States asked the FIRA panel to find that undertakings that, *inter alia*, required investors to (1) purchase goods of Canadian origin in preference to imported goods or to purchase from Canadian sources and (2) manufacture in Canada goods that would be imported otherwise, were inconsistent with *inter alia*, GATT, articles III.4,

14 GATT, "Canada—Administration of the Foreign Investment Review Act, Report of the Panel adopted by the GATT Council on 7 February 1984 (L/5504)," *Basic Instruments and Selected Documents: Thirtieth Supp.* (Geneva: GATT, 1984), at 140.

15 S. 2(2), FIRA, SC 1973, c. 46, as am.; repealed by s. 46, Investment Canada Act, RSC 1985, c. 28 (1st Supp.), as am.

16 S. 2.4, *supra*, note 10.

17 *Ibid.*

III.5, and XI.[18] Holding that it was not covered by its terms of reference, the FIRA Panel did not examine the issue of the domestic content requirements.[19] However, the FIRA panel did find that the requirements to purchase Canadian goods or from Canadian sources were inconsistent with Canada's national treatment obligations set out in article III.4 of the GATT.[20] The FIRA panel found further that such undertakings were not saved by additional language that conditioned the performance of the undertaking on Canadian goods being "competitively available" or "reasonably available."[21] The FIRA panel stated that:[22]

> ... in those cases where the imported and domestic product are offered on equivalent terms, adherence to the undertaking would entail giving preference to the domestic product. Whether or not the investor chooses to buy Canadian goods in given practical situations, is not at issue. The purpose of Article III.4 is not to protect the interests of the foreign investor but to ensure that goods originating in any Contracting Party benefit from treatment no less favourable than domestic ... goods, in respect of the requirements that affect their purchase .... The Panel considered that the alternative qualification "reasonably available ..." is *a fortiori* inconsistent with Article III.4, since the undertaking implies that preference has to be given ... when these are not available on entirely competitive terms.

In the Punta del Este Declaration,[23] which opened the Uruguay Round of the GATT negotiations, the assembled trade ministers agreed to (1) examine the operation of GATT articles related to the trade restrictive and distorting effects of investment measures and (2) elaborate, as appropriate, further provisions that may be necessary to avoid such adverse effects. On December 15, 1993, participants in the Uruguay Round negotiations reached an agreement to provide for a new framework to govern trade relations and to establish the World Trade Organization (WTO).[24] The TRIMS are addressed in part II:7 of the Final Act (the TRIMS Agreement).[25] In the preamble to the TRIMS Agreement, the members recognize that "certain investment measures can cause trade restrictive and distorting effects."[26] In article 2.1 of the TRIMS Agreement, the members agree that "Without prejudice to other rights and obligations under the GATT 1994, no Member

18 *Ibid.*, s. 3.1.

19 *Ibid.*, s. 5.3.

20 *Ibid.*, ss. 5.8 and 5.10.

21 *Ibid.*, ss. 5.9 and 5.11.

22 *Ibid.*; see also s. 5.11.

23 GATT, "Ministerial Declaration on the Uruguay Round: Declaration of 20 September 1986," *Basic Instruments and Selected Documents: Thirty-Third Supp.* (1987), at 19.

24 Final Act Embodying the Results of the Uruguay Round of Multilateral Trade Negotiations (the Final Act), MTN/FA, 15 December 1993, Special Distribution (UR-93-0246). Before accepting the Agreement Establishing the WTO (the GATT 1994) and thereby becoming Members of the WTO, participants who are not contracting parties to the GATT 1947, as subsequently am., must conclude negotiations for their accession to the GATT 1947. See MTN/FA I, art. 5 and MTN/FA II, art. II.4.

25 *Ibid.*, MTN/FA II-A1A-7.

26 *Ibid.*

shall apply any TRIM that is inconsistent with the provisions of Article III or Article XI of the GATT 1994."

Article III.1 of the GATT establishes the principle of national treatment (NT) and GATT, article XI sets out the general prohibition of quantitative restrictions. In particular, article III.4 of the GATT provides that:

The products of the territory of any contracting party imported into the territory of any other contracting party shall be accorded treatment no less favourable than that accorded to like products of national origin *in respect of all laws, regulations and requirements affecting their internal sale, offering for sale, purchase transportation, distribution or use. ...* (Italics added.)

Article III.5 of the GATT generally prohibits domestic sourcing requirements:

No contracting party shall establish or maintain any internal quantitative regulation relating to the mixture, processing or use of products in specified amounts or proportions which requires, directly or indirectly, that any specified amount or proportion of any product which is the subject of the regulation must be supplied *from domestic sources.* Moreover, no contracting party shall otherwise apply internal quantitative regulations in a manner contrary to the principles set forth in paragraph 1. (Italics added.)

Article III.4 and 5 of the GATT, therefore, would appear to proscribe domestic sourcing requirements. In accordance with article 2 of the TRIMS Agreement, an accompanying annex sets out an illustrative list of TRIMS that are inconsistent with article III.4 of the GATT. Not surprisingly, section 1(a) of the TRIMS Agreement indicates that domestic sourcing requirements are inconsistent with GATT, article III.4 if compliance with them is "necessary to obtain an advantage," and if they require "the purchase or use by an enterprise of products of domestic origin or from any domestic source. ..."[27]

More recently, the Organisation for Economic Co-operation and Development (OECD) has begun work on a multilateral agreement on investments, but as of the time of writing negotiations were not completed.[28]

D. Corporate Residency Requirements

In addition to the guidelines, the Canada Business Corporations Act (CBCA)[29] now requires the following: that a majority of the board of directors be resident Canadians;

---

27 Furthermore, art. 5.1 of the TRIMS Agreement provides that each member will notify, within 90 days of the establishment of the WTO on or before 1 July 1995, all non-conforming TRIMS to the Council for Trade in Goods, a unit of the WTO. Art. 5.2 further provides that each developed country Member shall eliminate all notified TRIMs within two years from the establishment of the WTO. In the case of developing countries and less-developed countries, art. 5.2 extends the time limit to five and seven years, respectively. A footnote to art. 5.1 also provides that in the case of TRIMS applied under discretionary authority each specific application shall be notified to the Council on Trade in Goods.

28 Hart, "A Multilateral Agreement on Foreign Direct Investment: Why Now" in Sauvé and Schwanen (eds.), *Investment Rules for the Global Economy: Enhancing Market Access Through Market Presence* (May 1996).

29 RSC, 1985, c. C-44, as am.

directors shall not transact business at a board meeting unless a majority of directors present are resident Canadians; a majority of members of each committee of the board must be resident Canadians; corporate records must be maintained in Canada; if the directors' records (which include the accounting records) are maintained outside Canada, "accounting records adequate to enable the directors to ascertain the financial position of the corporation with reasonable accuracy on a quarterly basis" must be available in Canada; the corporation must have a registered office in Canada; and shareholder meetings must be held in Canada, unless the shareholders unanimously agree to hold the meeting outside Canada.[30]

These requirements were adopted in the 1970s amid concerns over the level of foreign ownership and control of Canadian industry. After nearly 50 years of increased foreign direct investment, which was seen by the federal government as calling into question the economic independence of Canada, some argue that the residency requirements can help foreign-controlled firms understand the economic, political, and social environment of Canada, and that reducing or eliminating them could undermine the ability of the federal government to collect unpaid taxes and source deductions. The requirements are said to be an extremely significant ingredient in encouraging the board to ensure statutory compliance and in the enforcement of rights and liabilities under the Income Tax Act and all other legislation providing for directors' liability. Another factor in the introduction of the directors' residency requirements was the extraterritorial application of foreign laws.[31] However, some business people have complained that the residency requirement inhibits the ability of globally oriented Canadian companies to penetrate foreign markets. Others have pointed out that this requirement can also inhibit the inflow of investment to Canada. Furthermore, it makes other jurisdictions more attractive to investors who may feel that the residency requirements inhibit control over their company's decision making.

Article 1107 of the NAFTA, entitled "Senior Management and Boards of Directors" in the chapter on investment, expressly permits countries to require that a majority of the

---

30 *Ibid.*, ss. 105(3), 114(3), 115(2), 20(1), 20(5), 19(1), and 132.

31 The 1963 Cuban Assets Control Regulations, 31 CFR 515 passed under the US Trading with the Enemy Act, prohibited the subsidiaries of US corporations from trading with Cuba. Anyone caught violating a provision of the Act could be fined or imprisoned. In 1974, this Act affected a couple of Canadian subsidiaries. In the spring of 1974, it appeared that the US Government was about to block a sale of locomotives to Cuba by MLW Worthington Ltd. of Montreal, a subsidiary of Studebaker-Worthington of Harrison, NJ. It has been suggested that the two US directors on the subsidiary's board of directors only avoided violating US law by voting against the sale. In another case, in December 1974, a Canadian subsidiary manufacturing company, Cole Division of Litton Business Equipment Ltd., was unable to carry out an order for the sale of furniture to Cuba. At the time, the directors of the Canadian subsidiary of Litton were US citizens and residents. Apparently, Washington did not block the deal but, since the parent company, Litton Business Equipment Ltd., heavily depended on US defence contracts, they chose to interpret the law literally rather than risk trouble with Washington. Both cases were referred to when the CBCA was being considered for adoption. See Industry Canada, *Directors' and Other Corporate Residency Issues*, c. 3 (August 1995).

board of directors or any committee thereof of an enterprise of that party that is an investment of an investor of another party be of a particular nationality or resident in the territory of the party, provided that the requirement does not materially impair the ability of the investor to exercise control over its investment. As permitted by article 1108, the Canadian government has listed the residency requirement under the CBCA as an exception to the requirement in article 1107. Article XVII of the General Agreement on Trade in Service (GATS) makes a commitment to provide NT in service sectors covered by the agreement, subject to certain conditions and qualifications. Because it was considered that the board of director residency requirements might impose on foreign-owned or foreign-controlled Canadian incorporated service suppliers treatment "less favourable" than that accorded to Canadian-owned or Canadian-controlled suppliers, a qualification on NT was listed in the Canadian schedule to the GATS respecting board of director residency requirements. This qualification provides that a majority of the directors of federally incorporated corporations in Canada must be Canadian citizens or persons ordinarily resident in Canada. The exception allows Canada to keep the requirement even if it is non-conforming with the agreement.

In 1995, the Canadian government proposed a number of options for reforming these provisions.[32] However, at the time of writing no changes have been enacted.

III. TRANSFER PRICING NOT REFLECTING AN ARM'S-LENGTH PRICE

Transfer pricing is a versatile tool used by individuals and transnational enterprises in their international business transactions and investments for the avoidance of taxes, tariffs, and custom duties, and for many other purposes. Since often the pricing of goods and services transferred among the units of a transnational enterprise is not recorded in such a way as to correspond to an arm's-length price, the level of the transfer price will affect the profits and, hence, the taxable income, both of the selling and of the buying unit within the transnational enterprise. Thus, the tax authorities of both countries will seek to ascertain that no tax evasion has resulted from the artificial pricing. This is not easy to do due to the fungibility of international capital and the often imprecise and inaccurate manner in which accounting methods report income and loss. The many difficulties that the home and host countries encounter when auditing the accounts of the units of enterprises doing business in several countries encourage resorting to transfer pricing, which does not reflect an arm's-length price. Where it is not possible to establish the arm's-length price, the tax authorities will use other approximations such as cost plus reasonable profits, selling price minus reasonable profits or resale price, reasonable return on capital, or proportionate profits—that is, the total profits of the enterprise split according to the relative costs at its various units.

In general, the rationale for an enterprise engaged in international business to want to resort to transfer pricing for the following purposes:

1. To take advantage of differences in tax rates between jurisdictions. To gain the advantage of higher deductions in high tax jurisdictions, inflated prices may be paid to affiliates in low tax jurisdictions, thereby maximizing global after-tax profits.

32 *Ibid.*

2. To transfer profits from a profitable enterprise to one which would otherwise show a net loss, or expenses from the losing enterprise to one which would otherwise show a profit, through the transfer of goods, services, technology, money, property and employees, possibly at less than market value.

3. To take additional advantage of activities which benefit from lower tax rates, such as manufacturing and processing.

4. To take advantage of higher investment tax credits available in some states.

5. To avoid withholding taxes on dividends or branch profits taxes.

6. To avoid the application of custom duties by keeping the transfer prices of goods crossing international borders low. This may not be prevented by host country income taxes or anti-dumping provisions and custom valuation rules.

7. To circumvent exchange controls where profits remittance is precluded by controls on the export of currency.

8. To minimize taxable surplus and maximize exempt surplus accounts of affiliates.

9. To decrease apparent profits in an affiliate in order to deter labour demands for higher wages and benefits.

10. To minimize investment risks due to political factors in host states with unstable political or economic conditions.

11. To manipulate benefits to shareholders by selling to them or buying from them at inflated or deflated prices.

12. To circumvent profit or price control legislation.

The 1988 Draft United Nations Code of Conduct[33] on Transnational Corporations provides, in article 35 that:

In respect of their intra-corporate transactions, transnational corporations should not use pricing policies that are not based on relevant market prices, or, in the absence of such prices, the arm's-length principle, which have the effect of adversely affecting the tax revenues, the foreign exchange resources or other aspects of the economy of the countries in which they operate.

In Canada, transfer pricing is prohibited under the Income Tax Act administered by Revenue Canada. Revenue Canada has stated that "[i]n basic terms the taxpayer in Canada is expected to report taxable income on the basis of having charged fair prices for goods and services provided to non-resident affiliates, and of having paid no more than a fair price for goods and services received from non-resident affiliates. In this latter connection, it must be emphasized that the taxpayer should not absorb any duplication in the intercompany prices and other charges that are incurred."[34] Revenue Canada interprets sections 69(2) and (3) of the Income Tax Act as requiring that "the amount that the taxpayer in Canada has paid or agreed to pay a non-resident may not,

33 E/1988/39/Add 1, 1 February 1988. In 1990, it was referred to the UN ECOSOC and then to the UN assembly where it was generally felt that no decision should be taken until the outcome of the GATT Uruguay Round (UN doc. E/1990/94).

34 Revenue Canada *Interpretation Circular, 87-2, International Transfer Pricing and other International Issues* (27 February 1987).

for tax purposes, exceed a reasonable arms-length price ... and the amount a non-resident not dealing at arms-length has paid or agreed to pay may not, for tax purposes, be less than a reasonable arms-length price." To the extent possible, the taxpayer should use the arm's-length method of valuation. However, where the approach is "not practicable or proves unrealistic,"[35] or is not possible, the taxpayer may use a number of other methods.

Revenue Canada follows the valuation methods set forth by the OECD in 1979, with a strong preference for clearly defined and established intercompany agreements.[36] The 1995 OECD transfer pricing guidelines set forth clear restrictions on the use of the profit method for deterring transfer pricing. These guidelines limit the use of profit method to situations of last resort and indicate that it would only be acceptable if consistent with the OECD guidelines and the rather strict comparability standards set forth therein. In order to assist the taxpayer with these determinations, Revenue Canada provides a procedure by which an enterprise may apply for an advance pricing agreement to help determine acceptable transfer prices for the purposes of the Canadian Income Tax Act and, where appropriate, under international tax conventions that Canada has entered into with foreign governments.[37]

IV. INTERNATIONAL ECONOMIC BOYCOTTS

A. General

In 1978, the Canadian government adopted the following policy on international economic boycotts.

1. Boycott Activities Prohibited by the Present Policy

The types of activities that the Canadian government finds unacceptable are those that would, in connection with the provisions of any international economic boycott, require a Canadian firm or individual to:

1. engage in discrimination based on the race, national or ethnic origin or religion of any Canadian firm or individual;
2. refuse to purchase from or sell to any other Canadian firm or individual;
3. refuse to sell Canadian goods to any country;
4. refrain from purchases from any country; or
5. restrict commercial investment or other economic activity in any country.

---

35 *Ibid.*, paras. 10 and 11.

36 OECD, *Transfer Pricing and Multinational Enterprises* (1979). On 28 July 1995, the council of the OECD issued revised guidelines in a report entitled Organisation for Economic Co-operation and Development, Transfer Pricing and Multinational Enterprises and Tax Administrations (1995). In a press release, Revenue Canada announced that it would consider the OECD revisions in revising its policy; see Revenue Canada, *News Release 95-059 OECD Transfer Pricing Guidelines Released* (28 July 1995).

37 Revenue Canada, *Interpretation Circular 94-4, Advance Pricing Agreements (APA)* (Dec. 30, 1994).

2. Penalties

The present policy calls for the denial of government support and assistance with respect to a particular transaction for those enterprises that accept boycott provisions in contravention of government policy. In addition, the names of contravening enterprises are published in semi-annual reports tabled in Parliament. Present sanctions for failure to report or refusal to report under the Statistics Act call for a fine not exceeding $500 and three months in jail.[38] Under the Corporations and Labour Unions Returns Act the sanction is a fine of $50 for each day late in reporting.[39]

3. Guidelines for the Implementation of the Canadian Government Policy

1. Primary boycott undertakings continue to be acceptable and generally relate to the refusal of a boycotting country to accept any goods or components of a boycotted country, either directly or through third parties. Furthermore, a Canadian exporter, in shipping goods to a boycotting country, may comply with the shipping document requirements of that country with respect to (1) country of origin of the goods, (2) the name of the carrier, and (3) the route of shipment.

This information must be stated in positive, non-exclusionary terms except for the information with respect to the names of carrier, routes, or shipment that may continue to be negatively stated in conjunction to shipments to a boycotting country.

2. Negative certificates of origin are, as such, unacceptable.
3. Secondary boycott undertakings in general terms may require a Canadian enterprise, as a pre-condition for doing business in boycotting countries, to limit its commercial activities with respect to another country. Since this could involve a relationship separate and distinct from the transaction in question and would require the Canadian enterprise to restrict its commercial freedom, such undertakings are deemed to be at variance with the Canadian government policy.
4. Tertiary boycott undertakings, in general terms, may require an exporter to certify that goods or services are not procured in whole or in part from enterprises with which a boycotting country refuses to do business. Because Canadian enterprises could in this way be limited in their ability to do business with other Canadian enterprises, tertiary boycott undertakings are deemed to be at variance with the Canadian government policy.
5. Clauses requiring a person or firm to furnish information about another person's race, religion, sex, or national origin where such information is sought for boycott enforcement purposes are also deemed to be at variance with the Canadian government policy.
6. Umbrella boycott undertakings and fact-versus-intent clauses:
   a. Some general boycott clauses require Canadian enterprises to either abide by the laws and regulations of the country in which they are doing business, or

38 RSC 1985, c. S-19, s. 31.

39 RSC 1985, c. C-43, s. 9.

to abide by the general rules of the boycott; since there is reasonable doubt as to the intent of these clauses, Canadian enterprises entering into such undertakings are required, in order to receive continued support from the Canadian government, to include in the contract or supporting documentation an addendum provision along the following lines: "... that in meeting the terms of this contract, the sellers are not required to discriminate against any person on the basis of race, religion or national or ethnic origin, and are not required to refuse to purchase from or sell goods and/or services to any other Canadian company, agency or individual, sell Canadian goods and/or services to any country, or purchase goods and/or services from any country, except that it would be the right of the purchaser to refuse to accept goods, components and/or services of specified non-Canadian origin that would be prohibited entry if imported directly. ..."

b. Clauses that are statements of fact, for example, certification that the enterprise has no branch office or plant in a boycotted country, but that could be interpreted as having the effect of limiting an enterprise's future actions (that is, establishing a branch office or plant in the boycotted country) and thereby bring about those results which the policy was designed to prevent, require the provision by the Canadian exporter of a unilateral declaration to the Canadian government along the lines of the addendum in item a.

Firms providing statements of fact are required to attach an addendum to such clauses in order to indicate clearly that such statements of fact are not an indication of intent restricting the enterprise's future actions.

The "unilateral declaration" is also requested whenever Canadian enterprises encounter boycott clauses generally referred to as shipping clauses. These clauses, generally requiring certification that "... the carrying steamer is not included on country X's blacklist," are a standard feature of letter of credit and import documentation of several boycotting countries. While theoretically such undertakings might be viewed as having tertiary boycott connotations, the realities of Canadian shipping, whereby it has been determined that there are no Canadian registered bottoms engaged in trade in areas where economic boycotts are implemented, make it impossible for a Canadian enterprise to engage in discriminatory action against other Canadians in its choice of carrying vessel. Therefore, since these clauses neither limit the freedom of a Canadian enterprise to do business with other Canadian enterprises nor limit the freedom of Canadian enterprises to do business in a third country, it has been ruled that "shipping clauses" do not violate the Canadian government's policy. Nevertheless, to provide assurances on these points, Canadian enterprises encountering the shipping clause are required as a condition for receiving government services, to provide the "unilateral declaration."

The word "prohibited" in the "Status" column indicates that the fact certification or agreement would be considered to contravene the Canadian government's policy on international economic boycotts; the word "Okay" in the "Status" column indicates that the fact certification or agreement provision would not contravene Canadian government policy.

Certification of Fact

Fact Certified	Status
1. Goods are:	
a. of (for example, Canadian) origin ("positive")	Okay
b. not of Israeli origin ("negative")	Prohibited
c. not from blacklisted company	Prohibited (must be removed entirely)
d. not from company co-operating with Israel	Prohibited (must be removed entirely)
e. not manufactured by person in trade in Israel or with the government, nationals, or companies of Israel	Prohibited
2. Supplier/exporter/contractor:	
a. is not itself blacklisted or affiliated with blacklisted company	Okay (However, it would contravene the policy if a Canadian citizen were to make such a statement with respect to another Canadian company.)
b. has no direct/indirect connection with Israel	Okay (as long as it is factual and deals with past or present situation). Enterprise must provide to the Canadian government the addendum provision in the actual contract to ensure that it is not limiting its future business dealings with Israel.
3. Ship carrying goods is not:	
a. blacklisted	Okay (However, it requires the provision of a unilateral declaration.)
b. Israeli owned	Okay (primary boycott)
c. scheduled to call at Israeli port	Okay (primary boycott)
4. Insurer of goods is not blacklisted	Prohibited (must be removed entirely)

(The table is concluded on the next page.)

Agreements

Agreement Provision	Status
5. Will not send Israeli nationals to host Arab country to perform services	Okay (primary boycott)
6. Compliance with import laws of boycotting country	Okay (primary boycott)
7. Compliance with export laws of the boycotted country	Okay (primary boycott)
8. Supplier/exporter will abide by Arab boycott regulations	Not acceptable (unless amended by the inclusion of the standard addendum)
9. Contract and disputes will be governed by host Arab country laws.	Okay
10. Will comply with host Arab country laws	Not acceptable (unless amended by the inclusion of the standard addendum)
11. Customer has the right to prior approval of any subcontractors	Okay
12. Contract specifies permissible subcontractors, but none are "blacklisted"	Prohibited (inasmuch as selection could be done using the "blacklist" criteria. However, client has the right to "unilateral selection" of a supplier.)

Fact Certified	Status
13. Providing information re race, religion, national or ethnic origin, etc.	Prohibited

4. Provincial Legislation

At the provincial level, some provinces such as Ontario have passed legislation that condemns the following discriminatory business practices:[40]

1. A refusal to engage in business with a second person, where the refusal,
   (a) is on account of an attribute,
      (i) of the second person, or
      (ii) of a third person with whom the second person conducts, has conducted or may conduct business; and
   (b) is a condition of the engaging in business of the person making the refusal and another person.
2. A refusal or failure to employ, appoint or promote a second person or a dismissal or suspension of a second person from employment, where the refusal, failure, dismissal or suspension,
   (a) is on account of an attribute,
      (i) of the second person, or
      (ii) of a third person with whom the second person conducts, has conducted or may conduct business; and
   (b) is a condition of the engaging in business of the person making the refusal, failure, suspension or dismissal and another person.
3. Entering into a contract that includes a provision that one of the parties to the contract,
   (a) will refuse to engage in business with a second person; or
   (b) will refuse or fail to employ or promote or will dismiss or suspend from employment a second person, on account of an attribute of the second person or of a third person with whom the second person conducts, has conducted or may conduct business.

Furthermore:[41]

4. No person in Ontario shall seek or provide a statement, whether written or oral, to the effect that any goods or services supplied or rendered by any person or government do not originate in whole or in part in a specific location, territory or country for the purpose of engaging in or assisting in engaging in a discriminatory business practice as defined in section 4, but this subsection does not prohibit a person in Ontario from seeking or providing a statement, whether written or oral, to the effect that any goods or services supplied or rendered by any person or government originate in whole or in part in a specific location, territory or country.

However, the legislation does not apply to:[42]

2. A discriminatory business practice engaged in accordance with a policy of the Government of Canada directed toward trade with a country other than Canada or persons in a country other than Canada or of the Government of Ontario directed toward persons in Provinces or Territories other than Ontario.

---

40 S. 4 of Discriminatory Business Practices Act, RSO 1990, c. D.12, as am., SO 1989, c. 72, s. 26.

41 *Ibid.*, s. 5.

42 *Ibid.*, s. 2.

B. Export Development Corporation (EDC)

The EDC has adopted the following policy and practice:

The corporation will not provide any of the corporation's services in transactions where a Canadian enterprise would be required to:

1. engage in discrimination based on the race, national or ethnic origin or religion of any Canadian or other individual;
2. refuse to purchase from or sell to any other Canadian firm;
3. refuse to sell Canadian goods to any country;
4. refrain from purchasing from any country; or
5. restrict commercial investment or other economic activity in any country.

It is further agreed that the EDC must continue to recognize both a buyer's right to specify what he or she will purchase and a sovereign state's right to exclude the products or services of another country. These are primary boycott considerations recognized and accepted by the EDC and the Canadian government.

In line with this broad statement of policy, the EDC has adopted guidelines and procedures to ensure that its administration of policy remains consistent with its objectives and those of the Canadian government.

The procedure adopted for export credits insurance has been to attach the EDC's boycott endorsement to all contracts covering shipments to boycotting countries. This is necessary because export credits insurance contracts are signed in advance of arrangements to ship, making it impossible for the EDC to review either the exporter's commercial contract with the buyer or the shipping documents for boycott clauses unless and until a claim is made by the exporter. The endorsement makes it clear, however, that no claim will be honoured by the EDC if an unacceptable clause is discovered in shipping or other documents subsequent to the signing of the EDC's insurance contract. This effectively denies export credit insurance to any client who agrees to an unacceptable clause.

Since the EDC's boycott policy was formulated, the EDC has introduced other services for Canadian exporters—for example, performance guarantees, cross-consortium liability insurance, and surety bond insurance. As in the case with export credits insurance, the standard boycott endorsement is attached to all such policies that involve boycotting countries.

Statements of fact regarding past or present relations with a given country could be distinguished from statements of intent to discriminate. The former, if taken at face value, are acceptable because they impose no obligation on the Canadian enterprise to alter its future pattern of business dealings. The latter are clearly unacceptable inasmuch as they would limit an enterprise's freedom to do business in or with a given country in transactions unrelated to the deal in question. The EDC recognizes, however, that boycotting nations may pressure Canadian enterprises to limit their future dealings with a given country once a statement of fact has been made. As an additional assurance that Canadian enterprises making such statements had no intent to agree to unacceptable boycott provisions, the EDC requires them to sign the government's unilateral declaration. The declaration provides the EDC with a written commitment that the firms in question will not allow such statements to limit their future activities.

In instances where firms have encountered boycott clauses referred to as shipping clauses, the EDC's actions have been consistent with government policy.

V. TRADE SANCTIONS

Trade sanctions can be imposed by Canada on an *ad hoc* basis through three mechanisms. The first mechanism is the enactment of federal legislation specifically for that purpose. This does not occur frequently because of the time required to draft and pass such legislation. Sanctions can also be imposed under the United Nations Act.[43] This Act provides the Canadian federal government with the necessary authority to implement UN resolutions in Canada. This has rarely been used. Examples of implementation of economic and trade sanctions pursuant to the United Nations Act include the sanctions enacted with respect to Iraq in 1990.[44] The Iraq regulations prohibit the export from Canada knowingly of any goods to any person in Iraq, either directly or indirectly.

The third legislative basis, pursuant to which the federal government may enact trade or economic sanctions which can effect international distribution, is the Special Economic Measures Act (SEMA).[45] Section 4(1) of the Act authorizes the federal government to impose sanctions when there has been a "grave breach of international peace and security that has occurred that has resulted or is likely to result in a serious international crisis, or when Canada must implement a decision, resolution, or recommendation of an international organization of states or association of states of which Canada is a member, that calls on its members to take economic measures against a foreign state.[46] The sanctions imposed against Haiti were enacted under this legislation.[47]

The federal government may by order cause to be seized, frozen or sequestered any property situated in Canada that is held by or on behalf of a foreign state, any person in that foreign state, or a national of that foreign state who does not ordinarily reside in Canada.[48] The government may also make orders and regulations with respect to the restriction or prohibition of certain enumerated activities in relation to a foreign state.[49] The restricted and enumerated activities provision would seem to apply extraterritorially as it applies "with respect to the restriction or prohibition of any of the following activities, whether carried out in or outside Canada, in relation to a foreign state."[50] Section 4(2) of the SEMA contains a list of enumerated restricted or prohibited activities, which include:

---

43 United Nations Act, RSC, 1985, c. U-2.

44 United National Iraq Regulations, SOR/90-531, as am.

45 Special Economic Measures Act, SC 1992, c. 17.

46 *Ibid.*, s. 4(1).

47 Various regulations were adopted by the Canadian government relating to sanctions on Haiti. These include the Special Economic Measures (Haiti) Regulations, 1993, SOR/93-499, am. SOR/94-564.

48 S. 4(1)(b), *supra*, note 45.

49 *Ibid.*, s. 4(1)(a).

50 *Ibid.*, s. 4(2).

(a) any dealing by any person in Canada or Canadian outside Canada in any property wherever situated held by or on behalf of the foreign state, any person in that state, or a national of that state who does not ordinarily reside in Canada;

(b) the exportation, sale, supply or shipment by any person in Canada or Canadian outside Canada of any goods wherever situated to that foreign state;

(c) the transfer, provision or communication by any person in Canada or Canadian outside Canada of any technical data to that foreign state or any person in that foreign state;

(d) the importation, purchase, acquisition or shipment by any person in Canada or Canadian outside Canada of any goods that are exported, shipped or supplied from that foreign state;

(e) the provision or acquisition by any person in Canada or Canadian outside Canada of financial services or any other services to, from, or for the benefit of or on the direction or order of that foreign state;

(f) the docking in that foreign state of ships registered or licensed in Canada, or the docking in Canada by similar foreign ships; and

(g) the landing in that foreign state of aircraft registered in Canada or operated in connection with a Canadian air service or the landing in Canada by similar foreign aircraft.

The SEMA provides for the preservation of all secured and unsecured rights and interests held by persons other than the foreign state, persons in the foreign state, and nationals of the foreign state who do not ordinarily reside in Canada.[51] The SEMA also provides that the government can establish a system to resolve reasonable claims for compensation from any person who alleges to have suffered any loss or damages as a result of anything done or purported to have done under the SEMA.[52] Proceedings under the SEMA may only be commenced with the consent of the federal attorney general.[53]

The significance of international sanctions is that business enterprises should be aware of Canada's international political commitments and, to the extent that Canada has taken a position of opposing exports to specific jurisdictions, then manufacturers, distributors, and exporters should be sensitive to this and carefully review their existing distribution practices. Until the recent relaxation of controls on the export and import of goods from and to South Africa, it was good example of such sanctions. Sometimes products imported from the United States, for example, may be subject to one level of export control in the United States and another (not necessarily similar) level of export control in Canada. The re-export of the finished product is complicated thereby.

VI. BLOCKING LEGISLATION

As already noted, the Competition Act contains a number of provisions with respect to the implementation in Canada of foreign laws, judgments, decrees, orders, directives, instructions, and intimations of policy by persons or corporations doing business in

51 *Ibid.*, s. 5(3).

52 *Ibid.*, s. 6(3).

53 *Ibid.*, s. 12.

Canada.[54] The Foreign Extraterritorial Measures Act (FEMA)[55] allows the attorney general to prohibit or restrict the production of records or the giving of information where:[56]

> … a foreign tribunal has exercised, is exercising or is proposing or likely to exercise jurisdiction or powers of a kind or in a manner that has adversely affected or is likely to adversely affect significant Canadian interests in relation to international trade or commerce involving a business carried on in whole or in part of Canada or that otherwise has infringed or is likely to infringe Canadian sovereignty …

In September 1996, in response to the passage of the US Cuban Liberty and Democratic Solidarity (LIBERTAD) Act of 1996, which, unless suspended by the president, *inter alia*, permits US persons to sue in US courts those who "traffick" in the confiscated Cuban property of such US persons, the Canadian Parliament amended the FEMA.[57] Revised section 3(1) further prohibits or restricts the production of records and the giving of information where a foreign tribunal has exercised, is exercising, or is proposing or likely to exercise jurisdiction or powers that is or are related to the enforcement of a foreign trade law or a provision of a foreign trade law as may be set out in a schedule to FEMA.[58]

Revised section 2 defines "foreign trade law as:

> … a law of a foreign jurisdiction that directly or indirectly affects or is likely to affect trade or commerce between (a) Canada, a province, a Canadian citizen or resident of Canada, a corporation incorporated by or under a law of Canada or a province or a person carrying on business in Canada, and (b) any person or a foreign state …

The FEMA also allows the attorney general of Canada, with the concurrence of the secretary of state, to prohibit compliance with foreign measures. An order may be made where:[59]

> … a foreign state or a foreign tribunal has taken or is proposing or is likely to take measures affecting international trade or commerce of a kind or in a manner that has adversely affected or is likely to adversely affect significant Canadian interests in relation to international trade or commerce involving business carried on in whole or in part in Canada, or that otherwise has infringed or is likely to infringe Canadian sovereignty …

---

54 RSC 1985 (2nd Supp.), c. 19; chapter 16, *supra*, section II.

55 RSC 1985, c. F-29, as am. W.C. Graham, "The Foreign Extraterritorial Measures Act" (1986), 11 *Can. Bus. LJ* 410.

56 Ibid., s. 3(1).

57 With respect to the US legislation of 1996, see Pub. L 104-14, ss. 102(f), (g), and 204(d)(3), 12 March 1996, 110 Stat. 793, 794, 810 (22 USCA ss. 6003-5). With respect to the Canadian response, see Bill C-54, An Act to Amend the Foreign Extraterritorial Measures Act, SC 1996, c. 28.

58 *Ibid.*, s. 3(1).

59 See, *supra*, note 55, s. 5(1) and chapter 6, *supra*. This legislation was invoked for the first time on 31 October 1990 to force Canadian subsidiaries of American companies to ignore proposed US legislation prohibiting trade with Cuba. The legislation subsequently was vetoed by the US president.

The foreign measures include:[60]

> ... judgments and rulings made or to be made by the foreign state or foreign tribunal and directives, instructions, intimations of policy and other communications issued by or to be issued by the foreign state or foreign tribunal.

A causal link between the action of a foreign state and the object of the measures in Canada must exist. However, it need not be a direct link. Orders may be made to prohibit compliance "relating to such measures" where the instructions or communications of such measures are "from a person who is in a position to direct or influence the policies of the person in Canada."[61] Only two criteria must be met. First, there must be actual or likely measures of a foreign state. Second, these measures must be communicated to a person in Canada either directly by the foreign state or tribunal, or by a person with influence on the Canadian person. It seems clear that the communication may be of the measures themselves, and not the fact that they require the Canadian person to comply with them.

Thus, if a Canadian subsidiary were told by its US parent that US export control measures require the parent and its subsidiaries not to export certain goods to a particular state, an order could be made under the FEMA to prohibit the Canadian subsidiary from complying with such practice, whether or not the US law was aimed at foreign subsidiaries of the US parent. Section 5 could cover any contractual stipulation requiring a Canadian person or enterprise from exporting something to a state that is named or may be named. It would be sufficient if measures of a foreign state affected one of the contracting parties directly whether or not they were referred to expressly in the contract or required to be included in such a contract. These measures would still be "intimations of policy or other communications relating to such measures.[62]

"Submission clauses" would seem to be caught by section 5. Thus, where a Canadian person in a contract agrees to be governed by the laws of another state, as they existed at a certain date or will exist in the future, the attorney general could exclude the export restrictions.

Section 5 provides for two mechanisms: first, the attorney general may require information about the foreign measures from Canadian persons;[63] second, the attorney general may prohibit a person in Canada from complying with the foreign measures themselves, or any instructions or communications relating to them from any person with influence over the person in Canada.[64]

As of the time of writing, orders under the FEMA have been issued only in response to US legislation with respect to Cuba. In anticipation of the passage of the Cuban Democracy Act of 1992,[65] the Foreign Extraterritorial Measures (United States) Order,

---

60 *Ibid.*, s. 5(2).

61 *Ibid.*, s. 5(1)(b).

62 *Ibid.*

63 *Ibid.*, s. 5(1)(a).

64 *Ibid.*, s. 5(1)(b).

65 Pub. L 102-484, Div. A, Title XVII, 106 Stat. 2575 (22 USCA, ss. 6001, 6001 notes, and 6002 to 6010).

1992 (the 1992 Order)[66] was promulgated. The 1992 Order required notification to the federal attorney general by every Canadian corporation (whether federally or provincially incorporated) and every officer of a corporation who received, in respect of any trade or commerce between Canada and Cuba, any directives, instructions, intimations of policy, or other communication relating to the Cuban Democracy Act from a person who was in a position to direct or influence the policies of the corporation.[67] The 1992 Order further prohibited any compliance with the Cuban Democracy Act by corporations.[68] No prosecutions were ever initiated pursuant to the 1992 Order.

In 1996, in anticipation of the US legislation of 1996,[69] the 1992 Order was amended by the Foreign Extraterritorial Measures (United States) Order, 1992, amendment (the 1996 Order).[70] The 1996 Order is intended to more clearly apply to trade in services, including technology, in addition to goods.[71] It also broadens the definition of trade between Canada and Cuba by obliging US subsidiaries to deal on a "normal business basis" with "designated nationals" and "specially designated nationals" as those terms are used and applied in the US Cuban Assets Control Regulations.[72] The 1996 Order also expands the notification requirement to include corporate directors[73] and expands the prohibition on compliance to directors, officers, managers, and employees in a position of authority.[74] Finally, the 1996 Order attempts to make the notification requirement more effective by specifying the nature and scope of notification required.[75]

Section 8 of the FEMA also provides that the attorney general may declare judgments in proceedings under a foreign antitrust law by a foreign antitrust tribunal not to be recognized or enforced in Canada if such judgment has adversely affected or is likely to adversely affect significant Canadian interests in relation to international trade or commerce. The 1996 amendments to the FEMA in section 8(1.1) contain a similar provision with respect to judgments of foreign tribunals in relation to a foreign trade law listed in the schedule to the FEMA. In both instances, the attorney general can either order that the judgment not be recognized or enforced in Canada or, in respect of money damages, reduce the amount of such judgment. Similarly, in both cases, section 8(4) provides that the fact that the attorney general has not made an order should give rise to

---

66 SOR/92-584, *Can. Gaz.* pt. II, vol. 126, no. 22 (21 October 1992).

67 *Ibid.*, s. 3.

68 *Ibid.*, s. 4.

69 *Supra*, note 57.

70 SOR/96-84, *Can. Gaz.* pt. II, vol. 130, no. 2, (24 January 1996).

71 Department of Foreign Affairs and International Trade, *News Release No. 8—Canada Amends Order Blocking US Trade Restrictions* (18 January 1996).

72 31 CFR pt. 515.

73 *Supra*, note 70, s. 3(1).

74 *Ibid.*, s. 5.

75 *Ibid.*, s. 4, which provides that notice shall be sent by registered mail to the federal attorney general and set out the name and capacity of the person giving the notice; the name and capacity of the person from whom the communication originated; the date that the communication was received; and the period during which the communication is intended to be in effect.

no inference (adverse or otherwise) in Canadian courts. Section 8.1 of the amended FEMA further provides that in respect of a judgment satisfied outside Canada, the attorney general may order recovery of all amounts obtained from such judgment, on application by the party against whom judgment was given, whether Canadian citizen or resident, corporation incorporated in Canada, or a person carrying on business in Canada.

Section 7.1 specifically provides that:

> Any judgment given under the law of the United States entitled Cuban Liberty and Democratic Solidarity (LIBERTAD) Act of 1996 shall not be recognized or enforceable in any manner in Canada.

Section 9 allows the recovery of loss or damages and expenses in respect of a judgment that is subject to an order made pursuant to section 8. Section 9 also allows the recovery of loss or damages and expenses in respect of judgments satisfied outside Canada that are subject to an order made pursuant to section 8.1. In general, section 9 provides that when by order a foreign judgment is unenforceable, a party may recover any amount obtained pursuant to the judgment and after the 1996 amendments, all expenses relating to both the foreign and FEMA proceedings, including all solicitor-client costs or judicial or extrajudicial costs. Similarly, when by order the amount of damages awarded in a foreign judgment is reduced, a party may recover the excess of the amount paid under the judgment and the amount reduced by the order; an amount specified by the attorney general in respect of the expenses in the foreign proceeding; and the expenses in respect of the FEMA proceeding, including solicitor-client costs or judicial or extrajudicial costs, and such proportion of any loss or damages suffered by that party by reason of the enforcement of the judgment.

Section 9(1.1) of the amended FEMA permits a party, with the attorney general's consent, to initiate FEMA proceedings to recover expenses before final judgment is awarded in the foreign proceeding. With respect to recovery of loss or damages and expenses, section 9(2) authorizes a court to enforce its decisions by ordering the sale or seizure of shares of corporations incorporated in Canada. While section 9(2) always permitted seizure of such shares, the 1996 amendments now include any other property. Prior to the 1996 amendments, the test was whether the person obtaining the foreign judgment had a direct or beneficial interest in such shares. Today, the test is expanded to include "any person who controls, in law or in fact, that person."[76]

As a result of these amendments, the territorial scope of the FEMA has been clarified. At least with respect to foreign trade laws, the FEMA is intended to deal with foreign measures or trade laws that affect Canadian citizens, residents, and corporations incorporated in or doing business in Canada. In that the FEMA is concerned with the trade or commerce of Canada, it is also clear that the requisite effect is not necessarily one that would occur in Canada. However, orders made under section 5 may be made only with respect to "persons in Canada." This could mean a Canadian citizen or resident, a corporation incorporated in or carrying on business in Canada, as is the case for

76 *Supra*, note 55.

defining the scope of the "clawback" provision.[77] However, the clawback provision is wider since it gives the right to sue in Canada to any "Canadian citizen" and a "resident of Canada."[78] It would seem that the words "person in Canada" do not include Canadian citizens abroad.

VII. CORRUPT PRACTICES AND ILLICIT PAYMENTS

A. Introduction

The UN Draft International Agreement on Illicit Payments, in articles 1 and 2 provides that:[79]

> Art. 1: Each Contracting State undertakes to make the following acts punishable by appropriate criminal penalties under its national law:
>
> (a) The offering, promising or giving of any payment, gift or other advantage by any natural person, on his own behalf or on behalf of any enterprise or any other person whether juridical or natural, to or for the benefit of a public official as undue consideration for performing or refraining from the performance of his duties in connection with an international commercial transaction.
>
> (b) The soliciting, demanding, accepting or receiving, directly or indirectly, by a public official of any payment, gift or other advantage, as undue consideration for performing or refraining from the performance of his duties in connection with an international commercial transaction.
>
> Each Contracting State likewise undertakes to make the acts referred to in paragraph 1(a) of this article punishable by appropriate criminal penalties under its national law when committed by a

---

77 *Ibid.*, s. 9(1).

78 The clawback provision is not extraterritorial. It confers rights on Canadian citizens to sue before a court in Canada the person to whom damages were paid. It may be that, in a given case, it would be contrary to international law to do so because a precondition to enforcement jurisdiction is that a state must have prescriptive jurisdiction over the person.

79 E/AC 67/L3/Add 1. See also Draft United Nations Code of Conduct for Transnational Corporations, E/1988/39/Add. 1, 1 February 1988, art. 21: *Abstention from corrupt practices* 21:

> (a) Transnational corporations shall refrain, in their transactions, from the offering, promising or giving of any payment, gift or other advantage to or for the benefit of a public official as consideration for performing or refraining from the performance of his duties in connection with those transactions.
>
> (b) Transnational corporations shall maintain accurate records of any payments made by them, to any public official or intermediary. They shall make available these records to the competent authorities of the countries in which they operate, upon request, for investigations and proceedings concerning those payments.

OECD Declaration on International Investment and Multinational Enterprises (1976), as am., in 1979 and 1984. Annex, Guidelines for Multinational Enterprises, General Policies 7: "Not render—and they should not be solicited or expected to render—any bribe or other improper benefit, direct or indirect, to any public servant or holder of public office." See also in (1977), 15 *Int'l. Leg. Mat.* 967, at 972 and International Chamber of Commerce, *Report on Extortion and Bribery in Business*, 29 November 1977.

juridical person, or, in the case of a State which does not recognize criminal responsibility of juridical persons, to take appropriate measures, according to its national law, with the objective of comparable deterrent effects.

Art. 2: For the purpose of this Agreement:

(a) "Public official" means any person whether appointed or elected, whether permanently or temporarily, who, at the national, regional or local level holds a legislative, administrative, judicial or military office, or who, performing a public function, is an employee of a Government or of a public or governmental authority or agency or who otherwise performs a public function;

(b) International commercial transaction means [*inter alia*] any sale, contract or any other business transaction, actual or proposed with a national, regional or local Government or any authority or agency referred to in paragraph (a) of this article or any business transaction involving an application for governmental approval of a sale, contract or any other business transaction actual or proposed, relating to the supply or purchase of goods, services, capital or technology emanating from a State or States other than that in which those goods, services, capital or technology are to be delivered or rendered. It also means any application for or acquisition of proprietary interests or production rights from a Government by a foreign national or enterprise;

(c) "Intermediary" means any enterprise or any other person, whether juridical or natural, who negotiates with or otherwise deals with a public official on behalf of any other enterprise or any other person, whether juridical or natural, in connexion with an international commercial transaction.

Although this agreement has not yet been adopted, it expresses the concerns of the international community.

B. Canadian Legislation

Existing Canadian legislation with respect to public disclosure of payments made by business enterprises to foreign agents is non-existent.[80] The secrecy and confidentiality provisions of the Income Tax Act,[81] Statistics Act,[82] and other similar legislation preclude the public disclosure of information supplied in accordance with that legislation. Public disclosure of information supplied by management proxy circulars is required by the Canada Business Corporations Act[83] of corporations incorporated under the Act. The current regulations adopted under the Act do not require corporations to disclose information concerning payments made by them to foreign agents.

Provincial securities commissions, in the exercise of their statutory powers, do not seem to have taken any specific action in this direction.

---

80 Klotz, "Bribery of Foreign Officials—A Call for Change in the Law of Canada" (1994), 73 *Can. Bar Rev.* 467.

81 SC 1970-71-72, c. 63, as am., s. 241.

82 RSC 1985, c. S-19, as am., ss. 17 and 18.

83 RSC 1985, c. C-44, as am.

The Criminal Code[84] contains a very complete legal regime covering the corrupt practices of persons doing business with the government of Canada and with provincial governments.[85] The relevant sections deal with corrupt practices in Canada as a host country, but they do not deal with corrupt practices where Canada would be the home country—that is, contracts between a Canadian business corporation and a foreign government. The Criminal Code would have to be amended to include corrupt practices involved to obtain a contract with a foreign government.[86]

C. The 1996 Inter-American Convention Against Corruption

At an Organization of American States (OAS) meeting in Caracas on March 29, 1996, 21 member states, all from Latin America, signed the Inter-American Convention Against Corruption. The United States signed the convention on June 2, 1996 at a subsequent OAS meeting; however, at the time of writing, Canada had not yet signed it. The stated purposes of the Convention are to promote and strengthen the development by each party of the mechanisms needed to prevent, detect, punish, and eradicate corruption, and to promote, facilitate, and regulate cooperation to ensure the effectiveness of measures and actions to prevent, detect, punish, and eradicate corruption in the performance of public functions and acts of corruption specifically related to such performance.[87]

In article VI, the parties agree to adopt the necessary legislative or other measures to make each of the enumerated acts of corruption a criminal offence. In article VIII, the parties agree to prohibit and punish transnational bribery subject to the extent permitted by their respective constitutional laws and to provide assistance and cooperation with respect to the prosecution of transnational bribery in another state. Article IX provides that to the extent permitted by their own constitutional law, each party will create an offence of "illicit enrichment" constituted by a significant increase in the assets of a government official that he or she cannot reasonably explain in relation to his or her lawful earnings during the performance of his or her functions. In article XIII, the parties agree that each offence established by the convention shall be included as an indictable offence in any extradition treaty existing between or among member states. In article XVI, the parties agree not to invoke bankruptcy laws as a basis for refusing to provide assistance to a requesting state pursuant to the convention. Finally, article XXIII provides that the convention shall remain open for accession by non-members of the OAS.

D. The 1994 and 1996 OECD Council Recommendations

On May 27, 1994, the Council of the OECD adopted a non-binding recommendation on bribery in international business transactions. It was followed by another non-binding

---

84 RSC 1985 c. C-46, as am.

85 *Ibid.*, ss. 122-123.

86 See also s. 465(3) concerning conspiracies in Canada to effect a lawful purpose by unlawful means in a place outside Canada that is an offence by the law of such place and s. 465(4), in respect of conspiracies committed abroad.

87 Art. II(1) and (2).

recommendation adopted on April 11, 1996, on the tax deductibility of bribes to foreign public officials, which states that:

those member countries which do not disallow the deductibility of bribes to foreign public officials re-examine such treatment with the intention of denying this deductibility. Such action may be facilitated by the trend to treat bribes to foreign pubic officials as illegal.

E. The 1996 ICC Rules

The 1996 revised ICC Rules of Conduct to Combat Extortion and Bribery in International Business[88] prohibit extortion and bribery for any purpose and not just to obtain or retain business, making them more stringent than the previous ICC code published in 1977.

They now cover extortion and bribery in judicial proceedings, in tax matters, in environmental and other regulatory cases or in legislative proceedings. They contain these main provisions:

No enterprise may, directly or indirectly, offer or give a bribe and any demands for such a bribe must be rejected;

Enterprises should not kick back any portion of a contract payment to employees of the other contracting party;

Enterprises should do everything in their power to ensure that payments to agents represent no more than an appropriate remuneration for legitimate services;

All financial transacitons must be properly recorded, and there must be no "off the books" or secret accounts;

Enterprises should draw up their own codes, consistent with the ICC rules, to meet the particular circumstances of their business;

Corporate governing bodies should establish control systems aimed at preventing payments that infringe ICC rules. They should take appropriate action against directors or employees who contravene the rules.

Companies are invited to adopt these rules.

In 1996, the ICC also revised its Recommendation to Governments and International Organizations. The 1996 ICC Recommendation endorses the 1994 OECD Recommendation and urges its adoption by OECD members and non-member countries. The Revised Recommendation also urges cooperative enforcement of national laws in this area, with appropriate provision for safeguarding confidentiality.

The 1996 Recommendation encourages the adoption of national preventive measures relating to: disclosure procedures; economic regulations that use permits and authorizations; government procurement transactions; and political contributions. The ICC Recommendation urges the national adoption of: adequate mechanisms for surveillance and investigation; laws for the prosecution with appropriate penalties for those who offer, demand, solicit, or receive bribes; and laws for appropriate auditing of governments by independent professional auditors.

88 ICC, 1996 Revisions to the ICC Rules of Conduct (1996), part II.

VIII. CODES OF CONDUCT

A. Draft United Nations Code of Conduct on Transnational Corporations

The United Nations Draft[89] contains several important provisions dealing with consumer protection and environmental protection that transnational corporations must observe when manufacturing products for domestic or foreign consumption.

B. Private Codes of Conduct

Private codes of conduct adopted by most multinational corporations contain rules that are designed, *inter alia*, to ensure the improvement of standards and environmental protection as well as competitive conduct by them; for example, the Caterpillar Tractor Co. Code of Conduct,[90] which is one of the most comprehensive deals with human relationships, privacy of information about employees, ownership and investment, product quality and uniformity, competitive conduct, relationships with suppliers, sharing of technology, accounting records and financial reporting, intercompany pricing, currency transactions, differing business practices, public responsibility, observance of local laws, relationships with public officials, disclosure of information, inside information, international information flow, free enterprise world wide, and reporting code compliance.

IX. SELECTED BIBLIOGRAPHY

A. Books

Elliot (ed.), *Corruption and the Global Economy* (1996).

Fry and Radebaugh (eds.), *Investment in the North American Free Trade Area* (1991).

Graham, *Governments and Multinational Enterprises* (1996).

Graham and Richardson (eds.), *Global Competition Policy* (1996).

Guissinger, *Investment Incentives and Performance Requirements: Patterns of International Trade, Production and Investment* (1985).

Horn (ed.), *Legal Problems of Codes of Conduct for Multinational Enterprises* (1980).

Levitt, *Silent Surrender: The Multinational Corporation in Canada* (1970).

OECD, *Structure and Organisation of Multinational Enterprises* (1987).

Rubin and Hufbauer, *Emerging Standards of International Trade and Investment: Multinational Codes and Corporate Conduct* (1983).

Rugman, *Foreign Investment and NAFTA* (1994).

Rugman, *Multinationals and Canada-United States Free Trade* (1990).

---

89 *Supra*, note 33, arts. 39 to 45.

90 1 October 1974, revised 1 September 1977, 1 May 1985. See also Northern Telecom Code of Conduct.

Safarian, *The Performance of Foreign-Owned Firms in Canada* (1969).

Sarna, *Boycott and Blacklist* (1986).

Sauvant and Lavipour (eds.), *Controlling Multinational Enterprises: Problems, Strategies, Counter-Strategies* (1976).

Sauvé and Schwanen (eds.), *Investment Rules for the Global Economy: Enhacing Market Access Through Market Presence* (1996).

Waldmann, *Regulating International Business Through Codes of Conduct* (1980).

Wallace, *International Regulation of Multinational Corporations* (1976).

B. Articles

Baade, "The Legal Effects of Codes of Conduct for Multinational Enterprises," in *Legal Problems of Codes of Conduct for Multinational Enterprises*, vol. 1 (1980), at 3.

Coonrod, "The United Nations Code of Conduct for Transnational Corporations" (1977), 18 *Harv. Int'l. LJ* 273.

Elliot, "Combatting Corruption in the Western Hemisphere" in Walker (ed.), *Implementation of the Summit of the Americas: A Progress Report* (1996).

Graham, "The Foreign Extraterritorial Measures Act" (1986), 11 *Can. Bus. LJ* 410.

Klotz, "Bribery of Foreign Officials—A Call for Change in the Law of Canada" (1994), 73 *Can. Bar Rev.* 467.

Sanders, "Implementing International Codes of Conduct for Multinational Enterprises" (1982), 30 *Am. J of Comp. L* 241.

Warner and Rugman, "Recent US Protectionist R & D Policies: Are Canadian Multinationals Exempted?" (1994), 23 *Can. Bus. LJ* 395.

C. Documents

The CTC Reporter.

The Impact of Multinational Corporations on Development and on International Relations (New York: United Nations, 1974).

Transnational Corporations in World Development: A Re-examination (New York: United Nations, 1978).

Transnational Corporation: Issues Involved in the Formulation of a Code of Conduct (New York: United Nations, 1976).

CHAPTER EIGHTEEN

Government-Supported Export Insurance, Guarantees, and Financing: The Export Development Corporation

I. INTRODUCTION[1]

In Canada and other industrialized countries, the private sector's current production inputs and investments are financed through the private financial market. To the extent

1 Based in part on EDC 1995 Annual Report and the Report of the House of Commons Standing Committee on Foreign Affairs and International Trade, *Canadian SMEs in the World Economy: Developing Effective Business—Government Partnership for International Success*, June 1996.

that the national savings are insufficient, the financial system or individual enterprises generally have the capacity to raise funds in the international financial and capital markets. In this context, access to private domestic financing of exports is improving, particularly as the appetites of Canadian commercial banks and related organizations, such as Northstar, for aggressive export financing are increasing. Thus, government-supported export financing has been, with some exceptions, an insignificant factor in trade among industrialized countries.

Insurance of receivables does play a role in trade between developed economies, however, and the Export Development Bank insures a great deal of US receivables for Canadian exporters. As well, the Canadian Commercial Corporation (CCC) facilitates export sales of Canadian goods and services by means of government-to-government transactions. In these transactions, CCC assumes the role of prime contractor and undertakes to deliver products or services to a foreign customer with a back-to-back obligation from a Canadian supplier.[2]

In developing markets and transition economies government-supported export financing plays a more active role. For most developing and transition economies, their insufficient domestic savings and limited access to international financial and capital markets has meant that Canadian export sales to them are contingent on the availability of officially backed sources of funding.

Export financing, when supported by governments, has two fundamental characteristics. First, financing is made available to borrowers and buyers who do not normally have access to financial markets. Second, government intervention, particularly in the form of medium- and long-term financing at fixed interest rates may result in a form of subsidy if interest rates on export financing are below market rates.

All industrialized countries, several newly industrialized countries (for example, Brazil, Argentina, Korea, and India) and transition economies have government-supported programs for export financing. In general, financing is provided in accordance with the Organisation for Economic Co-operation and Development (OECD) ground rules, but recently concessional financing is on the decline due to stricter rules provided by the *Helsinki V*,[3] which requires that projects be deemed commercially unviable in order to receive concessional financing.

II. INTERNATIONAL GROUND RULES FOR EXPORT CREDITS AND MIXED CREDITS

Official export financing among OECD countries is subject to OECD Consensus guidelines on maximum maturity limits in a range of 8½ to 10 years, minimum cash downpayments of 15 percent, and minimum interest rates. These rates are subject to

2 CCC, *Annual Report 1994-95*. For a synopsis of the functions and programs of some of the key Canadian agencies (mostly government) that support exporters, see "A Road Map to Export Success" (Winter 1997), *EDC Today* 10.

3 Arrangement on Guidelines for Officially Supported Export Credits, doc. no. OCDE/GD (92)95, para. 8a)i) (Paris: OECD, 1992).

adjustment semi-annually to reflect changes in market interest rates. A system of commercial interest reference rates apply.

The consensus guidelines do not cover all sectors. For example, there is a separate agreement for nuclear power plants. Ships, other than offshore "rigs," are covered under another OECD understanding. Agriculture, however, is not covered by the agreement.

The OECD consensus also sets ground rules for the use of mixed credits aimed at reducing their disruptive effect on regular commercial transactions. These specify that mixed credit transactions must have a concessionality level of 35 percent and be subject to prior notification. The Development Assistance Committee (DAC) of the OECD has established guidelines for the use and reporting of "associated financing," which is any financing involving both export credits and official development assistance or other concessional liens. The DAC guidelines are aimed at ensuring that associated financing meets genuine development objectives.

The OECD consensus guidelines are not legally binding. As a result, countries sometimes depart from them to try to win a particular contract.

Although Canada has served notice that it will match financing at below-consensus rates where it makes economic sense, it remains firmly committed to the consensus and opposed to any spread of predatory financing practices that simply squander available resources.

III. THE FINANCING OF CANADIAN EXPORTS

A. Private Versus Government Sources

Over 90 percent of Canadian exports are delivered by the private sector (including Crown corporations) with essentially no government intervention in financing or marketing.

Private financial markets account for most of the financing of Canadian exports. They do this through direct loans to buyers, lines of credit, and other forms of trade financing. They also do it indirectly by financing Canadian exporters. Their involvement in medium- and long-term financing, particularly in developing markets, has been limited. Unlike banks in other industrialized countries, Canadian banks, in recent years, have not played an important role in the government's export financing program. Nonetheless, they have been very active internationally in other fields of banking. Their share in international banking with developing markets is significantly higher than Canada's share of world exports to those countries.

The bulk of government support is directed at exports to developing markets and transitional economies. It has been estimated that roughly one half of Canadian exports to developing markets are supported through government programs.

When it is used, government support is provided through the Export Development Corporation (EDC), which accounts for approximately 6.7 percent of exports, of which 1 percent is financed directly, and the Canadian Wheat Board, which accounts for 1 to 2 percent of exports. Other government agencies, such as the CCC, the Canadian Dairy Commission, the Canadian Saltfish Corporation, and the Freshwater Fish Marketing Corporation, acting as direct sellers, account for a further 1 to 2 percent of Canadian exports. Finally, the bilateral aid program of the Canadian International Development

Agency, finances 2 percent of total Canadian exports, or 15 percent of Canadian exports to developing countries. Provincial government programs also provide some support.

B. The Export Development Corporation[4]

1. Introduction

The EDC is a Crown corporation whose purpose is to support and develop Canada's export trade and Canadian capacity to engage in trade.[5]

The EDC helps Canadian exporters compete in world markets by providing a wide range of financial and risk management services, including export credit insurance, financing to foreign buyers of Canadian goods and services, and guarantees. It strives within its financial capacity to provide services that are internationally competitive so that, in the context of requirements for specific transactions, firms that are competitive in terms of price, quality, delivery, and service are also effectively competitive in terms of the availability of financial services.

The EDC is the successor to the Export Credits Insurance Corporation (ECIC), which was established by an Act of Parliament in 1944.

In the immediate post-war period, the demand for goods and services far outstripped availability, and, in the resulting seller's market, credit terms tended to be well within the financing capacity of commercial banks. This was reflected in the corporation's original program, export credits insurance, which provided protection against non-payment by foreign buyers, and thus facilitated bank financing.

By passing the Export Credits Insurance Act, Parliament anticipated the re-emergence of a buyer's market when normal trading conditions would reassert themselves, and the ability to provide credit terms would be a necessary competitive tool.

By 1960, the demand for long-term credit for capital projects led Parliament to amend the Act by adding a long-term financing facility to the corporation's powers. This service was established to help Canadian goods manufacturers and consulting engineers to retain their competitiveness in world markets.

Throughout the 1960s, the changing demand of Canadian exporters required several amendments to the Act to allow the corporation to increase its financial ceilings and augment its services. The culmination of these changes and diversification of services led to the decision to provide a new Act and a new corporation. Parliament passed the Export Development Act in June 1969; it was proclaimed on October 1, 1969.[6] Notably changed under the new Act was the EDC financing facility. All loans prior to October 1, 1969 were made for the government account and funded by borrowing from the Consolidated Revenue Fund. Under the Export Development Act, the loan service became the responsibility of the board of directors of the EDC. The government account remained for "national interest" lending to be administered by the EDC. The Act also added a new service: foreign investment insurance.

---

4 Based in part on Information Fact Sheet 90-02 (03-96), *EDC Corporate Profile*.

5 Export Development Act, RSC 1985, c. E-20, as am.

6 SC 1968-69, c. 39, as am.

The EDC's mandate was expanded by Parliament in 1993, providing the corporation with the ability to offer a wider range of financing and insurance products and services. The Export Development Act was amended to include provisions for streamlined pre-export financing, enhanced project financing, expanded lease financing services, and a broader range of account receivables insurance and foreign investment support facilities.[7]

The capital to operate the EDC comes from three sources: share capital paid-in by the government of Canada, retained earnings, and borrowed funds—the major source. By foregoing a return of its equity holding, the Government of Canada provides a subsidy to the EDC. Recently, the government has increased the capital of EDC by $50 million in recognition of the increasing demand on the EDC's facilities.

The EDC borrows by selling bonds in the international capital markets, and through private placements. Because it is a Crown corporation, fully backed by the government of Canada, the EDC can borrow money at the best possible market rates available. It also makes money on investments. Under the Export Development Act, it is permitted to invest funds in various safe instruments, and any money in its treasury that is not being used to fund loans at any point in time, is put to use in this manner. The fees collected from exporters constitute a fourth source of revenue for the EDC.

Should the EDC incur a loss on its lending operations, the Government of Canada is prepared to ask Parliament to approve appropriations for a loss makeup to the EDC, but this has not been necessary to date.

2. *EDC Programs*

a. Risks

Canadian exporters of goods face commercial and political risks. Commercial risks include inflation, which is of great importance in long-term contracts; repudiation of the contract by the buyer, payment delays; the insolvency or bankruptcy of the buyer; additional handling charges resulting from the interruption or diversion of a voyage; commercial disputes over the quality and suitability of the goods during or after the warranty period; and product liability suits by consumers.

Political risks include the imposition in the importing country of price controls, import restriction, foreign exchange controls, or of a moratorium on foreign exchange transactions, making it unlawful or impossible for the buyer to make the deferred payments in Canadian dollars or other restricted currency; the imposition in Canada of export controls after the contract is signed but prior to delay; the occurrence of war or insurrection in the importing country; war between Canada and the importing country; the cancellation of import or export licences; foreign exchange fluctuations where the contract price is specified in a foreign currency; and the seizure or confiscation of the goods by the importing country.

---

7 See also Export Development Corporation Exercise of Certain Powers Regulations, *Can. Gaz.* pt. II, vol. 128, no. 12, 15 June 1994.

The EDC's business is to provide exporters with tools that allow them to manage the risks they face while doing business internationally. Recently, the EDC has experienced a significant shift in the composition of its business volume away from sovereign risk toward commercial risk. The bulk of commercial risk is in industrialized countries, which now account for roughly half of total business volume.[8]

Commercial risks are always present even in a domestic transaction. However, their significance and probability of occurrence increase in international trade as Canadian exporters are often unable to obtain accurate credit information on foreign purchasers or importers. They may also find it either impossible or very expensive to collect their debts and seize foreign assets.

Political risks are peculiar to international trade and are particularly significant when dealing with less-developed or developing countries experiencing instability.

b. Programs

The EDC has four principal product areas, of which three are specifically designed to address the risks exporters face. They are credit insurance, contract bonding insurance, foreign investment insurance, and financing foreign purchasers.

i. CREDIT INSURANCE SERVICES Canadian firms of any size can insure their export sales against non-payment for foreign buyers. The EDC normally assumes 90 percent of the commercial and political risks, involving insolvency, default, repudiation, or cancellation of a contract by the buyer, as well as blockage of funds, war or rebellion, cancellation of import licences and the like in a foreign country, and cancellation of export permits in Canada.

Normally, the EDC covers both the commercial and political risks inherent in export transaction. However, in certain circumstances, the EDC is prepared to cover only the political risk.[9] In the case of two types of services involving the United States, the EDC covers only the commercial risk.[10]

Almost any kind of transaction involving the export of goods, services, or technology may be insured. Insurance is available to cover sales of general commodities and services normally made on short credit terms of up to 180 days, agricultural products sold on credit terms of up to three years and goods and services made on medium-term credit up to five years.

To facilitate the exporter's banking arrangements, the EDC will agree to pay any proceeds of a loss payable under an exporter's policy to a bank or other financial organization.

If a bank or other financial institution will agree to purchase an insured foreign receivable from an exporter on a limited recourse basis, the EDC is prepared to agree to the assignment of the exporter's rights and obligations under the policy to the bank or

8 EDC Corporate Plan, November 1995, at 11.

9 Based on Information Fact Sheet 99-05, *Global Comprehensive Insurance* and EDC Program Guide: *A Map of EDC's Risk Management Services.*

10 *Ibid.*

financial institution. However, should a loss be occasioned by any factor within the exporter's control, the bank or financial institution may exercise recourse to the exporter.

Credit insurance services that are available are as follows:

- *Global Comprehensive Insurance* provides cover to the exporter against both commercial and political risks inherent in export sales unless excluded by the EDC.
- *Export Credit Insurance* is essentially the same as Global Comprehensive Insurance except for some administrative features. It is especially tailored to meet the needs of small businesses and can cover shipments and contracts (coverage for services currently in development).
- *Global Political Insurance* provides cover to the exporter against specified political risks inherent in export sales made on short-term credit. An exporter is required to insure all export sales unless excluded by the EDC.
- *Selective Political Insurance* provides cover to the exporter against specified political risks inherent in sales made on short-term credit. An exporter may select the countries for which he or she wants cover, but all export sales to buyer in the selected countries must be insured.
- *Documentary Credit Insurance* provides coverage to Canadian banks against the risk of non-payment by a foreign bank. It is a fully selective policy covering all goods and services. However, 100 percent Canadian content is required for bulk agricultural commodities.
- *Medium-Term Bulk Agricultural Credits Insurance* provides cover to the exporter of bulk agricultural products against political and commercial risks inherent in export sales to foreign governments. Features include competitive premium rates, fast turn around times, and cover for credit terms of up to three years when warranted by international competition.
- *Sub-supplier Insurance* provides cover to a Canadian enterprise supplying goods or services to a Canadian exporter selling to a foreign buyer. Provided the export transaction is insured by the EDC, the sub-supplier can obtain the EDC cover against non-payment by the foreign buyer or the exporter as a result of commercial or political risks. Two policies are available: Specific Transaction Sub-supplier Insurance (Foreign Risks) and Specific Transaction Sub-supplier Insurance (Domestic Risks).
- *Equipment (Political Risk) Insurance* provides cover to exporters for equipment used on a foreign job site against political risk or actions by a foreign government that result in the loss of effective control over the equipment.
- *Specific Transaction Insurance* provides cover to the exporter for individual transactions involving goods and services, either from the effective date of contract of the shipment of goods until payment is received.

ii. CONTRACT BONDING The EDC has products that help protect exporters, banks, and surety companies against risks associated with letters of guarantee, performance bids, or surety bonds. Contract bonding offers the benefits of providing the exporter with collateral instead of tying up cash flow and giving unconditional coverage to the exporter's bank or other lenders.

The EDC offers several forms of bonding protection:

- *Bid Security Insurance* provides cover to the exporter against the arbitrary or improper call of an on-demand letter of credit or guarantee issued in favor of the buyer in support of a bid by the exporter.
- *Performance Security Insurance* provides cover to the exporter against a wrongful call be a foreign buyer of an advance payment or performance guarantee provided by the exporter's bank on behalf of the exporter.
- *Bid Security Guarantee* provides cover to banks and other financial Institutions against a call of security, usually in the form of a letter of guarantee, issued by a bank or financial institution on behalf of the Canadian exporter bidding on an export contract.
- *Performance Security Guarantee* provides cover to banks or other financial institutions against a call of security, usually in the form of an advance payment or performance guarantee, issued to a foreign buyer on behalf of a Canadian exporter.
- *Surety Bond Re-insurance* protects the surety company if the exporter defaults under the terms of a contract, reinsures the surety company for a portion of the risk for a percentage of the premium, and provides recourse from the exporter if paid out.
- *Surety Bond-Issuance* protects the buyer against exporter default. EDC issues bonds and acts as the surety.

iii. FOREIGN INVESTMENT INSURANCE Foreign investment insurance covers up to 90 percent of losses arising from three types of political risks: transfer of funds, expropriation or war, and revolution or insurrection. It provides up to 15 years of coverage and provides the backing often needed to attract other investors and lenders. It is designed to ensure that the EDC shares the Canadian company's risk if politically motivated conflict or action by the foreign government puts a project at risk. This allows for more flexible project structures.

iv. FINANCING FOREIGN PURCHASERS The EDC provides export financing for up to 85 percent of the contract value, at both fixed and floating rates of interest, to foreign buyers of Canadian goods, equipment, and services. Funds are disbursed directly by the EDC to Canadian exporters on behalf of the borrower—in effect providing the exporter with a cash sale.

The EDC has developed seven principal services to provide either buyer or supplier credit financing in support of exports of goods and services. These include individual loans, project loans for multiple contract lines of credit for banks or institutional buyers, note purchase agreements, simplified note purchases, forfeiting, and loans to Canadian buyers under the specialized credits program.[11]

- *A Loan* is a financing agreement in respect of a transaction where the terms of the financing have been agreed upon and the funds are disbursed under a Disbursement Procedures Agreement signed by the borrower/buyer, the exporter, and the EDC.

---

11 OECD *Export Credit Financing in OECD Member and Non-Member Countries* (looseleaf services, 1995), at 8.

- *A Direct Loan* is a financing agreement between the EDC and the buyer/borrower for a pre-determined transaction that may or may not involve a guarantor.
- *A Line of Credit* is a special version of a loan whereby a foreign borrower, usually a bank or financial institution, agrees to borrow from the EDC for a multiplicity of transactions for which neither the exporter(s) nor the buyer(s) may have yet been determined. An allocation occurs when the transaction, the buyer, and the exporter have been identified and approved for financing under the line of credit. A line of credit may require several disbursement procedures agreements, disbursement order or some other form of disbursement.
- *A Protocol* is a memorandum of understanding between the EDC and a foreign financial institution. Through a Supplier Credit Protocol, the EDC offers to consider the purchase of promissory notes issued to a Canadian exporter by a foreign buyer and guaranteed or avalized by the financial institution. Under a Buyer Credit Protocol, the EDC extends a loan to a foreign buyer. Repayment of the EDC loan is guaranteed by the foreign financial Institution.
- *A Loan Syndication* is a service whereby the EDC insures the credit risk of the buyer or borrower by either syndicating a loan itself or, in some special cases, by co-arranging loan syndication with commercial banks
- *The Note Purchase Program* consists of three facilities, each involving the purchase by the EDC (usually on a non-recourse basis) of promissory notes issued by foreign buyers to Canadian exporters for the purchase of Canadian goods and services. In case of complex transactions, the EDC and the exporter sign a Note Purchase Agreement in which the terms and conditions of the financing are established. In the case of straight-forward transactions, either a Simplified Note Purchase or Forfeiting may be appropriate. If a credit risk is greater than that described above, a first-class bank guarantee would be required and the Forfeiting facility would apply.
- *The Purchase of Receivables Program* offers financing arrangements in which the EDC provides insurance to the exporter by purchasing the exporter's receivables at a certain fixed discount. This method of support can be particularly useful in markets where extended terms are required.
- *The Pre-shipment Financing Program* provides specialized financing to Canadian companies to cover capital specific, up-front costs.
- *Leasing* is a program in which the EDC protects the exporter, buyer, or lessor by participating as a debt-provider for the lessor. The EDC can also act as the lessor under the revised Export Development Act.
- *Equity* protects the exporter/financier against all risks associated with venture assumed and may be used to encourage further equity/debt participation in a project.
- *The Project Finance Program* provides financing for large infrastructure projects as well as other large projects for which direct guarantee of project sponsor is not available.
- *The General Guarantee Framework Program* was designed to complement the EDC's direct lending programs by providing exporters whose annual export sales exceed $10 million with a choice of a direct loan from EDC or a loan from the bank partially guaranteed by the EDC. It is used mostly for non-OECD markets.

The EDC's medium-term financing facilities such as forfeiting, simplified note purchases, and allocations under lines of credit are available to exporters through the corporation's regional and district offices. This initiative is intended to provide better access to the EDC for exporters, especially to small- to medium-sized exporters requiring medium-term financing for proposed export transactions of $1 million or less. These exporters have the option of dealing directly with an EDC regional or district office or the corporation's head office in Ottawa.

When the EDC lends money to support a sale to another country, it does not disburse the money to the buyer. It is disbursed directly to the Canadian exporter. Then the EDC collects the principal and interest form the buyer over a period of years. The result is that every transaction supported by the EDC brings money into Canada and its funds at no time leave Canada.

Because the EDC operates on commercial principles, it will not lend money to a buyer unless it expects to get it back. Before the EDC makes a loan, it must be satisfied that the buyer is creditworthy and that the country in which he or she is located is an acceptable country risk. If the answer is negative on either count, the loan is not made. Rescheduling of loans may occur when a customer asks for more time to pay. Then, a new schedule of payment that gives him or her more time is set up.

3. Benefits to Canada

For the EDC, optimizing the Canadian content of exports is a major goal. This insures that the exports supported by the EDC create jobs in Canada. With this in mind, the EDC offers advice to exporters on how to meet and exceed Canadian content levels established for its services. The Canadian content level is determined at the time of application for export insurance or financing. Generally, goods and services should have a 50 percent Canadian content or better.

Other benefits to Canada are also taken into account when EDC determines whether a particular export transaction is eligible for support. These include technology transfer, research and development, and new investment in Canada resulting from the export.

4. Organization

The EDC has been restructured recently so that its products and services are sold and delivered by nine business teams focused on specific industry sectors. These include the Emerging Exporters Team, the Base and Semi-Manufactured Goods Team, The Consumer Goods Team, the Engineering and Professional Services Team, the Financial Institutions Team, the Forestry Team, the Industrial Equipment Team, the Information Technologies Team, and the Transportations Team. These sector-based teams are designed not only to develop a more thorough understanding of their specific industry sectors but also to provide greater autonomy to generate financial solutions for customers in all sectors and to make quicker decisions than in the past.[12]

---

12 EDC 1995 Annual Report, at 9.

5. *Small Exporters and SMEs*

In support of government policy, the EDC is committed to contributing to the competitiveness of Canadian exporters by providing services that are required by exporters of all sizes and types to succeed in international markets. The EDC is sensitive to the needs of smaller exporters, who represent about 85 percent of the corporation's customers by numbers if not by amount. This is an important emerging market as small- and medium-sized enterprises (SMEs) in both the goods and services sectors move into export markets.[13]

A key focus is to develop effective delivery mechanisms to each and support an expanding number of SMEs with a range of products and services that are tailored to their needs. The emerging exporters team, developed in 1995 is dedicated to providing streamlined service to smaller exporters having annual export sales up to $1 million. The team processes insurance applications, pre-qualifies transactions for line of credit financing, issues insurance policies, and approves foreign buyers—all by phone.

The EDC has also recently developed financing facilities tailored to meet the specific needs of small exporters. In concert with most of the major banks in Canada, the EDC has introduced the Master Accounts Receivable Guarantee (MARG) Program. This program was established to encourage banks to extend incremental operating lines of credit to exporters with total annual sales of less than $5 million, which are secured by their foreign accounts receivable. They have also introduced the *Small Exporter Guarantee Framework (SME Framework)* which was designed to complement the EDC's direct lending program by providing those exporters who have annual export sales of less than $10 million with a choice of direct loan from the EDC or a loan from the bank partially guaranteed by the EDC.

6. *Flexibility of Services*

The EDC's services are flexible and can be custom-tailored to the requirements of the exporter. In order to use the EDC's services to the best advantage, Canadian enterprises are encouraged to consult the EDC and their bankers about credit and financing considerations at the earliest possible date when they are developing their plans.

Most export credit agencies in other countries have what are called posted rates, in other words, the rates are the consensus minimums and they are non-negotiable. Because the EDC believes in a flexible negotiated approach, each transaction is negotiated individually with the goal of getting the interest rates above the consensus minimums whenever it can be done without jeopardizing the competitiveness of the Canadian exporter. A buyer looks at several factors when he or she is considering a purchase. The interest rate is only one of them. In a case where Canada has a strong commercial purpose—a good product, a good price, and so on—a buyer may accept a higher interest rate. The EDC credit officers are not mere order takers. They negotiate for months,

---

13 Report of the House of Commons Standing Committee on Foreign Affairs and International Trade, *Canadian SMEs in the World Economy: Developing Effective Business—Government Partnership for International Success*, June 1996.

sometimes years, to bring home a deal at the best possible return for Canada. Of course, unless the Canadian exporter is competitive too, the transaction will not go forward.

7. Confidentiality

Information provided to the EDC concerning an exporter's potential sale is always received in confidence. The EDC will not disclose an exporter's name or his or her potential involvement in a specific transaction until the sales arrangements are final and a financing agreement has been signed, unless it is done in the context of bank financing and with the exporter's expressed consent. In fact, the EDC will refrain even from indicating that it has been approached in respect of a transaction. The EDC will, as and when appropriate, take inquiries and forward them to the exporter for action as required.

In the case of credits insurance, the EDC makes known its participation only on request and when the exporter consents to the release of information.

The flexible, negotiated approach to export financing used by the EDC does not allow disclosure of interest rates on individual transaction. Otherwise, the last rate charged would tend to be the benchmark for the next negotiation; also, it would let the EDC's competitors know the kind of deals it is making.

For more information on the EDC:

Export Development Corporation
Corporate Communications Department
151 O'Connor Street
Ottawa, ON K1A 1K3
Tel: (613) 598-2500
Fax: (613) 237-2690
Internet: http://www.edc.ca

IV. GOVERNMENT-SUPPORTED EXPORT FINANCING AND THE GATT 1994

The Canadian government has maintained that it does not subsidize exports in contravention of article XVI, paragraphs 1 and 4 of the GATT 1994 and articles 5 and 6 of the 1994 Agreement on Subsidies and Countervailing Measures.[14] Yet, the preamble of the Export Development Act[15] mandates the EDC to "support and develop directly or indirectly Canada's export trade and Canadian capacity to engage in that trade."[16] Furthermore, although the EDC is required by the Financial Administration Act[17] to be self-sustaining in the long run without recourse to Parliament for funding, and support for exporters is based on commercial principles and disciplines, nevertheless, in creating

---

14 *General Agreement on Tariffs and Trade, Uruguay Round of Multilateral* Trade *Negotiations 1994*, Agreement on Subsidies and Countervailing Measures, pt. III, MTN/FA II-13, 5.

15 *Supra*, note 5.

16 *Ibid*., s. 10(1).

17 Financial Administration Act, RSC 1985, c. F-11, pt. X, as am.

the EDC, Parliament made provision for what is called national interest lending. If a proposed transaction presents a risk in excess of that normally undertaken by the EDC's board of directors or requires terms and conditions different from those normally offered by the EDC, but is judged to be in the national interest by the Secretary of State for Foreign Affairs, the Government of Canada may authorize the loan on the Canada account. In such cases, the funds for the loan come from the Consolidated Revenue Fund, rather than from the EDC's treasury. For corporate account lending, under the authority of the EDC's board of directors, the EDC's funds are used.

Thus, it would seem that Canada could violate the GATT principles and rules, for example, when government-supported export financing operates directly or indirectly to increase exports of any product from Canada and causes injury to the domestic industry of another member of the GATT, or nullification or impairment of the benefits accruing directly or indirectly to such other member, or serious prejudice to its interests. This would occur in the case of financing at below consensus minimum rates since paragraphs (j) and (k) of the Illustrative List of Export Subsidies found in Annex 1 of the Agreement on Subsidies and Countervailing Measures of the Uruguay Round of Multilateral Trade Negotiations 1994 prohibit:

> (j) The provision by governments (or special institutions controlled by governments) of export guarantee or insurance programs, of insurance or guarantee programs against increases in the costs of exported products or of exchange risk programs, at premium rates, which are manifestly inadequate to cover the long-term operating costs and losses of the programs.
>
> (k) The grant by governments (or special institutions controlled by and/or acting under the authority of governments) of export credit rates at below those which they actually have to pay for the funds so employed (or would have to pay if they borrowed on international capital markets in order to obtain funds on the same maturity and denominates in the same currency as the export credit), or the payment by them of all or part of the costs incurred by exporters of financial institutions in obtaining credits, in so far as they are used to secure a material advantage in the filed of export credit terms.
>
> Provided, however, that if a signatory is a party to an international undertaking on official export credits to which at least twelve original signatories to this Agreement are parties as of 1 January 1979 (or a successor undertaking which has been adopted by those original signatories) or if in practice a signatory applies the interest rates provisions of the relevant undertaking, an export credit practice which is in conformity with those provisions shall not be considered an export subsidy prohibited by this Agreement.

This proviso covers the OECD consensus guidelines and would exempt financing at consensus minimum rates.

V. SELECTED BIBLIOGRAPHY

A. Books

Arnold, *Up-date to Export Techniques* (2nd ed., 1989).

Canada, *So You Want to Export?* (Ottawa: Department of Foreign Affairs and International Trade, 1995).

Canada, Research and Publication Centre, *Handbooks of Grants and Subsidies, Federal and Provincial* (1986).

Canada, *Directory of Canadian Trading Houses* (Ottawa: Minister of Supply and Services; additional author: Business Opportunities Sourcing Systems, 1996).

Federal Business Development Bank, *Assistance to Business in Canada; ABC Federal/ Provincial: A Handbook of Business Assistance Programs Available from the Federal Government Including a Supplement of Provincial Programs Offered by Ontario* (4th ed., 1987).

Migra International Limited, *Canadian Export Guide* (looseleaf service, 1996).

Nimmo, *Export Guide: A Practical Approach* (6th ed., 1993).

OECD, *Export Credit Financing Systems in OECD Member and Non-member Countries* (looseleaf service, 1995).

Report of the House of Commons Standing Committee on Foreign Affairs and International Trade, *Canadian SMEs in the World Economy: Developing Effective Business-Government Partnership for International Success*, June 1996.

B. Periodicals

Canadian Commerce

Daily Commercial News

EDC Today

Export News

Export Digest

PART V

The Settlement of Trade Disputes

INTRODUCTION

A satisfactory mechanism for the resolution of trade disputes between states or private individuals is essential to the maintenance and development of a mutually profitable international trade relationship.

Differences must be resolved quickly, inexpensively, and effectively, in a manner that is fair to the parties and to the interests of the international community.

Chapters 19 and 20 deal with methods for the settlement of international trade disputes between states in the World Trade Organization (WTO) and under the North American Free Trade Agreement (NAFTA), whereas chapter 21 is concerned with the settlement of international commercial disputes between private parties or state enterprises and private parties by international commercial arbitration.

The major characteristics of the non-judicial process of arbitration, especially its flexibility, reflect the conciliatory attitude of the parties who do not wish to interrupt or jeopardize their international trade relationship during or after adjudication of their dispute.

CHAPTER NINETEEN

The WTO Rules and Procedures for the Settlement of Trade Disputes Between Members

I. INTRODUCTION

The GATT system of settlement of trade disputes, which has worked relatively well since its creation in 1948, has been revised on a number of occasions. Based on GATT, articles XXII and XXIII, the GATT dispute settlement mechanism evolved gradually to accommodate requirements that arose in specific cases. Many of the procedural practices which emerged were codified over the years.[1] During the Uruguay Round of Multilateral Trade Negotiations, launched on September 15, 1986 and concluded with the signing of the Marrakesh Agreement Establishing the World Trade Organization (WTO Agreement) on April 15, 1994, the GATT dispute settlement procedures underwent a comprehensive transformation. The result, the new WTO dispute settlement mechanism, is contained in the Understanding on Rules and Procedures Governing the Settlement of Disputes (DSU), which is Annex 2 to the WTO Agreement.

At the Uruguay Round Mid-term Review in December 1988 (the Mid-term Review), new procedures regarding the establishment and operation of panels were recommended for adoption by the CONTRACTING PARTIES on a trial basis from May 1, 1989 to the end of the Uruguay Round, in respect of complaints brought during that period under article XIII or XXIII and, eventually, on a permanent basis if found satisfactory at that time.[2] After the Mid-term Review, negotiations continued, addressing some more contentious issues dealing with the adoption of panel reports, the creation of an appellate mechanism, and the important question of implementation and withdrawal of concessions. Further revisions to the dispute settlement system were enshrined in the Understanding on Rules and Procedures Governing the Settlement of Disputes under Article XXII and XXIII of the GATT[3] annexed to the Draft Final Act Embodying the Results of the Uruguay Round of Multilateral Trade Negotiations of 20 December 1991

1 The major developments in the pre-WTO-GATT dispute settlement system were codified in Procedures under Article XXIII (decision of 5 April 1966), BISD, 14th Supp., at 18; Understanding Regarding Notification, Consultation, Dispute Settlement and Surveillance (adopted on 28 November 1979) (hereinafter the 1979 understanding), BISD, 26th Supp., at 21; and Improvements to the GATT Dispute Settlement Rules and Procedures (decision of 12 April 1989) (hereinafter the 1989 decision), BISD, 36th Supp., at 61.

2 See Mid-term Review Agreements, 21 April 1989, GATT, doc. MTN.TNC/11 (MIN), at 24-31 and BISD, 36th Supp. 61 (1990).

3 MTN.TNC/W/FA, s. 1-S.23.

(the so-called Dunkel Draft),[4] still applying only to disputes brought under GATT, articles XXII and XXIII. Nevertheless, the Dunkel Draft also contained a proposed text regarding Elements of an Integrated Dispute Settlement System[5] under a Multilateral Trade Organization.[6] Subsequently, in conjunction with institutional advances made in other areas of the multilateral trade negotiations, an integrated dispute settlement mechanism was created to govern disputes arising out of any of the WTO "covered agreements," including the GATT and the other multilateral agreements concerning trade in goods;[7] the General Agreement on Trade in Services (GATS);[8] the Agreement on Trade-Related Aspects of Intellectual Property Rights (TRIPS);[9] certain of the four Plurilateral Trade Agreements in Annex 4 to the WTO Agreement;[10] the WTO Agreement; and the DSU itself.

The overall objective was to make the dispute settlement system more flexible, binding, effective, and enforceable in the hope that the WTO members would eliminate resort to less legitimate methods of resolution of disputes, especially unilateral action in the form of retaliatory measures in national trade legislation. The DSU now contains a specific obligation, entitled "Strengthening of the Multilateral System,"[11] requiring WTO members to resort exclusively to the rules and procedures of the DSU for the settlement of WTO disputes. Mandating a multilateral determination of violation, nullification, or impairment, as well as of the reasonable time for implementation of recommendations and rulings and of the level of retaliation, this provision aims to preclude unilateral acts relating to the covered agreements on the part of WTO members.

WTO dispute settlement remains at the public interstate level, with governments as the only possible complainants and defendants. Thus, only a state that, like Canada, is a member[12] of the WTO may raise a complaint about the breach of the provisions of any of the "covered agreements" by another member.[13] No privatization of international

4 MTN.TNC/W/FA. The Dunkel Draft contained a consolidation of the results of the negotiations in almost all of the Uruguay Round Negotiating Groups.

5 *Ibid.*, T.1 to T.6.

6 See Agreement Establishing the Multilateral Trade Organization in the Dunkel Draft, at 91 to 101.

7 Annex 1A to the WTO Agreement.

8 Annex 1B to the WTO Agreement.

9 Annex 1C to the WTO Agreement.

10 As of 1 July 1996, the Agreement on Government Procurement is the only Plurilateral Trade Agreement to have been brought within the purview of the DSU.

11 DSU, art. 23.

12 Prior to the establishment of the WTO, GATT signatories were referred to as contracting parties. When the members of the GATT acted collectively they were referred to as CONTRACTING PARTIES with capital letters. This chapter is not concerned with disputes between a contracting party and the CONTRACTING PARTIES on the competence of the CONTRACTING PARTIES. Such disputes, which would involve the interpretation of the General Agreement, were settled by the council of the CONTRACTING PARTIES directly and not through panel procedures. Now, signatories of the WTO Agreement are referred to as WTO members.

13 Note that the EC has standing under the GATT-WTO, although it is not a state.

trade disputes has occurred. Even arbitration remains strictly state-to-state.[14] Affected private persons, whether Canadian citizens or permanent residents of Canada, have no standing under the DSU. No formal procedure exists for such private persons. They must approach the Department of Foreign Affairs and International Trade (DFAIT) or another department with the request to take up their case in accordance with the rules of the DSU. The decision is discretionary and not subject to review by the Federal Court. The WTO, as an international organization, cannot act on its own initiative through its director general to enforce compliance with the covered agreements.

II. THE PRE-WTO-GATT DISPUTE SETTLEMENT SYSTEM

A. General Survey of the GATT System

1. Relevant Provisions

The original GATT contains several articles with clauses dealing with the resolution of disputes.[15] However, articles XXII and XXIII, as supplemented successively by the 1979 Understanding Regarding Notification, Consultation, Dispute Settlement and Surveillance,[16] the 1982 Ministerial Declaration on Dispute Settlement, and the Decision of 12 April 1989 on Improvements to the GATT Dispute Settlement Rules and Procedures[17] are the most important because they contain the basic rules and procedures for pre-WTO-GATT dispute settlement.[18] Articles XXII and XXIII of the GATT 1994 still form the basis for disputes that now arise between WTO members under the GATT 1994 and under those Annex 1A agreements, where they have been incorporated *mutatis mutandis*. Other covered agreements contain specific equivalent or corresponding provisions.[19] Disputes arising between WTO members are now governed by the DSU, examined in section III, *infra*.

---

14 See DSU, art. 25.

15 E.g., arts. XIX (safeguards), XXVII (modification of schedules of concessions), and XXV:5 (waivers). For a complete list of the 19 clauses in the GATT that obligate the disputants to resolve differences by consultations, see Jackson, *World Trade and the Law of GATT* (1969), at 164. The text of the GATT may be found in IV BISD (1969).

16 BISD, 26th Supp. 210 (1978-79) (hereinafter the 1979 understanding).

17 BISD, 36th Supp. 61 (hereinafter the 1989 decision).

18 BISD, 29th Supp. 13 (1982) (hereinafter the Ministerial Declaration on Dispute Settlement). See also the 1984 decision that completed and clarified the 1979 understanding on certain questions and contains directives applicable on a one-year trial basis, especially with respect to a short roster of non-governmental experts qualified to serve as panelists: Action by Contracting Parties on Dispute Settlement Procedures, BISD, 31st Supp. 9 (1985).

19 The corresponding provisions to art. XXII of GATT 1994 in the covered agreements annexed to the 1994 Agreement Establishing the World Trade Organization (WTO Agreement) are: Agreement on Agriculture, art. 19; Agreement on the Application of Sanitary and Phytosanitary Measures, art. 11.1; Agreement on Textiles and Clothing, arts. 8:4 and 8:10; Agreement on Technical Barriers to Trade, art.

(The footnote is continued on the next page.)

2. *Brief Analysis of Relevant Provisions*

a. Consultations

GATT, article XXII, as amended in 1955, provided for consultations with respect to any matter affecting the operation of the GATT. Contracting parties were invited to solve their disputes by bilateral consultations and, if this failed, by the conciliatory intervention of the CONTRACTING PARTIES.[20] This is the diplomatic solution. Although working parties could be established under this article, contracting parties only resorted to this procedure infrequently between 1948 and 1995.

Both the 1979 understanding and the 1989 decision added that contracting parties would respond to requests for consultations promptly and would attempt to conclude them expeditiously with a view to reaching a mutually satisfactory solution.[21]

b. Nullification or Impairment

GATT article XXIII set out three causes of action on which a complaint may be based. A GATT contracting party could have recourse to the procedures provided for by article XXIII when it considered that any benefit accruing to it directly or indirectly under the GATT was being nullified or impaired or that the attainment of any objective of the GATT was being impeded as a result of:[22]

---

19 Continued ...
14.1; Agreement on Trade-Related Investment Measures, art. 8; Agreement on Implementation of Article VI of GATT 1994 (Anti-dumping Agreement), art. 17:2; Agreement on Implementation of Article VII of GATT 1994 (Customs Valuation Agreement), art. 19:1-2; Agreement on Preshipment Inspection, arts. 7 and 8; Agreement on Rules of Origin, arts. 7 and 8; Agreement on Import Licensing Procedures, art. 6; Agreement on Subsidies and Countervailing Measures, art. 30; Agreement on Safeguards, art. 14; Agreement on Trade-Related Aspects of Intellectual Property Rights (TRIPS Agreement), art. 64.1; and any corresponding provisions in Plurilateral Trade Agreements as determined by the competent bodies of each agreement and as notified to the Dispute Settlement Body (DSB). See also art. XXII of the General Agreement on Trade in Services (GATS).

20 BISD, 3rd Supp. 44 (1955). Art. XXII provides as follows:

> Consultation:
>
> 1. Each contracting party shall accord sympathetic consideration to, and shall afford adequate opportunity for consultation regarding, such representations as may be made by another contracting party with respect to any matter affecting the operation of this Agreement.
>
> 2. The CONTRACTING PARTIES may, at the request of a contracting party, consult with any contracting party or parties in respect of any matter for which it has not been possible to find a satisfactory solution through consultation under paragraph 1.

21 Para. 4. Note that any contracting party requesting consultations under art. XXII:2 had to inform the director general of the GATT to allow notification of all other contracting parties. 1958 Decision, BISD, 7th Supp. 24 (1959).

22 Art. XXIII:1.

(a) the failure of another contracting party to carry out its obligations under this Agreement;

(b) the application by another contracting party of any measure, whether or not it conflicts with the provisions of this Agreement; or

(c) the existence of any other situation.

Paragraph XXIII:1(a) has formed the basis of almost all GATT disputes. It involves so-called violation complaints, disputes arising due to the alleged violation or infringement of a GATT obligation. A *prima facie* presumption exists that a breach of the rules of the GATT nullifies or impairs benefits accruing to other contracting parties, thus having an adverse impact upon them. In such a case, it is up to the contracting party against which the complaint is made to rebut the charge.[23] The object is to stop the violation of agreed-upon rules in order to preserve the integrity of the GATT.

With respect to paragraph XXIII:1(b), involving so-called non-violation complaints, the complainant has to prove not necessarily that a breach of the rules has occurred, but that a benefit accruing to it under the GATT has been nullified or impaired. Paragraph XXIII:1(c), covering "situation complaints," has never been the foundation for a recommendation or ruling,[24] although it has formed the basis for parties' arguments.

In the GATT dispute settlement system, bilateral consultations between the disputants under articles XXII,[25] XXIII:1,[26] or XXXVIII:2 and 5[27] had to precede recourse to the dispute settlement procedures found in article XXIII:2. Thus, when the contracting parties were unable to resolve their dispute through consultation, negotiation, or conciliation,[28] the aggrieved party[29] could refer the matter to the GATT CONTRACTING PARTIES for prompt investigation. While GATT, article XXIII:2 makes no mention of panels or other adjudicatory mechanisms, the practice evolved on the basis of this provision that the aggrieved party could request the GATT council to appoint a panel to adjudicate such a dispute. Although there was no legal requirement, a request for the establishment of a panel was usually granted by the council in accordance with "standard practice" of the GATT, unless the request was opposed by the other party.

---

23 Now art. 3.8 of the Understanding on Rules and Procedures Governing the Settlement of Disputes (DSU), which is Annex 2 to the WTO Agreement. This provision was also included in the 1979 understanding, annex, para. 5. Note that the panel in *United States—Taxes on Petroleum and Certain Imported Substances*, BISD, 34th Supp. 136, at 157-58, stated, "while the CONTRACTING PARTIES had not explicitly decided whether the presumption that illegal measures cause nullification or impairment could be rebutted, the presumption had in practice operated as an irrefutable presumption."

24 For examination of how "non-violation" complaints are to be treated in WTO dispute settlement system, see section III.E.11, *infra*.

25 1960 decision, BISD, 9th Supp. 19 (1961).

26 1979 understanding, para. 6.

27 Art. XXXVII deals with commitments to less-developed contracting parties.

28 1979 understanding, para. 8.

29 Private persons had no standing under the GATT. They had to act through their governments. This remains the case under the WTO Agreement.

The GATT dispute settlement process gradually evolved and was codified in the 1979 Understanding, and subsequently in the 1989 Decision.[30] The use of the dispute settlement procedures was not to be intended or considered as a contentious act and all parties were to engage in these procedures in good faith in an effort to resolve the dispute.[31] The panel, pursuant to its terms of reference, was told to investigate the dispute in light of the rules of the GATT, hear the arguments of the parties concerned and make such findings as would assist the CONTRACTING PARTIES in making recommendations or rulings.[32] In the pre-WTO-GATT dispute settlement system, panels were to complete their reports within six months, although this time frame was exceeded on numerous occasions.[33] In cases of urgency, the panel was to deliver its report within three months following its establishment.[34]

It was always possible for the parties to the dispute to reach a settlement before the panel submitted its report to the council, in which case it was the end of the matter.[35]

The panel could,[36] if nullification or impairment was found, recommend that the offending measure be withdrawn,[37] or, if this could not be done immediately, that the injured party be compensated, for example, by lower tariffs until the withdrawal took place.[38] The report containing the findings and recommendations or rulings had to be given prompt consideration and approval by the council, which was empowered to act on behalf of the CONTRACTING PARTIES, in order to acquire legal force.[39] Adoption of the report and action taken pursuant to it within a reasonable period of time were decided by consensus.[40] Thus, any contracting party, including the party that was the

30 See section II.D, *infra.*

31 1979 understanding, para. 9. The function of art. XXIII:2 is to incite the parties to settle their dispute.

32 1979 understanding, para. 16.

33 1979 understanding, para. 20: The time required by panels varies with the particular case. See also 1982 Ministerial Declaration on Dispute Settlement, para. (vi). The panels were composed of three to five independent experts agreed upon by the parties to the dispute or selected by the director general: 1979 understanding, para. 11; annex, para. 6 (iii). See also 1984 decision, *supra*, note 18. The panel's composition and terms of reference, in principle, had to be determined within 30 days following the decision to establish it.

34 1979 understanding, para. 20.

35 1979 understanding, para. 17. The report of the panel could be confined to reporting that a solution has been reached.

36 1979 understanding, annex, paras. 3 and 6(viii) and 1982 Ministerial Declaration on Dispute Settlement, para. (v).

37 1979 understanding, annex, para. 4. Note that paras. 2 and 3 of the understanding provide for publication and notification of trade measures possibly in advance of implementation. Thus, if the measures were to violate the GATT obligations, a dispute could be avoided before it arose by consultations leading to the withdrawal of the measures.

38 1979 understanding, annex, para. 4.

39 1979 understanding, annex, para. 1, note 1.

40 1982 Ministerial Declaration on Dispute Settlement, para. (x).

object of the recommendations or rulings, could block the adoption of the report. However, obstruction in the process of dispute settlement was to be avoided.[41]

The CONTRACTING PARTIES were to keep under surveillance any matter on which they had made recommendations or rulings to make sure that implementation took place within a reasonable period of time.[42] If the recommendations or rulings were not implemented, the aggrieved contracting party could ask for the authorization of the council to take retaliatory action against the offending party.[43] While it never actually occurred and was only authorized once, this meant the suspension, on a discriminatory basis, of the application of concessions vis-à-vis the other member country concerned in order to restore the negotiated balance of rights and obligations under the GATT. Too, GATT, article XXIII:2 states: "[i]f the application to any contracting party of any concession or other obligation is in fact suspended, that contracting party shall then be free, not later than sixty days after such action is taken, to give written notice to the Executive Secretary to the CONTRACTING PARTIES of its intention to withdraw from this Agreement, and such withdrawal shall take effect upon the sixtieth day following the day on which such notice is received by him."[44]

As stated by one authority:[45]

> One of the basic objectives of any dispute procedure in GATT has been the effective resolution of the dispute rather than "punishment," or imposing a "sanction" or obtaining "compensation." The prime objective has been stated to be the "withdrawal" of a measure inconsistent with the General Agreement.

In spite of the progressive codification of the basic procedures for the settlement of the GATT disputes by third-party adjudication, consultations, and conciliation leading to an amicable settlement through diplomatic negotiations remained open to the contracting parties. Thus, a characteristic of the pre-WTO-GATT system of settlement of disputes was the conciliatory character of the procedures. The objective was to redress the contractual balance of rights and obligations between the disputants in particular and among the contracting parties in general.

---

41 *Ibid.*

42 1979 understanding, para. 22 and 1982 Ministerial Declaration on Dispute Settlement, para. (viii).

43 GATT, art. XXIII:2; 1979 understanding, para. 22; and annex, para. 4. This happened only once between 1948 and 1994 when, in 1952, the Netherlands was authorized to impose a discriminatory quota on imports of wheat flour from the United States following a dispute regarding US quotas on dairy products. The Netherlands did not retaliate: BISD, 3rd Supp. 46 (1955). In 1990, the United States asked the Council for authority to retaliate against Canada for its non-implementation of a panel report on import, distribution, and sale of alcoholic drinks by Canadian provincial marketing agencies adopted by the council on 22 March 1988 (BISD, 35th Supp. 37 (1988)). Retaliation is to take the form of suspension of concessions. Canada acknowledged that it was not in full compliance with the panel findings, but a negotiated arrangement was reached, obviating the need for authorization to retaliate.

44 GATT, art. XXIII:2.

45 Jackson, *World Trade and the Law of GATT* (1969), at 184.

3. *Developing Countries*

In 1966,[46] the CONTRACTING PARTIES adopted a decision, confirmed in 1979 and 1994[47] that established the procedure to be followed for consultations and conciliation between developed and developing contracting parties.

This procedure provides, *inter alia*, for the director general of the GATT (now WTO) to employ his or her good offices with a view to facilitating a solution, for setting up a panel with the task of examining the dispute or problem in order to recommend appropriate solutions, for compliance, and for short time limits for the carrying out of the different parts of this procedure.

If the dispute is not resolved through consultations and conciliation, either party to it may refer the matter to the CONTRACTING PARTIES.[48]

B. The Tokyo Round Codes

The non-tariff barriers agreements negotiated in the Tokyo Round also contained procedures for the settlement of disputes which applied only to GATT members having signed them. Some of them followed more or less the model of the 1979 understanding.[49] Others adopted new and more elaborate and rigorous procedures.[50] Still others established specific procedures although reference was made to articles XXII and XXIII of the GATT.[51] Finally, some were without detailed procedures.[52]

The procedures were operated by the committee administering the agreement concerned. For instance, the Code on Subsidies and Countervailing Measures provided that, when a signatory believed that any subsidy granted or maintained by another signatory either caused injury to its domestic industry, nullification or impairment of benefits accruing to it under the GATT, or serious prejudice to its interests, such signatory could request consultations with such other signatory. In the event that no mutually acceptable solution was reached, the next step was conciliation mediated by the administering committee. Once the matter was before the committee, the aggrieved party had the right to a proceeding before a panel. The committee, upon receipt of the panel report, could make recommendations to the parties and, if they were not followed within a reasonable

46 BISD, 14th Supp. 18 (1966).

47 DSU, *supra*, note 23, art. 3.12; 1979 understanding, paras. 7 and 8; and annex, paras. 2 and 3.

48 1982 Ministerial Declaration on Dispute Settlement, para. (i).

49 Agreement on Technical Barriers to Trade (Standards Code) and Agreement on Government Procurement; and Agreement on the Implementation of Article VII of the General Agreement on Tariffs and Trade (Code of Customs Valuation). See the GATT, *The Texts of the Tokyo Round Agreements* (1986).

50 Agreement on Interpretation of Articles VI, XVI, and XXIII of the General Agreement on Tariffs and Trade (Agreement on Subsidies and Countervailing Measures) and Agreement on Implementation of Article VI of the General Agreement on Tariffs and Trade (Anti-Dumping Agreement). See GATT, *The Texts of the Tokyo Round Agreements* (1986).

51 Agreement on Trade in Civil Aircraft; Agreement on Import Licensing Procedures. See GATT, *ibid.*

52 Bovine Meat Arrangement; Dairy Arrangement. See GATT, *ibid.*

period of time, authorize appropriate counter-measures. Strict time limits applied to each phase of the dispute settlement procedures.[53]

The dispute settlement procedures of the codes were used on occasion. Between 1979 and 1995, five of the twelve reports presented by panels established under the Code on Subsidies and Countervailing Measures were not adopted because they raised fundamental questions concerning the interpretation and application of certain articles of this code on which the administering committee disagreed.[54]

The existence of separate institutional arrangements and dispute settlement procedures under many of the Tokyo Round Codes led to a fragmented and complex GATT dispute settlement system. Code signatories could opt to bring disputes either to a Code Committee under the relevant Tokyo Round Code or to the GATT CONTRACTING PARTIES under the relevant provisions of GATT 1947. This raised the possibility of forum-shopping. It also presented the potential for "double jeopardy," because there was nothing barring a complainant unsuccessful in one forum from subsequently bringing the complaint in another forum.

All of the codes have now been superseded by the WTO Agreement. Those now constituting Multilateral Trade Agreements, in Annex 1A to the WTO Agreement, are thus subject to the integrated dispute settlement mechanism set out in the DSU. This is the case, for example, with the agreements on anti-dumping, subsidies and countervailing measures, technical barriers to trade, and import licensing procedures. The agreement on government procurement, as revised, is now a plurilateral trade agreement, in Annex 4 of the WTO Agreement, to which the provisions of the DSU apply as a result of a special committee decision.

C. Criticisms of the Pre-Uruguay Round System

Dissatisfaction with the GATT procedures[55] for the settlement of disputes resulted from a number of causes, especially fragmentation of the dispute settlement system, forum shopping, the lack of automatic access to panels, delays in appointing them and in establishing their terms of reference, and slow consideration of the cases due to the absence of strict time limits for the various stages of the procedure. Decision making by

53 Arts. 12, 13, 17, and 18.

54 See, e.g., 46 GATT FOCUS 2 (1987), Status Report—End of 1986.

55 For detailed analysis, see, e.g., Dam, *The GATT: Law and International Economic Organization* (1970); Hudec, *Adjudication of International Trade Disputes* (1978); Hudec, "GATT Dispute Settlement After the Tokyo Round: An Unfinished Business" (1980), 13 *Cornell Int'l. LJ* 145; Hudec, *The GATT Legal System and World Trade Diplomacy* (2nd ed., 1990); Hudec, *Enforcing International Trade Law: The Evolution of the GATT Legal System* (1993); Davey, "Dispute Settlement in GATT" (1987), 11 *Fordham Int'l. LJ* 51; Simmonds and Hill, *Law and Practice under the GATT* (1988); Bliss, "GATT Dispute Settlement Reform in the Uruguay Round: Problems and Prospects" (1987), 23 *Stan. J Int'l. L* 31; Long, *Law and Its Limitations in the GATT Multilateral Trade System* (1985); US International Trade Commission, *Review of the Effectiveness of Trade Dispute Settlement under the GATT and the Tokyo Round Agreements* (1985); McGovern, *International Trade Regulation* (1995); Jackson, *The World Trading System* (1989); and Jackson, *Restructuring the GATT System* (1990).

consensus, which allowed blockage by the losing party, and difficulties and delays in implementing panel reports were also undermining the system.

A better system of surveillance to ensure compliance with recommendations and rulings was needed which, ultimately, had to depend upon the political will of the GATT members to abide by the rules for the settlement of disputes. The lack of recourse available to the losing party had also been criticized.

Since the practice of the GATT had been to stress conciliation and negotiated settlements rather than the enforcement of obligations,[56] recommendations or rulings had been made only when the parties were unable to reach a mutually acceptable solution to their dispute. However, in recent years, especially since the *DISC* case,[57] the contracting parties seemed to have become more committed to the adjudicative process.

A more legalistic and rule-oriented procedure for the settlement of disputes would discourage the breach of the GATT rules, result in more precise decisions on the merits of disputes and ensure greater compliance with them than did the consensus system. Negotiated settlements favour countries that have considerable political and economic strength irrespective of the merits of the dispute. An adjudicative approach stresses fairness and is more likely to protect the rights of small countries.

Perhaps greater use should have been made of retaliation that, in the past, had meant only the re-establishment of the balance of concessions and advantages between the contracting parties concerned. Retaliatory measures should have taken the form of legal sanctions when the GATT rules were broken.[58] Unfortunately, a small country, especially if it is a developing country, has a limited capacity to retaliate against a major trading partner that fails to implement a panel recommendation.

The lack of agreement among the contracting parties on the nature of the panel rulings, whether they are binding on the parties to the dispute and constitute a precedent that can be relied upon in future disputes, had not enhanced the authority of the panels.

Although everyone agreed that the GATT system of settlement of disputes needed strengthening, it was obvious that improvements would not be fully successful as long as some of the contracting parties of the GATT were dissatisfied with the applicable substantive rules, especially those relating to subsidies. It was the lack of more rigorous substantive rules that resulted in a strain on the legal remedies.[59]

---

56 Long, *Law and Its Limitations in the GATT Multilateral Trade System* (1985), at 71: "In any proceedings, the Contracting Parties' main objective is to produce recommendations designed to protect this balance rather than have recourse to sanctions."

57 BISD, 23rd Supp. 98 (1975-76); J.H. Jackson, "The Jurisprudence of International Trade: The *DISC* Case in GATT" (1978), 72 *Am. J Int'l. L* 747; and R.E. Hudec, "Reforming GATT Adjudication Procedures: The Lessons of the *DISC* Case" (1987-88), 72 *Minn. L Rev.* 1443.

58 Note that the GATT obligations could be enforced by resorting to traditional remedies under international law. However, the practice had been "to rely mainly upon the provisions of GATT itself for legal redress in cases of violation or other disputes," Jackson, *World Trade and the Law of GATT* (1969), at 164.

59 See Hudec, "Transcending The Ostensible: Some Reflections on the Nature of Litigation Between Governments" (1987-88), 72 *Minn. L Rev.* 211. According to the US International Trade Commission in

(The footnote is continued on the next page.)

Of the many suggestions that were made to improve the pre-WTO system, the following should be mentioned: a mechanism for early warning; notification to the council of mutually agreed solutions where any GATT member could raise matters relating to such solutions; provision for going directly to the council and requesting a panel should the other party fail to respond to a request for consultations within an established time period; the enhancement of the consultation, mediation, and conciliation process, especially mediation by the director general; new options such as voluntary or mandatory binding arbitration to respond to the different nature of disputes provided the rights of third parties were not affected; automatic access to panels; strict time limits for the council when establishing panels; the holding of regular meetings of the council devoted exclusively to dispute settlement; the use of standard terms of reference by panels; the expansion and the regular updating of a roster of non-governmental panelists; the imposition of strict time limits on the work of panels and the examination and implementation of their reports by the council; the modification of the consensus rule, especially with respect to the adoption of the panel reports; the avoidance of differences of interpretation of the GATT rules by the panels; a more important role for the Secretariat and its legal staff; an appellate process; an improved followup procedure; a clarification of the procedure in disputes involving several complainants; and the right of intervention of third parties, including access to information.

Finally, it was also proposed that special and more favourable treatment should be accorded to developing countries that would include specialized legal assistance, supplementary training courses, and post-consultation review by the council, as long as these measures did not infringe the principle of equality of treatment. Many of these proposals were included in the 1989 decision. Others, notably the introduction of automaticity in the adoption of panel and appellate body reports and the establishment of the appellate body to review panel decisions were included in the 1991 Draft Final Act and introduced with the establishment of the WTO and the entrance into force of the DSU.

D. The 1989 Uruguay Round Mid-Term Review Decision

At the Mid-term Review, new procedures regarding the establishment and operation of panels were recommended for adoption by the CONTRACTING PARTIES on a trial basis from May 1, 1989 to the end of the Uruguay Round, in respect of complaints brought during that period under article XXII or XXIII and, eventually, on a permanent basis if found satisfactory at that time.[60] With one important exception, the procedures of the 1989 decision now apply only to disputes that arose between April 12, 1989 and the entrance into force of the WTO Agreement on January 1, 1995. The exception is that

59 Continued …

Review of the Effectiveness of Trade Dispute Settlement under the GATT and the Tokyo Round Agreements (1985), the difficulties were not due to any serious defects in the dispute settlement mechanism *per se*, but to the lack of political will on the part of the litigants to abide by GATT decisions.

60 See Mid-Term Review Agreements, 21 April 1989, GATT, doc. MTN.TNC/11 (MIN), at 24-31 and BISD, 36th Supp. 61 (1990).

the provisions of the 1989 decision still apply with respect to the consideration for adoption, surveillance, and implementation of Dispute Settlement Body (DSB) recommendations and rulings dealing with disputes concerning the so-called "situation complaints" referred to in article XXIII:1(c) of the GATT.[61]

Briefly, in addition to introducing provisions on notification, good offices, conciliation, mediation, arbitration, and technical assistance, the 1989 decision contained enhanced provisions laying down strict time frames for many procedural steps in the panel process. These included provisions for consultations and for panel procedures[62] (including establishment of a panel, its composition and terms of reference, and overall deadlines for panel examination). Provision was made for multiple complainants and for third-party practice. With respect to the various phases of a panel, the panels were to follow the suggested working procedures found in the July 1985 note of the office of legal affairs, unless the members of the panel agreed otherwise after consulting the parties to the dispute. As a general rule, the period in which the panel was to conduct its examination—from the time the composition and terms of reference of the panel had been agreed upon—to the time when the final report was provided to the parties to the dispute was not to exceed six months and, in cases of urgency, the panel had to aim to provide its report within three months as was the case pursuant to the 1979 understanding.[63]

Since panel procedures were to provide sufficient flexibility to ensure high-quality panel reports while not unduly delaying the panel process, no compulsory time limits were fixed. However, in no case was the period from the establishment of the panel to the submission of the report to the contracting parties to exceed nine months. This was stronger language than that found in the annex to the 1979 understanding.[64] These procedural improvements were carried on and enhanced in the WTO-DSU.

The 1989 decision retained the necessity for consensus in the adoption of panel reports. Thus, blocking the adoption of a panel report remained a possibility.

The 1989 decision contained an obligation on the part of the contracting party concerned to inform the DSB of its intention with respect to implementation of the recommendations or rulings when the panel report was accepted. If that party found it impracticable to comply immediately with the recommendations or rulings, it could have a reasonable period of time to do so. In order to incite the losing party to remove the offending measure as promptly as possible, the council monitored the implementation of recommendations and rulings. Thus, unless the council decided otherwise, this issue had to be on the agenda of the council meeting after six months following the adoption of the recommendations or rulings and had to remain on the agenda until it was resolved.

---

61 See DSU, *supra*, note 23, art. 26:2, and section III.E.11, *infra*. The DSU now governs these matters with respect to all other complaints (i.e., violation and non-violation complaints) arising after 1 January 1995.

62 Complaints of nullification or impairment were generally handled by panels. Matters of less contentious nature were entrusted to working parties.

63 1989 decision., para. 20.

64 *Ibid*., para. 6(ix).

III. THE WTO DISPUTE SETTLEMENT UNDERSTANDING

A. General

The WTO Understanding on Rules and Procedures Governing the Settlement of Disputes (the DSU) regulates the resolution of disputes arising among WTO members.[65]

In the DSU, WTO members "affirm their adherence to the principles for the management of disputes heretofore applied under articles XXII and XXIII of GATT 1947, and the rules and procedures as further elaborated and modified" in the DSU.[66] The WTO members recognize that the dispute settlement system of the WTO is a central element in providing security and predictability to the multilateral trading system, serving to protect the rights and obligations of members under the covered agreements, and to clarify the existing provisions of those agreements in accordance with customary rules of interpretation of public international law.[67] The DSU emphasizes that in their findings and recommendations, a panel, the appellate body, and the DSB cannot add to or diminish the rights and obligations provided in the covered agreements.[68] Moreover, the DSU stresses that the prompt settlement of disputes "is essential to the proper functioning of the WTO and the maintenance of a proper balance between the rights and obligations of Members."[69]

As under the GATT, the fundamental aim of the WTO dispute resolution mechanism remains to reach a positive and preferably mutually acceptable solution to a dispute. In the absence of a mutually acceptable solution reached through consultations, resort to a panel or to arbitration is available, with the primary objective being withdrawal of inconsistent measures pursuant to the terms of a panel report. Compensation will be provided only where the removal of the offending measure is not immediately possible. The last resort envisaged by the DSU is the temporary suspension of concessions or other obligations under the covered agreements that can be applied against the offending member, subject to DSB authorization and surveillance.[70]

The rules and procedures in the DSU build upon the reforms agreed to in the 1989 decision. As mentioned above, the 1989 decision already contained provisions on notification, consultations, good offices, conciliation, mediation, arbitration, improvements

65 Note that certain of the "covered agreements" contain provisions that are relevant for disputes arising under those particular agreements. These include Agreement on Subsidies and Countervailing Measures; Agreement on Implementation of Article VI of GATT 1994 (the Anti-dumping Agreement); Agreement on Technical Barriers to Trade; and Agreement on the Application of Sanitary and Phytosanitary Measures. App. 2 to the DSU, *supra*, note 23, enumerates these "Special or Additional Rules and Procedures Contained in the Covered Agreements."

66 *Ibid.*, art. 3:1.

67 *Ibid.*, art. 3:2. Note that the 1996 WTO Appellate Body Report in *United States—Standards for Reformulated and Conventional Gasoline* (WT/DS2/9) stated that art. 31 of the Vienna Convention on the Law of Treaties forms part of the "customary rules of interpretation of public international law."

68 *Ibid.*, arts. 3.2 and 19.2.

69 *Ibid.*, art. 3.3.

70 *Ibid.*, art. 3.7.

concerning the timing and procedures in the panel process, consideration and adoption of panel reports (although the consensus rule remained), technical assistance, and surveillance and implementation of recommendations and rulings. While some of these provisions were incorporated directly into the DSU, others were modified and enhanced in the DSU. In addition, the DSU added new provisions concerning the interim review of panel reports, the appellate review mechanism, and strengthening of the multilateral system.

The DSU applies only with respect to requests for consultations made on or after January 1, 1995. With respect to disputes for which the request for consultations was made under the GATT 1947, or under any predecessor agreement to the covered agreements prior to January 1, 1995, the relevant dispute settlement rules and procedures in effect immediately prior to January 1, 1995 continue to apply.[71] Certain provisions of the 1966 decision may also govern disputes involving developing countries.[72]

B. Procedural Innovation: Automaticity

Briefly, automaticity means that a decision is taken automatically, unless there is a consensus against it.

While the DSU provides that the DSB will ordinarily take its decisions by consensus,[73] one of the significant procedural innovations in the DSU is the enhanced automaticity it has introduced through the requirement of automaticity at certain points in the dispute settlement process. This requirement improves the efficacy of the procedures by rendering it more difficult for unwilling or losing parties to delay or block the proceedings. Automaticity is required in the DSB for the establishment of panels,[74] the adoption of panel[75] and appellate body reports,[76] and decisions concerning the surveillance of implementation of recommendations and rulings,[77] compensation, and the suspension of obligations.[78] A decision for these events is therefore taken automatically, unless there is a consensus decision to the contrary. This procedural evolution has therefore eradicated the ability of an unwilling losing party to block the establishment of a panel, to veto the

71 *Ibid.*, art. 3.11. This provision also applies to disputes in which the panel reports have not been adopted or fully implemented by 1 January 1995. Certain transitional arrangements and decisions have now terminated some of the dispute settlement provisions that were available in the pre-WTO-GATT system.

72 *Ibid.*, art. 3:12.

73 *Ibid.*, art. 2.4: consensus occurs "if no Member, present at the meeting of the DSB when the decision is taken, formally objects to the proposed decision." See also art. IX.1 of the WTO Agreement, codifying the practice of taking decisions by consensus that had developed and was followed under the GATT 1947. This provision states that unless otherwise provided, where a decision cannot be arrived at by consensus, the matter at issue shall be decided by voting.

74 *Ibid.*, art. 6.1.

75 *Ibid.*, art. 16.4.

76 *Ibid.*, art. 17.14.

77 *Ibid.*, art. 21.6.

78 *Ibid.*, art. 22.6.

adoption of a report or to block surveillance and implementation of DSB recommendations and rulings resulting from the adoption of a panel or appellate body report.

C. Integrated Dispute Settlement Mechanism

Along with procedural automaticity, another significant innovation in the DSU is the creation of an integrated dispute settlement mechanism. Whereas previously there was a patchwork of dispute settlement mechanisms under the GATT 1947 and the various Tokyo Round Codes, the new WTO has a single mechanism, administered by the DSB, which has responsibility for all the steps under disputes arising under the "covered agreements." The covered agreements embrace the following:[79]

(A) The Agreement Establishing the World Trade Organization
(B) Multilateral Trade Agreements
Annex 1A: Multilateral Agreements on Trade in Goods, which include the GATT 1994
Annex 1B: General Agreement on Trade in Services
Annex 1C: Agreement on Trade-Related Aspects of Intellectual Property Rights
Annex 2: Understanding on Rules and Procedures Governing the Settlement of Disputes
(C) Plurilateral Trade Agreements[80]
Annex 4: Agreement on Trade in Civil Aircraft
Agreement on Government Procurement
International Dairy Agreement
International Bovine Meat Agreement

The integrated dispute settlement mechanism is a corollary of the WTO single undertaking, whereby each WTO Member has undertaken to abide by all of the obligations contained in the WTO Agreement, including those in annexes 1, 2, and 3 of the WTO Agreement.[81] This integrated approach remedies many of the problems of the pre-WTO dispute settlement system, including forum-shopping.

In this integrated system, the DSU applies subject to the special or additional rules and procedures on dispute settlement contained in the covered agreements, identified in

79 *Ibid.*, app. I.

80 Note that in respect of the plurilateral trade agreements in Annex 4 to the WTO Agreement, the DSU, *ibid.*, only applies to the extent that the parties to each agreement adopt a decision setting out the terms for the application of the DSU to the individual agreement, including any special or additional rules or procedures, as notified to the DSB. To date, only the Agreement on Government Procurement has been explicitly made subject to the DSU; paras. XXII:2-7 of that agreement have been notified as special or additional dispute settlement procedures under app. 2 of the DSU. Where the dispute involves a Plurilateral Agreement, "only those Members that are parties to the Agreement may participate in decisions or actions taken by the DSB with respect to that dispute" (DSU, art. 2.1).

81 The plurilateral trade agreements in Annex 4 of the WTO Agreement are binding only upon their signatories.

Annex 2 to the DSU. These special or additional rules and procedures prevail over the DSU where differences exist.

D. The Dispute Settlement Body (DSB)

The DSB administers the rules and procedures of the DSU and all of the disputes arising under the covered agreements. Membership of the DSB is the same as that of the WTO General Council (that is, composed of all WTO members), but the DSB has its own chairperson and rules of procedure. The DSB exercises the authority of the General Council in its dispute settlement functions, meeting as often as necessary to carry out its functions within the relevant time frames.[82] In practice, the DSB meets approximately once a month or more often if necessary. The DSB administers all dispute settlement rules and procedures, including establishment of panels, consideration and adoption of panel and appellate reports, surveillance of implementation of rulings and recommendations, and authorization of suspension of concessions or other obligations under the covered agreements as retaliatory measures.[83]

Unlike the pre-WTO-GATT system, where different bodies had legal authority over the separate dispute settlement systems contained in the various agreements, under the WTO's integrated dispute settlement system contained in the DSU, one body is therefore empowered to deal with all the matters arising between the parties under any of the covered agreements. Another related advantage of the new DSU will be that the same panel will enjoy the authority to address all of the issues raised under any of the covered agreements. These factors streamline the dispute settlement process, and eliminate the possibility of forum shopping

E. The WTO Dispute Settlement Process

1. Notification

Parties may reach a mutually agreed solution to their dispute at any point in the dispute settlement procedures. Such mutually agreed solutions, as well as WTO arbitration awards,[84] must be notified to the DSB and to the relevant councils and committees, where any WTO member may raise any point relating to them.[85]

2. Consultations

The DSU stresses the importance of consultations in achieving the resolution of disputes. Each WTO member has undertaken to "accord sympathetic consideration to and afford adequate opportunity for consultation regarding any representations made by another Member concerning measures affecting the operation of any covered agreement taken within the territory of the former."[86]

---

82 DSU, art. 2.3.

83 *Ibid.*, art. 2.1.

84 *Ibid.*, art 25.3.

85 *Ibid.*, art. 3.6.

86 *Ibid.*, art. 4.2.

The WTO member requesting consultations must notify the DSB and the relevant councils and committees of the request. A request for consultations must be in writing, giving the reasons for the request and identifying the measure at issue and the legal basis for the complaint.[87]

A WTO member must respond to a request for consultations within 10 days and enter into consultations within 30 days of the request. If after 60 days of the request, there is no resolution of the dispute, the complaining party may request the establishment of a panel.[88] If any of these deadlines are missed or consultations are denied, the complaining party may then proceed directly to request that a panel be established.

Other WTO members with a "substantial trade interest" in consultations may participate in them if the requested member agrees that their claim is well-founded. Joining in consultations in this way permits such WTO members to become co-complainants if the dispute proceeds to the panel phase.

3. *Good Offices, Conciliation, and Mediation*

Good offices, conciliation, and mediation may be undertaken voluntarily at any time, even after a panel has been established, if the parties to the dispute agree.[89] They may also be terminated at any time. The director general, acting in an *ex officio* capacity, may offer good offices, conciliation, or mediation with a view to assisting WTO members to settle a dispute.[90] This is important when developing countries are involved.

4. *Arbitration*

The GATT system did not originally provide explicitly for arbitration, although it may have been available even in the absence of a specific provision. The concept of arbitration was explicitly introduced in the 1989 decision. Binding arbitration is now available as an alternative avenue of dispute resolution under the DSU where issues are "clearly defined by both parties."[91] Arbitration is also used at certain stages in disputes under the DSU, such as in the determination of a reasonable time for implementation in the absence of DSB approval of a period proposed by a member or agreement between the parties, and in the consideration of objections to the level of suspension of concessions proposed. Arbitration is also provided for in, for example, the Agreement on Subsidies and Countervailing Measures (article 8.5).

The possibility of resorting to binding arbitration is one of the more interesting features of the Uruguay Round improvements. It opens up new possibilities, although it is not clear how frequently WTO members will resort to arbitration, as opposed to the quasi-arbitral panel system.

---

87 *Ibid.*, art. 4.4 .

88 Shorter time limits are set in cases of urgency: *ibid.*, art. 4.8.

89 *Ibid.*, art. 5.1.

90 *Ibid.*, art. 5.6.

91 *Ibid.*, art. 25.1.

The parties to the arbitration must notify WTO members "sufficiently in advance of the actual commencement of the arbitration process."[92] Other WTO members are not affected by the arbitration and retain their rights under the GATT and the other covered agreements. They may become party to an arbitration proceeding only upon the agreement of the original parties to that arbitration.[93]

So far, arbitration has been serviced by the WTO Secretariat. There appears to have been no need to seek the services of the International Chamber of Commerce, the American Arbitration Association, or some other similar arbitral institution, although this route presumably remains open.

The parties to the arbitration agree upon the procedures to be followed. To date, these procedures have been *ad hoc*, although the parties could presumably choose to be governed by the 1985 UN Commission on International Trade Law (UNCITRAL) Model Law on Commercial Arbitration,[94] or the 1976 UNCITRAL Arbitration Rules.[95] There is no need for a choice of law clause since the arbitrator must apply the relevant provisions of the covered agreements to the merits of the dispute.

Parties must agree to abide by the arbitration award.[96] Arbitration awards must be notified to the DSB and to the relevant council or committee, where any WTO member may raise any point relating thereto.[97] The DSU provisions concerning surveillance of implementation[98] and compensation and suspension of concessions[99] apply to arbitration awards.[100] Should the arbitrator tribunal be limited to the remedies provided by the DSU and the covered agreements, or should it be able to award damages? How and where would a monetary award be enforced against a losing party? The fact that only states are involved in a WTO arbitration raises a host of interesting issues of public international law.

Canada has been involved in one GATT arbitration to date based on the provisions of the 1989 Decision.[101] The arbitration involved a dispute between Canada and the Europan Economic Community (EEC) on the issue of Canada's wheat rights under bilateral Quality and Ordinary Wheat Agreements concluded between Canada and the EEC on March 29, 1962. The parties agreed upon the arbitrator,[102] the questions to be examined, and the procedure to be followed, in an *ad hoc* manner. With respect to the issue of Canada's rights under the Agreement on Quality Wheat, the arbitrator noted that, in principle, a claim based on a bilateral agreement could not be brought under the

92 *Ibid.*, art. 25.3.

93 *Ibid.*, art. 25.2.

94 (1985), 24 *ILM* 1302.

95 (1976), 15 *ILM* 701.

96 DSU, *supra*, note 82, art. 25.3.

97 *Ibid.*, art. 25.3.

98 *Ibid.*, art. 21.

99 *Ibid.*, art. 22.

100 *Ibid.*, art. 25.4.

101 *Canada/European Communities—Article XVIII Rights*, 16 October 1990, BISD, 37th Supp. 80 (1990).

102 The arbitrator was Gardner Patterson, a former deputy director general of the GATT.

GATT multilateral dispute settlement procedures. However, an exception was warranted in this case "given the close connection of this particular bilateral agreement with the GATT, the fact that the Agreement was consistent with the objectives of the GATT, and that both parties joined in requesting recourse to the GATT Arbitration procedures." The arbitrator concluded that Canada maintained through the Agreement on Quality Wheat all the negotiating rights provided for in article XXVIII, or their equivalent. However, with respect to the Agreement on Ordinary Wheat, the arbitrator noted that Canada had never requested negotiations provided for under the agreement over three decades. The arbitrator reasoned: "a properly functioning multilateral international trading system does require that after a period silence must be considered acceptance of a state of affairs or abandonment of a claim. The predictability and stability that are the central features of the GATT system require that." He consequently held that Canada had relinquished any rights under the GATT that it might have possessed under it in 1962.

5. Establishment of Panel and Panel Procedures

The improvements and innovations made with respect to the panel procedures in the 1989 decision successfully remedied many of the criticisms addressed to past practice and developed a far more disciplined and streamlined dispute settlement process. The DSU has maintained and enhanced these provisions, furnishing strict time limits and precise rules for each phase in the process that are designed to increase confidence in the dispute settlement system and to guarantee implementation of its decisions.

Where consultations fail to resolve the dispute, the DSB will establish a panel at the request of the complaining party—at the latest at the DSB meeting following that at which the request first appears on the DSB agenda—unless the DSB decides by consensus not to establish a panel.[103] The DSU sets out specific rules and deadlines for deciding the terms of reference[104] and composition of panels.[105] The *ad hoc* panels are composed of three[106] individuals that may be, but are not necessarily, drawn from a roster maintained by the Secretariat. The selection of panelists raises many interesting issues, including the issue of nationality. Citizens of parties or third parties to a dispute shall not serve on a panel concerned with that dispute unless the parties agree otherwise. In addition, in a dispute between a developing country member and a developed country member the panel shall, if the developing country so requests, include at least one

---

103 DSU, *supra*, note 82, art. 6:1.

104 *Ibid.*, art. 7. The parties use the following standard terms of reference unless they agree otherwise within 20 days from the establishment of the panel:

> To examine, in the light of the relevant provisions in (name of the covered agreement(s) cited by the parties to the dispute), the matter referred to the DSB by (name of party) in document ... and to make such findings as will assist the DSB in making the recommendations or in giving the rulings provided for in that/those agreement(s).

105 *Ibid.*, art. 8.

106 Unless parties to the dispute agree, within 10 days from the establishment of the panel, to a panel composed of five panelists.

panelist from a developing country. If the parties are unable to agree upon the panelists within 20 days after the establishment of a panel, at the request of either party, the director general, in consultation with the chairperson of the DSB and the chairperson of the relevant council or committee, shall determine the composition of the panel.[107] These procedures do not differ greatly from those followed by arbitral institutions. Their less flexible nature and deadlines may have the result of encouraging disputants to achieve settlements in the consultation phase, particularly when coupled with the more effective procedures for adoption and implementation of panel recommendations.

The DSU adopts the special procedures for multiple complainants that were set out in the 1989 decision. Where more than one member requests the establishment of a panel related to the same matter, a single panel should, whenever possible, be established to examine these complaints.[108] The DSU contains enhanced provisions on third party practice. Third parties having a "substantial interest" in the matter under investigation can be heard before, and make written submissions to, the panel.[109] Third-party submissions are to be reflected in the panel report.[110] Third parties also receive submissions of the parties to the dispute to the first meeting of the panel.[111] The option remains open for third parties to have recourse to normal DSU procedures where they consider that a measure already subject to a panel proceeding nullifies or impairs benefits accruing to them under the covered agreements. Wherever possible, such a dispute will be referred to the original panel.[112]

The function of the panels is to assist the DSB in discharging its responsibilities under the DSU and covered agreements. Thus, "a panel should make an objective assessment of the matter before it, including the facts and the applicability of and conformity with the relevant covered agreements, and such other findings as will assist the DSB in making recommendations or rulings provided for in the covered agreements."[113] The DSU outlines some aspects of panel procedures[114] but is silent on many features of the panel process.

Once established, the panel must generally complete its work within six months. In no case should it take more than nine months from the date that the composition and terms of reference are set.[115] This language is stronger than that found in the annex to the 1979 understanding.[116] In practice, panels generally take about nine months to complete their work.

---

107 DSU, *supra*, note 82, art. 8.7.

108 *Ibid.*, art. 9.

109 *Ibid.*, art. 10.2.

110 *Ibid.*, art. 10.2.

111 *Ibid.*, art. 10.3.

112 *Ibid.*, art. 10.4.

113 *Ibid.*, art. 11.

114 *Ibid.*, art. 12 and app. 3.

115 *Ibid.*, arts. 12.9 and 20.

116 See 1979 understanding, para. 6(ix).

The DSU stipulates that the panel procedures should provide sufficient flexibility to ensure high-quality panel reports, while not unduly delaying the process.[117] Panels should fix the timetable for the panel process after consulting the parties[118] and set precise deadlines for written submissions, which the parties should respect.[119] A proposed timetable for panel work, which may be modified, is included in appendix 3 to the DSU. Appendix 3 to the DSU also contains working procedures for panels.

Parties to the dispute make written submissions to the panel, outlining the facts of the case and their arguments. The panel then holds a first substantive meeting with the parties where the parties present their oral arguments. This is followed by a special session with the third parties. The parties then make formal rebuttals at the second substantive meeting with the panel. The panel may request further written submissions from the parties. Written submissions to the panel are confidential.[120]

A panel may seek information and technical advice from any individual or body it deems appropriate, but must inform the authorities of a WTO member if the individual or body is within its territory.[121] A panel may also consult experts and request a written advisory report from an expert review group concerning a scientific or other technical matter raised by a party to the dispute.[122]

At the request of the complaining party, a panel may suspend its work at any time for a period not exceeding 12 months.[123]

Where one or more of the parties to the dispute is a developing country, the panel report must explicitly indicate how account has been taken of relevant provisions of differential and more favourable treatment for developing countries members that form part of the covered agreements that have been raised by the developing country member in the course of the dispute settlement process.[124]

The WTO Secretariat will continue to assist panels "especially on the legal, historical and procedural aspects of the matters dealt with."[125] It also provides a legal expert within the technical cooperation services to furnish legal advice and assistance to developing

---

117 DSU, *supra*, note 82, art. 12.2.

118 *Ibid.*, art. 12.3.

119 *Ibid.*, art. 12.5.

120 *Ibid.*, art. 18.2.

121 *Ibid.*, art. 13.1.

122 *Ibid.*, art. 13.2.

123 *Ibid.*, art. 12.12.

124 *Ibid.*, art. 12.11.

125 *Ibid.*, art. 27.1. Lowenfeld points out that the Secretariat has played a significant but little-known role in the GATT dispute settlement panel process and GATT staff members from both economic and legal offices have sat with panelists, prepared drafts of findings of fact, and, in some instances, drafted key sections of panel reports. He notes, "In many ways, this little-known role of the secretariat has been highly useful—providing an institutional memory and a safeguard in case one or more panelists were unprepared." See Lowenfeld, "Remedies along with Rights: Institutional Reform in the New GATT" (1994), 88 *Am. J Int'l. Law* 477, at 485.

country members.[126] The Secretariat conducts training courses for interested members concerning the dispute settlement procedures and practices outlined in the DSU.

6. *Interim Review*

In order to ensure that a panel is fully aware of all issues and concerns in a dispute, the parties have an opportunity to comment during the panel process upon the sections of the panel report summarizing the facts and arguments of the parties.[127] The parties subsequently receive the panel's "interim report,"[128] which includes the fact and argument sections, in addition to the panel's findings and conclusions. A party may comment upon the interim report and request that the panel review precise aspects of it. A party can request that a further meeting with the panel be held on the issues identified. If no parties submit comments within a period of time set by the panel, the interim report is considered the final report and is circulated to the WTO members.

The interim review stage allows the panel, in conjunction with the parties, to clarify issues, rectify errors, and avoid taking decisions on matters not essential to the case at hand. Parties may still reach a mutually agreed solution to the dispute after they have viewed the interim report. Several commentators have criticized the addition of the interim review stage as a retreat from the otherwise generally rule-oriented procedures under the DSU, arguing that it allows an additional opportunity for negotiated settlement between the parties once they have viewed the panel's stance on the issues under consideration.[129] The final report of the panel must include a discussion of the arguments made at the interim review stage.[130]

7. *Appellate Review*

The concept of appellate review of panel decisions by a permanent appellate body[131] is perhaps the most significant and innovative attribute of the new DSU. While it has been criticized as potentially reducing the authority and prestige of panels[132] because of the concern that the losing party will automatically appeal an unfavourable panel report, the creation of the appellate body could also have the positive effect of encouraging panels to be thorough and accurate in their legal reasoning. The addition of an appellate review was a *quid pro quo* for the introduction of the virtually automatic adoption of panel reports due to the requirement of negative consensus to block adoption.

---

126 DSU, *ibid.*, art. 27.2.

127 *Ibid.*, art. 15.1.

128 *Ibid.*, art. 15.2.

129 See, e.g., Pescatore, "The GATT Dispute Settlement Mechanism" (1993), 27 *JWT* 5, at 17 where he states that this constitutes a "veiled return from genuine dispute settlement to mere conciliation."

130 DSU, *supra*, note 82, art. 15.3.

131 *Ibid.*, art. 17.

132 Pierre Pescatore, "The GATT Dispute Settlement Mechanism: Its present situation and its prospects" (1993), 10 *J of Int'l. Arbitration* 27.

The appellate body is composed of seven members[133] "of recognised authority, with demonstrated expertise in law, international trade and the subject matter of the covered agreements generally," and who are "broadly representative of membership in the WTO"[134] and available at all times on short notice. A division of three is established to hear and decide any one appeal.[135]

The term of the appellate body members is four years (with the exception of three of the first appellate body members to be appointed, who serve two-year terms), with the possibility of one re-appointment.[136] The appellate body and its divisions make every effort to take their decisions by consensus. Where a consensus is not possible, a decision is to be taken by majority vote.[137] The appellate body has its own secretariat that is institutionally distinct from the WTO Secretariat.

The appellate body developed its working procedures for appellate review[138] in consultation with the chairperson of the DSB and the WTO director general. The working procedures consist of two parts. Part I[139] deals with internal matters among the appellate body members. Part II[140] deals with the process for appeals.

The appellate body divisions of three are composed on the basis of rotation, while taking into account the principles of random selection, unpredictability, and opportunity for all members to serve regardless of their national origin.[141] The approach of the appellate body to the issue of nationality in the composition of divisions therefore contrasts with the WTO approach with respect to panels. Regarding panels, citizens of WTO members whose governments are parties or third parties to a panel dispute are not to serve on a panel unless the parties to the dispute agree otherwise.[142]

An interesting element of appellate body decision making is the principle of "collegiality." To ensure consistency and coherence in decision making and to draw on the individual and collective expertise of the appellate body members, the appellate body members convene on a regular basis to discuss matters of policy, practice, and procedure. In addition, the division responsible for deciding each appeal is required to exchange views with the other four appellate body members before the division finalizes its report.

---

133 The DSB announced the first seven appellate body members in November 1995. They are J. Bacchus (USA); C. Beeby (New Zealand), C.D. Ehlermann (Germany), S. El-Naggar (Egypt), F. Feliciano (Philippines), J. Lacarte Muro (Uruguay); and M. Matsushita (Japan).

134 DSU, *supra*, note 82, art. 17.3.

135 *Ibid.*, art. 17.1.

136 *Ibid.*, art. 17.2.

137 Working Procedures for Appellate Review, WT/AB/WP/1, in effect 15 February 1996 (the Working Procedures), r. 3.2. DSU, *ibid.*, art. 17.9 confers upon the appellate body the authority to draw up its own working procedures.

138 *Ibid.*

139 Pt. I consists of rr. 2 to 15.

140 Pt. II consists of rr. 16 to 32.

141 DSU, *supra*, note 82, art. 17.1 and Working Procedures, r. 6:1-2.

142 DSU, *ibid.*, art. 8.3.

The appellate body has adopted rules of conduct to govern matters relating to conflicts of interest.[143] There are also rules governing incapacity,[144] replacement,[145] resignation,[146] and transition[147] of appellate body members.

Only parties to the dispute—not third parties—are permitted to appeal a panel report.[148] The right to appeal is automatic; there are no requirements for eligibility, such as obtaining leave to appeal. Third parties may make written submissions to, and be given an opportunity to be heard by, the appellate body.[149]

An appeal is limited to "issues of law covered in the panel report and legal interpretations developed by the panel."[150] The appellate body may uphold, modify, or reverse the legal findings and conclusions of the panel.[151]

An appeal is launched by notification to the DSB and simultaneous filing of a notice of appeal with the appellate body secretariat. The working procedures outline the timeframes and content requirements for the appellant's,[152] appellee(s), and third party(ies) submissions.[153] There is also a provision on multiple appeals.[154] Within 15 days after the date of filing of the notice of appeal, a party to the dispute other than the original appellant may join in the appeal, or appeal on the basis of other alleged errors in the issues of law covered in the panel report and legal interpretations developed by the panel.[155]

An oral hearing is held in each appeal, taking place as a general rule 30 days after the filing of the notice of appeal.[156] Further written submissions may be requested from the participants to the appeal at any time during the appellate proceedings.[157] Written submissions to the appellate body, as well as the proceedings of the appellate body, are confidential.[158]

---

143 Working Procedures, *supra*, note 137, rr. 8 to 11 and Annex II. Note that the final version of the *Rules of Conduct for the Understanding on Rules and Procedures Governing the Settlement of Disputes* was formally approved by the DSB on 3 December 1996. Pursuant to r. 8:2 of the Working Procedures, these rules of conduct were directly incorporated into the Working Procedures and supersede Annex II.

144 *Ibid.*, r. 12.

145 *Ibid.*, r. 13.

146 *Ibid.*, r. 14.

147 *Ibid.*, r. 15.

148 DSU, art. 17.3.

149 *Ibid.*, art. 17.3.

150 *Ibid.*, art. 17.6.

151 *Ibid.*, art. 17.13.

152 Working Procedures, *supra*, note 137, r. 21. The appellant's submission is to be filed within 10 days after the date of filing of the notice of appeal.

153 The appellee (Working Procedures, *ibid.*, r. 22) and third-party submissions (working procedures, r. 24) must be filed within 25 days after the filing of the notice of appeal.

154 *Ibid.*, r. 23.

155 *Ibid.*, r. 23.1.

156 *Ibid.*, r. 27.

157 *Ibid.*, r. 28.1.

158 DSU, *supra*, note 82, arts. 18.2 and 17.10.

The DSU sets stringent time limits for appeals. Generally, the period between the date that a party to the dispute formally notifies its intention to appeal and the circulation of the appellate body report shall not exceed 60 days. Where the appellate body considers that it cannot provide its report within the period, it must formally notify the DSB of the reasons for the delay together with an estimate of the period within which it will submit its report. In no case can the appeal process exceed 90 days.[159]

The major advantage of this new method of reviewing and rectifying errors of law made by panels is to surmount blockage and delay in the ultimate settlement of the dispute and to provide an additional safeguard against the possibility that a panel report could be faulty in reasoning or in result.

8. Consideration and Adoption of Panel and Appellate Body Reports

In order to provide sufficient time for WTO members to examine panel reports, such reports must not be considered for adoption by the DSB until 20 days after the date of their circulation to the WTO members.[160] WTO members having objections to the panel report must circulate their objections in writing at least 10 days prior to the DSB meeting at which the panel report will be considered.[161] The parties to the dispute have the right to participate fully in the consideration of the panel report by the DSB, and their views are to be fully recorded.[162]

Strict deadlines are imposed for the adoption of panel and appellate reports, lessening the possibility for a losing party to draw out the adoption process. These time limits, coupled with the major innovation of the automaticity rule for the adoption of reports, lead to greater automaticity in the adoption procedure. Thus, within 60 days of the circulation of a panel report where no appeal is lodged,[163] the DSB is to adopt the report unconditionally unless there is a consensus against adoption. Where a party notifies its intention to appeal, the panel report will not be considered for adoption by the DSB until the appeal has been completed.[164] In practice, where the panel report has been the subject of an appeal, the appellate body report is adopted by the DSB together with the panel report as modified by the appellate body report.

An appellate body report must be adopted unconditionally by the DSB within 30 days of its circulation to the WTO members, unless there is a consensus of the DSB against adoption.[165]

This represents a major improvement over the adoption procedures contained in the 1979 understanding and in the 1989 decision, which both continued the practice of adoption by consensus. In negotiating the 1989 decision, ministers declined to decide

---

159 *Ibid.*, art. 17.5.

160 *Ibid.*, art. 16.1.

161 *Ibid.*, art. 16.2.

162 *Ibid.*, art. 16.3.

163 *Ibid.*, art. 16.4.

164 *Ibid.*, art. 16.4.

165 *Ibid.*, art. 17.14.

that the parties to the dispute must either abstain or be excluded from the consensus (the so-called "consensus minus two" proposal). Thus, blocking of a panel report by the losing party remained a possibility. This possibility has now virtually disappeared with the requirement of negative consensus to block adoption in the DSU.

Unless agreed to by the parties, the period from the establishment of the panel until the DSB considers the panel or appellate report for adoption, as a general rule, must not exceed nine months where the report is not appealed, or 12 months where the report is appealed.[166]

If an adopted report holds that a challenged measure is inconsistent with a provision in a covered agreement, it is supposed to recommend that the offending state bring the measure into conformity with the pertinent agreement. A report can suggest ways in which the member can implement the recommendations.[167] Once adopted by the DSB, the findings and recommendations of panel and appellate body reports become recommendations and rulings of the DSB.

9. *Surveillance of Implementation of Recommendations and Rulings*

Recognizing that "prompt compliance with recommendations or rulings of the DSB is essential in order to ensure effective resolution of disputes to the benefit of all Members,"[168] the DSU provides for the surveillance of implementation of recommendations and rulings. At a DSB meeting within 30 days after the adoption of a panel or appellate body report, the member concerned must inform the DSB of its intentions concerning the implementation of recommendations and rulings. If immediate compliance is not possible, the member will have a "reasonable period of time" for implementation of the recommendations and rulings.

Unlike in the past, the determination of what constitutes a "reasonable period" is subject to DSB approval or agreement between the parties within 45 days of the report's adoption. If this proves impossible, the "reasonable period" will be determined by binding arbitration to take place within 90 days of the issuance of the report. The arbitrator will be chosen by the parties, or failing agreement, by the director general. The DSU offers a guideline of 15 months as a "reasonable period."[169]

If parties disagree over whether a measure taken to comply with a panel report is consistent with the agreement in question, the issue may be referred to a dispute settlement panel—if possible the panel that heard the original dispute.[170]

The DSB is charged with keeping the implementation of the report under surveillance, an issue which any WTO member can raise at any time following the report's adoption. Unless the DSB decides otherwise, the subject is to be put on the DSB agenda six months after the establishment of the "reasonable period" of time and is to remain on the agenda thereafter until the issue is resolved.[171]

166 *Ibid.*, art. 20.

167 *Ibid.*, art. 19.1.

168 *Ibid.*, art. 21.1.

169 *Ibid.*, art. 21.3(c).

170 *Ibid.*, art. 21.5.

171 *Ibid.*, art. 21.6.

10. Compensation and Suspension of Concessions

Precise provisions now govern resort to compensation and the temporary suspension of concessions where the losing party fails to comply with a panel or appellate body report within a reasonable period of time.[172] Compensation and the suspension of concessions or other obligations are temporary measures; "neither ... is preferred to full implementation of a recommendation to bring a measure into conformity with the covered agreements."[173] They are applied until such time as the measure found to be inconsistent with the covered agreement has been removed, or agreement has been reached on its phasing out, or the member that must implement recommendations or rulings provides a solution to the nullification or impairment of benefits. The payment of damages as a form of compensation is not contemplated by the DSU.

Article 22 of the DSU, which reiterates and reinforces the necessity for a multilateral approach to the suspension of concessions contained in GATT, article XXIII:2, requires that a WTO member request authorization from the DSB to suspend the application to the member concerned of concessions or other obligations under the covered agreements. Such authorization is automatic. Coupled with the requirement in article 23 of the DSU that members "have recourse to, and abide by" DSU rules and procedures and "obtain DSB authorization in accordance with ... [Article 22] before suspending concessions or other obligations under the covered agreements in response to the failure of the Member concerned to implement the recommendations and rulings ... ," this prohibits unilateral retaliation by a WTO member.

If the member concerned fails to bring a measure found to be inconsistent with any of the covered agreements into compliance therewith or otherwise to implement the DSB recommendations and rulings within a reasonable period of time, the member must, if so requested and no later than the expiry of that reasonable period of time, enter into negotiations with any party to the dispute with a view to developing mutually acceptable compensation. If no compensation can be agreed upon within 20 days after the expiry of the reasonable period of time, any party to the dispute may request authorization from the DSB to suspend the application to the member concerned of concessions or other obligations under the covered agreements.[174] Retaliation should occur in the sector(s) in which the panel or appellate body found violation or nullification or impairment. However, where this is considered not practical or effective, the DSU permits cross-retaliation in other sectors under the same agreement, or, in serious circumstances, under another covered agreement.[175] The amount of trade covered by the suspension must be appropriate in the circumstances, equivalent to the level of nullification or impairment caused by the offending measure.[176]

---

172 *Ibid.*, art. 22.

173 *Ibid.*, art. 22.1.

174 *Ibid.*, art. 22.2.

175 *Ibid.*, art. 22.3.

176 *Ibid.*, art. 22.4.

The request of the member for authorization to retaliate will be authorized by the DSB, unless there is a consensus to reject it.[177] However, where the member concerned objects to the level of retaliation proposed or claims that the principles and procedures dealing with cross-retaliation have not been followed, these issues may be referred to binding arbitration carried out, where possible, by the panel that originally examined the dispute, or by an arbitrator. The decision of the arbitral body is final.[178] The DSB is to be informed promptly of the arbitral decision and to grant, upon request, authorization to retaliate where the request is consistent with the arbitral decision, unless the DSB decides by consensus to reject the request.[179]

11. Non-Violation Complaints

The DSU sets out special procedures for so-called non-violation complaints[180]—that is, complaints concerning the application by another WTO member of a measure which does not conflict with provisions of a covered agreement, but that nevertheless nullifies or impairs the benefits accruing to a member under the relevant covered agreement or frustrates the attainment of any objective of that agreement. These provisions only relate to those covered agreements that incorporate article XXIII of the GATT 1994. For the time being, this does not include, for example, the TRIPS Agreement. The GATS contains its own distinct non-violation provisions.

In non-violation complaints under the DSU, where a panel or the appellate body determines that a measure nullifies or impairs benefits under, or impedes the attainment of objectives of, the relevant covered agreement without violating it, there is no obligation to withdraw the measure. In such cases, the panel or appellate body shall recommend that the WTO member concerned make a mutually satisfactory adjustment, which may include compensation.

Special procedures also apply with respect to so-called situation complaints, where a member considers that any benefit accruing to it under the relevant covered agreement is being impeded as a result of "the existence of any other situation." Such situation complaints are referred to in GATT, article XXIII.1(c), and are now subject to DSU, article 26.2. The DSU procedures only apply to such complaints up to and including the circulation of the panel report to WTO members. Thereafter, the provisions of the 1989 Decision apply to consideration and adoption of panel reports, and surveillance of implementation of recommendations and rulings. This conserves the necessity for consensus in the adoption of the report.

12. Strengthening of the Multilateral System

When WTO members seek the redress of a violation of obligations or other nullification or impairment of benefits under the covered agreements or an impediment to the attainment of any objective of the covered agreements, they shall have recourse to, and abide

177 *Ibid.*, art. 22.6.

178 *Ibid.*, art. 22.7.

179 *Ibid.*, art. 22.7.

180 *Ibid.*, art. 26.1. Non-violation complaints are referred to in GATT, art. XXIII.1(b).

by, the rules and procedures of the DSU.[181] Thus, the determination that a violation has occurred, that benefits have been impaired, or that attainment of an objective of the covered agreements has been impeded; the determination of the "reasonable period of time" for implementation of recommendations and rulings; and the determination of the level of suspension of concessions are to be made exclusively through recourse to the procedures set out in the DSU. These provisions discourage unilateral actions on the part of WTO members, thereby reinforcing the multilateral dispute settlement system.

13. Technical Assistance

The WTO Secretariat assists WTO members with respect to dispute settlement upon request. Additional legal advice and assistance by a qualified expert within the technical cooperation division may also be obtained by any developing country member. Training courses for interested contracting parties concerning WTO dispute settlement procedures and practices are provided by the Secretariat.

14. Overview of the WTO Dispute Settlement Process[182]

Consultations (Article 4)

- parties may request panel if no solution found within 60 days

[**Good offices, conciliation, or mediation** (Article 5)]

Establishment of Panel (Article 6)

- no later than at the DSB meeting following that at which the request for panel establishment is first made
  - terms of reference: standard terms unless special terms agreed within 20 days (article 7)
  - composition: to be agreed within 20 days or decided by director general at the request of a party (article 8)

Panel procedures (Article 12 and Appendix 3)

- written submissions; meetings with parties and meeting with third parties (article 10)
- interim review (article 15)
- release of final report to parties: in general not to exceed 6 months from the date that panel composition and terms of reference have been agreed (article 12.8)
- circulation of final report to WTO members: not to exceed 9 months from the establishment of the panel (article 12.9)

181 *Ibid.*, art. 23.

182 All references are to the DSU, *ibid.* These time periods may be changed by mutual agreement between the parties. Shorter time frames apply in cases of urgency.

Adoption of panel report by DSB
- within 60 days unless appealed (article 16.4)

OR

Appellate review (Article 17)[183]
- unless an appeal is notified within 60 days, the panel report will be put on the DSB agenda for adoption (article 16.4)
- in general, appellate proceedings are not to exceed 60 days; in no case are they to exceed 90 days (article 17.5)

Adoption of Appellate Body report and panel report as modified by Appellate Body report
- within 30 days (article 17.14)

Surveillance of implementation of recommendations and rulings (Article 21)
- Member concerned to inform DSB of intentions with respect to implementation within 30 days
- if immediate compliance impracticable, implementation to occur within defined "reasonable period of time"; determination of "reasonable period of time" generally not to exceed 15 months from the date of establishment of panel

Negotiation of compensation pending full implementation (Article 22)

Authorization of retaliation pending full implementation (Article 22)

IV. STATISTICAL DATA WITH RESPECT TO COMPLAINTS AND THEIR DISPOSAL

In practice, as under the GATT, a large number of WTO disputes concerning the interpretation or implementation of the covered agreements are settled through bilateral consultations. Under the GATT, for example, 196 complaints were filed from 1947 to 1994. Of these, 107 were referred to panels, resulting in the release of 91 panel reports, of which 79 were adopted.[184]

Figures since the establishment of the WTO reveal a greater propensity to resort to dispute settlement. These figures reveal that only a minority of disputes lead to the establishment of a panel and to the release of a final panel report (and now, appellate body report) although the number of panels established is growing. The other complaints are largely settled through bilateral consultations before a panel has been established.[185] As of mid-July 1996, in the approximately 18 months since the establishment of the WTO, 50 complaints have been filed—that is, approximately one-quarter of the total

183 Additional procedural provisions are set out in the working procedures for appellate review.

184 These figures do not include disputes under any of the Tokyo Round Agreements.

185 For a survey, see R.E. Hudec, *Enforcing International Trade Law: The Evolution of the GATT Legal System* (1993).

number of complaints filed throughout the GATT's 47-year history. Seven of these WTO complaints are under panel examination, and a panel has been requested in an eighth. Twenty-three are in the consultations phase. Three are the subject of a panel report that has just been released to the members (*Japan—Taxes on Alcoholic Beverages*, complaints by the European Communities, Canada, and the United States), and which has been appealed to the appellate body on August 8. Two complaints were the subject of panel and appellate body reports adopted simultaneously by the DSB on May 20, 1996 (in *United States—Standards for Reformulated and Conventional Gasoline*, complaints by Venezuela and Brazil) and are now in the implementation phase. The remaining complaints have been settled or are the subject of mutually agreed solutions notified in accordance with article 3.6 of the DSU, or are inactive (that is, although no mutually agreed solution has been notified and they have not been formally withdrawn, there does not appear to have been any further recent progress made).

The recent increase in resort to the dispute settlement procedures of the WTO seems to indicate that the WTO members have more confidence in the dispute settlement system and in the quality of the work of the panels, reinforced by the mechanism of appellate review. The new WTO system, with its greater automaticity, strict time frames, and more effective mechanisms for surveillance and implementation of dispute settlement rulings and recommendations also appears to provide a greater incentive for parties to reach bilateral settlements.

V. SOME GATT AND WTO DISPUTES INVOLVING CANADA

The published record does not reveal the full extent of the impact of GATT-WTO dispute settlement procedures upon Canada. In a number of instances, not formally recorded, negotiations were sufficient to remedy problems created by Canada or problems created by other states for Canadian exports. Similarly, in a number of instances, Canada, while not a complainant or the object of a complaint, may have had an interest in the outcome of various disputes between other contracting parties.

As far as can be ascertained, Canada has been the object of the following complaints:

1. Under GATT 1947 and the Tokyo Round Agreements

US 1962	Value for duty on import of potatoes[186]
EC 1965	Canada-USA Agreement on automotive parts[187]
US 1974	Article XIX, restrictions on cattle[188]
US 1975	Import quotas on eggs[189]
EC 1976	Withdrawal of tariff concessions under article XXVIII:3[190]
US 1982	Administration of Foreign Investment Review Act[191]

186 L/1927, BISD, 11th Supp. 55, 88 (1962) (settled).

187 L/2409, BISD, 13th Supp. 112 (1965) (working party) decision.

188 L/4118, retaliation under XIX.3 (1974).

189 L/4279, BISD, 23rd Supp. 91 (1977) (working party) decision.

190 L/4636, BISD, 25th Supp. 42 (1978).

191 L/5504, BISD, 30th Supp. 140 (1982-83).

EC 1983	Anti-dumping investigation of electrical generators from Italy[192]
SA 1984	Internal tax on gold coins[193]
EC 1985	Internal regulations on alcoholic beverages[194]
US 1986	Restrictions on exports of uranium[195]
EC 1986	Imposition of countervailing duties on imports of manufacturing beef from the EC[196]
EC 1986	Imposition of countervailing duty on pasta[197]
US 1987	Restrictions on export of unprocessed herring and salmon[198]
US 1988	Restrictions on import of ice cream and yoghurt[199]
US 1989	Injury determination on grain corn from the United States[200]
EC 1990	Article XVIII rights concerning ordinary and quality wheat (Award by Arbitrator)[201]
US 1990	Import, distribution, and sale of alcoholic beverages by provincial agencies[202]
EC 1993	Anti-dumping duties on certain steel products[203]
EC 1993	Anti-dumping duties on certain hot-rolled carbon steel plate[204]

2. Under the WTO Agreement

US 1996	Measures concerning the tax treatment and importation of certain periodicals[205]

Canada has initiated or joined the following complaints:

1. Under GATT 1947 and the Tokyo Round Agreements

US 1973	US tax legislation (DISC)[206]
EC 1974	Adequacy of compensation in Art. XXIV:6 negotiations[207]

192 Anti-dumping, unreported. The *ad hoc* group made no recommendation.

193 36 GATT FOCUS 6 (1985), 38 GATT FOCUS 1 (1986).

194 54 GATT FOCUS 1 (1988) and BISD, 35th Supp. 37 (1989).

195 L/6104. Resolved by art. 902 of Canada-US Free Trade Agreement.

196 SCM/85. Report by the panel (13 October 1987).

197 SCM/78. No ruling (Subsidies Code).

198 L/6132, 53 GATT FOCUS 7 (1988), 54 GATT FOCUS 2 (1988) and report by the panel: L/6268 (4 November 1987); (1988), 27 *Int'l. L Mat.* 1596, BISD, 35th Supp. 98 (1989).

199 L/6445, 59 GATT FOCUS 3 (1989), 66 GATT FOCUS 2 (1989), 2 TCT 7143 (1989), BISD, 36th Supp. 68 (1990).

200 SCM/95 (Subsidies Code).

201 BISD, 37th Supp. 80 (1990).

202 BISD, 39th Supp. 27 (1992).

203 No ruling.

204 No ruling.

205 WT/DS31.

206 L/4422, BISD, 23rd Supp. 98 (1977), 28 Supp. 114 (1981).

207 L/4107 C/M/105 (1975) (settled).

Japan 1979	Import restrictions on leather[208]
US 1980	Import prohibition on tuna and tuna products[209]
EC 1980	Discriminatory import restrictions on beef from Canada[210]
US 1981	Section 337 restraints on imports of automotive spring assemblies[211]
US 1983	Countervailing duty investigation on soft wood lumber[212]
EC 1984	Import restrictions on newsprint from Canada[213]
EC 1984	Export subsidy on boneless manufacturing beef[214]
US 1985	Import restrictions on products containing sugar[215]
EC 1985	Ban on importation of skins of certain seal pups and related products[216]
US 1986	US taxes on petroleum and certain imported petroleum substances[217]
US 1986	Customs user fee[218]
US 1986	Countervailing duty on imports of softwood lumber from Canada[219]
US 1987	Section 337 action on cellular mobile telephones[220]
Japan 1987	Imports of spruce-pine fir (SPF) dimension lumber[221]
US 1988	Restrictions on imports of ice cream[222]
US 1989	Countervailing duty on fresh, chilled, and frozen processed pork[223]
EC 1989	Subsidies for producers and processors of oil seeds[224]
US 1991	Measures affecting the export of pure and alloy magnesium[225]
US 1991	Measures affecting alcoholic and malt beverages[226]

208 L/5042, BISD, 27th Supp. 118 (1980).

209 L/5198, BISD, 29th Supp. 91 (1980-81).

210 L/5099 BISD, 28th Supp. 92 (1980-81).

211 L/5333, BISD, 30th Supp. 107 (1983).

212 SCM/40 (no ruling—Subsidies Code).

213 L/5680, BISD, 31st Supp. 114 (1985).

214 SCM/51 (Subsidies Code).

215 L/5783, 33 GATT FOCUS 8 (1985).

216 L/5940 (no ruling).

217 L/6085, 48 GATT FOCUS 1 (1987), BISD, 34th Supp. 136 (1988).

218 53 GATT FOCUS 7 (1988).

219 SCM/73, SCM/83 (Subsidies Code, settled). See Memorandum of Understanding on Softwood Lumber of 30 December 1986, Softwood Lumber Products Export Charge Act, RSC 1985, c. 12 (3rd Supp.), and Canada-US Free Trade Agreement 1989, art. 2009.

220 L/6213 (no ruling).

221 L/6262, L/6470; 2 TCT 7119 (1989), BISD, 36th Supp. 167 (1990).

222 L/6444.

223 DS7/1 and L/6721 (1990).

224 DS3/1 (no ruling).

225 SCM/174 (complaint withdrawn).

226 BISD, 39th Supp. (1992) 206.

EEC 1993	Regulations affecting the sale of imported bovine semen in Italy[227]
US 1993	Measures affecting the importation and internal sale of tobacco[228]

2. Under the WTO Agreement

EC 1995	Trade description of scallops[229]
Japan 1995	Taxes on alcoholic beverages[230]
Australia 1995	Measures affecting the importation of salmon[231]
EC 1995	Duties on imports of cereals[232]
Korea 1995	Measures concerning the shelf-life and physical treatment of bottled water[233]
Hungary 1996	Export subsidies in respect of agricultural products[234]
Brazil 1996	Export financing programme for aircraft[235]
EC 1996	Measures affecting livestock and meat (hormones)[236]

Canada has also reserved its rights to participate as a third party in *United States—The Cuban Liberty and Democratic Solidarity Act* (WT/DS38), a complaint brought by the EC against the US Helms-Burton legislation. This legislation imposes certain restrictions on goods of Cuban origin, and provides for the possible refusal of visas and the exclusion of non-US nationals from US territory, as well as the potential for a right of action for US citizens against non-US nationals and companies "trafficking" in confiscated Cuban property.

Canada was granted two waivers under article XXV:5 of the GATT 1947: "Delay in the Implementation of Certain Concessions in the Geneva (1967) Protocol"[237] and "CARIBCAN."[238]

The report of the working party that examined the Canada-US Free Trade Agreement was adopted on November 12, 1991.[239] The NAFTA is still under examination.[240] The WTO Committee on Regional Trade Agreements now also conducts periodic reviews of regional trade agreements.

---

227 Complaint settled.

228 DS/44R, adopted 4 October 1994.

229 WT/DS7. Mutually agreed solution notified on 5 July 1996.

230 WT/DS10.

231 WT/DS18.

232 WT/DS9 (settlement apparent).

233 WT/DS20. A mutually agreed solution was notified on 6 May 1996.

234 WT/DS35. However, Canada did not participate in the request for the establishment of a panel by Argentina, the United States, New Zealand, and Australia in January 1997.

235 WT/DS46.

236 WT/DS48. A panel was established in this dispute on 16 October 1996.

237 Decision of the Contracting Parties adopted 25 July 1968, L/3049, BISD, 16th Supp. 20 (1968).

238 Decision of the contracting parties adopted 28 November 1986, L/6102, BISD, 33rd Supp. 97 (1987).

239 L/6927, BISD, 38th Supp. 47 (1991).

240 See also WTO, *Report on Regionalism in the World Trading System* (1995).

VI. CONCLUSION

A strong, credible, and effective dispute settlement system that maintains the balance of rights and obligations of WTO members within the system and operates to provide legal remedies for violations of agreed-upon international norms is the keystone of a rule-oriented multilateral trade regime. The history of the GATT-WTO dispute settlement process reveals a strong tension between, and an effort to balance, the pragmatic handling of trade tensions through negotiation and compromise, on the one hand, and the legalistic settlement of disputes, on the other.

The new DSU provisions on automaticity in, *inter alia*, the establishment and composition of panels, and on adoption of panel and appellate body reports, coupled with strict time frames for each step of the process and the strengthened surveillance procedures to reinforce implementation of panel rulings make the new WTO dispute settlement system considerably more rule oriented. They furnish a stronger and more disciplined forum for WTO dispute settlement.

As in international law generally, there is technically no *stare decisis* in the GATT-WTO dispute resolution process.[241] However, GATT and WTO panel reports (and now WTO appellate body reports) have more recently come to be considered as having a persuasive force resembling precedent.[242] Adopted reports provide guidance concerning the interpretation and application of GATT-WTO principles. In its report on *Japan—Taxes on Alcoholic Beverages*,[243] the appellate body stated the following on the role of adopted GATT panel reports in the WTO legal system: "[a]dopted panel reports are an important part of the GATT *acquis*. They are often considered by subsequent panels. They create legitimate expectations among WTO members, and, therefore, should be taken into account where they are relevant to any dispute. However, they are not binding, except with respect to resolving the particular dispute between the parties to that dispute."

A review of the rules and procedures in the DSU is to be conducted within four years after the entry into force of the WTO Agreement. Following this review, the ministerial conference is to take a decision "whether to continue, modify or terminate such dispute settlement rules and procedures."[244]

---

241 See Jackson (1990), *supra*, note 55, at 67.

242 Jackson, *ibid*. More recently, Professor Jackson has argued that the legal effect of an adopted panel report under the GATT 1947 was a combination of (1) an obligation under international law binding on the parties in a particular case and (2) subsequent practice in the application of the treaty within the meaning of art. 31(3) of the Vienna Convention on the Law of Treaties (1969) 1155 UNTS 331. See Jackson, "The Legal Meaning of a GATT Dispute Settlement Report: Some Reflections" in Blokker and Muller (eds.), *Towards More Effective Supervision by International Organizations: Essays in Honour of Henry G. Schermers*, vol. I (1994), at 149-64. More recently, in *Japan—Taxes on Alcoholic Beverages* (AB-1996-2), the appellate body disagreed with the panel report's finding that "panel reports adopted by the GATT CONTRACTING PARTIES and the WTO Dispute Settlement Body constitute subsequent practice in a specific case" as the phrase "subsequent practice" is used in article 31 of the Vienna Convention.

243 AB-1996-2.

244 See "Decision on the Application and Review of the Understanding on Rules and Procedures Governing the Settlement of Disputes in WTO," *The Results of the Uruguay Round of Multilateral Trade Negotiations: The Legal Texts* (1994), at 465.

VII. SELECTED BIBLIOGRAPHY

A. Books

Dam, *The GATT: Law and International Economic Organization* (1970).

Grainger, *GATT Disputes: Consensus Without Concord* (1989).

Hallstrom, *The GATT Panels and the Formation of International Trade Law* (1995).

Hudec, *Adjudication of International Trade Disputes* (1978).

Hudec, *Enforcing International Trade Law: the Evolution of the GATT Legal System* (1993).

Hudec, *The GATT Legal System and World Trade Diplomacy* (2nd ed., 1990).

Jackson, *Restructuring the GATT System* (1990).

Jackson, *The World Trading System* (1989).

Jackson, *World Trade and the Law of GATT* (1969).

Long, *Law and Its Limitations in the GATT Multilateral Trade System* (1985).

McGovern, *International Trade Regulation* (1995).

Pescatore, Davey, and Lowenfeld, *Handbook of WTO/GATT Dispute Settlement* (1993).

Petersmann and Hilf (eds.), *The New GATT Round of Multilateral Trade Negotiations: Legal and Economic Problems* (2nd ed., 1991).

Rubin and Jones (eds.), *Conflict and Resolution in US-EC Trade Relations at the Opening of the Uruguay Round* (1989).

Simmonds and Hill (eds.), *Law and Practice under the GATT* (1989).

Steger and Hart (eds.), *In Whose Interest?: Due Process and Transparency in International Trade*, proceedings of a conference of the Centre for Trade Policy and Law (Ottawa: May 1990).

Trebilcock and Howse, *The Regulation of International Trade* (1995).

US Int. Trade Commission, pub. no. 1793, *Review of the Effectiveness of Trade Dispute Settlement under the GATT and the Tokyo Round Agreements, Report to the Committee on Finance, US Senate, as Investigation No. 332-212 under Section 332(g) of the Tariff Act of 1930* (1985).

B. Articles

Abbott, "The Uruguay Round and Dispute Resolution: Building a Private Interests System of Justice" (1992), 1 *Col. Bus. L Rev.* 111-49.

Bello and Holmer, "Settling Disputes in the GATT: The Past, Present and Future" (1990), 24 *Int'l. Lawyer* 519.

Bliss, "GATT Dispute Settlement Reform in the Uruguay Round: Problems and Prospects" (1987), 23 *Stan. J Int'l. L* 31.

Bronckers, "Non-judicial and Judicial Remedies in International Trade Disputes: Some Reflections at the Close of the Uruguay Round" (1990) 24 *J World Trade* 121.

Carasco, "The Foreign Investment Review Agency (FIRA) and the General Agreement on Tariffs and Trade (GATT): Incompatible?" (1983), 13 *Georgia J Int'l. & Comp. L* 441.

Castel, "The Uruguay Round and the Improvements to the GATT Dispute Settlement Rules and Procedures" (1989), 38 *Int'l. & Comp. LQ* 834.

Cheetham, "The Federal Government Proposals for Reform of the GATT Dispute Settlement System: Continued Momentum for a Rules-Oriented Approach to Dispute Settlement in International Trade Agreements" (1991), 22 *Rev. Gen. de Droit* 431.

Croley and Jackson, "WTO Procedures, Standard of Review, and Deference to National Governments" (1996), 90 *Am. J Int'l. Law* 193.

Davey, "Dispute Settlement and the GATT" (1987), 11 *Fordham Int'l. LJ* 51.

Hudec, "GATT Dispute Settlement After the Tokyo Round: An Unfinished Business" (1980), 13 *Cornell Int'l. LJ* 145.

Hudec, "Legal Issues in US-EC Trade Policy: GATT Litigation 1960-1985" in Baldwin, Hamilton, and Sapir (eds.), *Issues in US-EC Trade Relations* (1988), 17.

Hudec, "Reforming GATT Adjudication Procedures: The Lessons of the DISC Case" (1988), 72 *Minn. L Rev.* 1443.

Hudec, "Transcending the Ostensible: Some Reflections on the Nature of Litigation Between Governments" (1987), 72 *Minn. L Rev.* 211.

Ingersoll, "Current Efficacy of the GATT Dispute Settlement Process" (1987), 22 *Texas Int'l. LJ* 87.

Jackson, "Governmental Disputes in International Trade Relations: A Proposal in the Context of GATT" (1979), 13 *J World Trade L* 1.

Jackson, "The Jurisprudence of International Trade: The DISC Case in GATT" (1978), 72 *Am. J Int'l. L* 747.

Komuro, "The WTO Dispute Settlement Mechanism—Coverage and Procedures of the New Understanding" (1995),12 *J Int'l. Arb.* 81.

Lowenfeld, "Remedies Along with Rights: Institutional Reform in the New GATT" (1994), 88 *Am. J. Int'l Law* 477.

McRae, "Recourse to GATT for Resolving International Trade Disputes" in Saunders (ed.), *Trading Canada's Natural Resources* (1987), at 168.

Montana-Mora, "A GATT with Teeth: Law Wins over Politics in the Resolution of International Trade Disputes" (1993), 31 *Columbia J Transnat'l. Law* 103.

Ostrihansky, "Settlement of Interstate Trade Disputes—The Role of Law and Legal Procedures" (1991), 22 *Netherlands Yearbook of Int'l. Law* 163.

Ostrihanksy, "The Future of Dispute Settlement within the GATT: Conciliation v. Adjudication" (1991), *UN Decade of Int'l. Law* 125.

Parker, "Dispute Settlement in the GATT and the Canada-US Free Trade Agreement" (1989), 23 *J World Trade L* 83.

Pescatore, "The GATT Dispute Settlement Mechanism: Its Present Situation and Its Prospects" (1993), 27 *J World Trade* 5.

Petersmann, "Proposals for Improvements in the GATT Dispute Settlement System: a Survey and Comparative Analysis" in Dicke, Detlev C. and Ernst-Ulrich Petersmann (eds.), *Foreign Trade in the Present and a New International Economic Order* (1988), at 340.

Petersmann, "Strengthening GATT Procedures for Settling Disputes" (1988), *World Economy* 55.

Petersmann, "The Dispute Settlement System of the World Trade Organization and the Evolution of the GATT Dispute Settlement System Since 1948" (1994), 31 *Common Market Law Rev.* 1157.

Petersmann, "The Mid-Term Review Agreements of the Uruguay Round and the 1989 Improvements to the GATT Dispute Settlement Procedures" (1989), 32 *German Yearbook of Int'l. Law* 290.

Peterson, "The GATT and Restrictions on Foreign Investment: the United States Challenge to Canada's Foreign Investment Law" (1982), 1 *UCLA Pacific Basin LJ* 224.

Plank, "An Unofficial Description of How a GATT Panel Works and Does Not" (1987), 4 *J Int'l. Arb.* 53.

Price, "New Institutional Developments in GATT" (1992), 1 *Minn. J Global Trade* 87.

Thomas, "Litigation Process under the GATT Dispute Settlement System: Lessons for the World Trade Organization?" (1996), 30 *J of World Trade L* 53.

Van Bael, "The GATT Dispute Settlement Procedure" (1988), 22 *J World Trade L* 67.

CHAPTER TWENTY

The Settlement of Disputes Under Chapter 20 of the North American Free Trade Agreement

I. INTRODUCTION

The maintenance of a harmonious relationship between states bound by a bilateral international trade agreement requires procedures to avoid conflicts and, should they arise, to resolve them quickly and effectively to the satisfaction of the parties involved. Such procedures usually take the form of notification of trade measures that contracting states are planning to adopt that may affect the other, and consultation and direct negotiation with respect to such measures prior to their enactment, followed by mediation, good offices, or conciliation by third parties, when necessary. If the potential or actual conflict is not resolved, the dispute may be submitted to binding arbitration or some other method of settlement. Finally, should the losing party refuse to comply with the award or decision, sanctions such as compensation, retaliation, or termination of the agreement may be imposed.

As set out in chapter 2 of this book, the North American Free Trade Agreement (NAFTA) in fact adopts a complex and varied set of provisions to deal with dispute settlement. These provisions involve a variety of different procedures adopted within the treaty such as those dealing with anti-dumping and countervailing duty disputes in chapter 19 or the reference to the International Convention for the Settlement of Investment Disputes (ICSID) in chapter 11 to deal with investment disputes. In addition, the

NAFTA leaves it open to the parties to adopt other general dispute settlement procedures such as arbitration or alternative dispute settlement techniques. The NAFTA also requires the establishment of domestic dispute settlement procedures in such areas as government procurement and intellectual property. Beyond this, the NAFTA is complemented by dispute settlement procedures that exist under other treaties, such as the General Agreement on Tariffs and Trade (GATT) 1994 or international environmental treaties, which may be used by the parties in addition to the NAFTA provisions. The two side agreements on environmental and labour cooperation, reviewed in chapter 2 of this book, also establish special dispute settlement procedures.

In adopting this complex approach, the NAFTA follows the Free Trade Agreement (FTA),[1] which contained both general chapter 18 procedures, which dealt with institutional provisions and binational dispute settlement, as well as the chapter 19 procedures, which dealt specifically with anti-dumping and countervailing duty disputes and a range of other procedures throughout the treaty.[2]

Chapter 20 of the NAFTA is the central procedure for the settlement of disputes. This chapter is applicable unless more specific provisions exist. With very few exceptions,[3] all parts of the NAFTA are subject to the principle of compulsory dispute settlement: the applicable procedure may vary, but the principle is almost invariable.

II. INSTITUTIONAL PROVISIONS

Chapter 20 deals with the institutional provisions for the joint management of the NAFTA as well as with the avoidance or settlement of disputes between the parties regarding the interpretation or application of the agreement. The management of the NAFTA is entrusted to a free trade commission, composed of one cabinet level official from each of the parties. The commission must meet at least once a year and, in fact has met more frequently. The commission is charged with the supervision and management of disputes as well as the further development of the dispute settlement process. The commission oversees the many committees and working groups created under various NAFTA chapters, and is free to create others as it deems necessary. It may delegate authority to other bodies and seek the advice of outside experts.

---

1 SC 1988, c. 65, sched. A and regulations, *Can. Gaz.* 6 January 1989, extra no. 1, vol. 123.

2 See also a few provisions scattered throughout the Canada-US Free Trade Agreement (FTA), art. 303 (consultation with respect to rules of origin for goods); Annex 406.6 (consultation concerning the uniform application of rules of origin for goods); Annex 406.7 (appeals relating to rules of origin); Annex 406.9 (notification and consultation prior to major changes in the flow of trade); art. 709 (consultation on agricultural issues); Annex 705.4 (10 to 19) (institutional procedures and arbitration panels re local support for wheat); art. 1103 (emergency action and arbitration); art. 1406 (services and denial of benefits); Annex 1404.B, art. 4 (tourism and consultation); art. 1504 (temporary entry for business persons and dispute settlement); art. 1608 (investment disputes); and art. 1704 (financial services, notification, and consultation).

3 Chapter 15 on competition, decisions to deny temporary access to a service provider under chapter 16, proposed emergency action under chapter 8.

The commission is assisted by a secretariat, composed of three national sections. Each national section is headed by a secretary responsible for the administration of their office. The role of the secretariat is to provide whatever assistance the commission may require, to support the work of other NAFTA committees and working groups as directed by the commission, and to provide assistance to dispute settlement panels. This last task has proven to be the principal administrative function of the secretariat, apart from organizing meetings of the commission. It must be noted that the secretariat is strictly an intergovernmental body, it is subject to the commission in all respects and has no legal existence independent of the commission.[4] Nothing prevents the commission from expanding the role of the secretariat, but there seems to be no disposition to do so.

III. SETTLEMENT OF DISPUTES UNDER CHAPTER 20

The purpose of chapter 20 is the avoidance and settlement of any dispute, not covered by a more specific procedure, relating to the interpretation and application of the NAFTA. It also applies whenever a party considers that an actual or proposed measure of another party is or would be inconsistent with the obligations of the NAFTA, or would cause nullification or impairment in the sense of Annex 2004.[5]

Chapter 20 deals with situations where disputes arise under both the NAFTA and the GATT-WTO 1994. In principle, such disputes may be settled in either forum, according to the rules of that forum, at the discretion of the complaining party. Once the procedure for the settlement of a dispute has been initiated under the NAFTA or the GATT, the chosen forum must be used to the exclusion of the other.[6] In disputes concerning environmental issues, sanitary or phytosanitary standards, or standards in general, the responding party may insist upon chapter 20 procedures to the exclusion of the WTO.

A party that considers that any actual or proposed measure might affect the operation of the NAFTA may request consultations. The other party must enter into consultation and a third party may also be included, at the responding party's request. Consultations take place directly between the parties or within the framework of a regularly scheduled or a special meeting of the commission. Such a meeting must be convened, at the request of a party, should consultations not succeed. Consultations held under the aegis of articles 513 (rules of origin), 723 (sanitary and phytosanitary standards), and 914 (standards) take the place of formal consultations. The commission must respond within 10 days to a request for consultations and may have recourse to experts or good offices and mediation procedures in its efforts to assist the parties in reaching a satisfactory solution.

---

4 As described in chapter 2 of this book, the two commissions created by the labour and environmental side agreements in fact enjoy greater latitude than the NAFTA Secretariat.

5 North American Free Trade Implementation Act, SC 1993, c. 44. NAFTA is reprinted in (1993), 32 *ILM* 296.

6 NAFTA, art. 2005.

If a dispute is not resolved by consultative procedures, a party may call upon the commission to appoint an arbitral panel.[7] With certain differences, the arbitral panel procedure is essentially the panel of experts of the Canada-US Free Trade Agreement (FTA), which in turn was directly inspired by the GATT. On receipt of a request from a party, the commission must establish an arbitral panel.

Detailed rules of the NAFTA and special rules of procedure deal with the composition of panels, the general principles they must follow, and the time allotted for their proceedings. Panellists are normally chosen from a single roster maintained by the commission.[8] The panel of arbitrators must be composed of five members. Each party must select two from among the roster members having the nationality of the other party. The parties should then agree on a chairperson. If they fail to agree, the party chosen by lot may select a chairperson who does not hold the nationality of that party.[9] The rules of procedure ensure a right to at least one hearing before the panel as well as the opportunity to provide written submissions and rebuttals.[10] The proceedings of the panel are confidential.[11] Panellists must also comply with a code of conduct.[12]

The terms of reference of the panel, envisaged by article 2012.3, require the panel to make findings of fact, determinations of law, and recommendations about how the dispute may best be resolved. If nullification and impairment are alleged, this must be stated in the terms of reference. The panel process envisaged by chapter 20 and the rules of procedure are normally completed within a period of some five months after the constitution of the panel. As is the case with the WTO, the panel is required to present the parties with an initial report containing findings of fact, its determinations as to whether the measure at issue is or would be inconsistent with the obligations of the NAFTA or cause nullification and impairment, and its recommendations, if any, for resolution of the dispute. The panel must afford the parties opportunity to comment on its preliminary findings prior to completion of its report. Panellists may furnish separate opinions on matters not unanimously agreed, but these opinions are to remain anonymous. Normally, the commission is required to publish the final report within 15 days of submission.

---

7 The FTA, *supra*, note 1, explicitly distinguished binding arbitration from the expert panel proceedings. The NAFTA, while essentially continuing the expert panel proceeding, terms this proceeding an "arbitral panel" in order to reinforce its compulsory character. Nothing prevents the parties from adopting a formal interstate arbitral procedure but it is not explicitly mentioned as it was in the FTA.

8 NAFTA, arts. 2009 to 2012; Model Rules of Procedure for chapter 20 of the North American Free Trade Agreement are required by art. 2012.1. In fact, the parties have continued to use the rules of procedure for article 1905, special committees, issued for the FTA, *Can. Gaz.* pt. I, 29 January 1994, 774. The roster had not been appointed in 1996 when the United States initiated the first procedure. The parties were therefore obliged to select panelists at large.

9 In the first procedure under chapter 20 the parties chose a British national, Professor E. Lauterpacht.

10 FTA, *supra*, note 1, art. 1807.4.

11 *Ibid.*

12 Code of Conduct for Dispute Settlement Procedures Under Chapters 19 and 20 of the North American Free Trade Agreement, in *Can. Gaz.*, pt. I, 22 January 1994, 539.

The panel report is formally a recommendation to the commission, which, in turn, is required to agree on the means to resolve the dispute.[13] Whenever possible, resolution of the dispute is by removing or not implementing a measure at variance with the NAFTA or causing nullification or impairment, or, failing such a resolution, by awarding compensation.[14] If the commission cannot reach agreement on a mutually satisfactory resolution of the dispute within 30 days of receiving the panel's final report, or such other date as the commission may decide, and a party considers that its fundamental rights under the NAFTA or benefits anticipated under it are or would be impaired by the implementation or maintenance of the measure at issue, that party is free to suspend the application to the other party of benefits of equivalent effect until the parties have reached agreement on the resolution of the dispute.[15]

The remedies given to an aggrieved party—that is, compensation, remedial action, or suspension of the application of equivalent benefits—are substantially similar to those available under the GATT 1994.[16] Retaliation may not prove effective against the United States, given the relative size of the Mexican and Canadian economies and given the experience under the FTA, which shows that considerable time may be required to reach a final resolution of a dispute under the NAFTA, since the commission must negotiate a mutually satisfactory resolution of the dispute. Under normal circumstances, the solution to the dispute should conform to the recommendation of the panel. Under the FTA, all disputes were resolved either by maintaining the legislation vindicated by the panel or by negotiating a solution involving changes to the legislation or administrative decisions found to be in conflict with the treaty. The NAFTA does not require authorization before retaliation can take place, but should there be a dispute as to the proportionality or propriety of the retaliatory measures, these issues can be put to a panel.[17]

Comparison of the NAFTA process with the comparable GATT-WTO 1994 process poses interesting questions. Until the entry into force of the GATT 1994, one year later than the NAFTA, there was no doubt that the NAFTA offered more automatic and rapid procedures. In comparison to the WTO, the NAFTA time limits are short both with respect to the appointment of panelists and for the presentation of the initial report to the parties: in the latter case, three months from the formation of the panel may be too short for the panels to engage in fact finding and to consider all the parties' arguments. The NAFTA also has tight deadlines for the adoption of reports by the panels and by the commission. However, it must be noted that the GATT 1994 process now also has short deadlines and the formation of a panel is required unless there is a consensus among WTO members against it. The same rule applies to the adoption of the report, which in some respects makes it more enforceable than a NAFTA panel report since it enjoys the support of all 120 WTO members. In addition, the WTO process has been strengthened

13 NAFTA, art. 2018.1.

14 NAFTA, art. 2018.2.

15 NAFTA, art. 2019.

16 GATT, art. XXIII. Understanding Regarding Notification, Dispute Settlement and Surveillance.

17 NAFTA, art.2019.3.

by the adoption of an appellate process on points of law, recourse to which involves the commitment to be bound by the ruling of the appellate body.

The choice between the WTO or the NAFTA may be a difficult one. The NAFTA process will continue to be more manageable since it involves a small group of states; however, in some respects, the force of a WTO panel may be greater. It should be noted that within the first two years of NAFTA's existence, the United States had initiated both NAFTA and WTO proceedings against Canada. The decision as to choice of forum appears to depend essentially on the relative strength of the applicable NAFTA or GATT 1994 rules.

There is no provision in chapter 20 for participation by private parties or provinces and states.[18] This is consistent with principles of international law and GATT practice. When an issue of interpretation of the NAFTA arises in domestic judicial or administrative proceedings, the parties endeavour to agree on such interpretation within the commission at the behest of a party or of a domestic tribunal. If an agreement is reached, the party in whose territory the court or administrative body is located shall submit the agreed-upon interpretation to that body. If no agreement is reached, either party may submit its own views to the court or administrative body in accordance with the rules of that forum.[19] This provision can be seen as a modest opening to private parties. While it may have potential, it has yet to be invoked.

IV. FTA DISPUTES

Since the procedures of the NAFTA and the FTA are so close, it is appropriate to examine the five reports issued by five panels established under chapter 18 of the FTA. These five reports, without establishing formal precedents, have set the pattern subsequently followed under chapter 20 of the NAFTA. The five panels dealt with disputes involving Canadian landing requirements for West Coast salmon and herring;[20] US size requirements for the import of Canadian lobsters;[21] the inclusion of non-mortgage interest in the calculation of rules of origin;[22]allegations that the Canadian Wheat Board subsidized grain exports;[23] and the exclusion of UHT milk from Québec from the market in Puerto Rico.[24]

---

18 The labour and environmental side agreements both require that Canadian provinces agree to extend the agreements to their territories.

19 NAFTA, art. 2020.

20 *In the Matter of Canada's Landing Requirements for Pacific Coast Salmon and Herring*, final report, 16 October 1989; CDA-89-1807-01; (1989). QL, LEXIS.

21 *United States Regulations on Lobster*, final report, 22 May 1990; USA-89-1807-01; (1990). QL, LEXIS.

22 *Treatment of Non-Mortgage Interest under Article 304*, final report, 8 June 1992; USA-92-1807-01. QL, LEXIS.

23 *The Interpretation of and Canada's Compliance with Article 701.3 with Respect to Durum Wheat Sales*, final report, 8 February 1993, USA-93-1807-01. QL, LEXIS.

24 *Puerto Rico Regulations on the Import, Distribution and Sale of UHT Milk from Québec*, final report, 3 June 1993; USA-93-1807-01. QL, LEXIS.

Salmon and Herring

This dispute involved a complaint by the United States against Canadian fisheries regulations[25] that prohibited the export of unprocessed salmon and herring caught in Canadian waters. The Government of the United States argued that these measures constituted an export quota prohibited by the FTA and could not be justified under the general exceptions provided for in the treaty. The Government of Canada argued that the regulations constituted legitimate conservation measures forming part of a general scheme of fisheries management that could be justified under the provisions that incorporated the exceptions under the GATT, article XX(g). In response to the complaint and a GATT panel that had condemned the regulations,[26] the Government of Canada issued new regulations requiring the landing in Canada of all such fish caught in Canadian waters. The Government of the United States raised the same objections to the new regulations.

The panel decided that the primary effect of the measure was the regulation of export transactions, which placed a materially greater burden on export sales than on domestic sales. But the panel recognized that the measures also had a legitimate conservation objective. The panel concluded that any exception made for conservation purposes must be proportional to the conservation problem posed and that the issue in this case could not justify a 100 percent export ban. The panel suggested that at least 10 to 20 percent of the fish caught might be exported directly without compromising the conservation objectives. After some months of difficult negotiations, the commission reached agreement on a 25 percent export limit to be reached in a two-year period.

Lobster

The Government of Canada objected to US fisheries legislation that prohibited the sale, purchase, or transport of small live lobsters in or from the United States, arguing that this measure constituted an import quota prohibited by the NAFTA and the GATT. The United States responded that this was a conservation measure designed to protect lobster stocks and stressed that it was applied to all lobster—foreign and domestic—thus meeting the national treatment (NT) standard.

The majority of the panel agreed with the United States. Two panelists, apparently both Canadians, disagreed with this finding. The absence of unanimity may have weakened the force of the panel report but the result was that the US legislation remained unchanged.

Non-Mortgage Interest

This dispute involved the operation of a joint venture between General Motors and the Suzuki Motor Co. which produced automobiles in Ontario. It arose out of the refusal by

---

25 *Pacific Commercial Salmon Fishery Regulations*, CRC 1978, c. 823, s. 6 and *Pacific Herring Fishery Regulations*, CRC 1978, c. 825, s. 13(2).

26 *Canada—Measures Affecting Exports of Unprocessed Herring and Salmon*, GATT, BISD, 35th Supp. 98.

the US customs to accept non-mortgage interest charges as a part of the total calculation of Canadian value for purposes of the FTA rules of origin.

The panel report is based on a close reading of chapter 3 of the FTA. The unanimous opinion of the panel was that under US and Canadian law and internationally accepted accounting standards, non-mortgage interest formed part of the direct cost of processing and assembling as envisaged by article 304 of the FTA. This report was accepted without great controversy, but it should be noted that the production of the plant in question was subsequently subjected to more stringent rules under the NAFTA.[27]

Durum Wheat

This dispute arose out of the long-standing suspicion in the United States that the Canadian Wheat Board, which has a monopoly on the export of a variety of grains, including durum wheat used for making pasta, used its powers to covertly subsidize Canadian grain exports. This issue was so politically sensitive that the two governments went outside the regular roster of panellists to name particularly distinguished members, such as the former chief justice of Canada and a retired US attorney general.

The result was one that gave little satisfaction to the United States. The panel read the FTA, chapter 7 as requiring the prohibition of export subsidies and as prohibiting certain specific domestic subsidies. They held that the Wheat Board's acquisition costs were not among the prohibited domestic subsidies and that the Wheat Board's contribution to freight costs were outside the scope of article 701(3). However, in order to allay fears in the United States, the panel recommended that the Wheat Board open its books to scrutiny under a joint information-sharing scheme. This was subsequently done, but it has had little impact on US suspicions of the Canadian export monopoly.

As an interesting aside, the panel suggested that the FTA, chapter 18 would be better administered by a permanent group of judges rather than *ad hoc* panels. This suggestion was not taken up in the NAFTA, although NAFTA, chapter 20 envisages a single roster of some 30 experts, rather than the separate national lists that existed under the FTA.

UHT Milk

This dispute arose out of the closure of the market by the government of Puerto Rico to UHT milk from Québec. The product had been sold in Puerto Rico for many years without incident. However, one year after Puerto Rico adopted a new standard for milk production—the pasteurized milk ordinance that governed the production of milk throughout the United States—the producer was informed that it should conform to the new standard and, after a year of seemingly vain negotiations, the product was banned from the market on the ground that formal compliance or satisfactory evidence that the UHT milk was produced according to standards that were "essentially equivalent," had not been demonstrated.

The decision of the Government of Puerto Rico to close the market came at a moment when negotiations between the producer, the Embassy of Canada and authorities

27 See Paterson and Band, *International Trade & Investment Law in Canada* (2nd ed., 1994), at 2-68.

in Washington were still under way. Ultimately, it was this event that was determinative. The Government of Canada made several arguments: that the closure constituted a quota, that the manner of applying the new standard did not afford NT and that the producer had not been offered an opportunity to prove equivalence of the Québec and the US standards under the provisions of chapter 7 on agricultural standards. The panel rejected the first argument and declined in the circumstances to rule on the second. While many of the provisions on phytosanitary standards were deemed to be of a best efforts nature, the panel ruled that the Québec producer had a right to be afforded an opportunity to prove that its product was produced under conditions equivalent to the US standard. Closure of the market in the midst of negotiations, while not beyond the authority of Puerto Rico, did violate legitimate Canadian expectations that there would be a proper opportunity to provide appropriate evidence. The panel thus ruled that there had been nullification and impairment of legitimate Canadian expectations and recommended that the producer be given a proper opportunity to provide the evidence. This was successfully done in the ensuing two years and the product ultimately returned to the market in Puerto Rico.

V. NAFTA DISPUTES

In late 1995, the Government of the United States called for the establishment of a panel to consider the tariffs established by Canada on January 1, 1995 covering a range of agricultural commodities pursuant to the GATT 1994 Agreement on Agriculture. The United States alleged that these tariffs, some of which were over 200 percent, violated the NAFTA commitment of January 1, 1994 not to establish any new tariffs; it was also argued that the tariffs were subject to the phase-out principle and that no steps had been taken to begin this process. Canada responded with the argument that these tariffs were adopted under the GATT-WTO 1994 Agreement on Agriculture, an essential feature of which was the establishment of tariff equivalents for pre-existing agricultural quotas. Canada thus argued that the measures were justified by a new and separate treaty that reflected a separate negotiating process in which long-standing differences about the use of quotas on agricultural goods had been resolved by the international community in the Uruguay Round of Multilateral Trade Negotiations.

The issues posed were complex, involving arguments based on the NAFTA text, principles of treaty interpretation, the relationship of the NAFTA and WTO texts, and the relationship of separate but related trade negotiations. The issues were of great political sensitivity. They reflected longstanding unease in the United States over the Canadian supply management systems and the very strong desire of the Canadian federal and provincial governments to ensure the survival of these programs that would be seriously threatened by the removal of the tariff equivalents of the previous quotas. The process proved to be so sensitive for both governments that they took five months just to name the panelists and attempted to keep their names secret. The parties also chose a British professor of international law to chair the panel.[28] The central arguments of the

28 *Tariffs Applied by Canada to certain US-Origin Agricultural Products* (preliminary report, 15 July 1996, final report 2 December 1996, CDA-95-2008-01. QL, LEXIS.

United States were threefold. The Government of Canada, by entering into the NAFTA in 1994, had committed itself (1) not to raise tariffs, (2) not to impose new tariffs, and (3) to phase out all tariffs. By imposing these tariffs on agricultural goods, it was alleged that Canada had violated the most basic obligations of the NAFTA. On their face, these were simple, elegant, and powerful arguments. In reply, Canada did not deny the existence of the tariffs, but rather argued that they were justified by the WTO Agreement on Agriculture, which formed part of the general multilateral trade agreements that entered into force in 1995 and that enshrined the substance of the real negotiations on agriculture between the two countries. There was thus, in Canada's view, no contradiction between the two agreements, since the NAFTA had left the substance of agricultural trade to be negotiated in the subsequent multilateral negotiations. The panel in essence accepted the Canadian contention. The panel report is remarkable for its very close analysis of a number of complex issues, including the interrelationship of several agreements. In the panel's view, the central commitment was neither in the NAFTA nor in the WTO Agreement on Agriculture, but in the commitment made bewteen Canada and the United States in the 1988 FTA, article 710, which was designed to preserve the GATT rights of both countries in respect of agricultural trade in the face of future negotiations.

VI. ASSESSMENT OF THE PROCESS

There is little doubt that the principle of compulsory dispute settlement is a source of strength of the NAFTA. The same is true of the chapter 20 procedure. The very existence of the procedure is a guarantee that disputes can be resolved and there is a strong incentive to resolve them by negotiation. This in fact takes place in most cases and the small number of disputes that actually proceed under chapter 20 should be seen as a success rather than a failure of the process. It is also interesting to study the body of the NAFTA law that is slowly being developed under chapter 20. This law is of a hybrid character. It draws heavily upon the GATT law and in the long term will enrich and expand the total corpus of that law. It also displays a clear association with public international law, since several panels have felt compelled to examine the links with general principles of treaty law. These panels have done much to complete the law of the NAFTA.

While a positive assessment is certainly in order, some reservations and comments must be made both in comparison to the WTO and also concerning the actual working of the NAFTA procedure. The NAFTA dispute settlement system was clearly superior to that of the GATT before 1995. This remains true in the sense that the NAFTA provisions on dispute settlement are more complex and varied. Chapter 20 itself represents a tight and highly manageable procedure for NAFTA parties but, in the final analysis, implementation of panel reports remains a political decision often subject to lengthy negotiation. Furthermore, with the emergence of the WTO appellate body, which has already issued binding decisions in response to appeals on points of law, the WTO dispute settlement procedure comes closer to being both compulsory and binding. For these and other reasons, in some circumstances, there may be an advantage for the NAFTA parties to choose the WTO procedure over chapter 20. Under the NAFTA, implementation of panel reports is neither immediate nor automatic, although there is no instance of their having been set aside. Further, lengthy negotiations are necessary between the parties to a dispute before the recommendations of the panel will be implemented. In this situation, the bargaining power of the stronger party may prevail over the letter of the law. In conclusion, chapter 20 remains a valuable element of the NAFTA, but there will be situations where the parties to the NAFTA will look to other remedies.

VII. SELECTED BIBLIOGRAPHY

A. Books

Holbein and Musch, *North American Free Trade Agreements* (1992-).

Johnson, *The North American Free Trade Agreement* (1995).

Leycegui, Robson, and Stein, *Trading Punches: Trade Remedy Law and Disputes Under NAFTA* (1995).

Paterson and Band, *International Trade and Investment Law in Canada* (2nd ed., 1995).

Trebilcock and Howse, *The Regulation of International Trade* (1995).

B. Articles

"Alternative Dispute Resolution in Canada-United States Trade Relations: a Symposium" (1988), 40 *Me. L Rev.* 223.

Apuzzo and Kerr, "International Arbitration—The Dispute Settlement Procedures Chosen for the Canada-US Free Trade Agreement" (1988), 5 *J Int'l. Arb.* 7.

Castel, "The Settlement of Disputes Under the 1988 Canada-United States Free Trade Agreement" (1989), 83 *Am. J Int'l. L* 118.

de Mestral and Winter, "Dispute Settlement Under the North American Free Trade Agreement and the Treaty of European Union" (1994), 17 *J European Integration* 235.

Eklund, "A Primer on Arbitration of NAFTA Chapter Eleven Investor-State Disputes" (1994), 11 *J Int'l. Arb.* 135.

Ferguson, "Dispute Settlement Under the Canada-United States Free Trade Agreement" (1989), 47 *U of T Fac. L Rev.* 317.

Fried, "Dispute Settlement in International Trade: The Canada-US Free Trade Agreement" (1988), 15 *Private Investors Abroad* 1.

Gastle and Castel, "Should the North American Free Trade Agreement Dispute Settlement Mechanism in Anti-Dumping and Countervailing Duty Cases Be Reformed in the Light of Softwood Lumber III?" (1995), 26 *Law & Policy in Int'l. Business* 823-96.

Graham, "Dispute Resolution in the Canada-United States Free Trade Agreement: One Element of a Complex Relationship" (1992), 37 *McGill LJ* 544.

Horlick and deBusk, "Dispute Resolution Under NAFTA: Building on the US-Canada FTA, GATT and ICSID" (1993), 10 *J Int'l. Arb.* 51.

Hudec, "Dispute Resolution Under a North American Free Trade Area: The Importance of the Domestic Legal Setting" (1987), 12 *Can. US LJ* 329.

Huntington, "Settling Disputes Under NAFTA" (1993), 34 *Harv. Int'l. L* 407.

McDorman, "The Dispute Settlement Regime of the Free Trade Agreement" (1988), 2 *Nev. Int'l. Bus. L* 303.

Warner, *Round Two of the Canada-US Free Trade Agreement: The Case for Replacing Antidumping with Antitrust* (Ontario Centre for International Business, pub. no. 32, 1990).

CHAPTER TWENTY-ONE

The Settlement of International Commercial Disputes by Arbitration

I. INTRODUCTION

The phenomenal growth and the increasing complexity of international trade in recent years have resulted in arbitration becoming the preferred method of settlement of international commercial disputes.

It is now customary to include in an international commercial contract an arbitration clause whereby the parties consent to submit any dispute arising in connection with this contract to one or more individuals chosen by them. Even in the absence of such a clause, the parties may still, after a dispute has arisen, refer it to arbitration by means of a special submission or agreement.

The increase in the number of arbitrations of international trade disputes has also been stimulated by the preparation and adoption by public and private international organizations of special conventions,[1] model laws,[2] and model rules[3] dealing with various aspects of international commercial arbitration. Some of these, in turn, have been implemented by domestic legislation in many countries. Thus, any business enterprise or person involved in international trade should become thoroughly familiar with international commercial arbitration.[4] This is particularly important in Canada, where one-third of the gross national product is generated by the export of goods and services.

II. TYPES OF ARBITRATION

An arbitration may be *ad hoc* or institutional. In the case of an *ad hoc* arbitration, the parties initiate and proceed with the arbitration without the assistance of a permanent

1 E.g., 1923 Protocol on Arbitration Clauses (1924), 27 LNTS 158; 1927 Convention for the Execution of Foreign Arbitral Awards (1929-30), 92 LNTS 302; 1958 Convention on the Recognition and Enforcement of Foreign Arbitral Awards (1959), 330 UNTS 38 (hereinafter referred to as 1958 Convention); and 1961 European Convention on International Commercial Arbitration (1963-64), 484 UNTS 364.

2 E.g., UNCITRAL 1985 Model Law on International Commercial Arbitration (1985), 24 *Int'l. Leg. Mat.* 1302 (hereinafter referred to as Model Law).

3 E.g., UNCITRAL 1976 Arbitration Rules; 1988 Rules of Conciliation and Arbitration of the International Chamber of Commerce to be found in vol. II of this book.

4 In general, see David, *Arbitration in International Trade* (1985).

arbitral institution. Together with the arbitrators, they control the arbitration. Thus, the *ad hoc* arbitration clause must be drafted with great care. This is a very difficult task, because it is impossible to foresee and provide for all the procedural issues that may arise. Often, however, the legislation in force at the place of the arbitration will assist the parties.

In the case of international commercial arbitration, it is wiser to resort to supervised institutional arbitration where such issues are decided by reference to the arbitration rules of the institution to which the arbitration has been entrusted. There are more than 50 general purpose institutions in the world that administer the arbitral process. Many more are special-sector institutions.[5] Furthermore, it is also better to choose a permanent institution that will set the arbitration process in motion *and* supervise it until an award is made than one whose role is limited to constituting the arbitral tribunal.

Supervised institutional arbitration characterizes the approach to arbitration taken by the largest and most experienced institutions, such as the International Chamber of Commerce International Court of Arbitration,[6] the American Arbitration Association,[7] the London Court of International Arbitration,[8] and the Inter-American Commercial Arbitration Commission.[9] The services of these institutions are available in Canada[10] where they provide neutral and impartial arbitration.

In Canada, since 1986, international commercial arbitration may also be administered by the Quebec National and International Commercial Arbitration Centre in Quebec City,[11] the British Columbia International Commercial Arbitration Centre in Vancouver (also called the Vancouver Centre for Commercial Disputes),[12] and the Canadian Arbitration, Conciliation and Amicable Composition Centre in Ottawa.[13] Since March 1996, the Dispute Resolution Institute of North America, located in Detroit and Windsor, provides international commercial arbitration services to corporations from the North America Free Trade Agreement (NAFTA) countries. Because of their recent origin, these centres have had few occasions to administer international commercial arbitrations. Their role is to act as facilitators rather than supervisors. In 1995, the British Columbia International Arbitration Centre and the Quebec International Arbitration Centre have joined with the Mexico City International Chamber of Commerce and established a trilingual and tripartite body called the Commercial Arbitration and Mediation Centre for the Americas.

---

5 E.g., Federation of Oils, Seeds and Fats Association of London.

6 38 Cours Albert 1er, Paris 75008, France.

7 140 West 51st, New York, NY 10020, USA.

8 69 Cannon St., London, EC4 N5BC, UK.

9 1819 H Street NW, Federal Bar Building West, room 301, Washington, DC 20006, USA.

10 See Canadian Council for International Business, Secretariat, 55 Metcalfe Street, Suite 1160, Ottawa, ON, K1P 6N4.

11 500 Grande Allée est, Office 120, Québec, QC, G1R 2J7.

12 Suite 670, 999 Canada Place, World Trade Centre, Vancouver, BC, V6C 2E2.

13 14 Henderson Ave., Ottawa, ON, K1N 7P1. See also the Arbitrator's Institute of Canada and the Vancouver Maritime Arbitrator's Association.

III. ADVANTAGES

The advantages of international commercial arbitration are numerous but, on occasion, may depend upon the circumstances. Because party autonomy is the very foundation of arbitration, the parties may choose flexible procedural rules, the applicable substantive law, a convenient place for arbitration, a language understood by both, and more important, arbitrators known for their objectivity, skill, and expertise in the subject matter of the dispute. The involvement of the courts is minimal, especially in the case of institutional arbitration.

Secrecy, confidentiality and, often, low costs are other positive attributes of international commercial arbitration. The easy enforceability of arbitration agreements and awards is also an important consideration because it allows the parties to achieve greater certainty and predictability in their contractual relationship. Speedy resolution of the dispute is another advantage of arbitration provided there is no obstruction on the part of one of the parties and the alternative judicial process is inadequate, slow, cumbersome, and formalistic.

International commercial arbitration is not the same as domestic arbitration because it always involves at least two legal systems and consequently raises private international law issues. It has a specificity of its own that requires special rules. It must be flexible and free of the technicalities of the law of procedure and the law of evidence in force at the place of arbitration. It is this flexibility that makes arbitration attractive to the international business community when compared to the deficiencies or failures of the national judicial systems involved. The risk of an adverse decision and very rarely the risk of an erroneous decision are well worth taking.

Finally, the arbitral process does not close the door to continuous negotiation between the parties leading to an amicable settlement nor does it put an end to normal business dealings between them. Quite often, cases are settled before an award is made.

IV. CANADIAN SOURCES

A. Federal and Provincial Legislation

Since 1985, Canada has put in place special federal and provincial legislation that implements the 1958 UN Convention on the Recognition and Enforcement of Foreign Arbitral Awards and adopts the 1985 UN Commission on International Trade Law (UNCITRAL) Model Law on International Commercial Arbitration. These two international documents are designed to facilitate international commercial arbitration. They contain liberal provisions without ignoring basic requirements of procedural justice and due process of law. Party autonomy, arbitrator's discretion, and limited control by the courts are now the major characteristics of international commercial arbitration in Canada.[14] The new legislation also contains very adequate safeguards for efficient and impartial dispute settlement.

14 Art. 5 of the Model Law, *supra*, note 2, delimits clearly the extent of judicial supervision. There must be no court intervention except as provided in the Model Law. See also art. 6.

Two separate federal statutes adopt the text of each of these international documents to be found in a schedule preceded by a few general provisions dealing with, *inter alia*, interpretation, scope of application, courts, and publication. Slight modifications have been made to the Model Law, which is called the Commercial Arbitration Code.[15]

Provincial legislation is more varied. Ontario has only adopted the Model Law which incorporates the essence of the 1958 Convention, also appended as a schedule.[16] British Columbia has two statutes, one implementing the 1958 Convention to be found in a schedule,[17] and another adapting the provisions of the Model Law to the special needs of the province although the departures from the original are not fundamental.[18] In Quebec, the Code of Civil Procedure refers to the Model Law[19] and to the 1958 Convention[20] both as supplementary sources only, since most of the provisions of these documents are incorporated into the code, which applies to arbitration in general.[21] Almost all provinces and one territory have one statute only that covers both the 1958 Convention and the Model Law to be found in Schedules A and B.[22]

In interpreting the Model Law, recourse may be had to the Report of the UNCITRAL on the work of its 18th session (3 to 21 June 1985) and the analytical commentary contained in the Report of the Secretary General to the 18th session of the UNCITRAL.[23]

---

15 United Nations Foreign Arbitral Awards Convention Act, RSC 1985, c. 16 (2nd Supp.); Commercial Arbitration Act, RSC 1985, c. 17 (2nd Supp.), as am., by RSC 1985, c. 1 (4th Supp.), and SC 1993, c. 44, s. 50 (hereinafter referred to as federal Code); and Federal Court Rules, SOR/88-221, rr. 1025 1029 and 1040-1051.

16 International Commercial Arbitration Act, RSO 1990, c. I.9. This Act repeals the Foreign Arbitral Awards Act, SO 1986, c. 25.

17 Foreign Arbitral Awards Act, SBC 1985, c. 74.

18 International Commercial Arbitration Act, SBC 1986, c. 14, as am. by SBC 1988, c. 46, ss. 33 to 35. In *Quintette Coal Ltd. v. Nippon Steel Corp. et al.* (1988), 29 BCLR (2d) 233, [1989] 1 WWR 120, the BC SC held that ss. 16, 17, and 31(6) did not violate s. 96 (appointment of judges) of the Constitution Act, 1867, 30 & 31 Vict., c. 3, as am.

19 SQ 1986, c. 73, art. 940.6.

20 *Ibid.*, art. 948. The substance of a provision of the New York Convention is also found in the Quebec Civil Code, art. 2640.

21 See Code of Civil Procedure, arts. 940 to 951.2 and *Précis de procédure civile du Québec* (2 vols. 1994), vol. 2, at 577 to 612.

22 International Commercial Arbitration Act, SA 1986-87, c. I-6.6; SM 1986-7, c. 32, as am., 1993, c. 48, s. 50; SNB 1986, c. I-12.2; RSN 1990, c. I-15; SNWT 1986(1), c. 6; RSNS 1989, c. 234; and SPEI 1988, c. I-5. The Yukon and Saskatchewan have two statutes: the International Commercial Arbitration Act, SY 1987, c. 14; SS 1988-89, c. I-10.2 and the Enforcement of Foreign Arbitral Award Act, RSY 1986, c. 70, SS 1986, c. E-9.11, as am. by SS 1988, c. 8.

23 See, e.g., RSC 1985, c. 17 (2nd Supp.), as am. by RSC 1985, c. 1 (4th Supp.), s. 4(2) and Quebec Code of Civil Procedure, art. 940.6. These documents have been published in the *Can. Gaz.* pt. I, vol. 120, no. 40, supp. (1986).

Except for British Columbia and Quebec, all the statutes adopting the Model Law provide that it applies to international commercial agreements and awards whether made before or after the coming into force of the Act.[24] A similar provision exists in the legislation implementing the 1958 Convention,[25] with the exception of British Columbia, Quebec, Saskatchewan, and the Yukon.

B. The North American Free Trade Agreement

Chapter 11 of the NAFTA provides for the settlement of disputes between a party and a an inventor of another party by way of arbitration.[26]

C. Institutional Rules of Procedure

The Quebec National and International Arbitration Centre,[27] the British Columbia International Commercial Arbitration Centre,[28] and the Canadian Arbitration Conciliation and Amicable Composition Centre[29] located in Ottawa have adopted rules of procedure for international commercial arbitrations administered by them.

V. SCOPE OF APPLICATION OF THE FEDERAL AND PROVINCIAL LEGISLATION

A. International "Commercial" Arbitration

In all the common law provinces and the territories, and in the federal statute implementing it, the 1958 Convention applies only to the recognition and enforcement of awards respecting differences arising out of legal relationships, whether contractual or not, that are considered to be commercial under the law of the enacting province.[30] In British Columbia, the International Commercial Arbitration Act has adopted part of a definition found in a note accompanying article I(1) of the Model Law, which states:[31]

> The term "commercial" should be given a wide interpretation so as to cover matters arising from all relationships of a commercial nature, whether contractual or not. Relationships of a commercial nature include, but are not limited to, the following transactions: any trade transaction for the supply or exchange of goods or services; distribution agreement; commercial representation or agency; factoring; leasing; construction of works; consulting; engineering; licensing; investment;

---

24 E.g., The International Commercial Arbitration Act, SS 1988, c. I-10.2, s. 3(2) and International Commercial Arbitration Act, RSO 1990, c. I.9, s. 2(2).

25 E.g., United Nations Foreign Arbitral Awards Convention Act, RSC 1985, c. 16 (2nd Supp.), s. 4(2).

26 Arts. 1115 to 1139. An advisory committee on private commercial disputes has also been established pursuant to arts. 2001 and 2002, which is concerned with alternative dispute resolution, especially arbitration.

27 International Arbitration Rules.

28 Rules for International Commercial Arbitration and Conciliation Proceedings, discussed *infra*.

29 Arbitration Rules of the Canadian Arbitration, Conciliation and Amicable Composition Centre.

30 E.g., SBC 1985, c. 74, s. 3.

31 SBC 1986, c. 14, s. 1(6), as am. by SBC 1988, c. 46, s. 33.

financing; banking; insurance; exploitation agreement or concession; joint venture and other forms of industrial or business co-operation; carriage of goods or passengers by air, sea, rail or road.

In Quebec, the expression "matters of extraprovincial or international trade" is used when referring to the Model Law.[32] On the other hand, the provisions implementing the 1958 Convention are not limited to commercial relationships.[33] In the other common law provinces and territories, the legislation follows the Model Law and does not define the term "commercial."[34] The federal Code also applies to commercial arbitration,[35] but only in relation to matters where at least one of the parties to the arbitration is Her Majesty in right of Canada, a departmental corporation or a Crown corporation, or in relation to maritime or admiralty matters.[36]

B. "Domestic" Commercial Arbitration

The provisions of the federal Code apply to both international and domestic commercial arbitration[37] but, with some exceptions, only if the place of arbitration is in Canada.[38] This is not the case in the other provinces and territories where the Model Law is restricted in its application to "international" arbitration provided the place of arbitration is in the province[39] and also subject to the same exceptions.[40]

C. "International" Commercial Arbitration

In all the provinces and the territories that have adopted the Model Law,[41] an arbitration is international if:

---

32 Code of Civil Procedure, art. 940.6.

33 *Ibid.*, art. 948.

34 E.g., SA 1986, c. I-6.6, s. 4(2). See *Dunhill Personnel Systems Inc. v. Dunhill Temps Edmonton Ltd.* (1993), 13 Alta. LR (3d) 241, 144 AR 272 (QB) and *Borowski v. Fiedler (Heinrich) Perforiertechnik GmbH* (1994), 158 AR 213 (QB).

35 Note that SC 1993, c. 44, s. 50 has added s. 5(4) to the Arbitration Code, which declares that commercial arbitration includes claims under art. 1116 or 1117 of the NAFTA. The BC Act covers investment claims: s. 1(6)(p), *supra*, note 31.

36 *Supra*, note 15, s. 5(2).

37 Federal Code, art. 1. The word "international," which appears in para. (1) of art. 1 of the Model Law, *supra*, note 2, has been deleted from para. (1) of art. 1 of the code. See also paras. (3) and (4) of art. 1 of the Model Law, which contain a description of when arbitration is international have been deleted.

38 Art. 1(2): "The provisions of this law, except articles 8, 9, 35, and 36, apply only if the place of arbitration is in the territory of this State."

39 E.g., SA 1986, c. I-6.6, s. (2).

40 Arts. 8 (arbitration agreement and substantive claim before court); 9 (arbitration agreement and interim measures by court); 35 and 36 (recognition and enforcement of awards); SA 1986, c. I-6.6, art. 1(2); and the federal Code, art. 1(2).

41 See, e.g., SBC 1986, c. 14, ss. 1(3) and (4). For a discussion of this provision, see J. Blom, "Conflict of Laws Aspects of the International Commercial Arbitration Act" in Paterson and Thompson (eds.), *UNCITRAL Arbitration Model in Canada* (1987), 127.

(a) the parties to an arbitration agreement have, at the time of the conclusion of that agreement, their places of business in different states; or

(b) one of the following places is situated outside the State in which the parties have their places of business:

(i) the place of arbitration if determined in, or pursuant to, the arbitration agreement;

(ii) any place where a substantial part of the obligations of the commercial relationship is to be performed or the place with which the subject-matter of the dispute is most closely connected; or

(c) the parties have expressly agreed that the subject-matter of the arbitration agreement relates to more than one country.

(4) For the purposes of paragraph (3) of this article:

(a) if a party has more than one place of business, the place of business is that which has the closest relationship to the arbitration agreement;

(b) if a party does not have a place of business, reference is to be made to his habitual residence.

In some instances, it may be difficult to determine which place of business has the closest relationship to the arbitration agreement. In Ontario, despite article 1(3)(c) of the Model Law, an arbitration concluded there between parties that all have their places of business in Ontario is not international only because the parties have expressly agreed that the subject matter of the arbitration agreement relates to more than one country.[42]

D. "Interprovincial" Commercial Arbitration

In British Columbia[43] and Ontario,[44] an arbitration taking place there is not "international" when it has a relevant connection with two or more provinces. In the other provinces and the territories, there is no such express limitation and it is a matter of interpretation whether the word "state" in the Model Law means country, province, or territory.

VI. THE ARBITRATION AGREEMENT

Since the federal and provincial legislation implementing the Model Law only applies to an arbitration that takes place in one of the provinces or territories, the discussion that follows is based on this assumption. Other rules may prevail where the parties have derogated from the permissive provisions of the Model Law or chosen another set of arbitration rules, or where the place of arbitration is outside Canada.

---

42 SO 1990, c. I.9, s. 2(3).

43 SBC 1986, c. 14, s. 1(5). Interprovincial commercial arbitration is governed by the Commercial Arbitration Act, SBC 1986, c. 3, as am. by SBC 1988, c. 46; see especially ss. 7 to 17, which refer to the rules of the BC International Commercial Arbitration Centre.

44 RSO 1990, c. I.9, s. 1(7).

A. Definition and Form

Whether the arbitration is *ad hoc* or institutional, the most important document pertaining to it is the arbitration agreement. It is the beginning of the whole arbitral process. According to article 7 of the Model Law:[45]

> (1) "Arbitration agreement" is an agreement by the parties to submit to arbitration all or certain disputes which have arisen or which may arise between them in respect of a defined legal relationship, whether contractual or not. An arbitration agreement may be in the form of an arbitration clause in a contract or in the form of a separate agreement.
>
> (2) The arbitration agreement shall be in writing. An agreement is in writing if it is contained in a document signed by the parties or in an exchange of letters, telex, telegrams or other means of telecommunication which provide a record of the agreement, or in an exchange of statements of claim and defence in which the existence of an agreement is alleged by one party and not denied by another. The reference in a contract to a document containing an arbitration clause constitutes an arbitration agreement provided that the contract is in writing and the reference is such as to make that clause part of the contract.

This article widens and clarifies the definition found in article II of the 1958 Convention on which it is based.

B. Capacity of the Parties

The capacity of the parties to agree to arbitration is governed by the proper law of the agreement or the personal law of either party.[46]

C. Autonomy of the Arbitration Clause

The arbitration clause is deemed to be separate from and independent of the contract in which it is contained.[47] Thus, the fact that the contract is invalid does not deprive the arbitral tribunal of jurisdiction to decide the issue of invalidity of the clause and its potential consequences. This means that the tribunal can also decide whether the dispute falls within the scope of the arbitration clause.[48] However, if one party denies the existence of both the contract and the arbitration clause, the arbitration cannot proceed until this question has been settled by the relevant court.

---

45 SBC 1986, c. 14, s. 7 and Quebec Civil Code, arts. 2638 and 2640.

46 1958 Convention, art. V.1.(a); SBC 1986, c. 14, ss. 34(2)(a)(i) and 36(1)(a)(i); and Model Law, *supra*, note 2, arts. 34(2)(a)(i) and 36(1)(a)(i). The Model Law and the BC International Commercial Arbitration Act do not contain the words: "the law applicable to them."

47 *Harper v. Kvaerner Fjellstrand Shipping A.S.* (1991), 28 ACWS (3d) 994 (BCSC).

48 SBC 1986, c. 14, s. 16(1)(a): "An arbitration clause which forms part of a contract shall be treated as an agreement independent of the other terms of the contract and (b) a decision by the arbitral tribunal that the contract is null and void shall not entail *ipso jure* the invalidity of the arbitration clause." This provision is based on art. 16 of the Model Law, *supra*, note 2, and in Quebec, Civil Code, art. 2642. As to the scope of the clause, see *Globe Union Industrial Corp. v. G.A.P. Marketing Corp.* (1994), 100 BCLR (2d) 41 (SC).

D. Law Applicable to the Arbitration Agreement

The law applicable to the merits of the dispute[49] does not necessarily govern the validity and interpretation of the arbitration agreement. Of course, the parties may specifically stipulate the law governing the arbitration agreement. Since the award may be set aside if the arbitration agreement is invalid under the law to which the parties have subjected it or, failing any indication of that law, the law of the place of arbitration,[50] it could be argued that the law of the place of arbitration governs the arbitration agreement in the absence of an express choice.

E. Arbitrability and Scope of the Arbitration Agreement

The question whether some types of dispute can be settled by arbitration must be determined by the law applicable to the validity of the arbitration agreement. This is supported by article II.1 of the 1958 Convention. If there is any doubt as to the arbitrability of the types of dispute that could arise with respect to a particular contract being negotiated, it is advisable to examine all the potentially applicable national laws.

In the case of international commercial arbitration, the question likely to arise is whether the parties could submit to arbitration disputes that involve, for example, the law of competition, bankruptcy, patents, trade-marks, and securities. If the arbitral tribunal rejects a claim of non-arbitrability, the aggrieved party may still resist the enforcement of the award, in which case the relevant court applies its own law to determine whether the award relates to an arbitrable dispute.[51] Even if the subject matter of the dispute is arbitrable, there remains the question of whether the claim or claims come within the scope of the arbitration agreement. Generally, this issue is decided by the arbitral tribunal that interprets the arbitration agreement.[52]

F. Arbitration Agreement and the Courts

In British Columbia, it is provided that where a party to an arbitration agreement commences legal proceedings in a court against another party to the agreement in respect of a matter agreed to be submitted to arbitration, a party to the legal proceedings, before or after entering an appearance and before delivery of any pleadings or taking any other step in the proceedings, may apply to that court to stay the proceedings. Upon such an

---

49 For that law, see s. 28 of SBC 1986, c. 14 and Model Law, *ibid.*, art. 28.

50 SBC 1986, c. 14, s. 34(2)(a)(i) and s. 36(1)(a)(i). 1958 Convention, art. V.1(a).

51 See, e.g., 1958 Convention, art. V.2(a); SBC 1986, c. 14, ss. 1(8), 34(2)(b)(i) and 36(1)(b)(i); and Model Law, *supra*, note 2, arts. 1(5), 34(2)(b)(i), and 36(1)(b)(i).

52 See *Canada Packers Inc. v. Terra Nova Tankers Inc.* (1993), 11 OR (3d) 382 (Gen. Div.) (contractual and non-contractual relationships). See also *Kaverit Steel and Crane Ltd. v. Kone Corp.* (1992), 87 DLR (4th) 129, 85 Alta. LR (2d) 287, [1992] 3 WWR 716, 4 CPC (3d) 99, 40 CPR (3d) 161 (CA), leave to appeal to SCC refused; *Dunhill Personnel Systems Inc.*, *supra*, note 34; and *Onex Corp. v. Ball Corp.* (1994), 12 BLR (2d) 151 (Ont. Gen. Div.) (rectification of drafting mistake arbitrable).

application, the court shall make an order staying the legal proceedings unless it determines that the arbitration agreement is null and void, inoperative, or incapable of being performed.[53] While this matter is before the court, the arbitration may be commenced or continued and an award made. This provision is not restricted to agreements providing for arbitration in the province. Also, irrespective of the place of arbitration, it is not incompatible with an arbitration agreement for a party to request from a court, before or during arbitral proceedings, an interim measure of protection and for that court to grant it.[54]

G. The Elements of the Arbitration Clause or Agreement

1. Arbitration Pursuant to the Model Law or Rules of an Arbitral Institution

Here, as already noted, the arbitral institution provides the rules for, for example, solving procedural matters, preventing attempts to obstruct or delay proceedings, the service of documents, security for costs, deposits for the arbitrators' fees, and the facilities for the hearing with little or no resort to national courts.

The arbitration clause or agreement must define with precision the types of controversy to be submitted to arbitration, for example, "all disputes arising in connection with

53 Model Law (UNCITRAL 1985 Model Law on International Commercial Arbitration (1985), 24 *Int'l. Leg. Mat.* 1302), art. 8. E.g., *Gulf Canada Resources Ltd. v. Arochem International Inc.* (1992) (BC SC) (stay granted); *ODC Exhibit Systems Ltd. v. Lee* (1988), 41 BLR 286 (BCSC) (stay refused as claim not arising from conciliation agreement); *Stancroft Trust Ltd. v. Can-Asia Capital Co.* (1990), 43 BCLR (2d) 341 (CA); and *Boart Sweden AB v. Nya Strommes A.B.* (1988), 41 BLR 295 (Ont. HC) (proceedings stayed with respect to matters subject to the arbitration agreement); *Rio Algom Ltd. v. Sammi Steel Co. Ltd.* (1991), 47 CPC (2d) 251 (Ont. Gen. Div.); *Kaverit Steel & Crane Ltd. v. Kone Corp.* (1992), 87 DLR (4th) 129, 40 CPR (3d) 161 (Alta. CA); *Mind Star Toys Inc. v. Samsung Co.* (1992), 9 OR (3d) 374 (Gen. Div.); *BWV Investments Ltd. v. Saskerfco Products Inc.* (1994), 125 Sask R 286, 119 DLR (4th) 537 (CA) (stay granted); *Campbell v. Murphy* (1993), 15 OR (3d) 444 (Gen. Div.) (stay granted); *Automatic Systems Inc. v. Bracknell Corp.* (1994), 74 OAC 111, 18 OR (3d) 257, 113 DLR (4th) 449, 12 BLR (2d) 132 (CA) (stay granted); *Automatic Systems Inc. v. E.S. Fox Ltd.* (1994), 12 BLR (2d) 148, 13 CLR (2d) 165 (Ont. CA) (stay granted), noted Potter (1994-95), 24 CBLJ 429; *Kvaerner Enviropower Inc. v. Tamar Industries Ltd.*, [1995] 2 WWR 433 (Alta. CA)(stay granted); *Globe Union Industrial Corp. v. G.A.P. Marketing Corp.*, (1994) 100 BCLR (2d) 41 (SC) (stay granted); *North American Life Insurance Co. v. Canada Mortgage and Housing Corp.* (1994), 124 Sask. R 222 (QB) (stay granted); *Trade Fortune Inc. v. Amalgamated Mills Supplies Ltd.*, (1994), 113 DLR (4th) 116 (BC SC) (stay granted); *A.B.N. AMRO Bank Canada v. Krupp Mak Machinebau GmbH* (1995), 24 OR (3d) 450 (Gen. Div.) allowing leave to appeal to Div. Court (1994), 21 OR (3d) 511 (Gen. Div.); *Nanisivik Mines Ltd. v. F.C.R.S. Shipping Ltd.* (1994), 113 DLR (4th) 537 (FCA) (stay granted); *Canada Packers Inc. v. Terra Nova Tankers Inc.* (1993), 11 OR (3d) 382 (Gen. Div.); *BC Navigation S.A. (Trustee of) v. Campotex Shipping Services Ltd.* (1987), 16 TR 79 (TD); and *RuhrKohle Handel Inter GmbH v. Fednav Ltd.* (1991), 36 CPR (3d) 521 (Fed. TD), aff'd. [1992] 3 FC 98 (sub nom. *Ruhrvohle Handel Inter GmbH v. Federal Calumet (The)*) (CA).

54 *Ibid.*, s. 9. *Trade Fortune Inc. v. Amalgamated Mills Supplies Ltd.*, *ibid.*

the present contract." It should be worded neither too restrictively nor too widely. If reference is made to the rules of a particular arbitral institution or of a particular state, the words "presently in force" or "in force at the time this contract is signed" or "as the same may be in effect at the time of the arbitral proceedings" depending on the circumstances, should be added to avoid any ambiguity.

The arbitration clause as well as the arbitration agreement must be in writing. Also, care must be taken that the specific formal requirements of the law of the place of arbitration have been met.

2. *Sample Model Clauses*

A. *Standard ICC Arbitration Clause*

All disputes arising in connection with the present contract shall be finally settled under the Rules of Conciliation and Arbitration of the International Chamber of Commerce by one or more arbitrators appointed in accordance with the said Rules.

B. *Standard ICC Maritime Arbitration Clause*

All disputes arising from this contract/charter party shall be finally settled in accordance with the ICC-CMI International Arbitration Rules by one or more arbitrators appointed in accordance with the said Rules.

C. *Standard Quebec National and International Commercial Arbitration Centre Arbitration Clause*

Any dispute which arises in the course of or following the performance of the present contract will be definitively settled under the auspices of the Quebec National and International Commercial Arbitration Centre, by means of arbitration and to the exclusion of courts of law, in accordance with its International Arbitration Rules [or General Commercial Arbitration Rules] in force at the time this contract is signed and to which the parties declare they have adhered.

D. *Model British Columbia International Commercial Arbitration Centre Arbitration Clause*

All disputes arising out of or in connection with this contract or in respect of any defined legal relationship associated therewith or derived therefrom shall be referred to and finally resolved by arbitration under the Rules of the British Columbia International Commercial Arbitration Centre.

The appointing authority shall be the British Columbia International Commercial Arbitration Centre.

The case shall be administered by the British Columbia International Commercial Arbitration Centre in accordance with its "Procedures for Cases under the BCICAC Rules."

The place of arbitration shall be Vancouver, British Columbia, Canada.

The following matters also should be considered by parties for inclusion in the arbitration provisions of contracts:

- governing or proper law;
- procedural law;
- number of arbitrators;
- specific qualifications of the arbitrators or a presiding arbitrator including, but not limited to, language, technical training, nationality, and legal training; and
- language or languages of the arbitration.

E. *Standard Canadian Arbitration Conciliation and Amicable Composition Centre Arbitration Clause*

Any dispute, controversy, or claim arising out of or relating to this contract, or the breach, termination or validity thereof, shall be settled by arbitration in accordance with the Arbitration Rules of the Arbitration, Conciliation and Amicable Composition Centre in effect on the date of this agreement.

F. *Standard London Court of Arbitration Clause*

Any dispute arising out of or in connection with this contract, including any question regarding its existence, validity or termination, shall be referred to and finally resolved by arbitration under the Rules of the London Court of International Arbitration, which Rules are deemed to be incorporated by reference to this clause.

G. *Standard AAA International Arbitration Clause*

Any controversy or claim arising out of or relating to this contract shall be determined by arbitration in accordance with the International Arbitration Rules of the American Arbitration Association.

H. *North American Export Grain Association Free on Board Export Contract USA/Canada*

Buyer and seller agree that any controversy or claim arising out of, in connection with or relating to this contract, or the interpretation, performance or breach thereof, shall be settled by arbitration in the City of New York before the American Arbitration Association or its successors, pursuant to the Grain Arbitration Rules of the American Arbitration Association, as the same may be in effect at the time of such arbitration proceeding, which rules are hereby deemed incorporated herein and made a part hereof, and under the laws of the State of New York. The arbitration award shall be final and binding on both parties and judgment upon such arbitration award may be entered in the Supreme Court of the State of New York or any other Courts having jurisdiction thereof. Buyer and seller hereby recognize and expressly consent to the jurisdiction over each of them of the American Arbitration Association or its successors, and of all the Courts in the State of New York. Buyer and seller agree that this contract shall be deemed to have been made in New York State and be deemed to be performed there, any reference herein or elsewhere to the contrary notwithstanding.

I. *UNICTRAL Arbitration Rules (1976)*

(i) *Model Arbitration Clause*

Any dispute, controversy or claim arising out of or relating to this contract, or the breach, termination or invalidity thereof, shall be settled by arbitration in accordance with the UNCITRAL Arbitration Rules as at present in force.

Note—Parties may wish to consider adding:

(a) The appointing authority shall be … (name of institution or person);
(b) The number of arbitrators shall be … (one or three);
(c) The place of arbitration shall be … (town and country);
(d) The language(s) to be used in the arbitral proceedings shall be …

Parties wishing an arbitral institution to act as an appointing authority and administrator under the UNCITRAL Rules may use any of the following clauses depending upon the circumstances:

(ii) *ICC as appointing authority*

Any dispute, controversy or claim arising out of or relating to this contract, or the breach, termination or invalidity thereof, shall be settled by arbitration in accordance with the UNCITRAL Arbitration Rules as at present in force.

The appointing authority shall be the ICC acting in accordance with the rules adopted by the ICC for this purpose.

(iii) *AAA as appointing authority and administrator*

Any dispute, controversy or claim arising out of or relating to this contract, or the breach, termination, or invalidity thereof, shall be settled by arbitration in accordance with the UNCITRAL Arbitration Rules in effect on the date of this contract.

The appointing authority shall be the American Arbitration Association.

The case shall be administered by the American Arbitration Association in accordance with its "Procedures for Cases under the UNCITRAL Arbitration Rules."

Note: Parties may wish to consider adding:

(a) The number of arbitrators shall be … (one or three).
(b) The place of arbitration shall be … (town and country).
(c) The language(s) to be used in the arbitral proceedings shall be …

(iv) *AAA as appointing authority only*

Any dispute, controversy or claim arising out of or relating to this contract, or the breach, termination, or invalidity thereof, shall be settled by arbitration in accordance with the UNCITRAL Arbitration Rules in effect on the date of this contract.

The appointing authority shall be the American Arbitration Association.

Note: Parties may wish to consider adding:

(a) The number of arbitrators shall be … (one or three).
(b) The place of arbitration shall be … (town and country)
(c) The language(s) to be used in the arbitral proceedings shall be …

(v) *BCICAC as appointing authority and administrator*

Any dispute, controversy or claim arising out of or relating to this contract, or the breach, termination or invalidity of it shall be settled by arbitration in accordance with the UNCITRAL Arbitration Rules in effect on the date of this contract.

The appointing authority shall be the British Columbia International Commercial Arbitration Centre.

The case shall be administered by the British Columbia International Commercial Arbitration Centre in accordance with its "Procedures for Cases under the UNCITRAL Arbitration Rules."

The place of arbitration shall be Vancouver, British Columbia, Canada.

Note: Parties may wish to consider adding:

(a) The number of arbitrators shall be … (one or three).
(b) The language(s) to be used in the arbitral proceedings shall be …

(vi) *BCICAC as appointing authority only*

Any dispute, controversy or claim arising out of or relating to this contract, or the breach, termination, or invalidity of it, shall be settled by arbitration in accordance with the UNCITRAL Arbitration Rules in effect on the date of the contract.

The appointing authority shall be the British Columbia International Commercial Arbitration Centre.

Note: Parties may wish to consider adding:

(a) The number of arbitrators shall be … (one or three).

(b) The language(s) to be used in the arbitral proceedings shall be …

3. Other Provisions

Even if reference is made to the arbitration rules of a particular state or arbitral institution, the parties may derogate from these rules and add specific provisions of their own dealing with a number of matters.[55] Thus, with respect to the international character of the arbitration, the parties may expressly agree that the subject matter of the arbitration agreement relates to more than one country.[56]

In general, it is advisable to agree on the number of arbitrators (usually three), although a sole arbitrator may be less costly. The decision depends upon a number of factors such as the importance of the dispute, the number of parties involved, and the need for specialized expertise.[57] The nationality of the arbitrators may also be stipulated, for example, "all arbitrators shall be of Canadian nationality" or "none of the arbitrators may have the nationality of any of the parties"[58]—as well as the procedure for appointing the arbitrators,[59] for replacing and challenging them[60]—and the time limits for making such appointments. In general, the arbitrator's nationality is important when selecting a sole or third arbitrator as he or she should not be of the same nationality as one of the parties.

The parties should provide for an appointing authority if they refuse or are unable to agree on the appointment or if the chosen arbitrators are unable to agree on a chairperson.

---

55 This is authorized by the Model Law, *supra*, note 53; see arts. 1(1), 3, 7(2), 10, 11, 13, 17, 19, 20, 21, 22, 23, 24, 25, 26, 28, 29, and 31.

56 Model Law, *ibid.*, art. 1(3)(c) but see Ontario, International Commercial Arbitration Act, RSO 1990, c. I.9, s. 2(3), which states: "Despite article 1(3)(c) of the Model Law, an arbitration conducted in Ontario between parties that all have their places of business in Ontario is not international only because the parties have expressly agreed that the subject-matter of the arbitration agreement relates to more than one country."

57 Art. 2641 of the Civil Code of Quebec states that "A stipulation which places one party in a privileged position with respect to the designation of the arbitrators is null."

58 Compare Model Law, *supra*, note 53, art. 11(1): "No person shall be precluded by reason of his nationality from acting as an arbitrator, unless otherwise agreed by the parties" to SBC 1988, c. 46, s. 11(9). Ontario provides that a person of any nationality may be an arbitrator: RSO 1990, c. I.9, s. 5.

59 Model Law, *ibid.*, art. 11(2).

60 Model Law, *ibid.*, 13(1).

Since often complex questions of law arise in the course of an international commercial arbitration, it is recommended that the sole arbitrator or the chairperson of a three-member tribunal be legally trained. Technical expertise, residence in the place of arbitration, experience, and knowledge of foreign languages also should be taken into consideration.

It is important to stipulate an acceptable place of arbitration as this choice may determine the procedural law or rules applicable to the arbitration and the degree of assistance and intervention of the courts of that place.[61] The place of arbitration also indicates which rules are mandatory and which are permissive.

The place of arbitration should be in a state that is a party to the 1958 Convention or has adopted the Model Law in order to force the courts of that state to defer to arbitration when allowed to hear disputes with respect to a contract that contains an arbitration clause[62] and in order to facilitate the recognition and enforcement of the award in another signatory state where the defendant's assets are located.[63]

The language to be used in the arbitral proceedings should be stipulated in the arbitration agreement or clause,[64] for example:

> The language of the arbitration shall be English, but either party shall be free to make any submission in either English or French without providing a translation thereof.

The selection of the law applicable to the substance of the dispute is very important if one wishes to avoid the possiblity of a lengthy dispute on this question. A typical provision would be as follows:

> The substance of any dispute arising in connection with the present contract shall be decided in accordance with the law of France as of the date of signature of this contract or [as of the date of the arbitral proceeding], excluding its private international law rules.[65]

This choice of law clause does not determine the procedure to be used in the arbitral proceedings nor the law that gives the arbitration clause or agreement its validity. In order not to undermine the effect of specific provisions of the contract or in order to avoid unacceptable legal rules, the parties may wish to adopt a clause to that effect, for example:

> To the extent not provided for in the present contract, the substance of any dispute arising in connection with it shall be decided in accordance with the law of Ontario, as of the date of signature of the contract, excluding its private international law rules.

---

61 Model Law, *ibid.*, arts. 20 and 1(2). For instance, the BC International Commercial Arbitration Act, SBC 1986, c. 4, s. 1(2) states that the Act, except for ss. 8, 9, 35, and 36, applies only if the place of arbitration is in the province.

62 Art. II.3. Model Law, *supra*, note 53, art. 8.

63 Art. III. And see art. I.3 (reciprocity). Note that art. 1130 of the NAFTA states that unless the disputing parties provide otherwise, the tribunal shall hold an arbitration in the territory of a party who is a party to the 1958 Convention.

64 Model Law, *supra*, note 53, art. 22.

65 *Ibid.*, art. 28(1).

or

The law of Quebec shall apply to the substance of the dispute to the exclusion of article ... of the Civil Code.

It is not clear whether the arbitral tribunal will give effect to a clause whereby the parties selected "the widely accepted principles of law governing international commercial contracts" with no specific reference to a particular system of law although article 28(1) of the Model Law, by referring to *rules* of law, would seem to suggest that the parties are free to designate rules of law from various sources including instruments without the force of law. Whether there exists a *lex mercatoria* of international commercial contracts is not at all certain.[66] Of course, it is acceptable to refer to trade usages.[67] The parties may also wish to choose the same law as that applicable to the validity and effect of the arbitration agreement or clause.

If the parties desire to give the arbitral tribunal the maximum freedom to fashion its decision free from strict rules of law, they will authorize it to decide *ex aequo et bono* or as *amiable compositeur*,[68] for example:

The arbitral tribunal shall be entitled to decide according to equity and good conscience and shall not be required to follow the strict rules of law.

In general, the rules of procedure to be followed by the arbitral tribunal are those contained in the rules of the chosen arbitral institution. If some or all of them are not acceptable to the parties, they may adopt special rules, or refer to other rules in the arbitration agreement or clause.[69]

---

66 On the concept of *lex mercatoria*, see Craig, Park, and Paulsson, *International Chamber of Commerce Arbitration* (1984), c. 17.03 and c. 35 and O. Lando, "The *Lex Mercatoria* in International Commercial Arbitration" (1985), 34 *Int. & Comp. LQ* 747. See also chapter 3, *supra*.

67 Model Law, *supra*, note 53, art. 28(4).

68 *Ibid.*, 28(3).

69 *Ibid.*, art. 19(1). In Quebec, art. 2643, the Civil Code provides that subject to the peremptory provisions of law, the procedure of arbitration is governed by the contract or, failing that, by the Code of Civil Procedure. See also the Code of Civil Procedure, art. 940: "The provisions of this Title apply to an arbitration where the parties have not made stipulations to the contrary." However certain articles are peremptory:

940.5 (service of documents—where the object of the service is a judicial proceeding).

940.2 (court having jurisdiction).

941.3 (appointment of arbitrators, decision of court is final and without appeal).

942.7 (incidental cessation of arbitrator's appointment, decision of court is final and without appeal).

943.2 (competence of arbitrators, decision of court is final and without appeal).

945.8 (arbitration award, decision of court is final and without appeal).

946 to 947.4 (homologation of the arbitration award and annulment of the arbitration award).

The parties may give to the arbitral tribunal the power to order provisional relief or other interim measures.[70]

Other procedural or evidentiary matters on which the parties may reach an agreement are as follows: when written communications are deemed to be received;[71] the date of commencement of arbitral proceedings;[72] the period of time for submitting the statements of claim and defence;[73] whether the arbitral tribunal shall decide the case on the basis of documents alone;[74] whether either party shall, at the request of the other, make available documents or witnesses relevant to the major aspects of the contractual relationship issue; whether evidence should be on oath; the effect of default by one party;[75] whether the appointment of experts should be excluded;[76] whether any decision of the arbitral tribunal shall be made by a majority of all its members;[77] the time within which it should be made; whether a record of the proceedings should be kept; whether the award should be in writing and reasons on which it is based stated;[78] the type of relief to be given; the currency of the award; whether interest should be paid on the award; and, finally, whether costs should be apportioned in advance or excluded, for example:

Each party shall share equally the administrative expenses for conducting the arbitration and the arbitrators' fees.

4. *Ad Hoc Arbitration*

In the case of an *ad hoc* arbitration, the agreement to arbitrate or the arbitration clause is more difficult to draft since no arbitral institution is involved. It should clearly define the types of dispute and claims to be arbitrated; the law or rules applicable to the procedure to be followed by the arbitrators; the law to be applied to the substance of the dispute; the time limits and manner of making the award; and provide for the place of arbitration, the language to be used, the number of arbitrators, and the method for appointing and replacing them. The parties should declare that the arbitral award is final and binding and not subject to appeal to the courts.[79]

Ad hoc arbitration is cheaper because no administrative fees are payable to an institution, but the parties or the arbitrators must look after all administrative matters. If one of the parties does not cooperate, it may be necessary to resort to the courts of the place of arbitration more often than in the case of institutional arbitration. When the *ad*

---

70 Model Law, *ibid.*, art. 17. Art. 9 prevails over art. 17: *Trade Fortune Inv. v. Amalgamated Mills Supplies Ltd.*, *supra*, note 53.

71 Model Law, *ibid.*, art. 3.

72 *Ibid.*, art. 21.

73 *Ibid.*, art. 23.

74 *Ibid.*, art. 24.

75 *Ibid.*, art. 25.

76 *Ibid.*, art. 26.

77 *Ibid.*, art. 29.

78 *Ibid.*, art. 31(2).

79 For *ad hoc* arbitration, see Antaki and Prujiner (eds.), *International Commercial Arbitration* (1986), 43.

hoc arbitration takes place in Canada, the arbitration law and rules of the place of arbitration may be referred to by the parties as a supplementary source to be used in the absence of specific provisions in the arbitration clause or agreement.

VII. COMPOSITION OF THE ARBITRAL TRIBUNAL

The Model Law provides for the number of arbitrators[80] and the procedure for their appointment when the parties have not determined these questions.[81] The relevant court will assist the parties in case of delay or deadlock.[82] Any person approached to be an arbitrator must disclose any circumstances likely to give rise to justifiable doubts as to his or her independence or impartiality. The obligation to disclose exists throughout the course of the arbitral proceedings. An arbitrator may be challenged only if circumstances exist that give rise to justifiable doubt as to his or her independence or impartiality, or if he or she does not possess the qualifications agreed to by the parties.[83] If a challenge is not successful, the challenging party may, within 30 days after receiving notice of rejection of the challenge, request the relevant court to decide on the challenge, which decision is not subject to appeal.[84] While such request is pending, the arbitral tribunal, including the challenged arbitrator, may continue the arbitral proceedings and make an award. These provisions are intended to reduce the risks and effects of dilatory tactics. The Ontario Act provides that, unless the parties otherwise agree, if an arbitrator is replaced or removed in accordance with the Model Law, any hearing held prior to the replacement or removal shall start afresh. The parties may remove an arbitrator or a substitute arbitrator at any time prior to the final award, regardless of how the arbitrator was appointed.[85] The Model Law also deals with failure or impossibility to act on the part of an arbitrator.[86]

VIII. JURSIDICTION OF THE ARBITRAL TRIBUNAL AND INTERIM MEASURES

The arbitral tribunal may rule on its own jurisdiction, including any objections with respect to the existence and validity of the arbitration clause or agreement. The objections to the jurisdiction of the tribunal must be raised as early as possible.[87] The arbitral tribunal may rule on the plea of lack of jurisdiction as a preliminary question or in the award on the merits. If it rules, as a preliminary question, that it has jurisdiction, any

80 Three arbitrators: Model Law, *supra*, note 53, art. 10. Quebec Code of Civil Procedure, art. 941.

81 Model Law, *ibid.*, art. 11.

82 *Ibid.*, art. 11(3), (4), and (5).

83 *Ibid.*, art. 12 and Quebec Code of Civil Procedure, arts. 942 to 942.8.

84 *Ibid.*, art. 13(3). Note that in BC, SBC 1986, c. 14, s. 13(5), the Supreme Court may refuse to decide on the challenge of an arbitrator if under the procedure agreed upon by the parties, the aggrieved party had an opportunity to have the challenge decided upon by a body other than the arbitral tribunal.

85 RSO 1990, c. I.9, s. 4(2). See also SBC 1986, c. 14, s. 15.

86 Model Law, *supra*, note 53, art. 14. For the appointment of a substitute arbitrator, see art. 15.

87 *Ibid.*, art. 16(1) and (2) and Quebec Code of Civil Procedure, arts. 943 to 943.2.

party may request, within 30 days after having received notice of that ruling, the relevant court to decide the matter, which decision is not subject to appeal. Again, while such a request is pending, the arbitral tribunal may continue the arbitral proceedings and make an award.[88] The Model Law empowers the tribunal, if requested by a party, to order any party to take such interim measures of protection as the tribunal may consider necessary in respect of the subject matter of the dispute. This power is subject to contrary agreement by the parties. The measures in question are more limited in scope than those available through the courts since the jurisdiction of the tribunal does not extend to third parties[89] and no provision is made for their enforcement. However, the legislation adopting the Model Law usually declares that the order of the tribunal must be considered as if it were an award.[90]

IX. CONDUCT OF ARBITRAL PROCEEDINGS

The basic philosophy of the Model Law is that the parties must be treated with equality and each must be given a full opportunity of presenting his or her case.[91] Thus, the Model Law strives to achieve fairness, objectivity, and impartiality.

In the absence of express agreement with respect to the procedure to be followed by the arbitral tribunal in conducting the proceedings, it will conduct the arbitration in such a manner that it considers appropriate. The power conferred on the arbitral tribunal includes the power to determine the admissibility, relevance, materiality, and weight of any evidence.[92] This provision is important because it excludes the local rules of evidence of the place of arbitration. It is designed to facilitate international commercial arbitration.

Unless otherwise agreed by the parties, the arbitral tribunal shall determine the place of arbitration having regard to the circumstances of the case, including the convenience of the parties[93] and the language or languages to be used in the proceedings.[94]

The Model Law deals with the statements of claim and defence,[95] the hearings, and the written proceedings.[96] An oral hearing is not absolutely necessary. Unless otherwise agreed by the parties, if, without showing sufficient cause, any party fails to appear at a hearing or to produce documentary evidence, the arbitral tribunal may continue the

---

88 *Ibid.*, art. 16(3). If the tribunal rules on its jurisdiction in the award on the merits, judicial review is available pursuant to arts. 34 or 36.

89 *Ibid.*, art. 17.

90 International Commercial Arbitration Act, RSO 1990, c. I.9, s. 9.

91 Model Law, *supra*, note 53, art. 18.

92 *Ibid.*, art. 19. Quebec Code of Civil Procedure, art. 944.1.

93 *Ibid.*, art. 20(1). It may also meet elsewhere for certain purposes, e.g., inspection of goods, art. 20(2).

94 *Ibid.*, art. 22(1). It may order the translation of documentary evidence: art. 22(2).

95 *Ibid.*, art. 23. This applies to counterclaims and defences to counterclaims: art. 23(2).

96 *Ibid.*, art. 24. Quebec Code of Civil Procedure, arts. 944.3 and 944.4. Note that in BC, s. 24(5) of SBC 1986, c. 14, states: "Unless otherwise agreed by the parties, all oral hearings and meetings in arbitral proceedings are to be held in camera." The Model Law does not deal with the procedural aspects of the hearings, e.g., number of hearings.

proceedings and make the award on the evidence before it.[97] This is an important provision whose purpose is to prod an uncooperative party to expedite matters and to improve the chances of recognition and enforcement in another country of an award given by default. Experts may be appointed by the tribunal to report to it on specific issues to be determined by the tribunal and to participate in the hearings.[98]

Since it is often difficult to obtain evidence, the arbitral tribunal may request, from a competent court of the place of arbitration, assistance in taking evidence.[99]

X. MULTI-PARTY ARBITRATION

Where there are several parties to the same contract (for example, a joint venture) or a number of parties to a series of contracts involving the same project (for example, a turnkey construction contract and a series of related subcontracts), it is advisable, in order to save both time and money, to have all major disputes that may arise in connection with such contract or project decided by one arbitral tribunal in a single, comprehensive arbitration proceeding.

Multi-party arbitration avoids the danger of inconsistent results where related disputes are resolved in separate proceedings. Furthermore, all the relevant evidence is made available to the arbitral tribunal before which each of the various disputes is brought. To resort to multi-party arbitration, all parties[100] must agree to it either at the time the dispute or disputes arise, or at the time the parties enter into their various contractual arrangements. The multi-party arbitration agreement should include the following points:[101]

1. The right for any party adhering to the arrangement (the adhering party) to pursue any type of claim against any other adhering party regardless of whether or not they are parties of the same contract.

2. The right for any adhering party to intervene in any arbitration proceeding between two or more other adhering parties, again, regardless of whether or not they are parties of the same contract.

3. The right for any adhering party who is a defendant in an arbitration proceeding related to the project to involve one or more other adhering parties in the arbitration.

---

97 *Ibid.*, art. 25(c). This article also deals with failure to communicate the statement of claim or of defence.

98 *Ibid.*, art. 26. In British Columbia, SBC 1986, c. 14, s. 6(3) contains an additional provision to the effect that "Unless otherwise agreed by the parties, the expert shall, on the request of a party, make available to that party for examination all documents, goods or other property in the expert's possession with which he was provided in order to prepare his report." This is intended to enable the parties to question the experts more efficiently.

99 *Ibid.*, art. 27. For judicial assistance in Canada, see Castel, *Canadian Conflict of Laws* (3rd ed., 1994), 135.

100 In projects involving a large number of parties, it may be better to limit the multi-party arbitration agreement to those parties having a significant involvement in the project.

101 ICC, *Guide on Multi-party Arbitration Under the Rules of the ICC Court of Arbitration* (1982), at 5. See also, Craig, Park, and Paulsson, *supra*, note 66, 5.11, 8.14; G. Bernini, "Arbitration in Multi-party Business Disputes," 1980 Yearbook Commercial Arbitration 291; and B. von Hoffman, "International Construction Arbitration" in P. Sarcevic (ed.), *Essays on International Commercial Arbitration* (1989), 222, at 237.

4. The right for any adhering party to obtain the recognition of or compliance with any award on the part of all of the other adhering parties, whether or not they were parties to the arbitration proceeding, so long as they were given an adequate opportunity to become parties.

In all these cases, the adhering party must provide evidence of an actual interest.

It is worth noting that even in the absence of a multi-party arbitration clause, all the provinces and the territories have added, to the Model Law, a provision dealing with the consolidation of arbitration proceedings involving the same subject matter, but different parties or different issues between the same parties:[102]

The court, on application of the parties to two or more arbitration proceedings, may order

(a) the arbitration proceedings to be consolidated, on terms it considers just.

(b) The arbitration proceedings to be heard at the same time, or one immediately after another; or

(c) any of the arbitration proceedings to be stayed until after the determination of any other of them.

(2) Where the court orders arbitration proceedings to be consolidated pursuant to clause (1)(a) and the parties to the consolidated arbitration proceedings are in agreement as to the choice of the arbitral tribunal for that arbitration proceeding, the court shall appoint the arbitral tribunal chosen by the parties, but, if the parties cannot agree, the court may appoint the arbitral tribunal for that arbitration proceeding.

(3) Nothing in this section shall be construed as preventing the parties to two or more arbitration proceedings from agreeing to consolidate those arbitration proceedings and taking such steps as are necessary to effect that consolidation.

The court cannot order consolidation in all cases.

XI. MAKING OF AWARD AND TERMINATION OF PROCEEDINGS

The arbitral tribunal shall apply, to the substance of the dispute, the law expressly chosen by the parties or, in the absence of express choice, the law determined by the private international law rules that it considers relevant.[103] In some instances, it may be difficult for the tribunal to decide which private international law rules to apply, although it may be inclined to adopt those in force at the place of arbitration. In Canada, in the field of contracts, if the parties have not expressly chosen the applicable law, the courts will ascertain whether there exists an inferred or implied choice of law.[104] Otherwise, the courts will apply the system of law with which the transaction has its closest and most real connection.[105]

---

102 E.g., International Commercial Arbitration Act, SA 1986, c. I-6.6; RSO 1990, c. I.9, s. 7; SBC 1986, c. 14, s. 27(2).

103 Model Law (UNCITRAL 1985 Model Law on International Commercial Arbitration (1985), 24 *Int'l. Leg. Mat.* 1302), art. 28(3). The NAFTA provides that an arbitral tribunal established to settle disputes between a party and an investor of another party shall decide the issues in dispute in accordance with the Agreement and applicable rules of international law: art. 1131.

104 Castel, *supra*, note 99.

105 *Ibid.*, at 559. This is called the proper law doctrine.

In all the common law provinces and territories, the legislation has modified the Model Law in order to free the tribunal from being bound by any specific private international law rules. It is provided that: "Notwithstanding article 28(2) of the [Model Law], if the parties fail to make a designation pursuant to article 28(1) of the [Model Law] the arbitral tribunal shall apply the rules of law it considers to be appropriate given all the circumstances respecting the dispute."[106] This provision adopts the proper law doctrine.

The Model Law declares that the law or legal system of a given state shall be construed, unless otherwise expressed, as directly referring to the substantive law of that state.[107] This is designed to avoid the doctrine of *renvoi*, which has been rejected by most legal systems in the field of contracts.[108]

In all cases, the tribunal shall decide, in accordance with the terms of the contract, if one is involved, and shall take into account the usages of the trade applicable to the transaction.[109] Thus, the arbitral tribunal could rely on the Incoterms or on the International Chamber of Commerce (ICC) Uniform Customs and Practice for Documentary Credits or on the *lex mercatoria* if it exists.[110]

The Model Law also declares that in arbitral proceedings with more than one arbitrator, any decision is made by a majority of its members, unless otherwise agreed by the parties. However, questions of procedure may be decided by a presiding arbitrator if so authorized by the parties or by all members of the arbitral tribunal.[111]

A settlement reached by the parties during the arbitral proceedings may be recorded in the form of an award. This has been the international practice.[112] In all the common law provinces and territories, it is also provided that for the purpose of encouraging settlement of a dispute, an arbitral tribunal may, with the agreement of the parties, employ mediation, conciliation or other procedures at any time during the arbitral proceedings and, with the agreement of the parties, the members of the arbitral tribunal are not disqualified from resuming their roles as arbitrators by reason of the mediation, conciliation or other procedure.[113] The Model Law does not address the question of alternate dispute resolution.

The arbitral award must be made in writing and be signed by the arbitrator or arbitrators. It must state the reasons on which it is based, unless the parties have agreed

---

106 E.g., International Commercial Arbitration Act, SBC 1986, c. 14, s. 28(3); RSPEI 1988, c. I-5, s. 7; and RSO 1990, c. I.9, s. 6. Not so in the federal Code, which retains the original version.

107 Art. 28(1) (express choice). It is assumed that this rule applies also in the case of choice by the arbitrators under art. 28(2).

108 Castel, *supra*, note 99, at 569.

109 Model Law, *supra*, note 103, art. 28(4) and Quebec Code of Civil Procedure, art. 944.10.

110 As to the negation of a *lex mercatoria*, see *Amin Rasheed Shipping Corp. v. Kuwait Insurance Co., The Al Wahab*, [1983] 2 All ER 884, [1984] 1 C 50 (HL), which did not involve an arbitration. See also, *supra*, note 66.

111 Model Law, *supra*, note 103, art. 29 and Quebec Code of Civil Procedure, art. 944.11.

112 Model Law, *ibid.*, art. 30.

113 International Commercial Arbitration Act, SBC 1986, c. 14, s. 30(1); RSO 1990, c. I.9, s. 3; and SA 1986, c. I-6.6, s. 5.

otherwise. It must also state the date and place of arbitration.[114] In British Columbia, the arbitral tribunal may award interest and make an order for costs.[115] The arbitral tribunal may, at any time during the arbitral proceedings, make an interim arbitral award on any matter with respect to which it may make a final arbitral award.[116]

The arbitral proceedings are terminated by the final award or by an order of the arbitral tribunal in certain circumstances.[117] Provision is made for the correction and interpretation of the award and for an additional award to deal with claims presented in the arbitral proceedings but omitted from the award. The tribunal will only act if it considers the request to be justified.[118]

XII. RECOURSE AGAINST THE AWARD

An award may be set aside by the relevant court[119] at the place of arbitration on application by a party within three months of receipt of the award. The applying party must furnish proof of the existence of one or more of the following grounds: lack of capacity of any of the parties to conclude the arbitration agreement; lack of a valid arbitration agreement; lack of notice of the appointment of an arbitrator or of the arbitral proceedings; inability of the applicant party to present its case; award dealing with a dispute not contemplated by or not falling within the terms of the submission to arbitration or containing decisions on matters beyond the scope of the submission to arbitration; and composition of the arbitral tribunal or arbitral procedure not in accordance with the agreement of the parties, unless such agreement was in conflict with an imperative provision of the Model Law, or, failing agreement, to the Model Law. The award may also be set aside by the court if it finds that the subject matter of the dispute is not capable of settlement by arbitration under its law or the award is in conflict with its public policy. An error of law is not a ground for setting aside the award.[120]

Additional domestic grounds for setting aside an award are excluded. It should be noted that the setting aside of an award by the court of the place where it was given prevents its enforcement in all other jurisdictions.[121] This is not the case with respect to a refusal to recognize or enforce an award that is effective only in the state or states where the winning party sought such recognition or enforcement.

XIII. BRIEF ANALYSIS OF INSTITUTIONAL RULES OF PROCEDURE

When selecting an arbitral institution and its rules of procedure it is important to make sure that these rules are consistent with established international practice. The rules of

---

114 Model Law, *supra*, note 103, art. 31 and Quebec Code of Civil Procedure, arts. 945.2 and 945.3.

115 International Commercial Arbitration Act, SBC 1986, c. 14, ss. 31(7) and (8).

116 *Ibid.*, s. 31(6).

117 Model Law, *supra*, note 103, art. 32.

118 *Ibid.*, art. 33 and Quebec Code of Civil Procedure, arts. 945.6 and 945.7.

119 *Ibid.*, art. 34 and Quebec Code of Civil Procedure, *ibid.*, arts. 946 to 947.4 (homologation and annulment of the arbitration award).

120 *Quintette Coal Ltd. v. Nippon Steel Corp.* (1990), 47 BCLR (2d) 201 (SC) applying art. 34(2).

121 See Model Law, *supra*, note 103, art. 36(1)(a)(v) and 1958 Convention, art. V.1(e).

the Canadian centres meet this requirement because they incorporate the substance of the 1976 UNCITRAL Arbitration Rules, which are well known, accepted internationally, and have been found effective. However, they contain a few departures from the UNCITRAL rules in order to take into consideration the legislation in force at the place where the institution is located. The rules followed in Canada are also consistent with the Model Law, which is applicable nation wide.

Although, the 1988 Rules for the International Chamber of Commerce International Court of Arbitration are less influenced by the UNCITRAL rules, it is always possible for any arbitral institution to proceed under the original UNCITRAL rules if that is the wish of the parties.

In general, the British Columbia rules[122] deal with their interpretation and application,[123] the calculation of time, the composition of the arbitral tribunal, the jurisdiction of the tribunal, the conduct of arbitral proceedings, the making of the award, the termination of proceedings, and conciliation since, in many countries, parties prefer to reach a settlement by conciliation rather than by adjudication. The rules that provide a complete procedural code without ignoring party autonomy[124] are probably the best that can be found at the present time.

XIV. RECOGNITION AND ENFORCEMENT OF ARBITRATION AGREEMENTS AND FOREIGN AND INTERNATIONAL COMMERCIAL ARBITRAL AWARDS

For a Canadian business concern, it is very important to determine, before agreeing to be bound by an arbitration agreement or clause, whether an international commercial arbitral award made in Canada or abroad will be enforceable in Canada or abroad where the other party resides or maintains its assets should that party refuse to comply voluntarily with the terms of this award.

A. 1958 Convention

The federal Parliament and the legislatures[125] of all the provinces and territories have implemented the 1958 Convention on the Recognition and Enforcement of Foreign Arbitral Awards.[126]

---

122 Rules for International Commercial Arbitration and Conciliation Proceedings in the Vancouver Centre for Commercial Disputes. app. IV of Paterson and Thompson, *UNCITRAL Arbitration Model in Canada* (1987), 201 and comments by Thompson, "The Marriage of the UNCITRAL Model Arbitration Law and the UNCITRAL Arbitration Rules," *ibid.*, at 143.

123 The rules only apply to "international" commercial arbitrations.

124 See r. 1(3): "The parties to an arbitration under these Rules may modify, vary or amend the Rules by agreement in writing."

125 E.g., The United Nations Foreign Arbitral Awards Convention Act, RSC 1985, c. 16 (2nd Supp.); Foreign Arbitral Awards Act, SBC 1985; and Quebec Code of Civil Procedure, arts. 948 to 951.2.

126 For an analysis of the convention, see Gaja (ed.), *International Commercial Arbitration: The New York Convention* (1978); Graham, "The New York Convention of 1958: A Canadian Perspective" in Antaki

(The footnote is continued on the next page.)

The purpose of the 1958 Convention is to facilitate the recognition and enforcement of foreign arbitration agreements and arbitral awards respecting differences arising out of legal relationships, whether contractual or not, that are considered as commercial under the law of the recognizing and enforcing state.[127]

The legislation implementing the Convention applies to "foreign" domestic as well as "international" commercial arbitral awards whether the arbitration was *ad hoc* or institutional and whether it was ratified by a competent authority. This includes awards made in another province. Since reciprocity is not required by the legislation,[128] the "foreign" award need not have been made in a state that is a party to the 1958 Convention.

Article II of the 1958 Convention provides for the recognition of an arbitration clause in a contract or an arbitration agreement—that is, in writing, signed by the parties, or contained in an exchange of letters or telegrams—under which the parties undertake to submit to arbitration all or any differences that have arisen or may arise between them in respect of a defined legal relationship, whether contractual or not, that is considered commercial under the law of the recognizing state.[129] This provision applies to "international" arbitrations taking place in jurisdictions that have implemented the Convention. Also, the court of a contracting state, when seized of an action in a matter in respect of which the parties have made such an agreement, shall, at the request of one of the parties, refer the parties to arbitration, unless it finds that the said agreement is null and void, inoperative or incapable of being performed according to the law applicable to it.[130]

Article II of the 1958 Convention has become partly redundant since it is now duplicated in a more elaborate form in the Model Law adopted by the federal Parliament and all the provinces and territories.[131]

---

126 Continued ...

and Prujiner (eds.), *International Commercial Arbitration* (1986), 185; Graham, "International Commercial Arbitration: The Developing Canadian Profile" in Paterson and Thompson (eds.), *UNCITRAL Model Arbitration in Canada* (1987), 77; Cohen, "La reconnaissance et l'exécution au Canada des sentences arbitrales étrangères" (1987), 47 *R du B* 435; Lalonde, Buchanan, and Ross, "Domestic and International Commercial Arbitration in Quebec: Current Status and Perspectives for the Future" (1985), 45 *R du B* 705; Prujiner, "Les nouvelles règles de l'arbitrage au Québec," [1987] *Rev. de l'Arbitrage* 425; Tremblay, "Commentaires des articles du Code civil et du Code de procédure civile en matière d'arbitrage" (1988), 90 *R du N* 394, 536; Dorais, "L'arbitrage commercial-Développements législatifs" (1987), 47 *R du B* 273; and Brierley, "Une Loi nouvelle pour le Québec en matière d'arbitrage" (1987), 47 *R du B* 259.

127 E.g., RSC 1985, c. 16 (2nd Supp.), s. 4(1); SBC 1985, c. 74, s. 3. The 1958 Convention allows the signatories to enter a reservation to restrict it to differences arising out of relationships that are "commercial" in nature: art I.3. This is what Canada has done.

128 Arts. I.1 and 2 and Quebec Code of Civil Procedure, art. 948.

129 Arts. II.1 and 2 and, e.g., SC 1986, c. 21, s. 4(1).

130 Art. II.3 and, e.g., International Commercial Arbitration Act, SPEI 1986, c. 14, s. 10 and Quebec Code of Civil Procedure, art. 940.1.

131 E.g., Model Law, *supra*, note 103, arts. 7 and 8 and International Commercial Arbitration Act, SBC 1986, c. 14, ss. 7 and 8; see also, *supra*, note 53. The 1958 Convention still applies to non "international" commercial arbitration agreements.

Articles III, IV, V, and VI of the 1958 Convention deal with the rules of recognition and enforcement of foreign or international commercial arbitral awards. Since the only permissible grounds on which Canadian courts may refuse to recognize and enforce an award under the Convention have been adopted by the Model Law, they will be discussed in the next paragraph.

Article 1136.6 of the NAFTA provides that a disputing investor may seek enforcement of an arbitration award under the 1958 Convention. For this purpose, a claim that is submitted to arbitration by an investor of a contracting party shall be considered to arise out of a commercial relationship or transaction.

B. Model Law

In Canada, on the provincial level, an "international" commercial arbitral award, irrespective of the state in which it was made, thus excluding reciprocity, shall be recognized as binding and, on application in writing to a competent court, be enforced provided certain requirements have been met.[132] For example, an international commercial arbitral award made in France will be recognized and enforced in Ontario or in British Columbia. Except in these two provinces, the legislation also covers an "international" commercial arbitral award made in another province.[133] The Model Law does not cover foreign "domestic" commercial arbitral awards that are within the scope of the 1958 Convention, nor does it apply to "non commercial" foreign arbitral awards, which must be enforced at common law or pursuant to special provincial legislation.[134]

The federal Code[135] applies to both domestic and foreign commercial arbitral awards whether or not they are "international."

It should be mentioned that the Ontario statute stipulates that for the purpose of the recognition and enforcement of an international commercial arbitral award pursuant to the Model Law, an arbitral award includes a commercial arbitral award made outside Canada, even if the arbitration to which it relates is not international as defined in the

132 Model Law, *ibid.*, arts. 35 and 36. International Commercial Arbitration Act, SBC 1986, c. 14, s. 1(2), and ss. 35 and 36. The legislation of each province or territory designates a competent court, e.g., Supreme Court of British Columbia. A confirmed arbitral award may be enforced under the Model Law: *Schreter v. Gasmac Inc.* (1992), 89 DLR (4th) 365, 7 OR (3d) 608, 41 CPR (3d) 494, 6 BLR (2d) 71 (Gen. Div.), additional reasons at (1992), 89 DLR (4th) 380, 41 CPR (3d) 509.

133 International Commercial Arbitration Act, SBC 1986, c. 14, s. 1(5) and International Commercial Arbitration Act 1988, RSO 1990, c. I.9, s. 1(7).

134 E.g., the Reciprocal Enforcement of Judgments Act, RSA 1980, c. R-6 and the Court Order Enforcement Act, RSBC 1979, c. 75, ss. 30 to 41.

135 S. 5(2) of RSC 1985, c. 17 (2nd Supp.), as am., RSC 1985, c. 1 (4th Supp.), 1993, c. 44, s. 50, federal Code, art. 1(1) and (2) and Federal Court Rules 1040-1051, SOR/88-221. Since the phrase "commercial arbitration" in art.1(1) of the code includes a claim under art. 1116 or 1117 of chapter 11 of the NAFTA, it is submitted that an award may be enforced in accordance with the provisions of the code. See s. 5(4) of the Commercial Arbitration Act, *ibid.* See also Federal Court Rules, r. 1040, which refers to arts. 35 and 36 of the code.

Model Law.[136] No such provision exists in the relevant law of the other Canadian jurisdictions because the Model Law is restricted to "international" commercial arbitral awards. Since the Ontario Foreign Arbitral Awards Act 1986[137] implementing the 1958 Convention was repealed in 1988, provision had to be made for the recognition and enforcement of foreign commercial arbitral awards that are not international. Thus, in Ontario, the Model Law applies to both.

In Canada, the party relying on an international commercial arbitral award or applying for its enforcement must supply the duly authenticated original award or a duly certified copy together with the original arbitration agreement or a duly certified copy thereof.[138] If the award or agreement is not made in the English or French language, this party must supply a duly certified translation of it into one of these official languages.

According to article 36 of the Model Law:

> (1) Recognition or enforcement of an arbitral award, irrespective of the country in which it was made, may be refused only:
>
> (a) at the request of the party against whom it is invoked, if that party furnishes to the competent court where recognition or enforcement is sought proof that:
>
> (i) a party to the arbitration agreement referred to in article 7 was under some incapacity; or the said agreement is not valid under the law to which the parties have subjected it or, failing any indication thereon, under the law of the country where the award was made, or
>
> (ii) the party against whom the award is invoked was not given proper notice of the appointment of an arbitrator or of the arbitral proceedings or was otherwise unable to present his case, or
>
> (iii) the award deals with a dispute not contemplated by or not falling within the terms of the submission to arbitration, or it contains decisions on matters beyond the scope of the submission to arbitration, provided that, if the decisions on matters submitted to arbitration can be separated from those not so submitted, that part of the award which contains decisions on matters submitted to arbitration may be recognized and enforced,[139] or

136 International Commercial Arbitration Act, RSO 1990, c. I.9, s. 10.

137 SO 1986, c. 25.

138 Model Law, *supra*, note 103, art. 35(2) and Quebec Code of Civil Procedure, art. 949.1. In this province, the application for recognition and execution is made by way of motion for homologation to the court, which would have had competence in Quebec to decide the matter in dispute submitted to the arbitration. See also art. 946. International Commercial Arbitration Act, SBC 1986, c. 14, s. 35(2), which adds the words "unless the court orders otherwise." In *Schreter v. Gasmac Inc.*, *supra*, note 132, it was held that a proceeding to enforce a foreign arabitral award under the International Commercial Arbitration Act is properly commenced by an application rather than by an action.

139 *Dunhill Personnel Systems Inc. v. Dunhill Temps Edmonton Ltd.* (1993), 13 Alta. LR (3d) 241, 144 AR 272 (QB) and *Aamaco Transmissions Inc. v. Kunz* (1991), 97 Sask. R 5, 12 WAC 5. A failure to give reasons is not by itself a ground for refusing to enforce an award: *Schreter v. Gasmac Inc.*, *supra*, note 132.

(iv) the composition of the arbitral tribunal or the arbitral procedure was not in accordance with the agreement of the parties or, failing such agreement, was not in accordance with the law of the country where the arbitration took place, or

(v) the award has not yet become binding on the parties or has been set aside or suspended by a court of the country in which, or under the law of which, that award was made; or

(b) if the court finds that:

(i) the subject-matter of the dispute is not capable of settlement by arbitration under the law of this State,[140] or

(ii) the recognition or enforcement of the award would be contrary to the public policy of this State.[141]

(2) If an application for setting aside or suspension of an award has been made to a court referred to in paragraph (1)(a)(v) of this article, the court where recognition or enforcement is sought may, if it considers it proper, adjourn its decision and may also, on the application of the party claiming recognition or enforcement of the award, order the other party to provide appropriate security.

The burden of proof is on the person who is opposed to the recognition and enforcement of the arbitral award. These grounds are the same as those that may be invoked to set aside an award.[142] They are to be found in the 1958 Convention.[143] However, the grounds relating to arbitrability and public policy, in the case of recognition and enforcement, may lead to different results since the state of setting aside may not be the same as the state of enforcement.

The major advantage of the legislation now in place in Canada is that awards are recognized and enforced almost automatically without the necessity of bringing an action on them in the local courts to confirm them, as was the case before, and without a review of the merits of the dispute.[144]

Once an international commercial arbitral award is recognized by the court, it is enforceable in the same manner as a judgment or order of that court and it binds the

140 *Kanto Yakin Kogyo Kabushiki-Kaisha v. Can-Eng Manufacturing Ltd.* (1992), 7 OR (3d) 779, 4 BLR (2d) 108, 40 CPR (3d) 451 (Gen. Div.), aff'd. (1995), 60 CPR (3d) 417, 22 OR (3d) 576.

141 *Kanto Yakin Kogyo Kabushiki-Kaisha v. Can-Eng Manufacturing Ltd., ibid.* and *Schreter v. Gasmac Inc., supra,* note 132.

142 Model Law, *supra,* note 103, art. 34. The enforcing court will not examine the merits of an arbitral award: *Schreter v. Gasmac Inc., supra,* note 132, or set it aside for an error of law: *Quintette Coal Ltd. v. Nippon Steel Corp.* (1990), 50 BCLR (2d) 207, [1991] 1 WWR 219 (CA), leave to appeal to SCC refused (1990), 50 BCLR (2d) xxvii applying s. 34.

143 In Quebec, see Code of Civil Procedure, arts. 949, 950, and 951. For a good case decided under the 1958 Convention, see *Parsons & Whitemore Overseas Co. v. Société Générale de l'Industrie du Papier,* 508 F2d 969 (USCA 1974).

144 E.g., Quebec Code of Civil Procedure, arts. 948 and 951.1.

persons as between whom it was made and may be relied upon by any of them in any legal proceedings.[145]

XV. COSTS

In general, the costs of arbitration comprise the fees and expenses of the arbitrators, the administrative expenses for conducting the arbitration, the legal costs of the parties for presenting their arguments, and, in some instances, the fees and expenses of experts or witnesses. If the losing party refuses to comply with the terms of the award, additional costs may be incurred to force compliance.

In their award, the arbitrators must decide which costs are to be borne by the parties and in which proportion unless the parties have agreed in advance as to their apportionment.

Costs may be quite high especially when the arbitration is lengthy and complicated. Therefore, in the case of an *ad hoc* arbitration, it is advisable to settle the question of costs in advance. The costs of institutional arbitration are more predictable. They are usually set according to a schedule. For instance, in the case of the International Court of Arbitration of the ICC, the administrative charges, as well as the fees of the arbitrators are based on the amount in dispute in each case. This method permits a party to estimate the costs of an arbitration before it begins. It also discourages inflated claims or counterclaims. Even if a case becomes more complex than foreseen, there will be no increase in administrative charges. The fees of the arbitrators are generally within a set range based on the amount in dispute. They are not calculated on a per hour or *per diem* basis, which could provide a disincentive for rapid work. The fees will take into account the rapidity of the proceedings, the complexity of the dispute, and the time spent by the arbitrators. In exceptional cases, the fees may be fixed above or below the scale in order to ensure fairness to both the parties and the arbitrators.

The costs are paid out of an advance on costs payable equally by the claimant and the defendant. The arbitrators will not proceed until the advance on costs has been satisfied. If the dispute is settled amicably during the course of the proceedings the final costs may be set at an amount below that which would have been reached by applying the schedule.[146]

The administrative fees of the British Columbia International Commercial Arbitration Centre and the Quebec National and International Commercial Arbitration Centre are also based on the amount in dispute. On the other hand, the fees of the arbitrators are calculated on a per hour basis by the Quebec Centre, whereas the rules of the British Columbia Centre provide that they are set by the arbitral tribunal and must be reasonable, taking into account the amount in dispute, the complexity of the subject matter, the

---

145 E.g., International Commercial Arbitration Act, RSO 1990, c. I.9, s. 11. The legislation also applies to an arbitration to which the Crown is a party: s. 12. In Quebec, the arbitration award once homologated is executory as a judgment of the court: art. 951.2 of Code of Civil Procedure.

146 See Scales of Administrative Expenses and of Arbitrator's Fees of the International Court of Arbitration of the International Chamber of Commerce, ICC Rules of Conciliation and Arbitration in force as from 1 January 1988, 37.

time spent by the arbitrators, and any other relevant circumstances.[147] Thus, it is more difficult to estimate their amount in advance.

XVI. GENERAL CONCLUSION

Today, the Canadian legal environment is most favourable to international commercial arbitration. By adopting legislation that achieves a good balance between procedural fairness and party autonomy as well as speed in resolving disputes, under minimal judicial control and assistance, Canada has become a very attractive and convenient place for international commercial arbitration. Domestic and foreign business concerns engaged in international trade should take advantage of this situation, especially when the judicial system of their respective countries is seriously congested and sometimes inadequate. It is strongly recommended that an arbitration clause providing for *institutional* arbitration in Canada be inserted in every international or interprovincial commercial contract.

XVII. SELECTED BIBLIOGRAPHY

A. Books

Antaki and Prujiner (eds.), *International Commercial Arbitration* (1986).

Carbonneau (ed.), *Resolving Transnational Disputes Through International Arbitration* (1984).

Craig, Park, and Paulsson, *International Chamber of Commerce Arbitration* (2nd ed., 1990)

Dore, *Arbitration and Conciliation Under the UNCITRAL Rules: A Textual Analysis* (1986).

Dore, *Theory and Practice of Multiparty Commercial Arbitration* (1990).

Emond (ed.), *Commercial Dispute Resolution* (1989).

Gaillard and von Mehren (eds.), *International Arbitration Recent Developments* (1988).

Holtzmann and Neuhaus, *A Guide to the UNCITRAL Model Law on International Commercial Arbitration Legislative History and Commentary* (1989).

International Chamber of Commerce, *International Arbitration: Sixty Years of ICC Arbitration. A Look at the Future* (1984).

International Chamber of Commerce, *Inter-American Commercial Arbitration* (1990).

Mustill and Boyd, *The Law and Practice of Commercial Arbitration in England* (2nd ed., 1989).

Paterson and Thompson (eds.), *UNCITRAL Arbitration Model in Canada* (1987).

Redfern and Hunter, *Law and Practice of International Commercial Arbitration* (1986).

147 R. 37(3) of the rules.

Sanders (ed.), *New Trends in the Development of International Commercial Arbitration and the Role of Arbitral and Other Institutions (International Council for Commercial Arbitration* (Congress Series no. 1) (1983)

Sarcevic (ed.), *Essays on International Commercial Arbitration* (1989).

B. Articles

Branson and Wallace, "Choosing the Substantive Law to Apply in International Commercial Arbitration" (1986), 27 *Va. J Int'l. L* 39.

Brierley, "Canadian Acceptance of International Commercial Arbitration" (1988), 40 *Me. L Rev.* 287.

Castel, "The Enforcemnt of Agreements to Arbitrate and Arbitral Awards in Canada (1991), 17 *Can.-US LJ* 491.

Graham, "The Internationalization of Commercial Arbitration in Canada: A Preliminary Reaction" (1987-88), 13 *CBLJ* 2.

Hentzen, "The New Legislation on Arbitration in Canada" (1988), 22 *Int'l. L* 829.

Highet, "The Enigma of the Lex Mercatoria" (1989), 63 *Tul. L Rev.* 613.

Lalonde et al., "Domestic and International Commercial Arbitration in Québec: Current Status and Perspectives for the Future" (1985), 45 *R du B* 705.

Lando, "The Lex Mercatoria in International Commercial Arbitration" (1985), 34 *Int'l. & Comp. LQ* 747.

McNerney and Esplugues, "International Commercial Arbitration: The UNCITRAL Model Law" (1986), 9 *BC Int'l. & Comp. L Rev.* 47.

Sanders, "A Twenty Years' Review of the Convention on the Recognition and Enforcement of Foreign Arbitral Awards" (1979), 13 *Int'l. L* 269.

Springer, "The United Nations Convention on the Recognition and Enforcement of Foreign Arbitral Awards" (1969), *3 Int'l. L* 320.

Thompson, "A British Columbia Perspective on International Commercial Arbitration" (1987-88), 13 *Can. Bus. LJ* 72.

Thompson, "The UNCITRAL Arbitration Rules" (1976), 17 *Harv. Int'l. LJ* 141.

Ulmer, "Drafting the International Arbitration Clause" (1986), 20 *Int'l. L* 1335.

C. Periodicals

Arbitration International

ICC International Court of Arbitration Bulletin

World Arbitration Reporter

Yearbook of Commercial Arbitration

Index